Great Lives from History

Cumulative Indexes

Great Lives from History

Cumulative Indexes

Edited by

The Editors of Salem Press

SALEM PRESS
Pasadena, California Hackensack, New Jersey

Editor in Chief: Dawn P. Dawson
Editorial Director: Christina J. Moose *Production Editor:* Andrea E. Miller
Project Editor: Judy Selhorst *Design and Layout:* James Hutson
Photo Editor: Cynthia Breslin Beres

Cover photos: The Granger Collection, New York; Hulton Archive/Getty Images; Library of Congress; and Ullstein Bild.

∞ The paper used in these volumes conforms to the American National Standard for Permanence of Paper for Printed Library Materials, Z39.48-1992 (R1997).

Library of Congress Cataloging-in-Publication Data

Great lives from history. Cumulative indexes.
p. cm. — (Great lives from history)
ISBN 978-1-58765-356-8 (vol. 1 : alk. paper) 1. Great lives from history—Indexes. 2. Biography—Indexes.
CT120.G695 2008
920.02—dc22

2008030386

First Printing

PRINTED IN THE UNITED STATES OF AMERICA

Contents

Publisher's Note vii

Alphabetical List of Entries 1

Category Index 35

Agriculture 35
Anthropology and Sociology 35
Archaeology 36
Architecture 36
Art 36
Assassins and Murderers 38
Astronomy 38
Aviation and Space Exploration 40
Biology 40
Business and Industry 41
Cartography 42
Chemistry 42
Church Government and Reform 43
Civil Rights 44
Communications 44
Computer Science 44
Conservation and Environmentalism 44
Crime 44
Dance 45
Diplomacy 45
Earth Sciences 47
Economics 47
Education 48
Engineering 49
Exploration 50
Gangsters and Associates 51
Genetics 51
Geography 51
Government and Politics 52
Historiography 63
Invention and Technology 63
Journalism 64
Language and Linguistics 65
Law 65
Literature 66
Mathematics 71
Medicine 72
Military Affairs 73
Monarchy (20th century) 76
Music 76
Native American Affairs 78
Natural History 78
Outlaws and Gunslingers 78
Philanthropy and Patrons of the Arts 79
Philosophy 79
Photography 82
Physics 82
Physiology 83
Pirates 83
Psychology and Psychiatry 83
Racists and Hatemongers 84
Radio, Film, and Television 84
Religion and Theology 85
Scholarship 89
Science 90
Social Reform 90
Sports 92
Terrorists 93
Theater and Live Entertainment 93
Traitors and Spies 94
Warfare and Conquest 95
Witches and Occultists 97
Women's Rights 97

Chronological List of Entries 99

Geographical Index 171

Afghanistan 171
Albania 172
Algeria 172
Angola 172
Argentina 172
Armenia 172
Australia 172
Austria 172
Azerbaijan 173
Barbados 173
Belarus 173
Belgium 173
Bolivia 173
Bosnia 173
Brazil 173
Bulgaria 173
Burma 173
Byzantine Empire 173
Cambodia 173
Canada 173
Central African Republic 174
Chad 174
Chile 174
China 174
Colombia 175
Congo 175
Costa Rica 175
Croatia 175
Cuba 175
Czech Republic and Slovakia 175
Denmark 175
Dominican Republic 176

Ecuador 176
Egypt 176
El Salvador 176
England 176
Estonia 181
Ethiopia 181
Finland 181
France 181
Georgia, Republic of 185
Germany 185
Ghana 187
Greece 187
Guatemala 188
Guinea 188
Haiti 188
Hungary 188
Iceland 189
India and Sri Lanka 189
Indonesia 189
Iran 189
Iraq 190
Ireland and Northern Ireland 190
Israel/Palestine 190
Italy 191
Ivory Coast 193
Jamaica 193
Japan 193
Jordan 193
Kazakhstan 193
Kenya 193
Korea (North and South) . . . 193
Kuwait 193
Laos 193
Latvia 193
Lebanon 193
Liberia 193
Libya 193
Lithuania 193
Madagascar 194
Malawi 194
Malaysia 194
Mali 194
Martinique 194
Mexico 194
Mongolia 194
Morocco 194
Mozambique 194
Native America 194
Netherlands 194
New Zealand 195
Nicaragua 195
Nigeria 195
Norway 195
Oman 195
Ottoman Empire 195
Pakistan 196
Panama 196
Paraguay 196
Peru 196
Philippines 196
Poland 196
Portugal 196
Roman Empire 196
Roman Republic 197
Romania 197
Russia 197
Saudi Arabia 199
Scandinavia 199
Scotland 199
Senegal 199
Serbia and Montenegro 199
Sicily 199
Singapore 199
Slovenia 200
Somalia 200
South Africa 200
Soviet Union 200
Spain 200
Sudan 201
Sweden 201
Switzerland 202
Syria 202
Taiwan 202
Tanzania 202
Thailand 202
Tibet 202
Trinidad and Tobago 202
Tunisia 202
Turkey 202
Turkmenistan 203
Uganda 203
Ukraine 203
United States 203
Uzbekistan 212
Vatican City 212
Venezuela 212
Vietnam 212
Wales 212
Yugoslavia 212
Zambia 212
Zimbabwe 212

Subject and Personages Index 213

Publisher's Note

Salem Press's *Great Lives from History* series is a far-reaching view of of the most famous, and infamous, personages of history, in all areas of human endeavor, from the arts through political, religious, and science figures. Established in 2004 with *The Ancient World*, the series saw completion in 2009 with the final installment, *The 20th Century*. Each of the eight sets (27 volumes altogether) is arranged alphabetically by name of personage and includes the following finding aids: a Chronological List of Entries, a Category Index, a Geographical Index, a Personage Index, and a comprehensive Subject Index.

Here, for the first time, all of these indexes have been merged to form this one-volume set of the *Cumulative Indexes* to all 4,474 lives covered. Each of the five indexes from all eight sets has been merged with its fellows from the other sets, and for convenience the Subject and Personage indexes have been combined into one comprehensive Subject and Personages Index. The resulting merged indexes are further organized as follows:

- **Alphabetical List of Entries:** A complete list of all the lives, arranged alphabetically.
- **Category Index:** Lives by category, from *Agriculture* and *Art* through *Law* and *Government and Politics* to *Literature* to *Medicine*, *Social Reform*, and *Women's Rights*. Lives within each category are arranged alphabetically. Ample cross-references direct readers to other likely areas of interest.
- **Chronological List of Entries:** A complete list of all the lives, arranged chronologically. Subheads divide the personages covered into date ranges by birth year in order to speed the location of lives by period.
- **Geographical Index:** Lives by geographic locale, from *Afghanistan* to *Zimbabwe*. Cross-references direct readers to related locales: Those looking up *Russia*, for example, will also be directed to the lives listed under *Soviet Union*.
- **Subject and Personages Index:** A merging of the subject *and* personages indexes of all ten sets, this massive index includes persons, concepts, terms, battles, works of literature, inventions, organizations, artworks, musical compositions, and many other topics of discussion. More than 5,000 "see" and "see also" cross-references direct readers to related topics of interest.

In all five indexes, the page numbers for each entry are preceded by a set code indicating to which reference set the entry belongs:

- **Anc:** *Great Lives from History: The Ancient World* (2004, 2 vols.)
- **MA:** *Great Lives from History: The Middle Ages* (2005, 2 vols.)
- **Ren:** *Great Lives from History: The Renaissance & Early Modern Era* (2005, 2 vols.)
- **17th:** *Great Lives from History: The 17th Century* (2006, 2 vols.)
- **18th:** *Great Lives from History: The 18th Century* (2006, 2 vols.)
- **19th:** *Great Lives from History: The 19th Century* (2007, 4 vols.)
- **20th:** *Great Lives from History: The 20th Century* (2009, 10 vols.)
- **Notor:** *Great Lives from History: Notorious Lives* (2007, 3 vols.)

Finally, we refer the user to the first pages of the Category and Geographical indexes, where we have included tables of contents for those two indexes, and to the first page of the Subject and Personages Index, where additional user notes are provided.

Great Lives from History

Cumulative Indexes

Alphabetical List of Entries

A

Alvar Aalto, *20th:* 1
Aaron, *Anc:* 1
Hank Aaron, *20th:* 5
Sani Abacha, *Notor:* 1
Frank W. Abagnale, Jr., *Notor:* 3
Abahai, *17th:* 1
Pietro d'Abano, *MA:* 1
ʿAbbās the Great, *17th:* 4
Ferhat Abbas, *20th:* 7
ʿAbd al-Malik, *MA:* 3
ʿAbd al-Muʾmin, *MA:* 6
ʿAbd al-Raḥmān III al-Nāṣir, *MA:* 9
Abdelkader, *19th:* 1
Muhammad Muḥammad ʿAbduh, *19th:* 4
Abdülhamid II, *19th:* 7
Niels Henrik Abel, *19th:* 9
Peter Abelard, *MA:* 13
Ralph Abernathy, *20th:* 11
Fanny Abington, *18th:* 1
Abraham, *Anc:* 4
Isaac ben Judah Abravanel, *Ren:* 1
Abū Ḥanīfah, *MA:* 18
Abu Nidal, *Notor:* 4
Abul Wefa, *MA:* 21
Barbe Acarie, *Ren:* 3
Chinua Achebe, *20th:* 14
Dean Acheson, *20th:* 17
José de Acosta, *Ren:* 5
Lord Acton, *19th:* 12
Robert and James Adam, *18th:* 3
Adam de la Halle, *MA:* 24
Abigail Adams, *18th:* 7
Henry Adams, *19th:* 16
John Adams, *18th:* 11
John Quincy Adams, *19th:* 20
Samuel Adams, *18th:* 16
Jane Addams, *20th:* 22
Joseph Addison, *18th:* 20
Konrad Adenauer, *20th:* 26
Halide Edib Adıvar, *20th:* 29
Alfred Adler, *20th:* 33
Felix Adler, *19th:* 26
Joe Adonis, *Notor:* 6
Adrian IV, *MA:* 27
Adrian VI, *Ren:* 7
Aeschylus, *Anc:* 7
Aesop, *Anc:* 11
Æthelflæd, *MA:* 30
Afonso I (c. 1108-1185), *MA:* 33
Afonso I (c. 1455-1543), *Ren:* 9
Afonso de Albuquerque, *Ren:* 22
Elizabeth Cabot Agassiz, *19th:* 29
Louis Agassiz, *19th:* 31
Mehmet Ali Mehmet Ali Ağca, *Notor:* 8
Agesilaus II of Sparta, *Anc:* 14
Maria Gaetana Agnesi, *18th:* 24
Georgius Agricola, *Ren:* 11
Gnaeus Julius Agricola, *Anc:* 17
Marcus Vipsanius Agrippa, *Anc:* 20
Agrippina the Younger, *Anc:* 23
Aḥmad ibn Ḥanbal, *MA:* 36
Sir Sayyid Ahmad Khan, *19th:* 35
Ahmed III, *18th:* 26
Alvin Ailey, *20th:* 36
JoAnne Akalaitis, *20th:* 39
Akbar, *Ren:* 15
Said Akbar, *Notor:* 10
Akhenaton, *Anc:* 26
Anna Akhmatova, *20th:* 42
Akiba ben Joseph, *Anc:* 29
Akihito, *20th:* 46
ʿAlāʾ-ud-Dīn Muḥammad Khaljī, *MA:* 39
First Viscount Alanbrooke, *20th:* 50
Alaungpaya, *18th:* 29
Leon Battista Alberti, *Ren:* 18
Saint Albertus Magnus, *MA:* 42
Alboin, *MA:* 45
Madeleine Albright, *20th:* 54
Alcibiades of Athens, *Anc:* 33, *Notor:* 11
Alcmaeon, *Anc:* 36
Bronson Alcott, *19th:* 38
Louisa May Alcott, *19th:* 41
Alcuin, *MA:* 49
John Alden, *17th:* 7
Mateo Alemán, *Ren:* 25
Jean le Rond d'Alembert, *18th:* 31
Alexander I, *19th:* 45
Alexander II, *19th:* 48
Alexander III, *MA:* 56
Alexander VI, *Ren:* 27, *Notor:* 14
Alexander VII, *17th:* 9
Saint Alexander Nevsky, *MA:* 52
Alexander the Great, *Anc:* 39
Alexis, *17th:* 11
Alfonso X, *MA:* 59
Alfred the Great, *MA:* 63
Hannes Alfvén, *20th:* 58
Horatio Alger, *19th:* 51
Alhazen, *MA:* 66
Muhammad Ali, *20th:* 61
Ali Paşa Tepelenë, *19th:* 55
Ethan Allen, *18th:* 35
Lord Allenby, *20th:* 65
Salvador Allende, *20th:* 70
Alp Arslan, *MA:* 70
John Peter Altgeld, *19th:* 57
Duke of Alva, *Ren:* 31
Pedro de Alvarado, *Ren:* 34
Luis W. Alvarez, *20th:* 73
Amalasuntha, *MA:* 75
Viktor A. Ambartsumian, *20th:* 77
Saint Ambrose, *Anc:* 42
Amenhotep III, *Anc:* 45
Aldrich Ames, *Notor:* 16
Oakes Ames, *Notor:* 18
Lord Amherst, *18th:* 38
Idi Amin, *20th:* 80, *Notor:* 20
Amina Sarauniya Zazzua, *Ren:* 37
Yigal Amir, *Notor:* 22
Roald Amundsen, *20th:* 83

An Lushan, *MA:* 78
Ānanda, *Anc:* 49
Albert Anastasia, *Notor:* 23
Anaxagoras, *Anc:* 52
Anaximander, *Anc:* 55
Anaximenes of Miletus, *Anc:* 58
Hans Christian Andersen, *19th:* 61
Marian Anderson, *20th:* 87
John André, *18th:* 42
Andrea del Sarto, *Ren:* 39
Isabella Andreini, *Ren:* 42
Lancelot Andrewes, *17th:* 14
Saint Angela Merici, *Ren:* 44
Blessed Angela of Foligno, *MA:* 81
Mother Angelica, *20th:* 90
Fra Angelico, *MA:* 83
Sir Norman Angell, *20th:* 92
Maya Angelou, *20th:* 97
Sofonisba Anguissola, *Ren:* 46
Anna, Princess of the Byzantine Empire, *MA:* 86
Anna Comnena, *MA:* 89
Queen Anne, *18th:* 45
Anne of Austria, *17th:* 18
Anne of Brittany, *Ren:* 48
Anne of Cleves, *Ren:* 51
Saint Anselm, *MA:* 92
Lord Anson, *18th:* 49
Susan B. Anthony, *19th:* 65
Saint Anthony of Egypt, *Anc:* 60
Saint Anthony of Padua, *MA:* 95
Antigonus I Monophthalmos, *Anc:* 63
Antiochus the Great, *Anc:* 65
Antisthenes, *Anc:* 68
Ion Antonescu, *Notor:* 25
Antonia Minor, *Anc:* 71
Marc Antony, *Anc:* 73
Apache Kid, *Notor:* 27
Virginia Apgar, *20th:* 100
Guillaume Apollinaire, *20th:* 104
Apollonius of Perga, *Anc:* 76
Johnny Appleseed, *19th:* 68
Marshall Applewhite, *Notor:* 28
Corazon Aquino, *20th:* 107
Yasir Arafat, *20th:* 110
Eugene Aram, *Notor:* 30
Roscoe Arbuckle, *Notor:* 32
Diane Arbus, *20th:* 115
Archimedes, *Anc:* 80
Hannah Arendt, *20th:* 118
Aretaeus of Cappadocia, *Anc:* 84
Pietro Aretino, *Ren:* 53
Second Duke of Argyll, *18th:* 53
Oscar Arias Sánchez, *20th:* 121
Ludovico Ariosto, *Ren:* 56
Jean-Bertrand Aristide, *20th:* 124
Aristippus, *Anc:* 87
Aristophanes, *Anc:* 90
Aristotle, *Anc:* 94
Aristoxenus, *Anc:* 97
Sir Richard Arkwright, *18th:* 55
Arminius, *Anc:* 99
Jacobus Arminius, *Ren:* 59
Edwin H. Armstrong, *20th:* 127
Johnnie Armstrong, *Notor:* 35
Louis Armstrong, *20th:* 130
Neil Armstrong, *20th:* 134
Angélique Arnauld, *17th:* 20
Benedict Arnold, *18th:* 59, *Notor:* 36
Matthew Arnold, *19th:* 71
Thomas Arnold, *19th:* 76
Arnold of Villanova, *MA:* 98
Arnolfo di Cambio, *MA:* 102
Árpád, *MA:* 105
Svante August Arrhenius, *20th:* 138
Arria the Elder, *Anc:* 102
Arria the Younger, *Anc:* 103
Arsinoe II Philadelphus, *Anc:* 105
Artemisia I, *Anc:* 109
Chester A. Arthur, *19th:* 79
ʿAruj, *Notor:* 38
Āryabhaṭa the Elder, *MA:* 108
Dorothy Arzner, *20th:* 141
Shoko Asahara, *Notor:* 40
Asanga, *Anc:* 111
Francis Asbury, *18th:* 62
Asclepiades of Bithynia, *Anc:* 114
Mary Kay Ash, *20th:* 145
al-Ashʿarī, *MA:* 111
Ashikaga Takauji, *MA:* 115
Ashurbanipal, *Anc:* 117
Ashurnasirpal II, *Anc:* 120
Anne Askew, *Ren:* 62
Askia Daud, *Ren:* 64
Aśoka, *Anc:* 124
Aspasia of Miletus, *Anc:* 127
H. H. Asquith, *20th:* 149
Hafez al-Assad, *20th:* 153
Fred Astaire, *20th:* 155
Mary Astell, *18th:* 64
Luise Aston, *19th:* 83
John Jacob Astor, *19th:* 86
Nancy Astor, *20th:* 158
Aśvaghosa, *Anc:* 130
Atahualpa, *Ren:* 66
Atatürk, *20th:* 162
Saint Athanasius of Alexandria, *Anc:* 132
Atossa, *Anc:* 136
Mohammed Atta al-Sayed, *Notor:* 43
Attila, *Anc:* 138, *Notor:* 45
Clement Attlee, *20th:* 165
Margaret Atwood, *20th:* 169
Hubertine Auclert, *19th:* 89
W. H. Auden, *20th:* 172
John James Audubon, *19th:* 91
Saint Augustine, *Anc:* 142
Augustus, *Anc:* 145
Aung San Suu Kyi, *20th:* 174
Aurangzeb, *17th:* 23
Sri Aurobindo, *20th:* 177
Jane Austen, *19th:* 94
Stephen Fuller Austin, *19th:* 98
Averroës, *MA:* 118
Avicenna, *MA:* 123
Amedeo Avogadro, *19th:* 101
Avvakum Petrovich, *17th:* 26
Nnamdi Azikiwe, *20th:* 180

B

Walter Baade, *20th:* 184
Andreas Baader, *Notor:* 47
Baʿal Shem Tov, *18th:* 68
The Bāb, *19th:* 105
Charles Babbage, *19th:* 107
Bābur, *Ren:* 69
Johann Sebastian Bach, *18th:* 71
Isaac Backus, *18th:* 75
Francis Bacon, *Ren:* 72
Nathaniel Bacon, *17th:* 29
Roger Bacon, *MA:* 127
Sir Robert Stephenson Smyth Baden-Powell, *19th:* 110
Leo Baeck, *20th:* 186

Karl Ernst von Baer, *19th:* 114
Bahā'ullāh, *19th:* 117
Jean-Sylvain Bailly, *18th:* 77
Bobby Baker, *Notor:* 48
Mikhail Bakhtin, *20th:* 190
Jim Bakker, *Notor:* 50
Mikhail Bakunin, *19th:* 119
George Balanchine, *20th:* 193
Vasco Núñez de Balboa, *Ren:* 76
Emily Greene Balch, *20th:* 197
James Baldwin, *20th:* 201
Robert Baldwin, *19th:* 122
Stanley Baldwin, *20th:* 204
Arthur Balfour, *20th:* 208
Joe Ball, *Notor:* 52
John Ball, *MA:* 130
Lucille Ball, *20th:* 212
Robert D. Ballard, *20th:* 215
Honoré de Balzac, *19th:* 126
Ban Gu, *Anc:* 149
Ban Zhao, *Anc:* 152
George Bancroft, *19th:* 130
Hastings Kamuzu Banda, *20th:* 219
Sir Surendranath Banerjea, *20th:* 221
Margita Bangová, *Notor:* 54
Sir Joseph Banks, *18th:* 80
Benjamin Banneker, *18th:* 84
Sir Frederick G. Banting, *20th:* 224
Bao Dai, *20th:* 228
Barabbas, *Notor:* 55
Barbarossa, *Ren:* 79
Anna Barbauld, *18th:* 87
Samuel Barber, *20th:* 230
Klaus Barbie, *Notor:* 57
John Bardeen, *20th:* 234
Velma Margie Barfield, *Notor:* 59
Ma Barker, *Notor:* 61
Christiaan Barnard, *20th:* 236
Henry Barnard, *19th:* 135
Djuna Barnes, *20th:* 240
P. T. Barnum, *19th:* 138
Clyde Barrow, *Notor:* 62
Sydney Barrows, *Notor:* 64
Sir Charles Barry, *19th:* 142
Karl Barth, *20th:* 243
Roland Barthes, *20th:* 246
Béla Bartók, *20th:* 250
Clara Barton, *19th:* 145
Sir Edmund Barton, *19th:* 149
Mikhail Baryshnikov, *20th:* 253
Johann Bernhard Basedow, *18th:* 89
Omar al-Bashir, *Notor:* 66
Basil the Macedonian, *MA:* 133
John Baskerville, *18th:* 92
Nikolay Gennadiyevich Basov, *20th:* 256
Sam Bass, *Notor:* 68
Jean-Marie Bastien-Thiry, *Notor:* 69
Hester Bateman, *18th:* 95
Elizabeth Báthory, *Ren:* 81, *Notor:* 70
Bathsheba, *Anc:* 155
Fulgencio Batista y Zaldívar, *Notor:* 73
al-Battānī, *MA:* 137
Charles Baudelaire, *19th:* 152
L. Frank Baum, *19th:* 155
Richard Baxter, *17th:* 32
Chevalier de Bayard, *Ren:* 84
Baybars I, *MA:* 139
Bayezid II, *Ren:* 87
Pierre Bayle, *17th:* 36
Sir William Maddock Bayliss, *20th:* 259
Dorothea Beale, *19th:* 159
Charles A. Beard, *20th:* 262
Aubrey Beardsley, *19th:* 162
The Beatles, *20th:* 266
Beatrice of Nazareth, *MA:* 144
Lady Margaret Beaufort, *Ren:* 90
Pierre-Augustin Caron de Beaumarchais, *18th:* 97
Francis Beaumont, *Ren:* 92
Simone de Beauvoir, *20th:* 271
Lord Beaverbrook, *20th:* 275
Cesare Beccaria, *18th:* 100
Johann Joachim Becher, *17th:* 39
Dave Beck, *Notor:* 75
Elisabeth Becker, *Notor:* 76
Saint Thomas Becket, *MA:* 147
Samuel Beckett, *20th:* 279
Byron De La Beckwith, *Notor:* 78
The Becquerel Family, *19th:* 165
Saint Bede the Venerable, *MA:* 150
Catharine Beecher, *19th:* 168
Henry Ward Beecher, *19th:* 172
Ludwig van Beethoven, *19th:* 175
Menachem Begin, *20th:* 284
Aphra Behn, *17th:* 42
Emil von Behring, *19th:* 179
Alexander Graham Bell, *19th:* 182
Tom Bell, *Notor:* 80
Samuel Bellamy, *Notor:* 81
John Bellingham, *Notor:* 83
Giovanni Bellini, *Ren:* 97
Muhammad Muḥammad Bello, *19th:* 186
Saul Bellow, *20th:* 288
Pierre Belon, *Ren:* 101
Bambi Bembenek, *Notor:* 84
David Ben-Gurion, *20th:* 292
Benedict XIV, *18th:* 102
Ruth Benedict, *20th:* 296
Saint Benedict of Nursia, *MA:* 153
Edvard Beneš, *20th:* 299
Stephen Vincent Benét, *20th:* 303
Maurycy Beniowski, *Notor:* 85
Walter Benjamin, *20th:* 306
Benjamin of Tudela, *MA:* 157
James Gordon Bennett, *19th:* 188
Jeremy Bentham, *18th:* 104
Thomas Hart Benton, *19th:* 192
Carl Benz, *19th:* 197
Berenice II, *Anc:* 157
Alban Berg, *20th:* 309
David Berg, *Notor:* 87
Friedrich Bergius, *20th:* 313
Ingmar Bergman, *20th:* 316
Ingrid Bergman, *20th:* 321
Henri Bergson, *20th:* 323
Lavrenty Beria, *Notor:* 89
Vitus Jonassen Bering, *18th:* 108
George Berkeley, *18th:* 111
David Berkowitz, *Notor:* 91
Irving Berlin, *20th:* 327
Hector Berlioz, *19th:* 200
Claude Bernard, *19th:* 205
Saint Bernard of Clairvaux, *MA:* 160
Paul Bernardo, *Notor:* 93
Tim Berners-Lee, *20th:* 331
Sarah Bernhardt, *19th:* 208
Gian Lorenzo Bernini, *17th:* 45
The Bernoulli Family, *17th:* 48

Eduard Bernstein, *20th:* 334
Leonard Bernstein, *20th:* 337
Charlotte de Berry, *Notor:* 94
Annie Besant, *19th:* 211
Bess of Hardwick, *Ren:* 103
Friedrich Wilhelm Bessel, *19th:* 215
Sir Henry Bessemer, *19th:* 218
Hans Albrecht Bethe, *20th:* 341
Mary McLeod Bethune, *20th:* 345
Thomas Betterton, *17th:* 51
Friedrich von Beust, *19th:* 222
Aneurin Bevan, *20th:* 349
Lord Beveridge, *20th:* 352
Ernest Bevin, *20th:* 356
Jeff Bezos, *20th:* 360
Bhumibol Adulyadej, *20th:* 363
Benazir Bhutto, *20th:* 365
Zulfikar Ali Bhutto, *20th:* 368
Kenneth Bianchi, *Notor:* 95
John Biddle, *17th:* 53
Nicholas Biddle, *19th:* 225
Ambrose Bierce, *19th:* 228
Albert Bierstadt, *19th:* 232
Ronnie Biggs, *Notor:* 97
Theodore G. Bilbo, *Notor:* 99
Osama Bin Laden, *20th:* 371, *Notor:* 101
George Caleb Bingham, *19th:* 234
al-Bīrūnī, *MA:* 163
Otto von Bismarck, *19th:* 238
Georges Bizet, *19th:* 241
Vilhelm Bjerknes, *20th:* 374
Hugo L. Black, *20th:* 377
Joseph Black, *18th:* 115
Black Hawk, *19th:* 244
Harry A. Blackmun, *20th:* 382
Sir William Blackstone, *18th:* 118
Elizabeth Blackwell, *19th:* 247
James G. Blaine, *19th:* 251
Tony Blair, *20th:* 385
Robert Blake, *17th:* 55
William Blake, *18th:* 121
Louis Blanc, *19th:* 254
Blanche of Castile, *MA:* 166
Louis Blériot, *20th:* 388
Eugen Bleuler, *20th:* 391
William Bligh, *18th:* 126, *Notor:* 104
Tamsin Blight, *Notor:* 106
Aleksandr Blok, *20th:* 394
Lou Blonger, *Notor:* 107
Amelia Bloomer, *19th:* 257
Gebhard Leberecht von Blücher, *19th:* 260
Léon Blum, *20th:* 396
Anthony Blunt, *Notor:* 109
Boabdil, *Ren:* 105
Franz Boas, *20th:* 400
Giovanni Boccaccio, *MA:* 169
Luigi Boccherini, *18th:* 129
Umberto Boccioni, *20th:* 403
Bodhidharma, *Anc:* 160
Barbara Leigh Smith Bodichon, *19th:* 263
Sir Thomas Bodley, *Ren:* 108
Ivan Boesky, *Notor:* 110
Boethius, *MA:* 173
Germain Boffrand, *18th:* 132
Humphrey Bogart, *20th:* 406
Bohemond I, *MA:* 176
Jakob Böhme, *17th:* 59
Niels Bohr, *20th:* 408
Nicolas Boileau-Despréaux, *17th:* 63
Marie Anne Victorine Boivin, *19th:* 265
Jean-Bédel Bokassa, *Notor:* 113
Anne Boleyn, *Ren:* 111
First Viscount Bolingbroke, *18th:* 135
Simón Bolívar, *19th:* 267
Heinrich Böll, *20th:* 411
Saint Bonaventure, *MA:* 180
Margaret Bondfield, *20th:* 414
Dietrich Bonhoeffer, *20th:* 418
Saint Boniface, *MA:* 183
Boniface VIII, *MA:* 186, *Notor:* 115
Pierre Bonnard, *20th:* 421
Stede Bonnet, *Notor:* 117
Claude Alexandre de Bonneval, *18th:* 140
William H. Bonney, *Notor:* 118
Jules Bonnot, *Notor:* 120
Anne Bonny, *Notor:* 122
Daniel Boone, *18th:* 143
Edwin Booth, *19th:* 271
John Wilkes Booth, *Notor:* 123
William Booth, *19th:* 274
Lizzie Borden, *19th:* 277, *Notor:* 125
Sir Robert Laird Borden, *20th:* 423
Giovanni Alfonso Borelli, *17th:* 65
Björn Borg, *20th:* 426
Jorge Luis Borges, *20th:* 430
Cesare Borgia, *Ren:* 114, *Notor:* 127
Lucrezia Borgia, *Ren:* 117, *Notor:* 129
Boris I of Bulgaria, *MA:* 189
Norman Borlaug, *20th:* 434
Martin Bormann, *Notor:* 131
Max Born, *20th:* 437
Aleksandr Borodin, *19th:* 280
Francesco Borromini, *17th:* 67
Hieronymus Bosch, *Ren:* 120
Jacques-Bénigne Bossuet, *17th:* 70
James Boswell, *18th:* 146
Louis Botha, *20th:* 439
Walther Bothe, *20th:* 442
Sandro Botticelli, *Ren:* 123
Horatio W. Bottomley, *20th:* 445
Boudicca, *Anc:* 163
Louis-Antoine de Bougainville, *18th:* 150
Nadia Boulanger, *20th:* 449
Pierre Boulez, *20th:* 452
Joseph Boulogne, *18th:* 153
Matthew Boulton, *18th:* 156
Louyse Bourgeois, *17th:* 73
Saint Marguerite Bourgeoys, *17th:* 75
Habib Bourguiba, *20th:* 457
Margaret Bourke-White, *20th:* 460
Boutros Boutros-Ghali, *20th:* 464
Christopher John Boyce, *Notor:* 133
Belle Boyd, *Notor:* 135
Robert Boyle, *17th:* 78
Mrs. Anne Bracegirdle, *17th:* 82
Henry de Bracton, *MA:* 192
Mary Elizabeth Braddon, *19th:* 284
William Bradford, *17th:* 84
F. H. Bradley, *19th:* 288
Omar Nelson Bradley, *20th:* 468

Sir Donald G. Bradman, *20th:* 471
Anne Bradstreet, *17th:* 88
Mathew B. Brady, *19th:* 291
Sir Lawrence Bragg, *20th:* 474
Sophie Brahe, *Ren:* 126
Tycho Brahe, *Ren:* 128
Brahmagupta, *MA:* 195
Johannes Brahms, *19th:* 296
Louis Braille, *19th:* 299
Donato Bramante, *Ren:* 132
Constantin Brancusi, *20th:* 478
Louis D. Brandeis, *20th:* 482
Marlon Brando, *20th:* 486
Willy Brandt, *20th:* 490
Joseph Brant, *18th:* 159
Georges Braque, *20th:* 493
Fernand Braudel, *20th:* 497
Eva Braun, *Notor:* 137
Wernher von Braun, *20th:* 500
Bertolt Brecht, *20th:* 504
Arthur Bremer, *Notor:* 139
William J. Brennan, *20th:* 507
Margaret Brent, *17th:* 92
André Breton, *20th:* 510
Josef Breuer, *20th:* 514
Henri-Édouard-Prosper Breuil, *20th:* 517
Stephen G. Breyer, *20th:* 520
Leonid Brezhnev, *20th:* 523
Percy Williams Bridgman, *20th:* 526
John Bright, *19th:* 302
Saint Brigit, *MA:* 198
James Brindley, *18th:* 162
John R. Brinkley, *Notor:* 141
Benjamin Britten, *20th:* 529
Curly Bill Brocius, *Notor:* 143
Sir Isaac Brock, *19th:* 306
William Brodie, *Notor:* 145
Louis de Broglie, *20th:* 534
The Brontë Sisters, *19th:* 308
Gwendolyn Brooks, *20th:* 537
Henry Brougham, *19th:* 312
George Brown, *19th:* 316
Helen Gurley Brown, *20th:* 539
John Brown, *19th:* 319
Lancelot Brown, *18th:* 165
Molly Brown, *20th:* 542
Olympia Brown, *19th:* 323
Sir Thomas Browne, *17th:* 94
Elizabeth Barrett Browning, *19th:* 326
James Bruce, *18th:* 168
Robert Bruce, *MA:* 200
Anton Bruckner, *19th:* 329
Pieter Bruegel, the Elder, *Ren:* 135
Gro Harlem Brundtland, *20th:* 544
Isambard Kingdom Brunel, *19th:* 333
Marc Isambard Brunel, *19th:* 337
Filippo Brunelleschi, *MA:* 205
Leonardo Bruni, *MA:* 208
Emil Brunner, *20th:* 547
Giordano Bruno, *Ren:* 138
Marcus Junius Brutus, *Anc:* 166, *Notor:* 146
William Jennings Bryan, *20th:* 550
William Cullen Bryant, *19th:* 340
Martin Buber, *20th:* 554
Martin Bucer, *Ren:* 142
Louis Buchalter, *Notor:* 148
George Buchanan, *Ren:* 146
James Buchanan, *19th:* 343
Pearl S. Buck, *20th:* 557
First Duke of Buckingham, *17th:* 96
William F. Buckley, Jr., *20th:* 561
Buddha, *Anc:* 169
Warren Buffett, *20th:* 563
Comte de Buffon, *18th:* 171
Nikolay Ivanovich Bukharin, *20th:* 566
Charles Bulfinch, *19th:* 346
Bernhard von Bülow, *20th:* 569
Rudolf Bultmann, *20th:* 572
Ralph Bunche, *20th:* 574
Ted Bundy, *Notor:* 149
John Bunyan, *17th:* 100
Luis Buñuel, *20th:* 578
Angelo Buono, Jr., *Notor:* 151
Richard Burbage, *17th:* 104
Luther Burbank, *19th:* 350
Jacob Burckhardt, *19th:* 354
Warren E. Burger, *20th:* 581
Guy Burgess, *Notor:* 152
Hubert de Burgh, *MA:* 211
Jean Buridan, *MA:* 215
Edmund Burke, *18th:* 174
William Burke, *Notor:* 154
Jocelyn Burnell, *20th:* 584
Sir Macfarlane Burnet, *20th:* 587
Thomas Burnet, *17th:* 106
Frances Hodgson Burnett, *19th:* 357
Charles Burney, *18th:* 177
Fanny Burney, *18th:* 180
Daniel Hudson Burnham, *19th:* 360
Robert Burns, *18th:* 183
Aaron Burr, *19th:* 363, *Notor:* 155
Edgar Rice Burroughs, *20th:* 590
Sir Richard Francis Burton, *19th:* 368
Robert Burton, *17th:* 108
George H. W. Bush, *20th:* 594
Joseph Butler, *18th:* 187
Josephine Butler, *19th:* 371
Nicholas Murray Butler, *20th:* 597
R. A. Butler, *20th:* 602
Richard Girnt Butler, *Notor:* 157
Samuel Butler, *19th:* 374
Joey Buttafuoco, *Notor:* 159
Mary Butters, *Notor:* 160
Sir Thomas Fowell Buxton, *19th:* 376
Samuel Joseph Byck, *Notor:* 162
Richard Byrd, *20th:* 606
William Byrd, *Ren:* 148
Lord Byron, *19th:* 379

C

Álvar Núñez Cabeza de Vaca, *Ren:* 152
John Cabot, *Ren:* 155
Sebastian Cabot, *Ren:* 159
Juan Rodríguez Cabrillo, *Ren:* 161
Frances Xavier Cabrini, *19th:* 383
Francesca Caccini, *17th:* 111
Julius Caesar, *Anc:* 172
John Cairncross, *Notor:* 164
Calamity Jane, *19th:* 386
Alexander Calder, *20th:* 609
Fanny Calderón de la Barca, *19th:* 389
Pedro Calderón de la Barca, *17th:* 113

John C. Calhoun, *19th:* 392
Caligula, *Anc:* 176, *Notor:* 165
Maria Callas, *20th:* 612
Plutarco Elías Calles, *20th:* 615
William Calley, *Notor:* 168
Callimachus, *Anc:* 179
Jacques Callot, *17th:* 116
Albert Calmette, *20th:* 618
George Calvert, *17th:* 119
Roberto Calvi, *Notor:* 170
John Calvin, *Ren:* 163
Melvin Calvin, *20th:* 621
Jean-Jacques-Régis de Cambacérès, *19th:* 396
Richard Cameron, *17th:* 121
Simon Cameron, *Notor:* 171
Luís de Camões, *Ren:* 167
Tommaso Campanella, *17th:* 124
Alexander Campbell, *19th:* 399
Kim Campbell, *20th:* 624
Thomas Campion, *17th:* 127
Albert Camus, *20th:* 628
Canaletto, *18th:* 190
Felix Candela, *20th:* 631
George Canning, *19th:* 403
Annie Jump Cannon, *20th:* 635
Billy Cannon, *Notor:* 173
Canonicus, *17th:* 129
Antonio Canova, *19th:* 406
Canute the Great, *MA:* 221
Karel Čapek, *20th:* 638
Cao Cao, *Anc:* 182
Cao Xueqin, *18th:* 194
Al Capone, *20th:* 641, *Notor:* 175
Truman Capote, *20th:* 644
Caravaggio, *Ren:* 170
Gerolamo Cardano, *Ren:* 172
Lázaro Cárdenas, *20th:* 647
Fernando Henrique Cardoso, *20th:* 651
Benjamin N. Cardozo, *20th:* 653
William Carey, *19th:* 409
Sir Guy Carleton, *18th:* 196
Don Carlos, *19th:* 412
Chester F. Carlson, *20th:* 657
Thomas Carlyle, *19th:* 415
Rudolf Carnap, *20th:* 659
Andrew Carnegie, *19th:* 419
Lazare Carnot, *18th:* 200
Caroline, *18th:* 203
Giovanni da Pian del Carpini, *MA:* 226
Robert Carr, *17th:* 131
The Carracci Family, *Ren:* 175
Charles Carroll, *18th:* 205
Lewis Carroll, *19th:* 423
Kit Carson, *19th:* 426
Rachel Carson, *20th:* 662
Jimmy Carter, *20th:* 666
Jacques Cartier, *Ren:* 178
Henri Cartier-Bresson, *20th:* 671
Willis A. Carto, *Notor:* 177
Cartouche, *Notor:* 178
Enrico Caruso, *20th:* 675
George Washington Carver, *20th:* 678
Mary Ann Shadd Cary, *19th:* 431
Pablo Casals, *20th:* 681
Casanova, *18th:* 208
Sante Jeronimo Caserio, *Notor:* 180
Casimir the Great, *MA:* 229
Mary Cassatt, *19th:* 433
Butch Cassidy, *Notor:* 181
René Cassin, *20th:* 684
Gian Domenico Cassini, *17th:* 134
Cassiodorus, *MA:* 233
Ernst Cassirer, *20th:* 688
Cassius, *Anc:* 185
Paul Castellano, *Notor:* 183
Baldassare Castiglione, *Ren:* 181
Viscount Castlereagh, *19th:* 437
Fidel Castro, *20th:* 691, *Notor:* 185
Willa Cather, *20th:* 696
Catherine de Médicis, *Ren:* 184
Catherine of Aragon, *Ren:* 187
Catherine of Braganza, *17th:* 137
Saint Catherine of Genoa, *Ren:* 191
Saint Catherine of Siena, *MA:* 236
Catherine the Great, *18th:* 211
Catiline, *Anc:* 188, *Notor:* 188
George Catlin, *19th:* 441
Cato the Censor, *Anc:* 190
Cato the Younger, *Anc:* 194
Carrie Chapman Catt, *20th:* 701
Catullus, *Anc:* 196
Guido Cavalcanti, *MA:* 239
Georgiana Cavendish, *18th:* 215
Henry Cavendish, *18th:* 217
Thomas Cavendish, *Ren:* 193
Count Cavour, *19th:* 444
William Caxton, *Ren:* 196
George Cayley, *19th:* 447
Cædmon, *MA:* 219
Nicolae Ceauşescu, *20th:* 704, *Notor:* 190
William Cecil, *Ren:* 199
Benvenuto Cellini, *Ren:* 202
Aulus Cornelius Celsus, *Anc:* 199
Beatrice Cenci, *Notor:* 192
Vinton Gray Cerf, *20th:* 707
Miguel de Cervantes, *Ren:* 206
Aimé Césaire, *20th:* 709
Andrea Cesalpino, *Ren:* 211
Cetshwayo, *19th:* 450
Paul Cézanne, *19th:* 453
Cassie L. Chadwick, *Notor:* 193
Edwin Chadwick, *19th:* 456
Sir James Chadwick, *20th:* 714
Cassius Chaerea, *Notor:* 195
Marc Chagall, *20th:* 717
Houston Stewart Chamberlain, *Notor:* 196
Joseph Chamberlain, *19th:* 460
Neville Chamberlain, *20th:* 720
Wilt Chamberlain, *20th:* 725
Whittaker Chambers, *Notor:* 198
Samuel de Champlain, *17th:* 139
Chandragupta Maurya, *Anc:* 202
Coco Chanel, *20th:* 727
William Ellery Channing, *19th:* 464
Charles Chaplin, *20th:* 731
George Chapman, *Ren:* 213
Mark David Chapman, *Notor:* 200
Hester Chapone, *18th:* 221
Jean-Siméon Chardin, *18th:* 223
Charlemagne, *MA:* 242
Charles I, *17th:* 143
Charles II (1630-1685; King of England), *17th:* 147, *Notor:* 201
Charles II (1661-1700; King of Spain), *17th:* 151
Charles III, *18th:* 227
Charles IV, *MA:* 257
Charles V, *Ren:* 220

Charles VI (1685-1740; Holy Roman Emperor), *18th:* 229
Charles VI (1368-1422; King of France), *Notor:* 203
Charles VII, *Ren:* 224
Charles VIII, *Ren:* 227
Charles X Gustav, *17th:* 153
Charles XII, *18th:* 232
Charles XIV John, *19th:* 468
Ray Charles, *20th:* 735
Charles d'Orléans, *MA:* 247
Charles Martel, *MA:* 250
Charles the Bald, *MA:* 254
Charles the Bold, *Ren:* 217
Queen Charlotte, *18th:* 235
Henri Charrière, *Notor:* 204
Alain Chartier, *MA:* 260
Salmon P. Chase, *19th:* 470
Samuel Chase, *18th:* 237
François-René de Chateaubriand, *19th:* 474
Marquise du Châtelet, *18th:* 240
Geoffrey Chaucer, *MA:* 264
César Chávez, *20th:* 738
Anton Chekhov, *19th:* 478
Chen Duxiu, *20th:* 741
Chen Shu, *17th:* 156
Cheng I Sao, *Notor:* 205
G. K. Chesterton, *20th:* 744
Duchesse de Chevreuse, *17th:* 158
Chiang Kai-shek, *20th:* 746
Judy Chicago, *20th:* 750
Chikamatsu Monzaemon, *18th:* 243
Andrei Chikatilo, *Notor:* 207
Lydia Maria Child, *19th:* 482
Shirley Chisholm, *20th:* 753
Étienne François de Choiseul, *18th:* 246
Noam Chomsky, *20th:* 757
Chŏng Sŏn, *18th:* 248
Chongzhen, *17th:* 160
Frédéric Chopin, *19th:* 486
Kate Chopin, *19th:* 490
Jean Chrétien, *20th:* 761
Chrétien de Troyes, *MA:* 267
Christian VII, *Notor:* 208
Dame Agatha Christie, *20th:* 765
John Reginald Halliday Christie, *Notor:* 210
Christina, *17th:* 163
Christina of Markyate, *MA:* 270
Christine de Pizan, *MA:* 273
Henri Christophe, *19th:* 494
Saint Christopher, *Anc:* 205
Saint John Chrysostom, *Anc:* 208
Benjamin Church, *Notor:* 211
Sarah Churchill, *18th:* 250
Sir Winston Churchill, *20th:* 768
Cicero, *Anc:* 210
El Cid, *MA:* 278
Cimabue, *MA:* 282
Cimon, *Anc:* 213
André-Gustave Citroën, *20th:* 772
Cixi, *19th:* 496
Saint Clare of Assisi, *MA:* 284
First Earl of Clarendon, *17th:* 166
George Rogers Clark, *18th:* 253
William Clark, *19th:* 1359
Claude Lorrain, *17th:* 171
Georges Claude, *20th:* 775
Claudius I, *Anc:* 217
Carl von Clausewitz, *19th:* 499
Henry Clay, *19th:* 502
Cleisthenes of Athens, *Anc:* 221
Georges Clemenceau, *20th:* 778
Clement I, *Anc:* 223
Clement VII, *Ren:* 229, *Notor:* 212
Jacques Clément, *Notor:* 214
Cleomenes, *Anc:* 226
Cleopatra VII, *Anc:* 229
Grover Cleveland, *19th:* 507
Bill Clinton, *20th:* 783
DeWitt Clinton, *19th:* 512
Sir Henry Clinton, *18th:* 256
Hillary Rodham Clinton, *20th:* 788
Robert Clive, *18th:* 259
Clodia, *Anc:* 233
Saint Clotilda, *MA:* 287
Clovis, *MA:* 290
Dorothy Clutterbuck, *Notor:* 215
Ty Cobb, *20th:* 791
William Cobbett, *19th:* 517
Richard Cobden, *19th:* 520
Jean Cocteau, *20th:* 794
William Cody, *19th:* 524
Sebastian Coe, *20th:* 797
Ferdinand Julius Cohn, *19th:* 527
Roy Cohn, *Notor:* 217
Sir Edward Coke, *17th:* 174
Jean-Baptiste Colbert, *17th:* 180
Bessie Coleman, *20th:* 801
Samuel Taylor Coleridge, *19th:* 529
John Colet, *Ren:* 232
Colette, *20th:* 804
Schuyler Colfax, *Notor:* 219
Vincent Coll, *Notor:* 221
Frank Collin, *Notor:* 222
Michael Collins, *20th:* 807
Norman Collins, *20th:* 810
Joe Colombo, *Notor:* 224
Vittoria Colonna, *Ren:* 235
Charles W. Colson, *Notor:* 225
Samuel Colt, *19th:* 533
John Coltrane, *20th:* 814
Christopher Columbus, *Ren:* 237
Commodus, *Notor:* 227
Arthur Holly Compton, *20th:* 817
Anthony Comstock, *Notor:* 229
Auguste Comte, *19th:* 536
James Bryant Conant, *20th:* 820
The Great Condé, *17th:* 184
Étienne Bonnot de Condillac, *18th:* 263
Marquis de Condorcet, *18th:* 267
Confucius, *Anc:* 236
Joseph Conrad, *20th:* 824
John Constable, *19th:* 540
Learie Constantine, *20th:* 829
Constantine the Great, *Anc:* 239
Anne Conway, *17th:* 187
James Cook, *18th:* 270
Janet Cooke, *Notor:* 231
Jay Cooke, *19th:* 544
William Fothergill Cooke, *19th:* 547
Calvin Coolidge, *20th:* 832
D. B. Cooper, *Notor:* 233
James Fenimore Cooper, *19th:* 552
Nicolaus Copernicus, *Ren:* 241
Aaron Copland, *20th:* 836
John Singleton Copley, *18th:* 274
Charlotte Corday, *Notor:* 235
Arcangelo Corelli, *17th:* 190
Pierre Corneille, *17th:* 193
First Marquess Cornwallis, *18th:* 278

Carolina Coronado, *19th:* 556
Francisco Vásquez de Coronado, *Ren:* 245
Correggio, *Ren:* 249
Hernán Cortés, *Ren:* 252
Bill Cosby, *20th:* 840
William T. Cosgrave, *20th:* 843
Frank Costello, *Notor:* 237
John Cotton, *17th:* 196
Pierre de Coubertin, *20th:* 846
Charles E. Coughlin, *Notor:* 239
François Couperin, *18th:* 281
Gustave Courbet, *19th:* 559
Jacques Cousteau, *20th:* 849
Miles Coverdale, *Ren:* 255
Pêro da Covilhã, *Ren:* 259
Sir Noël Coward, *20th:* 853
Abraham Cowley, *17th:* 199
Hannah Cowley, *18th:* 284
Lucas Cranach, the Elder, *Ren:* 262
Hart Crane, *20th:* 858
Stephen Crane, *19th:* 562
Thomas Cranmer, *Ren:* 266
Richard Crashaw, *17th:* 202
Cheryl Crawford, *20th:* 861
Bettino Craxi, *Notor:* 241
Crazy Horse, *19th:* 566
Francis Crick, *20th:* 865
Benedetto Croce, *20th:* 869
David Crockett, *19th:* 571
Croesus, *Anc:* 244
Oliver Cromwell, *17th:* 204
Thomas Cromwell, *Ren:* 269
Walter Cronkite, *20th:* 872
Bing Crosby, *20th:* 874
Aleister Crowley, *Notor:* 242
Samuel Ajayi Crowther, *19th:* 574
Celia Cruz, *20th:* 877
Sor Juana Inés de la Cruz, *17th:* 208
Ctesibius of Alexandria, *Anc:* 247
Cuauhtémoc, *Ren:* 273
Paul Cuffe, *19th:* 576
E. E. Cummings, *20th:* 879
Andrew Cunanan, *Notor:* 245
Imogen Cunningham, *20th:* 883
Merce Cunningham, *20th:* 886
Marie and Pierre Curie, *20th:* 888
John Curtin, *20th:* 891
George Nathaniel Curzon, *20th:* 894
Caleb Cushing, *19th:* 578
Harvey Williams Cushing, *20th:* 898
Pauline Cushman, *Notor:* 246
George A. Custer, *19th:* 582, *Notor:* 248
Moll Cutpurse, *Notor:* 250
Georges Cuvier, *19th:* 585
Cypselus of Corinth, *Notor:* 251
Cyrano de Bergerac, *17th:* 211
Saint Cyril, *MA:* 294
Cyrus the Great, *Anc:* 248
Leon Czolgosz, *Notor:* 252

D

Jacques Daguerre, *19th:* 589
Jeffrey Dahmer, *Notor:* 255
Dai Zhen, *18th:* 287
Gottlieb Daimler, *19th:* 592
Dalai Lama, *20th:* 902
First Marquis of Dalhousie, *19th:* 595
Salvador Dalí, *20th:* 904
Bob Dalton, *Notor:* 257
Emmett Dalton, *Notor:* 258
John Dalton, *19th:* 597
William Dampier, *17th:* 215, *Notor:* 260
Enrico Dandolo, *MA:* 298
Alexandra Danilova, *20th:* 908
André-Louis Danjon, *20th:* 911
Dante, *MA:* 300
Georges Danton, *18th:* 289
Abraham Darby, *18th:* 292
Rubén Darío, *19th:* 601
Darius the Great, *Anc:* 251
François Darlan, *Notor:* 262
Joseph Darnand, *Notor:* 264
Richard Walther Darré, *Notor:* 266
Clarence Darrow, *20th:* 913
Charles Darwin, *19th:* 603
Jean Dauberval, *18th:* 295
John Davenport, *17th:* 218
David, *Anc:* 255
David I, *MA:* 304
David II, *MA:* 307
Jacques-Louis David, *19th:* 607
Lady Eleanor Davies, *17th:* 220
Robertson Davies, *20th:* 917
Bette Davis, *20th:* 919
Jefferson Davis, *19th:* 610
John Davis, *Ren:* 276
Richard Allen Davis, *Notor:* 267
Sir Humphry Davy, *19th:* 616
Lucy S. Dawidowicz, *20th:* 922
Dorothy Day, *20th:* 925
Moshe Dayan, *20th:* 929
Ferenc Deák, *19th:* 619
Alfred Deakin, *19th:* 623
Tino De Angelis, *Notor:* 268
Deborah, *Anc:* 258
Eugene V. Debs, *20th:* 932
Claude Debussy, *20th:* 936
Stephen Decatur, *19th:* 626
Richard Dedekind, *19th:* 629
John Dee, *Ren:* 278
Daniel Defoe, *18th:* 298
Lee de Forest, *20th:* 940
Deganawida, *Ren:* 281
Edgar Degas, *19th:* 632
Alcide De Gasperi, *20th:* 944
Léon Degrelle, *Notor:* 270
Aagje Deken, *18th:* 301
Thomas Dekker, *17th:* 223
F. W. de Klerk, *20th:* 948
Eugene de Kock, *Notor:* 271
Eugène Delacroix, *19th:* 635
Robert Delaunay, *20th:* 950
Léo Delibes, *19th:* 639
Frederick Delius, *20th:* 953
John DeLorean, *Notor:* 272
Agnes de Mille, *20th:* 957
Cecil B. DeMille, *20th:* 960
Democritus, *Anc:* 261
Demosthenes, *Anc:* 264
Jack Dempsey, *20th:* 964
Deng Xiaoping, *20th:* 968
Maurice Denis, *20th:* 972
Saint Denis, *Anc:* 268
Fourteenth Earl of Derby, *19th:* 642
Jacques Derrida, *20th:* 974
Albert DeSalvo, *Notor:* 274
René Descartes, *17th:* 226
Eamon de Valera, *20th:* 979
Phoolan Devi, *Notor:* 275

George Dewey, *19th:* 645
John Dewey, *20th:* 982
Melvil Dewey, *19th:* 649
Dhuoda, *MA:* 310
Sergei Diaghilev, *20th:* 985
Legs Diamond, *Notor:* 277
Diana, Princess of Wales, *20th:* 989
Diane de Poitiers, *Ren:* 283
Bartolomeu Dias, *Ren:* 286
Porfirio Díaz, *19th:* 652, *Notor:* 278
Charles Dickens, *19th:* 655
Emily Dickinson, *19th:* 658
John Dickinson, *18th:* 303
Denis Diderot, *18th:* 307
Dido, *Anc:* 271
John G. Diefenbaker, *20th:* 992
Otto Paul Hermann Diels, *20th:* 995
Rudolf Diesel, *19th:* 663
Marlene Dietrich, *20th:* 997
John Dillinger, *Notor:* 281
Joe DiMaggio, *20th:* 1001
Dio Cassius, *Anc:* 274
Diocles of Carystus, *Anc:* 277
Diocletian, *Anc:* 280
Diogenes, *Anc:* 283
Dionysius Exiguus, *MA:* 313
Diophantus, *Anc:* 286
Françoise Dior, *Notor:* 283
Pedanius Dioscorides, *Anc:* 289
Paul A. M. Dirac, *20th:* 1004
Walt Disney, *20th:* 1006
Benjamin Disraeli, *19th:* 666
Dorothea Dix, *19th:* 671
Thomas Dixon, Jr., *Notor:* 284
Milovan Djilas, *20th:* 1011
William Dodd, *Notor:* 286
Samuel K. Doe, *Notor:* 288
Bob Dole, *20th:* 1014
Elizabeth Dole, *20th:* 1018
Gerhard Domagk, *20th:* 1021
Saint Dominic, *MA:* 316
Domitian, *Notor:* 289
Donatello, *MA:* 319
Karl Dönitz, *Notor:* 292
Gaetano Donizetti, *19th:* 674
John Donne, *17th:* 230
Black Donnellys, *Notor:* 294
Bill Doolin, *Notor:* 296
Jimmy Doolittle, *20th:* 1023
Dorgon, *17th:* 234
Jacques Doriot, *Notor:* 298
Fyodor Dostoevski, *19th:* 677
Helen Gahagan Douglas, *20th:* 1026
Stephen A. Douglas, *19th:* 681
William O. Douglas, *20th:* 1029
Frederick Douglass, *19th:* 684
John Dowland, *Ren:* 289
Diane Downs, *Notor:* 299
Sir Arthur Conan Doyle, *19th:* 688
Draco, *Anc:* 293
Sir Francis Drake, *Ren:* 291, *Notor:* 301
Michael Drayton, *17th:* 237
Theodore Dreiser, *20th:* 1032
Carl Theodor Dreyer, *20th:* 1037
John Dryden, *17th:* 239
Du Fu, *MA:* 322
José Napoleon Duarte, *20th:* 1040
Alexander Dubček, *20th:* 1042
Joachim du Bellay, *Ren:* 294
W. E. B. Du Bois, *20th:* 1046
Duccio di Buoninsegna, *MA:* 326
Marcel Duchamp, *20th:* 1051
David Duke, *Notor:* 303
James Buchanan Duke, *19th:* 692
John Foster Dulles, *20th:* 1054
Alexandre Dumas, *père, 19th:* 695
Jean-Henri Dunant, *19th:* 699
Paul Laurence Dunbar, *19th:* 701
Isadora Duncan, *20th:* 1058
Katherine Dunham, *20th:* 1061
John Duns Scotus, *MA:* 329
John Dunstable, *MA:* 333
Joseph-François Dupleix, *18th:* 311
Eleuthère Irénée du Pont, *19th:* 705
John E. du Pont, *Notor:* 305
Albrecht Dürer, *Ren:* 297
First Earl of Durham, *19th:* 708
Émile Durkheim, *20th:* 1065
Claude Duval, *Notor:* 306
François Duvalier, *20th:* 1069, *Notor:* 307
Jean-Claude Duvalier, *Notor:* 309
Antonín Dvořák, *19th:* 711
Sir Anthony van Dyck, *17th:* 244
Reginald Dyer, *Notor:* 311
Bob Dylan, *20th:* 1072
Felix Dzerzhinsky, *Notor:* 312

E

James Buchanan Eads, *19th:* 715
Thomas Eakins, *19th:* 717
Amelia Earhart, *20th:* 1075
Wyatt Earp, *19th:* 720, *Notor:* 315
George Eastman, *20th:* 1078
Abba Eban, *20th:* 1082
Bernard Ebbers, *Notor:* 317
Félix Éboué, *20th:* 1085
Sir John Carew Eccles, *20th:* 1089
Dietrich Eckart, *Notor:* 319
Hugo Eckener, *20th:* 1092
Mary Baker Eddy, *19th:* 723
Marian Wright Edelman, *20th:* 1096
Sir Anthony Eden, *20th:* 1099
Maria Edgeworth, *19th:* 728
Thomas Alva Edison, *19th:* 731
Edward I, *MA:* 343
Edward II, *MA:* 347
Edward III, *MA:* 350
Edward IV, *Ren:* 301
Edward VI, *Ren:* 303
Edward VII, *20th:* 1104
Edward the Confessor, *MA:* 337
Edward the Elder, *MA:* 340
Jonathan Edwards, *18th:* 314
António Egas Moniz, *20th:* 1107
Egbert, *MA:* 353
Christian von Ehrenfels, *20th:* 1110
Eugen Ehrlich, *20th:* 1113
Paul Ehrlich, *20th:* 1115
John D. Ehrlichman, *Notor:* 320
Adolf Eichmann, *Notor:* 322
Gustave Eiffel, *19th:* 734
Ira Einhorn, *Notor:* 324
Albert Einstein, *20th:* 1118
Willem Einthoven, *20th:* 1122
Dwight D. Eisenhower, *20th:* 1125
Sergei Eisenstein, *20th:* 1129
Elagabalus, *Notor:* 326

Juan Sebastián de Elcano, *Ren:* 307
Eleanor of Aquitaine, *MA:* 355
Sir Edward Elgar, *20th:* 1132
Mircea Eliade, *20th:* 1136
Elijah ben Solomon, *18th:* 318
Charles William Eliot, *19th:* 737
George Eliot, *19th:* 740
John Eliot, *17th:* 247
T. S. Eliot, *20th:* 1139
Elizabeth I, *Ren:* 310
Elizabeth II, *20th:* 1143
Elizabeth of Bohemia, *17th:* 250
Saint Elizabeth of Hungary, *MA:* 359
Elizabeth Petrovna, *18th:* 321
Elizabeth Stuart, *17th:* 253
Duke Ellington, *20th:* 1145
Havelock Ellis, *20th:* 1148
Ruth Ellis, *Notor:* 327
Fanny Elssler, *19th:* 743
Paul Éluard, *20th:* 1151
Ralph Waldo Emerson, *19th:* 745
Empedocles, *Anc:* 295
Shūsaku Endō, *20th:* 1155
Friedrich Engels, *19th:* 750
Enheduanna, *Anc:* 298
Quintus Ennius, *Anc:* 301
Enver Paşa, *20th:* 1157
Epaminondas, *Anc:* 303
Nora Ephron, *20th:* 1161
Epicurus, *Anc:* 307
Sir Jacob Epstein, *20th:* 1165
Olaudah Equiano, *18th:* 324
Erasistratus, *Anc:* 310
Desiderius Erasmus, *Ren:* 314
Eratosthenes of Cyrene, *Anc:* 314
Louise Erdrich, *20th:* 1168
Ludwig Erhard, *20th:* 1173
Werner Erhard, *Notor:* 329
Erik XIV, *Notor:* 331
Max Ernst, *20th:* 1176
First Baron Erskine, *18th:* 326
Matthias Erzberger, *20th:* 1180
M. C. Escher, *20th:* 1183
Pablo Escobar, *Notor:* 332
Ferdinand Walsin Esterhazy, *Notor:* 334
Billie Sol Estes, *Notor:* 336
Ethelred II, the Unready, *MA:* 362
Rudolf Christoph Eucken, *20th:* 1185
Euclid, *Anc:* 317
Eudoxus of Cnidus, *Anc:* 320
Eugene of Savoy, *18th:* 330
Leonhard Euler, *18th:* 333
Eupalinus of Megara, *Anc:* 323
Euripides, *Anc:* 326
Eusebius of Caesarea, *Anc:* 330
Sir Arthur Evans, *19th:* 753
Herbert Vere Evatt, *20th:* 1188
John Evelyn, *17th:* 256
Ada Everleigh, *Notor:* 338
Chris Evert, *20th:* 1191
Julius Evola, *Notor:* 339
Judith Campbell Exner, *Notor:* 340
Jan van and Hubert van Eyck, *MA:* 365
Ezana, *Anc:* 333
Ezekiel, *Anc:* 335
Ezra, *Anc:* 338

F

Fabius, *Anc:* 342
David and Johannes Fabricius, *17th:* 259
Hieronymus Fabricius ab Aquapendente, *Ren:* 319
Fahd, *20th:* 1195
Daniel Gabriel Fahrenheit, *18th:* 336
Louis Faidherbe, *19th:* 756
Third Baron Fairfax, *17th:* 261
Faisal, *20th:* 1198
Faisal I, *20th:* 1202
Fakhr al-Dīn al-Rāzī, *MA:* 369
Albert B. Fall, *Notor:* 342
Manuel de Falla, *20th:* 1206
Jerry Falwell, *20th:* 1209
Frantz Fanon, *20th:* 1212
Michael Faraday, *19th:* 759
Wallace Dodd Fard, *Notor:* 344
Alessandro Farnese, *Ren:* 321
Farouk I, *20th:* 1215
David G. Farragut, *19th:* 762
Louis Farrakhan, *20th:* 1217
Beatrix Jones Farrand, *20th:* 1219
Father Divine, *Notor:* 346
Orval E. Faubus, *Notor:* 348
William Faulkner, *20th:* 1222
Dame Millicent Garrett Fawcett, *19th:* 766
Guy Fawkes, *Ren:* 324, *Notor:* 350
Faxian, *Anc:* 345
Gustav Theodor Fechner, *19th:* 770
Dianne Feinstein, *20th:* 1227
Jacqueline Félicie, *MA:* 372
Federico Fellini, *20th:* 1231
John Felton, *Notor:* 352
François de Salignac de La Mothe-Fénelon, *17th:* 265
Ferdinand II (1452-1516; Spanish king), *Ren:* 328
Ferdinand II (1578-1637; Holy Roman Emperor), *17th:* 267
Adam Ferguson, *18th:* 338
Pierre de Fermat, *17th:* 271
Enrico Fermi, *20th:* 1235
Nicholas Ferrar, *17th:* 274
Enzo Ferrari, *20th:* 1239
Geraldine Ferraro, *20th:* 1242
Johann Gottlieb Fichte, *18th:* 342
Marsilio Ficino, *Ren:* 332
Marshall Field, *19th:* 773
Stephen J. Field, *19th:* 777
Henry Fielding, *18th:* 346
Giuseppe Fieschi, *Notor:* 353
Millard Fillmore, *19th:* 781
Firdusi, *MA:* 375
Johann Bernhard Fischer von Erlach, *18th:* 350
Albert Fish, *Notor:* 355
Saint John Fisher, *Ren:* 335
Jim Fisk, *Notor:* 357
John Fitch, *18th:* 353
Lord Edward Fitzgerald, *18th:* 356
Ella Fitzgerald, *20th:* 1246
F. Scott Fitzgerald, *20th:* 1249
Maria Anne Fitzherbert, *18th:* 358
Gustave Flaubert, *19th:* 785
Heidi Fleiss, *Notor:* 359
Sir Alexander Fleming, *20th:* 1254
Williamina Paton Stevens Fleming, *19th:* 788
John Fletcher, *Ren:* 92, *17th:* 277

André-Hercule de Fleury, *18th:* 361
Abraham Flexner, *20th:* 1256
Baron Florey, *20th:* 1259
Pretty Boy Floyd, *Notor:* 360
Robert Fludd, *17th:* 280
Michel Fokine, *20th:* 1263
Lydia Folger Fowler, *19th:* 812
Jim Folsom, *Notor:* 362
Henry Fonda, *20th:* 1265
Lavinia Fontana, *Ren:* 338
Dame Margot Fonteyn, *20th:* 1268
Betty Ford, *20th:* 1272
Gerald R. Ford, *20th:* 1274
Henry Ford, *20th:* 1279
Larry C. Ford, *Notor:* 363
C. S. Forester, *20th:* 1283
Francesco Forgione, *20th:* 1286
Edwin Forrest, *19th:* 790
Nathan Bedford Forrest, *Notor:* 365
E. M. Forster, *20th:* 1288
William Edward Forster, *19th:* 793
Elisabeth Förster-Nietzsche, *Notor:* 367
Abe Fortas, *Notor:* 369
Charlotte Forten, *19th:* 796
Sir John Fortescue, *Ren:* 340
Bob Fosse, *20th:* 1291
Abby Kelley Foster, *19th:* 799
Stephen Collins Foster, *19th:* 802
Charles Fourier, *19th:* 805
Joseph Fourier, *19th:* 809
Charles James Fox, *18th:* 363
George Fox, *17th:* 283
Girolamo Fracastoro, *Ren:* 343
Jean-Honoré Fragonard, *18th:* 367
Anatole France, *19th:* 815
Francis I, *Ren:* 346
Francis Ferdinand, *20th:* 1294
Francis Joseph I, *19th:* 818
Saint Francis of Assisi, *MA:* 378
César Franck, *19th:* 821
Francisco Franco, *20th:* 1297, *Notor:* 371
Anne Frank, *20th:* 1301
Antoinette Frank, *Notor:* 373
Hans Michael Frank, *Notor:* 374
Martin Frankel, *Notor:* 376
Helen Frankenthaler, *20th:* 1304
Felix Frankfurter, *20th:* 1308
Aretha Franklin, *20th:* 1312
Benjamin Franklin, *18th:* 370
Sir John Franklin, *19th:* 825
Rosalind Franklin, *20th:* 1316
Sir James George Frazer, *20th:* 1319
Fredegunde, *MA:* 381
Frederick I, *18th:* 375
Frederick I Barbarossa, *MA:* 384
Frederick II, *MA:* 389
Frederick III, *Ren:* 350
Frederick V, *17th:* 293
Frederick Henry, *17th:* 286
Frederick the Great, *18th:* 378
Frederick William I, *18th:* 381
Frederick William, the Great Elector, *17th:* 290
Gottlob Frege, *19th:* 828
John C. Frémont, *19th:* 831
Girolamo Frescobaldi, *17th:* 295
Sigmund Freud, *20th:* 1323
Eugène Freyssinet, *20th:* 1326
Betty Friedan, *20th:* 1329
Milton Friedman, *20th:* 1332
Karl von Frisch, *20th:* 1335
Max Frisch, *20th:* 1338
Leo Frobenius, *20th:* 1341
Sir Martin Frobisher, *Ren:* 352
Friedrich Froebel, *19th:* 835
Jean Froissart, *MA:* 392
Erich Fromm, *20th:* 1345
Lynette Fromme, *Notor:* 377
Robert Frost, *20th:* 1348
Elizabeth Fry, *19th:* 839
Roger Fry, *20th:* 1351
Klaus Fuchs, *Notor:* 379
Leonhard Fuchs, *Ren:* 356
Athol Fugard, *20th:* 1354
Alberto Fujimori, *20th:* 1359, *Notor:* 382
Fujiwara Michinaga, *MA:* 396
Saint Fulbert of Chartres, *MA:* 399
Loie Fuller, *20th:* 1361
Margaret Fuller, *19th:* 841
R. Buckminster Fuller, *20th:* 1364
Robert Fulton, *19th:* 845
Fulvia, *Notor:* 384
Fyodor I, *Notor:* 385

G

Clark Gable, *20th:* 1368
Andrea Gabrieli, *Ren:* 359
Giovanni Gabrieli, *Ren:* 362
John Wayne Gacy, *Notor:* 387
James Gadsden, *19th:* 849
Yuri Gagarin, *20th:* 1370
Matilda Joslyn Gage, *19th:* 852
Thomas Gage, *18th:* 384
Thomas Gainsborough, *18th:* 387
Carmine Galante, *Notor:* 389
John Kenneth Galbraith, *20th:* 1374
Galen, *Anc:* 348
Galerius, *Notor:* 390
Galileo, *17th:* 298
Mavis Gallant, *20th:* 1377
Albert Gallatin, *19th:* 854
Joe Gallo, *Notor:* 392
Évariste Galois, *19th:* 857
Leopoldo Galtieri, *Notor:* 394
Francis Galton, *19th:* 860
Luigi Galvani, *18th:* 391
José de Gálvez, *18th:* 394
Vasco da Gama, *Ren:* 365
Léon Gambetta, *19th:* 864
Carlo Gambino, *Notor:* 396
George Gamow, *20th:* 1379
Abel Gance, *20th:* 1382
Indira Gandhi, *20th:* 1385
Mahatma Gandhi, *20th:* 1388
Greta Garbo, *20th:* 1392
Federico García Lorca, *20th:* 1395
Gabriel García Márquez, *20th:* 1398
Stephen Gardiner, *Ren:* 368
Erle Stanley Gardner, *20th:* 1403
Isabella Stewart Gardner, *20th:* 1406
James A. Garfield, *19th:* 867
Giuseppe Garibaldi, *19th:* 871
Judy Garland, *20th:* 1409
Marc Garneau, *20th:* 1412
Tony Garnier, *20th:* 1414
David Garrick, *18th:* 397
William Lloyd Garrison, *19th:* 874
Marcus Garvey, *20th:* 1417
Giovanna Garzoni, *17th:* 302
Pierre Gassendi, *17th:* 304

Bill Gates, *20th:* 1421
Antonio Gaudí, *20th:* 1423
Paul Gauguin, *19th:* 879
Charles de Gaulle, *20th:* 1427
Carl Friedrich Gauss, *19th:* 883
Gilbert Gauthe, *Notor:* 397
Joseph-Louis Gay-Lussac, *19th:* 886
Norman Bel Geddes, *20th:* 1431
Lou Gehrig, *20th:* 1434
Frank Gehry, *20th:* 1438
Hans Geiger, *20th:* 1440
Rudolf Geiger, *20th:* 1443
Ed Gein, *Notor:* 399
Jean Genet, *20th:* 1445
Genghis Khan, *MA:* 402, *Notor:* 400
Vito Genovese, *Notor:* 402
Genseric, *Anc:* 351
Giovanni Gentile, *20th:* 1448
Artemisia Gentileschi, *17th:* 307
Alberico Gentili, *Ren:* 372
Geoffrey of Monmouth, *MA:* 405
George I, *18th:* 400
George II, *18th:* 403
George III, *18th:* 408
George IV, *19th:* 890
George V, *20th:* 1451
George VI, *20th:* 1454
Henry George, *19th:* 894
Balthasar Gérard, *Notor:* 404
Théodore Géricault, *19th:* 898
Sophie Germain, *19th:* 901
Geronimo, *19th:* 904
Elbridge Gerry, *18th:* 412
Gershom ben Judah, *MA:* 408
George Gershwin, *20th:* 1458
Ira Gershwin, *20th:* 1462
Arnold Gesell, *20th:* 1465
Conrad Gesner, *Ren:* 375
Sir John Paul Getty, *20th:* 1468
Maḥmūd Ghāzān, *MA:* 411
al-Ghazzālī, *MA:* 415
Lorenzo Ghiberti, *MA:* 418
Gia Long, *19th:* 907
Alberto Giacometti, *20th:* 1470
Sam Giancana, *Notor:* 405
Edward Gibbon, *18th:* 415
James Gibbons, *19th:* 910
Orlando Gibbons, *17th:* 309
Josiah Willard Gibbs, *19th:* 913
Althea Gibson, *20th:* 1474
André Gide, *20th:* 1477
Vincent Gigante, *Notor:* 407
Sir Humphrey Gilbert, *Ren:* 378
W. S. Gilbert, *19th:* 916
William Gilbert, *Ren:* 381
Mildred Gillars, *Notor:* 409
Dizzy Gillespie, *20th:* 1480
Charlotte Perkins Gilman, *20th:* 1484
Gary Gilmore, *Notor:* 411
Étienne Gilson, *20th:* 1488
Vincenzo Gioberti, *19th:* 921
Giorgione, *Ren:* 383
Giotto, *MA:* 421
Jean Giraudoux, *20th:* 1492
Lillian Gish, *20th:* 1496
Salvatore Giuliano, *Notor:* 413
William Ewart Gladstone, *19th:* 924
John Glenn, *20th:* 1499
Christoph Gluck, *18th:* 418
August von Gneisenau, *19th:* 928
Arthur de Gobineau, *Notor:* 415
Jean-Luc Godard, *20th:* 1502
Robert H. Goddard, *20th:* 1507
Kurt Gödel, *20th:* 1510
First Earl of Godolphin, *18th:* 421
Nathuram Vinayak Godse, *Notor:* 416
Boris Godunov, *Ren:* 387
William Godwin, *18th:* 424
Joseph Goebbels, *20th:* 1513, *Notor:* 418
Magda Goebbels, *Notor:* 421
George Washington Goethals, *20th:* 1517
Johann Wolfgang von Goethe, *18th:* 428
Bernhard Goetz, *Notor:* 423
Vincent van Gogh, *19th:* 932
Nikolai Gogol, *19th:* 937
Sir George Goldie, *19th:* 940
Emma Goldman, *20th:* 1519, *Notor:* 424
Oliver Goldsmith, *18th:* 432
Baruch Goldstein, *Notor:* 427
Samuel Goldwyn, *20th:* 1523
Samuel Gompers, *19th:* 943
Luis de Góngora y Argote, *17th:* 312
Benny Goodman, *20th:* 1527
Charles Goodyear, *19th:* 946
Mikhail Gorbachev, *20th:* 1530
Nadine Gordimer, *20th:* 1534
Charles George Gordon, *19th:* 949
Al Gore, *20th:* 1538
William Crawford Gorgas, *20th:* 1541
Hermann Göring, *20th:* 1545, *Notor:* 428
Maxim Gorky, *20th:* 1549
Gośāla Maskarīputra, *Anc:* 355
Gottfried von Strassburg, *MA:* 423
John Gotti, *Notor:* 431
Glenn Gould, *20th:* 1553
Jay Gould, *Notor:* 433
Stephen Jay Gould, *20th:* 1555
Charles Gounod, *19th:* 952
Marie le Jars de Gournay, *17th:* 314
Francisco de Goya, *18th:* 436
Gracchi, *Anc:* 357
William Gilbert Grace, *19th:* 955
Baltasar Gracián y Morales, *17th:* 316
Billy Graham, *20th:* 1557
Katharine Graham, *20th:* 1560
Martha Graham, *20th:* 1563
Antonio Gramsci, *20th:* 1566
Cary Grant, *20th:* 1570
Ulysses S. Grant, *19th:* 958
Günter Grass, *20th:* 1573
Henry Grattan, *18th:* 440
Sammy Gravano, *Notor:* 434
Asa Gray, *19th:* 963
El Greco, *Ren:* 390
Horace Greeley, *19th:* 966
Thomas Hill Green, *19th:* 971
Graham Greene, *20th:* 1577
Nathanael Greene, *18th:* 443
Alan Greenspan, *20th:* 1581
Francis Greenway, *19th:* 974
Gregory VII, *MA:* 433
Gregory IX, *MA:* 436
Gregory XIII, *Ren:* 393
James Gregory, *17th:* 319
Gregory of Nazianzus, *Anc:* 361

Gregory of Nyssa, *Anc:* 363
Gregory of Tours, *MA:* 426
Gregory the Great, *MA:* 430
Sir Richard Grenville, *Ren:* 396
Wayne Gretzky, *20th:* 1585
Charles Grey, *19th:* 977
Sir Edward Grey, *20th:* 1587
Sir George Grey, *19th:* 981
Lady Jane Grey, *Ren:* 399
Jean-Baptiste Vaquette de Gribeauval, *18th:* 447
Edvard Grieg, *19th:* 984
Arthur Griffith, *20th:* 1591
D. W. Griffith, *20th:* 1593
Francesco Maria Grimaldi, *17th:* 321
Sarah and Angelina Grimké, *19th:* 988
Jacob and Wilhelm Grimm, *19th:* 992
Hans Jakob Christoffel von Grimmelshausen, *17th:* 324
Edmund Grindal, *Ren:* 402
Juan Gris, *20th:* 1597
Andrei Gromyko, *20th:* 1600
Walter Gropius, *20th:* 1602
Hugo Grotius, *17th:* 326
Sir William Robert Grove, *19th:* 996
Matthias Grünewald, *Ren:* 405
Guacanagarí, *Ren:* 408
Guarino Guarini, *17th:* 330
Gudea, *Anc:* 366
Heinz Guderian, *20th:* 1606
Otto von Guericke, *17th:* 333
Che Guevara, *20th:* 1609, *Notor:* 436
Daniel Guggenheim, *20th:* 1613
Francesco Guicciardini, *Ren:* 410
Guido d'Arezzo, *MA:* 439
Charlotte Guillard, *Ren:* 413
Charles-Édouard Guillaume, *20th:* 1616
Charles Julius Guiteau, *Notor:* 439
Guo Moruo, *20th:* 1619
Gustav I Vasa, *Ren:* 415
Gustavus II Adolphus, *17th:* 336
Johann Gutenberg, *MA:* 441
Guy de Chauliac, *MA:* 445
Madame Guyon, *17th:* 339
Gwenllian verch Gruffydd, *MA:* 448
Nell Gwyn, *17th:* 342

H

H. D., *20th:* 1623
George Habash, *20th:* 1626
Fritz Haber, *20th:* 1628
Jürgen Habermas, *20th:* 1632
Sir Robert Abbott Hadfield, *19th:* 1000
Hadrian, *Anc:* 370
Ernst Haeckel, *19th:* 1002
Hafiz, *MA:* 451
H. Rider Haggard, *19th:* 1006
Otto Hahn, *20th:* 1635
Samuel Hahnemann, *19th:* 1009
Haile Selassie I, *20th:* 1639
al-Ḥākim, *Notor:* 441
Richard Hakluyt, *Ren:* 419
Hakuin, *18th:* 450
H. R. Haldeman, *Notor:* 442
George Ellery Hale, *20th:* 1643
Matthew Hale (1609-1676), *17th:* 345
Matthew F. Hale (b. 1971), *Notor:* 444
Sarah Josepha Hale, *19th:* 1012
al-Ḥallāj, *MA:* 454
Mary A. Hallaren, *20th:* 1645
Edmond Halley, *17th:* 348
Frans Hals, *17th:* 352
William F. Halsey, *20th:* 1647
Fannie Lou Hamer, *20th:* 1651
Hamilcar Barca, *Anc:* 373
Alexander Hamilton, *18th:* 452
Sir William Rowan Hamilton, *19th:* 1015
Dag Hammarskjöld, *20th:* 1653
Oscar Hammerstein II, *20th:* 1657
Hammurabi, *Anc:* 376
Knut Hamsun, *20th:* 1660
John Hancock, *18th:* 457
Learned Hand, *20th:* 1663
George Frideric Handel, *18th:* 462
W. C. Handy, *20th:* 1667
Hanfeizi, *Anc:* 379
Marcus A. Hanna, *19th:* 1018
Hannibal, *Anc:* 382
Hanno, *Anc:* 385
Lorraine Hansberry, *20th:* 1669
Robert Philip Hanssen, *Notor:* 445
Karl von Hardenberg, *19th:* 1021
Keir Hardie, *19th:* 1025
John Wesley Hardin, *Notor:* 447
Warren G. Harding, *20th:* 1674
Thomas Hardy, *19th:* 1028
James Hargreaves, *18th:* 466
Alfred and Harold Harmsworth, *20th:* 1678
Adolf von Harnack, *20th:* 1681
Harold II, *MA:* 457
William Rainey Harper, *19th:* 1031
William Averell Harriman, *20th:* 1684
Barbara Harris, *20th:* 1689
Jean Harris, *Notor:* 448
Joel Chandler Harris, *19th:* 1036
Benjamin Harrison, *19th:* 1040
Frederic Harrison, *19th:* 1044
William Henry Harrison, *19th:* 1048
Harṣa, *MA:* 460
Lorenz Hart, *20th:* 1691
Hartmann von Aue, *MA:* 463
Nicolai Hartmann, *20th:* 1696
Hārūn al-Rashīd, *MA:* 467
William Harvey, *17th:* 355
al-Ḥasan al-Baṣrī, *MA:* 471
Hassan II, *20th:* 1699
Warren Hastings, *18th:* 469
Ichirō Hatoyama, *20th:* 1701
Hatshepsut, *Anc:* 388
Mohammad Hatta, *20th:* 1704
Václav Havel, *20th:* 1707
Robert Hawke, *20th:* 1710
Stephen Hawking, *20th:* 1712
Nicholas Hawksmoor, *18th:* 472
Nathaniel Hawthorne, *19th:* 1051
John Hay, *19th:* 1054
Víctor Raúl Haya de la Torre, *20th:* 1716
Ferdinand Vandeveer Hayden, *19th:* 1058
Joseph Haydn, *18th:* 476
F. A. Hayek, *20th:* 1720
Helen Hayes, *20th:* 1723
Rutherford B. Hayes, *19th:* 1061

Le Ly Hayslip, *20th:* 1727
Bill Haywood, *Notor:* 450
Rita Hayworth, *20th:* 1730
Linda Burfield Hazzard, *Notor:* 453
Patty Hearst, *Notor:* 454
William Randolph Hearst, *20th:* 1734
Sir Edward Heath, *20th:* 1738
Georg Wilhelm Friedrich Hegel, *19th:* 1065
Martin Heidegger, *20th:* 1742
Piet Hein, *17th:* 359
Heinrich Heine, *19th:* 1069
Ernst Heinkel, *20th:* 1746
Werner Heisenberg, *20th:* 1749
Saint Helena, *Anc:* 391
Lillian Hellman, *20th:* 1752
Hermann von Helmholtz, *19th:* 1073
Jan Baptista van Helmont, *17th:* 361
Claude-Adrien Helvétius, *18th:* 479
Felicia Dorothea Hemans, *19th:* 1076
Catharina van Hemessen, *Ren:* 421
Ernest Hemingway, *20th:* 1755
Hengist, *Anc:* 394
Sonja Henie, *20th:* 1759
George Hennard, *Notor:* 456
Henrietta Maria, *17th:* 364
Henry I, *MA:* 481
Henry II (1133-1189; King of England), *MA:* 483
Henry II (1519-1559; King of France), *Ren:* 423
Henry II the Saint, *MA:* 486
Henry III (1207-1272; King of England), *MA:* 490
Henry III (1551-1589; King of France), *Ren:* 426
Henry IV (1050-1106; Holy Roman Emperor), *MA:* 497
Henry IV (1367-1413; King of England), *MA:* 493
Henry IV (1553-1610; King of France), *Ren:* 429
Henry IV of Castile, *Ren:* 432
Henry V, *MA:* 501
Henry VI, *Ren:* 434
Henry VII, *Ren:* 438
Henry VIII, *Ren:* 441
Joseph Henry, *19th:* 1078
O. Henry, *19th:* 1081
Patrick Henry, *18th:* 482
Henry the Lion, *MA:* 473
Prince Henry the Navigator, *MA:* 477
Hans Werner Henze, *20th:* 1762
Audrey Hepburn, *20th:* 1766
Katharine Hepburn, *20th:* 1769
Heraclitus of Ephesus, *Anc:* 397
Heraclius, *MA:* 505
George Herbert, *17th:* 366
Johann Gottfried Herder, *18th:* 486
Aileen Clarke Hernandez, *20th:* 1773
Hero of Alexandria, *Anc:* 401
Herod Antipas, *Notor:* 458
Herod the Great, *Anc:* 403, *Notor:* 459
Herodotus, *Anc:* 407
Herophilus, *Anc:* 410
Juan de Herrera, *Ren:* 445
Robert Herrick, *17th:* 368
Édouard Herriot, *20th:* 1777
Caroline Lucretia Herschel, *18th:* 489
William Herschel, *18th:* 492
Gustav Hertz, *20th:* 1780
Gerhard Herzberg, *20th:* 1783
Aleksandr Herzen, *19th:* 1085
Theodor Herzl, *19th:* 1088
Hesiod, *Anc:* 413
Harry Hammond Hess, *20th:* 1785
Rudolf Hess, *Notor:* 460
Hermann Hesse, *20th:* 1787
Johannes and Elisabetha Hevelius, *17th:* 371
Georg von Hevesy, *20th:* 1792
Reinhard Heydrich, *Notor:* 462
Thor Heyerdahl, *20th:* 1795
Thomas Heywood, *17th:* 373
Hiawatha, *Ren:* 448
Wild Bill Hickok, *19th:* 1091
Miguel Hidalgo y Costilla, *19th:* 1094
Thomas Wentworth Higginson, *19th:* 1097
David Hilbert, *20th:* 1800
Saint Hilda of Whitby, *MA:* 509
Johann Lucas von Hildebrandt, *18th:* 494
Hildegard von Bingen, *MA:* 512
Henry Hill, *Notor:* 465
James Jerome Hill, *19th:* 1100
Octavia Hill, *19th:* 1103
Susanna Mildred Hill, *Notor:* 466
Sir Edmund Hillary, *20th:* 1802
Marie Hilley, *Notor:* 467
Heinrich Himmler, *20th:* 1807, *Notor:* 468
John Hinckley, Jr., *Notor:* 470
Paul Hindemith, *20th:* 1811
Paul von Hindenburg, *20th:* 1814
Hipparchus, *Anc:* 417
Hippocrates, *Anc:* 420
Hippolytus of Rome, *Anc:* 423
Hirohito, *20th:* 1818, *Notor:* 473
Hiroshige, *19th:* 1107
Hishikawa Moronobu, *17th:* 375
Alger Hiss, *20th:* 1822, *Notor:* 475
Alfred Hitchcock, *20th:* 1825
Adolf Hitler, *20th:* 1829, *Notor:* 477
Ho Chi Minh, *20th:* 1834
Ho Xuan Huong, *19th:* 1110
Thomas Hobbes, *17th:* 378
Oveta Culp Hobby, *20th:* 1838
Leonard T. Hobhouse, *20th:* 1841
David Hockney, *20th:* 1845
Dorothy Crowfoot Hodgkin, *20th:* 1849
Jimmy Hoffa, *Notor:* 480
Abbie Hoffman, *Notor:* 483
William Hogarth, *18th:* 497
Hōjō Ujimasa, *Ren:* 451
Paul-Henri-Dietrich d'Holbach, *18th:* 501
Hans Holbein, the Younger, *Ren:* 453
Billie Holiday, *20th:* 1852
John Philip Holland, *19th:* 1113
Doc Holliday, *Notor:* 485
H. H. Holmes, *Notor:* 486
Oliver Wendell Holmes, *19th:* 1116

Oliver Wendell Holmes, Jr., *20th:* 1856
Friedrich von Holstein, *19th:* 1119
Homer, *Anc:* 427
Winslow Homer, *19th:* 1122
Karla Homolka, *Notor:* 488
Soichiro Honda, *20th:* 1859
Honda Toshiaki, *18th:* 504
Hong Xiuquan, *19th:* 1127
Robert Hooke, *17th:* 383
Richard Hooker, *Ren:* 457
Thomas Hooker, *17th:* 386
Herbert Hoover, *20th:* 1862
J. Edgar Hoover, *20th:* 1866, *Notor:* 489
Bob Hope, *20th:* 1870
Harry Hopkins, *20th:* 1872
Edward Hopper, *20th:* 1876
Grace Murray Hopper, *20th:* 1879
Horace, *Anc:* 430
Karen Horney, *20th:* 1883
Vladimir Horowitz, *20th:* 1886
Jeremiah Horrocks, *17th:* 388
Elmyr de Hory, *Notor:* 492
Hosokawa Gracia, *Ren:* 459
François Hotman, *Ren:* 461
Harry Houdini, *20th:* 1889
Sir Godfrey Newbold Hounsfield, *20th:* 1892
Félix Houphouët-Boigny, *20th:* 1895
Bernardo Alberto Houssay, *20th:* 1899
Sam Houston, *19th:* 1130
Catherine Howard, *Ren:* 466
Elias Howe, *19th:* 1133
Julia Ward Howe, *19th:* 1137
Richard Howe, *18th:* 506
Samuel Gridley Howe, *19th:* 1141
William Howe, *18th:* 510
Enver and Nexhmije Hoxha, *Notor:* 493
Sir Fred Hoyle, *20th:* 1902
Hrosvitha, *MA:* 516
Hu Yaobang, *20th:* 1905
Hua Guofeng, *20th:* 1907
Huáscar, *Ren:* 469
L. Ron Hubbard, *20th:* 1909, *Notor:* 495
Edwin Powell Hubble, *20th:* 1912
James Oliver Huberty, *Notor:* 497
Balthasar Hubmaier, *Ren:* 472
Henry Hudson, *17th:* 390
Dolores Huerta, *20th:* 1915
Margaret Lindsay Huggins, *19th:* 1144
Charles Evans Hughes, *20th:* 1920
Howard Hughes, *20th:* 1925
Langston Hughes, *20th:* 1928
William Morris Hughes, *20th:* 1931
Victor Hugo, *19th:* 1146
Cordell Hull, *20th:* 1934
Humāyūn, *Ren:* 475
Alexander von Humboldt, *19th:* 1151
David Hume, *18th:* 514
Engelbert Humperdinck, *19th:* 1154
Hubert H. Humphrey, *20th:* 1938
Laud Humphreys, *Notor:* 498
Hun Sen, *20th:* 1942
E. Howard Hunt, *Notor:* 499
William Holman Hunt, *19th:* 1157
János Hunyadi, *MA:* 519
Zora Neale Hurston, *20th:* 1944
Jan Hus, *MA:* 522
Hussein I, *20th:* 1950
Qusay Saddam Hussein, *Notor:* 501
Saddam Hussein, *20th:* 1947, *Notor:* 503
Uday Hussein, *Notor:* 505
Edmund Husserl, *20th:* 1955
Robert M. Hutchins, *20th:* 1958
Anne Hutchinson, *17th:* 394
Thomas Hutchinson, *18th:* 518
Aldous Huxley, *20th:* 1961
Thomas Henry Huxley, *19th:* 1161
Christiaan Huygens, *17th:* 397
Hyder Ali, *18th:* 522
Hypatia, *Anc:* 434

I

Pierre Le Moyne d'Iberville, *17th:* 401
Ibn al-ʿArabī, *MA:* 526
Ibn Baṭṭūṭah, *MA:* 529
Ibn Gabirol, *MA:* 532
Ibn Khaldūn, *MA:* 536
Ibrāhīm Lodī, *Ren:* 478
İbrahim Paşa, *Ren:* 480
Henrik Ibsen, *19th:* 1165
al-Idrīsī, *MA:* 539
Ignatius of Antioch, *Anc:* 437
Saint Ignatius of Loyola, *Ren:* 482
Ihara Saikaku, *17th:* 403
Ii Naosuke, *19th:* 1168
Hayato Ikeda, *20th:* 1965
Imhotep, *Anc:* 439
Jean-Auguste-Dominique Ingres, *19th:* 1171
Innocent III, *MA:* 541
Innocent IV, *MA:* 545
Innocent XI, *17th:* 405
Eugène Ionesco, *20th:* 1968
Megan Louise Ireland, *Notor:* 508
Saint Irenaeus, *Anc:* 442
Saint Irene, *MA:* 548
Irish Invincibles, *Notor:* 509
Clifford Irving, *Notor:* 510
David Irving, *Notor:* 512
Henry Irving, *19th:* 1175
Washington Irving, *19th:* 1180
Isabella I, *Ren:* 328
Isabella II, *19th:* 1183
Isabella d'Este, *Ren:* 485
Isabella of France, *MA:* 552
Isaiah, *Anc:* 446
Saint Isidore of Seville, *MA:* 555
İsmet Paşa, *20th:* 1971
Isocrates, *Anc:* 450
Itō Hirobumi, *19th:* 1185
Itzcóatl, *MA:* 558
Ivan V, *Notor:* 514
Ivan VI, *Notor:* 515
Ivan the Great, *Ren:* 487
Ivan the Terrible, *Ren:* 492, *Notor:* 517
Charles Ives, *20th:* 1974
Izumo no Okuni, *17th:* 408

J

Abū Mūsā Jābir ibn Ḥayyān, *MA:* 562
Jack the Ripper, *Notor:* 519
Andrew Jackson, *19th:* 1189
Helen Hunt Jackson, *19th:* 1193

Jesse Jackson, *20th:* 1978
Shoeless Joe Jackson, *Notor:* 521
Stonewall Jackson, *19th:* 1197
François Jacob, *20th:* 1982
Mary Putnam Jacobi, *19th:* 1200
Jacopo della Quercia, *MA:* 566
Jahāngīr, *17th:* 410
al-Jāḥiẓ, *MA:* 568
Roman Jakobson, *20th:* 1986
Jamāl al-Dīn al-Afghānī, *19th:* 1203
James I, *17th:* 413
James I the Conqueror, *MA:* 571
James II, *17th:* 416
James III, *Ren:* 496
James IV, *Ren:* 498
James V, *Ren:* 501
Frank James, *19th:* 1211
Henry James, *19th:* 1206
Jesse James, *19th:* 1211, *Notor:* 523
William James, *19th:* 1213
Anna Jameson, *19th:* 1217
Leoš Janáček, *20th:* 1989
Pierre Janet, *20th:* 1993
Cornelius Otto Jansen, *17th:* 419
Wojciech Jaruzelski, *Notor:* 525
Karl Jaspers, *20th:* 1996
Jean Jaurès, *19th:* 1220
John Jay, *18th:* 524
Thomas Jefferson, *18th:* 528
Lord Jeffrey, *19th:* 1223
Edward Jenner, *18th:* 532
Jeremiah, *Anc:* 453
Saint Jerome, *Anc:* 456
Jesus, *Anc:* 458
Sarah Orne Jewett, *19th:* 1226
Jezebel, *Notor:* 527
Jiang Qing, *Notor:* 528
Jiang Zemin, *20th:* 2000
Francisco Jiménez de Cisneros, *Ren:* 503
Jimmu Tennō, *Anc:* 462
Jing Ke, *Notor:* 530
Jingū, *Anc:* 465,
Mohammed Ali Jinnah, *20th:* 2002
Joachim of Fiore, *MA:* 575
Joan of Arc, *MA:* 578
Joan the Mad, *Notor:* 531
Steve Jobs, *20th:* 2006
Jōchō, *MA:* 581
Alfred Jodl, *Notor:* 533
Joseph-Jacques-Césaire Joffre, *20th:* 2009
Robert Joffrey, *20th:* 2012
Saint Isaac Jogues, *17th:* 423
Johanan ben Zakkai, *Anc:* 468
John II, *Ren:* 511
John III, *Ren:* 513
John III Sobieski, *17th:* 427
John IV, *17th:* 430
John XXIII, *20th:* 2017
Augustus John, *20th:* 2014
King John, *MA:* 584, *Notor:* 534
John of Austria, *17th:* 425
John of Damascus, *MA:* 587
John Parricida, *Notor:* 536
John Paul II, *20th:* 2020
Saint John of the Cross, *Ren:* 507
John the Apostle, *Anc:* 471
Saint John the Baptist, *Anc:* 474
Andrew Johnson, *19th:* 1229
Lady Bird Johnson, *20th:* 2025
Lyndon B. Johnson, *20th:* 2027
Samuel Johnson, *18th:* 535
Frédéric Joliot and Irène Joliot-Curie, *20th:* 2032
Louis Jolliet, *17th:* 433
Bobby Jones, *20th:* 2036
Inigo Jones, *17th:* 436
Jim Jones, *Notor:* 537
John Paul Jones, *18th:* 539
Margaret Jones, *Notor:* 540
Mother Jones, *20th:* 2039
Ben Jonson, *17th:* 439
Janis Joplin, *20th:* 2043
Scott Joplin, *19th:* 1235
Barbara Jordan, *20th:* 2046
Michael Jordan, *20th:* 2050
Christine Jorgensen, *20th:* 2053
Joseph II, *18th:* 544
Chief Joseph, *19th:* 1238
Joséphine, *19th:* 1241
Flavius Josephus, *Anc:* 477, *Notor:* 541
Josquin des Prez, *Ren:* 515
James Joyce, *20th:* 2055
William Joyce, *Notor:* 542
Juan Carlos I, *20th:* 2060
Benito Juárez, *19th:* 1245
Judah ha-Levi, *MA:* 591
Judas Iscariot, *Notor:* 544
Julia III, *Anc:* 489
Julia Domna, *Anc:* 480
Julia Mamaea, *Anc:* 483
Julia Soaemias, *Anc:* 486
Julian of Norwich, *MA:* 595
Julius II, *Ren:* 518
Carl Jung, *20th:* 2062
Justin II, *Notor:* 546
Justinian I, *MA:* 598
Juvenal, *Anc:* 493

K

Theodore Kaczynski, *Notor:* 547
Franz Kafka, *20th:* 2066
Lazar Kaganovich, *Notor:* 549
Meir Kahane, *Notor:* 551
Damia al-Kāhina, *MA:* 604
Frida Kahlo, *20th:* 2069
Kalicho, *Ren:* 522
Kālidāsa, *Anc:* 496
Kamehameha I, *19th:* 1249
Heike Kamerlingh Onnes, *20th:* 2072
Engelbert Kämpfer, *17th:* 445
Wassily Kandinsky, *20th:* 2074
Kang Youwei, *19th:* 1252
Kangxi, *17th:* 448
Kanishka, *Anc:* 499
Immanuel Kant, *18th:* 548
Pyotr Leonidovich Kapitsa, *20th:* 2077
Fanya Kaplan, *Notor:* 552
Merzifonlu Kara Mustafa Paşa, *17th:* 451
Radovan Karadžić, *Notor:* 554
Herbert von Karajan, *20th:* 2081
Karīm Khān Zand, *18th:* 552
Joseph ben Ephraim Karo, *Ren:* 524
Alvin Karpis, *Notor:* 556
Kâtib Çelebî, *17th:* 454
Angelica Kauffmann, *18th:* 554
Wenzel Anton von Kaunitz, *18th:* 557
Yasunari Kawabata, *20th:* 2084
Yoshiko Kawashima, *Notor:* 558

John Kay, *18th:* 559
Nikos Kazantzakis, *20th:* 2087
Edmund Kean, *19th:* 1254
Tom Keating, *Notor:* 559
Buster Keaton, *20th:* 2090
John Keats, *19th:* 1259
Helen Keller, *20th:* 2093
Gene Kelly, *20th:* 2096
Machine Gun Kelly, *Notor:* 561
Ned Kelly, *Notor:* 562
Baron Kelvin, *19th:* 1264
Fanny Kemble, *19th:* 1267
Margery Kempe, *MA:* 607
Kenau Hasselaer, *Ren:* 526
John F. Kennedy, *20th:* 2098
Robert F. Kennedy, *20th:* 2102
James Kent, *19th:* 1271
Jomo Kenyatta, *20th:* 2106
Johannes Kepler, *17th:* 457
Aleksandr Fyodorovich Kerensky, *20th:* 2110
Jack Kerouac, *20th:* 2114
Albert Kesselring, *20th:* 2117
Jack Ketch, *Notor:* 565
Tom Ketchum, *Notor:* 566
Jack Kevorkian, *Notor:* 567
Francis Scott Key, *19th:* 1274
John Maynard Keynes, *20th:* 2120
Khadīja, *MA:* 610
Khieu Samphan, *Notor:* 569
Bohdan Khmelnytsky, *17th:* 461
Ayatollah Khomeini, *20th:* 2123, *Notor:* 571
Khosrow I, *MA:* 613
Nikita S. Khrushchev, *20th:* 2128, *Notor:* 574
al-Khwārizmī, *MA:* 617
William Kidd, *17th:* 464, *Notor:* 576
Søren Kierkegaard, *19th:* 1278
Jean-Claude Killy, *20th:* 2132
Kim Dae Jung, *20th:* 2136
Kim Il Sung, *20th:* 2138, *Notor:* 578
Kim Jong Il, *20th:* 2141, *Notor:* 581
Sante Kimes, *Notor:* 584
Billie Jean King, *20th:* 2143
Martin Luther King, Jr., *20th:* 2147
Rodney King, *Notor:* 585
Stephen King, *20th:* 2151
William Lyon Mackenzie King, *20th:* 2155
Mary Kingsley, *19th:* 1281
Eusebio Francisco Kino, *17th:* 467
Alfred Kinsey, *20th:* 2159
Rudyard Kipling, *19th:* 1284
Ernst Ludwig Kirchner, *20th:* 2164
Jeane Kirkpatrick, *20th:* 2167
Henry Kissinger, *20th:* 2170
Lord Kitchener, *20th:* 2173
Paul Klee, *20th:* 2176
Heinrich von Kleist, *19th:* 1289
Gustav Klimt, *20th:* 2180
Friedrich Gottlieb Klopstock, *18th:* 562
John Knox, *Ren:* 528
Kōbō Daishi, *MA:* 620,
Robert Koch, *19th:* 1291
Helmut Kohl, *20th:* 2182
Kuniaki Koiso, *Notor:* 587
Kōken, *MA:* 623
Oskar Kokoschka, *20th:* 2185
Käthe Kollwitz, *20th:* 2189
Jan Komenský, *17th:* 469
David Koresh, *Notor:* 589
Sergei Korolev, *20th:* 2191
Tadeusz Tadeusz Kościuszko, *18th:* 564
Kösem Sultan, *17th:* 472
Sofya Kovalevskaya, *19th:* 1295
Ignacy Krasicki, *18th:* 567
Lee Krasner, *20th:* 2195
Reginald Kray, *Notor:* 591
Ronald Kray, *Notor:* 593
Sir Hans Adolf Krebs, *20th:* 2199
Krishnadevaraya, *Ren:* 532
Ray Kroc, *20th:* 2201
August Krogh, *20th:* 2204
Paul Kruger, *19th:* 1298
Alfred Krupp, *19th:* 1301
Kublai Khan, *MA:* 626
Elisabeth Kübler-Ross, *20th:* 2207
Richard Kuklinski, *Notor:* 595
Béla Kun, *Notor:* 596
František Kupka, *20th:* 2211
Igor Vasilyevich Kurchatov, *20th:* 2214
Akira Kurosawa, *20th:* 2217
Mikhail Illarionovich Kutuzov, *18th:* 569
Lady Alice Kyteler, *MA:* 629, *Notor:* 598

L

Rudolf Laban, *20th:* 2221
Jean de La Bruyère, *17th:* 475
Jacques Lacan, *20th:* 2224
Madame de La Fayette, *17th:* 477
Jean Laffite, *Notor:* 600
Robert M. La Follette, *20th:* 2227
Henri-Marie La Fontaine, *20th:* 2231
Jean de La Fontaine, *17th:* 480
Selma Lagerlöf, *20th:* 2234
Joseph-Louis Lagrange, *18th:* 573
Fiorello Henry La Guardia, *20th:* 2237
Leonard Lake, *Notor:* 602
Lalibela, *MA:* 632
John Lambert, *17th:* 483
Joseph Lancaster, *19th:* 1304
Frederick William Lanchester, *20th:* 2240
Lev Davidovich Landau, *20th:* 2244
Ann Landers, *20th:* 2247
Francesco Landini, *MA:* 635
Henri Désiré Landru, *Notor:* 603
Karl Landsteiner, *20th:* 2250
Fritz Lang, *20th:* 2253
K. D. Lang, *20th:* 2256
Dorothea Lange, *20th:* 2260
Helene Lange, *19th:* 1307
Susanne K. Langer, *20th:* 2263
Samuel Pierpont Langley, *19th:* 1309
Lillie Langtry, *19th:* 1312
Sir Edwin Ray Lankester, *19th:* 1315
Lord Lansdowne, *20th:* 2266
Meyer Lansky, *Notor:* 604
Aemilia Lanyer, *Ren:* 535
Laozi, *Anc:* 502
Pierre-Simon Laplace, *19th:* 1317

Sophie von La Roche, *18th:* 577
François de La Rochefoucauld, *17th:* 487
Lyndon H. LaRouche, Jr., *Notor:* 606
Sieur de La Salle, *17th:* 490
Bartolomé de Las Casas, *Ren:* 537
Harold J. Laski, *20th:* 2269
Ferdinand Lassalle, *19th:* 1321
Orlando di Lasso, *Ren:* 540
Saint László I, *MA:* 637
Julia C. Lathrop, *20th:* 2272
Hugh Latimer, *Ren:* 543
Georges de La Tour, *17th:* 493
Benjamin Henry Latrobe, *19th:* 1325
William Laud, *17th:* 495
Estée Lauder, *20th:* 2275
Max von Laue, *20th:* 2278
Sir Wilfrid Laurier, *20th:* 2281
François Laval, *17th:* 498
Pierre Laval, *20th:* 2285, *Notor:* 609
Marie Laveau, *Notor:* 610
Rod Laver, *20th:* 2288
Anton Szandor LaVey, *Notor:* 612
Antoine-Laurent Lavoisier, *18th:* 579
Bonar Law, *20th:* 2292
John Law, *Notor:* 614
Henry Lawes, *17th:* 502
D. H. Lawrence, *20th:* 2295
Ernest Orlando Lawrence, *20th:* 2300
John Laird Mair Lawrence, *19th:* 1328
Richard Lawrence, *Notor:* 615
T. E. Lawrence, *20th:* 2303
Thomas Lawrence, *18th:* 583
Halldór Laxness, *20th:* 2308
Kenneth Lay, *Notor:* 617
Emma Lazarus, *19th:* 1331
Le Thanh Tong, *Ren:* 546
L. S. B. Leakey, *20th:* 2310
Mary Leakey, *20th:* 2315
Timothy Leary, *Notor:* 619
Henrietta Swan Leavitt, *20th:* 2317
Nicolas Leblanc, *18th:* 587
Gustave Le Bon, *20th:* 2320
Charles Le Brun, *17th:* 504
Le Corbusier, *20th:* 2323
Ann Lee, *18th:* 591
Charles Lee, *Notor:* 621
Daulton Lee, *Notor:* 623
Robert E. Lee, *19th:* 1334
Lee Kuan Yew, *20th:* 2326
First Duke of Leeds, *17th:* 506
Nick Leeson, *Notor:* 624
Antoni van Leeuwenhoek, *17th:* 509
Jacques Lefèvre d'Étaples, *Ren:* 548
Eva Le Gallienne, *20th:* 2330
Miguel López de Legazpi, *Ren:* 550
Fernand Léger, *20th:* 2334
Gottfried Wilhelm Leibniz, *17th:* 513
Earl of Leicester, *Ren:* 553
Leif Eriksson, *MA:* 640
Jacob Leisler, *17th:* 518
Georges Lemaître, *20th:* 2337
Henri Lemoine, *Notor:* 627
Ninon de Lenclos, *17th:* 520
Vladimir Ilich Lenin, *20th:* 2341, *Notor:* 628
Charlotte Lennox, *18th:* 594
Étienne Lenoir, *19th:* 1338
André Le Nôtre, *17th:* 523
Leo IX, *MA:* 644
Leo X, *Ren:* 557, *Notor:* 630
Leo XIII, *19th:* 1342
Leo Africanus, *Ren:* 555
Leonardo da Vinci, *Ren:* 561
Leonardo of Pisa, *MA:* 648
Leonidas, *Anc:* 505
Anna Leonowens, *19th:* 1346
Leopold I, *17th:* 526
Leopold II, *19th:* 1349, *Notor:* 632
Nathan F. Leopold, Jr., *Notor:* 634
Jean-Marie Le Pen, *Notor:* 636
Marc Lépine, *Notor:* 638
Duke de Lerma, *17th:* 530
Mikhail Lermontov, *19th:* 1352
Alain-René Lesage, *18th:* 596
Pierre Lescot, *Ren:* 565
Ferdinand de Lesseps, *19th:* 1356
Gotthold Ephraim Lessing, *18th:* 598
Mary Kay Letourneau, *Notor:* 640
Louis Le Vau, *17th:* 532
René Lévesque, *20th:* 2345
Levi ben Gershom, *MA:* 650
Claude Lévi-Strauss, *20th:* 2347
Dennis Levine, *Notor:* 642
Levni, *18th:* 602
Bernard Lewis, *20th:* 2351
C. S. Lewis, *20th:* 2353
Jerry Lewis, *20th:* 2357
John L. Lewis, *20th:* 2360
Meriwether Lewis, *19th:* 1359
Sinclair Lewis, *20th:* 2363
Michel de L'Hospital, *Ren:* 568
Li Bo, *MA:* 653
Li Hongzhang, *19th:* 1363
Li Peng, *20th:* 2367
Li Qingzhao, *MA:* 656
Willard F. Libby, *20th:* 2371
Roy Lichtenstein, *20th:* 2373
G. Gordon Liddy, *Notor:* 643
Trygve Lie, *20th:* 2375
Justus von Liebig, *19th:* 1366
Wilhelm Liebknecht, *19th:* 1370
Serge Lifar, *20th:* 2378
John Lilburne, *17th:* 534
Liliuokalani, *19th:* 1373
Lin Biao, *20th:* 2381
Lin Zexu, *19th:* 1376
Maya Ying Lin, *20th:* 2385
Abraham Lincoln, *19th:* 1380
Mary Todd Lincoln, *19th:* 1385
Jenny Lind, *19th:* 1387
Anne Morrow Lindbergh, *20th:* 2389
Charles A. Lindbergh, *20th:* 2392
John Walker Lindh, *Notor:* 645
Carolus Linnaeus, *18th:* 604
Jacques Lipchitz, *20th:* 2397
Hans Lippershey, *17th:* 537
Walter Lippmann, *20th:* 2400
Antônio Francisco Lisboa, *18th:* 608
Joseph Lister, *19th:* 1390
Franz Liszt, *19th:* 1393
Little Turtle, *18th:* 610
Sir Thomas Littleton, *Ren:* 570
Maksim Maksimovich Litvinov, *20th:* 2404
Liu Yin, *17th:* 540

Liu Shaoqi, *20th:* 2408
Second Earl of Liverpool, *19th:* 1397
Livia Drusilla, *Anc:* 508
David Livingstone, *19th:* 1400
Livy, *Anc:* 511
David Lloyd George, *20th:* 2411
Sir Andrew Lloyd Webber, *20th:* 2414
Nikolay Ivanovich Lobachevsky, *19th:* 1403
Lobengula, *19th:* 1406
John Locke, *17th:* 542
Belva A. Lockwood, *19th:* 1409
Sir Joseph Norman Lockyer, *19th:* 1412
Henry Cabot Lodge, *20th:* 2417
Richard A. Loeb, *Notor:* 647
Mikhail Vasilyevich Lomonosov, *18th:* 613
Jack London, *20th:* 2420
Huey Long, *20th:* 2424, *Notor:* 649
Harry Longabaugh, *Notor:* 651
Henry Wadsworth Longfellow, *19th:* 1416
Bill Longley, *Notor:* 653
Duchesse de Longueville, *17th:* 548
Byron Looper, *Notor:* 654
Anita Loos, *20th:* 2428
Roderigo Lopez, *Notor:* 655
Hendrik Antoon Lorentz, *20th:* 2431
Konrad Lorenz, *20th:* 2434
Pietro and Ambrogio Lorenzetti, *MA:* 659
Louis IX, *MA:* 666
Louis XI, *Ren:* 574
Louis XII, *Ren:* 577
Louis XIII, *17th:* 551
Louis XIV, *17th:* 554
Louis XV, *18th:* 615
Louis XVI, *18th:* 618
Joe Louis, *20th:* 2437
Louis the German, *MA:* 662
Marquis de Louvois, *17th:* 558
Countess of Lovelace, *19th:* 1420
Richard Lovelace, *17th:* 562
Juliette Gordon Low, *20th:* 2441
Amy Lowell, *20th:* 2444
Richard Lower, *17th:* 564
Lu Xun, *20th:* 2447
Seventh Earl of Lucan, *Notor:* 657
George Lucas, *20th:* 2450
Tommy Lucchese, *Notor:* 658
Clare Boothe Luce, *20th:* 2453
Henry R. Luce, *20th:* 2456
Lucian, *Anc:* 513
Lucky Luciano, *Notor:* 660
Shannon W. Lucid, *20th:* 2460
Lucretia, *Anc:* 517
Lucretius, *Anc:* 520
Erich Ludendorff, *20th:* 2462
Roger Ludlow, *17th:* 567
Saint Ludmilla, *MA:* 670
Ludwig II, *Notor:* 662
Lord Lugard, *20th:* 2465
György Lukács, *20th:* 2468
Raymond Lull, *MA:* 673
Jean-Baptiste Lully, *17th:* 569
Auguste and Louis Lumière, *20th:* 2471
Patrice Lumumba, *20th:* 2476
Jeffrey Lundgren, *Notor:* 664
Isaac ben Solomon Luria, *Ren:* 579
Victor Lustig, *Notor:* 665
Martin Luther, *Ren:* 582
Albert Lutuli, *20th:* 2478
Rosa Luxemburg, *20th:* 2482
Sir Charles Lyell, *19th:* 1423
Mary Lyon, *19th:* 1428
Dame Enid Muriel Lyons, *20th:* 2486
Joseph Aloysius Lyons, *20th:* 2489
Trofim Lysenko, *Notor:* 667
Lysippus, *Anc:* 523

M

Ma Yuan, *MA:* 677
Douglas MacArthur, *20th:* 2492
John MacArthur, *19th:* 1431
Catherine Macaulay, *18th:* 621
Thomas Babington Macaulay, *19th:* 1433
Joseph McCarthy, *20th:* 2497, *Notor:* 669
Mary McCarthy, *20th:* 2501
Barbara McClintock, *20th:* 2504
James W. McCord, Jr., *Notor:* 671
Cyrus Hall McCormick, *19th:* 1438
Carson McCullers, *20th:* 2507
Flora MacDonald, *18th:* 623
Jeffrey MacDonald, *Notor:* 673
Sir John Alexander Macdonald, *19th:* 1441
Ramsay MacDonald, *20th:* 2510
Alexander McGillivray, *18th:* 626
William Holmes McGuffey, *19th:* 1445
Joaquim Maria Machado de Assis, *19th:* 1449
Guillaume de Machaut, *MA:* 679
Samora Machel, *20th:* 2515
Niccolò Machiavelli, *Ren:* 587
Sir Alexander Mackenzie (c. 1764-1820), *18th:* 629
Alexander Mackenzie (1822-1892), *19th:* 1452
William Lyon Mackenzie, *19th:* 1454
Sir Halford John Mackinder, *20th:* 2518
William McKinley, *19th:* 1460
Catharine A. MacKinnon, *20th:* 2522
Colin Maclaurin, *18th:* 632
Donald Duart Maclean, *Notor:* 674
John J. R. Macleod, *20th:* 2526
Marshall McLuhan, *20th:* 2529
Virginia McMartin, *Notor:* 676
Daniel and Alexander Macmillan, *19th:* 1464
Edwin Mattison McMillan, *20th:* 2532
Harold Macmillan, *20th:* 2536
Daniel M'Naghten, *Notor:* 677
Robert McNamara, *20th:* 2541
Aimee Semple McPherson, *Notor:* 679
William Charles Macready, *19th:* 1467
Timothy McVeigh, *Notor:* 681
Francisco Madero, *20th:* 2544
Dolley Madison, *19th:* 1470

James Madison, *18th:* 636
Gaius Maecenas, *Anc:* 527
Ferdinand Magellan, *Ren:* 591
Muḥammad ibn ʿAbd al-Karīm al-Maghīlī, *Ren:* 595
René Magritte, *20th:* 2547
Datuk Seri Mahathir bin Mohamad, *20th:* 2551
The Mahdi, *19th:* 1473
Naguib Mahfouz, *20th:* 2553
Gustav Mahler, *20th:* 2558
Horst Mahler, *Notor:* 684
Mahmud I, *18th:* 639
Maḥmūd of Ghazna, *MA:* 683
Norman Mailer, *20th:* 2563
Madame de Maintenon, *17th:* 572
Sieur de Maisonneuve, *17th:* 574
John Major, *20th:* 2567
Malcolm X, *20th:* 2570
Georgi M. Malenkov, *20th:* 2573
François de Malherbe, *17th:* 577
Mary Mallon, *Notor:* 685
Sir Thomas Malory, *Ren:* 598
Marcello Malpighi, *17th:* 579
André Malraux, *20th:* 2576
Thomas Robert Malthus, *19th:* 1475
Lee Boyd Malvo, *Notor:* 765
Man Ray, *20th:* 2580
Manasseh ben Israel, *17th:* 582
The Mancini Sisters, *17th:* 585
Nelson Mandela, *20th:* 2583
Winnie Mandela, *Notor:* 686
Frederika Mandelbaum, *Notor:* 688
Benoit B. Mandelbrot, *20th:* 2588
Édouard Manet, *19th:* 1479
Meri Te Tai Mangakahia, *19th:* 1483
Wilma Mankiller, *20th:* 2591
Mary de la Rivière Manley, *18th:* 641
Horace Mann, *19th:* 1486
Thomas Mann, *20th:* 2594
Carl Gustaf Mannerheim, *20th:* 2598
Henry Edward Manning, *19th:* 1489
Daniel Mannix, *19th:* 1492
François Mansart, *17th:* 587
Jules Hardouin-Mansart, *17th:* 590
First Earl of Mansfield, *18th:* 643
Charles Manson, *Notor:* 689
Andrea Mantegna, *Ren:* 601
Manuel I, *Ren:* 605
Aldus Manutius, *Ren:* 608
Alessandro Manzoni, *19th:* 1495
Mao Zedong, *20th:* 2601, *Notor:* 691
Salvatore Maranzano, *Notor:* 694
Jean-Paul Marat, *18th:* 648, *Notor:* 696
Franz Marc, *20th:* 2606
Gabriel Marcel, *20th:* 2609
Carlos Marcello, *Notor:* 698
Rocky Marciano, *20th:* 2612
Guglielmo Marconi, *20th:* 2615
Ferdinand Marcos, *20th:* 2619, *Notor:* 699
Imelda Marcos, *Notor:* 702
Marcus Aurelius, *Anc:* 530
Luca Marenzio, *Ren:* 610
Margaret of Austria, *Ren:* 612
Margaret of Denmark, Norway, and Sweden, *MA:* 689
Margaret of Parma, *Ren:* 615
Andreas Sigismund Marggraf, *18th:* 651
Marguerite de Navarre, *Ren:* 617
Maria Celeste, *17th:* 593
Maria Theresa, *18th:* 653
Marie-Antoinette, *18th:* 657, *Notor:* 704
Marie de France, *MA:* 693
Marie de l'Incarnation, *17th:* 595
Marie de Médicis, *17th:* 598
Marie-Thérèse, *17th:* 600
Doña Marina, *Ren:* 621
Jacques Maritain, *20th:* 2624
Gaius Marius, *Anc:* 533
Dame Alicia Markova, *20th:* 2627
First Duke of Marlborough, *18th:* 660
Christopher Marlowe, *Ren:* 623
Marozia, *Notor:* 706
Jacques Marquette, *17th:* 603
George C. Marshall, *20th:* 2629
John Marshall, *19th:* 1498
Thurgood Marshall, *20th:* 2633
José Martí, *19th:* 1503
Martial, *Anc:* 536
Agnes Martin, *20th:* 2636
Harriet Martineau, *19th:* 1505
Jean Martinet, *Notor:* 707
Simone Martini, *MA:* 696
Andrew Marvell, *17th:* 605
Karl Marx, *19th:* 1508
Mary (mother of Jesus), *Anc:* 539
Mary I, *Ren:* 639
Mary II, *17th:* 610
Mary of Burgundy, *Ren:* 631
Mary of Guise, *Ren:* 633
Mary of Hungary, *Ren:* 636
Mary of Modena, *17th:* 607
Mary, Queen of Scots, *Ren:* 627
Masaccio, *MA:* 699
Tomáš Masaryk, *20th:* 2639
Masinissa, *Anc:* 542
George Mason, *18th:* 664
Massasoit, *17th:* 612
Joe Masseria, *Notor:* 708
William Ferguson Massey, *20th:* 2643
Léonide Massine, *20th:* 2646
al-Masʿūdī, *MA:* 703
Mata Hari, *Notor:* 710
Cotton Mather, *18th:* 667
Increase Mather, *18th:* 671
Robert Jay Mathews, *Notor:* 712
Matilda of Canossa, *MA:* 705
Henri Matisse, *20th:* 2649
Matsuo Bashō, *17th:* 615
Konosuke Matsushita, *20th:* 2653
Matthias I Corvinus, *Ren:* 642
Clorinda Matto de Turner, *19th:* 1512
Guy de Maupassant, *19th:* 1515
François Mauriac, *20th:* 2657
Maurice of Nassau, *17th:* 618
Frederick Denison Maurice, *19th:* 1518
Matthew Fontaine Maury, *19th:* 1522
Mausolus, *Anc:* 545
Maximilian, *19th:* 1525
Maximilian I, *Ren:* 646
Maximilian II, *Ren:* 650
James Clerk Maxwell, *19th:* 1528

Vladimir Mayakovsky, *20th:* 2659
Louis B. Mayer, *20th:* 2662
William J. and Charles H. Mayo, *20th:* 2665
Jules Mazarin, *17th:* 620
Ivan Stepanovich Mazepa, *17th:* 624
Giuseppe Mazzini, *19th:* 1531
Margaret Mead, *20th:* 2668
Gaston Bullock Means, *Notor:* 713
George Meany, *20th:* 2672
Mechthild von Magdeburg, *MA:* 708
Cosimo I de' Medici, *Ren:* 653
Cosimo II de' Medici, *17th:* 626
Lorenzo de' Medici, *Ren:* 655
Mehmed II, *MA:* 711, *Ren:* 659
Mehmed III, *Ren:* 661
Ulrike Meinhof, *Notor:* 715
Golda Meir, *20th:* 2674
Lise Meitner, *20th:* 2679
Philipp Melanchthon, *Ren:* 664
Second Viscount Melbourne, *19th:* 1534
Melisende, *MA:* 715
Andrew Mellon, *20th:* 2683
Herman Melville, *19th:* 1537
Menander (c. 210-c. 135 B.C.E.; Greco-Bactrian king), *Anc:* 550
Menander (c. 642-c. 291 B.C.E.; dramatist), *Anc:* 547
Rigoberta Menchú, *20th:* 2686
Mencius, *Anc:* 552
H. L. Mencken, *20th:* 2688
Gregor Mendel, *19th:* 1541
Dmitry Ivanovich Mendeleyev, *19th:* 1544
Erich Mendelsohn, *20th:* 2692
Felix Mendelssohn, *19th:* 1549
Moses Mendelssohn, *18th:* 675
Dorothy Reed Mendenhall, *20th:* 2695
Pierre Mendès-France, *20th:* 2698
Bernardino de Mendoza, *Ren:* 668
Ana de Mendoza y de la Cerda, *Ren:* 670
Menelik II, *19th:* 1552
Pedro Menéndez de Avilés, *Ren:* 672
Menes, *Anc:* 556
Josef Mengele, *Notor:* 717
Mengistu Haile Mariam, *20th:* 2701, *Notor:* 719
Menkaure, *Anc:* 558
Adah Isaacs Menken, *19th:* 1555
Menno Simons, *Ren:* 675
Gian Carlo Menotti, *20th:* 2703
Mentewab, *18th:* 677
Sir Robert Gordon Menzies, *20th:* 2707
Ramón Mercader, *Notor:* 721
Gerardus Mercator, *Ren:* 678
Ottmar Mergenthaler, *19th:* 1558
Maurice Merleau-Ponty, *20th:* 2710
Marin Mersenne, *17th:* 628
Thomas Merton, *20th:* 2713
Jacques Mesrine, *Notor:* 723
Valeria Messallina, *Anc:* 561
Olivier Messiaen, *20th:* 2715
Reinhold Messner, *20th:* 2718
Metacom, *17th:* 633
Ioannis Metaxas, *Notor:* 724
Saint Methodius, *MA:* 294
Metternich, *19th:* 1561
Tom Metzger, *Notor:* 726
Vsevolod Yemilyevich Meyerhold, *20th:* 2722
Mi Fei, *MA:* 718
Michelangelo, *Ren:* 682
Jules Michelet, *19th:* 1564
André and Édouard Michelin, *20th:* 2725
Albert A. Michelson, *19th:* 1567
James A. Michener, *20th:* 2728
Thomas Middleton, *17th:* 636
Ludwig Mies van der Rohe, *20th:* 2731
Mijailo Mijailovic, *Notor:* 727
Stanley Milgram, *Notor:* 729
Darius Milhaud, *20th:* 2735
Michael Milken, *Notor:* 731
James Mill, *19th:* 1571
John Stuart Mill, *19th:* 1574
Edna St. Vincent Millay, *20th:* 2738
Arthur Miller, *20th:* 2742
Kate Millett, *20th:* 2746
Robert Andrews Millikan, *20th:* 2750
Wilbur Mills, *Notor:* 733
A. A. Milne, *20th:* 2753
Slobodan Milošević, *20th:* 2756, *Notor:* 735
Miltiades the Younger, *Anc:* 563
John Milton, *17th:* 639
Minamoto Yoritomo, *MA:* 721
Peter Minuit, *17th:* 643
Comte de Mirabeau, *18th:* 679
Joan Miró, *20th:* 2759
Yukio Mishima, *20th:* 2763
John Mitchell, *Notor:* 737
Maria Mitchell, *19th:* 1580
William Mitchell, *20th:* 2765
Mithradates VI Eupator, *Anc:* 567
François Mitterrand, *20th:* 2769
Ratko Mladić, *Notor:* 739
Mobutu Sese Seko, *20th:* 2773, *Notor:* 740
Amedeo Modigliani, *20th:* 2776
Mohammad Reza Shah Pahlavi, *20th:* 2779, *Notor:* 742
Mohammed I Askia, *Ren:* 686
Khalid Shaikh Mohammed, *Notor:* 744
Molière, *17th:* 646
Molly Maguires, *Notor:* 745
Vyacheslav Mikhailovich Molotov, *20th:* 2783, *Notor:* 746
Theodor Mommsen, *19th:* 1582
George Monck, *17th:* 650
Piet Mondrian, *20th:* 2786
Claude Monet, *20th:* 2790
Gaspard Monge, *18th:* 682
Duke of Monmouth, *17th:* 653
Jean Monnet, *20th:* 2793
James Monroe, *19th:* 1586
Marilyn Monroe, *20th:* 2797
Mary Wortley Montagu, *18th:* 687
Michel Eyquem de Montaigne, *Ren:* 689
Eugenio Montale, *20th:* 2801
Marquis de Montalembert, *18th:* 690
Louis-Joseph de Montcalm, *18th:* 692
Montesquieu, *18th:* 695
Maria Montessori, *20th:* 2804

Claudio Monteverdi, *17th:* 656
Lola Montez, *19th:* 1590
Montezuma II, *Ren:* 693
Simon de Montfort, *MA:* 725
Jacques-Étienne and Joseph-Michel Montgolfier, *18th:* 698
Bernard Law Montgomery, *20th:* 2808
Duchesse de Montpensier, *17th:* 660
Montuhotep II, *Anc:* 570
Susanna Moodie, *19th:* 1593
Dwight L. Moody, *19th:* 1596
Sun Myung Moon, *20th:* 2811, *Notor:* 749
G. E. Moore, *20th:* 2814
Henry Moore, *20th:* 2818
Marianne Moore, *20th:* 2821
Bugs Moran, *Notor:* 751
Hannah More, *18th:* 702
Sir Thomas More, *Ren:* 697
Sir Henry Morgan, *Notor:* 753
J. P. Morgan, *19th:* 1599
Lewis Henry Morgan, *19th:* 1603
Thomas Hunt Morgan, *20th:* 2825
Hans Joachim Morgenthau, *20th:* 2828
Akio Morita, *20th:* 2831
Thomas Morley, *Ren:* 701
Philippe de Mornay, *Ren:* 703
Boris Ivanovich Morozov, *17th:* 663
Gouverneur Morris, *18th:* 705
Robert Morris, *18th:* 707
William Morris, *19th:* 1606
Toni Morrison, *20th:* 2834
Samuel F. B. Morse, *19th:* 1610
William Thomas Green Morton, *19th:* 1613
Gaetano Mosca, *20th:* 2838
Moses, *Anc:* 572
Grandma Moses, *20th:* 2841
Moses Maimonides, *MA:* 686
Moses de León, *MA:* 730
Sir Oswald Mosley, *Notor:* 755
Mohammad Mossadegh, *20th:* 2844
Robert Motherwell, *20th:* 2847
John R. Mott, *20th:* 2849
Lucretia Mott, *19th:* 1616
Mou Qizhong, *Notor:* 757
Louis Mountbatten, *20th:* 2853
Zacarias Moussaoui, *Notor:* 758
Wolfgang Amadeus Mozart, *18th:* 711
Mozi, *Anc:* 576
Robert Mugabe, *20th:* 2858, *Notor:* 761
Lodowick Muggleton, *17th:* 665
Muḥammad, *MA:* 733
Elijah Muhammad, *Notor:* 763
John Allen Muhammad, *Notor:* 765
Muḥammad ʿAlī Pasha, *19th:* 1620
John Muir, *19th:* 1623
Hermann Joseph Muller, *20th:* 2861
Kary B. Mullis, *20th:* 2864
Brian Mulroney, *20th:* 2866
Edvard Munch, *20th:* 2870
Alice Munro, *20th:* 2873
Murad IV, *17th:* 668
Murasaki Shikibu, *MA:* 738
Rupert Murdoch, *20th:* 2876
William Murdock, *18th:* 715
Joaquín Murieta, *Notor:* 767
Bartolomé Esteban Murillo, *17th:* 670
Johannes de Muris, *MA:* 741
Edward R. Murrow, *20th:* 2879
Mansa Mūsā, *MA:* 744
Yoweri Kaguta Museveni, *20th:* 2883
Benito Mussolini, *20th:* 2885, *Notor:* 769
Modest Mussorgsky, *19th:* 1626
Mustafa I, *17th:* 673
Mustafa III, *18th:* 719
Mutsuhito, *19th:* 1631
Gunnar Myrdal, *20th:* 2890

N

Vladimir Nabokov, *20th:* 2894
Nabu-rimanni, *Anc:* 579
Ralph Nader, *20th:* 2897
Nādir Shāh, *18th:* 722, *Notor:* 772
Naḥmanides, *MA:* 747
Sarojini Naidu, *20th:* 2900
Sir V. S. Naipaul, *20th:* 2903
James Naismith, *20th:* 2905
Nānak, *Ren:* 707
Nanny, *18th:* 724
Fridtjof Nansen, *20th:* 2907
Dadabhai Naoroji, *19th:* 1634
John Napier, *Ren:* 710
Napoleon I, *19th:* 1636
Napoleon III, *19th:* 1639
John Nash, *19th:* 1642
Paul Nash, *20th:* 2910
Thomas Nashe, *Ren:* 714
James Nasmyth, *19th:* 1646
Gamal Abdel Nasser, *20th:* 2914
Thomas Nast, *19th:* 1649
Carry Nation, *19th:* 1652
Giulio Natta, *20th:* 2919
Martina Navratilova, *20th:* 2922
Ne Win, *Notor:* 773
Nebuchadnezzar II, *Anc:* 582
Alexander Neckam, *MA:* 750
Jacques Necker, *18th:* 726
Louis-Eugène-Félix Néel, *20th:* 2926
Nefertari, *Anc:* 585
Nefertiti, *Anc:* 587
Jawaharlal Nehru, *20th:* 2929
Baby Face Nelson, *Notor:* 774
Leslie Nelson, *Notor:* 776
Lord Nelson, *19th:* 1656
Saint Philip Neri, *Ren:* 717
Walther Hermann Nernst, *20th:* 2934
Nero, *Anc:* 591, *Notor:* 777
Pablo Neruda, *20th:* 2937
Pier Luigi Nervi, *20th:* 2940
Nest verch Rhys ap Tewdwr, *MA:* 753
Bonnie Nettles, *Notor:* 779
John von Neumann, *20th:* 2943
Louise Nevelson, *20th:* 2947
John Newbery, *18th:* 730
Duchess of Newcastle, *17th:* 676
Simon Newcomb, *19th:* 1660
Thomas Newcomen, *18th:* 733
John Henry Newman, *19th:* 1663
Florence Newton, *Notor:* 781
Huey Newton, *Notor:* 782
Sir Isaac Newton, *17th:* 679
Michel Ney, *19th:* 1667

Nezahualcóyotl, *Ren:* 720
Charles Ng, *Notor:* 784
Ngo Dinh Diem, *20th:* 2951
Ngo Quyen, *MA:* 756
Nguyen Hue, *18th:* 736
Nguyen Van Thieu, *20th:* 2954
Madame Nhu, *Notor:* 786
Nichiren, *MA:* 758
Nicholas I, *19th:* 1670, *Notor:* 788
Nicholas V, *MA:* 768
Nicholas of Autrecourt, *MA:* 761
Nicholas of Cusa, *Ren:* 724
Nicholas the Great, *MA:* 764
Terry Nichols, *Notor:* 790
Ben Nicholson, *20th:* 2956
Jack Nicklaus, *20th:* 2959
Barthold Georg Niebuhr, *19th:* 1673
Reinhold Niebuhr, *20th:* 2962
Carl Nielsen, *20th:* 2965
Oscar Niemeyer, *20th:* 2967
Martin Niemöller, *20th:* 2971
Nicéphore Niépce, *19th:* 1676
Friedrich Nietzsche, *19th:* 1680
Eligiusz Niewiadomski, *Notor:* 792
Florence Nightingale, *19th:* 1684
Vaslav Nijinsky, *20th:* 2974
Nijō, *MA:* 771
Nikon, *17th:* 683
Chester W. Nimitz, *20th:* 2977
Kitarō Nishida, *20th:* 2981
Richard M. Nixon, *20th:* 2984, *Notor:* 793
Saparmurat Niyazov, *Notor:* 796
Niẓām al-Mulk, *MA:* 774
Njinga, *17th:* 687
Kwame Nkrumah, *20th:* 2988
Alfred Nobel, *19th:* 1689
Max Nordau, *20th:* 2992
Manuel Noriega, *Notor:* 797
Jessye Norman, *20th:* 2995
Lord North, *18th:* 738
Nostradamus, *Ren:* 728, *Notor:* 799
Robert Nozick, *20th:* 2999
Rudolf Nureyev, *20th:* 3001
Rebecca Nurse, *17th:* 689
Julius Nyerere, *20th:* 3004

O

Annie Oakley, *19th:* 1692
Titus Oates, *17th:* 692, *Notor:* 802
Dion O'Banion, *Notor:* 803
Hermann Oberth, *20th:* 3008
Milton Obote, *20th:* 3011
Álvaro Obregón, *20th:* 3013
William of Ockham, *MA:* 778
Daniel O'Connell, *19th:* 1695
Flannery O'Connor, *20th:* 3017
Sandra Day O'Connor, *20th:* 3020
Thomas Power O'Connor, *20th:* 3024
Oda Nobunaga, *Ren:* 732
Odoacer, *MA:* 782
Jacques Offenbach, *19th:* 1699
Ogata Kōrin, *17th:* 695
Ōgimachi, *Ren:* 735
James Edward Oglethorpe, *18th:* 742
Ogyū Sorai, *18th:* 746
Sadaharu Oh, *20th:* 3027
Bernardo O'Higgins, *19th:* 1703
Oichi, *Ren:* 737
Ōjin Tennō, *Anc:* 594
Georgia O'Keeffe, *20th:* 3031
Seán T. O'Kelly, *20th:* 3034
Saint Olaf, *MA:* 785
Olaf I, *MA:* 789
Johan van Oldenbarnevelt, *Ren:* 740
Claes Oldenburg, *20th:* 3037
Anne Oldfield, *18th:* 749
Saint Olga, *MA:* 792
Count-Duke of Olivares, *17th:* 697
Sir Laurence Olivier, *20th:* 3039
Frederick Law Olmsted, *19th:* 1706
Olympias, *Anc:* 597
Grace O'Malley, *Ren:* 743, *Notor:* 805
Omar Khayyám, *MA:* 795
Rory O'More, *17th:* 699
Jacqueline Kennedy Onassis, *20th:* 3045
Michael Ondaatje, *20th:* 3048
Eugene O'Neill, *20th:* 3051
Tip O'Neill, *20th:* 3055
Jan Hendrik Oort, *20th:* 3059
Aleksandr Ivanovich Oparin, *20th:* 3062
Opechancanough, *17th:* 702
J. Robert Oppenheimer, *20th:* 3065
Andrea Orcagna, *MA:* 798
Origen, *Anc:* 599
Duc d'Orléans, *18th:* 751
Aleksey Grigoryevich Orlov, *18th:* 755
Grigori Grigoryevich Orlov, *18th:* 757
José Clemente Orozco, *20th:* 3068
Daniel Ortega, *20th:* 3072
Katherine Davalos Ortega, *20th:* 3074
José Ortega y Gasset, *20th:* 3077
Arthur Orton, *Notor:* 806
George Orwell, *20th:* 3080
Thomas Mott Osborne, *20th:* 3085
Osceola, *19th:* 1709
Sir William Osler, *19th:* 1711
Osman I, *MA:* 800
Wilhelm Ostwald, *20th:* 3088
Lee Harvey Oswald, *Notor:* 807
Otto I, *MA:* 805
Nikolaus August Otto, *19th:* 1714
J. J. P. Oud, *20th:* 3092
Sir James Outram, *19th:* 1717
Ouyang Xiu, *MA:* 808
Ovid, *Anc:* 602
Robert Owen, *19th:* 1720
Jesse Owens, *20th:* 3095
Axel Oxenstierna, *17th:* 704

P

Pachacuti, *Ren:* 746
Johann Pachelbel, *17th:* 708
Niccolò Paganini, *19th:* 1724
Thomas Paine, *18th:* 759
Sophia Palaeologus, *Ren:* 749
Giovanni Pierluigi da Palestrina, *Ren:* 751
William Paley, *18th:* 763
Eusapia Palladino, *Notor:* 810
Andrea Palladio, *Ren:* 753
Alice Freeman Palmer, *19th:* 1727
Lord Palmerston, *19th:* 1731
Vijaya Lakshmi Pandit, *20th:* 3099

Emmeline Pankhurst, *20th:* 3102
Andreas Papandreou, *20th:* 3106
Franz von Papen, *20th:* 3109
Denis Papin, *17th:* 710
Pappus, *Anc:* 606
Paracelsus, *Ren:* 757
Mungo Park, *18th:* 765
Bonnie Parker, *Notor:* 811
Charlie Parker, *20th:* 3112
Dorothy Parker, *20th:* 3116
Matthew Parker, *Ren:* 761
Theodore Parker, *19th:* 1735
Sir Henry Parkes, *19th:* 1739
Francis Parkman, *19th:* 1742
Rosa Parks, *20th:* 3119
Parmenides, *Anc:* 608
Charles Stewart Parnell, *19th:* 1747
Catherine Parr, *Ren:* 764
Vernon Louis Parrington, *20th:* 3124
Dolly Parton, *20th:* 3127
Blaise Pascal, *17th:* 713
Boris Pasternak, *20th:* 3131
Louis Pasteur, *19th:* 1751
Vallabhbhai Jhaverbhai Patel, *20th:* 3135
Walter Pater, *19th:* 1755
A. B. Paterson, *19th:* 1758
William Paterson, *17th:* 716
Alan Paton, *20th:* 3138
Saint Patrick, *MA:* 811
George S. Patton, *20th:* 3142
Paul III, *Ren:* 767
Paul V, *17th:* 719
Paul VI, *20th:* 3148
Alice Paul, *20th:* 3145
Saint Paul, *Anc:* 611
Paul of Aegina, *MA:* 814
Wolfgang Pauli, *20th:* 3152
Linus Pauling, *20th:* 3155
Pausanias the Traveler, *Anc:* 618
Pausanias of Sparta, *Anc:* 615
Luciano Pavarotti, *20th:* 3159
Ante Pavelić, *Notor:* 813
Ivan Petrovich Pavlov, *20th:* 3162
Anna Pavlova, *20th:* 3166
Octavio Paz, *20th:* 3169
Víctor Paz Estenssoro, *20th:* 3172
Elizabeth Palmer Peabody, *19th:* 1761
Charles Peace, *Notor:* 815
Charles Willson Peale, *18th:* 768
Lester B. Pearson, *20th:* 3174
Robert Edwin Peary, *20th:* 3177
John Pecham, *MA:* 817
Gregory Peck, *20th:* 3181
Pedro I, *19th:* 1763
Pedro II, *19th:* 1766
Sir Robert Peel, *19th:* 1768
I. M. Pei, *20th:* 3183
Charles Sanders Peirce, *19th:* 1772
Nicolas-Claude Fabri de Peiresc, *17th:* 722
Pelé, *20th:* 3187
Henry Pelham, *18th:* 771
Pemisapan, *Ren:* 771
Thomas Joseph Pendergast, *Notor:* 817
Peng Dehuai, *20th:* 3191
William Penn, *17th:* 724
Dolly Pentreath, *Notor:* 818
Samuel Pepys, *17th:* 728
Leander Perez, *Notor:* 819
Javier Pérez de Cuéllar, *20th:* 3194
Pericles, *Anc:* 620
Frances Perkins, *20th:* 3198
Eva Perón, *20th:* 3201, *Notor:* 821
Juan Perón, *20th:* 3205, *Notor:* 823
H. Ross Perot, *20th:* 3208
Pérotin, *MA:* 824
Charles Perrault, *17th:* 731
Auguste Perret, *20th:* 3213
Fred Perry, *20th:* 3216
Matthew C. Perry, *19th:* 1776
Oliver Hazard Perry, *19th:* 1779
John J. Pershing, *20th:* 3219
Johann Heinrich Pestalozzi, *19th:* 1782
Philippe Pétain, *20th:* 3222, *Notor:* 825
Peter III, *18th:* 778
Saint Peter, *Anc:* 624
Peter the Cruel, *Notor:* 827
Peter the Great, *18th:* 774
Oscar Peterson, *20th:* 3226
Scott Peterson, *Notor:* 828
Marcel Petiot, *Notor:* 831
Symon Petlyura, *Notor:* 832
Petrarch, *MA:* 827
Petrus Peregrinus de Maricourt, *MA:* 820
Sir William Petty, *17th:* 733
Georg von Peuerbach, *Ren:* 773
Phaedrus, *Anc:* 628
Phalaris, *Notor:* 834
Pheidippides, *Anc:* 630
Phidias, *Anc:* 633
Kim Philby, *Notor:* 836
Philip II (1165-1223; King of France), *MA:* 835
Philip II (1527-1598; King of Spain), *Ren:* 778
Philip II of Macedonia, *Anc:* 637
Philip III, *17th:* 736
Philip IV, *17th:* 738
Philip IV the Fair, *MA:* 839
Philip V, *18th:* 781
Philip the Good, *MA:* 832
Philip the Magnanimous, *Ren:* 775
Philippa of Hainaut, *MA:* 842
Katherine Philips, *17th:* 741
Arthur Phillip, *18th:* 783
Wendell Phillips, *19th:* 1785
Philo of Alexandria, *Anc:* 640
Edith Piaf, *20th:* 3228
Jean Piaget, *20th:* 3231
Émile Picard, *20th:* 3234
Pablo Picasso, *20th:* 3237
Auguste and Jean-Felix Piccard, *20th:* 3240
Mary Pickford, *20th:* 3244
Giovanni Pico della Mirandola, *Ren:* 782
Susan La Flesche Picotte, *20th:* 3247
Franklin Pierce, *19th:* 1789
William Luther Pierce III, *Notor:* 838
Piero della Francesca, *Ren:* 785
Zebulon Pike, *19th:* 1793
Pontius Pilate, *Anc:* 643, *Notor:* 840
Józef Piłsudski, *20th:* 3250
Gifford Pinchot, *20th:* 3253
Pindar, *Anc:* 646
Lydia E. Pinkham, *19th:* 1796
Augusto Pinochet Ugarte, *20th:* 3257, *Notor:* 842

The Pinzón Brothers, *Ren:* 789
Luigi Pirandello, *20th:* 3260
Dominique Pire, *20th:* 3264
The Pirelli Family, *20th:* 3266
Henri Pirenne, *20th:* 3269
Tomé Pires, *Ren:* 792
Andrea Pisano, *MA:* 845
Nicola and Giovanni Pisano, *MA:* 847
Elena Cornaro Piscopia, *17th:* 743
Pisistratus, *Anc:* 649
Camille Pissarro, *19th:* 1799
William Pitt the Elder, *18th:* 786
William Pitt the Younger, *18th:* 789
Pittacus of Mytilene, *Anc:* 652
Pius II, *Ren:* 794
Pius V, *Ren:* 797
Pius VI, *18th:* 793
Pius IX, *19th:* 1802
Pius X, *20th:* 3272
Pius XI, *20th:* 3275
Pius XII, *20th:* 3278
Piye, *Anc:* 655
Francisco Pizarro, *Ren:* 800
Francis Place, *19th:* 1806
Max Planck, *20th:* 3282
Sylvia Plath, *20th:* 3285
Plato, *Anc:* 659
Plautus, *Anc:* 662
Gary Player, *20th:* 3288
Pliny the Elder, *Anc:* 665
Plotinus, *Anc:* 668
Plutarch, *Anc:* 670
Konstantin Petrovich Pobedonostsev, *19th:* 1810, *Notor:* 845
Pocahontas, *17th:* 745
Edgar Allan Poe, *19th:* 1813
Poggio, *MA:* 850
Henri Poincaré, *19th:* 1816
Raymond Poincaré, *20th:* 3292
Sidney Poitier, *20th:* 3296
Pol Pot, *20th:* 3298, *Notor:* 846
James K. Polk, *19th:* 1819
Jonathan Pollard, *Notor:* 849
Jackson Pollock, *20th:* 3301
Marco Polo, *MA:* 853
Polybius, *Anc:* 673
Polyclitus, *Anc:* 675
Polycrates of Samos, *Notor:* 850
Polygnotus, *Anc:* 678
Marquês de Pombal, *18th:* 795
Madame de Pompadour, *18th:* 798
Pompey the Great, *Anc:* 681
Georges Pompidou, *20th:* 3305
Juan Ponce de León, *Ren:* 803
Pontiac, *18th:* 801
Charles Ponzi, *Notor:* 852
Alexander Pope, *18th:* 805
Aleksandr Stepanovich Popov, *19th:* 1824
Poppaea Sabina, *Anc:* 685
Marguerite Porete, *MA:* 856
Porphyry, *Anc:* 687
Cole Porter, *20th:* 3308
James Porter, *Notor:* 854
Katherine Anne Porter, *20th:* 3310
Posidonius, *Anc:* 690
Grigori Aleksandrovich Potemkin, *18th:* 808
Beatrix Potter, *20th:* 3314
Francis Poulenc, *20th:* 3318
Nicolas Poussin, *17th:* 749
Adam Clayton Powell, Jr., *Notor:* 856
Colin Powell, *20th:* 3321
John Wesley Powell, *19th:* 1827
Lewis Powell (1844-1865), *Notor:* 858
Lewis F. Powell, Jr. (1907-1998), *20th:* 3325
Powhatan, *17th:* 752
Ludwig Prandtl, *20th:* 3327
Praxiteles, *Anc:* 694
William Hickling Prescott, *19th:* 1831
Elvis Presley, *20th:* 3330
Leontyne Price, *20th:* 3334
Thomas Pride, *17th:* 756
Joseph Priestley, *18th:* 811
Miguel Primo de Rivera, *Notor:* 860
Gavrilo Princip, *Notor:* 861
Priscian, *MA:* 859
Priscillian, *Anc:* 698
Proclus, *Anc:* 701
Joseph Profaci, *Notor:* 863
Sergei Prokofiev, *20th:* 3338
Sextus Propertius, *Anc:* 704
Protagoras, *Anc:* 707
Pierre-Joseph Proudhon, *19th:* 1834
Marcel Proust, *20th:* 3342
Psamtik I, *Anc:* 710
Michael Psellus, *MA:* 863
Ptolemy (astronomer), *Anc:* 712
Ptolemy Philadelphus, *Anc:* 715
Ptolemy Soter, *Anc:* 719
Giacomo Puccini, *20th:* 3346
Jean Pucelle, *MA:* 866
Samuel von Pufendorf, *17th:* 759
Yemelyan Ivanovich Pugachev, *18th:* 814
Augustus Welby Northmore Pugin, *19th:* 1838
Joseph Pulitzer, *19th:* 1841
Henry Purcell, *17th:* 763
E. B. Pusey, *19th:* 1844
Alexander Pushkin, *19th:* 1848
Puyi, *Notor:* 864
John Pym, *17th:* 767
Pyrrhon of Elis, *Anc:* 722
Pythagoras, *Anc:* 725
Pytheas, *Anc:* 729

Q

Muammar al-Qaddafi, *20th:* 3350, *Notor:* 867
Qāytbāy, *Ren:* 807
Qianlong, *18th:* 817
Qu Yuan, *Anc:* 732
William Clarke Quantrill, *Notor:* 869
John Quelch, *Notor:* 871
François Quesnay, *18th:* 820
Francisco Gómez de Quevedo y Villegas, *17th:* 770
Vidkun Quisling, *Notor:* 873

R

Rabanus Maurus, *MA:* 870
François Rabelais, *Ren:* 809
Isidor Isaac Rabi, *20th:* 3355
Rābiʿah al-ʿAdawiyah, *MA:* 873
Yitzhak Rabin, *20th:* 3358
Sergei Rachmaninoff, *20th:* 3361
Puniša Račić, *Notor:* 876

Jean Racine, *17th:* 773
John Rackham, *Notor:* 877
Ann Radcliffe, *18th:* 823
Dennis Rader, *Notor:* 879
Pierre Esprit Radisson, *17th:* 777
Sir Henry Raeburn, *19th:* 1852
Gilles de Rais, *Notor:* 880
Thenmuli Rajaratnam, *Notor:* 882
Sir Walter Ralegh, *Ren:* 813
Sir Chandrasekhara Venkata Raman, *20th:* 3364
Rāmānuja, *MA:* 876
Marquise de Rambouillet, *17th:* 779
Jean-Philippe Rameau, *18th:* 826
Ilich Ramírez Sánchez, *Notor:* 883
Ramses II, *Anc:* 735
Peter Ramus, *Ren:* 817
Mahadev Govind Ranade, *19th:* 1855
Ayn Rand, *20th:* 3367
A. Philip Randolph, *20th:* 3369
Ranjit Singh, *19th:* 1857
Leopold von Ranke, *19th:* 1860
Jeannette Rankin, *20th:* 3374
Raphael, *Ren:* 819
Knud Johan Victor Rasmussen, *20th:* 3377
Grigori Yefimovich Rasputin, *19th:* 1863, *Notor:* 885
Ratramnus, *MA:* 879
Robert Rauschenberg, *20th:* 3380
Walter Rauschenbusch, *20th:* 3382
François Ravaillac, *Notor:* 888
Maurice Ravel, *20th:* 3386
Jerry John Rawlings, *20th:* 3389
John Rawls, *20th:* 3391
James Earl Ray, *Notor:* 889
John Ray, *17th:* 782
Rammohan Ray, *19th:* 1866
Satyajit Ray, *20th:* 3394
Sam Rayburn, *20th:* 3397
Raymond of Peñafort, *MA:* 881
Guillaume-Thomas Raynal, *18th:* 829
al-Rāzī, *MA:* 884
Stenka Razin, *17th:* 784
Raziya, *MA:* 888
Mary Read, *Notor:* 891
Ronald Reagan, *20th:* 3400
André Rebouças, *19th:* 1869
Red Cloud, *19th:* 1871
Odilon Redon, *19th:* 1875
Walter Reed, *19th:* 1877
Regulus, *Anc:* 738
William H. Rehnquist, *20th:* 3405
First Baron Reith of Stonehaven, *20th:* 3410
Erich Maria Remarque, *20th:* 3413
Rembrandt, *17th:* 786
Frederic Remington, *19th:* 1881
Ernest Renan, *19th:* 1884
Janet Reno, *20th:* 3416
Jean Renoir, *20th:* 3420
Pierre-Auguste Renoir, *19th:* 1888
Madame Restell, *Notor:* 892
Walter P. Reuther, *20th:* 3424
Paul Revere, *18th:* 832
Sir Joshua Reynolds, *18th:* 836
Reza Shah Pahlavi, *20th:* 3428
Syngman Rhee, *20th:* 3430
Rheticus, *Ren:* 823
Cecil Rhodes, *19th:* 1891
Joachim von Ribbentrop, *Notor:* 894
David Ricardo, *19th:* 1896
Matteo Ricci, *Ren:* 825
Richard I, *MA:* 891
Richard II, *MA:* 893
Richard III, *Ren:* 828, *Notor:* 896
Ann Richards, *20th:* 3434
Ellen Swallow Richards, *19th:* 1899
Abby Sage Richardson, *19th:* 1902
Henry Hobson Richardson, *19th:* 1905
Samuel Richardson, *18th:* 841
Cardinal de Richelieu, *17th:* 790
Mordecai Richler, *20th:* 3438
Charles Richter, *20th:* 3440
Hyman G. Rickover, *20th:* 3443
Sally Ride, *20th:* 3447
Nicholas Ridley, *Ren:* 833
Leni Riefenstahl, *20th:* 3451
Louis Riel, *19th:* 1908
Cola di Rienzo, *MA:* 897
Rainer Maria Rilke, *20th:* 3454
Arthur Rimbaud, *19th:* 1912
Nikolay Rimsky-Korsakov, *19th:* 1915
Johnny Ringo, *Notor:* 898
Efraín Ríos Montt, *Notor:* 899
Albrecht Ritschl, *19th:* 1918
George Rivas, *Notor:* 901
Diego Rivera, *20th:* 3457
Rob Roy, *Notor:* 902
Jerome Robbins, *20th:* 3459
Bartholomew Roberts, *Notor:* 905
Paul Robeson, *20th:* 3462
Robespierre, *18th:* 844, *Notor:* 907
Robin Hood, *Notor:* 909
Frank Robinson, *20th:* 3467
Jackie Robinson, *20th:* 3470
Mary Robinson (1758?-1800), *18th:* 848
Mary Robinson (b. 1944), *20th:* 3474
Comte de Rochambeau, *18th:* 851
John D. Rockefeller, *19th:* 1921
John D. Rockefeller, Jr., *20th:* 3476
Nelson A. Rockefeller, *20th:* 3478
Knute Rockne, *20th:* 3481
George Lincoln Rockwell, *Notor:* 911
Norman Rockwell, *20th:* 3483
Richard Rodgers, *20th:* 3486
Auguste Rodin, *19th:* 1925
George Rodney, *18th:* 854
John Augustus Roebling, *19th:* 1928
John Roebuck, *18th:* 858
Edith Nourse Rogers, *20th:* 3489
Will Rogers, *20th:* 3491
Rollo, *MA:* 900
Charles Stewart Rolls, *20th:* 3496
Michael Romanov, *17th:* 794
Oscar Romero, *20th:* 3499
Erwin Rommel, *20th:* 3502
George Romney, *18th:* 862
Pierre de Ronsard, *Ren:* 837
Wilhelm Conrad Röntgen, *19th:* 1931
Eleanor Roosevelt, *20th:* 3506
Franklin D. Roosevelt, *20th:* 3509

Theodore Roosevelt, *20th:* 3515
Elihu Root, *20th:* 3519
Hermann Rorschach, *20th:* 3522
Pete Rose, *20th:* 3525
Saint Rose of Lima, *17th:* 796
Ethel Rosenberg, *Notor:* 913
Julius Rosenberg, *Notor:* 915
Betsy Ross, *18th:* 865
Sir James Clark Ross, *19th:* 1934
John Ross, *19th:* 1937
Nellie Tayloe Ross, *20th:* 3529
Sir Ronald Ross, *20th:* 3532
Christina Rossetti, *19th:* 1940
Gioacchino Rossini, *19th:* 1944
Sir Joseph Rotblat, *20th:* 3536
Mark Rothko, *20th:* 3539
The Rothschild Family, *19th:* 1947
Arnold Rothstein, *Notor:* 917
Georges Rouault, *20th:* 3541
Peyton Rous, *20th:* 3545
Henri Rousseau, *19th:* 1951
Jean-Jacques Rousseau, *18th:* 868
Darlie Routier, *Notor:* 918
F. Sherwood Rowland, *20th:* 3547
Mary White Rowlandson, *17th:* 798
Sir Frederick Henry Royce, *20th:* 3496
Josiah Royce, *20th:* 3550
Pete Rozelle, *20th:* 3553
Peter Paul Rubens, *17th:* 802
Jack Ruby, *Notor:* 919
Rudolf I, *MA:* 904
Rudolf II, *Ren:* 840
Eric Rudolph, *Notor:* 921
Muriel Rukeyser, *20th:* 3556
Jalāl al-Dīn Rūmī, *MA:* 908
Gerd von Rundstedt, *20th:* 3559
Prince Rupert, *17th:* 805
Rurik, *MA:* 911
Benjamin Rush, *18th:* 872
John Ruskin, *19th:* 1954
Bertrand Russell, *20th:* 3562
Bill Russell, *20th:* 3565
Henry Norris Russell, *20th:* 3570
John Russell, *19th:* 1958
Babe Ruth, *20th:* 3572
Ernest Rutherford, *20th:* 3576
Michiel Adriaanszoon de Ruyter, *17th:* 807

S

Sacagawea, *19th:* 1962
Nicola Sacco, *20th:* 3580, *Notor:* 924
Nelly Sachs, *20th:* 3583
Anwar el-Sadat, *20th:* 3587
Marquis de Sade, *18th:* 875, *Notor:* 926
Saʿdi, *MA:* 915
Carl Sagan, *20th:* 3590
Saʿīd ibn Sulṭān, *19th:* 1965
Saigō Takamori, *19th:* 1968
Ruth St. Denis, *20th:* 3593
Augustus Saint-Gaudens, *19th:* 1972
Louis de Saint-Just, *18th:* 877
Louis St. Laurent, *20th:* 3597
Camille Saint-Saëns, *20th:* 3600
Henri de Saint-Simon, *19th:* 1975
Andrei Sakharov, *20th:* 3602
Saladin, *MA:* 918
António de Oliveira Salazar, *20th:* 3606, *Notor:* 928
Yolanda Saldívar, *Notor:* 930
Salimbene, *MA:* 921
J. D. Salinger, *20th:* 3609
First Earl of Salisbury, *Ren:* 844
Third Marquis of Salisbury, *19th:* 1977
Jonas Salk, *20th:* 3613
Sallust, *Anc:* 742
Salome, *Notor:* 932
Sammu-ramat, *Anc:* 744
Samory Touré, *19th:* 1981
Pete Sampras, *20th:* 3616
Samuel, *Anc:* 747
José de San Martín, *19th:* 1984
George Sand, *19th:* 1987
Carl Sandburg, *20th:* 3619
Frederick Sanger, *20th:* 3622
Margaret Sanger, *20th:* 3625
Śaṅkara, *MA:* 924
Jacopo Sansovino, *Ren:* 847
Antonio López de Santa Anna, *19th:* 1990
George Santayana, *20th:* 3629
Santorio Santorio, *17th:* 810
Alberto Santos-Dumont, *20th:* 3632
Sappho, *Anc:* 750
La Saragossa, *19th:* 1993
John Singer Sargent, *19th:* 1996
Sargon II, *Anc:* 752
Domingo Faustino Sarmiento, *19th:* 2000
Nathalie Sarraute, *20th:* 3635
Jean-Paul Sartre, *20th:* 3638
Erik Satie, *20th:* 3641
Eisaku Satō, *20th:* 3645
Ferdinand de Saussure, *20th:* 3649
Jeanne Sauvé, *20th:* 3652
Thomas Savery, *17th:* 813
Friedrich Karl von Savigny, *19th:* 2003
Sir George Savile, *17th:* 815
Savitri Devi, *Notor:* 934
Girolamo Savonarola, *Ren:* 850
Elizabeth Sawyer, *Notor:* 935
Comte de Saxe, *18th:* 881
Saxo Grammaticus, *MA:* 927
Joseph Justus Scaliger, *Ren:* 855
Alessandro Scarlatti, *18th:* 883
Gerhard Johann David von Scharnhorst, *19th:* 2006
Max Scheler, *20th:* 3655
Friedrich Wilhelm Joseph von Schelling, *19th:* 2009
Wilhelm Schickard, *17th:* 818
Friedrich Schiller, *18th:* 887
Baldur von Schirach, *Notor:* 937
Friedrich Schleiermacher, *19th:* 2013
Heinrich Schliemann, *19th:* 2016
Bernhard Voldemar Schmidt, *20th:* 3659
Karl Schmidt-Rottluff, *20th:* 3661
Arnold Schoenberg, *20th:* 3664
Friedrich Hermann Schomberg, *17th:* 820
Arthur Schopenhauer, *19th:* 2019
Olive Schreiner, *19th:* 2023
Erwin Schrödinger, *20th:* 3668
Franz Schubert, *19th:* 2026
Dutch Schultz, *Notor:* 938
Charles M. Schulz, *20th:* 3672
Clara Schumann, *19th:* 2029
Robert Schumann, *19th:* 2031
Anna Maria van Schurman, *17th:* 823
Carl Schurz, *19th:* 2035

Heinrich Schütz, *17th:* 825
Karl Schwarzschild, *20th:* 3674
Albert Schweitzer, *20th:* 3678
Scipio Aemilianus, *Anc:* 755
Scipio Africanus, *Anc:* 758
Scopas, *Anc:* 761
Martin Scorsese, *20th:* 3681
Charlotte Angas Scott, *19th:* 2039
Dred Scott, *19th:* 2041
Sir George Gilbert Scott, *19th:* 2044
Sir Walter Scott, *19th:* 2047
Winfield Scott, *19th:* 2051
Edward Wyllis Scripps, *19th:* 2055
Madeleine de Scudéry, *17th:* 828
Glenn Theodore Seaborg, *20th:* 3684
Sebastian, *Ren:* 859
Richard John Seddon, *19th:* 2058
Hans von Seeckt, *20th:* 3688
Anaïs Ségalas, *19th:* 2062
Andrés Segovia, *20th:* 3691
Sei Shōnagon, *MA:* 930
Seki Kōwa, *17th:* 831
Seleucus I Nicator, *Anc:* 763
Peter Sellers, *20th:* 3695
Ignaz Philipp Semmelweis, *19th:* 2064
Maurice Sendak, *20th:* 3698
Seneca the Younger, *Anc:* 766
Léopold Senghor, *20th:* 3702
Sennacherib, *Anc:* 769
Mack Sennett, *20th:* 3706
Sequoyah, *19th:* 2067
Sergius I, *MA:* 933
Saint Sergius I, *MA:* 936
Junípero Serra, *18th:* 891
Michael Servetus, *Ren:* 861
Robert W. Service, *20th:* 3708
Sesostris III, *Anc:* 771
Sesshū, *Ren:* 865
Saint Elizabeth Seton, *19th:* 2071
Georges Seurat, *19th:* 2074
Dr. Seuss, *20th:* 3710
Madame de Sévigné, *17th:* 833
Samuel Sewall, *18th:* 893
Anna Seward, *18th:* 897
William H. Seward, *19th:* 2077
Anne Sexton, *20th:* 3713
Jane Seymour, *Ren:* 868
Caterina Sforza, *Ren:* 870
Ludovico Sforza, *Ren:* 872
Shabbetai Tzevi, *17th:* 835
First Earl of Shaftesbury, *17th:* 838
Shah Jahan, *17th:* 842
Shaka, *19th:* 2081
William Shakespeare, *Ren:* 876
Assata Olugbala Shakur, *Notor:* 940
Shāpūr II, *Anc:* 774
Granville Sharp, *18th:* 899
Anna Howard Shaw, *19th:* 2084
Clay Shaw, *Notor:* 941
George Bernard Shaw, *20th:* 3716
Daniel Shays, *18th:* 902
Fulton J. Sheen, *20th:* 3722
Mary Wollstonecraft Shelley, *19th:* 2088
Percy Bysshe Shelley, *19th:* 2092
Alan Shepard, *20th:* 3725
Jack Sheppard, *Notor:* 943
Sam Sheppard, *Notor:* 945
Richard Brinsley Sheridan, *18th:* 905
Roger Sherman, *18th:* 908
William Tecumseh Sherman, *19th:* 2097
Shi Huangdi, *Anc:* 779, *Notor:* 947
Fusako Shigenobu, *Notor:* 949
Harold Shipman, *Notor:* 950
Mother Shipton, *Notor:* 952
James Shirley, *17th:* 846
Dmitri Shostakovich, *20th:* 3728
Shōtoku Taishi, *MA:* 940
George P. Shultz, *20th:* 3731
Shunzhi, *17th:* 848
Muhammad Siad Barre, *20th:* 3734, *Notor:* 953
Jean Sibelius, *20th:* 3736
Sarah Siddons, *18th:* 912
Henry Sidgwick, *19th:* 2102
Sīdī al-Mukhtār al-Kuntī, *18th:* 914
Sir Philip Sidney, *Ren:* 881
Bugsy Siegel, *Notor:* 954
Justine Siegemundin, *17th:* 851
The Siemens Family, *19th:* 2105
Emmanuel-Joseph Sieyès, *18th:* 916
Siger of Brabant, *MA:* 942
Sigismund I, the Old, *Ren:* 885
Sigismund II Augustus, *Ren:* 887
Sigismund III Vasa, *17th:* 853
Norodom Sihanouk, *20th:* 3740
Beverly Sills, *20th:* 3744
Diego de Siloé, *Ren:* 890
Sima Guang, *MA:* 945
Sima Qian, *Anc:* 782
Sima Xiangru, *Anc:* 785
John Graves Simcoe, *18th:* 919
Saint Simeon Stylites, *Anc:* 789
William Joseph Simmons, *Notor:* 957
Simonides, *Anc:* 793
O. J. Simpson, *Notor:* 958
Frank Sinatra, *20th:* 3747
Upton Sinclair, *20th:* 3750
Miles Sindercombe, *Notor:* 961
Beant Singh, *Notor:* 962
Satwant Singh, *Notor:* 963
Elisabetta Sirani, *17th:* 856
Sirhan Sirhan, *Notor:* 965
Saint Siricius, *Anc:* 796
Sitting Bull, *19th:* 2108
Śivājī, *17th:* 858
Sixtus IV, *Ren:* 893
Sixtus V, *Ren:* 895
Jeffrey Skilling, *Notor:* 967
B. F. Skinner, *20th:* 3754
Otto Skorzeny, *Notor:* 969
Samuel Slater, *19th:* 2111
First Viscount Slim, *20th:* 3758
Claus Sluter, *MA:* 947
Pamela Ann Smart, *Notor:* 971
Adam Smith, *18th:* 921
Alfred E. Smith, *20th:* 3762
Bessie Smith, *20th:* 3765
Gerald L. K. Smith, *Notor:* 973
Jedediah Smith, *19th:* 2114
John Smith, *17th:* 861
Joseph Smith, *19th:* 2117
Madeleine Smith, *Notor:* 975
Margaret Chase Smith, *20th:* 3768
Susan Smith, *Notor:* 977
Theobald Smith, *20th:* 3772
Jan Christian Smuts, *20th:* 3775

Snorri Sturluson, *MA:* 950
Ruth Snyder, *Notor:* 979
Charles Sobraj, *Notor:* 980
Socrates, *Anc:* 799
Frederick Soddy, *20th:* 3778
Nathan Söderblom, *20th:* 3781
Valerie Solanas, *Notor:* 982
Solomon, *Anc:* 803
Solon, *Anc:* 807
Aleksandr Solzhenitsyn, *20th:* 3783
First Duke of Somerset, *Ren:* 898
Mary Somerville, *19th:* 2121
Anastasio Somoza García, *Notor:* 984
Sonni ʿAlī, *Ren:* 900
Susan Sontag, *20th:* 3788
Sophia, *17th:* 865
Sophocles, *Anc:* 809
Sophonisba of Numidia, *Anc:* 812
Georges Sorel, *20th:* 3792
Sorghaghtani Beki, *MA:* 954
George Soros, *20th:* 3795
Sosigenes, *Anc:* 815
Sōtatsu, *17th:* 868
Hernando de Soto, *Ren:* 902
John Philip Sousa, *20th:* 3798
David H. Souter, *20th:* 3802
Wole Soyinka, *20th:* 3804
Paul-Henri Spaak, *20th:* 3808
Lazzaro Spallanzani, *18th:* 925
Spartacus, *Anc:* 818
Richard Speck, *Notor:* 986
Albert Speer, *Notor:* 987
John Hanning Speke, *19th:* 2123
Herbert Spencer, *19th:* 2126
Edmund Spenser, *Ren:* 906
Mikhail Mikhaylovich Speransky, *19th:* 2129
Steven Spielberg, *20th:* 3811
Baruch Spinoza, *17th:* 871
Benjamin Spock, *20th:* 3814
Squanto, *17th:* 875
Madame de Staël, *18th:* 929
Georg Ernst Stahl, *18th:* 933
Joseph Stalin, *20th:* 3817, *Notor:* 990
Miles Standish, *17th:* 877
Leland Stanford, *19th:* 2132
First Earl Stanhope, *18th:* 937
Konstantin Stanislavsky, *20th:* 3821
Henry Morton Stanley, *19th:* 2136
Wendell Stanley, *20th:* 3824
Edwin M. Stanton, *19th:* 2142
Elizabeth Cady Stanton, *19th:* 2146
Johannes Stark, *20th:* 3827
Charles Starkweather, *Notor:* 993
Ernest Henry Starling, *20th:* 3830
Belle Starr, *Notor:* 994
Henry Starr, *Notor:* 996
Hermann Staudinger, *20th:* 3833
Alexandre Stavisky, *Notor:* 998
Richard Steele, *18th:* 941
Stefan Dušan, *MA:* 957
Edward Steichen, *20th:* 3837
Edith Stein, *20th:* 3840
Freiherr vom Stein, *19th:* 2151
Gertrude Stein, *20th:* 3845
John Steinbeck, *20th:* 3849
Gloria Steinem, *20th:* 3852
Jakob Steiner, *19th:* 2154
Charles Proteus Steinmetz, *19th:* 2156
Stendhal, *19th:* 2160
Nicolaus Steno, *17th:* 881
Stephen I, *MA:* 964
King Stephen, *MA:* 960
Saint Stephen, *Anc:* 821
Stephen Báthory, *Ren:* 910
Alexander H. Stephens, *19th:* 2164
George Stephenson, *19th:* 2167
Thaddeus Stevens, *19th:* 2171
Adlai E. Stevenson, *20th:* 3856
Robert Louis Stevenson, *19th:* 2173
Simon Stevin, *Ren:* 912
James Stewart, *20th:* 3860
Alfred Stieglitz, *20th:* 3864
Flavius Stilicho, *Anc:* 824
Henry L. Stimson, *20th:* 3869
Karlheinz Stockhausen, *20th:* 3872
Harlan Fiske Stone, *20th:* 3878
Lucy Stone, *19th:* 2177
J. B. Stoner, *Notor:* 999
Marie Stopes, *20th:* 3882
Joseph Story, *19th:* 2180
Harriet Beecher Stowe, *19th:* 2184
Strabo, *Anc:* 827
Antonio Stradivari, *18th:* 944
First Earl of Strafford, *17th:* 884
Johann Strauss, *19th:* 2188
Richard Strauss, *20th:* 3885
Igor Stravinsky, *20th:* 3888
George Edmund Street, *19th:* 2191
Julius Streicher, *Notor:* 1001
Barbra Streisand, *20th:* 3892
Gustav Stresemann, *20th:* 3895
August Strindberg, *20th:* 3898
Alfredo Stroessner, *Notor:* 1004
Robert Franklin Stroud, *Notor:* 1005
Barbara Strozzi, *17th:* 888
Gilbert Stuart, *18th:* 947
William Stukeley, *18th:* 952
Peter Stuyvesant, *17th:* 890
Su Dongpo, *MA:* 968
Sir John Suckling, *17th:* 893
Antonio José de Sucre, *19th:* 2195
Suger, *MA:* 971
Suharto, *20th:* 3901, *Notor:* 1007
Suiko, *MA:* 974
Sukarno, *20th:* 3904
Süleyman the Magnificent, *Ren:* 914
Lucius Cornelius Sulla, *Anc:* 830, *Notor:* 1010
Anne Sullivan, *20th:* 3908
Arthur Sullivan, *19th:* 916
Harry Stack Sullivan, *20th:* 3910
Louis Sullivan, *19th:* 2198
Duke de Sully, *17th:* 896
Sulpicia, *Anc:* 834
Charles Sumner, *19th:* 2201
Sun Yat-sen, *20th:* 3913
Billy Sunday, *20th:* 3916
Sundiata, *MA:* 977
Mary Surratt, *Notor:* 1012
Suryavarman II, *MA:* 980
Graham Vivian Sutherland, *20th:* 3920
Bertha von Suttner, *19th:* 2205
Willie Sutton, *Notor:* 1014
Aleksandr Vasilyevich Suvorov, *18th:* 954
Shinichi Suzuki, *20th:* 3922

Suzuki Harunobu, *18th:* 958
Jan Swammerdam, *17th:* 898
Joseph Wilson Swan, *19th:* 2209
Michael Swango, *Notor:* 1015
Emanuel Swedenborg, *18th:* 961
Jonathan Swift, *18th:* 964
Thomas Sydenham, *17th:* 901
Sylvester II, *MA:* 983

T

Ta Mok, *Notor:* 1017
al-Ṭabarī, *MA:* 988
Tacitus, *Anc:* 837
Tadano Makuzu, *19th:* 2212
Robert A. Taft, *20th:* 3925
William Howard Taft, *20th:* 3929
Rabindranath Tagore, *20th:* 3933
Táhirih, *19th:* 2214
Hippolyte Taine, *19th:* 2216
Taira Kiyomori, *MA:* 990
Taizong, *MA:* 993
Taksin, *18th:* 968
Marion Talbot, *20th:* 3937
Thomas Talbot, *19th:* 2219
Maria Tallchief, *20th:* 3940
Talleyrand, *19th:* 2221
Thomas Tallis, *Ren:* 918
Queen Tamara, *MA:* 998
Tamerlane, *MA:* 1000
Tanaquil, *Anc:* 840
Tancred, *MA:* 1003
Roger Brooke Taney, *19th:* 2225, *Notor:* 1018
Jun'ichirō Tanizaki, *20th:* 3944
Tao Qian, *Anc:* 843
Ida Tarbell, *20th:* 3947
Ṭāriq ibn-Ziyād, *MA:* 1005
Tarquins, *Anc:* 846
Niccolò Fontana Tartaglia, *Ren:* 920
Tascalusa, *Ren:* 922
Abel Janszoon Tasman, *17th:* 905
Torquato Tasso, *Ren:* 924
Helen Brooke Taussig, *20th:* 3950
Charles Taylor, *Notor:* 1021
Dame Elizabeth Taylor, *20th:* 3953
Frederick Winslow Taylor, *20th:* 3955
Zachary Taylor, *19th:* 2230
Peter Ilich Tchaikovsky, *19th:* 2233
Edward Teach, *Notor:* 1023
Sara Teasdale, *20th:* 3959
Tecumseh, *19th:* 2237
Pierre Teilhard de Chardin, *20th:* 3963
Kateri Tekakwitha, *17th:* 908
Georg Philipp Telemann, *18th:* 970
Thomas Telford, *19th:* 2240
Edward Teller, *20th:* 3968
Shirley Temple, *20th:* 3973
Alfred, Lord Tennyson, *19th:* 2244
Terence, *Anc:* 849
Mother Teresa, *20th:* 3975
Saint Teresa of Ávila, *Ren:* 928
Valentina Tereshkova, *20th:* 3978
Ellen Terry, *19th:* 2248
Megan Terry, *20th:* 3982
Tertullian, *Anc:* 853
Nikola Tesla, *19th:* 2252
Tewodros II, *19th:* 2255
William Makepeace Thackeray, *19th:* 2257
Thales of Miletus, *Anc:* 856
Than Shwe, *Notor:* 1026
Thanadelthur, *18th:* 974
U Thant, *20th:* 3986
Twyla Tharp, *20th:* 3989
Margaret Thatcher, *20th:* 3992
Harry Kendall Thaw, *Notor:* 1027
Sylvanus Thayer, *19th:* 2260
Themistocles, *Anc:* 859
Theodora, *MA:* 1008, *Notor:* 1028
Theodore of Mopsuestia, *Anc:* 862
Theodoret of Cyrrhus, *Anc:* 865
Theodoric the Great, *MA:* 1012
Theodosius the Great, *Anc:* 868
Theoleptus of Philadelphia, *MA:* 1016
Theophanes the Confessor, *MA:* 1020
Theophrastus, *Anc:* 872
Hugo Theorell, *20th:* 3997
Thespis, *Anc:* 876
Adolphe Thiers, *19th:* 2263
Clarence Thomas, *20th:* 3999
Norman Thomas, *20th:* 4002
Saint Thomas, *Anc:* 878
Theodore Thomas, *19th:* 2267
Thomas à Kempis, *MA:* 1022
Thomas Aquinas, *MA:* 1027
David Thompson, *19th:* 2271
Sir Joseph John Thomson, *20th:* 4007
Tom Thomson, *20th:* 4010
Henry David Thoreau, *19th:* 2274
Edward L. Thorndike, *20th:* 4013
Jim Thorpe, *20th:* 4016
Thucydides, *Anc:* 882
James Thurber, *20th:* 4020
Thutmose III, *Anc:* 885
Tianqi, *17th:* 911
Tippu Tib, *19th:* 2277
Tiberius, *Anc:* 888
Giovanni Battista Tiepolo, *18th:* 976
Tiglath-pileser III, *Anc:* 892
Tigranes the Great, *Anc:* 895
Bal Gangadhar Tilak, *20th:* 4023
Paul Tillich, *20th:* 4027
Benjamin Tillman, *Notor:* 1030
Tintoretto, *Ren:* 931
Marietta Robusti Tintoretto, *Ren:* 935
Alfred von Tirpitz, *20th:* 4030
Tirso de Molina, *17th:* 913
Devanampiya Dēvānaṃpiya Tissa, *Anc:* 898
Titian, *Ren:* 936
Tito, *20th:* 4034, *Notor:* 1032
Tiy, *Anc:* 901
Alexis de Tocqueville, *19th:* 2280
Sweeney Todd, *Notor:* 1033
Hideki Tojo, *Notor:* 1034
Tokugawa Ieyasu, *17th:* 915
Tokugawa Tsunayoshi, *17th:* 919
Tokugawa Yoshimune, *18th:* 980
Tokyo Rose, *Notor:* 1036
J. R. R. Tolkien, *20th:* 4038
Leo Tolstoy, *19th:* 2283
Clyde William Tombaugh, *20th:* 4041
Wolfe Tone, *18th:* 982
Ferdinand Julius Tönnies, *20th:* 4044
Tomás de Torquemada, *Ren:* 939, *Notor:* 1038

Evangelista Torricelli, *17th:* 921
Omar Torrijos, *20th:* 4048
Lennart Torstenson, *17th:* 924
Arturo Toscanini, *20th:* 4050
Henri de Toulouse-Lautrec, *19th:* 2287
Ahmed Sékou Touré, *20th:* 4053
Cyril Tourneur, *17th:* 928
Toussaint Louverture, *18th:* 985
Charles Hard Townes, *20th:* 4057
Arnold Toynbee, *20th:* 4059
Eiji Toyoda, *20th:* 4062
Toyotomi Hideyoshi, *Ren:* 943
Spencer Tracy, *20th:* 4066
Catharine Parr Traill, *19th:* 2291
Trajan, *Anc:* 903
Richard Trevithick, *19th:* 2294
Flora Tristan, *19th:* 2297
Ernst Troeltsch, *20th:* 4069
Anthony Trollope, *19th:* 2299
Frances Trollope, *19th:* 2303
Maarten and Cornelis Tromp, *17th:* 930
Leon Trotsky, *20th:* 4072, *Notor:* 1040
Trotula, *MA:* 1031
Pierre Trudeau, *20th:* 4076
François Truffaut, *20th:* 4080
Rafael Trujillo, *20th:* 4084, *Notor:* 1042
Harry S. Truman, *20th:* 4086
John Trumbull, *18th:* 988
Sojourner Truth, *19th:* 2306
Moïse Tshombe, *20th:* 4091
Konstantin Tsiolkovsky, *20th:* 4095
Marina Tsvetayeva, *20th:* 4098
Tu Duc, *19th:* 2310
Harriet Tubman, *19th:* 2312
William V. S. Tubman, *20th:* 4101
Barbara W. Tuchman, *20th:* 4104
Karla Faye Tucker, *Notor:* 1044
The Tudor Family, *Ren:* 946
Jethro Tull, *18th:* 990
Tupac Amaru II, *18th:* 993
Andrei Nikolayevich Tupolev, *20th:* 4108
Sir Charles Tupper, *19th:* 2316
Viscount de Turenne, *17th:* 933
Ivan Turgenev, *19th:* 2319
Anne-Robert-Jacques Turgot, *18th:* 996
Alan Mathison Turing, *20th:* 4112
Frederick Jackson Turner, *20th:* 4115
J. M. W. Turner, *19th:* 2322
Nat Turner, *19th:* 2326
Ted Turner, *20th:* 4118
Dick Turpin, *Notor:* 1045
Tutankhamen, *Anc:* 908
Desmond Tutu, *20th:* 4121
Mark Twain, *19th:* 2329
William Marcy Tweed, *19th:* 2333, *Notor:* 1047
John Tyler, *19th:* 2337
Wat Tyler, *MA:* 1033
William Tyndale, *Ren:* 949
John Tyndall, *Notor:* 1050

U

Walter Ulbricht, *20th:* 4125
Ulfilas, *Anc:* 911
Vasili Vasilievich Ulrikh, *Notor:* 1052
ʿUmar I, *MA:* 1037
Miguel de Unamuno y Jugo, *20th:* 4128
Unkei, *MA:* 1040
Urban II, *MA:* 1043
Urban VI, *Notor:* 1053
Urban VIII, *17th:* 936
Harold C. Urey, *20th:* 4132
Ur-Nammu, *Anc:* 914
James Ussher, *17th:* 938
ʿUthman dan Fodio, *19th:* 2342

V

Vaḥīd Bihbahānī, *18th:* 1000
Valdemar II, *MA:* 1047
Valentinus, *Anc:* 918
Paul Valéry, *20th:* 4136
Lorenzo Valla, *MA:* 1049
Vālmīki, *Anc:* 922
James Van Allen, *20th:* 4139
Sir John Vanbrugh, *18th:* 1002
Martin Van Buren, *19th:* 2344
George Vancouver, *18th:* 1006
Cornelius Vanderbilt, *19th:* 2348
Volkert van der Graaf, *Notor:* 1055
Sir Henry Vane the Younger, *17th:* 941
Bartolomeo Vanzetti, *Notor:* 1056
Vardhamāna, *Anc:* 924
Edgard Varèse, *20th:* 4142
Getúlio Vargas, *Notor:* 1059
Harold E. Varmus, *20th:* 4145
Marcus Terentius Varro, *Anc:* 927
Giorgio Vasari, *Ren:* 953
Vasily III, *Ren:* 957
Vasily Shuysky, *17th:* 943
Vasubandhu, *Anc:* 930
Vattagamani, *Anc:* 933
Sébastien Le Prestre de Vauban, *17th:* 946
Hank Vaughan, *Notor:* 1060
Ralph Vaughan Williams, *20th:* 4147
Marquis de Vauvenargues, *18th:* 1009
Nikolai Ivanovich Vavilov, *20th:* 4151
Thorstein Veblen, *20th:* 4154
Veerappan, *Notor:* 1062
Lope de Vega Carpio, *17th:* 949
Diego Velázquez, *17th:* 953
Jean de Venette, *MA:* 1053
Eleuthérios Venizélos, *20th:* 4157
Vercingetorix, *Anc:* 935
Giuseppe Verdi, *19th:* 2351
Charles Gravier de Vergennes, *18th:* 1011
Vergil, *Anc:* 938
Jan Vermeer, *17th:* 956
Jules Verne, *19th:* 2354
Paolo Veronese, *Ren:* 959
Marcus Verrius Flaccus, *Anc:* 941
Andrea del Verrocchio, *Ren:* 962
Hendrik Frensch Verwoerd, *Notor:* 1064
Andreas Vesalius, *Ren:* 965
Vespasian, *Anc:* 943
Amerigo Vespucci, *Ren:* 969
Giambattista Vico, *18th:* 1013
Queen Victoria, *19th:* 2359
Jorge Rafael Videla, *Notor:* 1066
Eugène François Vidocq, *Notor:* 1067

Iswar Chandra Vidyasagar, *19th:* 2363
António Vieira, *17th:* 959
Élisabeth Vigée-Lebrun, *18th:* 1016
Pancho Villa, *20th:* 4160, *Notor:* 1069
Heitor Villa-Lobos, *20th:* 4163
Giovanni Villani, *MA:* 1056
Geoffroi de Villehardouin, *MA:* 1059
François Villon, *Ren:* 973
Saint Vincent de Paul, *17th:* 962
Vincent of Beauvais, *MA:* 1063
Saint Vincent of Lérins, *Anc:* 947
Rudolf Virchow, *19th:* 2365
Luchino Visconti, *20th:* 4166
Francisco de Vitoria, *Ren:* 978
Philippe de Vitry, *MA:* 1065
Antonio Vivaldi, *18th:* 1019
Vivekananda, *19th:* 2368
Vlad III the Impaler, *Ren:* 981, *Notor:* 1072
Vladimir I, *MA:* 1068
Vladislav II, *Ren:* 983
Andrey Andreyevich Vlasov, *Notor:* 1074
Vo Nguyen Giap, *20th:* 4169
Sir Julius Vogel, *19th:* 2371
Alessandro Volta, *18th:* 1022
Voltaire, *18th:* 1026
Claus von Bülow, *Notor:* 1075
Anastase Vonsiatsky, *Notor:* 1077
Édouard Vuillard, *20th:* 4173
Andrey Vyshinsky, *Notor:* 1079

W

Joachim Wach, *20th:* 4177
Richard Wagner, *19th:* 2374
Winifred Wagner, *Notor:* 1081
Muḥammad ibn ʿAbd al-Wahhāb, *18th:* 1030
Edward Gibbon Wakefield, *19th:* 2378
Selman Abraham Waksman, *20th:* 4180
Lillian D. Wald, *20th:* 4184
Kurt Waldheim, *20th:* 4187
Lech Wałęsa, *20th:* 4191
Shāh Walī Allāh, *18th:* 1032
Alice Walker, *20th:* 4196
James J. Walker, *Notor:* 1082
Madam C. J. Walker, *20th:* 4199
William Walker, *Notor:* 1084
Rachel Wall, *Notor:* 1086
George C. Wallace, *20th:* 4203, *Notor:* 1087
Henry A. Wallace, *20th:* 4207
William Wallace, *MA:* 1072
Albrecht Wenzel von Wallenstein, *17th:* 966
John Wallis, *17th:* 969
Robert Walpole, *18th:* 1034
John Walter II, *19th:* 2380
Barbara Walters, *20th:* 4211
Walther von der Vogelweide, *MA:* 1075
Sam Walton, *20th:* 4213
Sir William Walton, *20th:* 4216
Wang Anshi, *MA:* 1079
Wang Kŏn, *MA:* 1081
Wang Bi, *Anc:* 950
Wang Chong, *Anc:* 953
Wang Fuzhi, *17th:* 972
Wang Jingwei, *20th:* 4220
Wang Wei, *MA:* 1085
Wang Xizhi, *Anc:* 955
Wang Yangming, *Ren:* 986
Wang Zhenyi, *18th:* 1038
Felix Wankel, *20th:* 4224
Lester Frank Ward, *19th:* 2384
Mary Ward, *17th:* 974
Montgomery Ward, *19th:* 2386
Andy Warhol, *20th:* 4226
Carolyn Warmus, *Notor:* 1090
Jack Warner, *20th:* 4230
Earl Warren, *20th:* 4232
Mercy Otis Warren, *18th:* 1041
Robert Penn Warren, *20th:* 4236
Earl of Warwick, *Ren:* 989
Booker T. Washington, *19th:* 2390
George Washington, *18th:* 1043
Muddy Waters, *20th:* 4240
James D. Watson, *20th:* 4242
Thomas J. Watson, Jr., *20th:* 4246
Thomas J. Watson, Sr., *20th:* 4246
James Watt, *18th:* 1048
Antoine Watteau, *18th:* 1051
Anthony Wayne, *18th:* 1054
John Wayne, *20th:* 4250
Randy Weaver, *Notor:* 1091
Beatrice and Sidney Webb, *20th:* 4253
Carl Maria von Weber, *19th:* 2395
Max Weber, *20th:* 4258
Anton von Webern, *20th:* 4262
Daniel Webster, *19th:* 2398
John Webster, *17th:* 976
Noah Webster, *19th:* 2402
Josiah Wedgwood, *18th:* 1057
Alfred Wegener, *20th:* 4266
Joseph Weil, *Notor:* 1094
Simone Weil, *20th:* 4269
Kurt Weill, *20th:* 4273
Steven Weinberg, *20th:* 4277
August Weismann, *19th:* 2406
Carl Weiss, *Notor:* 1095
Hymie Weiss, *Notor:* 1096
Chaim Weizmann, *20th:* 4279
Orson Welles, *20th:* 4283
Duke of Wellington, *19th:* 2409
H. G. Wells, *20th:* 4287
Ida B. Wells-Barnett, *20th:* 4290
Wenceslaus, *MA:* 1088
W. C. Wentworth, *19th:* 2412
Max Wertheimer, *20th:* 4293
Charles Wesley, *18th:* 1061
John Wesley, *18th:* 1064
Horst Wessel, *Notor:* 1097
Benjamin West, *18th:* 1068
Mae West, *20th:* 4297
George Westinghouse, *19th:* 2416
Rogier van der Weyden, *MA:* 1092
Edith Wharton, *20th:* 4300
Phillis Wheatley, *18th:* 1070
Charles Wheatstone, *19th:* 547
George Hoyt Whipple, *20th:* 4304
James McNeill Whistler, *19th:* 2420
Dan White, *Notor:* 1099
Walter White, *20th:* 4307
George Whitefield, *18th:* 1073
Alfred North Whitehead, *20th:* 4311
Charles Whitman, *Notor:* 1101
Walt Whitman, *19th:* 2423
Eli Whitney, *18th:* 1076

Gertrude Vanderbilt Whitney, *20th:* 4315
John Greenleaf Whittier, *19th:* 2428
Sir Frank Whittle, *20th:* 4318
Widukind, *MA:* 1094
Norbert Wiener, *20th:* 4321
Elie Wiesel, *20th:* 4324
Simon Wiesenthal, *20th:* 4328
Hazel Wightman, *20th:* 4333
William Wilberforce, *18th:* 1079
Jonathan Wild, *Notor:* 1102
Oscar Wilde, *19th:* 2432
Laura Ingalls Wilder, *20th:* 4336
Charles Wilkes, *19th:* 2435
John Wilkes, *18th:* 1083
Sir George Hubert Wilkins, *20th:* 4339
Maurice Wilkins, *20th:* 4342
James Wilkinson, *Notor:* 1103
John Wilkinson, *18th:* 1086
Emma Willard, *19th:* 2438
Frances Willard, *19th:* 2442
William II, *20th:* 4346
William III, *17th:* 979
William IV, *19th:* 2445
William of Auvergne, *MA:* 1097
William of Auxerre, *MA:* 1101
William of Moerbeke, *MA:* 1105
William of Rubrouck, *MA:* 1107
William of Saint-Amour, *MA:* 1110
William of Saint-Thierry, *MA:* 1114
William the Conqueror, *MA:* 1117
William the Silent, *Ren:* 993
George Washington Williams, *19th:* 2449
Roger Williams, *17th:* 982
Tennessee Williams, *20th:* 4350
Thomas Willis, *17th:* 985
Edmund Wilson, *20th:* 4354
Edward O. Wilson, *20th:* 4358
Sir Harold Wilson, *20th:* 4360
James Wilson, *18th:* 1090
Woodrow Wilson, *20th:* 4364
Johann Joachim Winckelmann, *18th:* 1095
Duke of Windsor, *20th:* 4368
Oprah Winfrey, *20th:* 4372
Gerrard Winstanley, *17th:* 988
John Winthrop, *17th:* 990
Henry Wirz, *Notor:* 1105
Isaac Mayer Wise, *19th:* 2453
Stephen Samuel Wise, *20th:* 4376
John Witherspoon, *18th:* 1098
Ludwig Wittgenstein, *20th:* 4378
Władysław II Jagiełło and Jadwiga, *MA:* 1120
Peg Woffington, *18th:* 1102
Friedrich Wöhler, *19th:* 2456
Max Wolf, *20th:* 4382
James Wolfe, *18th:* 1104
Thomas Wolfe, *20th:* 4383
Wolfram von Eschenbach, *MA:* 1123
Mary Wollstonecraft, *18th:* 1108
Cardinal Thomas Wolsey, *Ren:* 996
Grant Wood, *20th:* 4387
Victoria Woodhull, *19th:* 2459
Tiger Woods, *20th:* 4390
Robert Burns Woodward, *20th:* 4393
Virginia Woolf, *20th:* 4397
William Wordsworth, *19th:* 2462
Fanny Bullock Workman, *19th:* 2466
Adam Worth, *Notor:* 1107
Sir Christopher Wren, *17th:* 994
Frances Wright, *19th:* 2469
Frank Lloyd Wright, *20th:* 4400
Orville and Wilbur Wright, *20th:* 4403
Wu Hou, *MA:* 1127
Wudi, *Anc:* 958
Wilhelm Wundt, *20th:* 4407
Aileen Carol Wuornos, *Notor:* 1108
John Wyclif, *MA:* 1130
Andrew Wyeth, *20th:* 4410
Joan Wytte, *Notor:* 1110

X

Xanthippe, *Anc:* 962
Saint Francis Xavier, *Ren:* 1000
Iannis Xenakis, *20th:* 4414
Xenophanes, *Anc:* 965
Xenophon, *Anc:* 968
Xerxes I, *Anc:* 971
Xia Gui, *MA:* 1134
Xiaozong, *Ren:* 1003
Xie Lingyun, *Anc:* 975
Xuanzang, *MA:* 1136
Xunzi, *Anc:* 978

Y

Genrikh Yagoda, *Notor:* 1112
Rosalyn Yalow, *20th:* 4419
Ahmad Zaki Yamani, *20th:* 4422
Yan Liben, *MA:* 1140
Yaqut, *MA:* 1143
Andrea Yates, *Notor:* 1113
Chuck Yeager, *20th:* 4425
William Butler Yeats, *20th:* 4428
Boris Yeltsin, *20th:* 4431
Nikolay Ivanovich Yezhov, *Notor:* 1115
Yo Fei, *MA:* 1145
Charlotte Mary Yonge, *19th:* 2472
Yonglo, *MA:* 1147
Yongzheng, *18th:* 1113
Dominique You, *Notor:* 1117
Brigham Young, *19th:* 2474
Cole Younger, *Notor:* 1118
Ramzi Yousef, *Notor:* 1121
Alexander and Demetrios Ypsilantis, *19th:* 2478
Yuan Shikai, *Notor:* 1122
Yui Shōsetsu, *17th:* 998
Hideki Yukawa, *20th:* 4436
Yakov Mikhailovich Yurovsky, *Notor:* 1124
Felix Yusupov, *Notor:* 1126

Z

Saʿd Zaghlūl, *20th:* 4439
Babe Didrikson Zaharias, *20th:* 4442
Marie Elizabeth Zakrzewska, *19th:* 2481
Giuseppe Zangara, *Notor:* 1128
Darryl F. Zanuck, *20th:* 4445
Emiliano Zapata, *20th:* 4448, *Notor:* 1129
Zara Yaqob, *Ren:* 1006
Abu Musab al-Zarqawi, *Notor:* 1132

Ayman al-Zawahiri, *Notor:* 1135
Zeami Motokiyo, *MA:* 1152
Zeng Guofan, *19th:* 2483
John Peter Zenger, *18th:* 1116
Zeno of Citium, *Anc:* 981
Zeno of Elea, *Anc:* 984
Zenobia, *Anc:* 986
Ferdinand von Zeppelin, *20th:* 4452
Clara Zetkin, *20th:* 4455
Zhang Zhidong, *19th:* 2486
Zhao Ziyang, *20th:* 4459
Andrey Aleksandrovich Zhdanov, *Notor:* 1137
Zheng Chenggong, *17th:* 1001
Zheng He, *MA:* 1156
Zhengde, *Ren:* 1008
Zhou Enlai, *20th:* 4461
Zhu De, *20th:* 4465
Zhu Xi, *MA:* 1159
Zhuangzi, *Anc:* 989
Georgy Zhukov, *20th:* 4469
Mohammad Zia-ul-Haq, *20th:* 4473
Grigory Yevseyevich Zinovyev, *Notor:* 1138
Count von Zinzendorf, *18th:* 1119
Jan Žižka, *MA:* 1162
Émile Zola, *19th:* 2489
Zoroaster, *Anc:* 992
Zoser, *Anc:* 996
Francisco de Zurbarán, *17th:* 1003
Ellen Taaffe Zwilich, *20th:* 4475
Huldrych Zwingli, *Ren:* 1010
Vladimir Zworykin, *20th:* 4479

Category Index

List of Categories

Agriculture 35
Anthropology and Sociology 35
Archaeology 36
Architecture 36
Art 36
Assassins and Murderers. . . . 38
Astronomy 39
Aviation and Space Exploration 40
Biology. 40
Business and Industry 41
Cartography 42
Chemistry 42
Church Government and Reform 43
Civil Rights 44
Communications 44
Computer Science 44
Conservation and Environmentalism 44
Crime 44
Dance 45
Diplomacy 45
Earth Sciences 47
Economics 47
Education 48
Engineering 49
Exploration. 50
Gangsters and Associates . . . 51
Genetics 51
Geography 51
Government and Politics. . . . 52
Historiography 63
Invention and Technology . . . 63
Journalism 64
Language and Linguistics . . . 65
Law 65
Literature. 66
Mathematics 71
Medicine 72
Military Affairs 73
Monarchy (20th century) . . . 76
Music 76
Native American Affairs. . . . 78
Natural History. 78
Outlaws and Gunslingers . . . 78
Philanthropy and Patrons of the Arts. 79
Philosophy 79
Photography 82
Physics 82
Physiology 83
Pirates 83
Psychology and Psychiatry . . . 83
Racists and Hatemongers . . . 84
Radio, Film, and Television. . . 84
Religion and Theology. 85
Scholarship. 89
Science 90
Social Reform 90
Sports 92
Terrorists. 93
Theater and Live Entertainment. 93
Traitors and Spies 94
Warfare and Conquest 95
Witches and Occultists. 97
Women's Rights 97

Agriculture

Johnny Appleseed, *19th:* 68
Bhumibol Adulyadej, *20th:* 363
Norman Borlaug, *20th:* 434
Luther Burbank, *19th:* 350
George Washington Carver, *20th:* 678
Fritz Haber, *20th:* 1628
Justus von Liebig, *19th:* 1366
Trofim Lysenko, *Notor:* 667
Cyrus Hall McCormick, *19th:* 1438
Thomas Robert Malthus, *19th:* 1475
Gifford Pinchot, *20th:* 3253
Jethro Tull, *18th:* 990
Nikolai Ivanovich Vavilov, *20th:* 4151
Henry A. Wallace, *20th:* 4207
Eli Whitney, *18th:* 1076

American Indian Affairs. *See* **Native American Affairs**

Anthropology and Sociology

Ruth Benedict, *20th:* 296
Franz Boas, *20th:* 400
Auguste Comte, *19th:* 536
Charles Darwin, *19th:* 603
Katherine Dunham, *20th:* 1061
Émile Durkheim, *20th:* 1065
Eugen Ehrlich, *20th:* 1113
Adam Ferguson, *18th:* 338
Sir James George Frazer, *20th:* 1319
Leo Frobenius, *20th:* 1341
Arnold Gesell, *20th:* 1465
Jürgen Habermas, *20th:* 1632
Fredereic Harrison, *19th:* 1044
Georg Wilhelm Friedrich Hegel, *19th:* 1065
Thor Heyerdahl, *20th:* 1795
Leonard T. Hobhouse, *20th:* 1841
Laud Humphreys, *Notor:* 498
Zora Neale Hurston, *20th:* 1944
Jomo Kenyatta, *20th:* 2106
Alfred Kinsey, *20th:* 2159
L. S. B. Leakey, *20th:* 2310
Mary Leakey, *20th:* 2315
Gustave Le Bon, *20th:* 2320
Claude Lévi-Strauss, *20th:* 2347
Harriet Martineau, *19th:* 1505
Margaret Mead, *20th:* 2668
Knud Johan Victor Rasmussen, *20th:* 3377
Henri de Saint-Simon, *19th:* 1975
Herbert Spencer, *19th:* 2126
Marion Talbot, *20th:* 3937
Alexis de Tocqueville, *19th:* 2280

Ferdinand Julius Tönnies, *20th:* 4044
Ernst Troeltsch, *20th:* 4069
Thorstein Veblen, *20th:* 4154
Giambattista Vico, *18th:* 1013
Lester Frank Ward, *19th:* 2384
Max Weber, *20th:* 4258

ARCHAEOLOGY

Henri-Édouard-Prosper Breuil, *20th:* 517
Thor Heyerdahl, *20th:* 1795
L. S. B. Leakey, *20th:* 2310
Mary Leakey, *20th:* 2315
Gustave Le Bon, *20th:* 2320
Rudolf Virchow, *19th:* 2365
William Stukeley, *18th:* 952
Johann Joachim Winckelmann, *18th:* 1095

ARCHITECTURE

Alvar Aalto, *20th:* 1
ʿAbd al-Malik, *MA:* 3
Robert and James Adam, *18th:* 3
Marcus Vipsanius Agrippa, *Anc:* 20
Leon Battista Alberti, *Ren:* 18
Alexander VII, *17th:* 9
Amenhotep III, *Anc:* 45
Arnolfo di Cambio, *MA:* 102
Ashurbanipal, *Anc:* 117
Ashurnasirpal II, *Anc:* 120
Sir Charles Barry, *19th:* 142
Gian Lorenzo Bernini, *17th:* 45
Bess of Hardwick, *Ren:* 103
Germain Boffrand, *18th:* 132
Francesco Borromini, *17th:* 67
Donato Bramante, *Ren:* 132
Lancelot Brown, *18th:* 165
Filippo Brunelleschi, *MA:* 205
Charles Bulfinch, *19th:* 346
Daniel Hudson Burnham, *19th:* 360
Felix Candela, *20th:* 631
Gustave Eiffel, *19th:* 734
Eupalinus of Megara, *Anc:* 323
Beatrix Jones Farrand, *20th:* 1219
Johann Bernhard Fischer von Erlach, *18th:* 350
John Fitch, *18th:* 353
Eugène Freyssinet, *20th:* 1326
R. Buckminster Fuller, *20th:* 1364
Tony Garnier, *20th:* 1414
Antonio Gaudí, *20th:* 1423
Frank Gehry, *20th:* 1438
Maḥmūd Ghāzān, *MA:* 411
Giotto, *MA:* 421
Francis Greenway, *19th:* 974
Walter Gropius, *20th:* 1602
Guarino Guarini, *17th:* 330
Nicholas Hawksmoor, *18th:* 472
Juan de Herrera, *Ren:* 445
Johann Lucas von Hildebrandt, *18th:* 494
Robert Hooke, *17th:* 383
Imhotep, *Anc:* 439
Inigo Jones, *17th:* 436
Justinian I, *MA:* 598
Khosrow I, *MA:* 613
Lalibela, *MA:* 632
Benjamin Henry Latrobe, *19th:* 1325
Charles Le Brun, *17th:* 504
Le Corbusier, *20th:* 2323
André Le Nôtre, *17th:* 523
Pierre Lescot, *Ren:* 565
Louis Le Vau, *17th:* 532
Maya Ying Lin, *20th:* 2385
Antônio Francisco Lisboa, *18th:* 608
François Mansart, *17th:* 587
Jules Hardouin-Mansart, *17th:* 590
Mausolus, *Anc:* 545
Melisende, *MA:* 715
Erich Mendelsohn, *20th:* 2692
Menkaure, *Anc:* 558
Michelangelo, *Ren:* 682
Ludwig Mies van der Rohe, *20th:* 2731
William Morris, *19th:* 1606
John Nash, *19th:* 1642
Pier Luigi Nervi, *20th:* 2940
Jack Nicklaus, *20th:* 2959
Oscar Niemeyer, *20th:* 2967
Frederick Law Olmsted, *19th:* 1706
J. J. P. Oud, *20th:* 3092
Andrea Palladio, *Ren:* 753
I. M. Pei, *20th:* 3183
Auguste Perret, *20th:* 3213
Augustus Welby Northmore Pugin, *19th:* 1838
Qāytbāy, *Ren:* 807
Ramses II, *Anc:* 735
Raphael, *Ren:* 819
Henry Hobson Richardson, *19th:* 1905
Jacopo Sansovino, *Ren:* 847
Sir George Gilbert Scott, *19th:* 2044
Shah Jahan, *17th:* 842
Diego de Siloé, *Ren:* 890
Sixtus V, *Ren:* 895
Sixtus IV, *Ren:* 893
Simon Stevin, *Ren:* 912
George Edmund Street, *19th:* 2191
William Stukeley, *18th:* 952
Suger, *MA:* 971
Louis Sullivan, *19th:* 2198
Suryavarman II, *MA:* 980
Tarquins, *Anc:* 846
Sir John Vanbrugh, *18th:* 1002
Giorgio Vasari, *Ren:* 953
John Wilkinson, *18th:* 1086
Sir Christopher Wren, *17th:* 994
Frank Lloyd Wright, *20th:* 4400
Iannis Xenakis, *20th:* 4414
Xerxes I, *Anc:* 971
Zoser, *Anc:* 996

ART. *See also* **ARCHITECTURE; DANCE; LITERATURE; MUSIC; PHILANTHROPHY AND PATRONS OF THE ARTS; PHOTOGRAPHY; RADIO, FILM, AND TELEVISION; THEATER AND LIVE ENTERTAINMENT**

Fanny Abington, *18th:* 1
Leon Battista Alberti, *Ren:* 18
Alexander VII, *17th:* 9
Andrea del Sarto, *Ren:* 39
Fra Angelico, *MA:* 83
Sofonisba Anguissola, *Ren:* 46
Guillaume Apollinaire, *20th:* 104
Arnolfo di Cambio, *MA:* 102
John James Audubon, *19th:* 91
Hester Bateman, *18th:* 95
Aubrey Beardsley, *19th:* 162

Giovanni Bellini, *Ren:* 97
Sarah Bernhardt, *19th:* 208
Gian Lorenzo Bernini, *17th:* 45
Albert Bierstadt, *19th:* 232
George Caleb Bingham, *19th:* 234
William Blake, *18th:* 121
Umberto Boccioni, *20th:* 403
Barbara Leigh Smith Bodichon, *19th:* 263
Pierre Bonnard, *20th:* 421
Hieronymus Bosch, *Ren:* 120
Sandro Botticelli, *Ren:* 123
Matthew Boulton, *18th:* 156
Constantin Brancusi, *20th:* 478
Georges Braque, *20th:* 493
Henri-Édouard-Prosper Breuil, *20th:* 517
Lancelot Brown, *18th:* 165
Pieter Bruegel, the Elder, *Ren:* 135
Samuel Butler, *19th:* 374
Alexander Calder, *20th:* 609
Jacques Callot, *17th:* 116
Canaletto, *18th:* 190
Antonio Canova, *19th:* 406
Caravaggio, *Ren:* 170
The Carracci Family, *Ren:* 175
Henri Cartier-Bresson, *20th:* 671
Mary Cassatt, *19th:* 433
George Catlin, *19th:* 441
Benvenuto Cellini, *Ren:* 202
Paul Cézanne, *19th:* 453
Marc Chagall, *20th:* 717
Jean-Siméon Chardin, *18th:* 223
Chen Shu, *17th:* 156
Judy Chicago, *20th:* 750
Chŏng Sŏn, *18th:* 248
Cimabue, *MA:* 282
Claude Lorrain, *17th:* 171
John Constable, *19th:* 540
John Singleton Copley, *18th:* 274
Correggio, *Ren:* 249
Gustave Courbet, *19th:* 559
Lucas Cranach, the Elder, *Ren:* 262
Salvador Dalí, *20th:* 904
Jacques-Louis David, *19th:* 607
Edgar Degas, *19th:* 632
Eugène Delacroix, *19th:* 635
Robert Delaunay, *20th:* 950
Maurice Denis, *20th:* 972
Walt Disney, *20th:* 1006
Donatello, *MA:* 319
Duccio di Buoninsegna, *MA:* 326
Marcel Duchamp, *20th:* 1051
Albrecht Dürer, *Ren:* 297
Sir Anthony van Dyck, *17th:* 244
Thomas Eakins, *19th:* 717
Sir Jacob Epstein, *20th:* 1165
Max Ernst, *20th:* 1176
M. C. Escher, *20th:* 1183
Jan van and Hubert van Eyck, *MA:* 365
Filippo Brunelleschi, *MA:* 205
Lavinia Fontana, *Ren:* 338
Jean-Honoré Fragonard, *18th:* 367
Helen Frankenthaler, *20th:* 1304
Roger Fry, *20th:* 1351
Thomas Gainsborough, *18th:* 387
Isabella Stewart Gardner, *20th:* 1406
Giovanna Garzoni, *17th:* 302
Paul Gauguin, *19th:* 879
Norman Bel Geddes, *20th:* 1431
Artemisia Gentileschi, *17th:* 307
Théodore Géricault, *19th:* 898
Lorenzo Ghiberti, *MA:* 418
Alberto Giacometti, *20th:* 1470
Giorgione, *Ren:* 383
Giotto, *MA:* 421
Vincent van Gogh, *19th:* 932
Francisco de Goya, *18th:* 436
Baltasar Gracián y Morales, *17th:* 316
El Greco, *Ren:* 390
Juan Gris, *20th:* 1597
Matthias Grünewald, *Ren:* 405
Charlotte Guillard, *Ren:* 413
Hakuin, *18th:* 450
Frans Hals, *17th:* 352
Catharina van Hemessen, *Ren:* 421
Hiroshige, *19th:* 1107
Hishikawa Moronobu, *17th:* 375
David Hockney, *20th:* 1845
William Hogarth, *18th:* 497
Hans Holbein, the Younger, *Ren:* 453
Winslow Homer, *19th:* 1122
Edward Hopper, *20th:* 1876
Elmyr de Hory, *Notor:* 492
William Holman Hunt, *19th:* 1157
Jean-Auguste-Dominique Ingres, *19th:* 1171
Jacopo della Quercia, *MA:* 566
Jōchō, *MA:* 581
Augustus John, *20th:* 2014
Frida Kahlo, *20th:* 2069
Wassily Kandinsky, *20th:* 2074
Angelica Kauffmann, *18th:* 554
Tom Keating, *Notor:* 559
Ernst Ludwig Kirchner, *20th:* 2164
Paul Klee, *20th:* 2176
Gustav Klimt, *20th:* 2180
Kōbō Daishi, *MA:* 620
Oskar Kokoschka, *20th:* 2185
Käthe Kollwitz, *20th:* 2189
Lee Krasner, *20th:* 2195
František Kupka, *20th:* 2211
Georges de La Tour, *17th:* 493
Thomas Lawrence, *18th:* 583
Charles Le Brun, *17th:* 504
Fernand Léger, *20th:* 2334
André Le Nôtre, *17th:* 523
Leonardo da Vinci, *Ren:* 561
Pierre Lescot, *Ren:* 565
Levni, *18th:* 602
Roy Lichtenstein, *20th:* 2373
Maya Ying Lin, *20th:* 2385
Jacques Lipchitz, *20th:* 2397
Antônio Francisco Lisboa, *18th:* 608
Liu Yin, *17th:* 540
Pietro and Ambrogio Lorenzetti, *MA:* 659
George Lucas, *20th:* 2450
Lysippus, *Anc:* 523
Ma Yuan, *MA:* 677
René Magritte, *20th:* 2547
André Malraux, *20th:* 2576
Man Ray, *20th:* 2580
Édouard Manet, *19th:* 1479
Andrea Mantegna, *Ren:* 601
Aldus Manutius, *Ren:* 608
Franz Marc, *20th:* 2606
Marie de Médicis, *17th:* 598
Agnes Martin, *20th:* 2636
Simone Martini, *MA:* 696
Masaccio, *MA:* 699

Henri Matisse, *20th:* 2649
Mi Fei, *MA:* 718
Michelangelo, *Ren:* 682
Kate Millett, *20th:* 2746
Joan Miró, *20th:* 2759
Amedeo Modigliani, *20th:* 2776
Piet Mondrian, *20th:* 2786
Claude Monet, *20th:* 2790
Henry Moore, *20th:* 2818
William Morris, *19th:* 1606
Grandma Moses, *20th:* 2841
Robert Motherwell, *20th:* 2847
Edvard Munch, *20th:* 2870
Bartolomé Esteban Murillo, *17th:* 670
Paul Nash, *20th:* 2910
Thomas Nast, *19th:* 1649
Nero, *Anc:* 591, *Notor:* 777
Louise Nevelson, *20th:* 2947
Ben Nicholson, *20th:* 2956
Ogata Kōrin, *17th:* 695
Georgia O'Keeffe, *20th:* 3031
Claes Oldenburg, *20th:* 3037
Andrea Orcagna, *MA:* 798
José Clemente Orozco, *20th:* 3068
Walter Pater, *19th:* 1755
Charles Willson Peale, *18th:* 768
Phidias, *Anc:* 633
Pablo Picasso, *20th:* 3237
Piero della Francesca, *Ren:* 785
Andrea Pisano, *MA:* 845
Nicola and Giovanni Pisano, *MA:* 847
Camille Pissarro, *19th:* 1799
Jackson Pollock, *20th:* 3301
Polyclitus, *Anc:* 675
Polygnotus, *Anc:* 678
Nicolas Poussin, *17th:* 749
Praxiteles, *Anc:* 694
Jean Pucelle, *MA:* 866
Sir Henry Raeburn, *19th:* 1852
Raphael, *Ren:* 819
Robert Rauschenberg, *20th:* 3380
Odilon Redon, *19th:* 1875
Rembrandt, *17th:* 786
Frederic Remington, *19th:* 1881
Pierre-Auguste Renoir, *19th:* 1888
Sir Joshua Reynolds, *18th:* 836
Diego Rivera, *20th:* 3457
Norman Rockwell, *20th:* 3483
Auguste Rodin, *19th:* 1925
George Romney, *18th:* 862
Betsy Ross, *18th:* 865
Mark Rothko, *20th:* 3539
Georges Rouault, *20th:* 3541
Henri Rousseau, *19th:* 1951
Peter Paul Rubens, *17th:* 802
John Ruskin, *19th:* 1954
Augustus Saint-Gaudens, *19th:* 1972
John Singer Sargent, *19th:* 1996
Karl Schmidt-Rottluff, *20th:* 3661
Charles M. Schulz, *20th:* 3672
Anna Maria van Schurman, *17th:* 823
Scopas, *Anc:* 761
Maurice Sendak, *20th:* 3698
Sesshū, *Ren:* 865
Georges Seurat, *19th:* 2074
Dr. Seuss, *20th:* 3710
Diego de Siloé, *Ren:* 890
Elisabetta Sirani, *17th:* 856
Claus Sluter, *MA:* 947
Sōtatsu, *17th:* 868
Gilbert Stuart, *18th:* 947
Su Dongpo, *MA:* 968
Graham Vivian Sutherland, *20th:* 3920
Suzuki Harunobu, *18th:* 958
Hippolyte Taine, *19th:* 2216
Tom Thomson, *20th:* 4010
James Thurber, *20th:* 4020
Giovanni Battista Tiepolo, *18th:* 976
Tintoretto, *Ren:* 931
Marietta Robusti Tintoretto, *Ren:* 935
Titian, *Ren:* 936
Henri de Toulouse-Lautrec, *19th:* 2287
J. M. W. Turner, *19th:* 2322
Unkei, *MA:* 1040
Giorgio Vasari, *Ren:* 953
Diego Velázquez, *17th:* 953
Jan Vermeer, *17th:* 956
Paolo Veronese, *Ren:* 959
Andrea del Verrocchio, *Ren:* 962
Élisabeth Vigée-Lebrun, *18th:* 1016
Édouard Vuillard, *20th:* 4173
Wang Wei, *MA:* 1085
Wang Xizhi, *Anc:* 955
Andy Warhol, *20th:* 4226
Antoine Watteau, *18th:* 1051
Josiah Wedgwood, *18th:* 1057
Benjamin West, *18th:* 1068
Rogier van der Weyden, *MA:* 1092
James McNeill Whistler, *19th:* 2420
Gertrude Vanderbilt Whitney, *20th:* 4315
Johann Joachim Winckelmann, *18th:* 1095
Grant Wood, *20th:* 4387
Wu Hou, *MA:* 1127
Andrew Wyeth, *20th:* 4410
Xia Gui, *MA:* 1134
Yan Liben, *MA:* 1140
Francisco de Zurbarán, *17th:* 1003

Assassins and Murderers

Mehmet Ali Ağca, *Notor:* 8
Said Akbar (?-1951), *Notor:* 10
Yigal Amir, *Notor:* 22
Eugene Aram, *Notor:* 30
Roscoe Arbuckle, *Notor:* 32
Joe Ball, *Notor:* 52
Velma Margie Barfield, *Notor:* 59
Jean-Marie Bastien-Thiry, *Notor:* 69
Elizabeth Báthory, *Ren:* 81, *Notor:* 70
Byron De La Beckwith, *Notor:* 78
John Bellingham, *Notor:* 83
Bambi Bembenek, *Notor:* 84
David Berkowitz, *Notor:* 91
Paul Bernardo, *Notor:* 93
Kenneth Bianchi, *Notor:* 95
John Wilkes Booth, *Notor:* 123
Lizzie Borden, *19th:* 277, *Notor:* 125
Arthur Bremer, *Notor:* 139
Marcus Junius Brutus, *Anc:* 166, *Notor:* 146
Ted Bundy, *Notor:* 149
Angelo Buono, Jr., *Notor:* 151
William Burke, *Notor:* 154
Aaron Burr, *19th:* 363, *Notor:* 155
Samuel Joseph Byck, *Notor:* 162

William Calley, *Notor:* 168
Sante Jeronimo Caserio, *Notor:* 180
Beatrice Cenci, *Notor:* 192
Cassius Chaerea, *Notor:* 195
Mark David Chapman, *Notor:* 200
Andrei Chikatilo, *Notor:* 207
John Reginald Halliday Christie, *Notor:* 210
Jacques Clément, *Notor:* 214
Charlotte Corday, *Notor:* 235
Andrew Cunanan, *Notor:* 245
Leon Czolgosz, *Notor:* 252
Jeffrey Dahmer, *Notor:* 255
Richard Allen Davis, *Notor:* 267
Albert DeSalvo, *Notor:* 274
Diane Downs, *Notor:* 299
John E. du Pont, *Notor:* 305
Reginald Dyer, *Notor:* 311
Ira Einhorn, *Notor:* 324
Ruth Ellis, *Notor:* 327
John Felton, *Notor:* 352
Giuseppe Fieschi, *Notor:* 353
Albert Fish, *Notor:* 355
Antoinette Frank, *Notor:* 373
Lynette Fromme, *Notor:* 377
John Wayne Gacy, *Notor:* 387
Ed Gein, *Notor:* 399
Balthasar Gérard, *Notor:* 404
Gary Gilmore, *Notor:* 411
Nathuram Vinayak Godse, *Notor:* 416
Bernhard Goetz, *Notor:* 423
Charles Julius Guiteau, *Notor:* 439
Jean Harris, *Notor:* 448
Linda Burfield Hazzard, *Notor:* 453
George Hennard, *Notor:* 456
Marie Hilley, *Notor:* 467
John Hinckley, Jr., *Notor:* 470
H. H. Holmes, *Notor:* 486
Karla Homolka, *Notor:* 488
James Oliver Huberty, *Notor:* 497
Irish Invincibles, *Notor:* 509
Jack the Ripper, *Notor:* 519
Jing Ke, *Notor:* 530
John Parricida, *Notor:* 536
Theodore Kaczynski, *Notor:* 547
Fanya Kaplan, *Notor:* 552
Ned Kelly, *Notor:* 562
Jack Ketch, *Notor:* 565
Sante Kimes, *Notor:* 584
Leonard Lake, *Notor:* 602
Henri Désiré Landru, *Notor:* 603
Richard Lawrence, *Notor:* 615
Nathan F. Leopold, Jr., *Notor:* 634
Marc Lépine, *Notor:* 638
Richard A. Loeb, *Notor:* 647
Byron Looper, *Notor:* 654
Seventh Earl of Lucan, *Notor:* 657
Jeffrey Lundgren, *Notor:* 664
Molly Maguires, *Notor:* 745
Jeffrey MacDonald, *Notor:* 673
Daniel M'Naghten, *Notor:* 677
Mary Mallon, *Notor:* 685
Lee Boyd Malvo, *Notor:* 765
Charles Manson, *Notor:* 689
Ramón Mercader, *Notor:* 721
Mijailo Mijailovic, *Notor:* 727
John Allen Muhammad, *Notor:* 765
Leslie Nelson, *Notor:* 776
Charles Ng, *Notor:* 784
Eligiusz Niewiadomski, *Notor:* 792
Lee Harvey Oswald, *Notor:* 807
Bonnie Parker, *Notor:* 811
Charles Peace, *Notor:* 815
Scott Peterson, *Notor:* 828
Marcel Petiot, *Notor:* 831
Lewis Powell (1884-1865), *Notor:* 858
Gavrilo Princip, *Notor:* 861
Puniša Račić, *Notor:* 876
Dennis Rader, *Notor:* 879
Gilles de Rais, *Notor:* 880
Thenmuli Rajaratnam, *Notor:* 882
François Ravaillac, *Notor:* 888
James Earl Ray, *Notor:* 889
Richard III, *Ren:* 828, *Notor:* 896
George Rivas, *Notor:* 901
Darlie Routier, *Notor:* 918
Jack Ruby, *Notor:* 919
Eric Rudolph, *Notor:* 921
Nicola Sacco, *20th:* 3580, *Notor:* 924
Yolanda Saldívar, *Notor:* 930
Clay Shaw, *Notor:* 941
Sam Sheppard, *Notor:* 945
Harold Shipman, *Notor:* 950
O. J. Simpson, *Notor:* 958
Beant Singh, *Notor:* 962
Satwant Singh, *Notor:* 963
Sirhan Sirhan, *Notor:* 965
Pamela Ann Smart, *Notor:* 971
Madeleine Smith, *Notor:* 975
Susan Smith, *Notor:* 977
Ruth Snyder, *Notor:* 979
Charles Sobraj, *Notor:* 980
Richard Speck, *Notor:* 986
Charles Starkweather, *Notor:* 993
Robert Franklin Stroud, *Notor:* 1005
Mary Surratt, *Notor:* 1012
Michael Swango, *Notor:* 1015
Harry Kendall Thaw, *Notor:* 1027
Sweeney Todd, *Notor:* 1033
Karla Faye Tucker, *Notor:* 1044
Volkert van der Graaf, *Notor:* 1055
Bartolomeo Vanzetti, *Notor:* 1056
Vlad III the Impaler, *Ren:* 981, *Notor:* 1072
Claus von Bülow, *Notor:* 1075
Carolyn Warmus, *Notor:* 1090
Carl Weiss, *Notor:* 1095
Dan White, *Notor:* 1099
Charles Whitman, *Notor:* 1101
Henry Wirz, *Notor:* 1105
Aileen Carol Wuornos, *Notor:* 1108
Andrea Yates, *Notor:* 1113
Yakov Mikhailovich Yurovsky, *Notor:* 1124
Felix Yusupov, *Notor:* 1126
Giuseppe Zangara, *Notor:* 1128

ASTRONOMY. *See also* AVIATION AND SPACE EXPLORATION; PHYSICS

Abul Wefa, *MA:* 21
Saint Albertus Magnus, *MA:* 42
Hannes Alfvén, *20th:* 58
Alhazen, *MA:* 66
Viktor A. Ambartsumian, *20th:* 77
Anaximander, *Anc:* 55
Apollonius of Perga, *Anc:* 76
Svante August Arrhenius, *20th:* 138
Āryabhaṭa the Elder, *MA:* 108

Avicenna, *MA:* 123
Walter Baade, *20th:* 184
Roger Bacon, *MA:* 127
Jean-Sylvain Bailly, *18th:* 77
Benjamin Banneker, *18th:* 84
al-Battānī, *MA:* 137
The Bernoulli Family, *17th:* 48
Friedrich Wilhelm Bessel, *19th:* 215
al-Bīrūnī, *MA:* 163
Giovanni Alfonso Borelli, *17th:* 65
Sophie Brahe, *Ren:* 126
Tycho Brahe, *Ren:* 128
Brahmagupta, *MA:* 195
Giordano Bruno, *Ren:* 138
Jocelyn Burnell, *20th:* 584
Robert Burton, *17th:* 108
Annie Jump Cannon, *20th:* 635
Gian Domenico Cassini, *17th:* 134
James Cook, *18th:* 270
Nicolaus Copernicus, *Ren:* 241
André-Louis Danjon, *20th:* 911
John Dee, *Ren:* 278
Albert Einstein, *20th:* 1118
Eudoxus of Cnidus, *Anc:* 320
David and Johannes Fabricius, *17th:* 259
Williamina Paton Stevens Fleming, *19th:* 788
Girolamo Fracastoro, *Ren:* 343
Galileo, *17th:* 298
George Gamow, *20th:* 1379
Pierre Gassendi, *17th:* 304
Carl Friedrich Gauss, *19th:* 883
James Gregory, *17th:* 319
Francesco Maria Grimaldi, *17th:* 321
George Ellery Hale, *20th:* 1643
Edmond Halley, *17th:* 348
Sir William Rowan Hamilton, *19th:* 1015
Stephen Hawking, *20th:* 1712
Caroline Lucretia Herschel, *18th:* 489
William Herschel, *18th:* 492
Gerhard Herzberg, *20th:* 1783
Johannes and Elisabetha Hevelius, *17th:* 371
Hipparchus, *Anc:* 417
Jeremiah Horrocks, *17th:* 388
Sir Fred Hoyle, *20th:* 1902
Edwin Powell Hubble, *20th:* 1912
Margaret Lindsay Huggins, *19th:* 1144
Christiaan Huygens, *17th:* 397
Hypatia, *Anc:* 434
Johannes Kepler, *17th:* 457
al-Khwārizmī, *MA:* 617
Samuel Pierpont Langley, *19th:* 1309
Pierre-Simon Laplace, *19th:* 1317
Henrietta Swan Leavitt, *20th:* 2317
Georges Lemaître, *20th:* 2337
Levi ben Gershom, *MA:* 650
Sir Joseph Norman Lockyer, *19th:* 1412
Albert A. Michelson, *19th:* 1567
Maria Mitchell, *19th:* 1580
Nabu-rimanni, *Anc:* 579
Simon Newcomb, *19th:* 1660
Nostradamus, *Ren:* 728, *Notor:* 799
Hermann Oberth, *20th:* 3008
Jan Hendrik Oort, *20th:* 3059
Petrus Peregrinus de Maricourt, *MA:* 820
Georg von Peuerbach, *Ren:* 773
Ptolemy (astronomer), *Anc:* 712
Pythagoras, *Anc:* 725
Pytheas, *Anc:* 729
Rheticus, *Ren:* 823
Matteo Ricci, *Ren:* 825
Henry Norris Russell, *20th:* 3570
Carl Sagan, *20th:* 3590
Wilhelm Schickard, *17th:* 818
Bernhard Voldemar Schmidt, *20th:* 3659
Karl Schwarzschild, *20th:* 3674
Sosigenes, *Anc:* 815
Simon Stevin, *Ren:* 912
Sylvester II, *MA:* 983
Clyde William Tombaugh, *20th:* 4041
Harold C. Urey, *20th:* 4132
James Van Allen, *20th:* 4139
Wang Zhenyi, *18th:* 1038
Max Wolf, *20th:* 4382

Aviation and Space Exploration

Neil Armstrong, *20th:* 134
Louis Blériot, *20th:* 388
Wernher von Braun, *20th:* 500
Richard Byrd, *20th:* 606
George Cayley, *19th:* 447
Bessie Coleman, *20th:* 801
Jimmy Doolittle, *20th:* 1023
Amelia Earhart, *20th:* 1075
Hugo Eckener, *20th:* 1092
Yuri Gagarin, *20th:* 1370
Marc Garneau, *20th:* 1412
John Glenn, *20th:* 1499
Robert H. Goddard, *20th:* 1507
William F. Halsey, *20th:* 1647
Ernst Heinkel, *20th:* 1746
Harry Hammond Hess, *20th:* 1785
Howard Hughes, *20th:* 1925
Albert Kesselring, *20th:* 2117
Sergei Korolev, *20th:* 2191
Anne Morrow Lindbergh, *20th:* 2389
Charles A. Lindbergh, *20th:* 2392
Shannon W. Lucid, *20th:* 2460
William Mitchell, *20th:* 2765
Auguste and Jean-Felix Piccard, *20th:* 3240
Ludwig Prandtl, *20th:* 3327
Sally Ride, *20th:* 3447
Alberto Santos-Dumont, *20th:* 3632
Alan Shepard, *20th:* 3725
Valentina Tereshkova, *20th:* 3978
Konstantin Tsiolkovsky, *20th:* 4095
Andrei Nikolayevich Tupolev, *20th:* 4108
James Van Allen, *20th:* 4139
Sir Frank Whittle, *20th:* 4318
Orville and Wilbur Wright, *20th:* 4403
Chuck Yeager, *20th:* 4425
Ferdinand von Zeppelin, *20th:* 4452

Biology. ***See also* Agriculture; Genetics; Medicine; Physiology**

José de Acosta, *Ren:* 5
Elizabeth Cabot Agassiz, *19th:* 29
Louis Agassiz, *19th:* 31
Saint Albertus Magnus, *MA:* 42

John James Audubon, *19th:* 91
Karl Ernst von Baer, *19th:* 114
Jean-Sylvain Bailly, *18th:* 77
Sir Frederick G. Banting, *20th:* 224
Sir William Maddock Bayliss, *20th:* 259
Pierre Belon, *Ren:* 101
Claude Bernard, *19th:* 205
Norman Borlaug, *20th:* 434
Comte de Buffon, *18th:* 171
Sir Macfarlane Burnet, *20th:* 587
Samuel Butler, *19th:* 374
Albert Calmette, *20th:* 618
Melvin Calvin, *20th:* 621
Rachel Carson, *20th:* 662
Andrea Cesalpino, *Ren:* 211
Ferdinand Julius Cohn, *19th:* 527
Francis Crick, *20th:* 865
Georges Cuvier, *19th:* 585
Charles Darwin, *19th:* 603
Gerhard Domagk, *20th:* 1021
Paul Ehrlich, *20th:* 1115
John Evelyn, *17th:* 256
Sir Alexander Fleming, *20th:* 1254
Baron Florey, *20th:* 1259
Rosalind Franklin, *20th:* 1316
Karl von Frisch, *20th:* 1335
Leonhard Fuchs, *Ren:* 356
Luigi Galvani, *18th:* 391
Stephen Jay Gould, *20th:* 1555
Asa Gray, *19th:* 963
Ernst Haeckel, *19th:* 1002
William Harvey, *17th:* 355
Georg von Hevesy, *20th:* 1792
Dorothy Crowfoot Hodgkin, *20th:* 1849
Bernardo Alberto Houssay, *20th:* 1899
Sir Fred Hoyle, *20th:* 1902
Alexander von Humboldt, *19th:* 1151
Thomas Henry Huxley, *19th:* 1161
François Jacob, *20th:* 1982
Robert Koch, *19th:* 1291
Sir Hans Adolf Krebs, *20th:* 2199
August Krogh, *20th:* 2204
Karl Landsteiner, *20th:* 2250
Sir Edwin Ray Lankester, *19th:* 1315
Antoni van Leeuwenhoek, *17th:* 509
Leonardo da Vinci, *Ren:* 561
Carolus Linnaeus, *18th:* 604
Konrad Lorenz, *20th:* 2434
Shannon W. Lucid, *20th:* 2460
John J. R. Macleod, *20th:* 2526
Marcello Malpighi, *17th:* 579
Barbara McClintock, *20th:* 2504
Gregor Mendel, *19th:* 1541
Thomas Hunt Morgan, *20th:* 2825
Hermann Joseph Muller, *20th:* 2861
Kary B. Mullis, *20th:* 2864
Fridtjof Nansen, *20th:* 2907
Aleksandr Ivanovich Oparin, *20th:* 3062
Louis Pasteur, *19th:* 1751
Linus Pauling, *20th:* 3155
Ivan Petrovich Pavlov, *20th:* 3162
Jean Piaget, *20th:* 3231
Aleksandr Stepanovich Popov, *19th:* 1824
John Ray, *17th:* 782
Peyton Rous, *20th:* 3545
Jonas Salk, *20th:* 3613
Frederick Sanger, *20th:* 3622
The Siemens Family, *19th:* 2105
Theobald Smith, *20th:* 3772
Mary Somerville, *19th:* 2121
Lazzaro Spallanzani, *18th:* 925
Herbert Spencer, *19th:* 2126
Wendell Stanley, *20th:* 3824
Hermann Staudinger, *20th:* 3833
Marie Stopes, *20th:* 3882
Jan Swammerdam, *17th:* 898
Joseph Wilson Swan, *19th:* 2209
Emanuel Swedenborg, *18th:* 961
Theophrastus, *Anc:* 872
Hugo Theorell, *20th:* 3997
Catharine Parr Traill, *19th:* 2291
Harold E. Varmus, *20th:* 4145
Nikolai Ivanovich Vavilov, *20th:* 4151
Rudolf Virchow, *19th:* 2365
Selman Abraham Waksman, *20th:* 4180
James D. Watson, *20th:* 4242
August Weismann, *19th:* 2406
George Westinghouse, *19th:* 2416
Thomas Willis, *17th:* 985
Edward O. Wilson, *20th:* 4358
Rosalyn Yalow, *20th:* 4419

BUSINESS AND INDUSTRY

Robert and James Adam, *18th:* 3
Abigail Adams, *18th:* 7
Oakes Ames, *Notor:* 18
Sir Richard Arkwright, *18th:* 55
Mary Kay Ash, *20th:* 145
John Jacob Astor, *19th:* 86
Jim Bakker, *Notor:* 50
Lucille Ball, *20th:* 212
P. T. Barnum, *19th:* 138
Sydney Barrows, *Notor:* 64
Hester Bateman, *18th:* 95
Lord Beaverbrook, *20th:* 275
Jeff Bezos, *20th:* 360
Nicholas Biddle, *19th:* 225
Louis Blériot, *20th:* 388
Ivan Boesky, *Notor:* 110
Horatio W. Bottomley, *20th:* 445
Matthew Boulton, *18th:* 156
Mrs. Anne Bracegirdle, *17th:* 82
Helen Gurley Brown, *20th:* 539
Warren Buffett, *20th:* 563
Roberto Calvi, *Notor:* 170
Al Capone, *20th:* 641, *Notor:* 175
Andrew Carnegie, *19th:* 419
Coco Chanel, *20th:* 727
André-Gustave Citroën, *20th:* 772
Georges Claude, *20th:* 775
Samuel Colt, *19th:* 533
Jay Cooke, *19th:* 544
William Fothergill Cooke, *19th:* 547
Bing Crosby, *20th:* 874
Paul Cuffe, *19th:* 576
Abraham Darby, *18th:* 292
Tino De Angelis, *Notor:* 268
John DeLorean, *Notor:* 272
Walt Disney, *20th:* 1006
James Buchanan Duke, *19th:* 692
Eleuthère Irénée du Pont, *19th:* 705
James Buchanan Eads, *19th:* 715
George Eastman, *20th:* 1078
Bernard Ebbers, *Notor:* 317
Billie Sol Estes, *Notor:* 336
Ada Everleigh, *Notor:* 338

Faisal, *20th:* 1198
Enzo Ferrari, *20th:* 1239
Marshall Field, *19th:* 773
Jim Fisk, *Notor:* 357
Henry Ford, *20th:* 1279
Martin Frankel, *Notor:* 376
Benjamin Franklin, *18th:* 370
Bill Gates, *20th:* 1421
Norman Bel Geddes, *20th:* 1431
Samuel Goldwyn, *20th:* 1523
Jay Gould, *Notor:* 433
Katharine Graham, *20th:* 1560
Daniel Guggenheim, *20th:* 1613
John Hancock, *18th:* 457
James Hargreaves, *18th:* 466
Alfred and Harold Harmsworth, *20th:* 1678
Bill Haywood, *Notor:* 450
William Randolph Hearst, *20th:* 1734
James Jerome Hill, *19th:* 1100
Oveta Culp Hobby, *20th:* 1838
Soichiro Honda, *20th:* 1859
L. Ron Hubbard, *20th:* 1909, *Notor:* 495
Howard Hughes, *20th:* 1925
Megan Louise Ireland, *Notor:* 508
Steve Jobs, *20th:* 2006
Bobby Jones, *20th:* 2036
Ray Kroc, *20th:* 2201
Alfred Krupp, *19th:* 1301
Estée Lauder, *20th:* 2275
Antoine-Laurent Lavoisier, *18th:* 579
John Law, *Notor:* 614
Kenneth Lay, *Notor:* 617
Nick Leeson, *Notor:* 624
Ferdinand de Lesseps, *19th:* 1356
Dennis Levine, *Notor:* 642
Henry R. Luce, *20th:* 2456
John MacArthur, *19th:* 1431
Daniel and Alexander Macmillan, *19th:* 1464
Robert McNamara, *20th:* 2541
Konosuke Matsushita, *20th:* 2653
Louis B. Mayer, *20th:* 2662
Andrew Mellon, *20th:* 2683
Ottmar Mergenthaler, *19th:* 1558
Michael Milken, *Notor:* 731
Jean Monnet, *20th:* 2793
J. P. Morgan, *19th:* 1599
Akio Morita, *20th:* 2831
Mou Qizhong, *Notor:* 757
Rupert Murdoch, *20th:* 2876
Jacques Necker, *18th:* 726
John Newbery, *18th:* 730
Katherine Davalos Ortega, *20th:* 3074
William Paterson, *17th:* 716
H. Ross Perot, *20th:* 3208
Lydia E. Pinkham, *19th:* 1796
Pirelli Family, *20th:* 3266
Charles Ponzi, *Notor:* 852
Paul Revere, *18th:* 832
Cecil Rhodes, *19th:* 1891
John D. Rockefeller, *19th:* 1921
John D. Rockefeller, Jr., *20th:* 1921
Nelson A. Rockefeller, *20th:* 3478
Charles Stewart Rolls, *20th:* 3496
Betsy Ross, *18th:* 865
The Rothschild Family, *19th:* 1947
Sir Frederick Henry Royce, *20th:* 3496
Pete Rozelle, *20th:* 3553
Eisaku Satō, *20th:* 3645
Daniel Shays, *18th:* 902
Jeffrey Skilling, *Notor:* 967
Samuel Slater, *19th:* 2111
Leland Stanford, *19th:* 2132
Joseph Wilson Swan, *19th:* 2209
Frederick Winslow Taylor, *20th:* 3955
Tippu Tib, *19th:* 2277
Eiji Toyoda, *20th:* 4062
Anne-Robert-Jacques Turgot, *18th:* 996
Ted Turner, *20th:* 4118
Cornelius Vanderbilt, *19th:* 2348
Madam C. J. Walker, *20th:* 4199
Sam Walton, *20th:* 4213
Montgomery Ward, *19th:* 2386
Jack Warner, *20th:* 4230
Thomas J. Watson, Jr., *20th:* 4246
Thomas J. Watson, Sr., *20th:* 4246
Josiah Wedgwood, *18th:* 1057
George Westinghouse, *19th:* 2416
Eli Whitney, *18th:* 1076
Oprah Winfrey, *20th:* 4372
Ahmad Zaki Yamani, *20th:* 4422
Darryl F. Zanuck, *20th:* 4445
John Peter Zenger, *18th:* 1116

Cartography

Roald Amundsen, *20th:* 83
Anaximander, *Anc:* 55
William Bligh, *18th:* 126, *Notor:* 104
Álvar Núñez Cabeza de Vaca, *Ren:* 152
John Cabot, *Ren:* 155
Juan Rodríguez Cabrillo, *Ren:* 161
Jacques Cartier, *Ren:* 178
James Cook, *18th:* 270
al-Idrīsī, *MA:* 539
Antoine-Laurent Lavoisier, *18th:* 579
Gerardus Mercator, *Ren:* 678
Robert Edwin Peary, *20th:* 3177
Wilhelm Schickard, *17th:* 818
George Vancouver, *18th:* 1006
Amerigo Vespucci, *Ren:* 969

Chemistry

Svante August Arrhenius, *20th:* 138
Amedeo Avogadro, *19th:* 101
Johann Joachim Becher, *17th:* 39
The Becquerel Family, *19th:* 165
Friedrich Bergius, *20th:* 313
Joseph Black, *18th:* 115
Robert Boyle, *17th:* 78
Melvin Calvin, *20th:* 621
Henry Cavendish, *18th:* 217
Georges Claude, *20th:* 775
James Bryant Conant, *20th:* 820
Marie and Pierre Curie, *20th:* 888
John Dalton, *19th:* 597
Sir Humphry Davy, *19th:* 616
Otto Paul Hermann Diels, *20th:* 995
Gerhard Domagk, *20th:* 1021
Eleuthère Irénée du Pont, *19th:* 705
Paul Ehrlich, *20th:* 1115
Michael Faraday, *19th:* 759
Sir Alexander Fleming, *20th:* 1254
Baron Florey, *20th:* 1259

Rosalind Franklin, *20th:* 1316
Joseph-Louis Gay-Lussac, *19th:* 886
Josiah Willard Gibbs, *19th:* 913
Fritz Haber, *20th:* 1628
Otto Hahn, *20th:* 1635
Jan Baptista van Helmont, *17th:* 361
Gerhard Herzberg, *20th:* 1783
Georg von Hevesy, *20th:* 1792
Dorothy Crowfoot Hodgkin, *20th:* 1849
Abū Mūsā Jābir ibn Ḥayyān, *MA:* 562
Frédéric Joliot and Irène Joliot-Curie, *20th:* 2032
Sir Hans Adolf Krebs, *20th:* 2199
Karl Landsteiner, *20th:* 2250
Antoine-Laurent Lavoisier, *18th:* 579
Nicolas Leblanc, *18th:* 587
Willard F. Libby, *20th:* 2371
Justus von Liebig, *19th:* 1366
Mikhail Vasilyevich Lomonosov, *18th:* 613
Shannon W. Lucid, *20th:* 2460
Auguste and Louis Lumière, *20th:* 2471
John J. R. Macleod, *20th:* 2526
Edwin Mattison McMillan, *20th:* 2532
Andreas Sigismund Marggraf, *18th:* 651
Dmitry Ivanovich Mendeleyev, *19th:* 1544
Gaspard Monge, *18th:* 682
Kary B. Mullis, *20th:* 2864
Giulio Natta, *20th:* 2919
Walther Hermann Nernst, *20th:* 2934
Aleksandr Ivanovich Oparin, *20th:* 3062
Wilhelm Ostwald, *20th:* 3088
Paracelsus, *Ren:* 757
Louis Pasteur, *19th:* 1751
Linus Pauling, *20th:* 3155
Ellen Swallow Richards, *19th:* 1899
John Roebuck, *18th:* 858
F. Sherwood Rowland, *20th:* 3547
Benjamin Rush, *18th:* 872
Jonas Salk, *20th:* 3613
Frederick Sanger, *20th:* 3622
Frederick Soddy, *20th:* 3778
Lazzaro Spallanzani, *18th:* 925
Georg Ernst Stahl, *18th:* 933
Wendell Stanley, *20th:* 3824
Hermann Staudinger, *20th:* 3833
Marie Stopes, *20th:* 3882
Hugo Theorell, *20th:* 3997
Harold C. Urey, *20th:* 4132
Alessandro Volta, *18th:* 1022
Selman Abraham Waksman, *20th:* 4180
Chaim Weizmann, *20th:* 4279
Maurice Wilkins, *20th:* 4342
Thomas Willis, *17th:* 985
Edward O. Wilson, *20th:* 4358
Friedrich Wöhler, *19th:* 2456
Robert Burns Woodward, *20th:* 4393
Rosalyn Yalow, *20th:* 4419

CHURCH GOVERNMENT AND REFORM. *See also* **RELIGION AND THEOLOGY**

Barbe Acarie, *Ren:* 3
Adrian IV, *MA:* 27
Saint Ambrose, *Anc:* 42
Anne Askew, *Ren:* 62
Saint Athanasius of Alexandria, *Anc:* 132
John Ball, *MA:* 130
Saint Thomas Becket, *MA:* 147
Saint Bernard of Clairvaux, *MA:* 160
Anne Boleyn, *Ren:* 111
Boniface VIII, *MA:* 186, *Notor:* 115
Saint Boniface, *MA:* 183
Martin Bucer, *Ren:* 142
George Buchanan, *Ren:* 146
John Calvin, *Ren:* 163
Catherine of Aragon, *Ren:* 187
Saint Catherine of Siena, *MA:* 236
Clement VII, *Ren:* 229, *Notor:* 212
John Colet, *Ren:* 232
Nicolaus Copernicus, *Ren:* 241
Mary Baker Eddy, *19th:* 723
Eusebius of Caesarea, *Anc:* 330
Guy Fawkes, *Ren:* 324, *Notor:* 350
Saint Fulbert of Chartres, *MA:* 399
Henry Grattan, *18th:* 440
Gregory VII, *MA:* 433
Gregory IX, *MA:* 436
Gregory the Great, *MA:* 430
Barbara Harris, *20th:* 1689
Henry II the Saint, *MA:* 486
Hippolytus of Rome, *Anc:* 423
François Hotman, *Ren:* 461
Balthasar Hubmaier, *Ren:* 472
Jan Hus, *MA:* 522
Ignatius of Antioch, *Anc:* 437
Innocent III, *MA:* 541
Innocent IV, *MA:* 545
Innocent XI, *17th:* 405
Cornelius Otto Jansen, *17th:* 419
John XXIII, *20th:* 2017
Saint John of the Cross, *Ren:* 507
John Paul II, *20th:* 2020
John Knox, *Ren:* 528
Hugh Latimer, *Ren:* 543
Leo IX, *MA:* 644
Leo XIII, *19th:* 1342
Martin Luther, *Ren:* 582
Marguerite de Navarre, *Ren:* 617
Menno Simons, *Ren:* 675
Sun Myung Moon, *20th:* 2811, *Notor:* 749
Moses, *Anc:* 572
Saint Philip Neri, *Ren:* 717
Nicholas V, *MA:* 768
Nicholas the Great, *MA:* 764
Matthew Parker, *Ren:* 761
Paul III, *Ren:* 767
Paul V, *17th:* 719
Paul VI, *20th:* 3148
John Pecham, *MA:* 817
Philip the Magnanimous, *Ren:* 775
Pius V, *Ren:* 797
Pius IX, *19th:* 1802
Pius X, *20th:* 3272
Pius XI, *20th:* 3275
Pius XII, *20th:* 3278
Cardinal de Richelieu, *17th:* 790
Nicholas Ridley, *Ren:* 833
Oscar Romero, *20th:* 3499
Girolamo Savonarola, *Ren:* 850

Saint Sergius I, *MA:* 936
Samuel Sewall, *18th:* 893
Saint Siricius, *Anc:* 796
Joseph Smith, *19th:* 2117
Saint Teresa of Ávila, *Ren:* 928
Tomás de Torquemada, *Ren:* 939, *Notor:* 1038
Desmond Tutu, *20th:* 4121
Urban II, *MA:* 1043
Valentinus, *Anc:* 918
Vardhamāna, *Anc:* 924
Stephen Samuel Wise, *20th:* 4376
Brigham Young, *19th:* 2474
Huldrych Zwingli, *Ren:* 1010

Civil Rights. ***See also*** **Women's Rights**

Ralph Abernathy, *20th:* 11
Maya Angelou, *20th:* 97
Aung San Suu Kyi, *20th:* 174
James Baldwin, *20th:* 201
Mary McLeod Bethune, *20th:* 345
Hugo L. Black, *20th:* 377
Louis D. Brandeis, *20th:* 482
René Cassin, *20th:* 684
César Chávez, *20th:* 738
Shirley Chisholm, *20th:* 753
Hillary Rodham Clinton, *20th:* 788
Bessie Coleman, *20th:* 801
Helen Gahagan Douglas, *20th:* 1026
W. E. B. Du Bois, *20th:* 1046
Marian Wright Edelman, *20th:* 1096
Frantz Fanon, *20th:* 1212
Louis Farrakhan, *20th:* 1217
Father Divine, *Notor:* 346
Mahatma Gandhi, *20th:* 1388
Marcus Garvey, *20th:* 1417
Fannie Lou Hamer, *20th:* 1651
Lorraine Hansberry, *20th:* 1669
Aileen Clarke Hernandez, *20th:* 1773
Dolores Huerta, *20th:* 1915
Barbara Jordan, *20th:* 2046
Martin Luther King, Jr., *20th:* 2147
Malcolm X, *20th:* 2570
Thurgood Marshall, *20th:* 2633
Toni Morrison, *20th:* 2834
Rosa Parks, *20th:* 3119
Sidney Poitier, *20th:* 3296
A. Philip Randolph, *20th:* 3369
Ann Richards, *20th:* 3434
Paul Robeson, *20th:* 3462
Eleanor Roosevelt, *20th:* 3506
Andrei Sakharov, *20th:* 3602
Mother Teresa, *20th:* 3975
Desmond Tutu, *20th:* 4121
Alice Walker, *20th:* 4196
Madam C. J. Walker, *20th:* 4199
Ida B. Wells-Barnett, *20th:* 4290
Walter White, *20th:* 4307
Oprah Winfrey, *20th:* 4372

Communications

Mother Angelica, *20th:* 90
Tim Berners-Lee, *20th:* 331
Louis Braille, *19th:* 299
Vinton Gray Cerf, *20th:* 707
William Fothergill Cooke, *19th:* 547
Walter Cronkite, *20th:* 872
First Marquis of Dalhousie, *19th:* 595
Joseph Goebbels, *20th:* 1513, *Notor:* 418
Katharine Graham, *20th:* 1560
Steve Jobs, *20th:* 2006
Henry R. Luce, *20th:* 2456
Marshall McLuhan, *20th:* 2529
Guglielmo Marconi, *20th:* 2615
Samuel F. B. Morse, *19th:* 1610
Rupert Murdoch, *20th:* 2876
Aleksandr Stepanovich Popov, *19th:* 1824
Pete Rozelle, *20th:* 3553
Ted Turner, *20th:* 4118
Barbara Walters, *20th:* 4211
Charles Wheatstone, *19th:* 547
Oprah Winfrey, *20th:* 4372

Computer Science

Tim Berners-Lee, *20th:* 331
Jeff Bezos, *20th:* 360
Vinton Gray Cerf, *20th:* 707
Bill Gates, *20th:* 1421
Grace Murray Hopper, *20th:* 1879
Steve Jobs, *20th:* 2006
Alan Mathison Turing, *20th:* 4112
Norbert Wiener, *20th:* 4321

Conservation and Environmentalism

Johnny Appleseed, *19th:* 68
Gro Harlem Brundtland, *20th:* 544
Rachel Carson, *20th:* 662
George Washington Carver, *20th:* 678
Jacques Cousteau, *20th:* 849
Al Gore, *20th:* 1538
Octavia Hill, *19th:* 1103
Lady Bird Johnson, *20th:* 2025
Charles A. Lindbergh, *20th:* 2392
John Muir, *19th:* 1623
Frederick Law Olmsted, *19th:* 1706
Gifford Pinchot, *20th:* 3253
Ellen Swallow Richards, *19th:* 1899
F. Sherwood Rowland, *20th:* 3547
Thanadelthur, *18th:* 974
Theophrastus, *Anc:* 872
Henry David Thoreau, *19th:* 2274
Montgomery Ward, *19th:* 2386

Crime. ***See also*** **Assassins and Murderers; Gangsters and Associates; Law; Outlaws and Gunslingers; Pirates; Racists and hatemongers; Terrorists; Traitors and Spies**

Frank W. Abagnale, Jr., *Notor:* 3
Oakes Ames, *Notor:* 18
Jim Bakker, *Notor:* 50
Margita Bangová, *Notor:* 54
Sydney Barrows, *Notor:* 64
Sam Bass, *Notor:* 68
Paul Bernardo, *Notor:* 93
Osama Bin Laden, *20th:* 371, *Notor:* 101
Lou Blonger, *Notor:* 107
Ivan Boesky, *Notor:* 110
Lizzie Borden, *19th:* 277, *Notor:* 125
John R. Brinkley, *Notor:* 141
William Brodie, *Notor:* 145
Joey Buttafuoco, *Notor:* 159

William Calley, *Notor:* 168
Roberto Calvi, *Notor:* 170
Billy Cannon, *Notor:* 173
Al Capone, *20th:* 641, *Notor:* 185
Cartouche, *Notor:* 178
Cassie L. Chadwick, *Notor:* 193
Henri Charrière, *Notor:* 204
Janet Cooke, *Notor:* 231
Moll Cutpurse, *Notor:* 250
Tino De Angelis, *Notor:* 268
John DeLorean, *Notor:* 272
Phoolan Devi, *Notor:* 275
William Dodd, *Notor:* 286
Karl Dönitz, *Notor:* 292
François Duvalier, *20th:* 1069, *Notor:* 307
Bernard Ebbers, *Notor:* 317
Billie Sol Estes, *Notor:* 336
Ada Everleigh, *Notor:* 338
Father Divine, *Notor:* 346
Giuseppe Fieschi, *Notor:* 353
Jim Fisk, *Notor:* 357
Heidi Fleiss, *Notor:* 359
Martin Frankel, *Notor:* 376
Gilbert Gauthe, *Notor:* 397
Joseph Goebbels, *20th:* 1513, *Notor:* 418
Hermann Göring, *20th:* 1545, *Notor:* 428
Jay Gould, *Notor:* 433
Francis Greenway, *19th:* 974
George Habash, *20th:* 1626
O. Henry, *19th:* 1081
Rudolf Hess, *Notor:* 460
Susanna Mildred Hill, *Notor:* 466
Heinrich Himmler, *20th:* 1807, *Notor:* 468
Adolf Hitler, *20th:* 1829, *Notor:* 477
Elmyr de Hory, *Notor:* 492
Saddam Hussein, *20th:* 501, *Notor:* 503
Megan Louise Ireland, *Notor:* 508
Clifford Irving, *Notor:* 510
Shoeless Joe Jackson, *Notor:* 521
Jesse and Frank James, *19th:* 1211
Alfred Jodl, *Notor:* 533
Tom Keating, *Notor:* 559
Rodney King, *Notor:* 585
Lyndon H. LaRouche, Jr., *Notor:* 606
John Law, *Notor:* 614
Kenneth Lay, *Notor:* 617
Nick Leeson, *Notor:* 624
Henri Lemoine, *Notor:* 627
Mary Kay Letourneau, *Notor:* 640
Dennis Levine, *Notor:* 642
Victor Lustig, *Notor:* 665
James W. McCord, Jr., *Notor:* 671
Aimee Semple McPherson, *Notor:* 679
Molly Maguires, *Notor:* 745
Frederika Mandelbaum, *Notor:* 688
Gaston Bullock Means, *Notor:* 713
Jacques Mesrine, *Notor:* 723
Michael Milken, *Notor:* 731
Mou Qizhong, *Notor:* 757
Baby Face Nelson, *Notor:* 774
Nostradamus, *Ren:* 728, *Notor:* 799
Titus Oates, *17th:* 692, *Notor:* 802
Arthur Orton, *Notor:* 806
Thomas Mott Osborne, *20th:* 3085
Eusapia Palladino, *Notor:* 810
Charles Ponzi, *Notor:* 852
James Porter, *Notor:* 854
Pol Pot, *20th:* 3298, *Notor:* 846
Grigori Yefimovich Rasputin, *19th:* 1863, *Notor:* 885
Joachim von Ribbentrop, *Notor:* 894
Louis Riel, *19th:* 1908
George Rivas, *Notor:* 901
Marquis de Sade, *18th:* 875, *Notor:* 926
Jack Sheppard, *Notor:* 943
Jeffrey Skilling, *Notor:* 967
Alexandre Stavisky, *Notor:* 998
Willie Sutton, *Notor:* 1014
Nat Turner, *19th:* 2326
William Marcy Tweed, *19th:* 2333, *Notor:* 1047
Veerappan, *Notor:* 1062
Eugène François Vidocq, *Notor:* 1067
Pancho Villa, *20th:* 4160, *Notor:* 1069
Joseph Weil, *Notor:* 1094
Simon Wiesenthal, *20th:* 4328
Jonathan Wild, *Notor:* 1102
Emiliano Zapata, *20th:* 4448, *Notor:* 1129

DANCE

Alvin Ailey, *20th:* 36
Maya Angelou, *20th:* 97
Fred Astaire, *20th:* 155
George Balanchine, *20th:* 193
Mikhail Baryshnikov, *20th:* 253
Merce Cunningham, *20th:* 886
Alexandra Danilova, *20th:* 908
Jean Dauberval, *18th:* 295
Agnes de Mille, *20th:* 957
Sergei Diaghilev, *20th:* 985
Isadora Duncan, *20th:* 1058
Michel Fokine, *20th:* 1263
Dame Margot Fonteyn, *20th:* 1268
Bob Fosse, *20th:* 1291
Loie Fuller, *20th:* 1361
Martha Graham, *20th:* 1563
Robert Joffrey, *20th:* 2012
Gene Kelly, *20th:* 2096
Rudolf Laban, *20th:* 2221
Serge Lifar, *20th:* 2378
Dame Alicia Markova, *20th:* 2627
Léonide Massine, *20th:* 2646
Vaslav Nijinsky, *20th:* 2974
Rudolf Nureyev, *20th:* 3001
Anna Pavlova, *20th:* 3166
Jerome Robbins, *20th:* 3459
Ruth St. Denis, *20th:* 3593
Maria Tallchief, *20th:* 3940
Twyla Tharp, *20th:* 3989

DIPLOMACY. ***See also* GOVERNMENT AND POLITICS**

Ferhat Abbas, *20th:* 7
Dean Acheson, *20th:* 17
John Adams, *18th:* 11
Konrad Adenauer, *20th:* 26
Adrian IV, *MA:* 27
Afonso I (c. 1455-1543), *Ren:* 9
First Viscount Alanbrooke, *20th:* 50
Madeleine Albright, *20th:* 54
John Alden, *17th:* 7
Saint Alexander Nevsky, *MA:* 52

Duke of Alva, *Ren:* 31
Sir Norman Angell, *20th:* 92
Yasir Arafat, *20th:* 110
Second Duke of Argyll, *18th:* 53
Oscar Arias Sánchez, *20th:* 121
H. H. Asquith, *20th:* 149
Atatürk, *20th:* 162
Clement Attlee, *20th:* 165
Aurangzeb, *17th:* 23
Arthur Balfour, *20th:* 208
George Bancroft, *19th:* 130
Fanny Calderón de la Barca, *19th:* 389
Menachem Begin, *20th:* 284
David Ben-Gurion, *20th:* 292
Edvard Beneš, *20th:* 299
Friedrich von Beust, *19th:* 222
Ernest Bevin, *20th:* 356
Otto von Bismarck, *19th:* 238
Tony Blair, *20th:* 385
Sir Thomas Bodley, *Ren:* 108
First Viscount Bolingbroke, *18th:* 135
Sir Robert Laird Borden, *20th:* 423
Louis Botha, *20th:* 439
Boutros Boutros-Ghali, *20th:* 464
Willy Brandt, *20th:* 490
Joseph Brant, *18th:* 159
Leonid Brezhnev, *20th:* 523
Robert Bruce, *MA:* 200
Gro Harlem Brundtland, *20th:* 544
Bernhard von Bülow, *20th:* 569
Ralph Bunche, *20th:* 574
George H. W. Bush, *20th:* 594
George Canning, *19th:* 403
Canonicus, *17th:* 129
Jimmy Carter, *20th:* 666
René Cassin, *20th:* 684
Baldassare Castiglione, *Ren:* 181
Viscount Castlereagh, *19th:* 437
François-René de Chateaubriand, *19th:* 474
Étienne François de Choiseul, *18th:* 246
Sir Winston Churchill, *20th:* 768
Georges Clemenceau, *20th:* 778
Bill Clinton, *20th:* 783
Robert Clive, *18th:* 259
James Bryant Conant, *20th:* 820
Carolina Coronado, *19th:* 556
Pierre de Coubertin, *20th:* 846
Pêro da Covilhã, *Ren:* 259
George Nathaniel Curzon, *20th:* 894
Caleb Cushing, *19th:* 578
Moshe Dayan, *20th:* 929
Alcide De Gasperi, *20th:* 944
Eamon de Valera, *20th:* 979
John Foster Dulles, *20th:* 1054
Abba Eban, *20th:* 1082
Sir Anthony Eden, *20th:* 1099
Elizabeth II, *20th:* 1143
Matthias Erzberger, *20th:* 1180
Herbert Vere Evatt, *20th:* 1188
Faisal, *20th:* 1198
Faisal I, *20th:* 1202
Benjamin Franklin, *18th:* 370
James Gadsden, *19th:* 849
Albert Gallatin, *19th:* 854
Indira Gandhi, *20th:* 1385
Stephen Gardiner, *Ren:* 368
Charles de Gaulle, *20th:* 1427
First Earl of Godolphin, *18th:* 421
Mikhail Gorbachev, *20th:* 1530
Sir Edward Grey, *20th:* 1587
Arthur Griffith, *20th:* 1591
Andrei Gromyko, *20th:* 1600
Dag Hammarskjöld, *20th:* 1653
Karl von Hardenberg, *19th:* 1021
William Averell Harriman, *20th:* 1684
Hassan II, *20th:* 1699
Mohammad Hatta, *20th:* 1704
Václav Havel, *20th:* 1707
Robert Hawke, *20th:* 1710
John Hay, *19th:* 1054
Sir Edward Heath, *20th:* 1738
Piet Hein, *17th:* 359
Frederick Henry, *17th:* 286
Édouard Herriot, *20th:* 1777
Theodor Herzl, *19th:* 1088
Alger Hiss, *20th:* 1822, *Notor:* 475
Friedrich von Holstein, *19th:* 1119
Charles Evans Hughes, *20th:* 1920
William Morris Hughes, *20th:* 1931
Cordell Hull, *20th:* 1934
Hussein I, *20th:* 1950
Washington Irving, *19th:* 1180
İsmet Paşa, *20th:* 1971
James IV, *Ren:* 498
James V, *Ren:* 501
John Jay, *18th:* 524
Thomas Jefferson, *18th:* 528
Kalicho, *Ren:* 522
Wenzel Anton von Kaunitz, *18th:* 557
John F. Kennedy, *20th:* 2098
Jeane Kirkpatrick, *20th:* 2167
Henry Kissinger, *20th:* 2170
Helmut Kohl, *20th:* 2182
Lord Lansdowne, *20th:* 2266
Pierre Laval, *20th:* 2285, *Notor:* 609
Bonar Law, *20th:* 2292
Ferdinand de Lesseps, *19th:* 1356
Li Hongzhang, *19th:* 1363
Trygve Lie, *20th:* 2375
Maksim Maksimovich Litvinov, *20th:* 2404
David Lloyd George, *20th:* 2411
Marquis de Louvois, *17th:* 558
Albert Lutuli, *20th:* 2478
Alexander McGillivray, *18th:* 626
John Major, *20th:* 2567
First Duke of Marlborough, *18th:* 660
Jacques Marquette, *17th:* 603
Mary of Burgundy, *Ren:* 631
Massasoit, *17th:* 612
Increase Mather, *18th:* 671
Jules Mazarin, *17th:* 620
Lorenzo de' Medici, *Ren:* 655
Golda Meir, *20th:* 2674
Pierre Mendès-France, *20th:* 2698
Bernardino de Mendoza, *Ren:* 668
Metacom, *17th:* 633
Metternich, *19th:* 1561
Peter Minuit, *17th:* 643
Jean Monnet, *20th:* 2793
Hans Joachim Morgenthau, *20th:* 2828
Philippe de Mornay, *Ren:* 703
Gouverneur Morris, *18th:* 705
Brian Mulroney, *20th:* 2866
Fridtjof Nansen, *20th:* 2907
Jawaharlal Nehru, *20th:* 2929
Pablo Neruda, *20th:* 2937

Nezahualcóyotl, *Ren:* 720
Nicholas V, *MA:* 768
Richard M. Nixon, *20th:* 2984, *Notor:* 793
Kwame Nkrumah, *20th:* 2988
Lord North, *18th:* 738
Oda Nobunaga, *Ren:* 732
Johan van Oldenbarnevelt, *Ren:* 740
Count-Duke of Olivares, *17th:* 697
Axel Oxenstierna, *17th:* 704
Lord Palmerston, *19th:* 1731
Vijaya Lakshmi Pandit, *20th:* 3099
Franz von Papen, *20th:* 3109
Vallabhbhai Jhaverbhai Patel, *20th:* 3135
Octavio Paz, *20th:* 3169
Lester B. Pearson, *20th:* 3174
Javier Pérez de Cuéllar, *20th:* 3194
Matthew C. Perry, *19th:* 1776
Józef Piłsudski, *20th:* 3250
William Pitt the Elder, *18th:* 786
William Pitt the Younger, *18th:* 789
Pocahontas, *17th:* 745
Pontiac, *18th:* 801
Colin Powell, *20th:* 3321
Powhatan, *17th:* 752
Isidor Isaac Rabi, *20th:* 3355
Yitzhak Rabin, *20th:* 3358
Rammohan Ray, *19th:* 1866
Ronald Reagan, *20th:* 3400
Joachim von Ribbentrop, *Notor:* 894
Cardinal de Richelieu, *17th:* 790
Paul Robeson, *20th:* 3462
Mary Robinson (b. 1944), *20th:* 3474
Nelson A. Rockefeller, *20th:* 3478
Peter Paul Rubens, *17th:* 802
Anwar el-Sadat, *20th:* 3587
Louis St. Laurent, *20th:* 3597
First Earl of Salisbury, *Ren:* 844
Third Marquis of Salisbury, *19th:* 1977
Domingo Faustino Sarmiento, *19th:* 2000
Eisaku Satō, *20th:* 3645
Léopold Senghor, *20th:* 3702
William H. Seward, *19th:* 2077
George P. Shultz, *20th:* 3731
Sīdī al-Mukhtār al-Kuntī, *18th:* 914
Margaret Chase Smith, *20th:* 3768
Jan Christian Smuts, *20th:* 3775
Sophia, *17th:* 865
Paul-Henri Spaak, *20th:* 3808
Squanto, *17th:* 875
First Earl Stanhope, *18th:* 937
Henry L. Stimson, *20th:* 3869
Gustav Stresemann, *20th:* 3895
Duke de Sully, *17th:* 896
William Howard Taft, *20th:* 3929
Talleyrand, *19th:* 2221
Tascalusa, *Ren:* 922
Shirley Temple, *20th:* 3973
U Thant, *20th:* 3986
Margaret Thatcher, *20th:* 3992
Omar Torrijos, *20th:* 4048
Pierre Trudeau, *20th:* 4076
Harry S. Truman, *20th:* 4086
Eleuthérios Venizélos, *20th:* 4157
Charles Gravier de Vergennes, *18th:* 1011
Kurt Waldheim, *20th:* 4187
George Washington, *18th:* 1043
Daniel Webster, *19th:* 2398
Chaim Weizmann, *20th:* 4279
William III, *17th:* 979
Sir Harold Wilson, *20th:* 4360
Woodrow Wilson, *20th:* 4364
Władysław II Jagiełło and Jadwiga, *MA:* 1120
Ahmad Zaki Yamani, *20th:* 4422
Zara Yaqob, *Ren:* 1006
Zhou Enlai, *20th:* 4461

EARTH SCIENCES. ***See also*** **AGRICULTURE; ASTRONOMY; CONSERVATION AND ENVIRONMENTALISM; GEOGRAPHY**

Louis Agassiz, *19th:* 31
Georgius Agricola, *Ren:* 11
Luis W. Alvarez, *20th:* 73
Jean Sylvain Bailly, *18th:* 77
Robert D. Ballard, *20th:* 215
Sir Henry Bessemer, *19th:* 218
Vilhelm Bjerknes, *20th:* 374
Comte de Buffon, *18th:* 171
Thomas Burnet, *17th:* 106
Jacques Cousteau, *20th:* 849
William Dampier, *17th:* 215, *Notor:* 260
Rudolf Geiger, *20th:* 1443
Stephen Jay Gould, *20th:* 1555
Sir Robert Abbott Hadfield, *19th:* 1000
Harry Hammond Hess, *20th:* 1785
Robert Hooke, *17th:* 383
Alexander von Humboldt, *19th:* 1151
Thomas Henry Huxley, *19th:* 1161
Sir Charles Lyell, *19th:* 1423
Matthew Fontaine Maury, *19th:* 1522
Fridtjof Nansen, *20th:* 2907
Auguste and Jean-Felix Piccard, *20th:* 3240
John Wesley Powell, *19th:* 1827
Charles Richter, *20th:* 3440
Lazzaro Spallanzani, *18th:* 925
Nicolaus Steno, *17th:* 881
Pierre Teilhard de Chardin, *20th:* 3963
Theophrastus, *Anc:* 872
Alfred Wegener, *20th:* 4266
Sir Frank Whittle, *20th:* 4318
Sir George Hubert Wilkins, *20th:* 4339

ECONOMICS. ***See also*** **BUSINESS AND INDUSTRY**

Clement Attlee, *20th:* 165
Emily Greene Balch, *20th:* 197
Eduard Bernstein, *20th:* 334
Lord Beveridge, *20th:* 352
Ernest Bevin, *20th:* 356
Warren Buffett, *20th:* 563
Nikolay Ivanovich Bukharin, *20th:* 566
R. A. Butler, *20th:* 602
Jean-Baptiste Colbert, *17th:* 180
Deng Xiaoping, *20th:* 968
Ludwig Erhard, *20th:* 1173
Milton Friedman, *20th:* 1332
John Kenneth Galbraith, *20th:* 1374

José de Gálvez, *18th:* 394
Henry George, *19th:* 894
Emma Goldman, *20th:* 1519, *Notor:* 424
Alan Greenspan, *20th:* 1581
F. A. Hayek, *20th:* 1720
Honda Toshiaki, *18th:* 504
Hu Yaobang, *20th:* 1905
John Maynard Keynes, *20th:* 2120
Harold J. Laski, *20th:* 2269
Antoine-Laurent Lavoisier, *18th:* 579
John Law, *Notor:* 614
Vladimir Ilich Lenin, *20th:* 2341, *Notor:* 628
Thomas Robert Malthus, *19th:* 1475
Karl Marx, *19th:* 1508
George Meany, *20th:* 2672
Pierre Mendès-France, *20th:* 2698
James Mill, *19th:* 1571
John Stuart Mill, *19th:* 1574
Jean Monnet, *20th:* 2793
Robert Morris, *18th:* 707
Gunnar Myrdal, *20th:* 2890
Jacques Necker, *18th:* 726
Sir William Petty, *17th:* 733
William Pitt the Elder, *18th:* 786
François Quesnay, *18th:* 820
Ayn Rand, *20th:* 3367
David Ricardo, *19th:* 1896
Adam Smith, *18th:* 921
Herbert Spencer, *19th:* 2126
Tadano Makuzu, *19th:* 2212
Frederick Winslow Taylor, *20th:* 3955
Anne-Robert-Jacques Turgot, *18th:* 996
Thorstein Veblen, *20th:* 4154
Beatrice and Sidney Webb, *20th:* 4253
Clara Zetkin, *20th:* 4455

EDUCATION. ***See also*** **HISTORIOGRAPHY; SCHOLARSHIP**

José de Acosta, *Ren:* 5
Abigail Adams, *18th:* 7
Jane Addams, *20th:* 22
Felix Adler, *19th:* 26
Elizabeth Cabot Agassiz, *19th:* 29
Louis Agassiz, *19th:* 31
Sir Sayyid Ahmad Khan, *19th:* 35
Alvin Ailey, *20th:* 36
Saint Albertus Magnus, *MA:* 42
Bronson Alcott, *19th:* 38
Alcuin, *MA:* 49
Alfred the Great, *MA:* 63
Saint Angela Merici, *Ren:* 44
Maya Angelou, *20th:* 97
Anne of Brittany, *Ren:* 48
Saint Anthony of Padua, *MA:* 95
Thomas Arnold, *19th:* 76
Mary Astell, *18th:* 64
Nnamdi Azikiwe, *20th:* 180
Isaac Backus, *18th:* 75
Roger Bacon, *MA:* 127
Emily Greene Balch, *20th:* 197
Anna Barbauld, *18th:* 87
Henry Barnard, *19th:* 135
Karl Barth, *20th:* 243
Johann Bernhard Basedow, *18th:* 89
Dorothea Beale, *19th:* 159
Lady Margaret Beaufort, *Ren:* 90
Catharine Beecher, *19th:* 168
Mary McLeod Bethune, *20th:* 345
Lord Beveridge, *20th:* 352
Barbara Leigh Smith Bodichon, *19th:* 263
Sir Thomas Bodley, *Ren:* 108
Nadia Boulanger, *20th:* 449
Saint Marguerite Bourgeoys, *17th:* 75
Nicholas Murray Butler, *20th:* 597
R. A. Butler, *20th:* 602
William Byrd, *Ren:* 148
Melvin Calvin, *20th:* 621
William Carey, *19th:* 409
Lazare Carnot, *18th:* 200
George Washington Carver, *20th:* 678
Mary Ann Shadd Cary, *19th:* 431
Catherine of Aragon, *Ren:* 187
Hester Chapone, *18th:* 221
Judy Chicago, *20th:* 750
Shirley Chisholm, *20th:* 753
John Colet, *Ren:* 232
Arthur Holly Compton, *20th:* 817
James Bryant Conant, *20th:* 820
Marquis de Condorcet, *18th:* 267
George Nathaniel Curzon, *20th:* 894
Alexandra Danilova, *20th:* 908
Lucy S. Dawidowicz, *20th:* 922
John Dewey, *20th:* 982
Melvil Dewey, *19th:* 649
John Dowland, *Ren:* 289
W. E. B. Du Bois, *20th:* 1046
Katherine Dunham, *20th:* 1061
Marian Wright Edelman, *20th:* 1096
Charles William Eliot, *19th:* 737
Desiderius Erasmus, *Ren:* 314
Jerry Falwell, *20th:* 1209
François de Salignac de La Mothe-Fénelon, *17th:* 265
Saint John Fisher, *Ren:* 335
André-Hercule de Fleury, *18th:* 361
Abraham Flexner, *20th:* 1256
William Edward Forster, *19th:* 793
Charlotte Forten, *19th:* 796
Friedrich Froebel, *19th:* 835
Roger Fry, *20th:* 1351
Saint Fulbert of Chartres, *MA:* 399
Giovanni Gentile, *20th:* 1448
Arnold Gesell, *20th:* 1465
Oliver Goldsmith, *18th:* 432
Baltasar Gracián y Morales, *17th:* 316
Billy Graham, *20th:* 1557
Thomas Hill Green, *19th:* 971
Walter Gropius, *20th:* 1602
William Rainey Harper, *19th:* 1031
Honda Toshiaki, *18th:* 504
Samuel Gridley Howe, *19th:* 1141
Robert M. Hutchins, *20th:* 1958
Saint Ignatius of Loyola, *Ren:* 482
Saint Isidore of Seville, *MA:* 555
James I the Conqueror, *MA:* 571
James IV, *Ren:* 498
Francisco Jiménez de Cisneros, *Ren:* 503
Robert Joffrey, *20th:* 2012
Barbara Jordan, *20th:* 2046
Helen Keller, *20th:* 2093
Jan Komenský, *17th:* 469
Rudolf Laban, *20th:* 2221
Joseph Lancaster, *19th:* 1304

Susanne K. Langer, *20th:* 2263
Harold J. Laski, *20th:* 2269
Julia C. Lathrop, *20th:* 2272
Anna Leonowens, *19th:* 1346
Mary Kay Letourneau, *Notor:* 640
Henry Wadsworth Longfellow, *19th:* 1416
Juliette Gordon Low, *20th:* 2441
Mary Lyon, *19th:* 1428
William Holmes McGuffey, *19th:* 1445
Catharine A. MacKinnon, *20th:* 2522
Virginia McMartin, *Notor:* 676
Madame de Maintenon, *17th:* 572
Horace Mann, *19th:* 1486
Jules Hardouin-Mansart, *17th:* 590
Marie de l'Incarnation, *17th:* 595
Increase Mather, *18th:* 671
Frederick Denison Maurice, *19th:* 1518
Philipp Melanchthon, *Ren:* 664
Robert Andrews Millikan, *20th:* 2750
Maria Montessori, *20th:* 2804
Hannah More, *18th:* 702
Thomas Morley, *Ren:* 701
Boris Ivanovich Morozov, *17th:* 663
Naḥmanides, *MA:* 747
James Naismith, *20th:* 2905
Nānak, *Ren:* 707
Robert Nozick, *20th:* 2999
Alice Freeman Palmer, *19th:* 1727
Elizabeth Palmer Peabody, *19th:* 1761
Charles Willson Peale, *18th:* 768
Johann Heinrich Pestalozzi, *19th:* 1782
Elena Cornaro Piscopia, *17th:* 743
Rabanus Maurus, *MA:* 870
Peter Ramus, *Ren:* 817
Ellen Swallow Richards, *19th:* 1899
Sally Ride, *20th:* 3447
Knute Rockne, *20th:* 3481
Jean-Jacques Rousseau, *18th:* 868
Carl Sagan, *20th:* 3590
Margaret Sanger, *20th:* 3625
Domingo Faustino Sarmiento, *19th:* 2000
Anna Maria van Schurman, *17th:* 823
Saint Elizabeth Seton, *19th:* 2071
Dr. Seuss, *20th:* 3710
Henry Sidgwick, *19th:* 2102
Elisabetta Sirani, *17th:* 856
B. F. Skinner, *20th:* 3754
Squanto, *17th:* 875
Leland Stanford, *19th:* 2132
Konstantin Stanislavsky, *20th:* 3821
Charles Proteus Steinmetz, *19th:* 2156
Harlan Fiske Stone, *20th:* 3878
Marie Stopes, *20th:* 3882
Anne Sullivan, *20th:* 3908
Shinichi Suzuki, *20th:* 3922
Sylvester II, *MA:* 983
Marion Talbot, *20th:* 3937
Twyla Tharp, *20th:* 3989
Sylvanus Thayer, *19th:* 2260
Edward L. Thorndike, *20th:* 4013
Miguel de Unamuno y Jugo, *20th:* 4128
Iswar Chandra Vidyasagar, *19th:* 2363
Saint Vincent de Paul, *17th:* 962
Vincent of Beauvais, *MA:* 1063
Vivekananda, *19th:* 2368
Booker T. Washington, *19th:* 2390
Noah Webster, *19th:* 2402
Ida B. Wells-Barnett, *20th:* 4290
Simon Wiesenthal, *20th:* 4328
Emma Willard, *19th:* 2438
Isaac Mayer Wise, *19th:* 2453
John Witherspoon, *18th:* 1098
Wilhelm Wundt, *20th:* 4407
Yaqut, *MA:* 1143
Yui Shōsetsu, *17th:* 998

ENGINEERING. ***See also* ARCHITECTURE; INVENTION AND TECHNOLOGY; PHYSICS**

Archimedes, *Anc:* 80
Edwin H. Armstrong, *20th:* 127
John Bardeen, *20th:* 234
Johann Joachim Becher, *17th:* 39
Carl Benz, *19th:* 197
Wernher von Braun, *20th:* 500
James Brindley, *18th:* 162
Isambard Kingdom Brunel, *19th:* 333
Marc Isambard Brunel, *19th:* 337
Filippo Brunelleschi, *MA:* 205
Felix Candela, *20th:* 631
Vinton Gray Cerf, *20th:* 707
André-Gustave Citroën, *20th:* 772
Samuel Colt, *19th:* 533
William Fothergill Cooke, *19th:* 547
Gottlieb Daimler, *19th:* 592
Rudolf Diesel, *19th:* 663
James Buchanan Eads, *19th:* 715
Gustave Eiffel, *19th:* 734
Enzo Ferrari, *20th:* 1239
Eugène Freyssinet, *20th:* 1326
R. Buckminster Fuller, *20th:* 1364
Robert Fulton, *19th:* 845
Robert H. Goddard, *20th:* 1507
George Washington Goethals, *20th:* 1517
Otto von Guericke, *17th:* 333
Ernst Heinkel, *20th:* 1746
Juan de Herrera, *Ren:* 445
John Philip Holland, *19th:* 1113
Sir Godfrey Newbold Hounsfield, *20th:* 1892
Sergei Korolev, *20th:* 2191
Frederick William Lanchester, *20th:* 2240
Samuel Pierpont Langley, *19th:* 1309
Benjamin Henry Latrobe, *19th:* 1325
Leonardo da Vinci, *Ren:* 561
André and Édouard Michelin, *20th:* 2725
Gaspard Monge, *18th:* 682
Jacques-Étienne and Joseph-Michel Montgolfier, *18th:* 698
Samuel F. B. Morse, *19th:* 1610
James Nasmyth, *19th:* 1646
Pier Luigi Nervi, *20th:* 2940
Thomas Newcomen, *18th:* 733
Thomas Paine, *18th:* 759
Denis Papin, *17th:* 710
Petrus Peregrinus de Maricourt, *MA:* 820
Auguste and Jean-Felix Piccard, *20th:* 3240

André Rebouças, *19th:* 1869
First Baron Reith of Stonehaven, *20th:* 3410
Hyman G. Rickover, *20th:* 3443
John Augustus Roebling, *19th:* 1928
Thomas Savery, *17th:* 813
Charles Proteus Steinmetz, *19th:* 2156
George Stephenson, *19th:* 2167
Simon Stevin, *Ren:* 912
Emanuel Swedenborg, *18th:* 961
Frederick Winslow Taylor, *20th:* 3955
Thomas Telford, *19th:* 2240
Nikola Tesla, *19th:* 2252
Sylvanus Thayer, *19th:* 2260
Richard Trevithick, *19th:* 2294
Konstantin Tsiolkovsky, *20th:* 4095
Andrei Nikolayevich Tupolev, *20th:* 4108
Sébastien Le Prestre de Vauban, *17th:* 946
Felix Wankel, *20th:* 4224
Charles Wheatstone, *19th:* 547
Sir Frank Whittle, *20th:* 4318
Simon Wiesenthal, *20th:* 4328
John Wilkinson, *18th:* 1086
Sir Christopher Wren, *17th:* 994
Ferdinand von Zeppelin, *20th:* 4452
Vladimir Zworykin, *20th:* 4479

ENTERTAINMENT. *See* DANCE; MUSIC; RADIO, FILM, AND TELEVISION; SPORTS; THEATER AND LIVE ENTERTAINMENT

ENVIRONMENTALISM. *See* CONSERVATION AND ENVIRONMENTALISM

EXPLORATION. *See also* AVIATION AND SPACE EXPLORATION; GEOGRAPHY
Afonso de Albuquerque, *Ren:* 22
Pedro de Alvarado, *Ren:* 34
Roald Amundsen, *20th:* 83
Johnny Appleseed, *19th:* 68
Vasco Núñez de Balboa, *Ren:* 76
Robert D. Ballard, *20th:* 215
Sir Joseph Banks, *18th:* 80
Benjamin of Tudela, *MA:* 157
Vitus Jonassen Bering, *18th:* 108
Albert Bierstadt, *19th:* 232
William Bligh, *18th:* 126, *Notor:* 104
Daniel Boone, *18th:* 143
Louis-Antoine de Bougainville, *18th:* 150
James Bruce, *18th:* 168
Sir Richard Francis Burton, *19th:* 368
Richard Byrd, *20th:* 606
Álvar Núñez Cabeza de Vaca, *Ren:* 152
John Cabot, *Ren:* 155
Sebastian Cabot, *Ren:* 159
Juan Rodríguez Cabrillo, *Ren:* 161
Calamity Jane, *19th:* 386
Giovanni da Pian del Carpini, *MA:* 226
Kit Carson, *19th:* 426
Jacques Cartier, *Ren:* 178
Thomas Cavendish, *Ren:* 193
Samuel de Champlain, *17th:* 139
André-Gustave Citroën, *20th:* 772
William Clark, *19th:* 1359
Christopher Columbus, *Ren:* 237
James Cook, *18th:* 270
Francisco Vásquez de Coronado, *Ren:* 245
Hernán Cortés, *Ren:* 252
Pêro da Covilhã, *Ren:* 259
David Crockett, *19th:* 571
Samuel Ajayi Crowther, *19th:* 574
William Dampier, *17th:* 215, *Notor:* 260
John Davis, *Ren:* 276
Bartolomeu Dias, *Ren:* 286
Sir Francis Drake, *Ren:* 291, *Notor:* 301
Juan Sebastián de Elcano, *Ren:* 307
Sir John Franklin, *19th:* 825
John C. Frémont, *19th:* 831
Sir Martin Frobisher, *Ren:* 352
Vasco da Gama, *Ren:* 365
Sir Humphrey Gilbert, *Ren:* 378
Hanno, *Anc:* 385
Ferdinand Vandeveer Hayden, *19th:* 1058
Prince Henry the Navigator, *MA:* 477
Thor Heyerdahl, *20th:* 1795
Sir Edmund Hillary, *20th:* 1802
Henry Hudson, *17th:* 390
Alexander von Humboldt, *19th:* 1151
Ibn Baṭṭūṭah, *MA:* 529
John II, *Ren:* 511
John III, *Ren:* 513
Louis Jolliet, *17th:* 433
Mary Kingsley, *19th:* 1281
Eusebio Francisco Kino, *17th:* 467
Sieur de La Salle, *17th:* 490
Bartolomé de Las Casas, *Ren:* 537
Miguel López de Legazpi, *Ren:* 550
Leif Eriksson, *MA:* 640
Leo Africanus, *Ren:* 555
Meriwether Lewis, *19th:* 1359
David Livingstone, *19th:* 1400
Sir Alexander Mackenzie, *18th:* 629
Ferdinand Magellan, *Ren:* 591
Marco Polo, *MA:* 853
Jacques Marquette, *17th:* 603
al-Masʿūdī, *MA:* 703
Pedro Menéndez de Avilés, *Ren:* 672
Peter Minuit, *17th:* 643
John Muir, *19th:* 1623
Fridtjof Nansen, *20th:* 2907
Mungo Park, *18th:* 765
Pausanias the Traveler, *Anc:* 618
Robert Edwin Peary, *20th:* 3177
Zebulon Pike, *19th:* 1793
The Pinzón Brothers, *Ren:* 789
Francisco Pizarro, *Ren:* 800
Juan Ponce de León, *Ren:* 803
John Wesley Powell, *19th:* 1827
Pytheas, *Anc:* 729
Pierre Esprit Radisson, *17th:* 777
Sir Walter Ralegh, *Ren:* 813
Knud Johan Victor Rasmussen, *20th:* 3377
Sir James Clark Ross, *19th:* 1934

Sacagawea, *19th:* 1962
Heinrich Schliemann, *19th:* 2016
Sebastian, *Ren:* 859
Jedediah Smith, *19th:* 2114
John Smith, *17th:* 861
Hernando de Soto, *Ren:* 902
John Hanning Speke, *19th:* 2123
Miles Standish, *17th:* 877
Henry Morton Stanley, *19th:* 2136
Abel Janszoon Tasman, *17th:* 905
David Thompson, *19th:* 2271
Alexis de Tocqueville, *19th:* 2280
George Vancouver, *18th:* 1006
Amerigo Vespucci, *Ren:* 969
Alfred Wegener, *20th:* 4266
Charles Wilkes, *19th:* 2435
Sir George Hubert Wilkins, *20th:* 4339
William of Rubrouck, *MA:* 1107
Fanny Bullock Workman, *19th:* 2466
Xuanzang, *MA:* 1136
Zheng He, *MA:* 1156

FILM. *See* RADIO, FILM, AND TELEVISION

GANGSTERS AND ASSOCIATES. *See also* OUTLAWS AND GUNSLINGERS
Joe Adonis, *Notor:* 6
Albert Anastasia, *Notor:* 23
Ma Barker, *Notor:* 61
Louis Buchalter, *Notor:* 148
Al Capone, *20th:* 641, *Notor:* 175
Paul Castellano, *Notor:* 183
Joe Colombo, *Notor:* 224
Frank Costello, *Notor:* 237
Legs Diamond, *Notor:* 277
John Dillinger, *Notor:* 281
Pablo Escobar, *Notor:* 332
Judith Campbell Exner, *Notor:* 340
Pretty Boy Floyd, *Notor:* 360
Carmine Galante, *Notor:* 389
Joe Gallo, *Notor:* 392
Carlo Gambino, *Notor:* 396
Vito Genovese, *Notor:* 402
Sam Giancana, *Notor:* 405
Vincent Gigante, *Notor:* 407
Salvatore Giuliano, *Notor:* 413
John Gotti, *Notor:* 431
Sammy Gravano, *Notor:* 434
Henry Hill, *Notor:* 465
Jimmy Hoffa, *Notor:* 480
Alvin Karpis, *Notor:* 556
Machine Gun Kelly, *Notor:* 561
Reginald Kray, *Notor:* 591
Ronald Kray, *Notor:* 593
Richard Kuklinski, *Notor:* 595
Meyer Lansky, *Notor:* 604
Tommy Lucchese, *Notor:* 658
Lucky Luciano, *Notor:* 660
Salvatore Maranzano, *Notor:* 694
Carlos Marcello, *Notor:* 698
Joe Masseria, *Notor:* 708
Bugs Moran, *Notor:* 751
Dion O'Banion, *Notor:* 803
Joseph Profaci, *Notor:* 863
Arnold Rothstein, *Notor:* 917
Dutch Schultz, *Notor:* 938
Bugsy Siegel, *Notor:* 954
Hymie Weiss, *Notor:* 1096
Adam Worth, *Notor:* 1107

GENETICS
Virginia Apgar, *20th:* 100
Norman Borlaug, *20th:* 434
Sir Macfarlane Burnet, *20th:* 587
Francis Crick, *20th:* 865
Rosalind Franklin, *20th:* 1316
George Gamow, *20th:* 1379
Barbara McClintock, *20th:* 2504
Gregor Mendel, *19th:* 1541
Thomas Hunt Morgan, *20th:* 2825
Hermann Joseph Muller, *20th:* 2861
Kary B. Mullis, *20th:* 2864
Peyton Rous, *20th:* 3545
Frederick Sanger, *20th:* 3622
Wendell Stanley, *20th:* 3824
Harold E. Varmus, *20th:* 4145
Nikolai Ivanovich Vavilov, *20th:* 4151
James D. Watson, *20th:* 4242
Maurice Wilkins, *20th:* 4342

GEOGRAPHY. *See also* EXPLORATION
José de Acosta, *Ren:* 5
Roald Amundsen, *20th:* 83
Anaximander, *Anc:* 55
Pierre Belon, *Ren:* 101
Benjamin of Tudela, *MA:* 157
al-Bīrūnī, *MA:* 163
Daniel Boone, *18th:* 143
Fernand Braudel, *20th:* 497
James Bruce, *18th:* 168
Sir Richard Francis Burton, *19th:* 368
Álvar Núñez Cabeza de Vaca, *Ren:* 152
Sebastian Cabot, *Ren:* 159
Kâtib Çelebî, *17th:* 454
James Cook, *18th:* 270
Pêro da Covilhã, *Ren:* 259
Juan Sebastián de Elcano, *Ren:* 307
Eratosthenes of Cyrene, *Anc:* 314
David and Johannes Fabricius, *17th:* 259
Rudolf Geiger, *20th:* 1443
Sir Humphrey Gilbert, *Ren:* 378
Richard Hakluyt, *Ren:* 419
Hanno, *Anc:* 385
Ferdinand Vandeveer Hayden, *19th:* 1058
Honda Toshiaki, *18th:* 504
Alexander von Humboldt, *19th:* 1151
al-Idrīsī, *MA:* 539
John II, *Ren:* 511
al-Khwārizmī, *MA:* 617
Eusebio Francisco Kino, *17th:* 467
Miguel López de Legazpi, *Ren:* 550
Leo Africanus, *Ren:* 555
Sir Halford John Mackinder, *20th:* 2518
al-Masʿūdī, *MA:* 703
Matthew Fontaine Maury, *19th:* 1522
Gerardus Mercator, *Ren:* 678
John Muir, *19th:* 1623
Pausanias the Traveler, *Anc:* 618
Robert Edwin Peary, *20th:* 3177
Petrus Peregrinus de Maricourt, *MA:* 820
Tomé Pires, *Ren:* 792
John Wesley Powell, *19th:* 1827
Ptolemy (astronomer), *Anc:* 712

Pytheas, *Anc:* 729
Pierre Esprit Radisson, *17th:* 777
Matteo Ricci, *Ren:* 825
Wilhelm Schickard, *17th:* 818
Simon Stevin, *Ren:* 912
Strabo, *Anc:* 827
Thomas Talbot, *19th:* 2219
Abel Janszoon Tasman, *17th:* 905
David Thompson, *19th:* 2271
Tippu Tib, *19th:* 2277
Amerigo Vespucci, *Ren:* 969
William of Rubrouck, *MA:* 1107
Edward O. Wilson, *20th:* 4358
Fanny Bullock Workman, *19th:* 2466
Yaqut, *MA:* 1143

Geology. ***See*** **Earth Sciences**

Government and Politics. ***See also*** **Diplomacy; Law; Monarchy; Traitors and Spies**
Abahai, *17th:* 1
Sani Abacha, *Notor:* 1
Ferhat Abbas, *20th:* 7
ʿAbbās the Great, *17th:* 4
ʿAbd al-Malik, *MA:* 3
ʿAbd al-Muʾmin, *MA:* 6
ʿAbd al-Raḥmān III al-Nāṣir, *MA:* 9
Abdelkader, *19th:* 1
Abdülhamid II, *19th:* 7
Isaac ben Judah Abravanel, *Ren:* 1
Chinua Achebe, *20th:* 14
Dean Acheson, *20th:* 17
Halide Edib Adıvar, *20th:* 29
Abigail Adams, *18th:* 7
John Adams, *18th:* 11
John Quincy Adams, *19th:* 20
Samuel Adams, *18th:* 16
Konrad Adenauer, *20th:* 26
Adrian VI, *Ren:* 7
Æthelflæd, *MA:* 30
Afonso I (c. 1108-1185), *MA:* 33
Afonso I (c. 1455-1543), *Ren:* 9
Agesilaus II, *Anc:* 14
Gnaeus Julius Agricola, *Anc:* 17
Marcus Vipsanius Agrippa, *Anc:* 20
Agrippina the Younger, *Anc:* 23
Ahmed III, *18th:* 26
Akbar (1542-1605), *Ren:* 15
Akhenaton, *Anc:* 26
Akihito, *20th:* 46
ʿAlāʾ-ud-Dīn Muḥammad Khaljī, *MA:* 39
Alaungpaya, *18th:* 29
Alboin, *MA:* 45
Madeleine Albright, *20th:* 54
Afonso de Albuquerque, *Ren:* 22
Alcibiades of Athens, *Anc:* 33, *Notor:* 11
John Alden, *17th:* 7
Alexander I, *19th:* 45
Alexander II, *19th:* 48
Alexander VI, *Ren:* 27, *Notor:* 14
Alexander VII, *17th:* 9
Saint Alexander Nevsky, *MA:* 52
Alexander the Great, *Anc:* 39
Alexis, *17th:* 11
Alfonso X, *MA:* 59
Alfred the Great, *MA:* 63
Ali Paşa Tepelenë, *19th:* 55
Ethan Allen, *18th:* 35
Salvador Allende, *20th:* 70
Alp Arslan, *MA:* 70
John Peter Altgeld, *19th:* 57
Amalasuntha, *MA:* 75
Saint Ambrose, *Anc:* 42
Amenhotep III, *Anc:* 45
Lord Amherst, *18th:* 38
Idi Amin, *20th:* 80, *Notor:* 20
Amina Sarauniya Zazzua, *Ren:* 37
Sir Norman Angell, *20th:* 92
Anna, Princess of the Byzantine Empire, *MA:* 86
Queen Anne, *18th:* 45
Anne of Austria, *17th:* 18
Anne of Brittany, *Ren:* 48
Anne of Cleves, *Ren:* 51
Lord Anson, *18th:* 49
Antigonus I Monophthalmos, *Anc:* 63
Ion Antonescu, *Notor:* 25
Antonia the Younger, *Anc:* 71
Marc Antony, *Anc:* 73
Corazon Aquino, *20th:* 107
Yasir Arafat, *20th:* 110
Second Duke of Argyll, *18th:* 53
Oscar Arias Sánchez, *20th:* 121
Jean-Bertrand Aristide, *20th:* 124
Árpád, *MA:* 105
Arria the Elder, *Anc:* 102
Arria the Younger, *Anc:* 103
Arsinoe II Philadelphus, *Anc:* 105
Artemisia I, *Anc:* 109
Chester A. Arthur, *19th:* 79
Ashikaga Takauji, *MA:* 115
Ashurbanipal, *Anc:* 117
Ashurnasirpal II, *Anc:* 120
Askia Daud, *Ren:* 64
Aśoka, *Anc:* 124
Aspasia of Miletus, *Anc:* 127
H. H. Asquith, *20th:* 149
Hafez al-Assad, *20th:* 153
Mary Astell, *18th:* 64
Nancy Astor, *20th:* 158
Atahualpa, *Ren:* 66
Atatürk, *20th:* 162
Atossa, *Anc:* 136
Attila, *Anc:* 138, *Notor:* 45
Clement Attlee, *20th:* 165
Augustus, *Anc:* 145
Aung San Suu Kyi, *20th:* 174
Aurangzeb, *17th:* 23
Sri Aurobindo, *20th:* 177
Stephen Fuller Austin, *19th:* 98
Nnamdi Azikiwe, *20th:* 180
Bābur, *Ren:* 69
Isaac Backus, *18th:* 75
Francis Bacon, *Ren:* 72
Nathaniel Bacon, *17th:* 29
Jean-Sylvain Bailly, *18th:* 77
Bobby Baker, *Notor:* 48
Robert Baldwin, *19th:* 122
Stanley Baldwin, *20th:* 204
Arthur Balfour, *20th:* 208
John Ball, *MA:* 130
Hastings Kamuzu Banda, *20th:* 219
Sir Surendranath Banerjea, *20th:* 221
Bao Dai, *20th:* 228
Barbarossa, *Ren:* 79
Anna Barbauld, *18th:* 87
Klaus Barbie, *Notor:* 57
Sir Edmund Barton, *19th:* 149
Omar al-Bashir, *Notor:* 66

Basil the Macedonian, *MA:* 133
Fulgencio Batista y Zaldívar, *Notor:* 73
Richard Baxter, *17th:* 32
Baybars I, *MA:* 139
Bayezid II, *Ren:* 87
Lady Margaret Beaufort, *Ren:* 90
Pierre-Augustin Caron de Beaumarchais, *18th:* 97
Lord Beaverbrook, *20th:* 275
Johann Joachim Becher, *17th:* 39
Dave Beck, *Notor:* 75
Saint Thomas Becket, *MA:* 147
Menachem Begin, *20th:* 284
Muḥammad Bello, *19th:* 186
David Ben-Gurion, *20th:* 292
Edvard Beneš, *20th:* 299
Benedict XIV, *18th:* 102
Thomas Hart Benton, *19th:* 192
Berenice II, *Anc:* 157
Lavrenty Beria, *Notor:* 89
Eduard Bernstein, *20th:* 334
Bess of Hardwick, *Ren:* 103
Friedrich von Beust, *19th:* 222
Aneurin Bevan, *20th:* 349
Ernest Bevin, *20th:* 356
Bhumibol Adulyadej, *20th:* 363
Benazir Bhutto, *20th:* 365
Zulfikar Ali Bhutto, *20th:* 368
Nicholas Biddle, *19th:* 225
Theodore G. Bilbo, *Notor:* 99
Osama Bin Laden, *20th:* 371, *Notor:* 101
Otto von Bismarck, *19th:* 238
Black Hawk, *19th:* 244
James G. Blaine, *19th:* 251
Tony Blair, *20th:* 385
Robert Blake, *17th:* 55
Blanche of Castile, *MA:* 166
Léon Blum, *20th:* 396
Boabdil, *Ren:* 105
Bohemond I, *MA:* 176
Jean-Bédel Bokassa, *Notor:* 113
Anne Boleyn, *Ren:* 111
First Viscount Bolingbroke, *18th:* 135
Simón Bolívar, *19th:* 267
Margaret Bondfield, *20th:* 414
Claude Alexandre de Bonneval, *18th:* 140
Sir Robert Laird Borden, *20th:* 423
Cesare Borgia, *Ren:* 114, *Notor:* 127
Lucrezia Borgia, *Ren:* 117, *Notor:* 129
Boris I of Bulgaria, *MA:* 189
Martin Bormann, *Notor:* 131
Louis Botha, *20th:* 439
Habib Bourguiba, *20th:* 457
Boutros Boutros-Ghali, *20th:* 464
William Bradford, *17th:* 84
Willy Brandt, *20th:* 490
Joseph Brant, *18th:* 159
Margaret Brent, *17th:* 92
Leonid Brezhnev, *20th:* 523
John Bright, *19th:* 302
Henry Brougham, *19th:* 312
George Brown, *19th:* 316
Robert Bruce, *MA:* 200
Gro Harlem Brundtland, *20th:* 544
Leonardo Bruni, *MA:* 208
Marcus Junius Brutus, *Anc:* 166, *Notor:* 146
William Jennings Bryan, *20th:* 550
George Buchanan, *Ren:* 146
James Buchanan, *19th:* 343
First Duke of Buckingham, *17th:* 96
William F. Buckley, Jr., *20th:* 561
Nikolay Ivanovich Bukharin, *20th:* 566
Bernhard von Bülow, *20th:* 569
Hubert de Burgh, *MA:* 211
Edmund Burke, *18th:* 174
Aaron Burr, *19th:* 363, *Notor:* 155
George H. W. Bush, *20th:* 594
Josephine Butler, *19th:* 371
R. A. Butler, *20th:* 602
Sebastian Cabot, *Ren:* 159
Julius Caesar, *Anc:* 172
John C. Calhoun, *19th:* 392
Caligula, *Anc:* 176, *Notor:* 165
Plutarco Elías Calles, *20th:* 615
George Calvert, *17th:* 119
Jean-Jacques-Régis de Cambacérès, *19th:* 396
Simon Cameron, *Notor:* 171
Kim Campbell, *20th:* 624
George Canning, *19th:* 403
Canonicus, *17th:* 129
Canute the Great, *MA:* 221
Cao Cao, *Anc:* 182
Lázaro Cárdenas, *20th:* 647
Fernando Henrique Cardoso, *20th:* 651
Sir Guy Carleton, *18th:* 196
Don Carlos, *19th:* 412
Lazare Carnot, *18th:* 200
Caroline, *18th:* 203
Robert Carr, *17th:* 131
Charles Carroll, *18th:* 205
Jimmy Carter, *20th:* 666
Casimir the Great, *MA:* 229
René Cassin, *20th:* 684
Cassiodorus, *MA:* 233
Cassius, *Anc:* 185
Baldassare Castiglione, *Ren:* 181
Viscount Castlereagh, *19th:* 437
Fidel Castro, *20th:* 691, *Notor:* 185
Catherine de Médicis, *Ren:* 184
Catherine the Great, *18th:* 211
Catherine of Braganza, *17th:* 137
Catiline, *Anc:* 188, *Notor:* 188
Cato the Censor, *Anc:* 190
Cato the Younger, *Anc:* 194
Carrie Chapman Catt, *20th:* 701
Georgiana Cavendish, *18th:* 215
Count Cavour, *19th:* 444
Nicolae Ceaușescu, *Notor:* 190
William Cecil, *Ren:* 199
Aimé Césaire, *20th:* 709
Cetshwayo, *19th:* 450
Joseph Chamberlain, *19th:* 460
Neville Chamberlain, *20th:* 720
Samuel de Champlain, *17th:* 139
Chandragupta Maurya, *Anc:* 202
Charlemagne, *MA:* 242
Charles I, *17th:* 143
Charles II (1630-1685; King of England), *17th:* 147, *Notor:* 201
Charles II (1661-1700; King of Spain), *17th:* 151
Charles III, *18th:* 227
Charles IV, *MA:* 257
Charles V, *Ren:* 220
Charles VI (1368-1422; King of France), *Notor:* 203

Charles VI (1685-1740; Holy Roman Emperor), *18th:* 229
Charles VII, *Ren:* 224
Charles VIII, *Ren:* 227
Charles X Gustav, *17th:* 153
Charles XII, *18th:* 232
Charles XIV John, *19th:* 468
Charles d'Orléans, *MA:* 247
Charles Martel, *MA:* 250
Charles the Bald, *MA:* 254
Charles the Bold, *Ren:* 217
Queen Charlotte, *18th:* 235
Alain Chartier, *MA:* 260
Salmon P. Chase, *19th:* 470
Samuel Chase, *18th:* 237
Geoffrey Chaucer, *MA:* 264
Chen Duxiu, *20th:* 741
Duchesse de Chevreuse, *17th:* 158
Chiang Kai-shek, *20th:* 746
Shirley Chisholm, *20th:* 753
Étienne François de Choiseul, *18th:* 246
Chongzhen, *17th:* 160
Jean Chrétien, *20th:* 761
Christian VII, *Notor:* 208
Christina, *17th:* 163
Henri Christophe, *19th:* 494
Sarah Churchill, *18th:* 250
Sir Winston Churchill, *20th:* 768
Cicero, *Anc:* 210
Cimon, *Anc:* 213
Cixi, *19th:* 496
First Earl of Clarendon, *17th:* 166
George Rogers Clark, *18th:* 253
Claudius I, *Anc:* 217
Henry Clay, *19th:* 502
Cleisthenes of Athens, *Anc:* 221
Georges Clemenceau, *20th:* 778
Cleomenes, *Anc:* 226
Cleopatra VII, *Anc:* 229
Grover Cleveland, *19th:* 507
Bill Clinton, *20th:* 783
DeWitt Clinton, *19th:* 512
Hillary Rodham Clinton, *20th:* 788
Robert Clive, *18th:* 259
Clodia, *Anc:* 233
Saint Clotilda, *MA:* 287
Clovis, *MA:* 290
Richard Cobden, *19th:* 520
Sebastian Coe, *20th:* 797
Roy Cohn, *Notor:* 217
Sir Edward Coke, *17th:* 174
Jean-Baptiste Colbert, *17th:* 180
Schuyler Colfax, *Notor:* 219
Michael Collins, *20th:* 807
Charles W. Colson, *Notor:* 225
Commodus, *Notor:* 227
Anthony Comstock, *Notor:* 229
Marquis de Condorcet, *18th:* 267
Learie Constantine, *20th:* 829
Constantine the Great, *Anc:* 239
Jay Cooke, *19th:* 544
Calvin Coolidge, *20th:* 832
First Marquess Cornwallis, *18th:* 278
William T. Cosgrave, *20th:* 843
Bettino Craxi, *Notor:* 241
David Crockett, *19th:* 571
Oliver Cromwell, *17th:* 204
Thomas Cromwell, *Ren:* 269
Cuauhtémoc, *Ren:* 273
John Curtin, *20th:* 891
George Nathaniel Curzon, *20th:* 894
Caleb Cushing, *19th:* 578
Cypselus of Corinth, *Notor:* 251
Cyrus the Great, *Anc:* 248
Dalai Lama, *20th:* 902
First Marquis of Dalhousie, *19th:* 595
Enrico Dandolo, *MA:* 298
Georges Danton, *18th:* 289
Darius the Great, *Anc:* 251
Joseph Darnand, *Notor:* 264
Richard Walther Darré, *Notor:* 266
John Davenport, *17th:* 218
David I, *MA:* 304
David II, *MA:* 307
Jefferson Davis, *19th:* 610
Moshe Dayan, *20th:* 929
Ferenc Deák, *19th:* 619
Alfred Deakin, *19th:* 623
Eugene V. Debs, *20th:* 932
John Dee, *Ren:* 278
Deganawida, *Ren:* 281
Alcide De Gasperi, *20th:* 944
F. W. de Klerk, *20th:* 948
Eugene de Kock, *Notor:* 271
Demosthenes, *Anc:* 264
Deng Xiaoping, *20th:* 968
Fourteenth Earl of Derby, *19th:* 642
Eamon de Valera, *20th:* 979
Diane de Poitiers, *Ren:* 283
Porfirio Díaz, *19th:* 652, *Notor:* 278
John Dickinson, *18th:* 303
Dido, *Anc:* 271
John G. Diefenbaker, *20th:* 992
Diocletian, *Anc:* 280
Benjamin Disraeli, *19th:* 666
Milovan Djilas, *20th:* 1011
Samuel K. Doe, *Notor:* 288
Bob Dole, *20th:* 1014
Elizabeth Dole, *20th:* 1018
Domitian, *Notor:* 289
Dorgon, *17th:* 234
Jacques Doriot, *Notor:* 298
Helen Gahagan Douglas, *20th:* 1026
Stephen A. Douglas, *19th:* 681
Draco, *Anc:* 293
José Napoleon Duarte, *20th:* 1040
Alexander Dubček, *20th:* 1042
John Foster Dulles, *20th:* 1054
Joseph-François Dupleix, *18th:* 311
First Earl of Durham, *19th:* 708
François Duvalier, *20th:* 1069, *Notor:* 307
Jean-Claude Duvalier, *Notor:* 309
Felix Dzerzhinsky, *Notor:* 312
Earl of Warwick, *Ren:* 989
Abba Eban, *20th:* 1082
Félix Éboué, *20th:* 1085
Sir Anthony Eden, *20th:* 1099
Edward I, *MA:* 343
Edward II, *MA:* 347
Edward III, *MA:* 350
Edward IV, *Ren:* 301
Edward VI, *Ren:* 303
Edward VII, *20th:* 1104
Edward the Confessor, *MA:* 337
Edward the Elder, *MA:* 340
Egbert, *MA:* 353
John D. Ehrlichman, *Notor:* 320
Dwight D. Eisenhower, *20th:* 1125

Elagabalus, *Notor:* 326
Eleanor of Aquitaine, *MA:* 355
Elizabeth I, *Ren:* 310
Elizabeth II, *20th:* 1143
Elizabeth Petrovna, *18th:* 321
Elizabeth Stuart, *17th:* 253
Friedrich Engels, *19th:* 750
Enver Paşa, *20th:* 1157
Epaminondas, *Anc:* 303
Ludwig Erhard, *20th:* 1173
Erik XIV, *Notor:* 331
First Baron Erskine, *18th:* 326
Matthias Erzberger, *20th:* 1180
Ethelred II, the Unready, *MA:* 362
Eugene of Savoy, *18th:* 330
Herbert Vere Evatt, *20th:* 1188
Ezana, *Anc:* 333
Fabius, *Anc:* 342
Fahd, *20th:* 1195
Louis Faidherbe, *19th:* 756
Third Baron Fairfax, *17th:* 261
Faisal, *20th:* 1198
Faisal I, *20th:* 1202
Albert B. Fall, *Notor:* 342
Jerry Falwell, *20th:* 1209
Frantz Fanon, *20th:* 1212
Alessandro Farnese, *Ren:* 321
Farouk I, *20th:* 1215
Louis Farrakhan, *20th:* 1217
Orval E. Faubus, *Notor:* 348
Guy Fawkes, *Ren:* 324, *Notor:* 350
Dianne Feinstein, *20th:* 1227
Ferdinand II (1452-1516; Spanish king), *Ren:* 328
Ferdinand II (1578-1637; Holy Roman Emperor), *17th:* 267
Geraldine Ferraro, *20th:* 1242
Millard Fillmore, *19th:* 781
Lord Edward Fitzgerald, *18th:* 356
Maria Anne Fitzherbert, *18th:* 358
André-Hercule de Fleury, *18th:* 361
Jim Folsom, *Notor:* 362
Betty Ford, *20th:* 1272
Gerald R. Ford, *20th:* 1274
William Edward Forster, *19th:* 793
Abe Fortas, *Notor:* 369
Sir John Fortescue, *Ren:* 340
Charles James Fox, *18th:* 363
Francis I, *Ren:* 346
Francis Ferdinand, *20th:* 1294
Francis Joseph I, *19th:* 818
Francisco Franco, *20th:* 1297, *Notor:* 371
Hans Michael Frank, *Notor:* 374
Benjamin Franklin, *18th:* 370
Fredegunde, *MA:* 381
Frederick I, *18th:* 375
Frederick I Barbarossa, *MA:* 384
Frederick II, *MA:* 389
Frederick III, *Ren:* 350
Frederick V, *17th:* 293
Frederick Henry, *17th:* 286
Frederick the Great, *18th:* 378
Frederick William I, *18th:* 381
Frederick William, the Great Elector, *17th:* 290
John C. Frémont, *19th:* 831
Alberto Fujimori, *20th:* 1359, *Notor:* 382
Fujiwara Michinaga, *MA:* 396
Fyodor I, *Notor:* 385
Thomas Gage, *18th:* 384
John Kenneth Galbraith, *20th:* 1374
Galerius, *Notor:* 390
Albert Gallatin, *19th:* 854
Leopoldo Galtieri, *Notor:* 394
José de Gálvez, *18th:* 394
Léon Gambetta, *19th:* 864
Indira Gandhi, *20th:* 1385
Mahatma Gandhi, *20th:* 1388
Stephen Gardiner, *Ren:* 368
James A. Garfield, *19th:* 867
Giuseppe Garibaldi, *19th:* 871
Charles de Gaulle, *20th:* 1427
Genghis Khan, *MA:* 402, *Notor:* 400
Genseric, *Anc:* 351
Giovanni Gentile, *20th:* 1448
Alberico Gentili, *Ren:* 372
George I, *18th:* 400
George II, *18th:* 403
George III, *18th:* 408
George IV, *19th:* 890
George V, *20th:* 1451
George VI, *20th:* 1454
Elbridge Gerry, *18th:* 412
Maḥmūd Ghāzān, *MA:* 411
Gia Long, *19th:* 907
Sir Humphrey Gilbert, *Ren:* 378
Vincenzo Gioberti, *19th:* 921
William Ewart Gladstone, *19th:* 924
John Glenn, *20th:* 1499
First Earl of Godolphin, *18th:* 421
Boris Godunov, *Ren:* 387
William Godwin, *18th:* 424
Joseph Goebbels, *20th:* 1513, *Notor:* 418
Magda Goebbels, *Notor:* 421
Sir George Goldie, *19th:* 940
Mikhail Gorbachev, *20th:* 1530
Al Gore, *20th:* 1538
Hermann Göring, *20th:* 1545, *Notor:* 428
Maxim Gorky, *20th:* 1549
Gracchi, *Anc:* 357
Ulysses S. Grant, *19th:* 958
Henry Grattan, *18th:* 440
Horace Greeley, *19th:* 966
Alan Greenspan, *20th:* 1581
Sir Richard Grenville, *Ren:* 396
Charles Grey, *19th:* 977
Lady Jane Grey, *Ren:* 399
Sir Edward Grey, *20th:* 1587
Sir George Grey, *19th:* 981
Arthur Griffith, *20th:* 1591
Andrei Gromyko, *20th:* 1600
Hugo Grotius, *17th:* 326
Guacanagarí, *Ren:* 408
Gudea, *Anc:* 366
Che Guevara, *20th:* 1609, *Notor:* 436
Francesco Guicciardini, *Ren:* 410
Guo Moruo, *20th:* 1619
Gustav I Vasa, *Ren:* 415
Gustavus II Adolphus, *17th:* 336
Nell Gwyn, *17th:* 342
George Habash, *20th:* 1626
Hadrian, *Anc:* 370
Haile Selassie I, *20th:* 1639
al-Ḥākim, *Notor:* 441
H. R. Haldeman, *Notor:* 442
Matthew Hale (1609-1676), *17th:* 345
Mary A. Hallaren, *20th:* 1645
Fannie Lou Hamer, *20th:* 1651

Hamilcar Barca, *Anc:* 373
Alexander Hamilton, *18th:* 452
Dag Hammarskjöld, *20th:* 1653
Hammurabi, *Anc:* 376
John Hancock, *18th:* 457
Marcus A. Hanna, *19th:* 1018
Karl von Hardenberg, *19th:* 1021
Keir Hardie, *19th:* 1025
Warren G. Harding, *20th:* 1674
Harold II, *MA:* 457
Alfred and Harold Harmsworth, *20th:* 1678
William Averell Harriman, *20th:* 1684
Benjamin Harrison, *19th:* 1040
William Henry Harrison, *19th:* 1048
Harṣa, *MA:* 460
Hārūn al-Rashīd, *MA:* 467
Hassan II, *20th:* 1699
Warren Hastings, *18th:* 469
Ichirō Hatoyama, *20th:* 1701
Hatshepsut, *Anc:* 388
Mohammad Hatta, *20th:* 1704
Václav Havel, *20th:* 1707
Robert Hawke, *20th:* 1710
Víctor Raúl Haya de la Torre, *20th:* 1716
Rutherford B. Hayes, *19th:* 1061
Sir Edward Heath, *20th:* 1738
Henrietta Maria, *17th:* 364
Henry I, *MA:* 481
Henry II (1133-1189; King of England), *MA:* 483
Henry II (1519-1559; King of France), *Ren:* 423
Henry II the Saint, *MA:* 486
Henry III (1207-1272; King of England), *MA:* 490
Henry III (1551-1589; King of France), *Ren:* 426
Henry IV (1050-1106; Holy Roman Emperor), *MA:* 497
Henry IV (1367-1413; King of England), *MA:* 493
Henry IV (1553-1610; King of France), *Ren:* 429
Henry IV of Castile, *Ren:* 432
Henry V, *MA:* 501
Henry VI, *Ren:* 434
Henry VII, *Ren:* 438
Henry VIII, *Ren:* 441
Patrick Henry, *18th:* 482
Henry the Lion, *MA:* 473
Heraclius, *MA:* 505
Herod the Great, *Anc:* 403, *Notor:* 459
Édouard Herriot, *20th:* 1777
Rudolf Hess, *Notor:* 460
Reinhard Heydrich, *Notor:* 462
Hiawatha, *Ren:* 448
Miguel Hidalgo y Costilla, *19th:* 1094
Heinrich Himmler, *20th:* 1807, *Notor:* 468
Paul von Hindenburg, *20th:* 1814
Hirohito, *20th:* 1818, *Notor:* 473
Alger Hiss, *20th:* 1822, *Notor:* 475
Adolf Hitler, *20th:* 1829, *Notor:* 477
Ho Chi Minh, *20th:* 1834
Oveta Culp Hobby, *20th:* 1838
Hōjō Ujimasa, *Ren:* 451
Honda Toshiaki, *18th:* 504
Hong Xiuquan, *19th:* 1127
Thomas Hooker, *17th:* 386
Herbert Hoover, *20th:* 1862
J. Edgar Hoover, *20th:* 1866, *Notor:* 489
Harry Hopkins, *20th:* 1872
Hosokawa Gracia, *Ren:* 459
François Hotman, *Ren:* 461
Félix Houphouët-Boigny, *20th:* 1895
Sam Houston, *19th:* 1130
Catherine Howard, *Ren:* 466
Richard Howe, *18th:* 506
Enver and Nexhmije Hoxha, *Notor:* 493
Hu Yaobang, *20th:* 1905
Hua Guofeng, *20th:* 1907
Huáscar, *Ren:* 469
Charles Evans Hughes, *20th:* 1920
William Morris Hughes, *20th:* 1931
Cordell Hull, *20th:* 1934
Humāyūn, *Ren:* 475
Hubert H. Humphrey, *20th:* 1938
Hun Sen, *20th:* 1942
E. Howard Hunt, *Notor:* 499
János Hunyadi, *MA:* 519
Hussein I, *20th:* 1950
Qusay Saddam Hussein, *Notor:* 501
Saddam Hussein, *20th:* 1947, *Notor:* 503
Uday Hussein, *Notor:* 505
Anne Hutchinson, *17th:* 394
Thomas Hutchinson, *18th:* 518
Hyder Ali, *18th:* 522
Pierre Le Moyne d'Iberville, *17th:* 401
Ibrāhīm Lodī, *Ren:* 478
İbrahim Paşa, *Ren:* 480
Ii Naosuke, *19th:* 1168
Hayato Ikeda, *20th:* 1965
Innocent XI, *17th:* 405
Saint Irene, *MA:* 548
Isabella I, *Ren:* 328
Isabella II, *19th:* 1183
Isabella d'Este, *Ren:* 485
Isabella of France, *MA:* 552
Saint Isidore of Seville, *MA:* 555
Itō Hirobumi, *19th:* 1185
Itzcóatl, *MA:* 558
Ivan V, *Notor:* 514
Ivan VI, *Notor:* 515
Ivan the Great, *Ren:* 487
Ivan the Terrible, *Ren:* 492, *Notor:* 517
Andrew Jackson, *19th:* 1189
Jesse Jackson, *20th:* 1978
Jahāngīr, *17th:* 410
Jamāl al-Dīn al-Afghānī, *19th:* 1203
James I, *17th:* 413
James I the Conqueror, *MA:* 571
James II, *17th:* 416
James III, *Ren:* 496
James IV, *Ren:* 498
James V, *Ren:* 501
Wojciech Jaruzelski, *Notor:* 525
Jean Jaurès, *19th:* 1220
John Jay, *18th:* 524
Thomas Jefferson, *18th:* 528
Jiang Zemin, *20th:* 2000
Jiang Qing, *Notor:* 528
Francisco Jiménez de Cisneros, *Ren:* 503

Jimmu Tennō, *Anc:* 462
Jingū, *Anc:* 465
Mohammed Ali Jinnah, *20th:* 2002
Joan of Arc, *MA:* 578
Joan the Mad, *Notor:* 531
Alfred Jodl, *Notor:* 533
King John, *MA:* 584, *Notor:* 534
John II, *Ren:* 511
John III, *Ren:* 513
John III Sobieski, *17th:* 427
John IV, *17th:* 430
John of Austria, *17th:* 425
Andrew Johnson, *19th:* 1229
Lady Bird Johnson, *20th:* 2025
Lyndon B. Johnson, *20th:* 2027
Barbara Jordan, *20th:* 2046
Chief Joseph, *19th:* 1238
Joseph II, *18th:* 544
Joséphine, *19th:* 1241
Juan Carlos I, *20th:* 2060
Benito Juárez, *19th:* 1245
Julia Domna, *Anc:* 480
Julia III, *Anc:* 489
Julia Mamaea, *Anc:* 483
Julia Soaemias, *Anc:* 486
Justin II, *Notor:* 546
Justinian I, *MA:* 598
Lazar Kaganovich, *Notor:* 549
Damia al-Kāhina, *MA:* 604
Kamehameha I, *19th:* 1249
Kang Youwei, *19th:* 1252
Kangxi, *17th:* 448
Kanishka, *Anc:* 499
Merzifonlu Kara Mustafa Paşa, *17th:* 451
Radovan Karadžić, *Notor:* 554
Karīm Khān Zand, *18th:* 552
Kâtib Çelebî, *17th:* 454
Wenzel Anton von Kaunitz, *18th:* 557
John F. Kennedy, *20th:* 2098
Robert F. Kennedy, *20th:* 2102
Jomo Kenyatta, *20th:* 2106
Aleksandr Fyodorovich Kerensky, *20th:* 2110
Khieu Samphan, *Notor:* 569
Bohdan Khmelnytsky, *17th:* 461
Ayatollah Khomeini, *20th:* 2123, *Notor:* 571
Khosrow I, *MA:* 613
Nikita S. Khrushchev, *20th:* 2128, *Notor:* 574
William Kidd, *17th:* 464, *Notor:* 576
Kim Dae Jung, *20th:* 2136
Kim Il Sung, *20th:* 2138, *Notor:* 578
Kim Jong Il, *20th:* 2141, *Notor:* 581
William Lyon Mackenzie King, *20th:* 2155
Henry Kissinger, *20th:* 2170
Lord Kitchener, *20th:* 2173
Helmut Kohl, *20th:* 2182
Kuniaki Koiso, *Notor:* 587
Kōken, *MA:* 623
Tadeusz Kościuszko, *18th:* 564
Kösem Sultan, *17th:* 472
Krishnadevaraya, *Ren:* 532
Paul Kruger, *19th:* 1298
Kublai Khan, *MA:* 626
Béla Kun, *Notor:* 596
Robert M. La Follette, *20th:* 2227
Henri-Marie La Fontaine, *20th:* 2231
Fiorello Henry La Guardia, *20th:* 2237
Lalibela, *MA:* 632
John Lambert, *17th:* 483
Lord Lansdowne, *20th:* 2266
Lyndon H. LaRouche, Jr., *Notor:* 606
Harold J. Laski, *20th:* 2269
Saint László I, *MA:* 637
Julia C. Lathrop, *20th:* 2272
William Laud, *17th:* 495
Sir Wilfrid Laurier, *20th:* 2281
Pierre Laval, *20th:* 2285, *Notor:* 609
Bonar Law, *20th:* 2292
John Laird Mair Lawrence, *19th:* 1328
Le Thanh Tong, *Ren:* 546
Lee Kuan Yew, *20th:* 2326
First Duke of Leeds, *17th:* 506
Earl of Leicester, *Ren:* 553
Jacob Leisler, *17th:* 518
Vladimir Ilich Lenin, *20th:* 2341, *Notor:* 628
Leo X, *Ren:* 557, *Notor:* 630
Leopold I, *17th:* 526
Leopold II, *19th:* 1349, *Notor:* 632
Duke de Lerma, *17th:* 530
René Lévesque, *20th:* 2345
Michel de L'Hospital, *Ren:* 568
Li Hongzhang, *19th:* 1363
Li Peng, *20th:* 2367
G. Gordon Liddy, *Notor:* 643
Trygve Lie, *20th:* 2375
Wilhelm Liebknecht, *19th:* 1370
John Lilburne, *17th:* 534
Liliuokalani, *19th:* 1373
Lin Biao, *20th:* 2381
Lin Zexu, *19th:* 1376
Abraham Lincoln, *19th:* 1380
Mary Todd Lincoln, *19th:* 1385
Walter Lippmann, *20th:* 2400
Maksim Maksimovich Litvinov, *20th:* 2404
Liu Shaoqi, *20th:* 2408
Second Earl of Liverpool, *19th:* 1397
Livia Drusilla, *Anc:* 508
David Lloyd George, *20th:* 2411
Lobengula, *19th:* 1406
Henry Cabot Lodge, *20th:* 2417
Huey Long, *20th:* 2424, *Notor:* 649
Duchesse de Longueville, *17th:* 548
Byron Looper, *Notor:* 654
Louis IX, *MA:* 666
Louis XI, *Ren:* 574
Louis XII, *Ren:* 577
Louis XIII, *17th:* 551
Louis XIV, *17th:* 554
Louis XV, *18th:* 615
Louis XVI, *18th:* 618
Louis the German, *MA:* 662
Marquis de Louvois, *17th:* 558
Lu Xun, *20th:* 2447
Clare Boothe Luce, *20th:* 2453
Lucretia, *Anc:* 517
Erich Ludendorff, *20th:* 2462
Roger Ludlow, *17th:* 567
Saint Ludmilla, *MA:* 670
Ludwig II, *Notor:* 662
Lord Lugard, *20th:* 2465

Patrice Lumumba, *20th:* 2476
Albert Lutuli, *20th:* 2478
Rosa Luxemburg, *20th:* 2482
Dame Enid Muriel Lyons, *20th:* 2486
Joseph Aloysius Lyons, *20th:* 2489
John MacArthur, *19th:* 1431
Catherine Macaulay, *18th:* 621
Thomas Babington Macaulay, *19th:* 1433
Joseph McCarthy, *20th:* 2497, *Notor:* 669
Sir John Alexander Macdonald, *19th:* 1441
Flora MacDonald, *18th:* 623
Ramsay MacDonald, *20th:* 2510
Alexander McGillivray, *18th:* 626
Samora Machel, *20th:* 2515
Niccolò Machiavelli, *Ren:* 587
Alexander Mackenzie, *19th:* 1452
William Lyon Mackenzie, *19th:* 1454
Sir Halford John Mackinder, *20th:* 2518
William McKinley, *19th:* 1460
Harold Macmillan, *20th:* 2536
Robert McNamara, *20th:* 2541
Francisco Madero, *20th:* 2544
Dolley Madison, *19th:* 1470
James Madison, *18th:* 636
Gaius Maecenas, *Anc:* 527
Datuk Seri Mahathir bin Mohamad, *20th:* 2551
The Mahdi, *19th:* 1473
Mahmud I, *18th:* 639
Sieur de Maisonneuve, *17th:* 574
John Major, *20th:* 2567
Georgi M. Malenkov, *20th:* 2573
André Malraux, *20th:* 2576
Manasseh ben Israel, *17th:* 582
The Mancini Sisters, *17th:* 585
Nelson Mandela, *20th:* 2583
Winnie Mandela, *Notor:* 686
Meri Te Tai Mangakahia, *19th:* 1483
Wilma Mankiller, *20th:* 2591
Mary de la Rivière Manley, *18th:* 641
Horace Mann, *19th:* 1486
Carl Gustaf Mannerheim, *20th:* 2598
Daniel Mannix, *19th:* 1492
Manuel I, *Ren:* 605
Mao Zedong, *20th:* 2601, *Notor:* 691
Jean-Paul Marat, *18th:* 648, *Notor:* 696
Ferdinand Marcos, *20th:* 2619, *Notor:* 699
Imelda Marcos, *Notor:* 702
Marcus Aurelius, *Anc:* 530
Margaret of Austria, *Ren:* 612
Margaret of Denmark, Norway, and Sweden, *MA:* 689
Margaret of Parma, *Ren:* 615
Marguerite de Navarre, *Ren:* 617
Maria Theresa, *18th:* 653
Mengistu Haile Mariam, *Notor:* 719
Marie-Antoinette, *18th:* 657, *Notor:* 704
Marie de Médicis, *17th:* 598
Marie-Thérèse, *17th:* 600
Gaius Marius, *Anc:* 533
Marozia, *Notor:* 706
José Martí, *19th:* 1503
Jean Martinet, *Notor:* 707
Andrew Marvell, *17th:* 605
Mary I, *Ren:* 639
Mary II, *17th:* 610
Mary of Burgundy, *Ren:* 631
Mary of Guise, *Ren:* 633
Mary of Hungary, *Ren:* 636
Mary of Modena, *17th:* 607
Mary, Queen of Scots, *Ren:* 627
Tomáš Masaryk, *20th:* 2639
Masinissa, *Anc:* 542
George Mason, *18th:* 664
Massasoit, *17th:* 612
William Ferguson Massey, *20th:* 2643
Matilda of Canossa, *MA:* 705
Matthias I Corvinus, *Ren:* 642
Maurice of Nassau, *17th:* 618
Maximilian, *19th:* 1525
Maximilian I, *Ren:* 646
Maximilian II, *Ren:* 650
Jules Mazarin, *17th:* 620
Ivan Stepanovich Mazepa, *17th:* 624
Giuseppe Mazzini, *19th:* 1531
George Meany, *20th:* 2672
Cosimo I de' Medici, *Ren:* 653
Cosimo II de' Medici, *17th:* 626
Lorenzo de' Medici, *Ren:* 655
Mehmed II, *MA:* 711, *Ren:* 659
Mehmed III, *Ren:* 661
Golda Meir, *20th:* 2674
Second Viscount Melbourne, *19th:* 1534
Melisende, *MA:* 715
Menander (c 210-c. 135 B.C.E. Greco-Bactrian king), *Anc:* 550
Rigoberta Menchú, *20th:* 2686
Pierre Mendès-France, *20th:* 2698
Bernardino de Mendoza, *Ren:* 668
Ana de Mendoza y de la Cerda, *Ren:* 670
Menelik II, *19th:* 1552
Menes, *Anc:* 556
Mengistu Haile Mariam, *20th:* 2701, *Notor:* 719
Mentewab, *18th:* 677
Sir Robert Gordon Menzies, *20th:* 2707
Valeria Messallina, *Anc:* 561
Metacom, *17th:* 633
Ioannis Metaxas, *Notor:* 724
Metternich, *19th:* 1561
Wilbur Mills, *Notor:* 733
Slobodan Milošević, *20th:* 2756, *Notor:* 735
Minamoto Yoritomo, *MA:* 721
Peter Minuit, *17th:* 643
Comte de Mirabeau, *18th:* 679
John Mitchell, *Notor:* 737
Mithradates VI Eupator, *Anc:* 567
François Mitterrand, *20th:* 2769
Mobutu Sese Seko, *20th:* 2773, *Notor:* 740
Mohammed I Askia, *Ren:* 686
Mohammad Reza Shah Pahlavi, *20th:* 2779, *Notor:* 742
Vyacheslav Mikhailovich Molotov, *20th:* 2783, *Notor:* 746
George Monck, *17th:* 650

Duke of Monmouth, *17th:* 653
Jean Monnet, *20th:* 2793
James Monroe, *19th:* 1586
Michel Eyquem de Montaigne, *Ren:* 689
Montezuma II, *Ren:* 693
Simon de Montfort, *MA:* 725
Duchesse de Montpensier, *17th:* 660
Montuhotep II, *Anc:* 570
Sun Myung Moon, *20th:* 2811, *Notor:* 749
Sir Thomas More, *Ren:* 697
Hans Joachim Morgenthau, *20th:* 2828
Philippe de Mornay, *Ren:* 703
Boris Ivanovich Morozov, *17th:* 663
Gouverneur Morris, *18th:* 705
Robert Morris, *18th:* 707
Gaetano Mosca, *20th:* 2838
Moses, *Anc:* 572
Mohammad Mossadegh, *20th:* 2844
Louis Mountbatten, *20th:* 2853
Robert Mugabe, *20th:* 2858, *Notor:* 761
Muḥammad, *MA:* 733
Muḥammad ʿAlī Pasha, *19th:* 1620
Brian Mulroney, *20th:* 2866
Murad IV, *17th:* 668
Mansa Mūsā, *MA:* 744
Yoweri Kaguta Museveni, *20th:* 2883
Benito Mussolini, *20th:* 2885, *Notor:* 769
Mustafa I, *17th:* 673
Mustafa III, *18th:* 719
Mutsuhito, *19th:* 1631
Ralph Nader, *20th:* 2897
Nādir Shāh, *18th:* 722, *Notor:* 772
Sarojini Naidu, *20th:* 2900
Dadabhai Naoroji, *19th:* 1634
Napoleon I, *19th:* 1636
Napoleon III, *19th:* 1639
Gamal Abdel Nasser, *20th:* 2914
Ne Win, *Notor:* 773
Nebuchadnezzar II, *Anc:* 582
Jacques Necker, *18th:* 726
Nefertari, *Anc:* 585
Nefertiti, *Anc:* 587
Jawaharlal Nehru, *20th:* 2929
Nero, *Anc:* 591, *Notor:* 777
Nest verch Rhys ap Tewdwr, *MA:* 753
Huey Newton, *Notor:* 782
Nezahualcóyotl, *Ren:* 720
Ngo Dinh Diem, *20th:* 2951
Ngo Quyen, *MA:* 756
Nguyen Hue, *18th:* 736
Nguyen Van Thieu, *20th:* 2954
Madame Nhu, *Notor:* 786
Nicholas I, *19th:* 1670, *Notor:* 788
Nicholas of Cusa, *Ren:* 724
Nikon, *17th:* 683
Richard M. Nixon, *20th:* 2984, *Notor:* 793
Niẓām al-Mulk, *MA:* 774
Njinga, *17th:* 687
Kwame Nkrumah, *20th:* 2988
Manuel Noriega, *Notor:* 797
Lord North, *18th:* 738
Nostradamus, *Ren:* 728, *Notor:* 799
Julius Nyerere, *20th:* 3004
Titus Oates, *17th:* 692, *Notor:* 802
Milton Obote, *20th:* 3011
Álvaro Obregón, *20th:* 3013
Thomas Power O'Connor, *20th:* 3024
Oda Nobunaga, *Ren:* 732
Odoacer, *MA:* 782
Ōgimachi, *Ren:* 735
James Edward Oglethorpe, *18th:* 742
Ogyū Sorai, *18th:* 746
Bernardo O'Higgins, *19th:* 1703
Oichi, *Ren:* 737
Ōjin Tennō, *Anc:* 594
Seán T. O'Kelly, *20th:* 3034
Saint Olaf, *MA:* 785
Olaf I, *MA:* 789
Johan van Oldenbarnevelt, *Ren:* 740
Saint Olga, *MA:* 792
Count-Duke of Olivares, *17th:* 697
Olympias, *Anc:* 597
Grace O'Malley, *Ren:* 743, *Notor:* 805
Rory O'More, *17th:* 699
Jacqueline Kennedy Onassis, *20th:* 3045
Tip O'Neill, *20th:* 3055
Opechancanough, *17th:* 702
Duc d'Orléans, *18th:* 751
Aleksey Grigoryevich Orlov, *18th:* 755
Grigori Grigoryevich Orlov, *18th:* 757
Daniel Ortega, *20th:* 3072
Katherine Davalos Ortega, *20th:* 3074
Osman I, *MA:* 800
Otto I, *MA:* 805
Sir James Outram, *19th:* 1717
Axel Oxenstierna, *17th:* 704
Pachacuti, *Ren:* 746
Thomas Paine, *18th:* 759
Sophia Palaeologus, *Ren:* 749
Lord Palmerston, *19th:* 1731
Vijaya Lakshmi Pandit, *20th:* 3099
Andreas Papandreou, *20th:* 3106
Franz von Papen, *20th:* 3109
Sir Henry Parkes, *19th:* 1739
Charles Stewart Parnell, *19th:* 1747
Catherine Parr, *Ren:* 764
Vallabhbhai Jhaverbhai Patel, *20th:* 3135
Alice Paul, *20th:* 3145
Ante Pavelić, *Notor:* 813
Víctor Paz Estenssoro, *20th:* 3172
Lester B. Pearson, *20th:* 3174
Pedro I, *19th:* 1763
Pedro II, *19th:* 1766
Sir Robert Peel, *19th:* 1768
Henry Pelham, *18th:* 771
Pemisapan, *Ren:* 771
Thomas Joseph Pendergast, *Notor:* 817
Peng Dehuai, *20th:* 3191
William Penn, *17th:* 724
Samuel Pepys, *17th:* 728
Leander Perez, *Notor:* 819

Javier Pérez de Cuéllar, *20th:* 3194
Pericles, *Anc:* 620
Frances Perkins, *20th:* 3198
Eva Perón, *20th:* 3201, *Notor:* 821
Juan Perón, *20th:* 3205, *Notor:* 823
H. Ross Perot, *20th:* 3208
Charles Perrault, *17th:* 731
Peter III, *18th:* 778
Peter the Cruel, *Notor:* 827
Peter the Great, *18th:* 774
Symon Petlyura, *Notor:* 832
Sir William Petty, *17th:* 733
Phalaris, *Notor:* 834
Philip II (1165-1223; King of France), *MA:* 835
Philip II (1527-1598; King of Spain), *Ren:* 778
Philip II of Macedonia, *Anc:* 637
Philip III, *17th:* 736
Philip IV, *17th:* 738
Philip IV the Fair, *MA:* 839
Philip V, *18th:* 781
Arthur Phillip, *18th:* 783
Philip the Good, *MA:* 832
Philip the Magnanimous, *Ren:* 775
Philippa of Hainaut, *MA:* 842
Franklin Pierce, *19th:* 1789
Pontius Pilate, *Anc:* 643, *Notor:* 840
Józef Piłsudski, *20th:* 3250
Gifford Pinchot, *20th:* 3253
Augusto Pinochet Ugarte, *20th:* 3257, *Notor:* 842
Pisistratus, *Anc:* 649
William Pitt the Elder, *18th:* 786
William Pitt the Younger, *18th:* 789
Pittacus of Mytilene, *Anc:* 652
Pius II, *Ren:* 794
Pius VI, *18th:* 793
Piye, *Anc:* 655
Francis Place, *19th:* 1806
Konstantin Petrovich Pobedonostsev, *19th:* 1810, *Notor:* 845
Raymond Poincaré, *20th:* 3292
Pol Pot, *20th:* 3298, *Notor:* 846
James K. Polk, *19th:* 1819
Polycrates of Samos, *Notor:* 850
Marquês de Pombal, *18th:* 795
Madame de Pompadour, *18th:* 798
Pompey the Great, *Anc:* 681
Georges Pompidou, *20th:* 3305
Pontiac, *18th:* 801
Poppaea Sabina, *Anc:* 685
Grigori Aleksandrovich Potemkin, *18th:* 808
Adam Clayton Powell, Jr., *Notor:* 856
Colin Powell, *20th:* 3321
Powhatan, *17th:* 752
Miguel Primo de Rivera, *Notor:* 860
Psamtik I, *Anc:* 710
Michael Psellus, *MA:* 863
Ptolemy Philadelphus, *Anc:* 715
Ptolemy Soter, *Anc:* 719
Yemelyan Ivanovich Pugachev, *18th:* 814
Puyi, *Notor:* 864
John Pym, *17th:* 767
Muammar al-Qaddafi, *20th:* 3350, *Notor:* 867
Qāytbāy, *Ren:* 807
Qianlong, *18th:* 817
Qu Yuan, *Anc:* 732
Yitzhak Rabin, *20th:* 3358
Pierre Esprit Radisson, *17th:* 777
Sir Walter Ralegh, *Ren:* 813
Ramses II, *Anc:* 735
Mahadev Govind Ranade, *19th:* 1855
Ayn Rand, *20th:* 3367
Jeannette Rankin, *20th:* 3374
Grigori Yefimovich Rasputin, *19th:* 1863, *Notor:* 885
Jerry John Rawlings, *20th:* 3389
John Rawls, *20th:* 3391
Sam Rayburn, *20th:* 3397
Guillaume-Thomas Raynal, *18th:* 829
Stenka Razin, *17th:* 784
Raziya, *MA:* 888
Ronald Reagan, *20th:* 3400
André Rebouças, *19th:* 1869
Red Cloud, *19th:* 1871
Janet Reno, *20th:* 3416
Paul Revere, *18th:* 832
Reza Shah Pahlavi, *20th:* 2779, *Notor:* 742
Syngman Rhee, *20th:* 3430
Cecil Rhodes, *19th:* 1891
Joachim von Ribbentrop, *Notor:* 894
Richard I, *MA:* 891
Richard II, *MA:* 893
Richard III, *Ren:* 828, *Notor:* 896
Ann Richards, *20th:* 3434
Cardinal de Richelieu, *17th:* 790
Louis Riel, *19th:* 1908
Cola di Rienzo, *MA:* 897
Efraín Ríos Montt, *Notor:* 899
Robespierre, *18th:* 844, *Notor:* 907
Mary Robinson (b. 1944), *20th:* 3474
Nelson A. Rockefeller, *20th:* 3478
George Rodney, *18th:* 854
Edith Nourse Rogers, *20th:* 3489
Rollo, *MA:* 900
Michael Romanov, *17th:* 794
Eleanor Roosevelt, *20th:* 3506
Franklin D. Roosevelt, *20th:* 3509
Theodore Roosevelt, *20th:* 3515
Elihu Root, *20th:* 3519
John Ross, *19th:* 1937
Nellie Tayloe Ross, *20th:* 3529
Rudolf I, *MA:* 904
Rudolf II, *Ren:* 840
Rurik, *MA:* 911
John Russell, *19th:* 1958
Anwar el-Sadat, *20th:* 3587
Saʿīd ibn Sulṭān, *19th:* 1965
Saigō Takamori, *19th:* 1968
Louis de Saint-Just, *18th:* 877
Louis St. Laurent, *20th:* 3597
Saladin, *MA:* 918
António de Oliveira Salazar, *20th:* 3606, *Notor:* 928
First Earl of Salisbury, *Ren:* 844
Third Marquis of Salisbury, *19th:* 1977
Sammu-ramat, *Anc:* 744
Samory Touré, *19th:* 1981
Samuel, *Anc:* 747
Antonio López de Santa Anna, *19th:* 1990
Sargon II, *Anc:* 752

Domingo Faustino Sarmiento, *19th:* 2000
Eisaku Satō, *20th:* 3645
Jeanne Sauvé, *20th:* 3652
Sir George Savile, *17th:* 815
Girolamo Savonarola, *Ren:* 850
Baldur von Schirach, *Notor:* 937
Carl Schurz, *19th:* 2035
Scipio Aemilianus, *Anc:* 755
Scipio Africanus, *Anc:* 758
Glenn Theodore Seaborg, *20th:* 3684
Richard John Seddon, *19th:* 2058
Seki Kōwa, *17th:* 831
Seleucus I Nicator, *Anc:* 763
Seneca the Younger, *Anc:* 766
Léopold Senghor, *20th:* 3702
Sennacherib, *Anc:* 769
Sergius I, *MA:* 933
Sesostris III, *Anc:* 771
William H. Seward, *19th:* 2077
Jane Seymour, *Ren:* 868
Caterina Sforza, *Ren:* 870
Ludovico Sforza, *Ren:* 872
First Earl of Shaftesbury, *17th:* 838
Shah Jahan, *17th:* 842
Shaka, *19th:* 2081
Shāpūr II, *Anc:* 774
Daniel Shays, *18th:* 902
Richard Brinsley Sheridan, *18th:* 905
Roger Sherman, *18th:* 908
Shi Huangdi, *Anc:* 779, *Notor:* 947
Shōtoku Taishi, *MA:* 940
George P. Shultz, *20th:* 3731
Muhammad Siad Barre, *20th:* 3734, *Notor:* 953
Sir Philip Sidney, *Ren:* 881
Emmanuel-Joseph Sieyès, *18th:* 916
Sigismund I, the Old, *Ren:* 885
Sigismund II Augustus, *Ren:* 887
Sigismund III Vasa, *17th:* 853
Norodom Sihanouk, *20th:* 3740
Sima Guang, *MA:* 945
Sima Xiangru, *Anc:* 785
John Graves Simcoe, *18th:* 919
Upton Sinclair, *20th:* 3750
Sitting Bull, *19th:* 2108
Śivājī, *17th:* 858
Sixtus V, *Ren:* 895
Adam Smith, *18th:* 921
Alfred E. Smith, *20th:* 3762
John Smith, *17th:* 861
Margaret Chase Smith, *20th:* 3768
Jan Christian Smuts, *20th:* 3775
Solomon, *Anc:* 803
Solon, *Anc:* 807
First Duke of Somerset, *Ren:* 898
Anastasio Somoza García, *Notor:* 984
Sonni ʿAlī, *Ren:* 900
Sophia, *17th:* 865
Sophonisba of Numidia, *Anc:* 812
Georges Sorel, *20th:* 3792
Sorghaghtani Beki, *MA:* 954
George Soros, *20th:* 3795
Paul-Henri Spaak, *20th:* 3808
Albert Speer, *Notor:* 987
Mikhail Mikhaylovich Speransky, *19th:* 2129
Baruch Spinoza, *17th:* 871
Madame de Staël, *18th:* 929
Joseph Stalin, *20th:* 3817, *Notor:* 990
Miles Standish, *17th:* 877
First Earl Stanhope, *18th:* 937
Edwin M. Stanton, *19th:* 2142
Richard Steele, *18th:* 941
Stefan Dušan, *MA:* 957
Freiherr vom Stein, *19th:* 2151
Stephen I, *MA:* 964
King Stephen, *MA:* 960
Stephen Báthory, *Ren:* 910
Alexander H. Stephens, *19th:* 2164
Thaddeus Stevens, *19th:* 2171
Adlai E. Stevenson, *20th:* 3856
Simon Stevin, *Ren:* 912
Henry L. Stimson, *20th:* 3869
First Earl of Strafford, *17th:* 884
Gustav Stresemann, *20th:* 3895
Alfredo Stroessner, *Notor:* 1004
Peter Stuyvesant, *17th:* 890
Sir John Suckling, *17th:* 893
Su Dongpo, *MA:* 968
Suger, *MA:* 971
Suharto, *20th:* 3901, *Notor:* 1007
Suiko, *MA:* 974
Sukarno, *20th:* 3904
Süleyman the Magnificent, *Ren:* 914
Lucius Cornelius Sulla, *Anc:* 830, *Notor:* 1010
Duke de Sully, *17th:* 896
Charles Sumner, *19th:* 2201
Sun Yat-sen, *20th:* 3913
Sundiata, *MA:* 977
Suryavarman II, *MA:* 980
Sylvester II, *MA:* 983
Ta Mok, *Notor:* 1017
Tacitus, *Anc:* 837
Robert A. Taft, *20th:* 3925
William Howard Taft, *20th:* 3929
Taira Kiyomori, *MA:* 990
Taizong, *MA:* 993
Taksin, *18th:* 968
Talleyrand, *19th:* 2221
Queen Tamara, *MA:* 998
Tamerlane, *MA:* 1000
Tanaquil, *Anc:* 840
Roger Brooke Taney, *19th:* 2225, *Notor:* 1018
Tarquins, *Anc:* 846
Tascalusa, *Ren:* 922
Charles Taylor, *Notor:* 1021
Zachary Taylor, *19th:* 2230
Shirley Temple, *20th:* 3973
Valentina Tereshkova, *20th:* 3978
Tewodros II, *19th:* 2255
Than Shwe, *Notor:* 1026
Thanadelthur, *18th:* 974
U Thant, *20th:* 3986
Margaret Thatcher, *20th:* 3992
Theodora, *MA:* 1008, *Notor:* 1028
Theodoric the Great, *MA:* 1012
Theodosius the Great, *Anc:* 868
Adolphe Thiers, *19th:* 2263
Norman Thomas, *20th:* 4002
Thutmose III, *Anc:* 885
Tianqi, *17th:* 911
Tiberius, *Anc:* 888
Tiglath-pileser III, *Anc:* 892
Tigranes the Great, *Anc:* 895
Bal Gangadhar Tilak, *20th:* 4023
Benjamin Tillman, *Notor:* 1030
Dēvānaṃpiya Tissa, *Anc:* 898
Tito, *20th:* 4034, *Notor:* 1032

Tiy, *Anc:* 901
Hideki Tojo, *Notor:* 1034
Tokugawa Ieyasu, *17th:* 915
Tokugawa Tsunayoshi, *17th:* 919
Tokugawa Yoshimune, *18th:* 980
Wolfe Tone, *18th:* 982
Tomás de Torquemada, *Ren:* 939, *Notor:* 1038
Omar Torrijos, *20th:* 4048
Ahmed Sékou Touré, *20th:* 4053
Toussaint Louverture, *18th:* 985
Toyotomi Hideyoshi, *Ren:* 943
Trajan, *Anc:* 903
Leon Trotsky, *20th:* 4072, *Notor:* 1040
Pierre Trudeau, *20th:* 4076
Rafael Trujillo, *20th:* 4084, *Notor:* 1042
Harry S. Truman, *20th:* 4086
Moïse Tshombe, *20th:* 4091
Tu Duc, *19th:* 2310
William V. S. Tubman, *20th:* 4101
The Tudor Family, *Ren:* 946
Sir Charles Tupper, *19th:* 2316
Anne-Robert-Jacques Turgot, *18th:* 996
Tutankhamen, *Anc:* 908
Desmond Tutu, *20th:* 4121
William Marcy Tweed, *19th:* 2333, *Notor:* 1047
John Tyler, *19th:* 2337
Walter Ulbricht, *20th:* 4125
Vasili Vasilievich Ulrikh, *Notor:* 1052
ᶜUmar I, *MA:* 1037
Urban VIII, *17th:* 936
Ur-Nammu, *Anc:* 914
ᶜUthman dan Fodio, *19th:* 2342
Vaḥīd Bihbahānī, *18th:* 1000
Valdemar II, *MA:* 1047
Martin Van Buren, *19th:* 2344
Sir Henry Vane the Younger, *17th:* 941
Getúlio Vargas, *Notor:* 1059
Vasily Shuysky, *17th:* 943
Vasily III, *Ren:* 957
Jean de Venette, *MA:* 1053
Eleuthérios Venizélos, *20th:* 4157
Vercingetorix, *Anc:* 935
Charles Gravier de Vergennes, *18th:* 1011
Vespasian, *Anc:* 943
Queen Victoria, *19th:* 2359
Jorge Rafael Videla, *Notor:* 1066
António Vieira, *17th:* 959
Pancho Villa, *20th:* 4160, *Notor:* 1069
Vlad III the Impaler, *Ren:* 981, *Notor:* 1072
Vladimir I, *MA:* 1068
Vladislav II, *Ren:* 983
Vo Nguyen Giap, *20th:* 4169
Sir Julius Vogel, *19th:* 2371
Anastase Vonsiatsky, *Notor:* 1077
Andrey Vyshinsky, *Notor:* 1079
Muḥammad ibn ᶜAbd al-Wahhāb, *18th:* 1030
Edward Gibbon Wakefield, *19th:* 2378
Kurt Waldheim, *20th:* 4187
Lech Wałęsa, *20th:* 4191
James J. Walker, *Notor:* 1082
William Walker, *Notor:* 1084
George C. Wallace, *20th:* 4203, *Notor:* 1087
Henry A. Wallace, *20th:* 4207
Albrecht Wenzel von Wallenstein, *17th:* 966
Robert Walpole, *18th:* 1034
Wang Jingwei, *20th:* 4220
Wang Anshi, *MA:* 1079
Wang Kŏn, *MA:* 1081
Wang Wei, *MA:* 1085
Wang Yangming, *Ren:* 986
Mercy Otis Warren, *18th:* 1041
George Washington, *18th:* 1043
Daniel Webster, *19th:* 2398
Chaim Weizmann, *20th:* 4279
Duke of Wellington, *19th:* 2409
Wenceslaus, *MA:* 1088
W. C. Wentworth, *19th:* 2412
Widukind, *MA:* 1094
William Wilberforce, *18th:* 1079
John Wilkes, *18th:* 1083
William II, *20th:* 4346
William III, *17th:* 979
William IV, *19th:* 2445
William the Conqueror, *MA:* 1117
William the Silent, *Ren:* 993
Roger Williams, *17th:* 982
Sir Harold Wilson, *20th:* 4360
James Wilson, *18th:* 1090
Woodrow Wilson, *20th:* 4364
Duke of Windsor, *20th:* 4368
Gerrard Winstanley, *17th:* 988
John Winthrop, *17th:* 990
John Witherspoon, *18th:* 1098
Władysław II Jagiełło and Jadwiga, *MA:* 1120
Mary Wollstonecraft, *18th:* 1108
Cardinal Thomas Wolsey, *Ren:* 996
Victoria Woodhull, *19th:* 2459
Wu Hou, *MA:* 1127
Wudi, *Anc:* 958
Xiaozong, *Ren:* 1003
Genrikh Yagoda, *Notor:* 1112
Ahmad Zaki Yamani, *20th:* 4422
Zara Yaqob, *Ren:* 1006
Boris Yeltsin, *20th:* 4431
Nikolay Ivanovich Yezhov, *Notor:* 1115
Yonglo, *MA:* 1147
Yongzheng, *18th:* 1113
Alexander and Demetrios Ypsilantis, *19th:* 2478
Yuan Shikai, *Notor:* 1122
Saᶜd Zaghlūl, *20th:* 4439
Zeng Guofan, *19th:* 2483
Zenobia, *Anc:* 986
Zhang Zhidong, *19th:* 2486
Zhao Ziyang, *20th:* 4459
Andrey Aleksandrovich Zhdanov, *Notor:* 1137
Zheng Chenggong, *17th:* 1001
Zhengde, *Ren:* 1008
Zhou Enlai, *20th:* 4461
Zhu De, *20th:* 4465
Zhu Xi, *MA:* 1159
Georgy Zhukov, *20th:* 4469
Mohammad Zia-ul-Haq, *20th:* 4473
Grigory Yevseyevich Zinovyev, *Notor:* 1138
Zoser, *Anc:* 996
Huldrych Zwingli, *Ren:* 1010

Gunslingers. ***See*** **Outlaws and Gunslingers**

HISTORIOGRAPHY

José de Acosta, *Ren:* 5
Lord Acton, *19th:* 12
Henry Adams, *19th:* 16
Alfonso X, *MA:* 59
Anna Comnena, *MA:* 89
Aśvaghosa, *Anc:* 130
Saint Athanasius of Alexandria, *Anc:* 132
Isaac Backus, *18th:* 75
Jean-Sylvain Bailly, *18th:* 77
Ban Gu, *Anc:* 149
George Bancroft, *19th:* 130
Pierre Bayle, *17th:* 36
Charles A. Beard, *20th:* 262
Saint Bede the Venerable, *MA:* 150
Pierre Belon, *Ren:* 101
Benjamin of Tudela, *MA:* 157
Walter Benjamin, *20th:* 306
Eduard Bernstein, *20th:* 334
al-Bīrūnī, *MA:* 163
Jacques-Bénigne Bossuet, *17th:* 70
Henry de Bracton, *MA:* 192
Fernand Braudel, *20th:* 497
Leonardo Bruni, *MA:* 208
George Buchanan, *Ren:* 146
Jacob Burckhardt, *19th:* 354
Thomas Carlyle, *19th:* 415
Giovanni da Pian del Carpini, *MA:* 226
Cassiodorus, *MA:* 233
Ernst Cassirer, *20th:* 688
Aulus Cornelius Celsus, *Anc:* 199
Auguste Comte, *19th:* 536
Benedetto Croce, *20th:* 869
Lucy S. Dawidowicz, *20th:* 922
Dio Cassius, *Anc:* 274
Eusebius of Caesarea, *Anc:* 330
Firdusi, *MA:* 375
Jean Froissart, *MA:* 392
Edward Gibbon, *18th:* 415
Étienne Gilson, *20th:* 1488
Oliver Goldsmith, *18th:* 432
Antonio Gramsci, *20th:* 1566
Gregory of Tours, *MA:* 426
Francesco Guicciardini, *Ren:* 410
Guo Moruo, *20th:* 1619
Guy de Chauliac, *MA:* 445
Richard Hakluyt, *Ren:* 419
Adolf von Harnack, *20th:* 1681
Herodotus, *Anc:* 407
Hrosvitha, *MA:* 516
Thomas Hutchinson, *18th:* 518
Ibn Khaldūn, *MA:* 536
Joachim of Fiore, *MA:* 575
Flavius Josephus, *Anc:* 477, *Notor:* 541
Kâtib Çelebî, *17th:* 454
Le Thanh Tong, *Ren:* 546
Leo Africanus, *Ren:* 555
Bernard Lewis, *20th:* 2351
Livy, *Anc:* 511
Mikhail Vasilyevich Lomonosov, *18th:* 613
Catherine Macaulay, *18th:* 621
Thomas Babington Macaulay, *19th:* 1433
Niccolò Machiavelli, *Ren:* 587
al-Masʿūdī, *MA:* 703
Jules Michelet, *19th:* 1564
James Mill, *19th:* 1571
Theodor Mommsen, *19th:* 1582
Barthold Georg Niebuhr, *19th:* 1673
Francis Parkman, *19th:* 1742
Vernon Louis Parrington, *20th:* 3124
Nicolas-Claude Fabri de Peiresc, *17th:* 722
Henri Pirenne, *20th:* 3269
Polybius, *Anc:* 673
William Hickling Prescott, *19th:* 1831
Michael Psellus, *MA:* 863
Leopold von Ranke, *19th:* 1860
Guillaume-Thomas Raynal, *18th:* 829
Ernest Renan, *19th:* 1884
Sallust, *Anc:* 742
Saxo Grammaticus, *MA:* 927
Joseph Justus Scaliger, *Ren:* 855
Friedrich Schiller, *18th:* 887
Heinrich Schliemann, *19th:* 2016
Sima Guang, *MA:* 945
Sima Qian, *Anc:* 782
Snorri Sturluson, *MA:* 950
Aleksandr Solzhenitsyn, *20th:* 3783
Strabo, *Anc:* 827
William Stukeley, *18th:* 952
al-Ṭabarī, *MA:* 988
Tacitus, *Anc:* 837
Hippolyte Taine, *19th:* 2216
Theophanes the Confessor, *MA:* 1020
Thucydides, *Anc:* 882
Arnold Toynbee, *20th:* 4059
Barbara W. Tuchman, *20th:* 4104
Frederick Jackson Turner, *20th:* 4115
Jean de Venette, *MA:* 1053
Andreas Vesalius, *Ren:* 965
Giambattista Vico, *18th:* 1013
Giovanni Villani, *MA:* 1056
Geoffroi de Villehardouin, *MA:* 1059
Vincent of Beauvais, *MA:* 1063
Joachim Wach, *20th:* 4177
Mercy Otis Warren, *18th:* 1041
George Washington Williams, *19th:* 2449
Johann Joachim Winckelmann, *18th:* 1095
Yaqut, *MA:* 1143

INDUSTRY. ***See* BUSINESS AND INDUSTRY**

INVENTION AND TECHNOLOGY. ***See also* ENGINEERING; PHYSICS**

Luis W. Alvarez, *20th:* 73
Archimedes, *Anc:* 80
Sir Richard Arkwright, *18th:* 55
Edwin H. Armstrong, *20th:* 127
Neil Armstrong, *20th:* 134
Charles Babbage, *19th:* 107
Robert D. Ballard, *20th:* 215
John Bardeen, *20th:* 234
John Baskerville, *18th:* 92
Nikolay Gennadiyevich Basov, *20th:* 256
Johann Joachim Becher, *17th:* 39
Alexander Graham Bell, *19th:* 182
Friedrich Bergius, *20th:* 313
Tim Berners-Lee, *20th:* 331
Sir Henry Bessemer, *19th:* 218
Jeff Bezos, *20th:* 360

Vilhelm Bjerknes, *20th:* 374
Walther Bothe, *20th:* 442
Matthew Boulton, *18th:* 156
Louis Braille, *19th:* 299
Wernher von Braun, *20th:* 500
Percy Williams Bridgman, *20th:* 526
Jean Buridan, *MA:* 215
Jacques Callot, *17th:* 116
Chester F. Carlson, *20th:* 657
George Washington Carver, *20th:* 678
William Caxton, *Ren:* 196
George Cayley, *19th:* 447
Vinton Gray Cerf, *20th:* 707
Georges Claude, *20th:* 775
William Fothergill Cooke, *19th:* 547
Jacques Cousteau, *20th:* 849
Ctesibius of Alexandria, *Anc:* 247
Jacques Daguerre, *19th:* 589
André-Louis Danjon, *20th:* 911
Abraham Darby, *18th:* 292
Lee de Forest, *20th:* 940
Jimmy Doolittle, *20th:* 1023
George Eastman, *20th:* 1078
Hugo Eckener, *20th:* 1092
Thomas Alva Edison, *19th:* 731
Daniel Gabriel Fahrenheit, *18th:* 336
Enzo Ferrari, *20th:* 1239
Henry Ford, *20th:* 1279
Benjamin Franklin, *18th:* 370
Bill Gates, *20th:* 1421
Hans Geiger, *20th:* 1440
Robert H. Goddard, *20th:* 1507
Charles Goodyear, *19th:* 946
Jean-Baptiste Vaquette de Gribeauval, *18th:* 447
Sir William Robert Grove, *19th:* 996
Otto von Guericke, *17th:* 333
Johann Gutenberg, *MA:* 441
George Ellery Hale, *20th:* 1643
James Hargreaves, *18th:* 466
Ernst Heinkel, *20th:* 1746
Hero of Alexandria, *Anc:* 401
Soichiro Honda, *20th:* 1859
Robert Hooke, *17th:* 383
Grace Murray Hopper, *20th:* 1879
Sir Godfrey Newbold Hounsfield, *20th:* 1892
Elias Howe, *19th:* 1133
Christiaan Huygens, *17th:* 397
Hypatia, *Anc:* 434
Steve Jobs, *20th:* 2006
Pyotr Leonidovich Kapitsa, *20th:* 2077
John Kay, *18th:* 559
Sergei Korolev, *20th:* 2191
Frederick William Lanchester, *20th:* 2240
Ernest Orlando Lawrence, *20th:* 2300
Antoni van Leeuwenhoek, *17th:* 509
Étienne Lenoir, *19th:* 1338
Leonardo da Vinci, *Ren:* 561
Levi ben Gershom, *MA:* 650
Hans Lippershey, *17th:* 537
George Lucas, *20th:* 2450
Auguste and Louis Lumière, *20th:* 2471
Cyrus Hall McCormick, *19th:* 1438
Manasseh ben Israel, *17th:* 582
Aldus Manutius, *Ren:* 608
Konosuke Matsushita, *20th:* 2653
Ottmar Mergenthaler, *19th:* 1558
André and Édouard Michelin, *20th:* 2725
Jacques-Étienne and Joseph-Michel Montgolfier, *18th:* 698
Akio Morita, *20th:* 2831
Samuel F. B. Morse, *19th:* 1610
William Murdock, *18th:* 715
John Napier, *Ren:* 710
James Nasmyth, *19th:* 1646
Giulio Natta, *20th:* 2919
Thomas Newcomen, *18th:* 733
Nicéphore Niépce, *19th:* 1676
Alfred Nobel, *19th:* 1689
Nikolaus August Otto, *19th:* 1714
Denis Papin, *17th:* 710
Petrus Peregrinus de Maricourt, *MA:* 820
Auguste and Jean-Felix Piccard, *20th:* 3240
Pirelli Family, *20th:* 3266
Aleksandr Stepanovich Popov, *19th:* 1824
Hyman G. Rickover, *20th:* 3443
Charles Stewart Rolls, *20th:* 3496
Frederick Henry Royce, *20th:* 3496
Thomas Savery, *17th:* 813
Bernhard Voldemar Schmidt, *20th:* 3659
Karl Schwarzschild, *20th:* 3674
The Siemens Family, *19th:* 2105
Simon Stevin, *Ren:* 912
Joseph Wilson Swan, *19th:* 2209
Emanuel Swedenborg, *18th:* 961
Frederick Winslow Taylor, *20th:* 3955
Lennart Torstenson, *17th:* 924
Charles Hard Townes, *20th:* 4057
Konstantin Tsiolkovsky, *20th:* 4095
Jethro Tull, *18th:* 990
Andrei Nikolayevich Tupolev, *20th:* 4108
James Van Allen, *20th:* 4139
Felix Wankel, *20th:* 4224
Thomas J. Watson, Jr., *20th:* 4246
Thomas J. Watson, Sr., *20th:* 4246
James Watt, *18th:* 1048
Josiah Wedgwood, *18th:* 1057
George Westinghouse, *19th:* 2416
Charles Wheatstone, *19th:* 547
Eli Whitney, *18th:* 1076
Sir Frank Whittle, *20th:* 4318
John Wilkinson, *18th:* 1086
Sir Christopher Wren, *17th:* 994
Orville and Wilbur Wright, *20th:* 4403
Ferdinand von Zeppelin, *20th:* 4452
Jan Žižka, *MA:* 1162
Vladimir Zworykin, *20th:* 4479

Journalism

Sir Norman Angell, *20th:* 92
Hubertine Auclert, *19th:* 89
Sir Surendranath Banerjea, *20th:* 221
Lord Beaverbrook, *20th:* 275
James Gordon Bennett, *19th:* 188
Ambrose Bierce, *19th:* 228
Amelia Bloomer, *19th:* 257
Horatio W. Bottomley, *20th:* 445

Margaret Bourke-White, *20th:* 460
George Brown, *19th:* 316
Helen Gurley Brown, *20th:* 539
William Cullen Bryant, *19th:* 340
William F. Buckley, Jr., *20th:* 561
Karel Čapek, *20th:* 638
Truman Capote, *20th:* 644
Henri Cartier-Bresson, *20th:* 671
Willa Cather, *20th:* 696
G. K. Chesterton, *20th:* 744
William Cobbett, *19th:* 517
Janet Cooke, *Notor:* 231
Walter Cronkite, *20th:* 872
Samuel Ajayi Crowther, *19th:* 574
Robertson Davies, *20th:* 917
Dorothy Day, *20th:* 925
Frederick Douglass, *19th:* 684
Theodore Dreiser, *20th:* 1032
W. E. B. Du Bois, *20th:* 1046
Dietrich Eckart, *Notor:* 319
Nora Ephron, *20th:* 1161
Betty Friedan, *20th:* 1329
Margaret Fuller, *19th:* 841
Gabriel García Márquez, *20th:* 1398
William Lloyd Garrison, *19th:* 874
Marcus Garvey, *20th:* 1417
Charlotte Perkins Gilman, *20th:* 1484
Maxim Gorky, *20th:* 1549
Katharine Graham, *20th:* 1560
Horace Greeley, *19th:* 966
Graham Greene, *20th:* 1577
Sarah Josepha Hale, *19th:* 1012
Alfred and Harold Harmsworth, *20th:* 1678
William Randolph Hearst, *20th:* 1734
Aleksandr Herzen, *19th:* 1085
Leonard T. Hobhouse, *20th:* 1841
Lord Jeffrey, *19th:* 1223
Ann Landers, *20th:* 2247
René Lévesque, *20th:* 2345
Walter Lippmann, *20th:* 2400
Sir Joseph Norman Lockyer, *19th:* 1412
Jack London, *20th:* 2420
Clare Boothe Luce, *20th:* 2453
Henry R. Luce, *20th:* 2456
Rosa Luxemburg, *20th:* 2482
William Lyon Mackenzie, *19th:* 1454
Norman Mailer, *20th:* 2563
Jean-Paul Marat, *18th:* 648, *Notor:* 696
José Martí, *19th:* 1503
Clorinda Matto de Turner, *19th:* 1512
H. L. Mencken, *20th:* 2688
Eugenio Montale, *20th:* 2801
Edward R. Murrow, *20th:* 2879
Sir V. S. Naipaul, *20th:* 2903
Thomas Nast, *19th:* 1649
Max Nordau, *20th:* 2992
Thomas Power O'Connor, *20th:* 3024
Jacqueline Kennedy Onassis, *20th:* 3045
José Ortega y Gasset, *20th:* 3077
Pierre-Joseph Proudhon, *19th:* 1834
Joseph Pulitzer, *19th:* 1841
Mordecai Richler, *20th:* 3438
Jean-Paul Sartre, *20th:* 3638
Jeanne Sauvé, *20th:* 3652
Edward Wyllis Scripps, *19th:* 2055
Susan Sontag, *20th:* 3788
Gloria Steinem, *20th:* 3852
Julius Streicher, *Notor:* 1001
Ida Tarbell, *20th:* 3947
James Thurber, *20th:* 4020
Bal Gangadhar Tilak, *20th:* 4023
Mark Twain, *19th:* 2329
John Walter II, *19th:* 2380
Barbara Walters, *20th:* 4211
Ida B. Wells-Barnett, *20th:* 4290
Laura Ingalls Wilder, *20th:* 4336
George Washington Williams, *19th:* 2449
Edmund Wilson, *20th:* 4354
Oprah Winfrey, *20th:* 4372
Virginia Woolf, *20th:* 4397

LANGUAGE AND LINGUISTICS

Mikhail Bakhtin, *20th:* 190
Roland Barthes, *20th:* 246
William Carey, *19th:* 409
Noam Chomsky, *20th:* 757
Saint Cyril, *MA:* 294
John Eliot, *17th:* 247
Albert Gallatin, *19th:* 854
Jacob and Wilhelm Grimm, *19th:* 992
Roman Jakobson, *20th:* 1986
Jacques Lacan, *20th:* 2224
Claude Lévi-Strauss, *20th:* 2347
Saint Methodius, *MA:* 294
Priscian, *MA:* 859
Ferdinand de Saussure, *20th:* 3649
Sequoyah, *19th:* 2067
Squanto, *17th:* 875
Noah Webster, *19th:* 2402
Fanny Bullock Workman, *19th:* 2466

LAW

Abū Ḥanīfah, *MA:* 18
Dean Acheson, *20th:* 17
John Adams, *18th:* 11
Aḥmad ibn Ḥanbal, *MA:* 36
Alexis, *17th:* 11
Chester A. Arthur, *19th:* 79
Avicenna, *MA:* 123
Sir Edmund Barton, *19th:* 149
Cesare Beccaria, *18th:* 100
Jeremy Bentham, *18th:* 104
Hugo L. Black, *20th:* 377
Harry A. Blackmun, *20th:* 382
Sir William Blackstone, *18th:* 118
Henry de Bracton, *MA:* 192
Louis D. Brandeis, *20th:* 482
William J. Brennan, *20th:* 507
Margaret Brent, *17th:* 92
Stephen G. Breyer, *20th:* 520
Henry Brougham, *19th:* 312
William Jennings Bryan, *20th:* 550
Warren E. Burger, *20th:* 581
Aaron Burr, *19th:* 363, *Notor:* 155
Jean-Jacques-Régis de Cambacérès, *19th:* 396
Benjamin N. Cardozo, *20th:* 653
Charles Carroll, *18th:* 205
Mary Ann Shadd Cary, *19th:* 431
Casimir the Great, *MA:* 229
René Cassin, *20th:* 684
Salmon P. Chase, *19th:* 470
Samuel Chase, *18th:* 237

Cicero, *Anc:* 210
Cleisthenes of Athens, *Anc:* 221
Bill Clinton, *20th:* 783
Hillary Rodham Clinton, *20th:* 788
Sir Edward Coke, *17th:* 174
Clarence Darrow, *20th:* 913
Deganawida, *Ren:* 281
Demosthenes, *Anc:* 264
John Dickinson, *18th:* 303
Bob Dole, *20th:* 1014
William O. Douglas, *20th:* 1029
Draco, *Anc:* 293
Wyatt Earp, *19th:* 720, *Notor:* 315
Edward I, *MA:* 343
Eugen Ehrlich, *20th:* 1113
Elijah ben Solomon, *18th:* 318
First Baron Erskine, *18th:* 326
Herbert Vere Evatt, *20th:* 1188
Stephen J. Field, *19th:* 777
Henry Fielding, *18th:* 346
Sir John Fortescue, *Ren:* 340
Felix Frankfurter, *20th:* 1308
Erle Stanley Gardner, *20th:* 1403
Genghis Khan, *MA:* 402, *Notor:* 400
Alberico Gentili, *Ren:* 372
Gershom ben Judah, *MA:* 408
Maḥmūd Ghāzān, *MA:* 411
al-Ghazzālī, *MA:* 415
Hugo Grotius, *17th:* 326
Matthew Hale (1609-1676), *17th:* 345
Hammurabi, *Anc:* 376
Learned Hand, *20th:* 1663
Henry I, *MA:* 481
Henry II (1133-1189; King of England), *MA:* 483
Patrick Henry, *18th:* 482
Hiawatha, *Ren:* 448
Wild Bill Hickok, *19th:* 1091
Alger Hiss, *20th:* 1822, *Notor:* 475
Oliver Wendell Holmes, Jr., *20th:* 1856
J. Edgar Hoover, *20th:* 1866, *Notor:* 489
François Hotman, *Ren:* 461
Hu Yaobang, *20th:* 1905
Charles Evans Hughes, *20th:* 1920
John Jay, *18th:* 524
Lord Jeffrey, *19th:* 1223
Barbara Jordan, *20th:* 2046
Robert F. Kennedy, *20th:* 2102
James Kent, *19th:* 1271
Francis Scott Key, *19th:* 1274
Henri-Marie La Fontaine, *20th:* 2231
Le Thanh Tong, *Ren:* 546
Michel de L'Hospital, *Ren:* 568
Sir Thomas Littleton, *Ren:* 570
Belva A. Lockwood, *19th:* 1409
Roger Ludlow, *17th:* 567
Catharine A. MacKinnon, *20th:* 2522
First Earl of Mansfield, *18th:* 643
John Marshall, *19th:* 1498
Thurgood Marshall, *20th:* 2633
Boris Ivanovich Morozov, *17th:* 663
Gouverneur Morris, *18th:* 705
Ralph Nader, *20th:* 2897
Rebecca Nurse, *17th:* 689
Sandra Day O'Connor, *20th:* 3020
Johan van Oldenbarnevelt, *Ren:* 740
Nicolas-Claude Fabri de Peiresc, *17th:* 722
Wendell Phillips, *19th:* 1785
Lewis F. Powell, Jr. (1907-1998), *20th:* 3325
Samuel von Pufendorf, *17th:* 759
Mahadev Govind Ranade, *19th:* 1855
William H. Rehnquist, *20th:* 3405
Janet Reno, *20th:* 3416
Louis St. Laurent, *20th:* 3597
Friedrich Karl von Savigny, *19th:* 2003
Sebastian, *Ren:* 859
Samuel Sewall, *18th:* 893
Granville Sharp, *18th:* 899
Roger Sherman, *18th:* 908
Solon, *Anc:* 807
David H. Souter, *20th:* 3802
Mikhail Mikhaylovich Speransky, *19th:* 2129
Edwin M. Stanton, *19th:* 2142
Stefan Dušan, *MA:* 957
Henry L. Stimson, *20th:* 3869
Harlan Fiske Stone, *20th:* 3878
Joseph Story, *19th:* 2180
Süleyman the Magnificent, *Ren:* 914
Robert A. Taft, *20th:* 3925
William Howard Taft, *20th:* 3929
Roger Brooke Taney, *19th:* 2225, *Notor:* 1018
Theodoric the Great, *MA:* 1012
Clarence Thomas, *20th:* 3999
Tokugawa Tsunayoshi, *17th:* 919
Ur-Nammu, *Anc:* 914
Vaḥīd Bihbahānī, *18th:* 1000
Francisco de Vitoria, *Ren:* 978
Earl Warren, *20th:* 4232
Daniel Webster, *19th:* 2398
Simon Wiesenthal, *20th:* 4328
James Wilson, *18th:* 1090
Saʿd Zaghlūl, *20th:* 4439

LINGUISTICS. *See* LANGUAGE AND LINGUISTICS

LITERATURE. *See also* JOURNALISM; LANGUAGE AND LINGUISTICS; PHILOSOPHY; THEATER AND LIVE ENTERTAINMENT

Chinua Achebe, *20th:* 14
José de Acosta, *Ren:* 5
Adam de la Halle, *MA:* 24
Abigail Adams, *18th:* 7
Henry Adams, *19th:* 16
Joseph Addison, *18th:* 20
Halide Edib Adıvar, *20th:* 29
Aeschylus, *Anc:* 7
Aesop, *Anc:* 11
Sir Sayyid Ahmad Khan, *19th:* 35
Anna Akhmatova, *20th:* 42
Louisa May Alcott, *19th:* 41
Alcuin, *MA:* 49
Mateo Alemán, *Ren:* 25
Alfonso X, *MA:* 59
Alfred the Great, *MA:* 63
Horatio Alger, *19th:* 51
Hans Christian Andersen, *19th:* 61
Isabella Andreini, *Ren:* 42
Maya Angelou, *20th:* 97
Guillaume Apollinaire, *20th:* 104
Pietro Aretino, *Ren:* 53

Ludovico Ariosto, *Ren:* 56
Aristophanes, *Anc:* 90
Matthew Arnold, *19th:* 71
Ashurbanipal, *Anc:* 117
Anne Askew, *Ren:* 62
Mary Astell, *18th:* 64
Aśvaghosa, *Anc:* 130
Margaret Atwood, *20th:* 169
W. H. Auden, *20th:* 172
Jane Austen, *19th:* 94
Avvakum Petrovich, *17th:* 26
Bābur, *Ren:* 69
Francis Bacon, *Ren:* 72
Mikhail Bakhtin, *20th:* 190
James Baldwin, *20th:* 201
Honoré de Balzac, *19th:* 126
Ban Zhao, *Anc:* 152
Anna Barbauld, *18th:* 87
Fanny Calderón de la Barca, *19th:* 389
Djuna Barnes, *20th:* 240
Roland Barthes, *20th:* 246
Charles Baudelaire, *19th:* 152
L. Frank Baum, *19th:* 155
Pierre-Augustin Caron de Beaumarchais, *18th:* 97
Francis Beaumont, *Ren:* 92
Simone de Beauvoir, *20th:* 271
Samuel Beckett, *20th:* 279
Saint Bede the Venerable, *MA:* 150
Aphra Behn, *17th:* 42
Saul Bellow, *20th:* 288
Pierre Belon, *Ren:* 101
Ruth Benedict, *20th:* 296
Stephen Vincent Benét, *20th:* 303
Walter Benjamin, *20th:* 306
Sarah Bernhardt, *19th:* 208
Ambrose Bierce, *19th:* 228
William Blake, *18th:* 121
Aleksandr Blok, *20th:* 394
Léon Blum, *20th:* 396
Giovanni Boccaccio, *MA:* 169
Boethius, *MA:* 173
Nicolas Boileau-Despréaux, *17th:* 63
Heinrich Böll, *20th:* 411
Saint Boniface, *MA:* 183
Jorge Luis Borges, *20th:* 430
Jacques-Bénigne Bossuet, *17th:* 70
James Boswell, *18th:* 146
Henry de Bracton, *MA:* 192
Mary Elizabeth Braddon, *19th:* 284
William Bradford, *17th:* 84
Anne Bradstreet, *17th:* 88
Bertolt Brecht, *20th:* 504
André Breton, *20th:* 510
Saint Brigit, *MA:* 198
The Brontë Sisters, *19th:* 308
Gwendolyn Brooks, *20th:* 537
Elizabeth Barrett Browning, *19th:* 326
Leonardo Bruni, *MA:* 208
William Cullen Bryant, *19th:* 340
Martin Buber, *20th:* 554
George Buchanan, *Ren:* 146
Pearl S. Buck, *20th:* 557
William F. Buckley, Jr., *20th:* 561
John Bunyan, *17th:* 100
Frances Hodgson Burnett, *19th:* 357
Fanny Burney, *18th:* 180
Robert Burns, *18th:* 183
Edgar Rice Burroughs, *20th:* 590
Robert Burton, *17th:* 108
Samuel Butler, *19th:* 374
Lord Byron, *19th:* 379
Julius Caesar, *Anc:* 172
Callimachus, *Anc:* 179
Luís de Camões, *Ren:* 167
Tommaso Campanella, *17th:* 124
Thomas Campion, *17th:* 127
Albert Camus, *20th:* 628
Cao Cao, *Anc:* 182
Cao Xueqin, *18th:* 194
Karel Čapek, *20th:* 638
Truman Capote, *20th:* 644
Lewis Carroll, *19th:* 423
Rachel Carson, *20th:* 662
Casanova, *18th:* 208
Baldassare Castiglione, *Ren:* 181
Willa Cather, *20th:* 696
Catullus, *Anc:* 196
Guido Cavalcanti, *MA:* 239
Georgiana Cavendish, *18th:* 215
Cædmon, *MA:* 219
Benvenuto Cellini, *Ren:* 202
Miguel de Cervantes, *Ren:* 206
Aimé Césaire, *20th:* 709
George Chapman, *Ren:* 213
Hester Chapone, *18th:* 221
Charles d'Orléans, *MA:* 247
Alain Chartier, *MA:* 260
François-René de Chateaubriand, *19th:* 474
Geoffrey Chaucer, *MA:* 264
Anton Chekhov, *19th:* 478
Chen Duxiu, *20th:* 741
G. K. Chesterton, *20th:* 744
Chikamatsu Monzaemon, *18th:* 243
Lydia Maria Child, *19th:* 482
Kate Chopin, *19th:* 490
Chrétien de Troyes, *MA:* 267
Dame Agatha Christie, *20th:* 765
Christine de Pizan, *MA:* 273
Saint John Chrysostom, *Anc:* 208
Sir Winston Churchill, *20th:* 768
Cicero, *Anc:* 210
First Earl of Clarendon, *17th:* 166
Claudius I, *Anc:* 217
Jean Cocteau, *20th:* 794
Samuel Taylor Coleridge, *19th:* 529
Colette, *20th:* 804
Norman Collins, *20th:* 810
Vittoria Colonna, *Ren:* 235
Joseph Conrad, *20th:* 824
James Fenimore Cooper, *19th:* 552
Carolina Coronado, *19th:* 556
Miles Coverdale, *Ren:* 255
Sir Noël Coward, *20th:* 853
Abraham Cowley, *17th:* 199
Hannah Cowley, *18th:* 284
Hart Crane, *20th:* 858
Stephen Crane, *19th:* 562
Richard Crashaw, *17th:* 202
Benedetto Croce, *20th:* 869
Sor Juana Inés de la Cruz, *17th:* 208
E. E. Cummings, *20th:* 879
Salvador Dalí, *20th:* 904
Dante, *MA:* 300
Rubén Darío, *19th:* 601
Clarence Darrow, *20th:* 913
David, *Anc:* 255
Lady Eleanor Davies, *17th:* 220
Robertson Davies, *20th:* 917

Cyrano de Bergerac, *17th:* 211
Daniel Defoe, *18th:* 298
Aagje Deken, *18th:* 301
Thomas Dekker, *17th:* 223
Agnes de Mille, *20th:* 957
Jacques Derrida, *20th:* 974
Dhuoda, *MA:* 310
Sergei Diaghilev, *20th:* 985
Charles Dickens, *19th:* 655
Emily Dickinson, *19th:* 658
Denis Diderot, *18th:* 307
Benjamin Disraeli, *19th:* 666
Milovan Djilas, *20th:* 1011
William Dodd, *Notor:* 286
John Donne, *17th:* 230
Fyodor Dostoevski, *19th:* 677
Sir Arthur Conan Doyle, *19th:* 688
Michael Drayton, *17th:* 237
Theodore Dreiser, *20th:* 1032
John Dryden, *17th:* 239
Du Fu, *MA:* 322
Joachim du Bellay, *Ren:* 294
Alexandre Dumas, *père*, *19th:* 695
Paul Laurence Dunbar, *19th:* 701
Dietrich Eckart, *Notor:* 319
Maria Edgeworth, *19th:* 728
Christian von Ehrenfels, *20th:* 1110
Eleanor of Aquitaine, *MA:* 355
Mircea Eliade, *20th:* 1136
George Eliot, *19th:* 740
T. S. Eliot, *20th:* 1139
Paul Éluard, *20th:* 1151
Ralph Waldo Emerson, *19th:* 745
Shūsaku Endō, *20th:* 1155
Enheduanna, *Anc:* 298
Quintus Ennius, *Anc:* 301
Nora Ephron, *20th:* 1161
Olaudah Equiano, *18th:* 324
Desiderius Erasmus, *Ren:* 314
Eratosthenes of Cyrene, *Anc:* 314
Louise Erdrich, *20th:* 1168
Rudolf Christoph Eucken, *20th:* 1185
Euripides, *Anc:* 326
Frantz Fanon, *20th:* 1212
William Faulkner, *20th:* 1222
François de Salignac de La Mothe-Fénelon, *17th:* 265
Henry Fielding, *18th:* 346
Firdusi, *MA:* 375
F. Scott Fitzgerald, *20th:* 1249
Gustave Flaubert, *19th:* 785
John Fletcher, *Ren:* 92, *17th:* 277
C. S. Forester, *20th:* 1283
E. M. Forster, *20th:* 1288
Girolamo Fracastoro, *Ren:* 343
Anatole France, *19th:* 815
Anne Frank, *20th:* 1301
Sir James George Frazer, *20th:* 1319
Sigmund Freud, *20th:* 1323
Max Frisch, *20th:* 1338
Jean Froissart, *MA:* 392
Robert Frost, *20th:* 1348
Athol Fugard, *20th:* 1354
Mavis Gallant, *20th:* 1377
George Gamow, *20th:* 1379
Federico García Lorca, *20th:* 1395
Erle Stanley Gardner, *20th:* 1403
Jean Genet, *20th:* 1445
Geoffrey of Monmouth, *MA:* 405
Gershom ben Judah, *MA:* 408
Conrad Gesner, *Ren:* 375
Edward Gibbon, *18th:* 415
André Gide, *20th:* 1477
Charlotte Perkins Gilman, *20th:* 1484
Jean Giraudoux, *20th:* 1492
William Godwin, *18th:* 424
Joseph Goebbels, *20th:* 1513, *Notor:* 418
Johann Wolfgang von Goethe, *18th:* 428
Nikolai Gogol, *19th:* 937
Emma Goldman, *20th:* 1519, *Notor:* 424
Oliver Goldsmith, *18th:* 432
Luis de Góngora y Argote, *17th:* 312
Nadine Gordimer, *20th:* 1534
Maxim Gorky, *20th:* 1549
Gottfried von Strassburg, *MA:* 423
Marie le Jars de Gournay, *17th:* 314
Baltasar Gracián y Morales, *17th:* 316
Antonio Gramsci, *20th:* 1566
Günter Grass, *20th:* 1573
Graham Greene, *20th:* 1577
Gregory of Nazianzus, *Anc:* 361
Jacob and Wilhelm Grimm, *19th:* 992
Hans Jakob Christoffel von Grimmelshausen, *17th:* 324
Charlotte Guillard, *Ren:* 413
Guo Moruo, *20th:* 1619
Johann Gutenberg, *MA:* 441
Madame Guyon, *17th:* 339
Gwenllian verch Gruffydd, *MA:* 448
H. D., *20th:* 1623
Hafiz, *MA:* 451
H. Rider Haggard, *19th:* 1006
Sarah Josepha Hale, *19th:* 1012
Knut Hamsun, *20th:* 1660
Lorraine Hansberry, *20th:* 1669
Thomas Hardy, *19th:* 1028
Joel Chandler Harris, *19th:* 1036
Hartmann von Aue, *MA:* 463
Václav Havel, *20th:* 1707
Nathaniel Hawthorne, *19th:* 1051
Le Ly Hayslip, *20th:* 1727
Heinrich Heine, *19th:* 1069
Lillian Hellman, *20th:* 1752
Ernest Hemingway, *20th:* 1755
O. Henry, *19th:* 1081
George Herbert, *17th:* 366
Johann Gottfried Herder, *18th:* 486
Robert Herrick, *17th:* 368
Hesiod, *Anc:* 413
Hermann Hesse, *20th:* 1787
Thor Heyerdahl, *20th:* 1795
Thomas Heywood, *17th:* 373
Thomas Wentworth Higginson, *19th:* 1097
Saint Hilda of Whitby, *MA:* 509
Hildegard von Bingen, *MA:* 512
Ho Xuan Huong, *19th:* 1110
Oliver Wendell Holmes, *19th:* 1116
Homer, *Anc:* 427
Horace, *Anc:* 430
Julia Ward Howe, *19th:* 1137
Hrosvitha, *MA:* 516
L. Ron Hubbard, *20th:* 1909, *Notor:* 495
Langston Hughes, *20th:* 1928

Victor Hugo, *19th:* 1146
Zora Neale Hurston, *20th:* 1944
Aldous Huxley, *20th:* 1961
Ibn Gabirol, *MA:* 532
Ihara Saikaku, *17th:* 403
Eugène Ionesco, *20th:* 1968
Clifford Irving, *Notor:* 510
Washington Irving, *19th:* 1180
Saint Isidore of Seville, *MA:* 555
Helen Hunt Jackson, *19th:* 1193
al-Jāḥiẓ, *MA:* 568
Roman Jakobson, *20th:* 1986
James I the Conqueror, *MA:* 571
Henry James, *19th:* 1206
Anna Jameson, *19th:* 1217
Sarah Orne Jewett, *19th:* 1226
John of Damascus, *MA:* 587
Samuel Johnson, *18th:* 535
Ben Jonson, *17th:* 439
James Joyce, *20th:* 2055
Judah ha-Levi, *MA:* 591
Julian of Norwich, *MA:* 595
Carl Jung, *20th:* 2062
Juvenal, *Anc:* 493
Franz Kafka, *20th:* 2066
Engelbert Kämpfer, *17th:* 445
Wassily Kandinsky, *20th:* 2074
Kâtib Çelebî, *17th:* 454
Yasunari Kawabata, *20th:* 2084
Nikos Kazantzakis, *20th:* 2087
John Keats, *19th:* 1259
Helen Keller, *20th:* 2093
Margery Kempe, *MA:* 607
Jack Kerouac, *20th:* 2114
Martin Luther King, Jr., *20th:* 2147
Stephen King, *20th:* 2151
Rudyard Kipling, *19th:* 1284
Paul Klee, *20th:* 2176
Heinrich von Kleist, *19th:* 1289
Friedrich Gottlieb Klopstock, *18th:* 562
Kōbō Daishi, *MA:* 620
Ignacy Krasicki, *18th:* 567
Jean de La Bruyère, *17th:* 475
Madame de La Fayette, *17th:* 477
Jean de La Fontaine, *17th:* 480
Selma Lagerlöf, *20th:* 2234
Aemilia Lanyer, *Ren:* 535
Sophie von La Roche, *18th:* 577
François de La Rochefoucauld, *17th:* 487
D. H. Lawrence, *20th:* 2295
T. E. Lawrence, *20th:* 2303
Halldór Laxness, *20th:* 2308
Emma Lazarus, *19th:* 1331
Jacques Lefèvre d'Étaples, *Ren:* 548
Ninon de Lenclos, *17th:* 520
Charlotte Lennox, *18th:* 594
Anna Leonowens, *19th:* 1346
Mikhail Lermontov, *19th:* 1352
Alain-René Lesage, *18th:* 596
Gotthold Ephraim Lessing, *18th:* 598
C. S. Lewis, *20th:* 2353
Sinclair Lewis, *20th:* 2363
Li Bo, *MA:* 653
Li Qingzhao, *MA:* 656
Anne Morrow Lindbergh, *20th:* 2389
Charles A. Lindbergh, *20th:* 2392
Liu Yin, *17th:* 540
Mikhail Vasilyevich Lomonosov, *18th:* 613
Jack London, *20th:* 2420
Henry Wadsworth Longfellow, *19th:* 1416
Anita Loos, *20th:* 2428
Richard Lovelace, *17th:* 562
Amy Lowell, *20th:* 2444
Lu Xun, *20th:* 2447
Clare Boothe Luce, *20th:* 2453
Lucian, *Anc:* 513
Lucretius, *Anc:* 520
György Lukács, *20th:* 2468
Raymond Lull, *MA:* 673
Mary McCarthy, *20th:* 2501
Carson McCullers, *20th:* 2507
Joaquim Maria Machado de Assis, *19th:* 1449
Guillaume de Machaut, *MA:* 679
Niccolò Machiavelli, *Ren:* 587
Naguib Mahfouz, *20th:* 2553
Norman Mailer, *20th:* 2563
François de Malherbe, *17th:* 577
Sir Thomas Malory, *Ren:* 598
André Malraux, *20th:* 2576
Mary de la Rivière Manley, *18th:* 641
Thomas Mann, *20th:* 2594
Aldus Manutius, *Ren:* 608
Alessandro Manzoni, *19th:* 1495
Jean-Paul Marat, *18th:* 648, *Notor:* 696
Gabriel Marcel, *20th:* 2609
Marcus Aurelius, *Anc:* 530
Marguerite de Navarre, *Ren:* 617
Marie de France, *MA:* 693
Christopher Marlowe, *Ren:* 623
José Martí, *19th:* 1503
Martial, *Anc:* 536
Harriet Martineau, *19th:* 1505
Andrew Marvell, *17th:* 605
Matsuo Bashō, *17th:* 615
Matthias I Corvinus, *Ren:* 642
Clorinda Matto de Turner, *19th:* 1512
Guy de Maupassant, *19th:* 1515
François Mauriac, *20th:* 2657
Vladimir Mayakovsky, *20th:* 2659
Mechthild von Magdeburg, *MA:* 708
Lorenzo de' Medici, *Ren:* 655
Herman Melville, *19th:* 1537
Menander (c. 642-c. 291 B.C.E.; dramatist), *Anc:* 547
Rigoberta Menchú, *20th:* 2686
H. L. Mencken, *20th:* 2688
Thomas Merton, *20th:* 2713
Michelangelo, *Ren:* 682
James A. Michener, *20th:* 2728
Thomas Middleton, *17th:* 636
Edna St. Vincent Millay, *20th:* 2738
Arthur Miller, *20th:* 2742
Kate Millett, *20th:* 2746
A. A. Milne, *20th:* 2753
John Milton, *17th:* 639
Yukio Mishima, *20th:* 2763
Molière, *17th:* 646
Mary Wortley Montagu, *18th:* 687
Michel Eyquem de Montaigne, *Ren:* 689
Eugenio Montale, *20th:* 2801
Duchesse de Montpensier, *17th:* 660
Susanna Moodie, *19th:* 1593
Marianne Moore, *20th:* 2821
Hannah More, *18th:* 702

Sir Thomas More, *Ren:* 697
Toni Morrison, *20th:* 2834
Moses de León, *MA:* 730
Robert Motherwell, *20th:* 2847
Lodowick Muggleton, *17th:* 665
Alice Munro, *20th:* 2873
Murasaki Shikibu, *MA:* 738
Vladimir Nabokov, *20th:* 2894
Sarojini Naidu, *20th:* 2900
Sir V. S. Naipaul, *20th:* 2903
Thomas Nashe, *Ren:* 714
Pablo Neruda, *20th:* 2937
John Newbery, *18th:* 730
Duchess of Newcastle, *17th:* 676
Nijō, *MA:* 771
Max Nordau, *20th:* 2992
Nostradamus, *Ren:* 728, *Notor:* 799
Flannery O'Connor, *20th:* 3017
Omar Khayyám, *MA:* 795
Michael Ondaatje, *20th:* 3048
George Orwell, *20th:* 3080
Ouyang Xiu, *MA:* 808
Ovid, *Anc:* 602
Thomas Paine, *18th:* 759
Dorothy Parker, *20th:* 3116
Catherine Parr, *Ren:* 764
Boris Pasternak, *20th:* 3131
A. B. Paterson, *19th:* 1758
Alan Paton, *20th:* 3138
Pausanias the Traveler, *Anc:* 618
Octavio Paz, *20th:* 3169
Samuel Pepys, *17th:* 728
Petrus Peregrinus de Maricourt, *MA:* 820
Charles Perrault, *17th:* 731
Petrarch, *MA:* 827
Phaedrus, *Anc:* 628
Katherine Philips, *17th:* 741
Pindar, *Anc:* 646
Luigi Pirandello, *20th:* 3260
Pius II, *Ren:* 794
Sylvia Plath, *20th:* 3285
Plautus, *Anc:* 662
Plutarch, *Anc:* 670
Edgar Allan Poe, *19th:* 1813
Poggio, *MA:* 850
Alexander Pope, *18th:* 805
Marguerite Porete, *MA:* 856
Katherine Anne Porter, *20th:* 3310
Beatrix Potter, *20th:* 3314
Priscian, *MA:* 859
Marcel Proust, *20th:* 3342
Alexander Pushkin, *19th:* 1848
Qu Yuan, *Anc:* 732
Francisco Gómez de Quevedo y Villegas, *17th:* 770
François Rabelais, *Ren:* 809
Rābiʿah al-ʿAdawiyah, *MA:* 873
Jean Racine, *17th:* 773
Ann Radcliffe, *18th:* 823
Sir Walter Ralegh, *Ren:* 813
Peter Ramus, *Ren:* 817
Ayn Rand, *20th:* 3367
Ratramnus, *MA:* 879
Guillaume-Thomas Raynal, *18th:* 829
Erich Maria Remarque, *20th:* 3413
Paul Revere, *18th:* 832
Samuel Richardson, *18th:* 841
Mordecai Richler, *20th:* 3438
Charles Richter, *20th:* 3440
Rainer Maria Rilke, *20th:* 3454
Arthur Rimbaud, *19th:* 1912
Mary Robinson (1758?-1800), *18th:* 848
Will Rogers, *20th:* 3491
Christina Rossetti, *19th:* 1940
Jean-Jacques Rousseau, *18th:* 868
Mary White Rowlandson, *17th:* 798
Muriel Rukeyser, *20th:* 3556
Jalāl al-Dīn Rūmī, *MA:* 908
Bertrand Russell, *20th:* 3562
Nelly Sachs, *20th:* 3583
Marquis de Sade, *18th:* 875, *Notor:* 926
Saʿdi, *MA:* 915
Salimbene, *MA:* 921
J. D. Salinger, *20th:* 3609
George Sand, *19th:* 1987
Carl Sandburg, *20th:* 3619
George Santayana, *20th:* 3629
Sappho, *Anc:* 750
Nathalie Sarraute, *20th:* 3635
Jean-Paul Sartre, *20th:* 3638
Ferdinand de Saussure, *20th:* 3649
Saxo Grammaticus, *MA:* 927
Joseph Justus Scaliger, *Ren:* 855
Friedrich Schiller, *18th:* 887
Olive Schreiner, *19th:* 2023
Scipio Aemilianus, *Anc:* 755
Sir Walter Scott, *19th:* 2047
Madeleine de Scudéry, *17th:* 828
Anaïs Ségalas, *19th:* 2062
Sei Shōnagon, *MA:* 930
Maurice Sendak, *20th:* 3698
Seneca the Younger, *Anc:* 766
Léopold Senghor, *20th:* 3702
Robert W. Service, *20th:* 3708
Madame de Sévigné, *17th:* 833
Samuel Sewall, *18th:* 893
Anna Seward, *18th:* 897
Anne Sexton, *20th:* 3713
Sextus Propertius, *Anc:* 704
William Shakespeare, *Ren:* 876
George Bernard Shaw, *20th:* 3716
Mary Wollstonecraft Shelley, *19th:* 2088
Percy Bysshe Shelley, *19th:* 2092
Richard Brinsley Sheridan, *18th:* 905
James Shirley, *17th:* 846
Sir Philip Sidney, *Ren:* 881
Sima Xiangru, *Anc:* 785
Sima Guang, *MA:* 945
Simonides, *Anc:* 793
Upton Sinclair, *20th:* 3750
John Smith, *17th:* 861
Snorri Sturluson, *MA:* 950
Solon, *Anc:* 807
Aleksandr Solzhenitsyn, *20th:* 3783
Susan Sontag, *20th:* 3788
Sophocles, *Anc:* 809
Wole Soyinka, *20th:* 3804
Edmund Spenser, *Ren:* 906
Madame de Staël, *18th:* 929
Richard Steele, *18th:* 941
Edward Steichen, *20th:* 3837
Gertrude Stein, *20th:* 3845
John Steinbeck, *20th:* 3849
Stendhal, *19th:* 2160
Robert Louis Stevenson, *19th:* 2173
August Strindberg, *20th:* 3898
Su Dongpo, *MA:* 968

Sir John Suckling, *17th:* 893
Sulpicia, *Anc:* 834
Bertha von Suttner, *19th:* 2205
Jonathan Swift, *18th:* 964
Tadano Makuzu, *19th:* 2212
Rabindranath Tagore, *20th:* 3933
Hippolyte Taine, *19th:* 2216
Jun'ichirō Tanizaki, *20th:* 3944
Tao Qian, *Anc:* 843
Torquato Tasso, *Ren:* 924
Sara Teasdale, *20th:* 3959
Pierre Teilhard de Chardin, *20th:* 3963
Alfred, Lord Tennyson, *19th:* 2244
Terence, *Anc:* 849
Megan Terry, *20th:* 3982
Tertullian, *Anc:* 853
William Makepeace Thackeray, *19th:* 2257
Theophrastus, *Anc:* 872
Thespis, *Anc:* 876
Henry David Thoreau, *19th:* 2274
James Thurber, *20th:* 4020
Tirso de Molina, *17th:* 913
Alexis de Tocqueville, *19th:* 2280
J. R. R. Tolkien, *20th:* 4038
Leo Tolstoy, *19th:* 2283
Cyril Tourneur, *17th:* 928
Catharine Parr Traill, *19th:* 2291
Flora Tristan, *19th:* 2297
Anthony Trollope, *19th:* 2299
Frances Trollope, *19th:* 2303
John Trumbull, *18th:* 988
Marina Tsvetayeva, *20th:* 4098
Ivan Turgenev, *19th:* 2319
Mark Twain, *19th:* 2329
William Tyndale, *Ren:* 949
Miguel de Unamuno y Jugo, *20th:* 4128
Paul Valéry, *20th:* 4136
Vālmīki, *Anc:* 922
Giorgio Vasari, *Ren:* 953
Marquis de Vauvenargues, *18th:* 1009
Lope de Vega Carpio, *17th:* 949
Vergil, *Anc:* 938
Jules Verne, *19th:* 2354
António Vieira, *17th:* 959
Geoffroi de Villehardouin, *MA:* 1059
François Villon, *Ren:* 973
Vincent of Beauvais, *MA:* 1063
Philippe de Vitry, *MA:* 1065
Sir Julius Vogel, *19th:* 2371
Voltaire, *18th:* 1026
Alice Walker, *20th:* 4196
Walther von der Vogelweide, *MA:* 1075
Wang Wei, *MA:* 1085
Wang Zhenyi, *18th:* 1038
Mercy Otis Warren, *18th:* 1041
Robert Penn Warren, *20th:* 4236
John Webster, *17th:* 976
Simone Weil, *20th:* 4269
H. G. Wells, *20th:* 4287
John Wesley, *18th:* 1064
Mae West, *20th:* 4297
Edith Wharton, *20th:* 4300
Phillis Wheatley, *18th:* 1070
Walt Whitman, *19th:* 2423
John Greenleaf Whittier, *19th:* 2428
Elie Wiesel, *20th:* 4324
Oscar Wilde, *19th:* 2432
Laura Ingalls Wilder, *20th:* 4336
Tennessee Williams, *20th:* 4350
Edmund Wilson, *20th:* 4354
Wolfram von Eschenbach, *MA:* 1123
Mary Wollstonecraft, *18th:* 1108
Virginia Woolf, *20th:* 4397
William Wordsworth, *19th:* 2462
Xenophanes, *Anc:* 965
Xenophon, *Anc:* 968
Xie Lingyun, *Anc:* 975
Xuanzang, *MA:* 1136
Zara Yaqob, *Ren:* 1006
William Butler Yeats, *20th:* 4428
Charlotte Mary Yonge, *19th:* 2472
Zeami Motokiyo, *MA:* 1152
John Peter Zenger, *18th:* 1116
Zhuangzi, *Anc:* 989
Émile Zola, *19th:* 2489

MATHEMATICS

Niels Henrik Abel, *19th:* 9
Abul Wefa, *MA:* 21
Maria Gaetana Agnesi, *18th:* 24
Jean le Rond d'Alembert, *18th:* 31
Alhazen, *MA:* 66
Viktor A. Ambartsumian, *20th:* 77
Apollonius of Perga, *Anc:* 76
Archimedes, *Anc:* 80
Āryabhaṭa the Elder, *MA:* 108
Charles Babbage, *19th:* 107
Roger Bacon, *MA:* 127
Benjamin Banneker, *18th:* 84
al-Battānī, *MA:* 137
George Berkeley, *18th:* 111
Tim Berners-Lee, *20th:* 331
The Bernoulli Family, *17th:* 48
Friedrich Wilhelm Bessel, *19th:* 215
al-Bīrūnī, *MA:* 163
Niels Bohr, *20th:* 408
Giovanni Alfonso Borelli, *17th:* 65
Max Born, *20th:* 437
Tycho Brahe, *Ren:* 128
Brahmagupta, *MA:* 195
Gerolamo Cardano, *Ren:* 172
Rudolf Carnap, *20th:* 659
Lazare Carnot, *18th:* 200
Lewis Carroll, *19th:* 423
Gian Domenico Cassini, *17th:* 134
Vinton Gray Cerf, *20th:* 707
Marquise du Châtelet, *18th:* 240
Marquis de Condorcet, *18th:* 267
James Cook, *18th:* 270
Richard Dedekind, *19th:* 629
John Dee, *Ren:* 278
René Descartes, *17th:* 226
Diophantus, *Anc:* 286
Paul A. M. Dirac, *20th:* 1004
Albert Einstein, *20th:* 1118
Eratosthenes of Cyrene, *Anc:* 314
M. C. Escher, *20th:* 1183
Euclid, *Anc:* 317
Eudoxus of Cnidus, *Anc:* 320
Leonhard Euler, *18th:* 333
Pierre de Fermat, *17th:* 271
Enrico Fermi, *20th:* 1235
Joseph Fourier, *19th:* 809
Gottlob Frege, *19th:* 828
Galileo, *17th:* 298
Évariste Galois, *19th:* 857
Francis Galton, *19th:* 860
Pierre Gassendi, *17th:* 304
Carl Friedrich Gauss, *19th:* 883
Sophie Germain, *19th:* 901

Kurt Gödel, *20th:* 1510
James Gregory, *17th:* 319
Sir William Rowan Hamilton, *19th:* 1015
Stephen Hawking, *20th:* 1712
Werner Heisenberg, *20th:* 1749
Hermann von Helmholtz, *19th:* 1073
Hero of Alexandria, *Anc:* 401
Caroline Lucretia Herschel, *18th:* 489
William Herschel, *18th:* 492
David Hilbert, *20th:* 1800
Hipparchus, *Anc:* 417
Grace Murray Hopper, *20th:* 1879
Christiaan Huygens, *17th:* 397
Hypatia, *Anc:* 434
Johannes Kepler, *17th:* 457
al-Khwārizmī, *MA:* 617
Sofya Kovalevskaya, *19th:* 1295
Joseph-Louis Lagrange, *18th:* 573
Lev Davidovich Landau, *20th:* 2244
Max von Laue, *20th:* 2278
Gottfried Wilhelm Leibniz, *17th:* 513
Georges Lemaître, *20th:* 2337
Leonardo of Pisa, *MA:* 648
Levi ben Gershom, *MA:* 650
Nikolay Ivanovich Lobachevsky, *19th:* 1403
Countess of Lovelace, *19th:* 1420
Colin Maclaurin, *18th:* 632
Benoit B. Mandelbrot, *20th:* 2588
Lise Meitner, *20th:* 2679
Marin Mersenne, *17th:* 628
Gaspard Monge, *18th:* 682
John Napier, *Ren:* 710
John von Neumann, *20th:* 2943
Simon Newcomb, *19th:* 1660
Omar Khayyám, *MA:* 795
Pappus, *Anc:* 606
Blaise Pascal, *17th:* 713
Sir William Petty, *17th:* 733
Georg von Peuerbach, *Ren:* 773
Émile Picard, *20th:* 3234
Piero della Francesca, *Ren:* 785
Elena Cornaro Piscopia, *17th:* 743
Henri Poincaré, *19th:* 1816
Ptolemy (astronomer), *Anc:* 712
Pythagoras, *Anc:* 725
Rheticus, *Ren:* 823
Matteo Ricci, *Ren:* 825
Bertrand Russell, *20th:* 3562
Wilhelm Schickard, *17th:* 818
Erwin Schrödinger, *20th:* 3668
Charlotte Angas Scott, *19th:* 2039
Seki Kōwa, *17th:* 831
Mary Somerville, *19th:* 2121
Sosigenes, *Anc:* 815
Jakob Steiner, *19th:* 2154
Simon Stevin, *Ren:* 912
Sylvester II, *MA:* 983
Niccolò Fontana Tartaglia, *Ren:* 920
Sir Joseph John Thomson, *20th:* 4007
Evangelista Torricelli, *17th:* 921
Alan Mathison Turing, *20th:* 4112
John Wallis, *17th:* 969
Wang Zhenyi, *18th:* 1038
Steven Weinberg, *20th:* 4277
Alfred North Whitehead, *20th:* 4311

MEDICINE. *See also* **BIOLOGY; CHEMISTRY; GENETICS; PHYSIOLOGY; PSYCHOLOGY AND PSYCHIATRY**

Pietro d'Abano, *MA:* 1
Alfred Adler, *20th:* 33
Georgius Agricola, *Ren:* 11
Alcmaeon, *Anc:* 36
Alhazen, *MA:* 66
Virginia Apgar, *20th:* 100
Aretaeus of Cappadocia, *Anc:* 84
Arnold of Villanova, *MA:* 98
Asclepiades, *Anc:* 114
Averroës, *MA:* 118
Avicenna, *MA:* 123
Baʿal Shem Tov, *18th:* 68
Sir Frederick G. Banting, *20th:* 224
Christiaan Barnard, *20th:* 236
Clara Barton, *19th:* 145
Sir William Maddock Bayliss, *20th:* 259
Johann Joachim Becher, *17th:* 39
Emil von Behring, *19th:* 179
Claude Bernard, *19th:* 205
The Bernoulli Family, *17th:* 48
Elizabeth Blackwell, *19th:* 247
Eugen Bleuler, *20th:* 391
Marie Anne Victorine Boivin, *19th:* 265
Giovanni Alfonso Borelli, *17th:* 65
Louyse Bourgeois, *17th:* 73
Josef Breuer, *20th:* 514
John R. Brinkley, *Notor:* 141
Sir Thomas Browne, *17th:* 94
Gro Harlem Brundtland, *20th:* 544
Sir Macfarlane Burnet, *20th:* 587
Robert Burton, *17th:* 108
Albert Calmette, *20th:* 618
Gerolamo Cardano, *Ren:* 172
Aulus Cornelius Celsus, *Anc:* 199
Andrea Cesalpino, *Ren:* 211
Harvey Williams Cushing, *20th:* 898
Diocles of Carystus, *Anc:* 277
Pedanius Dioscorides, *Anc:* 289
Gerhard Domagk, *20th:* 1021
António Egas Moniz, *20th:* 1107
Paul Ehrlich, *20th:* 1115
Willem Einthoven, *20th:* 1122
Erasistratus, *Anc:* 310
Hieronymus Fabricius ab Aquapendente, *Ren:* 319
Jacqueline Félicie, *MA:* 372
Sir Alexander Fleming, *20th:* 1254
Baron Florey, *20th:* 1259
Robert Fludd, *17th:* 280
Larry C. Ford, *Notor:* 363
Lydia Folger Fowler, *19th:* 812
Girolamo Fracastoro, *Ren:* 343
Sigmund Freud, *20th:* 1323
Leonhard Fuchs, *Ren:* 356
Galen, *Anc:* 348
Luigi Galvani, *18th:* 391
Arnold Gesell, *20th:* 1465
Conrad Gesner, *Ren:* 375
William Gilbert, *Ren:* 381
William Crawford Gorgas, *20th:* 1541
Guy de Chauliac, *MA:* 445
Samuel Hahnemann, *19th:* 1009
William Harvey, *17th:* 355

Linda Burfield Hazzard, *Notor:* 453
Jan Baptista van Helmont, *17th:* 361
Herophilus, *Anc:* 410
Georg von Hevesy, *20th:* 1792
Hippocrates, *Anc:* 420
Oliver Wendell Holmes, *19th:* 1116
Sir Godfrey Newbold Hounsfield, *20th:* 1892
Bernardo Alberto Houssay, *20th:* 1899
Imhotep, *Anc:* 439
Mary Putnam Jacobi, *19th:* 1200
Edward Jenner, *18th:* 532
Engelbert Kämpfer, *17th:* 445
Jack Kevorkian, *Notor:* 567
Robert Koch, *19th:* 1291
Sir Hans Adolf Krebs, *20th:* 2199
Elisabeth Kübler-Ross, *20th:* 2207
Karl Landsteiner, *20th:* 2250
Gustave Le Bon, *20th:* 2320
Leonardo da Vinci, *Ren:* 561
Joseph Lister, *19th:* 1390
Konrad Lorenz, *20th:* 2434
Richard Lower, *17th:* 564
John J. R. Macleod, *20th:* 2526
Moses Maimonides, *MA:* 686
Marcello Malpighi, *17th:* 579
William J. and Charles H. Mayo, *20th:* 2665
Dorothy Reed Mendenhall, *20th:* 2695
Mary Wortley Montagu, *18th:* 687
Maria Montessori, *20th:* 2804
William Thomas Green Morton, *19th:* 1613
Hermann Joseph Muller, *20th:* 2861
Kary B. Mullis, *20th:* 2864
Naḥmanides, *MA:* 747
Florence Nightingale, *19th:* 1684
Max Nordau, *20th:* 2992
Nostradamus, *Ren:* 728, *Notor:* 799
Sir William Osler, *19th:* 1711
Paracelsus, *Ren:* 757
Louis Pasteur, *19th:* 1751
Paul of Aegina, *MA:* 814
Linus Pauling, *20th:* 3155
Sir William Petty, *17th:* 733
Susan La Flesche Picotte, *20th:* 3247
William Luther Pierce III, *Notor:* 838
Lydia E. Pinkham, *19th:* 1796
François Quesnay, *18th:* 820
François Rabelais, *Ren:* 809
Grigori Yefimovich Rasputin, *19th:* 1863, *Notor:* 885
al-Rāzī, *MA:* 884
Walter Reed, *19th:* 1877
Madame Restell, *Notor:* 892
John Roebuck, *18th:* 858
Sir Ronald Ross, *20th:* 3532
Sir Joseph Rotblat, *20th:* 3536
Peyton Rous, *20th:* 3545
Benjamin Rush, *18th:* 872
Jonas Salk, *20th:* 3613
Margaret Sanger, *20th:* 3625
Santorio Santorio, *17th:* 810
Albert Schweitzer, *20th:* 3678
Ignaz Philipp Semmelweis, *19th:* 2064
Michael Servetus, *Ren:* 861
Justine Siegemundin, *17th:* 851
Benjamin Spock, *20th:* 3814
Georg Ernst Stahl, *18th:* 933
Wendell Stanley, *20th:* 3824
Ernest Henry Starling, *20th:* 3830
Nicolaus Steno, *17th:* 881
Marie Stopes, *20th:* 3882
Jan Swammerdam, *17th:* 898
Thomas Sydenham, *17th:* 901
Sylvester II, *MA:* 983
Helen Brooke Taussig, *20th:* 3950
Trotula, *MA:* 1031
Sir Charles Tupper, *19th:* 2316
Harold E. Varmus, *20th:* 4145
Andreas Vesalius, *Ren:* 965
Rudolf Virchow, *19th:* 2365
Selman Abraham Waksman, *20th:* 4180
Lillian D. Wald, *20th:* 4184
George Hoyt Whipple, *20th:* 4304
Thomas Willis, *17th:* 985
Rosalyn Yalow, *20th:* 4419
Marie Elizabeth Zakrzewska, *19th:* 2481

METALLURGY. ***See*** **EARTH SCIENCES**

METEOROLOGY. ***See*** **EARTH SCIENCES**

MILITARY AFFAIRS. ***See also*** **WARFARE AND CONQUEST**

Sani Abacha, *Notor:* 1
ʿAbbās the Great, *17th:* 4
ʿAbd al-Raḥmān III al-Nāṣir, *MA:* 9
Abdelkader, *19th:* 1
Samuel Adams, *18th:* 16
Afonso I (c. 1108-1185), *MA:* 33
Agesilaus II, *Anc:* 14
Gnaeus Julius Agricola, *Anc:* 17
Marcus Vipsanius Agrippa, *Anc:* 20
Akbar (1542-1605), *Ren:* 15
First Viscount Alanbrooke, *20th:* 50
Alboin, *MA:* 45
Afonso de Albuquerque, *Ren:* 22
Alcibiades of Athens, *Anc:* 33, *Notor:* 11
Alexander the Great, *Anc:* 39
Alexis, *17th:* 11
Alfred the Great, *MA:* 63
Ethan Allen, *18th:* 35
Lord Allenby, *20th:* 65
Alp Arslan, *MA:* 70
Duke of Alva, *Ren:* 31
Pedro de Alvarado, *Ren:* 34
Luis W. Alvarez, *20th:* 73
Lord Amherst, *18th:* 38
Amina Sarauniya Zazzua, *Ren:* 37
An Lushan, *MA:* 78
John André, *18th:* 42
Lord Anson, *18th:* 49
Antigonus I Monophthalmos, *Anc:* 63
Antiochus the Great, *Anc:* 65
Ion Antonescu, *Notor:* 25
Marc Antony, *Anc:* 73
Second Duke of Argyll, *18th:* 53
Arminius, *Anc:* 99
Benedict Arnold, *18th:* 59, *Notor:* 36
Árpád, *MA:* 105

Artemisia I, *Anc:* 109
Ashikaga Takauji, *MA:* 115
Ashurnasirpal II, *Anc:* 120
Atatürk, *20th:* 162
Attila, *Anc:* 138, *Notor:* 45
Stephen Fuller Austin, *19th:* 98
Bābur, *Ren:* 69
Sir Robert Stephenson Smyth Baden-Powell, *19th:* 110
Vasco Núñez de Balboa, *Ren:* 76
Barbarossa, *Ren:* 79
Basil the Macedonian, *MA:* 133
Chevalier de Bayard, *Ren:* 84
Baybars I, *MA:* 139
Bayezid II, *Ren:* 87
Lord Beaverbrook, *20th:* 275
Elisabeth Becker, *Notor:* 76
Osama Bin Laden, *20th:* 371, *Notor:* 101
Robert Blake, *17th:* 55
William Bligh, *18th:* 126, *Notor:* 104
Gebhard Leberecht von Blücher, *19th:* 260
Simón Bolívar, *19th:* 267
Daniel Boone, *18th:* 143
Cesare Borgia, *Ren:* 114, *Notor:* 127
Boudicca, *Anc:* 163
Joseph Boulogne, *18th:* 153
Omar Nelson Bradley, *20th:* 468
Joseph Brant, *18th:* 159
Sir Isaac Brock, *19th:* 306
Robert Bruce, *MA:* 200
Marcus Junius Brutus, *Anc:* 166, *Notor:* 146
Sir Richard Francis Burton, *19th:* 368
Richard Byrd, *20th:* 606
Juan Rodríguez Cabrillo, *Ren:* 161
Julius Caesar, *Anc:* 172
Plutarco Elías Calles, *20th:* 615
William Calley, *Notor:* 168
Canute the Great, *MA:* 221
Cao Cao, *Anc:* 182
Sir Guy Carleton, *18th:* 196
Kit Carson, *19th:* 426
Casimir the Great, *MA:* 229
Cassius, *Anc:* 185
Fidel Castro, *20th:* 691, *Notor:* 185
Chandragupta Maurya, *Anc:* 202
Charles VII, *Ren:* 224
Charles VIII, *Ren:* 227
Charles XIV John, *19th:* 468
Charles Martel, *MA:* 250
Chiang Kai-shek, *20th:* 746
Sir Winston Churchill, *20th:* 768
El Cid, *MA:* 278
Cimon, *Anc:* 213
George Rogers Clark, *18th:* 253
Claudius I, *Anc:* 217
Carl von Clausewitz, *19th:* 499
Cleomenes, *Anc:* 226
Sir Henry Clinton, *18th:* 256
Robert Clive, *18th:* 259
The Great Condé, *17th:* 184
Constantine the Great, *Anc:* 239
First Marquess Cornwallis, *18th:* 278
Hernán Cortés, *Ren:* 252
Croesus, *Anc:* 244
George A. Custer, *19th:* 582, *Notor:* 248
Cyrano de Bergerac, *17th:* 211
Cyrus the Great, *Anc:* 248
Darius the Great, *Anc:* 251
David I, *MA:* 304
David II, *MA:* 307
Moshe Dayan, *20th:* 929
Deborah, *Anc:* 258
Stephen Decatur, *19th:* 626
George Dewey, *19th:* 645
Bob Dole, *20th:* 1014
Karl Dönitz, *Notor:* 292
Jimmy Doolittle, *20th:* 1023
Sir Francis Drake, *Ren:* 291, *Notor:* 301
Reginald Dyer, *Notor:* 311
Edward I, *MA:* 343
Edward III, *MA:* 350
Edward the Elder, *MA:* 340
Egbert, *MA:* 353
Adolf Eichmann, *Notor:* 322
Dwight D. Eisenhower, *20th:* 1125
Epaminondas, *Anc:* 303
Fabius, *Anc:* 342
Louis Faidherbe, *19th:* 756
Third Baron Fairfax, *17th:* 261
Alessandro Farnese, *Ren:* 321
David G. Farragut, *19th:* 762
Ferdinand II (1452-1516; Spanish king), *Ren:* 328
Lord Edward Fitzgerald, *18th:* 356
Nathan Bedford Forrest, *Notor:* 365
Francis I, *Ren:* 346
Francisco Franco, *20th:* 1297, *Notor:* 371
Hans Michael Frank, *Notor:* 374
Frederick Henry, *17th:* 286
Frederick William I, *18th:* 381
Frederick William, the Great Elector, *17th:* 290
Sir Martin Frobisher, *Ren:* 352
James Gadsden, *19th:* 849
Thomas Gage, *18th:* 384
Vasco da Gama, *Ren:* 365
Anastasio Somoza García, *Notor:* 984
Giuseppe Garibaldi, *19th:* 871
Marc Garneau, *20th:* 1412
Genseric, *Anc:* 351
Sir Humphrey Gilbert, *Ren:* 378
August von Gneisenau, *19th:* 928
Joseph Goebbels, *20th:* 1513, *Notor:* 418
Charles George Gordon, *19th:* 949
Hermann Göring, *20th:* 1545, *Notor:* 428
Ulysses S. Grant, *19th:* 958
Nathanael Greene, *18th:* 443
Sir Richard Grenville, *Ren:* 396
Jean-Baptiste Vaquette de Gribeauval, *18th:* 447
Heinz Guderian, *20th:* 1606
Gustavus II Adolphus, *17th:* 336
Gwenllian verch Gruffydd, *MA:* 448
Mary A. Hallaren, *20th:* 1645
William F. Halsey, *20th:* 1647
Hamilcar Barca, *Anc:* 373
Alexander Hamilton, *18th:* 452
Hammurabi, *Anc:* 376
Hannibal, *Anc:* 382
Harold II, *MA:* 457
William Henry Harrison, *19th:* 1048

Hārūn al-Rashīd, *MA:* 467
Piet Hein, *17th:* 359
Hengist, *Anc:* 394
Henry I, *MA:* 481
Henry V, *MA:* 501
Rudolf Hess, *Notor:* 460
Reinhard Heydrich, *Notor:* 462
Thomas Wentworth Higginson, *19th:* 1097
Heinrich Himmler, *20th:* 1807, *Notor:* 468
Paul von Hindenburg, *20th:* 1814
Adolf Hitler, *20th:* 1829, *Notor:* 477
Ho Chi Minh, *20th:* 1834
Oveta Culp Hobby, *20th:* 1838
Sam Houston, *19th:* 1130
Richard Howe, *18th:* 506
William Howe, *18th:* 510
Huáscar, *Ren:* 469
Humāyūn, *Ren:* 475
Isabella I, *Ren:* 328
Itzcóatl, *MA:* 558
Andrew Jackson, *19th:* 1189
Stonewall Jackson, *19th:* 1197
Jimmu Tennō, *Anc:* 462
Jingū, *Anc:* 465
Joan of Arc, *MA:* 578
Alfred Jodl, *Notor:* 533
Joseph-Jacques-Césaire Joffre, *20th:* 2009
John III Sobieski, *17th:* 427
John of Austria, *17th:* 425
John Paul Jones, *18th:* 539
Julius II, *Ren:* 518
Kamehameha I, *19th:* 1249
Merzifonlu Kara Mustafa Paşa, *17th:* 451
Albert Kesselring, *20th:* 2117
Khosrow I, *MA:* 613
William Kidd, *17th:* 464, *Notor:* 576
Lord Kitchener, *20th:* 2173
Kuniaki Koiso, *Notor:* 587
Tadeusz Kościuszko, *18th:* 564
Krishnadevaraya, *Ren:* 532
Mikhail Illarionovich Kutuzov, *18th:* 569
Saint László I, *MA:* 637
T. E. Lawrence, *20th:* 2303
Robert E. Lee, *19th:* 1334
Earl of Leicester, *Ren:* 553
Leonidas, *Anc:* 505
Leopold I, *17th:* 526
Lin Biao, *20th:* 2381
John Walker Lindh, *Notor:* 645
Little Turtle, *18th:* 610
Louis XIII, *17th:* 551
Marquis de Louvois, *17th:* 558
Erich Ludendorff, *20th:* 2462
Douglas MacArthur, *20th:* 2492
Alexander McGillivray, *18th:* 626
Robert McNamara, *20th:* 2541
Maḥmūd of Ghazna, *MA:* 683
Gaius Marius, *Anc:* 533
First Duke of Marlborough, *18th:* 660
George C. Marshall, *20th:* 2629
Jean Martinet, *Notor:* 707
Masinissa, *Anc:* 542
Matthias I Corvinus, *Ren:* 642
Maurice of Nassau, *17th:* 618
Mausolus, *Anc:* 545
Mehmed II, *Notor:* 711, *Ren:* 659
Bernardino de Mendoza, *Ren:* 668
Miltiades the Younger, *Anc:* 563
William Mitchell, *20th:* 2765
Vyacheslav Mikhailovich Molotov, *20th:* 2783, *Notor:* 746
George Monck, *17th:* 650
Duke of Monmouth, *17th:* 653
Marquis de Montalembert, *18th:* 690
Louis-Joseph de Montcalm, *18th:* 692
Bernard Law Montgomery, *20th:* 2808
Montuhotep II, *Anc:* 570
Philippe de Mornay, *Ren:* 703
Louis Mountbatten, *20th:* 2853
Murad IV, *17th:* 668
Nādir Shāh, *18th:* 722, *Notor:* 772
John Napier, *Ren:* 710
Napoleon I, *19th:* 1636
Ne Win, *Notor:* 773
Nebuchadnezzar II, *Anc:* 582
Lord Nelson, *19th:* 1656
Michel Ney, *19th:* 1667
Ngo Quyen, *MA:* 756
Nguyen Van Thieu, *20th:* 2954
Chester W. Nimitz, *20th:* 2977
Manuel Noriega, *Notor:* 797
Oda Nobunaga, *Ren:* 732
James Edward Oglethorpe, *18th:* 742
Bernardo O'Higgins, *19th:* 1703
Olaf I, *MA:* 789
Grace O'Malley, *Ren:* 743, *Notor:* 805
Grigori Grigoryevich Orlov, *18th:* 757
Daniel Ortega, *20th:* 3072
Osman I, *MA:* 800
Pachacuti, *Ren:* 746
George S. Patton, *20th:* 3142
Pausanias of Sparta, *Anc:* 615
Peng Dehuai, *20th:* 3191
Matthew C. Perry, *19th:* 1776
Oliver Hazard Perry, *19th:* 1779
John J. Pershing, *20th:* 3219
Philippe Pétain, *20th:* 3222, *Notor:* 825
Pheidippides, *Anc:* 630
Philip II of Macedonia, *Anc:* 637
Arthur Phillip, *18th:* 783
Zebulon Pike, *19th:* 1793
Piye, *Anc:* 655
Pol Pot, *20th:* 3298, *Notor:* 846
Pompey the Great, *Anc:* 681
Pontiac, *18th:* 801
Colin Powell, *20th:* 3321
Thomas Pride, *17th:* 756
Ptolemy Soter, *Anc:* 719
Muammar al-Qaddafi, *20th:* 3350, *Notor:* 867
Qāytbāy, *Ren:* 807
William Clarke Quantrill, *Notor:* 869
Yitzhak Rabin, *20th:* 3358
Gilles de Rais, *Notor:* 880
Sir Walter Ralegh, *Ren:* 813
Ramses II, *Anc:* 735
Jerry John Rawlings, *20th:* 3389
Stenka Razin, *17th:* 784
Regulus, *Anc:* 738
Paul Revere, *18th:* 832
Joachim von Ribbentrop, *Notor:* 894
Richard I, *MA:* 891

Hyman G. Rickover, *20th:* 3443
George Rodney, *18th:* 854
Edith Nourse Rogers, *20th:* 3489
Erwin Rommel, *20th:* 3502
Gerd von Rundstedt, *20th:* 3559
Rurik, *MA:* 911
Michiel Adriaanszoon de Ruyter, *17th:* 807
Anwar el-Sadat, *20th:* 3587
Louis de Saint-Just, *18th:* 877
Saladin, *MA:* 918
José de San Martín, *19th:* 1984
Antonio López de Santa Anna, *19th:* 1990
La Saragossa, *19th:* 1993
Sargon II, *Anc:* 752
Comte de Saxe, *18th:* 881
Gerhard Johann David von Scharnhorst, *19th:* 2006
Friedrich Hermann Schomberg, *17th:* 820
Scipio Aemilianus, *Anc:* 755
Scipio Africanus, *Anc:* 758
Winfield Scott, *19th:* 2051
Hans von Seeckt, *20th:* 3688
Seleucus I Nicator, *Anc:* 763
Sesostris III, *Anc:* 771
Shāpūr II, *Anc:* 774
Daniel Shays, *18th:* 902
William Tecumseh Sherman, *19th:* 2097
Sir Philip Sidney, *Ren:* 881
John Graves Simcoe, *18th:* 919
Śivājī, *17th:* 858
Otto Skorzeny, *Notor:* 969
First Viscount Slim, *20th:* 3758
Margaret Chase Smith, *20th:* 3768
Sonni ʿAlī, *Ren:* 900
Spartacus, *Anc:* 818
Miles Standish, *17th:* 877
Stefan Dušan, *MA:* 957
Flavius Stilicho, *Anc:* 824
Henry L. Stimson, *20th:* 3869
Antonio José de Sucre, *19th:* 2195
Lucius Cornelius Sulla, *Anc:* 830, *Notor:* 1010
Duke de Sully, *17th:* 896
Aleksandr Vasilyevich Suvorov, *18th:* 954
Taira Kiyomori, *MA:* 990
Thomas Talbot, *19th:* 2219
Tancred, *MA:* 1003
Tarquins, *Anc:* 846
Niccolò Fontana Tartaglia, *Ren:* 920
Charles Taylor, *Notor:* 1021
Zachary Taylor, *19th:* 2230
Than Shwe, *Notor:* 1026
Sylvanus Thayer, *19th:* 2260
Themistocles, *Anc:* 859
Theodosius the Great, *Anc:* 868
Thutmose III, *Anc:* 885
Tiglath-pileser III, *Anc:* 892
Alfred von Tirpitz, *20th:* 4030
Lennart Torstenson, *17th:* 924
Toyotomi Hideyoshi, *Ren:* 943
Trajan, *Anc:* 903
Maarten and Cornelis Tromp, *17th:* 930
Rafael Trujillo, *20th:* 4084, *Notor:* 1042
Tupac Amaru II, *18th:* 993
Viscount de Turenne, *17th:* 933
ʿUmar I, *MA:* 1037
Ur-Nammu, *Anc:* 914
Vasily III, *Ren:* 957
Sébastien Le Prestre de Vauban, *17th:* 946
Vercingetorix, *Anc:* 935
Jorge Rafael Videla, *Notor:* 1066
Andrey Andreyevich Vlasov, *Notor:* 1074
Vo Nguyen Giap, *20th:* 4169
Kurt Waldheim, *20th:* 4187
William Walker, *Notor:* 1084
Albrecht Wenzel von Wallenstein, *17th:* 966
Earl of Warwick, *Ren:* 989
George Washington, *18th:* 1043
Anthony Wayne, *18th:* 1054
Duke of Wellington, *19th:* 2409
William the Silent, *Ren:* 993
William Wallace, *MA:* 1072
William the Conqueror, *MA:* 1117
Henry Wirz, *Notor:* 1105
Władysław II Jagiełło and Jadwiga, *MA:* 1120
James Wolfe, *18th:* 1104
Xerxes I, *Anc:* 971
Chuck Yeager, *20th:* 4425
Yo Fei, *MA:* 1145
Yuan Shikai, *Notor:* 1122
Yui Shōsetsu, *17th:* 998
Zenobia, *Anc:* 986
Zhu De, *20th:* 4465
Georgy Zhukov, *20th:* 4469
Mohammad Zia-ul-Haq, *20th:* 4473
Jan Žižka, *MA:* 1162

Monarchy (20th century). ***See also*** **Government and Politics**

Akihito, *20th:* 46
Bhumibol Adulyadej, *20th:* 363
Diana, Princess of Wales, *20th:* 989
Edward VII, *20th:* 1104
Elizabeth II, *20th:* 1143
Faisal, *20th:* 1198
Francis Ferdinand, *20th:* 1294
George V, *20th:* 1451
George VI, *20th:* 1454
Haile Selassie I, *20th:* 1639
Hassan II, *20th:* 1699
Hirohito, *20th:* 1818, *Notor:* 473
Hussein I, *20th:* 1950
Juan Carlos I, *20th:* 2060
William II, *20th:* 4346
Duke of Windsor, *20th:* 4368

Murderers. ***See*** **Assassins and Murderers**

Music

Fanny Abington, *18th:* 1
Adam de la Halle, *MA:* 24
Jean le Rond d'Alembert, *18th:* 31
Marian Anderson, *20th:* 87
Isabella Andreini, *Ren:* 42
Aristoxenus, *Anc:* 97
Louis Armstrong, *20th:* 130
W. H. Auden, *20th:* 172
Johann Sebastian Bach, *18th:* 71
Samuel Barber, *20th:* 230
Béla Bartók, *20th:* 250
The Beatles, *20th:* 266
Pierre-Augustin Caron de Beaumarchais, *18th:* 97
Ludwig van Beethoven, *19th:* 175

Alban Berg, *20th:* 309
Irving Berlin, *20th:* 327
Hector Berlioz, *19th:* 200
Leonard Bernstein, *20th:* 337
Georges Bizet, *19th:* 241
Luigi Boccherini, *18th:* 129
Aleksandr Borodin, *19th:* 280
Nadia Boulanger, *20th:* 449
Pierre Boulez, *20th:* 452
Joseph Boulogne, *18th:* 153
Johannes Brahms, *19th:* 296
Benjamin Britten, *20th:* 529
Anton Bruckner, *19th:* 329
Charles Burney, *18th:* 177
Robert Burns, *18th:* 183
Samuel Butler, *19th:* 374
William Byrd, *Ren:* 148
Francesca Caccini, *17th:* 111
Maria Callas, *20th:* 612
Thomas Campion, *17th:* 127
Enrico Caruso, *20th:* 675
Pablo Casals, *20th:* 681
Ray Charles, *20th:* 735
Frédéric Chopin, *19th:* 486
John Coltrane, *20th:* 814
Aaron Copland, *20th:* 836
Arcangelo Corelli, *17th:* 190
François Couperin, *18th:* 281
Sir Noël Coward, *20th:* 853
Bing Crosby, *20th:* 874
Celia Cruz, *20th:* 877
Claude Debussy, *20th:* 936
Léo Delibes, *19th:* 639
Frederick Delius, *20th:* 953
Sergei Diaghilev, *20th:* 985
Gaetano Donizetti, *19th:* 674
John Dowland, *Ren:* 289
John Dunstable, *MA:* 333
Antonín Dvořák, *19th:* 711
Bob Dylan, *20th:* 1072
Sir Edward Elgar, *20th:* 1132
Duke Ellington, *20th:* 1145
Fanny Elssler, *19th:* 743
Manuel de Falla, *20th:* 1206
Ella Fitzgerald, *20th:* 1246
Bob Fosse, *20th:* 1291
Stephen Collins Foster, *19th:* 802
César Franck, *19th:* 821
Aretha Franklin, *20th:* 1312
Girolamo Frescobaldi, *17th:* 295
Andrea Gabrieli, *Ren:* 359
Giovanni Gabrieli, *Ren:* 362
Judy Garland, *20th:* 1409
George Gershwin, *20th:* 1458
Ira Gershwin, *20th:* 1462
Orlando Gibbons, *17th:* 309
W. S. Gilbert, *19th:* 916
Dizzy Gillespie, *20th:* 1480
Christoph Gluck, *18th:* 418
Benny Goodman, *20th:* 1527
Glenn Gould, *20th:* 1553
Charles Gounod, *19th:* 952
Edvard Grieg, *19th:* 984
Guido d'Arezzo, *MA:* 439
Oscar Hammerstein II, *20th:* 1657
George Frideric Handel, *18th:* 462
W. C. Handy, *20th:* 1667
Lorenz Hart, *20th:* 1691
Joseph Haydn, *18th:* 476
Hans Werner Henze, *20th:* 1762
Caroline Lucretia Herschel, *18th:* 489
William Herschel, *18th:* 492
Hildegard von Bingen, *MA:* 512
Paul Hindemith, *20th:* 1811
Billie Holiday, *20th:* 1852
Vladimir Horowitz, *20th:* 1886
Engelbert Humperdinck, *19th:* 1154
Charles Ives, *20th:* 1974
Izumo no Okuni, *17th:* 408
Leoš Janáček, *20th:* 1989
John IV, *17th:* 430
Janis Joplin, *20th:* 2043
Scott Joplin, *19th:* 1235
Josquin des Prez, *Ren:* 515
Herbert von Karajan, *20th:* 2081
Francis Scott Key, *19th:* 1274
Francesco Landini, *MA:* 635
K. D. Lang, *20th:* 2256
Orlando di Lasso, *Ren:* 540
Henry Lawes, *17th:* 502
Jenny Lind, *19th:* 1387
Franz Liszt, *19th:* 1393
Sir Andrew Lloyd Webber, *20th:* 2414
Jean-Baptiste Lully, *17th:* 569
Guillaume de Machaut, *MA:* 679
Gustav Mahler, *20th:* 2558
Margaret of Austria, *Ren:* 612
Felix Mendelssohn, *19th:* 1549
Gian Carlo Menotti, *20th:* 2703
Marin Mersenne, *17th:* 628
Olivier Messiaen, *20th:* 2715
Darius Milhaud, *20th:* 2735
Claudio Monteverdi, *17th:* 656
Thomas Morley, *Ren:* 701
Wolfgang Amadeus Mozart, *18th:* 711
Johannes de Muris, *MA:* 741
Modest Mussorgsky, *19th:* 1626
Carl Nielsen, *20th:* 2965
Jessye Norman, *20th:* 2995
Jacques Offenbach, *19th:* 1699
Johann Pachelbel, *17th:* 708
Niccolò Paganini, *19th:* 1724
Giovanni Pierluigi da Palestrina, *Ren:* 751
Charlie Parker, *20th:* 3112
Dolly Parton, *20th:* 3127
Luciano Pavarotti, *20th:* 3159
Pérotin, *MA:* 824
Oscar Peterson, *20th:* 3226
Edith Piaf, *20th:* 3228
Pindar, *Anc:* 646
Cole Porter, *20th:* 3308
Francis Poulenc, *20th:* 3318
Elvis Presley, *20th:* 3330
Leontyne Price, *20th:* 3334
Sergei Prokofiev, *20th:* 3338
Giacomo Puccini, *20th:* 3346
Henry Purcell, *17th:* 763
Pythagoras, *Anc:* 725
Sergei Rachmaninoff, *20th:* 3361
Jean-Philippe Rameau, *18th:* 826
Maurice Ravel, *20th:* 3386
Nikolay Rimsky-Korsakov, *19th:* 1915
Jerome Robbins, *20th:* 3459
Richard Rodgers, *20th:* 3486
Gioacchino Rossini, *19th:* 1944
Camille Saint-Saëns, *20th:* 3600
Erik Satie, *20th:* 3641
Alessandro Scarlatti, *18th:* 883
Arnold Schoenberg, *20th:* 3664
Franz Schubert, *19th:* 2026
Clara Schumann, *19th:* 2029
Robert Schumann, *19th:* 2031
Heinrich Schütz, *17th:* 825
Albert Schweitzer, *20th:* 3678

Andrés Segovia, *20th:* 3691
Dmitri Shostakovich, *20th:* 3728
Jean Sibelius, *20th:* 3736
Beverly Sills, *20th:* 3744
Sima Xiangru, *Anc:* 785
Frank Sinatra, *20th:* 3747
Bessie Smith, *20th:* 3765
John Philip Sousa, *20th:* 3798
Simon Stevin, *Ren:* 912
Karlheinz Stockhausen, *20th:* 3872
Antonio Stradivari, *18th:* 944
Johann Strauss, *19th:* 2188
Richard Strauss, *20th:* 3885
Igor Stravinsky, *20th:* 3888
Barbra Streisand, *20th:* 3892
Barbara Strozzi, *17th:* 888
Arthur Sullivan, *19th:* 916
Shinichi Suzuki, *20th:* 3922
Rabindranath Tagore, *20th:* 3933
Thomas Tallis, *Ren:* 918
Peter Ilich Tchaikovsky, *19th:* 2233
Georg Philipp Telemann, *18th:* 970
Theodore Thomas, *19th:* 2267
Arturo Toscanini, *20th:* 4050
Edgard Varèse, *20th:* 4142
Ralph Vaughan Williams, *20th:* 4147
Giuseppe Verdi, *19th:* 2351
Heitor Villa-Lobos, *20th:* 4163
Philippe de Vitry, *MA:* 1065
Antonio Vivaldi, *18th:* 1019
Richard Wagner, *19th:* 2374
Sir William Walton, *20th:* 4216
Wang Wei, *MA:* 1085
Muddy Waters, *20th:* 4240
Carl Maria von Weber, *19th:* 2395
Anton von Webern, *20th:* 4262
Kurt Weill, *20th:* 4273
Charles Wesley, *18th:* 1061
Horst Wessel, *Notor:* 1097
Iannis Xenakis, *20th:* 4414
Ellen Taaffe Zwilich, *20th:* 4475

Native American Affairs

Atahualpa, *Ren:* 66
Black Hawk, *19th:* 244
Joseph Brant, *18th:* 159
Canonicus, *17th:* 129
Crazy Horse, *19th:* 566
Cuauhtémoc, *Ren:* 273
Deganawida, *Ren:* 281
Geronimo, *19th:* 904
Hiawatha, *Ren:* 448
Huáscar, *Ren:* 469
Itzcóatl, *MA:* 558
Chief Joseph, *19th:* 1238
Kalicho, *Ren:* 522
Kamehameha I, *19th:* 1249
Liliuokalani, *19th:* 1373
Little Turtle, *18th:* 610
Wilma Mankiller, *20th:* 2591
Doña Marina, *Ren:* 621
Massasoit, *17th:* 612
Metacom, *17th:* 633
Montezuma II, *Ren:* 693
Nezahualcóyotl, *Ren:* 720
Opechancanough, *17th:* 702
Osceola, *19th:* 1709
Pachacuti, *Ren:* 746
Pemisapan, *Ren:* 771
Pocahontas, *17th:* 745
Pontiac, *18th:* 801
Powhatan, *17th:* 752
Red Cloud, *19th:* 1871
John Ross, *19th:* 1937
Sacagawea, *19th:* 1962
Sequoyah, *19th:* 2067
Sitting Bull, *19th:* 2108
Squanto, *17th:* 875
Tascalusa, *Ren:* 922
Tecumseh, *19th:* 2237
Kateri Tekakwitha, *17th:* 908
Thanadelthur, *18th:* 974

Natural History

Elizabeth Cabot Agassiz, *19th:* 29
Anaxagoras, *Anc:* 52
Anaximander, *Anc:* 55
Aristotle, *Anc:* 94
Comte de Buffon, *18th:* 171
Rachel Carson, *20th:* 662
Empedocles, *Anc:* 295
Karl von Frisch, *20th:* 1335
Stephen Jay Gould, *20th:* 1555
Thomas Henry Huxley, *19th:* 1161
Engelbert Kämpfer, *17th:* 445
Lucretius, *Anc:* 520
Pliny the Elder, *Anc:* 665
John Ray, *17th:* 782
Pierre Teilhard de Chardin, *20th:* 3963
August Weismann, *19th:* 2406
Edward O. Wilson, *20th:* 4358

Oceanography. ***See*** **Earth Sciences**

Outlaws and Gunslingers. ***See also*** **Gangsters and Associates**

Apache Kid, *Notor:* 27
Johnnie Armstrong, *Notor:* 35
Clyde Barrow, *Notor:* 62
Tom Bell, *Notor:* 80
Ronnie Biggs, *Notor:* 97
William H. Bonney, *Notor:* 118
Curly Bill Brocius, *Notor:* 143
Butch Cassidy, *Notor:* 181
Bob Dalton, *Notor:* 257
Emmett Dalton, *Notor:* 258
Black Donnellys, *Notor:* 294
Bill Doolin, *Notor:* 296
Claude Duval, *Notor:* 306
Wyatt Earp, *19th:* 720, *Notor:* 315
John Wesley Hardin, *Notor:* 447
Doc Holliday, *Notor:* 485
Jesse James, *19th:* 1211, *Notor:* 523
Ned Kelly, *Notor:* 562
Tom Ketchum, *Notor:* 566
Harry Longabaugh, *Notor:* 651
Bill Longley, *Notor:* 653
Joaquín Murieta, *Notor:* 767
Johnny Ringo, *Notor:* 898
Rob Roy, *Notor:* 902
Robin Hood, *Notor:* 909
Belle Starr, *Notor:* 994
Henry Starr, *Notor:* 996
Dick Turpin, *Notor:* 1045
Hank Vaughan, *Notor:* 1060
Cole Younger, *Notor:* 1118

Patrons of the Arts. ***See*** **Philanthropy and Patrons of the Arts**

PHILANTHROPY AND PATRONS OF THE ARTS

ʿAbbās the Great, *17th:* 4
ʿAbd al-Muʾmin, *MA:* 6
ʿAbd al-Raḥmān III al-Nāṣir, *MA:* 9
Fanny Abington, *18th:* 1
Akbar (1542-1605), *Ren:* 15
Alexander VI, *Ren:* 27, *Notor:* 14
Alexander VII, *17th:* 9
Alfonso X, *MA:* 59
Anne of Brittany, *Ren:* 48
Ashurbanipal, *Anc:* 117
Ashurnasirpal II, *Anc:* 120
Christiaan Barnard, *20th:* 236
Hester Bateman, *18th:* 95
Bess of Hardwick, *Ren:* 103
Thomas Betterton, *17th:* 51
Bhumibol Adulyadej, *20th:* 363
Lucrezia Borgia, *Ren:* 117, *Notor:* 129
Molly Brown, *20th:* 542
Warren Buffett, *20th:* 563
Jacques Callot, *17th:* 116
Andrew Carnegie, *19th:* 419
Jimmy Carter, *20th:* 666
Catherine of Aragon, *Ren:* 187
Chŏng Sŏn, *18th:* 248
Christina, *17th:* 163
Jean-Baptiste Colbert, *17th:* 180
Vittoria Colonna, *Ren:* 235
Sergei Diaghilev, *20th:* 985
Diane de Poitiers, *Ren:* 283
George Eastman, *20th:* 1078
Elizabeth I (queen of England), *Ren:* 310
Eugene of Savoy, *18th:* 330
Henry Ford, *20th:* 1279
Francis I, *Ren:* 346
Frederick I, *18th:* 375
Isabella Stewart Gardner, *20th:* 1406
Bill Gates, *20th:* 1421
Sir John Paul Getty, *20th:* 1468
Maḥmūd Ghāzān, *MA:* 411
Marie le Jars de Gournay, *17th:* 314
Billy Graham, *20th:* 1557
Daniel Guggenheim, *20th:* 1613
Le Ly Hayslip, *20th:* 1727
Henry II (1519-1559; King of France), *Ren:* 423
Audrey Hepburn, *20th:* 1766
Saint Hilda of Whitby, *MA:* 509
Bob Hope, *20th:* 1870
Samuel Gridley Howe, *19th:* 1141
Isabella d'Este, *Ren:* 485
Jahāngīr, *17th:* 410
James III, *Ren:* 496
John IV, *17th:* 430
Julia Domna, *Anc:* 480
Julius II, *Ren:* 518
Kanishka, *Anc:* 499
Khosrow I, *MA:* 613
Lee Krasner, *20th:* 2195
Krishnadevaraya, *Ren:* 532
Ann Landers, *20th:* 2247
Estée Lauder, *20th:* 2275
Thomas Lawrence, *18th:* 583
Charles Le Brun, *17th:* 504
Ninon de Lenclos, *17th:* 520
Leo X, *Ren:* 557, *Notor:* 630
Levni, *18th:* 602
Jerry Lewis, *20th:* 2357
Juliette Gordon Low, *20th:* 2441
Cyrus Hall McCormick, *19th:* 1438
Gaius Maecenas, *Anc:* 527
Henry Edward Manning, *19th:* 1489
Marguerite de Navarre, *Ren:* 617
Marie de Médicis, *17th:* 598
Mary of Hungary, *Ren:* 636
Matthias I Corvinus, *Ren:* 642
Jules Mazarin, *17th:* 620
Cosimo I de' Medici, *Ren:* 653
Cosimo II de' Medici, *17th:* 626
Lorenzo de' Medici, *Ren:* 655
Melisende, *MA:* 715
Menkaure, *Anc:* 558
Mentewab, *18th:* 677
J. P. Morgan, *19th:* 1599
Nero, *Anc:* 591, *Notor:* 777
Nicholas V, *MA:* 768
Alfred Nobel, *19th:* 1689
Count-Duke of Olivares, *17th:* 697
Charles Willson Peale, *18th:* 768
Gregory Peck, *20th:* 3181
Nicolas-Claude Fabri de Peiresc, *17th:* 722
Charles Perrault, *17th:* 731
Philip IV, *17th:* 738
Philip the Good, *MA:* 832
Pisistratus, *Anc:* 649
Pius VI, *18th:* 793
Madame de Pompadour, *18th:* 798
Qāytbāy, *Ren:* 807
Marquise de Rambouillet, *17th:* 779
John D. Rockefeller, *19th:* 1921
John D. Rockefeller, Jr., *20th:* 3476
Rudolf II, *Ren:* 840
Ludovico Sforza, *Ren:* 872
Shah Jahan, *17th:* 842
Sigismund I, the Old, *Ren:* 885
Sigismund II Augustus, *Ren:* 887
Beverly Sills, *20th:* 3744
Elisabetta Sirani, *17th:* 856
Sixtus IV, *Ren:* 893
Nathan Söderblom, *20th:* 3781
George Soros, *20th:* 3795
Leland Stanford, *19th:* 2132
Tamerlane, *MA:* 1000
Dame Elizabeth Taylor, *20th:* 3953
Mother Teresa, *20th:* 3975
Tutankhamen, *Anc:* 908
Urban VIII, *17th:* 936
Madam C. J. Walker, *20th:* 4199
Sam Walton, *20th:* 4213
Gertrude Vanderbilt Whitney, *20th:* 4315
Oprah Winfrey, *20th:* 4372
Zenobia, *Anc:* 986

PHILOSOPHY. ***See also*** **RELIGION AND THEOLOGY**

Pietro d'Abano, *MA:* 1
Muḥammad ʿAbduh, *19th:* 4
Peter Abelard, *MA:* 13
Isaac ben Judah Abravanel, *Ren:* 1
Leon Battista Alberti, *Ren:* 18
Saint Albertus Magnus, *MA:* 42
Alcmaeon, *Anc:* 36
Bronson Alcott, *19th:* 38
Jean le Rond d'Alembert, *18th:* 31
Anaxagoras, *Anc:* 52
Anaximenes, *Anc:* 58
Anisthenes, *Anc:* 68

Saint Anselm, *MA:* 92
Hannah Arendt, *20th:* 118
Aristippus, *Anc:* 87
Aristotle, *Anc:* 94
Aristoxenus, *Anc:* 97
Asanga, *Anc:* 111
al-Ashʿarī, *MA:* 111
Aspasia of Miletus, *Anc:* 127
Mary Astell, *18th:* 64
Saint Augustine, *Anc:* 142
Sri Aurobindo, *20th:* 177
Averroës, *MA:* 118
Avicenna, *MA:* 123
Francis Bacon, *Ren:* 72
Roger Bacon, *MA:* 127
Leo Baeck, *20th:* 186
Mikhail Bakhtin, *20th:* 190
Mikhail Bakunin, *19th:* 119
Ban Zhao, *Anc:* 152
Roland Barthes, *20th:* 246
Pierre Bayle, *17th:* 36
Simone de Beauvoir, *20th:* 271
Walter Benjamin, *20th:* 306
Jeremy Bentham, *18th:* 104
Henri Bergson, *20th:* 323
George Berkeley, *18th:* 111
Louis Blanc, *19th:* 254
Boethius, *MA:* 173
Jakob Böhme, *17th:* 59
First Viscount Bolingbroke, *18th:* 135
Dietrich Bonhoeffer, *20th:* 418
F. H. Bradley, *19th:* 288
Louis D. Brandeis, *20th:* 482
Percy Williams Bridgman, *20th:* 526
Sir Thomas Browne, *17th:* 94
Giordano Bruno, *Ren:* 138
Martin Buber, *20th:* 554
Buddha, *Anc:* 169
Rudolf Bultmann, *20th:* 572
Ralph Bunche, *20th:* 574
Jean Buridan, *MA:* 215
Edmund Burke, *18th:* 174
Robert Burton, *17th:* 108
Joseph Butler, *18th:* 187
Tommaso Campanella, *17th:* 124
Albert Camus, *20th:* 628
Rudolf Carnap, *20th:* 659
Ernst Cassirer, *20th:* 688
Cato the Younger, *Anc:* 194
Andrea Cesalpino, *Ren:* 211
Marquise du Châtelet, *18th:* 240
Cicero, *Anc:* 210
Auguste Comte, *19th:* 536
Étienne Bonnot de Condillac, *18th:* 263
Marquis de Condorcet, *18th:* 267
Confucius, *Anc:* 236
Anne Conway, *17th:* 187
Benedetto Croce, *20th:* 869
Dai Zhen, *18th:* 287
Sir Humphry Davy, *19th:* 616
John Dee, *Ren:* 278
Democritus, *Anc:* 261
Jacques Derrida, *20th:* 974
René Descartes, *17th:* 226
John Dewey, *20th:* 982
Denis Diderot, *18th:* 307
Diogenes, *Anc:* 283
John Duns Scotus, *MA:* 329
Émile Durkheim, *20th:* 1065
Christian von Ehrenfels, *20th:* 1110
Eugen Ehrlich, *20th:* 1113
Elizabeth of Bohemia, *17th:* 250
Empedocles, *Anc:* 295
Epicurus, *Anc:* 307
Desiderius Erasmus, *Ren:* 314
Rudolf Christoph Eucken, *20th:* 1185
Fakhr al-Dīn al-Rāzī, *MA:* 369
Gustav Theodor Fechner, *19th:* 770
Adam Ferguson, *18th:* 338
Johann Gottlieb Fichte, *18th:* 342
Marsilio Ficino, *Ren:* 332
Robert Fludd, *17th:* 280
Girolamo Fracastoro, *Ren:* 343
Benjamin Franklin, *18th:* 370
Erich Fromm, *20th:* 1345
Galen, *Anc:* 348
Pierre Gassendi, *17th:* 304
Giovanni Gentile, *20th:* 1448
Conrad Gesner, *Ren:* 375
al-Ghazzālī, *MA:* 415
William Gilbert, *Ren:* 381
Étienne Gilson, *20th:* 1488
Vincenzo Gioberti, *19th:* 921
Kurt Gödel, *20th:* 1510
William Godwin, *18th:* 424
Gośāla Maskarīputra, *Anc:* 355
Baltasar Gracián y Morales, *17th:* 316
Thomas Hill Green, *19th:* 971
Jürgen Habermas, *20th:* 1632
Hakuin, *18th:* 450
al-Ḥallāj, *MA:* 454
Hanfeizi, *Anc:* 379
Frederic Harrison, *19th:* 1044
Nicolai Hartmann, *20th:* 1696
F. A. Hayek, *20th:* 1720
Georg Wilhelm Friedrich Hegel, *19th:* 1065
Martin Heidegger, *20th:* 1742
Claude-Adrien Helvétius, *18th:* 479
Heraclitus of Ephesus, *Anc:* 397
Johann Gottfried Herder, *18th:* 486
Hippolytus of Rome, *Anc:* 423
Thomas Hobbes, *17th:* 378
Leonard T. Hobhouse, *20th:* 1841
Paul-Henri-Dietrich d'Holbach, *18th:* 501
David Hume, *18th:* 514
Edmund Husserl, *20th:* 1955
Ibn al-ʿArabī, *MA:* 526
Ibn Gabirol, *MA:* 532
Isocrates, *Anc:* 450
François Jacob, *20th:* 1982
Jamāl al-Dīn al-Afghānī, *19th:* 1203
William James, *19th:* 1213
Karl Jaspers, *20th:* 1996
Judah ha-Levi, *MA:* 591
Julian of Norwich, *MA:* 595
Kang Youwei, *19th:* 1252
Immanuel Kant, *18th:* 548
Joseph ben Ephraim Karo, *Ren:* 524
Søren Kierkegaard, *19th:* 1278
Jan Komenský, *17th:* 469
Jacques Lacan, *20th:* 2224
Susanne K. Langer, *20th:* 2263
Laozi, *Anc:* 502
Ferdinand Lassalle, *19th:* 1321
Gottfried Wilhelm Leibniz, *17th:* 513
Ninon de Lenclos, *17th:* 520

Gotthold Ephraim Lessing, *18th:* 598
Levi ben Gershom, *MA:* 650
Claude Lévi-Strauss, *20th:* 2347
John Locke, *17th:* 542
Lucretius, *Anc:* 520
György Lukács, *20th:* 2468
Raymond Lull, *MA:* 673
Isaac ben Solomon Luria, *Ren:* 579
Martin Luther, *Ren:* 582
Trofim Lysenko, *Notor:* 667
Catherine Macaulay, *18th:* 621
Niccolò Machiavelli, *Ren:* 587
Moses Maimonides, *MA:* 686
Gabriel Marcel, *20th:* 2609
Marguerite de Navarre, *Ren:* 617
Jacques Maritain, *20th:* 2624
Karl Marx, *19th:* 1508
Tomáš Masaryk, *20th:* 2639
Giuseppe Mazzini, *19th:* 1531
Mencius, *Anc:* 552
Moses Mendelssohn, *18th:* 675
Maurice Merleau-Ponty, *20th:* 2710
Marin Mersenne, *17th:* 628
Jules Michelet, *19th:* 1564
James Mill, *19th:* 1571
John Stuart Mill, *19th:* 1574
Michel Eyquem de Montaigne, *Ren:* 689
Montesquieu, *18th:* 695
G. E. Moore, *20th:* 2814
Moses de León, *MA:* 730
Mozi, *Anc:* 576
Naḥmanides, *MA:* 747
Duchess of Newcastle, *17th:* 676
Nicholas of Autrecourt, *MA:* 761
Nicholas of Cusa, *Ren:* 724
Friedrich Nietzsche, *19th:* 1680
Kitarō Nishida, *20th:* 2981
Robert Nozick, *20th:* 2999
William of Ockham, *MA:* 778
Ogyū Sorai, *18th:* 746
José Ortega y Gasset, *20th:* 3077
Ouyang Xiu, *MA:* 808
Thomas Paine, *18th:* 759
William Paley, *18th:* 763
Paracelsus, *Ren:* 757
Theodore Parker, *19th:* 1735
Parmenides, *Anc:* 608
Blaise Pascal, *17th:* 713
Octavio Paz, *20th:* 3169
Charles Sanders Peirce, *19th:* 1772
Nicolas-Claude Fabri de Peiresc, *17th:* 722
Philo of Alexandria, *Anc:* 640
Giovanni Pico della Mirandola, *Ren:* 782
Elena Cornaro Piscopia, *17th:* 743
Plato, *Anc:* 659
Plotinus, *Anc:* 668
Porphyry, *Anc:* 687
Posidonius, *Anc:* 690
Joseph Priestley, *18th:* 811
Proclus, *Anc:* 701
Protagoras, *Anc:* 707
Pierre-Joseph Proudhon, *19th:* 1834
Michael Psellus, *MA:* 863
Samuel von Pufendorf, *17th:* 759
Pyrrhon of Elis, *Anc:* 722
Pythagoras, *Anc:* 725
Peter Ramus, *Ren:* 817
Ayn Rand, *20th:* 3367
John Rawls, *20th:* 3391
Guillaume-Thomas Raynal, *18th:* 829
al-Rāzī, *MA:* 884
David Ricardo, *19th:* 1896
Jean-Jacques Rousseau, *18th:* 868
Josiah Royce, *20th:* 3550
Bertrand Russell, *20th:* 3562
Śaṅkara, *MA:* 924
George Santayana, *20th:* 3629
Jean-Paul Sartre, *20th:* 3638
Max Scheler, *20th:* 3655
Friedrich Wilhelm Joseph von Schelling, *19th:* 2009
Friedrich Schiller, *18th:* 887
Arthur Schopenhauer, *19th:* 2019
Anna Maria van Schurman, *17th:* 823
Albert Schweitzer, *20th:* 3678
Seneca the Younger, *Anc:* 766
Henry Sidgwick, *19th:* 2102
Siger of Brabant, *MA:* 942
Adam Smith, *18th:* 921
Socrates, *Anc:* 799
Herbert Spencer, *19th:* 2126
Baruch Spinoza, *17th:* 871
Madame de Staël, *18th:* 929
Edith Stein, *20th:* 3840
Sylvester II, *MA:* 983
Pierre Teilhard de Chardin, *20th:* 3963
Thales of Miletus, *Anc:* 856
Theophrastus, *Anc:* 872
Thomas Aquinas, *MA:* 1027
Paul Tillich, *20th:* 4027
Tokugawa Tsunayoshi, *17th:* 919
Arnold Toynbee, *20th:* 4059
Ernst Troeltsch, *20th:* 4069
Miguel de Unamuno y Jugo, *20th:* 4128
Valentinus, *Anc:* 918
Paul Valéry, *20th:* 4136
Lorenzo Valla, *MA:* 1049
Vasubandhu, *Anc:* 930
Marquis de Vauvenargues, *18th:* 1009
Giambattista Vico, *18th:* 1013
Francisco de Vitoria, *Ren:* 978
Voltaire, *18th:* 1026
Joachim Wach, *20th:* 4177
Wang Bi, *Anc:* 950
Wang Chong, *Anc:* 953
Wang Fuzhi, *17th:* 972
Wang Yangming, *Ren:* 986
Lester Frank Ward, *19th:* 2384
Max Weber, *20th:* 4258
Simone Weil, *20th:* 4269
Max Wertheimer, *20th:* 4293
Alfred North Whitehead, *20th:* 4311
Elie Wiesel, *20th:* 4324
William of Auvergne, *MA:* 1097
William of Auxerre, *MA:* 1101
William of Moerbeke, *MA:* 1105
Ludwig Wittgenstein, *20th:* 4378
Xanthippe, *Anc:* 962
Xenophanes, *Anc:* 965
Xenophon, *Anc:* 968
Xie Lingyun, *Anc:* 975
Xunzi, *Anc:* 978
Zeno of Elea, *Anc:* 984
Zeno of Citium, *Anc:* 981
Zhu Xi, *MA:* 1159
Zhuangzi, *Anc:* 989

PHOTOGRAPHY

Diane Arbus, *20th:* 115
Margaret Bourke-White, *20th:* 460
Mathew B. Brady, *19th:* 291
Lewis Carroll, *19th:* 423
Henri Cartier-Bresson, *20th:* 671
Jacques Cousteau, *20th:* 849
Imogen Cunningham, *20th:* 883
Jacques Daguerre, *19th:* 589
George Eastman, *20th:* 1078
Margaret Lindsay Huggins, *19th:* 1144
Dorothea Lange, *20th:* 2260
Auguste and Louis Lumière, *20th:* 2471
Man Ray, *20th:* 2580
Samuel F. B. Morse, *19th:* 1610
Nicéphore Niépce, *19th:* 1676
Aleksandr Stepanovich Popov, *19th:* 1824
Leni Riefenstahl, *20th:* 3451
Wilhelm Conrad Röntgen, *19th:* 1931
Bernhard Voldemar Schmidt, *20th:* 3659
Karl Schwarzschild, *20th:* 3674
Edward Steichen, *20th:* 3837
Alfred Stieglitz, *20th:* 3864
Joseph Wilson Swan, *19th:* 2209

PHYSICS. ***See also*** **ENGINEERING; INVENTION AND TECHNOLOGY; MATHEMATICS**

Saint Albertus Magnus, *MA:* 42
Jean le Rond d'Alembert, *18th:* 31
Hannes Alfvén, *20th:* 58
Alhazen, *MA:* 66
Luis W. Alvarez, *20th:* 73
Viktor A. Ambartsumian, *20th:* 77
Svante August Arrhenius, *20th:* 138
Amedeo Avogadro, *19th:* 101
Roger Bacon, *MA:* 127
John Bardeen, *20th:* 234
Johann Joachim Becher, *17th:* 39
The Becquerel Family, *19th:* 165
George Berkeley, *18th:* 111
Tim Berners-Lee, *20th:* 331
The Bernoulli Family, *17th:* 48
Hans Albrecht Bethe, *20th:* 341
Vilhelm Bjerknes, *20th:* 374
Niels Bohr, *20th:* 408
Giovanni Alfonso Borelli, *17th:* 65
Max Born, *20th:* 437
Walther Bothe, *20th:* 442
Robert Boyle, *17th:* 78
Sir Lawrence Bragg, *20th:* 474
Percy Williams Bridgman, *20th:* 526
Louis de Broglie, *20th:* 534
Jean Buridan, *MA:* 215
Jocelyn Burnell, *20th:* 584
Henry Cavendish, *18th:* 217
Sir James Chadwick, *20th:* 714
Marquise du Châtelet, *18th:* 240
Arthur Holly Compton, *20th:* 817
William Fothergill Cooke, *19th:* 547
Francis Crick, *20th:* 865
Marie and Pierre Curie, *20th:* 888
John Dalton, *19th:* 597
Democritus, *Anc:* 261
René Descartes, *17th:* 226
Paul A. M. Dirac, *20th:* 1004
Albert Einstein, *20th:* 1118
Willem Einthoven, *20th:* 1122
Leonhard Euler, *18th:* 333
Michael Faraday, *19th:* 759
Gustav Theodor Fechner, *19th:* 770
Enrico Fermi, *20th:* 1235
Joseph Fourier, *19th:* 809
Benjamin Franklin, *18th:* 370
Galileo, *17th:* 298
Luigi Galvani, *18th:* 391
George Gamow, *20th:* 1379
Pierre Gassendi, *17th:* 304
Joseph-Louis Gay-Lussac, *19th:* 886
Hans Geiger, *20th:* 1440
Sophie Germain, *19th:* 901
Josiah Willard Gibbs, *19th:* 913
William Gilbert, *Ren:* 381
Robert H. Goddard, *20th:* 1507
Francesco Maria Grimaldi, *17th:* 321
Sir William Robert Grove, *19th:* 996
Otto von Guericke, *17th:* 333
Charles-Édouard Guillaume, *20th:* 1616
Otto Hahn, *20th:* 1635
Stephen Hawking, *20th:* 1712
Werner Heisenberg, *20th:* 1749
Hermann von Helmholtz, *19th:* 1073
Joseph Henry, *19th:* 1078
Gustav Hertz, *20th:* 1780
Gerhard Herzberg, *20th:* 1783
Georg von Hevesy, *20th:* 1792
David Hilbert, *20th:* 1800
Dorothy Crowfoot Hodgkin, *20th:* 1849
Robert Hooke, *17th:* 383
Sir Fred Hoyle, *20th:* 1902
Christiaan Huygens, *17th:* 397
Frédéric Joliot and Irène Joliot-Curie, *20th:* 2032
Heike Kamerlingh Onnes, *20th:* 2072
Pyotr Leonidovich Kapitsa, *20th:* 2077
Baron Kelvin, *19th:* 1264
Johannes Kepler, *17th:* 457
Igor Vasilyevich Kurchatov, *20th:* 2214
Lev Davidovich Landau, *20th:* 2244
Samuel Pierpont Langley, *19th:* 1309
Pierre-Simon Laplace, *19th:* 1317
Max von Laue, *20th:* 2278
Ernest Orlando Lawrence, *20th:* 2300
Henrietta Swan Leavitt, *20th:* 2317
Georges Lemaître, *20th:* 2337
Sir Joseph Norman Lockyer, *19th:* 1412
Mikhail Vasilyevich Lomonosov, *18th:* 613
Hendrik Antoon Lorentz, *20th:* 2431
Colin Maclaurin, *18th:* 632
Edwin Mattison McMillan, *20th:* 2532
Benoit B. Mandelbrot, *20th:* 2588
Guglielmo Marconi, *20th:* 2615
James Clerk Maxwell, *19th:* 1528

Lise Meitner, *20th:* 2679
Marin Mersenne, *17th:* 628
Albert A. Michelson, *19th:* 1567
Robert Andrews Millikan, *20th:* 2750
Gaspard Monge, *18th:* 682
Louis-Eugène-Félix Néel, *20th:* 2926
Walther Hermann Nernst, *20th:* 2934
John von Neumann, *20th:* 2943
Hermann Oberth, *20th:* 3008
J. Robert Oppenheimer, *20th:* 3065
Wilhelm Ostwald, *20th:* 3088
Denis Papin, *17th:* 710
Blaise Pascal, *17th:* 713
Wolfgang Pauli, *20th:* 3152
Petrus Peregrinus de Maricourt, *MA:* 820
Max Planck, *20th:* 3282
Henri Poincaré, *19th:* 1816
Aleksandr Stepanovich Popov, *19th:* 1824
Ludwig Prandtl, *20th:* 3327
Joseph Priestley, *18th:* 811
Isidor Isaac Rabi, *20th:* 3355
Sir Chandrasekhara Venkata Raman, *20th:* 3364
Charles Richter, *20th:* 3440
Sally Ride, *20th:* 3447
Wilhelm Conrad Röntgen, *19th:* 1931
Sir Joseph Rotblat, *20th:* 3536
Henry Norris Russell, *20th:* 3570
Ernest Rutherford, *20th:* 3576
Carl Sagan, *20th:* 3590
Andrei Sakharov, *20th:* 3602
Bernhard Voldemar Schmidt, *20th:* 3659
Erwin Schrödinger, *20th:* 3668
Karl Schwarzschild, *20th:* 3674
Glenn Theodore Seaborg, *20th:* 3684
Mary Somerville, *19th:* 2121
Johannes Stark, *20th:* 3827
Edward Teller, *20th:* 3968
Sir Joseph John Thomson, *20th:* 4007
Evangelista Torricelli, *17th:* 921
Charles Hard Townes, *20th:* 4057
Harold C. Urey, *20th:* 4132
James Van Allen, *20th:* 4139
Alessandro Volta, *18th:* 1022
Steven Weinberg, *20th:* 4277
Charles Wheatstone, *19th:* 547
Maurice Wilkins, *20th:* 4342
Rosalyn Yalow, *20th:* 4419
Hideki Yukawa, *20th:* 4436

PHYSIOLOGY. ***See also*** **BIOLOGY; MEDICINE**
Virginia Apgar, *20th:* 100
Sir William Maddock Bayliss, *20th:* 259
Claude Bernard, *19th:* 205
Josef Breuer, *20th:* 514
Sir John Carew Eccles, *20th:* 1089
António Egas Moniz, *20th:* 1107
Paul Ehrlich, *20th:* 1115
Willem Einthoven, *20th:* 1122
Luigi Galvani, *18th:* 391
Hermann von Helmholtz, *19th:* 1073
Bernardo Alberto Houssay, *20th:* 1899
Sir Hans Adolf Krebs, *20th:* 2199
August Krogh, *20th:* 2204
Karl Landsteiner, *20th:* 2250
Richard Lower, *17th:* 564
John J. R. Macleod, *20th:* 2526
Marcello Malpighi, *17th:* 579
Dorothy Reed Mendenhall, *20th:* 2695
Peyton Rous, *20th:* 3545
Santorio Santorio, *17th:* 810
Lazzaro Spallanzani, *18th:* 925
Ernest Henry Starling, *20th:* 3830
Nicolaus Steno, *17th:* 881
Jan Swammerdam, *17th:* 898
Helen Brooke Taussig, *20th:* 3950
Selman Abraham Waksman, *20th:* 4180
George Hoyt Whipple, *20th:* 4304
Thomas Willis, *17th:* 985

PIRATES
William Dampier, *17th:* 215, *Notor:* 260
ʿAruj, *Notor:* 38
Samuel Bellamy, *Notor:* 81
Maurycy Beniowski, *Notor:* 85
Charlotte de Berry, *Notor:* 94
Stede Bonnet, *Notor:* 117
Anne Bonny, *Notor:* 122
Cheng I Sao, *Notor:* 205
Francis Drake, *Ren:* 291, *Notor:* 301
William Kidd, *17th:* 464, *Notor:* 576
Jean Laffite, *Notor:* 600
Sir Henry Morgan, *Notor:* 753
Grace O'Malley, *Ren:* 743, *Notor:* 805
John Quelch, *Notor:* 871
John Rackham, *Notor:* 877
Mary Read, *Notor:* 891
Bartholomew Roberts, *Notor:* 905
Edward Teach, *Notor:* 1023
Rachel Wall, *Notor:* 1086
Dominique You, *Notor:* 1117

POLITICS. ***See*** **GOVERNMENT AND POLITICS**

PSYCHOLOGY AND PSYCHIATRY
Alfred Adler, *20th:* 33
Saint Albertus Magnus, *MA:* 42
Eugen Bleuler, *20th:* 391
Josef Breuer, *20th:* 514
Noam Chomsky, *20th:* 757
John Dewey, *20th:* 982
Christian von Ehrenfels, *20th:* 1110
Havelock Ellis, *20th:* 1148
Frantz Fanon, *20th:* 1212
Gustav Theodor Fechner, *19th:* 770
Sigmund Freud, *20th:* 1323
Erich Fromm, *20th:* 1345
Francis Galton, *19th:* 860
Arnold Gesell, *20th:* 1465
Georg Wilhelm Friedrich Hegel, *19th:* 1065
Oliver Wendell Holmes, *19th:* 1116
Karen Horney, *20th:* 1883
William James, *19th:* 1213
Pierre Janet, *20th:* 1993
Karl Jaspers, *20th:* 1996

Carl Jung, *20th:* 2062
Alfred Kinsey, *20th:* 2159
Elisabeth Kübler-Ross, *20th:* 2207
Jacques Lacan, *20th:* 2224
Timothy Leary, *Notor:* 619
Gustave Le Bon, *20th:* 2320
Konrad Lorenz, *20th:* 2434
Stanley Milgram, *Notor:* 729
Friedrich Nietzsche, *19th:* 1680
Ivan Petrovich Pavlov, *20th:* 3162
Jean Piaget, *20th:* 3231
Hermann Rorschach, *20th:* 3522
B. F. Skinner, *20th:* 3754
Herbert Spencer, *19th:* 2126
Benjamin Spock, *20th:* 3814
Harry Stack Sullivan, *20th:* 3910
Edward L. Thorndike, *20th:* 4013
Max Weber, *20th:* 4258
Max Wertheimer, *20th:* 4293
Wilhelm Wundt, *20th:* 4407

Publishing. *See* **Journalism; Literature**

Racists and Hatemongers

Byron De La Beckwith, *Notor:* 78
Theodore G. Bilbo, *Notor:* 99
Richard Girnt Butler, *Notor:* 157
Willis A. Carto, *Notor:* 177
Houston Stewart Chamberlain, *Notor:* 196
Frank Collin, *Notor:* 222
Charles E. Coughlin, *Notor:* 239
Léon Degrelle, *Notor:* 270
Françoise Dior, *Notor:* 283
Thomas Dixon, Jr., *Notor:* 284
David Duke, *Notor:* 303
Julius Evola, *Notor:* 339
Nathan Bedford Forrest, *Notor:* 365
Elisabeth Förster-Nietzsche, *Notor:* 367
Arthur de Gobineau, *Notor:* 415
Matthew F. Hale (b. 1971), *Notor:* 444
J. Edgar Hoover, *20th:* 1866, *Notor:* 489
David Irving, *Notor:* 512
Meir Kahane, *Notor:* 551
Jean-Marie Le Pen, *Notor:* 636
Joseph McCarthy, *20th:* 2497, *Notor:* 669
Robert Jay Mathews, *Notor:* 712
Tom Metzger, *Notor:* 726
Titus Oates, *17th:* 692, *Notor:* 802
William Luther Pierce III, *Notor:* 838
Savitri Devi, *Notor:* 934
William Joseph Simmons, *Notor:* 957
Gerald L. K. Smith, *Notor:* 973
Valerie Solanas, *Notor:* 982
Roger Brooke Taney, *19th:* 2225, *Notor:* 1018
Benjamin Tillman, *Notor:* 1030
John Tyndall, *Notor:* 1050
Hendrik Frensch Verwoerd, *Notor:* 1064
Winifred Wagner, *Notor:* 1081
Randy Weaver, *Notor:* 1091

Radio, Film, and Television

Mother Angelica, *20th:* 90
Maya Angelou, *20th:* 97
Edwin H. Armstrong, *20th:* 127
Dorothy Arzner, *20th:* 141
Fred Astaire, *20th:* 155
Lucille Ball, *20th:* 212
Mikhail Baryshnikov, *20th:* 253
The Beatles, *20th:* 266
Ingmar Bergman, *20th:* 316
Ingrid Bergman, *20th:* 321
Humphrey Bogart, *20th:* 406
Marlon Brando, *20th:* 486
Luis Buñuel, *20th:* 578
Ray Charles, *20th:* 735
Jean Cocteau, *20th:* 794
Norman Collins, *20th:* 810
Bill Cosby, *20th:* 840
Jacques Cousteau, *20th:* 849
Sir Noël Coward, *20th:* 853
Bing Crosby, *20th:* 874
Salvador Dalí, *20th:* 904
Bette Davis, *20th:* 919
Lee de Forest, *20th:* 940
Cecil B. DeMille, *20th:* 960
Marlene Dietrich, *20th:* 997
Carl Theodor Dreyer, *20th:* 1037
Sergei Eisenstein, *20th:* 1129
Nora Ephron, *20th:* 1161
Federico Fellini, *20th:* 1231
Henry Fonda, *20th:* 1265
Bob Fosse, *20th:* 1291
Clark Gable, *20th:* 1368
Abel Gance, *20th:* 1382
Greta Garbo, *20th:* 1392
Erle Stanley Gardner, *20th:* 1403
Judy Garland, *20th:* 1409
Lillian Gish, *20th:* 1496
Jean-Luc Godard, *20th:* 1502
Joseph Goebbels, *20th:* 1513, *Notor:* 418
Samuel Goldwyn, *20th:* 1523
Glenn Gould, *20th:* 1553
Cary Grant, *20th:* 1570
D. W. Griffith, *20th:* 1593
Helen Hayes, *20th:* 1723
Rita Hayworth, *20th:* 1730
Sonja Henie, *20th:* 1759
Audrey Hepburn, *20th:* 1766
Katharine Hepburn, *20th:* 1769
Alfred Hitchcock, *20th:* 1825
Bob Hope, *20th:* 1870
Howard Hughes, *20th:* 1925
Buster Keaton, *20th:* 2090
Gene Kelly, *20th:* 2096
Stephen King, *20th:* 2151
Akira Kurosawa, *20th:* 2217
Fritz Lang, *20th:* 2253
Jerry Lewis, *20th:* 2357
George Lucas, *20th:* 2450
Auguste and Louis Lumière, *20th:* 2471
Louis B. Mayer, *20th:* 2662
Marilyn Monroe, *20th:* 2797
Toni Morrison, *20th:* 2834
Edward R. Murrow, *20th:* 2879
Sir Laurence Olivier, *20th:* 3039
Dolly Parton, *20th:* 3127
Gregory Peck, *20th:* 3181
Edith Piaf, *20th:* 3228
Mary Pickford, *20th:* 3244
Sidney Poitier, *20th:* 3296
Aleksandr Stepanovich Popov, *19th:* 1824
Cole Porter, *20th:* 3308
Elvis Presley, *20th:* 3330
Satyajit Ray, *20th:* 3394
Ronald Reagan, *20th:* 3400

First Baron Reith of Stonehaven, *20th:* 3410
Jean Renoir, *20th:* 3420
Leni Riefenstahl, *20th:* 3451
Jerome Robbins, *20th:* 3459
Will Rogers, *20th:* 3491
Charles M. Schulz, *20th:* 3672
Martin Scorsese, *20th:* 3681
Peter Sellers, *20th:* 3695
Mack Sennett, *20th:* 3706
Fulton J. Sheen, *20th:* 3722
Frank Sinatra, *20th:* 3747
Steven Spielberg, *20th:* 3811
James Stewart, *20th:* 3860
Barbra Streisand, *20th:* 3892
Dame Elizabeth Taylor, *20th:* 3953
Shirley Temple, *20th:* 3973
Spencer Tracy, *20th:* 4066
François Truffaut, *20th:* 4080
Ted Turner, *20th:* 4118
Luchino Visconti, *20th:* 4166
Jack Warner, *20th:* 4230
John Wayne, *20th:* 1370
Orson Welles, *20th:* 4283
Mae West, *20th:* 4297
Sir George Hubert Wilkins, *20th:* 4339
Oprah Winfrey, *20th:* 4372
Darryl F. Zanuck, *20th:* 4445

RELIGION AND THEOLOGY. ***See also*** **CHURCH GOVERNMENT AND REFORM; PHILOSOPHY**

Aaron, *Anc:* 1
ʿAbbās the Great, *17th:* 4
ʿAbd al-Raḥmān III al-Nāṣir, *MA:* 9
Peter Abelard, *MA:* 13
Ralph Abernathy, *20th:* 11
Abraham, *Anc:* 4
Isaac ben Judah Abravanel, *Ren:* 1
Abū Ḥanīfah, *MA:* 18
Barbe Acarie, *Ren:* 3
José de Acosta, *Ren:* 5
Adrian IV, *MA:* 27
Adrian VI, *Ren:* 7
Afonso I (c. 1455-1543), *Ren:* 9
Maria Gaetana Agnesi, *18th:* 24
Aḥmad ibn Ḥanbal, *MA:* 36
Sir Sayyid Ahmad Khan, *19th:* 35
Akbar (1542-1605), *Ren:* 15
Akhenaton, *Anc:* 26
Akiba ben Joseph, *Anc:* 29
Saint Albertus Magnus, *MA:* 42
Alcuin, *MA:* 49
Alexander III, *MA:* 56
Alexander VI, *Ren:* 27, *Notor:* 14
Alexander VII, *17th:* 9
Alexis, *17th:* 11
Saint Ambrose, *Anc:* 42
Amenhotep III, *Anc:* 45
Ānanda, *Anc:* 49
Lancelot Andrewes, *17th:* 14
Saint Angela Merici, *Ren:* 44
Blessed Angela of Foligno, *MA:* 81
Mother Angelica, *20th:* 90
Anna, Princess of the Byzantine Empire, *MA:* 86
Saint Anselm, *MA:* 92
Saint Anthony, *Anc:* 60
Saint Anthony of Padua, *MA:* 95
Marshall Applewhite, *Notor:* 28
Jacobus Arminius, *Ren:* 59
Angélique Arnauld, *17th:* 20
Arnold of Villanova, *MA:* 98
Asanga, *Anc:* 111
Francis Asbury, *18th:* 62
al-Ashʿarī, *MA:* 111
Anne Askew, *Ren:* 62
Aśoka, *Anc:* 124
Aśvaghosa, *Anc:* 130
Saint Athanasius of Alexandria, *Anc:* 132
Saint Augustine, *Anc:* 142
Sri Aurobindo, *20th:* 177
Averroës, *MA:* 118
Avvakum Petrovich, *17th:* 26
Baʿal Shem Tov, *18th:* 68
The Bāb, *19th:* 105
Isaac Backus, *18th:* 75
Roger Bacon, *MA:* 127
Leo Baeck, *20th:* 186
Bahāʾullāh, *19th:* 117
Jim Bakker, *Notor:* 50
John Ball, *MA:* 130
Barabbas, *Notor:* 55
Anna Barbauld, *18th:* 87
Karl Barth, *20th:* 243
Bathsheba, *Anc:* 155
Richard Baxter, *17th:* 32
Baybars I, *MA:* 139
Pierre Bayle, *17th:* 36
Beatrice of Nazareth, *MA:* 144
Saint Thomas Becket, *MA:* 147
Saint Bede the Venerable, *MA:* 150
Henry Ward Beecher, *19th:* 172
Muḥammad Bello, *19th:* 186
Benedict XIV, *18th:* 102
Saint Benedict of Nursia, *MA:* 153
Benjamin of Tudela, *MA:* 157
David Berg, *Notor:* 87
George Berkeley, *18th:* 111
Saint Bernard of Clairvaux, *MA:* 160
Annie Besant, *19th:* 211
John Biddle, *17th:* 53
Bodhidharma, *Anc:* 160
Boethius, *MA:* 173
Jakob Böhme, *17th:* 59
Saint Bonaventure, *MA:* 180
Dietrich Bonhoeffer, *20th:* 418
Saint Boniface, *MA:* 183
Boniface VIII, *MA:* 186, *Notor:* 115
William Booth, *19th:* 274
Boris I of Bulgaria, *MA:* 189
Jacques-Bénigne Bossuet, *17th:* 70
Saint Marguerite Bourgeoys, *17th:* 75
Saint Brigit, *MA:* 198
Olympia Brown, *19th:* 323
Emil Brunner, *20th:* 547
William Jennings Bryan, *20th:* 550
Martin Buber, *20th:* 554
Martin Bucer, *Ren:* 142
George Buchanan, *Ren:* 146
Buddha, *Anc:* 169
Rudolf Bultmann, *20th:* 572
John Bunyan, *17th:* 100
Thomas Burnet, *17th:* 106
Robert Burton, *17th:* 108
Joseph Butler, *18th:* 187
John Calvin, *Ren:* 163
Richard Cameron, *17th:* 121
Tommaso Campanella, *17th:* 124

Alexander Campbell, *19th:* 399
William Carey, *19th:* 409
Giovanni da Pian del Carpini, *MA:* 226
Charles Carroll, *18th:* 205
Catherine of Aragon, *Ren:* 187
Saint Catherine of Genoa, *Ren:* 191
Saint Catherine of Siena, *MA:* 236
William Ellery Channing, *19th:* 464
Charlemagne, *MA:* 242
Charles V, *Ren:* 220
G. K. Chesterton, *20th:* 744
Christina of Markyate, *MA:* 270
Saint Christopher, *Anc:* 205
Saint John Chrysostom, *Anc:* 208
Saint Clare of Assisi, *MA:* 284
Clement I, *Anc:* 223
Clement VII, *Ren:* 227, *Notor:* 212
Jacques Clément, *Notor:* 214
Saint Clotilda, *MA:* 287
Clovis, *MA:* 290
Samuel Taylor Coleridge, *19th:* 529
John Colet, *Ren:* 232
Vittoria Colonna, *Ren:* 235
Auguste Comte, *19th:* 536
Constantine the Great, *Anc:* 239
John Cotton, *17th:* 196
Miles Coverdale, *Ren:* 255
Thomas Cranmer, *Ren:* 266
Thomas Cromwell, *Ren:* 269
Samuel Ajayi Crowther, *19th:* 574
Saint Cyril, *MA:* 294
Dalai Lama, *20th:* 902
John Davenport, *17th:* 218
David, *Anc:* 255
Lady Eleanor Davies, *17th:* 220
Dorothy Day, *20th:* 925
Deborah, *Anc:* 258
Alcide De Gasperi, *20th:* 944
Saint Denis, *Anc:* 268
Diane de Poitiers, *Ren:* 283
Dionysius Exiguus, *MA:* 313
William Dodd, *Notor:* 286
Saint Dominic, *MA:* 316
John Duns Scotus, *MA:* 329
Mary Baker Eddy, *19th:* 723
Edward VI, *Ren:* 303
Jonathan Edwards, *18th:* 314
Mircea Eliade, *20th:* 1136
Elijah ben Solomon, *18th:* 318
John Eliot, *17th:* 247
Saint Elizabeth of Hungary, *MA:* 359
Shūsaku Endō, *20th:* 1155
Enheduanna, *Anc:* 298
Desiderius Erasmus, *Ren:* 314
Werner Erhard, *Notor:* 329
Rudolf Christoph Eucken, *20th:* 1185
Eusebius of Caesarea, *Anc:* 330
Jan van and Hubert van Eyck, *MA:* 365
Ezana, *Anc:* 333
Ezekiel, *Anc:* 335
Ezra, *Anc:* 338
David and Johannes Fabricius, *17th:* 259
Fakhr al-Dīn al-Rāzī, *MA:* 369
Jerry Falwell, *20th:* 1209
Wallace Dodd Fard, *Notor:* 344
Louis Farrakhan, *20th:* 1217
Father Divine, *Notor:* 346
Faxian, *Anc:* 345
François de Salignac de La Mothe-Fénelon, *17th:* 265
Nicholas Ferrar, *17th:* 274
Marsilio Ficino, *Ren:* 332
Saint John Fisher, *Ren:* 335
André-Hercule de Fleury, *18th:* 361
Robert Fludd, *17th:* 280
Francesco Forgione, *20th:* 1286
George Fox, *17th:* 283
Saint Francis of Assisi, *MA:* 378
Frederick V, *17th:* 293
Mahatma Gandhi, *20th:* 1388
Stephen Gardiner, *Ren:* 368
Gilbert Gauthe, *Notor:* 397
Gershom ben Judah, *MA:* 408
al-Ghazzālī, *MA:* 415
James Gibbons, *19th:* 910
Orlando Gibbons, *17th:* 309
Étienne Gilson, *20th:* 1488
Vincenzo Gioberti, *19th:* 921
Gośāla Maskarīputra, *Anc:* 355
Baltasar Gracián y Morales, *17th:* 316
Billy Graham, *20th:* 1557
Henry Grattan, *18th:* 440
El Greco, *Ren:* 390
Gregory VII, *MA:* 433
Gregory IX, *MA:* 436
Gregory XIII, *Ren:* 393
Gregory of Nazianzus, *Anc:* 361
Gregory of Nyssa, *Anc:* 363
Gregory of Tours, *MA:* 426
Gregory the Great, *MA:* 430
Edmund Grindal, *Ren:* 402
Gustav I Vasa, *Ren:* 415
Madame Guyon, *17th:* 339
Hakuin, *18th:* 450
al-Ḥallāj, *MA:* 454
Adolf von Harnack, *20th:* 1681
Barbara Harris, *20th:* 1689
Harṣa, *MA:* 460
al-Ḥasan al-Baṣrī, *MA:* 471
Saint Helena, *Anc:* 391
Claude-Adrien Helvétius, *18th:* 479
Henry IV (1553-1610; King of France), *Ren:* 429
Henry VIII, *Ren:* 441
Prince Henry the Navigator, *MA:* 477
George Herbert, *17th:* 366
Herod Antipas, *Notor:* 458
Herod the Great, *Anc:* 403, *Notor:* 459
Miguel Hidalgo y Costilla, *19th:* 1094
Saint Hilda of Whitby, *MA:* 509
Hildegard von Bingen, *MA:* 512
Hippolytus of Rome, *Anc:* 423
Paul-Henri-Dietrich d'Holbach, *18th:* 501
Richard Hooker, *Ren:* 457
Thomas Hooker, *17th:* 386
Hosokawa Gracia, *Ren:* 459
Hrosvitha, *MA:* 516
L. Ron Hubbard, *20th:* 1909, *Notor:* 495
Balthasar Hubmaier, *Ren:* 472
Jan Hus, *MA:* 522
Anne Hutchinson, *17th:* 394
Thomas Henry Huxley, *19th:* 1161

Ibn al-ʿArabī, *MA:* 526
Ibn Gabirol, *MA:* 532
Ignatius of Antioch, *Anc:* 437
Saint Ignatius of Loyola, *Ren:* 482
Innocent III, *MA:* 541
Innocent IV, *MA:* 545
Innocent XI, *17th:* 405
Saint Irenaeus, *Anc:* 442
Saint Irene, *MA:* 548
Isaiah, *Anc:* 446
Saint Isidore of Seville, *MA:* 555
al-Jāḥiẓ, *MA:* 568
Cornelius Otto Jansen, *17th:* 419
Jeremiah, *Anc:* 453
Saint Jerome, *Anc:* 456
Jesus, *Anc:* 458
Jezebel, *Notor:* 527
Francisco Jiménez de Cisneros, *Ren:* 503
Mohammed Ali Jinnah, *20th:* 2002
Joachim of Fiore, *MA:* 575
Joan of Arc, *MA:* 578
Saint Isaac Jogues, *17th:* 423
Johanan ben Zakkai, *Anc:* 468
John III, *Ren:* 513
John XXIII, *20th:* 2017
John of Damascus, *MA:* 587
Saint John of the Cross, *Ren:* 507
John Paul II, *20th:* 2020
John the Apostle, *Anc:* 471
Saint John the Baptist, *Anc:* 474
Jim Jones, *Notor:* 537
Judah ha-Levi, *MA:* 591
Judas Iscariot, *Notor:* 544
Julian of Norwich, *MA:* 595
Julius II, *Ren:* 518
Justinian I, *MA:* 598
Kanishka, *Anc:* 499
Joseph ben Ephraim Karo, *Ren:* 524
Margery Kempe, *MA:* 607
Khadīja, *MA:* 610
Ayatollah Khomeini, *20th:* 2123, *Notor:* 571
Søren Kierkegaard, *19th:* 1278
Martin Luther King, Jr., *20th:* 2147
Eusebio Francisco Kino, *17th:* 467
John Knox, *Ren:* 528
Kōbō Daishi, *MA:* 620
Jan Komenský, *17th:* 469
David Koresh, *Notor:* 589
Ignacy Krasicki, *18th:* 567
Bartolomé de Las Casas, *Ren:* 537
Saint László I, *MA:* 637
Hugh Latimer, *Ren:* 543
William Laud, *17th:* 495
François Laval, *17th:* 498
Ann Lee, *18th:* 591
Jacques Lefèvre d'Étaples, *Ren:* 548
Leo IX, *MA:* 644
Leo X, *Ren:* 557, *Notor:* 630
Leo XIII, *19th:* 1342
Levi ben Gershom, *MA:* 650
Bernard Lewis, *20th:* 2351
C. S. Lewis, *20th:* 2353
David Livingstone, *19th:* 1400
Louis IX, *MA:* 666
Saint Ludmilla, *MA:* 670
Raymond Lull, *MA:* 673
Jeffrey Lundgren, *Notor:* 664
Isaac ben Solomon Luria, *Ren:* 579
Martin Luther, *Ren:* 582
Muḥammad ibn ʿAbd al-Karīmal-Maghīlī, *Ren:* 595
The Mahdi, *19th:* 1473
Moses Maimonides, *MA:* 686
Madame de Maintenon, *17th:* 572
Sieur de Maisonneuve, *17th:* 574
Malcolm X, *20th:* 2570
Manasseh ben Israel, *17th:* 582
Henry Edward Manning, *19th:* 1489
Daniel Mannix, *19th:* 1492
Charles Manson, *Notor:* 689
Gabriel Marcel, *20th:* 2609
Maria Celeste, *17th:* 593
Marie de l'Incarnation, *17th:* 595
Jacques Maritain, *20th:* 2624
Jacques Marquette, *17th:* 603
Mary, *Anc:* 539
Mary I, *Ren:* 639
Mary of Guise, *Ren:* 633
Mary, Queen of Scots, *Ren:* 627
Cotton Mather, *18th:* 667
Increase Mather, *18th:* 671
François Mauriac, *20th:* 2657
Frederick Denison Maurice, *19th:* 1518
Maximilian II, *Ren:* 650
Jules Mazarin, *17th:* 620
Aimee Semple McPherson, *Notor:* 679
Mechthild von Magdeburg, *MA:* 708
Mehmed II, *MA:* 711, *Ren:* 659
Philipp Melanchthon, *Ren:* 664
Melisende, *MA:* 715
Menander (c 210-c. 135 B.C.E.; Greco-Bactrian king), *Anc:* 550
Moses Mendelssohn, *18th:* 675
Bernardino de Mendoza, *Ren:* 668
Ana de Mendoza y de la Cerda, *Ren:* 670
Menno Simons, *Ren:* 675
Marin Mersenne, *17th:* 628
Thomas Merton, *20th:* 2713
Saint Methodius, *MA:* 294
Mohammed I Askia, *Ren:* 686
Dwight L. Moody, *19th:* 1596
Sun Myung Moon, *20th:* 2811, *Notor:* 749
Hannah More, *18th:* 702
Sir Thomas More, *Ren:* 697
Philippe de Mornay, *Ren:* 703
Moses, *Anc:* 572
Moses de León, *MA:* 730
John R. Mott, *20th:* 2849
Mozi, *Anc:* 576
Lodowick Muggleton, *17th:* 665
Muḥammad, *MA:* 733
Elijah Muhammad, *Notor:* 763
Naḥmanides, *MA:* 747
Nānak, *Ren:* 707
John Napier, *Ren:* 710
Nebuchadnezzar II, *Anc:* 582
Alexander Neckam, *MA:* 750
Nefertiti, *Anc:* 587
Saint Philip Neri, *Ren:* 717
Bonnie Nettles, *Notor:* 779
John Henry Newman, *19th:* 1663
Nezahualcóyotl, *Ren:* 720
Nichiren, *MA:* 758
Nicholas of Autrecourt, *MA:* 761
Nicholas of Cusa, *Ren:* 724

Nicholas the Great, *MA:* 764
Reinhold Niebuhr, *20th:* 2962
Martin Niemöller, *20th:* 2971
Nikon, *17th:* 683
Kitarō Nishida, *20th:* 2981
Max Nordau, *20th:* 2992
Titus Oates, *17th:* 692, *Notor:* 802
William of Ockham, *MA:* 778
Saint Olaf, *MA:* 785
Olaf I, *MA:* 789
Saint Olga, *MA:* 792
Origen, *Anc:* 599
Johann Pachelbel, *17th:* 708
Thomas Paine, *18th:* 759
Sophia Palaeologus, *Ren:* 749
William Paley, *18th:* 763
Matthew Parker, *Ren:* 761
Blaise Pascal, *17th:* 713
Saint Patrick, *MA:* 811
Paul III, *Ren:* 767
Paul V, *17th:* 719
Paul VI, *20th:* 3148
Saint Paul, *Anc:* 611
John Pecham, *MA:* 817
William Penn, *17th:* 724
Saint Peter, *Anc:* 624
Philip II (1527-1598; King of Spain), *Ren:* 778
Philip IV, *17th:* 738
Philip the Magnanimous, *Ren:* 775
Giovanni Pico della Mirandola, *Ren:* 782
Pontius Pilate, *Anc:* 643, *Notor:* 840
Elena Cornaro Piscopia, *17th:* 743
Pius II, *Ren:* 794
Pius V, *Ren:* 797
Pius VI, *18th:* 793
Pius IX, *19th:* 1802
Pius X, *20th:* 3272
Pius XI, *20th:* 3275
Pius XII, *20th:* 3278
Marguerite Porete, *MA:* 856
James Porter, *Notor:* 854
Joseph Priestley, *18th:* 811
Priscillian, *Anc:* 698
Michael Psellus, *MA:* 863
E. B. Pusey, *19th:* 1844
Rabanus Maurus, *MA:* 870
Rābiʿah al-ʿAdawiyah, *MA:* 873
Rāmānuja, *MA:* 876
Grigori Yefimovich Rasputin, *19th:* 1863, *Notor:* 885
Ratramnus, *MA:* 879
Walter Rauschenbusch, *20th:* 3382
John Ray, *17th:* 782
Rammohan Ray, *19th:* 1866
Raymond of Peñafort, *MA:* 881
Ernest Renan, *19th:* 1884
Matteo Ricci, *Ren:* 825
Cardinal de Richelieu, *17th:* 790
Nicholas Ridley, *Ren:* 833
Albrecht Ritschl, *19th:* 1918
Oscar Romero, *20th:* 3499
Saint Rose of Lima, *17th:* 796
Josiah Royce, *20th:* 3550
Jalāl al-Dīn Rūmī, *MA:* 908
Saladin, *MA:* 918
Salome, *Notor:* 932
Samuel, *Anc:* 747
Śaṅkara, *MA:* 924
Girolamo Savonarola, *Ren:* 850
Wilhelm Schickard, *17th:* 818
Friedrich Schleiermacher, *19th:* 2013
Anna Maria van Schurman, *17th:* 823
Heinrich Schütz, *17th:* 825
Albert Schweitzer, *20th:* 3678
Sergius I, *MA:* 933
Saint Sergius I, *MA:* 936
Junípero Serra, *18th:* 891
Michael Servetus, *Ren:* 861
Samuel Sewall, *18th:* 893
Jane Seymour, *Ren:* 868
Shabbetai Tzevi, *17th:* 835
Granville Sharp, *18th:* 899
Fulton J. Sheen, *20th:* 3722
Shōtoku Taishi, *MA:* 940
Sīdī al-Mukhṭār al-Kuntī, *18th:* 914
Siger of Brabant, *MA:* 942
Saint Simeon Stylites, *Anc:* 789
Saint Siricius, *Anc:* 796
Sixtus IV, *Ren:* 893
Sixtus V, *Ren:* 895
Joseph Smith, *19th:* 2117
Nathan Söderblom, *20th:* 3781
Solomon, *Anc:* 803
First Duke of Somerset, *Ren:* 898
Sorghaghtani Beki, *MA:* 954
Baruch Spinoza, *17th:* 871
Edith Stein, *20th:* 3840
Nicolaus Steno, *17th:* 881
Stephen I, *MA:* 964
Saint Stephen, *Anc:* 821
Suger, *MA:* 971
Billy Sunday, *20th:* 3916
Emanuel Swedenborg, *18th:* 961
Sylvester II, *MA:* 983
al-Ṭabarī, *MA:* 988
Táhirih, *19th:* 2214
Tarquins, *Anc:* 846
Pierre Teilhard de Chardin, *20th:* 3963
Kateri Tekakwitha, *17th:* 908
Mother Teresa, *20th:* 3975
Saint Teresa of Ávila, *Ren:* 928
Tertullian, *Anc:* 853
Theodora, *MA:* 1008, *Notor:* 1028
Theodore of Mopsuestia, *Anc:* 862
Theodoret of Cyrrhus, *Anc:* 865
Theoleptus of Philadelphia, *MA:* 1016
Theophanes the Confessor, *MA:* 1020
Saint Thomas, *Anc:* 878
Thomas à Kempis, *MA:* 1022
Thomas Aquinas, *MA:* 1027
Paul Tillich, *20th:* 4027
Tirso de Molina, *17th:* 913
Dēvānampiya Tissa, *Anc:* 898
Tiy, *Anc:* 901
Tomás de Torquemada, *Ren:* 939, *Notor:* 1038
Ernst Troeltsch, *20th:* 4069
Desmond Tutu, *20th:* 4121
William Tyndale, *Ren:* 949
Ulfilas, *Anc:* 911
ʿUmar I, *MA:* 1037
Urban II, *MA:* 1043
Urban VI, *Notor:* 1053
Urban VIII, *17th:* 936
James Ussher, *17th:* 938
ʿUthman dan Fodio, *19th:* 2342
Vaḥīd Bihbahānī, *18th:* 1000
Valentinus, *Anc:* 918
Lorenzo Valla, *MA:* 1049

Vardhamāna, *Anc:* 924
Vasily III, *Ren:* 957
Vattagamani, *Anc:* 933
Jean de Venette, *MA:* 1053
Iswar Chandra Vidyasagar, *19th:* 2363
António Vieira, *17th:* 959
Saint Vincent de Paul, *17th:* 962
Saint Vincent of Lérins, *Anc:* 947
Francisco de Vitoria, *Ren:* 978
Vivekananda, *19th:* 2368
Vladimir I, *MA:* 1068
Joachim Wach, *20th:* 4177
Muḥammad ibn ʿAbd al-Wahhāb, *18th:* 1030
Shāh Walī Allāh, *18th:* 1032
Mary Ward, *17th:* 974
Max Weber, *20th:* 4258
Charles Wesley, *18th:* 1061
John Wesley, *18th:* 1064
Rogier van der Weyden, *MA:* 1092
George Whitefield, *18th:* 1073
Elie Wiesel, *20th:* 4324
William of Auvergne, *MA:* 1097
William of Auxerre, *MA:* 1101
William of Saint-Amour, *MA:* 1110
William of Saint-Thierry, *MA:* 1114
Roger Williams, *17th:* 982
Isaac Mayer Wise, *19th:* 2453
Stephen Samuel Wise, *20th:* 4376
John Witherspoon, *18th:* 1098
Władysław II Jagiełło and Jadwiga, *MA:* 1120
Cardinal Thomas Wolsey, *Ren:* 996
Wu Hou, *MA:* 1127
John Wyclif, *MA:* 1130
Saint Francis Xavier, *Ren:* 1000
Xenophanes, *Anc:* 965
Xuanzang, *MA:* 1136
Zara Yaqob, *Ren:* 1006
Brigham Young, *19th:* 2474
Zhuangzi, *Anc:* 989
Count von Zinzendorf, *18th:* 1119
Jan Žižka, *MA:* 1162
Zoroaster, *Anc:* 992
Huldrych Zwingli, *Ren:* 1010

SCHOLARSHIP. ***See also*** **EDUCATION; LITERATURE; PHILOSOPHY**

José de Acosta, *Ren:* 5
Leon Battista Alberti, *Ren:* 18
Saint Albertus Magnus, *MA:* 42
Hannah Arendt, *20th:* 118
Angélique Arnauld, *17th:* 20
Leo Baeck, *20th:* 186
Mikhail Bakhtin, *20th:* 190
Ban Zhao, *Anc:* 152
Karl Barth, *20th:* 243
Roland Barthes, *20th:* 246
Béla Bartók, *20th:* 250
Johann Joachim Becher, *17th:* 39
Walter Benjamin, *20th:* 306
Sir William Blackstone, *18th:* 118
Franz Boas, *20th:* 400
Nicolas Boileau-Despréaux, *17th:* 63
Fernand Braudel, *20th:* 497
Percy Williams Bridgman, *20th:* 526
Sir Thomas Browne, *17th:* 94
Emil Brunner, *20th:* 547
George Buchanan, *Ren:* 146
Nikolay Ivanovich Bukharin, *20th:* 566
Charles Burney, *18th:* 177
Fernando Henrique Cardoso, *20th:* 651
Benjamin N. Cardozo, *20th:* 653
William Caxton, *Ren:* 196
Miles Coverdale, *Ren:* 255
Benedetto Croce, *20th:* 869
Dai Zhen, *18th:* 287
Lucy S. Dawidowicz, *20th:* 922
Jacques Derrida, *20th:* 974
Denis Diderot, *18th:* 307
John Dowland, *Ren:* 289
Mircea Eliade, *20th:* 1136
Elijah ben Solomon, *18th:* 318
T. S. Eliot, *20th:* 1139
David and Johannes Fabricius, *17th:* 259
Adam Ferguson, *18th:* 338
Marsilio Ficino, *Ren:* 332
Abraham Flexner, *20th:* 1256
Felix Frankfurter, *20th:* 1308
Sir James George Frazer, *20th:* 1319
Leo Frobenius, *20th:* 1341
Roger Fry, *20th:* 1351
Pierre Gassendi, *17th:* 304
Gershom ben Judah, *MA:* 408
Conrad Gesner, *Ren:* 375
Edward Gibbon, *18th:* 415
Étienne Gilson, *20th:* 1488
Charlotte Guillard, *Ren:* 413
Guo Moruo, *20th:* 1619
Hakuin, *18th:* 450
Adolf von Harnack, *20th:* 1681
Johannes and Elisabetha Hevelius, *17th:* 371
William Hogarth, *18th:* 497
Oliver Wendell Holmes, Jr., *20th:* 1856
Honda Toshiaki, *18th:* 504
François Hotman, *Ren:* 461
Balthasar Hubmaier, *Ren:* 472
Saint Jerome, *Anc:* 456
Samuel Johnson, *18th:* 535
Flavius Josephus, *Anc:* 477, *Notor:* 541
Engelbert Kämpfer, *17th:* 445
Joseph ben Ephraim Karo, *Ren:* 524
Kâtib Çelebî, *17th:* 454
Susanne K. Langer, *20th:* 2263
Harold J. Laski, *20th:* 2269
Timothy Leary, *Notor:* 619
Jacques Lefèvre d'Étaples, *Ren:* 548
Bernard Lewis, *20th:* 2351
Manasseh ben Israel, *17th:* 582
Aldus Manutius, *Ren:* 608
Marguerite de Navarre, *Ren:* 617
Cotton Mather, *18th:* 667
Margaret Mead, *20th:* 2668
Philipp Melanchthon, *Ren:* 664
Maurice Merleau-Ponty, *20th:* 2710
Michel Eyquem de Montaigne, *Ren:* 689
Hans Joachim Morgenthau, *20th:* 2828
Thomas Morley, *Ren:* 701
Gaetano Mosca, *20th:* 2838
Robert Nozick, *20th:* 2999

Ogyū Sorai, *18th:* 746
Origen, *Anc:* 599
Nicolas-Claude Fabri de Peiresc, *17th:* 722
Henri Pirenne, *20th:* 3269
Tomé Pires, *Ren:* 792
Elena Cornaro Piscopia, *17th:* 743
Alexander Pope, *18th:* 805
Porphyry, *Anc:* 687
Joseph Priestley, *18th:* 811
Rabanus Maurus, *MA:* 870
Peter Ramus, *Ren:* 817
Carl Sandburg, *20th:* 3619
Joseph Justus Scaliger, *Ren:* 855
Wilhelm Schickard, *17th:* 818
Anna Maria van Schurman, *17th:* 823
Sīdī al-Mukhṭār al-Kuntī, *18th:* 914
Sima Xiangru, *Anc:* 785
William Stukeley, *18th:* 952
Su Dongpo, *MA:* 968
Norman Thomas, *20th:* 4002
J. R. R. Tolkien, *20th:* 4038
Barbara W. Tuchman, *20th:* 4104
Frederick Jackson Turner, *20th:* 4115
Miguel de Unamuno y Jugo, *20th:* 4128
Marcus Terentius Varro, *Anc:* 927
Marcus Verrius Flaccus, *Anc:* 941
Vincent of Beauvais, *MA:* 1063
Beatrice and Sidney Webb, *20th:* 4253

SCIENCE. ***See also*** **AGRICULTURE; ARCHAEOLOGY; ASTRONOMY; AVIATION AND SPACE EXPLORATION; BIOLOGY; CHEMISTRY; COMPUTER SCIENCE; EARTH SCIENCES; ENGINEERING; GENETICS; GEOGRAPHY; INVENTION AND TECHNOLOGY; MATHEMATICS; MEDICINE; NATURAL HISTORY; PHYSICS; PHYSIOLOGY; PSYCHOLOGY AND PSYCHIATRY; SCHOLARSHIP**
José de Acosta, *Ren:* 5
Saint Albertus Magnus, *MA:* 42
Anaxagoras, *Anc:* 52
Anaximenes, *Anc:* 58
Archimedes, *Anc:* 80
Aristotle, *Anc:* 94
Francis Bacon, *Ren:* 72
Roger Bacon, *MA:* 127
al-Bīrūnī, *MA:* 163
Democritus, *Anc:* 261
Empedocles, *Anc:* 295
William Gilbert, *Ren:* 381
Pliny the Elder, *Anc:* 665
Thales of Miletus, *Anc:* 856

SOCIAL REFORM. ***See also*** **CIVIL RIGHTS; CONSERVATION AND ENVIRONMENTALISM; WOMEN'S RIGHTS**
Jane Addams, *20th:* 22
Halide Edib Adıvar, *20th:* 29
Felix Adler, *19th:* 26
Maria Gaetana Agnesi, *18th:* 24
John Peter Altgeld, *19th:* 57
Saint Angela Merici, *Ren:* 44
Sir Norman Angell, *20th:* 92
Susan B. Anthony, *19th:* 65
Corazon Aquino, *20th:* 107
Oscar Arias Sánchez, *20th:* 121
Thomas Arnold, *19th:* 76
Nancy Astor, *20th:* 158
Aung San Suu Kyi, *20th:* 174
Mikhail Bakunin, *19th:* 119
Emily Greene Balch, *20th:* 197
Arthur Balfour, *20th:* 208
John Ball, *MA:* 130
Klaus Barbie, *Notor:* 57
Clara Barton, *19th:* 145
Richard Baxter, *17th:* 32
Simone de Beauvoir, *20th:* 271
Cesare Beccaria, *18th:* 100
Jeremy Bentham, *18th:* 104
Annie Besant, *19th:* 211
Mary McLeod Bethune, *20th:* 345
Aneurin Bevan, *20th:* 349
Ernest Bevin, *20th:* 356
Benazir Bhutto, *20th:* 365
Zulfikar Ali Bhutto, *20th:* 368
Léon Blum, *20th:* 396
Margaret Bondfield, *20th:* 414
William Booth, *19th:* 274
Louis Braille, *19th:* 299
Louis D. Brandeis, *20th:* 482
Willy Brandt, *20th:* 490
William J. Brennan, *20th:* 507
John Brown, *19th:* 319
Molly Brown, *20th:* 542
Pearl S. Buck, *20th:* 557
Ralph Bunche, *20th:* 574
Sir Thomas Fowell Buxton, *19th:* 376
Frances Xavier Cabrini, *19th:* 383
Carrie Chapman Catt, *20th:* 701
Edwin Chadwick, *19th:* 456
Neville Chamberlain, *20th:* 720
César Chávez, *20th:* 738
Lydia Maria Child, *19th:* 482
Shirley Chisholm, *20th:* 753
Noam Chomsky, *20th:* 757
Hillary Rodham Clinton, *20th:* 788
Michael Collins, *20th:* 807
Marquis de Condorcet, *18th:* 267
Learie Constantine, *20th:* 829
Paul Cuffe, *19th:* 576
George Nathaniel Curzon, *20th:* 894
Dalai Lama, *20th:* 902
Georges Danton, *18th:* 289
Dorothy Day, *20th:* 925
Eugene V. Debs, *20th:* 932
John Dewey, *20th:* 982
Diana, Princess of Wales, *20th:* 989
Dorothea Dix, *19th:* 671
Bob Dole, *20th:* 1014
Helen Gahagan Douglas, *20th:* 1026
Frederick Douglass, *19th:* 684
W. E. B. Du Bois, *20th:* 1046
Jean-Henri Dunant, *19th:* 699
Marian Wright Edelman, *20th:* 1096
Albert Einstein, *20th:* 1118
Saint Elizabeth of Hungary, *MA:* 359

Havelock Ellis, *20th:* 1148
Friedrich Engels, *19th:* 750
Olaudah Equiano, *18th:* 324
First Baron Erskine, *18th:* 326
Frantz Fanon, *20th:* 1212
Louis Farrakhan, *20th:* 1217
Dame Millicent Garrett Fawcett, *19th:* 766
Guy Fawkes, *Ren:* 324, *Notor:* 350
Francesco Forgione, *20th:* 1286
Charlotte Forten, *19th:* 796
Abby Kelley Foster, *19th:* 799
Charles Fourier, *19th:* 805
Betty Friedan, *20th:* 1329
Elizabeth Fry, *19th:* 839
Margaret Fuller, *19th:* 841
John Kenneth Galbraith, *20th:* 1374
Indira Gandhi, *20th:* 1385
Mahatma Gandhi, *20th:* 1388
William Lloyd Garrison, *19th:* 874
Henry George, *19th:* 894
William Godwin, *18th:* 424
Emma Goldman, *20th:* 1519, *Notor:* 424
Samuel Gompers, *19th:* 943
Mikhail Gorbachev, *20th:* 1530
Al Gore, *20th:* 1538
Billy Graham, *20th:* 1557
Antonio Gramsci, *20th:* 1566
Henry Grattan, *18th:* 440
Horace Greeley, *19th:* 966
Sarah and Angelina Grimké, *19th:* 988
Che Guevara, *20th:* 1609, *Notor:* 436
Haile Selassie I, *20th:* 1639
Fannie Lou Hamer, *20th:* 1651
Dag Hammarskjöld, *20th:* 1653
Keir Hardie, *19th:* 1025
Barbara Harris, *20th:* 1689
Kenau Hasselaer, *Ren:* 526
Václav Havel, *20th:* 1707
Patty Hearst, *Notor:* 454
Audrey Hepburn, *20th:* 1766
Aileen Clarke Hernandez, *20th:* 1773
Édouard Herriot, *20th:* 1777
Aleksandr Herzen, *19th:* 1085
Theodor Herzl, *19th:* 1088
Thomas Wentworth Higginson, *19th:* 1097
Hildegard von Bingen, *MA:* 512
Octavia Hill, *19th:* 1103
Dorothy Crowfoot Hodgkin, *20th:* 1849
Abbie Hoffman, *Notor:* 483
Harry Hopkins, *20th:* 1872
François Hotman, *Ren:* 461
Dolores Huerta, *20th:* 1915
Hubert H. Humphrey, *20th:* 1938
Helen Hunt Jackson, *19th:* 1193
Jesse Jackson, *20th:* 1978
Mother Jones, *20th:* 2039
Christine Jorgensen, *20th:* 2053
Juan Carlos I, *20th:* 2060
Helen Keller, *20th:* 2093
Kim Dae Jung, *20th:* 2136
Martin Luther King, Jr., *20th:* 2147
William Lyon Mackenzie King, *20th:* 2155
Henri-Marie La Fontaine, *20th:* 2231
Ann Landers, *20th:* 2247
Lyndon H. LaRouche, Jr., *Notor:* 606
Bartolomé de Las Casas, *Ren:* 537
Julia C. Lathrop, *20th:* 2272
Emma Lazarus, *19th:* 1331
John L. Lewis, *20th:* 2360
Sinclair Lewis, *20th:* 2363
John Lilburne, *17th:* 534
Huey Long, *20th:* 2424, *Notor:* 649
Catharine A. MacKinnon, *20th:* 2522
Datuk Seri Mahathir bin Mohamad, *20th:* 2551
Manasseh ben Israel, *17th:* 582
Nelson Mandela, *20th:* 2583
Wilma Mankiller, *20th:* 2591
Henry Edward Manning, *19th:* 1489
Jean-Paul Marat, *18th:* 348, *Notor:* 696
Marguerite de Navarre, *Ren:* 617
Clorinda Matto de Turner, *19th:* 1512
Maximilian I, *Ren:* 646
George Meany, *20th:* 2672
Rigoberta Menchú, *20th:* 2686
Dorothy Reed Mendenhall, *20th:* 2695
Thomas Merton, *20th:* 2713
Maria Montessori, *20th:* 2804
Hannah More, *18th:* 702
Lucretia Mott, *19th:* 1616
Yoweri Kaguta Museveni, *20th:* 2883
Gunnar Myrdal, *20th:* 2890
Ralph Nader, *20th:* 2897
Sir V. S. Naipaul, *20th:* 2903
Nanny, *18th:* 724
Carry Nation, *19th:* 1652
Huey Newton, *Notor:* 782
Reinhold Niebuhr, *20th:* 2962
Martin Niemöller, *20th:* 2971
Daniel O'Connell, *19th:* 1695
Tip O'Neill, *20th:* 3055
Daniel Ortega, *20th:* 3072
Arthur Orton, *Notor:* 806
Thomas Mott Osborne, *20th:* 3085
Robert Owen, *19th:* 1720
Vijaya Lakshmi Pandit, *20th:* 3099
Theodore Parker, *19th:* 1735
Rosa Parks, *20th:* 3119
Alan Paton, *20th:* 3138
Paul VI, *20th:* 3148
Linus Pauling, *20th:* 3155
Víctor Paz Estenssoro, *20th:* 3172
Frances Perkins, *20th:* 3198
Peter the Great, *18th:* 774
Wendell Phillips, *19th:* 1785
Dominique Pire, *20th:* 3264
Francis Place, *19th:* 1806
Marquise de Rambouillet, *17th:* 779
Mahadev Govind Ranade, *19th:* 1855
A. Philip Randolph, *20th:* 3369
Jeannette Rankin, *20th:* 3374
Walter Rauschenbusch, *20th:* 3382
Rammohan Ray, *19th:* 1866
Stenka Razin, *17th:* 784

Walter P. Reuther, *20th:* 3424
Reza Shah Pahlavi, *20th:* 2779, *Notor:* 742
Ann Richards, *20th:* 3434
Ellen Swallow Richards, *19th:* 1899
Cola di Rienzo, *MA:* 897
Paul Robeson, *20th:* 3462
Robespierre, *18th:* 844, *Notor:* 907
Mary Robinson (b. 1944), *20th:* 3474
George Lincoln Rockwell, *Notor:* 911
Oscar Romero, *20th:* 3499
Sir Joseph Rotblat, *20th:* 3536
Muriel Rukeyser, *20th:* 3556
Benjamin Rush, *18th:* 872
John Ruskin, *19th:* 1954
Bertrand Russell, *20th:* 3562
Nicola Sacco, *20th:* 3580, *Notor:* 924
Louis de Saint-Just, *18th:* 877
Henri de Saint-Simon, *19th:* 1975
Andrei Sakharov, *20th:* 3602
Margaret Sanger, *20th:* 3625
Jean-Paul Sartre, *20th:* 3638
Eisaku Satō, *20th:* 3645
Albert Schweitzer, *20th:* 3678
Dred Scott, *19th:* 2041
Samuel Sewall, *18th:* 893
Granville Sharp, *18th:* 899
Anna Howard Shaw, *19th:* 2084
Daniel Shays, *18th:* 902
Upton Sinclair, *20th:* 3750
Nathan Söderblom, *20th:* 3781
Aleksandr Solzhenitsyn, *20th:* 3783
Susan Sontag, *20th:* 3788
Georges Sorel, *20th:* 3792
Benjamin Spock, *20th:* 3814
Gloria Steinem, *20th:* 3852
Thaddeus Stevens, *19th:* 2171
Adlai E. Stevenson, *20th:* 3856
Lucy Stone, *19th:* 2177
Marie Stopes, *20th:* 3882
Harriet Beecher Stowe, *19th:* 2184
Barbra Streisand, *20th:* 3892
Anne Sullivan, *20th:* 3908
Charles Sumner, *19th:* 2201
Bertha von Suttner, *19th:* 2205
Jonathan Swift, *18th:* 964
Rabindranath Tagore, *20th:* 3933
Edward Teller, *20th:* 3968
Mother Teresa, *20th:* 3975
Norman Thomas, *20th:* 4002
Ahmed Sékou Touré, *20th:* 4053
Leon Trotsky, *20th:* 4072, *Notor:* 1040
Sojourner Truth, *19th:* 2306
Harriet Tubman, *19th:* 2312
William V. S. Tubman, *20th:* 4101
Tupac Amaru II, *18th:* 993
Nat Turner, *19th:* 2326
Desmond Tutu, *20th:* 4121
Wat Tyler, *MA:* 1033
Iswar Chandra Vidyasagar, *19th:* 2363
Pancho Villa, *20th:* 4160, *Notor:* 1069
Saint Vincent de Paul, *17th:* 962
Anastase Vonsiatsky, *Notor:* 1077
Winifred Wagner, *Notor:* 1081
Lillian D. Wald, *20th:* 4184
Lech Wałęsa, *20th:* 4191
Booker T. Washington, *19th:* 2390
Beatrice and Sidney Webb, *20th:* 4253
H. G. Wells, *20th:* 4287
Ida B. Wells-Barnett, *20th:* 4290
Phillis Wheatley, *18th:* 1070
George Whitefield, *18th:* 1073
Elie Wiesel, *20th:* 4324
Simon Wiesenthal, *20th:* 4328
William Wilberforce, *18th:* 1079
John Wilkes, *18th:* 1083
Frances Willard, *19th:* 2442
Gerrard Winstanley, *17th:* 988
Stephen Samuel Wise, *20th:* 4376
Mary Wollstonecraft, *18th:* 1108
Victoria Woodhull, *19th:* 2459
Frances Wright, *19th:* 2469
Marie Elizabeth Zakrzewska, *19th:* 2481
Emiliano Zapata, *20th:* 4448, *Notor:* 1129
John Peter Zenger, *18th:* 1116
Clara Zetkin, *20th:* 4455
Zhao Ziyang, *20th:* 4459
Grigory Yevseyevich Zinovyev, *Notor:* 1138
Count von Zinzendorf, *18th:* 1119

Social Sciences. ***See*** **Anthropology and Sociology; Archaeology; Communications; Diplomacy; Economics; Education; Government and Politics; Historiography; Natural History; Psychology and Psychiatry**

Sociology. ***See*** **Anthropology and Sociology**

Space Exploration. ***See*** **Aviation and Space Exploration**

Spies. ***See*** **Traitors and Spies**

Sports
Hank Aaron, *20th:* 5
Muhammad Ali, *20th:* 61
Björn Borg, *20th:* 426
Sir Donald G. Bradman, *20th:* 471
Billy Cannon, *Notor:* 173
Wilt Chamberlain, *20th:* 725
Ty Cobb, *20th:* 791
Sebastian Coe, *20th:* 797
Learie Constantine, *20th:* 829
Pierre de Coubertin, *20th:* 846
Jack Dempsey, *20th:* 964
Joe DiMaggio, *20th:* 1001
Sir Arthur Conan Doyle, *19th:* 688
Chris Evert, *20th:* 1191
Enzo Ferrari, *20th:* 1239
Lou Gehrig, *20th:* 1434
Althea Gibson, *20th:* 1474
William Gilbert Grace, *19th:* 955
Wayne Gretzky, *20th:* 1585
Sonja Henie, *20th:* 1759
Sir Edmund Hillary, *20th:* 1802
Shoeless Joe Jackson, *Notor:* 521
Bobby Jones, *20th:* 2036
Michael Jordan, *20th:* 2050

Jean-Claude Killy, *20th:* 2132
Billie Jean King, *20th:* 2143
Rod Laver, *20th:* 2288
Joe Louis, *20th:* 2437
Rocky Marciano, *20th:* 2612
Reinhold Messner, *20th:* 2718
James Naismith, *20th:* 2905
Martina Navratilova, *20th:* 2922
Jack Nicklaus, *20th:* 2959
Annie Oakley, *19th:* 1692
Sadaharu Oh, *20th:* 3027
Jesse Owens, *20th:* 3095
A. B. Paterson, *19th:* 1758
Pelé, *20th:* 3187
Fred Perry, *20th:* 3216
Gary Player, *20th:* 3288
Paul Robeson, *20th:* 3462
Frank Robinson, *20th:* 3467
Jackie Robinson, *20th:* 3470
Knute Rockne, *20th:* 3481
Pete Rose, *20th:* 3525
Pete Rozelle, *20th:* 3553
Bill Russell, *20th:* 3565
Babe Ruth, *20th:* 3572
Pete Sampras, *20th:* 3616
Billy Sunday, *20th:* 3916
Jim Thorpe, *20th:* 4016
Tiger Woods, *20th:* 4390
Fanny Bullock Workman, *19th:* 2466
Babe Didrikson Zaharias, *20th:* 4442

TECHNOLOGY. ***See*** **INVENTION AND TECHNOLOGY**

TELEVISION. ***See*** **RADIO, FILM, AND TELEVISION**

TERRORISTS
Larry C. Ford, *Notor:* 363
Abu Nidal, *Notor:* 4
Shoko Asahara, *Notor:* 40
Mohammed Atta al-Sayed, *Notor:* 43
Andreas Baader, *Notor:* 47
Osama Bin Laden, *20th:* 371, *Notor:* 101
D. B. Cooper, *Notor:* 233
Baruch Goldstein, *Notor:* 427
Irish Invincibles, *Notor:* 509
Timothy McVeigh, *Notor:* 681
Horst Mahler, *Notor:* 684
Ulrike Meinhof, *Notor:* 715
Khalid Shaikh Mohammed, *Notor:* 744
Zacarias Moussaoui, *Notor:* 758
Terry Nichols, *Notor:* 790
Ilich Ramírez Sánchez, *Notor:* 883
Eric Rudolph, *Notor:* 921
Fusako Shigenobu, *Notor:* 949
Ramzi Yousef, *Notor:* 1121
Abu Musab al-Zarqawi, *Notor:* 1132
Ayman al-Zawahiri, *Notor:* 1135
Patty Hearst, *Notor:* 454
Thenmuli Rajaratnam, *Notor:* 882

THEATER AND LIVE ENTERTAINMENT. ***See also*** **DANCE; MUSIC; RADIO, FILM, AND TELEVISION**
Fanny Abington, *18th:* 1
Adam de la Halle, *MA:* 24
Aeschylus, *Anc:* 7
JoAnne Akalaitis, *20th:* 39
Aristophanes, *Anc:* 90
Fred Astaire, *20th:* 155
Lucille Ball, *20th:* 212
P. T. Barnum, *19th:* 138
Francis Beaumont, *Ren:* 92
Samuel Beckett, *20th:* 279
Aphra Behn, *17th:* 42
Ingmar Bergman, *20th:* 316
Ingrid Bergman, *20th:* 321
Sarah Bernhardt, *19th:* 208
Thomas Betterton, *17th:* 51
Humphrey Bogart, *20th:* 406
Edwin Booth, *19th:* 271
Mrs. Anne Bracegirdle, *17th:* 82
Marlon Brando, *20th:* 486
Bertolt Brecht, *20th:* 504
Richard Burbage, *17th:* 104
Fanny Burney, *18th:* 180
Pedro Calderón de la Barca, *17th:* 113
Charles Chaplin, *20th:* 731
George Chapman, *Ren:* 213
Ray Charles, *20th:* 735
Anton Chekhov, *19th:* 478
Chikamatsu Monzaemon, *18th:* 243
William Cody, *19th:* 524
Bessie Coleman, *20th:* 801
Pierre Corneille, *17th:* 193
Bill Cosby, *20th:* 840
Sir Noël Coward, *20th:* 853
Hannah Cowley, *18th:* 284
Cheryl Crawford, *20th:* 861
Bing Crosby, *20th:* 874
Celia Cruz, *20th:* 877
Robertson Davies, *20th:* 917
Bette Davis, *20th:* 919
Thomas Dekker, *17th:* 223
Agnes de Mille, *20th:* 957
Sergei Diaghilev, *20th:* 985
Walt Disney, *20th:* 1006
Helen Gahagan Douglas, *20th:* 1026
John Dryden, *17th:* 239
Alexandre Dumas, *père*, *19th:* 695
Katherine Dunham, *20th:* 1061
Sergei Eisenstein, *20th:* 1129
Fanny Elssler, *19th:* 743
Nora Ephron, *20th:* 1161
Euripides, *Anc:* 326
Henry Fielding, *18th:* 346
John Fletcher, *Ren:* 92, *17th:* 277
Henry Fonda, *20th:* 1265
Edwin Forrest, *19th:* 790
Bob Fosse, *20th:* 1291
Athol Fugard, *20th:* 1354
Loie Fuller, *20th:* 1361
Federico García Lorca, *20th:* 1395
Judy Garland, *20th:* 1409
David Garrick, *18th:* 397
Norman Bel Geddes, *20th:* 1431
Jean Genet, *20th:* 1445
W. S. Gilbert, *19th:* 916
Jean Giraudoux, *20th:* 1492
Lillian Gish, *20th:* 1496
Johann Wolfgang von Goethe, *18th:* 428
Nell Gwyn, *17th:* 342
Knut Hamsun, *20th:* 1660
Lorraine Hansberry, *20th:* 1669
Harṣa, *MA:* 460
Lorenz Hart, *20th:* 1691
Václav Havel, *20th:* 1707
Helen Hayes, *20th:* 1723

Rita Hayworth, *20th:* 1730
Hans Werner Henze, *20th:* 1762
Katharine Hepburn, *20th:* 1769
Thomas Heywood, *17th:* 373
Bob Hope, *20th:* 1870
Harry Houdini, *20th:* 1889
Hrosvitha, *MA:* 516
Henrik Ibsen, *19th:* 1165
Ihara Saikaku, *17th:* 403
Eugène Ionesco, *20th:* 1968
Henry Irving, *19th:* 1175
Izumo no Okuni, *17th:* 408
Inigo Jones, *17th:* 436
Ben Jonson, *17th:* 439
Scott Joplin, *19th:* 1235
Kālidāsa, *Anc:* 496
Edmund Kean, *19th:* 1254
Gene Kelly, *20th:* 2096
Fanny Kemble, *19th:* 1267
Stephen King, *20th:* 2151
Heinrich von Kleist, *19th:* 1289
Jean de La Fontaine, *17th:* 480
Francesco Landini, *MA:* 635
Lillie Langtry, *19th:* 1312
Eva Le Gallienne, *20th:* 2330
Charlotte Lennox, *18th:* 594
Alain-René Lesage, *18th:* 596
Gotthold Ephraim Lessing, *18th:* 598
Jerry Lewis, *20th:* 2357
Serge Lifar, *20th:* 2378
Jenny Lind, *19th:* 1387
Sir Andrew Lloyd Webber, *20th:* 2414
Anita Loos, *20th:* 2428
Jean-Baptiste Lully, *17th:* 569
Guillaume de Machaut, *MA:* 679
William Charles Macready, *19th:* 1467
Christopher Marlowe, *Ren:* 623
Léonide Massine, *20th:* 2646
Vladimir Mayakovsky, *20th:* 2659
Louis B. Mayer, *20th:* 2662
Menander (c. 642-c. 291 B.C.E.; dramatist), *Anc:* 547
Adah Isaacs Menken, *19th:* 1555
Vsevolod Yemilyevich Meyerhold, *20th:* 2722
Thomas Middleton, *17th:* 636
Darius Milhaud, *20th:* 2735
Arthur Miller, *20th:* 2742
A. A. Milne, *20th:* 2753
Molière, *17th:* 646
Marilyn Monroe, *20th:* 2797
Lola Montez, *19th:* 1590
Toni Morrison, *20th:* 2834
Rupert Murdoch, *20th:* 2876
Thomas Nashe, *Ren:* 714
Vaslav Nijinsky, *20th:* 2974
Jessye Norman, *20th:* 2995
Annie Oakley, *19th:* 1692
Anne Oldfield, *18th:* 749
Sir Laurence Olivier, *20th:* 3039
Eugene O'Neill, *20th:* 3051
Dolly Parton, *20th:* 3127
Luciano Pavarotti, *20th:* 3159
Anna Pavlova, *20th:* 3166
Gregory Peck, *20th:* 3181
Oscar Peterson, *20th:* 3226
Katherine Philips, *17th:* 741
Edith Piaf, *20th:* 3228
Mary Pickford, *20th:* 3244
Luigi Pirandello, *20th:* 3260
Plautus, *Anc:* 662
Sidney Poitier, *20th:* 3296
Cole Porter, *20th:* 3308
Sergei Prokofiev, *20th:* 3338
Giacomo Puccini, *20th:* 3346
Henry Purcell, *17th:* 763
Sergei Rachmaninoff, *20th:* 3361
Jean Racine, *17th:* 773
Satyajit Ray, *20th:* 3394
Jean Renoir, *20th:* 3420
Abby Sage Richardson, *19th:* 1902
Jerome Robbins, *20th:* 3459
Paul Robeson, *20th:* 3462
Mary Robinson (1758?-1800), *18th:* 848
Richard Rodgers, *20th:* 3486
Will Rogers, *20th:* 3491
Nathalie Sarraute, *20th:* 3635
Friedrich Schiller, *18th:* 887
Peter Sellers, *20th:* 3695
Maurice Sendak, *20th:* 3698
Mack Sennett, *20th:* 3706
William Shakespeare, *Ren:* 876
James Shirley, *17th:* 846
Sarah Siddons, *18th:* 912
Sima Xiangru, *Anc:* 785
Frank Sinatra, *20th:* 3747
Sophocles, *Anc:* 809
Wole Soyinka, *20th:* 3804
Konstantin Stanislavsky, *20th:* 3821
Richard Steele, *18th:* 941
Barbra Streisand, *20th:* 3892
August Strindberg, *20th:* 3898
Sir John Suckling, *17th:* 893
Arthur Sullivan, *19th:* 916
Maria Tallchief, *20th:* 3940
Shirley Temple, *20th:* 3973
Terence, *Anc:* 849
Ellen Terry, *19th:* 2248
Megan Terry, *20th:* 3982
Twyla Tharp, *20th:* 3989
Thespis, *Anc:* 876
Theodore Thomas, *19th:* 2267
Tirso de Molina, *17th:* 913
Cyril Tourneur, *17th:* 928
Sir John Vanbrugh, *18th:* 1002
Lope de Vega Carpio, *17th:* 949
Philippe de Vitry, *MA:* 1065
Voltaire, *18th:* 1026
Mercy Otis Warren, *18th:* 1041
John Webster, *17th:* 976
Kurt Weill, *20th:* 4273
Orson Welles, *20th:* 4283
Mae West, *20th:* 4297
Oscar Wilde, *19th:* 2432
Tennessee Williams, *20th:* 4350
Peg Woffington, *18th:* 1102
Zeami Motokiyo, *MA:* 1152

THEOLOGY. *See* **RELIGION AND THEOLOGY**

TRAITORS AND SPIES

Alcibiades of Athens, *Anc:* 33, *Notor:* 11
Aldrich Ames, *Notor:* 16
Benedict Arnold, *18th:* 59, *Notor:* 36
Anthony Blunt, *Notor:* 109
Christopher John Boyce, *Notor:* 133
Belle Boyd, *Notor:* 135
Guy Burgess, *Notor:* 152
Aaron Burr, *19th:* 363, *Notor:* 155
John Cairncross, *Notor:* 164

Catiline, *Anc:* 188, *Notor:* 188
Whittaker Chambers, *Notor:* 198
Benjamin Church, *Notor:* 211
Pauline Cushman, *Notor:* 246
François Darlan, *Notor:* 262
Ferdinand Walsin Esterhazy, *Notor:* 334
Klaus Fuchs, *Notor:* 379
Fulvia, *Notor:* 384
Mildred Gillars, *Notor:* 409
Robert Philip Hanssen, *Notor:* 445
Alger Hiss, *20th:* 1822, *Notor:* 475
Flavius Josephus, *Anc:* 477, *Notor:* 541
William Joyce, *Notor:* 542
Judas Iscariot, *Notor:* 544
Yoshiko Kawashima, *Notor:* 558
Pierre Laval, *20th:* 2285, *Notor:* 609
Charles Lee, *Notor:* 621
Daulton Lee, *Notor:* 623
John Walker Lindh, *Notor:* 645
Roderigo Lopez, *Notor:* 655
Donald Duart Maclean, *Notor:* 674
Mata Hari, *Notor:* 710
Sir Oswald Mosley, *Notor:* 755
Philippe Pétain, *20th:* 3222, *Notor:* 825
Kim Philby, *Notor:* 836
Jonathan Pollard, *Notor:* 849
Vidkun Quisling, *Notor:* 873
Ethel Rosenberg, *Notor:* 913
Julius Rosenberg, *Notor:* 915
Miles Sindercombe, *Notor:* 961
Tokyo Rose, *Notor:* 1036
Andrey Andreyevich Vlasov, *Notor:* 1074
James Wilkinson, *Notor:* 1103
Emma Goldman, *20th:* 1519, *Notor:* 424

WARFARE AND CONQUEST. ***See also*** **MILITARY AFFAIRS**

Abahai, *17th:* 1
ʿAbbās the Great, *17th:* 4
ʿAbd al-Malik, *MA:* 3
ʿAbd al-Muʾmin, *MA:* 6
Æthelflæd, *MA:* 30
Afonso I (c. 1108-1185), *MA:* 33
Agesilaus II, *Anc:* 14
Gnaeus Julius Agricola, *Anc:* 17
Marcus Vipsanius Agrippa, *Anc:* 20
Akbar (1542-1605), *Ren:* 15
ʿAlāʾ-ud-Dīn Muḥammad Khaljī, *MA:* 39
Alaungpaya, *18th:* 29
Alboin, *MA:* 45
Alcibiades of Athens, *Anc:* 33, *Notor:* 11
Saint Alexander Nevsky, *MA:* 52
Alexander the Great, *Anc:* 39
Alfred the Great, *MA:* 63
Ali Paşa Tepelenë, *19th:* 55
Ethan Allen, *18th:* 35
Lord Allenby, *20th:* 65
Alp Arslan, *MA:* 70
Lord Amherst, *18th:* 38
Amina Sarauniya Zazzua, *Ren:* 37
An Lushan, *MA:* 78
John André, *18th:* 42
Lord Anson, *18th:* 49
Antigonus I Monophthalmos, *Anc:* 63
Antiochus the Great, *Anc:* 65
Marc Antony, *Anc:* 73
Yasir Arafat, *20th:* 110
Second Duke of Argyll, *18th:* 53
Arminius, *Anc:* 99
Árpád, *MA:* 105
Artemisia I, *Anc:* 109
Ashurnasirpal II, *Anc:* 120
Askia Daud, *Ren:* 64
Atahualpa, *Ren:* 66
Attila, *Anc:* 138, *Notor:* 45
Aurangzeb, *17th:* 23
Osama Bin Laden, *20th:* 371, *Notor:* 101
Black Hawk, *19th:* 244
Robert Blake, *17th:* 55
Boabdil, *Ren:* 105
Bohemond I, *MA:* 176
Claude Alexandre de Bonneval, *18th:* 140
Daniel Boone, *18th:* 143
Cesare Borgia, *Ren:* 114, *Notor:* 127
Louis Botha, *20th:* 439
Boudicca, *Anc:* 163
Louis-Antoine de Bougainville, *18th:* 150
Omar Nelson Bradley, *20th:* 468
Joseph Brant, *18th:* 159
Sir Isaac Brock, *19th:* 306
Marcus Junius Brutus, *Anc:* 166, *Notor:* 146
Sebastian Cabot, *Ren:* 159
Julius Caesar, *Anc:* 172
Canonicus, *17th:* 129
Cao Cao, *Anc:* 182
Sir Guy Carleton, *18th:* 196
Lazare Carnot, *18th:* 200
Cassius, *Anc:* 185
Cetshwayo, *19th:* 450
Chandragupta Maurya, *Anc:* 202
Charlemagne, *MA:* 242
Charles VIII, *Ren:* 227
Charles X Gustav, *17th:* 153
Étienne François de Choiseul, *18th:* 246
El Cid, *MA:* 278
Cimon, *Anc:* 213
George Rogers Clark, *18th:* 253
Claudius I, *Anc:* 217
Cleomenes, *Anc:* 226
Sir Henry Clinton, *18th:* 256
Robert Clive, *18th:* 259
Clovis, *MA:* 290
Michael Collins, *20th:* 807
The Great Condé, *17th:* 184
Constantine the Great, *Anc:* 239
Hernán Cortés, *Ren:* 252
Crazy Horse, *19th:* 566
Croesus, *Anc:* 244
Oliver Cromwell, *17th:* 204
Cuauhtémoc, *Ren:* 273
Cyrus the Great, *Anc:* 248
Darius the Great, *Anc:* 251
Moshe Dayan, *20th:* 929
Deborah, *Anc:* 258
Milovan Djilas, *20th:* 1011
Jimmy Doolittle, *20th:* 1023
Dorgon, *17th:* 234
Joseph-François Dupleix, *18th:* 311
Dwight D. Eisenhower, *20th:* 1125
Elizabeth Petrovna, *18th:* 321

Enver Paşa, *20th:* 1157
Epaminondas, *Anc:* 303
Eugene of Savoy, *18th:* 330
Fabius, *Anc:* 342
Third Baron Fairfax, *17th:* 261
Faisal I, *20th:* 1202
Lord Edward Fitzgerald, *18th:* 356
Frederick the Great, *18th:* 378
Thomas Gage, *18th:* 384
Genghis Khan, *MA:* 402, *Notor:* 400
Genseric, *Anc:* 351
Geronimo, *19th:* 904
Maḥmūd Ghāzān, *MA:* 411
Gia Long, *19th:* 907
Sir Humphrey Gilbert, *Ren:* 378
Hermann Göring, *20th:* 1545, *Notor:* 428
Nathanael Greene, *18th:* 443
Sir Richard Grenville, *Ren:* 396
Guacanagarí, *Ren:* 408
Heinz Guderian, *20th:* 1606
Gustavus II Adolphus, *17th:* 336
George Habash, *20th:* 1626
William F. Halsey, *20th:* 1647
Hamilcar Barca, *Anc:* 373
Hammurabi, *Anc:* 376
Hannibal, *Anc:* 382
Harṣa, *MA:* 460
Hārūn al-Rashīd, *MA:* 467
Piet Hein, *17th:* 359
Hengist, *Anc:* 394
Prince Henry the Navigator, *MA:* 477
Heraclius, *MA:* 505
Paul von Hindenburg, *20th:* 1814
Adolf Hitler, *20th:* 1829, *Notor:* 477
Ho Chi Minh, *20th:* 1834
Hōjō Ujimasa, *Ren:* 451
Richard Howe, *18th:* 506
William Howe, *18th:* 510
Humāyūn, *Ren:* 475
Saddam Hussein, *20th:* 1947, *Notor:* 503
Hyder Ali, *18th:* 522
Pierre Le Moyne d'Iberville, *17th:* 401
Ibrāhīm Lodī, *Ren:* 478
İbrahim Paşa, *Ren:* 480
Ivan the Terrible, *Ren:* 492, *Notor:* 517
Jahāngīr, *17th:* 410
James I the Conqueror, *MA:* 571
James III, *Ren:* 496
James IV, *Ren:* 498
James V, *Ren:* 501
János Hunyadi, *MA:* 519
Jimmu Tennō, *Anc:* 462
Jingū, *Anc:* 465
Joseph-Jacques-Césaire Joffre, *20th:* 2009
John III Sobieski, *17th:* 427
John Paul Jones, *18th:* 539
Damia al-Kāhina, *MA:* 604
Merzifonlu Kara Mustafa Paşa, *17th:* 451
Karīm Khān Zand, *18th:* 552
Albert Kesselring, *20th:* 2117
Bohdan Khmelnytsky, *17th:* 461
Khosrow I, *MA:* 613
Kim Il Sung, *20th:* 2138, *Notor:* 578
Lord Kitchener, *20th:* 2173
Tadeusz Kościuszko, *18th:* 564
Krishnadevaraya, *Ren:* 532
Kublai Khan, *MA:* 626
Mikhail Illarionovich Kutuzov, *18th:* 569
John Lambert, *17th:* 483
Bartolomé de Las Casas, *Ren:* 537
T. E. Lawrence, *20th:* 2303
Le Thanh Tong, *Ren:* 546
Miguel López de Legazpi, *Ren:* 550
Leonidas, *Anc:* 505
Leopold I, *17th:* 526
Little Turtle, *18th:* 610
Lobengula, *19th:* 1406
Louis XII, *Ren:* 577
Douglas MacArthur, *20th:* 2492
Samora Machel, *20th:* 2515
Francisco Madero, *20th:* 2544
The Mahdi, *19th:* 1473
Mahmud I, *18th:* 639
Maḥmūd of Ghazna, *MA:* 683
Mao Zedong, *20th:* 2601, *Notor:* 691
Doña Marina, *Ren:* 621
Gaius Marius, *Anc:* 533
First Duke of Marlborough, *18th:* 660
George C. Marshall, *20th:* 2629
Mary of Guise, *Ren:* 633
Masinissa, *Anc:* 542
Maurice of Nassau, *17th:* 618
Mausolus, *Anc:* 545
Ivan Stepanovich Mazepa, *17th:* 624
Mehmed II, *MA:* 711, *Ren:* 659
Mehmed III, *Ren:* 661
Menelik II, *19th:* 1552
Metacom, *17th:* 633
Slobodan Milošević, *20th:* 2756, *Notor:* 735
Miltiades the Younger, *Anc:* 563
Minamoto Yoritomo, *MA:* 721
Mobutu Sese Seko, *20th:* 2773, *Notor:* 740
George Monck, *17th:* 650
Duke of Monmouth, *17th:* 653
Marquis de Montalembert, *18th:* 690
Louis-Joseph de Montcalm, *18th:* 692
Duchesse de Montpensier, *17th:* 660
Montuhotep II, *Anc:* 570
Murad IV, *17th:* 668
Nādir Shāh, *18th:* 722, *Notor:* 772
Nanny, *18th:* 724
Nebuchadnezzar II, *Anc:* 582
Ngo Quyen, *MA:* 756
Nguyen Hue, *18th:* 736
Nguyen Van Thieu, *20th:* 2954
Odoacer, *MA:* 782
Oichi, *Ren:* 737
Grace O'Malley, *Ren:* 743, *Notor:* 805
Rory O'More, *17th:* 699
Opechancanough, *17th:* 702
Osceola, *19th:* 1709
Osman I, *MA:* 800
Pachacuti, *Ren:* 746
Pausanias of Sparta, *Anc:* 615
Pemisapan, *Ren:* 771
Pheidippides, *Anc:* 630
Philip II of Macedonia, *Anc:* 637
Józef Piłsudski, *20th:* 3250
Piye, *Anc:* 655

Francisco Pizarro, *Ren:* 800
Pompey the Great, *Anc:* 681
Grigori Aleksandrovich Potemkin, *18th:* 808
Thomas Pride, *17th:* 756
Ptolemy Soter, *Anc:* 719
Yemelyan Ivanovich Pugachev, *18th:* 814
Qāytbāy, *Ren:* 807
Pierre Esprit Radisson, *17th:* 777
Ramses II, *Anc:* 735
Ranjit Singh, *19th:* 1857
Stenka Razin, *17th:* 784
Regulus, *Anc:* 738
Comte de Rochambeau, *18th:* 851
George Rodney, *18th:* 854
Erwin Rommel, *20th:* 3502
Prince Rupert, *17th:* 805
Michiel Adriaanszoon de Ruyter, *17th:* 807
Sargon II, *Anc:* 752
Comte de Saxe, *18th:* 881
Friedrich Hermann Schomberg, *17th:* 820
Scipio Aemilianus, *Anc:* 755
Scipio Africanus, *Anc:* 758
Sebastian, *Ren:* 859
Hans von Seeckt, *20th:* 3688
Seleucus I Nicator, *Anc:* 763
Sesostris III, *Anc:* 771
Shaka, *19th:* 2081
Shāpūr II, *Anc:* 774
Sigismund I, the Old, *Ren:* 885
Sigismund II Augustus, *Ren:* 887
John Graves Simcoe, *18th:* 919
Sitting Bull, *19th:* 2108
Śivājī, *17th:* 858
First Viscount Slim, *20th:* 3758
Jan Christian Smuts, *20th:* 3775
Sonni ʿAlī, *Ren:* 900
Hernando de Soto, *Ren:* 902
Spartacus, *Anc:* 818
Simon Stevin, *Ren:* 912
Flavius Stilicho, *Anc:* 824
Lucius Cornelius Sulla, *Anc:* 830, *Notor:* 1010
Suryavarman II, *MA:* 980
Taksin, *18th:* 968
Tamerlane, *MA:* 1000
Ṭāriq ibn-Ziyād, *MA:* 1005
Tarquins, *Anc:* 846
Tascalusa, *Ren:* 922
Tecumseh, *19th:* 2237
Tewodros II, *19th:* 2255
Thanadelthur, *18th:* 974
Themistocles, *Anc:* 859
Theodosius the Great, *Anc:* 868
Thutmose III, *Anc:* 885
Tiglath-pileser III, *Anc:* 892
Tippu Tib, *19th:* 2277
Tito, *20th:* 4034, *Notor:* 1032
Tokugawa Ieyasu, *17th:* 915
Wolfe Tone, *18th:* 982
Lennart Torstenson, *17th:* 924
Samory Touré, *19th:* 1981
Toussaint Louverture, *18th:* 985
Trajan, *Anc:* 903
Maarten and Cornelis Tromp, *17th:* 930
Viscount de Turenne, *17th:* 933
ʿUmar I, *MA:* 1037
Ur-Nammu, *Anc:* 914
ʿUthman dan Fodio, *19th:* 2342
Valdemar II, *MA:* 1047
Vasily III, *Ren:* 957
Vercingetorix, *Anc:* 935
Pancho Villa, *20th:* 4160, *Notor:* 1069
Geoffroi de Villehardouin, *MA:* 1059
Vlad III the Impaler, *Ren:* 981, *Notor:* 1072
Vladimir I, *MA:* 1068
Vo Nguyen Giap, *20th:* 4169
Muḥammad ibn ʿAbd al-Wahhāb, *18th:* 1030
Kurt Waldheim, *20th:* 4187
Albrecht Wenzel von Wallenstein, *17th:* 966
Wang Kŏn, *MA:* 1081
George Washington, *18th:* 1043
Anthony Wayne, *18th:* 1054
Widukind, *MA:* 1094
James Wolfe, *18th:* 1104
Xerxes I, *Anc:* 971
Chuck Yeager, *20th:* 4425
Yo Fei, *MA:* 1145
Emiliano Zapata, *20th:* 4448, *Notor:* 1129
Zeng Guofan, *19th:* 2483
Zenobia, *Anc:* 986
Zheng Chenggong, *17th:* 1001
Georgy Zhukov, *20th:* 4469
Jan Žižka, *MA:* 1162

WITCHES AND OCCULTISTS

Tamsin Blight, *Notor:* 106
Mary Butters, *Notor:* 160
Dorothy Clutterbuck, *Notor:* 215
Aleister Crowley, *Notor:* 242
Margaret Jones, *Notor:* 540
Lady Alice Kyteler, *MA:* 629, *Notor:* 598
Marie Laveau, *Notor:* 610
Anton Szandor LaVey, *Notor:* 612
Florence Newton, *Notor:* 781
Dolly Pentreath, *Notor:* 818
Elizabeth Sawyer, *Notor:* 935
Mother Shipton, *Notor:* 952
Joan Wytte, *Notor:* 1110

WOMEN'S RIGHTS. ***See also* CIVIL RIGHTS**

Abigail Adams, *18th:* 7
Jane Addams, *20th:* 22
Halide Edib Adıvar, *20th:* 29
Agrippina the Younger, *Anc:* 23
Amalasuntha, *MA:* 75
Saint Angela Merici, *Ren:* 44
Maya Angelou, *20th:* 97
Susan B. Anthony, *19th:* 65
Antonia Minor, *Anc:* 71
Arria the Elder, *Anc:* 102
Arria the Younger, *Anc:* 103
Arsinoe II Philadelphus, *Anc:* 105
Artemisia I, *Anc:* 109
Aspasia of Miletus, *Anc:* 127
Mary Astell, *18th:* 64
Luise Aston, *19th:* 83
Nancy Astor, *20th:* 158
Atossa, *Anc:* 136
Margaret Atwood, *20th:* 169
Hubertine Auclert, *19th:* 89
Ban Zhao, *Anc:* 152
Dorothea Beale, *19th:* 159
Simone de Beauvoir, *20th:* 271
Catharine Beecher, *19th:* 168
Benazir Bhutto, *20th:* 365
Elizabeth Blackwell, *19th:* 247
Amelia Bloomer, *19th:* 257

Barbara Leigh Smith Bodichon, *19th:* 263
Margaret Bondfield, *20th:* 414
Mrs. Anne Bracegirdle, *17th:* 82
Eva Braun, *Notor:* 137
Helen Gurley Brown, *20th:* 539
Molly Brown, *20th:* 542
Olympia Brown, *19th:* 323
Gro Harlem Brundtland, *20th:* 544
Pearl S. Buck, *20th:* 557
Josephine Butler, *19th:* 371
Kim Campbell, *20th:* 624
Mary Ann Shadd Cary, *19th:* 431
Catherine of Aragon, *Ren:* 187
Carrie Chapman Catt, *20th:* 701
Hester Chapone, *18th:* 221
Judy Chicago, *20th:* 750
Shirley Chisholm, *20th:* 753
Cleopatra VII, *Anc:* 229
Hillary Rodham Clinton, *20th:* 788
Clodia, *Anc:* 233
Bessie Coleman, *20th:* 801
Hannah Cowley, *18th:* 284
Deborah, *Anc:* 258
Dido, *Anc:* 271
Dame Millicent Garrett Fawcett, *19th:* 766
Betty Ford, *20th:* 1272
Abby Kelley Foster, *19th:* 799
Lydia Folger Fowler, *19th:* 812
Betty Friedan, *20th:* 1329
Elizabeth Fry, *19th:* 839
Matilda Joslyn Gage, *19th:* 852
Gershom ben Judah, *MA:* 408
Charlotte Perkins Gilman, *20th:* 1484
William Godwin, *18th:* 424
Emma Goldman, *20th:* 1519, *Notor:* 424
Sarah and Angelina Grimké, *19th:* 988
Mary A. Hallaren, *20th:* 1645
Fannie Lou Hamer, *20th:* 1651
Lorraine Hansberry, *20th:* 1669
Hatshepsut, *Anc:* 388
Saint Helena, *Anc:* 391
Aileen Clarke Hernandez, *20th:* 1773
Oveta Culp Hobby, *20th:* 1838
Julia Ward Howe, *19th:* 1137
Dolores Huerta, *20th:* 1915
Mary Putnam Jacobi, *19th:* 1200
John III Sobieski, *17th:* 427
Mother Jones, *20th:* 2039
Julia III, *Anc:* 489
Julia Domna, *Anc:* 480
Julia Mamaea, *Anc:* 483
Julia Soaemias, *Anc:* 486
Billie Jean King, *20th:* 2143
Jeane Kirkpatrick, *20th:* 2167
Lady Alice Kyteler, *MA:* 629, *Notor:* 598
Helene Lange, *19th:* 1307
Aemilia Lanyer, *Ren:* 535
Ninon de Lenclos, *17th:* 520
Livia Drusilla, *Anc:* 508
Belva A. Lockwood, *19th:* 1409
Lucretia, *Anc:* 517
Mary Lyon, *19th:* 1428
Catherine Macaulay, *18th:* 621
Catharine A. MacKinnon, *20th:* 2522
Madame de Maintenon, *17th:* 572
Meri Te Tai Mangakahia, *19th:* 1483
Wilma Mankiller, *20th:* 2591
Marguerite de Navarre, *Ren:* 617
Marie de l'Incarnation, *17th:* 595
Harriet Martineau, *19th:* 1505
Clorinda Matto de Turner, *19th:* 1512
Margaret Mead, *20th:* 2668
Valeria Messallina, *Anc:* 561
Edna St. Vincent Millay, *20th:* 2738
Kate Millett, *20th:* 2746
Mary Wortley Montagu, *18th:* 687
Duchesse de Montpensier, *17th:* 660
Hannah More, *18th:* 702
Toni Morrison, *20th:* 2834
Lucretia Mott, *19th:* 1616
Sarojini Naidu, *20th:* 2900
Carry Nation, *19th:* 1652
Nefertari, *Anc:* 585
Nefertiti, *Anc:* 587
Rebecca Nurse, *17th:* 689
Olympias, *Anc:* 597
Alice Freeman Palmer, *19th:* 1727
Emmeline Pankhurst, *20th:* 3102
Alice Paul, *20th:* 3145
Elena Cornaro Piscopia, *17th:* 743
Poppaea Sabina, *Anc:* 685
Jeannette Rankin, *20th:* 3374
Ann Richards, *20th:* 3434
Abby Sage Richardson, *19th:* 1902
Mary Robinson (1758?-1800), *18th:* 848
Mary Robinson (b. 1944), *20th:* 3474
Edith Nourse Rogers, *20th:* 3489
Eleanor Roosevelt, *20th:* 3506
Sammu-ramat, *Anc:* 744
Margaret Sanger, *20th:* 3625
Sappho, *Anc:* 750
Olive Schreiner, *19th:* 2023
Anna Maria van Schurman, *17th:* 823
Anne Sexton, *20th:* 3713
Anna Howard Shaw, *19th:* 2084
Henry Sidgwick, *19th:* 2102
Margaret Chase Smith, *20th:* 3768
Susan Sontag, *20th:* 3788
Elizabeth Cady Stanton, *19th:* 2146
Gloria Steinem, *20th:* 3852
Lucy Stone, *19th:* 2177
Harriet Beecher Stowe, *19th:* 2184
Sulpicia, *Anc:* 834
Tadano Makuzu, *19th:* 2212
Tanaquil, *Anc:* 840
Theodora, *MA:* 1008, *Notor:* 1028
Tiy, *Anc:* 901
Flora Tristan, *19th:* 2297
Frances Trollope, *19th:* 2303
Vivekananda, *19th:* 2368
Alice Walker, *20th:* 4196
Ida B. Wells-Barnett, *20th:* 4290
Emma Willard, *19th:* 2438
Frances Willard, *19th:* 2442
Oprah Winfrey, *20th:* 4372
Mary Wollstonecraft, *18th:* 1108
Victoria Woodhull, *19th:* 2459
Frances Wright, *19th:* 2469
Xanthippe, *Anc:* 962
Marie Elizabeth Zakrzewska, *19th:* 2481
Zenobia, *Anc:* 986
Clara Zetkin, *20th:* 4455

Chronological List of Entries

The arrangement of personages in this list is chronological on the basis of birth years. Where the birth year is unknown, then other vital years appear, and the subject is placed in relative order. More general dates precede specific dates. When birth dates are the same, then the names are placed alphabetically. All personages appearing in this list are the subjects of articles in the *Great Lives from History* series.

3100 - 1101 B.C.E.

Menes (c. 3100-c. 3000 B.C.E.) *Anc:* 556
Zoser (c. 2700-c. 2650 B.C.E.) *Anc:* 996
Imhotep (fl. 27th cent. B.C.E.) *Anc:* 439
Menkaure (2532-2503 B.C.E.) *Anc:* 558
Enheduanna (c. 2320-c. 2250 B.C.E.) *Anc:* 298
Ur-Nammu (late 22d cent.-2095 B.C.E.) *Anc:* 914
Gudea (c. 2120-c. 2070 B.C.E.) *Anc:* 366
Montuhotep II (2055-2004 B.C.E.) *Anc:* 570
Abraham (c. 2050-c. 1950 B.C.E.) *Anc:* 4
Sesostris III (d. 1843 B.C.E.) *Anc:* 771
Hammurabi (c. 1810-1750 B.C.E.) *Anc:* 376
Hatshepsut (c. 1525-c. 1482 B.C.E.) *Anc:* 388
Thutmose III (late 16th cent.-1450 B.C.E.) *Anc:* 885
Tiy (c. 1410-c. 1340 B.C.E.) *Anc:* 901
Amenhotep III (c. 1403-c. 1353 B.C.E.) *Anc:* 45
Aaron (c. 1395-c. 1272 B.C.E.) *Anc:* 1
Akhenaton (c. 1364-c. 1334 B.C.E.) *Anc:* 26
Nefertiti (c. 1364-c. 1334 B.C.E.) *Anc:* 587
Tutankhamen (c. 1370-c. 1352 B.C.E.) *Anc:* 908
Nefertari (c. 1307-c. 1265 B.C.E.) *Anc:* 585
Moses (c. 1300-c. 1200 B.C.E.) *Anc:* 572
Ramses II (c. 1300-1213 B.C.E.) *Anc:* 735
Deborah (fl. c. 1200-1125 B.C.E.) *Anc:* 258

1100 - 601 B.C.E.

Samuel (c. 1090-c. 1020 B.C.E.) *Anc:* 747
David (c. 1030-c. 962 B.C.E.) *Anc:* 255
Bathsheba (fl. 10th cent. B.C.E.) *Anc:* 155
Ashurnasirpal II (c. 915-859 B.C.E.) *Anc:* 120
Dido (mid-9th cent.-late 9th/early 8th cent. B.C.E.) *Anc:* 271
Sammu-ramat (c. 840-after 807 B.C.E.) *Anc:* 744
Jezebel (c. 800-853 B.C.E.) *Notor:* 527
Homer (c. early 8th cent.-c. late 8th cent. B.C.E.) *Anc:* 427
Tiglath-pileser III (early 8th cent.-727 B.C.E.) *Anc:* 892
Piye (c. 769-716 B.C.E.) *Anc:* 655
Isaiah (c. 760-c. 701-680 B.C.E.) *Anc:* 446
Sargon II (second half of 8th cent.-705 B.C.E.) *Anc:* 752
Sennacherib (c. 735-Jan., 681 B.C.E.) *Anc:* 769
Hesiod (fl. c. 700 B.C.E.) *Anc:* 413
Draco (fl. perhaps 7th cent. B.C.E.) *Anc:* 293
Cypselus of Corinth (early 7th cent.-627 B.C.E.) *Notor:* 251
Lucius Tarquinius Priscus (7th cent.-579 B.C.E.) *Anc:* 846
Ashurbanipal (c. 685-627 B.C.E.) *Anc:* 117
Psamtik I (c. 684-610 B.C.E.) *Anc:* 710
Tanaquil (fl. mid- to late 7th cent. B.C.E.) *Anc:* 840
Jeremiah (c. 645-after 587 B.C.E.) *Anc:* 453
Pittacus of Mytilene (c. 645-c. 570 B.C.E.) *Anc:* 652
Nebuchadnezzar II (c. 630-562 B.C.E.) *Anc:* 582
Sappho (c. 630-c. 580 B.C.E.) *Anc:* 750
Solon (c. 630-c. 560 B.C.E.) *Anc:* 807
Zoroaster (c. 628-c. 551 B.C.E.) *Anc:* 992
Ezekiel (c. 627-c. 570 B.C.E.) *Anc:* 335
Thales of Miletus (c. 624-c. 548 B.C.E.) *Anc:* 856
Aesop (c. 620-c. 560 B.C.E.) *Anc:* 11
Pisistratus (c. 612-527 B.C.E.) *Anc:* 649
Anaximander (c. 610-c. 547 B.C.E.) *Anc:* 55
Phalaris (c. 610-600-544 B.C.E.) *Notor:* 834
Laozi (604-6th cent. B.C.E.) *Anc:* 502
Cyrus the Great (c. 601-590 to c. 530 B.C.E.) *Anc:* 248

600 - 501 B.C.E.

Ānanda (fl. 6th cent. B.C.E.) *Anc:* 49
Gośāla Maskarīputra (6th cent.-c. 467 B.C.E.) *Anc:* 355
Lucius Tarquinius Superbus (6th cent.-after 510 B.C.E.) *Anc:* 846
Lucretia (6th cent.-c. 509 B.C.E.) *Anc:* 517
Vardhamāna (c. 599-527 B.C.E.) *Anc:* 924
Croesus (c. 595-546 B.C.E.) *Anc:* 244
Pythagoras (c. 580-c. 500 B.C.E.) *Anc:* 725
Eupalinus of Megara (c. 575-c. 500 B.C.E.) *Anc:* 323
Cleomenes I (d. c. 490 B.C.E.) *Anc:* 226
Cleisthenes of Athens (c. 570-after 507 B.C.E.) *Anc:* 221
Xenophanes (c. 570-c. 478 B.C.E.) *Anc:* 965
Buddha (c. 566-c. 486 B.C.E.) *Anc:* 169
Simonides (c. 556-c. 467 B.C.E.) *Anc:* 793
Miltiades the Younger (c. 554-489 B.C.E.) *Anc:* 563
Confucius (551-479 B.C.E.) *Anc:* 236
Darius the Great (550-486 B.C.E.) *Anc:* 251
Atossa (c. 545-possibly c. 479 B.C.E.) *Anc:* 136
Heraclitus of Ephesus (c. 540-c. 480) *Anc:* 397
Thespis (before 535-after 501 B.C.E.) *Anc:* 876
Ezra (fl. late 6th/early 5th cent. B.C.E.) *Anc:* 338
Artemisia I (late 6th cent.-probably mid-5th cent. B.C.E.) *Anc:* 109
Pausanias of Sparta (late 6th cent.-c. 470 B.C.E.) *Anc:* 615
Aeschylus (525-524 to 456-455 B.C.E.) *Anc:* 7
Themistocles (c. 524-c. 460 B.C.E.) *Anc:* 859
Hanno (c. 520-510 B.C.E.) *Anc:* 385
Xerxes I (c. 519-465 B.C.E.) *Anc:* 971
Pindar (518-438 B.C.E.) *Anc:* 646
Pheidippides (probably c. 515-perhaps 490 B.C.E.) *Anc:* 630
Parmenides (c. 515-perhaps after 436 B.C.E.) *Anc:* 608
Alcmaeon (c. 510-c. 430 B.C.E.) *Anc:* 36
Cimon (c. 510-c. 451 B.C.E.) *Anc:* 213
Leonidas (c. 510-Aug. 20, 480 B.C.E.) *Anc:* 505

500 - 401 B.C.E.

Vālmīki (fl. c. 500 B.C.E.) *Anc:* 922
Anaxagoras (c. 500-c. 428 B.C.E.) *Anc:* 52
Polygnotus (c. 500-c. 440? B.C.E.) *Anc:* 678
Sophocles (c. 496-406 B.C.E.) *Anc:* 809
Pericles (c. 495-429 B.C.E.) *Anc:* 620
Empedocles (c. 490-c. 430 B.C.E.) *Anc:* 295
Phidias (c. 490-c. 430 B.C.E.) *Anc:* 633
Zeno of Elea (c. 490-c. 440 B.C.E.) *Anc:* 984
Euripides (c. 485-406 B.C.E.) *Anc:* 326
Protagoras (c. 485-c. 410 B.C.E.) *Anc:* 707
Herodotus (c. 484-c. 425 B.C.E.) *Anc:* 407
Aspasia of Miletus (c. 475-after 428 B.C.E.) *Anc:* 127
Mozi (c. 470-c. 391 B.C.E.) *Anc:* 576
Socrates (c. 470-399 B.C.E.) *Anc:* 799
Democritus (c. 460-c. 370 B.C.E.) *Anc:* 261
Hippocrates (c. 460-c. 370 B.C.E.) *Anc:* 420
Polyclitus (c. 460-c. 410 B.C.E.) *Anc:* 675
Thucydides (c. 459-c. 402 B.C.E.) *Anc:* 882
Alcibiades of Athens (c. 450-404 B.C.E.) *Anc:* 33, *Notor:* 11
Aristophanes (c. 450-c. 385 B.C.E.) *Anc:* 90
Xanthippe (c. 445-early to mid-4th cent. B.C.E.) *Anc:* 962
Agesilaus II of Sparta (c. 444-c. 360 B.C.E.) *Anc:* 14
Antisthenes (c. 444-c. 365 B.C.E.) *Anc:* 68
Isocrates (436-338 B.C.E.) *Anc:* 450
Aristippus (c. 435-365 B.C.E.) *Anc:* 87
Xenophon (c. 431-c. 354 B.C.E.) *Anc:* 968
Mausolus (d. 353 B.C.E.) *Anc:* 545
Plato (c. 427-347 B.C.E.) *Anc:* 659
Scopas (possibly as early as 420-late 4th cent. B.C.E.) *Anc:* 761
Diogenes (c. 412-403 to c. 324-321 B.C.E.) *Anc:* 283
Epaminondas (c. 410-362 B.C.E.) *Anc:* 303

400 - 301 B.C.E.

Eudoxus of Cnidus (c. 390-c. 337 B.C.E.) *Anc:* 320
Lysippus (c. 390-c. 300 B.C.E.) *Anc:* 523
Demosthenes (384-322 B.C.E.) *Anc:* 264
Antigonus I Monophthalmos (382-301 B.C.E.) *Anc:* 63
Philip II of Macedonia (382-336 B.C.E.) *Anc:* 637
Olympias (c. 375-316 B.C.E.) *Anc:* 597

Diocles of Carystus (c. 375-c. 295 B.C.E.) *Anc:* 277
Aristoxenus (375-360 B.C.E.) *Anc:* 97
Mencius (c. 372-c. 289 B.C.E.) *Anc:* 552
Theophrastus (c. 372-c. 287 B.C.E.) *Anc:* 872
Praxiteles (c. 370-c. 330 B.C.E.) *Anc:* 694
Cleomenes II (d. c. 309 B.C.E.) *Anc:* 227
Ptolemy Soter (367/366-283/282 B.C.E.) *Anc:* 719
Zhuangzi (c. 365-c. 290 B.C.E.) *Anc:* 989
Pyrrhon of Elis (c. 360-c. 272 B.C.E.) *Anc:* 722
Seleucus I Nicator (358 or 354-Aug./Sept., 281 B.C.E.) *Anc:* 763
Alexander the Great (356-June 10 or 13, 323 B.C.E.) *Anc:* 39
Pytheas (c. 350-325 to after 300 B.C.E.) *Anc:* 729
Chandragupta Maurya (c. 346-298 B.C.E.) *Anc:* 202
Qu Yuan (c. 343-278 B.C.E.) *Anc:* 732
Menander, dramatist (c. 342-c. 291 B.C.E.) *Anc:* 547
Epicurus (341-270 B.C.E.) *Anc:* 307
Herophilus (c. 335-c. 280 B.C.E.) *Anc:* 410
Zeno of Citium (c. 335-c. 263 B.C.E.) *Anc:* 981
Euclid (c. 330-c. 270 B.C.E.) *Anc:* 317
Erasistratus (c. 325-c. 250 B.C.E.) *Anc:* 310
Arsinoe II Philadelphus (c. 316-July, 270 B.C.E.) *Anc:* 105
Ptolemy Philadelphus (Feb., 308-246 B.C.E.) *Anc:* 715
Xunzi (c. 307-c. 235 B.C.E.) *Anc:* 978
Callimachus (c. 305-c. 240 B.C.E.) *Anc:* 179
Aśoka (c. 302-c. 232 B.C.E.) *Anc:* 124

300 - 201 B.C.E.

Jimmu Tennō (possibly 3d cent.-possibly late 3d cent. B.C.E.) *Anc:* 462
Regulus (c. 300-c. 249 B.C.E.) *Anc:* 738
Ctesibius of Alexandria (fl. c. 290-probably after 250 B.C.E.) *Anc:* 247
Eratosthenes of Cyrene (c. 285-c. 205 B.C.E.) *Anc:* 314
Hanfeizi (280-233 B.C.E.) *Anc:* 379
Fabius (c. 275-203 B.C.E.) *Anc:* 342
Hamilcar Barca (c. 275-winter, 229/228 B.C.E.) *Anc:* 373
Berenice II (c. 273-221 B.C.E.) *Anc:* 157
Cleomenes III (d. 219 B.C.E.) *Anc:* 228
Dēvānaṃpiya Tissa (d. 207 B.C.E.) *Anc:* 898
Sophonisba (d. c. 203 B.C.E.) *Anc:* 812
Apollonius of Perga (c. 262-c. 190 B.C.E.) *Anc:* 76
Shi Huangdi (259-210 B.C.E.) *Anc:* 779, *Notor:* 947
Plautus (c. 254-184 B.C.E.) *Anc:* 662
Jing Ke (mid-3d cent.-early 227 B.C.E.) *Notor:* 530
Hannibal (247-182 B.C.E.) *Anc:* 382
Antiochus the Great (c. 242-187 B.C.E.) *Anc:* 65
Quintus Ennius (239-169 B.C.E.?) *Anc:* 301
Masinissa (c. 238-148 B.C.E.) *Anc:* 542
Scipio Africanus (236-184/183 B.C.E.) *Anc:* 758
Cato the Censor (234-149 B.C.E.) *Anc:* 190
Menander, Greco-Bactrian king (c. 210-c. 135 B.C.E.) *Anc:* 550

200 - 101 B.C.E.

Polybius (c. 200-c. 118 B.C.E.) *Anc:* 673
Terence (c. 190-159 B.C.E.) *Anc:* 849
Hipparchus (190-after 127 B.C.E.) *Anc:* 417
Scipio Aemilianus (185/184-129 B.C.E.) *Anc:* 755
Sima Xiangru (179-117 B.C.E.) *Anc:* 785
Tiberius Sempronius Gracchus (163-June, 133 B.C.E.) *Anc:* 357
Gaius Marius (157-Jan. 13, 86 B.C.E.) *Anc:* 533
Wudi (156-87 B.C.E.) *Anc:* 958
Gaius Sempronius Gracchus (153-121 B.C.E.) *Anc:* 357
Sima Qian (145-86 B.C.E.) *Anc:* 782
Tigranes the Great (c. 140-c. 55 B.C.E.) *Anc:* 895
Lucius Cornelius Sulla (138-78 B.C.E.) *Anc:* 830, *Notor:* 1010
Mithradates VI Eupator (c. 134-63 B.C.E.) *Anc:* 567
Spartacus (late 2d cent.-71 B.C.E.) *Anc:* 818
Vattagamani (late 2d cent.-77 B.C.E.) *Anc:* 933
Asclepiades of Bithynia (124-c. 44 B.C.E.) *Anc:* 114
Marcus Terentius Varro (116-27 B.C.E.) *Anc:* 927
Catiline (c. 108-early 62 B.C.E.) *Anc:* 188, *Notor:* 188
Cicero (Jan. 3, 106-Dec. 7, 43 B.C.E.) *Anc:* 210
Pompey the Great (Sept. 29, 106-Sept. 28, 48 B.C.E.) *Anc:* 681

100 B.C.E. - 1 C.E.

Judas Iscariot (1st cent. B.C.E.-c. 30 C.E.) *Notor:* 544
Barabbas (early 1st cent.-1st cent. C.E.) *Notor:* 55
Nabu-rimanni (early 1st cent.-late 1st cent. B.C.E.) *Anc:* 579
Julius Caesar (July 12/13, 100-Mar. 15, 44 B.C.E.) *Anc:* 172
Lucretius (c. 98-Oct. 15, 55 B.C.E.) *Anc:* 520
Clodia (c. 95-after 45 B.C.E.) *Anc:* 233
Cato the Younger (95-46 B.C.E.) *Anc:* 194
Sosigenes (c. 90-1st cent. B.C.E.) *Anc:* 815
Sallust (86-35 B.C.E.) *Anc:* 742
Catullus (c. 85-c. 54 B.C.E.) *Anc:* 196
Marcus Junius Brutus (85-Oct. 23, 42 B.C.E.) *Anc:* 166, *Notor:* 146
Fulvia (c. 85/80-40 B.C.E.) *Notor:* 384
Marc Antony (c. 82-30 B.C.E.) *Anc:* 73
Cassius (d. 42 B.C.E.) *Anc:* 185
Vercingetorix (c. 75-c. 46 B.C.E.) *Anc:* 935
Herod the Great (73-spring, 4 B.C.E.) *Anc:* 403, *Notor:* 459
Gaius Maecenas (c. 70-8 B.C.E.) *Anc:* 527
Vergil (Oct. 15, 70-Sept. 21, 19 B.C.E.) *Anc:* 938
Cleopatra VII (69-Aug. 3, 30 B.C.E.) *Anc:* 229
Horace (Dec. 8, 65-Nov. 27, 8 B.C.E.) *Anc:* 430
Strabo (64 or 63 B.C.E.-after 23 C.E.) *Anc:* 827
Marcus Vipsanius Agrippa (c. 63-Mar., 12 B.C.E.) *Anc:* 20
Augustus (Sept. 23, 63 B.C.E.-Aug. 19, 14 C.E.) *Anc:* 145
Marcus Verrius Flaccus (c. 60 B.C.E.-c. 22 C.E.) *Anc:* 941
Livia Drusilla (Jan. 30, 58 B.C.E.-29 C.E.) *Anc:* 508
Sextus Propertius (c. 57-48 B.C.E.-d. c. 16 B.C.E.-2 C.E.) *Anc:* 704
Ovid (Mar. 20, 43 B.C.E.-17 C.E.) *Anc:* 602
Tiberius (Nov. 16, 42 B.C.E.-Mar. 16, 37 C.E.) *Anc:* 888
Julia III (39 B.C.E.-14 C.E.) *Anc:* 489
Antonia Minor (Jan. 31, 36 B.C.E.-May 1, 37 C.E.) *Anc:* 71
Sulpicia (fl. late 1st cent. B.C.E.) *Anc:* 834
Aulus Cornelius Celsus (c. 25 B.C.E.-c. 50 C.E.) *Anc:* 199
Mary (b. 22 B.C.E.) *Anc:* 539
Herod Antipas (before 20 B.C.E.-after 39 C.E.) *Notor:* 458
Philo of Alexandria (c. 20 B.C.E.-c. 45 C.E.) *Anc:* 640
Arminius (c. 17 B.C.E.-19 C.E.) *Anc:* 99
Phaedrus (c. 15 B.C.E.-c. 55 C.E.) *Anc:* 628
Pontius Pilate (c. 10 B.C.E.-after 36 C.E.) *Anc:* 643, *Notor:* 840
Claudius I (Aug. 1, 10 B.C.E.-Oct. 13, 54 C.E.) *Anc:* 217
Saint John the Baptist (c. 7 B.C.E.-c. 27 C.E.) *Anc:* 474
Jesus (c. 6 B.C.E.-30 C.E.) *Anc:* 458
Seneca the Younger (c. 4 B.C.E.-Apr., 65 C.E.) *Anc:* 766

1 C.E. - 100 C.E.

Boudicca (1st cent.-60) *Anc:* 163
Saint Thomas (c. early 1st cent.-second half of 1st cent.) *Anc:* 878
Arria the Elder (c. 1-42) *Anc:* 102
Cassius Chaerea (c. 1-41 C.E.) *Notor:* 195
Johanan ben Zakkai (c. 1 -c. 80) *Anc:* 468
Saint Stephen (c. 5-c. 36) *Anc:* 821
Vespasian (Nov. 17, 9-June 23, 79) *Anc:* 943
Saint Paul (c. 10-c. 64) *Anc:* 611
John the Apostle (c. 10-c. 100) *Anc:* 471
Saint Peter (d. 64) *Anc:* 624
Caligula (Aug. 31, 12-Jan. 24, 41) *Anc:* 176, *Notor:* 165
Salome (c. 15-1st cent.) *Notor:* 932
Agrippina the Younger (Nov. 6, c. 15-Mar. 59) *Anc:* 23
Valeria Messallina (c. 20-48) *Anc:* 561
Pliny the Elder (probably 23-Aug. 25, 79) *Anc:* 665
Wang Chong (27-c. 100) *Anc:* 953
Ignatius of Antioch (c. 30-Dec. 20, 107) *Anc:* 437
Poppaea Sabina (31-65) *Anc:* 685
Ban Gu (32-92) *Anc:* 149
Flavius Josephus (c. 37-c. 100) *Anc:* 477, *Notor:* 541
Nero (Dec. 15, 37-Jun. 9, 68) *Anc:* 591, *Notor:* 777
Martial (Mar. 1, 38-41-c. 103) *Anc:* 536
Akiba ben Joseph (c. 40-c. 135) *Anc:* 29
Pedanius Dioscorides (c. 40-c. 90) *Anc:* 289
Clement I (d. c. 99) *Anc:* 223
Gnaeus Julius Agricola (June 13, 40-Aug. 23, 93) *Anc:* 17
Ban Zhao (c. 45-c. 120) *Anc:* 152
Plutarch (c. 46-after 120) *Anc:* 670
Domitian (Oct. 24, 51-Sept. 18, 96) *Notor:* 289
Trajan (c. 53-c. Aug. 8, 117) *Anc:* 903

Tacitus (c. 56-c. 120) *Anc:* 837
Juvenal (c. 60-c. 130) *Anc:* 493
Hero of Alexandria (fl. 62-late 1st cent.) *Anc:* 401
Hadrian (Jan. 24, 76-July 10, 138) *Anc:* 370
Aśvaghosa (c. 80-c. 150) *Anc:* 130
Kanishka (late 1st or 2d cent.-c. 152) *Anc:* 499

101 C.E. - 200 C.E.

Aretaeus of Cappadocia (b. probably 2d cent.) *Anc:* 84
Valentinus (probably early 2d cent.-c. 165) *Anc:* 918
Julia Mamaea (2d cent.-Mar. 10, 235) *Anc:* 483
Ptolemy, astronomer (c. 100-c. 178) *Anc:* 712
Pausanias the Traveler (c. 110-115 to c. 180) *Anc:* 618
Lucian (c. 120-c. 180) *Anc:* 513
Saint Irenaeus (between 120 and 140-c. 202) *Anc:* 442
Marcus Aurelius (Apr. 26, 121-Mar. 17, 180 C.E.) *Anc:* 530
Galen (129-c. 199) *Anc:* 348
Dio Cassius (c. 150-c. 235) *Anc:* 274
Cao Cao (155-220) *Anc:* 182
Commodus (Aug. 31, 161-Dec. 31, 192) *Notor:* 227
Julia Domna (c. 167-217) *Anc:* 480
Hippolytus of Rome (c. 170-c. 235) *Anc:* 423
Julia Soaemias (c. 180-222) *Anc:* 486
Origen (c. 185-c. 254 C.E.) *Anc:* 599

201 C.E. - 300 C.E.

Saint Christopher (possibly 3d cent.-c. 250) *Anc:* 205
Saint Denis (d. c. 250) *Anc:* 268
Elagabalus (203/204-Mar. 11, 222) *Notor:* 326
Plotinus (205-270) *Anc:* 668
Wang Bi (226-249) *Anc:* 950
Porphyry (c. 234-c. 305) *Anc:* 687
Zenobia (c. 240-after 274) *Anc:* 986
Diocletian (c. 245-Dec. 3, 316) *Anc:* 280
Saint Helena (c. 248-c. 328) *Anc:* 391
Diophantus (fl. c. 250) *Anc:* 286
Galerius (c. 250-May, 311) *Notor:* 390
Saint Anthony of Egypt (c. 251-probably Jan. 17, 356) *Anc:* 60
Eusebius of Caesarea (c. 260-May 30, 339) *Anc:* 330
Constantine the Great (Feb. 17/27, c. 272-285-May 22, 337) *Anc:* 239
Saint Athanasius of Alexandria (c. 293-May 2, 373) *Anc:* 132

301 C.E. - 400 C.E.

Jingū (early 4th cent.-late 4th cent.) *Anc:* 465,
Pappus (c. 300-c. 350) *Anc:* 606
Wang Xizhi (c. 303-c. 350) *Anc:* 955
Ezana (c. 307-c. 379) *Anc:* 333
Shāpūr II (309-379) *Anc:* 774
Ulfilas (311-383) *Anc:* 911
Gregory of Nazianzus (329/330-389/390) *Anc:* 361
Saint Jerome (331-347 to probably 420) *Anc:* 456
Gregory of Nyssa (c. 335-c. 394) *Anc:* 363
Saint Siricius (c. 335/340-Nov. 26, 399) *Anc:* 796
Saint Ambrose (339-Apr. 4, 397) *Anc:* 42
Kālidāsa (c. 340-c. 400) *Anc:* 496
Priscillian (c. 340-385) *Anc:* 698
Theodosius the Great (Jan. 11, 346 or 347-Jan. 17, 395) *Anc:* 868
Theodore of Mopsuestia (c. 350-428) *Anc:* 862
Saint John Chrysostom (c. 354-Sept. 14, 407) *Anc:* 208
Saint Augustine (Nov. 13, 354-Aug. 28, 430) *Anc:* 142
Asanga (c. 365-c. 440) *Anc:* 111
Flavius Stilicho (c. 365-Aug. 22, 408) *Anc:* 824
Tao Qian (365-427) *Anc:* 843
Hypatia (c. 370-Mar., 415) *Anc:* 434
Ōjin Tennō (late 4th cent.-early 5th cent.) *Anc:* 594
Saint Vincent of Lérins (late 4th cent.-c. 450) *Anc:* 947
Xie Lingyun (385-433) *Anc:* 975
Genseric (c. 390-477) *Anc:* 351
Saint Simeon Stylites (c. 390-459) *Anc:* 789
Theodoret of Cyrrhus (c. 393-c. 458) *Anc:* 865
Vasubandhu (c. 400-c. 480) *Anc:* 930

401 C.E. - 500 C.E.

Bodhidharma (5th cent.-6th cent.) *Anc:* 160
Priscian (5th cent.-6th cent.) *MA:* 859
Attila (c. 406-453) *Anc:* 138, *Notor:* 45
Proclus (c. 410-485) *Anc:* 701
Saint Patrick (between 418 and 422-Mar. 17, 493) *MA:* 811
Hengist (c. 420-c. 488) *Anc:* 394
Odoacer (c. 435-about Mar. 15, 493) *MA:* 782
Dionysius Exiguus (latter half of 5th cent.-first half of 6th cent.) *MA:* 313
Saint Brigit (c. 450-Feb. 1, 525) *MA:* 198
Theodoric the Great (c. 454-Aug. 30, 526) *MA:* 1012
Clovis (c. 466-Nov. 27, 511) *MA:* 290
Saint Clotilda (c. 474-June 3, 545) *MA:* 287
Āryabhaṭa the Elder (c. 476-c. 550) *MA:* 108
Saint Benedict of Nursia (c. 480-c. 547) *MA:* 153
Justinian I (probably May 11, 483-Nov. 14, 565) *MA:* 598
Cassiodorus (c. 490-c. 585) *MA:* 233
Amalasuntha (c. 495-Apr. 30, 535) *MA:* 75
Theodora (c. 497-June 28, 548) *MA:* 1008, *Notor:* 1028

501 C.E. - 600 C.E.

Alboin (6th cent.-572) *MA:* 45
Khosrow I (c. 510-579) *MA:* 613
Justin II (c. 520-Oct. 5, 578) *Notor:* 546
Gregory of Tours (Nov. 30, 539-Nov. 17, 594) *MA:* 426
Gregory the Great (c. 540-Mar. 12, 604) *MA:* 430
Fredegunde (c. 550-597) *MA:* 381
Khadīja (c. 554-619) *MA:* 610
Suiko (554-Apr. 15, 628) *MA:* 974
Saint Isidore of Seville (c. 560-Apr. 4, 636) *MA:* 555
Sergius I (d. Dec. 9, 638) *MA:* 933
Muḥammad (c. 570-June 8, 632) *MA:* 733
Shōtoku Taishi (574-Apr. 8, 622) *MA:* 940
Heraclius (c. 575-Feb. 11, 641) *MA:* 505
ʿUmar I (c. 586-Nov. 3, 644) *MA:* 1037
Harṣa (c. 590-c. 647) *MA:* 460
Brahmagupta (c. 598-c. 660) *MA:* 195
Taizong (Jan. 23, 599-May, 649) *MA:* 993
Yan Liben (c. 600-673) *MA:* 1140

601 C.E. - 700 C.E.

Cædmon (early 7th cent.-c. 680) *MA:* 219
Xuanzang (c. 602-664) *MA:* 1136
Saint Hilda of Whitby (614-Nov. 17, 689) *MA:* 509
Paul of Aegina (c. 625-c. 690) *MA:* 814
Wu Hou (625-Dec. 16, 705) *MA:* 1127
Saint Sergius I (635-Sept. 8, 701) *MA:* 936
al-Ḥasan al-Baṣrī (642-728) *MA:* 471
ʿAbd al-Malik (c. 646-Oct., 705) *MA:* 3
Damia al-Kāhina (c. 650-c. 702) *MA:* 604
Saint Boniface (c. 675-June 5, 754) *MA:* 183
John of Damascus (c. 675-Dec. 4, 749) *MA:* 587
Charles Martel (c. 688-Oct. 22, 741) *MA:* 250
Abū Ḥanīfah (c. 699-767) *MA:* 18
Ṭāriq ibn-Ziyād (before 700-c. 720) *MA:* 1005
Śaṅkara (c. 700-c. 750) *MA:* 924

701 C.E. - 800 C.E.

Widukind (8th cent.-c. 807) *MA:* 1094
Li Bo (701-762) *MA:* 653
Wang Wei (701-761) *MA:* 1085
An Lushan (703-757) *MA:* 78
Du Fu (712-770) *MA:* 322
Rābiʿah al-ʿAdawiyah (c. 717-801) *MA:* 873
Kōken (718-770) *MA:* 623
Abū Mūsā Jābir ibn Ḥayyān (721-815) *MA:* 562
Alcuin (c. 735-May 19, 804) *MA:* 49
Charlemagne (Apr. 2, 742-Jan. 28, 814) *MA:* 242

Saint Irene (c. 752-Aug. 9, 803) *MA:* 548
Theophanes the Confessor (c. 752-c. 818) *MA:* 1020
Hārūn al-Rashīd (Feb., 766-Mar. 24, 809) *MA:* 467
Egbert (c. 770-839) *MA:* 353
Kōbō Daishi (July 27, 774-Apr. 22, 835) *MA:* 620,
al-Jāḥiẓ (c. 776-868) *MA:* 568
al-Khwārizmī (c. 780-c. 850) *MA:* 617
Rabanus Maurus (c. 780-Feb. 4, 856) *MA:* 870
Aḥmad ibn Ḥanbal (Dec., 780-July, 855) *MA:* 36

801 C.E. - 900 C.E.

Ratramnus (early 9th cent.-c. 868) *MA:* 879
Rurik (9th cent.-879) *MA:* 911
Dhuoda (c. 805-c. 843) *MA:* 310
Basil the Macedonian (812 or 813-Aug. 29, 886) *MA:* 133
Nicholas the Great (c. 819/822-Nov. 13, 867) *MA:* 764
Charles the Bald (June 13, 823-Oct. 6, 877) *MA:* 254
Saint Methodius (c. 825-Apr. 6, 884) *MA:* 294
Saint Cyril (c. 827-Feb. 14, 869) *MA:* 294
Boris I of Bulgaria (830-May 15, 907) *MA:* 189
al-Ṭabarī (c. 839-923) *MA:* 988
Alfred the Great (849-Oct. 26, 899) *MA:* 63
Árpád (c. 850-907) *MA:* 105
al-Ḥallāj (c. 858-Mar. 26, 922) *MA:* 454
al-Battānī (858-929) *MA:* 137
Saint Ludmilla (c. 860-Sept. 15, 921) *MA:* 670
Rollo (c. 860-c. 932) *MA:* 900
al-Rāzī (c. 864-925) *MA:* 369
Æthelflæd (c. 870-June 12, 918) *MA:* 30
Edward the Elder (870?-July 17, 924) *MA:* 340
al-Ashʿarī (873 or 874-935 or 936) *MA:* 111
Wang Kŏn (877-943) *MA:* 1081
Marozia (c. 890-c. 936) *Notor:* 706
al-Masʿūdī (c. 890-956) *MA:* 703
Saint Olga (890-969) *MA:* 792
ʿAbd al-Raḥmān III al-Nāṣir (Jan., 891-Oct. 15, 961) *MA:* 9
Ngo Quyen (c. 898-944) *MA:* 756

901 C.E. - 1000

Otto I (Nov. 23, 912-May 7, 973) *MA:* 805
Hrosvitha (c. 930/935-c. 1002) *MA:* 516
Firdusi (932/941-between 1020 and 1025) *MA:* 375
Abul Wefa (June 10, 940-July 15, 998) *MA:* 21
Sylvester II (c. 945-May 12, 1003) *MA:* 983
Vladimir I (c. 956-July 15, 1015) *MA:* 1068
Saint Fulbert of Chartres (c. 960-Apr. 10, 1028) *MA:* 399
Anna, Princess of the Byzantine Empire (Mar. 13, 963-1011) *MA:* 86
Alhazen (965-1039) *MA:* 66
Sei Shōnagon (c. 966 or 967-1013) *MA:* 930
Fujiwara Michinaga (966-Jan. 3, 1028) *MA:* 396
Olaf I (c. 968-Sept. 9, 1000) *MA:* 789
Ethelred II, the Unready (968?-Apr. 23, 1016) *MA:* 362
Leif Eriksson (c. 970-c. 1035) *MA:* 640
Maḥmūd of Ghazna (c. 971-1030) *MA:* 683, *MA:* 683
Henry II the Saint (May 6, 973-July 13, 1024) *MA:* 486
al-Bīrūnī (Sept., 973-Dec. 13, 1048) *MA:* 163
Stephen I (975-Aug. 15, 1038) *MA:* 964
Murasaki Shikibu (c. 978-c. 1030) *MA:* 738
Avicenna (Aug. or Sept., 980-1037) *MA:* 123
al-Ḥākim (Aug. 14, 985-Feb. 13, 1021?) *Notor:* 441
Guido d'Arezzo (c. 991-1050) *MA:* 439
Canute the Great (c. 995-Nov. 12, 1035) *MA:* 221
Saint Olaf (c. 995-July 29, 1030) *MA:* 785

1001 - 1100

Jōchō (d. 1057) *MA:* 581
Trotula (c. 11th cent.-1097) *MA:* 1031
Leo IX (June 21, 1002-Apr. 19, 1054) *MA:* 644
Edward the Confessor (c. 1005-Jan. 5, 1066) *MA:* 337
Ouyang Xiu (1007-1072) *MA:* 808
Rāmānuja (c. 1017-1137) *MA:* 876

Michael Psellus (c. 1018-1078) *MA:* 863
Niẓām al-Mulk (1018 or 1019-Oct. 14, 1092) *MA:* 774
Sima Guang (1019-1086) *MA:* 945
Gregory VII (c. 1020-May 25, 1085) *MA:* 433
Ibn Gabirol (c. 1020-c. 1057) *MA:* 532
Wang Anshi (1021-1086) *MA:* 1079
Harold II (c. 1022-Oct. 14, 1066) *MA:* 457
William the Conqueror (c. 1028-Sept. 9, 1087) *MA:* 1117
Alp Arslan (c. 1030-Nov., 1072, or Jan., 1073) *MA:* 70
Su Dongpo (Dec. 19, 1036-July 28, 1101) *MA:* 968
Saint László I (June 27, 1040-July 29, 1095) *MA:* 637
Urban II (1042-July 29, 1099) *MA:* 1043
El Cid (c. 1043-July 10, 1099) *MA:* 278
Matilda of Canossa (1046-July 24, 1115) *MA:* 705
Omar Khayyám (May 18, 1048?-Dec. 4, 1123?) *MA:* 795
Henry IV of Germany (Nov. 11, 1050-Aug. 7, 1106) *MA:* 497
Bohemond I (c. 1052-Mar. 7, 1111) *MA:* 176
Mi Fei (1052-1107) *MA:* 718
al-Ghazzālī (1058-Dec. 18, 1111) *MA:* 415
Henry I (c. Sept., 1068-Dec. 1, 1135) *MA:* 481
Judah ha-Levi (c. 1075-July, 1141) *MA:* 591
Tancred (c. 1078-Dec. 12, 1112) *MA:* 1003
Peter Abelard (1079-Apr. 21, 1142) *MA:* 13
Nest verch Rhys ap Tewdwr (c. 1080-c. 1136) *MA:* 753
David I (between 1080 and 1085-May 24, 1153) *MA:* 304
Suger (1081-Jan. 13, 1151) *MA:* 971
Anna Comnena (Dec. 1, 1083-after 1148) *MA:* 89
Li Qingzhao (c. 1084-1155) *MA:* 656
Gwenllian verch Gruffydd (c. 1085-1136) *MA:* 448
William of Saint-Thierry (c. 1085-Sept. 8, 1147 or 1148) *MA:* 1114
Suryavarman II (d. 1150) *MA:* 980
Saint Bernard of Clairvaux (1090-Aug. 20, 1153) *MA:* 160
ʿAbd al-Muʾmin (1094-May 2, 1163) *MA:* 6
Christina of Markyate (c. 1096-1160) *MA:* 270
King Stephen (c. 1097-Oct. 25, 1154) *MA:* 960
Hildegard von Bingen (1098-Sept. 17, 1179) *MA:* 512
Geoffrey of Monmouth (c. 1100-1154) *MA:* 405
al-Idrīsī (1100-between 1164 and 1166) *MA:* 539

1101 - 1200

Benjamin of Tudela (12th cent.-1173) *MA:* 157
Yo Fei (1103-1141) *MA:* 1145
Alexander III (c. 1105-Aug. 30, 1181) *MA:* 56
Afonso I (c. 1108-Dec. 6, 1185) *MA:* 33
Enrico Dandolo (1108?-1205) *MA:* 298
Adrian IV (c. 1110-Sept. 1, 1159) *MA:* 27
Taira Kiyomori (1118-Mar. 21, 1181) *MA:* 990
Saint Thomas Becket (Dec. 21, 1118-Dec. 29, 1170) *MA:* 147
Eleanor of Aquitaine (c. 1122-Apr. 1, 1204) *MA:* 355
Frederick I Barbarossa (c. 1123-June 10, 1190) *MA:* 384
Averroës (1126-1198) *MA:* 118
Henry the Lion (1129-Aug. 6, 1195) *MA:* 473
Zhu Xi (Oct. 18, 1130-Apr. 23, 1200) *MA:* 1159
Henry II (Mar. 5, 1133-July 6, 1189) *MA:* 483
Joachim of Fiore (c. 1135-1202) *MA:* 575
Moses Maimonides (Mar. 30, 1135-Dec. 13, 1204) *MA:* 686
Saladin (1138-Mar. 4, 1193) *MA:* 918
Minamoto Yoritomo (1147-Feb. 9, 1199) *MA:* 721
Fakhr al-Dīn al-Rāzī (1148 or 1149-1210) *MA:* 369
Lalibela (c. mid-12th cent.-c. 1221) *MA:* 632
Chrétien de Troyes (c. 1150-c. 1190) *MA:* 267
Marie de France (c. 1150-c. 1215) *MA:* 693
Saxo Grammaticus (c. 1150-c. 1220) *MA:* 927
Unkei (c. 1150-1223) *MA:* 1040
William of Auxerre (c. 1150-Nov. 3, 1231) *MA:* 1101
Geoffroi de Villehardouin (1150-c. 1213) *MA:* 1059
Pérotin (1155-1160 to 1200-1205) *MA:* 824
Genghis Khan (between 1155 and 1162-Aug. 18, 1227) *MA:* 402, *Notor:* 400
Alexander Neckam (Sept. 8, 1157-probably Mar. 31, 1217) *MA:* 750
Richard I (Sept. 8, 1157-Apr. 6, 1199) *MA:* 891
Queen Tamara (1159-1212) *MA:* 998
Hartmann von Aue (c. 1160-1165-c. 1210-1220) *MA:* 463
Innocent III (1160 or 1161-July 16, 1216) *MA:* 541
Ma Yuan (c. 1165-c. 1225) *MA:* 677
Ibn al-ʿArabī (July 28, 1165-Nov. 16, 1240) *MA:* 526
King John (Dec. 24, 1166-Oct. 18, 1216) *MA:* 584, *Notor:* 534
Saint Dominic (c. 1170-Aug. 6, 1221) *MA:* 316

Gregory IX (c. 1170-Aug. 22, 1241) *MA:* 436
Leonardo of Pisa (c. 1170-c. 1240) *MA:* 648
Walther von der Vogelweide (c. 1170-c. 1230) *MA:* 1075
Wolfram von Eschenbach (c. 1170-c. 1217) *MA:* 1123
Valdemar II (May 9, 1170-Mar. 28, 1241) *MA:* 1047
Hubert de Burgh (late 1100's-May 12, 1243) *MA:* 211
Sorghaghtani Beki (late 1100's-Feb. or Mar., 1252) *MA:* 954
Raymond of Peñafort (c. 1175-Jan. 6, 1275) *MA:* 881
Snorri Sturluson (1178 or 1179-Sept. 22, 1241) *MA:* 950
Yaqut (1179-1229) *MA:* 1143
Giovanni da Pian del Carpini (c. 1180-Aug. 1, 1252) *MA:* 226
Innocent IV (c. 1180-Dec. 7, 1254) *MA:* 545
Xia Gui (c. 1180-1230) *MA:* 1134
Saint Francis of Assisi (c. 1181-Oct. 3, 1226) *MA:* 378
Blanche of Castile (Mar. 4, 1188-Nov. 26 or 27, 1252) *MA:* 166
Vincent of Beauvais (c. 1190-1264) *MA:* 1063
William of Auvergne (c. 1190-Mar. 30, 1249) *MA:* 1097
Naḥmanides (1194-1270) *MA:* 747
Saint Clare of Assisi (July 16, 1194-Aug. 11, 1253) *MA:* 284
Frederick II (Dec. 26, 1194-Dec. 13, 1250) *MA:* 389
Saint Anthony of Padua (Aug. 15, 1195-June 13, 1231) *MA:* 95
Raziya (d. 1240) *MA:* 888
Saint Albertus Magnus (c. 1200-Nov. 15, 1280) *MA:* 42
Saʿdi (c. 1200-c. 1291) *MA:* 915
William of Saint-Amour (c. 1200-Sept. 13, 1272) *MA:* 1110
Beatrice of Nazareth (1200-1268) *MA:* 144

1201 - 1300

Robin Hood (fl. 13th cent.?) *Notor:* 909
Henry de Bracton (early 13th cent.-1268) *MA:* 192
Petrus Peregrinus de Maricourt (early 13th cent.-13th cent.) *MA:* 820
Saint Elizabeth of Hungary (1207-Nov. 17, 1231) *MA:* 359
Henry III (Oct. 1, 1207-Nov. 16, 1272) *MA:* 490
Simon de Montfort (c. 1208-Aug. 4, 1265) *MA:* 725
James I the Conqueror (Feb. 2, 1208-July 27, 1276) *MA:* 571
Gottfried von Strassburg (fl. c. 1210) *MA:* 423
Mechthild von Magdeburg (c. 1210-c. 1297) *MA:* 708
Louis IX (Apr. 25, 1214-Aug. 25, 1270) *MA:* 666
Sundiata (c. 1215-c. 1255) *MA:* 977
William of Moerbeke (c. 1215-c. 1286) *MA:* 1105
William of Rubrouck (c. 1215-c. 1295) *MA:* 1107
Kublai Khan (1215-1294) *MA:* 626
Saint Bonaventure (1217 or 1221-July 15, 1274) *MA:* 180
Rudolf I (May 1, 1218-July 15, 1291) *MA:* 904
Saint Alexander Nevsky (c. 1220-Nov. 14, 1263) *MA:* 52
Roger Bacon (c. 1220-c. 1292) *MA:* 127
Nicola Pisano (c. 1220-between 1278 and 1284) *MA:* 847
Salimbene (Oct. 9, 1221-c. 1290) *MA:* 921
Alfonso X (Nov. 23, 1221-Apr. 4, 1284) *MA:* 59
Nichiren (Mar. 30, 1222-Nov. 14, 1282) *MA:* 758
Baybars I (c. 1223-July 1, 1277) *MA:* 139
Thomas Aquinas (1224 or 1225-Mar. 7, 1274) *MA:* 1027
John Pecham (c. 1230-Dec. 8, 1292) *MA:* 817
Boniface VIII (c. 1235-Oct. 11, 1303) *MA:* 186, *Notor:* 115
Raymond Lull (c. 1235-early 1316) *MA:* 673
Siger of Brabant (c. 1235-c. 1282) *MA:* 942
Arnold of Villanova (c. 1239-Sept. 6, 1311) *MA:* 98
Edward I (June 17, 1239-July 7, 1307) *MA:* 343
Cimabue (c. 1240-c. 1302) *MA:* 282
Arnolfo di Cambio (c. 1245-between 1302 and 1310) *MA:* 102
Blessed Angela of Foligno (1248-Jan. 4, 1309) *MA:* 81
Pietro d'Abano (c. 1250-1316) *MA:* 1
Adam de la Halle (c. 1250-c. 1285-1288) *MA:* 24
Giovanni Pisano (c. 1250-between 1314 and 1318) *MA:* 847
Moses de León (1250-1305) *MA:* 730
ʿAlāʾ-ud-Dīn Muḥammad Khaljī (d. 1316) *MA:* 39
Marco Polo (c. 1254-Jan. 8, 1324) *MA:* 853
Duccio di Buoninsegna (c. 1255-Aug. 3, 1319) *MA:* 326
Marguerite Porete (c. 1255-1280-June 1, 1310) *MA:* 856
Osman I (c. 1258-1326) *MA:* 800

Nijō (1258-after 1306) *MA:* 771
Guido Cavalcanti (c. 1259-Aug. 27 or 28, 1300) *MA:* 239
Dante (May or June, 1265-Sept. 13 or 14, 1321) *MA:* 300
Giotto (c. 1266-Jan. 8, 1337) *MA:* 421
John Duns Scotus (c. Mar., 1266-Nov. 8, 1308) *MA:* 329
Philip IV the Fair (1268-Nov. 29, 1314) *MA:* 839
Andrea Pisano (c. 1270-1290-c. 1348) *MA:* 845
William Wallace (c. 1270-Aug. 23, 1305) *MA:* 1072
Maḥmūd Ghāzān (Nov. 5, 1271-May 11, 1304) *MA:* 411
Robert Bruce (July 11, 1274-June 7, 1329) *MA:* 200
Giovanni Villani (c. 1275-1348) *MA:* 1056
Jacqueline Félicie (c. 1280-after 1322) *MA:* 372
Pietro Lorenzetti (c. 1280-1348) *MA:* 659
Mansa Mūsā (c. 1280-1337) *MA:* 744
Lady Alice Kyteler (1280-after 1324) *MA:* 629, *Notor:* 598
Simone Martini (c. 1284-1344) *MA:* 696
Edward II (Apr. 25, 1284-Sept. 21, 1327) *MA:* 347
William of Ockham (c. 1285-1347 or 1349) *MA:* 778
Levi ben Gershom (1288-probably Apr. 20, 1344) *MA:* 650
Guy de Chauliac (c. 1290-July 25, 1368) *MA:* 445
Ambrogio Lorenzetti (c. 1290-1348) *MA:* 659
Jean Pucelle (c. 1290-1334) *MA:* 866
John Parricida (1290-Dec. 13, 1312 or 1313) *Notor:* 536
Philippe de Vitry (Oct. 31, 1291-June 9, 1361) *MA:* 1065
Isabella of France (c. 1292-Aug. 23, 1358) *MA:* 552
Jean Buridan (c. 1295-c. 1358) *MA:* 215
Johannes de Muris (c. 1300-c. 1351) *MA:* 741
Nicholas of Autrecourt (c. 1300-after 1350) *MA:* 761

1301 - 1400

Wat Tyler (14th cent.-June 15, 1381) *MA:* 1033
Ibn Baṭṭūṭah (Feb. 24, 1304-c. 1377) *MA:* 529
Petrarch (July 20, 1304-July 18, 1374) *MA:* 827
Ashikaga Takauji (1305-June 7, 1358) *MA:* 115
Jean de Venette (1307 or 1308-1368 or 1369) *MA:* 1053
Andrea Orcagna (c. 1308-c. 1368) *MA:* 798
Stefan Dušan (1308-Dec. 20, 1355) *MA:* 957
Casimir the Great (Apr. 30, 1310-Nov. 5, 1370) *MA:* 229
Philippa of Hainaut (c. 1312-Aug. 15, 1369) *MA:* 842
Edward III (Nov. 13, 1312-June 21, 1377) *MA:* 350
Cola di Rienzo (1313-Oct. 8, 1354) *MA:* 897
Giovanni Boccaccio (June or July, 1313-Dec. 21, 1375) *MA:* 169
Charles IV (May 14, 1316-Nov. 29, 1378) *MA:* 257
Urban VI (c. 1318-Oct. 15, 1389) *Notor:* 1053
Hafiz (c. 1320-1389 or 1390) *MA:* 451
David II (Mar. 5, 1324-Feb. 22, 1371) *MA:* 307
Francesco Landini (c. 1325-Sept. 2, 1397) *MA:* 635
John Wyclif (c. 1328-Dec. 31, 1384) *MA:* 1130
John Ball (1331-July 15, 1381) *MA:* 130
Ibn Khaldūn (May 27, 1332-Mar. 17, 1406) *MA:* 536
Peter the Cruel (Aug., 30, 1334-Mar. 23, 1369) *Notor:* 827
Tamerlane (1336-1405) *MA:* 1000
Jean Froissart (c. 1337?-1404) *MA:* 392
Claus Sluter (c. 1340-1350-c. 1405-1406) *MA:* 947
Julian of Norwich (1342-after 1416) *MA:* 595
Geoffrey Chaucer (c. 1343-Oct. 25?, 1400) *MA:* 264
Saint Catherine of Siena (Mar. 25, 1347-Apr. 29, 1380) *MA:* 236
Władysław II Jagiełło (c. 1351-June 1, 1434) *MA:* 1120
Margaret of Denmark, Norway, and Sweden (1353-Oct. 28, 1412) *MA:* 689
Wenceslaus (Feb. 26, 1361-Aug. 16, 1419) *MA:* 1088
Zeami Motokiyo (1363-1443) *MA:* 1152
Yonglo (May 2, 1363-Aug. 5, 1424) *MA:* 1147
Christine de Pizan (c. 1365-c. 1430) *MA:* 273
Richard II (Jan. 6, 1367-Feb., 1400) *MA:* 893
Henry IV of England (Apr. 3, 1367-Mar. 20, 1413) *MA:* 493
Charles VI (Dec. 3, 1368-Oct. 21, 1422) *Notor:* 203
Leonardo Bruni (c. 1370-Mar. 9, 1444) *MA:* 208
Zheng He (c. 1371-between 1433 and 1436) *MA:* 1156
Jan Hus (1372 or 1373-July 6, 1415) *MA:* 522
Margery Kempe (c. 1373-c. 1440) *MA:* 607
Jadwiga (1373 or 1374-July 17, 1399) *MA:* 1120
Jacopo della Quercia (c. 1374-Oct. 20, 1438) *MA:* 566
Filippo Brunelleschi (1377-Apr. 15, 1446) *MA:* 205
Lorenzo Ghiberti (c. 1378-Dec. 1, 1455) *MA:* 418

Thomas à Kempis (1379-Aug. 8, 1471) *MA:* 1022
Poggio (Feb. 11, 1380-Oct. 30, 1459) *MA:* 850
Itzcóatl (c. 1382-1440) *MA:* 558
Alain Chartier (c. 1385-c. 1430) *MA:* 260
Sir John Fortescue (c. 1385-c. 1479) *Ren:* 340
Donatello (c. 1386-Dec. 13, 1466) *MA:* 319
Henry V (Sept. 16?, 1387-Aug. 31, 1422) *MA:* 501
Hubert van Eyck (before 1390-probably Sept. 18, 1426) *MA:* 365
John Dunstable (c. 1390-Dec. 24, 1453) *MA:* 333
Jan van Eyck (c. 1390-July 9, 1441) *MA:* 365
Pachacuti (c. 1391-1471) *Ren:* 746
Johann Gutenberg (1394-1399-probably Feb. 3, 1468) *MA:* 441
Prince Henry the Navigator (Mar. 4, 1394-Nov. 13, 1460) *MA:* 477
Charles d'Orléans (Nov. 24, 1394-Jan. 4, 1465) *MA:* 247
Philip the Good (July 31, 1396-June 15, 1467) *MA:* 832
Nicholas V (Nov. 15, 1397-Mar. 24, 1455) *MA:* 768
Rogier van der Weyden (1399 or 1400-June 18, 1464) *MA:* 1092
Zara Yaqob (1399-1468) *Ren:* 1006

1401 - 1450

Nicholas of Cusa (1401-Aug. 11, 1464) *Ren:* 724
Masaccio (Dec. 21, 1401-1428) *MA:* 699
Nezahualcóyotl (1402-1472) *Ren:* 720
Charles VII (Feb. 22, 1403-July 22, 1461) *Ren:* 224
Leon Battista Alberti (Feb. 14, 1404-Apr., 1472) *Ren:* 18
Gilles de Rais (Sept. or Oct., 1404-Oct. 26, 1440) *Notor:* 880
Pius II (Oct. 18, 1405-Aug. 14/15, 1464) *Ren:* 794
János Hunyadi (c. 1407-Aug. 11, 1456) *MA:* 519
Lorenzo Valla (1407-Aug. 1, 1457) *MA:* 1049
Joan of Arc (c. 1412-May 30, 1431) *MA:* 578
Qāytbāy (1414-Aug. 8, 1496) *Ren:* 807
Sixtus IV (July 21, 1414-Aug. 12, 1484) *Ren:* 893
Frederick III (Sept. 21, 1415-Aug. 19, 1493) *Ren:* 350
Piero della Francesca (c. 1420-Oct. 12, 1492) *Ren:* 785
Sesshū (1420-1506) *Ren:* 865
Tomás de Torquemada (1420-Sept. 16, 1498) *Ren:* 939, *Notor:* 1038
Henry VI (Dec. 6, 1421-May 21, 1471) *Ren:* 434
William Caxton (c. 1422-c. 1491) *Ren:* 196
Sir Thomas Littleton (1422-Aug. 23, 1481) *Ren:* 570
Georg von Peuerbach (May 30, 1423-Apr. 8, 1461) *Ren:* 773
Louis XI (July 3, 1423-Aug. 30, 1483) *Ren:* 574
Sonni ʿAlī (c. early 15th cent.-Nov. 6, 1492) *Ren:* 900
Sir Thomas Malory (early 15th cent.-Mar. 14, 1471) *Ren:* 598
Henry IV of Castile (Jan. 6, 1425-Dec. 11, 1474) *Ren:* 432
Earl of Warwick (Nov. 22, 1428-Apr. 14, 1471) *Ren:* 989
Giovanni Bellini (c. 1430-1516) *Ren:* 97
Andrea Mantegna (c. 1431-Sept. 13, 1506) *Ren:* 601
François Villon (1431-1463?) *Ren:* 973
Alexander VI (Jan. 1, 1431-Aug. 18, 1503) *Ren:* 27, *Notor:* 14
Vlad III the Impaler (late 1431-Dec., 1476) *Ren:* 981, *Notor:* 1072
Mehmed II (Mar. 30, 1432-May 3, 1481) *MA:* 711, *Ren:* 659
Marsilio Ficino (Oct. 19, 1433-Oct. 1, 1499) *Ren:* 332
Andrea del Verrocchio (1435-Oct. 7, 1488) *Ren:* 962
Francisco Jiménez de Cisneros (1436-Nov. 8, 1517) *Ren:* 503
Isaac ben Judah Abravanel (1437-Nov., 1508) *Ren:* 1
Muḥammad ibn ʿAbd al-Karīm al-Maghīlī (c. 1440-between 1503 and 1506) *Ren:* 595
Martín Alonso Pinzón (c. 1440-Mar. 20, 1493) *Ren:* 789
Ivan the Great (Jan. 22, 1440-Oct. 27, 1505) *Ren:* 487
Mohammed I Askia (c. 1442-1538) *Ren:* 686
Le Thanh Tong (1442-1497) *Ren:* 546
Edward IV (Apr. 28, 1442-Apr. 9, 1483) *Ren:* 301
Matthias I Corvinus (Feb. 24, 1443-Apr. 6, 1490) *Ren:* 642
Julius II (Dec. 5, 1443-Feb. 21, 1513) *Ren:* 518
Lady Margaret Beaufort (May 31, 1443-June 29, 1509) *Ren:* 90
Sandro Botticelli (c. 1444-May 17, 1510) *Ren:* 123
Donato Bramante (1444-Apr. 11, 1514) *Ren:* 132
Pêro da Covilhã (c. 1447-after 1526) *Ren:* 259
Saint Catherine of Genoa (1447-Sept. 15, 1510) *Ren:* 191
Bayezid II (Dec., 1447 or Jan., 1448-May 26, 1512) *Ren:* 87
Sophia Palaeologus (c. 1449-Apr. 7, 1503) *Ren:* 749

Lorenzo de' Medici (Jan. 1, 1449-Apr. 8, 1492) *Ren:* 655
Guacanagarí (c. mid-15th cent.-c. early 16th cent.) *Ren:* 408
Hieronymus Bosch (c. 1450-Aug. 9, 1516) *Ren:* 120
John Cabot (c. 1450-c. 1498) *Ren:* 155
Bartolomeu Dias (c. 1450-May 29, 1500) *Ren:* 286
Josquin des Prez (c. 1450-1455-Aug. 27, 1521) *Ren:* 515
Aldus Manutius (c. 1450-Feb. 6, 1515) *Ren:* 608

1451 - 1500

Isabella I (Apr. 22, 1451-Nov. 26, 1504) *Ren:* 328
James III (July 10, 1451, or May, 1452-June 11, 1488) *Ren:* 496
Christopher Columbus (between Aug. 25 and Oct. 31, 1451-May 20, 1506) *Ren:* 237
Ferdinand II (Mar. 10, 1452-Jan. 23, 1516) *Ren:* 328
Leonardo da Vinci (Apr. 15, 1452-May 2, 1519) *Ren:* 561
Girolamo Savonarola (Sept. 21, 1452-May 23, 1498) *Ren:* 850
Richard III (Oct. 2, 1452-Aug. 22, 1485) *Ren:* 828, *Notor:* 896
Afonso de Albuquerque (1453-Dec. 15, 1515) *Ren:* 22
Amerigo Vespucci (Mar. 9, 1454-Feb. 22, 1512) *Ren:* 969
John II (Mar. 3, 1455-Oct. 25, 1495) *Ren:* 511
Vladislav II (Mar. 1, 1456-Mar. 13, 1516) *Ren:* 983
Henry VII (Jan. 28, 1457-Apr. 21, 1509) *Ren:* 438
Mary of Burgundy (Feb. 13, 1457-Mar. 27, 1482) *Ren:* 631
Adrian VI (Mar. 2, 1459-Sept. 14, 1523) *Ren:* 7
Maximilian I (Mar. 22, 1459-Jan. 12, 1519) *Ren:* 646
Afonso I (c. late 1450's or early 1460's-1543) *Ren:* 9
Vasco da Gama (c. 1460-Dec. 24, 1524) *Ren:* 365
Jacques Lefèvre d'Étaples (c. 1460-1536) *Ren:* 548
Juan Ponce de León (c. 1460-July, 1521) *Ren:* 803
Vicente Yáñez Pinzón (c. 1462-c. 1523) *Ren:* 789
Caterina Sforza (1462 or 1463-May 20, 1509) *Ren:* 870
Louis XII (June 27, 1462-Jan. 1, 1515) *Ren:* 577
Giovanni Pico della Mirandola (Feb. 24, 1463-Nov. 17, 1494) *Ren:* 782
Boabdil (c. 1464-1527 or 1538) *Ren:* 105
John Colet (probably 1466-Sept. 16, 1519) *Ren:* 232
Desiderius Erasmus (Oct. 28, 1466?-July 12, 1536) *Ren:* 314
Montezuma II (1467-June 30, 1520) *Ren:* 693
Sigismund I, the Old (Jan. 1, 1467-Apr. 1, 1548) *Ren:* 885
Tomé Pires (c. 1468-c. 1540) *Ren:* 792
Paul III (Feb. 29, 1468-Nov. 10, 1549) *Ren:* 767
Saint John Fisher (1469-June 22, 1535) *Ren:* 335
Nānak (Apr. 15, 1469-1539) *Ren:* 707
Niccolò Machiavelli (May 3, 1469-June 21, 1527) *Ren:* 587
Manuel I (May 31, 1469-Dec. 13, 1521) *Ren:* 605
Saint Angela Merici (Mar. 21, 1470, or 1474-Jan. 27, 1540) *Ren:* 44
Charles VIII (June 30, 1470-Apr. 7, 1498) *Ren:* 227
Xiaozong (July 30, 1470-June 8, 1505) *Ren:* 1003
Cardinal Thomas Wolsey (1471 or 1472-Nov. 29, 1530) *Ren:* 996
Lucas Cranach, the Elder (1472-Oct. 16, 1553) *Ren:* 262
Wang Yangming (Nov. 30, 1472-Jan. 9, 1529) *Ren:* 986
ʿAruj (c. 1473-1518) *Notor:* 38
Chevalier de Bayard (c. 1473-Apr. 30, 1524) *Ren:* 84
Nicolaus Copernicus (Feb. 19, 1473-May 24, 1543) *Ren:* 241
James IV (Mar. 17, 1473-Sept. 9, 1513) *Ren:* 498
Sebastian Cabot (c. 1474-1557) *Ren:* 159
Isabella d'Este (May 18, 1474-Feb. 13, 1539) *Ren:* 485
Bartolomé de Las Casas (Aug., 1474-July 17, 1566) *Ren:* 537
Ludovico Ariosto (Sept. 8, 1474-July 6, 1533) *Ren:* 56
Ibrāhīm Lodī (late 15th cent.-Apr. 21, 1526) *Ren:* 478
Matthias Grünewald (c. 1475-Aug., 1528) *Ren:* 405
Vasco Núñez de Balboa (1475-Jan., 1519) *Ren:* 76
Cesare Borgia (1475 or 1476-Mar. 12, 1507) *Ren:* 114, *Notor:* 127
Michelangelo (Mar. 6, 1475-Feb. 18, 1564) *Ren:* 682
Leo X (Dec. 11, 1475-Dec. 1, 1521) *Ren:* 557, *Notor:* 630
Giorgione (c. 1477-1510) *Ren:* 383
Anne of Brittany (Jan., 25, 1477-Jan., 9, 1514) *Ren:* 48
Girolamo Fracastoro (c. 1478-Aug. 6, 1553) *Ren:* 343
Francisco Pizarro (c. 1478-June 26, 1541) *Ren:* 800
Sir Thomas More (Feb. 7, 1478-July 6, 1535) *Ren:* 697

Clement VII (May 26, 1478-Sept. 25, 1534) *Ren:* 229, *Notor:* 212
Baldassare Castiglione (Dec. 6, 1478-Feb. 2, 1529) *Ren:* 181
Vasily III (possibly Mar. 25 or 26, 1479-Dec. 3, 1533) *Ren:* 957
Joan the Mad (Nov. 6, 1479-Apr. 12, 1555) *Notor:* 531
Krishnadevaraya (d. 1529) *Ren:* 532
Balthasar Hubmaier (c. 1480-Mar. 10, 1528) *Ren:* 472
Ferdinand Magellan (c. 1480-Apr. 27, 1521) *Ren:* 591
Margaret of Austria (Jan. 10, 1480-Dec. 1, 1530) *Ren:* 612
Lucrezia Borgia (Apr. 18, 1480-June 24, 1519) *Ren:* 117, *Notor:* 129
Francisco de Vitoria (c. 1483-Aug. 12, 1546) *Ren:* 978
Bābur (Feb. 14, 1483-Dec. 26, 1530) *Ren:* 69
Raphael (Apr. 6, 1483-Apr. 6, 1520) *Ren:* 819
Martin Luther (Nov. 10, 1483-Feb. 18, 1546) *Ren:* 582
Huldrych Zwingli (Jan. 1, 1484-Oct. 11, 1531) *Ren:* 1010
Charlotte Guillard (c. mid 1480's?-between Apr. 18 and July 20, 1557) *Ren:* 413
Leo Africanus (c. 1485-c. 1554) *Ren:* 555
Thomas Cromwell (1485?-July 28, 1540) *Ren:* 269
Hugh Latimer (between 1485 and 1492-Oct. 16, 1555) *Ren:* 543
Pedro de Alvarado (1485-1541) *Ren:* 34
Hernán Cortés (1485-Dec. 2, 1547) *Ren:* 252
The Tudor Family (Reigned 1485-1603) *Ren:* 946
Catherine of Aragon (Dec. 16, 1485-Jan. 7, 1536) *Ren:* 187
Jacopo Sansovino (July 2, 1486-Nov. 27, 1570) *Ren:* 847
Andrea del Sarto (July 16, 1486-Sept. 28, 1530) *Ren:* 39
Juan Sebastián de Elcano (c. 1487-Aug. 4, 1526) *Ren:* 307
Miles Coverdale (c. 1488-Jan. 20, 1568) *Ren:* 255
Joseph ben Ephraim Karo (1488-Mar. 24, 1575) *Ren:* 524
Mother Shipton (1488-1561) *Notor:* 952
Correggio (c. 1489-c. Mar. 5, 1534) *Ren:* 249
Thomas Cranmer (July 2, 1489-Mar. 21, 1556) *Ren:* 266
Johnnie Armstrong (c. 1490's-1530) *Notor:* 35
Álvar Núñez Cabeza de Vaca (c. 1490-c. 1560) *Ren:* 152
Titian (c. 1490-Aug. 27, 1576) *Ren:* 936
Jacques Cartier (c. 1491-Sept. 1, 1557) *Ren:* 178
Saint Ignatius of Loyola (1491-July 31, 1556) *Ren:* 482
Zhengde (1491-1521) *Ren:* 1008
Henry VIII (June 28, 1491-Jan. 28, 1547) *Ren:* 441
Martin Bucer (Nov. 11, 1491-Feb. 28, 1551) *Ren:* 142
Vittoria Colonna (1492-Feb. 25, 1547) *Ren:* 235
Marguerite de Navarre (Apr. 11, 1492-Dec. 21, 1549) *Ren:* 617
Pietro Aretino (Apr. 19 or 20, 1492-Oct. 21, 1556) *Ren:* 53
Stephen Gardiner (c. 1493-Nov. 12, 1555) *Ren:* 368
İbrahim Paşa (1493 or 1494-Mar. 15, 1536) *Ren:* 480
Paracelsus (Nov. 11 or Dec. 17, 1493-Sept. 24, 1541) *Ren:* 757
William Tyndale (c. 1494-Oct. 6, 1536) *Ren:* 949
Süleyman the Magnificent (1494 or 1495-Sept. 5 or 6, 1566) *Ren:* 914
Georgius Agricola (Mar. 24, 1494-Nov. 21, 1555) *Ren:* 11
Francis I (Sept. 12, 1494-Mar. 31, 1547) *Ren:* 346
Cuauhtémoc (c. 1495-Feb. 28, 1525) *Ren:* 273
Huáscar (c. 1495-1532) *Ren:* 469
Diego de Siloé (c. 1495-Oct. 22, 1563) *Ren:* 890
Hernando de Soto (c. 1496-May 21, 1542) *Ren:* 902
Menno Simons (1496-Jan. 31, 1561) *Ren:* 675
Gustav I Vasa (May 12, 1496-Sept. 29, 1560) *Ren:* 415
Hans Holbein, the Younger (1497 or 1498-1543) *Ren:* 453
Philipp Melanchthon (Feb. 16, 1497-Apr. 19, 1560) *Ren:* 664
Diane de Poitiers (Sept. 3, 1499-Apr. 25, 1566) *Ren:* 283
Barbarossa (d. 1546) *Ren:* 79
Anne Boleyn (c. 1500-1501-May 19, 1536) *Ren:* 111
Juan Rodríguez Cabrillo (c. 1500-Jan. 3, 1543) *Ren:* 161
Nicholas Ridley (c. 1500-Oct. 16, 1555) *Ren:* 833
Niccolò Fontana Tartaglia (c. 1500-Dec. 13, 1557) *Ren:* 920
Tascalusa (c. 1500-Oct. 18, 1540) *Ren:* 922
Charles V (Feb. 24, 1500-Sept. 21, 1556) *Ren:* 220
Benvenuto Cellini (Nov. 3, 1500-Feb. 13, 1571) *Ren:* 202

1501 - 1520

Leonhard Fuchs (Jan. 17, 1501-May 10, 1566) *Ren:* 356
Gerolamo Cardano (Sept. 24, 1501-Sept. 21, 1576) *Ren:* 172
Atahualpa (c. 1502-Aug. 29, 1533) *Ren:* 66
Doña Marina (c. 1502-1527 or 1528) *Ren:* 621
Gregory XIII (Jan. 7, 1502-Apr. 10, 1585) *Ren:* 393
John III (June 6, 1502-June 11, 1557) *Ren:* 513
Nostradamus (Dec. 14, 1503-July 1 or 2, 1566) *Ren:* 728, *Notor:* 799
Pius V (Jan. 17, 1504-May 1, 1572) *Ren:* 797
Philip the Magnanimous (Nov. 13, 1504-Mar. 31, 1567) *Ren:* 775
Matthew Parker (Aug. 6, 1504-May 17, 1575) *Ren:* 761
Michel de L'Hospital (c. 1505-Mar. 13, 1573) *Ren:* 568
Mary of Hungary (Sept. 17, 1505-Oct. 18, 1558) *Ren:* 636
First Duke of Somerset (c. 1506-Jan. 22, 1552) *Ren:* 898
George Buchanan (Feb., 1506-Sept. 29, 1582) *Ren:* 146
Saint Francis Xavier (Apr. 7, 1506-Dec. 3, 1552) *Ren:* 1000
Duke of Alva (Oct. 29, 1507-Dec. 11, 1582) *Ren:* 31
Humāyūn (1508-Jan., 1556) *Ren:* 475
Andrea Palladio (Nov. 30, 1508-Aug., 1580) *Ren:* 753
Jane Seymour (c. 1509-Oct. 24, 1537) *Ren:* 868
John Calvin (July 10, 1509-May 27, 1564) *Ren:* 163
Miguel López de Legazpi (c. 1510-Aug. 20, 1572) *Ren:* 550
Pierre Lescot (1510?-Sept. 10, 1578) *Ren:* 565
Francisco Vásquez de Coronado (1510-Sept. 22, 1554) *Ren:* 245
Michael Servetus (1511-Oct. 27, 1553) *Ren:* 861
Giorgio Vasari (July 30, 1511-June 27, 1574) *Ren:* 953
Catherine Parr (c. 1512-Sept. 5, 1548) *Ren:* 764
Gerardus Mercator (Mar. 5, 1512-Dec. 2, 1594) *Ren:* 678
James V (Apr. 10, 1512-Dec. 14, 1542) *Ren:* 501
John Knox (c. 1514-Nov. 24, 1572) *Ren:* 528
Rheticus (Feb. 16, 1514-Dec. 5, 1574) *Ren:* 823
Andreas Vesalius (Dec. 31, 1514-Oct. 15, 1564) *Ren:* 965
Peter Ramus (1515-Aug. 26, 1572) *Ren:* 817
Saint Teresa of Ávila (Mar. 28, 1515-Oct. 4, 1582) *Ren:* 928
Saint Philip Neri (July 21, 1515-May 26, 1595) *Ren:* 717
Anne of Cleves (Sept. 22, 1515-July 16, 1557) *Ren:* 51
Mary of Guise (Nov. 22, 1515-June 11, 1560) *Ren:* 633
Mary I (Feb. 18, 1516-Nov. 17, 1558) *Ren:* 639
Conrad Gesner (Mar. 26, 1516-Dec. 13, 1565) *Ren:* 375
Pierre Belon (c. 1517-Apr. 1565 or 1564) *Ren:* 101
Ōgimachi (1517-1593) *Ren:* 735
Tintoretto (c. 1518-May 31, 1594) *Ren:* 931
Edmund Grindal (1519?-July 6, 1583) *Ren:* 402
Pedro Menéndez de Avilés (Feb. 15, 1519-Sept. 17, 1574) *Ren:* 672
Henry II (Mar. 31, 1519-July 10, 1559) *Ren:* 423
Cosimo I de' Medici (June 12, 1519-Apr. 21, 1574) *Ren:* 653
Andrea Gabrieli (c. 1520-1586) *Ren:* 359
Sigismund II Augustus (Aug. 1, 1520-July 7, 1572) *Ren:* 887
William Cecil (Sept. 13, 1520-Aug. 4, 1598) *Ren:* 199

1521 - 1540

Pemisapan (d. June 1, 1586) *Ren:* 771
Anne Askew (c. 1521-July 16, 1546) *Ren:* 62
Catherine Howard (c. 1521-Feb. 13, 1542) *Ren:* 466
Sixtus V (Dec. 13, 1521-Aug. 27, 1590) *Ren:* 895
Joachim du Bellay (1522-Jan. 1, 1560) *Ren:* 294
Margaret of Parma (1522-Jan. 18, 1586) *Ren:* 615
Luís de Camões (c. 1524-June 10, 1580) *Ren:* 167
François Hotman (Aug. 23, 1524-Feb. 12, 1590) *Ren:* 461
Pierre de Ronsard (Sept. 11, 1524-Dec. 27, 1585) *Ren:* 837
Askia Daud (c. early 16th cent.-July or Aug., 1582) *Ren:* 64
Pieter Bruegel, the Elder (c. 1525-Sept. 5, 1569) *Ren:* 135
Hiawatha (c. 1525-c. 1575) *Ren:* 448
Giovanni Pierluigi da Palestrina (c. 1525-Feb. 2, 1594) *Ren:* 751

Roderigo Lopez (1525-June 7, 1594) *Notor:* 655
Andrea Cesalpino (probably June 5, 1525-Feb. 23 or Mar. 15, 1603) *Ren:* 211
Kenau Hasselaer (1526-1588) *Ren:* 526
Bess of Hardwick (c. 1527-Feb. 13, 1608) *Ren:* 103
Philip II (May 21, 1527-Sept. 13, 1598) *Ren:* 778
John Dee (July 13, 1527-Dec., 1608) *Ren:* 278
Maximilian II (July 31, 1527-Oct. 12, 1576) *Ren:* 650
Catharina van Hemessen (1528-after 1587) *Ren:* 421
Paolo Veronese (1528-Apr. 19, 1588) *Ren:* 959
Juan de Herrera (c. 1530-Jan. 15, 1597) *Ren:* 445
Grace O'Malley (1530-1603) *Ren:* 743, *Notor:* 805
Ivan the Terrible (Aug. 25, 1530-Mar. 18, 1584) *Ren:* 492, *Notor:* 517
Amina Sarauniya Zazzua (c. 1532-c. 1610) *Ren:* 37
Sofonisba Anguissola (c. 1532-Nov., 1625) *Ren:* 46
Orlando di Lasso (1532-June 14, 1594) *Ren:* 540
Michel Eyquem de Montaigne (Feb. 28, 1533-Sept. 13, 1592) *Ren:* 689
William the Silent (Apr. 24, 1533-July 10, 1584) *Ren:* 993
Elizabeth I (Sept. 7, 1533-Mar. 24, 1603) *Ren:* 310
Stephen Báthory (Sept. 27, 1533-Dec. 12, 1586) *Ren:* 910
Erik XIV (Dec. 13, 1533-Feb. 26, 1577) *Notor:* 331
Isaac ben Solomon Luria (1534-Aug. 5, 1572) *Ren:* 579
Oda Nobunaga (June, 1534-June 21, 1582) *Ren:* 732
Sir Martin Frobisher (c. 1535-Nov. 22, 1594) *Ren:* 352
Toyotomi Hideyoshi (Feb. 6, 1537-Sept. 18, 1598) *Ren:* 943
Hieronymus Fabricius ab Aquapendente (May 20, 1537-May 21, 1619) *Ren:* 319
Lady Jane Grey (Oct., 1537-Feb. 12, 1554) *Ren:* 399
Edward VI (Oct. 12, 1537-July 6, 1553) *Ren:* 303
Hōjō Ujimasa (1538-Aug. 12, 1590) *Ren:* 451
Sir Humphrey Gilbert (c. 1539-Sept. 9, 1583) *Ren:* 378
Sir Francis Drake (c. 1540-Jan. 28, 1596) *Ren:* 291, *Notor:* 301
José de Acosta (1540-Feb. 15, 1600) *Ren:* 5
Ana de Mendoza y de la Cerda (June 29, 1540-Feb. 2, 1592) *Ren:* 670
Joseph Justus Scaliger (Aug. 5, 1540-Jan. 21, 1609) *Ren:* 855

1541 - 1560

El Greco (1541-Apr. 7, 1614) *Ren:* 390
Bernardino de Mendoza (Feb. 21, 1541-Aug. 3, 1604) *Ren:* 668
Sir Richard Grenville (c. June 15, 1542-c. Sept. 3, 1591) *Ren:* 396
Saint John of the Cross (June 24, 1542-Dec. 14, 1591) *Ren:* 507
Akbar (Oct. 15, 1542-Oct. 16, 1605) *Ren:* 15
Mary, Queen of Scots (Dec. 8, 1542-Feb. 8, 1587) *Ren:* 627
William Byrd (1543-July 4, 1623) *Ren:* 148
Tokugawa Ieyasu (Jan. 31, 1543-June 1, 1616) *17th:* 915
Torquato Tasso (Mar. 11, 1544-Apr. 25, 1595) *Ren:* 924
William Gilbert (May 24, 1544-Dec. 10, 1603) *Ren:* 381
Opechancanough (c. 1545-1644 or 1646) *17th:* 702
Sir Thomas Bodley (Mar. 2, 1545-Jan. 28, 1613) *Ren:* 108
Alessandro Farnese (Aug. 27, 1545-Dec. 2-3, 1592) *Ren:* 321
Tycho Brahe (Dec. 14, 1546-Oct. 24, 1601) *Ren:* 128
Mateo Alemán (Sept. 28, 1547-c. 1614) *Ren:* 25
Miguel de Cervantes (Sept. 29, 1547-Apr. 23, 1616) *Ren:* 206
Giordano Bruno (1548-Feb. 17, 1600) *Ren:* 138
Oichi (1548-June 14, 1583) *Ren:* 737
Simon Stevin (1548-Feb., 1620) *Ren:* 912
Philippe de Mornay (Nov. 5, 1549-Nov. 11, 1623) *Ren:* 703
Kalicho (c. mid-1500's-late 1577) *Ren:* 522
John Davis (c. 1550-Dec. 29 or 30, 1605) *Ren:* 276
Deganawida (c. 1550-c. 1600) *Ren:* 281
Powhatan (c. 1550-Apr., 1618) *17th:* 752
John Napier (1550-Apr. 4, 1617) *Ren:* 710
Boris Godunov (c. 1551-Apr. 23, 1605) *Ren:* 387
Henry III (Sept. 19, 1551-Aug. 2, 1589) *Ren:* 426
Richard Hakluyt (c. 1552-Nov. 23, 1616) *Ren:* 419
Sir Walter Ralegh (c. 1552-Oct. 29, 1618) *Ren:* 813
Edmund Spenser (c. 1552-Jan. 13, 1599) *Ren:* 906
Lavinia Fontana (1552-Aug. 11, 1614) *Ren:* 338
Vasily Shuysky (1552-Sept. 12, 1612) *17th:* 943
Alberico Gentili (Jan. 14, 1552-June 19, 1608) *Ren:* 372
Sir Edward Coke (Feb. 1, 1552-Sept. 3, 1634) *17th:* 174
Rudolf II (July 18, 1552-Jan. 20, 1612) *Ren:* 840

Paul V (Sept. 17, 1552-Jan. 28, 1621) *17th:* 719
Matteo Ricci (Oct. 6, 1552-May 11, 1610) *Ren:* 825
Luca Marenzio (1553-Aug. 22, 1599) *Ren:* 610
Duke de Lerma (1553-May 17, 1625) *17th:* 530
Henry IV (Dec. 13, 1553-May 14, 1610) *Ren:* 429
Marietta Robusti Tintoretto (c. 1554-c. 1590) *Ren:* 935
Sebastian (Jan. 20, 1554-Aug. 4, 1578) *Ren:* 859
Richard Hooker (Mar., 1554-Nov. 2, 1600) *Ren:* 457
Sir Philip Sidney (Nov. 30, 1554-Oct. 17, 1586) *Ren:* 881
Lancelot Andrewes (1555-Sept. 26, 1626) *17th:* 14
François de Malherbe (1555-Oct. 6, 1628) *17th:* 577
Ludovico Carracci (baptized Apr. 21, 1555-Nov. 13, 1619) *Ren:* 175
Sophie Brahe (Sept. 22, 1556, or Aug. 24, 1559-1643) *Ren:* 126
Balthasar Gérard (1557-July 24, 1584) *Notor:* 404
Thomas Morley (1557 or 1558-Oct., 1602) *Ren:* 701
Fyodor I (May 31, 1557-Jan. 17, 1598) *Notor:* 385
Agostino Carracci (Aug. 16, 1557-Feb. 23, 1602) *Ren:* 175
George Chapman (c. 1559-May 12, 1634) *Ren:* 213
Duke de Sully (Dec. 13, 1559-Dec. 22, 1641) *17th:* 896
Henry Hudson (1560's?-1611) *17th:* 390
Elizabeth Báthory (Aug. 7, 1560-Aug. 21, 1614) *Ren:* 81, *Notor:* 70
Thomas Cavendish (baptized Sept. 19, 1560-c. May, 1592) *Ren:* 193
Jacobus Arminius (Oct. 10, 1560-Oct. 19, 1609) *Ren:* 59
Annibale Carracci (Nov. 3, 1560-July 15, 1609) *Ren:* 175

1561 - 1580

Francis Bacon (Jan. 22, 1561-Apr. 9, 1626) *Ren:* 72
Santorio Santorio (Mar. 29, 1561-Feb. 22 or Mar. 6, 1636) *17th:* 810
Luis de Góngora y Argote (July 11, 1561-May 23, 1627) *17th:* 312
Isabella Andreini (1562-July 10, 1604) *Ren:* 42
John Dowland (1562 or 1563-probably Feb. 20, 1626, London) *Ren:* 289
Lope de Vega Carpio (Nov. 25, 1562-Aug. 27, 1635) *17th:* 949
Louyse Bourgeois (c. 1563-Dec., 1636) *17th:* 73
Michael Drayton (1563-Dec. 23, 1631) *17th:* 237
Hosokawa Gracia (1563-July 16, 1600) *Ren:* 459
First Earl of Salisbury (June 1, 1563-May 24, 1612) *Ren:* 844
Christopher Marlowe (Feb. 6, 1564-May 30, 1593) *Ren:* 623
Galileo (Feb. 15, 1564-Jan. 8, 1642) *17th:* 298
David Fabricius (Mar. 9, 1564-May 7, 1617) *17th:* 259
William Shakespeare (Apr. 23, 1564-Apr. 23, 1616) *Ren:* 876
Canonicus (c. 1565-June 4, 1647) *17th:* 129
Marie le Jars de Gournay (Oct. 6, 1565-July 13, 1645) *17th:* 314
Barbe Acarie (Feb. 1, 1566-Apr. 18, 1618) *Ren:* 3
Mehmed III (May 26, 1566-Dec. 22, 1603) *Ren:* 661
James I (June 19, 1566-Mar. 27, 1625) *17th:* 413
Sigismund III Vasa (June 20, 1566-Apr. 30, 1632) *17th:* 853
Jacques Clément (c. 1567-Aug. 1, 1589) *Notor:* 214
Samuel de Champlain (c. 1567/1570-Dec. 25, 1635) *17th:* 139
Thomas Campion (Feb. 12, 1567-Mar. 1, 1620) *17th:* 127
Claudio Monteverdi (May 15, 1567-Nov. 29, 1643) *17th:* 656
Thomas Nashe (Nov., 1567-1601) *Ren:* 714
Maurice of Nassau (Nov. 14, 1567-Apr. 23, 1625) *17th:* 618
Urban VIII (Baptized Apr. 5, 1568-July 29, 1644) *17th:* 936
Tommaso Campanella (Sept. 5, 1568-May 21, 1639) *17th:* 124
Aemilia Lanyer (Jan. 27, 1569-1645) *Ren:* 535
Jahāngīr (Aug. 31, 1569-Oct. 28, 1627) *17th:* 410
Hans Lippershey (c. 1570-c. 1619) *17th:* 537
Guy Fawkes (Apr. 13, 1570-Jan. 31, 1606) *Ren:* 324, *Notor:* 350
Izumo no Okuni (1571-1658) *17th:* 408
ʿAbbās the Great (Jan. 27, 1571-Jan. 19, 1629) *17th:* 4
Caravaggio (Autumn, 1571-July 18, 1610) *Ren:* 170
Johannes Kepler (Dec. 27, 1571-Nov. 15, 1630) *17th:* 457
Thomas Dekker (c. 1572-Aug., 1632) *17th:* 223
John Donne (between Jan. 24 and June 19, 1572-Mar. 31, 1631) *17th:* 230
Thomas Heywood (c. 1573-Aug., 1641) *17th:* 373

Marie de Médicis (Apr. 26, 1573-July 3, 1642) *17th:* 598
Ben Jonson (June 11, 1573-Aug. 6, 1637) *17th:* 439
Inigo Jones (July 15, 1573-June 21, 1652) *17th:* 436
William Laud (Oct. 7, 1573-Jan. 10, 1645) *17th:* 495
Robert Fludd (Baptized Jan. 17, 1574-Sept. 8, 1637) *17th:* 280
Cyril Tourneur (c. 1575-Feb. 28, 1626) *17th:* 928
Jakob Böhme (Apr. 24, 1575-Nov. 17, 1624) *17th:* 59
John Webster (c. 1577/1580-before 1634) *17th:* 976
Beatrice Cenci (Feb. 6, 1577-Sept. 11, 1599) *Notor:* 192
Robert Burton (Feb. 8, 1577-Jan. 25, 1640) *17th:* 108
Peter Paul Rubens (June 28, 1577-May 30, 1640) *17th:* 802
Piet Hein (Nov. 15, 1577-June 18, 1629) *17th:* 359
François Ravaillac (1578-May 27, 1610) *Notor:* 888
William Harvey (Apr. 1, 1578-June 3, 1657) *17th:* 355
Ferdinand II (July 9, 1578-Feb. 15, 1637) *17th:* 267
George Calvert (1579 or 1580-Apr. 15, 1632) *17th:* 119
John Fletcher (Dec., 1579-Aug., 1625) *Ren:* 92, *17th:* 277
Sōtatsu (unknown-c. 1643) *17th:* 868
Elizabeth Sawyer (c. 1580?-Apr. 19, 1621) *Notor:* 935
Peter Minuit (c. 1580-June, 1638) *17th:* 643
Massasoit (c. 1580-1661) *17th:* 612
Tirso de Molina (1580?-Feb., 1648) *17th:* 913
John Smith (Baptized Jan. 9, 1580-June 21, 1631) *17th:* 861
Jan Baptista van Helmont (Jan. 12, 1580-Dec. 30, 1644) *17th:* 361
Thomas Middleton (Baptized Apr. 18, 1580-July 4, 1627) *17th:* 636
Francisco Gómez de Quevedo y Villegas (Sept. 17, 1580-Sept. 8, 1645) *17th:* 770
Nicolas-Claude Fabri de Peiresc (Dec. 1, 1580-June 24, 1637) *17th:* 722

1581 - 1600

James Ussher (Jan. 4, 1581-Mar. 21, 1656) *17th:* 938
Saint Vincent de Paul (Apr. 24, 1581-Sept. 27, 1660) *17th:* 962
Njinga (1582-Dec. 17, 1663) *17th:* 687
Frans Hals (c. 1583-Sept. 1, 1666) *17th:* 352
Orlando Gibbons (1583-June 5, 1625) *17th:* 309
Hugo Grotius (Apr. 10, 1583-Aug. 28, 1645) *17th:* 326
Axel Oxenstierna (June 16, 1583-Aug. 28, 1654) *17th:* 704
Girolamo Frescobaldi (Sept., 1583-Mar. 1, 1643) *17th:* 295
Albrecht Wenzel von Wallenstein (Sept. 24, 1583-Feb. 25, 1634) *17th:* 966
Francis Beaumont (c. 1584-Mar. 6, 1616) *Ren:* 92
Moll Cutpurse (c. 1584-July 26, 1659) *Notor:* 250
Miles Standish (c. 1584-Oct. 3, 1656) *17th:* 877
Frederick Henry (Jan. 29, 1584-Mar. 14, 1647) *17th:* 286
John Pym (May 20, 1584-Dec. 8, 1643) *17th:* 767
John Cotton (Dec. 4, 1584-Dec. 23, 1652) *17th:* 196
Kösem Sultan (1585-Sept. 2, 1651) *17th:* 472
Mary Ward (Jan. 23, 1585-Jan. 30, 1645) *17th:* 974
Cardinal de Richelieu (Sept. 9, 1585-Dec. 4, 1642) *17th:* 790
Heinrich Schütz (Baptized Oct. 9, 1585-Nov. 6, 1672) *17th:* 825
Saint Rose of Lima (Apr. 20 or 30, 1586-Aug. 24, 1617) *17th:* 796
Thomas Hooker (probably July 7, 1586-July 7, 1647) *17th:* 386
Robert Carr (c. 1587-July 17, 1645) *17th:* 131
Count-Duke of Olivares (Jan. 6, 1587-July 22, 1645) *17th:* 697
Johannes Fabricius (Jan. 8, 1587-Mar. 19, 1616) *17th:* 259
Francesca Caccini (Sept. 18, 1587-after June, 1641) *17th:* 111
Marquise de Rambouillet (1588-Dec. 27, 1655) *17th:* 779
John Winthrop (Jan. 22, 1588-Apr. 5, 1649) *17th:* 990
Thomas Hobbes (Apr. 5, 1588-Dec. 4, 1679) *17th:* 378
Marin Mersenne (Sept. 8, 1588-Sept. 1, 1648) *17th:* 628
Squanto (c. 1590-Nov., 1622) *17th:* 875
Lady Eleanor Davies (1590-July 5, 1652) *17th:* 220
Boris Ivanovich Morozov (1590-Nov. 11, 1661) *17th:* 663
William Bradford (Mar., 1590-May 9, 1657) *17th:* 84
Roger Ludlow (Baptized Mar. 7, 1590-June, 1666) *17th:* 567
Cosimo II de' Medici (May 12, 1590-Feb. 28, 1621) *17th:* 626

Mustafa I (1591-Jan. 20, 1639) *17th:* 673
Angélique Arnauld (1591-Aug. 6, 1661) *17th:* 20
Anne Hutchinson (Baptized July 20, 1591-Aug. 20, 1643) *17th:* 394
Robert Herrick (Baptized Aug. 24, 1591-Oct., 1674) *17th:* 368
Rory O'More (c. 1592-in or after 1666) *17th:* 699
Jacques Callot (1592-Mar. 25, 1635) *17th:* 116
Shah Jahan (Jan. 5, 1592-Jan. 22, 1666) *17th:* 842
Pierre Gassendi (Jan. 22, 1592-Oct. 24, 1655) *17th:* 304
Nicholas Ferrar (Feb. 22, 1592-Dec. 4, 1637) *17th:* 274
Jan Komenský (Mar. 28, 1592-Nov. 15, 1670) *17th:* 469
Wilhelm Schickard (Apr. 22, 1592-Oct. 24, 1635) *17th:* 818
First Duke of Buckingham (Aug. 28, 1592-Aug. 23, 1628) *17th:* 96
Abahai (Nov. 28, 1592-Sept. 21, 1643) *17th:* 1
Georges de La Tour (Mar. 13, 1593-Jan. 30, 1652) *17th:* 493
George Herbert (Apr. 3, 1593-Mar. 1, 1633) *17th:* 366
First Earl of Strafford (Apr. 13, 1593-May 12, 1641) *17th:* 884
Artemisia Gentileschi (July 8, 1593-1652 or 1653) *17th:* 307
Gustavus II Adolphus (Dec. 9, 1594-Nov. 6, 1632) *17th:* 336
John Felton (c. 1595-Nov. 28, 1628) *Notor:* 352
Bohdan Khmelnytsky (c. 1595-Aug. 16, 1657) *17th:* 461
Pocahontas (c. 1596-Mar., 1617) *17th:* 745
Henry Lawes (Baptized Jan. 5, 1596-Oct. 21, 1662) *17th:* 502
René Descartes (Mar. 31, 1596-Feb. 11, 1650) *17th:* 226
Michael Romanov (July 22, 1596-July 23, 1645) *17th:* 794
Elizabeth Stuart (Aug. 19, 1596-Feb. 13, 1662) *17th:* 253
Frederick V (Aug. 26, 1596-Nov. 29, 1632) *17th:* 293
James Shirley (Baptized Sept. 7, 1596-Oct. 29, 1666) *17th:* 846
John Davenport (Apr., 1597-Mar. 15, 1670) *17th:* 218
François Mansart (Jan. 23, 1598-Sept. 23, 1666) *17th:* 587
Maarten Tromp (Apr. 23, 1598-Aug. 10, 1653) *17th:* 930
Francisco de Zurbarán (Baptized Nov. 7, 1598-Aug. 27, 1664) *17th:* 1003
Gian Lorenzo Bernini (Dec. 7, 1598-Nov. 28, 1680) *17th:* 45
John Alden (c. 1599-Sept. 12, 1687) *17th:* 7
Alexander VII (Feb. 13, 1599-May 22, 1667) *17th:* 9
Sir Anthony van Dyck (Mar. 22, 1599-Dec. 9, 1641) *17th:* 244
Oliver Cromwell (Apr. 25, 1599-Sept. 3, 1658) *17th:* 204
Diego Velázquez (Baptized June 6, 1599-Aug. 6, 1660) *17th:* 953
Robert Blake (late Aug.?, 1599-Aug. 7, 1657) *17th:* 55
Francesco Borromini (Sept. 25, 1599-Aug. 2, 1667) *17th:* 67
Marie de l'Incarnation (Oct. 28, 1599-Apr. 30, 1672) *17th:* 595
Margaret Brent (c. 1600-c. 1671) *17th:* 92
Margaret Jones (c. 1600-June 15, 1648) *Notor:* 540
Florence Newton (c. 1600?-probably 1661) *Notor:* 781
Giovanna Garzoni (1600-Feb., 1670) *17th:* 302
Claude Lorrain (1600-Nov. 23, 1682) *17th:* 171
Pedro Calderón de la Barca (Jan. 17, 1600-May 25, 1681) *17th:* 113
Maria Celeste (Aug. 12, 1600-Apr. 2, 1634) *17th:* 593
Charles I (Nov. 19, 1600-Jan. 30, 1649) *17th:* 143
Duchesse de Chevreuse (Dec., 1600-Aug. 12, 1679) *17th:* 158

1601 - 1610

Baltasar Gracián y Morales (Jan. 8, 1601-Dec. 6, 1658) *17th:* 316
Pierre de Fermat (Aug. 17, 1601-Jan. 12, 1665) *17th:* 271
Anne of Austria (Sept. 22, 1601-Jan. 20, 1666) *17th:* 18
Louis XIII (Sept. 27, 1601-May 14, 1643) *17th:* 551
Jules Mazarin (July 14, 1602-Mar. 9, 1661) *17th:* 620
Otto von Guericke (Nov. 20, 1602-May 11, 1686) *17th:* 333
Abel Janszoon Tasman (c. 1603-1659) *17th:* 905
Roger Williams (c. 1603-between Jan. 16 and Mar. 15, 1683) *17th:* 982

Lennart Torstenson (Aug. 17, 1603-Apr. 7, 1651) *17th:* 924
Manasseh ben Israel (c. 1604-Nov. 20, 1657) *17th:* 582
John IV (Mar. 18, 1604-Nov. 6, 1656) *17th:* 430
John Eliot (Baptized Aug. 5, 1604-May 21, 1690) *17th:* 247
Thomas Pride (c. 1605-Oct. 23, 1658) *17th:* 756
Nikon (1605-Aug. 27, 1681) *17th:* 683
Yui Shōsetsu (1605-Sept., 1651) *17th:* 998
Philip IV (Apr. 8, 1605-Sept. 17, 1665) *17th:* 738
Sir Thomas Browne (Oct. 19, 1605-Oct. 19, 1682) *17th:* 94
Tianqi (Dec. 23, 1605-Sept. 30, 1627) *17th:* 911
Pierre Corneille (June 6, 1606-Oct. 1, 1684) *17th:* 193
Rembrandt (July 15, 1606-Oct. 4, 1669) *17th:* 786
Saint Isaac Jogues (Jan. 10, 1607-Oct. 18, 1646) *17th:* 423
Michiel Adriaanszoon de Ruyter (Mar. 24, 1607-Apr. 29, 1676) *17th:* 807
Anna Maria van Schurman (Nov. 5, 1607-May 14, 1678) *17th:* 823
Madeleine de Scudéry (Nov. 15, 1607-June 2, 1701) *17th:* 828
Giovanni Alfonso Borelli (Jan. 28, 1608-Dec. 31, 1679) *17th:* 65
António Vieira (Feb. 6, 1608-July 18, 1697) *17th:* 959
Evangelista Torricelli (Oct. 15, 1608-Oct. 25, 1647) *17th:* 921
George Monck (Dec. 6, 1608-Jan. 3, 1670) *17th:* 650
John Milton (Dec. 9, 1608-Nov. 8, 1674) *17th:* 639
Kâtib Çelebî (Feb., 1609-Sept. 24, 1657) *17th:* 454
Sir John Suckling (Baptized Feb. 10, 1609-1642) *17th:* 893
First Earl of Clarendon (Feb. 18, 1609-Dec. 9, 1674) *17th:* 166
Lodowick Muggleton (July, 1609-Mar. 14, 1698) *17th:* 665
Matthew Hale (Nov. 1, 1609-Dec. 25, 1676) *17th:* 345
Henrietta Maria (Nov. 25 or 26, 1609-Sept. 10, 1669) *17th:* 364
Peter Stuyvesant (c. 1610-Feb., 1672) *17th:* 890

1611 - 1620

Johannes Hevelius (Jan. 28, 1611-Jan. 28, 1687) *17th:* 371
Chongzhen (Feb. 6, 1611-Apr. 25, 1644) *17th:* 160
Innocent XI (May 16, 1611-Aug. 12, 1689) *17th:* 405
Viscount de Turenne (Sept. 11, 1611-July 27, 1675) *17th:* 933
Richard Crashaw (c. 1612-Aug. 21, 1649) *17th:* 202
Anne Bradstreet (1612?-Sept. 16, 1672) *17th:* 88
Louis Le Vau (1612-Oct. 11, 1670) *17th:* 532
Third Baron Fairfax (Jan. 17, 1612-Nov. 12, 1671) *17th:* 261
Sieur de Maisonneuve (Baptized Feb. 15, 1612-Sept. 9, 1676) *17th:* 574
Murad IV (July 27, 1612-Feb. 9, 1640) *17th:* 668
Dorgon (Nov. 17, 1612-Dec. 31, 1650) *17th:* 234
André Le Nôtre (Mar. 12, 1613-Sept. 15, 1700) *17th:* 523
Sir Henry Vane the Younger (Baptized May 26, 1613-June 14, 1662) *17th:* 941
François de La Rochefoucauld (Sept. 15, 1613-Mar. 16 or 17, 1680) *17th:* 487
John Lilburne (c. 1615-Aug. 29, 1657) *17th:* 534
John Biddle (Baptized Jan. 14, 1615-Sept. 22, 1662) *17th:* 53
Richard Baxter (Nov. 12, 1615-Dec. 8, 1691) *17th:* 32
Friedrich Hermann Schomberg (Dec., 1615, or Jan., 1616-July 1, 1690) *17th:* 820
John Wallis (Dec. 3, 1616-Nov. 8, 1703) *17th:* 969
Abraham Cowley (1618-July 28, 1667) *17th:* 199
Hishikawa Moronobu (1618-1694) *17th:* 375
Liu Yin (1618-July 21, 1664) *17th:* 540
Richard Lovelace (1618-1656 or 1657) *17th:* 562
Bartolomé Esteban Murillo (Baptized Jan. 1, 1618-Mar. 28, 1682) *17th:* 670
Francesco Maria Grimaldi (Apr. 2, 1618-Dec. 28, 1663) *17th:* 321
Aurangzeb (Nov. 3, 1618-Mar. 3, 1707) *17th:* 23
Elizabeth of Bohemia (Dec. 26, 1618-Feb. 8, 1680) *17th:* 250
Barbara Strozzi (1619-Nov. 11, 1677) *17th:* 888
Jeremiah Horrocks (c. 1619-Jan. 3, 1641) *17th:* 388
Cyrano de Bergerac (Mar. 6, 1619-July 28, 1655) *17th:* 211
Duchesse de Longueville (Aug. 28, 1619-Apr. 15, 1679) *17th:* 548
Jean-Baptiste Colbert (Aug. 29, 1619-Sept. 6, 1683) *17th:* 180

John Lambert (Baptized Sept. 7, 1619-Mar., 1684) *17th:* 483
Wang Fuzhi (Oct. 7, 1619-Feb. 18, 1692) *17th:* 972
Prince Rupert (Dec. 17, 1619-Nov. 29, 1682) *17th:* 805
Jean Martinet (c. 1620?-1672) *Notor:* 707
Miles Sindercombe (c. 1620?-Feb. 13, 1657) *Notor:* 961
Avvakum Petrovich (1620 or 1621-Apr. 14, 1682) *17th:* 26
Frederick William, the Great Elector (Feb. 16, 1620-May 9, 1688) *17th:* 290
Saint Marguerite Bourgeoys (Apr. 17, 1620-Jan. 12, 1700) *17th:* 75
John Evelyn (Oct. 31, 1620-Feb. 27, 1706) *17th:* 256
Ninon de Lenclos (Nov. 10, 1620-Oct. 17, 1705) *17th:* 520

1621 - 1630

Thomas Willis (Jan. 27, 1621-Nov. 11, 1675) *17th:* 985
Rebecca Nurse (Baptized Feb. 21, 1621-July 19, 1692) *17th:* 689
Hans Jakob Christoffel von Grimmelshausen (Mar. 17, 1621?-Aug. 17, 1676) *17th:* 324
Andrew Marvell (Mar. 31, 1621-Aug. 16, 1678) *17th:* 605
Jean de La Fontaine (July 8, 1621-Apr. 13, 1695) *17th:* 480
First Earl of Shaftesbury (July 22, 1621-Jan. 21, 1683) *17th:* 838
The Great Condé (Sept. 8, 1621-Dec. 11, 1686) *17th:* 184
Molière (Baptized Jan. 15, 1622-Feb. 17, 1673) *17th:* 646
Charles X Gustav (Nov. 8, 1622-Feb. 13, 1660) *17th:* 153
Duchess of Newcastle (1623-Dec. 15, 1673) *17th:* 676
François Laval (Apr. 30, 1623-May 6, 1708) *17th:* 498
Sir William Petty (May 26, 1623-Dec. 16, 1687) *17th:* 733
Blaise Pascal (June 19, 1623-Aug. 19, 1662) *17th:* 713
Guarino Guarini (Jan. 17, 1624-Mar. 6, 1683) *17th:* 330
George Fox (July, 1624-Jan. 13, 1691) *17th:* 283
Zheng Chenggong (Aug. 28, 1624-June 23, 1662) *17th:* 1001
Thomas Sydenham (Baptized Sept. 10, 1624-Dec. 29, 1689) *17th:* 901
Gian Domenico Cassini (June 8, 1625-Sept. 14, 1712) *17th:* 134
Madame de Sévigné (Feb. 5, 1626-Apr. 17, 1696) *17th:* 833
Christina (Dec. 8, 1626-Apr. 19, 1689) *17th:* 163
Robert Boyle (Jan. 25, 1627-Dec. 31, 1691) *17th:* 78
Śivājī (Apr. 6, 1627-Apr. 3, 1680), *17th:* 858
Duchesse de Montpensier (May 29, 1627-Apr. 5, 1693) *17th:* 660
Jacques-Bénigne Bossuet (Sept. 27, 1627-Apr. 12, 1704) *17th:* 70
John Ray (Nov. 29, 1627-Jan. 17, 1705) *17th:* 782
Charles Perrault (Jan. 12, 1628-May 16, 1703) *17th:* 731
Marcello Malpighi (Mar. 10, 1628-Nov. 29, 1694) *17th:* 579
John Bunyan (Baptized Nov. 30, 1628-Aug. 31, 1688) *17th:* 100
Alexis (Mar. 19, 1629-Feb. 8, 1676) *17th:* 11
John of Austria (Apr. 7, 1629-Sept. 17, 1679) *17th:* 425
Christiaan Huygens (Apr. 14, 1629-July 8, 1695) *17th:* 397
John III Sobieski (Aug. 17, 1629-June 17, 1696) *17th:* 427
Cornelis Tromp (Sept. 9, 1629-May 29, 1691) *17th:* 930
Stenka Razin (c. 1630-June 16, 1671) *17th:* 784
Charles II of England (May 29, 1630-Feb. 6, 1685) *17th:* 147, *Notor:* 201
Jack Ketch (d. Nov., 1686) *Notor:* 565

1631 - 1640

Katherine Philips (Jan. 1, 1631-June 22, 1664) *17th:* 741
Richard Lower (Baptized Jan. 29, 1631-Jan. 17, 1691) *17th:* 564
John Dryden (Aug. 19, 1631-May 12, 1700) *17th:* 239
Anne Conway (Dec. 14, 1631-Feb. 18, 1679) *17th:* 187
Samuel von Pufendorf (Jan. 8, 1632-Oct. 26, 1694) *17th:* 759
First Duke of Leeds (Feb. 20, 1632-July 26, 1712) *17th:* 506
John Locke (Aug. 29, 1632-Oct. 28, 1704) *17th:* 542
Sir Christopher Wren (Oct. 20, 1632-Feb. 25, 1723) *17th:* 994
Antoni van Leeuwenhoek (Oct. 24, 1632-Aug. 26, 1723) *17th:* 509
Jan Vermeer (Baptized Oct. 31, 1632-Dec., 1675) *17th:* 956
Baruch Spinoza (Nov. 24, 1632-Feb. 21, 1677) *17th:* 871
Jean-Baptiste Lully (Nov. 29, 1632-Mar. 22, 1687) *17th:* 569
Samuel Pepys (Feb. 23, 1633-May 26, 1703) *17th:* 728
Sébastien Le Prestre de Vauban (May 15, 1633-Mar. 30, 1707) *17th:* 946
Sir George Savile (Nov. 11, 1633-Apr. 5, 1695) *17th:* 815
Merzifonlu Kara Mustafa Paşa (1634 or 1635-Dec. 25, 1683) *17th:* 451
Madame de La Fayette (Baptized Mar. 18, 1634-May 25, 1693) *17th:* 477
Thomas Betterton (c. 1635-Apr. 28, 1710) *17th:* 51
Thomas Burnet (c. 1635-Sept. 27, 1715) *17th:* 106
Sir Henry Morgan (c. 1635-Aug. 25, 1688) *Notor:* 753
Johann Joachim Becher (May 6, 1635-Oct., 1682) *17th:* 39
Robert Hooke (July 18, 1635-Mar. 3, 1703) *17th:* 383
Madame de Maintenon (Nov. 27, 1635-Apr. 15, 1719) *17th:* 572
Pierre Esprit Radisson (c. 1636-buried c. June 21, 1710) *17th:* 777
Charlotte de Berry (1636-?) *Notor:* 94
Laura Mancini (1636-Feb. 8, 1657) *17th:* 585
Justine Siegemundin (1636 or 1650-1705) *17th:* 851
Nicolas Boileau-Despréaux (Nov. 1, 1636-Mar. 13, 1711) *17th:* 63
Mary White Rowlandson (c. 1637-Jan. 5, 1711) *17th:* 798
Jan Swammerdam (Feb. 12, 1637-Feb. 17, 1680) *17th:* 898
Jacques Marquette (June 1, 1637-May 18, 1675) *17th:* 603
Elisabetta Sirani (1638-Aug., 1665) *17th:* 856
Nicolaus Steno (Jan. 11, 1638-Dec. 5, 1686) *17th:* 881
Shunzhi (Mar. 15, 1638-Feb. 5, 1661) *17th:* 848
Louis XIV (Sept. 5, 1638-Sept. 1, 1715) *17th:* 554
Marie-Thérèse (Sept. 10, 1638-July 30, 1683) *17th:* 600
James Gregory (Nov., 1638-Oct., 1675) *17th:* 319
Catherine of Braganza (Nov. 25, 1638-Dec. 31, 1705) *17th:* 137
Metacom (c. 1639-Aug. 12, 1676) *17th:* 633
Olympia Mancini (1639-1708) *17th:* 585
Marquis de Louvois (Jan. 18, 1639-July 16, 1691) *17th:* 558
Ivan Stepanovich Mazepa (Mar. 20, 1639-Oct. 2, 1709) *17th:* 624
Increase Mather (June 21, 1639-Aug. 23, 1723) *18th:* 671
Jean Racine (Baptized Dec. 22, 1639-Apr. 21, 1699) *17th:* 773
Jacob Leisler (Baptized Mar. 31, 1640-May 16, 1691) *17th:* 518
Leopold I (June 9, 1640-May 5, 1705) *17th:* 526
Aphra Behn (July?, 1640-Apr. 16, 1689) *17th:* 42

1641 - 1650

Ihara Saikaku (1642-Sept. 9, 1693) *17th:* 403
Seki Kōwa (Mar., 1642-Oct. 24, 1708) *17th:* 831
Sir Isaac Newton (Dec. 25, 1642-Mar. 20, 1727) *17th:* 679
Claude Duval (1643-Jan. 21, 1670) *Notor:* 306
Sieur de La Salle (Nov. 22, 1643-Mar. 19, 1687) *17th:* 490
Antonio Stradivari (1644?-Dec. 18, 1737) *18th:* 944
Matsuo Bashō (1644-Oct. 12, 1694) *17th:* 615
William Penn (Oct. 14, 1644-July 30, 1718) *17th:* 724

William Kidd (c. 1645-May 23, 1701) *17th:* 464, *Notor:* 576
First Earl of Godolphin (baptized June 15, 1645-Sept. 15, 1712) *18th:* 421
Eusebio Francisco Kino (Aug. 10, 1645-Mar. 15, 1711) *17th:* 467
Jean de La Bruyère (Aug. 16, 1645-May 10, 1696) *17th:* 475
Louis Jolliet (Baptized Sept. 21, 1645-May, 1700) *17th:* 433
Tokugawa Tsunayoshi (Feb. 23, 1646-Feb. 19, 1709) *17th:* 919
Jules Hardouin-Mansart (c. Apr. 16, 1646-May 11, 1708) *17th:* 590
Elena Cornaro Piscopia (June 5, 1646-July 26, 1684) *17th:* 743
Hortense Mancini (June 6, 1646-July 16, 1699) *17th:* 585
Gottfried Wilhelm Leibniz (July 1, 1646-Nov. 14, 1716) *17th:* 513
Elisabetha Hevelius (c. 1647-1693) *17th:* 371
Nathaniel Bacon (Jan. 2, 1647-Oct. 26, 1676) *17th:* 29
Denis Papin (Aug. 22, 1647-c. 1712) *17th:* 710
Pierre Bayle (Nov. 18, 1647-Dec. 28, 1706) *17th:* 36
Richard Cameron (c. 1648-July 22, 1680) *17th:* 121
Madame Guyon (Apr. 13, 1648-June 9, 1717) *17th:* 339
Sor Juana Inés de la Cruz (Nov., 1648-Apr. 17, 1695) *17th:* 208
Marie-Anne Mancini (1649-June 20, 1714) *17th:* 585
Duke of Monmouth (Apr. 9, 1649-July 15, 1685) *17th:* 653
Titus Oates (Sept. 15, 1649-July 12 or 13, 1705) *17th:* 692, *Notor:* 802
Thomas Savery (c. 1650-May, 1715) *17th:* 813
Nell Gwyn (Feb. 2, 1650-Nov. 14, 1687) *17th:* 342
First Duke of Marlborough (May 26, 1650-June 16, 1722) *18th:* 660
William III (Nov. 14, 1650-Mar. 19, 1702) *17th:* 979

1651 - 1660

William Dampier (Aug.?, 1651-Mar., 1715) *17th:* 215, *Notor:* 260
François de Salignac de La Mothe-Fénelon (Aug. 6, 1651-Jan. 7, 1715) *17th:* 265
Engelbert Kämpfer (Sept. 16, 1651-Nov. 2, 1716) *17th:* 445
Samuel Sewall (Mar. 28, 1652-Jan. 1, 1730) *18th:* 893
Chikamatsu Monzaemon (1653-Jan. 6, 1725) *18th:* 243
Arcangelo Corelli (Feb. 17, 1653-Jan. 8, 1713) *17th:* 190
André-Hercule de Fleury (June 22, 1653-Jan. 29, 1743) *18th:* 361
Johann Pachelbel (Baptized Sept. 1, 1653-Mar. 3, 1706) *17th:* 708
Kangxi (May 4, 1654-Dec. 20, 1722) *17th:* 448
Jakob I Bernoulli (Jan. 6, 1655-Aug. 16, 1705) *17th:* 48
Kateri Tekakwitha (1656-Apr. 17, 1680) *17th:* 908
Johann Bernhard Fischer von Erlach (baptized July 20, 1656-Apr. 5, 1723) *18th:* 350
Edmond Halley (Nov. 8, 1656-June 14, 1742) *17th:* 348
Frederick I (July 11, 1657-Feb. 25, 1713) *18th:* 375
Sophia (Sept. 27, 1657-July 14, 1704) *17th:* 865
Ogata Kōrin (1658-1716) *17th:* 695
William Paterson (Apr., 1658-Jan. 22, 1719) *17th:* 716
Mary of Modena (Oct. 5, 1658-May 7, 1718) *17th:* 607
Henry Purcell (1659-Nov. 21, 1695) *17th:* 763
Daniel Defoe (1660-Apr. 26, 1731) *18th:* 298
Chen Shu (Mar. 13, 1660-Apr. 17, 1735) *17th:* 156
Alessandro Scarlatti (May 2, 1660-Oct. 22, 1725) *18th:* 883
George I (May 28, 1660-June 11, 1727) *18th:* 400
Sarah Churchill (June 5, 1660-Oct. 18, 1744) *18th:* 250
Georg Ernst Stahl (Oct. 21, 1660-May 14, 1734) *18th:* 933

1661 - 1670

Levni (unknown-1732) *18th:* 602
Nicholas Hawksmoor (c. 1661-Mar. 25, 1736) *18th:* 472
Pierre Le Moyne d'Iberville (Baptized July 20, 1661-July 9, 1706) *17th:* 401
Charles II of Spain (Nov. 6, 1661-Nov. 1, 1700) *17th:* 151
Mrs. Anne Bracegirdle (c. 1663-Sept. 12, 1748) *17th:* 82

Thomas Newcomen (Jan. or Feb., 1663-Aug. 5, 1729) *18th:* 733
Cotton Mather (Feb. 12, 1663-Feb. 13, 1728) *18th:* 667
Sir John Vanbrugh (baptized Jan. 24, 1664-Mar. 26, 1726) *18th:* 1002
John Quelch (c. 1665-June 30, 1704) *Notor:* 871
Queen Anne (Feb. 6, 1665-Aug. 1, 1714) *18th:* 45
Ogyū Sorai (Feb. 16, 1666-Jan. 19, 1728) *18th:* 746
Ivan V (Sept. 6, 1666-Feb. 8, 1696) *Notor:* 514
Mary Astell (Nov. 12, 1666-May 9, 1731) *18th:* 64
Germain Boffrand (May 16, 1667-Mar. 19, 1754) *18th:* 132
Johann I Bernoulli (Aug. 6, 1667-Jan. 1, 1748) *17th:* 48
Jonathan Swift (Nov. 30, 1667-Oct. 19, 1745) *18th:* 964
Alain-René Lesage (May 8, 1668-Nov. 17, 1747) *18th:* 596
Giambattista Vico (June 23, 1668-Jan. 23, 1744) *18th:* 1013
François Couperin (Nov. 10, 1668-Sept. 11, 1733) *18th:* 281
Johann Lucas von Hildebrandt (Nov. 14, 1668-Nov. 16, 1745) *18th:* 494
Mary de la Rivière Manley (c. 1670-July 11, 1724) *18th:* 641

1671 - 1680

Rob Roy (baptized Mar. 7, 1671-Dec. 28, 1734) *Notor:* 902
John Law (Apr. 21, 1671-Mar. 21, 1729) *Notor:* 614
Richard Steele (baptized Mar. 12, 1672-Sept. 1, 1729) *18th:* 941
Joseph Addison (May 1, 1672-June 17, 1719) *18th:* 20
Peter the Great (June 9, 1672-Feb. 8, 1725) *18th:* 774
First Earl Stanhope (1673-Feb. 5, 1721) *18th:* 937
Ahmed III (Dec. 30, 1673-July 1, 1736) *18th:* 26
Jethro Tull (baptized Mar. 30, 1674-Feb. 21, 1741) *18th:* 990
Dolly Pentreath (c. 1675-Dec., 1777) *Notor:* 818
Benedict XIV (Mar. 31, 1675-May 3, 1758) *18th:* 102
Claude Alexandre de Bonneval (July 14, 1675-Mar. 23, 1747) *18th:* 140
Chŏng Sŏn (Jan. 3, 1676-Mar. 24, 1759) *18th:* 248
Robert Walpole (Aug. 26, 1676-Mar. 18, 1745) *18th:* 1034
Abraham Darby (c. 1678-Mar. 8, 1717) *18th:* 292
Antonio Vivaldi (Mar. 4, 1678-July 28, 1741) *18th:* 1019
First Viscount Bolingbroke (Sept. 16, 1678-Dec. 12, 1751) *18th:* 135
Yongzheng (Dec. 13, 1678-Oct. 8, 1735) *18th:* 1113
Second Duke of Argyll (Oct. 10, 1680-Oct. 4, 1743) *18th:* 53

1681 - 1690

Nanny (unknown-1750's) *18th:* 724
Georg Philipp Telemann (Mar. 14, 1681-June 25, 1767) *18th:* 970
Vitus Jonassen Bering (Aug. 12, 1681-Dec. 19, 1741) *18th:* 108
Jonathan Wild (c. 1682-May 24, 1725) *Notor:* 1102
Bartholomew Roberts (May 17, 1682-Feb. 10, 1722) *Notor:* 905
Charles XII (June 17, 1682-Nov. 30, 1718) *18th:* 232
Anne Oldfield (1683-Oct. 30, 1730) *18th:* 749
Caroline (Mar. 1, 1683-Nov. 20, 1737) *18th:* 203
Jean-Philippe Rameau (baptized Sept. 25, 1683-Sept. 12, 1764) *18th:* 826
George II (Nov. 10, 1683-Oct. 25, 1760) *18th:* 403
Philip V (Dec. 19, 1683-July 9, 1746) *18th:* 781
Antoine Watteau (Oct. 10, 1684-July 18, 1721) *18th:* 1051
Tokugawa Yoshimune (Nov. 27, 1684-July 12, 1751) *18th:* 980
Mary Read (c. 1685-Apr. 28, 1721) *Notor:* 891
Hakuin (1685/1686-1768/1769) *18th:* 450
George Frideric Handel (Feb. 23, 1685-Apr. 14, 1759) *18th:* 462
George Berkeley (Mar. 12, 1685-Jan. 14, 1753) *18th:* 111
Johann Sebastian Bach (Mar. 21, 1685-July 28, 1750) *18th:* 71

Charles VI (Oct. 1, 1685-Oct. 20, 1740) *18th:* 229
Daniel Gabriel Fahrenheit (May 24, 1686-Sept. 16, 1736) *18th:* 336
William Stukeley (Nov. 7, 1687-Mar. 3, 1765) *18th:* 952
Stede Bonnet (1688-Dec. 10, 1718) *Notor:* 117
Emanuel Swedenborg (Jan. 29, 1688-Mar. 29, 1772) *18th:* 961
Alexander Pope (May 21, 1688-May 30, 1744) *18th:* 805
Frederick William I (Aug. 15, 1688-May 31, 1740) *18th:* 381
Nādir Shāh (Oct. 22, 1688-June 19, 1747) *18th:* 722, *Notor:* 772
Samuel Bellamy (1689-Apr. 26, 1717) *Notor:* 81
Montesquieu (Jan. 18, 1689-Feb. 10, 1755) *18th:* 695
Mary Wortley Montagu (baptized May 26, 1689-Aug. 21, 1762) *18th:* 687
Samuel Richardson (baptized Aug. 19, 1689-July 4, 1761) *18th:* 841

1691 - 1700

Joseph Butler (May 18, 1692-June 16, 1752) *18th:* 187
Cartouche (1693-Nov. 28, 1721) *Notor:* 178
François Quesnay (June 4, 1694-Dec. 16, 1774) *18th:* 820
Henry Pelham (Sept. 24, 1694-Mar. 6, 1754) *18th:* 771
Voltaire (Nov. 21, 1694-May 30, 1778) *18th:* 1026
Giovanni Battista Tiepolo (Mar. 5, 1696-Mar. 27, 1770) *18th:* 976
Mahmud I (Aug. 2, 1696-Dec. 13, 1754) *18th:* 639
Comte de Saxe (Oct. 28, 1696-Nov. 30, 1750) *18th:* 881
James Edward Oglethorpe (Dec. 22, 1696-June 30, 1785) *18th:* 742
Anne Bonny (c. 1697-after 1720) *Notor:* 122
Thanadelthur (c. 1697-Feb. 5, 1717) *18th:* 974
John Peter Zenger (1697-July 28, 1746) *18th:* 1116
Joseph-François Dupleix (Jan. 1, 1697-Nov. 10, 1763) *18th:* 311
Lord Anson (Apr. 23, 1697-June 6, 1762) *18th:* 49
Canaletto (Oct. 18, 1697-Apr. 20, 1768) *18th:* 190
William Hogarth (Nov. 10, 1697-Oct. 26, 1764) *18th:* 497
Colin Maclaurin (Feb., 1698-Jan. 14, 1746) *18th:* 632
Baʿal Shem Tov (Aug. 27, 1698-May 23, 1760) *18th:* 68
Marquês de Pombal (May 13, 1699-May 8, 1782) *18th:* 795
Jean-Siméon Chardin (Nov. 2, 1699-Dec. 6, 1779) *18th:* 223
Mentewab (c. 1700-1772) *18th:* 677
John Rackham (c. 1700-Nov. 17, 1720) *Notor:* 877
Count von Zinzendorf (May 26, 1700-May 9, 1760) *18th:* 1119

1701 - 1710

Jack Sheppard (1702-Nov. 16, 1724) *Notor:* 943
Muḥammad ibn ʿAbd al-Wahhāb (1703-1792) *18th:* 1030
Shāh Walī Allāh (Feb. 21, 1703-1762) *18th:* 1032
John Wesley (June 17, 1703-Mar. 2, 1791) *18th:* 1064
Jonathan Edwards (Oct. 5, 1703-Mar. 22, 1758) *18th:* 314
Eugene Aram (1704-Aug. 6, 1759) *Notor:* 30
John Kay (July 16, 1704-c. 1780-1781) *18th:* 559
Vaḥīd Bihbahānī (1705/1706-1791/1790) *18th:* 1000
First Earl of Mansfield (Mar. 2, 1705-Mar. 20, 1793) *18th:* 643
Dick Turpin (probably Sept., 1705-Apr. 7, 1739) *Notor:* 1045
Benjamin Franklin (Jan. 17, 1706-Apr. 17, 1790) *18th:* 370
John Baskerville (baptized Jan. 28, 1706-Jan. 8, 1775) *18th:* 92
Marquise du Châtelet (Dec. 17, 1706-Sept. 10, 1749) *18th:* 240
Leonhard Euler (Apr. 15, 1707-Sept. 18, 1783) *18th:* 333
Henry Fielding (Apr. 22, 1707-Oct. 8, 1754) *18th:* 346
Carolus Linnaeus (May 23, 1707-Jan. 10, 1778) *18th:* 604
Comte de Buffon (Sept. 7, 1707-Apr. 16, 1788) *18th:* 171

Charles Wesley (Dec. 18, 1707-Mar. 29, 1788) *18th:* 1061
Hester Bateman (baptized Oct. 7, 1708-Sept. 16, 1794) *18th:* 95
William Pitt the Elder (Nov. 15, 1708-May 11, 1778) *18th:* 786
Andreas Sigismund Marggraf (Mar. 3, 1709-Aug. 7, 1782) *18th:* 651
Samuel Johnson (Sept. 18, 1709-Dec. 13, 1784) *18th:* 535
Elizabeth Petrovna (Dec. 29, 1709-Jan. 5, 1762) *18th:* 321
Louis XV (Feb. 15, 1710-May 10, 1774) *18th:* 615

1711 - 1720

Wenzel Anton von Kaunitz (Feb. 2, 1711-June 27, 1794) *18th:* 557
David Hume (May 7, 1711-Aug. 25, 1776) *18th:* 514
Thomas Hutchinson (Sept. 9, 1711-June 3, 1780) *18th:* 518
Qianlong (Sept. 25, 1711-Feb. 7, 1799) *18th:* 817
Mikhail Vasilyevich Lomonosov (Nov. 19, 1711-Apr. 15, 1765) *18th:* 613
Frederick the Great (Jan. 24, 1712-Aug. 17, 1786) *18th:* 378
Louis-Joseph de Montcalm (Feb. 28, 1712-Sept. 14, 1759) *18th:* 692
Jean-Jacques Rousseau (June 28, 1712-July 2, 1778) *18th:* 868
Guillaume-Thomas Raynal (Apr. 12, 1713-Mar. 6, 1796) *18th:* 829
John Newbery (baptized July 19, 1713-Dec. 22, 1767) *18th:* 730
Denis Diderot (Oct. 5, 1713-July 31, 1784) *18th:* 307
Junípero Serra (Nov. 24, 1713-Aug. 28, 1784) *18th:* 891
Alaungpaya (c. 1714-Apr. 13, 1760?) *18th:* 29
Christoph Gluck (July 2, 1714-Nov. 15, 1787) *18th:* 418
George Whitefield (Dec. 16, 1714-Sept. 30, 1770) *18th:* 1073
Cao Xueqin (1715?-Feb. 12, 1763) *18th:* 194
Claude-Adrien Helvétius (Jan. 26, 1715-Dec. 26, 1771) *18th:* 479
Marquis de Vauvenargues (Aug. 6, 1715-May 28, 1747) *18th:* 1009
Jean-Baptiste Vaquette de Gribeauval (Sept. 15, 1715-May 9, 1789) *18th:* 447
Étienne Bonnot de Condillac (Sept. 30, 1715-Aug. 2, 1780) *18th:* 263
James Brindley (1716-Sept. 27, 1772) *18th:* 162
Charles III (Jan. 20, 1716-Dec. 14, 1788) *18th:* 227
Lancelot Brown (baptized Aug. 30, 1716-Feb. 6, 1783) *18th:* 165
Mustafa III (Jan. 28, 1717-Jan. 21, 1774) *18th:* 719
Lord Amherst (Jan. 29, 1717-Aug. 3, 1797) *18th:* 38
David Garrick (Feb. 19, 1717-Jan. 20, 1779) *18th:* 397
Maria Theresa (May 13, 1717-Nov. 29, 1780) *18th:* 653
Jean le Rond d'Alembert (Nov. 17, 1717-Oct. 29, 1783) *18th:* 31
Johann Joachim Winckelmann (Dec. 9, 1717-June 8, 1768) *18th:* 1095
Pius VI (Dec. 27, 1717-Aug. 29, 1799) *18th:* 793
George Rodney (baptized Feb. 13, 1718-May 24, 1792) *18th:* 854
Maria Gaetana Agnesi (May 16, 1718-Jan. 9, 1799) *18th:* 24
John Roebuck (baptized Sept. 17, 1718-July 17, 1794) *18th:* 858
Étienne François de Choiseul (June 28, 1719-May 8, 1785) *18th:* 246
Charles Gravier de Vergennes (Dec. 28, 1719-Feb. 13, 1787) *18th:* 1011
Pontiac (c. 1720-Apr. 20, 1769) *18th:* 801
José de Gálvez (Jan. 2, 1720-June 17, 1787) *18th:* 394
James Hargreaves (baptized Jan. 8, 1720-Apr. 22, 1778) *18th:* 466
Elijah ben Solomon (Apr. 23, 1720-Oct. 9, 1797) *18th:* 318
Peg Woffington (Oct. 18, 1720?-Mar. 28, 1760) *18th:* 1102

1721 - 1730

Thomas Gage (1721-Apr. 2, 1787) *18th:* 384
Roger Sherman (Apr. 19, 1721-July 23, 1793) *18th:* 908
Madame de Pompadour (Dec. 29, 1721-Apr. 15, 1764) *18th:* 798
Hyder Ali (1722-Dec. 7, 1782) *18th:* 522
Flora MacDonald (1722-Mar. 4, 1790) *18th:* 623
Samuel Adams (Sept. 27, 1722-Oct. 2, 1803) *18th:* 16
Adam Smith (baptized June 5, 1723-July 17, 1790) *18th:* 921
Adam Ferguson (June 20, 1723-Feb. 22, 1816) *18th:* 338
Sir William Blackstone (July 10, 1723-Feb. 14, 1780) *18th:* 118
Sir Joshua Reynolds (July 16, 1723-Feb. 23, 1792) *18th:* 836
Johann Bernhard Basedow (Sept. 11, 1723-July 25, 1790) *18th:* 89
Paul-Henri-Dietrich d'Holbach (Dec., 1723-Jan. 21, 1789) *18th:* 501
Isaac Backus (Jan. 9, 1724-Nov. 20, 1806) *18th:* 75
Dai Zhen (Jan. 19, 1724-July 1, 1777) *18th:* 287
Immanuel Kant (Apr. 22, 1724-Feb. 12, 1804) *18th:* 548
Friedrich Gottlieb Klopstock (July 2, 1724-Mar. 14, 1803) *18th:* 562
Sir Guy Carleton (Sept. 3, 1724-Nov. 10, 1808) *18th:* 196
Suzuki Harunobu (1725?-1770) *18th:* 958
Casanova (Apr. 2, 1725-June 4, 1798) *18th:* 208
Comte de Rochambeau (July 1, 1725-May 10, 1807) *18th:* 851
Robert Clive (Sept. 29, 1725-Nov. 22, 1774) *18th:* 259
John Wilkes (Oct. 17, 1725-Dec. 26, 1797) *18th:* 1083
George Mason (Dec. 11, 1725-Oct. 7, 1792) *18th:* 664
Richard Howe (Mar. 8, 1726-Aug. 5, 1799) *18th:* 506
Charles Burney (Apr. 7, 1726-Apr. 12, 1814) *18th:* 177
James Wolfe (Jan. 2, 1727-Sept. 13, 1759) *18th:* 1104
Anne-Robert-Jacques Turgot (May 10, 1727-Mar. 18, 1781) *18th:* 996
Thomas Gainsborough (baptized May 14, 1727-Aug. 2, 1788) *18th:* 387
Hester Chapone (Oct. 27, 1727-Dec. 25, 1801) *18th:* 221
John Wilkinson (1728-July 14, 1808) *18th:* 1086
Peter III (Feb. 21, 1728-July 18, 1762) *18th:* 778
Joseph Black (Apr. 16, 1728-Dec., 6, 1799) *18th:* 115
Robert Adam (July 3, 1728-Mar. 3, 1792) *18th:* 3
Matthew Boulton (Sept. 3, 1728-Aug. 18, 1809) *18th:* 156
Mercy Otis Warren (Sept. 25, 1728-Oct. 19, 1814) *18th:* 1041
James Cook (Oct. 27, 1728-Feb. 14, 1779) *18th:* 270
Oliver Goldsmith (Nov. 10, 1728 or 1730-Apr. 4, 1774) *18th:* 432
Charlotte Lennox (c. 1729-Jan. 4, 1804) *18th:* 594
Sīdī al-Mukhṭār al-Kuntī (1729-1811) *18th:* 914
Edmund Burke (Jan. 12, 1729-July 9, 1797) *18th:* 174
Lazzaro Spallanzani (Jan. 12, 1729-Feb. 11, 1799) *18th:* 925
Gotthold Ephraim Lessing (Jan. 22, 1729-Feb. 15, 1781) *18th:* 598
Catherine the Great (May 2, 1729-Nov. 17, 1796) *18th:* 211
William Dodd (May 29, 1729-June 27, 1777) *Notor:* 286
William Howe (Aug. 10, 1729-July 12, 1814) *18th:* 510
Moses Mendelssohn (Sept. 6, 1729-Jan. 4, 1786) *18th:* 675
Louis-Antoine de Bougainville (Nov. 12, 1729-Aug. 31, 1811) *18th:* 150
Aleksandr Vasilyevich Suvorov (Nov. 24, 1729-May 18, 1800) *18th:* 954
Sir Henry Clinton (Apr. 16, 1730-Dec. 23, 1795) *18th:* 256
Josiah Wedgwood (baptized July 12, 1730-Jan. 3, 1795) *18th:* 1057
James Bruce (Dec. 14, 1730-Apr. 27, 1794) *18th:* 168

1731 - 1740

Catherine Macaulay (Apr. 2, 1731-June 22, 1791) *18th:* 621
Henry Cavendish (Oct. 10, 1731-Feb. 24, 1810) *18th:* 217
Benjamin Banneker (Nov. 9, 1731-Oct. 9, 1806) *18th:* 84
Sophie von La Roche (Dec. 6, 1731-Feb. 18, 1807) *18th:* 577

Pierre-Augustin Caron de Beaumarchais (Jan. 24, 1732-May 18, 1799) *Ren:* 92
Charles Lee (Feb. 6, 1732-Oct. 2, 1782) *Notor:* 621
George Washington (Feb. 22, 1732-Dec. 14, 1799) *18th:* 1043
Joseph Haydn (Mar. 31, 1732-May 31, 1809) *18th:* 476
Jean-Honoré Fragonard (Apr. 5, 1732-Aug. 22, 1806) *18th:* 367
Lord North (Apr. 13, 1732-Aug. 5, 1792) *18th:* 738
James Adam (July 21, 1732-Oct. 20, 1794) *18th:* 3
Jacques Necker (Sept. 30, 1732-Apr. 9, 1804) *18th:* 726
John Dickinson (Nov. 8, 1732-Feb. 14, 1808) *18th:* 303
Warren Hastings (Dec. 6, 1732-Aug. 22, 1818) *18th:* 469
Sir Richard Arkwright (Dec. 23, 1732-Aug. 3, 1792) *18th:* 55
Joseph Priestley (Mar. 13, 1733-Feb. 6, 1804) *18th:* 811
Robert Morris (Jan. 31, 1734-May 8, 1806) *18th:* 707
Taksin (Apr. 17, 1734-Apr. 6, 1782) *18th:* 968
Benjamin Church (Aug. 24, 1734-Jan., 1778) *Notor:* 211
Daniel Boone (Nov. 2, 1734-Sept. 26, 1820) *18th:* 143
George Romney (Dec. 26, 1734-Nov. 15, 1802) *18th:* 862
Paul Revere (Jan. 1, 1735-May 10, 1818) *18th:* 832
Ignacy Krasicki (Feb. 3, 1735-Mar. 14, 1801) *18th:* 567
John Adams (Oct. 30, 1735-July 4, 1826) *18th:* 11
Granville Sharp (Nov. 10, 1735-July 6, 1813) *18th:* 899
James Watt (Jan. 19, 1736-Aug. 25, 1819) *18th:* 1048
Joseph-Louis Lagrange (Jan. 25, 1736-Apr. 10, 1813) *18th:* 573
Ann Lee (Feb. 29, 1736-Sept. 8, 1784) *18th:* 591
Patrick Henry (May 29, 1736-June 6, 1799) *18th:* 482
Jean-Sylvain Bailly (Sept. 15, 1736-Nov. 12, 1793) *18th:* 77
Fanny Abington (1737-Mar. 4, 1815) *18th:* 1
John Hancock (Jan. 12, 1737-Oct. 8, 1793) *18th:* 457
Thomas Paine (Jan. 29, 1737-June 8, 1809) *18th:* 759
Edward Gibbon (May 8, 1737-Jan. 16, 1794) *18th:* 415
Luigi Galvani (Sept. 9, 1737-Dec. 4, 1798) *18th:* 391
Charles Carroll (Sept. 19, 1737-Nov. 14, 1832) *18th:* 205
Aleksey Grigoryevich Orlov (Oct. 5, 1737-Jan. 5, 1808) *18th:* 755
Antônio Francisco Lisboa (c. 1738-Nov. 18, 1814) *18th:* 608
Ethan Allen (Jan. 21, 1738-Feb. 12, 1789) *18th:* 35
Cesare Beccaria (Mar. 15, 1738-Nov. 28, 1794) *18th:* 100
George III (June 4, 1738-Jan. 29, 1820) *18th:* 408
John Singleton Copley (July 3, 1738-Sept. 9, 1815) *18th:* 274
Benjamin West (Oct. 10, 1738-Mar. 11, 1820) *18th:* 1068
Arthur Phillip (Oct. 11, 1738-Aug. 31, 1814) *18th:* 783
William Herschel (Nov. 15, 1738-Aug. 25, 1822) *18th:* 492
First Marquess Cornwallis (Dec. 31, 1738-Oct. 5, 1805) *18th:* 278
Joseph Boulogne (c. 1739-June 9 or 10, 1799) *18th:* 153
Grigori Aleksandrovich Potemkin (Sept. 24, 1739-Oct. 16, 1791) *18th:* 808
Tupac Amaru II (c. 1740-May 18, 1781) *18th:* 993
Marquis de Sade (June 2, 1740-Dec. 2, 1814) *18th:* 875, *Notor:* 926
Ivan VI (Aug. 23, 1740-July 16, 1764) *Notor:* 515
Joseph-Michel Montgolfier (Aug. 26, 1740-June 26, 1810) *18th:* 698

1741 - 1750

Benedict Arnold (Jan. 14, 1741-June 14, 1801) *18th:* 59, *Notor:* 36
Joseph II (Mar. 13, 1741-Feb. 20, 1790) *18th:* 544
Charles Willson Peale (Apr. 15, 1741-Feb. 22, 1827) *18th:* 768
Samuel Chase (Apr. 17, 1741-June 19, 1811) *18th:* 237
William Brodie (Sept. 28, 1741-Oct. 1, 1788) *Notor:* 145
Angelica Kauffmann (Oct. 30, 1741-Nov. 5, 1807) *18th:* 554
Aagje Deken (Dec. 10, 1741-Nov. 14, 1804) *18th:* 301
Yemelyan Ivanovich Pugachev (c. 1742-Jan. 21, 1775) *18th:* 814

Joseph Brant (1742-Nov. 24, 1807) *18th:* 159
Nathanael Greene (Aug. 7, 1742-June 19, 1786) *18th:* 443
Jean Dauberval (Aug. 19, 1742-Feb. 14, 1806) *18th:* 295
James Wilson (Sept. 14, 1742-Aug. 21, 1798) *18th:* 1090
Nicolas Leblanc (Dec. 6, 1742-Jan. 16, 1806) *18th:* 587
Anna Seward (Dec. 12, 1742-Mar. 25, 1809) *18th:* 897
Gebhard Leberecht von Blücher (Dec. 16, 1742-Sept. 12, 1819) *19th:* 260
Toussaint Louverture (1743-Apr. 7, 1803) *18th:* 985
John Fitch (Jan. 21, 1743-July 2, 1798) *18th:* 353
Sir Joseph Banks (Feb. 13, 1743-June 19, 1820) *18th:* 80
Luigi Boccherini (Feb. 19, 1743-May 28, 1805) *18th:* 129
Hannah Cowley (Mar. 4, 1743-Mar. 11, 1809) *18th:* 284
Thomas Jefferson (Apr. 13, 1743-July 4, 1826) *18th:* 528
Jean-Paul Marat (May 24, 1743-July 13, 1793) *18th:* 648, *Notor:* 696
Anna Barbauld (June 20, 1743-Mar. 9, 1825) *18th:* 87
William Paley (July, 1743-May 25, 1805) *18th:* 763
Antoine-Laurent Lavoisier (Aug. 26, 1743-May 8, 1794) *18th:* 579
Marquis de Condorcet (Sept. 17, 1743-Mar. 29, 1794) *18th:* 267
Ali Paşa Tepelenë (c. 1744-Feb. 5, 1822) *19th:* 55
Honda Toshiaki (1744-1821/1822) *18th:* 504
Mayer Amschel Rothschild (Feb. 23, 1744-Sept. 19, 1812) *19th:* 1947
Queen Charlotte (May 19, 1744-Nov. 17, 1818) *18th:* 235
Elbridge Gerry (July 17, 1744-Nov. 23, 1814) *18th:* 412
Johann Gottfried Herder (Aug. 25, 1744-Dec. 18, 1803) *18th:* 486
Olaudah Equiano (c. 1745-Mar. 31, 1797) *18th:* 324
Anthony Wayne (Jan. 1, 1745-Dec. 15, 1796) *18th:* 1054
Jacques-Étienne Montgolfier (Jan. 6, 1745-Aug. 2, 1799) *18th:* 698
Hannah More (Feb. 2, 1745-Sept. 7, 1833) *18th:* 702
Alessandro Volta (Feb. 18, 1745-Mar. 5, 1827) *18th:* 1022
Francis Asbury (Aug. 20, 1745-Mar. 31, 1816) *18th:* 62
Mikhail Illarionovich Kutuzov (Sept. 16, 1745-Apr. 28, 1813) *18th:* 569
John Jay (Dec. 12, 1745-May 17, 1829) *18th:* 524
Benjamin Rush (Jan. 4, 1746-Apr. 19, 1813) *18th:* 872
Johann Heinrich Pestalozzi (Jan. 12, 1746-Feb. 17, 1827) *19th:* 1782
Tadeusz Kościuszko (Feb. 4, 1746-Oct. 15, 1817) *18th:* 564
Francisco de Goya (Mar. 30, 1746-Apr. 16, 1828) *18th:* 436
Gaspard Monge (May 10, 1746-July 28, 1818) *18th:* 682
Henry Grattan (baptized July 3, 1746-June 4, 1820) *18th:* 440
Maurycy Beniowski (Sept. 20, 1746-May 23, 1786) *Notor:* 85
Daniel Shays (c. 1747-Sept. 29, 1825) *18th:* 902
Duc d'Orléans (Apr. 13, 1747-Nov. 6, 1793) *18th:* 751
John Paul Jones (July 6, 1747-July 18, 1792) *18th:* 539
Jeremy Bentham (Feb. 15, 1748-June 6, 1832) *18th:* 104
Emmanuel-Joseph Sieyès (May 3, 1748-June 20, 1836) *18th:* 916
Jacques-Louis David (Aug. 30, 1748-Dec. 29, 1825) *19th:* 607
Charles James Fox (Jan. 24, 1749-Sept. 13, 1806) *18th:* 363
Christian VII (Jan. 29, 1749-Mar. 13, 1808) *Notor:* 208
Comte de Mirabeau (Mar. 9, 1749-Apr. 2, 1791) *18th:* 679
Pierre-Simon Laplace (Mar. 23, 1749-Mar. 5, 1827) *19th:* 1317
Edward Jenner (May 17, 1749-Jan. 26, 1823) *18th:* 532
Johann Wolfgang von Goethe (Aug. 28, 1749-Mar. 22, 1832) *18th:* 428
First Baron Erskine (Jan., 10, 1750-Nov. 17, 1823) *18th:* 326
Caroline Lucretia Herschel (Mar. 16, 1750-Jan. 9, 1848) *18th:* 489
John Trumbull (Apr. 24, 1750-May 11, 1831) *18th:* 988
John André (May 2, 1750-Oct. 2, 1780) *18th:* 42
Karl von Hardenberg (May 31, 1750-Nov. 26, 1822) *19th:* 1021

1751 - 1760

James Madison (Mar. 16, 1751-June 28, 1836) *18th:* 636

Richard Brinsley Sheridan (baptized Nov. 4, 1751-July 7, 1816) *18th:* 905

Little Turtle (c. 1752-July 14, 1812) *18th:* 610

Nguyen Hue (c. 1752-1792) *18th:* 736

Betsy Ross (Jan. 1, 1752-Jan. 30, 1836) *18th:* 865

Gouverneur Morris (Jan. 31, 1752-Nov. 6, 1816) *18th:* 705

John Graves Simcoe (Feb. 25, 1752-Oct. 26, 1806) *18th:* 919

Fanny Burney (June 13, 1752-Jan. 6, 1840) *18th:* 180

John Nash (Sept. 1752-May 13, 1835) *19th:* 1642

George Rogers Clark (Nov. 19, 1752-Feb. 13, 1818) *18th:* 253

Phillis Wheatley (1753?-Dec. 5, 1784) *18th:* 1070

Miguel Hidalgo y Costilla (May 8, 1753-July 30, 1811) *19th:* 1094

Lazare Carnot (May 13, 1753-Aug. 2, 1823) *18th:* 200

Jean-Jacques-Régis de Cambacérès (Oct. 18, 1753-Mar. 8, 1824) *19th:* 396

Talleyrand (Feb. 2, 1754-May 17, 1838) *19th:* 2221

William Murdock (Aug. 21, 1754-Nov. 15, 1839) *18th:* 715

Louis XVI (Aug. 23, 1754-Jan. 21, 1793) *18th:* 618

William Bligh (Sept. 9, 1754-Dec. 7, 1817) *18th:* 126, *Notor:* 104

ʿUthman dan Fodio (Dec., 1754-Apr., 1817) *19th:* 2342

Alexander Hamilton (Jan. 11, 1755-July 12, 1804) *18th:* 452

Samuel Hahnemann (Apr. 10, 1755-July 2, 1843) *19th:* 1009

Élisabeth Vigée-Lebrun (Apr. 16, 1755-Mar. 30, 1842) *18th:* 1016

Sarah Siddons (July 5, 1755-June 8, 1831) *18th:* 912

John Marshall (Sept. 24, 1755-July 6, 1835) *19th:* 1498

Marie-Antoinette (Nov. 2, 1755-Oct. 16, 1793) *18th:* 657, *Notor:* 704

Gerhard Johann David von Scharnhorst (Nov. 12, 1755-June 28, 1813) *19th:* 2006

Gilbert Stuart (Dec. 3, 1755-July 9, 1828) *18th:* 947

Wolfgang Amadeus Mozart (Jan. 27, 1756-Dec. 5, 1791) *18th:* 711

Aaron Burr (Feb. 6, 1756-Sept. 14, 1836) *19th:* 363, *Notor:* 155

William Godwin (Mar. 3, 1756-Apr. 7, 1836) *18th:* 424

Sir Henry Raeburn (Mar. 4, 1756-July 8, 1823) *19th:* 1852

Maria Anne Fitzherbert (July 26, 1756-Mar. 27, 1837) *18th:* 358

Sweeney Todd (Oct. 16, 1756-Jan. 25, 1802) *Notor:* 1033

Georgiana Cavendish (June 7, 1757-Mar. 30, 1806) *18th:* 215

George Vancouver (June 22, 1757-May 10, 1798) *18th:* 1006

Thomas Telford (Aug. 9, 1757-Sept. 2, 1834) *19th:* 2240

Freiherr vom Stein (Oct. 26, 1757-June 29, 1831) *19th:* 2151

Antonio Canova (Nov. 1, 1757-Oct. 13, 1822) *19th:* 406

William Blake (Nov. 28, 1757-Aug. 12, 1827) *18th:* 121

Kamehameha I (c. 1758-May 8, 1819) *19th:* 1249

James Monroe (Apr. 28, 1758-July 4, 1831) *19th:* 1586

Robespierre (May 6, 1758-July 28, 1794) *18th:* 844, *Notor:* 907

Lord Nelson (Sept. 29, 1758-Oct. 21, 1805) *19th:* 1656

Noah Webster (Oct. 16, 1758-May 28, 1843) *19th:* 2402

Mary Robinson (Nov. 27, 1758?-Dec. 26, 1800) *18th:* 848

Alexander McGillivray (c. 1759-Feb. 17, 1793) *18th:* 626

Paul Cuffe (Jan. 17, 1759-Sept. 7, 1817) *19th:* 576

Robert Burns (Jan. 25, 1759-July 21, 1796) *18th:* 183

Mary Wollstonecraft (Apr. 27, 1759-Sept. 10, 1797) *18th:* 1108

William Pitt the Younger (May 28, 1759-Jan. 23, 1806) *18th:* 789

William Wilberforce (Aug. 24, 1759-July 29, 1833) *18th:* 1079

Georges Danton (Oct. 26, 1759-Apr. 5, 1794) *18th:* 289

Friedrich Schiller (Nov. 10, 1759-May 9, 1805) *18th:* 887

Rachel Wall (1760-Oct. 8, 1789) *Notor:* 1086

Henri de Saint-Simon (Oct. 17, 1760-May 19, 1825) *19th:* 1975

August von Gneisenau (Oct. 27, 1760-Aug. 23, 1831) *19th:* 928

1761 - 1770

Albert Gallatin (Jan. 29, 1761-Aug. 12, 1849) *19th:* 854
William Carey (Aug. 17, 1761-June 9, 1834) *19th:* 409
Gia Long (Feb. 8, 1762-Jan. 25 or Feb. 3, 1820) *19th:* 907
Johann Gottlieb Fichte (May 19, 1762-Jan. 29, 1814) *18th:* 342
George IV (Aug. 12, 1762-June 26, 1830) *19th:* 890
Tadano Makuzu (1763-July 26, 1825) *19th:* 2212
Charles XIV John (Jan. 26, 1763-Mar. 8, 1844) *19th:* 468
William Cobbett (Mar. 9, 1763-June 18, 1835) *19th:* 517
Wolfe Tone (June 20, 1763-Nov. 19, 1798) *18th:* 982
John Jacob Astor (July 17, 1763-Mar. 29, 1848) *19th:* 86
James Kent (July 31, 1763-Dec. 12, 1847) *19th:* 1271
Charles Bulfinch (Aug. 8, 1763-Apr. 4, 1844) *19th:* 346
Lord Edward Fitzgerald (Oct. 15, 1763-June 4, 1798) *18th:* 356
Sir Alexander Mackenzie (c. 1764-Mar. 12, 1820) *18th:* 629
Charles Grey (Mar. 13, 1764-July 17, 1845) *19th:* 977
Benjamin Henry Latrobe (May 1, 1764-Sept. 3, 1820) *19th:* 1325
Ann Radcliffe (July 9, 1764-Feb. 7, 1823) *18th:* 823
Nicéphore Niépce (Mar. 7, 1765-July 5, 1833) *19th:* 1676
William IV (Aug. 21, 1765-June 20, 1837) *19th:* 2445
Robert Fulton (Nov. 14, 1765-Feb. 24, 1815) *19th:* 845
Eli Whitney (Dec. 8, 1765-Jan. 8, 1825) *18th:* 1076
Thomas Robert Malthus (Feb. 13, 1766-Dec. 23, 1834) *19th:* 1475
Madame de Staël (Apr. 22, 1766-July 14, 1817) *18th:* 929
John MacArthur (Aug. 18, 1766-Apr. 11, 1834) *19th:* 1431
John Dalton (Sept. 6, 1766-July 27, 1844) *19th:* 597
Black Hawk (1767-Oct. 3, 1838) *19th:* 244
Andrew Jackson (Mar. 15, 1767-June 8, 1845) *19th:* 1189
John Quincy Adams (July 11, 1767-Feb. 23, 1848) *19th:* 20
Louis de Saint-Just (Aug. 25, 1767-July 28, 1794) *18th:* 877
Henri Christophe (Oct. 6, 1767-Oct. 8, 1820) *19th:* 494
Wang Zhenyi (1768-1797) *18th:* 1038
Maria Edgeworth (Jan. 1, 1768-May 22, 1849) *19th:* 728
Tecumseh (Mar., 1768-Oct. 5, 1813) *19th:* 2237
Joseph Fourier (Mar. 21, 1768-May 16, 1830) *19th:* 809
Dolley Madison (May 20, 1768-July 12, 1849) *19th:* 1470
Samuel Slater (June 9, 1768-Apr. 21, 1835) *19th:* 2111
Charlotte Corday (July 27, 1768-July 17, 1793) *Notor:* 235
François-René de Chateaubriand (Sept. 4, 1768-July 4, 1848) *19th:* 474
Friedrich Schleiermacher (Nov. 21, 1768-Feb. 12, 1834) *19th:* 2013
Muḥammad ʿAlī Pasha (1769-Aug. 2, 1849) *19th:* 1620
Michel Ney (Jan. 10, 1769-Dec. 7, 1815) *19th:* 1667
Thomas Lawrence (Apr. 13, 1769-Jan. 7, 1830) *18th:* 583
Marc Isambard Brunel (Apr. 25, 1769-Dec. 12, 1849) *19th:* 337
Duke of Wellington (May 1, 1769-Sept. 14, 1852) *19th:* 2409
Viscount Castlereagh (June 18, 1769-Aug. 12, 1822) *19th:* 437
Napoleon I (Aug. 15, 1769-May 5, 1821) *19th:* 1636
Georges Cuvier (Aug. 23, 1769-May 13, 1832) *19th:* 585
Alexander von Humboldt (Sept. 14, 1769-May 6, 1859) *19th:* 1151
Sir Isaac Brock (Oct. 6, 1769-Oct. 13, 1812) *19th:* 306
Sequoyah (c. 1770-Aug., 1843) *19th:* 2067
William Wordsworth (Apr. 7, 1770-Apr. 23, 1850) *19th:* 2462
George Canning (Apr. 11, 1770-Aug. 8, 1827) *19th:* 403
Second Earl of Liverpool (June 7, 1770-Dec. 4, 1828) *19th:* 1397
William Clark (Aug. 1, 1770-Sept. 1, 1838) *19th:* 1359
Georg Wilhelm Friedrich Hegel (Aug. 27, 1770-Nov. 14, 1831) *19th:* 1065
Ludwig van Beethoven (baptized Dec. 17, 1770-Mar. 26, 1827) *19th:* 175

1771 - 1780

Richard Trevithick (Apr. 13, 1771-Apr. 22, 1833) *19th:* 2294
Robert Owen (May 14, 1771-Nov. 17, 1858) *19th:* 1720
Eleuthère Irénée du Pont (June 24, 1771-Oct. 31, 1834) *19th:* 705
Thomas Talbot (July 19, 1771-Feb. 5, 1853) *19th:* 2219
Sir Walter Scott (Aug. 15, 1771-Sept. 21, 1832) *19th:* 2047
Mungo Park (Sept. 10, 1771-c. Jan., 1806) *18th:* 765
Francis Place (Nov. 3, 1771-Jan. 1, 1854) *19th:* 1806
Dominique You (c. 1772-Nov. 15, 1830) *Notor:* 1117
Mikhail Mikhaylovich Speransky (Jan. 12, 1772-Feb. 23, 1839) *19th:* 2129
Charles Fourier (Apr. 7, 1772-Oct. 10, 1837) *19th:* 805
David Ricardo (Apr. 18, 1772-Sept. 11, 1823) *19th:* 1896
Rammohan Ray (May 22, 1772-Sept. 27, 1833) *19th:* 1866
Samuel Taylor Coleridge (Oct. 21, 1772-July 25, 1834) *19th:* 529
William Henry Harrison (Feb. 9, 1773-Apr. 4, 1841) *19th:* 1048
James Mill (Apr. 6, 1773-June 23, 1836) *19th:* 1571
Marie Anne Victorine Boivin (Apr. 9, 1773-May 16, 1841) *19th:* 265
Metternich (May 15, 1773-June 11, 1859) *19th:* 1561
Lord Jeffrey (Oct. 23, 1773-Jan. 26, 1850) *19th:* 1223
George Cayley (Dec. 27, 1773-Dec. 15, 1857) *19th:* 447
Meriwether Lewis (Aug. 18, 1774-Oct. 11, 1809) *19th:* 1359
Saint Elizabeth Seton (Aug. 28, 1774-Jan. 4, 1821) *19th:* 2071
Salomon Mayer Rothschild (Sept. 9, 1774-July 27, 1855) *19th:* 1947
Johnny Appleseed (Sept. 26, 1774-Mar. 18?, 1845) *19th:* 68
Mary Butters (late 1700's-early 1800's) *Notor:* 160
Cheng I Sao (1775-1844) *Notor:* 205
Joan Wytte (1775-1813) *Notor:* 1110
Friedrich Wilhelm Joseph von Schelling (Jan. 27, 1775-Aug. 20, 1854) *19th:* 2009
J. M. W. Turner (Apr. 23, 1775-Dec. 19, 1851) *19th:* 2322
Eugène François Vidocq (July 23 or 24, 1775-May 11, 1857) *Notor:* 1067
Daniel O'Connell (Aug. 6, 1775-May 15, 1847) *19th:* 1695
Jane Austen (Dec. 16, 1775-July 18, 1817) *19th:* 94
Ho Xuan Huong (c. 1776-1820?) *19th:* 1110
John Bellingham (1776-May 18, 1812) *Notor:* 83
John Walter II (Feb. 23, 1776-July 28, 1847) *19th:* 2380
Sophie Germain (Apr. 1, 1776-June 27, 1831) *19th:* 901
John Constable (June 11, 1776-Mar. 31, 1837) *19th:* 540
Amedeo Avogadro (Aug. 9, 1776-July 9, 1856) *19th:* 101
Barthold Georg Niebuhr (Aug. 27, 1776-Jan. 2, 1831) *19th:* 1673
Roger Brooke Taney (Mar. 17, 1777-Oct. 12, 1864) *19th:* 2225, *Notor:* 1018
Henry Clay (Apr. 12, 1777-June 29, 1852) *19th:* 502
Carl Friedrich Gauss (Apr. 30, 1777-Feb. 23, 1855) *19th:* 883
Nathan Mayer Rothschild (Sept. 16, 1777-July 28, 1836) *19th:* 1947
Heinrich von Kleist (Oct. 18, 1777-Nov. 21, 1811) *19th:* 1289
Francis Greenway (Nov. 20, 1777-Sept. 26, 1837) *19th:* 974
Alexander I (Dec. 23, 1777-Dec. 1, 1825) *19th:* 45
José de San Martín (Feb. 25, 1778-Aug. 17, 1850) *19th:* 1984
Henry Brougham (Sept. 19, 1778-May 7, 1868) *19th:* 312
Joseph Lancaster (Nov. 25, 1778-Oct. 24, 1838) *19th:* 1304
Joseph-Louis Gay-Lussac (Dec. 6, 1778-May 9, 1850) *19th:* 886
Sir Humphry Davy (Dec. 17, 1778-May 29, 1829) *19th:* 616
Zebulon Pike (Jan. 5, 1779-Apr. 27, 1813) *19th:* 1793
Friedrich Karl von Savigny (Feb. 21, 1779-Oct. 25, 1861) *19th:* 2003
Frances Trollope (Mar. 10, 1779-Oct. 6, 1863) *19th:* 2303
Second Viscount Melbourne (Mar. 15, 1779-Nov. 24, 1848) *19th:* 1534
Francis Scott Key (Aug. 1, 1779-Jan. 11, 1843) *19th:* 1274
Joseph Story (Sept. 18, 1779-Sept. 10, 1845) *19th:* 2180

Jean Laffite (c. 1780-after 1822) *Notor:* 600
William Ellery Channing (Apr. 7, 1780-Oct. 2, 1842) *19th:* 464
Elizabeth Fry (May 21, 1780-Oct. 12, 1845) *19th:* 839
Carl von Clausewitz (June 1, 1780-Nov. 16, 1831) *19th:* 499
Jean-Auguste-Dominique Ingres (Aug. 29, 1780-Jan. 14, 1867) *19th:* 1171
Ranjit Singh (Nov. 13, 1780-June 27, 1839) *19th:* 1857
Mary Somerville (Dec. 26, 1780-Nov. 29, 1872) *19th:* 2121

1781 - 1790

Muḥammad Bello (1781-Oct. 26, 1837) *19th:* 186
George Stephenson (June 9, 1781-Aug. 12, 1848) *19th:* 2167
Daniel Webster (Jan. 18, 1782-Oct. 24, 1852) *19th:* 2398
Thomas Hart Benton (Mar. 14, 1782-Apr. 10, 1858) *19th:* 192
John C. Calhoun (Mar. 18, 1782-Mar. 31, 1850) *19th:* 392
Friedrich Froebel (Apr. 21, 1782-June 21, 1852) *19th:* 835
Niccolò Paganini (Oct. 27, 1782-May 27, 1840) *19th:* 1724
Martin Van Buren (Dec. 5, 1782-July 24, 1862) *19th:* 2344
Stendhal (Jan. 23, 1783-Mar. 23, 1842) *19th:* 2160
Washington Irving (Apr. 3, 1783-Nov. 28, 1859) *19th:* 1180
Simón Bolívar (July 24, 1783-Dec. 17, 1830) *19th:* 267
Friedrich Wilhelm Bessel (July 22, 1784-Mar. 17, 1846) *19th:* 215
Lord Palmerston (Oct. 20, 1784-Oct. 18, 1865) *19th:* 1731
Zachary Taylor (Nov. 24, 1784-July 9, 1850) *19th:* 2230
Jacob Grimm (Jan. 4, 1785-Sept. 30, 1863) *19th:* 992
Alessandro Manzoni (Mar. 7, 1785-May 22, 1873) *19th:* 1495
John James Audubon (Apr. 26, 1785-Jan. 27, 1851) *19th:* 91
Sylvanus Thayer (June 9, 1785-Sept. 7, 1872) *19th:* 2260
Oliver Hazard Perry (Aug. 20, 1785-Aug. 23, 1819) *19th:* 1779
La Saragossa (1786-1857) *19th:* 1993
Nicholas Biddle (Jan. 8, 1786-Feb. 27, 1844) *19th:* 225
Wilhelm Grimm (Feb. 24, 1786-Dec. 16, 1859) *19th:* 992
Sir Thomas Fowell Buxton (Apr. 1, 1786-Feb. 19, 1845) *19th:* 376
Sir John Franklin (Apr. 16, 1786-June 11, 1847) *19th:* 825
Winfield Scott (June 13, 1786-May 29, 1866) *19th:* 2051
David Crockett (Aug. 17, 1786-Mar. 6, 1836) *19th:* 571
Carl Maria von Weber (Nov. 18, 1786-June 5, 1826) *19th:* 2395
Shaka (c. 1787-Sept. 22, 1828) *19th:* 2081
Emma Willard (Feb. 23, 1787-Apr. 15, 1870) *19th:* 2438
Edmund Kean (Nov. 4, 1787-May 15, 1833) *19th:* 1254
Jacques Daguerre (Nov. 18, 1787-July 10, 1851) *19th:* 589
Sacagawea (c. 1788-Dec. 20, 1812) *19th:* 1962
Lord Byron (Jan. 22, 1788-Apr. 19, 1824) *19th:* 379
Sir Robert Peel (Feb. 5, 1788-July 2, 1850) *19th:* 1768
Arthur Schopenhauer (Feb. 22, 1788-Sept. 21, 1860) *19th:* 2019
Antoine-César Becquerel (Mar. 8, 1788-Jan. 18, 1878) *19th:* 165
Don Carlos (Mar. 29, 1788-Mar. 10, 1855) *19th:* 412
Carl Mayer Rothschild (Apr. 24, 1788-Mar. 10, 1855) *19th:* 1947
James Gadsden (May 15, 1788-Dec. 26, 1858) *19th:* 849
Alexander Campbell (Sept. 12, 1788-Mar. 4, 1866) *19th:* 399
Sarah Josepha Hale (Oct. 24, 1788-Apr. 30, 1879) *19th:* 1012
Jules Michelet (Aug. 21, 1789-Feb. 9, 1874) *19th:* 1564
James Fenimore Cooper (Sept. 15, 1789-Sept. 14, 1851) *19th:* 552
John Tyler (Mar. 29, 1790-Jan. 18, 1862) *19th:* 2337
W. C. Wentworth (Aug. 13, 1790-Mar. 20, 1872) *19th:* 2412
John Ross (Oct. 3, 1790-Aug. 1, 1866) *19th:* 1937
Giuseppe Fieschi (Dec. 3, 1790-Feb. 19, 1836) *Notor:* 353

1791 - 1800

Saʿīd ibn Sulṭān (1791-Oct. 19, 1856) *19th:* 1965
James Buchanan (Apr. 23, 1791-June 1, 1868) *19th:* 343
Samuel F. B. Morse (Apr. 27, 1791-Apr. 2, 1872) *19th:* 1610
Michael Faraday (Sept. 22, 1791-Aug. 25, 1867) *19th:* 759
Charles Babbage (Dec. 26, 1791-Oct. 18, 1871) *19th:* 107
William Burke (1792-Jan. 28, 1829) *Notor:* 154
Alexander Ypsilantis (1792-Jan. 31, 1828) *19th:* 2478
Gioacchino Rossini (Feb. 29, 1792-Nov. 13, 1868) *19th:* 1944
Karl Ernst von Baer (Feb. 29, 1792-Nov. 28, 1876) *19th:* 114
Thaddeus Stevens (Apr. 4, 1792-Aug. 11, 1868) *19th:* 2171
First Earl of Durham (Apr. 12, 1792-July 28, 1840) *19th:* 708
Pius IX (May 13, 1792-Feb. 7, 1878) *19th:* 1802
James Mayer Rothschild (May 15, 1792-Nov. 15, 1868) *19th:* 1947
Percy Bysshe Shelley (Aug. 4, 1792-July 8, 1822) *19th:* 2092
John Russell (Aug. 18, 1792-May 28, 1878) *19th:* 1958
Sarah Grimké (Nov. 26, 1792-Dec. 23, 1873) *19th:* 988
Nikolay Ivanovich Lobachevsky (Dec. 1, 1792-Feb. 24, 1856) *19th:* 1403
Lucretia Mott (Jan. 3, 1793-Nov. 11, 1880) *19th:* 1616
Sam Houston (Mar. 2, 1793-July 26, 1863) *19th:* 1130
William Charles Macready (Mar. 3, 1793-Apr. 27, 1873) *19th:* 1467
Felicia Dorothea Hemans (Sept. 25, 1793-May 16, 1835) *19th:* 1076
Stephen Fuller Austin (Nov. 3, 1793-Dec. 27, 1836) *19th:* 98
Demetrios Ypsilantis (Dec. 25, 1793-1832) *19th:* 2478
Marie Laveau (1794-June 15, 1881) *Notor:* 610
Antonio López de Santa Anna (Feb. 21, 1794-June 21, 1876) *19th:* 1990
Matthew C. Perry (Apr. 10, 1794-Mar. 4, 1858) *19th:* 1776
Anna Jameson (May 19, 1794-Mar. 17, 1860) *19th:* 1217
Cornelius Vanderbilt (May 27, 1794-Jan. 4, 1877) *19th:* 2348
William Cullen Bryant (Nov. 3, 1794-June 12, 1878) *19th:* 340
Dred Scott (c. 1795-Sept. 17, 1858) *19th:* 2041
Antonio José de Sucre (Feb. 3, 1795-June 4, 1830) *19th:* 2195
William Lyon Mackenzie (Mar. 12, 1795-Aug. 28, 1861) *19th:* 1454
Sir Charles Barry (May 23, 1795-May 12, 1860) *19th:* 142
Thomas Arnold (June 13, 1795-June 12, 1842) *19th:* 76
James Gordon Bennett (Sept. 1, 1795-June 1, 1872) *19th:* 188
Frances Wright (Sept. 6, 1795-Dec. 13, 1852) *19th:* 2469
John Keats (Oct. 31, 1795-Feb. 23, 1821) *19th:* 1259
Thomas Carlyle (Dec. 4, 1795-Feb. 5, 1881) *19th:* 415
Leopold von Ranke (Dec. 21, 1795-May 23, 1886) *19th:* 1860
Jakob Steiner (Mar. 18, 1796-Apr. 1, 1863) *19th:* 2154
Edward Gibbon Wakefield (Mar. 20, 1796-May 16, 1862) *19th:* 2378
Horace Mann (May 4, 1796-Aug. 2, 1859) *19th:* 1486
William Hickling Prescott (May 4, 1796-Jan. 28, 1859) *19th:* 1831
Nicholas I (July 6, 1796-Mar. 2, 1855) *19th:* 1670, *Notor:* 788
George Catlin (July 26, 1796-Dec. 23, 1872) *19th:* 441
Sojourner Truth (c. 1797-Nov. 26, 1883) *19th:* 2306
Hiroshige (1797-Oct. 12, 1858) *19th:* 1107
Franz Schubert (Jan. 31, 1797-Nov. 19, 1828) *19th:* 2026
Mary Lyon (Feb. 28, 1797-Mar. 5, 1849) *19th:* 1428
Adolphe Thiers (Apr. 15, 1797-Sept. 3, 1877) *19th:* 2263
Mary Wollstonecraft Shelley (Aug. 30, 1797-Feb. 1, 1851) *19th:* 2088
Sir Charles Lyell (Nov. 14, 1797-Feb. 22, 1875) *19th:* 1423
Gaetano Donizetti (Nov. 29, 1797-Apr. 8, 1848) *19th:* 674
Heinrich Heine (Dec. 13, 1797-Feb. 17, 1856) *19th:* 1069
Joseph Henry (Dec. 17, 1797-May 13, 1878) *19th:* 1078

Tamsin Blight (1798-Oct. 6, 1856) *Notor:* 106
Auguste Comte (Jan. 19, 1798-Sept. 5, 1857) *19th:* 536
Charles Wilkes (Apr. 3, 1798-Feb. 8, 1877) *19th:* 2435
Eugène Delacroix (Apr. 26, 1798-Aug. 13, 1863) *19th:* 635
Pedro I (Oct. 12, 1798-Sept. 24, 1834) *19th:* 1763
Jedediah Smith (Jan. 6, 1799-May 27, 1831) *19th:* 2114
Simon Cameron (Mar. 8, 1799-June 26, 1889) *Notor:* 171
Fourteenth Earl of Derby (Mar. 29, 1799-Oct. 23, 1869) *19th:* 642
Honoré de Balzac (May 20, 1799-Aug. 18, 1850) *19th:* 126
Alexander Pushkin (June 6, 1799-Feb. 10, 1837) *19th:* 1848
Bronson Alcott (Nov. 29, 1799-Mar. 4, 1888) *19th:* 38
Richard Lawrence (1800 or 1801-June 13, 1861) *Notor:* 615
Millard Fillmore (Jan. 7, 1800-Mar. 8, 1874) *19th:* 781
Caleb Cushing (Jan. 17, 1800-Jan. 2, 1879) *19th:* 578
Edwin Chadwick (Jan. 24, 1800-July 6, 1890) *19th:* 456
John Brown (May 9, 1800-Dec. 2, 1859) *19th:* 319
Friedrich Wöhler (July 31, 1800-Sept. 23, 1882) *19th:* 2456
E. B. Pusey (Aug. 22, 1800-Sept. 16, 1882) *19th:* 1844
Catharine Beecher (Sept. 6, 1800-May 12, 1878) *19th:* 168
William Holmes McGuffey (Sept. 23, 1800-May 4, 1873) *19th:* 1445
Nat Turner (Oct. 2, 1800-Nov. 11, 1831) *19th:* 2326
George Bancroft (Oct. 3, 1800-Jan. 17, 1891) *19th:* 130
Thomas Babington Macaulay (Oct. 25, 1800-Dec. 28, 1859) *19th:* 1433
Charles Goodyear (Dec. 29, 1800-July 1, 1860) *19th:* 946

1801 - 1810

John Henry Newman (Feb. 21, 1801-Aug. 11, 1890) *19th:* 1663
Vincenzo Gioberti (Apr. 5, 1801-Oct. 26, 1852) *19th:* 921
Gustav Theodor Fechner (Apr. 19, 1801-Nov. 18, 1887) *19th:* 770
William H. Seward (May 16, 1801-Oct. 10, 1872) *19th:* 2077
Brigham Young (June 1, 1801-Aug. 29, 1877) *19th:* 2474
David G. Farragut (July 5, 1801-Aug. 14, 1870) *19th:* 762
Samuel Gridley Howe (Nov. 10, 1801-Jan. 9, 1876) *19th:* 1141
Catharine Parr Traill (Jan. 9, 1802-Aug. 28, 1899) *19th:* 2291
Sir Charles Wheatstone (Feb. 6, 1802-Oct. 19, 1875) *19th:* 547
Lydia Maria Child (Feb. 11, 1802-Oct. 20, 1880) *19th:* 482
Victor Hugo (Feb. 26, 1802-May 22, 1885) *19th:* 1146
Dorothea Dix (Apr. 4, 1802-July 17, 1887) *19th:* 671
Harriet Martineau (June 12, 1802-June 27, 1876) *19th:* 1505
Alexandre Dumas, *père* (July 24, 1802-Dec. 5, 1870) *19th:* 695
Niels Henrik Abel (Aug. 5, 1802-Apr. 6, 1829) *19th:* 9
Sir James Outram (Jan. 29, 1803-Mar. 11, 1863) *19th:* 1717
Flora Tristan (Apr. 7, 1803-Nov. 14, 1844) *19th:* 2297
Justus von Liebig (May 12, 1803-Apr. 18, 1873) *19th:* 1366
Ralph Waldo Emerson (May 25, 1803-Apr. 27, 1882) *19th:* 745
Ferenc Deák (Oct. 17, 1803-Jan. 28, 1876) *19th:* 619
Susanna Moodie (Dec. 6, 1803-Apr. 8, 1885) *19th:* 1593
Hector Berlioz (Dec. 11, 1803-Mar. 8, 1869) *19th:* 200
Osceola (c. 1804-Jan. 30, 1838) *19th:* 1709
Robert Baldwin (May 12, 1804-Dec. 9, 1858) *19th:* 122
Elizabeth Palmer Peabody (May 16, 1804-Jan. 3, 1894) *19th:* 1761
Richard Cobden (June 3, 1804-Apr. 2, 1865) *19th:* 520
George Sand (July 1, 1804-June 8, 1876) *19th:* 1987
Nathaniel Hawthorne (July 4, 1804-May 19, 1864) *19th:* 1051
Franklin Pierce (Nov. 23, 1804-Oct. 8, 1869) *19th:* 1789

Benjamin Disraeli (Dec. 21, 1804-Apr. 19, 1881) *19th:* 666
Fanny Calderón de la Barca (Dec. 23, 1804-Feb. 3, 1882) *19th:* 389
Angelina Grimké (Feb. 20, 1805-Oct. 26, 1879) *19th:* 988
Hans Christian Andersen (Apr. 2, 1805-Aug. 4, 1875) *19th:* 61
Frederick Denison Maurice (Apr. 29, 1805-Apr. 1, 1872) *19th:* 1518
Giuseppe Mazzini (June 22, 1805-Mar. 10, 1872) *19th:* 1531
Alexis de Tocqueville (July 29, 1805-Apr. 16, 1859) *19th:* 2280
Sir William Rowan Hamilton (Aug. 3/4, 1805-Sept. 2, 1865) *19th:* 1015
Ferdinand de Lesseps (Nov. 19, 1805-Dec. 7, 1894) *19th:* 1356
William Lloyd Garrison (Dec. 10, 1805-May 24, 1879) *19th:* 874
Joseph Smith (Dec. 23, 1805-June 27, 1844) *19th:* 2117
Samuel Ajayi Crowther (c. 1806-Dec. 31, 1891) *19th:* 574
Matthew Fontaine Maury (Jan. 14, 1806-Feb. 1, 1873) *19th:* 1522
Elizabeth Barrett Browning (Mar. 6, 1806-June 29, 1861) *19th:* 326
Edwin Forrest (Mar. 9, 1806-Dec. 12, 1872) *19th:* 790
Benito Juárez (Mar. 21, 1806-July 19, 1872) *19th:* 1245
Isambard Kingdom Brunel (Apr. 9, 1806-Sept. 15, 1859) *19th:* 333
William Fothergill Cooke (May 4, 1806-June 25, 1879) *19th:* 547
John Stuart Mill (May 20, 1806-May 7, 1873) *19th:* 1574
John Augustus Roebling (June 12, 1806-July 22, 1869) *19th:* 1928
Robert E. Lee (Jan. 19, 1807-Oct. 12, 1870) *19th:* 1334
Henry Wadsworth Longfellow (Feb. 27, 1807-Mar. 24, 1882) *19th:* 1416
Louis Agassiz (May 28, 1807-Dec. 14, 1873) *19th:* 31
Giuseppe Garibaldi (July 4, 1807-June 2, 1882) *19th:* 871
John Greenleaf Whittier (Dec. 17, 1807-Sept. 7, 1892) *19th:* 2428
Salmon P. Chase (Jan. 13, 1808-May 7, 1873) *19th:* 470
Napoleon III (Apr. 20, 1808-Jan. 9, 1873) *19th:* 1639
Henry Edward Manning (July 15, 1808-Jan. 14, 1892) *19th:* 1489
James Nasmyth (Aug. 19, 1808-May 7, 1890) *19th:* 1646
Abdelkader (Sept. 6, 1808-May 25/26, 1883) *19th:* 1
Andrew Johnson (Dec. 29, 1808-July 31, 1875) *19th:* 1229
Louis Braille (Jan. 4, 1809-Jan. 6, 1852) *19th:* 299
Friedrich von Beust (Jan. 13, 1809-Oct. 24, 1886) *19th:* 222
Pierre-Joseph Proudhon (Jan. 15, 1809-Jan. 19, 1865) *19th:* 1834
Edgar Allan Poe (Jan. 19, 1809-Oct. 7, 1849) *19th:* 1813
Felix Mendelssohn (Feb. 3, 1809-Nov. 4, 1847) *19th:* 1549
Charles Darwin (Feb. 12, 1809-Apr. 19, 1882) *19th:* 603
Abraham Lincoln (Feb. 12, 1809-Apr. 15, 1865) *19th:* 1380
Cyrus Hall McCormick (Feb. 15, 1809-May 13, 1884) *19th:* 1438
Nikolai Gogol (Mar. 31, 1809-Mar. 4, 1852) *19th:* 937
Alfred, Lord Tennyson (Aug. 6, 1809-Oct. 6, 1892) *19th:* 2244
Oliver Wendell Holmes (Aug. 29, 1809-Oct. 7, 1894) *19th:* 1116
Fanny Kemble (Nov. 27, 1809-Jan. 15, 1893) *19th:* 1267
Kit Carson (Dec. 24, 1809-May 23, 1868) *19th:* 426
William Ewart Gladstone (Dec. 29, 1809-May 19, 1898) *19th:* 924
Abby Kelley Foster (Jan. 15, 1810-Jan. 14, 1887) *19th:* 799
Frédéric Chopin (Mar. 1, 1810-Oct. 17, 1849) *19th:* 486
Leo XIII (Mar. 2, 1810-July 20, 1903) *19th:* 1342
Theodore Parker (Apr. 24, 1810-May 10, 1860) *19th:* 1735
Margaret Fuller (May 23, 1810-July 19, 1850) *19th:* 841
Robert Schumann (June 8, 1810-July 29, 1856) *19th:* 2031
Fanny Elssler (June 23, 1810-Nov. 27, 1884) *19th:* 743
P. T. Barnum (July 5, 1810-Apr. 7, 1891) *19th:* 138
Count Cavour (Aug. 10, 1810-June 6, 1861) *19th:* 444
Asa Gray (Nov. 18, 1810-Jan. 30, 1888) *19th:* 963

1811 - 1820

Charles Sumner (Jan. 6, 1811-Mar. 11, 1874) *19th:* 2201
Henry Barnard (Jan. 24, 1811-July 5, 1900) *19th:* 135
Horace Greeley (Feb. 3, 1811-Nov. 29, 1872) *19th:* 966
Domingo Faustino Sarmiento (Feb. 14, 1811-Sept. 11, 1888) *19th:* 2000
George Caleb Bingham (Mar. 20, 1811-July 7, 1879) *19th:* 234
Harriet Beecher Stowe (June 14, 1811-July 1, 1896) *19th:* 2184
Sir William Robert Grove (July 11, 1811-Aug. 1, 1896) *19th:* 996
Sir George Gilbert Scott (July 13, 1811-Mar. 27, 1878) *19th:* 2044
William Makepeace Thackeray (July 18, 1811-Dec. 24, 1863) *19th:* 2257
Franz Liszt (Oct. 22, 1811-July 31, 1886) *19th:* 1393
Évariste Galois (Oct. 25, 1811-May 31, 1832) *19th:* 857
Louis Blanc (Oct. 29, 1811-Dec. 6, 1882) *19th:* 254
John Bright (Nov. 16, 1811-Mar. 27, 1889) *19th:* 302
Zeng Guofan (Nov. 26, 1811-Mar. 12, 1872) *19th:* 2483
Wendell Phillips (Nov. 29, 1811-Feb. 2, 1884) *19th:* 1785
Charles Dickens (Feb. 7, 1812-June 9, 1870) *19th:* 655
Alexander H. Stephens (Feb. 11, 1812-Mar. 4, 1883) *19th:* 2164
Augustus Welby Northmore Pugin (Mar. 1, 1812-Sept. 14, 1852) *19th:* 1838
Aleksandr Herzen (Apr. 6, 1812-Jan. 21, 1870) *19th:* 1085
Sir George Grey (Apr. 14, 1812-Sept. 19, 1898) *19th:* 981
First Marquis of Dalhousie (Apr. 22, 1812-Dec. 19, 1860) *19th:* 595
Alfred Krupp (Apr. 26, 1812-July 14, 1887) *19th:* 1301
Madame Restell (May 6, 1812-Apr. 1, 1878) *Notor:* 892
Sir Henry Bessemer (Jan. 19, 1813-Mar. 15, 1898) *19th:* 218
John C. Frémont (Jan. 21, 1813-July 13, 1890) *19th:* 831
David Livingstone (Mar. 19, 1813-May 1, 1873) *19th:* 1400
Stephen A. Douglas (Apr. 23, 1813-June 3, 1861) *19th:* 681
Søren Kierkegaard (May 5, 1813-Nov. 11, 1855) *19th:* 1278
Richard Wagner (May 22, 1813-Feb. 13, 1883) *19th:* 2374
Henry Ward Beecher (June 24, 1813-Mar. 8, 1887) *19th:* 172
Claude Bernard (July 12, 1813-Feb. 10, 1878) *19th:* 205
Daniel Macmillan (Sept. 13, 1813-June 27, 1857) *19th:* 1464
Giuseppe Verdi (Oct. 10, 1813-Jan. 27, 1901) *19th:* 2351
Táhirih (1814/1820-1852) *19th:* 2214
Daniel M'Naghten (1814-1865) *Notor:* 677
Hong Xiuquan (Jan. 1, 1814-June 1, 1864) *19th:* 1127
Mikhail Bakunin (May 30, 1814-July 1, 1876) *19th:* 119
Anaïs Ségalas (Sept. 21, 1814-Aug. 31, 1893) *19th:* 2062
Mikhail Lermontov (Oct. 15, 1814-July 27, 1841) *19th:* 1352
Luise Aston (Nov. 26, 1814-Dec. 21, 1871) *19th:* 83
Edwin M. Stanton (Dec. 19, 1814-Dec. 24, 1869) *19th:* 2142
Sir John Alexander Macdonald (Jan. 11, 1815-June 6, 1891) *19th:* 1441
Otto von Bismarck (Apr. 1, 1815-July 30, 1898) *19th:* 238
Anthony Trollope (Apr. 24, 1815-Dec. 6, 1882) *19th:* 2299
Sir Henry Parkes (May 27, 1815-Apr. 27, 1896) *19th:* 1739
Elizabeth Cady Stanton (Nov. 12, 1815-Oct. 26, 1902) *19th:* 2146
Ii Naosuke (Nov. 29, 1815-Mar. 24, 1860) *19th:* 1168
Countess of Lovelace (Dec. 10, 1815-Nov. 27, 1852) *19th:* 1420
James Donnelly (Mar. 7, 1816-Feb. 4, 1880) *Notor:* 294
Charlotte Brontë (Apr. 21, 1816-Mar. 31, 1855) *19th:* 308
Arthur de Gobineau (July 14, 1816-Oct. 13, 1882) *Notor:* 415
Stephen J. Field (Nov. 4, 1816-Apr. 9, 1899) *19th:* 777
Werner Siemens (Dec. 13, 1816-Dec. 6, 1892) *19th:* 2105

Frederick Douglass (Feb., 1817?-Feb. 20, 1895) *19th:* 684
Henry David Thoreau (July 12, 1817-May 6, 1862) *19th:* 2274
Sir Sayyid Ahmad Khan (Oct. 17, 1817-Mar. 27, 1898) *19th:* 35
Bahāʾullāh (Nov. 12, 1817-May 29, 1892) *19th:* 117
Theodor Mommsen (Nov. 30, 1817-Nov. 1, 1903) *19th:* 1582
Tewodros II (c. 1818-Apr. 13, 1868) *19th:* 2255
Alexander II (Apr. 29, 1818-Mar. 13, 1881) *19th:* 48
Karl Marx (May 5, 1818-Mar. 14, 1883) *19th:* 1508
Jacob Burckhardt (May 25, 1818-Aug. 8, 1897) *19th:* 354
Amelia Bloomer (May 27, 1818-Dec. 30, 1894) *19th:* 257
Louis Faidherbe (June 3, 1818-Sept. 29, 1889) *19th:* 756
Charles Gounod (June 17, 1818-Oct. 18, 1893) *19th:* 952
Ignaz Philipp Semmelweis (July 1, 1818-Aug. 13, 1865) *19th:* 2064
William Edward Forster (July 11, 1818-Apr. 5, 1886) *19th:* 793
Emily Brontë (July 30, 1818-Dec. 19, 1848) *19th:* 308
Maria Mitchell (Aug. 1, 1818-June 28, 1889) *19th:* 1580
Lucy Stone (Aug. 13, 1818-Oct. 18, 1893) *19th:* 2177
Ivan Turgenev (Nov. 9, 1818-Sept. 3, 1883) *19th:* 2319
Lewis Henry Morgan (Nov. 21, 1818-Dec. 17, 1881) *19th:* 1603
George Brown (Nov. 29, 1818-May 9, 1880) *19th:* 316
Mary Todd Lincoln (Dec. 13, 1818-July 16, 1882) *19th:* 1385
John Ruskin (Feb. 8, 1819-Jan. 20, 1900) *19th:* 1954
Lydia E. Pinkham (Feb. 9, 1819-May 17, 1883) *19th:* 1796
Isaac Mayer Wise (Mar. 29, 1819-Mar. 26, 1900) *19th:* 2453
Queen Victoria (May 24, 1819-Jan. 22, 1901) *19th:* 2359
Julia Ward Howe (May 27, 1819-Oct. 17, 1910) *19th:* 1137
Walt Whitman (May 31, 1819-Mar. 26, 1892) *19th:* 2423
Gustave Courbet (June 10, 1819-Dec. 31, 1877) *19th:* 559
Jacques Offenbach (June 20, 1819-Oct. 5, 1880) *19th:* 1699
Elias Howe (July 9, 1819-Oct. 3, 1867) *19th:* 1133
Herman Melville (Aug. 1, 1819-Sept. 28, 1891) *19th:* 1537
William Thomas Green Morton (Aug. 9, 1819-July 15, 1868) *19th:* 1613
Clara Schumann (Sept. 13, 1819-May 20, 1896) *19th:* 2029
The Bāb (Oct. 20, 1819-July 9, 1850) *19th:* 105
George Eliot (Nov. 22, 1819-Dec. 22, 1880) *19th:* 740
Harriet Tubman (c. 1820-Mar. 10, 1913) *19th:* 2312
Anne Brontë (Jan. 17, 1820-May 28, 1849) *19th:* 308
William Tecumseh Sherman (Feb. 8, 1820-Feb. 14, 1891) *19th:* 2097
Susan B. Anthony (Feb. 15, 1820-Mar. 13, 1906) *19th:* 65
Alexandre-Edmond Becquerel (Mar. 24, 1820-May 11, 1891) *19th:* 165
Herbert Spencer (Apr. 27, 1820-Dec. 8, 1903) *19th:* 2126
Florence Nightingale (May 12, 1820-Aug. 13, 1910) *19th:* 1684
James Buchanan Eads (May 23, 1820-Mar. 8, 1887) *19th:* 715
Iswar Chandra Vidyasagar (Sept. 26, 1820-July 29, 1891) *19th:* 2363
Jenny Lind (Oct. 6, 1820-Nov. 2, 1887) *19th:* 1387
Friedrich Engels (Nov. 28, 1820-Aug. 5, 1895) *19th:* 750
Carolina Coronado (Dec. 12, 1820-Jan. 15, 1911) *19th:* 556

1821 - 1830

Elizabeth Blackwell (Feb. 3, 1821-May 31, 1910) *19th:* 247
Lola Montez (Feb. 17, 1821-Jan. 17, 1861) *19th:* 1590
Charles Baudelaire (Apr. 9, 1821-Aug. 31, 1867) *19th:* 152
Sir Charles Tupper (July 2, 1821-Oct., 30, 1915) *19th:* 2316
Nathan Bedford Forrest (July 13, 1821-Oct. 29, 1877) *Notor:* 365

Mary Baker Eddy (July 16, 1821-Dec. 3, 1910) *19th:* 723
Jay Cooke (Aug. 10, 1821-Feb. 18, 1905) *19th:* 544
Hermann von Helmholtz (Aug. 31, 1821-Sept. 8, 1894) *19th:* 1073
Rudolf Virchow (Oct. 13, 1821-Sept. 5, 1902) *19th:* 2365
Fyodor Dostoevski (Nov. 11, 1821-Feb. 9, 1881) *19th:* 677
Gustave Flaubert (Dec. 12, 1821-May 8, 1880) *19th:* 785
Clara Barton (Dec. 25, 1821-Apr. 12, 1912) *19th:* 145
Red Cloud (1822-Dec. 10, 1909) *19th:* 1871
Heinrich Schliemann (Jan. 6, 1822-Dec. 26, 1890) *19th:* 2016
Étienne Lenoir (Jan. 12, 1822-Aug. 4, 1900) *19th:* 1338
Alexander Mackenzie (Jan. 28, 1822-Apr. 17, 1892) *19th:* 1452
Francis Galton (Feb. 16, 1822-Jan. 17, 1911) *19th:* 860
Albrecht Ritschl (Mar. 25, 1822-Mar. 20, 1889) *19th:* 1918
Frederick Law Olmsted (Apr. 26, 1822-Aug. 28, 1903) *19th:* 1706
Ulysses S. Grant (Apr. 27, 1822-July 23, 1885) *19th:* 958
Lydia Folger Fowler (May 5, 1822-Jan. 26, 1879) *19th:* 812
Gregor Mendel (July 22, 1822-Jan. 6, 1884) *19th:* 1541
Rutherford B. Hayes (Oct. 4, 1822-Jan. 17, 1893) *19th:* 1061
Elizabeth Cabot Agassiz (Dec. 5, 1822-June 27, 1907) *19th:* 29
César Franck (Dec. 10, 1822-Nov. 8, 1890) *19th:* 821
Matthew Arnold (Dec. 24, 1822-Apr. 15, 1888) *19th:* 71
Louis Pasteur (Dec. 27, 1822-Sept. 28, 1895) *19th:* 1751
Mathew B. Brady (c. 1823-Jan. 15, 1896) *19th:* 291
Li Hongzhang (Feb. 15, 1823-Nov. 7, 1901) *19th:* 1363
Ernest Renan (Feb. 28, 1823-Oct. 2, 1892) *19th:* 1884
Schuyler Colfax (Mar. 23, 1823-Jan. 13, 1885) *Notor:* 219
William Marcy Tweed (Apr. 3, 1823-Apr. 12, 1878) *19th:* 2333, *Notor:* 1047
William Siemens (Apr. 4, 1823-Nov. 19, 1883) *19th:* 2105
Mary Surratt (May or June, 1823-July 7, 1865) *Notor:* 1012
Charlotte Mary Yonge (Aug. 11, 1823-Mar. 24, 1901) *19th:* 2472
Johannah Donnelly (Sept. 22, 1823-Feb. 4, 1880) *Notor:* 294
Mary Ann Shadd Cary (Oct. 9, 1823-June 5, 1893) *19th:* 431
Henry Wirz (Nov. 25, 1823-Nov. 10, 1865) *Notor:* 1105
Thomas Wentworth Higginson (Dec. 22, 1823-May 9, 1911) *19th:* 1097
Stonewall Jackson (Jan. 21, 1824-May 10, 1863) *19th:* 1197
Leland Stanford (Mar. 9, 1824-June 20, 1893) *19th:* 2132
William Walker (May 8, 1824-Sept. 12, 1860) *Notor:* 1084
George Edmund Street (June 20, 1824-Dec. 18, 1881) *19th:* 2191
Baron Kelvin (June 26, 1824-Dec. 17, 1907) *19th:* 1264
Anton Bruckner (Sept. 4, 1824-Oct. 11, 1896) *19th:* 329
Tom Bell (1825-Oct. 4, 1856) *Notor:* 80
Ferdinand Lassalle (Apr. 11, 1825-Aug. 31, 1864) *19th:* 1321
Thomas Henry Huxley (May 4, 1825-June 29, 1895) *19th:* 1161
Dadabhai Naoroji (Sept. 4, 1825-June 30, 1917) *19th:* 1634
Paul Kruger (Oct. 10, 1825-July 14, 1904) *19th:* 1298
Johann Strauss (Oct. 25, 1825-June 3, 1899) *19th:* 2188
Pedro II (Dec. 2, 1825-Dec. 5, 1891) *19th:* 1766
Cetshwayo (c. 1826-Feb. 8, 1884) *19th:* 450
Matilda Joslyn Gage (Mar. 24, 1826-Mar. 18, 1898) *19th:* 852
Wilhelm Liebknecht (Mar. 29, 1826-Aug. 7, 1900) *19th:* 1370
Stephen Collins Foster (July 4, 1826-Jan. 13, 1864) *19th:* 802
Friedrich Siemens (Dec. 8, 1826-May 24, 1904) *19th:* 2105
Saigō Takamori (1827/1828-Sept. 24, 1877) *19th:* 1968
William Holman Hunt (Apr. 2, 1827-Sept. 7, 1910) *19th:* 1157
Joseph Lister (Apr. 5, 1827-Feb. 10, 1912) *19th:* 1390
Barbara Leigh Smith Bodichon (Apr. 8, 1827-June 11, 1891) *19th:* 263
John Hanning Speke (May 4, 1827-Sept. 15, 1864) *19th:* 2123

Konstantin Petrovich Pobedonostsev (May 21, 1827-Mar. 23, 1907) *19th:* 1810, *Notor:* 845
Ferdinand Julius Cohn (Jan. 24, 1828-June 25, 1898) *19th:* 527
Jules Verne (Feb. 8, 1828-Mar. 24, 1905) *19th:* 2354
Henrik Ibsen (Mar. 20, 1828-May 23, 1906) *19th:* 1165
Josephine Butler (Apr. 13, 1828-Dec. 30, 1906) *19th:* 371
Hippolyte Taine (Apr. 21, 1828-Mar. 5, 1893) *19th:* 2216
Leo Tolstoy (Sept. 9, 1828-Nov. 20, 1910) *19th:* 2283
Joseph Wilson Swan (Oct. 31, 1828-May 27, 1914) *19th:* 2209
Carl Schurz (Mar. 2, 1829-May 14, 1906) *19th:* 2035
Karl Siemens (Mar. 3, 1829-Mar. 21, 1906) *19th:* 2105
William Booth (Apr. 10, 1829-Aug. 20, 1912) *19th:* 274
Geronimo (June, 1829-Feb. 17, 1909) *19th:* 904
Marie Elizabeth Zakrzewska (Sept. 6, 1829-May 12, 1902) *19th:* 2481
Ferdinand Vandeveer Hayden (Sept. 7, 1829-Dec. 22, 1887) *19th:* 1058
Tu Duc (Sept. 22, 1829-July 9, 1883) *19th:* 2310
Chester A. Arthur (Oct. 5, 1829-Nov. 18, 1886) *19th:* 79
Frederika Mandelbaum (c. 1830-Feb. 26, 1894) *Notor:* 688
Samory Touré (c. 1830-June 2, 1900) *19th:* 1981
Albert Bierstadt (Jan. 7, 1830-Feb. 18, 1902) *19th:* 232
James G. Blaine (Jan. 31, 1830-Jan. 27, 1893) *19th:* 251
Third Marquis of Salisbury (Feb. 3, 1830-Aug. 22, 1903) *19th:* 1977
Mother Jones (May 1, 1830-Nov. 30, 1930) *20th:* 2039
Camille Pissarro (July 10, 1830-Nov. 13, 1903) *19th:* 1799
Francis Joseph I (Aug. 18, 1830-Nov. 21, 1916) *19th:* 818
Porfirio Díaz (Sept. 15, 1830-July 2, 1915) *19th:* 652, *Notor:* 278
Isabella II (Oct. 10, 1830-Apr. 10, 1904) *19th:* 1183
Helen Hunt Jackson (Oct. 15, 1830-Aug. 12, 1885) *19th:* 1193
Belva A. Lockwood (Oct. 24, 1830-May 19, 1917) *19th:* 1409
Christina Rossetti (Dec. 5, 1830-Dec. 29, 1894) *19th:* 1940
Emily Dickinson (Dec. 10, 1830-May 15, 1886) *19th:* 658

1831 - 1840

Sitting Bull (Mar., 1831-Dec. 15, 1890) *19th:* 2108
Dorothea Beale (Mar. 21, 1831-Nov. 9, 1906) *19th:* 159
James Clerk Maxwell (June 13, 1831-Nov. 5, 1879) *19th:* 1528
Richard Dedekind (Oct. 6, 1831-Feb. 12, 1916) *19th:* 629
Frederic Harrison (Oct. 18, 1831-Jan. 14, 1923) *19th:* 1044
Anna Leonowens (Nov. 6, 1831-Jan. 19, 1915) *19th:* 1346
James A. Garfield (Nov. 19, 1831-Sept. 19, 1881) *19th:* 867
Joaquín Murieta (c. 1832-July 25, 1853) *Notor:* 767
Édouard Manet (Jan. 23, 1832-Apr. 30, 1883) *19th:* 1479
Lewis Carroll (Jan. 27, 1832-Jan. 14, 1898) *19th:* 423
Charles Peace (May 14, 1832-Feb. 25, 1879) *Notor:* 815
Nikolaus August Otto (June 10, 1832-Jan. 26, 1891) *19th:* 1714
Maximilian (July 6, 1832-June 19, 1867) *19th:* 1525
Wilhelm Wundt (Aug. 16, 1832-Aug. 31, 1920) *20th:* 4407
Louisa May Alcott (Nov. 29, 1832-Mar. 6, 1888) *19th:* 41
Gustave Eiffel (Dec. 15, 1832-Dec. 27, 1923) *19th:* 734
Charles George Gordon (Jan. 28, 1833-Jan. 26, 1885) *19th:* 949
Johannes Brahms (May 7, 1833-Apr. 3, 1897) *19th:* 296
Pauline Cushman (June 10, 1833-Dec. 2, 1893) *Notor:* 246
Benjamin Harrison (Aug. 20, 1833-Mar. 13, 1901) *19th:* 1040
Alfred Nobel (Oct. 21, 1833-Dec. 10, 1896) *19th:* 1689
Aleksandr Borodin (Nov. 12, 1833-Feb. 27, 1887) *19th:* 280
Edwin Booth (Nov. 13, 1833-June 7, 1893) *19th:* 271
Lord Acton (Jan. 10, 1834-June 19, 1902) *19th:* 12

August Weismann (Jan. 17, 1834-Nov. 5, 1914) *19th:* 2406
Dmitry Ivanovich Mendeleyev (Feb. 8, 1834-Feb. 2, 1907) *19th:* 1544
Ernst Haeckel (Feb. 16, 1834-Aug. 9, 1919) *19th:* 1002
Gottlieb Daimler (Mar. 17, 1834-Mar. 6, 1900) *19th:* 592
Charles William Eliot (Mar. 20, 1834-Aug. 22, 1926) *19th:* 737
Arthur Orton (Mar. 20, 1834-Apr. 2, 1898) *Notor:* 806
William Morris (Mar. 24, 1834-Oct. 3, 1896) *19th:* 1606
John Wesley Powell (Mar. 24, 1834-Sept. 23, 1902) *19th:* 1827
Jim Fisk (Apr. 1, 1834-Jan. 7, 1872) *Notor:* 357
James McNeill Whistler (July 10, 1834-July 17, 1903) *19th:* 2420
Edgar Degas (July 19, 1834-Sept. 27, 1917) *19th:* 632
James Gibbons (July 23, 1834-Mar. 24, 1921) *19th:* 910
Marshall Field (Aug. 18, 1834-Jan. 16, 1906) *19th:* 773
Samuel Pierpont Langley (Aug. 22, 1834-Feb. 27, 1906) *19th:* 1309
Olympia Brown (Jan. 5, 1835-Oct. 23, 1926) *19th:* 323
Sir Julius Vogel (Feb. 24, 1835-Mar. 12, 1899) *19th:* 2371
Simon Newcomb (Mar. 12, 1835-July 11, 1909) *19th:* 1660
Leopold II (Apr. 9, 1835-Dec. 17, 1909) *19th:* 1349, *Notor:* 632
Pius X (June 2, 1835-Aug. 20, 1914) *20th:* 3272
Adah Isaacs Menken (June 15, 1835-Aug. 10, 1868) *19th:* 1555
Mary Elizabeth Braddon (Oct. 4, 1835-Feb. 4, 1915) *19th:* 284
Camille Saint-Saëns (Oct. 9, 1835-Dec. 16, 1921) *20th:* 3600
Theodore Thomas (Oct. 11, 1835-Jan. 4, 1905) *19th:* 2267
Andrew Carnegie (Nov. 25, 1835-Aug. 11, 1919) *19th:* 419
Cixi (Nov. 29, 1835-Nov. 15, 1908) *19th:* 496
Mark Twain (Nov. 30, 1835-Apr. 21, 1910) *19th:* 2329
Samuel Butler (Dec. 4, 1835-June 18, 1902) *19th:* 374
Lobengula (c. 1836-Jan., 1894) *19th:* 1406
Léo Delibes (Feb. 21, 1836-Jan. 16, 1891) *19th:* 639
Winslow Homer (Feb. 24, 1836-Sept. 29, 1910) *19th:* 1122
Thomas Hill Green (Apr. 7, 1836-Mar. 26, 1882) *19th:* 971
Sir Joseph Norman Lockyer (May 17, 1836-Aug. 16, 1920) *19th:* 1412
Jay Gould (May 27, 1836-Dec. 2, 1892) *Notor:* 433
Joseph Chamberlain (July 8, 1836-July 2, 1914) *19th:* 460
W. S. Gilbert (Nov. 18, 1836-May 29, 1911) *19th:* 916
Tippu Tib (c. 1837-June 14, 1905) *19th:* 2277
Dwight L. Moody (Feb. 5, 1837-Dec. 22, 1899) *19th:* 1596
Grover Cleveland (Mar. 18, 1837-June 24, 1908) *19th:* 507
J. P. Morgan (Apr. 17, 1837-Mar. 31, 1913) *19th:* 1599
Friedrich von Holstein (Apr. 24, 1837-May 8, 1909) *19th:* 1119
Wild Bill Hickok (May 27, 1837-Aug. 2, 1876) *19th:* 1091
William Clarke Quantrill (July 31, 1837-June 6, 1865) *Notor:* 869
Charlotte Forten (Aug. 17, 1837-July 22, 1914) *19th:* 796
Zhang Zhidong (Sept. 2, 1837-Oct. 4, 1909) *19th:* 2486
Marcus A. Hanna (Sept. 24, 1837-Feb. 15, 1904) *19th:* 1018
Abby Sage Richardson (Oct. 14, 1837-Dec. 5, 1900) *19th:* 1902
George Dewey (Dec. 26, 1837-Jan. 16, 1917) *19th:* 645
Jamāl al-Dīn al-Afghānī (1838-Mar. 9, 1897) *19th:* 1203
André Rebouças (Jan. 13, 1838-May 9, 1898) *19th:* 1869
Henry Adams (Feb. 16, 1838-Mar. 27, 1918) *19th:* 16
Léon Gambetta (Apr. 2, 1838-Dec. 31, 1882) *19th:* 864
John Muir (Apr. 21, 1838-Dec. 24, 1914) *19th:* 1623
John Wilkes Booth (May 10, 1838-Apr. 26, 1865) *Notor:* 123
Henry Sidgwick (May 31, 1838-Aug. 28, 1900) *19th:* 2102
Ferdinand von Zeppelin (July 8, 1838-Mar. 8, 1917) *20th:* 4452
Liliuokalani (Sept. 2, 1838-Nov. 11, 1917) *19th:* 1373
James Jerome Hill (Sept. 16, 1838-May 29, 1916) *19th:* 1100
Victoria Woodhull (Sept. 23, 1838-June 10, 1927) *19th:* 2459
Henry Hobson Richardson (Sept. 29, 1838-Apr. 27, 1886) *19th:* 1905

John Hay (Oct. 8, 1838-July 1, 1905) *19th:* 1054
Georges Bizet (Oct. 25, 1838-June 3, 1875) *19th:* 241
Octavia Hill (Dec. 3, 1838-Aug. 13, 1912) *19th:* 1103
Paul Cézanne (Jan. 19, 1839-Oct. 22, 1906) *19th:* 453
Josiah Willard Gibbs (Feb. 11, 1839-Apr. 28, 1903) *19th:* 913
Modest Mussorgsky (Mar. 21, 1839-Mar. 28, 1881) *19th:* 1626
Joaquim Maria Machado de Assis (June 21, 1839-Sept. 29, 1908) *19th:* 1449
John D. Rockefeller (July 8, 1839-May 23, 1937) *19th:* 1921
Walter Pater (Aug. 4, 1839-July 30, 1894) *19th:* 1755
Henry George (Sept. 2, 1839-Oct. 29, 1897) *19th:* 894
Charles Sanders Peirce (Sept. 10, 1839-Apr. 19, 1914) *19th:* 1772
Frances Willard (Sept. 28, 1839-Feb. 18, 1898) *19th:* 2442
George A. Custer (Dec. 5, 1839-June 25, 1876) *19th:* 582, *Notor:* 248
Curly Bill Brocius (c. 1840-probably Mar. 24, 1882) *Notor:* 143
Chief Joseph (c. 1840-Sept. 21, 1904) *19th:* 1238
Émile Zola (Apr. 2, 1840-Sept. 28, 1902) *19th:* 2489
Isabella Stewart Gardner (Apr. 14, 1840-July 17, 1924) *20th:* 1406
Odilon Redon (Apr. 20, 1840-July 6, 1916) *19th:* 1875
Peter Ilich Tchaikovsky (May 7, 1840-Nov. 6, 1893) *19th:* 2233
Thomas Hardy (June 2, 1840-Jan. 11, 1928) *19th:* 1028
Thomas Nast (Sept. 27, 1840-Dec. 7, 1902) *19th:* 1649
Auguste Rodin (Nov. 12, 1840-Nov. 17, 1917) *19th:* 1925
Claude Monet (Nov. 14, 1840-Dec. 5, 1926) *20th:* 2790

1841 - 1850

Henry Morton Stanley (Jan. 28, 1841-May 10, 1904) *19th:* 2136
Pierre-Auguste Renoir (Feb. 25, 1841-Dec. 3, 1919) *19th:* 1888
John Philip Holland (Feb. 29, 1841-Aug. 12, 1914) *19th:* 1113
Oliver Wendell Holmes, Jr. (Mar. 8, 1841-Mar. 6, 1935) *20th:* 1856
Gustave Le Bon (May 7, 1841-Dec. 13, 1931) *20th:* 2320
Lester Frank Ward (June 18, 1841-Apr. 18, 1913) *19th:* 2384
Antonín Dvořák (Sept. 8, 1841-May 1, 1904) *19th:* 711
Charles Julius Guiteau (Sept. 8, 1841-June 30, 1882) *Notor:* 439
Georges Clemenceau (Sept. 28, 1841-Nov. 24, 1929) *20th:* 778
Itō Hirobumi (Oct. 14, 1841-Oct. 26, 1909) *19th:* 1185
Edward VII (Nov. 9, 1841-May 6, 1910) *20th:* 1104
Sir Wilfrid Laurier (Nov. 20, 1841-Feb. 17, 1919) *20th:* 2281
James Donnelly, Jr. (Dec. 8, 1841-May 15, 1897) *Notor:* 294
Crazy Horse (1842?-Sept. 5, 1877) *19th:* 566
William James (Jan. 11, 1842-Aug. 26, 1910) *19th:* 1213
Josef Breuer (Jan. 15, 1842-June 20, 1925) *20th:* 514
Mahadev Govind Ranade (Jan. 18, 1842-Jan. 16, 1901) *19th:* 1855
Arthur Sullivan (May 13, 1842-Nov. 22, 1900) *19th:* 916
Ambrose Bierce (June 24, 1842-Jan., 1914?) *19th:* 228
Mary Putnam Jacobi (Aug. 31, 1842-June 10, 1906) *19th:* 1200
Abdülhamid II (Sept. 21, 1842-Feb. 10, 1918) *19th:* 7
Ellen Swallow Richards (Dec. 3, 1842-Mar. 30, 1911) *19th:* 1899
Molly Maguires (formed 1843) *Notor:* 745
Frank James (Jan. 10, 1843-Feb. 18, 1915) *19th:* 1211
William McKinley (Jan. 29, 1843-Sept. 14, 1901) *19th:* 1460
Montgomery Ward (Feb. 17, 1843-Dec. 7, 1913) *19th:* 2386
Henry James (Apr. 15, 1843-Feb. 28, 1916) *19th:* 1206
Bertha von Suttner (June 9, 1843-June 21, 1914) *19th:* 2205
Edvard Grieg (June 15, 1843-Sept. 4, 1907) *19th:* 984
Robert Koch (Dec. 11, 1843-May 27, 1910) *19th:* 1291
Adam Worth (1844-Jan. 8, 1902) *Notor:* 1107
Cole Younger (Jan. 15, 1844-Mar. 21, 1916) *Notor:* 1118
Anthony Comstock (Mar. 7, 1844-Sept. 21, 1915) *Notor:* 229

Anatole France (Apr. 16, 1844-Oct. 12, 1924) *19th:* 815
Lewis Powell (Apr. 22, 1844-July 7, 1865) *Notor:* 858
Belle Boyd (May 4, 1844-June 11, 1900) *Notor:* 135
Henri Rousseau (May 21, 1844-Sept. 2, 1910) *19th:* 1951
Mary Cassatt (May 22, 1844-June 14, 1926) *19th:* 433
Thomas Eakins (July 25, 1844-June 25, 1916) *19th:* 717
The Mahdi (Aug. 12, 1844-June 22, 1885) *19th:* 1473
Menelik II (Aug. 17, 1844-Dec. 12, 1913) *19th:* 1552
Friedrich Nietzsche (Oct. 15, 1844-Aug. 25, 1900) *19th:* 1680
Sarah Bernhardt (Oct. 22, 1844-Mar. 26, 1923) *19th:* 208
Louis Riel (Oct. 22, 1844-Nov. 16, 1885) *19th:* 1908
Carl Benz (Nov. 25, 1844-Apr. 4, 1929) *19th:* 197
William Donnelly (1845-Mar. 7, 1897) *Notor:* 294
Lord Lansdowne (Jan. 14, 1845-June 3, 1927) *20th:* 2266
Elihu Root (Feb. 15, 1845-Feb. 7, 1937) *20th:* 3519
Wilhelm Conrad Röntgen (Mar. 27, 1845-Feb. 10, 1923) *19th:* 1931
Richard John Seddon (June 22, 1845-June 10, 1906) *19th:* 2058
Ludwig II (Aug. 24, 1845-June 13, 1886) *Notor:* 662
Rudolf Christoph Eucken (Jan. 5, 1846-Sept. 14, 1926) *20th:* 1185
F. H. Bradley (Jan. 30, 1846-Sept. 18, 1924) *19th:* 288
William Cody (Feb. 26, 1846-Jan. 10, 1917) *19th:* 524
Sir George Goldie (May 20, 1846-Aug. 20, 1925) *19th:* 940
Charles Stewart Parnell (June 27, 1846-Oct. 6, 1891) *19th:* 1747
Elisabeth Förster-Nietzsche (July 10, 1846-Nov. 8, 1935) *Notor:* 367
Daniel Hudson Burnham (Sept. 4, 1846-June 1, 1912) *19th:* 360
George Westinghouse (Oct. 6, 1846-Mar. 12, 1914) *19th:* 2416
Carry Nation (Nov. 25, 1846-June 9, 1911) *19th:* 1652
John Donnelly (1847/1848-Feb. 4, 1880) *Notor:* 294
Thomas Alva Edison (Feb. 11, 1847-Oct. 18, 1931) *19th:* 731
Anna Howard Shaw (Feb. 14, 1847-July 2, 1919) *19th:* 2084
Ellen Terry (Feb. 27, 1847-July 21, 1928) *19th:* 2248
Alexander Graham Bell (Mar. 3, 1847-Aug. 2, 1922) *19th:* 182
Joseph Pulitzer (Apr. 10, 1847-Oct. 29, 1911) *19th:* 1841
Dame Millicent Garrett Fawcett (June 11, 1847-Aug. 5, 1929) *19th:* 766
Benjamin Tillman (Aug. 11, 1847-July 3, 1918) *Notor:* 1030
Jesse James (Sept. 5, 1847-Apr. 3, 1882) *19th:* 1211, *Notor:* 523
Annie Besant (Oct. 1, 1847-Sept. 20, 1933) *19th:* 211
Paul von Hindenburg (Oct. 2, 1847-Aug. 2, 1934) *20th:* 1814
Georges Sorel (Nov. 2, 1847-Aug. 30, 1922) *20th:* 3792
Ferdinand Walsin Esterhazy (Dec. 16, 1847-May 21, 1923) *Notor:* 334
John Peter Altgeld (Dec. 30, 1847-Mar. 12, 1902) *19th:* 57
Belle Starr (Feb. 5, 1848-Feb. 3, 1889) *Notor:* 994
Augustus Saint-Gaudens (Mar. 1, 1848-Aug. 3, 1907) *19th:* 1972
Wyatt Earp (Mar. 19, 1848-Jan. 13, 1929) *19th:* 720, *Notor:* 315
Helene Lange (Apr. 9, 1848-May 13, 1930) *19th:* 1307
Hubertine Auclert (Apr. 10, 1848-Apr. 4, 1914) *19th:* 89
Paul Gauguin (June 7, 1848-May 8, 1903) *19th:* 879
William Gilbert Grace (July 18, 1848-Oct. 23, 1915) *19th:* 955
Arthur Balfour (July 25, 1848-Mar. 19, 1930) *20th:* 208
Margaret Lindsay Huggins (Aug. 14, 1848-May 24, 1915) *19th:* 1144
Thomas Power O'Connor (Oct. 5, 1848-Nov. 18, 1929) *20th:* 3024
Gottlob Frege (Nov. 8, 1848-July 26, 1925) *19th:* 828
Sir Surendranath Banerjea (Nov. 10, 1848-Aug. 6, 1925) *20th:* 221
Joel Chandler Harris (Dec. 9, 1848-July 3, 1908) *19th:* 1036
Giovanni Battista Pirelli (Dec. 27, 1848-Oct. 20, 1932) *20th:* 3266
Muḥammad ʿAbduh (c. 1849-July 11, 1905) *19th:* 4
Sir Edmund Barton (Jan. 18, 1849-Jan. 7, 1920) *19th:* 149
August Strindberg (Jan. 22, 1849-May 14, 1912) *20th:* 3898
Luther Burbank (Mar. 7, 1849-Apr. 11, 1926) *19th:* 350
Alfred von Tirpitz (Mar. 19, 1849-Mar. 6, 1930) *20th:* 4030
Patrick Donnelly (Apr. 15, 1849-May 18, 1914) *Notor:* 294

Hank Vaughan (Apr. 27, 1849-June 15, 1893) *Notor:* 1060
Bernhard von Bülow (May 3, 1849-Oct. 28, 1929) *20th:* 569
Lou Blonger (May 13, 1849-Apr. 20, 1924) *Notor:* 107
Sir William Osler (July 12, 1849-Dec. 29, 1919) *19th:* 1711
Emma Lazarus (July 22, 1849-Nov. 19, 1887) *19th:* 1331
Sarah Orne Jewett (Sept. 3, 1849-June 24, 1909) *19th:* 1226
Ivan Petrovich Pavlov (Sept. 26, 1849-Feb. 27, 1936) *20th:* 3162
George Washington Williams (Oct. 16, 1849-Aug. 2, 1891) *19th:* 2449
Frances Hodgson Burnett (Nov. 24, 1849-Oct. 29, 1924) *19th:* 357
Eduard Bernstein (Jan. 6, 1850-Dec. 18, 1932) *20th:* 334
Sofya Kovalevskaya (Jan. 15, 1850-Feb. 10, 1891) *19th:* 1295
Samuel Gompers (Jan. 27, 1850-Dec. 13, 1924) *19th:* 943
Tomáš Masaryk (Mar. 7, 1850-Sept. 14, 1937) *20th:* 2639
Johnny Ringo (May 3, 1850-July 12 or 13, 1882) *Notor:* 898
Henry Cabot Lodge (May 12, 1850-Nov. 9, 1924) *20th:* 2417
Lord Kitchener (June 24, 1850-June 5, 1916) *20th:* 2173
Frances Xavier Cabrini (July 15, 1850-Dec. 22, 1917) *19th:* 383
Guy de Maupassant (Aug. 5, 1850-July 6, 1893) *19th:* 1515
Michael Donnelly (Sept., 1850-Dec. 9, 1879) *Notor:* 294
Robert Louis Stevenson (Nov. 13, 1850-Dec. 3, 1894) *19th:* 2173

1851 - 1860

Kate Chopin (Feb. 8, 1851-Aug. 22, 1904) *19th:* 490
Adolf von Harnack (May 7, 1851-June 10, 1930) *20th:* 1681
Sir Arthur Evans (July 8, 1851-July 11, 1941) *19th:* 753
Sam Bass (July 21, 1851-July 21, 1878) *Notor:* 68
Felix Adler (Aug. 13, 1851-Apr. 24, 1933) *19th:* 26
Doc Holliday (Aug. 14, 1851-Nov. 8, 1887) *Notor:* 485
Walter Reed (Sept. 13, 1851-Nov. 22, 1902) *19th:* 1877
Bill Longley (Oct. 6, 1851-Oct. 11, 1878) *Notor:* 653
Melvil Dewey (Dec. 10, 1851-Dec. 26, 1931) *19th:* 649
Joseph-Jacques-Césaire Joffre (Jan. 12, 1852-Jan. 3, 1931) *20th:* 2009
Calamity Jane (May 1, 1852?-Aug. 1, 1903) *19th:* 386
Antonio Gaudí (June 25, 1852-June 10, 1926) *20th:* 1423
H. H. Asquith (Sept. 12, 1852-Feb. 15, 1928) *20th:* 149
Mutsuhito (Nov. 3, 1852-July 30, 1912) *19th:* 1631
Clorinda Matto de Turner (Nov. 11, 1852-Oct. 25, 1909) *19th:* 1512
Antoine-Henri Becquerel (Dec. 15, 1852-Aug. 25, 1908) *19th:* 165
Albert A. Michelson (Dec. 19, 1852-May 9, 1931) *19th:* 1567
José Martí (Jan. 28, 1853-May 19, 1895) *19th:* 1503
Vincent van Gogh (Mar. 30, 1853-July 29, 1890) *19th:* 932
John Wesley Hardin (May 26, 1853-Aug. 19, 1895) *Notor:* 447
Cecil Rhodes (July 5, 1853-Mar. 26, 1902) *19th:* 1891
Hendrik Antoon Lorentz (July 18, 1853-Feb. 4, 1928) *20th:* 2431
Wilhelm Ostwald (Sept. 2, 1853-Apr. 4, 1932) *20th:* 3088
Heike Kamerlingh Onnes (Sept. 21, 1853-Feb. 21, 1926) *20th:* 2072
Lillie Langtry (Oct. 13, 1853-Feb. 12, 1929) *19th:* 1312
Robert Donnelly (Nov. 9, 1853-June 14, 1911) *Notor:* 294
Sir James George Frazer (Jan. 1, 1854-May 7, 1941) *20th:* 1319
Eusapia Palladino (Jan. 21, 1854-May 16, 1918) *Notor:* 810
Paul Ehrlich (Mar. 14, 1854-Aug. 20, 1915) *20th:* 1115
Emil von Behring (Mar. 15, 1854-Mar. 31, 1917) *19th:* 179
Henri-Marie La Fontaine (Apr. 22, 1854-May 14, 1943) *20th:* 2231

Henri Poincaré (Apr. 29, 1854-July 17, 1912) *19th:* 1816
Ottmar Mergenthaler (May 11, 1854-Oct. 28, 1899) *19th:* 1558
Edward Wyllis Scripps (June 18, 1854-Mar. 12, 1926) *19th:* 2055
Sir Robert Laird Borden (June 26, 1854-June 10, 1937) *20th:* 423
Leoš Janáček (July 3, 1854-Aug. 12, 1928) *20th:* 1989
George Eastman (July 12, 1854-Mar. 14, 1932) *20th:* 1078
Thomas Donnelly (Aug. 30, 1854-Feb. 4, 1880) *Notor:* 294
Engelbert Humperdinck (Sept. 1, 1854-Sept. 27, 1921) *19th:* 1154
William Crawford Gorgas (Oct. 3, 1854-July 4, 1920) *20th:* 1541
Oscar Wilde (Oct. 16, 1854-Nov. 30, 1900) *19th:* 2432
Arthur Rimbaud (Oct. 20, 1854-Nov. 10, 1891) *19th:* 1912
John Philip Sousa (Nov. 6, 1854-Mar. 6, 1932) *20th:* 3798
Ned Kelly (Dec., 1854-Nov. 11, 1880) *Notor:* 562
Alice Freeman Palmer (Feb. 21, 1855-Dec. 6, 1902) *19th:* 1727
Andrew Mellon (Mar. 24, 1855-Aug. 26, 1937) *20th:* 2683
Olive Schreiner (Mar. 24, 1855-Dec. 10, 1920) *19th:* 2023
Robert M. La Follette (June 14, 1855-June 18, 1925) *20th:* 2227
Ferdinand Julius Tönnies (July 26, 1855-Apr. 9, 1936) *20th:* 4044
Houston Stewart Chamberlain (Sept. 9, 1855-Jan. 9, 1927) *Notor:* 196
Josiah Royce (Nov. 20, 1855-Sept. 14, 1916) *20th:* 3550
John Singer Sargent (Jan. 12, 1856-Apr. 15, 1925) *19th:* 1996
Frederick Winslow Taylor (Mar. 20, 1856-Mar. 21, 1915) *20th:* 3955
William Ferguson Massey (Mar. 26, 1856-May 10, 1925) *20th:* 2643
Booker T. Washington (Apr. 5, 1856-Nov. 14, 1915) *19th:* 2390
Philippe Pétain (Apr. 24, 1856-July 23, 1951) *20th:* 3222, *Notor:* 825
Sigmund Freud (May 6, 1856-Sept. 23, 1939) *20th:* 1323
Robert Edwin Peary (May 6, 1856-Feb. 20, 1920) *20th:* 3177
L. Frank Baum (May 15, 1856-May 6, 1919) *19th:* 155
H. Rider Haggard (June 22, 1856-May 14, 1925) *19th:* 1006
Daniel Guggenheim (July 9, 1856-Sept. 28, 1930) *20th:* 1613
Nikola Tesla (July 9, 1856-Jan. 7, 1943) *19th:* 2252
Bal Gangadhar Tilak (July 23, 1856-Aug. 1, 1920) *20th:* 4023
Émile Picard (July 24, 1856-Dec. 11, 1941) *20th:* 3234
William Rainey Harper (July 26, 1856-Jan. 10, 1906) *19th:* 1031
George Bernard Shaw (July 26, 1856-Nov. 2, 1950) *20th:* 3716
Alfred Deakin (Aug. 3, 1856-Oct. 7, 1919) *19th:* 623
Keir Hardie (Aug. 15, 1856-Sept. 26, 1915) *19th:* 1025
Louis Sullivan (Sept. 3, 1856-Apr. 14, 1924) *19th:* 2198
Jenny Donnelly (Oct., 1856-Sept. 3, 1917) *Notor:* 294
Louis D. Brandeis (Nov. 13, 1856-Oct. 5, 1941) *20th:* 482
Sir Joseph John Thomson (Dec. 18, 1856-Aug. 30, 1940) *20th:* 4007
James Buchanan Duke (Dec. 23, 1856-Oct. 10, 1925) *19th:* 692
Woodrow Wilson (Dec. 28, 1856-Feb. 3, 1924) *20th:* 4364
Sir Robert Stephenson Smyth Baden-Powell (Feb. 22, 1857-Jan. 8, 1941) *19th:* 110
Clarence Darrow (Apr. 18, 1857-Mar. 13, 1938) *20th:* 913
Eugen Bleuler (Apr. 30, 1857-July 15, 1939) *20th:* 391
Sir Ronald Ross (May 13, 1857-Sept. 16, 1932) *20th:* 3532
Williamina Paton Stevens Fleming (May 15, 1857-May 21, 1911) *19th:* 788
Pius XI (May 31, 1857-Feb. 10, 1939) *20th:* 3275
Sir Edward Elgar (June 2, 1857-Feb. 23, 1934) *20th:* 1132
Saʿd Zaghlūl (July, 1857-Aug. 23, 1927) *20th:* 4439
Clara Zetkin (July 5, 1857-June 20, 1933) *20th:* 4455
William Howard Taft (Sept. 15, 1857-Mar. 8, 1930) *20th:* 3929
Konstantin Tsiolkovsky (Sept. 17, 1857-Sept. 19, 1935) *20th:* 4095
Cassie L. Chadwick (Oct. 10, 1857-Oct. 10, 1907) *Notor:* 193
Ida Tarbell (Nov. 5, 1857-Jan. 6, 1944) *20th:* 3947
Ferdinand de Saussure (Nov. 26, 1857-Feb. 22, 1913) *20th:* 3649
Joseph Conrad (Dec. 3, 1857-Aug. 3, 1924) *20th:* 824

Bill Doolin (1858-Aug. 24, 1896) *Notor:* 296
Lord Lugard (Jan. 22, 1858-Apr. 11, 1945) *20th:* 2465
Beatrice Webb (Jan. 22, 1858-Apr. 30, 1943) *20th:* 4253
Rudolf Diesel (Mar. 18, 1858-Sept. 29, 1913) *19th:* 663
Kang Youwei (Mar. 19, 1858-Mar. 31, 1927) *19th:* 1252
Gaetano Mosca (Apr. 1, 1858-Nov. 8, 1941) *20th:* 2838
Émile Durkheim (Apr. 15, 1858-Nov. 15, 1917) *20th:* 1065
Max Planck (Apr. 23, 1858-Oct. 4, 1947) *20th:* 3282
Charlotte Angas Scott (June 8, 1858-Nov. 10, 1931) *19th:* 2039
George Washington Goethals (June 29, 1858-Jan. 21, 1928) *20th:* 1517
Julia C. Lathrop (June 29, 1858-Apr. 15, 1932) *20th:* 2272
Franz Boas (July 9, 1858-Dec. 21, 1942) *20th:* 400
Emmeline Pankhurst (July 14, 1858-June 14, 1928) *20th:* 3102
Marion Talbot (July 31, 1858-Oct. 20, 1948) *20th:* 3937
Bonar Law (Sept. 16, 1858-Oct. 30, 1923) *20th:* 2292
Theodore Roosevelt (Oct. 27, 1858-Jan. 6, 1919) *20th:* 3515
Selma Lagerlöf (Nov. 20, 1858-Mar. 16, 1940) *20th:* 2234
Sir Robert Abbott Hadfield (Nov. 28, 1858-Sept. 30, 1940) *19th:* 1000
Giacomo Puccini (Dec. 22, 1858-Nov. 29, 1924) *20th:* 3346
Fanny Bullock Workman (Jan. 8, 1859-Jan. 22, 1925) *19th:* 2466
Carrie Chapman Catt (Jan. 9, 1859-Mar. 9, 1947) *20th:* 701
George Nathaniel Curzon (Jan. 11, 1859-Mar. 20, 1925) *20th:* 894
William II (Jan. 27, 1859-June 4, 1941) *20th:* 4346
Havelock Ellis (Feb. 2, 1859-July 8, 1939) *20th:* 1148
Svante August Arrhenius (Feb. 19, 1859-Oct. 2, 1927) *20th:* 138
Aleksandr Stepanovich Popov (Mar. 16, 1859-Jan. 13, 1906) *19th:* 1824
Edmund Husserl (Apr. 8, 1859-Apr. 27, 1938) *20th:* 1955
Sir Arthur Conan Doyle (May 22, 1859-July 7, 1930) *19th:* 688
Pierre Janet (May 30, 1859-Feb. 24, 1947) *20th:* 1993
Christian von Ehrenfels (June 20, 1859-Sept. 8, 1932) *20th:* 1110
Édouard Michelin (June 23, 1859-Aug. 25, 1940) *20th:* 2725
Sidney Webb (July 13, 1859-Oct. 13, 1947) *20th:* 4253
Theobald Smith (July 31, 1859-Dec. 10, 1934) *20th:* 3772
Knut Hamsun (Aug. 4, 1859-Feb. 19, 1952) *20th:* 1660
Jean Jaurès (Sept. 3, 1859-July 31, 1914) *19th:* 1220
Yuan Shikai (Sept. 16, 1859-June 6, 1916) *Notor:* 1122
Thomas Mott Osborne (Sept. 23, 1859-Oct. 20, 1926) *20th:* 3085
Henri Bergson (Oct. 18, 1859-Jan. 4, 1941) *20th:* 323
John Dewey (Oct. 20, 1859-June 1, 1952) *20th:* 982
William H. Bonney (Nov. 23, 1859-July 14, 1881) *Notor:* 118
Georges Seurat (Dec. 2, 1859-Mar. 29, 1891) *19th:* 2074
Apache Kid (c. 1860-after 1894) *Notor:* 27
John J. Pershing (Jan. 13, 1860-July 15, 1948) *20th:* 3219
Anton Chekhov (Jan. 29, 1860-July 15, 1904) *19th:* 478
William Jennings Bryan (Mar. 19, 1860-July 26, 1925) *20th:* 550
Horatio W. Bottomley (Mar. 23, 1860-May 26, 1933) *20th:* 445
Sir William Maddock Bayliss (May 2, 1860-Aug. 27, 1924) *20th:* 259
Theodor Herzl (May 2, 1860-July 3, 1904) *19th:* 1088
Willem Einthoven (May 21, 1860-Sept. 28, 1927) *20th:* 1122
Charlotte Perkins Gilman (July 3, 1860-Aug. 17, 1935) *20th:* 1484
Gustav Mahler (July 7, 1860-May 18, 1911) *20th:* 2558
Lizzie Borden (July 19, 1860-June 1, 1927) *19th:* 277, *Notor:* 125
Annie Oakley (Aug. 13, 1860-Nov. 3, 1926) *19th:* 1692
Raymond Poincaré (Aug. 20, 1860-Oct. 15, 1934) *20th:* 3292
Jane Addams (Sept. 6, 1860-May 21, 1935) *20th:* 22
Grandma Moses (Sept. 7, 1860-Dec. 13, 1961) *20th:* 2841
Juliette Gordon Low (Oct. 31, 1860-Jan. 18, 1927) *20th:* 2441

1861 - 1870

Charles-Édouard Guillaume (Feb. 15, 1861-June 13, 1938) *20th:* 1616
Sir Halford John Mackinder (Feb. 15, 1861-Mar. 6, 1947) *20th:* 2518
Lord Allenby (Apr. 23, 1861-May 14, 1936) *20th:* 65
Rabindranath Tagore (May 7, 1861-Aug. 7, 1941) *20th:* 3933
H. H. Holmes (May 16, 1861-May 7, 1896) *Notor:* 486
William J. Mayo (June 29, 1861-July 28, 1939) *20th:* 2665
George Washington Carver (July 12, 1861[?]-Jan. 5, 1943) *20th:* 678
Walter Rauschenbusch (Oct. 4, 1861-July 25, 1918) *20th:* 3382
Frederic Remington (Oct. 4, 1861-Dec. 26, 1909) *19th:* 1881
Fridtjof Nansen (Oct. 10, 1861-May 13, 1930) *20th:* 2907
James Naismith (Nov. 6, 1861-Nov. 28, 1939) *20th:* 2905
Frederick Jackson Turner (Nov. 14, 1861-Mar. 14, 1932) *20th:* 4115
Albert B. Fall (Nov. 26, 1861-Nov. 30, 1944) *Notor:* 342
Loie Fuller (Jan. 15, 1862-Jan. 1, 1928) *20th:* 1361
David Hilbert (Jan. 23, 1862-Feb. 14, 1943) *20th:* 1800
Edith Wharton (Jan. 24, 1862-Aug. 11, 1937) *20th:* 4300
Frederick Delius (Jan. 29, 1862-June 10, 1934) *20th:* 953
Vilhelm Bjerknes (Mar. 14, 1862-Apr. 9, 1951) *20th:* 374
Nicholas Murray Butler (Apr. 2, 1862-Dec. 7, 1947) *20th:* 597
Charles Evans Hughes (Apr. 11, 1862-Aug. 27, 1948) *20th:* 1920
Sir Edward Grey (Apr. 25, 1862-Sept. 7, 1933) *20th:* 1587
Gustav Klimt (July 14, 1862-Feb. 6, 1918) *20th:* 2180
Ida B. Wells-Barnett (July 16, 1862-Mar. 25, 1931) *20th:* 4290
Claude Debussy (Aug. 22, 1862-Mar. 25, 1918) *20th:* 936
O. Henry (Sept. 11, 1862-June 5, 1910) *19th:* 1081
Eugen Ehrlich (Sept. 14, 1862-May 2, 1922) *20th:* 1113
William Morris Hughes (Sept. 25, 1862-Oct. 28, 1952) *20th:* 1931
Louis Botha (Sept. 27, 1862-Aug. 27, 1919) *20th:* 439
Mary Kingsley (Oct. 13, 1862-June 3, 1900) *19th:* 1281
Auguste Lumière (Oct. 19, 1862-Apr. 10, 1954) *20th:* 2471
Billy Sunday (Nov. 19, 1862-Nov. 6, 1935) *20th:* 3916
Henri Pirenne (Dec. 23, 1862-Oct. 24, 1935) *20th:* 3269
Pierre de Coubertin (Jan. 1, 1863-Sept. 2, 1937) *20th:* 846
Vivekananda (Jan. 12, 1863-July 4, 1902) *19th:* 2368
David Lloyd George (Jan. 17, 1863-Mar. 26, 1945) *20th:* 2411
Konstantin Stanislavsky (Jan. 17, 1863-Aug. 7, 1938) *20th:* 3821
Sir Frederick Henry Royce (Mar. 27, 1863-Apr. 22, 1933) *20th:* 3496
William Randolph Hearst (Apr. 29, 1863-Aug. 14, 1951) *20th:* 1734
Max Wolf (June 21, 1863-Oct. 3, 1932) *20th:* 4382
Albert Calmette (July 12, 1863-Oct. 29, 1933) *20th:* 618
Henry Ford (July 30, 1863-Apr. 7, 1947) *20th:* 1279
Tom Ketchum (Oct. 31, 1863-Apr. 26, 1901) *Notor:* 566
Annie Jump Cannon (Dec. 11, 1863-Apr. 13, 1941) *20th:* 635
Edvard Munch (Dec. 12, 1863-Jan. 23, 1944) *20th:* 2870
George Santayana (Dec. 16, 1863-Sept. 26, 1952) *20th:* 3629
Francis Ferdinand (Dec. 18, 1863-June 28, 1914) *20th:* 1294
Alfred Stieglitz (Jan. 1, 1864-July 13, 1946) *20th:* 3864
Thomas Dixon, Jr. (Jan. 11, 1864-Apr. 3, 1946) *Notor:* 284
A. B. Paterson (Feb. 17, 1864-Feb. 2, 1941) *19th:* 1758
Daniel Mannix (Mar. 4, 1864-Nov. 6, 1963) *19th:* 1492
Max Weber (Apr. 21, 1864-June 14, 1920) *20th:* 4258
Richard Strauss (June 11, 1864-Sept. 8, 1949) *20th:* 3885
Walther Hermann Nernst (June 25, 1864-Nov. 18, 1941) *20th:* 2934

Eleuthérios Venizélos (Aug. 23, 1864-Mar. 18, 1936) *20th:* 4157
Leonard T. Hobhouse (Sept. 8, 1864-June 21, 1929) *20th:* 1841
Miguel de Unamuno y Jugo (Sept. 29, 1864-Dec. 31, 1936) *20th:* 4128
Louis Lumière (Oct. 5, 1864-June 6, 1948) *20th:* 2471
Reginald Dyer (Oct. 9, 1864-July 23, 1927) *Notor:* 311
Henri de Toulouse-Lautrec (Nov. 24, 1864-Sept. 9, 1901) *19th:* 2287
Ernst Troeltsch (Feb. 17, 1865-Feb. 1, 1923) *20th:* 4069
Erich Ludendorff (Apr. 9, 1865-Dec. 20, 1937) *20th:* 2462
Charles Proteus Steinmetz (Apr. 9, 1865-Oct. 26, 1923) *19th:* 2156
John R. Mott (May 25, 1865-Jan. 31, 1955) *20th:* 2849
George V (June 3, 1865-Jan. 20, 1936) *20th:* 1451
William Butler Yeats (June 13, 1865-Jan. 28, 1939) *20th:* 4428
Susan La Flesche Picotte (June 17, 1865-Sept. 18, 1915) *20th:* 3247
Carl Nielsen (July 9, 1865-Oct. 3, 1931) *20th:* 2965
Alfred Harmsworth (July 15, 1865-Aug. 14, 1922) *20th:* 1678
Charles H. Mayo (July 19, 1865-May 26, 1939) *20th:* 2665
Warren G. Harding (Nov. 2, 1865-Aug. 2, 1923) *20th:* 1674
Jean Sibelius (Dec. 8, 1865-Sept. 20, 1957) *20th:* 3736
Rudyard Kipling (Dec. 30, 1865-Jan. 18, 1936) *19th:* 1284
Nathan Söderblom (Jan. 15, 1866-July 12, 1931) *20th:* 3781
Benedetto Croce (Feb. 25, 1866-Nov. 20, 1952) *20th:* 869
Butch Cassidy (Apr. 13, 1866-possibly Nov. 7, 1908) *Notor:* 181
Anne Sullivan (Apr. 14, 1866-Oct. 20, 1936) *20th:* 3908
Ernest Henry Starling (Apr. 17, 1866-May 2, 1927) *20th:* 3830
Hans von Seeckt (Apr. 22, 1866-Dec. 27, 1936) *20th:* 3688
Erik Satie (May 17, 1866-July 1, 1925) *20th:* 3641
Beatrix Potter (July 28, 1866-Dec. 22, 1943) *20th:* 3314
H. G. Wells (Sept. 21, 1866-Aug. 13, 1946) *20th:* 4287
Thomas Hunt Morgan (Sept. 25, 1866-Dec. 4, 1945) *20th:* 2825
Ramsay MacDonald (Oct. 12, 1866-Nov. 9, 1937) *20th:* 2510
Sun Yat-sen (Nov. 12, 1866-Mar. 12, 1925) *20th:* 3913
Abraham Flexner (Nov. 13, 1866-Sept. 21, 1959) *20th:* 1256
Wassily Kandinsky (Dec. 4, 1866-Dec. 13, 1944) *20th:* 2074
Roger Fry (Dec. 14, 1866-Sept. 9, 1934) *20th:* 1351
Emily Greene Balch (Jan. 8, 1867-Jan. 9, 1961) *20th:* 197
Rubén Darío (Jan. 18, 1867-Feb. 6, 1916) *19th:* 601
Laura Ingalls Wilder (Feb. 7, 1867-Feb. 10, 1957) *20th:* 4336
Lillian D. Wald (Mar. 10, 1867-Sept. 1, 1940) *20th:* 4184
Harry Longabaugh (spring, 1867-possibly Nov. 7, 1908) *Notor:* 651
Arturo Toscanini (Mar. 25, 1867-Jan. 16, 1957) *20th:* 4050
Wilbur Wright (Apr. 16, 1867-May 30, 1912) *20th:* 4403
Carl Gustaf Mannerheim (June 4, 1867-Jan. 27, 1951) *20th:* 2598
Frank Lloyd Wright (June 8, 1867-Apr. 9, 1959) *20th:* 4400
Luigi Pirandello (June 28, 1867-Dec. 10, 1936) *20th:* 3260
Käthe Kollwitz (July 8, 1867-Apr. 22, 1945) *20th:* 2189
Molly Brown (July 18, 1867-Oct. 26, 1932) *20th:* 542
Stanley Baldwin (Aug. 3, 1867-Dec. 14, 1947) *20th:* 204
Henry L. Stimson (Sept. 21, 1867-Oct. 20, 1950) *20th:* 3869
Pierre Bonnard (Oct. 3, 1867-Jan. 23, 1947) *20th:* 421
Józef Piłsudski (Dec. 5, 1867-May 12, 1935) *20th:* 3250
Madam C. J. Walker (Dec. 23, 1867-May 25, 1919) *20th:* 4199
Linda Burfield Hazzard (1868-1938) *Notor:* 453
Salvatore Maranzano (1868-Sept. 10, 1931) *Notor:* 694
W. E. B. Du Bois (Feb. 23, 1868-Aug. 27, 1963) *20th:* 1046
Robert Andrews Millikan (Mar. 22, 1868-Dec. 19, 1953) *20th:* 2750
Dietrich Eckart (Mar. 23, 1868-Dec. 26, 1923) *Notor:* 319
Maxim Gorky (Mar. 28, 1868-June 18, 1936) *20th:* 1549

Harold Harmsworth (Apr. 26, 1868-Nov. 26, 1940) *20th:* 1678
Meri Te Tai Mangakahia (May 22, 1868-Oct. 10, 1920) *19th:* 1483
Karl Landsteiner (June 14, 1868-June 26, 1943) *20th:* 2250
George Ellery Hale (June 29, 1868-Feb. 21, 1938) *20th:* 1643
Henrietta Swan Leavitt (July 4, 1868-Dec. 12, 1921) *20th:* 2317
Hugo Eckener (Aug. 10, 1868-Aug. 14, 1954) *20th:* 1092
Frederick William Lanchester (Oct. 23, 1868-Mar. 8, 1946) *20th:* 2240
Édouard Vuillard (Nov. 11, 1868-June 21, 1940) *20th:* 4173
Scott Joplin (Nov. 24, 1868-Apr. 1, 1917) *19th:* 1235
Fritz Haber (Dec. 9, 1868-Jan. 29, 1934) *20th:* 1628
Bill Haywood (Feb. 4, 1869-May 18, 1928) *Notor:* 450
Neville Chamberlain (Mar. 18, 1869-Nov. 9, 1940) *20th:* 720
Harvey Williams Cushing (Apr. 8, 1869-Oct. 7, 1939) *20th:* 898
Henri Désiré Landru (Apr. 12, 1869-Feb. 25, 1922) *Notor:* 603
Bob Dalton (May 13, 1869-Oct. 5, 1892) *Notor:* 257
Emma Goldman (June 27, 1869-May 14, 1940) *20th:* 1519, *Notor:* 424
Tony Garnier (Aug. 13, 1869-Jan. 19, 1948) *20th:* 1414
Mary Mallon (Sept. 23, 1869-Nov. 11, 1938) *Notor:* 685
Mahatma Gandhi (Oct. 2, 1869-Jan. 30, 1948) *20th:* 1388
André Gide (Nov. 22, 1869-Feb. 19, 1951) *20th:* 1477
Eligiusz Niewiadomski (Dec. 1, 1869-Jan. 31, 1923) *Notor:* 792
Henri Matisse (Dec. 31, 1869-Nov. 3, 1954) *20th:* 2649
Grigori Yefimovich Rasputin (c. 1870-Dec. 30, 1916) *19th:* 1863, *Notor:* 885
Miguel Primo de Rivera (Jan. 8, 1870-Mar. 16, 1930) *Notor:* 860
Alfred Adler (Feb. 7, 1870-May 28, 1937) *20th:* 33
Albert Fish (May 19, 1870-Jan. 16, 1936) *Notor:* 355
Benjamin N. Cardozo (May 24, 1870-July 9, 1938) *20th:* 653
Jan Christian Smuts (May 24, 1870-Sept. 11, 1950) *20th:* 3775
Kitarō Nishida (June 17, 1870-June 7, 1945) *20th:* 2981
Maria Montessori (Aug. 31, 1870-May 6, 1952) *20th:* 2804
Georges Claude (Sept. 24, 1870-May 23, 1960) *20th:* 775
Maurice Denis (Nov. 25, 1870-Nov. 13, 1943) *20th:* 972

1871 - 1880

Ma Barker (c. 1871-Jan. 16, 1935) *Notor:* 61
Harry Kendall Thaw (Feb. 12, 1871-Feb. 22, 1947) *Notor:* 1027
Rosa Luxemburg (Mar. 5, 1871-Jan. 15, 1919) *20th:* 2482
Georges Rouault (May 27, 1871-Feb. 13, 1958) *20th:* 3541
Ioannis Metaxas (Apr. 12, 1871-Jan. 29, 1941) *Notor:* 724
Emmett Dalton (May 3, 1871-July 13, 1937) *Notor:* 258
Marcel Proust (July 10, 1871-Nov. 18, 1922) *20th:* 3342
Vernon Louis Parrington (Aug. 3, 1871-June 16, 1929) *20th:* 3124
Orville Wright (Aug. 19, 1871-Jan. 30, 1948) *20th:* 4403
Theodore Dreiser (Aug. 27, 1871-Dec. 28, 1945) *20th:* 1032
Ernest Rutherford (Aug. 30, 1871-Oct. 19, 1937) *20th:* 3576
František Kupka (Sept. 23, 1871-June 24, 1958) *20th:* 2211
Cordell Hull (Oct. 2, 1871-July 23, 1955) *20th:* 1934
Paul Valéry (Oct. 30, 1871-July 20, 1945) *20th:* 4136
Stephen Crane (Nov. 1, 1871-June 5, 1900) *19th:* 562
Learned Hand (Jan. 27, 1872-Aug. 18, 1961) *20th:* 1663
Piet Mondrian (Mar. 7, 1872-Feb. 1, 1944) *20th:* 2786
Sergei Diaghilev (Mar. 31, 1872-Aug. 19, 1929) *20th:* 985
Arthur Griffith (Mar. 31, 1872-Aug. 12, 1922) *20th:* 1591
Léon Blum (Apr. 9, 1872-Mar. 30, 1950) *20th:* 396

Bertrand Russell (May 18, 1872-Feb. 2, 1970) *20th:* 3562
Beatrix Jones Farrand (June 19, 1872-Feb. 27, 1959) *20th:* 1219
Paul Laurence Dunbar (June 27, 1872-Feb. 9, 1906) *19th:* 701
Thomas Joseph Pendergast (July 22, 1872-Jan. 26, 1945) *Notor:* 817
Louis Blériot (July 1, 1872-Aug. 2, 1936) *20th:* 388
Édouard Herriot (July 5, 1872-Mar. 26, 1957) *20th:* 1777
Roald Amundsen (July 16, 1872-June 18, 1928[?]) *20th:* 83
Sri Aurobindo (Aug. 15, 1872-Dec. 5, 1950) *20th:* 177
Aubrey Beardsley (Aug. 21, 1872-Mar. 16, 1898) *19th:* 162
Harlan Fiske Stone (Oct. 11, 1872-Apr. 22, 1946) *20th:* 3878
Ralph Vaughan Williams (Oct. 12, 1872-Aug. 26, 1958) *20th:* 4147
Sir Norman Angell (Dec. 26, 1872-Oct. 7, 1967) *20th:* 92
Leon Czolgosz (1873-Oct. 29, 1901) *Notor:* 252
Colette (Jan. 28, 1873-Aug. 3, 1954) *20th:* 804
Enrico Caruso (Feb. 25, 1873-Aug. 2, 1921) *20th:* 675
Margaret Bondfield (Mar. 17, 1873-June 16, 1953) *20th:* 414
Sergei Rachmaninoff (Apr. 1, 1873-Mar. 28, 1943) *20th:* 3361
Leo Baeck (May 23, 1873-Nov. 2, 1956) *20th:* 186
Leo Frobenius (June 29, 1873-Aug. 9, 1938) *20th:* 1341
Alberto Santos-Dumont (July 20, 1873-July 24, 1932) *20th:* 3632
Lee de Forest (Aug. 26, 1873-June 30, 1961) *20th:* 940
Sante Jeronimo Caserio (Sept. 8, 1873-Aug. 16, 1894) *Notor:* 180
Karl Schwarzschild (Oct. 9, 1873-May 11, 1916) *20th:* 3674
Francisco Madero (Oct. 30, 1873-Feb. 22, 1913) *20th:* 2544
G. E. Moore (Nov. 4, 1873-Oct. 24, 1958) *20th:* 2814
W. C. Handy (Nov. 16, 1873-Mar. 28, 1958) *20th:* 1667
Willa Cather (Dec. 7, 1873-Apr. 24, 1947) *20th:* 696
Henry Starr (Dec. 2, 1873-Feb. 22, 1921) *Notor:* 996
Alfred E. Smith (Dec. 30, 1873-Oct. 4, 1944) *20th:* 3762
Robert W. Service (Jan. 16, 1874-Sept. 11, 1958) *20th:* 3708
John D. Rockefeller, Jr. (Jan. 29, 1874-May 11, 1960) *20th:* 3476
Gertrude Stein (Feb. 3, 1874-July 27, 1946) *20th:* 3845
Amy Lowell (Feb. 9, 1874-May 12, 1925) *20th:* 2444
Vsevolod Yemilyevich Meyerhold (Feb. 9, 1874-Feb. 2, 1940) *20th:* 2722
Auguste Perret (Feb. 12, 1874-Feb. 25, 1954) *20th:* 3213
Thomas J. Watson, Sr. (Feb. 17, 1874-June 19, 1956) *20th:* 4246
Stephen Samuel Wise (Mar. 17, 1874-Apr. 19, 1949) *20th:* 4376
Harry Houdini (Mar. 24, 1874-Oct. 31, 1926) *20th:* 1889
Johannes Stark (Apr. 15, 1874-June 21, 1957) *20th:* 3827
Guglielmo Marconi (Apr. 25, 1874-July 20, 1937) *20th:* 2615
G. K. Chesterton (May 29, 1874-June 14, 1936) *20th:* 744
Ernst Cassirer (July 28, 1874-Apr. 13, 1945) *20th:* 688
Herbert Hoover (Aug. 10, 1874-Oct. 20, 1964) *20th:* 1862
Max Scheler (Aug. 22, 1874-May 19, 1928) *20th:* 3655
Edward L. Thorndike (Aug. 31, 1874-Aug. 9, 1949) *20th:* 4013
Arnold Schoenberg (Sept. 13, 1874-July 13, 1951) *20th:* 3664
Dorothy Reed Mendenhall (Sept. 22, 1874-July 31, 1964) *20th:* 2695
Charles Ives (Oct. 20, 1874-May 19, 1954) *20th:* 1974
August Krogh (Nov. 15, 1874-Sept. 13, 1949) *20th:* 2204
Charles A. Beard (Nov. 27, 1874-Sept. 1, 1948) *20th:* 262
Chaim Weizmann (Nov. 27, 1874-Nov. 9, 1952) *20th:* 4279
António Egas Moniz (Nov. 29, 1874-Dec. 13, 1955) *20th:* 1107
Sir Winston Churchill (Nov. 30, 1874-Jan. 24, 1965) *20th:* 768
William Lyon Mackenzie King (Dec. 17, 1874-July 22, 1950) *20th:* 2155
Joseph Weil (1875 or 1877-Feb. 26, 1976) *Notor:* 1094
Gertrude Vanderbilt Whitney (Jan. 9, 1875-Apr. 18, 1942) *20th:* 4315
Albert Schweitzer (Jan. 14, 1875-Sept. 4, 1965) *20th:* 3678

D. W. Griffith (Jan. 22, 1875-July 23, 1948) *20th:* 1593
Ludwig Prandtl (Feb. 4, 1875-Aug. 15, 1953) *20th:* 3327
Maurice Ravel (Mar. 7, 1875-Dec. 28, 1937) *20th:* 3386
Syngman Rhee (Mar. 26, 1875-July 19, 1965) *20th:* 3430
Giovanni Gentile (May 30, 1875-Apr. 15, 1944) *20th:* 1448
Thomas Mann (June 6, 1875-Aug. 12, 1955) *20th:* 2594
Mary Mcleod Bethune (July 10, 1875-May 18, 1955) *20th:* 345
Carl Jung (July 26, 1875-June 6, 1961) *20th:* 2062
Edgar Rice Burroughs (Sept. 1, 1875-Mar. 19, 1950) *20th:* 590
Matthias Erzberger (Sept. 20, 1875-Aug. 26, 1921) *20th:* 1180
Aleister Crowley (Oct. 12, 1875-Dec. 1, 1947) *Notor:* 242
Vallabhbhai Jhaverbhai Patel (Oct. 31, 1875-Dec. 15, 1950) *20th:* 3135
Rainer Maria Rilke (Dec. 4, 1875-Dec. 29, 1926) *20th:* 3454
Gerd von Rundstedt (Dec. 12, 1875-Feb. 24, 1953) *20th:* 3559
Jack London (Jan. 12, 1876-Nov. 22, 1916) *20th:* 2420
Otto Paul Hermann Diels (Jan. 23, 1876-Mar. 7, 1954) *20th:* 995
Ada Everleigh (Feb. 15, 1876-Jan. 5, 1960) *Notor:* 338
Constantin Brancusi (Feb. 19, 1876-Mar. 16, 1957) *20th:* 478
Pius XII (Mar. 2, 1876-Oct. 9, 1958) *20th:* 3278
Maksim Maksimovich Litvinov (July 17, 1876-Dec. 31, 1951) *20th:* 2404
Mata Hari (Aug. 7, 1876-Oct. 15, 1917) *Notor:* 710
John J. R. Macleod (Sept. 6, 1876-Mar. 16, 1935) *20th:* 2526
Jules Bonnot (Oct. 14, 1876-Apr. 28, 1912) *Notor:* 120
Manuel de Falla (Nov. 23, 1876-Nov. 14, 1946) *20th:* 1206
Nellie Tayloe Ross (Nov. 29, 1876-Dec. 19, 1977) *20th:* 3529
Mohammed Ali Jinnah (Dec. 25, 1876-Sept. 11, 1948) *20th:* 2002
Pablo Casals (Dec. 29, 1876-Oct. 22, 1973) *20th:* 681
Henri-Édouard-Prosper Breuil (Feb. 28, 1877-Aug. 14, 1961) *20th:* 517
Isadora Duncan (May 26, 1877-Sept. 14, 1927) *20th:* 1058
Hermann Hesse (July 2, 1877-Aug. 9, 1962) *20th:* 1787
Tom Thomson (Aug. 4, 1877-July 8, 1917) *20th:* 4010
Charles Stewart Rolls (Aug. 28, 1877-July 12, 1910) *20th:* 3496
Frederick Soddy (Sept. 2, 1877-Sept. 22, 1956) *20th:* 3778
Felix Dzerzhinsky (Sept. 11, 1877-July 20, 1926) *Notor:* 312
Plutarco Elías Calles (Sept. 25, 1877-Oct. 19, 1945) *20th:* 615
Theodore G. Bilbo (Oct. 18, 1877-Aug. 21, 1947) *Notor:* 99
Henry Norris Russell (Oct. 25, 1877-Feb. 18, 1957) *20th:* 3570
Augustus John (Jan. 4, 1878-Oct. 31, 1961) *20th:* 2014
Carl Sandburg (Jan. 6, 1878-July 22, 1967) *20th:* 3619
André-Gustave Citroën (Feb. 5, 1878-July 3, 1935) *20th:* 772
Martin Buber (Feb. 8, 1878-June 13, 1965) *20th:* 554
Reza Shah Pahlavi (Mar. 16, 1878-July 26, 1944) *20th:* 2779, *Notor:* 742
Gustav Stresemann (May 10, 1878-Oct. 3, 1929) *20th:* 3895
Pancho Villa (June 5, 1878-July 20, 1923) *20th:* 4160, *Notor:* 1069
Yakov Mikhailovich Yurovsky (June 19, 1878-Aug. 2, 1938) *Notor:* 1124
George Hoyt Whipple (Aug. 28, 1878-Feb. 1, 1976) *20th:* 4304
Upton Sinclair (Sept. 20, 1878-Nov. 25, 1968) *20th:* 3750
Joseph Stalin (Dec. 18, 1878-Mar. 5, 1953) *20th:* 3817, *Notor:* 990
Joe Masseria (1879-Apr. 15, 1931) *Notor:* 708
E. M. Forster (Jan. 1, 1879-June 7, 1970) *20th:* 1288
Ruth St. Denis (Jan. 20, 1879-July 21, 1968) *20th:* 3593
Sarojini Naidu (Feb. 13, 1879-Mar. 2, 1949) *20th:* 2900
Lord Beveridge (Mar. 5, 1879-Mar. 16, 1963) *20th:* 352
Otto Hahn (Mar. 8, 1879-July 28, 1968) *20th:* 1635
Albert Einstein (Mar. 14, 1879-Apr. 18, 1955) *20th:* 1118
Edward Steichen (Mar. 27, 1879-Mar. 25, 1973) *20th:* 3837
Bernhard Voldemar Schmidt (Mar. 30, 1879-Dec. 1, 1935) *20th:* 3659
Symon Petlyura (May 10, 1879-May 25, 1926) *Notor:* 832

Nancy Astor (May 19, 1879-May 2, 1964) *20th:* 158
Lord Beaverbrook (May 25, 1879-June 9, 1964) *20th:* 275
Knud Johan Victor Rasmussen (June 7, 1879-Dec. 21, 1933) *20th:* 3377
Gaston Bullock Means (July 11, 1879-Dec. 12, 1938) *Notor:* 713
Eugène Freyssinet (July 13, 1879-June 8, 1962) *20th:* 1326
Emiliano Zapata (Aug. 8, 1879-Apr. 10, 1919) *20th:* 4448, *Notor:* 1129
Margaret Sanger (Sept. 14, 1879-Sept. 6, 1966) *20th:* 3625
Joseph Aloysius Lyons (Sept. 15, 1879-Apr. 7, 1939) *20th:* 2489
Peyton Rous (Oct. 5, 1879-Feb. 16, 1970) *20th:* 3545
Chen Duxiu (Oct. 8, 1879-May 27, 1942) *20th:* 741
Max von Laue (Oct. 9, 1879-Apr. 23, 1960) *20th:* 2278
Franz von Papen (Oct. 29, 1879-May 2, 1969) *20th:* 3109
Will Rogers (Nov. 4, 1879-Aug. 15, 1935) *20th:* 3491
Leon Trotsky (Nov. 7, 1879-Aug. 21, 1940) *20th:* 4072, *Notor:* 1040
Rudolf Laban (Dec. 15, 1879-July 1, 1958) *20th:* 2221
Paul Klee (Dec. 18, 1879-June 29, 1940) *20th:* 2176
William Mitchell (Dec. 29, 1879-Feb. 19, 1936) *20th:* 2765
Susanna Mildred Hill (c. 1880-unknown) *Notor:* 466
William Joseph Simmons (1880-May 18, 1945) *Notor:* 957
Mack Sennett (Jan. 17, 1880-Nov. 5, 1960) *20th:* 3706
Dorothy Clutterbuck (Jan. 19, 1880-Jan. 12, 1951) *Notor:* 215
Douglas MacArthur (Jan. 26, 1880-Apr. 5, 1964) *20th:* 2492
John L. Lewis (Feb. 12, 1880-June 11, 1969) *20th:* 2360
Álvaro Obregón (Feb. 19, 1880-July 17, 1928) *20th:* 3013
Frances Perkins (Apr. 10, 1880-May 14, 1965) *20th:* 3198
Max Wertheimer (Apr. 16, 1880-Oct. 12, 1943) *20th:* 4293
Michel Fokine (Apr. 23, 1880-Aug. 22, 1942) *20th:* 1263
Kuniaki Koiso (Mar. 22, 1880-Nov. 3, 1950) *Notor:* 587
Ernst Ludwig Kirchner (May 6, 1880-June 15, 1938) *20th:* 2164
William T. Cosgrave (June 6, 1880-Nov. 16, 1965) *20th:* 843
Jeannette Rankin (June 11, 1880-May 18, 1973) *20th:* 3374
Arnold Gesell (June 21, 1880-May 29, 1961) *20th:* 1465
Helen Keller (June 27, 1880-June 1, 1968) *20th:* 2093
Guillaume Apollinaire (Aug. 26, 1880-Nov. 9, 1918) *20th:* 104
H. L. Mencken (Sept. 12, 1880-Jan. 29, 1956) *20th:* 2688
Marie Stopes (Oct. 15, 1880-Oct. 2, 1958) *20th:* 3882
Alfred Wegener (Nov. 1, 1880-Nov. 1930) *20th:* 4266
Sir Jacob Epstein (Nov. 10, 1880-Aug. 19, 1959) *20th:* 1165
Aleksandr Blok (Nov. 28, 1880-Aug. 7, 1921) *20th:* 394
George C. Marshall (Dec. 31, 1880-Oct. 16, 1959) *20th:* 2629

1881 - 1890

Piero Pirelli (Jan. 27, 1881-Aug. 7, 1956) *20th:* 3266
Fernand Léger (Feb. 4, 1881-Aug. 17, 1955) *20th:* 2334
Anna Pavlova (Feb. 12, 1881-Jan. 23, 1931) *20th:* 3166
Ernest Bevin (Mar. 9, 1881-Apr. 14, 1951) *20th:* 356
Edith Nourse Rogers (Mar. 19, 1881-Sept. 10, 1960) *20th:* 3489
Hermann Staudinger (Mar. 23, 1881-Sept. 8, 1965) *20th:* 3833
Béla Bartók (Mar. 25, 1881-Sept. 26, 1945) *20th:* 250
Alcide De Gasperi (Apr. 3, 1881-Aug. 19, 1954) *20th:* 944
Pierre Teilhard de Chardin (May 1, 1881-Apr. 10, 1955) *20th:* 3963
Aleksandr Fyodorovich Kerensky (May 2, 1881-June 11, 1970) *20th:* 2110
Atatürk (May 19, 1881-Nov. 10, 1938) *20th:* 162
James J. Walker (June 19, 1881-Nov. 18, 1946) *Notor:* 1082
Sir Alexander Fleming (Aug. 6, 1881-Mar. 11, 1955) *20th:* 1254
François Darlan (Aug. 7, 1881-Dec. 24, 1942) *Notor:* 262
Lu Xun (Sept. 25, 1881-Oct. 19, 1936) *20th:* 2447

Pablo Picasso (Oct. 25, 1881-Apr. 8, 1973) *20th:* 3237
Enver Paşa (Nov. 22, 1881-Aug. 4, 1922) *20th:* 1157
John XXIII (Nov. 25, 1881-June 3, 1963) *20th:* 2017
Irish Invincibles (formed late 1881) *Notor:* 509
Father Divine (c. 1882-Sept. 10, 1965) *Notor:* 346
Sam Rayburn (Jan. 6, 1882-Nov. 16, 1961) *20th:* 3397
Arnold Rothstein (Jan. 17, 1882-Nov. 6, 1928) *Notor:* 917
A. A. Milne (Jan. 18, 1882-Jan. 31, 1956) *20th:* 2753
Virginia Woolf (Jan. 25, 1882-Mar. 28, 1941) *20th:* 4397
Franklin D. Roosevelt (Jan. 30, 1882-Apr. 12, 1945) *20th:* 3509
Louis St. Laurent (Feb. 1, 1882-July 25, 1973) *20th:* 3597
James Joyce (Feb. 2, 1882-Jan. 13, 1941) *20th:* 2055
Nicolai Hartmann (Feb. 20, 1882-Oct. 9, 1950) *20th:* 1696
Charles Ponzi (Mar. 3, 1882-Jan. 18, 1949) *Notor:* 852
Percy Williams Bridgman (Apr. 21, 1882-Aug. 20, 1961) *20th:* 526
Alberto Pirelli (Apr. 28, 1882-Oct. 19, 1971) *20th:* 3266
Georges Braque (May 13, 1882-Aug. 31, 1963) *20th:* 493
Mohammad Mossadegh (May 19, 1882-Mar. 5, 1967) *20th:* 2844
Ion Antonescu (June 15, 1882-June 1, 1946) *Notor:* 25
Igor Stravinsky (June 17, 1882-Apr. 6, 1971) *20th:* 3888
Edward Hopper (July 22, 1882-May 15, 1967) *20th:* 1876
Seán T. O'Kelly (Aug. 25, 1882-Nov. 23, 1966) *20th:* 3034
Samuel Goldwyn (Aug. 27, 1882-Jan. 31, 1974) *20th:* 1523
Hans Geiger (Sept. 30, 1882-Sept. 24, 1945) *20th:* 1440
Robert H. Goddard (Oct. 5, 1882-Aug. 10, 1945) *20th:* 1507
Eamon de Valera (Oct. 14, 1882-Aug. 29, 1975) *20th:* 979
Umberto Boccioni (Oct. 19, 1882-Aug. 17, 1916) *20th:* 403
Jean Giraudoux (Oct. 29, 1882-Jan. 31, 1944) *20th:* 1492
William F. Halsey (Oct. 30, 1882-Aug. 16, 1959) *20th:* 1647
Felix Frankfurter (Nov. 15, 1882-Feb. 22, 1965) *20th:* 1308
Jacques Maritain (Nov. 18, 1882-Apr. 28, 1973) *20th:* 2624
Max Born (Dec. 11, 1882-Jan. 5, 1970) *20th:* 437
Ichirō Hatoyama (Jan. 1, 1883-Mar. 7, 1959) *20th:* 1701
Clement Attlee (Jan. 3, 1883-Oct. 8, 1967) *20th:* 165
Nikos Kazantzakis (Feb. 18, 1883-Oct. 26, 1957) *20th:* 2087
Karl Jaspers (Feb. 23, 1883-Feb. 26, 1969) *20th:* 1996
Imogen Cunningham (Apr. 12, 1883-June 23, 1976) *20th:* 883
Getúlio Vargas (Apr. 19, 1883-Aug. 24, 1954) *Notor:* 1059
Wang Jingwei (May 4, 1883-Nov. 10, 1944) *20th:* 4220
José Ortega y Gasset (May 9, 1883-Oct. 18, 1955) *20th:* 3077
Walter Gropius (May 18, 1883-July 5, 1969) *20th:* 1602
John Maynard Keynes (June 5, 1883-Apr. 21, 1946) *20th:* 2120
Pierre Laval (June 28, 1883-Oct. 15, 1945) *20th:* 2285, *Notor:* 609
Franz Kafka (July 3, 1883-June 3, 1924) *20th:* 2066
First Viscount Alanbrooke (July 23, 1883-June 17, 1963) *20th:* 50
Benito Mussolini (July 29, 1883-Apr. 28, 1945) *20th:* 2885, *Notor:* 769
Coco Chanel (Aug. 19, 1883-Jan. 10, 1971) *20th:* 727
Grigory Yevseyevich Zinovyev (Sept. 23, 1883-Aug. 25, 1935) *Notor:* 1138
José Clemente Orozco (Nov. 23, 1883-Sept. 7, 1949) *20th:* 3068
Anton von Webern (Dec. 3, 1883-Sept. 15, 1945) *20th:* 4262
Andrey Vyshinsky (Dec. 10, 1883-Nov. 22, 1954) *Notor:* 1079
Edgard Varèse (Dec. 22, 1883-Nov. 6, 1965) *20th:* 4142
Halide Edib Adıvar (1884-Jan. 9, 1964) *20th:* 29
Auguste Piccard (Jan. 28, 1884-Mar. 24, 1962) *20th:* 3240
Jean-Felix Piccard (Jan. 28, 1884-Jan. 28, 1963) *20th:* 3240
Harry S. Truman (May 8, 1884-Dec. 26, 1972) *20th:* 4086
Edvard Beneš (May 28, 1884-Sept. 3, 1948) *20th:* 299
Étienne Gilson (June 13, 1884-Sept. 19, 1978) *20th:* 1488

Louis B. Mayer (July 12, 1884-Oct. 29, 1957) *20th:* 2662
Amedeo Modigliani (July 12, 1884-Jan. 24, 1920) *20th:* 2776
Sara Teasdale (Aug. 8, 1884-Jan. 29, 1933) *20th:* 3959
Rudolf Bultmann (Aug. 20, 1884-July 30, 1976) *20th:* 572
İsmet Paşa (Sept. 24, 1884-Dec. 25, 1973) *20th:* 1971
Friedrich Bergius (Oct. 11, 1884-Mar. 30, 1949) *20th:* 313
Eleanor Roosevelt (Oct. 11, 1884-Nov. 7, 1962) *20th:* 3506
Norman Thomas (Nov. 20, 1884-Dec. 19, 1968) *20th:* 4002
Karl Schmidt-Rottluff (Dec. 1, 1884-Aug. 10, 1976) *20th:* 3661
Félix Éboué (Dec. 26, 1884-May 17, 1944) *20th:* 1085
Hideki Tojo (Dec. 30, 1884-Dec. 23, 1948) *Notor:* 1034
John Curtin (Jan. 8, 1885-July 5, 1945) *20th:* 891
Alice Paul (Jan. 11, 1885-July 9, 1977) *20th:* 3145
Sinclair Lewis (Feb. 7, 1885-Jan. 10, 1951) *20th:* 2363
Alban Berg (Feb. 9, 1885-Dec. 24, 1935) *20th:* 309
Julius Streicher (Feb. 12, 1885-Oct. 16, 1946) *Notor:* 1001
Chester W. Nimitz (Feb. 24, 1885-Feb. 20, 1966) *20th:* 2977
Robert Delaunay (Apr. 12, 1885-Oct. 25, 1941) *20th:* 950
György Lukács (Apr. 13, 1885-June 4, 1971) *20th:* 2468
Faisal I (May 20, 1885-Sept. 8, 1933) *20th:* 1202
John R. Brinkley (July 8, 1885-May 26, 1942) *Notor:* 141
Georg von Hevesy (Aug. 1, 1885-July 5, 1966) *20th:* 1792
D. H. Lawrence (Sept. 11, 1885-Mar. 2, 1930) *20th:* 2295
Karen Horney (Sept. 16, 1885-Dec. 4, 1952) *20th:* 1883
Niels Bohr (Oct. 7, 1885-Nov. 18, 1962) *20th:* 408
François Mauriac (Oct. 11, 1885-Sept. 1, 1970) *20th:* 2657
George S. Patton (Nov. 11, 1885-Dec. 21, 1945) *20th:* 3142
Albert Kesselring (Nov. 20, 1885-July 16, 1960) *20th:* 2117
Béla Kun (Feb. 20, 1886-Nov. 30, 1939) *Notor:* 596
Hugo L. Black (Feb. 27, 1886-Sept. 25, 1971) *20th:* 377
Oskar Kokoschka (Mar. 1, 1886-Feb. 22, 1980) *20th:* 2185
Felix Yusupov (Mar. 23, 1886-Sept. 27, 1967) *Notor:* 1126
Ludwig Mies van der Rohe (Mar. 27, 1886-Aug. 7, 1969) *20th:* 2731
Karl Barth (May 10, 1886-Dec. 10, 1968) *20th:* 243
Jun'ichirō Tanizaki (July 24, 1886-July 30, 1965) *20th:* 3944
Paul Tillich (Aug. 20, 1886-Oct. 22, 1965) *20th:* 4027
H. D. (Sept. 10, 1886-Sept. 27, 1961) *20th:* 1623
David Ben-Gurion (Oct. 16, 1886-Dec. 1, 1973) *20th:* 292
Karl von Frisch (Nov. 20, 1886-June 12, 1982) *20th:* 1335
Alexandre Stavisky (Nov. 20, 1886-Jan. 8, 1934) *Notor:* 998
Zhu De (Dec. 12 or 18, 1886-July 6, 1976) *20th:* 4465
Ty Cobb (Dec. 18, 1886-July 17, 1961) *20th:* 791
Hazel Wightman (Dec. 20, 1886-Dec. 5, 1974) *20th:* 4333
Fanya Kaplan (1887-Sept. 3, 1918) *Notor:* 552
Heitor Villa-Lobos (Mar. 5, 1887-Nov. 17, 1959) *20th:* 4163
Erich Mendelsohn (Mar. 21, 1887-Sept. 15, 1953) *20th:* 2692
Juan Gris (Mar. 23, 1887-May 11, 1927) *20th:* 1597
Roscoe Arbuckle (Mar. 24, 1887-June 29, 1933) *Notor:* 32
Bernardo Alberto Houssay (Apr. 10, 1887-Sept. 21, 1971) *20th:* 1899
Francesco Forgione (May 25, 1887-Sept. 23, 1968) *20th:* 1286
Ruth Benedict (June 5, 1887-Sept. 17, 1948) *20th:* 296
Marc Chagall (July 7, 1887-Mar. 28, 1985) *20th:* 717
Shoeless Joe Jackson (July 16, 1887-Dec. 5, 1951) *Notor:* 521
Vidkun Quisling (July 18, 1887-Oct. 24, 1945) *Notor:* 873
Gustav Hertz (July 22, 1887-Oct. 30, 1975) *20th:* 1780
Marcel Duchamp (July 28, 1887-Oct. 2, 1968) *20th:* 1051
Erwin Schrödinger (Aug. 12, 1887-Jan. 4, 1961) *20th:* 3668
Marcus Garvey (Aug. 17, 1887-June 10, 1940) *20th:* 1417
Nadia Boulanger (Sept. 16, 1887-Oct. 22, 1979) *20th:* 449
René Cassin (Oct. 5, 1887-Feb. 20, 1976) *20th:* 684
Le Corbusier (Oct. 6, 1887-Aug. 27, 1965) *20th:* 2323

Chiang Kai-shek (Oct. 31, 1887-Apr. 5, 1975) *20th:* 746
Marianne Moore (Nov. 15, 1887-Feb. 5, 1972) *20th:* 2821
Georgia O'Keeffe (Nov. 15, 1887-Mar. 6, 1986) *20th:* 3031
Bernard Law Montgomery (Nov. 17, 1887-Mar. 24, 1976) *20th:* 2808
Nikolai Ivanovich Vavilov (Nov. 26, 1887-Jan. 26, 1943) *20th:* 4151
Jack the Ripper (fl. 1888) *Notor:* 519
Ernst Heinkel (Jan. 24, 1888-Jan. 30, 1958) *20th:* 1746
John Foster Dulles (Feb. 25, 1888-May 24, 1959) *20th:* 1054
Knute Rockne (Mar. 8, 1888-Mar. 31, 1931) *20th:* 3481
Anita Loos (Apr. 26, 1888-Aug. 18, 1981) *20th:* 2428
Irving Berlin (May 11, 1888-Sept. 22, 1989) *20th:* 327
Jim Thorpe (May 22, 1888-Mar. 28, 1953) *20th:* 4016
Heinz Guderian (June 17, 1888-May 15, 1954) *20th:* 1606
Selman Abraham Waksman (July 22, 1888-Aug. 16, 1973) *20th:* 4180
T. E. Lawrence (Aug. 16, 1888-May 19, 1935) *20th:* 2303
T. S. Eliot (Sept. 26, 1888-Jan. 4, 1965) *20th:* 1139
Henry A. Wallace (Oct. 7, 1888-Nov. 18, 1965) *20th:* 4207
Nikolay Ivanovich Bukharin (Oct. 9, 1888-Mar. 15, 1938) *20th:* 566
Eugene O'Neill (Oct. 16, 1888-Nov. 27, 1953) *20th:* 3051
Richard Byrd (Oct. 25, 1888-Mar. 11, 1957) *20th:* 606
Sir George Hubert Wilkins (Oct. 31, 1888-Dec. 1, 1958) *20th:* 4339
Sir Chandrasekhara Venkata Raman (Nov. 7, 1888-Nov. 21, 1970) *20th:* 3364
Jean Monnet (Nov. 9, 1888-Mar. 16, 1979) *20th:* 2793
Andrei Nikolayevich Tupolev (Nov. 10, 1888-Dec. 23, 1972) *20th:* 4108
Carl Theodor Dreyer (Feb. 3, 1889-Mar. 20, 1968) *20th:* 1037
Arnold Toynbee (Apr. 14, 1889-Oct. 22, 1975) *20th:* 4059
A. Philip Randolph (Apr. 15, 1889-May 16, 1979) *20th:* 3369
Charles Chaplin (Apr. 16, 1889-Dec. 25, 1977) *20th:* 731
Adolf Hitler (Apr. 20, 1889-Apr. 30, 1945) *20th:* 1829, *Notor:* 477
Ludwig Wittgenstein (Apr. 26, 1889-Apr. 29, 1951) *20th:* 4378
António de Oliveira Salazar (Apr. 28, 1889-July 27, 1970) *20th:* 3606, *Notor:* 928
Paul Nash (May 11, 1889-July 11, 1946) *20th:* 2910
Anna Akhmatova (June 23, 1889-Mar. 5, 1966) *20th:* 42
Jean Cocteau (July 5, 1889-Oct. 11, 1963) *20th:* 794
Vasili Vasilievich Ulrikh (July 13, 1889-May 7, 1951) *Notor:* 1052
Ante Pavelić (July 14, 1889-Dec. 28, 1959) *Notor:* 813
Erle Stanley Gardner (July 17, 1889-Mar. 11, 1970) *20th:* 1403
First Baron Reith of Stonehaven (July 20, 1889-June 16, 1971) *20th:* 3410
Vladimir Zworykin (July 30, 1889-July 29, 1982) *20th:* 4479
Robert A. Taft (Sept. 8, 1889-July 31, 1953) *20th:* 3925
Walter Lippmann (Sept. 23, 1889-Dec. 14, 1974) *20th:* 2400
Martin Heidegger (Sept. 26, 1889-May 26, 1976) *20th:* 1742
Abel Gance (Oct. 25, 1889-Nov. 10, 1981) *20th:* 1382
Jawaharlal Nehru (Nov. 14, 1889-May 27, 1964) *20th:* 2929
Edwin Powell Hubble (Nov. 20, 1889-Sept. 28, 1953) *20th:* 1912
Gabriel Marcel (Dec. 7, 1889-Oct. 8, 1973) *20th:* 2609
Emil Brunner (Dec. 23, 1889-Apr. 6, 1966) *20th:* 547
Victor Lustig (Jan. 4, 1890-Mar. 11, 1947) *Notor:* 665
Karel Čapek (Jan. 9, 1890-Dec. 25, 1938) *20th:* 638
Robert Franklin Stroud (Jan. 28, 1890-Nov. 21, 1963) *Notor:* 1005
J. J. P. Oud (Feb. 9, 1890-Apr. 5, 1963) *20th:* 3092
Boris Pasternak (Feb. 10, 1890-May 30, 1960) *20th:* 3131
Vyacheslav Mikhailovich Molotov (Mar. 9, 1890-Nov. 8, 1986) *20th:* 2783, *Notor:* 746
Vaslav Nijinsky (Mar. 12, 1890-Apr. 8, 1950) *20th:* 2974
Sir Lawrence Bragg (Mar. 31, 1890-July 1, 1971) *20th:* 474
André-Louis Danjon (Apr. 6, 1890-Apr. 21, 1967) *20th:* 911
Alfred Jodl (May 10, 1890-Oct. 16, 1946) *Notor:* 533
Katherine Anne Porter (May 15, 1890-Sept. 18, 1980) *20th:* 3310
Ho Chi Minh (May 19, 1890-Sept. 3, 1969) *20th:* 1834

Harry Hopkins (Aug. 17, 1890-Jan. 29, 1946) *20th:* 1872
Man Ray (Aug. 27, 1890-Nov. 18, 1976) *20th:* 2580
Dame Agatha Christie (Sept. 15, 1890-Jan. 12, 1976) *20th:* 765
Aimee Semple McPherson (Oct. 9, 1890-Sept. 27, 1944) *Notor:* 679
Dwight D. Eisenhower (Oct. 14, 1890-Mar. 28, 1969) *20th:* 1125
Michael Collins (Oct. 16, 1890-Aug. 22, 1922) *20th:* 807
Charles de Gaulle (Nov. 22, 1890-Nov. 9, 1970) *20th:* 1427
Fritz Lang (Dec. 5, 1890-Aug. 2, 1976) *20th:* 2253
Edwin H. Armstrong (Dec. 18, 1890-Jan. 31, 1954) *20th:* 127
Hermann Joseph Muller (Dec. 21, 1890-Apr. 5, 1967) *20th:* 2861

1891 - 1900

Genrikh Yagoda (1891-Mar. 15, 1938) *Notor:* 1112
Zora Neale Hurston (Jan. 7, 1891-Jan. 28, 1960) *20th:* 1944
Walther Bothe (Jan. 8, 1891-Feb. 8, 1957) *20th:* 442
Antonio Gramsci (Jan. 23, 1891-Apr. 27, 1937) *20th:* 1566
Frank Costello (Jan. 26, 1891-Feb. 18, 1973) *Notor:* 237
Grant Wood (Feb. 13, 1891-Feb. 12, 1942) *20th:* 4387
Wallace Dodd Fard (Feb. 25, 1891-after 1934) *Notor:* 344
Max Ernst (Apr. 2, 1891-Apr. 1, 1976) *20th:* 1176
Nicola Sacco (Apr. 22, 1891-Aug. 23, 1927) *20th:* 3580, *Notor:* 924
Sergei Prokofiev (Apr. 23, 1891-Mar. 5, 1953) *20th:* 3338
Rudolf Carnap (May 18, 1891-Sept. 14, 1970) *20th:* 659
Cole Porter (June 9, 1891-Oct. 15, 1964) *20th:* 3308
Pier Luigi Nervi (June 21, 1891-Jan. 9, 1979) *20th:* 2940
Leander Perez (July 16, 1891-Mar. 19, 1969) *Notor:* 819
First Viscount Slim (Aug. 6, 1891-Dec. 14, 1970) *20th:* 3758
Bugs Moran (Aug. 21, 1891-Feb. 25, 1957) *Notor:* 751
Jacques Lipchitz (Aug. 22, 1891-May 26, 1973) *20th:* 2397
Karl Dönitz (Sept. 16, 1891-Dec. 24, 1984) *Notor:* 292
Edith Stein (Oct. 12, 1891-Aug. 9, 1942) *20th:* 3840
Sir James Chadwick (Oct. 20, 1891-July 24, 1974) *20th:* 714
Rafael Trujillo (Oct. 24, 1891-May 30, 1961) *20th:* 4084, *Notor:* 1042
Charles E. Coughlin (Oct. 25, 1891-Oct. 27, 1979) *Notor:* 239
Sir Frederick G. Banting (Nov. 14, 1891-Feb. 21, 1941) *20th:* 224
William Averell Harriman (Nov. 15, 1891-July 26, 1986) *20th:* 1684
Erwin Rommel (Nov. 15, 1891-Oct. 14, 1944) *20th:* 3502
Nelly Sachs (Dec. 10, 1891-May 12, 1970) *20th:* 3583
J. R. R. Tolkien (Jan. 3, 1892-Sept. 2, 1973) *20th:* 4038
Martin Niemöller (Jan. 14, 1892-Mar. 6, 1984) *20th:* 2971
Harry Stack Sullivan (Feb. 21, 1892-Jan. 14, 1949) *20th:* 3910
Edna St. Vincent Millay (Feb. 22, 1892-Oct. 19, 1950) *20th:* 2738
Mary Pickford (Apr. 8, 1892-May 29, 1979) *20th:* 3244
Tito (May 7, 1892-May 4, 1980) *20th:* 4034, *Notor:* 1032
Djuna Barnes (June 12, 1892-June 18, 1982) *20th:* 240
Reinhold Niebuhr (June 21, 1892-June 1, 1971) *20th:* 2962
Pearl S. Buck (June 26, 1892-Mar. 6, 1973) *20th:* 557
Dion O'Banion (July 8, 1892-Nov. 10, 1924) *Notor:* 803
Walter Benjamin (July 15, 1892-Sept. 26, 1940) *20th:* 306
Haile Selassie I (July 23, 1892-Aug. 27, 1975) *20th:* 1639
Jack Warner (Aug. 2, 1892-Sept. 9, 1978) *20th:* 4230
Louis de Broglie (Aug. 15, 1892-Mar. 19, 1987) *20th:* 534
Arthur Holly Compton (Sept. 10, 1892-Mar. 15, 1962) *20th:* 817
Marina Tsvetayeva (Oct. 8, 1892-Aug. 31, 1941) *20th:* 4098

Guo Moruo (Nov. 16, 1892-June 12, 1978) *20th:* 1619
Francisco Franco (Dec. 4, 1892-Nov. 20, 1975) *20th:* 1297, *Notor:* 371
Hermann Göring (Jan. 12, 1893-Oct. 15, 1946) *20th:* 1545, *Notor:* 428
Bessie Coleman (Jan. 26, 1893-Apr. 30, 1926) *20th:* 801
Omar Nelson Bradley (Feb. 12, 1893-Apr. 8, 1981) *20th:* 468
Andrés Segovia (Feb. 21, 1893-June 2, 1987) *20th:* 3691
Walter Baade (Mar. 24, 1893-June 25, 1960) *20th:* 184
James Bryant Conant (Mar. 26, 1893-Feb. 11, 1978) *20th:* 820
Dean Acheson (Apr. 11, 1893-Oct. 12, 1971) *20th:* 17
Joan Miró (Apr. 20, 1893-Dec. 25, 1983) *20th:* 2759
Norman Bel Geddes (Apr. 27, 1893-May 8, 1958) *20th:* 1431
Harold C. Urey (Apr. 29, 1893-Jan. 5, 1981) *20th:* 4132
Joachim von Ribbentrop (Apr. 30, 1893-Oct. 16, 1946) *Notor:* 894
Harold J. Laski (June 30, 1893-Mar. 24, 1950) *20th:* 2269
Walter Ulbricht (June 30, 1893-Aug. 1, 1973) *20th:* 4125
Walter White (July 1, 1893-Mar. 21, 1955) *20th:* 4307
Vladimir Mayakovsky (July 19, 1893-Apr. 14, 1930) *20th:* 2659
Mae West (Aug. 17, 1893-Nov. 22, 1980) *20th:* 4297
Dorothy Parker (Aug. 22, 1893-June 7, 1967) *20th:* 3116
Huey Long (Aug. 30, 1893-Sept. 10, 1935) *20th:* 2424, *Notor:* 649
Lillian Gish (Oct. 14, 1893-Feb. 27, 1993) *20th:* 1496
Lazar Kaganovich (Nov. 22, 1893-July 25, 1991) *Notor:* 549
Mao Zedong (Dec. 26, 1893-Sept. 9, 1976) *20th:* 2601, *Notor:* 691
Jomo Kenyatta (c. 1894-Aug. 22, 1978) *20th:* 2106
Norman Rockwell (Feb. 3, 1894-Nov. 8, 1978) *20th:* 3483
Harold Macmillan (Feb. 10, 1894-Dec. 29, 1986) *20th:* 2536
Aleksandr Ivanovich Oparin (Mar. 2, 1894-Apr. 21, 1980) *20th:* 3062
Ben Nicholson (Apr. 10, 1894-Feb. 6, 1982) *20th:* 2956
Bessie Smith (Apr. 15, 1894-Sept. 26, 1937) *20th:* 3765
Nikita S. Khrushchev (Apr. 17, 1894-Sept. 11, 1971) *20th:* 2128, *Notor:* 574
Rudolf Hess (Apr. 26, 1894-Aug. 17, 1987) *Notor:* 460
Martha Graham (May 11, 1894-Apr. 1, 1991) *20th:* 1563
Dave Beck (June 16, 1894-Dec. 26, 1993) *Notor:* 75
Alfred Kinsey (June 23, 1894-Aug. 25, 1956) *20th:* 2159
Duke of Windsor (June 23, 1894-May 28, 1972) *20th:* 4368
Hermann Oberth (June 25, 1894-Dec. 29, 1989) *20th:* 3008
Pyotr Leonidovich Kapitsa (July 9, 1894-Apr. 8, 1984) *20th:* 2077
Georges Lemaître (July 17, 1894-June 20, 1966) *20th:* 2337
Gavrilo Princip (July 25, 1894-Apr. 28, 1918) *Notor:* 861
Aldous Huxley (July 26, 1894-Nov. 22, 1963) *20th:* 1961
George Meany (Aug. 16, 1894-Jan. 10, 1980) *20th:* 2672
Rudolf Geiger (Aug. 24, 1894-Jan. 22, 1981) *20th:* 1443
Jean Renoir (Sept. 15, 1894-Feb. 12, 1979) *20th:* 3420
E. E. Cummings (Oct. 14, 1894-Sept. 3, 1962) *20th:* 879
Norbert Wiener (Nov. 26, 1894-Mar. 18, 1964) *20th:* 4321
Konosuke Matsushita (Nov. 27, 1894-Apr. 27, 1989) *20th:* 2653
James Thurber (Dec. 8, 1894-Nov. 2, 1961) *20th:* 4020
Sir Robert Gordon Menzies (Dec. 20, 1894-May 15, 1978) *20th:* 2707
J. Edgar Hoover (Jan. 1, 1895-May 2, 1972) *20th:* 1866, *Notor:* 489
Babe Ruth (Feb. 6, 1895-Aug. 16, 1948) *20th:* 3572
Víctor Raúl Haya de la Torre (Feb. 22, 1895-Aug. 2, 1979) *20th:* 1716
Ruth Snyder (Mar. 27, 1895-Jan. 12, 1928) *Notor:* 979
Nikolay Ivanovich Yezhov (May 1, 1895-probably Feb. 2, 1940) *Notor:* 1115
Lorenz Hart (May 2, 1895-Nov. 22, 1943) *20th:* 1691
Fulton J. Sheen (May 8, 1895-Dec. 9, 1979) *20th:* 3722
Edmund Wilson (May 8, 1895-June 12, 1972) *20th:* 4354
Lázaro Cárdenas (May 21, 1895-Oct. 19, 1970) *20th:* 647

Dorothea Lange (May 26, 1895-Oct. 11, 1965) *20th:* 2260
Jack Dempsey (June 24, 1895-May 31, 1983) *20th:* 964
Richard Walther Darré (July 14, 1895-Sept. 5, 1953) *Notor:* 266
R. Buckminster Fuller (July 12, 1895-July 1, 1983) *20th:* 1364
Oscar Hammerstein II (July 12, 1895-Aug. 23, 1960) *20th:* 1657
Machine Gun Kelly (July 17, 1895-July 17, 1954) *Notor:* 561
Léonide Massine (Aug. 8, 1895-Mar. 16, 1979) *20th:* 2646
Buster Keaton (Oct. 4, 1895-Feb. 1, 1966) *20th:* 2090
Juan Perón (Oct. 8, 1895-July 1, 1974) *20th:* 3205, *Notor:* 823
Gerhard Domagk (Oct. 30, 1895-Apr. 24, 1964) *20th:* 1021
Paul Hindemith (Nov. 16, 1895-Dec. 28, 1963) *20th:* 1811
Mikhail Bakhtin (Nov. 17, 1895-Mar. 7, 1975) *20th:* 190
William V. S. Tubman (Nov. 29, 1895-July 23, 1971) *20th:* 4101
Paul Éluard (Dec. 14, 1895-Nov. 18, 1952) *20th:* 1151
George VI (Dec. 14, 1895-Feb. 6, 1952) *20th:* 1454
Susanne K. Langer (Dec. 20, 1895-July 17, 1985) *20th:* 2263
Joe Ball (Jan. 7, 1896-Sept. 24, 1938) *Notor:* 52
Anastasio Somoza García (Feb. 1, 1896-Sept. 29, 1956) *Notor:* 984
André Breton (Feb. 19, 1896-Sept. 28, 1966) *20th:* 510
Andrey Aleksandrovich Zhdanov (Feb. 26, 1896-Aug. 31, 1948) *Notor:* 1137
Trygve Lie (July 16, 1896-Dec. 30, 1968) *20th:* 2375
Jean Piaget (Aug. 9, 1896-Sept. 16, 1980) *20th:* 3231
F. Scott Fitzgerald (Sept. 24, 1896-Dec. 21, 1940) *20th:* 1249
Roman Jakobson (Oct. 11, 1896-July 18, 1982) *20th:* 1986
Eugenio Montale (Oct. 12, 1896-Sept. 12, 1981) *20th:* 2801
Sir Oswald Mosley (Nov. 16, 1896-Dec. 3, 1980) *Notor:* 755
Georgy Zhukov (Dec. 1, 1896-June 18, 1974) *20th:* 4469
Ira Gershwin (Dec. 6, 1896-Aug. 17, 1983) *20th:* 1462
Jimmy Doolittle (Dec. 14, 1896-Sept. 27, 1993) *20th:* 1023
Legs Diamond (1897-Dec. 18, 1931) *Notor:* 277
Dorothy Arzner (Jan. 3, 1897-Oct. 1, 1979) *20th:* 141
Marcel Petiot (Jan. 17, 1897-May 25, 1946) *Notor:* 831
Ludwig Erhard (Feb. 4, 1897-May 5, 1977) *20th:* 1173
Louis Buchalter (Feb. 6, 1897-Mar. 4, 1944) *Notor:* 148
Marian Anderson (Feb. 27, 1897-Apr. 8, 1993) *20th:* 87
Joseph Darnand (Mar. 19, 1897-Oct. 10, 1945) *Notor:* 264
Lester B. Pearson (Apr. 23, 1897-Dec. 27, 1972) *20th:* 3174
Sir Anthony Eden (June 12, 1897-Jan. 14, 1977) *20th:* 1099
Winifred Wagner (June 23, 1897-Mar. 5, 1980) *Notor:* 1081
Dame Enid Muriel Lyons (July 9, 1897-Sept. 2, 1981) *20th:* 2486
Irène Joliot-Curie (Sept. 12, 1897-Mar. 17, 1956) *20th:* 2032
William Faulkner (Sept. 25, 1897-July 6, 1962) *20th:* 1222
Paul VI (Sept. 26, 1897-Aug. 6, 1978) *20th:* 3148
Joseph Profaci (Oct. 2, 1897-June 7, 1962) *Notor:* 863
Elijah Muhammad (Oct. 7, 1897-Feb. 25, 1975) *Notor:* 763
Joseph Goebbels (Oct. 29, 1897-May 1, 1945) *20th:* 1513, *Notor:* 418
Dorothy Day (Nov. 8, 1897-Nov. 29, 1980) *20th:* 925
Aneurin Bevan (Nov. 15, 1897-July 6, 1960) *20th:* 349
Lucky Luciano (Nov. 24, 1897-Jan. 26, 1962) *Notor:* 660
Vito Genovese (Nov. 27 1897-Feb. 14, 1969) *Notor:* 402
Margaret Chase Smith (Dec. 14, 1897-May 29, 1995) *20th:* 3768
Hastings Kamuzu Banda (c. 1898-Nov. 25, 1997) *20th:* 219
Albert Lutuli (c. 1898-July 21, 1967) *20th:* 2478
Liu Shaoqi (1898-Nov. 12, 1969) *20th:* 2408
Hymie Weiss (1898-Oct. 11, 1926) *Notor:* 1096
Sergei Eisenstein (Jan. 23, 1898-Feb. 11, 1948) *20th:* 1129
Joachim Wach (Jan. 25, 1898-Aug. 27, 1955) *20th:* 4177
Alvar Aalto (Feb. 3, 1898-May 11, 1976) *20th:* 1
Bertolt Brecht (Feb. 10, 1898-Aug. 14, 1956) *20th:* 504
Enzo Ferrari (Feb. 18, 1898-Aug. 14, 1988) *20th:* 1239

Gerald L. K. Smith (Feb. 27, 1898-Apr. 15, 1976) *Notor:* 973
Zhou Enlai (Mar. 5, 1898-Jan. 8, 1976) *20th:* 4461
Henry R. Luce (Apr. 3, 1898-Feb. 28, 1967) *20th:* 2456
Paul Robeson (Apr. 9, 1898-Jan. 23, 1976) *20th:* 3462
Golda Meir (May 3, 1898-Dec. 8, 1978) *20th:* 2674
Julius Evola (May 19, 1898-June 11, 1974) *Notor:* 339
Helen Brooke Taussig (May 24, 1898-May 20, 1986) *20th:* 3950
Federico García Lorca (June 5, 1898-Aug. 19, 1936) *20th:* 1395
Anastase Vonsiatsky (June 12, 1898-1965) *Notor:* 1077
M. C. Escher (June 17, 1898-Mar. 27, 1972) *20th:* 1183
Erich Maria Remarque (June 22, 1898-Sept. 25, 1970) *20th:* 3413
Stephen Vincent Benét (July 22, 1898-Mar. 13, 1943) *20th:* 303
Alexander Calder (July 22, 1898-Nov. 11, 1976) *20th:* 609
Henry Moore (July 30, 1898-Aug. 31, 1986) *20th:* 2818
Hyman G. Rickover (Aug. 24, 1898, or Jan. 27, 1900-July 8, 1986) *20th:* 3443
Baron Florey (Sept. 24, 1898-Feb. 21, 1968) *20th:* 1259
Jacques Doriot (Sept. 26, 1898-Feb. 22, 1945) *Notor:* 298
George Gershwin (Sept. 26, 1898-July 11, 1937) *20th:* 1458
Trofim Lysenko (Sept. 29, 1898-Nov. 20, 1976) *Notor:* 667
William O. Douglas (Oct. 16, 1898-Jan. 19, 1980) *20th:* 1029
Shinichi Suzuki (Oct. 17, 1898-Jan. 26, 1998) *20th:* 3922
Peng Dehuai (c. Oct. 24, 1898-Nov. 29, 1974) *20th:* 3191
René Magritte (Nov. 21, 1898-Aug. 15, 1967) *20th:* 2547
C. S. Lewis (Nov. 29, 1898-Nov. 22, 1963) *20th:* 2353
Gunnar Myrdal (Dec. 6, 1898-May 17, 1987) *20th:* 2890
Francis Poulenc (Jan. 7, 1899-Jan. 30, 1963) *20th:* 3318
Eva Le Gallienne (Jan. 11, 1899-June 3, 1991) *20th:* 2330
Al Capone (Jan. 17, 1899-Jan. 25, 1947) *20th:* 641, *Notor:* 175
Robert M. Hutchins (Jan. 17, 1899-May 14, 1977) *20th:* 1958
Paul-Henri Spaak (Jan. 25, 1899-July 31, 1972) *20th:* 3808
Lavrenty Beria (Mar. 29, 1899-Dec. 23, 1953) *Notor:* 89
John Reginald Halliday Christie (Apr. 8, 1899-July 15, 1953) *Notor:* 210
Vladimir Nabokov (Apr. 23, 1899-July 2, 1977) *20th:* 2894
Duke Ellington (Apr. 29, 1899-May 24, 1974) *20th:* 1145
F. A. Hayek (May 8, 1899-Mar. 23, 1992) *20th:* 1720
Fred Astaire (May 10, 1899-June 22, 1987) *20th:* 155
Yasunari Kawabata (June 11, 1899-Apr. 16, 1972) *20th:* 2084
Hart Crane (July 21, 1899-Apr. 27, 1932) *20th:* 858
Ernest Hemingway (July 21, 1899-July 2, 1961) *20th:* 1755
Alfred Hitchcock (Aug. 13, 1899-Apr. 29, 1980) *20th:* 1825
Jorge Luis Borges (Aug. 24, 1899-June 14, 1986) *20th:* 430
C. S. Forester (Aug. 27, 1899-Apr. 2, 1966) *20th:* 1283
Sir Macfarlane Burnet (Sept. 3, 1899-Aug. 31, 1985) *20th:* 587
Louise Nevelson (Sept. 23 or Oct. 16, 1899-Apr. 17, 1988) *20th:* 2947
Ferhat Abbas (Oct. 24, 1899-Dec. 24, 1985) *20th:* 7
Hayato Ikeda (Dec. 3, 1899-Aug. 13, 1965) *20th:* 1965
Humphrey Bogart (Dec. 25, 1899-Jan. 14, 1957) *20th:* 406
Puniša Račić (c. 1900?-1945) *Notor:* 876
Adlai E. Stevenson (Feb. 5, 1900-July 14, 1965) *20th:* 3856
Luis Buñuel (Feb. 22, 1900-July 29, 1983) *20th:* 578
Kurt Weill (Mar. 2, 1900-Apr. 3, 1950) *20th:* 4273
Frédéric Joliot (Mar. 19, 1900-Aug. 14, 1958) *20th:* 2032
Erich Fromm (Mar. 23, 1900-Mar. 18, 1980) *20th:* 1345
Spencer Tracy (Apr. 5, 1900-June 10, 1967) *20th:* 4066
Wolfgang Pauli (Apr. 25, 1900-Dec. 14, 1958) *20th:* 3152
Charles Richter (Apr. 26, 1900-Sept. 30, 1985) *20th:* 3440

Jan Hendrik Oort (Apr. 28, 1900-Nov. 5, 1992) *20th:* 3059
Ayatollah Khomeini (May 17, 1900, or Sept. 24, 1902-June 3, 1989) *20th:* 2123, *Notor:* 571
Hans Michael Frank (May 23, 1900-Oct. 16, 1946) *Notor:* 374
Martin Bormann (June 17, 1900-May 2, 1945) *Notor:* 131
Louis Mountbatten (June 25, 1900-Aug. 27, 1979) *20th:* 2853
Nathalie Sarraute (July 18, 1900-Oct. 19, 1999) *20th:* 3635
Vijaya Lakshmi Pandit (Aug. 18, 1900-Dec. 1, 1990) *20th:* 3099
Sir Hans Adolf Krebs (Aug. 25, 1900-Nov. 22, 1981) *20th:* 2199
Giuseppe Zangara (Sept. 7, 1900-Mar. 20, 1933) *Notor:* 1128
Andrey Andreyevich Vlasov (Sept. 14, 1900-Aug. 1, 1946) *Notor:* 1074
Thomas Wolfe (Oct. 3, 1900-Sept. 15, 1938) *20th:* 4383
Heinrich Himmler (Oct. 7, 1900-May 23, 1945) *20th:* 1807, *Notor:* 468
Helen Hayes (Oct. 10, 1900-Mar. 17, 1993) *20th:* 1723
Aaron Copland (Nov. 14, 1900-Dec. 2, 1990) *20th:* 836
Helen Gahagan Douglas (Nov. 25, 1900-June 28, 1980) *20th:* 1026
Mildred Gillars (Nov. 29, 1900-June 25, 1988) *Notor:* 409

1901 - 1910

Ngo Dinh Diem (Jan. 3, 1901-Nov. 2, 1963) *20th:* 2951
Fulgencio Batista y Zaldívar (Jan. 16, 1901-Aug. 6, 1973) *Notor:* 73
Clark Gable (Feb. 1, 1901-Nov. 16, 1960) *20th:* 1368
Linus Pauling (Feb. 28, 1901-Aug. 19, 1994) *20th:* 3155
Eisaku Satō (Mar. 27, 1901-June 3, 1975) *20th:* 3645
Jacques Lacan (Apr. 13, 1901-Sept. 9, 1981) *20th:* 2224
Hirohito (Apr. 29, 1901-Jan. 7, 1989) *20th:* 1818, *Notor:* 473
Sukarno (June 6, 1901-June 21, 1970) *20th:* 3904
Willie Sutton (June 30, 1901-Nov. 2, 1980) *Notor:* 1014
Louis Armstrong (Aug. 4, 1901-July 6, 1971) *20th:* 130
Ernest Orlando Lawrence (Aug. 8, 1901-Aug. 27, 1958) *20th:* 2300
Hendrik Frensch Verwoerd (Sept. 8, 1901-Sept. 6, 1966) *Notor:* 1064
Learie Constantine (Sept. 21, 1901-July 1, 1971) *20th:* 829
Enrico Fermi (Sept. 29, 1901-Nov. 28, 1954) *20th:* 1235
Alberto Giacometti (Oct. 10, 1901-Jan. 11, 1966) *20th:* 1470
André Malraux (Nov. 3, 1901-Nov. 23, 1976) *20th:* 2576
Magda Goebbels (Nov. 11, 1901-May 1, 1945) *Notor:* 421
Walt Disney (Dec. 5, 1901-Dec. 15, 1966) *20th:* 1006
Werner Heisenberg (Dec. 5, 1901-Feb. 1, 1976) *20th:* 1749
Margaret Mead (Dec. 16, 1901-Nov. 15, 1978) *20th:* 2668
Marlene Dietrich (Dec. 27, 1901-May 6, 1992) *20th:* 997
Georgi M. Malenkov (Jan. 8, 1902-Jan. 14, 1988) *20th:* 2573
Langston Hughes (Feb. 1, 1902-May 22, 1967) *20th:* 1928
Charles A. Lindbergh (Feb. 4, 1902-Aug. 26, 1974) *20th:* 2392
Albert Anastasia (Feb. 26, 1902-Oct. 25, 1957) *Notor:* 23
John Steinbeck (Feb. 27, 1902-Dec. 20, 1968) *20th:* 3849
Bobby Jones (Mar. 17, 1902-Dec. 18, 1971) *20th:* 2036
Sir William Walton (Mar. 29, 1902-Mar. 8, 1983) *20th:* 4216
Halldór Laxness (Apr. 23, 1902-Feb. 8, 1998) *20th:* 2308
Barbara McClintock (June 16, 1902-Sept. 2, 1992) *20th:* 2504
Richard Rodgers (June 28, 1902-Dec. 30, 1979) *20th:* 3486

Meyer Lansky (July 4, 1902-Jan. 15, 1983) *Notor:* 604
Dutch Schultz (Aug. 6, 1902-Oct. 24, 1935) *Notor:* 938
Paul A. M. Dirac (Aug. 8, 1902-Oct. 20, 1984) *20th:* 1004
Mohammad Hatta (Aug. 12, 1902-Mar. 14, 1980) *20th:* 1704
Felix Wankel (Aug. 13, 1902-Oct. 9, 1988) *20th:* 4224
Leni Riefenstahl (Aug. 22, 1902-Sept. 8, 2003) *20th:* 3451
Fernand Braudel (Aug. 24, 1902-Nov. 28, 1985) *20th:* 497
Darryl F. Zanuck (Sept. 5, 1902-Dec. 22, 1979) *20th:* 4445
Cheryl Crawford (Sept. 24, 1902-Oct. 7, 1986) *20th:* 861
Ray Kroc (Oct. 5, 1902-Jan. 14, 1984) *20th:* 2201
Joe Adonis (Nov. 22, 1902-Nov. 26, 1972) *Notor:* 6
R. A. Butler (Dec. 9, 1902-Mar. 8, 1982) *20th:* 602
Alan Paton (Jan. 11, 1903-Apr. 12, 1988) *20th:* 3138
Igor Vasilyevich Kurchatov (Jan. 12, 1903-Feb. 7, 1960) *20th:* 2214
Sir John Carew Eccles (Jan. 27, 1903-May 2, 1997) *20th:* 1089
Giulio Natta (Feb. 26, 1903-May 2, 1979) *20th:* 2919
Clare Boothe Luce (Apr. 10, 1903-Oct. 9, 1987) *20th:* 2453
Benjamin Spock (May 2, 1903-Mar. 15, 1998) *20th:* 3814
Bing Crosby (May 3, 1903-Oct. 14, 1977) *20th:* 874
Bob Hope (May 29, 1903-July 27, 2003) *20th:* 1870
Lou Gehrig (June 19, 1903-June 2, 1941) *20th:* 1434
John Dillinger (June 22, 1903-July 22, 1934) *Notor:* 281
George Orwell (June 25, 1903-Jan. 21, 1950) *20th:* 3080
Hugo Theorell (July 6, 1903-Aug. 15, 1982) *20th:* 3997
Habib Bourguiba (Aug. 3, 1903-Apr. 6, 2000) *20th:* 457
L. S. B. Leakey (Aug. 7, 1903-Oct. 1, 1972) *20th:* 2310
Graham Vivian Sutherland (Aug. 24, 1903-Feb. 17, 1980) *20th:* 3920
Mark Rothko (Sept. 25, 1903-Feb. 25, 1970) *20th:* 3539
Vladimir Horowitz (Oct. 1, 1903-Nov. 5, 1989) *20th:* 1886
Konrad Lorenz (Nov. 7, 1903-Feb. 27, 1989) *20th:* 2434
John von Neumann (Dec. 28, 1903-Feb. 8, 1957) *20th:* 2943
Cary Grant (Jan. 18, 1904-Nov. 29, 1986) *20th:* 1570
George Balanchine (Jan. 22, 1904-Apr. 30, 1983) *20th:* 193
Pretty Boy Floyd (Feb. 3, 1904-Oct. 22, 1934) *Notor:* 360
Hans Joachim Morgenthau (Feb. 17, 1904-July 19, 1980) *20th:* 2828
Dr. Seuss (Mar. 2, 1904-Sept. 24, 1991) *20th:* 3710
George Gamow (Mar. 4, 1904-Aug. 20, 1968) *20th:* 1379
Reinhard Heydrich (Mar. 7, 1904-June 4, 1942) *Notor:* 462
B. F. Skinner (Mar. 20, 1904-Aug. 18, 1990) *20th:* 3754
J. Robert Oppenheimer (Apr. 22, 1904-Feb. 18, 1967) *20th:* 3065
Margaret Bourke-White (June 14, 1904-Aug. 27, 1971) *20th:* 460
Pablo Neruda (July 12, 1904-Sept. 23, 1973) *20th:* 2937
Ralph Bunche (Aug. 7, 1904-Dec. 9, 1971) *20th:* 574
Wendell Stanley (Aug. 16, 1904-June 15, 1971) *20th:* 3824
Deng Xiaoping (Aug. 22, 1904-Feb. 19, 1997) *20th:* 968
Graham Greene (Oct. 2, 1904-Apr. 3, 1991) *20th:* 1577
Alger Hiss (Nov. 11, 1904-Nov. 15, 1996) *20th:* 1822, *Notor:* 475
Nathan F. Leopold, Jr. (Nov. 19, 1904-Aug. 30, 1971) *Notor:* 634
Nnamdi Azikiwe (Nov. 16, 1904-May 11, 1996) *20th:* 180
Alexandra Danilova (Nov. 20, 1904-July 13, 1997) *20th:* 908
Louis-Eugène-Félix Néel (Nov. 22, 1904-Nov. 17, 2000) *20th:* 2926
Gerhard Herzberg (Dec. 25, 1904-Mar. 3, 1999) *20th:* 1783
Faisal (c. 1905-Mar. 25, 1975) *20th:* 1198
Oveta Culp Hobby (Jan. 19, 1905-Aug. 16, 1995) *20th:* 1838
Ayn Rand (Feb. 2, 1905-Mar. 6, 1982) *20th:* 3367
Albert Speer (Mar. 19, 1905-Sept. 1, 1981) *Notor:* 987
Serge Lifar (Apr. 2, 1905-Dec. 15, 1986) *20th:* 2378
Robert Penn Warren (Apr. 24, 1905-Sept. 15, 1989) *20th:* 4236

Henry Fonda (May 16, 1905-Aug. 12, 1982) *20th:* 1265
Richard A. Loeb (June 11, 1905-Jan. 28, 1936) *Notor:* 647
Lillian Hellman (June 20, 1905-June 30, 1984) *20th:* 1752
Jean-Paul Sartre (June 21, 1905-Apr. 15, 1980) *20th:* 3638
Dag Hammarskjöld (July 29, 1905-Sept. 18, 1961) *20th:* 1653
Agnes de Mille (Sept. 18, 1905-Oct. 7, 1993) *20th:* 957
Greta Garbo (Sept. 18, 1905-Apr. 15, 1990) *20th:* 1392
Savitri Devi (Sept. 30, 1905-Oct. 22, 1982) *Notor:* 934
Henri Lemoine (fl. 1905) *Notor:* 627
Félix Houphouët-Boigny (Oct. 18, 1905-Dec. 7, 1993) *20th:* 1895
Howard Hughes (Dec. 24, 1905-Apr. 5, 1976) *20th:* 1925
Elmyr de Hory (1906-Dec. 11, 1976) *Notor:* 492
Dietrich Bonhoeffer (Feb. 4, 1906-Apr. 9, 1945) *20th:* 418
Clyde William Tombaugh (Feb. 4, 1906-Jan. 17, 1997) *20th:* 4041
Puyi (Feb. 7, 1906-Oct. 17, 1967) *Notor:* 864
Bugsy Siegel (Feb. 28, 1906-June 20, 1947) *Notor:* 954
Adolf Eichmann (Mar. 19, 1906-May 31, 1962) *Notor:* 322
Samuel Beckett (Apr. 13, 1906-Dec. 22, 1989) *20th:* 279
William Joyce (Apr. 24, 1906-Jan. 3, 1946) *Notor:* 542
William J. Brennan (Apr. 25, 1906-July 24, 1997) *20th:* 507
Kurt Gödel (Apr. 28, 1906-Jan. 14, 1978) *20th:* 1510
Harry Hammond Hess (May 24, 1906-Aug. 25, 1969) *20th:* 1785
Anne Morrow Lindbergh (June 22, 1906-Feb. 7, 2001) *20th:* 2389
Léon Degrelle (June 15, 1906-Mar. 31, 1994) *Notor:* 270
Hans Albrecht Bethe (July 2, 1906-Mar. 6, 2005) *20th:* 341
Ed Gein (Aug. 27, 1906-July 26, 1984) *Notor:* 399
Dmitri Shostakovich (Sept. 25, 1906-Aug. 9, 1975) *20th:* 3728
Léopold Senghor (Oct. 9, 1906-Dec. 20, 2001) *20th:* 3702
Hannah Arendt (Oct. 14, 1906-Dec. 4, 1975) *20th:* 118
Luchino Visconti (Nov. 2, 1906-Mar. 17, 1976) *20th:* 4166
Henri Charrière (Nov. 16, 1906-July 29, 1973) *Notor:* 204
Soichiro Honda (Nov. 17, 1906-Aug. 5, 1991) *20th:* 1859
Carl Weiss (Dec. 6, 1906-Sept. 8, 1935) *Notor:* 1095
Grace Murray Hopper (Dec. 9, 1906-Jan. 1, 1992) *20th:* 1879
Leonid Brezhnev (Dec. 19, 1906-Nov. 10, 1982) *20th:* 523
Virginia McMartin (c. 1907-Dec. 18, 1995) *Notor:* 676
Pierre Mendès-France (Jan. 11, 1907-Oct. 18, 1982) *20th:* 2698
Sergei Korolev (Jan. 12, 1907-Jan. 14, 1966) *20th:* 2191
Hideki Yukawa (Jan. 23, 1907-Sept. 8, 1981) *20th:* 4436
James A. Michener (Feb. 3, 1907[?]-Oct. 16, 1997) *20th:* 2728
W. H. Auden (Feb. 21, 1907-Sept. 29, 1973) *20th:* 172
Mircea Eliade (Mar. 9, 1907-Apr. 22, 1986) *20th:* 1136
Baldur von Schirach (Mar. 9, 1907-Aug. 8, 1974) *Notor:* 937
François Duvalier (Apr. 14, 1907-Apr. 21, 1971) *20th:* 1069, *Notor:* 307
Mary A. Hallaren (May 4, 1907-Feb. 13, 2005) *20th:* 1645
Katharine Hepburn (May 12, 1907-June 29, 2003) *20th:* 1769
Sir Laurence Olivier (May 22, 1907-June 11, 1989) *20th:* 3039
Yoshiko Kawashima (May 24, 1907-Mar. 25, 1948) *Notor:* 558
Rachel Carson (May 27, 1907-Apr. 14, 1964) *20th:* 662
Sir Frank Whittle (June 1, 1907-Aug. 8, 1996) *20th:* 4318
Frida Kahlo (July 6, 1907-July 13, 1954) *20th:* 2069
Walter P. Reuther (Sept. 1, 1907-May 9, 1970) *20th:* 3424
Horst Wessel (Sept. 9, 1907-Feb. 23, 1930) *Notor:* 1097
Warren E. Burger (Sept. 17, 1907-June 25, 1995) *20th:* 581
Edwin Mattison McMillan (Sept. 18, 1907-Sept. 7, 1991) *20th:* 2532
Anthony Blunt (Sept. 26, 1907-Mar. 26, 1983) *Notor:* 109

Víctor Paz Estenssoro (Oct. 2, 1907-June 7, 2001) *20th:* 3172
Norman Collins (Oct. 3, 1907-Sept. 6, 1982) *20th:* 810
Lewis F. Powell, Jr. (Nov. 19, 1907-Aug. 25, 1998) *20th:* 3325
Lin Biao (Dec. 5, 1907-Sept. 13, 1971) *20th:* 2381
Oscar Niemeyer (b. Dec. 15, 1907) *20th:* 2967
Simone de Beauvoir (Jan. 9, 1908-Apr. 14, 1986) *20th:* 271
Edward Teller (Jan. 15, 1908-Sept. 9, 2003) *20th:* 3968
Lev Davidovich Landau (Jan. 22, 1908-Apr. 1, 1968) *20th:* 2244
Maurice Merleau-Ponty (Mar. 14, 1908-May 4, 1961) *20th:* 2710
Bette Davis (Apr. 5, 1908-Oct. 8, 1989) *20th:* 919
Herbert von Karajan (Apr. 5, 1908-July 16, 1989) *20th:* 2081
Edward R. Murrow (Apr. 25, 1908-Apr. 27, 1965) *20th:* 2879
James Stewart (May 20, 1908-July 2, 1997) *20th:* 3860
John Bardeen (May 23, 1908-Jan. 30, 1991) *20th:* 234
Hannes Alfvén (May 30, 1908-Apr. 2, 1995) *20th:* 58
Otto Skorzeny (June 12, 1908-July 5, 1975) *Notor:* 969
Sam Giancana (June 15, 1908-June 19, 1975) *Notor:* 405
Salvador Allende (June 26, 1908-Sept. 11, 1973) *20th:* 70
Estée Lauder (July 1, 1908-Apr. 24, 2004) *20th:* 2275
Thurgood Marshall (July 2, 1908-Jan. 24, 1993) *20th:* 2633
Nelson A. Rockefeller (July 8, 1908-Jan. 26, 1979) *20th:* 3478
Vincent Coll (July 20, 1908-Feb. 8, 1932) *Notor:* 221
Alvin Karpis (Aug. 10, 1908-Aug. 26, 1979) *Notor:* 556
Henri Cartier-Bresson (Aug. 22, 1908-Aug. 2, 2004) *20th:* 671
Sir Donald G. Bradman (Aug. 27, 1908-Feb. 25, 2001) *20th:* 471
Lyndon B. Johnson (Aug. 27, 1908-Jan. 22, 1973) *20th:* 2027
Viktor A. Ambartsumian (Sept. 18, 1908-Aug. 12, 1996) *20th:* 77
Jim Folsom (Oct. 9, 1908-Nov. 21, 1987) *Notor:* 362
John Kenneth Galbraith (Oct. 15, 1908-Apr. 29, 2006) *20th:* 1374
Enver Hoxha (Oct. 16, 1908-Apr. 11, 1985) *Notor:* 493
Lee Krasner (Oct. 27, 1908-June 19, 1984) *20th:* 2195
Sir Joseph Rotblat (Nov. 4, 1908-Aug. 31, 2005) *20th:* 3536
Harry A. Blackmun (Nov. 12, 1908-Mar. 4, 1999) *20th:* 382
Joseph McCarthy (Nov. 14, 1908-May 2, 1957) *20th:* 2497, *Notor:* 669
Claude Lévi-Strauss (b. Nov. 28, 1908) *20th:* 2347
Adam Clayton Powell, Jr. (Nov. 29, 1908-Apr. 4, 1972) *Notor:* 856
Baby Face Nelson (Dec. 6, 1908-Nov. 27, 1934) *Notor:* 774
Olivier Messiaen (Dec. 10, 1908-Apr. 27, 1992) *20th:* 2715
Willard F. Libby (Dec. 17, 1908-Sept. 8, 1980) *20th:* 2371
Simon Wiesenthal (Dec. 31, 1908-Sept. 20, 2005) *20th:* 4328
U Thant (Jan. 22, 1909-Nov. 25, 1974) *20th:* 3986
Simone Weil (Feb. 3, 1909-Aug. 24, 1943) *20th:* 4269
Clyde Barrow (Mar. 24, 1909-May 23, 1934) *Notor:* 62
Fred Perry (May 18, 1909-Feb. 2, 1995) *20th:* 3216
Wilbur Mills (May 24, 1909-May 2, 1992) *Notor:* 733
Benny Goodman (May 30, 1909-June 13, 1986) *20th:* 1527
Virginia Apgar (June 7, 1909-Aug. 7, 1974) *20th:* 100
Katherine Dunham (June 22, 1909-May 21, 2006) *20th:* 1061
Andrei Gromyko (July 18, 1909-July 2, 1989) *20th:* 1600
Kwame Nkrumah (Sept. 21, 1909-Apr. 27, 1972) *20th:* 2988
Eugène Ionesco (Nov. 26, 1909-Mar. 28, 1994) *20th:* 1968
Muhammad Siad Barre (c. 1910-Jan. 2, 1995) *20th:* 3734, *Notor:* 953
Orval E. Faubus (Jan. 7, 1910-Dec. 14, 1994) *Notor:* 348
Felix Candela (Jan. 27, 1910-Dec. 7, 1997) *20th:* 631
Carlos Marcello (Feb. 6, 1910-Mar. 3, 1993) *Notor:* 698
Dominique Pire (Feb. 10, 1910-Jan. 30, 1969) *20th:* 3264
Carmine Galante (Feb. 21, 1910-July 12, 1979) *Notor:* 389
Samuel Barber (Mar. 9, 1910-Jan. 23, 1981) *20th:* 230
Akira Kurosawa (Mar. 23, 1910-Sept. 6, 1998) *20th:* 2217
Nathuram Vinayak Godse (May 19, 1910-Nov. 15, 1949) *Notor:* 416

Jacques Cousteau (June 11, 1910-June 25, 1997) *20th:* 849
Abe Fortas (June 19, 1910-Apr. 5, 1982) *Notor:* 369
Mother Teresa (Aug. 26, 1910-Sept. 5, 1997) *20th:* 3975
Bonnie Parker (Oct. 1, 1910-May 23, 1934) *Notor:* 811
Dame Alicia Markova (Dec. 1, 1910-Dec. 2, 2004) *20th:* 2627
Jean Genet (Dec. 19, 1910-Apr. 15, 1986) *20th:* 1445

1911 - 1920

Ronald Reagan (Feb. 6, 1911-June 5, 2004) *20th:* 3400
L. Ron Hubbard (Mar. 13, 1911-Jan. 24, 1986) *20th:* 1909, *Notor:* 495
Josef Mengele (Mar. 16, 1911-Feb. 7, 1979) *Notor:* 717
Jack Ruby (Mar. 25, 1911-Jan. 3, 1967) *Notor:* 919
Tennessee Williams (Mar. 26, 1911-Feb. 25, 1983) *20th:* 4350
Melvin Calvin (Apr. 8, 1911-Jan. 8, 1997) *20th:* 621
Guy Burgess (Apr. 16, 1911-Aug. 30, 1963) *Notor:* 152
Max Frisch (May 15, 1911-Apr. 4, 1991) *20th:* 1338
Ne Win (May 24, 1911-Dec. 5, 2002) *Notor:* 773
Hubert H. Humphrey (May 27, 1911-Jan. 13, 1978) *20th:* 1938
Milovan Djilas (June 12, 1911-Apr. 20, 1995) *20th:* 1011
Luis W. Alvarez (June 13, 1911-Sept. 1, 1988) *20th:* 73
Babe Didrikson Zaharias (June 26, 1911-Sept. 27, 1956) *20th:* 4442
Georges Pompidou (July 5, 1911-Apr. 2, 1974) *20th:* 3305
Gian Carlo Menotti (July 7, 1911-Feb. 1, 2007) *20th:* 2703
Marshall McLuhan (July 21, 1911-Dec. 31, 1980) *20th:* 2529
Lucille Ball (Aug. 6, 1911-Apr. 26, 1989) *20th:* 212
Vo Nguyen Giap (Aug. 25, 1911) *20th:* 4169
Naguib Mahfouz (Dec. 11, 1911-Aug. 30, 2006) *20th:* 2553
Klaus Fuchs (Dec. 29, 1911-Jan. 28, 1988) *Notor:* 379
Kim Philby (Jan. 1, 1912-May 11, 1988) *Notor:* 836
Jackson Pollock (Jan. 28, 1912-Aug. 11, 1956) *20th:* 3301
Barbara W. Tuchman (Jan. 30, 1912-Feb. 6, 1989) *20th:* 4104
Eva Braun (Feb. 6, 1912-Apr. 30, 1945) *Notor:* 137
Agnes Martin (Mar. 22, 1912-Dec. 16, 2004) *20th:* 2636
Wernher von Braun (Mar. 23, 1912-June 16, 1977) *20th:* 500
Kim Il Sung (Apr. 15, 1912-July 8, 1994) *20th:* 2138, *Notor:* 578
Glenn Theodore Seaborg (Apr. 19, 1912-Feb. 25, 1999) *20th:* 3684
Mary McCarthy (June 21, 1912-Oct. 25, 1989) *20th:* 2501
Alan Mathison Turing (June 23, 1912-June 7, 1954) *20th:* 4112
Milton Friedman (July 31, 1912-Nov. 16, 2006) *20th:* 1332
Gene Kelly (Aug. 23, 1912-Feb. 2, 1996) *20th:* 2096
Alfredo Stroessner (Nov. 3, 1912-Aug. 16, 2006) *Notor:* 1004
Tip O'Neill (Dec. 9, 1912-Jan. 5, 1994) *20th:* 3055
Lady Bird Johnson (Dec. 22, 1912-July 11, 2007) *20th:* 2025
Richard M. Nixon (Jan. 9, 1913-Apr. 22, 1994) *20th:* 2984, *Notor:* 793
Rosa Parks (Feb. 4, 1913-Oct. 24, 2005) *20th:* 3119
Mary Leakey (Feb. 6, 1913-Dec. 9, 1996) *20th:* 2315
Jimmy Hoffa (Feb. 14, 1913-possibly July 30, 1975) *Notor:* 480
Clay Shaw (Mar. 17, 1913-Aug. 14, 1974) *Notor:* 941
Donald Duart Maclean (May 25, 1913-Mar. 6, 1983) *Notor:* 674
Aimé Césaire (June 25, 1913-Apr. 17, 2008) *20th:* 709
Gerald R. Ford (July 14, 1913-Dec. 26, 2006) *20th:* 1274
John Cairncross (July 25, 1913-Oct. 8, 1995) *Notor:* 164
Menachem Begin (Aug. 16, 1913-Mar. 9, 1992) *20th:* 284
Robertson Davies (Aug. 28, 1913-Dec. 2, 1995) *20th:* 917
Jesse Owens (Sept. 12, 1913-Mar. 31, 1980) *20th:* 3095
Eiji Toyoda (b. Sept. 12, 1913) *20th:* 4062

John Mitchell (Sept. 15, 1913-Nov. 9, 1988) *Notor:* 737
Klaus Barbie (Oct. 25, 1913-Sept. 25, 1991) *Notor:* 57
Bao Dai (Oct. 22, 1913-July 30, 1997) *20th:* 228
Albert Camus (Nov. 7, 1913-Jan. 4, 1960) *20th:* 628
Benjamin Britten (Nov. 22, 1913-Dec. 4, 1976) *20th:* 529
Muriel Rukeyser (Dec. 15, 1913-Feb. 12, 1980) *20th:* 3556
Willy Brandt (Dec. 18, 1913-Oct. 8, 1992) *20th:* 490
Jiang Qing (1914-May 14, 1991) *Notor:* 528
Thomas J. Watson, Jr. (Jan. 14, 1914-Dec. 31, 1993) *20th:* 4246
Ramón Mercader (Feb. 7, 1914-Oct. 18, 1978) *Notor:* 721
Norman Borlaug (b. Mar. 25, 1914) *20th:* 434
Joe Louis (May 13, 1914-Apr. 12, 1981) *20th:* 2437
James Van Allen (Sept. 7, 1914-Aug. 9, 2006) *20th:* 4139
Thor Heyerdahl (Oct. 6, 1914-Apr. 18, 2002) *20th:* 1795
Jonas Salk (Oct. 28, 1914-June 23, 1995) *20th:* 3613
Joe DiMaggio (Nov. 25, 1914-Mar. 8, 1999) *20th:* 1001
Tino De Angelis (b. 1915) *Notor:* 268
Robert Motherwell (Jan. 24, 1915-July 16, 1991) *20th:* 2847
Thomas Merton (Jan. 31, 1915-Dec. 10, 1968) *20th:* 2713
Abba Eban (Feb. 2, 1915-Nov. 17, 2002) *20th:* 1082
Muddy Waters (Apr. 4, 1915-Apr. 30, 1983) *20th:* 4240
Billie Holiday (Apr. 7, 1915-July 17, 1959) *20th:* 1852
Orson Welles (May 6, 1915-Oct. 10, 1985) *20th:* 4283
Moshe Dayan (May 20, 1915-Oct. 16, 1981) *20th:* 929
Saul Bellow (June 10, 1915-Apr. 5, 2005) *20th:* 288
Lucy S. Dawidowicz (June 16, 1915-Dec. 5, 1990) *20th:* 922
Paul Castellano (June 20, 1915-Dec. 16, 1985) *Notor:* 183
Sir Fred Hoyle (June 24, 1915-Aug. 20, 2001) *20th:* 1902
Charles Hard Townes (b. July 28, 1915) *20th:* 4057
Ingrid Bergman (Aug. 29, 1915-Aug. 29, 1982) *20th:* 321
Ethel Rosenberg (Sept. 28, 1915-June 19, 1953) *Notor:* 913
Arthur Miller (Oct. 17, 1915-Feb. 10, 2005) *20th:* 2742
Roland Barthes (Nov. 12, 1915-Mar. 26, 1980) *20th:* 246
Hu Yaobang (Nov. 20, 1915-Apr. 15, 1989) *20th:* 1905
Augusto Pinochet Ugarte (Nov. 25, 1915-Dec. 10, 2006) *20th:* 3257, *Notor:* 842
Frank Sinatra (Dec. 12, 1915-May 14, 1998) *20th:* 3747
Edith Piaf (Dec. 19, 1915-Oct. 11, 1963) *20th:* 3228
Sir Harold Wilson (Mar. 11, 1916-May 24, 1995) *20th:* 4360
Gregory Peck (Apr. 15, 1916-June 12, 2003) *20th:* 3181
Bernard Lewis (b. May 31, 1916) *20th:* 2351
Francis Crick (June 8, 1916-July 28, 2004) *20th:* 865
Robert McNamara (b. June 9, 1916) *20th:* 2541
Tokyo Rose (July 4, 1916-Sept. 26, 2006) *Notor:* 1036
François Mitterrand (Oct. 26, 1916-Jan. 8, 1996) *20th:* 2769
Walter Cronkite (b. Nov. 4, 1916) *20th:* 872
Maurice Wilkins (Dec. 15, 1916-Oct. 5, 2004) *20th:* 4342
Carson McCullers (Feb. 19, 1917-Sept. 29, 1967) *20th:* 2507
Tom Keating (Mar., 1917-Feb. 12, 1984) *Notor:* 559
Robert Burns Woodward (Apr. 10, 1917-July 8, 1979) *20th:* 4393
Ella Fitzgerald (Apr. 25, 1917-June 15, 1996) *20th:* 1246
I. M. Pei (b. Apr. 26, 1917) *20th:* 3183
John F. Kennedy (May 29, 1917-Nov. 22, 1963) *20th:* 2098
Gwendolyn Brooks (June 7, 1917-Dec. 3, 2000) *20th:* 537
Katharine Graham (June 16, 1917-July 17, 2001) *20th:* 1560
Andrew Wyeth (b. July 12, 1917) *20th:* 4410
Oscar Romero (Aug. 15, 1917-Mar. 24, 1980) *20th:* 3499
Ferdinand Marcos (Sept. 11, 1917-Sept. 28, 1989) *20th:* 2619, *Notor:* 699
Fannie Lou Hamer (Oct. 6, 1917-Mar. 14, 1977) *20th:* 1651
Dizzy Gillespie (Oct. 21, 1917-Jan. 6, 1993) *20th:* 1480
Indira Gandhi (Nov. 19, 1917-Oct. 31, 1984) *20th:* 1385
Heinrich Böll (Dec. 21, 1917-July 16, 1985) *20th:* 411
Gamal Abdel Nasser (Jan. 15, 1918-Sept. 28, 1970) *20th:* 2914
Nicolae Ceauşescu (Jan. 26, 1918-Dec. 25, 1989) *20th:* 704, *Notor:* 190

Richard Girnt Butler (Feb. 23, 1918-Sept. 8, 2004) *Notor:* 157
George Lincoln Rockwell (Mar. 9, 1918-Aug. 25, 1967) *Notor:* 911
Sam Walton (Mar. 29, 1918-Apr. 5, 1992) *20th:* 4213
Betty Ford (b. Apr. 8, 1918) *20th:* 1272
Mary Kay Ash (May 12, 1918-Nov. 22, 2001) *20th:* 145
Julius Rosenberg (May 12, 1918-June 19, 1953) *Notor:* 915
Ann Landers (July 4, 1918-June 22, 2002) *20th:* 2247
Ingmar Bergman (July 14, 1918-July 30, 2007) *20th:* 316
Nelson Mandela (b. July 18, 1918) *20th:* 2583
Frederick Sanger (b. Aug. 13, 1918) *20th:* 3622
Leonard Bernstein (Aug. 25, 1918-Oct. 14, 1990) *20th:* 337
E. Howard Hunt (Oct. 9, 1918-Jan. 23, 2007) *Notor:* 499
Jerome Robbins (Oct. 11, 1918-July 29, 1998) *20th:* 3459
Billy Graham (b. Nov. 7, 1918) *20th:* 1557
Aleksandr Solzhenitsyn (Dec. 11, 1918-Aug. 3, 2008) *20th:* 3783
Kurt Waldheim (Dec. 21, 1918-June 14, 2007) *20th:* 4187
Anwar el-Sadat (Dec. 25, 1918-Oct. 6, 1981) *20th:* 3587
J. D. Salinger (b. Jan. 1, 1919) *20th:* 3609
Jackie Robinson (Jan. 31, 1919-Oct. 24, 1972) *20th:* 3470
Andreas Papandreou (Feb. 5, 1919-June 23, 1996) *20th:* 3106
David Berg (Feb. 18, 1919-Nov., 1994) *Notor:* 87
Eva Perón (May 7, 1919-July 26, 1952) *20th:* 3201, *Notor:* 821
Dame Margot Fonteyn (May 18, 1919-Feb. 21, 1991) *20th:* 1268
Sir Edmund Hillary (July 20, 1919-Jan. 11, 2008) *20th:* 1802
Merce Cunningham (b. Aug. 16, 1919) *20th:* 886
George C. Wallace (Aug. 25, 1919-Sept. 13, 1998) *20th:* 4203, *Notor:* 1087
Sir Godfrey Newbold Hounsfield (Aug. 28, 1919-Aug. 12, 2004) *20th:* 1892
Zhao Ziyang (Oct. 17, 1919-Jan. 17, 2005) *20th:* 4459
Pierre Trudeau (Oct. 18, 1919-Sept. 28, 2000) *20th:* 4076
Mohammad Reza Shah Pahlavi (Oct. 26, 1919-July 27, 1980) *20th:* 2779, *Notor:* 742
Moïse Tshombe (Nov. 10, 1919-June 29, 1969) *20th:* 4091
Said Akbar (c. 1920's?-Oct. 16, 1951) *Notor:* 10
Sun Myung Moon (b. Jan. 6, 1920) *20th:* 2811, *Notor:* 749
Javier Pérez de Cuéllar (b. Jan. 19, 1920) *20th:* 3194
Federico Fellini (b. Jan. 20, 1920-Oct. 31, 1993) *20th:* 1231
Farouk I (Feb. 11, 1920-Mar. 18, 1965) *20th:* 1215
Roberto Calvi (Apr. 13, 1920-June 12, 1982) *Notor:* 170
John Paul II (May 18, 1920-Apr. 2, 2005) *20th:* 2020
François Jacob (b. June 17, 1920) *20th:* 1982
Rosalind Franklin (July 25, 1920-Apr. 16, 1958) *20th:* 1316
Charlie Parker (Aug. 29, 1920-Mar. 12, 1955) *20th:* 3112
Timothy Leary (Oct. 22, 1920-May 31, 1996) *Notor:* 619
Byron De La Beckwith (Nov. 9, 1920-Jan. 21, 2001) *Notor:* 78
George P. Shultz (b. Dec. 13, 1920) *20th:* 3731

1921 - 1930

Akio Morita (Jan. 26, 1921-Oct. 3, 1999) *20th:* 2831
Nexhmije Hoxha (Feb. 7, 1921) *Notor:* 493
Hua Guofeng (b. Feb. 16, 1921) *20th:* 1907
John Rawls (Feb. 21, 1921-Nov. 24, 2002) *20th:* 3391
Jean-Bédel Bokassa (Feb. 22, 1921-Nov. 3, 1996) *Notor:* 113
Satyajit Ray (May 2, 1921-Apr. 23, 1992) *20th:* 3394
Andrei Sakharov (May 21, 1921-Dec. 14, 1989) *20th:* 3602
Suharto (June 8, 1921-Jan. 27, 2008) *20th:* 3901, *Notor:* 1007
John Glenn (b. July 18, 1921) *20th:* 1499
Rosalyn Yalow (b. July 19, 1921) *20th:* 4419
Alexander Dubček (Nov. 27, 1921-Nov. 7, 1992) *20th:* 1042
Fahd (1922 or 1923-Aug. 1, 2005) *20th:* 1195
Ahmed Sékou Touré (Jan. 9, 1922-Mar. 26, 1984) *20th:* 4053

Helen Gurley Brown (b. Feb. 18, 1922) *20th:* 539
Yitzhak Rabin (Mar. 1, 1922-Nov. 4, 1995) *20th:* 3358
Jack Kerouac (Mar. 12, 1922-Oct. 21, 1969) *20th:* 2114
Julius Nyerere (Apr. 13, 1922-Oct. 14, 1999) *20th:* 3004
Jeanne Sauvé (Apr. 26, 1922-Jan. 26, 1993) *20th:* 3652
Iannis Xenakis (May 29, 1922-Feb. 4, 2001) *20th:* 4414
Judy Garland (June 10, 1922-June 22, 1969) *20th:* 1409
Mavis Gallant (b. Aug. 11, 1922) *20th:* 1377
René Lévesque (Aug. 24, 1922-Nov. 1, 1987) *20th:* 2345
Lyndon H. LaRouche, Jr. (Sept. 8, 1922) *Notor:* 606
Norodom Sihanouk (b. Oct. 31, 1922) *20th:* 3740
Christiaan Barnard (Nov. 8, 1922-Sept. 2, 2001) *20th:* 236
Boutros Boutros-Ghali (b. Nov. 14, 1922) *20th:* 464
Salvatore Giuliano (Nov. 16, 1922-July 6, 1950) *Notor:* 413
Charles M. Schulz (Nov. 26, 1922-Feb. 12, 2000) *20th:* 3672
Nikolay Gennadiyevich Basov (Dec. 14, 1922-July 1, 2001) *20th:* 256
Norman Mailer (Jan. 31, 1923-Nov. 10, 2007) *20th:* 2563
Chuck Yeager (b. Feb. 13, 1923) *20th:* 4425
Diane Arbus (Mar. 14, 1923-July 26, 1971) *20th:* 115
Shūsaku Endō (Mar. 27, 1923-Sept. 29, 1996) *20th:* 1155
Nguyen Van Thieu (Apr. 5, 1923-Sept. 29, 2001) *20th:* 2954
Mother Angelica (b. Apr. 28, 1923) *20th:* 90
Henry Kissinger (b. May 27, 1923) *20th:* 2170
Joe Colombo (b. June 16, 1923-May 22 or May 23, 1978) *Notor:* 224
Wojciech Jaruzelski (b. July 6, 1923) *Notor:* 525
Elisabeth Becker (b. July 20, 1923-July 4, 1946) *Notor:* 76
Bob Dole (b. July 22, 1923) *20th:* 1014
Rocky Marciano (Sept. 1, 1923-Aug. 31, 1969) *20th:* 2612
Lee Kuan Yew (b. Sept. 16, 1923) *20th:* 2326
Roy Lichtenstein (Oct. 27, 1923-Sept. 29, 1997) *20th:* 2373
Alan Shepard (Nov. 18, 1923-July 21, 1998) *20th:* 3725
Nadine Gordimer (b. Nov. 20, 1923) *20th:* 1534
Maria Callas (Dec. 2, 1923-Sept. 16, 1977) *20th:* 612
Sam Sheppard (Dec. 29, 1923-Apr. 6, 1970) *Notor:* 945
Bonnie Nettles (1924-June, 1985) *Notor:* 779
Madame Nhu (b. 1924) *Notor:* 786
James W. McCord, Jr. (b. Jan. 26, 1924) *Notor:* 671
Robert Mugabe (b. Feb. 21, 1924) *20th:* 2858, *Notor:* 761
Marlon Brando (Apr. 3, 1924-July 1, 2004) *20th:* 486
J. B. Stoner (Apr. 13, 1924-Apr. 23, 2005) *Notor:* 999
George H. W. Bush (b. June 12, 1924) *20th:* 594
James Baldwin (Aug. 2, 1924-Dec. 1, 1987) *20th:* 201
Mohammad Zia-ul-Haq (Aug. 12, 1924-Aug. 17, 1988) *20th:* 4473
Truman Capote (Sept. 30, 1924-Aug. 25, 1984) *20th:* 644
Jimmy Carter (b. Oct. 1, 1924) *20th:* 666
William H. Rehnquist (Oct. 1, 1924-Sept. 3, 2005) *20th:* 3405
Celia Cruz (Oct. 21, 1924-July 16, 2003) *20th:* 877
Benoit B. Mandelbrot (b. Nov. 20, 1924) *20th:* 2588
Shirley Chisholm (Nov. 30, 1924-Jan. 1, 2005) *20th:* 753
Milton Obote (Dec. 28, 1924-Oct. 10, 2005) *20th:* 3011
D. B. Cooper (mid-1920's-Nov. 24, 1971) *Notor:* 233
Idi Amin (c. 1925-Aug. 16, 2003) *20th:* 80, *Notor:* 20
John DeLorean (Jan. 6, 1925-Mar. 19, 2005) *Notor:* 272
Yukio Mishima (Jan. 14, 1925-Nov. 25, 1970) *20th:* 2763
Maria Tallchief (b. Jan. 24, 1925) *20th:* 3940
John D. Ehrlichman (Mar. 20, 1925-Feb. 14, 1999) *Notor:* 320
Flannery O'Connor (Mar. 25, 1925-Aug. 3, 1964) *20th:* 3017
Pierre Boulez (b. Mar. 26, 1925) *20th:* 452
Malcolm X (May 19, 1925-Feb. 21, 1965) *20th:* 2570
Pol Pot (May 19, 1925-Apr. 15, 1998) *20th:* 3298, *Notor:* 846
Patrice Lumumba (July 2, 1925-c. Jan. 17, 1961) *20th:* 2476
Frantz Fanon (July 20, 1925-Dec. 6, 1961) *20th:* 1212
George Habash (Aug. 2, 1925[?]-Jan. 26, 2008) *20th:* 1626
Jorge Rafael Videla (b. Aug. 2, 1925) *Notor:* 1066
Oscar Peterson (Aug. 15, 1925-Dec. 23, 2007) *20th:* 3226
Peter Sellers (Sept. 8, 1925-July 24, 1980) *20th:* 3695

Margaret Thatcher (b. Oct. 13, 1925) *20th:* 3992
Robert Rauschenberg (Oct. 22, 1925-May 12, 2008) *20th:* 3380
Robert F. Kennedy (Nov. 20, 1925-June 6, 1968) *20th:* 2102
José Napoleon Duarte (Nov. 23, 1925-Feb. 23, 1990) *20th:* 1040
William F. Buckley, Jr. (Nov. 24, 1925-Feb. 27, 2008) *20th:* 561
Kim Dae Jung (b. Dec. 3, 1925) *20th:* 2136
Datuk Seri Mahathir bin Mohamad (b. Dec. 20, 1925) *20th:* 2551
Ta Mok (1926-July 21, 2006) *Notor:* 1017
Pete Rozelle (Mar. 1, 1926-Dec. 6, 1996) *20th:* 3553
Alan Greenspan (b. Mar. 6, 1926) *20th:* 1581
Ralph Abernathy (Mar. 11, 1926-Apr. 17, 1990) *20th:* 11
Jerry Lewis (b. Mar. 16, 1926) *20th:* 2357
Aileen Clarke Hernandez (b. May 23, 1926) *20th:* 1773
Christine Jorgensen (May 30, 1926-May 3, 1989) *20th:* 2053
Marilyn Monroe (June 1, 1926-Aug. 5, 1962) *20th:* 2797
Efraín Ríos Montt (b. June 16, 1926) *Notor:* 899
Hans Werner Henze (b. July 1, 1926) *20th:* 1762
Elisabeth Kübler-Ross (July 8, 1926-Aug. 24, 2004) *20th:* 2207
Leopoldo Galtieri (July 15, 1926-Jan. 12, 2003) *Notor:* 394
Willis A. Carto (b. July 17, 1926) *Notor:* 177
Fidel Castro (b. Aug. 13, 1926 or 1927) *20th:* 691, *Notor:* 185
Jiang Zemin (b. Aug. 17, 1926) *20th:* 2000
John Coltrane (Sept. 23, 1926-July 17, 1967) *20th:* 814
Ruth Ellis (Oct. 9, 1926-July 13, 1955) *Notor:* 327
H. R. Haldeman (Oct. 27, 1926-Nov. 12, 1993) *Notor:* 442
Jeane Kirkpatrick (Nov. 19, 1926-Dec. 7, 2006) *20th:* 2167
Leontyne Price (b. Feb. 10, 1927) *20th:* 3334
Roy Cohn (Feb. 20, 1927-Aug. 2, 1986) *Notor:* 217
Sidney Poitier (b. Feb. 20, 1927) *20th:* 3296
César Chávez (Mar. 31, 1927-Apr. 23, 1993) *20th:* 738
Bob Fosse (June 23, 1927-Sept. 23, 1987) *20th:* 1291
F. Sherwood Rowland (b. June 28, 1927) *20th:* 3547
Althea Gibson (Aug. 25, 1927-Sept. 28, 2003) *20th:* 1474
Günter Grass (b. Oct. 16, 1927) *20th:* 1573
Jean-Marie Bastien-Thiry (Oct. 19, 1927-Mar. 11, 1963) *Notor:* 69
Bhumibol Adulyadej (b. Dec. 5, 1927) *20th:* 363
Bobby Baker (b. 1928) *Notor:* 48
Zulfikar Ali Bhutto (Jan. 5, 1928-Apr. 4, 1979) *20th:* 368
Gabriel García Márquez (b. Mar. 6, 1928) *20th:* 1398
James Earl Ray (Mar. 10, 1928-Apr. 23, 1998) *Notor:* 889
Vincent Gigante (Mar. 29, 1928-Dec. 19, 2005) *Notor:* 407
Maya Angelou (b. Apr. 4, 1928) *20th:* 97
James D. Watson (b. Apr. 6, 1928) *20th:* 4242
Shirley Temple (b. Apr. 23, 1928) *20th:* 3973
Jack Kevorkian (b. May 26, 1928) *Notor:* 567
Maurice Sendak (b. June 10, 1928) *20th:* 3698
Che Guevara (June 14, 1928-Oct. 9, 1967) *20th:* 1609, *Notor:* 436
Jean-Marie Le Pen (b. June 20, 1928) *Notor:* 636
Andy Warhol (Aug. 6, 1928-Feb. 22, 1987) *20th:* 4226
Karlheinz Stockhausen (Aug. 22, 1928-Dec. 5, 2007) *20th:* 3872
Elie Wiesel (b. Sept. 30, 1928) *20th:* 4324
Anne Sexton (Nov. 9, 1928-Oct. 4, 1974) *20th:* 3713
Li Peng (b. Oct., 1928) *20th:* 2367
Helen Frankenthaler (b. Dec. 12, 1928) *20th:* 1304
Robert Joffrey (Dec. 24, 1928-Mar. 25, 1988) *20th:* 2012
Martin Luther King, Jr. (Jan. 15, 1929-Apr. 4, 1968) *20th:* 2147
Claes Oldenburg (b. Jan. 28, 1929) *20th:* 3037
Omar Torrijos (Feb. 13, 1929-July 31, 1981) *20th:* 4048
Frank Gehry (b. Feb. 28, 1929) *20th:* 1438
Joe Gallo (Apr. 7, 1929-Apr. 7, 1972) *Notor:* 392
Audrey Hepburn (May 4, 1929-Jan. 20, 1993) *20th:* 1766
Beverly Sills (May 25, 1929-July 2, 2007) *20th:* 3744
Edward O. Wilson (b. June 10, 1929) *20th:* 4358
Anne Frank (June 12, 1929-Mar., 1945) *20th:* 1301
Jürgen Habermas (b. June 18, 1929) *20th:* 1632
Imelda Marcos (b. July 2, 1929) *Notor:* 702
Hassan II (July 9, 1929-July 23, 1999) *20th:* 1699
Jacqueline Kennedy Onassis (July 28, 1929-May 19, 1994) *20th:* 3045
Ronnie Biggs (b. Aug. 8, 1929) *Notor:* 97
Yasir Arafat (Aug. 24, 1929-Nov. 11, 2004) *20th:* 110
Robert Hawke (b. Dec. 9, 1929) *20th:* 1710
Samuel Joseph Byck (Jan. 30, 1930-Feb. 22, 1974) *Notor:* 162
Sandra Day O'Connor (b. Mar. 26, 1930) *20th:* 3020
Helmut Kohl (b. Apr. 3, 1930) *20th:* 2182

Dolores Huerta (b. Apr. 10, 1930) *20th:* 1915
Anton Szandor LaVey (Apr. 11, 1930-Oct. 29, 1997) *Notor:* 612
Lorraine Hansberry (May 19, 1930-Jan. 12, 1965) *20th:* 1669
Barbara Harris (b. June 12, 1930) *20th:* 1689
H. Ross Perot (b. June 27, 1930) *20th:* 3208
Ahmad Zaki Yamani (b. June 30, 1930) *20th:* 4422
Jacques Derrida (July 15, 1930-Oct. 8, 2004) *20th:* 974
Neil Armstrong (b. Aug. 5, 1930) *20th:* 134
George Soros (b. Aug. 12, 1930) *20th:* 3795
Warren Buffett (b. Aug. 30, 1930) *20th:* 563
Ray Charles (Sept. 23, 1930-June 10, 2004) *20th:* 735
Hafez al-Assad (Oct. 6, 1930-June 10, 2000) *20th:* 153
Laud Humphreys (Oct. 16, 1930-Aug. 23, 1988) *Notor:* 498
Clifford Irving (b. Nov. 5, 1930) *Notor:* 510
Chinua Achebe (b. Nov. 16, 1930) *20th:* 14
G. Gordon Liddy (b. Nov. 30, 1930) *Notor:* 643
Jean-Luc Godard (b. Dec. 3, 1930) *20th:* 1502

1931 - 1940

Alvin Ailey (Jan. 5, 1931-Dec. 1, 1989) *20th:* 36
Mordecai Richler (Jan. 27, 1931-July 3, 2001) *20th:* 3438
Boris Yeltsin (Feb. 1, 1931-Apr. 23, 2007) *20th:* 4431
Toni Morrison (b. Feb. 18, 1931) *20th:* 2834
Mikhail Gorbachev (b. Mar. 2, 1931) *20th:* 1530
Rupert Murdoch (b. Mar. 11, 1931) *20th:* 2876
Jim Jones (May 13, 1931-Nov. 18, 1978) *Notor:* 537
Marshall Applewhite (May 17, 1931-c. Mar. 26, 1997) *Notor:* 28
Fernando Henrique Cardoso (b. June 18, 1931) *20th:* 651
Alice Munro (b. July 10, 1931) *20th:* 2873
Khieu Samphan (b. July 27, 1931) *Notor:* 569
Albert DeSalvo (Sept. 3, 1931-Nov. 25, 1973) *Notor:* 274
Barbara Walters (b. Sept. 25, 1931) *20th:* 4211
Desmond Tutu (b. Oct. 7, 1931) *20th:* 4121
Charles W. Colson (b. Oct. 16, 1931) *Notor:* 225
François Truffaut (Feb. 6, 1932-Oct. 21, 1984) *20th:* 4080
Dame Elizabeth Taylor (b. Feb. 27, 1932) *20th:* 3953
Françoise Dior (Apr. 7, 1932-1993) *Notor:* 283
Athol Fugard (b. June 11, 1932) *20th:* 1354
Megan Terry (b. July 22, 1932) *20th:* 3982
Meir Kahane (Aug. 1, 1932-Nov. 5, 1990) *Notor:* 551
Sir V. S. Naipaul (b. Aug. 17, 1932) *20th:* 2903
Sir John Paul Getty (Sept. 7, 1932-Apr. 16, 2003) *20th:* 1468
Glenn Gould (Sept. 25, 1932-Oct. 4, 1982) *20th:* 1553
Sylvia Plath (Oct. 27, 1932-Feb. 11, 1963) *20th:* 3285
Velma Margie Barfield (Oct. 29, 1932-Nov. 2, 1984) *Notor:* 59
Susan Sontag (Jan. 16, 1933-Dec. 28, 2004) *20th:* 3788
Than Shwe (b. Feb. 2, 1933) *Notor:* 1026
Steven Weinberg (b. May 3, 1933) *20th:* 4277
Louis Farrakhan (b. May 11, 1933) *20th:* 1217
Marie Hilley (June 4, 1933-Feb. 26, 1987) *Notor:* 467
Dianne Feinstein (b. June 22, 1933) *20th:* 1227
Jerry Falwell (Aug. 11, 1933-May 15, 2007) *20th:* 1209
Stanley Milgram (Aug. 15, 1933-Dec. 20, 1984) *Notor:* 729
Ann Richards (Sept. 1, 1933-Sept. 13, 2006) *20th:* 3434
William Luther Pierce III (Sept. 11, 1933-July 23, 2002) *Notor:* 838
Samora Machel (Sept. 29, 1933-Oct. 19, 1986) *20th:* 2515
Reginald Kray (Oct. 24, 1933-Oct. 1, 2000) *Notor:* 591
Ronald Kray (Oct. 24, 1933-Mar. 17, 1995) *Notor:* 593
Akihito (b. Dec. 23, 1933) *20th:* 46
Jean Chrétien (b. Jan. 11, 1934) *20th:* 761
Judith Campbell Exner (Jan. 11, 1934-Sept. 24, 1999) *Notor:* 340
Hank Aaron (b. Feb. 5, 1934) *20th:* 5
Bill Russell (b. Feb. 12, 1934) *20th:* 3565
Bettino Craxi (Feb. 24, 1934-Jan. 19, 2000) *Notor:* 241
Ralph Nader (b. Feb. 27, 1934) *20th:* 2897
Yuri Gagarin (Mar. 9, 1934-Mar. 27, 1968) *20th:* 1370
Gloria Steinem (b. Mar. 25, 1934) *20th:* 3852
Wole Soyinka (b. July 13, 1934) *20th:* 3804
John Tyndall (July 14, 1934-July 19, 2005) *Notor:* 1050
Katherine Davalos Ortega (b. July 16, 1934) *20th:* 3074
Sante Kimes (b. July 24, 1934) *Notor:* 584
Kate Millett (b. Sept. 14, 1934) *20th:* 2746
Angelo Buono, Jr. (Oct. 5, 1934-Sept. 21, 2002) *Notor:* 151
Ulrike Meinhof (Oct. 7, 1934-May 9, 1976) *Notor:* 715
Carl Sagan (Nov. 9, 1934-Dec. 20, 1996) *20th:* 3590
Charles Manson (b. Nov. 12, 1934) *Notor:* 689

Seventh Earl of Lucan (Dec. 18, 1934-Declared legally dead Aug. 11, 1999) *Notor:* 657
James Porter (Jan. 2, 1935-Feb. 11, 2005) *Notor:* 854
Elvis Presley (Jan. 8, 1935-Aug. 16, 1977) *20th:* 3330
Dalai Lama (b. July 6, 1935) *20th:* 902
Geraldine Ferraro (b. Aug. 26, 1935) *20th:* 1242
Frank Robinson (b. Aug. 31, 1935) *20th:* 3467
Werner Erhard (b. Sept. 5, 1935) *Notor:* 329
Luciano Pavarotti (Oct. 12, 1935-Sept. 6, 2007) *20th:* 3159
Gary Player (b. Nov. 1, 1935) *20th:* 3288
Hussein I (Nov. 14, 1935-Feb. 7, 1999) *20th:* 1950
Margita Bangová (c. 1936) *Notor:* 54
Horst Mahler (b. Jan. 23, 1936) *Notor:* 684
Barbara Jordan (Feb. 21, 1936-Jan. 17, 1996) *20th:* 2046
F. W. de Klerk (b. Mar. 18, 1936) *20th:* 948
Valerie Solanas (Apr. 9, 1936-c. Apr. 25, 1988) *Notor:* 982
Elizabeth Dole (b. July 29, 1936) *20th:* 1018
Wilt Chamberlain (Aug. 21, 1936-Oct. 12, 1999) *20th:* 725
Winnie Mandela (b. Sept. 26, 1936) *Notor:* 686
Václav Havel (b. Oct. 5, 1936) *20th:* 1707
Andrei Chikatilo (Oct., 16, 1936-Feb. 14, 1994) *Notor:* 207
Abbie Hoffman (Nov. 30, 1936-Apr. 12, 1989) *Notor:* 483
Jacques Mesrine (Dec. 28, 1936-Nov. 2, 1979) *Notor:* 723
Mengistu Haile Mariam (b. 1937) *20th:* 2701, *Notor:* 719
Ivan Boesky (b. Mar. 6, 1937) *Notor:* 110
Valentina Tereshkova (b. Mar. 6, 1937) *20th:* 3978
Colin Powell (b. Apr. 5, 1937) *20th:* 3321
Saddam Hussein (Apr. 28, 1937-Dec. 30, 2006) *Notor:* 501
Abu Nidal (May, 1937-Aug. 16, 2002) *Notor:* 4
Madeleine Albright (b. May 15, 1937) *20th:* 54
JoAnne Akalaitis (b. June 29, 1937) *20th:* 39
David Hockney (b. July 9, 1937) *20th:* 1845
Bill Cosby (b. July 12, 1937) *20th:* 840
Billy Cannon (b. Aug. 2, 1937) *Notor:* 173
Juan Carlos I (b. Jan. 5, 1938) *20th:* 2060
Manuel Noriega (b. Feb. 11, 1938) *Notor:* 797
Rudolf Nureyev (Mar. 17, 1938-Jan. 6, 1993) *20th:* 3001
Tom Metzger (b. Apr. 9, 1938) *Notor:* 726
Janet Reno (b. July 21, 1938) *20th:* 3416
Alberto Fujimori (b. July 28, 1938) *20th:* 1359, *Notor:* 382
Rod Laver (b. Aug. 9, 1938) *20th:* 2288
Stephen G. Breyer (b. Aug. 15, 1938) *20th:* 520
Robert Nozick (Nov. 16, 1938-Jan. 23, 2002) *20th:* 2999
Ted Turner (b. Nov. 19, 1938) *20th:* 4118
Charles Starkweather (Nov. 24, 1938-June 25, 1959) *Notor:* 993
John E. du Pont (b. c. 1939) *Notor:* 305
Jim Bakker (b. Jan. 2, 1939) *Notor:* 50
Brian Mulroney (b. Mar. 20, 1939) *20th:* 2866
Gro Harlem Brundtland (b. Apr. 20, 1939) *20th:* 544
Ellen Taaffe Zwilich (b. Apr. 30, 1939) *20th:* 4475
Marian Wright Edelman (b. June 6, 1939) *20th:* 1096
Judy Chicago (b. July 20, 1939) *20th:* 750
David H. Souter (b. Sept. 17, 1939) *20th:* 3802
Lee Harvey Oswald (Oct. 18, 1939-Nov. 24, 1963) *Notor:* 807
Margaret Atwood (b. Nov. 18, 1939) *20th:* 169
Harold E. Varmus (b. Dec. 18, 1939) *20th:* 4145
Mou Qizhong (b. 1940 or 1941) *Notor:* 757
Jack Nicklaus (b. Jan. 21, 1940) *20th:* 2959
Saparmurat Niyazov (b. Feb. 19, 1940) *Notor:* 796
Ira Einhorn (b. Mar. 15, 1940) *Notor:* 324
Sadaharu Oh (b. May 10, 1940) *20th:* 3027
Ringo Starr (b. July 7, 1940) *20th:* 266
John Lennon (Oct. 9, 1940-Dec. 8, 1980) *20th:* 266
Pelé (b. Oct. 23, 1940) *20th:* 3187
John Gotti (Oct. 27, 1940-June 10, 2002) *Notor:* 431
Gary Gilmore (Dec. 4, 1940-Jan. 17, 1977) *Notor:* 411

1941 - 1950

Kim Jong Il (b. Feb. 16, 1941) *20th:* 2141, *Notor:* 581
Pete Rose (b. Apr. 14, 1941) *20th:* 3525
Nora Ephron (b. May 19, 1941) *20th:* 1161
Aldrich Ames (b. June 16, 1941) *Notor:* 16
Charles Whitman (June 24, 1941-Aug. 1, 1966) *Notor:* 1101
Twyla Tharp (b. July 1, 1941) *20th:* 3989
Slobodan Milošević (Aug. 20, 1941-Mar. 11, 2006) *20th:* 2756, *Notor:* 735

Bernard Ebbers (b. Aug. 27, 1941) *Notor:* 317
Stephen Jay Gould (Sept. 10, 1941-May 20, 2002) *20th:* 1555
Oscar Arias Sánchez (b. Sept. 13, 1941) *20th:* 121
Jesse Jackson (b. Oct. 8, 1941) *20th:* 1978
Richard Speck (Dec. 6, 1941-Dec. 5, 1991) *Notor:* 986
Muammar al-Qaddafi (b. 1942) *20th:* 3350, *Notor:* 867
Stephen Hawking (b. Jan. 8, 1942) *20th:* 1712
Muhammad Ali (b. Jan. 17, 1942) *20th:* 61
Huey Newton (Feb. 17, 1942-Aug. 22, 1989) *Notor:* 782
John Wayne Gacy (Mar. 17, 1942-May 10, 1994) *Notor:* 387
Aretha Franklin (b. Mar. 25, 1942) *20th:* 1312
Kenneth Lay (Apr. 15, 1942-July 5, 2006) *Notor:* 617
Barbra Streisand (b. Apr. 24, 1942) *20th:* 3892
Theodore Kaczynski (b. May 22, 1942) *Notor:* 547
Paul McCartney (b. June 18, 1942) *20th:* 266
Robert D. Ballard (b. June 30, 1942) *20th:* 215
James Oliver Huberty (Oct. 11, 1942-July 18, 1984) *Notor:* 497
Martin Scorsese (b. Nov. 17, 1942) *20th:* 3681
Shannon W. Lucid (b. Jan. 14, 1943) *20th:* 2460
Janis Joplin (Jan. 19, 1943-Oct. 4, 1970) *20th:* 2043
George Harrison (Feb. 25, 1943-Nov. 29, 2001) *20th:* 266
Ratko Mladić (Mar. 12, 1943) *Notor:* 739
John Major (b. Mar. 29, 1943) *20th:* 2567
Andreas Baader (May 6, 1943-Oct. 18, 1977) *Notor:* 47
William Calley (b. June 8, 1943) *Notor:* 168
Henry Hill (b. June 11, 1943) *Notor:* 465
Vinton Gray Cerf (b. June 23, 1943) *20th:* 707
Jocelyn Burnell (b. July 15, 1943) *20th:* 584
Jean-Claude Killy (b. Aug. 30, 1943) *20th:* 2132
Sani Abacha (Sept. 20, 1943-June 8, 1998) *Notor:* 1
Lech Wałęsa (b. Sept. 29, 1943) *20th:* 4191
Jeffrey MacDonald (b. Oct. 12, 1943) *Notor:* 673
Billie Jean King (b. Nov. 22, 1943) *20th:* 2143
Yoweri Kaguta Museveni (b. 1944) *20th:* 2883
Omar al-Bashir (b. Jan. 1, 1944) *Notor:* 66
Alice Walker (b. Feb. 9, 1944) *20th:* 4196
Sirhan Sirhan (b. Mar. 19, 1944) *Notor:* 965
Charles Sobraj (b. Apr. 6, 1944) *Notor:* 980
Robert Philip Hanssen (b. Apr. 18, 1944) *Notor:* 445
George Lucas (b. May 14, 1944) *20th:* 2450
Mary Robinson (b. May 21, 1944) *20th:* 3474
Reinhold Messner (b. Sept. 17, 1944) *20th:* 2718
Frank Collin (b. Nov. 3, 1944) *Notor:* 222
Kary B. Mullis (b. Dec. 28, 1944) *20th:* 2864
Gilbert Gauthe (b. 1945) *Notor:* 397
Dennis Rader (b. Mar. 9, 1945) *Notor:* 879
Sammy Gravano (b. Mar. 12, 1945) *Notor:* 434
Aung San Suu Kyi (b. June 19, 1945) *20th:* 174
Radovan Karadžić (b. June 19, 1945) *Notor:* 554
Fusako Shigenobu (b. Sept. 3, 1945) *Notor:* 949
Jessye Norman (b. Sept. 15, 1945) *20th:* 2995
Daniel Ortega (b. Nov. 11, 1945) *20th:* 3072
Wilma Mankiller (b. Nov. 18, 1945) *20th:* 2591
Dolly Parton (b. Jan. 19, 1946) *20th:* 3127
Harold Shipman (June 14, 1946-Jan. 13, 2004) *Notor:* 950
Michael Milken (b. July 4, 1946) *Notor:* 731
Leonard Lake (July 20, 1946-June 6, 1985) *Notor:* 602
Bill Clinton (b. Aug. 19, 1946) *20th:* 783
Catharine A. MacKinnon (b. Oct. 7, 1946) *20th:* 2522
Dan White (Sept. 2, 1946-Oct. 21, 1985) *Notor:* 1099
Ted Bundy (Nov. 24, 1946-Jan. 24, 1989) *Notor:* 149
Steven Spielberg (b. Dec. 18, 1946) *20th:* 3811
Kim Campbell (b. Mar. 10, 1947) *20th:* 624
Jerry John Rawlings (b. June 22, 1947) *20th:* 3389
O. J. Simpson (b. July 9, 1947) *Notor:* 958
Assata Olugbala Shakur (b. July 16, 1947) *Notor:* 940
Stephen King (b. Sept. 21, 1947) *20th:* 2151
Hillary Rodham Clinton (b. Oct. 26, 1947) *20th:* 788
Randy Weaver (b. Jan. 3, 1948) *Notor:* 1091
Mikhail Baryshnikov (b. Jan. 28, 1948) *20th:* 253
Charles Taylor (b. Jan. 28, 1948) *Notor:* 1021
Eugene de Kock (b. Jan. 29, 1948) *Notor:* 271
Sir Andrew Lloyd Webber (b. Mar. 22, 1948) *20th:* 2414
Al Gore (b. Mar. 31, 1948) *20th:* 1538
Frank W. Abagnale, Jr. (b. Apr. 27, 1948) *Notor:* 3
Clarence Thomas (b. June 23, 1948) *20th:* 3999
Lynette Fromme (b. Oct. 22, 1948) *Notor:* 377
Pablo Escobar (Jan. 12, 1949-Dec. 2, 1993) *Notor:* 332
Marc Garneau (b. Feb. 23, 1949) *20th:* 1412
Ilich Ramírez Sánchez (b. Oct. 12, 1949) *Notor:* 883
Le Ly Hayslip (b. Dec. 19, 1949) *20th:* 1727
Beant Singh (c. 1950?-Oct. 31, 1984) *Notor:* 962
Jeffrey Lundgren (May 3, 1950-Oct. 24, 2006) *Notor:* 664
Samuel K. Doe (May 6, 1950-Sept. 9, 1990) *Notor:* 288
David Duke (b. July 1, 1950) *Notor:* 303
Arthur Bremer (b. Aug. 21, 1950) *Notor:* 139
Larry C. Ford (Sept. 29, 1950-Mar. 2, 2000) *Notor:* 363

1951 - 1960

Kenneth Bianchi (b. May 22, 1951) *Notor:* 95
Sally Ride (b. May 26, 1951) *20th:* 3447
Ayman al-Zawahiri (b. June 19, 1951) *Notor:* 1135
Jean-Claude Duvalier (b. July 3, 1951) *Notor:* 309
Daulton Lee (b. 1952) *Notor:* 623
Sydney Barrows (b. Jan. 14, 1952) *Notor:* 64
Veerappan (Jan. 18, 1952-Oct. 18, 2004) *Notor:* 1062
Dennis Levine (b. 1953) *Notor:* 642
Robert Jay Mathews (Jan. 16, 1953-Dec. 8, 1984) *Notor:* 712
Christopher John Boyce (b. Feb. 16, 1953) *Notor:* 133
Tony Blair (b. May 6, 1953) *20th:* 385
David Berkowitz (b. June 1, 1953) *Notor:* 91
Benazir Bhutto (June 21, 1953-Dec. 27, 2007) *20th:* 365
Jean-Bertrand Aristide (b. July 15, 1953) *20th:* 124
Jeffrey Skilling (b. Nov. 25, 1953) *Notor:* 967
Oprah Winfrey (b. Jan. 29, 1954) *20th:* 4372
Patty Hearst (b. Feb. 20, 1954) *Notor:* 454
Richard Allen Davis (b. June 2, 1954) *Notor:* 267
Louise Erdrich (b. June 7, 1954) *20th:* 1168
Janet Cooke (b. July 23, 1954) *Notor:* 231
Jonathan Pollard (b. Aug. 7, 1954) *Notor:* 849
Michael Swango (b. Oct. 21, 1954) *Notor:* 1015
Martin Frankel (b. Nov. 21, 1954) *Notor:* 376
Chris Evert (b. Dec. 21, 1954) *20th:* 1191
Steve Jobs (b. Feb. 24, 1955) *20th:* 2006
Terry Nichols (b. Apr. 1, 1955) *Notor:* 790
Shoko Asahara (b. May 2, 1955) *Notor:* 40
Mark David Chapman (b. May 10, 1955) *Notor:* 200
John Hinckley, Jr. (b. May 29, 1955) *Notor:* 470
Tim Berners-Lee (b. June 8, 1955) *20th:* 331
Diane Downs (b. Aug. 7, 1955) *Notor:* 299
Bill Gates (b. Oct. 28, 1955) *20th:* 1421
Aileen Carol Wuornos (Feb. 29, 1956-Oct. 9, 2002) *Notor:* 1108
Joey Buttafuoco (b. Mar. 11, 1956) *Notor:* 159
Björn Borg (b. June 5, 1956) *20th:* 426
Sebastian Coe (b. Sept. 29, 1956) *20th:* 797
George Hennard (Oct. 15, 1956-Oct. 16, 1991) *Notor:* 456
Martina Navratilova (b. Oct. 18, 1956) *20th:* 2922
Baruch Goldstein (Dec. 9 or 12, 1956-Feb. 25, 1994) *Notor:* 427
Osama Bin Laden (b. Mar. 10, 1957) *20th:* 371, *Notor:* 101
Mehmet Ali Ağca (b. Jan. 9, 1958) *Notor:* 8
Bambi Bembenek (b. Aug. 15, 1958) *Notor:* 84
Rigoberta Menchú (b. Jan. 9, 1959) *20th:* 2686
David Koresh (Aug. 17, 1959-Apr. 19, 1993) *Notor:* 589
Maya Ying Lin (b. Oct. 5, 1959) *20th:* 2385
Karla Faye Tucker (Nov. 18, 1959-Feb. 3, 1998) *Notor:* 1044
Jeffrey Dahmer (May 21, 1960-Nov. 28, 1994) *Notor:* 255
Yolanda Saldívar (b. Sept. 19, 1960) *Notor:* 930
Charles Ng (b. Dec. 24, 1960) *Notor:* 784
John Allen Muhammad (b. Dec. 31, 1960) *Notor:* 765

1961 - 1985

Wayne Gretzky (b. Jan. 26, 1961) *20th:* 1585
Diana, Princess of Wales (July 1, 1961-Aug. 31, 1997) *20th:* 989
K. D. Lang (b. Nov. 2, 1961) *20th:* 2256
Satwant Singh (1962-Jan. 6, 1989) *Notor:* 963
Mary Kay Letourneau (b. Jan. 30, 1962) *Notor:* 640
Michael Jordan (b. Feb. 17, 1963) *20th:* 2050
Phoolan Devi (Aug. 10, 1963-July 25, 2001) *Notor:* 275
Byron Looper (b. 1964) *Notor:* 654
Carolyn Warmus (b. Jan. 8, 1964) *Notor:* 1090
Jeff Bezos (b. Jan. 12, 1964) *20th:* 360
Khalid Shaikh Mohammed (b. Mar. 1, 1964, or Apr. 14, 1965) *Notor:* 744
Uday Hussein (June 18, 1964-July 22, 2003) *Notor:* 505
Andrea Yates (b. July 2, 1964) *Notor:* 1113
Paul Bernardo (b. Aug. 27, 1964) *Notor:* 93
Marc Lépine (Oct. 26, 1964-Dec. 6, 1989) *Notor:* 638
Rodney King (b. Apr. 2, 1965) *Notor:* 585
Heidi Fleiss (b. Dec. 30, 1965) *Notor:* 359
Qusay Saddam Hussein (May 17, 1966-July 22, 2003) *Notor:* 501
Eric Rudolph (b. Sept. 19, 1966) *Notor:* 921
Abu Musab al-Zarqawi (Oct. 20, 1966-June 7, 2006) *Notor:* 1132
Nick Leeson (b. Feb. 25, 1967) *Notor:* 624
Pamela Ann Smart (b. Aug. 16, 1967) *Notor:* 971

Timothy McVeigh (Apr. 28, 1968-June 11, 2001) *Notor:* 681
Ramzi Yousef (b. May 20, 1968) *Notor:* 1121
Zacarias Moussaoui (b. May 30, 1968) *Notor:* 758
Mohammed Atta al-Sayed (Sept. 1, 1968-Sept. 11, 2001) *Notor:* 43
Volkert van der Graaf (b. July 9, 1969) *Notor:* 1055
Andrew Cunanan (Aug. 31, 1969-July 23, 1997) *Notor:* 245
Antoinette Frank (b. Jan. 1, 1970) *Notor:* 373
Darlie Routier (b. Jan. 4, 1970) *Notor:* 918
Karla Homolka (b. May 4, 1970) *Notor:* 488
George Rivas (b. May 6, 1970) *Notor:* 901
Yigal Amir (b. May 23, 1970) *Notor:* 22
Matthew F. Hale (b. July 27, 1971) *Notor:* 444
Pete Sampras (b. Aug. 12, 1971) *20th:* 3616
Susan Smith (b. Sept. 26, 1971) *Notor:* 977
Scott Peterson (b. Oct. 24, 1972) *Notor:* 828
Thenmuli Rajaratnam (b. 1974?-May 21, 1991) *Notor:* 882
Tiger Woods (b. Dec. 30, 1975) *20th:* 4390
Mijailo Mijailovic (b. Dec. 6, 1978) *Notor:* 727
John Walker Lindh (b. Feb. 9, 1981) *Notor:* 645
Lee Boyd Malvo (b. Feb. 18, 1985) *Notor:* 765

Geographical Index

List of Countries and Regions

Afghanistan 171
Albania. 172
Algeria 172
Angola 172
Argentina 172
Armenia 172
Australia. 172
Austria 172
Azerbaijan 173
Barbados. 173
Belarus 173
Belgium 173
Bolivia 173
Bosnia. 173
Brazil 173
Bulgaria 173
Burma. 173
Byzantine Empire. . . . 173
Cambodia 173
Canada 173
Central African Republic 174
Chad. 174
Chile. 174
China 174
Colombia 175
Congo. 175
Costa Rica 175
Croatia 175
Cuba 175
Czech Republic and Slovakia. 175
Denmark. 175
Dominican Republic 176
Ecuador 176
Egypt 176
El Salvador. 176
England 176
Estonia 181
Ethiopia 181
Finland 181
France. 181
Georgia, Republic of 185
Germany. 185
Ghana 187
Greece 187
Guatemala 188
Guinea 188
Haiti 188
Hungary 188
Iceland 189
India and Sri Lanka 189
Indonesia 189
Iran 189
Iraq 190
Ireland and Northern Ireland 190
Israel/Palestine 190
Italy 191
Ivory Coast. 193
Jamaica. 193
Japan. 193
Jordan. 193
Kazakhstan 193
Kenya 193
Korea (North and South) 193
Kuwait 193
Laos 193
Latvia 193
Lebanon 193
Liberia 193
Libya 193
Lithuania 193
Madagascar 194
Malawi 194
Malaysia. 194
Mali 194
Martinique 194
Mexico 194
Mongolia 194
Morocco 194
Mozambique. 194
Native America 194
Netherlands 194
New Zealand 195
Nicaragua 195
Nigeria 195
Norway. 195
Oman 195
Ottoman Empire. 195
Pakistan 196
Panama. 196
Paraguay. 196
Peru 196
Philippines 196
Poland. 196
Portugal 196
Roman Empire 196
Roman Republic. 197
Romania 197
Russia. 197
Saudi Arabia. 199
Scandinavia 199
Scotland 199
Senegal. 199
Serbia and Montenegro 199
Sicily 199
Singapore 199
Slovenia 200
Somalia. 200
South Africa 200
Soviet Union 200
Spain. 200
Sudan 201
Sweden. 201
Switzerland. 202
Syria 202
Taiwan 202
Tanzania. 202
Thailand 202
Tibet. 202
Trinidad and Tobago. 202
Tunisia 202
Turkey 202
Turkmenistan 203
Uganda 203
Ukraine. 203
United States 203
Uzbekistan 212
Vatican City 212
Venezuela. 212
Vietnam 212
Wales 212
Yugoslavia 212
Zambia 212
Zimbabwe. 212

Afghanistan
Osama Bin Laden, *20th:* 371, *Notor:* 101
al-Bīrūnī, *MA:* 163
Cyrus the Great, *Anc:* 248
Darius the Great, *Anc:* 251
Humāyūn, *Ren:* 475
Maḥmūd of Ghazna, *MA:* 683
Menander (Greco-Bactrian king), *Anc:* 550
Khalid Shaikh Mohammed, *Notor:* 744
Shāpūr II, *Anc:* 774
Xerxes I, *Anc:* 971

Africa. *See* **Algeria; Angola; Central African Republic; Chad; Congo; Egypt; Ethiopia; Ghana; Guinea; Ivory Coast; Kenya; Liberia; Libya; Madagascar; Malawi;**

MALI; MOROCCO; NIGERIA; OMAN; OTTOMAN EMPIRE; ROMAN EMPIRE; ROMAN REPUBLIC; SENEGAL; SOMALIA; SOUTH AFRICA; SUDAN; TANZANIA; TUNISIA; UGANDA; ZAMBIA; ZIMBABWE

ALBANIA
Ali Paşa Tepelenë, *19th:* 55
Enver and Nexhmije Hoxha, *Notor:* 493
Shabbetai Tzevi, *17th:* 835

ALGERIA
Ferhat Abbas, *20th:* 7
ʿAbd al-Muʾmin, *MA:* 6
Abdelkader, *19th:* 1
ʿAruj, *Notor:* 38
Saint Augustine, *Anc:* 142
Barbarossa, *Ren:* 79
Bernardo Alberto Houssay, *20th:* 1899
Damia al-Kāhina, *MA:* 604
Muḥammad ibn ʿAbd al-Karīm al-Maghīlī, *Ren:* 595
Masinissa, *Anc:* 542
Sophonisba of Numidia, *Anc:* 812
Ṭāriq ibn-Ziyād, *MA:* 1005

AMERICAN COLONIES. ***See*** **UNITED STATES**

ANGOLA
Afonso I, *Ren:* 9
Njinga, *17th:* 687

ARGENTINA
Jorge Luis Borges, *20th:* 430
Leopoldo Galtieri, *Notor:* 394
Che Guevara, *20th:* 1609, *Notor:* 436
Eva Perón, *20th:* 3201, *Notor:* 821
Juan Perón, *20th:* 3205, *Notor:* 823
José de San Martín, *19th:* 1984
Domingo Faustino Sarmiento, *19th:* 2000
Jorge Rafael Videla, *Notor:* 1066

ARMENIA
Viktor A. Ambartsumian, *20th:* 77
Tigranes the Great, *Anc:* 895

ASIA. ***See*** **AFGHANISTAN; ARMENIA; BURMA; BYZANTINE EMPIRE; CAMBODIA; CHINA; INDIA AND SRI LANKA; INDONESIA; JAPAN; KAZAKHSTAN; KOREA; LAOS; MALAYSIA; MONGOLIA; PAKISTAN; PHILIPPINES; SINGAPORE; THAILAND; TURKEY; TURKMENISTAN; UZBEKISTAN; VIETNAM**

ASIA MINOR. ***See*** **BYZANTINE EMPIRE; OTTOMAN EMPIRE; TURKEY**

ASSYRIA. ***See*** **IRAQ**

AUSTRALIA
Sir Edmund Barton, *19th:* 149
Sir Donald G. Bradman, *20th:* 471
Sir Lawrence Bragg, *20th:* 474
Sir Macfarlane Burnet, *20th:* 587
John Curtin, *20th:* 891
Alfred Deakin, *19th:* 623
Sir John Carew Eccles, *20th:* 1089
Herbert Vere Evatt, *20th:* 1188
Baron Florey, *20th:* 1259
Francis Greenway, *19th:* 974
Sir George Grey, *19th:* 981
Robert Hawke, *20th:* 1710
William Morris Hughes, *20th:* 1931
Megan Louise Ireland, *Notor:* 508
Ned Kelly, *Notor:* 562
Rod Laver, *20th:* 2288
Dame Enid Muriel Lyons, *20th:* 2486
Joseph Aloysius Lyons, *20th:* 2489
Daniel Mannix, *19th:* 1492
Sir Robert Gordon Menzies, *20th:* 2707
Rupert Murdoch, *20th:* 2876
Sir Henry Parkes, *19th:* 1739
A. B. Paterson, *19th:* 1758
Abel Janszoon Tasman, *17th:* 905
W. C. Wentworth, *19th:* 2412
Sir George Hubert Wilkins, *20th:* 4339

AUSTRIA
Alfred Adler, *20th:* 33
Alban Berg, *20th:* 309
Friedrich von Beust, *19th:* 222
Josef Breuer, *20th:* 514
Anton Bruckner, *19th:* 329
Martin Buber, *20th:* 554
Charles IV, *MA:* 257
Charles VI, *18th:* 229
Christian von Ehrenfels, *20th:* 1110
Eugen Ehrlich, *20th:* 1113
Fanny Elssler, *19th:* 743
Eugene of Savoy, *18th:* 330
Ferdinand II (1578-1637; Holy Roman Emperor), *17th:* 267
Johann Bernhard Fischer von Erlach, *18th:* 350
Francis Ferdinand, *20th:* 1294
Francis Joseph I, *19th:* 818
Frederick III, *Ren:* 350
Frederick V, *17th:* 293
Sigmund Freud, *20th:* 1323
Karl von Frisch, *20th:* 1335
Kurt Gödel, *20th:* 1510
Joseph Haydn, *18th:* 476
F. A. Hayek, *20th:* 1720
Theodor Herzl, *19th:* 1088
Johann Lucas von Hildebrandt, *18th:* 494
Adolf Hitler, *20th:* 1829, *Notor:* 477
Joseph II, *18th:* 544
Herbert von Karajan, *20th:* 2081
Wenzel Anton von Kaunitz, *18th:* 557
Gustav Klimt, *20th:* 2180
Oskar Kokoschka, *20th:* 2185
František Kupka, *20th:* 2211
Karl Landsteiner, *20th:* 2250
Fritz Lang, *20th:* 2253
Leopold I, *17th:* 526
Konrad Lorenz, *20th:* 2434
Gustav Mahler, *20th:* 2558
Maria Theresa, *18th:* 653
Marie-Antoinette, *18th:* 657, *Notor:* 704

Maximilian, *19th:* 1525
Maximilian II, *Ren:* 650
Lise Meitner, *20th:* 2679
Gregor Mendel, *19th:* 1541
Metternich, *19th:* 1561
Wolfgang Amadeus Mozart, *18th:* 711
Rudolf Nureyev, *20th:* 3001
Georg von Peuerbach, *Ren:* 773
Isidor Isaac Rabi, *20th:* 3355
Rheticus, *Ren:* 823
Rudolf II, *Ren:* 840
Arnold Schoenberg, *20th:* 3664
Erwin Schrödinger, *20th:* 3668
Franz Schubert, *19th:* 2026
Johann Strauss, *19th:* 2188
Bertha von Suttner, *19th:* 2205
Kurt Waldheim, *20th:* 4187
Anton von Webern, *20th:* 4262
Simon Wiesenthal, *20th:* 4328
Ludwig Wittgenstein, *20th:* 4378

AZERBAIJAN
Lev Davidovich Landau, *20th:* 2244

BARBADOS
Stede Bonnet, *Notor:* 117

BELARUS
Menachem Begin, *20th:* 284
Marc Chagall, *20th:* 717
Andrei Gromyko, *20th:* 1600
Chaim Weizmann, *20th:* 4279

BELGIUM. ***See also*** **NETHERLANDS**
Beatrice of Nazareth, *MA:* 144
Catharina van Hemessen, *Ren:* 421
Charles IV, *MA:* 257
Charles Martel, *MA:* 250
Léon Degrelle, *Notor:* 270
Sir Anthony van Dyck, *17th:* 244
Jan and Hubert van Eyck, *MA:* 365
Jean Froissart, *MA:* 392
Frans Hals, *17th:* 352
Jan Baptista van Helmont, *17th:* 361
Audrey Hepburn, *20th:* 1766
Cornelius Otto Jansen, *17th:* 419
Henri-Marie La Fontaine, *20th:* 2231
Orlando di Lasso, *Ren:* 540
Georges Lemaître, *20th:* 2337
Leopold II, *19th:* 1349, *Notor:* 632
René Magritte, *20th:* 2547
Margaret of Austria, *Ren:* 612
Mary of Burgundy, *Ren:* 631
Mary of Hungary, *Ren:* 636
Gerardus Mercator, *Ren:* 678
Dominique Pire, *20th:* 3264
Marguerite Porete, *MA:* 856
Peter Paul Rubens, *17th:* 802
Siger of Brabant, *MA:* 942
Paul-Henri Spaak, *20th:* 3808
Simon Stevin, *Ren:* 912
Andreas Vesalius, *Ren:* 965
Rogier van der Weyden, *MA:* 1092
William of Moerbeke, *MA:* 1105
Adam Worth, *Notor:*1107

BIAFRA. ***See*** **NIGERIA**

BOHEMIA. ***See*** **AUSTRIA; CZECH REPUBLIC AND SLOVAKIA**

BOLIVIA
Che Guevara, *20th:* 1609, *Notor:* 436
Víctor Paz Estenssoro, *20th:* 3172

BOSNIA
Ratko Mladić, *Notor:* 739
Gavrilo Princip, *Notor:* 861

BRAZIL
Fernando Henrique Cardoso, *20th:* 651
Antônio Francisco Lisboa, *18th:* 608
Joaquim Maria Machado de Assis, *19th:* 1449
Oscar Niemeyer, *20th:* 2967
Pedro I, *19th:* 1763
Pedro II, *19th:* 1766
Pelé, *20th:* 3187
André Rebouças, *19th:* 1869
Alberto Santos-Dumont, *20th:* 3632
Getúlio Vargas, *Notor:* 1059
António Vieira, *17th:* 959
Heitor Villa-Lobos, *20th:* 4163

BRITISH ISLES. ***See*** **ENGLAND; IRELAND AND NORTHERN IRELAND; SCOTLAND; WALES**

BULGARIA
Boris I of Bulgaria, *MA:* 189
Charles IV, *MA:* 257

BURMA
Alaungpaya, *18th:* 29
Aung San Suu Kyi, *20th:* 174
Ne Win, *Notor:* 773
Than Shwe, *Notor:* 1026
U Thant, *20th:* 3986

BYZANTINE EMPIRE
Anna, Princess of the Byzantine Empire, *MA:* 86
Anna Comnena, *MA:* 89
Basil the Macedonian, *MA:* 133
Saint Cyril, *MA:* 294
Saint Methodius, *MA:* 294
Heraclius, *MA:* 505
Saint Irene, *MA:* 548
Justin II, *Notor:* 546
Justinian I, *MA:* 598
Paul of Aegina, *MA:* 814
Priscian, *MA:* 859
Michael Psellus, *MA:* 863
Sergius I, *MA:* 933
Theodora, *MA:* 1008, *Notor:* 1028
Theophanes the Confessor, *MA:* 1020

CAMBODIA
Hun Sen, *20th:* 1942
Khieu Samphan, *Notor:* 569
Pol Pot, *20th:* 3298, *Notor:* 846
Norodom Sihanouk, *20th:* 3740
Suryavarman II, *MA:* 980
Ta Mok, *Notor:* 1017

CANADA
Lord Amherst, *18th:* 38
Margaret Atwood, *20th:* 169
Robert Baldwin, *19th:* 122

Margita Bangová, *Notor:* 54
Sir Frederick G. Banting, *20th:* 224
Lord Beaverbrook, *20th:* 275
Saul Bellow, *20th:* 288
Paul Bernardo, *Notor:* 93
Sir Robert Laird Borden, *20th:* 423
Saint Marguerite Bourgeoys, *17th:* 75
Joseph Brant, *18th:* 159
Sir Isaac Brock, *19th:* 306
George Brown, *19th:* 316
Kim Campbell, *20th:* 624
Sir Guy Carleton, *18th:* 196
Mary Ann Shadd Cary, *19th:* 431
Samuel de Champlain, *17th:* 139
Jean Chrétien, *20th:* 761
Sir Henry Clinton, *18th:* 256
Charles E. Coughlin, *Notor:* 239
Robertson Davies, *20th:* 917
John G. Diefenbaker, *20th:* 992
Black Donnellys, *Notor:* 294
First Earl of Durham, *19th:* 708
Bernard Ebbers, *Notor:* 317
John Kenneth Galbraith, *20th:* 1374
Mavis Gallant, *20th:* 1377
Marc Garneau, *20th:* 1412
Sir Humphrey Gilbert, *Ren:* 378
Glenn Gould, *20th:* 1553
Wayne Gretzky, *20th:* 1585
Gerhard Herzberg, *20th:* 1783
Karla Homolka, *Notor:* 488
William Howe, *18th:* 510
Pierre Le Moyne d'Iberville, *17th:* 401
Anna Jameson, *19th:* 1217
Saint Isaac Jogues, *17th:* 423
William Lyon Mackenzie King, *20th:* 2155
K. D. Lang, *20th:* 2256
Sieur de La Salle, *17th:* 490
Sir Wilfrid Laurier, *20th:* 2281
François Laval, *17th:* 498
Bonar Law, *20th:* 2292
Anna Leonowens, *19th:* 1346
Marc Lépine, *Notor:* 638
René Lévesque, *20th:* 2345
Sir John Alexander Macdonald, *19th:* 1441
Sir Alexander Mackenzie (c. 1764-1820), *18th:* 629
Alexander Mackenzie (1822-1892), *19th:* 1452
William Lyon Mackenzie, *19th:* 1454
Marshall McLuhan, *20th:* 2529
Sieur de Maisonneuve, *17th:* 574
Marie de l'Incarnation, *17th:* 595
Agnes Martin, *20th:* 2636
Louis-Joseph de Montcalm, *18th:* 692
Susanna Moodie, *19th:* 1593
Brian Mulroney, *20th:* 2866
Alice Munro, *20th:* 2873
James Naismith, *20th:* 2905
Simon Newcomb, *19th:* 1660
Michael Ondaatje, *20th:* 3048
Sir William Osler, *19th:* 1711
Lester B. Pearson, *20th:* 3174
Oscar Peterson, *20th:* 3226
Mary Pickford, *20th:* 3244
Pierre Esprit Radisson, *17th:* 777
Mordecai Richler, *20th:* 3438
Louis Riel, *19th:* 1908
Louis St. Laurent, *20th:* 3597
Jeanne Sauvé, *20th:* 3652
Mack Sennett, *20th:* 3706
Robert W. Service, *20th:* 3708
John Graves Simcoe, *18th:* 919
Thomas Talbot, *19th:* 2219
Thanadelthur, *18th:* 974
David Thompson, *19th:* 2271
Tom Thomson, *20th:* 4010
Catharine Parr Traill, *19th:* 2291
Pierre Trudeau, *20th:* 4076
Sir Charles Tupper, *19th:* 2316
George Vancouver, *18th:* 1006
James Wolfe, *18th:* 1104

Caribbean. ***See*** **Barbados; Cuba; Dominican Republic; Haiti; Jamaica; Martinique; Native America; Trinidad and Tobago**

Central African Republic
Jean-Bédel Bokassa, *Notor:* 113

Central America. ***See*** **Costa Rica; El Salvador; Guatemala; Native America; Nicaragua; Panama**

Central Asia. ***See*** **Afghanistan; Armenia; Byzantine Empire; Kazakhstan; Mongolia; Turkey; Turkmenistan; Uzbekistan**

Chad
Félix Éboué, *20th:* 1085

Chile
Salvador Allende, *20th:* 70
Pablo Neruda, *20th:* 2937
Bernardo O'Higgins, *19th:* 1703
Augusto Pinochet Ugarte, *20th:* 3257, *Notor:* 842

China. ***See also*** **Taiwan; Tibet**
Abahai, *17th:* 1
An Lushan, *MA:* 78
Ban Gu, *Anc:* 149
Ban Zhao, *Anc:* 152
Bodhidharma, *Anc:* 160
Pearl S. Buck, *20th:* 557
Cao Cao, *Anc:* 182
Cao Xueqin, *18th:* 194
Chen Duxiu, *20th:* 741
Chen Shu, *17th:* 156
Cheng I Sao, *Notor:* 205
Chiang Kai-shek, *20th:* 746
Chongzhen, *17th:* 160
Cixi, *19th:* 496
Confucius, *Anc:* 236
Dai Zhen, *18th:* 287
Deng Xiaoping, *20th:* 968
Dorgon, *17th:* 234
Du Fu, *MA:* 322
Faxian, *Anc:* 345
Genghis Khan, *MA:* 402, *Notor:* 400
Guo Moruo, *20th:* 1619
Hanfeizi, *Anc:* 379
Hong Xiuquan, *19th:* 1127
Hu Yaobang, *20th:* 1905

Hua Guofeng, *20th:* 1907
Jiang Qing, *Notor:* 528
Jiang Zemin, *20th:* 2000
Jing Ke, *Notor:* 530
Kang Youwei, *19th:* 1252
Kangxi, *17th:* 448
Yoshiko Kawashima, *Notor:* 558
Kublai Khan, *MA:* 626
Laozi, *Anc:* 502
Li Bo, *MA:* 653
Li Hongzhang, *19th:* 1363
Li Peng, *20th:* 2367
Li Qingzhao, *MA:* 656
Lin Biao, *20th:* 2381
Lin Zexu, *19th:* 1376
Liu Shaoqi, *20th:* 2408
Liu Yin, *17th:* 540
Lu Xun, *20th:* 2447
Henry R. Luce, *20th:* 2456
Ma Yuan, *MA:* 677
Mao Zedong, *20th:* 2601, *Notor:* 691
Mencius, *Anc:* 552
Mi Fei, *MA:* 718
Mou Qizhong, *Notor:* 757
Mozi, *Anc:* 576
Ouyang Xiu, *MA:* 808
I. M. Pei, *20th:* 3183
Peng Dehuai, *20th:* 3191
Puyi, *Notor:* 864
Qianlong, *18th:* 817
Qu Yuan, *Anc:* 732
Matteo Ricci, *Ren:* 825
Shi Huangdi, *Anc:* 779, *Notor:* 947
Shunzhi, *17th:* 848
Sima Guang, *MA:* 945
Sima Qian, *Anc:* 782
Sima Xiangru, *Anc:* 785
Sorghaghtani Beki, *MA:* 954
Su Dongpo, *MA:* 968
Sun Yat-sen, *20th:* 3913
Taizong, *MA:* 993
Tao Qian, *Anc:* 843
Tianqi, *17th:* 911
Wang Anshi, *MA:* 1079
Wang Bi, *Anc:* 950
Wang Chong, *Anc:* 953
Wang Fuzhi, *17th:* 972
Wang Jingwei, *20th:* 4220
Wang Wei, *MA:* 1085
Wang Xizhi, *Anc:* 955
Wang Yangming, *Ren:* 986
Wang Zhenyi, *18th:* 1038
Wu Hou, *MA:* 1127
Wudi, *Anc:* 958
Xia Gui, *MA:* 1134
Xiaozong, *Ren:* 1003
Xie Lingyun, *Anc:* 975
Xuanzang, *MA:* 1136
Xunzi, *Anc:* 978
Yan Liben, *MA:* 1140
Yo Fei, *MA:* 1145
Yonglo, *MA:* 1147
Yongzheng, *18th:* 1113
Yuan Shikai, *Notor:* 1122
Zeng Guofan, *19th:* 2483
Zhang Zhidong, *19th:* 2486
Zhao Ziyang, *20th:* 4459
Zheng Chenggong, *17th:* 1001
Zheng He, *MA:* 1156
Zhengde, *Ren:* 1008
Zhou Enlai, *20th:* 4461
Zhu De, *20th:* 4465
Zhu Xi, *MA:* 1159
Zhuangzi, *Anc:* 989

COLOMBIA
Simón Bolívar, *19th:* 267
Pablo Escobar, *Notor:* 332
Gabriel García Márquez, *20th:* 1398

CONGO
Mobutu Sese Seko, *20th:* 2773, *Notor:* 740
Patrice Lumumba, *20th:* 2476
Moïse Tshombe, *20th:* 4091

COSTA RICA
Oscar Arias Sánchez, *20th:* 121

CROATIA
Ante Pavelić, *Notor:* 813
Tito, *20th:* 4034, *Notor:* 1032

CUBA
Fulgencio Batista y Zaldívar, *Notor:* 73
Fidel Castro, *20th:* 691, *Notor:* 185
Celia Cruz, *20th:* 877
Che Guevara, *20th:* 1609, *Notor:* 436
José Martí, *19th:* 1503

CZECH REPUBLIC AND SLOVAKIA
Edvard Beneš, *20th:* 299
Maurycy Beniowski, *Notor:* 85
Karel Čapek, *20th:* 638
Charles IV, *MA:* 257
Saint Cyril, *MA:* 294
Alexander Dubček, *20th:* 1042
Antonín Dvořák, *19th:* 711
Elizabeth Stuart, *17th:* 253
Frederick V, *17th:* 293
Genseric, *Anc:* 351
Kurt Gödel, *20th:* 1510
Václav Havel, *20th:* 1707
Jan Hus, *MA:* 522
Edmund Husserl, *20th:* 1955
Leoš Janáček, *20th:* 1989
Franz Kafka, *20th:* 2066
Jan Komenský, *17th:* 469
František Kupka, *20th:* 2211
Rudolf Laban, *20th:* 2221
Saint László I, *MA:* 637
Leopold I, *17th:* 526
Saint Ludmilla, *MA:* 670
Victor Lustig, *Notor:* 665
Tomáš Masaryk, *20th:* 2639
Maximilian II, *Ren:* 650
Saint Methodius, *MA:* 294
Martina Navratilova, *20th:* 2922
Rainer Maria Rilke, *20th:* 3454
Rudolf II, *Ren:* 840
Prince Rupert, *17th:* 805
Vladislav II, *Ren:* 983
Albrecht Wenzel von Wallenstein, *17th:* 966
Wenceslaus, *MA:* 1088
Max Wertheimer, *20th:* 4293
Jan Žižka, *MA:* 1162

CZECHOSLOVAKIA. ***See*** **CZECH REPUBLIC AND SLOVAKIA**

DENMARK
Hans Christian Andersen, *19th:* 61
Vitus Jonassen Bering, *18th:* 108
Niels Bohr, *20th:* 408

Sophie Brahe, *Ren:* 126
Tycho Brahe, *Ren:* 128
Canute the Great, *MA:* 221
Christian VII, *Notor:* 208
Carl Theodor Dreyer, *20th:* 1037
Søren Kierkegaard, *19th:* 1278
August Krogh, *20th:* 2204
Margaret of Denmark, Norway, and Sweden, *MA:* 689
Theodor Mommsen, *19th:* 1582
Barthold Georg Niebuhr, *19th:* 1673
Carl Nielsen, *20th:* 2965
Knud Johan Victor Rasmussen, *20th:* 3377
Saxo Grammaticus, *MA:* 927
Nicolaus Steno, *17th:* 881
Valdemar II, *MA:* 1047

DOMINICAN REPUBLIC
Rafael Trujillo, *20th:* 4084, *Notor:* 1042

DUTCH EAST INDIES. *See* **INDONESIA**

EAST ASIA. *See* **CHINA; JAPAN; KOREA; MONGOLIA**

ECUADOR
Simón Bolívar, *19th:* 267

EGYPT
Aaron, *Anc:* 1
Muḥammad ʿAbduh, *19th:* 4
Akhenaton, *Anc:* 26
Alhazen, *MA:* 66
Amenhotep III, *Anc:* 45
Saint Anthony, *Anc:* 60
Apollonius of Perga, *Anc:* 76
Arsinoe II Philadelphus, *Anc:* 105
Saint Athanasius of Alexandria, *Anc:* 132
Mohammed Atta al-Sayed, *Notor:* 43
Baybars I, *MA:* 139
Berenice II, *Anc:* 157
Boutros Boutros-Ghali, *20th:* 464
Callimachus, *Anc:* 179
Cleopatra VII, *Anc:* 229
Ctesibius of Alexandria, *Anc:* 247
Darius the Great, *Anc:* 251
Eratosthenes of Cyrene, *Anc:* 314
Euclid, *Anc:* 317
Farouk I, *20th:* 1215
Hatshepsut, *Anc:* 388
Hero of Alexandria, *Anc:* 401
Herophilus, *Anc:* 410
Hypatia, *Anc:* 434
Ibn Khaldūn, *MA:* 536
Imhotep, *Anc:* 439
Naguib Mahfouz, *20th:* 2553
Moses Maimonides, *MA:* 686
al-Masʿūdī, *MA:* 703
Menes, *Anc:* 556
Menkaure, *Anc:* 558
Montuhotep II, *Anc:* 570
Moses, *Anc:* 572
Muḥammad ʿAlī Pasha, *19th:* 1620
Gamal Abdel Nasser, *20th:* 2914
Nefertari, *Anc:* 585
Nefertiti, *Anc:* 587
Origen, *Anc:* 599
Pappus, *Anc:* 606
Philo of Alexandria, *Anc:* 640
Piye, *Anc:* 655
Plotinus, *Anc:* 668
Psamtik I, *Anc:* 710
Ptolemy (astronomer), *Anc:* 712
Ptolemy Philadelphus, *Anc:* 715
Ptolemy Soter, *Anc:* 719
Qāytbāy, *Ren:* 807
Ramses II, *Anc:* 735
Anwar el-Sadat, *20th:* 3587
Sesostris III, *Anc:* 771
Shabbetai Tzevi, *17th:* 835
Sosigenes, *Anc:* 815
Thutmose III, *Anc:* 885
Tiy, *Anc:* 901
Tutankhamen, *Anc:* 908
Xerxes I, *Anc:* 971
Saʿd Zaghlūl, *20th:* 4439
Ayman al-Zawahiri, *Notor:* 1135
Zenobia, *Anc:* 986
Zoser, *Anc:* 996

EL SALVADOR
José Napoleon Duarte, *20th:* 1040
Oscar Romero, *20th:* 3499

ENGLAND
Fanny Abington, *18th:* 1
Lord Acton, *19th:* 12
Robert and James Adam, *18th:* 3
Joseph Addison, *18th:* 20
Adrian IV, *MA:* 27
Æthelflæd, *MA:* 30
First Viscount Alanbrooke, *20th:* 50
Alcuin, *MA:* 49
John Alden, *17th:* 7
Alfred the Great, *MA:* 63
Lord Allenby, *20th:* 65
Lord Amherst, *18th:* 38
John André, *18th:* 42
Lancelot Andrewes, *17th:* 14
Sir Norman Angell, *20th:* 92
Queen Anne, *18th:* 45
Anne of Cleves, *Ren:* 51
Saint Anselm, *MA:* 92
Lord Anson, *18th:* 49
Eugene Aram, *Notor:* 30
Second Duke of Argyll, *18th:* 53
Sir Richard Arkwright, *18th:* 55
Matthew Arnold, *19th:* 71
Thomas Arnold, *19th:* 76
Francis Asbury, *18th:* 62
Anne Askew, *Ren:* 62
H. H. Asquith, *20th:* 149
Mary Astell, *18th:* 64
Nancy Astor, *20th:* 158
Clement Attlee, *20th:* 165
W. H. Auden, *20th:* 172
Jane Austen, *19th:* 94
Charles Babbage, *19th:* 107
Francis Bacon, *Ren:* 72
Nathaniel Bacon, *17th:* 29
Roger Bacon, *MA:* 127
Sir Robert Stephenson Smyth Baden-Powell, *19th:* 110
Leo Baeck, *20th:* 186
Stanley Baldwin, *20th:* 204
Arthur Balfour, *20th:* 208
John Ball, *MA:* 130
Sir Joseph Banks, *18th:* 80
Anna Barbauld, *18th:* 87
Sir Charles Barry, *19th:* 142
John Baskerville, *18th:* 92
Hester Bateman, *18th:* 95
Richard Baxter, *17th:* 32

Sir William Maddock Bayliss, *20th:* 259
Dorothea Beale, *19th:* 159
Aubrey Beardsley, *19th:* 162
The Beatles, *20th:* 266
Lady Margaret Beaufort, *Ren:* 90
Francis Beaumont, *Ren:* 92
Lord Beaverbrook, *20th:* 275
Johann Joachim Becher, *17th:* 39
Saint Thomas Becket, *MA:* 147
Saint Bede the Venerable, *MA:* 150
Aphra Behn, *17th:* 42
John Bellingham, *Notor:* 83
Jeremy Bentham, *18th:* 104
Tim Berners-Lee, *20th:* 331
Charlotte de Berry, *Notor:* 94
Annie Besant, *19th:* 211
Bess of Hardwick, *Ren:* 103
Sir Henry Bessemer, *19th:* 218
Thomas Betterton, *17th:* 51
Aneurin Bevan, *20th:* 349
Lord Beveridge, *20th:* 352
Ernest Bevin, *20th:* 356
John Biddle, *17th:* 53
Ronnie Biggs, *Notor:* 97
Sir William Blackstone, *18th:* 118
Tony Blair, *20th:* 385
Robert Blake, *17th:* 55
William Blake, *18th:* 121
William Bligh, *18th:* 126, *Notor:* 104
Tamsin Blight, *Notor:* 106
Anthony Blunt, *Notor:* 109
Barbara Leigh Smith Bodichon, *19th:* 263
Sir Thomas Bodley, *Ren:* 108
Anne Boleyn, *Ren:* 111
First Viscount Bolingbroke, *18th:* 135
Margaret Bondfield, *20th:* 414
Saint Boniface, *MA:* 183
William Booth, *19th:* 274
James Boswell, *18th:* 146
Horatio W. Bottomley, *20th:* 445
Boudicca, *Anc:* 163
Matthew Boulton, *18th:* 156
Robert Boyle, *17th:* 78
Mrs. Anne Bracegirdle, *17th:* 82
Henry de Bracton, *MA:* 192
Mary Elizabeth Braddon, *19th:* 284
William Bradford, *17th:* 84
F. H. Bradley, *19th:* 288
Anne Bradstreet, *17th:* 88
Sir Lawrence Bragg, *20th:* 474
Margaret Brent, *17th:* 92
John Bright, *19th:* 302
James Brindley, *18th:* 162
Benjamin Britten, *20th:* 529
The Brontë Sisters, *19th:* 308
Lancelot Brown, *18th:* 165
Sir Thomas Browne, *17th:* 94
Elizabeth Barrett Browning, *19th:* 326
Isambard Kingdom Brunel, *19th:* 333
Marc Isambard Brunel, *19th:* 337
First Duke of Buckingham, *17th:* 96
John Bunyan, *17th:* 100
Richard Burbage, *17th:* 104
Guy Burgess, *Notor:* 152
Hubert de Burgh, *MA:* 211
Edmund Burke, *18th:* 174
Thomas Burnet, *17th:* 106
Frances Hodgson Burnett, *19th:* 357
Charles Burney, *18th:* 177
Fanny Burney, *18th:* 180
Sir Richard Francis Burton, *19th:* 368
Robert Burton, *17th:* 108
Joseph Butler, *18th:* 187
Josephine Butler, *19th:* 371
R. A. Butler, *20th:* 602
Samuel Butler, *19th:* 374
Sir Thomas Fowell Buxton, *19th:* 376
William Byrd, *Ren:* 148
Lord Byron, *19th:* 379
Sebastian Cabot, *Ren:* 159
John Cairncross, *Notor:* 164
George Calvert, *17th:* 119
Thomas Campion, *17th:* 127
George Canning, *19th:* 403
Canute the Great, *MA:* 221
William Carey, *19th:* 409
Sir Guy Carleton, *18th:* 196
Thomas Carlyle, *19th:* 415
Caroline, *18th:* 203
Robert Carr, *17th:* 131
Lewis Carroll, *19th:* 423
Catherine of Aragon, *Ren:* 187
Catherine of Braganza, *17th:* 137
Georgiana Cavendish, *18th:* 215
Henry Cavendish, *18th:* 217
Thomas Cavendish, *Ren:* 193
William Caxton, *Ren:* 196
George Cayley, *19th:* 447
Cædmon, *MA:* 219
William Cecil, *Ren:* 199
Edwin Chadwick, *19th:* 456
Sir James Chadwick, *20th:* 714
Houston Stewart Chamberlain, *Notor:* 196
Joseph Chamberlain, *19th:* 460
Neville Chamberlain, *20th:* 720
Charles Chaplin, *20th:* 731
George Chapman, *Ren:* 213
Hester Chapone, *18th:* 221
Charles I, *17th:* 143
Charles II (of England), *17th:* 147, *Notor:* 201
Charles d'Orléans, *MA:* 247
Queen Charlotte, *18th:* 235
Geoffrey Chaucer, *MA:* 264
G. K. Chesterton, *20th:* 744
Dame Agatha Christie, *20th:* 765
John Reginald Halliday Christie, *Notor:* 210
Christina of Markyate, *MA:* 270
Sarah Churchill, *18th:* 250
Sir Winston Churchill, *20th:* 768
First Earl of Clarendon, *17th:* 166
Sir Henry Clinton, *18th:* 256
Robert Clive, *18th:* 259
Dorothy Clutterbuck, *Notor:* 215
William Cobbett, *19th:* 517
Richard Cobden, *19th:* 520
Sebastian Coe, *20th:* 797
Sir Edward Coke, *17th:* 174
Samuel Taylor Coleridge, *19th:* 529
John Colet, *Ren:* 232
Norman Collins, *20th:* 810
Joseph Conrad, *20th:* 824
John Constable, *19th:* 540
Anne Conway, *17th:* 187
James Cook, *18th:* 270
First Marquess Cornwallis, *18th:* 278

John Cotton, *17th:* 196
Miles Coverdale, *Ren:* 255
Sir Noël Coward, *20th:* 853
Abraham Cowley, *17th:* 199
Hannah Cowley, *18th:* 284
Thomas Cranmer, *Ren:* 266
Richard Crashaw, *17th:* 202
Francis Crick, *20th:* 865
Oliver Cromwell, *17th:* 204
Thomas Cromwell, *Ren:* 269
Aleister Crowley, *Notor:* 242
George Nathaniel Curzon, *20th:* 894
Moll Cutpurse, *Notor:* 250
John Dalton, *19th:* 597
William Dampier, *17th:* 215, *Notor:* 260
Abraham Darby, *18th:* 292
Charles Darwin, *19th:* 603
John Davenport, *17th:* 218
Lady Eleanor Davies, *17th:* 220
John Davis, *Ren:* 276
Sir Humphry Davy, *19th:* 616
John Dee, *Ren:* 278
Daniel Defoe, *18th:* 298
Thomas Dekker, *17th:* 223
Frederick Delius, *20th:* 953
Fourteenth Earl of Derby, *19th:* 642
Diana, Princess of Wales, *20th:* 989
Charles Dickens, *19th:* 655
Paul A. M. Dirac, *20th:* 1004
Benjamin Disraeli, *19th:* 666
William Dodd, *Notor:* 286
John Donne, *17th:* 230
John Dowland, *Ren:* 289
Sir Francis Drake, *Ren:* 291, *Notor:* 301
Michael Drayton, *17th:* 237
John Dryden, *17th:* 239
John Dunstable, *MA:* 333
First Earl of Durham, *19th:* 708
Claude Duval, *Notor:* 306
Sir Anthony Eden, *20th:* 1099
Maria Edgeworth, *19th:* 728
Edward I, *MA:* 343
Edward II, *MA:* 347
Edward III, *MA:* 350
Edward IV, *Ren:* 301
Edward VI, *Ren:* 303
Edward VII, *20th:* 1104
Edward the Confessor, *MA:* 337
Edward the Elder, *MA:* 340
Egbert, *MA:* 353
Eleanor of Aquitaine, *MA:* 355
Sir Edward Elgar, *20th:* 1132
John Eliot, *17th:* 247
George Eliot, *19th:* 740
T. S. Eliot, *20th:* 1139
Elizabeth I (queen of England), *Ren:* 310
Elizabeth II, *20th:* 1143
Elizabeth Stuart, *17th:* 253
Havelock Ellis, *20th:* 1148
Ruth Ellis, *Notor:* 327
Sir Jacob Epstein, *20th:* 1165
Ethelred II, the Unready, *MA:* 362
Sir Arthur Evans, *19th:* 753
John Evelyn, *17th:* 256
Third Baron Fairfax, *17th:* 261
Michael Faraday, *19th:* 759
Dame Millicent Garrett Fawcett, *19th:* 766
Guy Fawkes, *Ren:* 324, *Notor:* 350
John Felton, *Notor:* 352
Nicholas Ferrar, *17th:* 274
Henry Fielding, *18th:* 346
Saint John Fisher, *Ren:* 335
Maria Anne Fitzherbert, *18th:* 358
John Fletcher, *Ren:* 92, *17th:* 277
Baron Florey, *20th:* 1259
Robert Fludd, *17th:* 280
Dame Margot Fonteyn, *20th:* 1268
C. S. Forester, *20th:* 1283
E. M. Forster, *20th:* 1288
William Edward Forster, *19th:* 793
Sir John Fortescue, *Ren:* 340
William Fothergill Cooke, *19th:* 547
Charles James Fox, *18th:* 363
George Fox, *17th:* 283
Sir John Franklin, *19th:* 825
Rosalind Franklin, *20th:* 1316
Sir Martin Frobisher, *Ren:* 352
Elizabeth Fry, *19th:* 839
Roger Fry, *20th:* 1351
Klaus Fuchs, *Notor:* 379
Thomas Gage, *18th:* 384
Thomas Gainsborough, *18th:* 387
Francis Galton, *19th:* 860
Stephen Gardiner, *Ren:* 368
David Garrick, *18th:* 397
George I, *18th:* 400
George II, *18th:* 403
George III, *18th:* 408
George IV, *19th:* 890
George V, *20th:* 1451
George VI, *20th:* 1454
Sir John Paul Getty, *20th:* 1468
Edward Gibbon, *18th:* 415
Orlando Gibbons, *17th:* 309
Sir Humphrey Gilbert, *Ren:* 378
W. S. Gilbert, *19th:* 916
William Gilbert, *Ren:* 381
William Ewart Gladstone, *19th:* 924
First Earl of Godolphin, *18th:* 421
William Godwin, *18th:* 424
Sir George Goldie, *19th:* 940
Oliver Goldsmith, *18th:* 432
Charles George Gordon, *19th:* 949
William Gilbert Grace, *19th:* 955
Cary Grant, *20th:* 1570
Thomas Hill Green, *19th:* 971
Graham Greene, *20th:* 1577
Sir Richard Grenville, *Ren:* 396
Charles Grey, *19th:* 977
Sir Edward Grey, *20th:* 1587
Sir George Grey, *19th:* 981
Lady Jane Grey, *Ren:* 399
Edmund Grindal, *Ren:* 402
Nell Gwyn, *17th:* 342
Sir Robert Abbott Hadfield, *19th:* 1000
H. Rider Haggard, *19th:* 1006
Richard Hakluyt, *Ren:* 419
Matthew Hale, *17th:* 345
Edmond Halley, *17th:* 348
George Frideric Handel, *18th:* 462
Thomas Hardy, *19th:* 1028
James Hargreaves, *18th:* 466
Alfred and Harold Harmsworth, *20th:* 1678
Harold II, *MA:* 457
Frederic Harrison, *19th:* 1044
William Harvey, *17th:* 355
Warren Hastings, *18th:* 469
Stephen Hawking, *20th:* 1712
Nicholas Hawksmoor, *18th:* 472

F. A. Hayek, *20th:* 1720
Sir Edward Heath, *20th:* 1738
Felicia Dorothea Hemans, *19th:* 1076
Hengist, *Anc:* 394
Henrietta Maria, *17th:* 364
Henry I, *MA:* 481
Henry II, *MA:* 483
Henry III, *MA:* 490
Henry IV (of England), *MA:* 493
Henry V, *MA:* 501
Henry VI, *Ren:* 434
Henry VII, *Ren:* 438
Henry VIII, *Ren:* 441
Audrey Hepburn, *20th:* 1766
George Herbert, *17th:* 366
Robert Herrick, *17th:* 368
Caroline Lucretia Herschel, *18th:* 489
William Herschel, *18th:* 492
Thomas Heywood, *17th:* 373
Saint Hilda of Whitby, *MA:* 509
Octavia Hill, *19th:* 1103
Alfred Hitchcock, *20th:* 1825
Thomas Hobbes, *17th:* 378
Leonard T. Hobhouse, *20th:* 1841
David Hockney, *20th:* 1845
Dorothy Crowfoot Hodgkin, *20th:* 1849
William Hogarth, *18th:* 497
Robert Hooke, *17th:* 383
Richard Hooker, *Ren:* 457
Thomas Hooker, *17th:* 386
Jeremiah Horrocks, *17th:* 388
Sir Godfrey Newbold Hounsfield, *20th:* 1892
Catherine Howard, *Ren:* 466
Richard Howe, *18th:* 506
William Howe, *18th:* 510
Sir Fred Hoyle, *20th:* 1902
Henry Hudson, *17th:* 390
Margaret Lindsay Huggins, *19th:* 1144
William Morris Hughes, *20th:* 1931
William Holman Hunt, *19th:* 1157
Anne Hutchinson, *17th:* 394
Aldous Huxley, *20th:* 1961
Thomas Henry Huxley, *19th:* 1161
David Irving, *Notor:* 512
Henry Irving, *19th:* 1175
Isabella of France, *MA:* 552
Jack the Ripper, *Notor:* 519
James I, *17th:* 413
James II, *17th:* 416
Henry James, *19th:* 1206
Edward Jenner, *18th:* 532
King John, *MA:* 584, *Notor:* 534
Samuel Johnson, *18th:* 535
Inigo Jones, *17th:* 436
Ben Jonson, *17th:* 439
William Joyce, *Notor:* 542
Julian of Norwich, *MA:* 595
John Kay, *18th:* 559
Edmund Kean, *19th:* 1254
Tom Keating, *Notor:* 559
John Keats, *19th:* 1259
Fanny Kemble, *19th:* 1267
Margery Kempe, *MA:* 607
Jack Ketch, *Notor:* 565
John Maynard Keynes, *20th:* 2120
William Kidd, *17th:* 464, *Notor:* 576
Mary Kingsley, *19th:* 1281
Rudyard Kipling, *19th:* 1284
Reginald Kray, *Notor:* 591
Ronald Kray, *Notor:* 593
Sir Hans Adolf Krebs, *20th:* 2199
Lady Alice Kyteler, *MA:* 629, *Notor:* 598
Rudolf Laban, *20th:* 2221
John Lambert, *17th:* 483
Joseph Lancaster, *19th:* 1304
Frederick William Lanchester, *20th:* 2240
Lillie Langtry, *19th:* 1312
Sir Edwin Ray Lankester, *19th:* 1315
Lord Lansdowne, *20th:* 2266
Aemilia Lanyer, *Ren:* 535
Harold J. Laski, *20th:* 2269
Hugh Latimer, *Ren:* 543
William Laud, *17th:* 495
Bonar Law, *20th:* 2292
Henry Lawes, *17th:* 502
D. H. Lawrence, *20th:* 2295
John Laird Mair Lawrence, *19th:* 1328
T. E. Lawrence, *20th:* 2303
Thomas Lawrence, *18th:* 583
L. S. B. Leakey, *20th:* 2310
Ann Lee, *18th:* 591
First Duke of Leeds, *17th:* 506
Nick Leeson, *Notor:* 624
Eva Le Gallienne, *20th:* 2330
Earl of Leicester, *Ren:* 553
Charlotte Lennox, *18th:* 594
Anna Leonowens, *19th:* 1346
Bernard Lewis, *20th:* 2351
C. S. Lewis, *20th:* 2353
John Lilburne, *17th:* 534
Joseph Lister, *19th:* 1390
Sir Thomas Littleton, *Ren:* 570
Second Earl of Liverpool, *19th:* 1397
David Lloyd George, *20th:* 2411
Sir Andrew Lloyd Webber, *20th:* 2414
John Locke, *17th:* 542
Sir Joseph Norman Lockyer, *19th:* 1412
Roderigo Lopez, *Notor:* 655
Countess of Lovelace, *19th:* 1420
Richard Lovelace, *17th:* 562
Richard Lower, *17th:* 564
Seventh Earl of Lucan, *Notor:* 657
Roger Ludlow, *17th:* 567
Lord Lugard, *20th:* 2465
Sir Charles Lyell, *19th:* 1423
John MacArthur, *19th:* 1431
Catherine Macaulay, *18th:* 621
Thomas Babington Macaulay, *19th:* 1433
Ramsay MacDonald, *20th:* 2510
Sir Halford John Mackinder, *20th:* 2518
Donald Duart Maclean, *Notor:* 674
Harold Macmillan, *20th:* 2536
Daniel M'Naghten, *Notor:* 677
William Charles Macready, *19th:* 1467
John Major, *20th:* 2567
Sir Thomas Malory, *Ren:* 598
Thomas Robert Malthus, *19th:* 1475
Mary de la Rivière Manley, *18th:* 641
Henry Edward Manning, *19th:* 1489
First Earl of Mansfield, *18th:* 643

Dame Alicia Markova, *20th:* 2627
First Duke of Marlborough, *18th:* 660
Christopher Marlowe, *Ren:* 623
Harriet Martineau, *19th:* 1505
Andrew Marvell, *17th:* 605
Mary I, *Ren:* 639
Mary II, *17th:* 610
Mary of Modena, *17th:* 607
Frederick Denison Maurice, *19th:* 1518
Second Viscount Melbourne, *19th:* 1534
Thomas Middleton, *17th:* 636
James Mill, *19th:* 1571
John Stuart Mill, *19th:* 1574
A. A. Milne, *20th:* 2753
John Milton, *17th:* 639
George Monck, *17th:* 650
Duke of Monmouth, *17th:* 653
Mary Wortley Montagu, *18th:* 687
Simon de Montfort, *MA:* 725
Bernard Law Montgomery, *20th:* 2808
Susanna Moodie, *19th:* 1593
G. E. Moore, *20th:* 2814
Henry Moore, *20th:* 2818
Hannah More, *18th:* 702
Sir Thomas More, *Ren:* 697
Thomas Morley, *Ren:* 701
William Morris, *19th:* 1606
Sir Oswald Mosley, *Notor:* 755
Louis Mountbatten, *20th:* 2853
Lodowick Muggleton, *17th:* 665
Sir V. S. Naipaul, *20th:* 2903
John Nash, *19th:* 1642
Paul Nash, *20th:* 2910
Thomas Nashe, *Ren:* 714
Alexander Neckam, *MA:* 750
Lord Nelson, *19th:* 1656
John Newbery, *18th:* 730
Duchess of Newcastle, *17th:* 676
Thomas Newcomen, *18th:* 733
John Henry Newman, *19th:* 1663
Sir Isaac Newton, *17th:* 679
Ben Nicholson, *20th:* 2956
Florence Nightingale, *19th:* 1684
Lord North, *18th:* 738
Rebecca Nurse, *17th:* 689
Titus Oates, *17th:* 692, *Notor:* 802
William of Ockham, *MA:* 778
James Edward Oglethorpe, *18th:* 742
Anne Oldfield, *18th:* 749
Sir Laurence Olivier, *20th:* 3039
Arthur Orton, *Notor:* 806
George Orwell, *20th:* 3080
William Paley, *18th:* 763
Lord Palmerston, *19th:* 1731
Emmeline Pankhurst, *20th:* 3102
Matthew Parker, *Ren:* 761
Catherine Parr, *Ren:* 764
Walter Pater, *19th:* 1755
William Paterson, *17th:* 716
Charles Peace, *Notor:* 815
John Pecham, *MA:* 817
Sir Robert Peel, *19th:* 1768
Henry Pelham, *18th:* 771
William Penn, *17th:* 724
Dolly Pentreath, *Notor:* 818
Samuel Pepys, *17th:* 728
Fred Perry, *20th:* 3216
Sir William Petty, *17th:* 733
Kim Philby, *Notor:* 836
Philippa of Hainaut, *MA:* 842
Katherine Philips, *17th:* 741
Arthur Phillip, *18th:* 783
William Pitt the Elder, *18th:* 786
William Pitt the Younger, *18th:* 789
Francis Place, *19th:* 1806
Alexander Pope, *18th:* 805
Beatrix Potter, *20th:* 3314
Thomas Pride, *17th:* 756
Joseph Priestley, *18th:* 811
Augustus Welby Northmore Pugin, *19th:* 1838
Henry Purcell, *17th:* 763
E. B. Pusey, *19th:* 1844
John Pym, *17th:* 767
John Quelch, *Notor:* 871
John Rackham, *Notor:* 877
Ann Radcliffe, *18th:* 823
Pierre Esprit Radisson, *17th:* 777
Sir Walter Ralegh, *Ren:* 813
John Ray, *17th:* 782
Mary Read, *Notor:* 891
First Baron Reith of Stonehaven, *20th:* 3410
Sir Joshua Reynolds, *18th:* 836
Cecil Rhodes, *19th:* 1891
David Ricardo, *19th:* 1896
Richard I, *MA:* 891
Richard II, *MA:* 893
Richard III, *Ren:* 828, *Notor:* 896
Samuel Richardson, *18th:* 841
Nicholas Ridley, *Ren:* 833
Robin Hood, *Notor:* 909
Mary Robinson (1758?-1800), *18th:* 848
George Rodney, *18th:* 854
John Roebuck, *18th:* 858
Charles Stewart Rolls, *20th:* 3496
George Romney, *18th:* 862
Sir James Clark Ross, *19th:* 1934
Sir Ronald Ross, *20th:* 3532
Christina Rossetti, *19th:* 1940
Sir Joseph Rotblat, *20th:* 3536
Mary White Rowlandson, *17th:* 798
Frederick Henry Royce, *20th:* 3496
Prince Rupert, *17th:* 805
John Ruskin, *19th:* 1954
John Russell, *19th:* 1958
Ernest Rutherford, *20th:* 3576
First Earl of Salisbury, *Ren:* 844
Third Marquis of Salisbury, *19th:* 1977
Frederick Sanger, *20th:* 3622
Thomas Savery, *17th:* 813
Sir George Savile, *17th:* 815
Elizabeth Sawyer, *Notor:* 935
Friedrich Hermann Schomberg, *17th:* 820
Charlotte Angas Scott, *19th:* 2039
Sir George Gilbert Scott, *19th:* 2044
Peter Sellers, *20th:* 3695
Robert W. Service, *20th:* 3708
Samuel Sewall, *18th:* 893
Anna Seward, *18th:* 897
Jane Seymour, *Ren:* 868
First Earl of Shaftesbury, *17th:* 838
William Shakespeare, *Ren:* 876
Granville Sharp, *18th:* 899
George Bernard Shaw, *20th:* 3716
Percy Bysshe Shelley, *19th:* 2092
Mary Wollstonecraft Shelley, *19th:* 2088
Jack Sheppard, *Notor:* 943

Harold Shipman, *Notor:* 950
Mother Shipton, *Notor:* 952
James Shirley, *17th:* 846
Sarah Siddons, *18th:* 912
Henry Sidgwick, *19th:* 2102
Sir Philip Sidney, *Ren:* 881
John Graves Simcoe, *18th:* 919
Miles Sindercombe, *Notor:* 961
First Viscount Slim, *20th:* 3758
John Smith, *17th:* 861
Frederick Soddy, *20th:* 3778
First Duke of Somerset, *Ren:* 898
John Hanning Speke, *19th:* 2123
Herbert Spencer, *19th:* 2126
Edmund Spenser, *Ren:* 906
Miles Standish, *17th:* 877
First Earl Stanhope, *18th:* 937
Ernest Henry Starling, *20th:* 3830
Richard Steele, *18th:* 941
King Stephen, *MA:* 960
George Stephenson, *19th:* 2167
Marie Stopes, *20th:* 3882
First Earl of Strafford, *17th:* 884
George Edmund Street, *19th:* 2191
William Stukeley, *18th:* 952
Sir John Suckling, *17th:* 893
Arthur Sullivan, *19th:* 916
Graham Vivian Sutherland, *20th:* 3920
Joseph Wilson Swan, *19th:* 2209
Thomas Sydenham, *17th:* 901
Thomas Tallis, *Ren:* 918
Dame Elizabeth Taylor, *20th:* 3953
Edward Teach, *Notor:* 1023
Alfred, Lord Tennyson, *19th:* 2244
Ellen Terry, *19th:* 2248
William Makepeace Thackeray, *19th:* 2257
Margaret Thatcher, *20th:* 3992
David Thompson, *19th:* 2271
Sir Joseph John Thomson, *20th:* 4007
Sweeney Todd, *Notor:* 1033
J. R. R. Tolkien, *20th:* 4038
Cyril Tourneur, *17th:* 928
Arnold Toynbee, *20th:* 4059
Catharine Parr Traill, *19th:* 2291
Richard Trevithick, *19th:* 2294
Anthony Trollope, *19th:* 2299
Frances Trollope, *19th:* 2303
The Tudor Family, *Ren:* 946
Jethro Tull, *18th:* 990
Alan Mathison Turing, *20th:* 4112
J. M. W. Turner, *19th:* 2322
Dick Turpin, *Notor:* 1045
Wat Tyler, *MA:* 1033
William Tyndale, *Ren:* 949
John Tyndall, *Notor:* 1050
James Ussher, *17th:* 938
Sir John Vanbrugh, *18th:* 1002
George Vancouver, *18th:* 1006
Sir Henry Vane the Younger, *17th:* 941
Ralph Vaughan Williams, *20th:* 4147
Queen Victoria, *19th:* 2359
Sir Julius Vogel, *19th:* 2371
Edward Gibbon Wakefield, *19th:* 2378
John Wallis, *17th:* 969
Robert Walpole, *18th:* 1034
John Walter II, *19th:* 2380
Sir William Walton, *20th:* 4216
Mary Ward, *17th:* 974
Earl of Warwick, *Ren:* 989
Beatrice and Sidney Webb, *20th:* 4253
John Webster, *17th:* 976
Josiah Wedgwood, *18th:* 1057
Duke of Wellington, *19th:* 2409
H. G. Wells, *20th:* 4287
Charles Wesley, *18th:* 1061
John Wesley, *18th:* 1064
Charles Wheatstone, *19th:* 547
George Whitefield, *18th:* 1073
Alfred North Whitehead, *20th:* 4311
Sir Frank Whittle, *20th:* 4318
William Wilberforce, *18th:* 1079
Jonathan Wild, *Notor:* 1102
Oscar Wilde, *19th:* 2432
John Wilkes, *18th:* 1083
Maurice Wilkins, *20th:* 4342
John Wilkinson, *18th:* 1086
William III, *17th:* 979
William IV, *19th:* 2445
William the Conqueror, *MA:* 1117
Roger Williams, *17th:* 982
Thomas Willis, *17th:* 985
Sir Harold Wilson, *20th:* 4360
Duke of Windsor, *20th:* 4368
Gerrard Winstanley, *17th:* 988
John Winthrop, *17th:* 990
Ludwig Wittgenstein, *20th:* 4378
James Wolfe, *18th:* 1104
Mary Wollstonecraft, *18th:* 1108
Cardinal Thomas Wolsey, *Ren:* 996
Virginia Woolf, *20th:* 4397
Adam Worth, *Notor:* 1107
Sir Christopher Wren, *17th:* 994
John Wyclif, *MA:* 1130
Joan Wytte, *Notor:* 1110
Charlotte Mary Yonge, *19th:* 2472

ESTONIA

Karl Ernst von Baer, *19th:* 114
Adolf von Harnack, *20th:* 1681
Bernhard Voldemar Schmidt, *20th:* 3659

ETHIOPIA

Ezana, *Anc:* 333
Haile Selassie I, *20th:* 1639
Lalibela, *MA:* 632
Mengistu Haile Mariam, *20th:* 2701, *Notor:* 719
Menelik II, *19th:* 1552
Mentewab, *18th:* 677
Tewodros II, *19th:* 2255
Zara Yaqob, *Ren:* 1006

FINLAND

Alvar Aalto, *20th:* 1
Carl Gustaf Mannerheim, *20th:* 2598
Jean Sibelius, *20th:* 3736

FLANDERS. ***See*** **BELGIUM; NETHERLANDS**

FRANCE. ***See also*** **MARTINIQUE**

Peter Abelard, *MA:* 13
Barbe Acarie, *Ren:* 3
Adam de la Halle, *MA:* 24
Jean le Rond d'Alembert, *18th:* 31
Angélique Arnauld, *17th:* 20

Anne of Austria, *17th:* 18
Anne of Brittany, *Ren:* 48
Guillaume Apollinaire, *20th:* 104
Arnold of Villanova, *MA:* 98
Hubertine Auclert, *19th:* 89
Jean-Sylvain Bailly, *18th:* 77
Honoré de Balzac, *19th:* 126
Djuna Barnes, *20th:* 240
Roland Barthes, *20th:* 246
Jean-Marie Bastien-Thiry, *Notor:* 69
Charles Baudelaire, *19th:* 152
Chevalier de Bayard, *Ren:* 84
Pierre Bayle, *17th:* 36
Pierre-Augustin Caron de Beaumarchais, *18th:* 97
Simone de Beauvoir, *20th:* 271
The Becquerel Family, *19th:* 165
Pierre Belon, *Ren:* 101
Henri Bergson, *20th:* 323
Hector Berlioz, *19th:* 200
Claude Bernard, *19th:* 205
Saint Bernard of Clairvaux, *MA:* 160
Sarah Bernhardt, *19th:* 208
Georges Bizet, *19th:* 241
Louis Blanc, *19th:* 254
Blanche of Castile, *MA:* 166
Louis Blériot, *20th:* 388
Léon Blum, *20th:* 396
Germain Boffrand, *18th:* 132
Nicolas Boileau-Despréaux, *17th:* 63
Marie Anne Victorine Boivin, *19th:* 265
Saint Bonaventure, *MA:* 180
Pierre Bonnard, *20th:* 421
Claude Alexandre de Bonneval, *18th:* 140
Jules Bonnot, *Notor:* 120
Jacques-Bénigne Bossuet, *17th:* 70
Louis-Antoine de Bougainville, *18th:* 150
Nadia Boulanger, *20th:* 449
Pierre Boulez, *20th:* 452
Joseph Boulogne, *18th:* 153
Louyse Bourgeois, *17th:* 73
Saint Marguerite Bourgeoys, *17th:* 75
Louis Braille, *19th:* 299
Constantin Brancusi, *20th:* 478
Georges Braque, *20th:* 493
Fernand Braudel, *20th:* 497
André Breton, *20th:* 510
Henri-Édouard-Prosper Breuil, *20th:* 517
Louis de Broglie, *20th:* 534
Comte de Buffon, *18th:* 171
Jean Buridan, *MA:* 215
Jacques Callot, *17th:* 116
Albert Calmette, *20th:* 618
John Calvin, *Ren:* 163
Jean-Jacques-Régis de Cambacérès, *19th:* 396
Albert Camus, *20th:* 628
Lazare Carnot, *18th:* 200
Jacques Cartier, *Ren:* 178
Henri Cartier-Bresson, *20th:* 671
Cartouche, *Notor:* 178
Sante Jeronimo Caserio, *Notor:* 180
René Cassin, *20th:* 684
Catherine de Médicis, *Ren:* 184
Paul Cézanne, *19th:* 453
Marc Chagall, *20th:* 717
Samuel de Champlain, *17th:* 139
Coco Chanel, *20th:* 727
Jean-Siméon Chardin, *18th:* 223
Charlemagne, *MA:* 242
Charles VI, *Notor:* 203
Charles VII, *Ren:* 224
Charles VIII, *Ren:* 227
Charles XIV John, *19th:* 468
Charles d'Orléans, *MA:* 247
Charles Martel, *MA:* 250
Charles the Bald, *MA:* 254
Charles the Bold, *Ren:* 217
Henri Charrière, *Notor:* 204
Alain Chartier, *MA:* 260
François-René de Chateaubriand, *19th:* 474
Marquise du Châtelet, *18th:* 240
Duchesse de Chevreuse, *17th:* 158
Étienne François de Choiseul, *18th:* 246
Chrétien de Troyes, *MA:* 267
Christine de Pizan, *MA:* 273
André-Gustave Citroën, *20th:* 772
Georges Claude, *20th:* 775
Claude Lorrain, *17th:* 171
Georges Clemenceau, *20th:* 778
Jacques Clément, *Notor:* 214
Saint Clotilda, *MA:* 287
Clovis, *MA:* 290
Jean Cocteau, *20th:* 794
Jean-Baptiste Colbert, *17th:* 180
Colette, *20th:* 804
Auguste Comte, *19th:* 536
The Great Condé, *17th:* 184
Étienne Bonnot de Condillac, *18th:* 263
Marquis de Condorcet, *18th:* 267
Charlotte Corday, *Notor:* 235
Pierre Corneille, *17th:* 193
Pierre de Coubertin, *20th:* 846
François Couperin, *18th:* 281
Gustave Courbet, *19th:* 559
Jacques Cousteau, *20th:* 849
Marie and Pierre Curie, *20th:* 888
Georges Cuvier, *19th:* 585
Cyrano de Bergerac, *17th:* 211
Jacques Daguerre, *19th:* 589
André-Louis Danjon, *20th:* 911
Georges Danton, *18th:* 289
François Darlan, *Notor:* 262
Joseph Darnand, *Notor:* 264
Jean Dauberval, *18th:* 295
Jacques-Louis David, *19th:* 607
Claude Debussy, *20th:* 936
Edgar Degas, *19th:* 632
Eugène Delacroix, *19th:* 635
Robert Delaunay, *20th:* 950
Léo Delibes, *19th:* 639
Maurice Denis, *20th:* 972
Saint Denis, *Anc:* 268
Jacques Derrida, *20th:* 974
René Descartes, *17th:* 226
Dhuoda, *MA:* 310
Diane de Poitiers, *Ren:* 283
Denis Diderot, *18th:* 307
Françoise Dior, *Notor:* 283
Jacques Doriot, *Notor:* 298
Joachim du Bellay, *Ren:* 294
Marcel Duchamp, *20th:* 1051
Alexandre Dumas, *père*, *19th:* 695
Joseph-François Dupleix, *18th:* 311
Émile Durkheim, *20th:* 1065
Gustave Eiffel, *19th:* 734
Eleanor of Aquitaine, *MA:* 355
Paul Éluard, *20th:* 1151

Ferdinand Walsin Esterhazy, *Notor:* 334
Eugene of Savoy, *18th:* 330
Louis Faidherbe, *19th:* 756
Jacqueline Félicie, *MA:* 372
Pierre de Fermat, *17th:* 271
Giuseppe Fieschi, *Notor:* 353
Gustave Flaubert, *19th:* 785
André-Hercule de Fleury, *18th:* 361
Charles Fourier, *19th:* 805
Joseph Fourier, *19th:* 809
Jean-Honoré Fragonard, *18th:* 367
Anatole France, *19th:* 815
Francis I, *Ren:* 346
César Franck, *19th:* 821
François de Salignac de La Mothe-Fénelon, *17th:* 265
Fredegunde, *MA:* 381
Eugène Freyssinet, *20th:* 1326
Saint Fulbert of Chartres, *MA:* 399
Évariste Galois, *19th:* 857
Léon Gambetta, *19th:* 864
Abel Gance, *20th:* 1382
Tony Garnier, *20th:* 1414
Pierre Gassendi, *17th:* 304
Paul Gauguin, *19th:* 879
Charles de Gaulle, *20th:* 1427
Joseph-Louis Gay-Lussac, *19th:* 886
Jean Genet, *20th:* 1445
Balthasar Gérard, *Notor:* 404
Théodore Géricault, *19th:* 898
Sophie Germain, *19th:* 901
Gershom ben Judah, *MA:* 408
André Gide, *20th:* 1477
Étienne Gilson, *20th:* 1488
Jean Giraudoux, *20th:* 1492
Arthur de Gobineau, *Notor:* 415
Jean-Luc Godard, *20th:* 1502
Charles Gounod, *19th:* 952
Marie le Jars de Gournay, *17th:* 314
Gregory of Tours, *MA:* 426
Jean-Baptiste Vaquette de Gribeauval, *18th:* 447
Charlotte Guillard, *Ren:* 413
Charles-Édouard Guillaume, *20th:* 1616
Guy de Chauliac, *MA:* 445
Madame Guyon, *17th:* 339
Claude-Adrien Helvétius, *18th:* 479
Henrietta Maria, *17th:* 364
Henry I, *MA:* 481
Henry II (1133-1189; King of England), *MA:* 483
Henry II (1519-1559; King of France), *Ren:* 423
Henry III, *Ren:* 426
Henry IV, *Ren:* 429
Édouard Herriot, *20th:* 1777
Paul-Henri-Dietrich d'Holbach, *18th:* 501
François Hotman, *Ren:* 461
Victor Hugo, *19th:* 1146
Pierre Le Moyne d'Iberville, *17th:* 401
Jean-Auguste-Dominique Ingres, *19th:* 1171
Eugène Ionesco, *20th:* 1968
Isabella of France, *MA:* 552
François Jacob, *20th:* 1982
James I the Conqueror, *MA:* 571
Pierre Janet, *20th:* 1993
Jean Jaurès, *19th:* 1220
Joan of Arc, *MA:* 578
Joseph-Jacques-Césaire Joffre, *20th:* 2009
Saint Isaac Jogues, *17th:* 423
Frédéric Joliot and Irène Joliot-Curie, *20th:* 2032
Joséphine, *19th:* 1241
Josquin des Prez, *Ren:* 515
Jean-Claude Killy, *20th:* 2132
Jean de La Bruyère, *17th:* 475
Jacques Lacan, *20th:* 2224
Madame de La Fayette, *17th:* 477
Jean Laffite, *Notor:* 600
Jean de La Fontaine, *17th:* 480
Joseph-Louis Lagrange, *18th:* 573
Henri Désiré Landru, *Notor:* 603
Pierre-Simon Laplace, *19th:* 1317
François de La Rochefoucauld, *17th:* 487
Sieur de La Salle, *17th:* 490
Georges de La Tour, *17th:* 493
François Laval, *17th:* 498
Pierre Laval, *20th:* 2285, *Notor:* 609
Antoine-Laurent Lavoisier, *18th:* 579
John Law, *Notor:* 614
Nicolas Leblanc, *18th:* 587
Gustave Le Bon, *20th:* 2320
Charles Le Brun, *17th:* 504
Jacques Lefèvre d'Étaples, *Ren:* 548
Fernand Léger, *20th:* 2334
Henri Lemoine, *Notor:* 627
Ninon de Lenclos, *17th:* 520
Étienne Lenoir, *19th:* 1338
André Le Nôtre, *17th:* 523
Leo IX, *MA:* 644
Jean-Marie Le Pen, *Notor:* 636
Alain-René Lesage, *18th:* 596
Pierre Lescot, *Ren:* 565
Ferdinand de Lesseps, *19th:* 1356
Louis Le Vau, *17th:* 532
Levi ben Gershom, *MA:* 650
Claude Lévi-Strauss, *20th:* 2347
Michel de L'Hospital, *Ren:* 568
Serge Lifar, *20th:* 2378
Duchesse de Longueville, *17th:* 548
Louis IX, *MA:* 666
Louis XI, *Ren:* 574
Louis XII, *Ren:* 577
Louis XIII, *17th:* 551
Louis XIV, *17th:* 554
Louis XV, *18th:* 615
Louis XVI, *18th:* 618
Marquis de Louvois, *17th:* 558
Jean-Baptiste Lully, *17th:* 569
Auguste and Louis Lumière, *20th:* 2471
Victor Lustig, *Notor:* 665
Guillaume de Machaut, *MA:* 679
Madame de Maintenon, *17th:* 572
Sieur de Maisonneuve, *17th:* 574
François de Malherbe, *17th:* 577
André Malraux, *20th:* 2576
Man Ray, *20th:* 2580
The Mancini Sisters, *17th:* 585
Benoit B. Mandelbrot, *20th:* 2588
Édouard Manet, *19th:* 1479
François Mansart, *17th:* 587
Jules Hardouin Mansart, *17th:* 590
Jean-Paul Marat, *18th:* 648, *Notor:* 696

Gabriel Marcel, *20th:* 2609
Margaret of Austria, *Ren:* 612
Marguerite de Navarre, *Ren:* 617
Marie-Antoinette, *18th:* 657, *Notor:* 704
Marie de France, *MA:* 693
Marie de l'Incarnation, *17th:* 595
Marie de Médicis, *17th:* 598
Marie-Thérèse, *17th:* 600
Jacques Maritain, *20th:* 2624
Jacques Marquette, *17th:* 603
Jean Martinet, *Notor:* 707
Mary of Burgundy, *Ren:* 631
Mary of Guise, *Ren:* 633
Mary of Modena, *17th:* 607
Henri Matisse, *20th:* 2649
Guy de Maupassant, *19th:* 1515
François Mauriac, *20th:* 2657
Jules Mazarin, *17th:* 620
Pierre Mendès-France, *20th:* 2698
Maurice Merleau-Ponty, *20th:* 2710
Marin Mersenne, *17th:* 628
Jacques Mesrine, *Notor:* 723
Olivier Messiaen, *20th:* 2715
Jules Michelet, *19th:* 1564
André and Édouard Michelin, *20th:* 2725
Darius Milhaud, *20th:* 2735
Comte de Mirabeau, *18th:* 679
François Mitterrand, *20th:* 2769
Molière, *17th:* 646
Claude Monet, *20th:* 2790
Gaspard Monge, *18th:* 682
Jean Monnet, *20th:* 2793
Michel Eyquem de Montaigne, *Ren:* 689
Marquis de Montalembert, *18th:* 690
Louis-Joseph de Montcalm, *18th:* 692
Montesquieu, *18th:* 695
Jacques-Étienne and Joseph-Michel Montgolfier, *18th:* 698
Duchesse de Montpensier, *17th:* 660
Philippe de Mornay, *Ren:* 703
Johannes de Muris, *MA:* 741
Napoleon I, *19th:* 1636
Napoleon III, *19th:* 1639
Louis-Eugène-Félix Néel, *20th:* 2926
Michel Ney, *19th:* 1667
Nicholas of Autrecourt, *MA:* 761
Nicéphore Niépce, *19th:* 1676
Nostradamus, *Ren:* 728, *Notor:* 799
Jacques Offenbach, *19th:* 1699
Duc d'Orléans, *18th:* 751
Denis Papin, *17th:* 710
Blaise Pascal, *17th:* 713
Louis Pasteur, *19th:* 1751
Nicolas-Claude Fabri de Peiresc, *17th:* 722
Petrus Peregrinus de Maricourt, *MA:* 820
Pérotin, *MA:* 824
Charles Perrault, *17th:* 731
Auguste Perret, *20th:* 3213
Philippe Pétain, *20th:* 3222, *Notor:* 825
Marcel Petiot, *Notor:* 831
Philip II, *MA:* 835
Philip IV the Fair, *MA:* 839
Philip the Good, *MA:* 832
Philippa of Hainaut, *MA:* 842
Edith Piaf, *20th:* 3228
Émile Picard, *20th:* 3234
Camille Pissarro, *19th:* 1799
Henri Poincaré, *19th:* 1816
Raymond Poincaré, *20th:* 3292
Madame de Pompadour, *18th:* 798
Georges Pompidou, *20th:* 3305
Marguerite Porete, *MA:* 856
Francis Poulenc, *20th:* 3318
Nicolas Poussin, *17th:* 749
Pierre-Joseph Proudhon, *19th:* 1834
Marcel Proust, *20th:* 3342
Jean Pucelle, *MA:* 866
Pytheas, *Anc:* 729
François Quesnay, *18th:* 820
François Rabelais, *Ren:* 809
Jean Racine, *17th:* 773
Pierre Esprit Radisson, *17th:* 777
Gilles de Rais, *Notor:* 880
Marquise de Rambouillet, *17th:* 779
Jean-Philippe Rameau, *18th:* 826
Peter Ramus, *Ren:* 817
Ratramnus, *MA:* 879
François Ravaillac, *Notor:* 888
Maurice Ravel, *20th:* 3386
Guillaume-Thomas Raynal, *18th:* 829
Odilon Redon, *19th:* 1875
Ernest Renan, *19th:* 1884
Jean Renoir, *20th:* 3420
Pierre-Auguste Renoir, *19th:* 1888
Cardinal de Richelieu, *17th:* 790
Arthur Rimbaud, *19th:* 1912
Robespierre, *18th:* 844, *Notor:* 907
Comte de Rochambeau, *18th:* 851
Auguste Rodin, *19th:* 1925
Rollo, *MA:* 900
Pierre de Ronsard, *Ren:* 837
Georges Rouault, *20th:* 3541
Henri Rousseau, *19th:* 1951
Jean-Jacques Rousseau, *18th:* 868
Marquis de Sade, *18th:* 875, *Notor:* 926
Louis de Saint-Just, *18th:* 877
Camille Saint-Saëns, *20th:* 3600
Henri de Saint-Simon, *19th:* 1975
George Sand, *19th:* 1987
Nathalie Sarraute, *20th:* 3635
Jean-Paul Sartre, *20th:* 3638
Erik Satie, *20th:* 3641
Comte de Saxe, *18th:* 881
Joseph Justus Scaliger, *Ren:* 855
Friedrich Hermann Schomberg, *17th:* 820
Albert Schweitzer, *20th:* 3678
Madeleine de Scudéry, *17th:* 828
Anaïs Ségalas, *19th:* 2062
Georges Seurat, *19th:* 2074
Madame de Sévigné, *17th:* 833
Emmanuel-Joseph Sieyès, *18th:* 916
Siger of Brabant, *MA:* 942
Claus Sluter, *MA:* 947
Charles Sobraj, *Notor:* 980
Georges Sorel, *20th:* 3792
Madame de Staël, *18th:* 929
First Earl Stanhope, *18th:* 937
Alexandre Stavisky, *Notor:* 998
Gertrude Stein, *20th:* 3845
Stendhal, *19th:* 2160
Suger, *MA:* 971

Duke de Sully, *17th:* 896
Sylvester II, *MA:* 983
Hippolyte Taine, *19th:* 2216
Talleyrand, *19th:* 2221
Tancred, *MA:* 1003
Pierre Teilhard de Chardin, *20th:* 3963
Adolphe Thiers, *19th:* 2263
Alexis de Tocqueville, *19th:* 2280
Henri de Toulouse-Lautrec, *19th:* 2287
Flora Tristan, *19th:* 2297
François Truffaut, *20th:* 4080
Viscount de Turenne, *17th:* 933
Anne-Robert-Jacques Turgot, *18th:* 996
Urban II, *MA:* 1043
Paul Valéry, *20th:* 4136
Edgard Varèse, *20th:* 4142
Sébastien Le Prestre de Vauban, *17th:* 946
Marquis de Vauvenargues, *18th:* 1009
Jean de Venette, *MA:* 1053
Vercingetorix, *Anc:* 935
Charles Gravier de Vergennes, *18th:* 1011
Jules Verne, *19th:* 2354
Eugène François Vidocq, *Notor:* 1067
Élisabeth Vigée-Lebrun, *18th:* 1016
Geoffroi de Villehardouin, *MA:* 1059
François Villon, *Ren:* 973
Saint Vincent de Paul, *17th:* 962
Vincent of Beauvais, *MA:* 1063
Saint Vincent of Lérins, *Anc:* 947
Philippe de Vitry, *MA:* 1065
Voltaire, *18th:* 1026
Édouard Vuillard, *20th:* 4173
Antoine Watteau, *18th:* 1051
Simone Weil, *20th:* 4269
William of Auvergne, *MA:* 1097
William of Auxerre, *MA:* 1101
William of Saint-Amour, *MA:* 1110
William of Saint-Thierry, *MA:* 1114
William the Conqueror, *MA:* 1117
Iannis Xenakis, *20th:* 4414
Émile Zola, *19th:* 2489

GEORGIA, REPUBLIC OF

Viktor A. Ambartsumian, *20th:* 77
Vladimir Mayakovsky, *20th:* 2659
Joseph Stalin, *20th:* 3817, *Notor:* 990

GERMANY

Konrad Adenauer, *20th:* 26
Georgius Agricola, *Ren:* 11
Saint Albertus Magnus, *MA:* 42
Anne of Cleves, *Ren:* 51
Hannah Arendt, *20th:* 118
Arminius, *Anc:* 99
Luise Aston, *19th:* 83
Walter Baade, *20th:* 184
Andreas Baader, *Notor:* 47
Johann Sebastian Bach, *18th:* 71
Leo Baeck, *20th:* 186
Karl Ernst von Baer, *19th:* 114
Klaus Barbie, *Notor:* 57
Johann Bernhard Basedow, *18th:* 89
Johann Joachim Becher, *17th:* 39
Ludwig van Beethoven, *19th:* 175
Emil von Behring, *19th:* 179
Walter Benjamin, *20th:* 306
Carl Benz, *19th:* 197
Friedrich Bergius, *20th:* 313
Eduard Bernstein, *20th:* 334
Friedrich Wilhelm Bessel, *19th:* 215
Hans Albrecht Bethe, *20th:* 341
Otto von Bismarck, *19th:* 238
Gebhard Leberecht von Blücher, *19th:* 260
Franz Boas, *20th:* 400
Jakob Böhme, *17th:* 59
Heinrich Böll, *20th:* 411
Dietrich Bonhoeffer, *20th:* 418
Saint Boniface, *MA:* 183
Martin Bormann, *Notor:* 131
Max Born, *20th:* 437
Walther Bothe, *20th:* 442
Johannes Brahms, *19th:* 296
Willy Brandt, *20th:* 490
Wernher von Braun, *20th:* 500
Bertolt Brecht, *20th:* 504
Martin Bucer, *Ren:* 142
Bernhard von Bülow, *20th:* 569
Rudolf Bultmann, *20th:* 572
Rudolf Carnap, *20th:* 659
Caroline, *18th:* 203
Ernst Cassirer, *20th:* 688
Houston Stewart Chamberlain, *Notor:* 196
Charlemagne, *MA:* 242
Charles IV, *MA:* 257
Charles VI, *18th:* 229
Christian VII, *Notor:* 208
Clovis, *MA:* 290
Ferdinand Julius Cohn, *19th:* 527
Lucas Cranach, the Elder, *Ren:* 262
Gottlieb Daimler, *19th:* 592
Richard Walther Darré, *Notor:* 266
Richard Dedekind, *19th:* 629
Otto Paul Hermann Diels, *20th:* 995
Rudolf Diesel, *19th:* 663
Marlene Dietrich, *20th:* 997
Gerhard Domagk, *20th:* 1021
Karl Dönitz, *Notor:* 292
Albrecht Dürer, *Ren:* 297
Dietrich Eckart, *Notor:* 319
Hugo Eckener, *20th:* 1092
Paul Ehrlich, *20th:* 1115
Adolf Eichmann, *Notor:* 322
Albert Einstein, *20th:* 1118
Elizabeth of Bohemia, *17th:* 250
Friedrich Engels, *19th:* 750
Ludwig Erhard, *20th:* 1173
Max Ernst, *20th:* 1176
Matthias Erzberger, *20th:* 1180
Rudolf Christoph Eucken, *20th:* 1185
David and Johannes Fabricius, *17th:* 259
Daniel Gabriel Fahrenheit, *18th:* 336
Gustav Theodor Fechner, *19th:* 770
Johann Gottlieb Fichte, *18th:* 342
Elisabeth Förster-Nietzsche, *Notor:* 367
Anne Frank, *20th:* 1301
Frederick I, *18th:* 375

Frederick I Barbarossa, *MA:* 384
Frederick III, *Ren:* 350
Frederick V, *17th:* 293
Frederick the Great, *18th:* 378
Frederick William I, *18th:* 381
Frederick William, the Great Elector, *17th:* 290
Gottlob Frege, *19th:* 828
Leo Frobenius, *20th:* 1341
Friedrich Froebel, *19th:* 835
Erich Fromm, *20th:* 1345
Klaus Fuchs, *Notor:* 379
Leonhard Fuchs, *Ren:* 356
Carl Friedrich Gauss, *19th:* 883
Hans Geiger, *20th:* 1440
Rudolf Geiger, *20th:* 1443
Genseric, *Anc:* 351
Gershom ben Judah, *MA:* 408
Christoph Gluck, *18th:* 418
August von Gneisenau, *19th:* 928
Joseph Goebbels, *20th:* 1513, *Notor:* 418
Magda Goebbels, *Notor:* 421
Johann Wolfgang von Goethe, *18th:* 428
Hermann Göring, *20th:* 1545, *Notor:* 428
Gottfried von Strassburg, *MA:* 423
Günter Grass, *20th:* 1573
Jacob and Wilhelm Grimm, *19th:* 992
Hans Jakob Christoffel von Grimmelshausen, *17th:* 324
Walter Gropius, *20th:* 1602
Matthias Grünewald, *Ren:* 405
Heinz Guderian, *20th:* 1606
Otto von Guericke, *17th:* 333
Johann Gutenberg, *MA:* 441
Fritz Haber, *20th:* 1628
Jürgen Habermas, *20th:* 1632
Ernst Haeckel, *19th:* 1002
Otto Hahn, *20th:* 1635
Samuel Hahnemann, *19th:* 1009
George Frideric Handel, *18th:* 462
Karl von Hardenberg, *19th:* 1021
Adolf von Harnack, *20th:* 1681
Nicolai Hartmann, *20th:* 1696
Hartmann von Aue, *MA:* 463
Georg Wilhelm Friedrich Hegel, *19th:* 1065
Martin Heidegger, *20th:* 1742
Heinrich Heine, *19th:* 1069
Ernst Heinkel, *20th:* 1746
Werner Heisenberg, *20th:* 1749
Hermann von Helmholtz, *19th:* 1073
Henry II the Saint, *MA:* 486
Henry IV (of Germany), *MA:* 497
Henry the Lion, *MA:* 473
Hans Werner Henze, *20th:* 1762
Johann Gottfried Herder, *18th:* 486
Caroline Lucretia Herschel, *18th:* 489
William Herschel, *18th:* 492
Gustav Hertz, *20th:* 1780
Gerhard Herzberg, *20th:* 1783
Rudolf Hess, *Notor:* 460
Hermann Hesse, *20th:* 1787
Johannes and Elisabetha Hevelius, *17th:* 371
Reinhard Heydrich, *Notor:* 462
David Hilbert, *20th:* 1800
Hildegard von Bingen, *MA:* 512
Heinrich Himmler, *20th:* 1807, *Notor:* 468
Paul Hindemith, *20th:* 1811
Paul von Hindenburg, *20th:* 1814
Adolf Hitler, *20th:* 1829, *Notor:* 477
Hans Holbein, the Younger, *Ren:* 453
Friedrich von Holstein, *19th:* 1119
Karen Horney, *20th:* 1883
Hrosvitha, *MA:* 516
Balthasar Hubmaier, *Ren:* 472
Alexander von Humboldt, *19th:* 1151
Engelbert Humperdinck, *19th:* 1154
Jan Hus, *MA:* 522
Edmund Husserl, *20th:* 1955
Karl Jaspers, *20th:* 1996
Alfred Jodl, *Notor:* 533
Joseph II, *18th:* 544
Engelbert Kämpfer, *17th:* 445
Immanuel Kant, *18th:* 548
Johannes Kepler, *17th:* 457
Albert Kesselring, *20th:* 2117
Ernst Ludwig Kirchner, *20th:* 2164
Henry Kissinger, *20th:* 2170
Heinrich von Kleist, *19th:* 1289
Friedrich Gottlieb Klopstock, *18th:* 562
Robert Koch, *19th:* 1291
Helmut Kohl, *20th:* 2182
Käthe Kollwitz, *20th:* 2189
Sir Hans Adolf Krebs, *20th:* 2199
Alfred Krupp, *19th:* 1301
Rudolf Laban, *20th:* 2221
Fritz Lang, *20th:* 2253
Helene Lange, *19th:* 1307
Sophie von La Roche, *18th:* 577
Ferdinand Lassalle, *19th:* 1321
Orlando di Lasso, *Ren:* 540
Max von Laue, *20th:* 2278
Gottfried Wilhelm Leibniz, *17th:* 513
Jacob Leisler, *17th:* 518
Leo IX, *MA:* 644
Leopold I, *17th:* 526
Gotthold Ephraim Lessing, *18th:* 598
Justus von Liebig, *19th:* 1366
Wilhelm Liebknecht, *19th:* 1370
Hans Lippershey, *17th:* 537
Louis the German, *MA:* 662
Erich Ludendorff, *20th:* 2462
Ludwig II, *Notor:* 662
Martin Luther, *Ren:* 582
Rosa Luxemburg, *20th:* 2482
Horst Mahler, *Notor:* 684
Thomas Mann, *20th:* 2594
Franz Marc, *20th:* 2606
Andreas Sigismund Marggraf, *18th:* 651
Karl Marx, *19th:* 1508
Maximilian I, *Ren:* 646
Maximilian II, *Ren:* 650
Mechthild von Magdeburg, *MA:* 708
Ulrike Meinhof, *Notor:* 715
Philipp Melanchthon, *Ren:* 664
Erich Mendelsohn, *20th:* 2692
Felix Mendelssohn, *19th:* 1549
Moses Mendelssohn, *18th:* 675
Josef Mengele, *Notor:* 717
Albert A. Michelson, *19th:* 1567
Ludwig Mies van der Rohe, *20th:* 2731

Theodor Mommsen, *19th:* 1582
Hans Joachim Morgenthau, *20th:* 2828
Walther Hermann Nernst, *20th:* 2934
Nicholas of Cusa, *Ren:* 724
Barthold Georg Niebuhr, *19th:* 1673
Martin Niemöller, *20th:* 2971
Friedrich Nietzsche, *19th:* 1680
Max Nordau, *20th:* 2992
Hermann Oberth, *20th:* 3008
Odoacer, *MA:* 782
Wilhelm Ostwald, *20th:* 3088
Otto I, *MA:* 805
Nikolaus August Otto, *19th:* 1714
Johann Pachelbel, *17th:* 708
Franz von Papen, *20th:* 3109
Philip the Magnanimous, *Ren:* 775
Max Planck, *20th:* 3282
Ludwig Prandtl, *20th:* 3327
Samuel von Pufendorf, *17th:* 759
Rabanus Maurus, *MA:* 870
Leopold von Ranke, *19th:* 1860
Erich Maria Remarque, *20th:* 3413
Joachim von Ribbentrop, *Notor:* 894
Leni Riefenstahl, *20th:* 3451
Rainer Maria Rilke, *20th:* 3454
Albrecht Ritschl, *19th:* 1918
John Augustus Roebling, *19th:* 1928
Erwin Rommel, *20th:* 3502
Wilhelm Conrad Röntgen, *19th:* 1931
The Rothschild Family, *19th:* 1947
Peter Paul Rubens, *17th:* 802
Rudolf I, *MA:* 904
Rudolf II, *Ren:* 840
Gerd von Rundstedt, *20th:* 3559
Nelly Sachs, *20th:* 3583
Friedrich Karl von Savigny, *19th:* 2003
Comte de Saxe, *18th:* 881
Gerhard Johann David von Scharnhorst, *19th:* 2006
Max Scheler, *20th:* 3655
Friedrich Wilhelm Joseph von Schelling, *19th:* 2009
Wilhelm Schickard, *17th:* 818
Friedrich Schiller, *18th:* 887
Baldur von Schirach, *Notor:* 937
Friedrich Schleiermacher, *19th:* 2013
Heinrich Schliemann, *19th:* 2016
Bernhard Voldemar Schmidt, *20th:* 3659
Karl Schmidt-Rottluff, *20th:* 3661
Friedrich Hermann Schomberg, *17th:* 820
Arthur Schopenhauer, *19th:* 2019
Clara Schumann, *19th:* 2029
Robert Schumann, *19th:* 2031
Carl Schurz, *19th:* 2035
Heinrich Schütz, *17th:* 825
Karl Schwarzschild, *20th:* 3674
Albert Schweitzer, *20th:* 3678
Hans von Seeckt, *20th:* 3688
Justine Siegemundin, *17th:* 851
The Siemens Family, *19th:* 2105
Otto Skorzeny, *Notor:* 969
Albert Speer, *Notor:* 987
Georg Ernst Stahl, *18th:* 933
Johannes Stark, *20th:* 3827
Hermann Staudinger, *20th:* 3833
Edith Stein, *20th:* 3840
Freiherr vom Stein, *19th:* 2151
Nicolaus Steno, *17th:* 881
Karlheinz Stockhausen, *20th:* 3872
Richard Strauss, *20th:* 3885
Julius Streicher, *Notor:* 1001
Gustav Stresemann, *20th:* 3895
Georg Philipp Telemann, *18th:* 970
Thomas à Kempis, *MA:* 1022
Paul Tillich, *20th:* 4027
Alfred von Tirpitz, *20th:* 4030
Ferdinand Julius Tönnies, *20th:* 4044
Ernst Troeltsch, *20th:* 4069
Walter Ulbricht, *20th:* 4125
Rudolf Virchow, *19th:* 2365
Joachim Wach, *20th:* 4177
Richard Wagner, *19th:* 2374
Winifred Wagner, *Notor:* 1081
Walther von der Vogelweide, *MA:* 1075
Felix Wankel, *20th:* 4224
Carl Maria von Weber, *19th:* 2395
Max Weber, *20th:* 4258
Alfred Wegener, *20th:* 4266
Kurt Weill, *20th:* 4273
August Weismann, *19th:* 2406
Wenceslaus, *MA:* 1088
Max Wertheimer, *20th:* 4293
Horst Wessel, *Notor:* 1097
Widukind, *MA:* 1094
William II, *20th:* 4346
Johann Joachim Winckelmann, *18th:* 1095
Friedrich Wöhler, *19th:* 2456
Max Wolf, *20th:* 4382
Wolfram von Eschenbach, *MA:* 1123
Wilhelm Wundt, *20th:* 4407
Marie Elizabeth Zakrzewska, *19th:* 2481
John Peter Zenger, *18th:* 1116
Ferdinand von Zeppelin, *20th:* 4452
Clara Zetkin, *20th:* 4455
Count von Zinzendorf, *18th:* 1119

GHANA

W. E. B. Du Bois, *20th:* 1046
Jerry John Rawlings, *20th:* 3389

GREECE

Aeschylus, *Anc:* 7
Aesop, *Anc:* 11
Agesilaus II, *Anc:* 14
Alcibiades of Athens, *Anc:* 33, *Notor:* 11
Alcmaeon, *Anc:* 36
Alexander the Great, *Anc:* 39
Ali Paşa Tepelenë, *19th:* 55
Anaxagoras, *Anc:* 52
Anaximander, *Anc:* 55
Anaximenes, *Anc:* 58
Anisthenes, *Anc:* 68
Antigonus I Monophthalmos, *Anc:* 63
Archimedes, *Anc:* 80
Aristippus, *Anc:* 87
Aristophanes, *Anc:* 90
Aristotle, *Anc:* 94
Aristoxenus, *Anc:* 97
Artemisia I, *Anc:* 109

Aspasia of Miletus, *Anc:* 127
Atatürk, *20th:* 162
Barbarossa, *Ren:* 79
Basil the Macedonian, *MA:* 133
Maria Callas, *20th:* 612
Callimachus, *Anc:* 179
Cimon, *Anc:* 213
Cleisthenes of Athens, *Anc:* 221
Cleomenes, *Anc:* 226
Cypselus of Corinth, *Notor:* 251
Saint Cyril, *MA:* 294
Democritus, *Anc:* 261
Demosthenes, *Anc:* 264
Dio Cassius, *Anc:* 274
Diocles of Carystus, *Anc:* 277
Diogenes, *Anc:* 283
Diophantus, *Anc:* 286
Draco, *Anc:* 293
Empedocles, *Anc:* 295
Epaminondas, *Anc:* 303
Epicurus, *Anc:* 307
Erasistratus, *Anc:* 310
Eratosthenes of Cyrene, *Anc:* 314
Euclid, *Anc:* 317
Eudoxus of Cnidus, *Anc:* 320
Eupalinus of Megara, *Anc:* 323
Euripides, *Anc:* 326
Fulvia, *Notor:* 384
Gregory of Nazianzus, *Anc:* 361
Gregory of Nyssa, *Anc:* 363
Heraclitus of Ephesus, *Anc:* 397
Herodotus, *Anc:* 407
Herophilus, *Anc:* 410
Hesiod, *Anc:* 413
Hipparchus, *Anc:* 417
Hippocrates, *Anc:* 420
Homer, *Anc:* 427
İbrahim Paşa, *Ren:* 480
Saint Irenaeus, *Anc:* 442
Isocrates, *Anc:* 450
John of Damascus, *MA:* 587
Nikos Kazantzakis, *20th:* 2087
Leonidas, *Anc:* 505
Lysippus, *Anc:* 523
Menander (dramatist), *Anc:* 547
Menander (Greco-Bactrian king), *Anc:* 550
Ioannis Metaxas, *Notor:* 724
Saint Methodius, *MA:* 294
Miltiades the Younger, *Anc:* 563
Olympias, *Anc:* 597
Andreas Papandreou, *20th:* 3106
Parmenides, *Anc:* 608
Pausanias of Sparta, *Anc:* 615
Pausanias the Traveler, *Anc:* 618
Pericles, *Anc:* 620
Phaedrus, *Anc:* 628
Pheidippides, *Anc:* 630
Phidias, *Anc:* 633
Philip II of Macedonia, *Anc:* 637
Pindar, *Anc:* 646
Pisistratus, *Anc:* 649
Pittacus of Mytilene, *Anc:* 652
Plato, *Anc:* 659
Plutarch, *Anc:* 670
Polybius, *Anc:* 673
Polyclitus, *Anc:* 675
Polycrates of Samos, *Notor:* 850
Polygnotus, *Anc:* 678
Porphyry, *Anc:* 687
Posidonius, *Anc:* 690
Praxiteles, *Anc:* 694
Proclus, *Anc:* 701
Protagoras, *Anc:* 707
Ptolemy Soter, *Anc:* 719
Pyrrhon of Elis, *Anc:* 722
Pythagoras, *Anc:* 725
Sappho, *Anc:* 750
Savitri Devi, *Notor:* 934
Scopas, *Anc:* 761
Seleucus I Nicator, *Anc:* 763
Simonides, *Anc:* 793
Socrates, *Anc:* 799
Solon, *Anc:* 807
Sophocles, *Anc:* 809
Stefan Dušan, *MA:* 957
Strabo, *Anc:* 827
Mother Teresa, *20th:* 3975
Thales of Miletus, *Anc:* 856
Themistocles, *Anc:* 859
Theodore of Mopsuestia, *Anc:* 862
Theophrastus, *Anc:* 872
Thespis, *Anc:* 876
Thucydides, *Anc:* 882
Eleuthérios Venizélos, *20th:* 4157
Xanthippe, *Anc:* 962
Iannis Xenakis, *20th:* 4414
Xenophanes, *Anc:* 965
Xenophon, *Anc:* 968
Yaqut, *MA:* 1143
Alexander and Demetrios Ypsilantis, *19th:* 2478
Zeno of Citium, *Anc:* 981
Zeno of Elea, *Anc:* 984

Guatemala

Pedro de Alvarado, *Ren:* 34
Juan Rodríguez Cabrillo, *Ren:* 161
Che Guevara, *20th:* 1609, *Notor:* 436
Rigoberta Menchú, *20th:* 2686
Efraín Ríos Montt, *Notor:* 899

Guinea

Ahmed Sékou Touré, *20th:* 4053

Haiti

Jean-Bertrand Aristide, *20th:* 124
Henri Christophe, *19th:* 494
Jean-Claude Duvalier, *Notor:* 309
François Duvalier, *20th:* 1069, *Notor:* 307
Guacanagarí, *Ren:* 408
Toussaint Louverture, *18th:* 985
Dominique You, *Notor:* 1117

Hungary

Árpád, *MA:* 105
Attila, *Anc:* 138, *Notor:* 45
Béla Bartók, *20th:* 250
Elizabeth Báthory, *Ren:* 81, *Notor:* 70
Maurycy Beniowski, *Notor:* 85
Charles IV, *MA:* 257
Charles VI, *18th:* 229
Ferenc Deák, *19th:* 619
Saint Elizabeth of Hungary, *MA:* 359
Georg von Hevesy, *20th:* 1792
Elmyr de Hory, *Notor:* 492
Harry Houdini, *20th:* 1889
János Hunyadi, *MA:* 519
Béla Kun, *Notor:* 596
Leopold I, *17th:* 526
Franz Liszt, *19th:* 1393
György Lukács, *20th:* 2468
Mary of Hungary, *Ren:* 636
Matthias I Corvinus, *Ren:* 642
John von Neumann, *20th:* 2943
Max Nordau, *20th:* 2992

Rudolf II, *Ren:* 840
Ignaz Philipp Semmelweis, *19th:* 2064
George Soros, *20th:* 3795
Stephen Báthory, *Ren:* 910
Stephen I, *MA:* 964
Edward Teller, *20th:* 3968
Theodoric the Great, *MA:* 1012
Vladislav II, *Ren:* 983

ICELAND
Halldór Laxness, *20th:* 2308
Leif Eriksson, *MA:* 640
Snorri Sturluson, *MA:* 950

INDIA AND SRI LANKA
Raziya, *MA:* 888
Akbar, *Ren:* 15
ʿAlāʾ-ud-Dīn Muḥammad Khaljī, *MA:* 39
Ānanda, *Anc:* 49
Āryabhaṭa the Elder, *MA:* 108
Asanga, *Anc:* 111
Aśoka, *Anc:* 124
Aśvaghosa, *Anc:* 130
Aurangzeb, *17th:* 23
Sri Aurobindo, *20th:* 177
Bābur, *Ren:* 69
Sir Surendranath Banerjea, *20th:* 221
Zulfikar Ali Bhutto, *20th:* 368
Bodhidharma, *Anc:* 160
Brahmagupta, *MA:* 195
Buddha, *Anc:* 169
Sir Richard Francis Burton, *19th:* 368
Chandragupta Maurya, *Anc:* 202
Robert Clive, *18th:* 259
First Marquess Cornwallis, *18th:* 278
Phoolan Devi, *Notor:* 275
Reginald Dyer, *Notor:* 311
Indira Gandhi, *20th:* 1385
Mahatma Gandhi, *20th:* 1388
Nathuram Vinayak Godse, *Notor:* 416
Gośāla Maskarīputra, *Anc:* 355
Harṣa, *MA:* 460
Warren Hastings, *18th:* 469
Humāyūn, *Ren:* 475
Hyder Ali, *18th:* 522
Ibrāhīm Lodī, *Ren:* 478
Jahāngīr, *17th:* 410
Mohammed Ali Jinnah, *20th:* 2002
Kālidāsa, *Anc:* 496
Kanishka, *Anc:* 499
Sir Sayyid Ahmad Khan, *19th:* 35
William Kidd, *17th:* 464, *Notor:* 576
Rudyard Kipling, *19th:* 1284
Krishnadevaraya, *Ren:* 532
Maḥmūd of Ghazna, *MA:* 683
Menander (Greco-Bactrian king), *Anc:* 550
Sarojini Naidu, *20th:* 2900
Nānak, *Ren:* 707
Dadabhai Naoroji, *19th:* 1634
Jawaharlal Nehru, *20th:* 2929
Michael Ondaatje, *20th:* 3048
Vijaya Lakshmi Pandit, *20th:* 3099
Thenmuli Rajaratnam, *Notor:* 882
Sir Chandrasekhara Venkata Raman, *20th:* 3364
Rāmānuja, *MA:* 876
Mahadev Govind Ranade, *19th:* 1855
Rammohan Ray, *19th:* 1866
Satyajit Ray, *20th:* 3394
Sir Ronald Ross, *20th:* 3532
Śaṅkara, *MA:* 924
Shah Jahan, *17th:* 842
Beant Singh, *Notor:* 962
Ranjit Singh, *19th:* 1857
Satwant Singh, *Notor:* 963
Śivājī, *17th:* 858
Rabindranath Tagore, *20th:* 3933
Mother Teresa, *20th:* 3975
Bal Gangadhar Tilak, *20th:* 4023
Dēvānaṃpiya Tissa, *Anc:* 898
Vālmīki, *Anc:* 922
Vardhamāna, *Anc:* 924
Vasubandhu, *Anc:* 930
Vattagamani, *Anc:* 933
Veerappan, *Notor:* 1062
Iswar Chandra Vidyasagar, *19th:* 2363
Vivekananda, *19th:* 2368
Shāh Walī Allāh, *18th:* 1032
Mohammad Zia-ul-Haq, *20th:* 4473

INDONESIA
Mohammad Hatta, *20th:* 1704
Suharto, *20th:* 3901, *Notor:* 1007
Sukarno, *20th:* 3904
Abel Janszoon Tasman, *17th:* 905

IRAN
ʿAbbās the Great, *17th:* 4
Abul Wefa, *MA:* 21
Alp Arslan, *MA:* 70
Antiochus the Great, *Anc:* 65
Atossa, *Anc:* 136
Avicenna, *MA:* 123
The Bāb, *19th:* 105
Bahāʾullāh, *19th:* 117
al-Bīrūnī, *MA:* 163
Cyrus the Great, *Anc:* 248
Darius the Great, *Anc:* 251
Fakhr al-Dīn al-Rāzī, *MA:* 369
Firdusi, *MA:* 375
Maḥmūd Ghāzān, *MA:* 411
al-Ghazzālī, *MA:* 415
Hafiz, *MA:* 451
al-Ḥallāj, *MA:* 454
Hārūn al-Rashīd, *MA:* 467
Abū Mūsā Jābir ibn Ḥayyān, *MA:* 562
Jamāl al-Dīn al-Afghānī, *19th:* 1203
Karīm Khān Zand, *18th:* 552
Ayatollah Khomeini, *20th:* 2123, *Notor:* 571
Maḥmūd of Ghazna, *MA:* 683
Mohammad Reza Shah Pahlavi, *20th:* 2779, *Notor:* 742
Mohammad Mossadegh, *20th:* 2844
Nādir Shāh, *18th:* 722, *Notor:* 772
Niẓām al-Mulk, *MA:* 774
Omar Khayyám, *MA:* 795
al-Rāzī, *MA:* 884
Reza Shah Pahlavi, *20th:* 2779, *Notor:* 742
Saʿdi, *MA:* 915
Shāpūr II, *Anc:* 774
al-Ṭabarī, *MA:* 988
Táhirih, *19th:* 2214
Vaḥīd Bihbahānī, *18th:* 1000
Xerxes I, *Anc:* 971
Zoroaster, *Anc:* 992

Iraq

Abū Ḥanīfah, *MA:* 18
Abu Nidal, *Notor:* 4
Abul Wefa, *MA:* 21
Aḥmad ibn Ḥanbal, *MA:* 36
Alhazen, *MA:* 66
Alp Arslan, *MA:* 70
al-Ashʿarī, *MA:* 111
Ashurbanipal, *Anc:* 117
Ashurnasirpal II, *Anc:* 120
al-Battānī, *MA:* 137
Cyrus the Great, *Anc:* 248
Darius the Great, *Anc:* 251
Enheduanna, *Anc:* 298
Ezra, *Anc:* 338
Faisal I, *20th:* 1202
Gudea, *Anc:* 366
al-Ḥallāj, *MA:* 454
Hammurabi, *Anc:* 376
al-Ḥasan al-Baṣrī, *MA:* 471
Qusay Saddam Hussein, *Notor:* 501
Saddam Hussein, *20th:* 1947, *Notor:* 503
Uday Hussein, *Notor:* 505
Abū Mūsā Jābir ibn Ḥayyān, *MA:* 562
al-Jāḥiẓ, *MA:* 568
Khosrow I, *MA:* 613
al-Khwārizmī, *MA:* 617
Nabu-rimanni, *Anc:* 579
Nebuchadnezzar II, *Anc:* 582
Rābiʿah al-ʿAdawiyah, *MA:* 873
Saladin, *MA:* 918
Sammu-ramat, *Anc:* 744
Sargon II, *Anc:* 752
Seleucus I Nicator, *Anc:* 763
Sennacherib, *Anc:* 769
Shāpūr II, *Anc:* 774
Tiglath-pileser III, *Anc:* 892
Ur-Nammu, *Anc:* 914
Vaḥīd Bihbahānī, *18th:* 1000
Xerxes I, *Anc:* 971
Zenobia, *Anc:* 986

Ireland and Northern Ireland

Queen Anne, *18th:* 45
Samuel Beckett, *20th:* 279
George Berkeley, *18th:* 111
Anne Bonny, *Notor:* 122
Saint Brigit, *MA:* 198
Edmund Burke, *18th:* 174
William Burke, *Notor:* 154
Jocelyn Burnell, *20th:* 584
Mary Butters, *Notor:* 160
Alexander Campbell, *19th:* 399
Sir Guy Carleton, *18th:* 196
Caroline, *18th:* 203
Viscount Castlereagh, *19th:* 437
Queen Charlotte, *18th:* 235
Michael Collins, *20th:* 807
First Marquess Cornwallis, *18th:* 278
William T. Cosgrave, *20th:* 843
Eamon de Valera, *20th:* 979
Lord Edward Fitzgerald, *18th:* 356
George I, *18th:* 400
George II, *18th:* 403
George III, *18th:* 408
Oliver Goldsmith, *18th:* 432
Henry Grattan, *18th:* 440
Arthur Griffith, *20th:* 1591
Sir William Rowan Hamilton, *19th:* 1015
Alfred and Harold Harmsworth, *20th:* 1678
John Philip Holland, *19th:* 1113
Irish Invincibles, *Notor:* 509
Anna Jameson, *19th:* 1217
Mother Jones, *20th:* 2039
James Joyce, *20th:* 2055
Baron Kelvin, *19th:* 1264
Lord Kitchener, *20th:* 2173
Lady Alice Kyteler, *MA:* 629, *Notor:* 598
C. S. Lewis, *20th:* 2353
Mary Mallon, *Notor:* 685
Daniel Mannix, *19th:* 1492
Lola Montez, *19th:* 1590
Florence Newton, *Notor:* 781
Daniel O'Connell, *19th:* 1695
Thomas Power O'Connor, *20th:* 3024
Seán T. O'Kelly, *20th:* 3034
Grace O'Malley, *Ren:* 743, *Notor:* 805
Rory O'More, *17th:* 699
Charles Stewart Parnell, *19th:* 1747
Saint Patrick, *MA:* 811
Sir William Petty, *17th:* 733
Mary Robinson (b. 1944), *20th:* 3474
Friedrich Hermann Schomberg, *17th:* 820
George Bernard Shaw, *20th:* 3716
Richard Brinsley Sheridan, *18th:* 905
Jonathan Swift, *18th:* 964
Thomas Talbot, *19th:* 2219
Wolfe Tone, *18th:* 982
James Ussher, *17th:* 938
Duke of Wellington, *19th:* 2409
Oscar Wilde, *19th:* 2432
Peg Woffington, *18th:* 1102
William Butler Yeats, *20th:* 4428

Israel/Palestine

Abraham, *Anc:* 4
Abu Nidal, *Notor:* 4
Akiba ben Joseph, *Anc:* 29
Yigal Amir, *Notor:* 22
Barabbas, *Notor:* 55
Bathsheba, *Anc:* 155
Menachem Begin, *20th:* 284
David Ben-Gurion, *20th:* 292
Martin Buber, *20th:* 554
Cyrus the Great, *Anc:* 248
Darius the Great, *Anc:* 251
David, *Anc:* 255
Moshe Dayan, *20th:* 929
Deborah, *Anc:* 258
Abba Eban, *20th:* 1082
Ezekiel, *Anc:* 335
Ezra, *Anc:* 338
Baruch Goldstein, *Notor:* 427
George Habash, *20th:* 1626
Herod Antipas, *Notor:* 458
Herod the Great, *Anc:* 403, *Notor:* 459
Isaiah, *Anc:* 446
Jeremiah, *Anc:* 453
Saint Jerome, *Anc:* 456
Jesus, *Anc:* 458
Jezebel, *Notor:* 527
Johanan ben Zakkai, *Anc:* 468
John of Damascus, *MA:* 587
John the Apostle, *Anc:* 471
Saint John the Baptist, *Anc:* 474

Flavius Josephus, *Anc:* 477, *Notor:* 541
Judas Iscariot, *Notor:* 544
Meir Kahane, *Notor:* 551
Joseph ben Ephraim Karo, *Ren:* 524
Isaac ben Solomon Luria, *Ren:* 579
Mary, *Anc:* 539
Golda Meir, *20th:* 2674
Melisende, *MA:* 715
Moses, *Anc:* 572
Naḥmanides, *MA:* 747
Saint Paul, *Anc:* 611
Saint Peter, *Anc:* 624
Yitzhak Rabin, *20th:* 3358
Salome, *Notor:* 932
Samuel, *Anc:* 747
Solomon, *Anc:* 803
Saint Stephen, *Anc:* 821
Saint Thomas, *Anc:* 878
Chaim Weizmann, *20th:* 4279
Xerxes I, *Anc:* 971
Zenobia, *Anc:* 986

ITALY. ***See also*** **ROMAN EMPIRE; ROMAN REPUBLIC; VATICAN CITY**
Pietro d Abano, *MA:* 1
Isaac ben Judah Abravanel, *Ren:* 1
Joe Adonis, *Notor:* 6
Adrian IV, *MA:* 27
Adrian VI, *Ren:* 7
Maria Gaetana Agnesi, *18th:* 24
Leon Battista Alberti, *Ren:* 18
Alboin, *MA:* 45
Alexander III, *MA:* 56
Alexander VI, *Ren:* 27, *Notor:* 14
Alexander VII, *17th:* 9
Amalasuntha, *MA:* 75
Andrea del Sarto, *Ren:* 39
Isabella Andreini, *Ren:* 42
Saint Angela Merici, *Ren:* 44
Blessed Angela of Foligno, *MA:* 81
Fra Angelico, *MA:* 83
Sofonisba Anguissola, *Ren:* 46
Saint Anselm, *MA:* 92
Saint Anthony of Padua, *MA:* 95
Guillaume Apollinaire, *20th:* 104
Pietro Aretino, *Ren:* 53
Ludovico Ariosto, *Ren:* 56
Arnold of Villanova, *MA:* 98
Arnolfo di Cambio, *MA:* 102
Amedeo Avogadro, *19th:* 101
Cesare Beccaria, *18th:* 100
Giovanni Bellini, *Ren:* 97
Benedict XIV, *18th:* 102
Saint Benedict of Nursia, *MA:* 153
Gian Lorenzo Bernini, *17th:* 45
Giovanni Boccaccio, *MA:* 169
Luigi Boccherini, *18th:* 129
Umberto Boccioni, *20th:* 403
Boethius, *MA:* 173
Bohemond I, *MA:* 176
Saint Bonaventure, *MA:* 180
Boniface VIII, *MA:* 186, *Notor:* 115
Giovanni Alfonso Borelli, *17th:* 65
Cesare Borgia, *Ren:* 114, *Notor:* 127
Lucrezia Borgia, *Ren:* 117, *Notor:* 129
Francesco Borromini, *17th:* 67
Sandro Botticelli, *Ren:* 123
Donato Bramante, *Ren:* 132
Filippo Brunelleschi, *MA:* 205
Leonardo Bruni, *MA:* 208
Giordano Bruno, *Ren:* 138
John Cabot, *Ren:* 155
Francesca Caccini, *17th:* 111
Roberto Calvi, *Notor:* 170
Tommaso Campanella, *17th:* 124
Canaletto, *18th:* 190
Antonio Canova, *19th:* 406
Caravaggio, *Ren:* 170
Gerolamo Cardano, *Ren:* 172
Giovanni da Pian del Carpini, *MA:* 226
The Carracci Family, *Ren:* 175
Enrico Caruso, *20th:* 675
Casanova, *18th:* 208
Gian Domenico Cassini, *17th:* 134
Cassiodorus, *MA:* 233
Baldassare Castiglione, *Ren:* 181
Saint Catherine of Genoa, *Ren:* 191
Saint Catherine of Siena, *MA:* 236
Catiline, *Anc:* 188, *Notor:* 188
Guido Cavalcanti, *MA:* 239
Count Cavour, *19th:* 444
Benvenuto Cellini, *Ren:* 202
Beatrice Cenci, *Notor:* 192
Andrea Cesalpino, *Ren:* 211
Cimabue, *MA:* 282
Saint Clare of Assisi, *MA:* 284
Claude Lorrain, *17th:* 171
Clement VII, *Ren:* 229, *Notor:* 212
Vittoria Colonna, *Ren:* 235
Christopher Columbus, *Ren:* 237
Arcangelo Corelli, *17th:* 190
Correggio, *Ren:* 249
Bettino Craxi, *Notor:* 241
Benedetto Croce, *20th:* 869
Saint Cyril, *MA:* 294
Enrico Dandolo, *MA:* 298
Dante, *MA:* 300
Alcide De Gasperi, *20th:* 944
Donatello, *MA:* 319
Gaetano Donizetti, *19th:* 674
Duccio di Buoninsegna, *MA:* 326
Eugene of Savoy, *18th:* 330
Julius Evola, *Notor:* 339
Hieronymus Fabricius ab Aquapendente, *Ren:* 319
Federico Fellini, *20th:* 1231
Enrico Fermi, *20th:* 1235
Enzo Ferrari, *20th:* 1239
Marsilio Ficino, *Ren:* 332
Lavinia Fontana, *Ren:* 338
Francesco Forgione, *20th:* 1286
Girolamo Fracastoro, *Ren:* 343
Saint Francis of Assisi, *MA:* 378
Frederick II, *MA:* 389
Girolamo Frescobaldi, *17th:* 295
Andrea Gabrieli, *Ren:* 359
Giovanni Gabrieli, *Ren:* 362
Galileo, *17th:* 298
Luigi Galvani, *18th:* 391
Giuseppe Garibaldi, *19th:* 871
Giovanna Garzoni, *17th:* 302
Vito Genovese, *Notor:* 402
Giovanni Gentile, *20th:* 1448
Artemisia Gentileschi, *17th:* 307
Alberico Gentili, *Ren:* 372
Lorenzo Ghiberti, *MA:* 418
Vincenzo Gioberti, *19th:* 921
Giorgione, *Ren:* 383
Giotto, *MA:* 421
Salvatore Giuliano, *Notor:* 413

Antonio Gramsci, *20th:* 1566
Gregory VII, *MA:* 433
Gregory IX, *MA:* 436
Gregory XIII, *Ren:* 393
Gregory the Great, *MA:* 430
Francesco Maria Grimaldi, *17th:* 321
Guarino Guarini, *17th:* 330
Francesco Guicciardini, *Ren:* 410
Guido d'Arezzo, *MA:* 439
Innocent III, *MA:* 541
Innocent IV, *MA:* 545
Innocent XI, *17th:* 405
Isabella d'Este, *Ren:* 485
Jacopo della Quercia, *MA:* 566
Joachim of Fiore, *MA:* 575
John XXIII, *20th:* 2017
John Paul II, *20th:* 2020
Juan Carlos I, *20th:* 2060
Julius II, *Ren:* 518
Eusebio Francisco Kino, *17th:* 467
Francesco Landini, *MA:* 635
Leo IX, *MA:* 644
Leo X, *Ren:* 557, *Notor:* 630
Leo XIII, *19th:* 1342
Leonardo da Vinci, *Ren:* 561
Leonardo of Pisa, *MA:* 648
Pietro and Ambrogio Lorenzetti, *MA:* 659
Jean-Baptiste Lully, *17th:* 569
Niccolò Machiavelli, *Ren:* 587
Marcello Malpighi, *17th:* 579
The Mancini Sisters, *17th:* 585
Andrea Mantegna, *Ren:* 601
Aldus Manutius, *Ren:* 608
Alessandro Manzoni, *19th:* 1495
Guglielmo Marconi, *20th:* 2615
Luca Marenzio, *Ren:* 610
Maria Celeste, *17th:* 593
Marie de Médicis, *17th:* 598
Marozia, *Notor:* 706
Simone Martini, *MA:* 696
Mary of Modena, *17th:* 607
Masaccio, *MA:* 699
Matilda of Canossa, *MA:* 705
Jules Mazarin, *17th:* 620
Giuseppe Mazzini, *19th:* 1531
Cosimo I de' Medici, *Ren:* 653
Cosimo II de' Medici, *17th:* 626
Lorenzo de' Medici, *Ren:* 655
Gian Carlo Menotti, *20th:* 2703
Reinhold Messner, *20th:* 2718
Saint Methodius, *MA:* 294
Michelangelo, *Ren:* 682
Amedeo Modigliani, *20th:* 2776
Eugenio Montale, *20th:* 2801
Maria Montessori, *20th:* 2804
Claudio Monteverdi, *17th:* 656
Gaetano Mosca, *20th:* 2838
Benito Mussolini, *20th:* 2885, *Notor:* 769
Giulio Natta, *20th:* 2919
Saint Philip Neri, *Ren:* 717
Pier Luigi Nervi, *20th:* 2940
Nicholas V, *MA:* 768
Nicholas the Great, *MA:* 764
Odoacer, *MA:* 782
Andrea Orcagna, *MA:* 798
Niccolò Paganini, *19th:* 1724
Sophia Palaeologus, *Ren:* 749
Giovanni Pierluigi da Palestrina, *Ren:* 751
Eusapia Palladino, *Notor:* 810
Andrea Palladio, *Ren:* 753
Paul III, *Ren:* 767
Paul V, *17th:* 719
Paul VI, *20th:* 3148
Luciano Pavarotti, *20th:* 3159
Petrarch, *MA:* 827
Giovanni Pico della Mirandola, *Ren:* 782
Piero della Francesca, *Ren:* 785
Luigi Pirandello, *20th:* 3260
Pirelli Family, *20th:* 3266
Andrea Pisano, *MA:* 845
Nicola Pisano and Giovanni Pisano, *MA:* 847
Elena Cornaro Piscopia, *17th:* 743
Pius II, *Ren:* 794
Pius V, *Ren:* 797
Pius VI, *18th:* 793
Pius IX, *19th:* 1802
Pius X, *20th:* 3272
Pius XI, *20th:* 3275
Pius XII, *20th:* 3278
Poggio, *MA:* 850
Marco Polo, *MA:* 853
Nicolas Poussin, *17th:* 749
Giacomo Puccini, *20th:* 3346
Raphael, *Ren:* 819
Matteo Ricci, *Ren:* 825
Cola di Rienzo, *MA:* 897
Gioacchino Rossini, *19th:* 1944
Nicola Sacco, *20th:* 3580, *Notor:* 924
Salimbene, *MA:* 921
Jacopo Sansovino, *Ren:* 847
Santorio Santorio, *17th:* 810
Girolamo Savonarola, *Ren:* 850
Alessandro Scarlatti, *18th:* 883
Saint Sergius I, *MA:* 936
Caterina Sforza, *Ren:* 870
Ludovico Sforza, *Ren:* 872
Elisabetta Sirani, *17th:* 856
Sixtus IV, *Ren:* 893
Sixtus V, *Ren:* 895
Lazzaro Spallanzani, *18th:* 925
Nicolaus Steno, *17th:* 881
Antonio Stradivari, *18th:* 944
Barbara Strozzi, *17th:* 888
Sylvester II, *MA:* 983
Tancred, *MA:* 1003
Niccolò Fontana Tartaglia, *Ren:* 920
Torquato Tasso, *Ren:* 924
Theodoric the Great, *MA:* 1012
Thomas Aquinas, *MA:* 1027
Giovanni Battista Tiepolo, *18th:* 976
Tintoretto, *Ren:* 931
Marietta Robusti Tintoretto, *Ren:* 935
Titian, *Ren:* 936
Evangelista Torricelli, *17th:* 921
Arturo Toscanini, *20th:* 4050
Trotula, *MA:* 1031
Urban II, *MA:* 1043
Urban VI, *Notor:* 1053
Urban VIII, *17th:* 936
Lorenzo Valla, *MA:* 1049
Giorgio Vasari, *Ren:* 953
Giuseppe Verdi, *19th:* 2351
Paolo Veronese, *Ren:* 959
Andrea del Verrocchio, *Ren:* 962
Amerigo Vespucci, *Ren:* 969
Giambattista Vico, *18th:* 1013
Giovanni Villani, *MA:* 1056
Luchino Visconti, *20th:* 4166
Antonio Vivaldi, *18th:* 1019
Alessandro Volta, *18th:* 1022

IVORY COAST
Félix Houphouët-Boigny, *20th:* 1895

JAMAICA
Anne Bonny, *Notor:* 122
Marcus Garvey, *20th:* 1417
Sir Henry Morgan, *Notor:* 753
Nanny, *18th:* 724
John Rackham, *Notor:* 877

JAPAN
Akihito, *20th:* 46
Shoko Asahara, *Notor:* 40
Ashikaga Takauji, *MA:* 115
Chikamatsu Monzaemon, *18th:* 243
Shūsaku Endō, *20th:* 1155
Fujiwara Michinaga, *MA:* 396
Hakuin, *18th:* 450
Ichirō Hatoyama, *20th:* 1701
Hirohito, *20th:* 1818, *Notor:* 473
Hiroshige, *19th:* 1107
Hishikawa Moronobu, *17th:* 375
Hōjō Ujimasa, *Ren:* 451
Soichiro Honda, *20th:* 1859
Honda Toshiaki, *18th:* 504
Hosokawa Gracia, *Ren:* 459
Ihara Saikaku, *17th:* 403
Ii Naosuke, *19th:* 1168
Hayato Ikeda, *20th:* 1965
Izumo no Okuni, *17th:* 408
Jimmu Tennō, *Anc:* 462
Jingū, *Anc:* 465
Jōchō, *MA:* 581
Yasunari Kawabata, *20th:* 2084
Kōbō Daishi, *MA:* 620
Kuniaki Koiso, *Notor:* 587
Kōken, *MA:* 623
Akira Kurosawa, *20th:* 2217
Matsuo Bashō, *17th:* 615
Konosuke Matsushita, *20th:* 2653
Minamoto Yoritomo, *MA:* 721
Yukio Mishima, *20th:* 2763
Akio Morita, *20th:* 2831
Murasaki Shikibu, *MA:* 738
Mutsuhito, *19th:* 1631
Nichiren, *MA:* 758
Nijō, *MA:* 771
Kitarō Nishida, *20th:* 2981
Oda Nobunaga, *Ren:* 732
Ogata Kōrin, *17th:* 695
Ōgimachi, *Ren:* 735
Ogyū Sorai, *18th:* 746
Sadaharu Oh, *20th:* 3027
Oichi, *Ren:* 737
Ōjin Tennō, *Anc:* 594
Saigō Takamori, *19th:* 1968
Eisaku Satō, *20th:* 3645
Sei Shōnagon, *MA:* 930
Seki Kōwa, *17th:* 831
Sesshū, *Ren:* 865
Fusako Shigenobu, *Notor:* 949
Shōtoku Taishi, *MA:* 940
Sōtatsu, *17th:* 868
Suiko, *MA:* 974
Suzuki Harunobu, *18th:* 958
Shinichi Suzuki, *20th:* 3922
Tadano Makuzu, *19th:* 2212
Taira Kiyomori, *MA:* 990
Jun'ichirō Tanizaki, *20th:* 3944
Hideki Tojo, *Notor:* 1034
Tokugawa Ieyasu, *17th:* 915
Tokugawa Tsunayoshi, *17th:* 919
Tokugawa Yoshimune, *18th:* 980
Tokyo Rose, *Notor:* 1036
Eiji Toyoda, *20th:* 4062
Toyotomi Hideyoshi, *Ren:* 943
Unkei, *MA:* 1040
Yui Shōsetsu, *17th:* 998
Hideki Yukawa, *20th:* 4436
Zeami Motokiyo, *MA:* 1152
Zheng Chenggong, *17th:* 1001

JORDAN
Yasir Arafat, *20th:* 110
Hussein I, *20th:* 1950
Abu Musab al-Zarqawi, *Notor:* 1132

KAZAKHSTAN
Dionysius Exiguus, *MA:* 313
Tamerlane, *MA:* 1000

KENYA
Jomo Kenyatta, *20th:* 2106
L. S. B. Leakey, *20th:* 2310
Mary Leakey, *20th:* 2315

KOREA (NORTH AND SOUTH)
Chŏng Sŏn, *18th:* 248
Kim Dae Jung, *20th:* 2136
Kim Il Sung, *20th:* 2138, *Notor:* 578
Kim Jong Il, *20th:* 2141, *Notor:* 581
Sun Myung Moon, *20th:* 2811, *Notor:* 749
Syngman Rhee, *20th:* 3430
Wang Kŏn, *MA:* 1081

KUWAIT
Ramzi Yousef, *Notor:* 1121

LAOS
Suryavarman II, *MA:* 980

LATVIA
Mikhail Baryshnikov, *20th:* 253
Sergei Eisenstein, *20th:* 1129
Nicolai Hartmann, *20th:* 1696
Wilhelm Ostwald, *20th:* 3088
Mark Rothko, *20th:* 3539
Vasili Vasilievich Ulrikh, *Notor:* 1052

LEBANON
Yasir Arafat, *20th:* 110

LIBERIA
Samuel K. Doe, *Notor:* 288
Samory Touré, *19th:* 1981
Charles Taylor, *Notor:* 1021
William V. S. Tubman, *20th:* 4101

LIBYA
Muammar al-Qaddafi, *20th:* 3350, *Notor:* 867

LITHUANIA
Elijah ben Solomon, *18th:* 318
Emma Goldman, *20th:* 1519, *Notor:* 424
Jacques Lipchitz, *20th:* 2397
Józef Piłsudski, *20th:* 3250
Stephen Báthory, *Ren:* 910

MACEDONIA. ***See* GREECE**

Madagascar
Maurycy Beniowski, *Notor:* 85

Malawi
Hastings Kamuzu Banda, *20th:* 219

Malaysia. ***See also*** **Singapore**
Datuk Seri Mahathir bin Mohamad, *20th:* 2551

Mali
Askia Daud, *Ren:* 64
Mohammed I Askia, *Ren:* 686
Mansa Mūsā, *MA:* 744
Sīdī al-Mukhṭār al-Kuntī, *18th:* 914
Sonni ʿAlī, *Ren:* 900
Sundiata, *MA:* 977

Manchuria. ***See*** **China**

Martinique
Aimé Césaire, *20th:* 709
Frantz Fanon, *20th:* 1212

Mesoamerica. ***See*** **Native America**

Mesopotamia. ***See*** **Iraq**

Mexico
Mateo Alemán, *Ren:* 25
Pedro de Alvarado, *Ren:* 34
Luis Buñuel, *20th:* 578
Fanny Calderón de la Barca, *19th:* 389
Plutarco Elías Calles, *20th:* 615
Felix Candela, *20th:* 631
Lázaro Cárdenas, *20th:* 647
Sor Juana Inés de la Cruz, *17th:* 208
Cuauhtémoc, *Ren:* 273
Porfirio Díaz, *19th:* 652, *Notor:* 278
Miguel Hidalgo y Costilla, *19th:* 1094
Itzcóatl, *MA:* 558
Benito Juárez, *19th:* 1245
Frida Kahlo, *20th:* 2069
Eusebio Francisco Kino, *17th:* 467
Francisco Madero, *20th:* 2544
Doña Marina, *Ren:* 621
Maximilian, *19th:* 1525
Montezuma II, *Ren:* 693
Nezahualcóyotl, *Ren:* 720
Álvaro Obregón, *20th:* 3013
José Clemente Orozco, *20th:* 3068
Octavio Paz, *20th:* 3169
Diego Rivera, *20th:* 3457
Antonio López de Santa Anna, *19th:* 1990
Junípero Serra, *18th:* 891
Pancho Villa, *20th:* 4160, *Notor:* 1069
Dominique You, *Notor:* 1117
Emiliano Zapata, *20th:* 4448, *Notor:* 1129

Middle East. ***See*** **Egypt; Iran; Iraq; Israel/Palestine; Jordan; Kuwait; Lebanon; Oman; Syria; Turkey**

Mongolia
Genghis Khan, *MA:* 402, *Notor:* 400

Moravia. ***See*** **Czech Republic and Slovakia**

Morocco
ʿAbd al-Muʾmin, *MA:* 6
Hassan II, *20th:* 1699
Ibn Baṭṭūṭah, *MA:* 529
al-Idrīsī, *MA:* 539
Boabdil, *Ren:* 105
Leo Africanus, *Ren:* 555

Mozambique
Samora Machel, *20th:* 2515

Native America
Atahualpa, *Ren:* 66
Black Hawk, *19th:* 244
Joseph Brant, *18th:* 159
Canonicus, *17th:* 129
Crazy Horse, *19th:* 566
Cuauhtémoc, *Ren:* 273
Deganawida, *Ren:* 281
Louise Erdrich, *20th:* 1168
Geronimo, *19th:* 904
Hiawatha, *Ren:* 448
Huáscar, *Ren:* 469
Itzcóatl, *MA:* 558
Chief Joseph, *19th:* 1238
Kalicho, *Ren:* 522
Kamehameha I, *19th:* 1249
Liliuokalani, *19th:* 1373
Little Turtle, *18th:* 610
Wilma Mankiller, *20th:* 2591
Doña Marina, *Ren:* 621
Massasoit, *17th:* 612
Metacom, *17th:* 633
Montezuma II, *Ren:* 693
Nezahualcóyotl, *Ren:* 720
Opechancanough, *17th:* 702
Osceola, *19th:* 1709
Pachacuti, *Ren:* 746
Pemisapan, *Ren:* 771
Susan La Flesche Picotte, *20th:* 3247
Pocahontas, *17th:* 745
Pontiac, *18th:* 801
Powhatan, *17th:* 752
Red Cloud, *19th:* 1871
John Ross, *19th:* 1937
Sacagawea, *19th:* 1962
Sequoyah, *19th:* 2067
Sitting Bull, *19th:* 2108
Squanto, *17th:* 875
Maria Tallchief, *20th:* 3940
Tascalusa, *Ren:* 922
Tecumseh, *19th:* 2237
Kateri Tekakwitha, *17th:* 908
Thanadelthur, *18th:* 974
Jim Thorpe, *20th:* 4016

Netherlands
Adrian VI, *Ren:* 7
Jacobus Arminius, *Ren:* 59
Pierre Bayle, *17th:* 36
Beatrice of Nazareth, *MA:* 144
The Bernoulli Family, *17th:* 48
Saint Boniface, *MA:* 183
Hieronymus Bosch, *Ren:* 120
Pieter Bruegel, the Elder, *Ren:* 135
Aagje Deken, *18th:* 301
Sir Anthony van Dyck, *17th:* 244

Willem Einthoven, *20th:* 1122
M. C. Escher, *20th:* 1183
Jan and Hubert van Eyck, *MA:* 365
Anne Frank, *20th:* 1301
Frederick Henry, *17th:* 286
Balthasar Gérard, *Notor:* 404
Vincent van Gogh, *19th:* 932
Hugo Grotius, *17th:* 326
Frans Hals, *17th:* 352
Piet Hein, *17th:* 359
Audrey Hepburn, *20th:* 1766
Christiaan Huygens, *17th:* 397
Cornelius Otto Jansen, *17th:* 419
Josquin des Prez, *Ren:* 515
Heike Kamerlingh Onnes, *20th:* 2072
Kenau Hasselaer, *Ren:* 526
Jan Komenský, *17th:* 469
Antoni van Leeuwenhoek, *17th:* 509
Hans Lippershey, *17th:* 537
Hendrik Antoon Lorentz, *20th:* 2431
Manasseh ben Israel, *17th:* 582
Margaret of Austria, *Ren:* 612
Margaret of Parma, *Ren:* 615
Mary of Burgundy, *Ren:* 631
Mary of Hungary, *Ren:* 636
Mata Hari, *Notor:* 710
Maurice of Nassau, *17th:* 618
Menno Simons, *Ren:* 675
Peter Minuit, *17th:* 643
Piet Mondrian, *20th:* 2786
Johan van Oldenbarnevelt, *Ren:* 740
Jan Hendrik Oort, *20th:* 3059
J. J. P. Oud, *20th:* 3092
Rembrandt, *17th:* 786
Peter Paul Rubens, *17th:* 802
Michiel Adriaanszoon de Ruyter, *17th:* 807
Friedrich Hermann Schomberg, *17th:* 820
Anna Maria van Schurman, *17th:* 823
Claus Sluter, *MA:* 947
Baruch Spinoza, *17th:* 871
Simon Stevin, *Ren:* 912
Peter Stuyvesant, *17th:* 890
Jan Swammerdam, *17th:* 898
Abel Janszoon Tasman, *17th:* 905
Thomas à Kempis, *MA:* 1022
Maarten and Cornelis Tromp, *17th:* 930
Jan Vermeer, *17th:* 956
Volkert van der Graaf, *Notor:* 1055
Rogier van der Weyden, *MA:* 1092
William III, *17th:* 979
William of Moerbeke, *MA:* 1105
William of Rubrouck, *MA:* 1107
William the Silent, *Ren:* 993

NEW ZEALAND
Sir George Grey, *19th:* 981
Sir Edmund Hillary, *20th:* 1802
Meri Te Tai Mangakahia, *19th:* 1483
William Ferguson Massey, *20th:* 2643
Ernest Rutherford, *20th:* 3576
Richard John Seddon, *19th:* 2058
Abel Janszoon Tasman, *17th:* 905
Sir Julius Vogel, *19th:* 2371
Edward Gibbon Wakefield, *19th:* 2378

NICARAGUA
Daniel Ortega, *20th:* 3072

NIGERIA
Sani Abacha, *Notor:* 1
Chinua Achebe, *20th:* 14
Amina Sarauniya Zazzua, *Ren:* 37
Nnamdi Azikiwe, *20th:* 180
Muḥammad Bello, *19th:* 186
Samuel Ajayi Crowther, *19th:* 574
Rubén Darío, *19th:* 601
Olaudah Equiano, *18th:* 324
Lord Lugard, *20th:* 2465
Mohammed I Askia, *Ren:* 686
Muhammad Siad Barre, *20th:* 3734, *Notor:* 953
Anastasio Somoza García, *Notor:* 984
Sonni ʿAlī, *Ren:* 900
Wole Soyinka, *20th:* 3804
ʿUthman dan Fodio, *19th:* 2342

NORTH AMERICA. ***See*** **CANADA; NATIVE AMERICA; UNITED STATES**

NORWAY
Niels Henrik Abel, *19th:* 9
Roald Amundsen, *20th:* 83
Vilhelm Bjerknes, *20th:* 374
Gro Harlem Brundtland, *20th:* 544
Canute the Great, *MA:* 221
Charles XIV John, *19th:* 468
Christian VII, *Notor:* 208
Edvard Grieg, *19th:* 984
Knut Hamsun, *20th:* 1660
Sonja Henie, *20th:* 1759
Thor Heyerdahl, *20th:* 1795
Henrik Ibsen, *19th:* 1165
Leif Eriksson, *MA:* 640
Trygve Lie, *20th:* 2375
Margaret of Denmark, Norway, and Sweden, *MA:* 689
Edvard Munch, *20th:* 2870
Fridtjof Nansen, *20th:* 2907
Saint Olaf, *MA:* 785
Olaf I, *MA:* 789
Vidkun Quisling, *Notor:* 873
Rollo, *MA:* 900

OMAN
Saʿīd ibn Sulṭān, *19th:* 1965

OTTOMAN EMPIRE
Abdelkader, *19th:* 1
Abdülhamid II, *19th:* 7
Ahmed III, *18th:* 26
Ali Paşa Tepelenë, *19th:* 55
Barbarossa, *Ren:* 79
Bayezid II, *Ren:* 87
İbrahim Paşa, *Ren:* 480
Jamāl al-Dīn al-Afghānī, *19th:* 1203
Merzifonlu Kara Mustafa Paşa, *17th:* 451
Joseph ben Ephraim Karo, *Ren:* 524
Kâtib Çelebî, *17th:* 454
Kösem Sultan, *17th:* 472
Levni, *18th:* 602
Isaac ben Solomon Luria, *Ren:* 579

Mahmud I, *18th:* 639
Mehmed II, *MA:* 711, *Ren:* 659
Mehmed III, *Ren:* 661
Muḥammad ʿAlī Pasha, *19th:* 1620
Murad IV, *17th:* 668
Mustafa I, *17th:* 673
Mustafa III, *18th:* 719
Shabbetai Tzevi, *17th:* 835
Süleyman the Magnificent, *Ren:* 914

Pakistan
Said Akbar, *Notor:* 10
ʿAlāʾ-ud-Dīn Muḥammad Khaljī, *MA:* 39
Benazir Bhutto, *20th:* 365
Zulfikar Ali Bhutto, *20th:* 368
Darius the Great, *Anc:* 251
Mohammed Ali Jinnah, *20th:* 2002
Kanishka, *Anc:* 499
Maḥmūd of Ghazna, *MA:* 683
Khalid Shaikh Mohammed, *Notor:* 744
Nānak, *Ren:* 707
Shah Jahan, *17th:* 842
Shāpūr II, *Anc:* 774
Xerxes I, *Anc:* 971
Mohammad Zia-ul-Haq, *20th:* 4473

Palestine. ***See* Israel/ Palestine**

Panama
Manuel Noriega, *Notor:* 797
Omar Torrijos, *20th:* 4048

Paraguay
Alfredo Stroessner, *Notor:* 1004

Persia. ***See* Iran**

Peru
José de Acosta, *Ren:* 5
Atahualpa, *Ren:* 66
Simón Bolívar, *19th:* 267
Alberto Fujimori, *20th:* 1359, *Notor:* 382
Víctor Raúl Haya de la Torre, *20th:* 1716
Huáscar, *Ren:* 469
Clorinda Matto de Turner, *19th:* 1512
Pachacuti, *Ren:* 746
Javier Pérez de Cuéllar, *20th:* 3194
Saint Rose of Lima, *17th:* 796
Tupac Amaru II, *18th:* 993

Philippines
Corazon Aquino, *20th:* 107
Miguel López de Legazpi, *Ren:* 550
Ferdinand Marcos, *20th:* 2619, *Notor:* 699
Imelda Marcos, *Notor:* 702

Poland
Baʿal Shem Tov, *18th:* 68
Leo Baeck, *20th:* 186
Menachem Begin, *20th:* 284
David Ben-Gurion, *20th:* 292
Friedrich Bergius, *20th:* 313
Dietrich Bonhoeffer, *20th:* 418
Max Born, *20th:* 437
Wernher von Braun, *20th:* 500
Casimir the Great, *MA:* 229
Ernst Cassirer, *20th:* 688
Charles IV, *MA:* 257
Frédéric Chopin, *19th:* 486
Carl von Clausewitz, *19th:* 499
Joseph Conrad, *20th:* 824
Nicolaus Copernicus, *Ren:* 241
Marie and Pierre Curie, *20th:* 888
Felix Dzerzhinsky, *Notor:* 312
Paul Ehrlich, *20th:* 1115
Hans Michael Frank, *Notor:* 374
Günter Grass, *20th:* 1573
Fritz Haber, *20th:* 1628
Henry III, *Ren:* 426
Johannes and Elisabetha Hevelius, *17th:* 371
Paul von Hindenburg, *20th:* 1814
Wojciech Jaruzelski, *Notor:* 525
John III Sobieski, *17th:* 427
John Paul II, *20th:* 2020
Bohdan Khmelnytsky, *17th:* 461
Tadeusz Kościuszko, *18th:* 564
Ignacy Krasicki, *18th:* 567
Saint László I, *MA:* 637
Rosa Luxemburg, *20th:* 2482
Benoit B. Mandelbrot, *20th:* 2588
Eligiusz Niewiadomski, *Notor:* 792
Józef Piłsudski, *20th:* 3250
Sir Joseph Rotblat, *20th:* 3536
Sigismund I, the Old, *Ren:* 885
Sigismund II Augustus, *Ren:* 887
Sigismund III Vasa, *17th:* 853
Edith Stein, *20th:* 3840
Stephen Báthory, *Ren:* 910
Chaim Weizmann, *20th:* 4279
Władysław II Jagiełło and Jadwiga, *MA:* 1120
Lech Wałęsa, *20th:* 4191

Portugal
Afonso I, *MA:* 33
Afonso de Albuquerque, *Ren:* 22
Juan Rodríguez Cabrillo, *Ren:* 161
Luís de Camões, *Ren:* 167
Catherine of Braganza, *17th:* 137
Pêro da Covilhã, *Ren:* 259
Bartolomeu Dias, *Ren:* 286
António Egas Moniz, *20th:* 1107
Vasco da Gama, *Ren:* 365
Prince Henry the Navigator, *MA:* 477
John II, *Ren:* 511
John III, *Ren:* 513
John IV, *17th:* 430
Roderigo Lopez, *Notor:* 655
Ferdinand Magellan, *Ren:* 591
Manuel I, *Ren:* 605
Pedro I, *19th:* 1763
Tomé Pires, *Ren:* 792
Marquês de Pombal, *18th:* 795
António de Oliveira Salazar, *20th:* 3606, *Notor:* 928
Sebastian, *Ren:* 859
António Vieira, *17th:* 959

Prussia. ***See* Germany; Poland; Russia**

Roman Empire. ***See also* Roman Republic**
Gnaeus Julius Agricola, *Anc:* 17
Marcus Vipsanius Agrippa, *Anc:* 20

Agrippina the Younger, *Anc:* 23
Saint Ambrose, *Anc:* 42
Antonia the Younger, *Anc:* 71
Marc Antony, *Anc:* 73
Aretaeus of Cappadocia, *Anc:* 84
Arria the Elder, *Anc:* 102
Arria the Younger, *Anc:* 103
Saint Athanasius of Alexandria, *Anc:* 132
Saint Augustine, *Anc:* 142
Augustus, *Anc:* 145
Julius Caesar, *Anc:* 172
Caligula, *Anc:* 176, *Notor:* 165
Aulus Cornelius Celsus, *Anc:* 199
Cassius Chaerea, *Notor:* 195
Saint Christopher, *Anc:* 205
Saint John Chrysostom, *Anc:* 208
Claudius I, *Anc:* 217
Clement I, *Anc:* 223
Commodus, *Notor:* 227
Constantine the Great, *Anc:* 239
Saint Denis, *Anc:* 268
Dio Cassius, *Anc:* 274
Diocletian, *Anc:* 280
Pedanius Dioscorides, *Anc:* 289
Domitian, *Notor:* 289
Elagabalus, *Notor:* 326
Eusebius of Caesarea, *Anc:* 330
Galen, *Anc:* 348
Galerius, *Notor:* 390
Gregory of Nazianzus, *Anc:* 361
Gregory of Nyssa, *Anc:* 363
Hadrian, *Anc:* 370
Saint Helena, *Anc:* 391
Hippolytus of Rome, *Anc:* 423
Ignatius of Antioch, *Anc:* 437
Saint Irenaeus, *Anc:* 442
Saint Jerome, *Anc:* 456
Flavius Josephus, *Anc:* 477, *Notor:* 541
Julia III, *Anc:* 489
Julia Domna, *Anc:* 480
Julia Mamaea, *Anc:* 483
Julia Soaemias, *Anc:* 486
Juvenal, *Anc:* 493
Livia Drusilla, *Anc:* 508
Livy, *Anc:* 511
Lucian, *Anc:* 513
Marcus Aurelius, *Anc:* 530
Martial, *Anc:* 536
Valeria Messallina, *Anc:* 561
Nero, *Anc:* 591, *Notor:* 777
Ovid, *Anc:* 602
Saint Paul, *Anc:* 611
Saint Peter, *Anc:* 624
Pontius Pilate, *Anc:* 643, *Notor:* 840
Pliny the Elder, *Anc:* 665
Poppaea Sabina, *Anc:* 685
Priscillian, *Anc:* 698
Sextus Propertius, *Anc:* 704
Pytheas, *Anc:* 729
Seneca the Younger, *Anc:* 766
Saint Siricius, *Anc:* 796
Flavius Stilicho, *Anc:* 824
Sulpicia, *Anc:* 834
Tacitus, *Anc:* 837
Tertullian, *Anc:* 853
Theodoret of Cyrrhus, *Anc:* 865
Theodosius the Great, *Anc:* 868
Tiberius, *Anc:* 888
Trajan, *Anc:* 903
Valentinus, *Anc:* 918
Vespasian, *Anc:* 943
Zenobia, *Anc:* 986

ROMAN REPUBLIC. *See also* ROMAN EMPIRE
Asclepiades, *Anc:* 114
Marcus Junius Brutus, *Anc:* 166, *Notor:* 146
Cassius, *Anc:* 185
Catiline, *Anc:* 188, *Notor:* 188
Cato the Censor, *Anc:* 190
Cato the Younger, *Anc:* 194
Catullus, *Anc:* 196
Cicero, *Anc:* 210
Clodia, *Anc:* 233
Quintus Ennius, *Anc:* 301
Fabius, *Anc:* 342
Fulvia, *Notor:* 384
Gracchi, *Anc:* 357
Horace, *Anc:* 430
Lucretia, *Anc:* 517
Lucretius, *Anc:* 520
Gaius Maecenas, *Anc:* 527
Gaius Marius, *Anc:* 533
Plautus, *Anc:* 662
Pompey the Great, *Anc:* 681
Regulus, *Anc:* 738
Sallust, *Anc:* 742
Scipio Aemilianus, *Anc:* 755
Scipio Africanus, *Anc:* 758
Spartacus, *Anc:* 818
Strabo, *Anc:* 827
Lucius Cornelius Sulla, *Anc:* 830, *Notor:* 1010
Tanaquil, *Anc:* 840
Tarquins, *Anc:* 846
Terence, *Anc:* 849
Marcus Terentius Varro, *Anc:* 927
Vergil, *Anc:* 938
Marcus Verrius Flaccus, *Anc:* 941

ROMANIA
Ion Antonescu, *Notor:* 25
Béla Bartók, *20th:* 250
Elizabeth Báthory, *Ren:* 81, *Notor:* 70
Constantin Brancusi, *20th:* 478
Nicolae Ceauşescu, *20th:* 704, *Notor:* 190
Mircea Eliade, *20th:* 1136
Eugène Ionesco, *20th:* 1968
Hermann Oberth, *20th:* 3008
Ulfilas, *Anc:* 911
Vlad III the Impaler, *Ren:* 981, *Notor:* 1072
Elie Wiesel, *20th:* 4324
Iannis Xenakis, *20th:* 4414

RUSSIA. *See also* SOVIET UNION
Anna Akhmatova, *20th:* 42
Alexander I, *19th:* 45
Alexander II, *19th:* 48
Saint Alexander Nevsky, *MA:* 52
Alexis, *17th:* 11
Viktor A. Ambartsumian, *20th:* 77
Avvakum Petrovich, *17th:* 26
Mikhail Bakhtin, *20th:* 190
Mikhail Bakunin, *19th:* 119
George Balanchine, *20th:* 193
Nikolay Gennadiyevich Basov, *20th:* 256
Lavrenty Beria, *Notor:* 89
Vitus Jonassen Bering, *18th:* 108
Aleksandr Blok, *20th:* 394
Aleksandr Borodin, *19th:* 280
Leonid Brezhnev, *20th:* 523

Nikolay Ivanovich Bukharin, *20th:* 566
Catherine the Great, *18th:* 211
Marc Chagall, *20th:* 717
Anton Chekhov, *19th:* 478
Saint Cyril, *MA:* 294
Alexandra Danilova, *20th:* 908
Sergei Diaghilev, *20th:* 985
Fyodor Dostoevski, *19th:* 677
Felix Dzerzhinsky, *Notor:* 312
Sergei Eisenstein, *20th:* 1129
Elizabeth Petrovna, *18th:* 321
Michel Fokine, *20th:* 1263
Fyodor I, *Notor:* 385
Yuri Gagarin, *20th:* 1370
George Gamow, *20th:* 1379
Boris Godunov, *Ren:* 387
Nikolai Gogol, *19th:* 937
Mikhail Gorbachev, *20th:* 1530
Maxim Gorky, *20th:* 1549
Andrei Gromyko, *20th:* 1600
Aleksandr Herzen, *19th:* 1085
David Hilbert, *20th:* 1800
Vladimir Horowitz, *20th:* 1886
Ivan V, *Notor:* 514
Ivan VI, *Notor:* 515
Ivan the Great, *Ren:* 487
Ivan the Terrible, *Ren:* 492, *Notor:* 517
Roman Jakobson, *20th:* 1986
Engelbert Kämpfer, *17th:* 445
Wassily Kandinsky, *20th:* 2074
Pyotr Leonidovich Kapitsa, *20th:* 2077
Fanya Kaplan, *Notor:* 552
Aleksandr Fyodorovich Kerensky, *20th:* 2110
Nikita S. Khrushchev, *20th:* 2128, *Notor:* 574
Käthe Kollwitz, *20th:* 2189
Sergei Korolev, *20th:* 2191
Sofya Kovalevskaya, *19th:* 1295
Igor Vasilyevich Kurchatov, *20th:* 2214
Mikhail Illarionovich Kutuzov, *18th:* 569
Lev Davidovich Landau, *20th:* 2244
Vladimir Ilich Lenin, *20th:* 2341, *Notor:* 628
Mikhail Lermontov, *19th:* 1352
Serge Lifar, *20th:* 2378
Maksim Maksimovich Litvinov, *20th:* 2404
Nikolay Ivanovich Lobachevsky, *19th:* 1403
Mikhail Vasilyevich Lomonosov, *18th:* 613
Rosa Luxemburg, *20th:* 2482
Trofim Lysenko, *Notor:* 667
Georgi M. Malenkov, *20th:* 2573
Dame Alicia Markova, *20th:* 2627
Léonide Massine, *20th:* 2646
Vladimir Mayakovsky, *20th:* 2659
Dmitry Ivanovich Mendeleyev, *19th:* 1544
Saint Methodius, *MA:* 294
Vsevolod Yemilyevich Meyerhold, *20th:* 2722
Vyacheslav Mikhailovich Molotov, *20th:* 2783, *Notor:* 746
Boris Ivanovich Morozov, *17th:* 663
Modest Mussorgsky, *19th:* 1626
Vladimir Nabokov, *20th:* 2894
Nicholas I, *19th:* 1670, *Notor:* 788
Vaslav Nijinsky, *20th:* 2974
Rudolf Nureyev, *20th:* 3001
Saint Olga, *MA:* 792
Aleksandr Ivanovich Oparin, *20th:* 3062
Aleksey Grigoryevich Orlov, *18th:* 755
Grigori Grigoryevich Orlov, *18th:* 757
Sophia Palaeologus, *Ren:* 749
Boris Pasternak, *20th:* 3131
Ivan Petrovich Pavlov, *20th:* 3162
Anna Pavlova, *20th:* 3166
Peter III, *18th:* 778
Peter the Great, *18th:* 774
Kim Philby, *Notor:* 836
Konstantin Petrovich Pobedonostsev, *19th:* 1810, *Notor:* 845
Aleksandr Stepanovich Popov, *19th:* 1824
Grigori Aleksandrovich Potemkin, *18th:* 808
Sergei Prokofiev, *20th:* 3338
Yemelyan Ivanovich Pugachev, *18th:* 814
Alexander Pushkin, *19th:* 1848
Sergei Rachmaninoff, *20th:* 3361
Ayn Rand, *20th:* 3367
Grigori Yefimovich Rasputin, *19th:* 1863, *Notor:* 885
Stenka Razin, *17th:* 784
Nikolay Rimsky-Korsakov, *19th:* 1915
Michael Romanov, *17th:* 794
Rurik, *MA:* 911
Andrei Sakharov, *20th:* 3602
Nathalie Sarraute, *20th:* 3635
Dmitri Shostakovich, *20th:* 3728
Aleksandr Solzhenitsyn, *20th:* 3783
Sophia, *17th:* 865
Mikhail Mikhaylovich Speransky, *19th:* 2129
Joseph Stalin, *20th:* 3817, *Notor:* 990
Konstantin Stanislavsky, *20th:* 3821
Igor Stravinsky, *20th:* 3888
Aleksandr Vasilyevich Suvorov, *18th:* 954
Queen Tamara, *MA:* 998
Peter Ilich Tchaikovsky, *19th:* 2233
Valentina Tereshkova, *20th:* 3978
Leo Tolstoy, *19th:* 2283
Leon Trotsky, *20th:* 4072, *Notor:* 1040
Konstantin Tsiolkovsky, *20th:* 4095
Marina Tsvetayeva, *20th:* 4098
Andrei Nikolayevich Tupolev, *20th:* 4108
Ivan Turgenev, *19th:* 2319
Vasili Vasilievich Ulrikh, *Notor:* 1052
Vasily III, *Ren:* 957
Vasily Shuysky, *17th:* 943
Nikolai Ivanovich Vavilov, *20th:* 4151
Vladimir I, *MA:* 1068
Andrey Andreyevich Vlasov, *Notor:* 1074

Andrey Vyshinsky, *Notor:* 1079
Selman Abraham Waksman, *20th:* 4180
Genrikh Yagoda, *Notor:* 1112
Boris Yeltsin, *20th:* 4431
Nikolay Ivanovich Yezhov, *Notor:* 1115
Yakov Mikhailovich Yurovsky, *Notor:* 1124
Felix Yusupov, *Notor:* 1126
Andrey Aleksandrovich Zhdanov, *Notor:* 1137
Georgy Zhukov, *20th:* 4469
Grigory Yevseyevich Zinovyev, *Notor:* 1138
Vladimir Zworykin, *20th:* 4479

SAUDI ARABIA
Faisal, *20th:* 1198
Fahdl, *20th:* 1195
ʿAbd al-Malik, *MA:* 3
Osama Bin Laden, *20th:* 371, *Notor:* 101
al-Ḥasan al-Baṣrī, *MA:* 471
Khadīja, *MA:* 610
T. E. Lawrence, *20th:* 2303
Muḥammad, *MA:* 733
ʿUmar I, *MA:* 1037
Muḥammad ibn ʿAbd al-Wahhāb, *18th:* 1030
Ahmad Zaki Yamani, *20th:* 4422

SCANDINAVIA. ***See also* DENMARK; FINLAND; ICELAND; NORWAY; SWEDEN**
Rurik, *MA:* 911

SCOTLAND
Robert and James Adam, *18th:* 3
Queen Anne, *18th:* 45
Second Duke of Argyll, *18th:* 53
Johnnie Armstrong, *Notor:* 35
Arthur Balfour, *20th:* 208
Alexander Graham Bell, *19th:* 182
James Gordon Bennett, *19th:* 188
Joseph Black, *18th:* 115
Tony Blair, *20th:* 385
James Boswell, *18th:* 146
William Brodie, *Notor:* 145
Henry Brougham, *19th:* 312
James Bruce, *18th:* 168
Robert Bruce, *MA:* 200
George Buchanan, *Ren:* 146
William Burke, *Notor:* 154
Robert Burns, *18th:* 183
Fanny Calderón de la Barca, *19th:* 389
Richard Cameron, *17th:* 121
Caroline, *18th:* 203
Robert Carr, *17th:* 131
Charles I, *17th:* 143
Charles II (of England), *17th:* 147, *Notor:* 201
Queen Charlotte, *18th:* 235
First Marquis of Dalhousie, *19th:* 595
David I, *MA:* 304
David II, *MA:* 307
Sir Arthur Conan Doyle, *19th:* 688
John Duns Scotus, *MA:* 329
Elizabeth Stuart, *17th:* 253
First Baron Erskine, *18th:* 326
Adam Ferguson, *18th:* 338
Sir Alexander Fleming, *20th:* 1254
Williamina Paton Stevens Fleming, *19th:* 788
Sir James George Frazer, *20th:* 1319
Klaus Fuchs, *Notor:* 379
George I, *18th:* 400
George II, *18th:* 403
George III, *18th:* 408
James Gregory, *17th:* 319
Keir Hardie, *19th:* 1025
David Hume, *18th:* 514
James I, *17th:* 413
James III, *Ren:* 496
James IV, *Ren:* 498
James V, *Ren:* 501
Lord Jeffrey, *19th:* 1223
William Kidd, *17th:* 464, *Notor:* 576
John Knox, *Ren:* 528
Bonar Law, *20th:* 2292
David Livingstone, *19th:* 1400
Flora MacDonald, *18th:* 623
Ramsay MacDonald, *20th:* 2510
Sir Alexander Mackenzie, *18th:* 629
William Lyon Mackenzie, *19th:* 1454
Colin Maclaurin, *18th:* 632
John J. R. Macleod, *20th:* 2526
Daniel and Alexander Macmillan, *19th:* 1464
First Earl of Mansfield, *18th:* 643
Mary, Queen of Scots, *Ren:* 627
Mary of Guise, *Ren:* 633
James Clerk Maxwell, *19th:* 1528
James Mill, *19th:* 1571
William Murdock, *18th:* 715
John Napier, *Ren:* 710
James Nasmyth, *19th:* 1646
Mungo Park, *18th:* 765
William Paterson, *17th:* 716
Sir Henry Raeburn, *19th:* 1852
First Baron Reith of Stonehaven, *20th:* 3410
John Roebuck, *18th:* 858
Rob Roy, *Notor:* 902
Sir Walter Scott, *19th:* 2047
Adam Smith, *18th:* 921
Madeleine Smith, *Notor:* 975
Mary Somerville, *19th:* 2121
Robert Louis Stevenson, *19th:* 2173
Thomas Telford, *19th:* 2240
William Wallace, *MA:* 1072
James Watt, *18th:* 1048
James Wilson, *18th:* 1090
John Witherspoon, *18th:* 1098
Frances Wright, *19th:* 2469

SENEGAL
Léopold Senghor, *20th:* 3702

SERBIA AND MONTENEGRO
Milovan Djilas, *20th:* 1011
Radovan Karadžić, *Notor:* 554
Slobodan Milošević, *20th:* 2756, *Notor:* 735
Puniša Račić, *Notor:* 876
Stefan Dušan, *MA:* 957

SICILY
Phalaris, *Notor:* 834

SINGAPORE
Lee Kuan Yew, *20th:* 2326

Slovakia. *See* **Czech Republic and Slovakia**

Slovenia
Saint Elizabeth of Hungary, *MA:* 359
Tito, *20th:* 4034, *Notor:* 1032

Somalia
Muhammad Siad Barre, *20th:* 3734, *Notor:* 953

South Africa
Christiaan Barnard, *20th:* 236
Louis Botha, *20th:* 439
Cetshwayo, *19th:* 450
F. W. de Klerk, *20th:* 948
Eugene de Kock, *Notor:* 271
Athol Fugard, *20th:* 1354
Nadine Gordimer, *20th:* 1534
Sir George Grey, *19th:* 981
Paul Kruger, *19th:* 1298
Lobengula, *19th:* 1406
Albert Lutuli, *20th:* 2478
Nelson Mandela, *20th:* 2583
Winnie Mandela, *Notor:* 686
Alan Paton, *20th:* 3138
Gary Player, *20th:* 3288
Cecil Rhodes, *19th:* 1891
Olive Schreiner, *19th:* 2023
Shaka, *19th:* 2081
Jan Christian Smuts, *20th:* 3775
Desmond Tutu, *20th:* 4121
Hendrik Frensch Verwoerd, *Notor:* 1064

South America. *See* **Argentina; Bolivia; Brazil; Chile; Colombia; Ecuador; Native America; Paraguay; Peru; Venezuela**

Southeast Asia. *See* **Burma; Cambodia; Indonesia; Laos; Malaysia; Philippines; Singapore; Thailand; Vietnam**

Soviet Union. *See also* **Azerbaijan; Belarus; Georgia, Republic of; Latvia; Russia; Ukraine**
Anna Akhmatova, *20th:* 42
Mikhail Bakhtin, *20th:* 190
George Balanchine, *20th:* 193
Mikhail Baryshnikov, *20th:* 253
Nikolay Gennadiyevich Basov, *20th:* 256
Aleksandr Blok, *20th:* 394
Leonid Brezhnev, *20th:* 523
Nikolay Ivanovich Bukharin, *20th:* 566
Guy Burgess, *Notor:* 152
Andrei Chikatilo, *Notor:* 207
Felix Dzerzhinsky, *Notor:* 312
Sergei Eisenstein, *20th:* 1129
Yuri Gagarin, *20th:* 1370
Maxim Gorky, *20th:* 1549
Andrei Gromyko, *20th:* 1600
Lazar Kaganovich, *Notor:* 549
Nikita S. Khrushchev, *20th:* 2128, *Notor:* 574
Sergei Korolev, *20th:* 2191
Igor Vasilyevich Kurchatov, *20th:* 2214
Lev Davidovich Landau, *20th:* 2244
Vladimir Ilich Lenin, *20th:* 2341, *Notor:* 628
Maksim Maksimovich Litvinov, *20th:* 2404
Georgi M. Malenkov, *20th:* 2573
Vladimir Mayakovsky, *20th:* 2659
Vsevolod Yemilyevich Meyerhold, *20th:* 2722
Vyacheslav Mikhailovich Molotov, *20th:* 2783, *Notor:* 746
Sun Myung Moon, *20th:* 2811, *Notor:* 749
Aleksandr Ivanovich Oparin, *20th:* 3062
Boris Pasternak, *20th:* 3131
Ivan Petrovich Pavlov, *20th:* 3162
Kim Philby, *Notor:* 836
Sergei Prokofiev, *20th:* 3338
Andrei Sakharov, *20th:* 3602
Dmitri Shostakovich, *20th:* 3728
Aleksandr Solzhenitsyn, *20th:* 3783
Joseph Stalin, *20th:* 3817, *Notor:* 990
Konstantin Stanislavsky, *20th:* 3821
Valentina Tereshkova, *20th:* 3978
Leon Trotsky, *20th:* 4072, *Notor:* 1040
Konstantin Tsiolkovsky, *20th:* 4095
Marina Tsvetayeva, *20th:* 4098
Andrei Nikolayevich Tupolev, *20th:* 4108
Vasili Vasilievich Ulrikh, *Notor:* 1052
Nikolai Ivanovich Vavilov, *20th:* 4151
Andrey Vyshinsky, *Notor:* 1079
Boris Yeltsin, *20th:* 4431
Yakov Mikhailovich Yurovsky, *Notor:* 1124
Andrey Aleksandrovich Zhdanov, *Notor:* 1137
Georgy Zhukov, *20th:* 4469
Grigory Yevseyevich Zinovyev, *Notor:* 1138

Spain
ʿAbd al-Muʾmin, *MA:* 6
ʿAbd al-Raḥmān III al-Nāṣir, *MA:* 9
Isaac ben Judah Abravanel, *Ren:* 1
José de Acosta, *Ren:* 5
Adrian VI, *Ren:* 7
Mateo Alemán, *Ren:* 25
Alfonso X, *MA:* 59
Duke of Alva, *Ren:* 31
Pedro de Alvarado, *Ren:* 34
Anne of Austria, *17th:* 18
Arnold of Villanova, *MA:* 98
Averroës, *MA:* 118
Vasco Núñez de Balboa, *Ren:* 76
Blanche of Castile, *MA:* 166
Boabdil, *Ren:* 105
Cesare Borgia, *Ren:* 114, *Notor:* 127
Luis Buñuel, *20th:* 578

Álvar Núñez Cabeza de Vaca, *Ren:* 152
Sebastian Cabot, *Ren:* 159
Juan Rodríguez Cabrillo, *Ren:* 161
Pedro Calderón de la Barca, *17th:* 113
Fanny Calderón de la Barca, *19th:* 389
Felix Candela, *20th:* 631
Don Carlos, *19th:* 412
Pablo Casals, *20th:* 681
Miguel de Cervantes, *Ren:* 206
Charles II (1630-1685; King of England), *17th:* 147, *Notor:* 201
Charles II (1661-1700; King of Spain), *17th:* 151
Charles III, *18th:* 227
Charles V, *Ren:* 220
Charles VI, *18th:* 229
Duchesse de Chevreuse, *17th:* 158
El Cid, *MA:* 278
Carolina Coronado, *19th:* 556
Francisco Vásquez de Coronado, *Ren:* 245
Hernán Cortés, *Ren:* 252
Salvador Dalí, *20th:* 904
Saint Dominic, *MA:* 316
Juan Sebastián de Elcano, *Ren:* 307
Manuel de Falla, *20th:* 1206
Alessandro Farnese, *Ren:* 321
Ferdinand II (1452-1516; Spanish king), *Ren:* 328
Francisco Franco, *20th:* 1297, *Notor:* 371
José de Gálvez, *18th:* 394
Federico García Lorca, *20th:* 1395
Antonio Gaudí, *20th:* 1423
Luis de Góngora y Argote, *17th:* 312
Francisco de Goya, *18th:* 436
Baltasar Gracián y Morales, *17th:* 316
El Greco, *Ren:* 390
Juan Gris, *20th:* 1597
Juan de Herrera, *Ren:* 445
Ibn al-ʿArabī, *MA:* 526
Ibn Gabirol, *MA:* 532
Ibn Khaldūn, *MA:* 536
al-Idrīsī, *MA:* 539
Saint Ignatius of Loyola, *Ren:* 482
Isabella I, *Ren:* 328
Isabella II, *19th:* 1183
Saint Isidore of Seville, *MA:* 555
James I the Conqueror, *MA:* 571
Francisco Jiménez de Cisneros, *Ren:* 503
Joan the Mad, *Notor:* 531
John of Austria, *17th:* 425
Saint John of the Cross, *Ren:* 507
Juan Carlos I, *20th:* 2060
Judah ha-Levi, *MA:* 591
Joseph ben Ephraim Karo, *Ren:* 524
Bartolomé de Las Casas, *Ren:* 537
Miguel López de Legazpi, *Ren:* 550
Leo Africanus, *Ren:* 555
Duke de Lerma, *17th:* 530
Raymond Lull, *MA:* 673
Moses Maimonides, *MA:* 686
Margaret of Parma, *Ren:* 615
Marie-Thérèse, *17th:* 600
Maximilian II, *Ren:* 650
Bernardino de Mendoza, *Ren:* 668
Ana de Mendoza y de la Cerda, *Ren:* 670
Pedro Menéndez de Avilés, *Ren:* 672
Ramón Mercader, *Notor:* 721
Joan Miró, *20th:* 2759
Moses de León, *MA:* 730
Bartolomé Esteban Murillo, *17th:* 670
Naḥmanides, *MA:* 747
Count-Duke of Olivares, *17th:* 697
José Ortega y Gasset, *20th:* 3077
Peter the Cruel, *Notor:* 827
Philip II, *Ren:* 778
Philip III, *17th:* 736
Philip IV, *17th:* 738
Philip V, *18th:* 781
Pablo Picasso, *20th:* 3237
The Pinzón Brothers, *Ren:* 789
Francisco Pizarro, *Ren:* 800
Juan Ponce de León, *Ren:* 803
Miguel Primo de Rivera, *Notor:* 860
Priscillian, *Anc:* 698
Francisco Gómez de Quevedo y Villegas, *17th:* 770
Raymond of Peñafort, *MA:* 881
George Santayana, *20th:* 3629
La Saragossa, *19th:* 1993
Andrés Segovia, *20th:* 3691
Junípero Serra, *18th:* 891
Michael Servetus, *Ren:* 861
Diego de Siloé, *Ren:* 890
Hernando de Soto, *Ren:* 902
Ṭāriq ibn-Ziyād, *MA:* 1005
Saint Teresa of Ávila, *Ren:* 928
Tirso de Molina, *17th:* 913
Tomás de Torquemada, *Ren:* 939, *Notor:* 1038
Miguel de Unamuno y Jugo, *20th:* 4128
Lope de Vega Carpio, *17th:* 949
Diego Velázquez, *17th:* 953
Francisco de Vitoria, *Ren:* 978
Saint Francis Xavier, *Ren:* 1000
Francisco de Zurbarán, *17th:* 1003

SRI LANKA. ***See*** **INDIA AND SRI LANKA**

SUDAN
Amina Sarauniya Zazzua, *Ren:* 37
Omar al-Bashir, *Notor:* 66
The Mahdi, *19th:* 1473

SWEDEN
Hannes Alfvén, *20th:* 58
Svante August Arrhenius, *20th:* 138
Ingmar Bergman, *20th:* 316
Ingrid Bergman, *20th:* 321
Björn Borg, *20th:* 426
Charles X Gustav, *17th:* 153
Charles XII, *18th:* 232
Charles XIV John, *19th:* 468
Christina, *17th:* 163
Erik XIV, *Notor:* 331
Greta Garbo, *20th:* 1392
Gustav I Vasa, *Ren:* 415
Gustavus II Adolphus, *17th:* 336
Dag Hammarskjöld, *20th:* 1653
Selma Lagerlöf, *20th:* 2234
Jenny Lind, *19th:* 1387

Carolus Linnaeus, *18th:* 604
Margaret of Denmark, Norway, and Sweden, *MA:* 689
Mijailo Mijailovic, *Notor:* 727
Peter Minuit, *17th:* 643
Gunnar Myrdal, *20th:* 2890
Alfred Nobel, *19th:* 1689
Axel Oxenstierna, *17th:* 704
Nelly Sachs, *20th:* 3583
Friedrich Hermann Schomberg, *17th:* 820
Sigismund III Vasa, *17th:* 853
Nathan Söderblom, *20th:* 3781
August Strindberg, *20th:* 3898
Emanuel Swedenborg, *18th:* 961
Hugo Theorell, *20th:* 3997
Lennart Torstenson, *17th:* 924

SWITZERLAND
Karl Barth, *20th:* 243
The Bernoulli Family, *17th:* 48
Eugen Bleuler, *20th:* 391
Emil Brunner, *20th:* 547
Jacob Burckhardt, *19th:* 354
Jean-Henri Dunant, *19th:* 699
Leonhard Euler, *18th:* 333
Max Frisch, *20th:* 1338
Conrad Gesner, *Ren:* 375
Alberto Giacometti, *20th:* 1470
Jean-Luc Godard, *20th:* 1502
Charles-Édouard Guillaume, *20th:* 1616
John Parricida, *Notor:* 536
Carl Jung, *20th:* 2062
Angelica Kauffmann, *18th:* 554
Paul Klee, *20th:* 2176
Elisabeth Kübler-Ross, *20th:* 2207
Le Corbusier, *20th:* 2323
Jacques Necker, *18th:* 726
Paracelsus, *Ren:* 757
Johann Heinrich Pestalozzi, *19th:* 1782
Jean Piaget, *20th:* 3231
Auguste and Jean-Felix Piccard, *20th:* 3240
Hermann Rorschach, *20th:* 3522
Ferdinand de Saussure, *20th:* 3649
Jakob Steiner, *19th:* 2154
Huldrych Zwingli, *Ren:* 1010

SYRIA
ʿAbd al-Malik, *MA:* 3
Alp Arslan, *MA:* 70
Hafez al-Assad, *20th:* 153
Cyrus the Great, *Anc:* 248
Darius the Great, *Anc:* 251
Elagabalus, *Notor:* 326
John of Damascus, *MA:* 587
Saladin, *MA:* 918
Seleucus I Nicator, *Anc:* 763
Saint Simeon Stylites, *Anc:* 789
Tancred, *MA:* 1003
Theodoret of Cyrrhus, *Anc:* 865
Xerxes I, *Anc:* 971
Yaqut, *MA:* 1143
Zenobia, *Anc:* 986

TAIWAN
Chiang Kai-shek, *20th:* 746

TANZANIA
Mary Leakey, *20th:* 2315
Julius Nyerere, *20th:* 3004
Saʿīd ibn Sulṭān, *19th:* 1965
Tippu Tib, *19th:* 2277

THAILAND
Bhumibol Adulyadej, *20th:* 363
Anna Leonowens, *19th:* 1346
Suryavarman II, *MA:* 980
Taksin, *18th:* 968

TIBET
Dalai Lama, *20th:* 902

TRANSYLVANIA. ***See*** **ROMANIA**

TRINIDAD AND TOBAGO
Learie Constantine, *20th:* 829
Sir V. S. Naipaul, *20th:* 2903

TUNISIA
Saint Augustine, *Anc:* 142
Habib Bourguiba, *20th:* 457
Dido, *Anc:* 271
Hamilcar Barca, *Anc:* 373
Hannibal, *Anc:* 382
Hanno, *Anc:* 385
Ibn Khaldūn, *MA:* 536
Masinissa, *Anc:* 542
Sophonisba of Numidia, *Anc:* 812
Terence, *Anc:* 849

TURKEY. ***See also*** **OTTOMAN EMPIRE**
Halide Edib Adıvar, *20th:* 29
Mehmet Ali Ağca, *Notor:* 8
Alp Arslan, *MA:* 70
Anaxagoras, *Anc:* 52
Anaximander, *Anc:* 55
Anaximenes, *Anc:* 58
Antigonus I Monophthalmos, *Anc:* 63
Antiochus the Great, *Anc:* 65
Apollonius of Perga, *Anc:* 76
Aretaeus of Cappadocia, *Anc:* 84
Aspasia of Miletus, *Anc:* 127
Atatürk, *20th:* 162
Barbarossa, *Ren:* 79
Basil the Macedonian, *MA:* 133
al-Battānī, *MA:* 137
Baybars I, *MA:* 139
Bayezid II, *Ren:* 87
Saint Christopher, *Anc:* 205
Saint John Chrysostom, *Anc:* 208
Croesus, *Anc:* 244
Cyrus the Great, *Anc:* 248
Darius the Great, *Anc:* 251
Dio Cassius, *Anc:* 274
Diogenes, *Anc:* 283
Pedanius Dioscorides, *Anc:* 289
Enver Paşa, *20th:* 1157
Eudoxus of Cnidus, *Anc:* 320
Galen, *Anc:* 348
Gregory of Nazianzus, *Anc:* 361
Gregory of Nyssa, *Anc:* 363
Saint Helena, *Anc:* 391
Herodotus, *Anc:* 407
Hipparchus, *Anc:* 417
Homer, *Anc:* 427
İbrahim Paşa, *Ren:* 480
Saint Irenaeus, *Anc:* 442
İsmet Paşa, *20th:* 1971
Jamāl al-Dīn al-Afghānī, *19th:* 1203
John the Apostle, *Anc:* 471
Joseph ben Ephraim Karo, *Ren:* 524
Kâtib Çelebî, *17th:* 454
Levni, *18th:* 602

Mausolus, *Anc:* 545
Mehmed II, *MA:* 711, *Ren:* 659
Mehmed III, *Ren:* 661
Melisende, *MA:* 715
Mithradates VI Eupator, *Anc:* 567
Osman I, *MA:* 800
Sophia Palaeologus, *Ren:* 749
Saint Paul, *Anc:* 611
Pausanias the Traveler, *Anc:* 618
Qāytbāy, *Ren:* 807
Jalāl al-Dīn Rūmī, *MA:* 908
Sennacherib, *Anc:* 769
Strabo, *Anc:* 827
Süleyman the Magnificent, *Ren:* 914
Theodore of Mopsuestia, *Anc:* 862
Theodoret of Cyrrhus, *Anc:* 865
Theoleptus of Philadelphia, *MA:* 1016
Ulfilas, *Anc:* 911
Xerxes I, *Anc:* 971
Zenobia, *Anc:* 986

TURKMENISTAN
al-Bīrūnī, *MA:* 163
Cyrus the Great, *Anc:* 248
Saparmurat Niyazov, *Notor:* 796

UGANDA
Idi Amin, *20th:* 80, *Notor:* 20
Lord Lugard, *20th:* 2465
Yoweri Kaguta Museveni, *20th:* 2883
Milton Obote, *20th:* 3011

UKRAINE
Anna Akhmatova, *20th:* 42
Baʿal Shem Tov, *18th:* 68
Leonid Brezhnev, *20th:* 523
Andrei Chikatilo, *Notor:* 207
Joseph Conrad, *20th:* 824
George Gamow, *20th:* 1379
Vladimir Horowitz, *20th:* 1886
John III Sobieski, *17th:* 427
Bohdan Khmelnytsky, *17th:* 461
Sergei Korolev, *20th:* 2191
Ivan Stepanovich Mazepa, *17th:* 624
Golda Meir, *20th:* 2674
Symon Petlyura, *Notor:* 832
Sergei Prokofiev, *20th:* 3338
Leon Trotsky, *20th:* 4072, *Notor:* 1040
Selman Abraham Waksman, *20th:* 4180
Grigory Yevseyevich Zinovyev, *Notor:* 1138

UNITED KINGDOM. ***See* ENGLAND; IRELAND AND NORTHERN IRELAND; SCOTLAND; WALES**

UNITED STATES
Hank Aaron, *20th:* 5
Frank W. Abagnale, Jr., *Notor:* 3
Ralph Abernathy, *20th:* 11
Dean Acheson, *20th:* 17
Abigail Adams, *18th:* 7
Henry Adams, *19th:* 16
John Adams, *18th:* 11
John Quincy Adams, *19th:* 20
Samuel Adams, *18th:* 16
Jane Addams, *20th:* 22
Felix Adler, *19th:* 26
Joe Adonis, *Notor:* 6
Elizabeth Cabot Agassiz, *19th:* 29
Louis Agassiz, *19th:* 31
Alvin Ailey, *20th:* 36
JoAnne Akalaitis, *20th:* 39
Madeleine Albright, *20th:* 54
Bronson Alcott, *19th:* 38
Louisa May Alcott, *19th:* 41
John Alden, *17th:* 7
Horatio Alger, *19th:* 51
Muhammad Ali, *20th:* 61
Ethan Allen, *18th:* 35
John Peter Altgeld, *19th:* 57
Luis W. Alvarez, *20th:* 73
Aldrich Ames, *Notor:* 16
Oakes Ames, *Notor:* 18
Albert Anastasia, *Notor:* 23
Marian Anderson, *20th:* 87
Mother Angelica, *20th:* 90
Maya Angelou, *20th:* 97
Susan B. Anthony, *19th:* 65
Apache Kid, *Notor:* 27
Virginia Apgar, *20th:* 100
Johnny Appleseed, *19th:* 68
Marshall Applewhite, *Notor:* 28
Roscoe Arbuckle, *Notor:* 32
Diane Arbus, *20th:* 115
Hannah Arendt, *20th:* 118
Louis Armstrong, *20th:* 130
Neil Armstrong, *20th:* 134
Benedict Arnold, *18th:* 59, *Notor:* 36
Chester A. Arthur, *19th:* 79
Dorothy Arzner, *20th:* 141
Francis Asbury, *18th:* 62
Mary Kay Ash, *20th:* 145
Fred Astaire, *20th:* 155
John Jacob Astor, *19th:* 86
Nancy Astor, *20th:* 158
W. H. Auden, *20th:* 172
John James Audubon, *19th:* 91
Stephen Fuller Austin, *19th:* 98
Isaac Backus, *18th:* 75
Nathaniel Bacon, *17th:* 29
Bobby Baker, *Notor:* 48
Jim Bakker, *Notor:* 50
George Balanchine, *20th:* 193
Emily Greene Balch, *20th:* 197
James Baldwin, *20th:* 201
Joe Ball, *Notor:* 52
Lucille Ball, *20th:* 212
Robert D. Ballard, *20th:* 215
George Bancroft, *19th:* 130
Benjamin Banneker, *18th:* 84
Samuel Barber, *20th:* 230
John Bardeen, *20th:* 234
Velma Margie Barfield, *Notor:* 59
Ma Barker, *Notor:* 61
Henry Barnard, *19th:* 135
Djuna Barnes, *20th:* 240
P. T. Barnum, *19th:* 138
Clyde Barrow, *Notor:* 62
Sydney Barrows, *Notor:* 64
Clara Barton, *19th:* 145
Mikhail Baryshnikov, *20th:* 253
Sam Bass, *Notor:* 68
L. Frank Baum, *19th:* 155
Charles A. Beard, *20th:* 262
Dave Beck, *Notor:* 75
Byron De La Beckwith, *Notor:* 78
Catharine Beecher, *19th:* 168
Henry Ward Beecher, *19th:* 172
Alexander Graham Bell, *19th:* 182
Tom Bell, *Notor:* 80
Samuel Bellamy, *Notor:* 81

Saul Bellow, *20th:* 288
Bambi Bembenek, *Notor:* 84
Ruth Benedict, *20th:* 296
Stephen Vincent Benét, *20th:* 303
James Gordon Bennett, *19th:* 188
Thomas Hart Benton, *19th:* 192
David Berg, *Notor:* 87
Ingrid Bergman, *20th:* 321
David Berkowitz, *Notor:* 91
Irving Berlin, *20th:* 327
Leonard Bernstein, *20th:* 337
Hans Albrecht Bethe, *20th:* 341
Mary McLeod Bethune, *20th:* 345
Jeff Bezos, *20th:* 360
Kenneth Bianchi, *Notor:* 95
Nicholas Biddle, *19th:* 225
Ambrose Bierce, *19th:* 228
Albert Bierstadt, *19th:* 232
Theodore G. Bilbo, *Notor:* 99
George Caleb Bingham, *19th:* 234
Hugo L. Black, *20th:* 377
Black Hawk, *19th:* 244
Harry A. Blackmun, *20th:* 382
Elizabeth Blackwell, *19th:* 247
James G. Blaine, *19th:* 251
Lou Blonger, *Notor:* 107
Amelia Bloomer, *19th:* 257
Franz Boas, *20th:* 400
Ivan Boesky, *Notor:* 110
Humphrey Bogart, *20th:* 406
William H. Bonney, *Notor:* 118
Daniel Boone, *18th:* 143
Edwin Booth, *19th:* 271
John Wilkes Booth, *Notor:* 123
Lizzie Borden, *19th:* 277, *Notor:* 125
Norman Borlaug, *20th:* 434
Margaret Bourke-White, *20th:* 460
Christopher John Boyce, *Notor:* 133
Belle Boyd, *Notor:* 135
William Bradford, *17th:* 84
Omar Nelson Bradley, *20th:* 468
Anne Bradstreet, *17th:* 88
Mathew B. Brady, *19th:* 291
Louis D. Brandeis, *20th:* 482
Marlon Brando, *20th:* 486
Joseph Brant, *18th:* 159
Wernher von Braun, *20th:* 500
Arthur Bremer, *Notor:* 139
William J. Brennan, *20th:* 507
Margaret Brent, *17th:* 92
Stephen G. Breyer, *20th:* 520
Percy Williams Bridgman, *20th:* 526
John R. Brinkley, *Notor:* 141
Curly Bill Brocius, *Notor:* 143
Gwendolyn Brooks, *20th:* 537
Helen Gurley Brown, *20th:* 539
John Brown, *19th:* 319
Molly Brown, *20th:* 542
Olympia Brown, *19th:* 323
William Jennings Bryan, *20th:* 550
William Cullen Bryant, *19th:* 340
Louis Buchalter, *Notor:* 148
James Buchanan, *19th:* 343
Pearl S. Buck, *20th:* 557
William F. Buckley, Jr., *20th:* 561
Warren Buffett, *20th:* 563
Charles Bulfinch, *19th:* 346
Ralph Bunche, *20th:* 574
Ted Bundy, *Notor:* 149
Angelo Buono, Jr., *Notor:* 151
Luther Burbank, *19th:* 350
Warren E. Burger, *20th:* 581
Frances Hodgson Burnett, *19th:* 357
Daniel Hudson Burnham, *19th:* 360
Aaron Burr, *19th:* 363, *Notor:* 155
Edgar Rice Burroughs, *20th:* 590
George H. W. Bush, *20th:* 594
Nicholas Murray Butler, *20th:* 597
Richard Girnt Butler, *Notor:* 157
Joey Buttafuoco, *Notor:* 159
Samuel Joseph Byck, *Notor:* 162
Richard Byrd, *20th:* 606
Frances Xavier Cabrini, *19th:* 383
Calamity Jane, *19th:* 386
Alexander Calder, *20th:* 609
John C. Calhoun, *19th:* 392
Maria Callas, *20th:* 612
William Calley, *Notor:* 168
Melvin Calvin, *20th:* 621
Simon Cameron, *Notor:* 171
Alexander Campbell, *19th:* 399
Felix Candela, *20th:* 631
Billy Cannon, *Notor:* 173
Canonicus, *17th:* 129
Al Capone, *20th:* 641, *Notor:* 175
Truman Capote, *20th:* 644
Benjamin N. Cardozo, *20th:* 653
Chester F. Carlson, *20th:* 657
Rudolf Carnap, *20th:* 659
Andrew Carnegie, *19th:* 419
Charles Carroll, *18th:* 205
Kit Carson, *19th:* 426
Rachel Carson, *20th:* 662
Jimmy Carter, *20th:* 666
Willis A. Carto, *Notor:* 177
George Washington Carver, *20th:* 678
Mary Ann Shadd Cary, *19th:* 431
Mary Cassatt, *19th:* 433
Butch Cassidy, *Notor:* 181
Paul Castellano, *Notor:* 183
Willa Cather, *20th:* 696
George Catlin, *19th:* 441
Carrie Chapman Catt, *20th:* 701
Vinton Gray Cerf, *20th:* 707
Cassie L. Chadwick, *Notor:* 193
Wilt Chamberlain, *20th:* 725
Whittaker Chambers, *Notor:* 198
William Ellery Channing, *19th:* 464
Charles Chaplin, *20th:* 731
Mark David Chapman, *Notor:* 200
Ray Charles, *20th:* 735
Salmon P. Chase, *19th:* 470
Samuel Chase, *18th:* 237
César Chávez, *20th:* 738
Judy Chicago, *20th:* 750
Lydia Maria Child, *19th:* 482
Shirley Chisholm, *20th:* 753
Noam Chomsky, *20th:* 757
Kate Chopin, *19th:* 490
Benjamin Church, *Notor:* 211
George Rogers Clark, *18th:* 253
William Clark, *19th:* 1359
Henry Clay, *19th:* 502
Grover Cleveland, *19th:* 507
Bill Clinton, *20th:* 783
DeWitt Clinton, *19th:* 512
Hillary Rodham Clinton, *20th:* 788
Ty Cobb, *20th:* 791
Roy Cohn, *Notor:* 217
Bessie Coleman, *20th:* 801
Schuyler Colfax, *Notor:* 219

Vincent Coll, *Notor:* 221
Frank Collin, *Notor:* 222
Joe Colombo, *Notor:* 224
Charles W. Colson, *Notor:* 225
Samuel Colt, *19th:* 533
John Coltrane, *20th:* 814
Arthur Holly Compton, *20th:* 817
Anthony Comstock, *Notor:* 229
James Bryant Conant, *20th:* 820
Janet Cooke, *Notor:* 231
Jay Cooke, *19th:* 544
Calvin Coolidge, *20th:* 832
D. B. Cooper, *Notor:* 233
James Fenimore Cooper, *19th:* 552
Aaron Copland, *20th:* 836
John Singleton Copley, *18th:* 274
Bill Cosby, *20th:* 840
Frank Costello, *Notor:* 237
John Cotton, *17th:* 196
Charles E. Coughlin, *Notor:* 239
Hart Crane, *20th:* 858
Stephen Crane, *19th:* 562
Cheryl Crawford, *20th:* 861
Crazy Horse, *19th:* 566
David Crockett, *19th:* 571
Walter Cronkite, *20th:* 872
Bing Crosby, *20th:* 874
Celia Cruz, *20th:* 877
Paul Cuffe, *19th:* 576
E. E. Cummings, *20th:* 879
Andrew Cunanan, *Notor:* 245
Imogen Cunningham, *20th:* 883
Merce Cunningham, *20th:* 886
Caleb Cushing, *19th:* 578
Harvey Williams Cushing, *20th:* 898
Pauline Cushman, *Notor:* 246
George A. Custer, *19th:* 582, *Notor:* 248
Leon Czolgosz, *Notor:* 252
Jeffrey Dahmer, *Notor:* 255
Bob Dalton, *Notor:* 257
Emmett Dalton, *Notor:* 258
Alexandra Danilova, *20th:* 908
Clarence Darrow, *20th:* 913
Bette Davis, *20th:* 919
Jefferson Davis, *19th:* 610
Richard Allen Davis, *Notor:* 267
Lucy S. Dawidowicz, *20th:* 922
Dorothy Day, *20th:* 925
Tino De Angelis, *Notor:* 268
Eugene V. Debs, *20th:* 932
Stephen Decatur, *19th:* 626
Lee de Forest, *20th:* 940
John DeLorean, *Notor:* 272
Agnes de Mille, *20th:* 957
Cecil B. DeMille, *20th:* 960
Jack Dempsey, *20th:* 964
Albert DeSalvo, *Notor:* 274
George Dewey, *19th:* 645
John Dewey, *20th:* 982
Melvil Dewey, *19th:* 649
Legs Diamond, *Notor:* 277
Emily Dickinson, *19th:* 658
John Dickinson, *18th:* 303
Marlene Dietrich, *20th:* 997
John Dillinger, *Notor:* 281
Joe DiMaggio, *20th:* 1001
Walt Disney, *20th:* 1006
Dorothea Dix, *19th:* 671
Thomas Dixon, Jr., *Notor:* 284
Bob Dole, *20th:* 1014
Elizabeth Dole, *20th:* 1018
Bill Doolin, *Notor:* 296
Jimmy Doolittle, *20th:* 1023
Helen Gahagan Douglas, *20th:* 1026
Stephen A. Douglas, *19th:* 681
William O. Douglas, *20th:* 1029
Frederick Douglass, *19th:* 684
Diane Downs, *Notor:* 299
Theodore Dreiser, *20th:* 1032
W. E. B. Du Bois, *20th:* 1046
David Duke, *Notor:* 303
James Buchanan Duke, *19th:* 692
John Foster Dulles, *20th:* 1054
Paul Laurence Dunbar, *19th:* 701
Isadora Duncan, *20th:* 1058
Katherine Dunham, *20th:* 1061
Eleuthère Irénée du Pont, *19th:* 705
John E. du Pont, *Notor:* 305
Bob Dylan, *20th:* 1072
James Buchanan Eads, *19th:* 715
Thomas Eakins, *19th:* 717
Amelia Earhart, *20th:* 1075
Wyatt Earp, *19th:* 720, *Notor:* 315
George Eastman, *20th:* 1078
Bernard Ebbers, *Notor:* 317
Mary Baker Eddy, *19th:* 723
Marian Wright Edelman, *20th:* 1096
Thomas Alva Edison, *19th:* 731
Jonathan Edwards, *18th:* 314
John D. Ehrlichman, *Notor:* 320
Ira Einhorn, *Notor:* 324
Albert Einstein, *20th:* 1118
Dwight D. Eisenhower, *20th:* 1125
Charles William Eliot, *19th:* 737
John Eliot, *17th:* 247
T. S. Eliot, *20th:* 1139
Duke Ellington, *20th:* 1145
Ralph Waldo Emerson, *19th:* 745
Nora Ephron, *20th:* 1161
Sir Jacob Epstein, *20th:* 1165
Louise Erdrich, *20th:* 1168
Werner Erhard, *Notor:* 329
Billie Sol Estes, *Notor:* 336
Ada Everleigh, *Notor:* 338
Chris Evert, *20th:* 1191
Judith Campbell Exner, *Notor:* 340
Albert B. Fall, *Notor:* 342
Jerry Falwell, *20th:* 1209
Frantz Fanon, *20th:* 1212
Wallace Dodd Fard, *Notor:* 344
David G. Farragut, *19th:* 762
Louis Farrakhan, *20th:* 1217
Beatrix Jones Farrand, *20th:* 1219
Father Divine, *Notor:* 346
Orval E. Faubus, *Notor:* 348
William Faulkner, *20th:* 1222
Dianne Feinstein, *20th:* 1227
Enrico Fermi, *20th:* 1235
Geraldine Ferraro, *20th:* 1242
Marshall Field, *19th:* 773
Stephen J. Field, *19th:* 777
Millard Fillmore, *19th:* 781
Albert Fish, *Notor:* 355
Jim Fisk, *Notor:* 357
John Fitch, *18th:* 353
Ella Fitzgerald, *20th:* 1246
F. Scott Fitzgerald, *20th:* 1249
Heidi Fleiss, *Notor:* 359
Williamina Paton Stevens Fleming, *19th:* 788
Abraham Flexner, *20th:* 1256
Pretty Boy Floyd, *Notor:* 360

Jim Folsom, *Notor:* 362
Henry Fonda, *20th:* 1265
Betty Ford, *20th:* 1272
Gerald R. Ford, *20th:* 1274
Henry Ford, *20th:* 1279
Larry C. Ford, *Notor:* 363
Edwin Forrest, *19th:* 790
Nathan Bedford Forrest, *Notor:* 365
Abe Fortas, *Notor:* 369
Charlotte Forten, *19th:* 796
Bob Fosse, *20th:* 1291
Abby Kelley Foster, *19th:* 799
Stephen Collins Foster, *19th:* 802
Lydia Folger Fowler, *19th:* 812
Antoinette Frank, *Notor:* 373
Martin Frankel, *Notor:* 376
Helen Frankenthaler, *20th:* 1304
Felix Frankfurter, *20th:* 1308
Aretha Franklin, *20th:* 1312
Benjamin Franklin, *18th:* 370
John C. Frémont, *19th:* 831
Betty Friedan, *20th:* 1329
Milton Friedman, *20th:* 1332
Erich Fromm, *20th:* 1345
Lynette Fromme, *Notor:* 377
Robert Frost, *20th:* 1348
Loie Fuller, *20th:* 1361
Margaret Fuller, *19th:* 841
R. Buckminster Fuller, *20th:* 1364
Robert Fulton, *19th:* 845
Clark Gable, *20th:* 1368
John Wayne Gacy, *Notor:* 387
James Gadsden, *19th:* 849
Matilda Joslyn Gage, *19th:* 852
Carmine Galante, *Notor:* 389
John Kenneth Galbraith, *20th:* 1374
Albert Gallatin, *19th:* 854
Joe Gallo, *Notor:* 392
Carlo Gambino, *Notor:* 396
George Gamow, *20th:* 1379
Greta Garbo, *20th:* 1392
Erle Stanley Gardner, *20th:* 1403
Isabella Stewart Gardner, *20th:* 1406
James A. Garfield, *19th:* 867
Judy Garland, *20th:* 1409
William Lloyd Garrison, *19th:* 874
Marcus Garvey, *20th:* 1417
Bill Gates, *20th:* 1421
Gilbert Gauthe, *Notor:* 397
Norman Bel Geddes, *20th:* 1431
Lou Gehrig, *20th:* 1434
Frank Gehry, *20th:* 1438
Ed Gein, *Notor:* 399
Vito Genovese, *Notor:* 402
Henry George, *19th:* 894
Geronimo, *19th:* 904
Elbridge Gerry, *18th:* 412
George Gershwin, *20th:* 1458
Ira Gershwin, *20th:* 1462
Arnold Gesell, *20th:* 1465
Sir John Paul Getty, *20th:* 1468
Sam Giancana, *Notor:* 405
James Gibbons, *19th:* 910
Josiah Willard Gibbs, *19th:* 913
Althea Gibson, *20th:* 1474
Vincent Gigante, *Notor:* 407
Mildred Gillars, *Notor:* 409
Dizzy Gillespie, *20th:* 1480
Charlotte Perkins Gilman, *20th:* 1484
Gary Gilmore, *Notor:* 411
Lillian Gish, *20th:* 1496
John Glenn, *20th:* 1499
Robert H. Goddard, *20th:* 1507
Kurt Gödel, *20th:* 1510
George Washington Goethals, *20th:* 1517
Bernhard Goetz, *Notor:* 423
Emma Goldman, *20th:* 1519, *Notor:* 424
Samuel Goldwyn, *20th:* 1523
Samuel Gompers, *19th:* 943
Benny Goodman, *20th:* 1527
Charles Goodyear, *19th:* 946
Al Gore, *20th:* 1538
William Crawford Gorgas, *20th:* 1541
John Gotti, *Notor:* 431
Jay Gould, *Notor:* 433
Stephen Jay Gould, *20th:* 1555
Billy Graham, *20th:* 1557
Katharine Graham, *20th:* 1560
Martha Graham, *20th:* 1563
Cary Grant, *20th:* 1570
Ulysses S. Grant, *19th:* 958
Sammy Gravano, *Notor:* 434
Asa Gray, *19th:* 963
Horace Greeley, *19th:* 966
Nathanael Greene, *18th:* 443
Alan Greenspan, *20th:* 1581
D. W. Griffith, *20th:* 1593
Sarah and Angelina Grimké, *19th:* 988
Walter Gropius, *20th:* 1602
Daniel Guggenheim, *20th:* 1613
Charles Julius Guiteau, *Notor:* 439
H. D., *20th:* 1623
H. R. Haldeman, *Notor:* 442
George Ellery Hale, *20th:* 1643
Matthew F. Hale, *Notor:* 444
Sarah Josepha Hale, *19th:* 1012
Mary A. Hallaren, *20th:* 1645
William F. Halsey, *20th:* 1647
Fannie Lou Hamer, *20th:* 1651
Alexander Hamilton, *18th:* 452
Oscar Hammerstein II, *20th:* 1657
John Hancock, *18th:* 457
Learned Hand, *20th:* 1663
W. C. Handy, *20th:* 1667
Marcus A. Hanna, *19th:* 1018
Lorraine Hansberry, *20th:* 1669
Robert Philip Hanssen, *Notor:* 445
John Wesley Hardin, *Notor:* 447
Warren G. Harding, *20th:* 1674
William Rainey Harper, *19th:* 1031
William Averell Harriman, *20th:* 1684
Barbara Harris, *20th:* 1689
Jean Harris, *Notor:* 448
Joel Chandler Harris, *19th:* 1036
Benjamin Harrison, *19th:* 1040
William Henry Harrison, *19th:* 1048
Lorenz Hart, *20th:* 1691
Nathaniel Hawthorne, *19th:* 1051
John Hay, *19th:* 1054
Ferdinand Vandeveer Hayden, *19th:* 1058
Helen Hayes, *20th:* 1723
Le Ly Hayslip, *20th:* 1727
Bill Haywood, *Notor:* 450
Rita Hayworth, *20th:* 1730
Linda Burfield Hazzard, *Notor:* 453
Patty Hearst, *Notor:* 454

William Randolph Hearst, *20th:* 1734
Lillian Hellman, *20th:* 1752
Ernest Hemingway, *20th:* 1755
George Hennard, *Notor:* 456
Joseph Henry, *19th:* 1078
O. Henry, *19th:* 1081
Patrick Henry, *18th:* 482
Katharine Hepburn, *20th:* 1769
Aileen Clarke Hernandez, *20th:* 1773
Harry Hammond Hess, *20th:* 1785
Wild Bill Hickok, *19th:* 1091
Thomas Wentworth Higginson, *19th:* 1097
Henry Hill, *Notor:* 465
James Jerome Hill, *19th:* 1100
Susanna Mildred Hill, *Notor:* 466
Marie Hilley, *Notor:* 467
John Hinckley, Jr., *Notor:* 470
Alger Hiss, *20th:* 1822, *Notor:* 475
Oveta Culp Hobby, *20th:* 1838
Jimmy Hoffa, *Notor:* 480
Abbie Hoffman, *Notor:* 483
Billie Holiday, *20th:* 1852
John Philip Holland, *19th:* 1113
Doc Holliday, *Notor:* 485
H. H. Holmes, *Notor:* 486
Oliver Wendell Holmes, *19th:* 1116
Oliver Wendell Holmes, Jr., *20th:* 1856
Winslow Homer, *19th:* 1122
Thomas Hooker, *17th:* 386
Herbert Hoover, *20th:* 1862
J. Edgar Hoover, *20th:* 1866, *Notor:* 489
Bob Hope, *20th:* 1870
Harry Hopkins, *20th:* 1872
Edward Hopper, *20th:* 1876
Grace Murray Hopper, *20th:* 1879
Karen Horney, *20th:* 1883
Vladimir Horowitz, *20th:* 1886
Harry Houdini, *20th:* 1889
Sam Houston, *19th:* 1130
Elias Howe, *19th:* 1133
Julia Ward Howe, *19th:* 1137
Samuel Gridley Howe, *19th:* 1141
L. Ron Hubbard, *20th:* 1909, *Notor:* 495
Edwin Powell Hubble, *20th:* 1912
James Oliver Huberty, *Notor:* 497
Dolores Huerta, *20th:* 1915
Charles Evans Hughes, *20th:* 1920
Howard Hughes, *20th:* 1925
Langston Hughes, *20th:* 1928
Cordell Hull, *20th:* 1934
Hubert H. Humphrey, *20th:* 1938
Laud Humphreys, *Notor:* 498
E. Howard Hunt, *Notor:* 499
Zora Neale Hurston, *20th:* 1944
Robert M. Hutchins, *20th:* 1958
Anne Hutchinson, *17th:* 394
Thomas Hutchinson, *18th:* 518
Clifford Irving, *Notor:* 510
Washington Irving, *19th:* 1180
Charles Ives, *20th:* 1974
Andrew Jackson, *19th:* 1189
Helen Hunt Jackson, *19th:* 1193
Jesse Jackson, *20th:* 1978
Shoeless Joe Jackson, *Notor:* 521
Stonewall Jackson, *19th:* 1197
Mary Putnam Jacobi, *19th:* 1200
Roman Jakobson, *20th:* 1986
Frank James, *19th:* 1211
Henry James, *19th:* 1206
Jesse James, *19th:* 1211, *Notor:* 523
William James, *19th:* 1213
John Jay, *18th:* 524
Thomas Jefferson, *18th:* 528
Sarah Orne Jewett, *19th:* 1226
Steve Jobs, *20th:* 2006
Robert Joffrey, *20th:* 2012
Andrew Johnson, *19th:* 1229
Lady Bird Johnson, *20th:* 2025
Lyndon B. Johnson, *20th:* 2027
Bobby Jones, *20th:* 2036
Jim Jones, *Notor:* 537
John Paul Jones, *18th:* 539
Margaret Jones, *Notor:* 540
Mother Jones, *20th:* 2039
Janis Joplin, *20th:* 2043
Scott Joplin, *19th:* 1235
Barbara Jordan, *20th:* 2046
Christine Jorgensen, *20th:* 2053
Chief Joseph, *19th:* 1238
Theodore Kaczynski, *Notor:* 547
Meir Kahane, *Notor:* 551
Kamehameha I, *19th:* 1249
Alvin Karpis, *Notor:* 556
Buster Keaton, *20th:* 2090
Helen Keller, *20th:* 2093
Gene Kelly, *20th:* 2096
Machine Gun Kelly, *Notor:* 561
John F. Kennedy, *20th:* 2098
Robert F. Kennedy, *20th:* 2102
James Kent, *19th:* 1271
Jack Kerouac, *20th:* 2114
Tom Ketchum, *Notor:* 566
Jack Kevorkian, *Notor:* 567
Francis Scott Key, *19th:* 1274
Sante Kimes, *Notor:* 584
Billie Jean King, *20th:* 2143
Martin Luther King, Jr., *20th:* 2147
Rodney King, *Notor:* 585
Stephen King, *20th:* 2151
Eusebio Francisco Kino, *17th:* 467
Alfred Kinsey, *20th:* 2159
Jeane Kirkpatrick, *20th:* 2167
Henry Kissinger, *20th:* 2170
David Koresh, *Notor:* 589
Tadeusz Kościuszko, *18th:* 564
Lee Krasner, *20th:* 2195
Ray Kroc, *20th:* 2201
Elisabeth Kübler-Ross, *20th:* 2207
Richard Kuklinski, *Notor:* 595
Jean Laffite, *Notor:* 600
Robert M. La Follette, *20th:* 2227
Fiorello Henry La Guardia, *20th:* 2237
Leonard Lake, *Notor:* 602
Ann Landers, *20th:* 2247
Karl Landsteiner, *20th:* 2250
Fritz Lang, *20th:* 2253
Dorothea Lange, *20th:* 2260
Susanne K. Langer, *20th:* 2263
Samuel Pierpont Langley, *19th:* 1309
Meyer Lansky, *Notor:* 604
Lyndon H. LaRouche, Jr., *Notor:* 606
Sieur de La Salle, *17th:* 490
Julia C. Lathrop, *20th:* 2272
Benjamin Henry Latrobe, *19th:* 1325
Estée Lauder, *20th:* 2275
Marie Laveau, *Notor:* 610
Anton Szandor LaVey, *Notor:* 612

Ernest Orlando Lawrence, *20th:* 2300
Richard Lawrence, *Notor:* 615
Kenneth Lay, *Notor:* 617
Emma Lazarus, *19th:* 1331
Timothy Leary, *Notor:* 619
Henrietta Swan Leavitt, *20th:* 2317
Ann Lee, *18th:* 591
Charles Lee, *Notor:* 621
Daulton Lee, *Notor:* 623
Robert E. Lee, *19th:* 1334
Eva Le Gallienne, *20th:* 2330
Jacob Leisler, *17th:* 518
Nathan F. Leopold, Jr., *Notor:* 634
Mary Kay Letourneau, *Notor:* 640
Dennis Levine, *Notor:* 642
Bernard Lewis, *20th:* 2351
Jerry Lewis, *20th:* 2357
John L. Lewis, *20th:* 2360
Meriwether Lewis, *19th:* 1359
Sinclair Lewis, *20th:* 2363
Willard F. Libby, *20th:* 2371
Roy Lichtenstein, *20th:* 2373
G. Gordon Liddy, *Notor:* 643
Liliuokalani, *19th:* 1373
Maya Ying Lin, *20th:* 2385
Abraham Lincoln, *19th:* 1380
Mary Todd Lincoln, *19th:* 1385
Anne Morrow Lindbergh, *20th:* 2389
Charles A. Lindbergh, *20th:* 2392
John Walker Lindh, *Notor:* 645
Walter Lippmann, *20th:* 2400
Little Turtle, *18th:* 610
Belva A. Lockwood, *19th:* 1409
Henry Cabot Lodge, *20th:* 2417
Richard A. Loeb, *Notor:* 647
Jack London, *20th:* 2420
Huey Long, *20th:* 2424, *Notor:* 649
Harry Longabaugh, *Notor:* 651
Henry Wadsworth Longfellow, *19th:* 1416
Bill Longley, *Notor:* 653
Byron Looper, *Notor:* 654
Anita Loos, *20th:* 2428
Joe Louis, *20th:* 2437
Juliette Gordon Low, *20th:* 2441
Amy Lowell, *20th:* 2444
George Lucas, *20th:* 2450
Tommy Lucchese, *Notor:* 658
Clare Boothe Luce, *20th:* 2453
Henry R. Luce, *20th:* 2456
Lucky Luciano, *Notor:* 660
Shannon W. Lucid, *20th:* 2460
Roger Ludlow, *17th:* 567
Jeffrey Lundgren, *Notor:* 664
Victor Lustig, *Notor:* 665
Mary Lyon, *19th:* 1428
Douglas MacArthur, *20th:* 2492
Joseph McCarthy, *20th:* 2497, *Notor:* 669
Mary McCarthy, *20th:* 2501
Barbara McClintock, *20th:* 2504
James W. McCord, Jr., *Notor:* 671
Cyrus Hall McCormick, *19th:* 1438
Carson McCullers, *20th:* 2507
Jeffrey MacDonald, *Notor:* 673
Alexander McGillivray, *18th:* 626
William Holmes McGuffey, *19th:* 1445
William McKinley, *19th:* 1460
Catharine A. MacKinnon, *20th:* 2522
Virginia McMartin, *Notor:* 676
Edwin Mattison McMillan, *20th:* 2532
Robert McNamara, *20th:* 2541
Aimee Semple McPherson, *Notor:* 679
Timothy McVeigh, *Notor:* 681
Dolley Madison, *19th:* 1470
James Madison, *18th:* 636
Molly Maguires, *Notor:* 745
Norman Mailer, *20th:* 2563
Malcolm X, *20th:* 2570
Mary Mallon, *Notor:* 685
Lee Boyd Malvo, *Notor:* 765
Man Ray, *20th:* 2580
Frederika Mandelbaum, *Notor:* 688
Benoit B. Mandelbrot, *20th:* 2588
Wilma Mankiller, *20th:* 2591
Horace Mann, *19th:* 1486
Charles Manson, *Notor:* 689
Salvatore Maranzano, *Notor:* 694
Carlos Marcello, *Notor:* 698
Rocky Marciano, *20th:* 2612
John Marshall, *19th:* 1498
George C. Marshall, *20th:* 2629
Thurgood Marshall, *20th:* 2633
Agnes Martin, *20th:* 2636
George Mason, *18th:* 664
Massasoit, *17th:* 612
Joe Masseria, *Notor:* 708
Cotton Mather, *18th:* 667
Increase Mather, *18th:* 671
Robert Jay Mathews, *Notor:* 712
Matthew Fontaine Maury, *19th:* 1522
Louis B. Mayer, *20th:* 2662
William J. and Charles H. Mayo, *20th:* 2665
Margaret Mead, *20th:* 2668
Gaston Bullock Means, *Notor:* 713
George Meany, *20th:* 2672
Golda Meir, *20th:* 2674
Andrew Mellon, *20th:* 2683
Herman Melville, *19th:* 1537
H. L. Mencken, *20th:* 2688
Dorothy Reed Mendenhall, *20th:* 2695
Adah Isaacs Menken, *19th:* 1555
Gian Carlo Menotti, *20th:* 2703
Ottmar Mergenthaler, *19th:* 1558
Thomas Merton, *20th:* 2713
Metacom, *17th:* 633
Tom Metzger, *Notor:* 726
Albert A. Michelson, *19th:* 1567
James A. Michener, *20th:* 2728
Ludwig Mies van der Rohe, *20th:* 2731
Stanley Milgram, *Notor:* 729
Michael Milken, *Notor:* 731
Edna St. Vincent Millay, *20th:* 2738
Arthur Miller, *20th:* 2742
Kate Millett, *20th:* 2746
Robert Andrews Millikan, *20th:* 2750
Wilbur Mills, *Notor:* 733
Peter Minuit, *17th:* 643
John Mitchell, *Notor:* 737
Maria Mitchell, *19th:* 1580
William Mitchell, *20th:* 2765
James Monroe, *19th:* 1586
Marilyn Monroe, *20th:* 2797

Dwight L. Moody, *19th:* 1596
Sun Myung Moon, *20th:* 2811, *Notor:* 749
Bugs Moran, *Notor:* 751
J. P. Morgan, *19th:* 1599
Lewis Henry Morgan, *19th:* 1603
Thomas Hunt Morgan, *20th:* 2825
Hans Joachim Morgenthau, *20th:* 2828
Gouverneur Morris, *18th:* 705
Robert Morris, *18th:* 707
Toni Morrison, *20th:* 2834
Samuel F. B. Morse, *19th:* 1610
William Thomas Green Morton, *19th:* 1613
Grandma Moses, *20th:* 2841
Robert Motherwell, *20th:* 2847
John R. Mott, *20th:* 2849
Lucretia Mott, *19th:* 1616
Zacarias Moussaoui, *Notor:* 758
Elijah Muhammad, *Notor:* 763
John Allen Muhammad, *Notor:* 765
John Muir, *19th:* 1623
Hermann Joseph Muller, *20th:* 2861
Kary B. Mullis, *20th:* 2864
Rupert Murdoch, *20th:* 2876
Joaquín Murieta, *Notor:* 767
Edward R. Murrow, *20th:* 2879
Ralph Nader, *20th:* 2897
James Naismith, *20th:* 2905
Thomas Nast, *19th:* 1649
Carry Nation, *19th:* 1652
Martina Navratilova, *20th:* 2922
Baby Face Nelson, *Notor:* 774
Leslie Nelson, *Notor:* 776
Bonnie Nettles, *Notor:* 779
John von Neumann, *20th:* 2943
Louise Nevelson, *20th:* 2947
Simon Newcomb, *19th:* 1660
Huey Newton, *Notor:* 782
Charles Ng, *Notor:* 784
Terry Nichols, *Notor:* 790
Jack Nicklaus, *20th:* 2959
Reinhold Niebuhr, *20th:* 2962
Chester W. Nimitz, *20th:* 2977
Richard M. Nixon, *20th:* 2984, *Notor:* 793
Jessye Norman, *20th:* 2995
Robert Nozick, *20th:* 2999
Rebecca Nurse, *17th:* 689
Annie Oakley, *19th:* 1692
Dion O'Banion, *Notor:* 803
Flannery O'Connor, *20th:* 3017
Sandra Day O'Connor, *20th:* 3020
James Edward Oglethorpe, *18th:* 742
Georgia O'Keeffe, *20th:* 3031
Claes Oldenburg, *20th:* 3037
Frederick Law Olmsted, *19th:* 1706
Jacqueline Kennedy Onassis, *20th:* 3045
Eugene O'Neill, *20th:* 3051
Tip O'Neill, *20th:* 3055
Opechancanough, *17th:* 702
J. Robert Oppenheimer, *20th:* 3065
Katherine Davalos Ortega, *20th:* 3074
Thomas Mott Osborne, *20th:* 3085
Osceola, *19th:* 1709
Lee Harvey Oswald, *Notor:* 807
Robert Owen, *19th:* 1720
Jesse Owens, *20th:* 3095
Thomas Paine, *18th:* 759
Alice Freeman Palmer, *19th:* 1727
Bonnie Parker, *Notor:* 811
Charlie Parker, *20th:* 3112
Dorothy Parker, *20th:* 3116
Theodore Parker, *19th:* 1735
Francis Parkman, *19th:* 1742
Rosa Parks, *20th:* 3119
Vernon Louis Parrington, *20th:* 3124
Dolly Parton, *20th:* 3127
George S. Patton, *20th:* 3142
Alice Paul, *20th:* 3145
Wolfgang Pauli, *20th:* 3152
Linus Pauling, *20th:* 3155
Elizabeth Palmer Peabody, *19th:* 1761
Charles Willson Peale, *18th:* 768
Robert Edwin Peary, *20th:* 3177
Gregory Peck, *20th:* 3181
I. M. Pei, *20th:* 3183
Charles Sanders Peirce, *19th:* 1772
Thomas Joseph Pendergast, *Notor:* 817
William Penn, *17th:* 724
Leander Perez, *Notor:* 819
Frances Perkins, *20th:* 3198
H. Ross Perot, *20th:* 3208
Matthew C. Perry, *19th:* 1776
Oliver Hazard Perry, *19th:* 1779
John J. Pershing, *20th:* 3219
Scott Peterson, *Notor:* 828
Wendell Phillips, *19th:* 1785
Mary Pickford, *20th:* 3244
Susan La Flesche Picotte, *20th:* 3247
Franklin Pierce, *19th:* 1789
William Luther Pierce III, *Notor:* 838
Zebulon Pike, *19th:* 1793
Gifford Pinchot, *20th:* 3253
Lydia E. Pinkham, *19th:* 1796
Sylvia Plath, *20th:* 3285
Pocahontas, *17th:* 745
Edgar Allan Poe, *19th:* 1813
Sidney Poitier, *20th:* 3296
James K. Polk, *19th:* 1819
Jonathan Pollard, *Notor:* 849
Jackson Pollock, *20th:* 3301
Pontiac, *18th:* 801
Charles Ponzi, *Notor:* 852
Cole Porter, *20th:* 3308
James Porter, *Notor:* 854
Katherine Anne Porter, *20th:* 3310
Adam Clayton Powell, Jr., *Notor:* 856
Colin Powell, *20th:* 3321
John Wesley Powell, *19th:* 1827
Lewis F. Powell, Jr. (1907-1998), *20th:* 3325
Lewis Powell (1844-1865), *Notor:* 858
William Hickling Prescott, *19th:* 1831
Elvis Presley, *20th:* 3330
Leontyne Price, *20th:* 3334
Joseph Profaci, *Notor:* 863
Joseph Pulitzer, *19th:* 1841
William Clarke Quantrill, *Notor:* 869
Isidor Isaac Rabi, *20th:* 3355
Dennis Rader, *Notor:* 879
Ayn Rand, *20th:* 3367
A. Philip Randolph, *20th:* 3369

Jeannette Rankin, *20th:* 3374
Robert Rauschenberg, *20th:* 3380
Walter Rauschenbusch, *20th:* 3382
John Rawls, *20th:* 3391
James Earl Ray, *Notor:* 889
Sam Rayburn, *20th:* 3397
Ronald Reagan, *20th:* 3400
Red Cloud, *19th:* 1871
Walter Reed, *19th:* 1877
William H. Rehnquist, *20th:* 3405
Frederic Remington, *19th:* 1881
Janet Reno, *20th:* 3416
Madame Restell, *Notor:* 892
Walter P. Reuther, *20th:* 3424
Paul Revere, *18th:* 832
Ann Richards, *20th:* 3434
Ellen Swallow Richards, *19th:* 1899
Abby Sage Richardson, *19th:* 1902
Henry Hobson Richardson, *19th:* 1905
Charles Richter, *20th:* 3440
Hyman G. Rickover, *20th:* 3443
Sally Ride, *20th:* 3447
Johnny Ringo, *Notor:* 898
George Rivas, *Notor:* 901
Jerome Robbins, *20th:* 3459
Paul Robeson, *20th:* 3462
Frank Robinson, *20th:* 3467
Jackie Robinson, *20th:* 3470
John D. Rockefeller, *19th:* 1921
John D. Rockefeller, Jr., *20th:* 3476
Nelson A. Rockefeller, *20th:* 3478
Knute Rockne, *20th:* 3481
George Lincoln Rockwell, *Notor:* 911
Norman Rockwell, *20th:* 3483
Richard Rodgers, *20th:* 3486
John Augustus Roebling, *19th:* 1928
Edith Nourse Rogers, *20th:* 3489
Will Rogers, *20th:* 3491
Eleanor Roosevelt, *20th:* 3506
Franklin D. Roosevelt, *20th:* 3509
Theodore Roosevelt, *20th:* 3515
Elihu Root, *20th:* 3519
Pete Rose, *20th:* 3525
Ethel Rosenberg, *Notor:* 913
Julius Rosenberg, *Notor:* 915
Betsy Ross, *18th:* 865
John Ross, *19th:* 1937
Nellie Tayloe Ross, *20th:* 3529
Mark Rothko, *20th:* 3539
Arnold Rothstein, *Notor:* 917
Peyton Rous, *20th:* 3545
Darlie Routier, *Notor:* 918
F. Sherwood Rowland, *20th:* 3547
Mary White Rowlandson, *17th:* 798
Josiah Royce, *20th:* 3550
Pete Rozelle, *20th:* 3553
Jack Ruby, *Notor:* 919
Eric Rudolph, *Notor:* 921
Muriel Rukeyser, *20th:* 3556
Benjamin Rush, *18th:* 872
Bill Russell, *20th:* 3565
Henry Norris Russell, *20th:* 3570
Babe Ruth, *20th:* 3572
Sacagawea, *19th:* 1962
Nicola Sacco, *20th:* 3580, *Notor:* 924
Carl Sagan, *20th:* 3590
Ruth St. Denis, *20th:* 3593
Augustus Saint-Gaudens, *19th:* 1972
Yolanda Saldívar, *Notor:* 930
J. D. Salinger, *20th:* 3609
Jonas Salk, *20th:* 3613
Pete Sampras, *20th:* 3616
Carl Sandburg, *20th:* 3619
Margaret Sanger, *20th:* 3625
George Santayana, *20th:* 3629
John Singer Sargent, *19th:* 1996
Arnold Schoenberg, *20th:* 3664
Dutch Schultz, *Notor:* 938
Charles M. Schulz, *20th:* 3672
Carl Schurz, *19th:* 2035
Martin Scorsese, *20th:* 3681
Charlotte Angas Scott, *19th:* 2039
Dred Scott, *19th:* 2041
Winfield Scott, *19th:* 2051
Edward Wyllis Scripps, *19th:* 2055
Glenn Theodore Seaborg, *20th:* 3684
Maurice Sendak, *20th:* 3698
Mack Sennett, *20th:* 3706
Sequoyah, *19th:* 2067
Junípero Serra, *18th:* 891
Saint Elizabeth Seton, *19th:* 2071
Dr. Seuss, *20th:* 3710
Samuel Sewall, *18th:* 893
William H. Seward, *19th:* 2077
Anne Sexton, *20th:* 3713
Assata Olugbala Shakur, *Notor:* 940
Anna Howard Shaw, *19th:* 2084
Clay Shaw, *Notor:* 941
Daniel Shays, *18th:* 902
Fulton J. Sheen, *20th:* 3722
Alan Shepard, *20th:* 3725
Sam Sheppard, *Notor:* 945
Roger Sherman, *18th:* 908
William Tecumseh Sherman, *19th:* 2097
George P. Shultz, *20th:* 3731
Bugsy Siegel, *Notor:* 954
Beverly Sills, *20th:* 3744
William Joseph Simmons, *Notor:* 957
O. J. Simpson, *Notor:* 958
Frank Sinatra, *20th:* 3747
Upton Sinclair, *20th:* 3750
Sirhan Sirhan, *Notor:* 965
Sitting Bull, *19th:* 2108
Jeffrey Skilling, *Notor:* 967
B. F. Skinner, *20th:* 3754
Samuel Slater, *19th:* 2111
Pamela Ann Smart, *Notor:* 971
Alfred E. Smith, *20th:* 3762
Bessie Smith, *20th:* 3765
Gerald L. K. Smith, *Notor:* 973
Jedediah Smith, *19th:* 2114
John Smith, *17th:* 861
Joseph Smith, *19th:* 2117
Margaret Chase Smith, *20th:* 3768
Susan Smith, *Notor:* 977
Theobald Smith, *20th:* 3772
Ruth Snyder, *Notor:* 979
Valerie Solanas, *Notor:* 982
Susan Sontag, *20th:* 3788
George Soros, *20th:* 3795
John Philip Sousa, *20th:* 3798
David H. Souter, *20th:* 3802
Richard Speck, *Notor:* 986
Steven Spielberg, *20th:* 3811
Benjamin Spock, *20th:* 3814
Squanto, *17th:* 875
Miles Standish, *17th:* 877

Leland Stanford, *19th:* 2132
Henry Morton Stanley, *19th:* 2136
Wendell Stanley, *20th:* 3824
Edwin M. Stanton, *19th:* 2142
Elizabeth Cady Stanton, *19th:* 2146
Charles Starkweather, *Notor:* 993
Belle Starr, *Notor:* 994
Henry Starr, *Notor:* 996
Edward Steichen, *20th:* 3837
Gertrude Stein, *20th:* 3845
John Steinbeck, *20th:* 3849
Gloria Steinem, *20th:* 3852
Charles Proteus Steinmetz, *19th:* 2156
Alexander H. Stephens, *19th:* 2164
Thaddeus Stevens, *19th:* 2171
Adlai E. Stevenson, *20th:* 3856
James Stewart, *20th:* 3860
Alfred Stieglitz, *20th:* 3864
Henry L. Stimson, *20th:* 3869
Harlan Fiske Stone, *20th:* 3878
Lucy Stone, *19th:* 2177
J. B. Stoner, *Notor:* 999
Joseph Story, *19th:* 2180
Harriet Beecher Stowe, *19th:* 2184
Igor Stravinsky, *20th:* 3888
Barbra Streisand, *20th:* 3892
Robert Franklin Stroud, *Notor:* 1005
Gilbert Stuart, *18th:* 947
Peter Stuyvesant, *17th:* 890
Anne Sullivan, *20th:* 3908
Harry Stack Sullivan, *20th:* 3910
Louis Sullivan, *19th:* 2198
Charles Sumner, *19th:* 2201
Billy Sunday, *20th:* 3916
Mary Surratt, *Notor:* 1012
Willie Sutton, *Notor:* 1014
Michael Swango, *Notor:* 1015
Robert A. Taft, *20th:* 3925
William Howard Taft, *20th:* 3929
Marion Talbot, *20th:* 3937
Maria Tallchief, *20th:* 3940
Roger Brooke Taney, *19th:* 2225, *Notor:* 1018
Ida Tarbell, *20th:* 3947
Helen Brooke Taussig, *20th:* 3950
Dame Elizabeth Taylor, *20th:* 3953
Frederick Winslow Taylor, *20th:* 3955
Zachary Taylor, *19th:* 2230
Sara Teasdale, *20th:* 3959
Tecumseh, *19th:* 2237
Edward Teller, *20th:* 3968
Shirley Temple, *20th:* 3973
Megan Terry, *20th:* 3982
Nikola Tesla, *19th:* 2252
Twyla Tharp, *20th:* 3989
Harry Kendall Thaw, *Notor:* 1027
Sylvanus Thayer, *19th:* 2260
Clarence Thomas, *20th:* 3999
Norman Thomas, *20th:* 4002
Theodore Thomas, *19th:* 2267
Henry David Thoreau, *19th:* 2274
Edward L. Thorndike, *20th:* 4013
Jim Thorpe, *20th:* 4016
James Thurber, *20th:* 4020
Paul Tillich, *20th:* 4027
Benjamin Tillman, *Notor:* 1030
Tokyo Rose, *Notor:* 1036
Clyde William Tombaugh, *20th:* 4041
Charles Hard Townes, *20th:* 4057
Spencer Tracy, *20th:* 4066
Harry S. Truman, *20th:* 4086
John Trumbull, *18th:* 988
Sojourner Truth, *19th:* 2306
Harriet Tubman, *19th:* 2312
Barbara W. Tuchman, *20th:* 4104
Karla Faye Tucker, *Notor:* 1044
Frederick Jackson Turner, *20th:* 4115
Nat Turner, *19th:* 2326
Ted Turner, *20th:* 4118
Mark Twain, *19th:* 2329
William Marcy Tweed, *19th:* 2333, *Notor:* 1047
John Tyler, *19th:* 2337
Harold C. Urey, *20th:* 4132
James Van Allen, *20th:* 4139
Martin Van Buren, *19th:* 2344
Cornelius Vanderbilt, *19th:* 2348
Sir Henry Vane the Younger, *17th:* 941
Bartolomeo Vanzetti, *Notor:* 1056
Edgard Varèse, *20th:* 4142
Harold E. Varmus, *20th:* 4145
Hank Vaughan, *Notor:* 1060
Thorstein Veblen, *20th:* 4154
Claus von Bülow, *Notor:* 1075
Anastase Vonsiatsky, *Notor:* 1077
Joachim Wach, *20th:* 4177
Selman Abraham Waksman, *20th:* 4180
Lillian D. Wald, *20th:* 4184
Alice Walker, *20th:* 4196
James J. Walker, *Notor:* 1082
Madam C. J. Walker, *20th:* 4199
William Walker, *Notor:* 1084
Rachel Wall, *Notor:* 1086
George C. Wallace, *20th:* 4203, *Notor:* 1087
Henry A. Wallace, *20th:* 4207
Barbara Walters, *20th:* 4211
Sam Walton, *20th:* 4213
Montgomery Ward, *19th:* 2386
Andy Warhol, *20th:* 4226
Carolyn Warmus, *Notor:* 1090
Jack Warner, *20th:* 4230
Earl Warren, *20th:* 4232
Mercy Otis Warren, *18th:* 1041
Robert Penn Warren, *20th:* 4236
Booker T. Washington, *19th:* 2390
George Washington, *18th:* 1043
Muddy Waters, *20th:* 4240
James D. Watson, *20th:* 4242
Thomas J. Watson, Jr., *20th:* 4246
Thomas J. Watson, Sr., *20th:* 4246
Anthony Wayne, *18th:* 1054
John Wayne, *20th:* 1370
Randy Weaver, *Notor:* 1091
Daniel Webster, *19th:* 2398
Noah Webster, *19th:* 2402
Joseph Weil, *Notor:* 1094
Kurt Weill, *20th:* 4273
Steven Weinberg, *20th:* 4277
Carl Weiss, *Notor:* 1095
Hymie Weiss, *Notor:* 1096
Orson Welles, *20th:* 4283
Ida B. Wells-Barnett, *20th:* 4290
Benjamin West, *18th:* 1068
Mae West, *20th:* 4297
George Westinghouse, *19th:* 2416
Edith Wharton, *20th:* 4300
Phillis Wheatley, *18th:* 1070
George Hoyt Whipple, *20th:* 4304
James McNeill Whistler, *19th:* 2420
Dan White, *Notor:* 1099
Walter White, *20th:* 4307

George Whitefield, *18th:* 1073
Charles Whitman, *Notor:* 1101
Walt Whitman, *19th:* 2423
Eli Whitney, *18th:* 1076
Gertrude Vanderbilt Whitney, *20th:* 4315
John Greenleaf Whittier, *19th:* 2428
Norbert Wiener, *20th:* 4321
Elie Wiesel, *20th:* 4324
Hazel Wightman, *20th:* 4333
Laura Ingalls Wilder, *20th:* 4336
Charles Wilkes, *19th:* 2435
James Wilkinson, *Notor:* 1103
Emma Willard, *19th:* 2438
Frances Willard, *19th:* 2442
George Washington Williams, *19th:* 2449
Roger Williams, *17th:* 982
Tennessee Williams, *20th:* 4350
Edmund Wilson, *20th:* 4354
Edward O. Wilson, *20th:* 4358
James Wilson, *18th:* 1090
Woodrow Wilson, *20th:* 4364
Oprah Winfrey, *20th:* 4372
John Winthrop, *17th:* 990
Henry Wirz, *Notor:* 1105
Isaac Mayer Wise, *19th:* 2453
Stephen Samuel Wise, *20th:* 4376
John Witherspoon, *18th:* 1098
Thomas Wolfe, *20th:* 4383
Grant Wood, *20th:* 4387
Victoria Woodhull, *19th:* 2459
Tiger Woods, *20th:* 4390
Robert Burns Woodward, *20th:* 4393
Fanny Bullock Workman, *19th:* 2466
Frances Wright, *19th:* 2469
Frank Lloyd Wright, *20th:* 4400
Orville and Wilbur Wright, *20th:* 4403
Aileen Carol Wuornos, *Notor:* 1108
Andrew Wyeth, *20th:* 4410
Rosalyn Yalow, *20th:* 4419
Andrea Yates, *Notor:* 1113
Chuck Yeager, *20th:* 4425
Dominique You, *Notor:* 1117
Brigham Young, *19th:* 2474
Cole Younger, *Notor:* 1118
Babe Didrikson Zaharias, *20th:* 4442
Marie Elizabeth Zakrzewska, *19th:* 2481
Giuseppe Zangara, *Notor:* 1128
Darryl F. Zanuck, *20th:* 4445
John Peter Zenger, *18th:* 1116
Ellen Taaffe Zwilich, *20th:* 4475
Vladimir Zworykin, *20th:* 4479

Uzbekistan
Alp Arslan, *MA:* 70
An Lushan, *MA:* 78
Avicenna, *MA:* 123
Cyrus the Great, *Anc:* 248
Tamerlane, *MA:* 1000

Vatican City
John XXIII, *20th:* 2017
John Paul II, *20th:* 2020
Paul VI, *20th:* 3148
Pius X, *20th:* 3272
Pius XI, *20th:* 3275
Pius XII, *20th:* 3278

Venezuela
Simón Bolívar, *19th:* 267
Ilich Ramírez Sánchez, *Notor:* 883
Antonio José de Sucre, *19th:* 2195

Vietnam
Bao Dai, *20th:* 228
Gia Long, *19th:* 907
Le Ly Hayslip, *20th:* 1727
Ho Chi Minh, *20th:* 1834
Ho Xuan Huong, *19th:* 1110
Le Thanh Tong, *Ren:* 546
Ngo Dinh Diem, *20th:* 2951
Ngo Quyen, *MA:* 756
Nguyen Hue, *18th:* 736
Nguyen Van Thieu, *20th:* 2954
Madame Nhu, *Notor:* 786
Charles Sobraj, *Notor:* 980
Suryavarman II, *MA:* 980
Tu Duc, *19th:* 2310
Vo Nguyen Giap, *20th:* 4169

Wales
Aneurin Bevan, *20th:* 349
Geoffrey of Monmouth, *MA:* 405
Sir William Robert Grove, *19th:* 996
Gwenllian verch Gruffydd, *MA:* 448
George Herbert, *17th:* 366
Augustus John, *20th:* 2014
T. E. Lawrence, *20th:* 2303
David Lloyd George, *20th:* 2411
Sir Henry Morgan, *Notor:* 753
Nest verch Rhys ap Tewdwr, *MA:* 753
Robert Owen, *19th:* 1720
Bartholomew Roberts, *Notor:* 905
Bertrand Russell, *20th:* 3562
Henry Morton Stanley, *19th:* 2136

West Indies. *See* Barbados; Cuba; Dominican Republic; Haiti; Jamaica; Martinique; Native America; Trinidad and Tobago

Yugoslavia
Milovan Djilas, *20th:* 1011
Slobodan Milošević, *20th:* 2756, *Notor:* 735

Zambia
Milton Obote, *20th:* 3011

Zimbabwe
Lobengula, *19th:* 1406
Albert Lutuli, *20th:* 2478
Robert Mugabe, *20th:* 2858, *Notor:* 761

Subject and Personages Index

The index below combines Personage and Subject index entries from all twenty-seven volumes of *Great Lives from History*, from *The Ancient World* (2004) through *The 20th Century* (2009) and *Notorious Lives* (2007). All personages whose names appear in **boldface type** in this index are the subjects of essays in one or more of the sets in *Great Lives from History*. Parenthetical information has been added where necessary to distinguish like-named individuals such as monarchs and persons with identical given and surnames.

Entries are filed by word (not letter). However, names of monarchs, popes, and others that incorporate Roman numerals consistently precede inverted names, and where individuals with the same name also bear the same Roman numeral—as is the case with many monarchs—we have added birth and death years in parentheses, along with an identifier. These names are arranged first by Roman numeral and then chronologically, regardless of additional names. Inverted names follow. For example:

Philip I the Handsome (1478-1506; king of Spain)
Philip II of Macedonia (382-336 b.c.e.)
Philip II (1165-1223; king of France)
Philip II the Bold (1342-1404; duke of Burgundy)
Philip II (1527-1598; king of Spain)
Philip III Arrhidaeus (d. 317 b.c.e.; king of Macedonia)
Philip III the Bold (1245-1285; king of France)
Philip III the Good (1396-1467; duke of Burgundy)
Philip III (1578-1621; king of Spain)
Philip IV the Fair (1268-1314; king of France)
Philip IV (1605-1665; king of Spain)
Philip V (238-179 b.c.e.; king of Macedonia)
Philip V (1683-1746; king of Spain)
Philip VI (1293-1350; king of France)
Philip, John
Philip, King. *See* Metacom
Philip, Prince (consort of Elizabeth II of Great Britain)
Philip of Anjou. *See* Philip V (king of Spain)
Philip of Jesus
Philip of Swabia
Philip the Magnanimous

Names of monarchs are not, however, always identified by birth and death years if they are already distinct:

Alfonso II, **Ren:** 28
Alfonso VI, **MA:** 279
Alfonso VIII, **MA:** 59, 316
Alfonso X, **MA:** 59-62
Alfonso XII, **19th:** 1184

Main entries are often followed by subentries, starting first with the set code (see the Publisher's Note that begins this volume) and followed by pages and/or subentries and their pages. The order of subentries is by set (*The Ancient World* through *The 20th Century*, followed by *Notorious Lives*), and the set codes are boldfaced to facilitate location of the discussion. Cross-references appear both to other entries within this index and to entries in the Category Index and Geographical Index earlier in this volume.

Finally, a word about geographic identifiers: Where acts, laws, agencies, associations, boards, bureaus, commissions, committees, conferences, councils, institutes, political parties, societies, and other entities in need of geographic distinctions are listed, we have endeavored to include geographic identifiers unless the entities are international. Most such entities that are not identified by nationality may be assumed to be U.S. entities.

A

À bout de souffle. See *Breathless*
A. D. (Millett), **20th:** 2748
À Edgar Poe (Redon), **19th:** 1875
A for Andromeda (television program), **20th:** 1904
À la recherche du temps perdu. See *Remembrance of Things Past*
À l'Échelle humaine. See *For All Mankind*
À l'heure de l'observatoire, les Amoureux (Man Ray), **20th:** 2581
A secreto agravio, secreta venganza. See *Secret Vengeance for Secret Insult*
Aachen Peace Congress (1748), **18th:** 557
Aalto, Alvar, **20th:** 1-4
Aaron, Anc: 1-4, 338, 573
Aaron, Hank, **20th:** 5-7, 3029
Aaron, Pietro, **Ren:** 517
Aaron's Rod (Lawrence), **20th:** 2297
AAW. *See* American Association for the Advancement of Women
Ab excessu divi Augusti (Tacitus), **Anc:** 19, 23, 104, 163, 508, 561, 685, 838
Ab urbe condita libri (Livy), **Anc:** 511, 517, 840

Abacha, Sani, **Notor:** 1-2
Abaelardus, Petrus. *See* Abelard, Peter
Abagnale, Frank W., Jr., **Notor:** 3-4
Abahai, **17th:** 1-3, 234, 848
Abailard, Pierre. *See* Abelard, Peter
ABAKO. *See* Alliance of the Bakongo
Abano, Pietro d', **MA:** 1-3
Abaqa, **MA:** 411
Abarbanel, Isaac. *See* Abravanel, Isaac ben Judah
ʿAbath al-Aqdār. See *Khufu's Wisdom*
ʿAbbās I (the Great), **17th:** 4-7, 411, 627, 668, 844
ʿAbbās II, **17th:** 844
Abbas, Ferhat, **20th:** 7-10
Abbas, Mahmoud, **20th:** 114
ʿAbbāsid caliphs, **MA:** 469
ʿAbbāsids, **MA:** 20-21, 70, 139, 467, 562, 568, 775
Abbesse de Jouarre, L' (Renan), **19th:** 1887
Abbey of Our Lady of Gethsemani, **20th:** 2713
Abbey Road (Beatles), **20th:** 269
Abbeychurch (Yonge), **19th:** 2472
Abbot, The (Scott), **19th:** 2048
Abbot, Francis E., **19th:** 1773
Abbot Suger on the Abbey Church of St. Denis and Its Art Treasures (Suger), **MA:** 973
ABC Evening News, The (television news program), **20th:** 4211
ABC of Communism, The (Bukharin and Preobrazhnesky), **20th:** 567
ʿAbd al-Hamid. *See* Abdülhamid II
ʿAbd al-Malik, **MA:** 3-6, 587
ʿAbd al-Muʾmin, **MA:** 6-9, 118
ʿAbd al-Qādir ibn Muḥyī ad-Dīn ibn Muṣṭafā al-Ḥasanī al-Jazāʿirī. *See* Abdelkader
ʿAbd al-Raḥmān III al-Nāṣir, **MA:** 9-12
ʿAbd al-Raḥmān al-Ghāfiqī, **MA:** 252
ʿAbd al-Raḥmān al-Nūjumī, **19th:** 1474
ʿAbd al-Wahhāb, Ibn. *See* Wahhāb, Muḥammad ibn ʿAbd al-
Abdelazer (Behn), **17th:** 43
Abdelkader, **19th:** 1-3
ʿAbduh, Muḥammad, **19th:** 4-6
Abdul Hamid. *See* Lindh, John Walker
Abdül Hamid II. *See* Abdülhamid II
Abdul Majid. *See* Mohammed, Khalid Shaikh
Abdulaziz Aziz, **19th:** 7, 1203
Abdulcelil Celebi. *See* Levni
Abdulcelil Levni. *See* Levni
Abdülhamid II, **19th:** 7-9, 1204
Abdullah (king of Transjordan), **20th:** 1202, 1950
Abdullah Ahmad Badawi, **20th:** 2552
Abdullah al-Fakʿasi al-Ghamdior. *See* Mohammed, Khalid Shaikh
Abdullahi, **19th:** 186, 2342
ʿAbdullahi ibn Muḥammad, **19th:** 1474
Abe Masahiro, **19th:** 1169
Abeille et architecte: Chronique, L'. See *Wheat and the Chaff, The*
Abel, Niels Henrik, **19th:** 9-12, 858, 885
Abel Gance, hier et demain (film), **20th:** 1383
Abel Sánchez (Unamuno), **20th:** 4130
Abelard, Peter, **MA:** 13-17, 28, 58, 161, 1115
Abelson, Philip, **20th:** 3684
Abenakis, **17th:** 612
Abendstunde eines Einsiedlers. See *Evening Hours of a Hermit*
Abentheuerliche Simplicissimus, Der. See *Simplicissimus*
Abernathy, Ralph, **20th:** 11-13, 1979, 2148
Abhandlung über den Ursprung der Sprache. See *Treatise upon the Origin of Language*
Abhayagiri, **Anc:** 934
Abhidharmakośa (Vasubandhu), **Anc:** 930
Abhidharmasamuccaya (Asanga), **Anc:** 113
Abhijñānaśākuntala (Kālidāsa), 496
Abington, Fanny, **18th:** 1-3
Abishag, **Anc:** 156
Abjuration, Act of (1581), **Ren:** 740
Abolition. *See* Antislavery; Slave trade; Slavery
Abolition of Slavery, Society for the. *See* Society for the Abolition of Slavery
Abolitionist movement, **19th:** Chester A. Arthur, 80; John Brown, 319; Mary Ann Shadd Cary, 431; William Ellery Channing, 466; Salmon P. Chase, 471; Lydia Maria Child, 482; Frederick Douglass, 685; England, 377; Abby Kelley Foster, 800; Matilda Joslyn Gage, 852; William Lloyd Garrison, 875; Grimké sisters, 989; Thomas Wentworth Higginson, 1098; Samuel Gridley Howe, 1142; Lucretia Mott, 1617; Theodore Parker, 1737; Wendell Phillips, 1786; Spain, 557; Elizabeth Cady Stanton, 2146; Lucy Stone, 2177; Sojourner Truth, 2307; Harriet Tubman, 2313
Aborigines, rights of, **19th:** 378
Abortion, **20th:** Ireland, 3474; legality of, 3853; Moral Majority, 1211; Nicaragua, 3073; Norway, 545; politics, 1228, 1244; Republican Party, 1016; Roman Catholic Church, 2023; Romania, 705; self-induced, 3625; U.S. Supreme Court, 383, 508, 522, 3022, 3326, 3407
About Behaviorism (Skinner), **20th:** 3756

About That (Mayakovsky), **20th:** 2660
About the House (Auden), **20th:** 173
Above the Barriers (Pasternak), **20th:** 3132
Abraham, Anc: 4-7, 916
Abraham (Hrosvitha), **MA:** 518
Abraham, Uritia, **Notor:** 307
Abraham Lincoln (Hay and Nicolay), **19th:** 1055
Abraham Lincoln: The Prairie Years (Sandburg), **20th:** 3620
Abraham Lincoln: The War Years (Sandburg), **20th:** 3621
Abram. *See* Abraham
Abravanel, Isaac ben Judah, Ren: 1-3
Abreu Freire, António Caetano de. *See* Egas Moniz, António
Abridgement of the Debates of Congress from 1789 to 1856 (Benton), **19th:** 195
Abriss der Logistik mit besonderer Berücksichtigung der Relationstheorie und ihrer Anwendungen. See *Introduction to Symbolic Logic and Its Applications*
Absalom, **Anc:** 256
Absalom, Absalom! (Faulkner), **20th:** 1224
Absalom and Achitophel (Dryden), **17th:** 241, 817
Absalon, **MA:** 927, 1047
Absentee, The (Edgeworth), **19th:** 729
Absinthe Drinker, The (Manet), **19th:** 1480
Absolute monarchy (France), **18th:** 617, 619, 751
Absolute Torch and Twang (Lang), **20th:** 2257
Absoluteness of Christianity and the History of Religions, The (Troeltsch), **20th:** 4070
Abstract expressionism, **20th:** 1846, 2196, 2606, 2636, 2847, 3303, 3539
Absurd, Theater of the, **20th:** 282, 1339, 1969
Abū ʿAbd Allāh Muḥammad ibn Jābir ibn Sinān al-Battānī al-Ḥarrānī al-Ṣabiʾ. *See* Battānī, al-
Abū ʿAbd Allāh Muḥammad XI. *See* Boabdil
Abu Abdallah. *See* Bin Laden, Osama; Zawahiri, Ayman al-
Abū al-Ḥasan. *See* Judah ha-Levi
Abū al-Ḥasan ʿAlī, **Ren:** 105, 329
Abū al-Mughīth al-Ḥusayn ibn Manṣūr al-Ḥallāj. *See* Ḥallāj, al-
Abū al-Rayḥān Muḥammad ibn Aḥmad al-Bīrūnī. *See* Bīrūnī, al-
Abū ʿAlī al-Ḥasan ibn al-Haytham. *See* Alhazen
Abū ʿAlī al-Ḥusayn ibn ʿAbd Allāh ibn Sīnā. *See* Avicenna
Abū ʿAlī Ḥasan ibn ʿAlī Abū ʿAlī. *See* Niẓām al-Mulk
Abū Bakr, **MA:** 734, 1037
Abū Bakr Muḥammad ibn al-ʿArabī al-Ḥātīmī al-Ṭaʾī. *See* Ibn al-ʿArabī
Abu Fatima. *See* Zawahiri, Ayman al-
Abū Hafs ʿUmar, **MA:** 7
Abū Ḥanīfah, MA: 18-21, 36
Abu Hassan (Weber), **19th:** 2395
Abū Ḥayyān al-Tawḥīdī, **MA:** 21
Abū ʿInān, **MA:** 536
Abū Isḥāq, **MA:** 451
Abu Jihad. *See* Wazir, Khalil al-
Abū Kāmil, **MA:** 619
Abu Mazen. *See* Abbas, Mahmoud
Abu Muhammad. *See* Zawahiri, Ayman al-
Abū Muḥammad al-Kūmi. *See* ʿAbd al-Muʾmin
Abu Nidal, 20th: 112; **Notor:** 4-6, 101
Abū ol-Qāsem Manṣūr. *See* Firdusi
Abu Sharif, Bassam, **Notor:** 883
Abū Ṭālib, **MA:** 611, 734, 1039
Abū-ul-Fath Jahāl-ud-Dīn Muḥammad Akbar. *See* Akbar
Abūʿ-Wafā. *See* Abul Wefa
Abū Yaʿqūb Yūsuf, **MA:** 8, 119
Abubakar Atiku, **19th:** 187
Abul Wefa, MA: 21-23, 137
Abury (Stukeley), **18th:** 953
Abydos, Battle of (989), **MA:** 87
Abyssinia, **Ren:** 260
Académie de France de Rome, **17th:** 182
Académie de l'art poétique (Deimier), **17th:** 578
Académie des Inscriptions et Belles-Lettres. *See* Academy of Humanities, France
Académie des Sciences. *See* Academy of Sciences, France
Académie d'Opéra, **17th:** 570
Académie Française, **17th:** 482, 504, 775, 780; **18th:** 78, 265, 267, 367, 574, 1027
Académie Royale de Musique, **17th:** 570
Académie Royale des Sciences, **17th:** 182, 398
Academy (Plato's), **Anc:** 94, 321, 659, 872, 981. *See also* Imperial Academy
Academy of Architects, France, **18th:** 133
Academy of Architecture, **17th:** 182
Academy of Fists, **18th:** 100
Academy of Humanities, France, **18th:** 78
Academy of Inscriptions, **17th:** 182
Academy of Sciences, France, **18th:** 25, 77, 171, 241, 267, 634, 700, 1050
Academy of Sciences, Italy, **18th:** 25
Academy of Sciences and Literature, Germany, **18th:** 263
Acadians, **17th:** 142
Acarie, Barbe, Ren: 3-5
Acarie Circle, **Ren:** 3
Accademia degli Unisoni, **17th:** 888
Accademia Reale, **17th:** 165
Accardo, Tony, **Notor:** 405

Acceleration Waltz (Strauss), **19th:** 2189
Accesa. *See* Andreini, Isabella
Acciaiuoli, Niccolò, **MA:** 169
Accommodationism, **20th:** 1047
Account of Colonel Crockett's Tour to the North and Down East, An (Crockett), **19th:** 572
Account of Corsica: The Journal of a Tour to That Island, An (Boswell), **18th:** 147
Account of Expeditions to the Sources of the Mississippi, An (Pike), **19th:** 1795
Account of Religion by Reason, An (Suckling), **17th:** 895
Account of the Destruction of the Jesuits in France, An (Alembert), **18th:** 33
Account of the Growth of Popery and Arbitrary Government in England, An (Marvell), **17th:** 606
Account of the Life of Mr. Richard Savage, An (Johnson), **18th:** 536
Accumulation of Capital, The (Luxemburg), **20th:** 2484
Accusatoria (Guicciardini), **Ren:** 411
Acetaria (Evelyn), **17th:** 257
Achaean League, **Anc:** 227
Achaeus, **Anc:** 65
Achamoth, **Anc:** 919
Achar Choeun. *See* Ta Mok
Acharnēs (Aristophanes), **Anc:** 90, 127
Achebe, Chinua, **20th:** 14-17
Acheson, Dean, **20th:** 17-21
Acheson-Lilienthal Report, **20th:** 3356
Achilles, **Anc:** 427
Achilli, Gracinto, **19th:** 1665
Achtung! Panzer! See *Attention! Tanks!* (Guderian)
Acis et Galaté (Lully), **17th:** 570
Aclea, Battle of (851), **MA:** 63
Acosta, José de, **Ren:** 5-7
Acquainted with the Night (Böll), **20th:** 412
Acquired immunodeficiency syndrome. *See* AIDS
Acre, Siege of (1191), **MA:** 837, 892
Acre fortress, storming of, **20th:** 285
Acroïnum, Battle of (741), **MA:** 1021
Across Arctic America (Rasmussen), **20th:** 3379
Across the Busy Years (Butler), **20th:** 600
Across the River and into the Trees (Hemingway), **20th:** 1757
Act for the Advancement of True Religion. *See* Advancement of True Religion, Act for
Act of ______. *See* ______, Act of
Acte additionnel, **19th:** 609
Actes and Monuments of These Latter and Perillous Dayes. See *Foxe's Book of Martyrs*
Actinomycin, **20th:** 4182
Action Committee for the United States of Europe, **20th:** 2795
Action Française, **20th:** 2624
Action Group, **20th:** 181
Actium, Battle of (31 B.C.E.), **Anc:** 21, 64, 71, 75, 146, 231, 527
Active Intellect, **MA:** 651
Active Liberty (Breyer), **20th:** 521
Active Service (Crane), **19th:** 564
Activism, peace, **20th:** Burma, 175; Catholicism, 927; Central America, 123; Christianity, 2973; International Peace Bureau, 2231; scientific community, 1120, 1851, 3156, 3537, 4344; Tibet, 903; Vietnam War, 610, 1561, 3815; world, 703, 2394, 3563; World War I, 598, 3375, 4003
Activism, social, **20th:** 669, 1521, 2094, 3752; Central America, 2686; European refugee villages, 3265; Green Revolution, 435; labor issues, 4270; women's issues, 3507
Acton, Lord, **19th:** 12-16
Actor Prepares, An (Stanislavsky), **20th:** 3822
Actors and acting, **18th:** Fanny Abington, 1-3; David Garrick, 397-400; Anne Oldfield, 749-751; Mary Robinson, 848-850; Sarah Siddons, 912-914; Peg Woffington, 1102-1104
Actors Studio Theatre, **20th:** 863
Actorum laboratorii chymici monacensis, seu, physicae subterraneae libri duo. See *Physica subterranea*
"Acts of Pilate" (forgeries), **Anc:** 645
Acts of the Witnesses, The (Muggleton), **17th:** 667
Acts of Thomas, The, **Anc:** 880
Ad Decimam, Battle of (532), **Anc:** 354
Ad filium (Cato), **Anc:** 192
Ad Helviam matrem de consolatione (Seneca), **Anc:** 767
Ad Marcellam (Porphyry), **Anc:** 688
Ad nationes (Tertullian), **Anc:** 853
Ad Parnassum (Klee), **20th:** 2178
Ad Vitellionem paralipomena, quibus astronomiae pars optica traditur. See *Optics* (Kepler)
Adad-nirari III, **Anc:** 745, 892
Adagia (Erasmus), **Ren:** 609
Adagio for Strings (Barber), **20th:** 231
Adam, Adolphe-Charles, **19th:** 639
Adam, James, **18th:** 3-7
Adam, Robert, **18th:** 3-7
Adam and Eve (Dürer), **Ren:** 298
Adam Bede (Eliot), **19th:** 741
Adam d'Arras. *See* Adam de la Halle
Adam de la Halle, **MA:** 24-26
Adam le Bossu. *See* Adam de la Halle
Adam, Where Art Thou? (Böll), **20th:** 412
Adamites, **Anc:** 700; **MA:** 1163
Adams, Abigail, **18th:** 7-11, 1042

Adams, Ansel, **20th:** 884
Adams, Charles. *See* Chambers, Whittaker
Adams, David Jackson. *See* Swango, Michael
Adams, Elizabeth, **Notor:** 359
Adams, Frank. *See* Abagnale, Frank W., Jr.
Adams, Henry, **19th:** 16-20; *The Education of Henry Adams*, 18
Adams, Henry Carter, **19th:** 28
Adams, John, **18th:** 7, 11-15, 139, 1042; diplomacy with English, 12; diplomacy with French, 12
Adams, John Quincy, **19th:** 16, 20-26, 503, 855; Monroe cabinet, 1587; James K. Polk, 1820; presidency, 1190; state of the union address, 23
Adams, Samuel, **18th:** 16-20, 276; American independence, 1041
Adams, Will, **17th:** 917
Adams-Onís Treaty (1819), **19th:** 22
Adam's Rib (film), **20th:** 4067
Adamus Exul, The (Grotius), **17th:** 327
Addams, Jane, **20th:** 22-25, 197, 599, 4185
Addis Ababa, Treaty of (1902), **19th:** 1554
Addison, Joseph, **18th:** 20-24, 434, 942; *The Tatler*, 21
Addled Parliament (1614), **17th:** 884
Address to the People on the Death of the Princess Charlotte, An (Shelley), **19th:** 2093
Address to the Public, An (Willard), **19th:** 2439
Addresses to the German Nation (Fichte), **18th:** 345
Adea Eurydice, **Anc:** 598
Adeimantus, **Anc:** 794
Adelaide of Burgundy, **MA:** 806
Adelchi (Manzoni), **19th:** 1496
Adelphoe (Terence), **Anc:** 850
Adenauer, Konrad, **20th:** 26-29
Adieux (Beauvoir), **20th:** 274
Adıvar, Halide Edib, **20th:** 29-32
Adler, Alfred, **20th:** 33-36, 1324
Adler, Dankmar, **19th:** 2198
Adler, Felix, **19th:** 26-29
ʾAdlī Pasha Yakan, **20th:** 4440
Admetus, and Other Poems (Lazarus), **19th:** 1331
Administration of Justice Act (1774), **18th:** 460
Admiral's Men, **Ren:** 214; **17th:** 440, 636
Admiralty (Royal Navy), **18th:** 50, 270; trial of John Hancock, 458
Adnotationes in Novum Testamentum (Valla), **MA:** 1051
Adobe Walls, Battle of (1864), **19th:** 429
Adolescence (Homer), **19th:** 1122
Adolphus, Gustavus II. *See* Gustavus II Adolphus
Adonais (Shelley), **19th:** 2096
Adone, Joe. *See* Adonis, Joe
Adonijah, **Anc:** 156, 256, 803
Adonis, **Anc:** 107
Adonis (La Fontaine), **17th:** 481
Adonis, Joe, **Notor:** 6-8, 237, 661, 709
Adoptionism, **MA:** 50
Adoration (Bosch), **Ren:** 121
Adoration of the Child (Bellini), **Ren:** 99
Adoration of the Golden Calf, The (Poussin), **17th:** 750
Adoration of the Magi (Botticelli), **Ren:** 124
Adoration of the Magi (Correggio), **Ren:** 249
Adoration of the Magi (Dürer), **Ren:** 298
Adoration of the Magi (Leonardo da Vinci), **Ren:** 562
Adoration of the Magi (Tiepolo), **18th:** 978
Adoration of the Shepherds, The (Caravaggio), **Ren:** 171
Adoration of the Shepherds (La Tour), **17th:** 494
Adorno, Caterinetta Fieschi. *See* Catherine of Genoa, Saint
Adorno, Giuliano, **Ren:** 191
Adorno, Theodor, **20th:** 1632
Adoula, Cyrille, **20th:** 576, 4092
Adriaanszoon de Ruyter, Michiel. *See* Ruyter, Michiel Adriaanszoon de
Adrian II, **MA:** 296
Adrian IV, **MA:** 27-29, 56, 272, 385
Adrian V, **MA:** 186
Adrian VI, **Ren:** 7-9, 54, 229, 410, 483
Adrianople, Battle of (378), **Anc:** 825, 868
Adrianople, Peace of (1568), **Ren:** 651
Adrianople, Treaty of (1713), **18th:** 27
Adul-Qādir. *See* Abdelkader
Advaita, **MA:** 925
Advanced Montessori Method, The (Montessori), **20th:** 2806
Advancement of Learning (Bacon), **Ren:** 73
Advancement of Science, The (Lankester), **19th:** 1316
Advancement of True Religion, Act for (1543), **Ren:** 62
Adventures in Radioisotope Research (Hevesy), **20th:** 1794
Adventures of Augie March, The (Bellow), **20th:** 288
Adventures of Captain Bonneville, U.S.A., The (Irving), **19th:** 1181
Adventures of Dollie, The (film), **20th:** 1594
Adventures of Huckleberry Finn (Twain), **19th:** 2330
Adventures of Ideas (Whitehead), **20th:** 4314
Adventures of Mr. Nicholas Wisdom (Krasicki), **18th:** 568
Adventures of Philip, The (Thackeray), **19th:** 2258-2259

Adventures of Rivella, The (Manley), **18th:** 642
Adventures of Sherlock Holmes, The (Doyle), **19th:** 688
Adventures of Telemachus, the Son of Ulysses, The (Fénelon), **17th:** 265
Adventures of the Dialectic (Merleau-Ponty), **20th:** 2711
Adventures of Tom Sawyer, The (Twain), **19th:** 2330
Adventurous Simplicissimus, The. See *Simplicissimus*
Adversus Apollinarem (Gregory of Nyssa), **Anc:** 364
Adversus haereses (Irenaeus), **Anc:** 444
Adversus haereticos. See *Commonitoria*
Advertisement Touching the Controversies of the Church of England, An, **Ren:** 72
Advertisements (Parker), **Ren:** 762
Advice to Young Men (Cobbett), **19th:** 518-519
Advis, Les (Gournay), **17th:** 315
Adwa, Battle of (1896), **19th:** 1554
Aegospotami, Battle of (405 B.C.E.), **Anc:** 35
Aeken, Jeroen van. *See* Bosch, Hieronymus
Ælfheah, martyrdom of, **MA:** 222, 364
Ælfled. *See* Æthelflæd
Ælfred. *See* Alfred the Great
Aelius, Lucius, **Anc:** 372
Aelle, **Anc:** 396
Aelst, Pieter Coecke van. *See* Coecke van Aelst, Pieter
Aemilia, **Anc:** 758
Aeneas, **Anc:** 172, 273
Aeneas, Anchises, and Ascanius Fleeing Troy (Bernini), **17th:** 45
Aeneid (Claude Lorrain), **17th:** 172
Aeneid (Vergil), **Anc:** 273, 302, 528, 604, 939
Aenigma fidei. See *Enigma of Faith, The*
Aeons (Gnosticism), **Anc:** 918
Aero-Design Division, **20th:** 4109
Aerodonetics (Lanchester), **20th:** 2242
Aerodromes, **19th:** 1311
Aerodynamics, **19th:** 1310; **20th:** 3328, 4108, 4405
Aerodynamics (Lanchester), **20th:** 2242
Aeronautics, **19th:** 448; **20th:** 501
Æsc. *See* Oisc
Aeschines, **Anc:** 129, 265
Aeschylus, Anc: 7-10, 92, 794, 810, 876
Aesop, Anc: 11-13, 628
Aesopea (Aesop), **Anc:** 12
Aesop's Fables. See *Aesopea*
Aesthetic movement, **19th:** 1755
Aesthetics, **18th:** Edmund Burke, 175; Immanuel Kant, 550; and manufacturing, 1060; Friedrich Schiller, 889; Johann Joachim Winckelmann, 1095
Aeterni patris. See *Scholastic Philosophy*
Æthelflæd, MA: 30-32, 65, 341
Æthelred II, the Unready. *See* Ethelred II, the Unready
Æthelstan, **MA:** 342
Aetia. See *Aitiōn*
Aetius, **Anc:** 140, 353
Aetnae (Aeschylus), **Anc:** 9
Affair in Trinidad (film), **20th:** 1732
Affair of the Placards (1534), **Ren:** 618
Affairs of the Poisons (1680), **17th:** 586
Affected Young Ladies, The (Molière), **17th:** 521, 647, 781
Affectionum quae dicuntur hystericae et hypochondriacae (Willis), **17th:** 986
Affirmative action, **20th:** 3022, 3407, 4001
Affluent Society, The (Galbraith), **20th:** 1375
Affonso. *See* Afonso I (c. 1455-1543; king of Kongo)
Afghan Civil War (1992-1996), **20th:** 373
Afghan War, First (1839-1842), **19th:** 1718
Afghānī, Jamāl al-Dīn al-. *See* Jamāl al-Dīn al-Afghānī
Afghanistan, **20th:**Soviet invasion of (1979-1989), 372. *See also* Geographical Index
Afghanistan War (beg. 2001), **20th:** 373, 3324; Canada, 763
AFL (football). *See* American Football League
AFL (labor). *See* AFL-CIO; American Federation of Labor
AFL-CIO, **20th:** 2673, 3426
Afonso I (c. 1108-1185; king of Portugal), **MA:** 33-36
Afonso I (c. 1455-1543; king of Kongo), **Ren:** 9-11
Afonso V, **Ren:** 22, 259, 511
Afonso VI, **17th:** 821
Afonso Henriques. *See* Afonso I (c. 1108-1185; king of Portugal)
Afonso the Conqueror. *See* Afonso I (c. 1108-1185; king of Portugal)
Africa, **Anc:** explorations of, 386-387; trade with Egypt, 334; **MA:** Portuguese exploration of, 479; **Ren:** Ottoman Empire and, 79; Portugal and, 513; Spain and, 79; **17th:** Colonization of, 687; **18th:** British exploration of, 765-768; Ethiopia, 677-679; Islam, 914; Scottish exploration of, 168-171; **19th:** explorations of, 1282, 1400, 2125; Great Britain in, 940; missions, 1401; partitioning of, 1350. *See also* Geographical Index
African Archives, **20th:** 1343
African National Congress, **20th:** 949, 2478, 2583
African Queen, The (film), **20th:** 407, 1771

African Slave Trade, The (Buxton), **19th:** 378, 574
African Slave Trade (Géricault), **19th:** 900
Africanus, Leo. *See* Leo Africanus
Africanus, Scipio. *See* Scipio Africanus
Africanus Numantinus, Publius Cornelius Scipio Aemilianus. *See* Scipio Aemilianus
Afrikaners, **19th:** 462
Afsluttende uvidenskabelig Efterskrift til de Philosophiske Smuler. See *Concluding Unscientific Postscript*
After All (Angell), **20th:** 95
After Dinner at Ornans (Courbet), **19th:** 559
After Me, Sleep (Ernst), **20th:** 1178
After Ninety (Cunningham), **20th:** 885
After Such Pleasures (Parker), **20th:** 3117
After the Fall (Miller), **20th:** 2743
Afterlife, Zoroastrian, **Anc:** 994
Aftermath (Longfellow), **19th:** 1419
Afternoon of a Faun (Debussy), **20th:** 986
Afzal Khan, **17th:** 859
Agade. *See* Akkad
Against All Heresies. See *Kata pasōn haireseōn elenkhos*
Against Apion. See *Contra Apionem*
Against Celsus. See *Contra Celsum*
Against Common Opinions. See *Pros tas koinas doxas*
Against Heresies. See *Adversus haereses*
Against Interpretation, and Other Essays (Sontag), **20th:** 3788
Against the Christians. See *Kata Christanōn*
Against the Grain (Paracelsus), **Ren:** 758
Against the Sophists. See *Kata tōn sophistōn*
Agamemnōn (Aeschylus), **Anc:** 9, 427, 653
Agamemnon (Milhaud), **20th:** 2735
Agarkar, Gopal Ganesh, **20th:** 4024
Agassi, Andre, **20th:** 3616
Agassiz, Elizabeth Cabot, **19th:** 29-31, 33
Agassiz, Louis, **19th:** 29, 31-35, 964-965
Agathe Tyche, **Anc:** 106
Agathocleia, **Anc:** 551
Agathocles, **Anc:** 106, 716
Agathon, **Notor:** 13
Ağca, Mehmet Ali, **Notor:** 8-10
Âge de raison, L'. See *Age of Reason, The* (Sartre)
Âge d'or, L'. See *Golden Age, The* (film)
Age of Anxiety, The (Auden), **20th:** 173
Age of Bronze, The (Rodin), **19th:** 1925
Age of Consent debate, **20th:** 4024
Age of Constantine the Great, The (Burckhardt), **19th:** 355
Age of Fallibility, The (Soros), **20th:** 3796
Age of Innocence, The (Wharton), **20th:** 4302
Age of Reason, The (Paine), **18th:** 760
Age of Reason, The (Sartre), **20th:** 3638
Age of Uncertainty, The (television special), **20th:** 1376
Agee, James, **20th:** 232
Ageladas, **Anc:** 633, 675
Ages of the World, The (Schelling), **19th:** 2011
Agesilaus. See *Logos eis Agēsilaon Basilea*
Agesilaus II of Sparta, **Anc:** 14-17, 304, 969
Agget, Neil, **20th:** 4122
Aggrey, Kwegyir, **20th:** 180
Agias (Pharsalus), **Anc:** 524
Agiatis, **Anc:** 228
Agincourt, Battle of (1415), **MA:** 247, 277, 503; **Ren:** 224
Aging, **20th:** 589; study of, 1501
Agis IV, **Anc:** 228
Agitators, **17th:** 535
Aglaophon, **Anc:** 678
Aglaura (Suckling), **17th:** 894
Agnadello, Battle of (1509), **Ren:** 84, 519
Agnes Grey (Brontë), **19th:** 310
Agnesi, Maria Gaetana, **18th:** 24-26
Agnew, Spiro T., **Notor:** 737
Agnolo, Andrea d'. *See* Andrea del Sarto
Agnolo, Donato d'. *See* Bramante, Donato
Agoge, **Anc:** 14
Agon (ballet), **20th:** 195
Agony in the Garden (Bellini), **Ren:** 98
Agony in the Garden (Cranach, the Elder), **Ren:** 262
Agony of Christianity, The (Unamuno), **20th:** 4130
Agoracritus, **Anc:** 635
Agram Treason Trials (1908), **20th:** 2641
Agrammes. *See* Dhanananda
Agramonte, Aristides, **19th:** 1879
Agrarian reform, Roman, **Anc:** 358
Agreement of the Free People (Lilburne, Walwyn, and Overton), **17th:** 535
Agreement of the People, **17th:** 535
Agricola, Georgius, **Ren:** 11-14
Agricola, Gnaeus Julius, **Anc:** 17-20, 163, 837; **Notor:** 290
Agricultural Adjustment Act of 1933, **20th:** 4207
Agricultural Revolution, **18th:** England, 990-993; United States, 1076-1079
Agricultural Society of India, **19th:** 411
Agricultural Workers Association, **20th:** 1915

Agriculture, **Anc:** Roman, 358, 929; Sumerian, 914; **MA:** China, 80; Sāsānian Empire, 615; Spain, 11; **18th:** Chinese, 818; and economics, 820; mixed farming, 990-993; Russian, 213; 19th: Australia, 1431; chemistry, 1368; horticulture, 351; Ohio, 69; reaper, 1439; **20th:** Africa, 435, 1086; breeding high-yield plants, 435; George Washington Carver, 678; China, 969, 4459; Egyptian land reform, 2915; Iranian land reform, 2780; Kenya, 2108; Mexico, 616; New Zealand, 2643; Soviet Union, 2129, 3818, 4151; Thailand, 363; United States, 4207. *See also* Category Index

Agrippa I, **Notor:** 458

Agrippa, Marcus Vipsanius, **Anc:** 20-23, 146, 231, 490, 527

Agrippina Landing at Brundisium with the Ashes of Germanicus (West), **18th:** 1068

Agrippina the Elder, **Anc:** 22-23, 72, 176, 561

Agrippina the Younger, **Anc:** 23-26, 71, 104, 219, 235, 561, 591, 685, 766; **Notor:** 777

Agudeza y Arte de ingenio. See *Mind's Wit and Art, The*

Aguinaldo, Emilio, **19th:** 647, 1055

Ah, but Your Land Is Beautiful (Paton), **20th:** 3140

Aharon. *See* Aaron

Ahaz, **Anc:** 448

Ahenobarbus, Lucius Domitius. *See* Nero

Ahi sā, **Anc:** 355, 925

Ahmad, Abu. *See* Zarqawi, Abu Musab al-

Aḥmad ibn Ḥanbal, **MA:** 36-39, 988

Aḥmad ibn Muḥammad. *See* Aḥmad ibn Ḥanbal

Ahmad Khan, Sir Sayyid, **19th:** 35-38

Ahmadnagar, **17th:** 843

Ahmadu Tal, **19th:** 187, 757

Ahmed I, **Ren:** 663; **17th:** 472, 673

Ahmed III, **18th:** 26-29, 233, 639; arts patronage, 603; Tulip Age, 28

Ahmed ʿArabi, **19th:** 5

Ahmed Pasha. *See* Bonneval, Claude Alexandre de

Ahmed Yesevi, **MA:** 1002

Ahmose I, **Anc:** 585

Ahmose-Nefertari, **Anc:** 585

Ahriman, **Anc:** 993

Ahuitzotl, **Ren:** 694

Ahura Mazda, **Anc:** 251, 567, 974, 993

Aias (Sophocles), **Anc:** 810

Aiax (Ennius), **Anc:** 301

Aïda (Verdi), **19th:** 2353

Aidan, Saint, **MA:** 509

Aidez l'Espagne (Miró), **20th:** 2761

Aidit, Dipa Nusantara, **20th:** 3906

AIDS, **20th:** Africa, 2586, 2884; Diana, Princess of Wales, 990; Ronald Reagan, 3402; Romania, 706

AIDS and Its Metaphors (Sontag), **20th:** 3790

Aids to Reflection (Coleridge), **19th:** 532

Aids to Scouting for N.C.O.s and Men. See *Scouting for Boys*

Aiionwatha. *See* Hiawatha

Aikin, Anna. *See* Barbauld, Anna

Aileen C. Hernandez Associates, **20th:** 1774

Ailey, Alvin, **20th:** 36-38, 2013

Aimeé Césaire (Césaire), **20th:** 710

Aīn Jalūt, Battle of (1260), **MA:** 140

Ainsworth, William Harrison, **Notor:** 944

Air brakes, **19th:** 2416

Air liquide, L'. See *Liquid Air, Oxygen, Nitrogen*

Air shows, **20th:** 802

Air traffic controllers strike (1981), **20th:** 3402

Airds Moss, Battle of (1680), **17th:** 123

Airplanes, **19th:** concept of, 448; **20th:** versus airships, 1095; bombers, 4110; breaking the sound barrier, 4427; development of, 3328, 3633, 4404; jets, 4319; monoplanes, 4108; prop-jets, 4110; racing, 1024, 1926; Rolls-Royce engines, 3497; supersonic, 4110. *See also* Aviation

Airships, **20th:** 3632, 4453; rigid, 1093, 1095; World War I, 389

ʿĀʾishah bint Abī Bakr, **MA:** 735

Aisin Gioro. *See* Puyi

Aisin Gioro Xianwangyu. *See* Kawashima, Yoshiko

Aisin Gioro Xianxi. *See* Kawashima, Yoshiko

Aitiōn (Callimachus), **Anc:** 180

Aitken, William Maxwell. *See* Beaverbrook, Lord

Aix-la-Chapelle, Treaty of (1748), **18th:** 312, 654, 773, 882

Ajax. See *Aias*

Ajwibatu. See *Shariʿa in Songhay*

Ak Koyunlu Dynasty, **MA:** 712

Akahige. See *Red Beard*

Akalaitis, JoAnne, **20th:** 39-42

Akatsuki no tera. See *Temple of Dawn, The*

Akbar (1542-1605; Mughal emperor of India), **Ren:** 15-18, 476; **17th:** 410

Akbar (d. 1704; Mughal prince), **17th:** 25

Akbar, Said, **Notor:** 10-11

Aké (Soyinka), **20th:** 3804

Akechi Mitsuhide, **Ren:** 460, 733

Akechi Tama. *See* Hosokawa Gracia

Akhenaton, **Anc:** 26-29, 46, 587, 735, 901, 908

Akhmatova, Anna, **20th:** 42-46; **Notor:** 1137

Akiba ben Joseph, **Anc:** 29-32

Akihito, **20th:** 46-50, 1818
Akins, Zoë, **20th:** 142
Akiva ben Joseph. *See* Akiba ben Joseph
Akkad, **Anc:** 366, 377
Akkumulation des Kapitals, Die. See *Accumulation of Capital, The*
Aku-Aku (Heyerdahl), **20th:** 1797
Akuffo, F. W., **20th:** 3389
Al Aaraaf, Tamerlane, and Minor Poems (Poe), **19th:** 1813
Al-Alamein, Second Battle of (1942), **20th:** 3504
Al-Beruni's India (al-Bīrūnī), **MA:** 164
Al-Buhaira, Battle of (1130), **MA:** 6
Al Jazeera (news organization), **20th:** 372
Al-Qādisīyah, Battle of (636), **MA:** 1038
Al-Qaeda, **20th:** 372; **Notor:** 43, 101, 758, 1133
ʿAlāʾ-ud-Dīn Muḥammad Khaljī, **MA:** 39-42
Alagherius, Durante. *See* Dante
Alam, Asadollah, **20th:** 2781
ʿĀlam Khān, **Ren:** 70, 478
Alamanni, **Anc:** 351; **MA:** 254, 288, 291, 662
ʿĀlamgīr I. *See* Aurangzeb
Alamo, **19th:** 572
Alanbrooke, first Viscount, **20th:** 50-53
Alans, **Anc:** 351
Alarcón, Hernando de, **Ren:** 246
Alaric I, **Anc:** 352, 825
Alaric II, **MA:** 293, 783
Alaska, **19th:** boundary dispute, 1056; purchase of, 2079
Alaska Syndicate, **20th:** 1614
Alastor (Shelley), **19th:** 2093
Alaungpaya, **18th:** 29-31
Alban, Viscount Saint. *See* Bacon, Francis
Albania. *See* Geographical Index
Albany and Susquehanna (railway), **19th:** 1601
Albany Congress (1754), **18th:** 372
Albategnius. *See* Battānī, al-
Albatenius. *See* Battānī, al-
Albemarle, first duke of. *See* Monck, George
Alberic I, **Notor:** 706
Alberic II, **Notor:** 707
Albert (prince consort of Queen Victoria of Great Britain), **19th:** 1535, 2360
Albert V (duke of Bavaria), **Ren:** 362, 541
Albert VI (duke of Austria), **Ren:** 351
Albert, Graf von Bollstädt. *See* Albertus Magnus, Saint
Albert Herring (Britten), **20th:** 531
Albert Memorial, **19th:** 2045
Albert of Cologne. *See* Albertus Magnus, Saint
Albert the Bear, **MA:** 474
Albert the Great. *See* Albertus Magnus, Saint
Alberti, Leon Battista, **MA:** 84, 207, 769, 850; **Ren:** 18-21, 132, 602, 782
Albertus Magnus, Saint, **MA:** 42-45, 1105
Albigensian Crusade (1209-1229), **MA:** 317, 571, 837
Albigensians, **Anc:** 700; **MA:** 57, 316, 543
Albina (Cowley), **18th:** 284
Albinus. *See* Alcuin
Alboin, **MA:** 45-48
Albrecht (duke of Prussia), **Ren:** 242
Albright, Madeleine, **20th:** 54-58, 784
Albumblade (Grieg), **19th:** 986
Albuquerque, Afonso de, **Ren:** 22-25
Alcacer-Seguer, capture of (1458), **MA:** 479
Alcáçovas, Treaty of (1479), **Ren:** 511
Alcaeus, **Anc:** 653, 750
Alcalá. *See* Polyglot Bible
Alcalá, Antonio José de Sucre. *See* Sucre, Antonio José de
Alcalde de Zalamea, El. See *Mayor of Zalamea, The*
Alcamenes, **Anc:** 635
Alcântara, Pedro de. *See* Pedro II
Alcântara Bourbon, Antonio Pedro de. *See* Pedro I
Alceste (Gluck and Calzabigi), **18th:** 419
Alceste (Lully and Quinault), **17th:** 570
Alchemist, The (Jonson), **17th:** 442
Alchemy, **MA:** Persia, 884; Spain, 562; **Ren:** 127, 824; **18th:** 580, 936
Alchemy of Finance, The (Soros), **20th:** 3796
Alcibiades of Athens, **Anc:** 33-35, 801, 884, 968; **Notor:** 11-13
Alcippus, **Anc:** 872
Alcmaeon, **Anc:** 36-38
ALCOA. *See* Aluminum Company of America
Alcoholism, Native Americans, **20th:** 1171, 3248
Alcools (Apollinaire), **20th:** 105
Alcott, Bronson, **19th:** 38-41, 842, 876, 1761
Alcott, Louisa May, **19th:** 40-44
Alcott House, **19th:** 40
Alcuin, **MA:** 49-51, 861, 870
Alden, John, **17th:** 7-9, 879
Alder, Kurt, **20th:** 996
Alderman (killer of Metacom), **17th:** 634
Aldhelm, **MA:** 219
Aldine Press, **Ren:** 608
Aldrich, Thomas, **Ren:** 762
Aldrin, Edwin E., Jr., **20th:** 136
Aleijadinho. *See* Lisboa, Antônio Francisco
Aleiya, **19th:** 1238
Aleksandr Nevsky. *See* Alexander Nevsky, Saint
Aleksandr Yaroslavich. *See* Alexander Nevsky, Saint

Alekseyev, Konstantin Sergeyevich. *See* Stanislavsky, Konstantin
Alemán, Mateo, **Ren:** 25-27
Alembert, Jean le Rond d', **18th:** 31-35, 267, 308
Alencar, José de, **19th:** 1450
Alençon, Marguerite d'. *See* Marguerite de Navarre
Aleph, and Other Stories, 1933-1969, The (Borges), **20th:** 432
Alessandri, Jorge, **20th:** 71
Aletheia (Parmenides), **Anc:** 609
Alēthon Diēgēmaton (Lucian), **Anc:** 515
Alexander (duke of Albany), **Ren:** 496, 498
Alexander I (1777-1825; czar of Russia), **19th:** 21, 45-48, 405, 1667, 1670; Mikhail Mikhaylovich Speransky, 2130; Freiherr vom Stein, 2152; **Notor:** 788, 813, 876
Alexander I (1893-1920; king of Greece), **20th:** 4158
Alexander II (d. 1073; pope), **MA:** 433, 706
Alexander II (1818-1881; czar of Russia), **19th:** 48-51, 1810; **Notor:** 845
Alexander III the Great (356-323 B.C.E.; king of Macedonia), **Anc:** 39-42, 63, 95, 107, 202, 266, 284, 523, 597, 639, 719, 763, 872
Alexander III (c. 1105-1181; pope), **MA:** 56-59, 386
Alexander III (1241-1286; king of Scotland), **MA:** 201, 346
Alexander III (1845-1894; czar of Russia), **19th:** 49, 1810; **Notor:** 845
Alexander IV (323-310 B.C.E.; son of Alexander the Great), **Anc:** 720
Alexander IV (1199-1261; pope), **MA:** 180, 727, 1111
Alexander VI (1431-1503; pope), **Ren:** 27-30, 88, 105, 115, 117, 228, 512, 518, 587, 767, 851; **Notor:** 14-15, 129-130
Alexander VII (1599-1667; pope), **17th:** 9-11, 46, 165, 406, 964
Alexander, Franz, **20th:** 1884
Alexander Graham Bell Association for the Deaf. *See* American Association to Promote Teaching of Speech to the Deaf
Alexander Nevsky (film), **20th:** 1129
Alexander Nevsky, Saint, **MA:** 52-55
Alexander of the North. *See* Charles XII
Alexander Severus, Marcus Aurelius, **Anc:** 484, 488
Alexander the Great (Racine), **17th:** 774
"Alexander's Ragtime Band" (Berlin), **20th:** 328
Alexandra (empress of Russia), **Notor:** 886, 1126
Alexandra Fedorovna, **19th:** 1863
Alexandre le Grand. See *Alexander the Great*
Alexandria, **Anc:** anti-Semitism in, 640; Arsinoe II Philadephus and, 107; astronomy at, 815; Christianity in, 133, 599; cultural center, 314; culture of, 132, 717; foundation of, 40; Library, 179, 314, 827; mathematics at, 76, 317; medicine at, 199; Museum, 314; science at, 80, 84; **MA:** 814
Alexandrian Donations, **Anc:** 75
Alexandrian War (48 B.C.E.), **Anc:** 174, 230
Alexiad (Anna Comnena), **MA:** 90
Alexianus, **Anc:** 484; **Notor:** 326
Alexis (czar of Russia), **17th:** 11-14, 28, 428, 463, 663, 683, 795, 865
Alexius I Comnenus, **MA:** 73, 89, 176, 1004
Alexius III Angelus, **MA:** 1017
Alexius IV Angelus, **MA:** 1059
Alf layla wa-layla. See *Arabian Nights' Entertainments, The*
Alfa Romeo Company, **20th:** 1239
Alfarrobeira, Battle of (1449), **MA:** 479
Alfonsín, Raúl, **Notor:** 1066
Alfonso (duke of Bisceglie), **Ren:** 118
Alfonso II, **Ren:** 28
Alfonso VI, **MA:** 279
Alfonso VIII, **MA:** 59, 316
Alfonso X, **MA:** 59-62
Alfonso XII, **19th:** 1184
Alfonso XIII, **20th:** 4130
Alfonso Borelli, Giovanni. *See* Borelli, Giovanni Alfonso
Alfonso the Wise. *See* Alfonso X
Alfred (Dvořák), **19th:** 712
Alfred Hitchcock Presents (television program), **20th:** 1827
Alfred the Great, **MA:** 30, 63-66, 340, 901
Alfthryth, **MA:** 362
Alfvén, Hannes, **20th:** 58-60
Alfvén waves, **20th:** 59
Algebra, **Anc:** 288, 318; **MA:** 617; **Ren:** Italy, 173, 920; Netherlands, 913; 18th: 335, 574, 684; **19th:** 858, 883. *See also* Mathematics
Algeciras Conference (1906), **19th:** 1121; **20th:** 780
Alger, Horatio, **19th:** 51-55; **20th:** 653
Algeria, **19th:** 757. *See also* Geographical Index
Algerian Memories (Workman and Workman), **19th:** 2467
Algerian People's Union, **20th:** 8
Algerian War (1954-1962), **20th:** 1428
Algerian Women in Their Quarters (Delacroix), **19th:** 637
Algériennes, poésies, Les (Ségalas), **19th:** 2062
Algerine War. *See* Barbary Wars
Algirdas, **MA:** 1120

Algonquians, **17th:** 141, 423, 499, 634, 799
Algonquin Round Table, **20th:** 3116
Algren, Nelson, **20th:** 273
Alhambra, The (Irving), **19th:** 1181
Alhazen, **Anc:** 79; **MA:** 66-70
Alhwini. *See* Alcuin
ʿAlī, **MA:** 3, 468, 472, 1039
Ali, Ben, **Notor:** 242
Ali, Drew, **Notor:** 763
Ali, Mohammed F. *See* Fard, Wallace Dodd
Ali, Muhammad, **20th:** 61-65, 2614
ʿAlī Muḥammad. *See* Bāb, the
Alī Muḥammad Mīrzā. *See* Bāb, the
Ali Paşa Tepelenë, **19th:** 55-57, 2479
ʿAlī Pasha, **Ren:** 88
ʿAlī the Great. *See* Sonni ʿAlī
Alia, Ramiz, **Notor:** 494
Aliae regulae (Guido d'Arezzo), **MA:** 440
Alianza Popular Revolucionaria Americana, **20th:** 1717
Alice's Adventures in Wonderland (Carroll), **19th:** 424
Alide (Lazarus), **19th:** 1331
Alien and Sedition Acts (1798), **18th:** 13, 238, 530, 637
Alighieri, Dante. *See* Dante
Alito, Samuel, **20th:** 3023
Alkabetz, Solomon, **Ren:** 524
Alkēstis (Euripides), **Anc:** 326, 810
Alkibiades. *See* Alcibiades of Athens
Alkmaeon. *See* Alcmaeon
All About Eve (film), **20th:** 921, 2798
All Fools (Chapman), **Ren:** 214
All for Love (Dryden), **17th:** 241
All God's Chillun Got Wings (O'Neill), **20th:** 3463
All in the Day's Work (Tarbell), **20th:** 3949
All-India Conference, **20th:** 222
All My Pretty Ones (Sexton), **20th:** 3714
All My Sons (Miller), **20th:** 2742
All Quiet on the Western Front (Remarque), **20th:** 3413
All Rivers Run to the Sea (Wiesel), **20th:** 4326
All-Stars (music group), **20th:** 132
All That Jazz (film), **20th:** 1292
All the King's Men (Warren), **20th:** 4238
All the Way Around and Back (Ives), **20th:** 1975
Allan, Maud, **Notor:** 933
Allan Quatermain (Haggard), **19th:** 1007
Allegory, **Anc:** 689; fables and, 629; Scripture as, 641
Allegory of Inclination (Artemisia), **17th:** 307
Allegory of Love, The (Lewis), **20th:** 2354
Allegory of Painting (Artemisia), **17th:** 308
Allegory of Painting, The (Vermeer), **17th:** 957
Allegory of Redemption (Cranachs), **Ren:** 264
Allegory of the Law and the Gospel (Cranach, the Elder), **Ren:** 264
Allegri, Antonio. *See* Correggio
Allegro (Rodgers and Hammerstein), **20th:** 1659
Allen, Ethan, **18th:** 35-38, 60
Allen, Paul, **20th:** 1421
Allen, William, **19th:** 1572
Allenby, Lord (Edmund Henry Hynman Allenby), **20th:** 65-69, 2305, 4440
Allende, Ignacio, **19th:** 1095
Allende, Salvador, **20th:** 70-73, 2172, 2939, 3257; **Notor:** 842
Alleyne, Ellen. *See* Rossetti, Christina
Allgemeine Psychopathologie. See *General Psychopathology*
Allgemeiner Deutscher Arbeiterverein. *See* General German Workers' Association
Alliance for Labor Action, **20th:** 3427
Alliance of the Bakongo, **20th:** 4091
Alligator Man. *See* Ball, Joe
Allison, Clay, **Notor:** 316
Allouez, Claude-Jean, **17th:** 433, 603
Alma do Brasil (Villa-Lobos), **20th:** 4164
Almagest. See *Mathēmatikē syntaxis*
Almagestum novum (Riccioli), **17th:** 322
Almagro, Diego de, **Ren:** 801
Almanacs, **18th:** Benjamin Banneker, 85; Benjamin Franklin, 371; Roger Sherman, 908
Almayer's Folly (Conrad), **20th:** 825
Almeida, Dom Francisco de, **Ren:** 22
Almohad Empire, **MA:** 6, 7, 33, 118, 571, 686
Almond for a Parrat, An (Nashe), **Ren:** 714
Almoravids, **MA:** 6, 33, 118, 280; art, 8
ALN. *See* National Liberation Army
Alo, Vincent, **Notor:** 237
"Aloha 'Oe" (Liliuokalani), **19th:** 1375
Alompra. *See* Alaungpaya
Alone (Byrd), **20th:** 607
Alonso, Giovanni Francesco Antonio. *See* Borelli, Giovanni Alfonso
Alp Arslan, **MA:** 70-75, 774, 795
Alphabets, **Anc:** Gothic, 911; Latin, 217; Phoenician, 273
Alpher, Ralph, **20th:** 1380
Alps and Sanctuaries (Butler), **19th:** 375
Alsace, Burgundy and, **Ren:** 218. *See also* Burgundy
Also sprach Zarathustra. See *Thus Spake Zarathustra*
Altair 8800, **20th:** 1421

Altamira, cave paintings at, **20th:** 518
Altar of Artemis (Praxiteles), **Anc:** 694
Altar of Victory, **Anc:** 43
Alte Feste, Battle of the (1632), **17th:** 338, 926
Altenberg, Peter, **20th:** 2185
Altgeld, John Peter, **19th:** 57-60
Altillo Chapel, El, **20th:** 633
Altmann, Klaus. *See* Barbie, Klaus
Altmark, Truce of (1629), **17th:** 337, 705
Altneuland. See *Old-New Land*
Altorf (Wright), **19th:** 2469
Altruism, **20th:** 4358
Altuniya, Ikhtiar al-Dīn, **MA:** 889
Aluminum Company of America, **20th:** 2683
Alva, duke of, **Ren:** 31-33, 85, 703, 740
Alvarado, Hernando de, **Ren:** 247
Alvarado, Juan de, **Ren:** 161
Alvarado, Pedro de, **Ren:** 34-37, 161
Alvares, Francisco, **Ren:** 261
Álvarez, Juan de Yepes y. *See* John of the Cross, Saint
Alvarez, Luis W., **20th:** 73-76
Alvarez, Walter, **20th:** 75
Álvarez de Toledo, Fernando. *See* Alva, duke of
Alvin Ailey American Dance Theater, **20th:** 37
Always (film), **20th:** 3812
Alwin, Patricio, **Notor:** 843
Aly Khan, **20th:** 1732
Alyattes, **Anc:** 244
Alzira (Verdi), **19th:** 2351
Amadas, Philip, **Ren:** 771
Amadeo, **19th:** 1184
Amadeus (film), **20th:** 3990
Amahl and the Night Visitors (Menotti), **20th:** 2705
Amalasuntha, **MA:** 75-78, 1014
Amalgamated Association of Iron and Steel Workers, **19th:** 420
Amalgamation Party, **19th:** 343
Amalric I, **MA:** 918
Aman. *See* Cao Cao
Aman Andom, **20th:** 2702
Amanohashidate (Sesshū), **Ren:** 866
Amarcord (film), **20th:** 1233
Amarna Letters, **Anc:** 902
Amarna period, **Anc:** 588
Amasia, Treaty of (1555), **Ren:** 916
Amasis II, **Notor:** 850
Amaterasu, **Anc:** 462, 465; **MA:** 623, 975
Amati, Niccolò, **18th:** 944
Amatruda, Catherine S., **20th:** 1466
Amaya, Mario, **Notor:** 983
Amazon (Toulouse-Lautrec), **19th:** 2287
Amazon.com, **20th:** 361
Ambartsumian, Viktor A., **20th:** 77-79
Ambassadors, The (James), **19th:** 1209
Amberley and of Ardsalla, Viscount. *See* Russell, John
Amblève, Battle of (716), **MA:** 251
Ambrose, Lyda Catherine, **Notor:** 1109
Ambrose, Saint, **Anc:** 42-45, 142, 391, 424, 600, 699, 796, 870
Ambrosius. *See* Ambrose, Saint
Ambrosius, Aurelius, **Anc:** 42, 395
Ameinias, **Anc:** 608
Ameixal, Battle of (1663), **17th:** 426
Amelia (Fielding), **18th:** 349
Amelia Goes to the Ball (Menotti), **20th:** 2704
Amen, **Anc:** 388, 571, 656, 711, 735
Amen-Ra, **Anc:** 26, 45, 588
Amenhotep II, **Anc:** 887
Amenhotep III, **Anc:** 27, 45-49, 901, 908
Amenhotep IV. *See* Akhenaton
Amerasians, **20th:** 559
America (Blake), **18th:** 122
America and the New Epoch (Steinmetz), **19th:** 2158
American, The (James), **19th:** 1207
American and American Indian conflicts, **18th:** 253, 610, 1056
American and Foreign Anti-Slavery Society, **19th:** 800
American Anti-Slavery Society, **19th:** 66, 483, 876, 2146
American Association for International Conciliation, **20th:** 598
American Association for the Advancement of Women, **19th:** 1581
American Association of University Women, **19th:** 1728, 1900; **20th:** 3937
American Association to Promote Teaching of Speech to the Deaf, **19th:** 184
American Ballet Center, **20th:** 2013
American Ballet Theatre, **20th:** 253, 958
American Beaver and His Works, The (Morgan), **19th:** 1605
American-British conflicts, **18th:** 198, 206, 253, 257, 386, 507, 518, 1043, 1054
American-British diplomacy, **18th:** 12, 372, 540
American Capitalism (Galbraith), **20th:** 1375
American Civil Liberties Union, **20th:** 4003
American College, The (Flexner), **20th:** 1257
American colonies. *See* Colonialism
American Colonization Society, **19th:** 577, 875, 1501
American Communist Party, **20th:** 1867
American Democracy, The (Laski), **20th:** 2270
American Democrat, The (Cooper), **19th:** 554
American Dictionary of the English Language, An (Webster), **19th:** 2404

American Dilemma, An (Myrdal), **20th:** 575, 2890
American Dream, An (Mailer), **20th:** 2563
American Equal Rights Association, **19th:** 2178
American Ethnological Society, **19th:** 856
American Exodus, An (Taylor and Lange), **20th:** 2261
American Federation of Labor, **19th:** 27, 943; **20th:** 2361, 2672, 3426
American Federation of Labor-Congress of Industrial Organizations. *See* AFL-CIO
American Football League, **20th:** 3554
American Foreign Policy in the Making, 1932-1940 (Beard), **20th:** 265
American-French diplomacy, **18th:** 373, 413, 706, 1011
American frontier, **18th:** California, 892; idea of, 145; Kentucky, 143; Northwest Territory, 1056; Ohio Valley and Great Lakes, 611; Spanish Louisiana, 525
American Frugal Housewife, The (Child), **19th:** 482, 484
American Fur Company, **19th:** 87
American Gothic (Wood), **20th:** 4388
American Government and Politics (Beard), **20th:** 262
American Graffiti (film), **20th:** 2450
American High School Today, The (Conant), **20th:** 823
American in Paris, An (film), **20th:** 1464, 2097
American in Paris, An (Gershwin), **20th:** 1459
American independence, **18th:** 1041; John Adams, 11-15; Edmund Burke, 174; Charles Carroll, 206; Charles James Fox, 364; Benjamin Franklin, 370-375; George III, 410; Elbridge Gerry, 412-414; Alexander Hamilton, 452-456; John Jay, 524; James Madison, 636-638; Gouverneur Morris, 705-707; Robert Morris, 707-711; Thomas Paine, 761; comte de Rochambeau, 853; Benjamin Rush, 872-874; George Washington, 1043-1047; John Wilkes, 1085; John Witherspoon, 1098-1102
American Independent Party, **20th:** 4206
American Indian-American conflicts, **18th:** 253, 610, 1056
American Indian-British alliance, **18th:** 40, 144, 159, 626
American Indian-British conflicts, **18th:** 385, 802
American Indian-British relations, **18th:** 744
American Indian-French relations, **18th:** 801
American Indian leaders, **18th:** Joseph Brant, 159-162; Little Turtle, 610-612; Alexander McGillivray, 626-629; Pontiac, 801-805
American Indian-Spanish alliance, **18th:** 627
American Indians, **18th:** and Lord Amherst, 40; and British colonial policy, 803; and Jonathan Edwards, 316; genocide, 803; and Junípero Serra, 892; **19th:** Foxes, 244; Iroquois, 1603; Lakota, 568, 1873, 2109; Nez Perce, 1240; Sauk, 244. *See also* Native Americans; *specific nations*
American Indians in the Pacific (Heyerdahl), **20th:** 1797
American Institute of Photography, **19th:** 292
American Israelite, The (newspaper), **19th:** 2454
American Journal of Education, **19th:** 136
American Language, The (Mencken), **20th:** 2689
American Library Association, **19th:** 649
American Magazine, The, **20th:** 3948
American Missionary Association, **19th:** 431
American Negro Theater, **20th:** 3296
American Notes (Dickens), **19th:** 655
American Party. *See* Know-Nothing Party
American Phrenological Journal, **19th:** 812
American Protective Association, **19th:** 911
American Railway Union, **20th:** 933
American Red Cross, **19th:** 146; **20th:** 1019
American Repertory Theatre, **20th:** 863, 2333
American Revolution, **18th:** John Adams, 11-15; Samuel Adams, 16-20; Ethan Allen, 35-38; Lord Amherst, 40; John André, 42-45; Benedict Arnold, 59-62; Isaac Backus, 75-77; Pierre-Augustin Cardon de Beaumarchais, 98; Joseph Brant, 159-162; Edmund Burke, 175; Charles Carroll, 205-208; Charles III, 227; Samuel Chase, 237-240; Sir Henry Clinton, 256-259; first Marquess Cornwallis, 278-281; John Dickinson, 303-307; French support, 98; George III, 409; Nathanael Greene, 443-447; Alexander Hamilton, 452-456; John Hancock, 457-462; Patrick Henry, 482-485; history, 1042; Richard Howe, 507, 511; Thomas Jefferson, 528-531; John Paul Jones, 539-543; Tadeusz Kościuszko, 564-566; George Mason, 664-667; Mohawks, 159; Robert Morris, 707-711; Lord North, 739; Thomas Paine, 759-762;

William Pitt the Younger, 789; Paul Revere, 832-836; comte de Rochambeau, 851-854; Betsy Ross, 865-867; Roger Sherman, 908-911; Charles Gravier de Vergennes, 1011; Mercy Otis Warren, 1041-1043; George Washington, 1043-1047; Anthony Wayne, 1054-1057; James Wilson, 1092; women's rights, 9. *See also* American independence; Lexington and Concord, Battle of
American Slavery as It Is (Weld), **19th:** 990
American Smelting and Refining Company, **20th:** 1614
American Society of Landscape Architects, **20th:** 1220
American Sociology Society, **19th:** 2385
American-Spanish relations, **18th:** 227, 524, 627
American Spirit, The (Beard), **20th:** 265
American System, **19th:** 503
American Taliban. *See* Lindh, John Walker
American Tobacco Company, **19th:** 692
American Tragedy, An (Dreiser), **20th:** 1034
American Unitarian Association, **19th:** 466
American Woman Suffrage Association, **19th:** 66, 1618, 2084, 2149, 2443
American Woman's Education Association, **19th:** 171
American Woman's Home, The (Beecher and Stowe), **19th:** 170-171
Americans for Democratic Action, **20th:** 3426
Americium, **20th:** 3685
Amerika (Mendelsohn), **20th:** 2693
Amériques (Varèse), **20th:** 4143
Amery, John, **Notor:** 298
Ames, Aldrich, **Notor:** 16-17
Ames, Louise B., **20th:** 1466
Ames, Maria del Rosario Casas, **Notor:** 17
Ames, Oakes, **Notor:** 18-19, 220
Ames, Rick. *See* Ames, Aldrich
Amethyst Ring, The (France), **19th:** 816
Amherst, Lord, **18th:** 38-42, 803, 1105
Amherst College, **19th:** 658; founding of, 2404
Ami du Peuple, L' (newspaper), **18th:** 648
Amida, Siege of (359), **Anc:** 776
Amiens, Mise of (1264), **MA:** 492, 669, 728
Amiens, Peace of (1802), **19th:** 1397, 2223
Amilcar Barca. *See* Hamilcar Barca
Amin (Jin prince), **17th:** 1
Amin, Idi, **20th:** 80-82, 2883, 3012; **Notor:** 20-22
Amīn, Muḥammad al-, **MA:** 468
Amin al-Sirr. *See* Abu Nidal
Amina Sarauniya Zazzua, **Ren:** 37-38
Amini, Ali, **20th:** 2780
Aminta (Tasso), **Ren:** 925
Amir, Mohammad El. *See* Atta al-Sayed, Mohammed
Amir, Yigal, **Notor:** 22-23
Amir Khusrau, **MA:** 40
Amis, Aphara. *See* Behn, Aphra
Amistad case, **19th:** 25, 341, 2181
Ammianus Marcellinus, **Anc:** 776
Ammonia, manufacture of, **20th:** 776, 1629
Ammonius Saccas, **Anc:** 668
Amoenitatum exoticarum (Kämpfer), **17th:** 446
Amon. *See* Amen-Ra
Amor brujo, El (Falla), **20th:** 1207
Amor Caritas (Saint-Gaudens), **19th:** 1973
Amor en los tiempos del cólera, El. See *Love in the Time of Cholera*
Amor, honor y poder (Calderón), **17th:** 113
Amor médico, El (Tirso), **17th:** 913
Amores (Ovid), **Anc:** 603
Amoretti (Spenser), **Ren:** 906
Amorosa visione, L' (Boccaccio), **MA:** 170
Amorous Fiammetta. See *Elegy of Lady Fiammetta, The*
Amorous Prince, The (Behn), **17th:** 43
Amorpha, Fugue in Two Colors (Kupka), **20th:** 2212
Amoskeag Manufacturing Company, **19th:** 2113
Amour fou, L'. See *Mad Love*
Amours, Les (Ronsard), **Ren:** 837
Amours de Psyché et de Cupidon, Les. See *Loves of Cupid and Psyche, The*
Amphictionic Council, **Anc:** 679
Amphitruo (Plautus), **Anc:** 663
Amphitryon (Kleist), **19th:** 1289
Amphitryon (Molière), **17th:** 648
Amphitryon 38 (Giraudoux), **20th:** 1494
ʿAmr al-Makki, **MA:** 454
ʿAmr ibn Saʿid al-Ashdaq, **MA:** 4
Amritsar, Treaty of (1809), **19th:** 1858
Amritsar Massacre (1919), **20th:** 2930, 3099
Āmuktamālyadā (Krishnadevaraya), **Ren:** 533
Amun. *See* Amen-Ra
Amundsen, Roald, **20th:** 83-86, 606
Amurao, Corazon, **Notor:** 986
Amyntas, **Anc:** 637, 650
An Lushan, **MA:** 78-80, 655, 1086
An Lushan Rebellion (755-763), **MA:** 78, 1086
Ana de Souza. *See* Njinga
Ana Nzinga Mbande, Ngola. *See* Njinga
Anabaptism, **Ren:** 472, 675, 1012
Anabasis. See *Kyrou anabasis*
Anacletus II, **MA:** 161

Anaconda Plan, **19th:** 2054
Anacreon, **Notor:** 851
Anagni, Treaty of (1175), **MA:** 386
Analects, The (Confucius), **Anc:** 236, 555, 950; **MA:** 1160
Analogy of Religion, Natural and Revealed, to the Constitution and Course of Nature, The (Butler), **18th:** 188
Analysis of Beauty, The (Hogarth), **18th:** 499
Analyst, The (Berkeley), **18th:** 112, 633
Analytic philosophy, **18th:** 550
Analytical Institutions (Agnesi), **18th:** 24
Analytical Theory of Heat, The (Fourier), **19th:** 810
Ānanda, **Anc:** 49-51, 170
Anandpal, **MA:** 684
Anarchism, **19th:** 120; United States, 59; **20th:** 1520, 3580
Anarchy, State, and Utopia (Nozick), **20th:** 2999, 3392
Anastasia. *See* Kösem Sultan
Anastasia (film), **20th:** 322, 1725
Anastasia, Albert, **Notor:** 7, 23-24, 183, 396, 403, 661, 709
Anathoth, shrine of, **Anc:** 453
Anatolius, Treaty of (443), **Anc:** 139
Anatomē (Diocles), **Anc:** 278
Anatome plantarum (Malpighi), **17th:** 581
Anatomical Exercises of Dr. William Harvey . . . Concerning the Motion of the Heart and Blood, The (Harvey), **17th:** 356
Anatomical Exercitations, Concerning the Generation of Living Creatures (Harvey), **17th:** 357
Anatomical studies, **17th:** England, 355, 564, 986; Germany, 852; Italy, 580; Netherlands, 881, 899
Anatomika (Herophilus), **Anc:** 410
Anatomy, **Anc:** Alexandrian, 84; Galen and, 348; Greek, 278, 311, 410; Roman, 201; **Ren:** Fabricius, 319; Guido Guidi, 211; Vesalius, 966; **19th:** 115, 586
Anatomy and Physiology of Capillaries, The (Krogh), **20th:** 2206
Anatomy Lesson of Dr. Tulp, The (Rembrandt), **17th:** 786
Anatomy of a Murder (film), **20th:** 3863
Anatomy of Melancholy, The (Burton), **17th:** 109
Anatomy of the Brain, The (Willis), **17th:** 564, 986
Anatomy of the World, An (Donne), **17th:** 232
Anaxagoras, **Anc:** 52-54, 326, 620, 633
Anaxandrides, **Anc:** 226, 505
Anaximander, **Anc:** 55-58, 397, 407, 858, 965
Anaximenes of Miletus, **Anc:** 58-60, 349, 858, 965
Anaya, Jorge Isaac, **Notor:** 394
ANC. *See* African National Congress
Anchorites, **Anc:** 62, 790
Anchors Aweigh (film), **20th:** 2097
Ancien Régime et la révolution, L'. See *Old Régime and the Revolution, The*
Anciennes Démocraties des Pays-Bas, Les. See *Belgian Democracy*
Ancient Society (Morgan), **19th:** 1605
Ancients and the Moderns, Quarrel of the, **17th:** 194, 732
& (Cummings), **20th:** 880
And Keep Your Powder Dry (Mead), **20th:** 2670
And the Sea Is Never Full (Wiesel), **20th:** 4326
And the Ship Sails On (film), **20th:** 1233
And the Walls Came Tumbling Down (Abernathy), **20th:** 13
And to Think That I Saw It on Mulberry Street (Seuss), **20th:** 3711
Andalusia, **Ren:** 105
Andalusian Dog, An (film), **20th:** 578, 906
Andersen, Hans Christian, **19th:** 61-64, 985
Anderson, Carl D., **20th:** 4436
Anderson, E. L. *See* Carto, Willis A.
Anderson, Marian, **20th:** 87-89
Anderson, Maxwell, **20th:** 4275
Anderson, Sherwood, **20th:** 1223
Anderson, Victor, **Notor:** 993
Anderson, William, **Notor:** 523, 870
Anderson School of Natural History, **19th:** 30, 34
Andō Hiroshige. *See* Hiroshige
Andō Tokutarō. *See* Hiroshige
Andom, Aman, **Notor:** 720
Andorra (Frisch), **20th:** 1339
André, John, **18th:** 42-45, 61; **Notor:** 37
Andrea d'Agnolo. *See* Andrea del Sarto
Andrea del Sarto, **Ren:** 39-41
Andrea di Pietro della Gondola. *See* Palladio, Andrea
Andrei Shuysky, **17th:** 943
Andreini, Francesco, **Ren:** 42
Andreini, Isabella, **Ren:** 42-43
Andrew II, **MA:** 359
Andrew, Saint, **Anc:** 472, 624
Andrew of Moray, **MA:** 346
Andrewes, Lancelot, **17th:** 14-17, 202, 247, 366, 496
Andrews, Stephen Pearl, **19th:** 2459
Andria (Terence), **Anc:** 850
Andromacha (Ennius), **Anc:** 301
Andromachē (Euripides), **Anc:** 327
Andromache (Racine), **17th:** 774
Andromeda Breakthrough, The (television program), **20th:** 1904
Andromeda galaxy, **20th:** 184
Andronicus II Palaeologus, **MA:** 1018

Andronicus III Palaeologus, **MA:** 530, 958
Andropov, Yuri, **20th:** 1530
Andros, Sir Edmond, **17th:** 518; **18th:** 667, 672
Andrusovo, Treaty of (1667), **17th:** 452
Anecdota. See *Secret History of the Court of the Emperor Justinian*
Anegawa, Battle of (1570), **Ren:** 738
Anemia, pernicious, **20th:** 4305
Anesthesia, **19th:** 1614
Anesthesiology, **20th:** 101
Ange Pitou. See *Six Years Later*
Ángel exterminador, El. See *Exterminating Angel, The*
Angel of Assassination. *See* Corday, Charlotte
Angel Standing in the Sun, The (Turner), **19th:** 2324
Angel with a Lariat (Lang), **20th:** 2257
Angela Merici, Saint, **Ren:** 44-45
Angela of Foligno, Blessed, **MA:** 81-83
Angela Tertiary, Sister. *See* Angela Merici, Saint
Angelica, Mother, **20th:** 90-92
Angelico, Fra, **MA:** 83-86, 769
Angélique, Mother. *See* Arnauld, Angélique
Angell, Sir Norman, **20th:** 92-96
Angelo, Donato d'. *See* Bramante, Donato
Angelou, Maya, **20th:** 97-100
Angels (Bernini), **17th:** 46
Angels (Saint-Gaudens), **19th:** 1973
Angevins, **MA:** 584, 836
Angiography, cerebral, **20th:** 1108
Angkor, kingdom of, **MA:** 981
Angkor Wat, **MA:** 981
Anglican Church, **18th:** 1061-1064; antinomianism, 1062; Mary Astell, 66; Joseph Butler, 188; colonial America, 159; disestablishment in revolutionary America, 636; George I, 402; Jonathan Swift, 964; George Whitefield, 1074; William Wilberforce, 1079. *See also* Church of England
Anglicanism, **19th:** 1845; Africa, 574. *See also* Church of England
Anglici super quatuor libros sententiarum subtilissimae quaestiones earumdemque decisiones (Ockham), **MA:** 778
Anglo-Dutch War, First (1651-1652), **17th:** 57, 808, 931, 942
Anglo-Dutch War, Second (1665-1667), **17th:** 148, 169, 417, 650, 806, 808, 817, 892, 931
Anglo-Dutch War, Third (1672-1674), **17th:** 215, 417, 806, 808, 839, 931
Anglo-French Entente Cordiale (1904), **19th:** 1121; **20th:** 2267
Anglo-French War (1549-1550), **Ren:** 305, 899
Anglo-Irish Agreement (1938), **20th:** 980
Anglo-Irish Treaty (1921-1922), **20th:** 1592, 3035
Anglo-Japanese Treaty (1902), **20th:** 2267
Anglo-Mysore Wars (1767-1769, 1780-1784), **18th:** 522, 523
Anglo-Normans, **MA:** 448
Anglo-Saxon Chronicle, The, **Anc:** 394; **MA:** 65
Anglo-Saxons, **MA:** 183, 223; kings, 31, 65, 342, 354, 364; paganism, 183
Anglo-Zulu War. *See* Zulu War
Angola, **20th:** conflict with Mozambique, 3196; independence of, 3607. *See also* Geographical Index
Angora, Treaty of (1926), **20th:** 164
Angosciola, Sofonisba. *See* Anguissola, Sofonisba
Angoulême, Francis of. *See* Francis I (1494-1547; king of France)
Angoulême, Marguerite d'. *See* Marguerite de Navarre
Anguissola, Sofonisba, **Ren:** 46-48, 935
Angus, fifth earl of. *See* Douglas, Archibald
Anhalt-Zerbst, Sophie Friederike Auguste von. *See* Catherine the Great
Anicertus, **Anc:** 686
Aniello, Tommaso. *See* Masaniello
Anil's Ghost (Ondaatje), **20th:** 3049
Animadversions on the First Part of the Machina coelestis of the Honourable, Learned, and Deservedly Famous Astronomer Johannes Hevelius (Hooke), **17th:** 372
Animal Chemistry (Liebig), **19th:** 1368
Animal experimentation, **18th:** blood system, 926; frogs, 391, 1024; sexual behavior, 927
Animal Farm (Orwell), **20th:** 3083
Animals in That Country, The (Atwood), **20th:** 170
Animated Lines (Kupka), **20th:** 2212
Animism, **Anc:** 857
Ann, Mother. *See* Lee, Ann
Ann Vickers (Lewis), **20th:** 2365
Anna II, **Notor:** 515
Anna Bolena (Donizetti), **19th:** 675
Anna Christie (film), **20th:** 1393
Anna Comnena, **MA:** 89-92
Anna Ivanovna, **Notor:** 515
Anna Karenina (film), **20th:** 1393
Anna Karenina (novel by Tolstoy), **19th:** 2284
Anna Komnene. *See* Anna Comnena
Anna of Oldenburg, **Ren:** 676
Anna "Porphyrogenita." *See* Anna, Princess of the Byzantine Empire

Anna, Princess of the Byzantine Empire, **MA:** 86-89
Annales (Ennius), **Anc:** 302
Annales (Vellius), **Anc:** 508
Annals. See *Ab excessu divi Augusti*
Annals, Chinese, **Anc:** 149
Annals of the Old and New Testament, The (Ussher), **17th:** 939
Annam, Chinese invasion of, **MA:** 1150
Annan, Kofi, **20th:** 466
Annapolis Convention (1786), **18th:** Alexander Hamilton, 453; James Madison, 636
Anne (queen of Great Britain and Ireland), **18th:** 45-49, 66, 250, 423, 662
Anne Boleyn. *See* Boleyn, Anne
Anne de Bretagne. *See* Anne of Brittany
Anne de Pisseleu, **Ren:** 284
Anne of Austria, **Ren:** 636; **17th:** 18-20; and the Great Condé, 185; and Cosimo II de' Medici, 627; and Saint Isaac Jogues, 424; and Madame de La Fayette, 477; and François de La Rochefoucauld, 487; and the duchesse de Longueville, 549; and Louis XIII, 551; and Louis XIV, 554; and Madame de Maintenon, 572; and the Mancini sisters, 585; and François Mansart, 589; and Marie de Médicis, 598; and Marie-Thérèse, 601; and Jules Mazarin, 621; and the duchesse de Montpensier, 660; and Philip IV, 738; and Cardinal de Richelieu, 791; and Hercule Rohan, 158; and Viscount de Turenne, 933
Anne of Beaujeu, **Ren:** 48
Anne of Brittany, **Ren:** 48-50, 227, 577, 613
Anne of Cleves, **Ren:** 51-53, 267, 271, 369, 443, 455, 467, 765, 947
Anne of Geierstein (Scott), **19th:** 2049
Anne of Mecklenburg, **Ren:** 775
Anne Sullivan Macy (Henney), **20th:** 3909
Anneau d'améthyste, L'. See *Amethyst Ring, The*
Années de pèlerinage (Liszt), **19th:** 1394
Anniceris, **Anc:** 89
Annie, Count. *See* Vonsiatsky, Anastase
Annie Allen (Brooks), **20th:** 537
Annie Get Your Gun (Berlin), **20th:** 329
Anno Domini 2000 (Vogel), **19th:** 2372
Annual Register, The, **18th:** 174
Annual Reports (Mann), **19th:** 1487
Annunciation, The (Fra Angelico), **MA:** 84
Annunciation (Martini), **MA:** 698
Annus Domini (Rossetti), **19th:** 1941
Annus Mirabilis (Dryden), **17th:** 240
Another Country (Baldwin), **20th:** 203
Another Essay for Investigation of the Truth (Davenport), **17th:** 219
Another Mexico. See *Lawless Roads, The*
Another Side of Bob Dylan (Dylan), **20th:** 1073
Ans dem Leben der Bienen. See *Dancing Bees, The*
Anselm, Saint, **MA:** 92-95, 481
Ansichten eines Clowns. See *Clown, The*
Ansikte mot ansikte. See *Face to Face* (film)
Anson, George (Lord Anson), **18th:** 49-52
Answer of the Elders of the Severall Churches in New England, An (Davenport), **17th:** 219
Answer to Job (Jung), **20th:** 2064
Answered Prayers (Capote), **20th:** 646
ANT-1, **20th:** 4108
Antar (Rimsky-Korsakov), **19th:** 1915
Antarctic Mystery, An (Verne), **19th:** 2357
Antarctica, exploration of, **18th:** 271, 1006; **19th:** 1935, 2436; **20th:** 84, 607, 4340
Antérotique, L' (du Bellay), **Ren:** 295
Anthem (Rand), **20th:** 3367
Anthills of the Savannah (Achebe), **20th:** 16
Anthologia Anthropologica (Frazer), **20th:** 1320
Anthony, Susan B., **19th:** 65-68, 258, 800, 852, 1097, 1411, 1618, 2084, 2148, 2460; **20th:** 702, 933
Anthony of Egypt, Saint, **Anc:** 60-63, 134
Anthony of Padua, Saint, **MA:** 95-98
Anthrax, **19th:** 1293
Anthropogenie. See *Evolution of Man, The*
Anthropology, **19th:** 1605; **20th:** Great Britain, 1319; participant observer technique, 2669; United States, 296, 401. *See also* Category Index
Antibiotics, **20th:** development of, 1022, 4181; synthesis of, 4394
Antibodies, development of, **20th:** 3156
Antichrist, **Anc:** Hippolytus on, 424
Antichrist, The (Nietzsche), **19th:** 1682
Anticipations (Wells), **20th:** 4288
Anti-Corn Law League, **19th:** 302, 1770
Antidosis (Isocrates), **Anc:** 451
Anti-Federalist Party, **19th:** 365
Antigonē (Sophocles), **Anc:** 810
Antigonus I Monophthalmos, **Anc:** 63-65, 720, 763

Antigonus II Gonatas, **Anc:** 716, 982
Antigonus Cyclops. *See* Antigonus I Monophthalmos
Antigonus Doson, **Anc:** 228
Antikrists mirakler. See *Miracles of Antichrist, The*
Anti-Masonic Party, **19th:** 781
Antimoderne (Maritain), **20th:** 2625
Antinomianism, **17th:** 395; **18th:** 1062
Antinous, **Anc:** 371
Antinous of Belvedere (Brancusi), **20th:** 479
Antioch, Battle of (540), **MA:** 614
Antioch, Siege of (1097-1098), **MA:** 177
Antioch College, **19th:** 1487
Antiochus I Soter, **Anc:** 310, 716
Antiochus II, **Anc:** 717
Antiochus IV Epiphanes, **Anc:** 478
Antiochus and Stratonice (David), **19th:** 608
Antiochus and Stratonice (Ingres), **19th:** 1173
Antiochus of Ascalon, **Anc:** 927
"Antiochus the Aleuad" (Simonides), **Anc:** 793
Antiochus the Great, **Anc:** 65-68
Antipas. *See* Herod Antipas
Anti-Pass Day (1961), **20th:** 2480
Antipater (successor to Alexander the Great), **Anc:** 63, 267, 598, 720
Antipater of Idumaea, **Anc:** 403
Antipater of Sidon, **Anc:** 545
Antiphon, The (Barnes), **20th:** 241
Antipopes, **Anc:** 425
Antiquarianism, **Anc:** Egyptian, 711; Roman, 928
Antiquary, The (Scott), **19th:** 2048
Antiquitates Judaicae (Josephus), **Anc:** 249, 260, 338, 405, 478
Antiquités de Rome, Les. See *Ruines of Rome*
Antiquities of the Jews, The. See *Antiquitates Judaicae*
Antirent War (1839-1846), **19th:** 555
Anti-Semitism, **Anc:** 479; Ambrose and, 44; **MA:** 1099; **20th:** Dreyfus affair, 780; Germany, 688, 1513, 1548, 1808, 1829, 3828, 3842; Great Britain, 358; Italy, 1236, 1450; Poland, 284, 923; Soviet Union, 2575; totalitarianism, 119; United States, 484, 757, 1217, 1980; World War II, 3584
Antisepsis, **19th:** 1391, 2065
Antislavery, **18th:** Benjamin Banneker, 86; Olaudah Equiano, 324-326; Benjamin Franklin, 373; in literature, 88; Guillaume-Thomas Raynal, 830; Samuel Sewall, 893-896; Granville Sharp, 899-902; Toussaint-Louverture, 985; Phillis Wheatley, 1070-1073
Anti-Slavery Society, **19th:** 377
Antisthenes, **Anc:** 68-71, 88, 129, 284
Antitrust suits, **19th:** 693; **20th:** Eastman Kodak, 1080; film studios, 2664; Microsoft, 1422; Standard Oil, 3949; William Howard Taft, 3930; U.S. Supreme Court, 378
Antivivisection movement, **20th:** 3831
Antoku, **MA:** 721, 992
Antonello da Messina, **Ren:** 98
Antonescu, Ion, **Notor:** 25-26
Antonia Ghini (Fontana), **Ren:** 338
Antonia Minor, **Anc:** 71-73, 217
Antonia the Younger. *See* Antonia Minor
Antoninus. *See* Caracalla
Antoninus Pius, **Anc:** 372, 530
Antonius Hybrida, Gaius, **Notor:** 188
Antony (Dumas), **19th:** 696
Antony, Marc, **Anc:** 20, 71, 73-76, 145, 185, 212, 231, 404, 527, 591, 928; **Notor:** 147, 384
Antony and Cleopatra (Barber), **20th:** 231, 3336
Antony and Cleopatra (Shakespeare), **Anc:** 75
Antrim, Billy. *See* Bonney, William H.
Antrim, Kid. *See* Bonney, William H.
Ants, The (Wilson and Hölldobler), **20th:** 4359
Antwerp, Siege of (1585), **Ren:** 322
Antwort auf Hiob. See *Answer to Job*
Anuladevi, **Anc:** 899
Anuṣṭubh (poetic meter), **Anc:** 922
Anwar bin Ibrahim, **20th:** 2552
Anything for a Quiet Life (Middleton and Webster), **17th:** 636, 977
Anything We Love Can Be Saved (Walker), **20th:** 4198
Apache Kid, **Notor:** 27-28
Apache War, The (Remington), **19th:** 1881
Apaches, **17th:** 468; **19th:** 904
Apalachees, **Ren:** 903
Apama, **Anc:** 157
Aparajito. See *Unvanquished, The*
Apartheid, **20th:** 4121; end of, 949, 2583; in literature, 1356, 1535, 3139, 3806; Namibia, 3196; opposition to, 2479, 3006, 3466
Apeiron (Boundlessness), **Anc:** 56
Apfelbaum, Hirsh. *See* Zinovyev, Grigory Yevseyevich
Apgar, Virginia, **20th:** 100-103
Apgar score, **20th:** 101
Aphorisms (Bradley), **19th:** 289
Aphormai pros ta noēta (Porphyry), **Anc:** 688
Aphrodite, **Anc:** 696, 751
Aphrodite of Knidos (Praxiteles), **Anc:** 696
Apion, **Anc:** 640
Apocalypse Now (film), **20th:** 488
Apollinaire, Guillaume, **19th:** 1952; **20th:** 104-107, 510, 952, 1051

Apollinarianism, **Anc:** 361
Apollinaris of Laodicea, **Anc:** 863
Apollo, **Anc:** 221, 695
Apollo (ballet), **20th:** 194, 988, 2378
Apollo and Daphne (Bernini), **17th:** 45
Apollo Conducting Barbarossa's Bride, Beatrice of Burgundy (Tiepolo), **18th:** 978
Apollo Musagète (ballet), **20th:** 909
Apollo Sauroctonos (Praxiteles), **Anc:** 695
Apollo space program, **20th:** 136, 3726
Apollodorus (chronicler), **Anc:** 320
Apollodorus of Carystus, **Anc:** 850
Apollonius of Perga, **Anc:** 76-80, 318, 418, 435, 580, 607
Apollonius of Rhodes, **Anc:** 179, 315
Apollonius of Tyana, **Anc:** 460, 482
Apologetica disceptatio pro astrologia (Servetus), **Ren:** 862
Apologética historia de las Indias (Las Casas), **Ren:** 539
Apologeticus (Tertullian), **Anc:** 853
Apologia (Abelard), **MA:** 16
Apologia (Pico della Mirandola), **Ren:** 783
Apologia ad Constantinum (Athanasius), **Anc:** 134
Apologia Pro Vita Sua (Newman), **19th:** 1665
Apologia Roberti S.R.E. Cardinalis Bellarmini, pro responsione sua ad librum Jacobi. See *Apology for the Responsio*
Apologia Sōcratis (Plato), **Anc:** 660
Apologia Sōcratous (Xenophon), **Anc:** 968
Apologie, The (Melanchthon), **Ren:** 666
Apologie der Confession aus dem Latin verdeudschet. See *Apologie, The*
Apologie for the Oath of Allegiance, An. See *Triplicinodo triplex cuneus*
"Apologie pour celle qui escrit." See *Apology for the Woman Writing and Other Works*
Apologists, Christian, **Anc:** 331
Apology Against the Arians, An. See *Contra Arianos*
Apology for Actors, An (Heywood), **17th:** 374
Apology for His Flight. See *Oratio apologetica de fuga sua*
Apology for the Life of Mrs. Shamela Andrews, An (Fielding), **18th:** 348, 842
Apology for the Responsio (Bellarmine), **17th:** 16
Apology for the Royal Party, An (Evelyn), **17th:** 256
Apology for the Woman Writing and Other Works (Gournay), **17th:** 315
Apology of Socrates. See *Apologia Sōcratous*
Apology to Constantius, An. See *Apologia ad Constantinum*
Apomnēmoneumata (Xenophon), **Anc:** 87, 968
Apono, Petrus de. *See* Abano, Pietro d'
Apostle, the. *See* Bokassa, Jean-Bédel
Apostle Paul. *See* Paul, Saint
Apostles, **Anc:** 223, 624, 822
Apostles at the Tomb of the Virgin (Carracci), **Ren:** 176
Apostles Society, **19th:** 2102; **20th:** 2814
Apostolic Fathers, **Anc:** Clement, 224; Ignatius, 439
Apostolic tradition, **Anc:** 424
Apostólicos, **19th:** 412
Apostolikē paradosis (Hippolytus), **Anc:** 425
Apotelesmatika (Ptolemy), **Anc:** 714
Apotheosis of Henry IV and the Proclamation of the Regency of Marie de Médicis, The (Rubens), **17th:** 599
Apotheosis of Homer, The (Ingres), **19th:** 1172
Apotheosis of Spain (Tiepolo), **18th:** 978
Apoxyomenos (Lysippus), **Anc:** 524
Appalachian Spring (Copland), **20th:** 839
Apparitions (Liszt), **19th:** 1394
Appeal for the Indians, An (Child), **19th:** 485
Appeal in Favor of That Class of Americans Called Africans, An (Child), **19th:** 483
Appeal to the Christian Women of the South (Grimké), **19th:** 990
Appeal to the Coloured Citizens of the World (Walker), **19th:** 2327
"Appeal to the Public for Religious Liberty, Against the Oppressions of the Present Day" (Backus et al.), **18th:** 76
Appeal to the Slavs, An (Bakunin), **19th:** 119
Appearance and Reality (Bradley), **19th:** 289
Appearance or Presence of the Son of Man, The (Davies), **17th:** 220
Appellation of John Knox . . . to the Nobility, Estates, and Commonalty, The (Knox), **Ren:** 530
Appian, **Anc:** 814
Appius and Virginia (Webster and Heywood), **17th:** 977
Appius Claudius, **Anc:** 896
Apple Computer, **20th:** 2007
Appleseed, Johnny, **19th:** 68-71
Applewhite, Marshall, **Notor:** 28-30, 779
Appraisal (Wood), **20th:** 4388
Appreciations (Pater), **19th:** 1756
Apprenticeship of Duddy Kravitz, The (Richler), **20th:** 3438

Approach to Literature, An (Warren), **20th:** 4237
Approaches to the Great Settlement (Balch), **20th:** 199
Approaching Simone (Terry), **20th:** 3983
April (Denis), **20th:** 972
April Laws (1848), **19th:** 621
April Theses, **20th:** 2342
Apu Sansar. See *World of Apu, The*
Apulia, Nicolas de. *See* Pisano, Nicola
Aqa Sayyid Muḥammad Bāqir Bihbahānī. *See* Vaḥīd Bihbahānī
Aqiba ben Joseph. *See* Akiba ben Joseph
Aqueducts, **Anc:** Greek, 323-324; Roman, 219
Aquila, **Anc:** 30
Aquileia, schism of, **MA:** 938
Aquillius, Manius, **Anc:** 568
Aquinas, Saint Thomas. *See* Thomas Aquinas
Aquino, Benigno, Jr., **20th:** 107, 2621; **Notor:** 700, 702
Aquino, Corazon, **20th:** 107-109, 2622; **Notor:** 701-702
Arab-Israeli War (1948), **20th:** 286, 576, 929, 3358
Arab-Israeli War (1973), **20th:** 1952
Arab Socialist Union, **20th:** 2915
Arabesques (Gogol), **19th:** 937
Arabian Nights' Entertainments, The, **MA:** 469, 562; **19th:** 370
Arabs in History, The (Lewis), **20th:** 2352
Arabs Skirmishing in the Mountains (Delacroix), **19th:** 637
Arafat, Yasir, **20th:** 110-114; **Notor:** 4
Aragon, kings of, **MA:** 573
Aragon, Louis, **20th:** 1152
Arakan, Second Battle of (1944), **20th:** 3760
Aram, Eugene, **Notor:** 30-31
Arango, Doroteo. *See* Villa, Pancho
Arantes do Nascimento, Edson. *See* Pelé
Aranyer din Ratri. See *Days and Nights in the Forest*
Araros, **Anc:** 93
Aratus of Sicyon, **Anc:** 228
Arawaks, **Ren:** 238
Arbeiterinnen und Frauenfrage der Gegenwart. See *Working Women and the Contemporary Woman Question* (Zetkin)
Arbenz Guzmán, Jacobo, **20th:** 1609; **Notor:** 499
Arbitration, The. See *Epitrepontes*
Arboath, Declaration of (1320), **MA:** 204
Arbogast, **Anc:** 824, 870
Arbolancha, Don Pedro de, **Ren:** 77
Arbuckle, Roscoe "Fatty," 20th: 2090; Notor: 32-34
Arbus, Diane, **20th:** 115-117
Arcades Project, The (Benjamin), **20th:** 307
Arcadia, La (Lope de Vega), **17th:** 950
Arcadia (Sidney), **Ren:** 882
Arcadian Academy, **17th:** 191
Arcadian Shepherds, The (Poussin), **17th:** 750
Arcadius, **Anc:** 824
Arcana coelestia . . . . See *Heavenly Arcana, The*
Arcanum divinae sapientia. See *On Christian Marriage*
Arcanum 17 (Breton), **20th:** 512
Arcesilaus, **Anc:** 314
Archaeologiae philosophicae (Burnet), **17th:** 107
Archaeology, **18th:** 952-954, 1096; **19th:** Greece, 2017; Knossos, 753. *See also* Avebury; Ruins; Stonehenge; Category Index
Archelaus, **Notor:** 458
Archimedes, **Anc:** 80-84, 606
Architecture, **MA:** Byzantine Empire, 602; China, 1138; church, 971; Ethiopia, 633; Gothic, 973; India, 41; Italy, 104, 206, 422, 769, 798; Japan, 583; Jerusalem, 717; Mali, 745; Morocco, 8; Muslim, 5, 41; Persia, 413; Poland, 232; Transcaucasus, 999; **Ren:** Egypt, 807; England, 104; France, 284, 348, 424, 566; Inca Empire, 747; Italy, 19, 132, 558, 654, 683, 754, 821, 848, 894, 896, 962; Ottoman Empire, 916; Poland, 886; Spain, 445, 890; **17th:** Baroque, 995; England, 436, 994; France, 523, 532, 587, 590; Italy, 10, 68, 330, 937; Mughal Empire, 843-844; Poland, 855; Russia, 866; **18th:** Robert and James Adam, 3-7; and antiquities, 4; Austrian Baroque, 494-497; Baroque, 608; Germain Boffrand, 132-135; Lancelot Brown, 165-168; ecclesiastical, 351, 473, 496; Johann Bernhard Fischer von Erlach, 350-353; France, 132; Gothic, 134, 473; interior design, 132; Karīm Khān Zand, 552; Left Bank, 133; military, 201, 448, 565, 690; patronage, 322, 617, 800; prisons, 106; Scotland, 3; stage design, 190; Vienna, 351; **19th:** Australia, 975; England, 142, 1838, 2044, 2191; Gothic, 2192; neo-Gothic, 2044; picturesque, 1643; Romanesque, 1906; skyscrapers, 2199; United States, 346, 360, 1326, 1706, 1905, 2199. *See also* Category Index
Architecture of Leon Battista Alberti in Ten Books, The (Alberti), **Ren:** 19
Architettura civile (Guarini), **17th:** 331
Arcimboldo, Giuseppe, **Ren:** 841
Arctic, **19th:** exploration of, 825; **20th:** exploration of, 606, 2908, 3177, 3267, 3378, 4339; flight over, 85

Ardashīr I, **Anc:** 485, 774
Ardashīr II, **Anc:** 870
Arendt, Hannah, **20th:** 118-121
Areopagitica (Milton), **17th:** 640
Areopagus, **Anc:** 214, 621
Ares, **Anc:** 333
Aretaeus of Cappadocia, **Anc:** 84-87
Aretino, Leonardo. *See* Bruni, Leonardo
Aretino, Pietro, **Ren:** 53-56, 931
Argall, Samuel, **17th:** 746
Argentina, **19th:** and Uruguay, 871. *See also* Geographical Index
Arghūn, **MA:** 411
Arginusae, Battle of (406 B.C.E.), **Anc:** 128
Argos, **Anc:** 227
Arguments in Rhetoric Against Quintilian (Ramus), **Ren:** 817
Argyll, earl of. *See* Campbell, Archibald
Argyll, second duke of, **18th:** 53-54; Act of Union, 53; Jacobite Rebellion, 54; Scottish parliament, 53
Arhats, **Anc:** 111
Arianism, **Anc:** 43, 62, 134, 241, 330, 361, 363, 698, 796, 869, 911; Vandals and, 353; **MA:** 75, 173, 291, 381, 430, 1013; **Ren:** 138
Arianna, L' (Monteverdi), **17th:** 658
Arias, Arnulfo, **20th:** 4048; **Notor:** 797
Arias Sánchez, Oscar, **20th:** 121-124
Arie musicali per cantarsi (Frescobaldi), **17th:** 297
Ariel (Plath), **20th:** 3286
Arikaras, **19th:** 2114
Ariobarzanes I, **Anc:** 831, 895
Ariosto, Ludovico, **Ren:** 56-59, 118, 168
Aris, Michael, **20th:** 174
Arispe, Miguel Ramos, **19th:** 99
Aristarchus of Samos, **Anc:** 418, 713
Aristide, Jean-Bertrand, **20th:** 124-127
Aristides, **Anc:** 214, 616, 860
Aristippus, **Anc:** 87-89
Aristobulus, **Anc:** 403-404, 641
Aristocles of Messana, **Anc:** 723
Aristodemus, **Anc:** 827
Ariston (son of Sophocles), **Anc:** 811
Ariston of Chios, **Anc:** 314
Aristophanes, **Anc:** 9, 12, 90-93, 708, 811
Aristophon, **Anc:** 678
Aristotelicae animadversions (Ramus), **Ren:** 817
Aristotle, **Anc:** 9, 39, 94-97, 263, 277, 321, 452, 609, 659, 807, 812, 856, 872, 877; **MA:** 67, 123, 182, 563, 651, 752, 861, 864, 942, 1027-1028, 1064, 1098, 1105; Church ban on, 127; commentaries, 42, 119, 215, 761, 778, 1102
Aristoxenus, **Anc:** 97-99
Arithmetica (Zenger), **18th:** 1116
Arithmetica Infinitorum (Wallis), **17th:** 969
Arithmetical Inquisitions (Gauss), **19th:** 883
Arithmētika (Diophantus), **Anc:** 286, 435
Ājīvikas, **Anc:** 355
Arizona, **19th:** 721; John C. Frémont, 834; Geronimo's raid on, 905
Arjirópolis (Sarmiento), **19th:** 2001
Arjumand Banu Begum. *See* Mumtaz Mahal
Ark of the Covenant, **Anc:** 256, 747, 805
Arkhidamos (Diocles), **Anc:** 278
Arkhipelag GULag, 1918-1956. See *Gulag Archipelago, 1918-1956*
Arkwright, Sir Richard, **18th:** 55-59, 561
Arléssienne, L' (Bizet), **19th:** 242
Arléssienne, L' (Daudet), **19th:** 242
Arlington, first earl of, **17th:** 507, 839
Armageddon, **Anc:** 887
Armagnacs, **MA:** 502; **Ren:** 224
Armamentarium chirurgicum (Scultetus), **17th:** 566
Armance (Stendhal), **19th:** 2162
Arme Heinrich, Der (Hartmann), **MA:** 464
Armée Nouvelle, L'. See *Democracy and Military Service*
Armenia, **Anc:** Christianization of, 776; Rome and, 870, 895, 906; Sāsānians and, 774, 777. *See also* Geographical Index
Armenian Dashnak Party, **20th:** 2110
Armenians, Ottoman Empire, **19th:** 8
Armida (Dvořák), **19th:** 713
Armide (Gluck), **18th:** 420
Armies, **Anc:** Macedonian, 39; Roman, 359, 533, 535, 832; **17th:** Brandenburg-Prussia, 291; England, 205, 262; France, 184, 554; Netherlands, 619, 924; Sweden, 338; **18th:** U.S., 43, 443, 565, 708, 1043, 1054
Armies of the Night, The (Mailer), **20th:** 2564
Arminianism, **Ren:** 61; **17th:** 327, 767. *See also* Arminius, Jacobus
Arminius, **Anc:** 99-101
Arminius, Jacobus, **Ren:** 59-61, 741
Arms control, **20th:** 3687; nuclear weapons, 4133; Pugwash Conferences on Science and World Affairs, 3537
Armstrong, Edwin H., **20th:** 127-129
Armstrong, Johnnie, **Notor:** 35-36
Armstrong, Louis, **20th:** 130-133
Armstrong, Neil, **20th:** 134-138
Army, U.S., **18th:** 43, 443, 565, 708, 1043, 1054

Army Air Service, **20th:** 2766
Army Council, **17th:** 263
Army Life in a Black Regiment (Higginson), **19th:** 1098
Army-McCarthy hearings (1954), **20th:** 2499
Army of the Future, The (de Gaulle), **20th:** 1427
Army of the North (France), **18th:** 200
Arnald of Villanova. *See* Arnold of Villanova
Arnauld, Angélique, **17th:** 20-23
Arnaz, Desi, **20th:** 212
Arndt, Ernst, **19th:** 2152
Arnold, Benedict, **18th:** 59-62; **Notor:** 36-38, 211, 1103
Arnold, Matthew, **19th:** 71-75
Arnold, Samuel, **Notor:** 1013
Arnold, Thomas, **19th:** 76-79
Arnold of Brescia, **MA:** 28
Arnold of Villanova, **MA:** 98-101
Arnolfini Wedding, The (van Eyck), **MA:** 367
Arnolfo di Cambio, **MA:** 102-104, 848
Arnstein, Nicky, **Notor:** 665
Aroostook War (1838-1839), **19th:** 2053
Arosa, James. *See* Adonis, Joe
Arosa, Joe. *See* Adonis, Joe
Arouet, François-Marie. *See* Voltaire
Around the World in Eighty Days (Verne), **19th:** 2357
Arp, Hans, **20th:** 1176
Árpád, **MA:** 105-108
Árpád kings of Hungary, **MA:** 107, 638, 966
ARPANET, **20th:** 707
Arpino, Cavaliere d'. *See* Cesari, Giuseppe
Arpino, Gerald, **20th:** 2012
Arrabbiata, **Ren:** 853
Arrangement in Grey and Black, No. 1 (Whistler), **19th:** 2421
Arras, Siege of (1654), **17th:** 933
Arras, Treaty of (1435), **Ren:** 225
Arrêt burlesque, L' (Boileau-Despréaux), **17th:** 63
Arrhenius, Svante August, **20th:** 138-141, 1904, 3089
Arrhidaeus, **Anc:** 597
Arria the Elder, **Anc:** 102-103
Arria the Younger, **Anc:** 103-105
Arrian, **Anc:** 524
Arrow of God (Achebe), **20th:** 15
Arrowsmith (film), **20th:** 1724
Arrowsmith (novel by Lewis), **20th:** 2365
Arrowsmith, John, **19th:** 542
Arroyo, Gloria Macapagal, **Notor:** 701
Arruns, **Anc:** 841, 846
Ars amatoria (Ovid), **Anc:** 603
Ars conjectandi (Bernoulli), **17th:** 49
Ars de statica medicina sectionibus aphorismorum septem comprehensa. See *Medicina Statica*
Ars generalis ultima (Lull), **MA:** 674
Ars nova (Vitry), **MA:** 741, 1065
Ars novae musicae (Muris), **MA:** 741
Ars poetica (Horace), **Anc:** 432
Arshak II, **Anc:** 776
Arsinoe (Eratosthenes), **Anc:** 316
Arsinoe II Philadelphus, **Anc:** 105-108, 247, 716
Arsphenamine. *See* Salvarsan
Art, **MA:** Almoravid, 8; China, 677, 718, 1140; Flanders, 366; France, 326, 847, 866; Fujiwara style, 582; Ghaznavid Dynasty, 685; Gothic, 103, 326, 366, 845, 847, 1092; Heian period, 581; International Gothic, 420; Italy, 83, 103, 206, 282, 320, 326, 418, 421, 659, 700, 769, 798, 845, 847; Japan, 117, 581, 1040; Nara period, 582; Netherlands, 947, 1092; Renaissance, 418, 568, 846; Siena, 326, 567, 696; Spain, 60; **Ren:** Dürer's theory, 299; France, 217; Italy, 18, 29, 203, 231, 395, 486; Papal States, 520; Spain, 391; **18th:** American, 947-951; Baroque, 437; depiction of beauty, 1097; book design, 92; comical, 498; decorative, 4, 95-97, 132-135, 472-475, 494-497, 978; design, 865; English, 156, 839; engraving, 122, 832; everyday life, 190, 1051; expressionism, 368; French, 224; frescoes, 977; Greek, 1095; history, 1095-1098; human body, 1095; Korea, 248-249; landscape painting, 248, 390; Laocoön statue, 1095; musical instrument design, 944-947; Ottoman Empire, 602-604; pastel, 225; patronage, 322, 585, 799; pottery making, 1057-1061; printing, 92-94; printmaking, 958-960; realism, 190, 275, 1069; rococo, 133, 437, 617, 978, 1052; Romanticism, 124, 437, 1053, 1069; Russia, 613; satirical, 498; silversmithing, 95; still life, 224; **20th:** collections, 1407; criticism, 105, 1352; philosophy of, 2265. *See also* Expressionism; Impressionism; Neo-Impressionism; Painting; Pop art; Portraiture; Post-Impressionism; Sculpture; Category Index
Art de toucher le clavecin, L' (Couperin), **18th:** 282
Art défensif supérieur à l'offensif, L' (Montalembert), **18th:** 691
Art d'être grand-père, L' (Hugo), **19th:** 1149
Art du théâtre, L'. See *Art of Theatre, The*
Art Nouveau, **20th:** 2180, 2787
Art of Decorating Dry Good Windows and Interiors, The (Baum), **19th:** 156
Art of Love. See *Ars amatoria*

Art of Loving, The (Fromm), **20th:** 1347
Art of Money Getting, The (Barnum), **19th:** 140
Art of Poetry, The (Boileau-Despréaux), **17th:** 63
Art of Riding, The. See *Peri hippikēs*
Art of the Novel, The (James), **19th:** 1209
Art of Theatre, The (Bernhardt), **19th:** 210
Art of Travel (Galton), **19th:** 860
Art of War, The (Machiavelli), **Ren:** 588
Art patronage, **Ren:** England, 104, 188, 312; France, 50, 284, 348, 424, 619; Holy Roman Empire, 841; Hungary, 644; India, 17, 532; Italy, 236, 486, 654, 657, 874; Netherlands, 614; Papal States, 29, 231, 520, 558; Poland, 886, 888; Portugal, 606; Scotland, 496, 499; women and, 614, 618; **17th:** China, 450; England, 244; France, 182, 599, 723; Italy, 627, 937; Russia, 625; Ṣafavid Dynasty, 5; Spain, 739; **18th:** 130, 322, 585, 617, 799; **19th:** J. P. Morgan, 1602; Napoleon I, 609, 898; Napoleon III, 1480; Nicholas I, 1671
Art poétique, L'. See *Art of Poetry, The*
Art poétique français (Sébillet), **Ren:** 294
Artabanus, **Anc:** 972
Artabazanes, **Anc:** 253, 971
Artabazus, **Anc:** 615
Artamenes (Scudéry), **17th:** 662, 829
Artaud, Antonin, **Notor:** 193
Artaxerxes I, **Anc:** 339
Artaxerxes II, **Anc:** 304, 339, 744
Arte de ingenio (Gracián), **17th:** 317
Arte nuevo de hacer comedias en este tiempo, El. See *New Art of Writing Plays, The*
Artemidorus, **Anc:** 185
Artemis, **Anc:** 397
Artemis at Brauron (Praxiteles), **Anc:** 694
Artemisia I, Anc: 109-111, 545, 761
Artemisium, **Anc:** 761
Artemisium, Battle of (480 B.C.E.), **Anc:** 507
Arthaśāstra (Kauṭilya), **Anc:** 204
Arthur (legendary king), **MA:** 406
Arthur (prince of England), **Ren:** 187, 439, 441
Arthur, Chester A., 19th: 79-83; **Notor:** 632
Arthurian romance, **MA:** 463
Article IX (Japanese constitution), **20th:** 1702
Articles of Confederation (1781), **18th:** 413, 636, 710, 904, 909, 1092
Artificial intelligence, **20th:** 4113
Artificial Paradises (Baudelaire), **19th:** 153
Artikel. See *Luther's and Zwingli's Propositions for Debate*
Artillery, **17th:** China, 2; England, 651; France, 184, 946; Sweden, 925
Artis magnae, sive de regulis algebraicis. See *Great Art, The*
Artis medicae liber VII (Cesalpino), **Ren:** 212
Artis medicae pars prima (Cesalpino), **Ren:** 212
Artisans' and Laborers' Dwelling Act of 1875, **19th:** 669
Artist Hesitating Between the Arts of Music and Painting, The (Kauffman), **18th:** 554
Artist's Mother at Breakfast, The (Toulouse-Lautrec), **19th:** 2288
Artists Union, **20th:** 3539
Arts Theater, **20th:** 3261
ʿArūj, Ren: 79; **Notor:** 38-40
Arundel, Thomas, **MA:** 895
Arundel Mill and Castle (Constable), **19th:** 542
Arusmont, Frances d'. *See* Wright, Frances
Arverni, **Anc:** 935
Arya Asanga. *See* Asanga
Āryabhaṭa the Elder, MA: 108-111, 195
Aryabhatiya, The (Āryabhaṭa), **MA:** 108
Āryadeva, **Anc:** 112
Aryans, **20th:** 1808, 1830
Aryasanga. *See* Asanga
Arzner, Dorothy, 20th: 141-144
As I Lay Dying (Faulkner), **20th:** 1224
Asaf Khan, **17th:** 842
Asahara, Shoko, Notor: 40-42, 949
Asai Nagamasa, **Ren:** 737
Asanga, Anc: 111-114, 930
Asar-oos-sunnadeed (Ahmad Khan), **19th:** 36
Asbaje y Ramírez de Santillana, Juana Inéz. *See* Cruz, Sor Juana Inés de la
Asbury, Francis, 18th: 62-64
Ascanius and the Stag (Claude Lorrain), **17th:** 172
Ascension (Coltrane), **20th:** 815
Ascension (Tintoretto), **Ren:** 933
Ascension of Christ, An (Veronese), **Ren:** 960
Ascent of Mount Carmel, The (John of the Cross), **Ren:** 509
Ascent to Calvary, The (Denis), **20th:** 973
Asceticism, **Anc:** Christian, 60, 456, 474, 698, 789; Diogenes and, 283; Jain, 355, 925; Mohist, 577; **MA:** Buddhist, 620; France, 160; Germany, 1022; India, 877, 925; Italy, 154; Japan, 1155; Muslim, 874; women, 236, 271, 361, 857
Asch, Solomon, **Notor:** 729
Asclepiades of Bithynia, Anc: 114-117, 199
Asclepiads, **Anc:** 420
Asclepieions, **Anc:** 348, 421
Asclepius, **Anc:** 348, 440, 810
Ascorbic acid. *See* Vitamin C

Ascue, Anne. *See* Askew, Anne
Asdings, **Anc:** 351
Asdrubale Being Bitten by a Crab (Anguissola), **Ren:** 46
Ash, Mary Kay, **20th:** 145-148
Ash Wednesday (Eliot), **20th:** 1141
Ash Wednesday Supper, The (Bruno), **Ren:** 139
Ashani Sanket. See *Distant Thunder*
Ashʿarī, al-, **MA:** 111-114
Asharism, **MA:** 112, 370
Ashburn, Betsy. *See* Ross, Betsy
Ashcan school, **20th:** 1876
Ashcroft, John, **Notor:** 683
Ashdown, Battle of (871), **MA:** 63
Asher, Jacob ben, **Ren:** 524
Ashikaga shogunate, **MA:** 117; **Ren:** 733, 735, 865
Ashikaga Tadayoshi, **MA:** 115
Ashikaga Takauji, **MA:** 115-118
Ashikaga Yoshiaki, **Ren:** 732, 736
Ashikaga Yoshikazu, **MA:** 1153
Ashikaga Yoshimitsu, **MA:** 117, 1152
Ashikaga Yoshimochi, **MA:** 1153
Ashikaga Yoshinori, **MA:** 1153
Ashikari. See *Reed Cutter, The*
Ashington, Battle of (1016), **MA:** 223
Ashkenaz, **MA:** 408
Ashkenazi, Bezalel, **Ren:** 579
Ashley, Lord. *See* Shaftesbury, first earl of
Ashley, William, **19th:** 2114
Ashraf Refaat Nabith Henin. *See* Mohammed, Khalid Shaikh
Ashrāf Sayf al-Dīn Qāʾit Bāy, al-. *See* Qāytbāy
Ashton, Frederick, **20th:** 1268
Ashtoreth, **Anc:** 805
Ashur-nirari V, **Anc:** 892
Ashurbanipal, **Anc:** 117-120, 123, 378, 710
Ashurnasirpal II, **Anc:** 120-123
Ashvaghosha. *See* Aśvaghosa
Asian Drama (Myrdal), **20th:** 2891
Asivisopama Sutta, **Anc:** 899
Ask Your Mama (Hughes), **20th:** 1930
Askew, Anne, **Ren:** 62-64
Askia Daud, **Ren:** 64-66
Askia Dynasty, **Ren:** 688
Askia Ishaq I, **Ren:** 64
Askia, Moḥammad I. *See* Mohammed I Askia
Askia the Great. *See* Mohammed I Askia
Askiya Dāwūd. *See* Askia Daud
Asmodée (Mauriac), **20th:** 2658
Aśoka, **Anc:** 124-127, 131, 204, 898, 934
Aspasia of Miletus, **Anc:** 127-129
Aspects of the Novel (Forster), **20th:** 1289
Aspects of the Theory of Syntax (Chomsky), **20th:** 758
Aspida affair, **20th:** 3106
Aspirations of the World (Child), **19th:** 485
Aspis (Menander), **Anc:** 548
Aspromonte, Battle of (1862), **19th:** 873
Asquith, H. H., **20th:** 149-153, 210, 1588
Assad, Bashar al-, **20th:** 154
Assad, Hafez al-, **20th:** 112, 153-155, 1979
Assassinations and assassination attempts, **Anc:** Agrippina the Younger, 591, 686, 767; Antipater, 403; Julius Caesar, 174, 185; Caligula, 178, 218; Caracalla, 482; Ephialtes, 621; Gaius Sempronius Gracchus, 359; Tiberius Sempronius Gracchus, 358; Hasdrubal, 382; Hipparchus, 651; Huai Wang, 732; Julia Soaemias, 484; Philip II, 266, 597, 639; Philip II of Macedonia, 719; Pompey the Great, 683, 927; Sargon II, 754; Seleucus I Nicator, 716; Sennacherib, 770; Servius, 846; Tarquin the First, 846; Valentinian III, 353; Xerxes I, 973; **20th:** Abdullah, 1951; Salvador Allende, 72; Benigno Aquino, Jr., 108, 2622; Jean-Bertrand Aristide, 125; Atatürk, 164; Al Capone, 642; Fidel Castro, 692; Sánchez Cerro, 1718; Jean Chrétien, 763; Matthias Erzberger, 1182; Faisal, 1201; Francis Ferdinand, 1295, 1589; Henry Clay Frick, 1521; Indira Gandhi, 1387; Giovanni Gentile, 1450; Hassan II, 1699; Edward Heath, 1740; Adolf Hitler, 1809, 1832; Hussein I, 1952; John Paul II, 2022; John F. Kennedy, 1686, 2101, 4234; Robert F. Kennedy, 2105; Kim Dae Jung, 2136; Martin Luther King, Jr., 1979; Patrice Lumumba, 2477; William McKinley, 1521; Malcolm X, 2572; Hasan ʿAlī Mansur, 2125, 2781; Mao Zedong, 2383; Mobutu Sese Seko, 2774; Eduardo C. Mondlane, 2515; Louis Mountbatten, 2856; Gabriel Narutowicz, 3252; Nicholas II, 2111; Max Nordau, 2994; Álvaro Obregón, 616, 3016; Park Chung Hee, 2136; Yitzhak Rabin, 3360; Walter Charles Rand, 4025; Ali Razmara, 2779, 2845; Ronald Reagan, 3402; Oscar Romero, 3501; Anwar el-Sadat, 3589; Abdirashid Ali Shermarke, 3734; Calvo Sotelo, 1297; Sir Lee Stack, 4440; Leon Trotsky, 4075; Rafael Trujillo, 4085; Pancho Villa, 4162; George C. Wallace, 4206; Wang Jingwei, 4221; Zaho Ziyang, 4460
Assassins, **MA:** 141, 415, 775. *See also* Category Index
Assault on Reason, The (Gore), **20th:** 1540
Assertio septem sacramentorum (Henry VIII), **Ren:** 442

Assertion of the Seven Sacraments Against Martin Luther, An. See *Assertio septem sacramentorum*
Assisi, **MA:** 226
Asso, Raymond, **20th:** 3229
Associated Television Corporation, **20th:** 812
Association for the Advancement of the Medical Education of Women, **19th:** 1201
Association for the Advancement of Women, **19th:** 1139, 2442
Association for the Emancipation of Women, **19th:** 89
Association for the Rights of Women, **19th:** 89
Association of All Classes of All Nations, **19th:** 1722
Associations movement (1779-1780), **18th:** 364
Assommoir, L' (Zola), **19th:** 2490
Assumption (Sirani), **17th:** 857
Assumption of Mary, **Anc:** 540
Assumption of the Virgin (Annibale), **Ren:** 171
Assumption of the Virgin, The (Correggio), **Ren:** 250
Assumption of the Virgin (Fontana), **Ren:** 338
Assumption of the Virgin (Titian), **Ren:** 937
Assurbanipal. *See* Ashurbanipal
Assyria, **Anc:** Egypt and, 710, 753; government, 250; Jews and, 447, 453; Urartu and, 892. *See also* Mesopotamia
Astaire, Fred, **20th:** 155-158, 1410, 1463, 1731, 3309
Astarte (ballet), **20th:** 2013
Astarte, priesthood of **Anc:** 271
Astell, Mary, **18th:** 64-67, 687
Asteroids, **20th:** extinction of dinosaurs, 75; Trojan, 4382
Aston, Luise, **19th:** 83-85
Aston, Sir Walter, **17th:** 238
Astor, John Jacob, **19th:** 86-89, 856
Astor, Nancy, **20th:** 158-161
Astor, Waldorf, **20th:** 159
Astor House, **19th:** 88
Astor Place Riot (1848), **19th:** 792
Astoria (Irving), **19th:** 88, 1181
Astraea Redux (Dryden), **17th:** 240
Astrakhan, Russian conquest of, **Ren:** 494
Astrolabes, **Anc:** 418, 435
Astrology, **Anc:** 424; **MA:** 1, 128, 652; Muslim, 165; **Ren:** Denmark, 127; England, 279; France, 729; Hungary, 773. *See also* Astronomy
Astronauts, **20th:** first African American woman, 803; first man, 135, 1371; first man to walk on the moon, 3726; first woman, 2460; first woman on space shuttle, 3448; oldest, 1501
Astronomer, The (Vermeer), **17th:** 958
Astronomia magna. See *Great Astronomy*
Astronomia nova. See *New Astronomy* (Kepler)
Astronomia reformata (Riccioli), **17th:** 322
Astronomical Society, **18th:** 493
Astronomical tables, **18th:** 85
Astronomie cometicae synopsis (Halley), **17th:** 350
Astronomy, **Anc:** 424; Alexandrian, 434; Babylonian, 579; Greek, 857; Hellenic, 713; Hellenistic, 579; mapping, 417; mathematics and, 78; Pythagoras and, 727; **MA:** 217, 650, 751, 985; astrolabe, 821; France, 742; India, 109, 195; Iran, 124, 796; Iraq, 68, 137, 617; Persia, 21; **Ren:** Austria, 773, 823-824; Denmark, 126, 129; Italy, 139, 344; Netherlands, 913; Poland, 242; **17th:** England, 348, 388; France, 135, 304, 722; Germany, 259, 458, 818; Italy, 66, 134, 299, 921; Netherlands, 397; Poland, 371; Scotland, 319; **18th:** Benjamin Banneker, 84-87; China, 1039; Elijah ben Solomon, 318; Caroline Lucretia Herschel, 489-491; William Herschel, 492-493; Wang Zhenyi, 1038-1040; **19th:** astrophysics, 1413; England, 1145; France, 1318; Germany, 215, 884; United States, 788, 1309, 1580, 1661. *See also* Astrology; Category Index
Astrophel and Stella (Sidney), **Ren:** 881
Astrophysical Journal, The, **20th:** 1643
Astrophysical Observatory of the Smithsonian Institution, **19th:** 185
Astrophysics, **19th:** 1310, 1413; **20th:** 77, 635, 1644
Astrup, Eivind, **20th:** 3178
Asturian miners strike (1934), **20th:** 1297
Astyages, **Anc:** 248
ʿAṣud al-Dawla Abū Shujaʿ Muḥammad ibn Dāʾūd Cḥāghrï Beg. *See* Alp Arslan
Asuka emperors, **MA:** 976
Asurbanipal. *See* Ashurbanipal
Aśvaghosa, **Anc:** 130-132, 501
Aswān High Dam, **20th:** 1056, 2915
At Fault (Chopin), **19th:** 491
At the Hawk's Well (Yeats), **20th:** 4429
At the Sign of the Reine Pédauque (France), **19th:** 816
At the Top of My Voice (Mayakovsky), **20th:** 2660
Atahualpa, **Ren:** 66-68, 469, 801, 902
Atala (Chateaubriand), **19th:** 476
Atatürk, **20th:** 31, 68, 162-165, 1158, 1971, 4158
Atef, Mohammed, **Notor:** 102
Ateret Zequenim (Abravanel), **Ren:** 1
Ateştan gömlek. See *Shirt of Flame, The*
Athalaric, **MA:** 76, 1014

Athaliah (Racine), **17th:** 775
Athanaric, **Anc:** 868, 911
Athanasius of Alexandria, Saint, **Anc:** 60, 62, 132-135, 331, 333; **MA:** 292
Āthār al-bāqīyah ʿan al-qurūn al-khāliyah. See *Chronology of Ancient Nations, The*
Āthār assanadīd. See *Asar-oos-sunnadeed*
Atheism, **18th:** George Berkeley, 112; Denis Diderot, 307; Johann Gottlieb Fichte, 344; William Godwin, 425; Claude-Adrien Helvétius, 481; Paul-Henri-Dietrich d'Holbach, 502
Atheist's Tragedy, The (Tourneur), **17th:** 928
Athena Lemnia (Phidias), **Anc:** 634
Athena Promachos (Phidias), **Anc:** 634
Athenaeus of Attaleia, **Anc:** 84
Athenaeus of Naucratis, **Anc:** 610
Athenaiōn politeia (Aristotle), **Anc:** 807
Athenian Constitution, The. See *Athenaiōn politeia*
Athenian Empire, **Anc:** 215
Athenodorus, **Anc:** 194, 827
Athens, **Anc:** Macedonia and, 638; Sparta and, 215, 226, 621, 631, 859, 882, 969; Thebes and, 304
Athletics, **Anc:** Greek, 632; Roman, 591
Ätiologie, der Begriff, und die Prophylaxis des Kindbettfiebers, Die. See *Cause, Concept, and Prophylaxis of Childbed Fever, The*
Atkins, Susan, **Notor:** 690
Atkinson, Henry, **19th:** 245
Atlacatl, **Ren:** 36
Atlanta Braves, **20th:** 4119
Atlantic, The (magazine), **19th:** 1118
Atlántida, L' (Falla), **20th:** 1207
Atlantis (Frobenius), **20th:** 1343
Atlas of Representative Stellar Spectra (Huggins and Huggins), **19th:** 1145
Atlas Shrugged (Rand), **20th:** 3368
Atlas sive cosmographicae meditationes de fabrica mundi et fabricati figura. See *Historia mundi*
Atlee, Clement, **Notor:** 755
Atli. *See* Attila
Atmosphere and Environment X (Nevelson), **20th:** 2949
Atom Station, The (Laxness), **20th:** 2309
Atombombe und die Zukunft des Menschen, Die. See *Future of Mankind, The*
Atomic bomb, **20th:** *Bhagavad-Gita*, 3066; China, 2382; development of, 1637, 2944; Germany, 444, 1442; Hiroshima, 822, 1237, 4088; Nagasaki, 3685; Soviet Union, 1781, 2215; United States, 1237, 2302
Atomic theory, **19th:** 599, 887
Atomism, **Anc:** 115, 261, 356, 520, 610
Atoms, study of, **20th:** 714, 3577, 3969, 4008, 4436
Aton, **Anc:** 28, 588, 902, 908
Atonal music, **20th:** 310
Atossa, **Anc:** 136-138, 251, 971
Atotarho, **Ren:** 281, 448
Atrées (Xenakis), **20th:** 4416
Atsumori (Zeami), **MA:** 1154
Atta, Mohammed. *See* Atta al-Sayed, Mohammed
Atta al-Sayed, Mohammed, **Notor:** 43-44
Atta Troll (Heine), **19th:** 1071
Attaché in Madrid, The (Calderón), **19th:** 391
Attainder, Act of (1542), **Ren:** 765
Attalus I, **Anc:** 65
Attalus III, **Anc:** 359
Attar'athae, **Anc:** 791
Attempt at a Critique of All Revelation (Fichte), **18th:** 342
Attenborough, Richard, **Notor:** 210
Attention! Tanks! (Guderian), **20th:** 1606
Attic Nights. See *Noctes Atticae*
Attica State Prison riots (1971), **20th:** 3480
Atticus, Titus Pomponius, **Anc:** 211
Attila, **Anc:** 138-142; **MA:** 782, 1012; **Notor:** 45-46
Attila (Verdi), **19th:** 2351
Attila of the South. *See* Zapata, Emiliano
Attila the Hun. *See* Attila
Attlee, Clement, **20th:** 165-168, 358, 1389, 2932
Atwood, Charles B., **19th:** 361
Atwood, Margaret, **20th:** 169-171
Atzerodt, George A., **Notor:** 1013
Au bal de la chance. See *Wheel of Fortune, The*
Au bal du Moulin de la Galette (Toulouse-Lautrec), **19th:** 2289
Au Moulin Rouge (Toulouse-Lautrec), **19th:** 2289
Aubigné, Françoise d'. *See* Maintenon, Madame de
Aubrey, John, **18th:** 952
Auclert, Hubertine, **19th:** 89-91
Auden, W. H., **20th:** 172-174, 530
Audion tubes, **20th:** 127, 941
Auditorium Building, **19th:** 2198
Auditorium in the Old Burgtheater (Klimt), **20th:** 2180
Audomarus Talaeus. *See* Talon, Omer
Audubon, John James, **19th:** 91-94
Audubon Society, **19th:** 93
Auerstedt, Battle of (1806), **19th:** 260
Aufbau der realen Welt, Der (Hartmann), **20th:** 1697
Aufstieg und Fall der Stadt Mahagonny. See *Rise and Fall of the City of Mahagonny, The*

Aufzeichnungen des Malte Laurids Brigge, Die. See *Notebooks of Malte Laurids Brigge, The*
Augsburg, Diet of (1530), **Ren:** 143, 221, 666, 776
Augsburg, League of, **17th:** 407, 560, 979
Augsburg, Peace of (1555), **Ren:** 222, 651, 776-777
Augsburg, War of the League of (1689-1697), **17th:** 401, 407, 528, 555, 560, 611, 946, 979
Augsburg Confession (1530), **Ren:** 666, 798
Augsburg Interim (1548), **Ren:** 144, 222
August (Hamsun), **20th:** 1662
August, Prince, **19th:** 499
August, Sigismund. *See* Sigismund II Augustus
August 1956 (Nicholson), **20th:** 2957
Augusta. *See* Julia Domna
Augusta National Golf Club, **20th:** 2038
Augustine, Saint, **Anc:** 44, 142-144, 208, 332, 353, 518, 853, 947; **MA:** 96, 155, 1098
Augustine of Canterbury, **MA:** 431
Augustinians, **Ren:** 582
Augustinus (Jansen), **17th:** 420, 936
Augustus (Roman emperor), **Anc:** 20, 23, 71, 73, 145-148, 167, 176, 217, 230, 280, 404, 431, 489, 509, 511, 527, 602, 704, 842, 888, 938, 941; **Notor:** 147, 384, 458-459
Augustus II (king of Poland), **18th:** 232
Augustus, Tiberius Claudius Nero Caesar. *See* Tiberius
Auld Alliance, **MA:** 345
Aung San, **20th:** 174; 3986
Aung San Suu Kyi, **20th:** 174-177; **Notor:** 773, 1026
Aungzeya. *See* Alaungpaya
Aunt Jane's Nieces (Van Dyne), **19th:** 157
Aurangzeb, **17th:** 23-26, 843, 859
Aurelian, **Anc:** 281, 988
Aurelius, Marcus. *See* Marcus Aurelius
Aurelius Augustinus. *See* Augustine, Saint
Aurello, Toddo, **Notor:** 435
Aurier, G.-Albert, **19th:** 935
Aurillot, Barbara. *See* Acarie, Barbe
Aurobindo, Sri, **20th:** 177-180
Aurora, The (Böhme), **17th:** 60
Aurora Leigh (Browning), **19th:** 327
Aus dem Leben der Marionetten. See *From the Life of the Marionettes*
Aus dem Leben einer Frau (Aston), **19th:** 84
Aus dem Leben einer Jüdischen Familie. See *Life in a Jewish Family*
Aus dem Tagebuch einer Schnecke. See *From the Diary of a Snail*
Aus den Memoiren de Venetianers Jacob Casanova de Seingalt. See *Memoirs of Jacques Casanova de Seingalt, The*
Aus den sieben Tagen (Stockhausen), **20th:** 3875
Aus Italien (Strauss), **20th:** 3885
Aus meinem Leben. See *Autobiography of Goethe, The*; *Out of My Life*
Ausgleich (1867), **19th:** 621
Austen, Jane, **19th:** 94-98
Austerlitz, Battle of (1805), **18th:** 570; **19th:** 46, 469, 1636
Austin, James T., **19th:** 1786
Austin, Moses, **19th:** 98
Austin, Stephen Fuller, **19th:** 98-101
Australasian National Convention (1897), **19th:** 150
Australia, **17th:** 905; European exploration of, 216; **18th:** British colonization, 82, 783-785; James Cook, 271; **19th:** British exploration of, 981; Commonwealth of, 151, 624; penal colony, 974; settlement plans, 2379; wool industry, 1432. *See also* Geographical Index
Australia in World Affairs (Evatt), **20th:** 1189
Australian Natives Association, **19th:** 150
Australopithecus boisei, **20th:** 2313
Austria, **MA:** 258, 390, 768, 830; **Ren:** attack on Ottoman Empire, 663; **18th:** army, 330; conflicts with France, 330, 658, 881; conflicts with Ottomans, 230, 330, 639; relations with Prussia, 378, 557, 654; **20th:** annexation by Germany, 723, 1831. *See also* Geographical Index
Austria, Anne of. *See* Anne of Austria
Austria, John of. *See* John of Austria
Austrian-Ottoman War (1736-1739), **18th:** 230
Austrian-Russian alliance, **18th:** 570, 955
Austrian Succession, War of the (1740-1748), **18th:** 102, 378, 405, 447, 616, 654, 772, 801, 881
Austro-Hungarian Empire, **19th:** 223, 621, 820; **20th:** 1294
Austro-Prussian War (1866), **19th:** 819
Austro-Sardinian War (1859), **19th:** 699, 872; Napoleon III, 1640
Authoress of the Odyssey (Butler), **19th:** 375
Authority in the Modern State (Laski), **20th:** 2269
Auto-da-fé, **Ren:** 940
Autobiography (Chesterton), **20th:** 745
Autobiography (Milne), **20th:** 2754

Autobiography (Mill), **19th:** 1572, 1575
Autobiography of Alice B. Toklas, The (Stein), **20th:** 3847
Autobiography of an Idea, The (Sullivan), **19th:** 2199
Autobiography of Benjamin Franklin (Franklin), **18th:** 373
Autobiography of Goethe, The (Goethe), **18th:** 430
Autobiography of Malcolm X, The (Malcolm X), **20th:** 2570
Autobiography of Values (Lindbergh), **20th:** 2395
Autocrat of the Breakfast-Table, The (Holmes), **19th:** 1118
Autoeducazione nelle scuole elementari, L'. See *Advanced Montessori Method, The*
Automata. See *Peri automatopoietikes*
Automatisme psychologique, L' (Janet), **20th:** 1993
Automobiles, **19th:** 594; development of, 197, 1339; **20th:** Citroëns, 772; dymaxion car, 1366; Ferraris, 1240; Fords, 1280; Lanchesters, 2241; Mazdas, 4225; racing, 1239, 1280; Rolls-Royces, 3496; rotary engines, 4225; streamlining, 1432; tires, 2726, 3267; Toyotas, 4064; travel by, 2726
Autopact (1965), **20th:** 3176
Autos sacramentales, **17th:** 115, 949
Autre Monde, L' (Cyrano), **17th:** 211
Autumn and Winter Landscapes (Sesshū), **Ren:** 866
Autumn Harvest Uprising (1927), **20th:** 2381
Autumnal Leaves (Child), **19th:** 484
Auxentius, **Anc:** 912
Avare, L'. See *Miser, The*
Avars, **MA:** 46, 505, 934; Frankish invasion of, 244
Avebury, **18th:** 952-954
Avellaneda, Nicolas, **19th:** 2001
Avenir de la science, L'. See *Future of Science, The*
Aventine Secession (1924), **20th:** 945
Aventures de Télémaque, Les. See *Adventures of Telemachus, the Son of Ulysses, The*
Averroës, **MA:** 1, 118-122, 127, 318, 446, 526, 651, 674, 1028, 1106
Averroès et l'Averroïsme (Renan), **19th:** 1885
Averroists, **MA:** 943
Aves sin nido (Matto), **19th:** 1513
Avesta (Zoroaster), **Anc:** 993
Avianus, Flavius, **Anc:** 629
Aviation, **20th:** France, 388; Germany, 1746; military applications, 1648, 2767; speed records, 2392; theories, 2242; women, 1075; zeppelins, 1093. *See also* Airplanes; Space exploration; Category Index
Avicebron. *See* Ibn Gabirol
Avicenna, **MA:** 1, 123-127, 163, 445, 1102
Avidius Cassius, Gaius, **Anc:** 531
Avignon Papacy (1305-1378), **MA:** 237, 259, 522, 741. *See also* Babylonian Captivity of the Church
Ávila Camacho, Manuel, **20th:** 617
Avodah, Achdut Ha, **20th:** 2677
Avogadro, Amedeo, **19th:** 101-104
Avogadro's law, **19th:** 102
Avon, first earl of. *See* Eden, Sir Anthony
Avril, Prosper, **20th:** 125
Avrillot, Barbe-Jeanne. *See* Acarie, Barbe
Avro Arrow controversy, **20th:** 993
Avtobiograficheskiy ocherk. See *I Remember* (Pasternak)
Avvakum Petrovich, **17th:** 26-28, 685
Awakening, The (Chopin), **19th:** 492
Awashonks, **17th:** 634
Awful Rowing Towards God, The (Sexton), **20th:** 3715
Awful Truth, The (film), **20th:** 1571
Awkward Age, The (James), **19th:** 1207
Awlād Ḥāratinā. See *Children of Gebelawi*
Awolowo, Obafemi, **20th:** 181
Axayácatl, **Ren:** 693
Axel's Castle (Wilson), **20th:** 4355
Axis Sally. *See* Gillars, Mildred
Ay (Egyptian vizier), **Anc:** 28, 587, 908
Aya no tsuzumu. See *Damask Drum, The*
Ayacucho, Battle of (1824), **19th:** 2196
Ayatollah Khomeini. *See* Khomeini, Ayatollah
Aylesford, Battle of (c. 450), **Anc:** 395
Aylwin, Patricio, **20th:** 3258
Aymer of Valence, **MA:** 348
Ayonwatha. *See* Hiawatha
Ayres and Dialogues (Lawes), **17th:** 503
Ayscough, Anne. *See* Askew, Anne
Aytegin, Ikhtiar al-Dīn, **MA:** 889
Ayub Khan, **20th:** 368
Ayutla Rebellion, **19th:** 1245
Ayyad, Nidal, **Notor:** 1121
Ayyūb, Najm al-Dīn, **MA:** 918
Ayyubids, **MA:** 139; sultans, 920
Azalism, **19th:** 106
Aʿẓam, Qāʾīd-e. *See* Jinnah, Mohammed Ali
Azbuka kommunizma. See *ABC of Communism, The*
Azeglio, Massimo d', **19th:** 445
Azerbaijan, **20th:** 2779. *See also* Geographical Index
Azharot (Ibn Gabirol), **MA:** 532
Azikiwe, Nnamdi, **20th:** 180-183, 2988
Aziz, Fahd ibn Abdul. *See* Fahd

Azores, Portuguese occupation of, **MA:** 479
Azriyau, **Anc:** 893
Aztec Empire, **Ren:** 34, 252, 273, 621, 693, 722; **MA:** 558; education, 560; religion, 560; slavery, 559; trade, 559
Azul (Darío), **19th:** 601
Azuma kagami, **MA:** 1040
Azzam, Shaikh Abdullah, **Notor:** 1136
Azzolino, Decio, **17th:** 165

B

Baade, Walter, **20th:** 184-186
Baader, Andreas, **Notor:** 47-48, 684, 715
Baal, **Anc:** 373, 487
Baᶜal Shem Tov, **18th:** 68-70, 319; founder of Hasidism, 69; homeopathy, 69; pantheism, 69; study of nature, 68
Bāb, the, **19th:** 105-107, 117, 2214
Bab Ballads, The (Gilbert), **19th:** 916
Baba ᶜAruj. *See* ᶜArūj
Babangida, Ibrahim, **Notor:** 1
Bābar. *See* Bābur
Babbage, Charles, **19th:** 107-110, 1421
Babbitt (Lewis), **20th:** 2365
Bāber. *See* Bābur
Babes in Arms (film), **20th:** 1410
Babes in Arms (Rodgers and Hart), **20th:** 1693
Babes in the Bighouse (Terry), **20th:** 3983
Babeuf, Françoise-Noël, **Notor:** 697
Bābīism, **19th:** 105-106, 117
Babington, Anthony, **Ren:** 312
Babington plot (1586), **Ren:** 201, 629, 669
Babor, Karl, **20th:** 4329
Babrius, **Anc:** 629
Bābur, **Ren:** 15, 69-72, 475, 478, 708
Baby Doc. *See* Duvalier, Jean-Claude
Baby, Take a Bow (film), **20th:** 3973
Babylon, **Anc:** Assyria and, 118, 120; as Christian metaphor, 143; Cyrus the Great and, 249; Jews and, 453; Sammu-ramat and, 745
Babylone d'Allemagne (Toulouse-Lautrec), **19th:** 2289
Babylonia, **Anc:** culture, 4; government, 250
Babylōniaka (Berosus), **Anc:** 746
Babylonian captivity, **Anc:** 446
Babylonian Captivity of the Church, **MA:** 522, 1130. *See also* Avignon Papacy
Babylonian Exile, **Anc:** 336, 338, 468, 582
Bacall, Lauren, **20th:** 407
Bacchanal of the Andrians, The (Titian), **Ren:** 937
Bacchus, **Anc:** 512
Bacchus (Michelangelo), **Ren:** 682
Bacchus and Ariadne (Titian), **Ren:** 937
Bacchus et Ariadne (ballet), **20th:** 2379
Bacchylides, **Anc:** 793
Bach, Ambrosius, **17th:** 708
Bach, Johann Christoph, **17th:** 708
Bach, Johann Sebastian, **17th:** 708; **18th:** 71-74; **19th:** 177
Bach-dang River, Battle of (938), **MA:** 756
Bacharach, Burt, **20th:** 999
Bachianas brasileiras (Villa-Lobos), **20th:** 4164
Bachman, Richard. *See* King, Stephen
Bachmann, Augustus Quirnus. *See* Rivinus
Bachmann, Ingeborg, **20th:** 1763
Bacille Calmette-Guérin vaccine, **20th:** 620
Back to Methuselah (Shaw), **20th:** 3720
Back to the Future (film), **20th:** 3812
Backus, Isaac, **18th:** 75-77
Backwoods of Canada, The (Traill), **19th:** 2292
Bacon, Francis, **Ren:** 72-75, 382; Idols of the Tribe, 73; **17th:** 175, 227, 357, 378; influence on Robert Boyle, 78
Bacon, Nathaniel, **17th:** 29-32
Bacon, Roger, **MA:** 127-129, 821, 1109
Bacon's Laws, **17th:** 30
Bacon's Rebellion (1676), **17th:** 30
Bacteria (Cohn), **19th:** 528
Bacteriology, **19th:** 528, 1292, 1878; **20th:** 3773
Bactria, **Anc:** 66
Bad Axe, Battle of (1832), **19th:** 2231
Bad Faces, **19th:** 1872
Bad-Tempered Man, The. See *Dyskolos*
Bade, Josse, **Ren:** 549
Baden-Powell, Sir Robert Stephenson Smyth, **19th:** 110-114
Badoglio, Pietro, **20th:** 2888
Badr, Battle of (624), **MA:** 735
Badr ibn Sayf, **19th:** 1966
Baeck, Leo, **20th:** 186-190
Bæda. *See* Bede the Venerable, Saint
Baer, Karl Ernst von, **19th:** 114-117
Baghchesaray, Treaty of. *See* Bakchisaray, Treaty of (1681)
Baghdad, **MA:** 158, 470, 775; Mongol invasion of, 908, 916; **Ren:** Ottoman conquest of, 481
Baghdad School, **MA:** 21
Baglioni, Orazio, **Ren:** 203
Bagot, Sir Charles, **19th:** 124
Bagrationi Dynasty, **MA:** 998
Bahāʾ Allāh. *See* Bahāʾullāh
Bahāʾīism, **19th:** 105, 118
Bahāʾullāh, **19th:** 106, 117-119
Bahādur Shāh, **17th:** 25
Bahia, **17th:** 288
Bahram IV, **Anc:** 777
Bahrām Shāh, **MA:** 889

Bai hua jing, **MA:** 1128
Bailey, F. Lee, **Notor:** 275, 455, 945, 959
Bailey, Frederick Augustus Washington. *See* Douglass, Frederick
Bailey, Harvey, **Notor:** 556
Bailey, James Anthony, **19th:** 140
Baillie, Joanna, **19th:** 1077
Bailly, Jean-Sylvain, **18th:** 77-79
Baiser au lépreux, Le. See *Kiss for the Leper, A*
Baisers volés. See *Stolen Kisses*
Baisunqur Mīrzā, **Ren:** 69
Bajazet (Racine), **17th:** 775
Bajki i przypowieści. See *Polish Fables*
Bakchai (Euripides), **Anc:** 328
Bakchisaray, Treaty of (1681), **17th:** 453
Baker, Anderson K. *See* Father Divine
Baker, Bobby, **Notor:** 48-50
Baker, Frank "Home Run," **20th:** 792
Baker, George. *See* Father Divine
Baker, Mary Morse. *See* Eddy, Mary Baker
Baker, Robert Gene. *See* Baker, Bobby
Baker, Samuel White, **19th:** 2125
Baker v. Carr (1962), **20th:** 1310, 4234
Bakhtiar, Shapour, **Notor:** 743
Bakhtin, Mikhail, **20th:** 190-193
Bakker, Jim, **Notor:** 50-52
Bakker, Tammy Faye, **Notor:** 50
Bakkush, Abdul Hamid al-, **20th:** 3351
Bakr, Ahmed Hassan al-, **20th:** 1947
Bakst, Léon, **20th:** 985
Bakufu, **MA:** 722, 1040
Bakunin, Mikhail, **19th:** 119-122, 222, 679, 1086; **Notor:** 180
Bakuninism, **19th:** 120
Bakwa of Turunku, **Ren:** 37
Balaam and His Master and Other Sketches and Stories (Harris), **19th:** 1037
Balaganchik. See *Puppet Show, The*
Balaka. See *Flight of Swans, A*
Balakirev, Mily Alekseyevich, **19th:** 281, 1915
Balama, Revolt of the (1588), **Ren:** 65
Balance of Truth, The (Kâtib Çelebî), **17th:** 455
Balanchine, George, **20th:** 193-197, 254, 988, 2378, 3890; Alexandra Danilova, 908; Margot Fonteyn, 1269; Maria Tallchief, 3940
Balboa, Vasco Núñez de, **Ren:** 76-78, 800
Balch, Emily Greene, **20th:** 197-200
Balcony, The (Genet), **20th:** 1447
Bald Soprano, The (Ionesco), **20th:** 1969
Baldassare Castiglione (Raphael), **Ren:** 821
Baldwin I, **MA:** 1060
Baldwin II, **MA:** 715
Baldwin III, **MA:** 717
Baldwin, James, **20th:** 201-204
Baldwin, Robert, **19th:** 122-125, 1458
Baldwin, Stanley, **20th:** 204-208, 276, 349, 722, 897, 4369
Baldwin, William, **19th:** 1456
Bale, John, **Ren:** 63
Balfour, Arthur, **19th:** 462, 1090; **20th:** 160, 208-211
Balfour Declaration (1917), **19th:** 1090; **20th:** 210, 292, 2156, 2305, 2994, 4281
Balian de Adam. *See* Salimbene
Baliol, Edward de, **MA:** 307
Baliol, John de, **MA:** 201, 307, 346, 1073
Balkan Defense Pact (1934), **20th:** 164
Balkan Wars (1912-1913), **20th:** 4158
Balkh, **17th:** 844
Ball, Joe, **Notor:** 52-53
Ball, John, **MA:** 130-132, 894, 1033
Ball, Lucille, **20th:** 143, 212-215
Balla, Giacomo, **20th:** 403
Ballad of Reading Gaol, The (Wilde), **19th:** 2434
Ballad of the Sad Café, The (McCullers), **20th:** 2508
Ballade (Brahms), **19th:** 298
Ballads and Other Poems (Longfellow), **19th:** 1417
Ballads of a Bohemian (Service), **20th:** 3709
Ballads of a Cheechako (Service), **20th:** 3709
Ballance, John, **19th:** 2059
Ballantyne, James, **19th:** 2047
Ballantyne, John, **19th:** 2047
Ballard, Robert D., **20th:** 215-218
Ballet, **18th:** 295, 419; **19th:** Europe, 743; France, 633, 640; Russia, 2235; **20th:** modern, 2379; Paris, 986; Russia, 193, 253, 909, 985, 1263, 2646, 3002, 3166; Spain, 1207; United Kingdom, 1268, 2628; United States, 194, 886, 1264, 2012, 3461, 3940
Ballet d'action, **18th:** 296
Ballet Russe de Monte Carlo, **20th:** 194, 909, 2012, 2628, 2648, 3940, 3989
Ballet Theater, **20th:** 958
Ballets, Les, **20th:** 194
Ballets Russes, **20th:** 909, 985, 1263, 1270, 2378, 2627, 2646, 2974, 3166, 3318, 3339, 3643, 3888; George Balanchine, 194; Sergei Diaghilev, 986
Balli di Sfessania (Callot), **17th:** 118
Ballinger, Richard, **20th:** 3931
Ballmer, Steve, **20th:** 1421
Ballo, Muhammad. *See* Bello, Muḥammad
Ballo delle ingrate, Il (Monteverdi), **17th:** 658
Ballo in maschera, Un (Verdi), **19th:** 2352
Balloons, hot-air, **18th:** 699; **20th:** 3242, 3632, 4452

Ballot Act of 1872, **19th:** 304, 794
Ballou, Hosea, **19th:** 466
Ballou's Pictorial (magazine), **19th:** 1123
Balochi, Abdul Basit. *See* Yousef, Ramzi
Balthasar (France), **19th:** 815
Baltimore, first Lord. *See* Calvert, George
Baltimore Orioles, **20th:** 3468
Baltimore Sermon of 1819, **19th:** 466
Balzac, Honoré de, **19th:** 126-129; **Notor:** 1068
Bamberg Conference, **19th:** 223
Bambi (animated film), **20th:** 1008
Ban Biao, **Anc:** 149, 953
Ban Chao, **Anc:** 149, 152
Ban Gu, **Anc:** 149-152, 953
Ban Jieyu, **Anc:** 152
Ban La Tra Toan, **Ren:** 546
Ban Mengjian. *See* Ban Gu
Ban Zhao, **Anc:** 149, 152-154
Banca de Castilla. *See* Blanche of Castile
Bancroft, George, **19th:** 130-134
Banda, Hastings Kamuzu, **20th:** 219-220
Bandinelli, Roland. *See* Alexander III (c. 1105-1181; pope)
Bandit Augustin Lorenzo, The (Rivera), **20th:** 3458
Bandit Queen. *See* Devi, Phoolan; Starr, Belle
Bandolero, El (Tirso), **17th:** 914
Bandopadhyay, Iswar Chandra. *See* Vidyasagar, Iswar Chandra
Banerjea, Sir Surendranath, **20th:** 221-223
Banga, Mobutu Sese Seko Nkuku Ngbendu Wa Za. *See* Mobutu Sese Seko
Bangladesh, **20th:** independence of, 369, 2005; Liberation War (1971), 369, 1386
Bangová, Margita, **Notor:** 54-55
Bank of Crete scandal, **20th:** 3108
Bank of England, **17th:** 717
Bank of the Manhattan Company, **19th:** 364
Bank of the United States, **18th:** founding, 207, 454; Robert Morris, 710; James Wilson, 1092; **19th:** 344, 2226
Banking, **Anc:** 252; **19th:** England, 1398; Europe, 1948; France, 1836, 1976; investment, 1600-1601; New Zealand, 2060; robbery, 1211; United States, 193, 226, 344, 365, 472, 503, 544, 856, 2226, 2339, 2346
Banks, Sir Joseph, **18th:** 80-83, 270
Banks, Nathaniel, **19th:** 1199
Bannan, Benjamin, **Notor:** 745
Banneker, Benjamin, **18th:** 84-87
Banner (newspaper), **19th:** 317
Bannockburn, Battle of (1314), **MA:** 203, 348, 552
Banquet, The (Dante), **MA:** 302
Banquet céleste, Le (Messiaen), **20th:** 2716
Banquet of Antony and Cleopatra (Tiepolo), **18th:** 977
Banting, Sir Frederick G., **20th:** 224-227, 2526
Bantu Education Act of 1953, **20th:** 4121
Banville, John, **Notor:** 675
Banya. See *Bathhouse, The*
Bánzer Suárez, Hugo, **20th:** 3173
Bao Dai, **20th:** 228-230, 2951, 4170
Bao zhang dai fang lu (Mi Fei), **MA:** 719
Baoyun, **Anc:** 345
Bapheus, Battle of (1302), **MA:** 801
Baptism, **Anc:** Christian, 476; **Ren:** 473, 675, 863, 1013; **19th:** debate, 400
Baptism (Tintoretto), **Ren:** 933
Baptism of Christ (Piero), **Ren:** 785
Baptism of Christ (Sirani), **17th:** 857
Baptism of Christ (Verrocchio), **Ren:** 561, 963
Baptist Missionary Society, **19th:** 410
Baptistes. See *Tyrannical-Government Anatomized*
Baptists, **18th:** colonial America, 75; support for American Revolution, 76; Isaac Backus, 75; First Amendment, 76; religious freedom, 76
Bar at the Folies-Bergère, A (Manet), **19th:** 1481
Bar Kokhba, **Anc:** 31, 470
Barabbas, **Notor:** 55-57
Baraghani, Fāṭima. *See* Táhirih
Barak, **Anc:** 259
Barak, Ehud, **20th:** 113
Baranaparichay (Vidyasagar), **19th:** 2363
Barbados. *See* Geographical Index
Barbarelli, Giorgio. *See* Giorgione
Barbaro, Ermolao, **Ren:** 548
Barbarossa, **Ren:** 79-81, 915
Barbarossa, Khiḍr, **Notor:** 38
Barbary Wars (1801-1815), **19th:** 628; David G. Farragut, 763
Barbate, Battle of. *See* Guadalete, Battle of
Barbauld, Anna, **18th:** 87-89
Barber, Samuel, **20th:** 230-233, 2704, 3335
Barber of Seville, The (Beaumarchais), **18th:** 98
Barber of Seville, The (Rossini), **19th:** 1944
Barberini, Maffeo Vincenzo. *See* Urban VIII
Barbie, Klaus, **Notor:** 57-59, 814
Barbot, Clément, **Notor:** 308
Barbra Streisand Album, The (Streisand), **20th:** 3892
Barbra Streisand's Greatest Hits (Streisand), **20th:** 3893
Barca, Pedro Calderón de la. *See* Calderón de la Barca, Pedro
Barcelona, Treaty of (1493), **Ren:** 227
Barchester Towers (Trollope), **19th:** 2300

Barclay, Robert H., **19th:** 1779
Bardeen, John, **20th:** 234-236
Bardeen, Cooper, and Schrieffer theory, **20th:** 235
Bardiya. *See* Smerdis
Barebones Parliament (1653), **17th:** 484, 838
Barfield, Velma Margie, **Notor:** 59-60
Barghash, **19th:** 1967
Bari, Council of (1098), **MA:** 94
Baring-Gould, Sabine, **Notor:** 881
Bark, King. *See* Gustav I Vasa
Bark of Dante, The. See *Dante and Virgil Crossing the Styx*
Barker, Arizona Donnie. *See* Barker, Ma
Barker, Doc, **Notor:** 556
Barker, Frank, Jr., **Notor:** 169
Barker, Freddie, **Notor:** 556
Barker, Herman, **Notor:** 61
Barker, Kate. *See* Barker, Ma
Barker, Ma, **Notor:** 61-62, 556
Barkouf (Offenbach), **19th:** 1701
Barlaam the Calabrian, **MA:** 1018
Barlow, Joel, **19th:** 846
Barlowe, Arthur, **Ren:** 771
Barmakids, **MA:** 467, 562
Barmen Confession, **20th:** 245
Barn with Snow (O'Keeffe), **20th:** 3033
Barnabas, **Anc:** 223
Barnaby Rudge (Dickens), **19th:** 655
Barnard, Christiaan, **20th:** 236-239
Barnard, George G., **19th:** 2334
Barnard, Henry, **19th:** 135-137
Barnes, Djuna, **20th:** 240-243
Barnes, George Kelly, Jr. *See* Kelly, Machine Gun
Barnes, Robert, **Ren:** 256
Barnes, Thomas, **19th:** 2382
Barnes v. Costle (1977), **20th:** 2522
Barnet, Battle of (1471), **Ren:** 301, 991
Barnet, Jonathan, **Notor:** 122, 877
Barnett, Ross, **Notor:** 79, 100
Barney's Version (Richler), **20th:** 3439
Barnum, P. T., **19th:** 138-142, 1388
Barnum, Sarah. *See* Bernhardt, Sarah
Barnum and Bailey circus, **19th:** 140
Barnum's American Museum, **19th:** 139
Barometers, **18th:** 336
Baronius, Caesar, **17th:** 720
Baronne de Rothschild (Ingres), **19th:** 1173
Barons' Cause, **MA:** 727
Barop, Johann Arnold, **19th:** 837
Baroque-rococo art, **18th:** 437
Baroque style, **17th:** Africa, 688; architecture, 69, 330, 468, 532, 588, 591, 599, 625, 855, 866, 995; drama, 914; England, 202, 310, 763, 995; fashion, 688; female artists, 303, 308; female writers, 315; France, 212, 478, 493, 504, 532, 569, 578, 588, 591, 599, 749; Germany, 827; Italy, 10, 45, 69, 192, 295, 302, 308, 330, 528, 656, 937; literature, 212, 315, 317, 325, 478, 577, 640, 950, 961; music, 192, 296, 310, 571, 658, 763, 827; Netherlands, 802; North America, 468; origins, 802; painting, 303, 308, 493, 504, 671, 749, 802, 937, 955, 1003; poetry, 202, 209, 313; Poland, 855; Russia, 625, 866; Spain, 312, 317, 671, 914, 955, 1003; **18th:** architecture, 350, 472-475, 608, 1003; music, 282, 828
Barrack-Room Ballads and Other Verses (Kipling), **19th:** 1285
Barre, Jean-Baptiste, **19th:** 744
Barrie, James, **19th:** 1177
Barrier Treaty (1715), **18th:** 939
Barron, James, **19th:** 627
Barron, Moses, **20th:** 224
Barrow, Buck, **Notor:** 62, 812
Barrow, Clyde, **Notor:** 62-64, 811
Barrow, Isaac, **17th:** 923
Barrows, Sydney, **Notor:** 64, 66
Barry, Sir Charles, **19th:** 142-145
Barry, Elizabeth, **17th:** 83
Barry Lyndon (Thackeray), **19th:** 2258
Barrymore, Lionel, **20th:** 1594
Barrymore, Maurice, **19th:** 273
Barth, Heinrich, **19th:** 940
Barth, Karl, **20th:** 243-246, 418, 548, 1742
Barthes, Roland, **20th:** 246-249
Bartholdi, Frédéric Auguste, **19th:** 735
Bartholin, Thomas, **17th:** 881
Bartholomew Fair (Jonson), **17th:** 442
Bartholomew of Cremona, **MA:** 1108
Barthou, Louis, **Notor:** 813
Bartlett, Bob, **20th:** 3179
Bartók, Béla, **20th:** 250-253
Barton, Clara, **19th:** 145-148
Barton, Sir Edmund, **19th:** 149-152, 624
Barton, Elizabeth, **Ren:** 336
Barton, Frances. *See* Abington, Fanny
Baryonic stars, **20th:** 78
Baryshnikov, Mikhail, **20th:** 253-255, 3003, 3990
Baryshnikov on Broadway (television special), **20th:** 254
Bas Bleu (More), **18th:** 702
Base of the Rocky Mountains, Laramie Peak, The (Bierstadt), **19th:** 233
Baseball, **20th:** gambling on, 3527; integration of, 3471; Japan, 3027; United States, 791, 1001, 1435, 3468, 3526, 3572
Basedow, Johann Bernhard, **18th:** 89-92
Basel, Council of, **MA:** 768; **Ren:** 725
Basement, The (Millett), **20th:** 2748

Bashful Man at Court, The (Tirso), **17th:** 913
Bashir, Omar al-, **Notor:** 66-67
Bashkent, Battle of (1473), **MA:** 712
Bashō. *See* Matsuo Bashō
Basho no ronri, **20th:** 2982
BASIC (programming language), **20th:** 1421
Basic History of the United States, A (Beard), **20th:** 265
Basil I. *See* Basil the Macedonian
Basil II, **MA:** 87
Basil III. *See* Vasily III
Basil the Great, **Anc:** 361, 363
Basil the Macedonian, **MA:** 133-136, 296
Basileus. *See* Porphyry
Basilikon Doron (James I), **17th:** 413
Basis of Morality, The (Schopenhauer), **19th:** 2021
Baskerville, John, **18th:** 92-94
Basketball, **20th:** creation of game, 2905; United States, 725, 2050, 3566
Basoalto, Neftalí Ricardo Reyes. *See* Neruda, Pablo
Basov, Nikolay Gennadiyevich, **20th:** 256-258
Bass, Sam, **Notor:** 68-69
Bassano, Aemelia. *See* Lanyer, Aemilia
Bassianus, Varius Avitus. *See* Elagabalus
Bassus, Aufidius, **Anc:** 665
Bassus, Varius Avitus. *See* Elagabalus
Bastides, Don Pedro de, **Ren:** 76
Bastien-Thiry, Jean-Marie, **Notor:** 69-70
Bastille, Fall of the (1789), **18th:** 78, 289, 425, 619, 658, 681, 728, 753, 844, 918
Bataan, Battle of (1941-1942), **20th:** 2494
Ba-ta-clan (Offenbach), **19th:** 1700
Batavia. *See* Jakarta
Bateman, Hester, **18th:** 95-97
Bateman, Hezekiah, **19th:** 1176
Bates, Edward, **19th:** 715
Bateson, Gregory, **20th:** 2669
Bath of Pallas, The. See *Eis Loutra tēs Pallados*
Baʿth Party (Iraq), **20th:** 1947
Bathers, The (Courbet), **19th:** 560
Bathhouse, The (Mayakovsky), **20th:** 2660, 2723
Bathing Place, Asnieres, A (Seurat), **19th:** 2075
Bathing Woman, The (Ingres), **19th:** 1173
Báthory, Elizabeth, **Ren:** 81-84; **Notor:** 70-72. *See also* Vlad III the Impaler
Báthory, Karla, **Ren:** 81
Báthory, Stephen. *See* Stephen Báthory
Bathos, The (Hogarth), **18th:** 500
Bathsheba, **Anc:** 155-157, 256, 803
Bathshua. *See* Bathsheba
Bathyscaphe, **20th:** 3242
Batiates, Lentulus, **Anc:** 818
Batih, Battle of (1652), **17th:** 463
Batista y Zaldívar, Fulgencio, **20th:** 691; **Notor:** 73-74, 185, 437, 605
Batoche, Battle of (1885), **19th:** 1911
Batrachoi (Aristophanes), **Anc:** 9, 811
Battaglia di Legnano, La (Verdi), **19th:** 2352
Battaile of Agincourt, The (Drayton), **17th:** 238
Battambang Revolt (1967), **20th:** 3741
Battānī, al-, **MA:** 22, 137-139
Batteries, **18th:** 393, 1023; **19th:** 733
Battery, the. *See* Nettles, Bonnie
Battista Sforza (Piero), **Ren:** 787
Battle Between Carnival and Lent, The (Bruegel), **Ren:** 136
"Battle Hymn of the Republic, The," **19th:** 1139
Battle of _______. *See* _______, Battle of
Battle of Britain, The (Nash), **20th:** 2912
Battle of Jacob and the Angel, The (Denis), **20th:** 973
Battle of Marathon, The (Browning), **19th:** 326
Battle of the Centaurs, The (Michelangelo), **Ren:** 682
Battle of the Romans and Sabines, The (David), **19th:** 609
Battle of Trafalgar, The (Turner), **19th:** 2323
Battle-Pieces and Aspects of the War (Melville), **19th:** 1540
Battles of Coxinga, The (Chikamatsu), **18th:** 244
Batu Khan, **MA:** 53, 227, 403, 412, 955, 1108
Baudelaire, Charles, **19th:** 152-155, 1481
Baudricourt, Robert de, **MA:** 578
Bauer, Francis, **19th:** 1678
Bauer, Georg. *See* Agricola, Georgius
Bauer, Mayer Amschel. *See* Rothschild, Mayer Amschel
Baugé, Battle of (1521), **Ren:** 224
Bauhaus, **20th:** 1603, 2075
Baum, L. Frank, **19th:** 155-158
Bäumer, Gertrude, **19th:** 1308
Baumfree, Isabella. *See* Truth, Sojourner
Baur, Ferdinand Christian, **19th:** 1918
Bautzen, Battle of (1813), **19th:** 1674, 2161
Bavaria, **MA:** 251, 258, 386, 473, 486, 663, 805
Bavaria, duke of. *See* Rupert, Prince
Bawa, **19th:** 2342
Bax, Belfort, **Notor:** 976
Baxter, John. *See* Hunt, E. Howard
Baxter, Richard, **17th:** 32-36, 347
Bay, Qaʾit. *See* Qāytbāy
Bay of Pigs invasion (1961), **20th:** 2100, 2130, 3858
Bay Psalm Book, **17th:** 247

Bayar, Celal, **20th:** 1973
Bayard, Chevalier de, **Ren:** 84-87
Bayard, Nicholas, **17th:** 519
Baybars I, **MA:** 139-143
Baydu, **MA:** 411
Bayes's theorem, **19th:** 1319
Bayezid II, **MA:** 711; **Ren:** 87-90, 659, 808
Bayle, Pierre, **17th:** 36-39
Bayley, Elizabeth Ann. *See* Seton, Saint Elizabeth
Bayliss, Sir William Maddock, **20th:** 259-261, 3830
Bayn, Aphra. *See* Behn, Aphra
Bayn al-qaṣrayn. See *Palace Walk*
Bayou Folk (Chopin), **19th:** 491
Bazille, Jean Frédéric, **19th:** 1888
Bazin, André, **20th:** 4080
BBC. *See* British Broadcasting Corporation
BCG vaccine. *See* Bacille Calmette-Guérin vaccine
Beacon Hill Memorial Column, **19th:** 347
Beaconsfield, first earl of. *See* Disraeli, Benjamin
Beadle, George, **20th:** 2504
Beagle, HMS, **19th:** 605
Beale, Dorothea, **19th:** 159-161
Beals, Melba Pattillo, **Notor:** 349
Bean, John, **Notor:** 1050
Bean Eater, The (Carracci), **Ren:** 176
Bean Eaters, The (Brooks), **20th:** 537
Beanes, William, **19th:** 1275
Bear Flag revolt (1846), **19th:** 428, 832
Beard, Charles A., **20th:** 262-266
Beard, Mary, **20th:** 263
Beards, **Anc:** Egyptian, 440; kingship and, 366, 389
Beardsley, Aubrey, **19th:** 162-165
Beast in Me and Other Animals, The (Thurber), **20th:** 4021
Beat movement, **20th:** 2114
Beat to Quarters. See *Happy Return, The*
Beata Lodovica Albertoni (Bernini), **17th:** 46
Beatae Angelae de Fulginio visionum et instructionum liber. See *Memoriale*
Béatitudes, Les (Franck), **19th:** 823
Beatles, **20th:** 266-271
Beatles, The (Beatles), **20th:** 269
Beaton, David, **Ren:** 146
Beatrice Cenci (Sirani), **17th:** 857
Béatrice et Bénédict (Berlioz), **19th:** 203
Beatrice of Nazareth, **MA:** 144-147
Beatrijs van Tienen. *See* Beatrice of Nazareth
Beatrix, Blessed. *See* Beatrice of Nazareth
Beatson, William F., **19th:** 368
Beatty, Warren, **Notor:** 956
Beau Temps, Le (Man Ray), **20th:** 2581
Beauchamp of Hache, Viscount. *See* Somerset, first duke of
Beauclerk, Charles, **17th:** 343
Beaufort, Henry, **MA:** 502; **Ren:** 434
Beaufort, Lady Margaret, **Ren:** 90-92, 335, 438, 831
Beauharnais, Joséphine de. *See* Joséphine
Beauharnais, Viscountess de. *See* Joséphine
Beauharnais v. Illinois (1952), **20th:** 379
Beaujeu, sieur de, **17th:** 491
Beaumarchais, Pierre-Augustin Caron de, **18th:** 97-99
Beaumont, Francis, **Ren:** 92-97, 878; **17th:** 105, 278, 636, 846
Beaumont, Gustave de, **19th:** 2280
"Beautiful, Pitiless Lady, The." *See* "Belle Dame sans merci, La"
Beauty and the Beast (film), **20th:** 795
Beauvoir, Simone de, **20th:** 271-275, 3638
Beaux' Stratagem, The (Farquhar), **18th:** 1
Beaverbrook, Lord, **20th:** 95, 206, 275-278, 1680
Bebel, August, **19th:** 1370; **20th:** 335
Bebop, **20th:** 1481
Beccaria, Cesare, **18th:** 100-102
Becher, Johann Joachim, **17th:** 39-41; **18th:** 934
Beck, Dave, **Notor:** 75-76, 480
Beck, Martha, **Notor:** 1109
Becker, Elisabeth, **Notor:** 76-77
Becker, Hans, **20th:** 443, 715
Becker, Lydia, **19th:** 767; **20th:** 3103
Becker Psalter (Schütz), **17th:** 826
Becket (Tennyson), **19th:** 1177
Becket, Saint Thomas, **MA:** 57, 147-150, 357, 484
Becket, Thomas à. *See* Becket, Saint Thomas
Beckett, Samuel, **20th:** 242, 279-283, 432, 1472
Beckwith, Byron De La, **Notor:** 78-79
Beckwith, Charles, **Notor:** 194
Becquerel, Alexandre-Edmond, **19th:** 165-168
Becquerel, Antoine-César, **19th:** 165-168
Becquerel, Antoine-Henri, **19th:** 165-168; **20th:** 889
Bed (Rauschenberg), **20th:** 3380
Beda. *See* Bede the Venerable, Saint
Bedbug, The (Mayakovsky), **20th:** 2660, 2723
Bede the Venerable, Saint, **MA:** 150-153, 219, 861, 938
Bedell, William, **17th:** 939
Bedford, countess of. *See* Harington, Lucy
Bedford, earl of. *See* Francis, Lord Russell
Bednye lyudi. See *Poor Folk*
Bedroom (Oldenburg), **20th:** 3037
Beebe, William, **20th:** 3242
Beecher, Catharine, **19th:** 168-172, 989

Beecher, Harriet Elizabeth. *See* Stowe, Harriet Beecher
Beecher, Henry Ward, **19th:** 172-175, 2184, 2330, 2460
Beet Queen, The (Erdrich), **20th:** 1169
Beethoven, Ludwig van, **19th:** 175-179
Before the Gates of Kairouan (Klee), **20th:** 2177
Before Thy Throne I Now Appear (Bach), **18th:** 73
Begas, **Anc:** 333
Beggar in Jerusalem, A (Wiesel), **20th:** 4325
Beggar Maid, The (Munro), **20th:** 2874
Beggar's Bush, The (Fletcher and Massinger), **17th:** 279
Beggar's Opera, The (Gay), **18th:** 1
Beghards, **MA:** 708, 857, 1023
Begin, Menachem, **20th:** 284-288, 294, 3358, 3588
Beginners All-purpose Symbolic Instruction Code. *See* BASIC
Begriffsschrift (Frege), **19th:** 828
Beguines, **MA:** 144, 708, 856, 1023
Begum's Fortune, The (Verne), **19th:** 2356
Behan, John, **Notor:** 144
Behavior of Organisms, The (Skinner), **20th:** 3756
Behaviorism, **20th:** 3755, 4014
Beheading of Saint John the Baptist, The (Verrocchio), **Ren:** 963
Behemoth (Hobbes), **17th:** 381
Behind the Lines (Milne), **20th:** 2754
Behn, Aphra, **17th:** 42-44, 82
Behrens, Peter, **20th:** 2323, 2731
Behring, Emil von, **19th:** 179-182
Beiden Grundprobleme der Ethik, Die. See *Basis of Morality, The*
Beilis, Mendel, **20th:** 2111
Beim Häuten der Zwiebel. See *Peeling the Onion*
Being and Nothingness (Sartre), **20th:** 3639
Being and Some Philosophers (Gilson), **20th:** 1490
Being and Time (Heidegger), **20th:** 1742
Being There (film), **20th:** 3697
Beiträge zur Einleitung in das Alte Testament. See *Critical and Historical Introduction to the Canonical Scriptures of the Old Testament, A*
Béjart, Armande, **17th:** 648
Béjart, Madeleine, **17th:** 646
Bekentnisse des Hochstaplers Felix Krull. See *Confessions of Felix Krull, Confidence Man*
Bekes, Gáspár, **Ren:** 910
Béla I, **MA:** 637
Béla Kohn. *See* Kun, Béla
Belarus. *See* Geographical Index
Belasco, David, **20th:** 3244, 3594
Belaúnde Terry, Fernando, **20th:** 1718
Belches on Couches (Terry), **20th:** 3984
Belgian Democracy (Pirenne), **20th:** 3270
Belgium, **MA:** philosophy in, 1105; **19th:** independence of, 1732. *See also* Geographical Index
Belgrade, Siege of (1456), **MA:** 521, 712
Belgrade, Treaty of (1739), **18th:** 640, 720
Belinda (Edgeworth), **19th:** 729
Belinda, Aunt. *See* Braddon, Mary Elizabeth
Belinsky, Vissarion, **19th:** 119, 1353
Belisarius, **Anc:** 354; **MA:** 600, 614, 1010
Belisarius (David), **19th:** 608
Bell, Alexander Graham, **19th:** 182-185
Bell, Edward, **20th:** 447
Bell, Tom, **Notor:** 80-81
Bell Jar, The (Plath), **20th:** 3285
Bell P-59, **20th:** 4319
Bell Telephone Company, **19th:** 183
Bella (Giraudoux), **20th:** 1493
Bellamont, earl of. *See* Coote, Richard
Bellamy, Samuel, **Notor:** 81-82
Bellarmine, Robert, **Ren:** 192; **17th:** 16, 720
Bellasis, John, **17th:** 484
Bellay, Joachim du, **Ren:** 424, 837
"Belle Dame sans merci, La" (Chartier), **MA:** 262
Belle de jour (film), **20th:** 579
Belle et la bête, La. See *Beauty and the Beast*
Belle Hélène, La (Offenbach), **19th:** 1701
Belle of the Nineties (film), **20th:** 4298
Bellelli Family, The (Degas), **19th:** 632
Bellérophon (Lully and Corneille), **17th:** 570
Belle's Stratagem, The (Cowley), **18th:** 284
Bellingham, John, **Notor:** 83-84
Bellini, Giorgione, **Ren:** 383
Bellini, Giovanni, **Ren:** 97-101
Bellini, Jacopo, **Ren:** 97
Bello, Muḥammad, **19th:** 186-188, 2343
Bellow, Saul, **20th:** 288-291
Bells, The (Lewis), **19th:** 1176
Bells, The (Rachmaninoff), **20th:** 3362
Bells of Zlonice (Dvořák), **19th:** 712
Bellum Catilinae (Sallust), **Anc:** 742
Bellum Iugurthinum (Sallust), **Anc:** 743
Bellum Judaium (Josephus), **Anc:** 405, 468, 477
Belon, Pierre, **Ren:** 101-103
Belonger, Louis H. *See* Blonger, Lou
Belopoeïca (Hero of Alexandria), **Anc:** 401
Beloved (Morrison), **20th:** 2836

Belshazzar's Feast (Walton and Sitwell), **20th:** 4218
Beltway Sniper. *See* Malvo, Lee Boyd; Muhammad, John Allen
Belvedere Palace, **18th:** 495
Bembenek, Bambi, **Notor:** 84-85
Bembo, Pietro, **Ren:** 118, 235, 609
Ben Ali, Zine El Abidíne, **20th:** 459
Ben Bella, Ahmed, **20th:** 10, 110
Ben Eliezer, Israel. *See* Baʿal Shem Tov
Ben-Gurion, David, **20th:** 285, 292-295, 929, 2677, 3359, 4282
Ben Hur (film), **20th:** 2663
Ben Israel, Manasseh. *See* Manasseh ben Israel
Ben Khedda, Benyoussef, **20th:** 9
Ben-Zvi, Itzhak, **20th:** 292
Benavente y Martínez, Jacinto, **20th:** 2332
Benavides, Oscar R., **20th:** 1718
Bencivieni di Pepo. *See* Cimabue
Benckendorff, Alexander, **19th:** 1671
Beneath the Wheel. See *Prodigy, The*
Benedict XI, **Notor:** 116
Benedict XII, **MA:** 230, 763, 778
Benedict XIV, **18th:** 25, 102-104
Benedict, Ruth, **20th:** 296-299, 2668
Benedict of Nursia, Saint, **MA:** 153-156, 644
Benedict the Pole, **MA:** 227
Benedictine Rule, **MA:** 155, 284
Benedictines, **MA:** 144, 819, 1114
Benefactor, The (Sontag), **20th:** 3788
Beneš, Edvard, **20th:** 299-302, 639, 2641
Benét, Stephen Vincent, **20th:** 303-306
Bénévent, prince de. *See* Talleyrand
Benevento, Battle of (1266), **MA:** 302
Benevento, Concordat of (1156), **MA:** 56
Bengal, India, **18th:** British colonialism, 469; Robert Clive, 260; **20th:** partition of, 222, 4025
Bengalee (journal), **20th:** 221
Bénigne Bossuet, Jacques. *See* Bossuet, Jacques-Bénigne
Beniowski, Maurycy, **Notor:** 85-86
Benito Juárez Democratic Club, **20th:** 2544
Benizuri-e (crimson-print pictures), **18th:** 958
Benjamin, Judah P., **19th:** 715
Benjamin, Walter, **20th:** 306-309
Benjamin Banneker's Pennsylvania, Delaware, Maryland and Virginia Almanack and Ephemeris for the Year of Our Lord, 1792 (Banneker), **18th:** 85
Benjamin of Tudela, **MA:** 157-159
Bennet, Henry. *See* Arlington, first earl of
Bennett, Belva Ann. *See* Lockwood, Belva A.
Bennett, George, **19th:** 317
Bennett, James Gordon, **19th:** 188-192, 967
Bennett, Michèle, **Notor:** 310
Benny Goodman Story, The (film), **20th:** 1529
Benois, Aleksander, **20th:** 985
Benoist, François, **19th:** 639
Benoît, Jeanne Mathilde. *See* Sauvé, Jeanne
Beňovszký, Móric Ágost. *See* Beniowski, Maurycy
Benserade, Isaac de, **17th:** 781
Bentham, Jeremy, **18th:** 104-108; **19th:** 365, 456, 1572, 1574, 1721, 1807, 2103
Benthamites. *See* Utilitarianism
Benti, Tafari, **Notor:** 720
Bentinck, Lord George, **19th:** 643
Bentinck, William, **19th:** 1858
Bentivoglio, Enzo, **17th:** 295
Bentivoglio, Guido, **17th:** 295
Bentley, Thomas, **18th:** 1059
Benton, Thomas Hart, **19th:** 192-196, 831; **20th:** 3301
Benvenuto Cellini (Berlioz), **19th:** 202
Benvenuto di Giuseppe. *See* Cimabue
Benyowsky, Maurice Auguste. *See* Beniowski, Maurycy
Benz, Carl, **19th:** 197-200
Benz and Company, **19th:** 197
Beornwulf, **MA:** 353
Beowulf, **Anc:** 394
Beppo (Byron), **19th:** 381
Ber, Sonni ʿAlī. *See* Sonni ʿAlī
Berardelli, Alessandro, **Notor:** 924, 1057
Berav, Jacob, **Ren:** 524
Berbers, **MA:** 6, 604; Jews, 604
Bercher, Jean. *See* Dauberval, Jean
Berengar of Tours, **MA:** 400
Bérénice (Racine), **17th:** 774
Berenice II, **Anc:** 157-159, 180
Berenson, Bernard, **20th:** 1407
Berestechno, Battle of (1651), **17th:** 463
Berg, Alan, **Notor:** 713
Berg, Alban, **20th:** 309-313, 452, 3666
Berg, David, **Notor:** 87-88
Berg, Nicholas, **Notor:** 1133
Berger, Victor, **20th:** 4003
Bergerac, Cyrano de. *See* Cyrano de Bergerac
Bergius, Friedrich, **20th:** 313-316
Bergman, Ingmar, **20th:** 316-320
Bergman, Ingrid, **20th:** 321-323
Bergson, Henri, **20th:** 323-326, 403, 638, 1488, 2087, 2624
Bergsonian Philosophy and Thomism (Maritain), **20th:** 2625
Bergtekne, Den (Grieg), **19th:** 986
Berhan Mogassa. *See* Mentewab
Beria, Lavrenty, **20th:** 2128; **Notor:** 89-91, 380, 550, 748, 1116

Berigan, Bunny, **20th:** 1527
Bering, Vitus Jonassen, **18th:** 108-111
Bering Strait, **18th:** 109
Berke Khan, **MA:** 54
Berkeley, George, **18th:** 111-115; David Hume, 514; criticism of Isaac Newton, 633
Berkeley, Sir William, **17th:** 29, 703
Berkman, Alexander, **20th:** 1520, 1867; **Notor:** 425
Berkowitz, David, **Notor:** 91-92
Berkshire Hathaway, **20th:** 564
Berlage, Hendrik Petrus, **20th:** 3092
Berlin, Irving, **20th:** 156, 327-330
Berlin Academy, **18th:** 32, 334, 480, 573, 651
Berlin Conference of 1884-1885, **19th:** 7, 941, 1350
Berlin Society of Sciences, **17th:** 516
Berlin Wall, **20th:** building of, 4126; fall of, 2183
Berliner Abendblätter, **19th:** 1290
Berlioz, Hector, **19th:** 200-205
Bermannus sive de re metallica dialogus (Agricola), **Ren:** 12
Bernac, Pierre, **20th:** 3319
Bernadotte, Folke, **20th:** 576
Bernadotte, Jean-Baptiste-Jules. *See* Charles XIV John
Bernal, John Desmond, **20th:** 1849
Bernard, Claude, **19th:** 205-208, 2489
Bernard, Émile, **19th:** 934
Bernard, Henrietta-Rosine. *See* Bernhardt, Sarah
Bernard of Clairvaux, Saint, **MA:** 16, 160-163, 576, 1114
Bernardo, Paul, **Notor:** 93-94, 488
Berners-Lee, Tim, **20th:** 331-333, 709
Bernhardt, Sarah, **19th:** 208-211; **20th:** 2330; **Notor:** 933
Bernières de Louvigny, Jean de, **17th:** 499
Bernini, Gian Lorenzo, **17th:** 10, 45-47, 68, 303, 330, 532, 937, 995
Bernoulli family, **17th:** Daniel, 48-50; Jakob I, 48-50, 832; Johann I, 48-50
Bernstein, Carl, **20th:** 1162, 1562; **Notor:** 672, 738
Bernstein, Eduard, **20th:** 334-337, 2482
Bernstein, Leonard, **20th:** 337-340
Bernstorff, Andreas Peter, **Notor:** 209
Berosus, **Anc:** 746
Berry, Charlotte de, **Notor:** 94-95
Berry, Chuck, **20th:** 4240
Berry, duke of. *See* Louis XVI
Berson, Solomon, **20th:** 4420
Bertha's Christmas Vision (Alger), **19th:** 52
Berthelot, Philippe, **20th:** 1493
Berthold (elector of Mainz), **Ren:** 647
Berthollet, Claude Louis, **19th:** 886
Bertrand, Clay. *See* Shaw, Clay
Bérulle, Pierre de, **17th:** 962
Berwick, Battle of (1403), **MA:** 501
Beryllium-10, **20th:** 2533
Besant, Annie, **19th:** 211-214
Beside the Sea (Motherwell), **20th:** 2848
Bess of Hardwick, **Ren:** 103-105
Bessel, Friedrich Wilhelm, **19th:** 215-217
Bessemer, Sir Henry, **19th:** 218-221
Bessemer process, **19th:** 219, 420, 716, 1301
Bessus, **Anc:** 719
Best, Charles Herbert, **20th:** 225, 2526
Best Years of Our Lives, The (film), **20th:** 1525
Bestiary (Sutherland), **20th:** 3921
Besy. See *Possessed, The*
Bet yosef (Karo), **Ren:** 524
Betaille, Nicolas, **20th:** 1969
Bete Giorgis, **MA:** 633
Bete Medhane Alem, **MA:** 633
Bethany College, **19th:** 402
Bethe, Hans Albrecht, **20th:** 341-345, 3969; **Notor:** 380
Bethesda orphanage, **18th:** 1074
Bethléem (Gounod), **19th:** 954
Bethlehem Steel Company, **20th:** 3956
Bethlen, Gabriel, **17th:** 855
Bethmann Hollweg, Theobald von, **20th:** 1181
Bethsabee. *See* Bathsheba
Bethune, Mary McLeod, **20th:** 345-348
Béthune, Maximilien de. *See* Sully, duke de
Bethune-Cookman College, **20th:** 347
Betrachtungen eines Unpolitischen (Mann), **20th:** 2595
Betrothed, The (Manzoni), **19th:** 1496
Betrothed, The (Scott), **19th:** 2048
Bettelheim, Bruno, **20th:** 3699
Betterton, Thomas, **17th:** 51-53, 82
Betty Ford Center, **20th:** 1273
Between Past and Future (Arendt), **20th:** 119
Between the Acts (Woolf), **20th:** 4398
Beʿur ha-Gra (Elijah ben Solomon), **18th:** 319
Beust, Friedrich von, **19th:** 222-224
Bevan, Aneurin, **20th:** 349-351, 357
Beveridge, Lord, **20th:** 352-356
Beverwijk, Johann van, **17th:** 824
Bevin, Ernest, **20th:** 166, 354, 356-360, 1456, 2675
Bey, Qait. *See* Qāytbāy
Beyle, Marie-Henri. *See* Stendhal
Beyond Freedom and Dignity (Skinner), **20th:** 3756

Beyond Good and Evil (Nietzsche), **19th:** 1682
Beyond Tragedy (Niebuhr), **20th:** 2963
Beza, Theodore, **Ren:** 60, 165
Bezels of Wisdom, The (Ibn al-ʿArabī), **MA:** 527
Bezos, Jeff, **20th:** 360-362
Bhagavad Gita, The, **MA:** 877
Bhagavati Sūtra (Sudharma Svami), **Anc:** 355
Bhai Santokh Singh, **19th:** 1859
Bhakti, **MA:** 877
Bhanduka Upaska, **Anc:** 898
Bhāskara II, **MA:** 195
Bhaskaravarman, **MA:** 460
Bhikśuṇī Prātimokśa, **Anc:** 346
Bhonsle, Śivājī. *See* Śivājī
Bhumibol Adulyadej, **20th:** 363-364
Bhūmis, **Anc:** 113
Bhutto, Benazir, **20th:** 365-368, 4474; **Notor:** 1121
Bhutto, Mir Murtaza, **20th:** 366
Bhutto, Zulfikar Ali, **20th:** 365, 368-370, 4473
Bhutto Zardari, Bilawal, **20th:** 367
Biafra, **20th:** 15, 182
Bianchi, Charles P. *See* Ponzi, Charles
Bianchi, Kenneth, **Notor:** 95-96, 151
Bianchini, Giovanni, **Ren:** 773
Biathanatos (Donne), **17th:** 232
Bibb, Henry, **19th:** 431
Bible, **Anc:** Abraham in, 4; Bathsheba in, 155; David in, 255; Egypt in, 737; Ezekiel in, 335; Gothic, 911; history, 330; Jesus Christ in, 458; John the Baptist in, 474; Judges, 258; Moses in, 572; Nubuchadnezzar in, 582; Origen's commentaries, 599; Peter in, 624; Samuel in, 749; Sennacherib in, 770; Temple of Jerusalem, 804; Theodore of Mopsuestia on, 863; Tiglath-pileser in, 892; translations of, 457; **MA:** Billyng, 867; commentaries, 50, 432, 534, 651, 731, 751, 871; Gutenberg, 442; translations of, 219, 523, 1051, 1131; **Ren:** commentary on, 1, 143, 549; English translation of, 256, 267; King James version, 845; science and, 824; translation into English, 834, 950; translation into French, 550; translation into German, 583, 666; **17th:** Algonquian, 248; Hebrew, 583; Irish, 939; King James, 15, 247, 940; **19th:** translation of, 411, 575. *See also* Bishop's Bible; Great Bible; Polyglot Bible
Bible and Sword (Tuchman), **20th:** 4105
Bibliotheca universalis. See *Conrad Gesner: A Bio-Bibliography*
Biches, Les (ballet), **20th:** 3318
Bickerstaff, Isaac. *See* Steele, Richard
Bidatsu, **MA:** 975
Biddellians. *See* Unitarianism
Biddle, John, **17th:** 53-55
Biddle, Nicholas, **19th:** 190, 225-228
Bideno, Juan, **Notor:** 447
Bidwell, Marshall, **19th:** 122
Biedermann und die Brandstifter. See *Fire Raisers, The*
"Bienzong Lun" (Xie Lingyun), **Anc:** 976
Bierce, Ambrose, **19th:** 228-231
Bierstadt, Albert, **19th:** 232-234, 294
Bierut, Boleslaw, **Notor:** 77
Big bang theory, **20th:** 1380, 1713, 1902, 2339
Big Bankroll. *See* Rothstein, Arnold
Big Broadcast, The (film), **20th:** 876
Big Broadcast of 1938, The (film), **20th:** 1870
Big Brother and the Holding Company, **20th:** 2043
Big City, The (film), **20th:** 3395
Big Daddy. *See* Amin, Idi
Big Deal (Fosse), **20th:** 1292
Big Four (railroad developers), **19th:** 2133
Big Jim. *See* Fisk, James
Big Parade, The (film), **20th:** 2663
Big Paul. *See* Castellano, Paul
Big Sea, The (Hughes), **20th:** 1929
Big Shave, The (film), **20th:** 3681
Big Sur (Kerouac), **20th:** 2116
Big Trail, The (film), **20th:** 4250
Big Turtle. *See* Boone, Daniel
Bigelow, Henry Jacob, **19th:** 1614
Bigge, John Thomas, **19th:** 976
Bigger Grand Canyon, A (Hockney), **20th:** 1847
Bigger They Come, The (Gardner), **20th:** 1404
Biggs, Ronnie, **Notor:** 97-98
Bigi, Francesco di Cristoforo. *See* Franciabigio
Bigley, Elizabeth. *See* Chadwick, Cassie L.
Bigley, Ken, **Notor:** 1133
Bijapur, **17th:** 859
Bikini Killer. *See* Sobraj, Charles
Biko, Steve, **20th:** 4122
Bila Tserkva, Battle of (1651), **17th:** 463
Bilbo, Theodore G., **Notor:** 99-100, 999
Bildungsroman, **18th:** 429
Bill & Melinda Gates Foundation, **20th:** 565, 1422
Bill of Rights, English (1689), **17th:** 34
Bill of Rights, U.S., **18th:** 413, 460, 665
Bill 101 (Quebec), **20th:** 2345
Billiards at Half-Past Nine (Böll), **20th:** 412
Billy Budd (Britten), **20th:** 531
Billy Budd, Foretopman (Melville), **19th:** 1540
Billy Graham Evangelistic Association, **20th:** 1558

Billy the Kid. *See* Bonney, William H.
Billy the Kid (Copland), **20th:** 838
Bilney, Thomas, **Ren:** 543
Bin Laden, Osama, **20th:** 371-374; **Notor:** 101-103, 645, 744, 759, 884, 1071, 1121, 1133, 1135, 1136
Binding Law, Great. *See* Great Peace and Power and Law
Binet, Alfred, **19th:** 862
Bingham, George Caleb, **19th:** 234-237
Bingham, Sir Richard, **Ren:** 744
Bingham, Richard John. *See* Lucan, seventh earl of
Bingham Canyon, **20th:** 1614
Bingo Palace, The (Erdrich), **20th:** 1170
Bingshu Jieyao (Cao Cao), **Anc:** 183
Binh Xuyen, **20th:** 229, 2952
Binomial system of nomenclature, **18th:** 606
Biogenetic law, **19th:** 1004
Biographia Literaria (Coleridge), **19th:** 532
Biographical and Critical Miscellanies (Prescott), **19th:** 1833
Biographie industrielle et scientifique (Eiffel), **19th:** 736
Biographies of Child Development (Gesell and Castner), **20th:** 1466
Biographies of Illustrious Women. See *Lienü zhuan*
Biography, **Anc:** Chinese, 783; Greek tradition of, 18; history and, 150, 671; **18th:** 146-150, 536
Bioi paralleloi (Plutarch), **Anc:** 64, 127, 616, 671, 794, 807, 811, 818
Biological Aspects of Infectious Diseases (Burnet), **20th:** 587
Biological sciences, Greek, **Anc:** 38, 94, 297
Biologie der Ethik, Die. See *Morals and Evolution of Man*
Biology, **17th:** England, 564, 783, 903, 987; Italy, 66, 356, 580; Netherlands, 510, 899; **18th:** 925-928, 961; **19th:** birds, 92; botany, 964, 1152; classification methods, 586, 1003; embryology, 115, 1316; evolution, 604, 1162, 2128; experimental, 207; genetics, 1543; marine, 32; microbiology, 528, 1293, 1752, 2407. *See also* Category Index
Biometrika, **19th:** 862
Bion of Borysthenes, **Anc:** 314
Bion Prasis (Lucian), **Anc:** 514
Bipartisan Campaign Reform Act of 2001, **20th:** 1229
Biraima, Damel, **19th:** 757
Birbeck, Morris, **19th:** 2414
Birbeck College, **19th:** 1807
Bird, Robert Montgomery, **19th:** 792
Bird of Time, The (Naidu), **20th:** 2900
Birdland, **20th:** 3114
Birdman of Alcatraz. *See* Stroud, Robert Franklin
Birds, The. See *Ornithes*
Birds of America, The (Audubon), **19th:** 92
Birds of Paradise (Pollock), **20th:** 3303
Birgham, Treaty of (1290), **MA:** 201
Birkbeck, George, **19th:** 1807
Birmingham march (1963), **20th:** 2149
Birney, James G., **19th:** 471
Birr wa al-ithm, al- (Avicenna), **MA:** 123
Birth control, **19th:** 212; **20th:** 558, 1150, 3626; Great Britain, 3883; Roman Catholic Church, 3150
Birth Control (Sutherland), **20th:** 3883
Birth defects, study of, **20th:** 102
Birth of a Nation, The (film), **20th:** 1496, 1595, 2662
Birth of the Virgin (Andrea del Sarto), **Ren:** 39
Birth of the Virgin (Lorenzetti), **MA:** 661
Birth of the War-God, The. See *Kumārasambhava*
Birth of Tragedy Out of the Spirit of Music, The (Nietzsche), **19th:** 1682
Birth of Venus, The (Botticelli), **Ren:** 125
Birth Project, The (Chicago), **20th:** 752
Bīrūnī, al-, **MA:** 124, 163-165, 685, 703
Bisbee mine strike (1917), **20th:** 1308
Bishop, J. Michael, **20th:** 4145
Bishop, Nicholas, **17th:** 104
Bishop's Bible, **Ren:** 762
Bishops, Kings, and Saints of York, The (Alcuin), **MA:** 49
Bishops' War, First (1639), **17th:** 262, 562, 894, 941
Bishops' War, Second (1640), **17th:** 562
Bismarck, Otto von, **19th:** 223, 238-241, 819, 1119, 1323, 1371, 1641, 2367; Theodor Mommsen, 1583; **20th:** 569, 4347; **Notor:** 662
Bissandougou, Treaty of (1886), **19th:** 1982
Bits of Travel (Jackson), **19th:** 1195
Bitter Sweet (Coward), **20th:** 855
Bitzer, Billy "G. W.," **20th:** 1594
Biwa, **MA:** 773
Bizet, Georges, **19th:** 241-244
Bizzarrie poetiche (Fontei), **17th:** 888
Bjerknes, Vilhelm, **20th:** 374-377
Bjørnson, Bjørnstjerne, **19th:** 986
Black (Dumas), **19th:** 697
Black, Bill. *See* Longley, Bill
Black, Hugo L., **20th:** 377-381
Black, Joseph, **18th:** 115-117, 1049; discovery of oxygen, 116

Black Arrow, The (Stevenson), **19th:** 2174
Black Bart. *See* Roberts, Bartholomew
Black Beetles in Amber (Bierce), **19th:** 230
Black Bellamy. *See* Bellamy, Samuel
Black, Brown, and Beige (Ellington), **20th:** 1146
Black Cloud, The (Hoyle), **20th:** 1903
Black Death, **MA:** 217, 236, 308, 351, 445-446, 531, 595, 690, 698, 780, 799, 899, 1034, 1054
Black Decameron, The (Frobenius), **20th:** 1342
Black Donnellys, **Notor:** 294-295
Black Dwarf, The (Scott), **19th:** 2048
Black Fish (Braque), **20th:** 495
Black Folk (Du Bois), **20th:** 1049
Black Hand, **20th:** 1295
Black Hawk, **19th:** 244-247, 2052
Black Hawk War (1832), **19th:** 245, 2052, 2231
Black Hole of Calcutta (1756), **18th:** 260
Black holes, **20th:** 3676
Black Jack Ketchum. *See* Ketchum, Tom
Black Kettle, **Notor:** 248
Black Knight, The (Elgar), **20th:** 1134
Black Legend, **Ren:** 780
Black Mask, The (magazine), **20th:** 1403
Black Napoleon of the Sudan. *See* Samory Touré
Black Notebook, The (Mauriac), **20th:** 2658
Black Paintings, The (Goya), **18th:** 438
Black Patio Door (O'Keeffe), **20th:** 3032
Black Phalanx (Wilson), **19th:** 2450
Black Pope. *See* LaVey, Anton Szandor
Black Prince. *See* Edward the Black Prince
Black Reconstruction (Du Bois), **20th:** 1048
Black Riders and Other Lines, The (Crane), **19th:** 563
Black Sam. *See* Bellamy, Samuel
Black September (1970), **20th:** 111, 1627
Black Skin, White Masks (Fanon), **20th:** 1213
Black Star Line, **20th:** 1419
Black Tulip, The (Dumas), **19th:** 697
Black Warrior. *See* Tascalusa
Blackbeard. *See* Teach, Edward
Blackboard Jungle (film), **20th:** 3297
Blackfriars Theatre, **Ren:** 878; **17th:** 51, 104, 279, 442, 846, 977
Blackmail (film), **20th:** 1826
Blackmun, Harry A., **20th:** 382-384
Blacks, The (Genet), **20th:** 1447
Blacks, discrimination against, **19th:** 80, 577, 606, 686, 798, 2392
Blackstone, Sir William, **18th:** 104, 118-121
Blackwell, Elizabeth, **19th:** 247-250, 2481
Blackwell, Emily, **19th:** 249
Blaes, Gerard, **17th:** 898
Blagdon Controversy, **18th:** 703
Blaine, James G., **19th:** 251-253, 508, 1042
Blair, Francis Preston, **19th:** 1336
Blair, Tony, **20th:** 385-387, 2568
Blair Mountain, Battle of (1921), **20th:** 2041
Blaise Hamlet, **19th:** 1644
Blake, Joseph, **Notor:** 943
Blake, Robert, **17th:** 55-59, 651, 931
Blake, William, **18th:** 121-125
Blakely, David, **Notor:** 327
Blalock, Alfred, **20th:** 3950
Blalock-Taussig Shunt, **20th:** 3951
Blanc, Louis, **19th:** 254-257
Blanche of Castile, **MA:** 43, 166-169, 666
Blanco (Paz), **20th:** 3170
Bland-Allison Act (1878), **19th:** 1063
Blanton, Thomas, Jr., **Notor:** 79
Blasting caps, **19th:** 1689
Blaubart. See *Bluebeard* (Frisch)
Blaue Engel, Der. See *Blue Angel, The*
Blaue Licht, Das. See *Blue Light, The*
Blaue Reiter, **20th:** 1176, 2074, 2177, 2607, 2692
Blaue Reiter Almanac, The (Marc and Kandinsky, eds.), **20th:** 2607
Blavatsky, Helena, **19th:** 212
Bleak House (Dickens), **19th:** 655
Blechtrommel, Die. See *Tin Drum*
Bleda (Turkic king), **Notor:** 45
Blee, Tammy. *See* Blight, Tamsin
Bléneau, Battle of (1652), **17th:** 933
Blenheim, Battle of (1704), **18th:** 47, 661
Blenheim Palace, **18th:** 251, 473, 1004
Blenheim Park, **18th:** 166
Blériot, Louis, **20th:** 388-390
Bleuler, Eugen, **20th:** 391-394, 2062
Bligh, William, **18th:** 126-129; **19th:** 1432; **Notor:** 104-106
Blight, Tamsin, **Notor:** 106-107, 1110
Blight, Thomasina. *See* Blight, Tamsin
Blind Assassin, The (Atwood), **20th:** 170
Blind Beggar of Alexandria, The (Chapman), **Ren:** 214
Bliss, George, **19th:** 1135
Blithe Spirit (Coward), **20th:** 856
Blithedale Romance, The (Hawthorne), **19th:** 1052
Bloch, Ivan, **19th:** 2207
Bloch, Marc, **20th:** 497
Blok, Aleksandr, **20th:** 394-396

Blonde on Blonde (Dylan), **20th:** 1073
Blonger, Lou, **Notor:** 107-108
Blood, **18th:** circulation, 926; **20th:** preservation of, 3546; typing, 2250
Blood, Council of, **Ren:** 32
Blood, James Harvey, **19th:** 2459
Blood and Sand (film), **20th:** 1731
Blood Countess. *See* Báthory, Elizabeth
Blood Knot, The (Fugard), **20th:** 1355
Blood of a Poet, The (film), **20th:** 795
Blood of Others, The (Beauvoir), **20th:** 272
Blood Wedding (García Lorca), **20th:** 1396
Bloodletting Letter of 1539, The (Vesalius), **Ren:** 966
Bloody Blonde. *See* Snyder, Ruth
Bloody Cloak of Joseph, The (Velázquez), **17th:** 954
Bloody Czar of Franconia. *See* Streicher, Julius
Bloody Felix. *See* Dzerzhinsky, Felix
Bloody Mama. *See* Barker, Ma
Bloody Marsh, Battle of (1742), **18th:** 744
Bloody Mary. *See* Mary I
Bloody Sunday (1920), **20th:** 1591
Bloody Tenent Yet More Bloody, The (Williams), **17th:** 984
Bloom of Life, The (France), **19th:** 815
Bloomer, Amelia, **19th:** 257-259
Bloomer, Dexter, **19th:** 257
Bloomsbury Group, **20th:** 1288, 1353, 2815, 4397
Blossius, **Anc:** 357
Bloudy Tenent of Persecution, for Cause of Conscience, Discussed, The (Williams), **17th:** 983
Blucher (locomotive), **19th:** 2167
Blücher, Gebhard Leberecht von, **19th:** 260-262, 930, 2007
Blue and Black (Krasner), **20th:** 2197
Blue Angel, The (film), **20th:** 998
Blue baby syndrome, **20th:** 3950
Blue Cloak, The (Bruegel), **Ren:** 136
Blue Danube, The (Strauss), **19th:** 2189
Blue Light, The (film), **20th:** 3451
Blue Nile River exploration, **18th:** 168
Blue Ridge Broadcasting Corporation, **20th:** 1558
Blue Train (Coltrane), **20th:** 814
Bluebeard. *See* Rais, Gilles de
Bluebeard (Frisch), **20th:** 1340
Bluebeard of Gambais. *See* Landru, Henri Désiré
Bluebeard of Texas. *See* Ball, Joe
Blues music, **20th:** 131, 735, 1314, 1668, 1853, 3765, 4240
Blues Suite (ballet), **20th:** 37
Bluest Eye, The (Morrison), **20th:** 2835
Bluestockings, **18th:** 181, 221, 578, 702
Blum, Léon, **20th:** 396-400
Blum, Richard C., **20th:** 1230
Blunderer, The (Molière), **17th:** 647
Blunt, Anthony, **Notor:** 109-110, 152, 164, 674, 837
Bo. *See* Applewhite, Marshall
Bo Ne Win. *See* Ne Win
Boabdil, **Ren:** 105-107, 330
Boahen, Adu, **20th:** 3390
Boan. *See* Wang Yangming
Boas, Franz, **20th:** 296, 400-402, 1945, 2668
Bobrinsky, Aleksey Grigoryevich, **18th:** 757
Bocage, Le (Ronsard), **Ren:** 837
Boccaccio, Andrea, **Notor:** 128
Boccaccio, Giovanni, **MA:** 169-172, 239, 264; **Notor:** 116
Boccherini, Luigi, **18th:** 129-132
Bocchus, **Anc:** 533, 831
Boccia, Ferdinand, **Notor:** 238, 402
Boccioni, Umberto, **20th:** 403-405
Bock, Hieronymus, **Ren:** 357
Bocskay, István, **Ren:** 842
Boda, Mike, **20th:** 3581
Bodaidaruma. *See* Bodhidharma
Bodas de sangre. See *Blood Wedding*
Bodhi tree, **Anc:** 899
Bodhidharma, **Anc:** 160-162
Bodhisattvas, **Anc:** 112, 931
Bodichon, Barbara Leigh Smith, **19th:** 263-265
Bodine, Maria, **Notor:** 892
Bodleian Library, **Ren:** 109
Bodley, Sir Thomas, **Ren:** 108-111
Bodley Head publishers, **19th:** 163
Bodmer, Karl, **19th:** 232
Body of the Dead Christ in the Tomb, The (Holbein the Younger), **Ren:** 455
Body versus soul, **Anc:** 688
Boece (Chaucer), **MA:** 265
Boeotia, **Anc:** Hesiod and, 413; Sparta and, 14, 16; wars, 303
Boeotian League, **Anc:** 304, 621
Boer Wars (1880-1881, 1899-1902), **19th:** 111, 462, 689, 768, 1299, 1894, 1979, 2060; **20th:** 66, 440, 768, 1843, 2174, 2267; Canada, 2283; Liberal Party, 149
Boerhaave, Herman, **17th:** 511; **18th:** 337
Boesky, Ivan, **Notor:** 110-112, 731
Boesman and Lena (Fugard), **20th:** 1356
Boethius, **MA:** 173-176, 1014
Bœuf sur le toit, Le (ballet), **20th:** 2736
Boeyens, Adrian Florensz. *See* Adrian VI
Boffrand, Germain, **18th:** 132-135
Bogart, Humphrey, **20th:** 406-408, 1771
Bogatiri (Borodin), **19th:** 281

Boggs, Lilburn W., **19th:** 2475
Bogot, **17th:** 498
Bohème, La (Puccini), **20th:** 676, 3347
Bohemia, **MA:** Christianity, 670; education, 259; law, 258; **17th:** 97, 250, 254, 268, 293, 415, 495, 526, 737, 805, 966
Bohemond I, **MA:** 91, 176-179, 1003
Böhme, Jakob, **17th:** 59-62
Bohr, Niels, **20th:** 408-411, 3968; hafnium, 1792; Lise Meitner, 2680; model of the atom, 442, 714, 1749
Boileau-Despréaux, Nicolas, **17th:** 63-65, 482, 578, 732, 829
Bois-le-Duc, Siege of (1629), **17th:** 261
Boivin, Marie Anne Victorine, **19th:** 265-267
Bojaxhiu, Agnes Gonxha. *See* Teresa, Mother
Bokassa, Jean-Bédel (Bokassa I), **Notor:** 113-114
Bold Stroke for a Husband, A (Cowley), **18th:** 284
Bolero (Ravel), **20th:** 3387
Boleslav I (prince of Bohemia), **MA:** 671
Bolesław I Chrobry, **MA:** 222, 487, 1069
Boleyn, Anne, **Ren:** 51, 111-114, 189, 231, 256, 266, 270, 310, 335, 443, 466, 639, 765, 947
Bolingbroke, first Viscount, **18th:** 135-140
Bolívar, Simón, **19th:** 267-271, 1986, 2195
Bolivia, **19th:** independence of, 2196; **20th:** Che Guevara, 1611. *See also* Geographical Index
Böll, Heinrich, **20th:** 411-414
Bolling, Reynal C., **20th:** 2766
Bologna, Concordat of (1516), **Ren:** 348, 559
Bolotnikov, Ivan, **17th:** 944
Boltzmann, Ludwig, **20th:** 3090
Bolyai, János, **19th:** 1404
Bom Jesus de Matosinhos (Brazil), **18th:** 609
Bon, Gustave Le. *See* Le Bon, Gustave
Bon Man, **Ren:** 547
Bon-sens, Le. See *Common Sense* (Holbach)
Bonagratia of Bergamo, **MA:** 779
Bonanno, Joe, **Notor:** 224, 389, 863
Bonaparte, Charles Louis Napoleon. *See* Napoleon III
Bonaparte, Joseph, **19th:** 412, 1636, 1993, 2410
Bonaparte, Joséphine. *See* Joséphine
Bonaparte, Louis, **Notor:** 1068
Bonaparte, Lucien, **18th:** 131
Bonaparte, Napoleon. *See* Napoleon I
Bonaparte et la Revolution (film), **20th:** 1383
Bonastrug de Porta. *See* Naḥmanides
Bonaventure, Saint, **MA:** 97, 180-183, 1111
Bondfield, Margaret, **20th:** 414-417
Bondi, Herman, **20th:** 1902
Bones of the Cuttlefish (Montale), **20th:** 2801
Bonfini, Antonio, **Ren:** 644
Bonham, Thomas, **17th:** 176
Bonhoeffer, Dietrich, **20th:** 418-420
Bönickhausen, Gustave. *See* Eiffel, Gustave
Boniface VIII, **MA:** 99, 186-189, 302, 329, 841, 857; **Notor:** 115-116
Boniface, Saint, **MA:** 183-186
Boniface of Montferrat, **MA:** 1060
Bonifacious (Mather), **18th:** 669
Bonifacius, **Anc:** 352
Bonifatius. *See* Boniface, Saint
Bonn. *See* Bonny, Anne
Bonnard, Pierre, **20th:** 421-423, 972
Bonne d'enfants, La (Offenbach), **19th:** 1700
Bonnes, Les. See *Maids, The*
Bonnet, Stede, **Notor:** 117-118
Bonneval, Claude Alexandre de, **18th:** 140-142
Bonney, William H., **Notor:** 118-120
Bonnie Prince Charlie. *See* Charles Edward
Bonnot, Jules, **Notor:** 120-122
Bonny, Anne, **Notor:** 122-123, 877, 891
Bonny, James, **Notor:** 122
Bonpland, Aimé, **19th:** 1151
Bonus Army, **20th:** 2493
Booitjie and the Oubaas (Fugard), **20th:** 1357
Book, A (Barnes), **20th:** 240
Book of Common Prayer, **Ren:** 267, 305, 529, 835, 899
Book of Common Prayer (Mohawk version), **18th:** 161
Book of Contemplation (Lull), **MA:** 673
Book of Divine Works (Hildegard von Bingen), **MA:** 513
Book of Dreams (Kerouac), **20th:** 2115
Book of Folly, The (Sexton), **20th:** 3715
Book of Government, The (Niẓām al-Mulk), **MA:** 776
Book of Highlights (al-Ashʿarī), **MA:** 112
Book of Hours, The (Rilke), **20th:** 3454
Book of Images, The (Rilke), **20th:** 3455
Book of Job, The (Blake), **18th:** 123
Book of Kildare, **MA:** 199
Book of Large and Small Numbers (Yoshida), **17th:** 831
Book of Margery Kempe, The (Kempe), **MA:** 608
Book of Minerals (Albertus Magnus), **MA:** 44
Book of Mormon, **19th:** 2117, 2119

Book of My Life, The (Cardano), **Ren:** 174
Book of Nature (Swammerdam), **17th:** 899
Book of Redemption, The (Naḥmanides), **MA:** 749
Book of Repulsive Women, The (Barnes), **20th:** 240
Book of Roses, The (Parkman), **19th:** 1746
Book of Snobs, The (Thackeray), **19th:** 2259
Book of Songs (Heine), **19th:** 1070
Book of Spiritual Physick, The (al-Rāzī), **MA:** 886
Book of Squares, The (Leonardo of Pisa), **MA:** 649
Book of the City of Ladies, The (Christine de Pizan), **MA:** 275
Book of the Courtier, The (Castiglione), **Ren:** 182, 235, 384, 821
Book of the Duchess, The (Chaucer), **MA:** 264
Book of the Hamburgs, The (Baum), **19th:** 155
Book of the Kuzari (Judah ha-Levi), **MA:** 593
Book of the Pomegranate, The (Moses de León), **MA:** 731
Book of the Popes, The. See *Liber Pontificalis*
Book of the Three Virtues, The (Christine de Pizan), **MA:** 276
Book of the True Poem, The (Machaut), **MA:** 680
Book of the Visions and Instructions of Blessed Angela of Foligno, The. See *Memoriale*
Book of Theseus, The (Boccaccio), **MA:** 170
Book Without a Name (Petrarch), **MA:** 829
Booke of Ayres, A (Campion and Rosseter), **17th:** 127
Books, **18th:** censorship, 214, 238, 980; children's, 433, 730-732; design, 93; women writers, 1109. *See also* Printing; Libraries
Books of Opinions of Peter Lombard, The. See *Sentences*
Books on Personal Matters (Petrarch), **MA:** 830
Boone, Daniel, **18th:** 143-146
Boone's Station, Kentucky, **18th:** 144
Boonesborough, Kentucky, **18th:** 143
Booth, Cynthia, **20th:** 2313
Booth, Edwin, **19th:** 271-274, 1256
Booth, George, **17th:** 485
Booth, John Wilkes, **19th:** 272, 1383, 1386; **Notor:** 123-125, 147, 858, 1012
Booth, Junius Brutus, **19th:** 1256
Booth, William, **19th:** 274-277
Booth Theatre, **19th:** 272
Boothe, Ann Clare. *See* Luce, Clare Boothe
Borberg, Claus Cecil. *See* Von Bülow, Claus
Borbón, Carlos María Isidro de. *See* Carlos, Don
Borden, Abby Durfee Gray, **19th:** 277
Borden, Andrew J., **19th:** 277; **Notor:** 125
Borden, Emma Lenora, **19th:** 277; **Notor:** 125
Borden, Lizzie, **19th:** 277-280; **Notor:** 125-127
Borden, Sir Robert Laird, **20th:** 423-426
Borelli, Charles. *See* Ponzi, Charles
Borelli, Giovanni Alfonso, **17th:** 65-67, 362, 579, 986
Borg, Björn, **20th:** 426-429
Borges, Jorge Luis, **20th:** 430-434; **Notor:** 206, 1066
Borghese, Camillo. *See* Paul V
Borghese, Scipione, **17th:** 45
Borgia, Cesare, **Ren:** 28, 114-117, 588, 871; **Notor:** 14, 127-130
Borgia, Giovanni, **Notor:** 14, 127, 130
Borgia, Juan, **Ren:** 115, 117
Borgia, Lucrezia, **Ren:** 27, 56, 116, 117-119; **Notor:** 14, 15, 127, 129-131
Borgia, Rodrigo. *See* Alexander VI
Borinquén. *See* Puerto Rico
Boris I of Bulgaria, **MA:** 189-192, 767
Boris Godunov (Mussorgsky), **19th:** 1628
Boris Godunov (Pushkin), **19th:** 1849
Bořivoj, **MA:** 670
Borja y Doms, Rodrigo de. *See* Alexander VI
Borlaug, Norman, **20th:** 434-436
Bormann, Martin, **Notor:** 131-133
Born, Max, **20th:** 437-439; **Notor:** 379
Børn av tiden. See *Children of the Age*
Born-Haber cycle, **20th:** 438
Born-Oppenheimer approximation, **20th:** 438
Bornhöved, Battle of (1227), **MA:** 1048
Bornu, **Ren:** 556
Borodin, Aleksandr, **19th:** 280-283, 1915
Borodino, Battle of (1812), **19th:** 47, 499, 1668
Boron, discovery of, **19th:** 888
Borough, Edward, **Ren:** 764
Borough Road School, **19th:** 1305
Boroughbridge, Battle of (1322), **MA:** 348, 552
Borromini, Francesco, **17th:** 67-70, 330, 532, 937
Borujerdi, Ayatollah Mohammad-Hussein, **20th:** 2124; **Notor:** 571
Bosch, Hieronymus, **Ren:** 120-123, 135
Bosnia, **20th:** human rights, 2524; independence of, 2758; United Nations, 465. *See also* Geographical Index
Bosnian Crisis (1908-1909), **20th:** 1295

Boss of Bosses. *See* Gambino, Carlo
Boss Tweed. *See* Tweed, William Marcy
Bossuet, Jacques-Bénigne, **17th:** 70-73, 186, 265, 339, 488
Boston (Sinclair), **20th:** 3752
Boston Celtics, **20th:** 726, 3567
Boston Female Anti-Slavery Society, **19th:** 1786
Boston Five, **20th:** 3815
Boston Massacre (1770), **18th:** 17, 459, 520
Boston police strike (1919), **20th:** 832
Boston Port Act (1774), **18th:** 18, 443, 460
Boston Red Sox, **20th:** 3573
Boston Strangler. *See* DeSalvo, Albert
Boston Swindler. *See* Ponzi, Charles
Boston Tea Party (1773), **18th:** 11, 18, 409, 459, 483, 520, 833; poem by Mercy Otis Warren, 1041
Boston Theatre, **19th:** 347
Bostonians, The (James), **19th:** 1207
Boswell, Granny, **Notor:** 1110
Boswell, James, **18th:** 146-150, 538, 898
Boswell, Percy, **20th:** 2311
Boswell in Search of a Wife (Boswell), **18th:** 147
Boswell on the Grand Tour: Germany and Switzerland (Boswell), **18th:** 147
Boswell on the Grand Tour: Italy, Corsica, and France (Boswell), **18th:** 147
Boswell's London Journal, 1762-1763 (Boswell), **18th:** 146
Bosworth, Battle of (1485), **Ren:** 91, 438, 831, 946
Botany, **Anc:** Greece, 872; **Ren:** Germany, 356; Italy, 212; Switzerland, 376; **17th:** England, 200, 257, 782; Germany, 445; Italy, 581; Netherlands, 510, 899; **18th:** 80-83, 171, 604-607; **19th:** 528, 964; American West, 963; Venezuela, 1152
Boteler, Sir William, **17th:** 562
Botellier, Joaquín. *See* Murieta, Joaquín
Botha, Louis, **20th:** 439-442, 3776
Botha, Pieter W., **20th:** 2585; **Notor:** 271
Bothe, Walther, **20th:** 442-445, 715
Bothwell, fourth earl of. *See* Hepburn, James
Bothwell Bridge, Battle of (1679), **17th:** 122, 654
Botticelli, Sandro, **Ren:** 123-126
Bottomley, Horatio W., **20th:** 445-449
Boucher, François, **18th:** 367; portrait of Madame de Pompadour, 799
Boudicca, **Anc:** 163-165
Boudinot, Elias, **19th:** 1938
Boudu Saved from Drowning (film), **20th:** 3421
Bougainville, Louis-Antoine de, **18th:** 150-153
Bougainvillea vine, **18th:** 152
Boulanger, Georges, **20th:** 779
Boulanger, Nadia, **20th:** 449-452, 837
Boule (Athenian council), **Anc:** 222
Boulez, Pierre, **20th:** 452-456
Boulogne, count of. *See* Stephen (king of England)
Boulogne, Guy de, **Notor:** 1053
Boulogne, Joseph, **18th:** 153-155
Boulton, Matthew, **18th:** 156-158; William Murdock, 715; James Watt, 1049; **19th:** 2294
Boulton, Watt & Sons, **18th:** 716
Boundary theory, **20th:** 3328
Bounty, HMS, **18th:** 126; **Notor:** 104
Bourbon, Antonio Pedro de Alcântara. *See* Pedro I
Bourbon-Condé, Anne-Geneviève de. *See* Longueville, duchesse de
Bourbon dynasties, **Ren:** 184, 569; **17th:** 152, 184, 269, 426, 431, 527, 548, 622; **18th:** 246, 782, 918, 937
Bourbon Reforms, **18th:** 228
Bourbon Restoration, First (1814), **19th:** 397, 609
Bourbon Restoration, Second (1815), **19th:** 397, 609
Bourgeois, Louyse, **17th:** 73-75
Bourgeois gentilhomme, Le. See *Would-Be Gentleman, The*
Bourgeoys, Saint Marguerite, **17th:** 75-77, 576
Bourgogne, Marie de. *See* Mary of Burgundy
Bourguiba, Habib, **20th:** 457-460
Bourguignon, Louis-Dominique. *See* Cartouche
Bourke, Mary Teresa Winifred. *See* Robinson, Mary (president of Ireland)
Bourke-White, Margaret, **20th:** 460-463
Boursier, Louyse. *See* Bourgeois, Louyse
Boutique fantasque, La (ballet), **20th:** 2647
Bouton, Charles-Marie, **19th:** 589
Boutros-Ghali, Boutros, **20th:** 56, 464-468
Bouvard et Pécuchet (Flaubert), **19th:** 786
Bouvier de La Motte, Jeanne-Marie. *See* Guyon, Madame
Bouvines, Battle of (1214), **MA:** 166, 389, 586, 837
Bovelles, Charles de, **Ren:** 549
Bow, Clara, **20th:** 142
Bow and the Lyre, The (Paz), **20th:** 3170
Bow Street Runners. *See* Scotland Yard
Bowell, Mackenzie, **19th:** 2317
Bowers, Sam, **Notor:** 79
Bowie, James, **19th:** 791

Bowles, Samuel, **19th:** 660
Boxer, Barbara, **20th:** 1229
Boxer Rebellion (1900), **19th:** 498, 1055, 1253, 2487
Boxing, **20th:** 62, 964, 2438, 2614
Boy About to Take a Shower (Hockney), **20th:** 1846
Boy Peeling Fruit (Caravaggio), **Ren:** 170
Boy Scouts, **19th:** 112
Boy with a Basket of Fruit (Caravaggio), **Ren:** 170
Boy with a Squirrel (Copley), **18th:** 275
Boy with Baby Carriage (Rockwell), **20th:** 3484
Boyarinya Vera Sheloga (Rimsky-Korsakov), **19th:** 1916
Boyars, **17th:** 785
Boyce, Christopher John, **Notor:** 133-135, 623
Boycotts, **18th:** of British goods by American colonists, 18, 238, 458, 460; **20th:** Montgomery bus, 11, 2148
Boyd, Belle, **Notor:** 135-137
Boyd, Lord of Kilmarnock, **Ren:** 496
Boyes, William, **Notor:** 961
Boyhood on the Upper Mississippi (Lindbergh), **20th:** 2395
Boyle, Richard, **17th:** 885
Boyle, Robert, **17th:** 37, 48, 78-81, 257, 306, 335, 383, 514, 544, 564, 814, 901, 923
Boyle's law, **17th:** 79
Boylston Hall and Market, **19th:** 348
Boyne, Battle of the (1690), **17th:** 418, 611, 822
Boys from Brazil, The (film), **20th:** 3044
Boys from Syracuse, The (Rodgers and Hart), **20th:** 3487
Boys Town (film), **20th:** 4066
Boy's Will, A (Frost), **20th:** 1349
Bozeman Trail, **19th:** 567, 1872
Bozeman Trail War. *See* Red Cloud's War
Bra-ket notation, **20th:** 1005
Bracebridge Hall (Irving), **19th:** 1180
Bracegirdle, Mrs. Anne, **17th:** 51, 82-83
Bracton, Henry de, **MA:** 192-194
Bracton on the Laws and Customs of England (Bracton), **MA:** 193
Braddock, James, **20th:** 2438
Braddon, Mary Elizabeth, **19th:** 284-288
Bradford, Sarah, **19th:** 2315
Bradford, William, **17th:** 84-87, 130, 613, 876, 878
Bradlaugh, Charles, **19th:** 211; **20th:** 445
Bradlee, Ben, **Notor:** 231
Bradley, Christopher, **Notor:** 222
Bradley, F. H., **19th:** 288-291; **20th:** 1842
Bradley, Jim, **Notor:** 447
Bradley, Omar Nelson, **20th:** 468-471, 3143
Bradman, Sir Donald G., **20th:** 471-474
Bradstreet, Anne, **17th:** 88-91
Brady, Ed, **20th:** 1521
Brady, James, **Notor:** 471
Brady, Mathew B., **19th:** 291-295
Brady, Mrs. E. *See* Goldman, Emma
Brady, William, **Notor:** 119
Bragança Dynasty. *See* Braganza Dynasty
Braganza, duke of. *See* John IV
Braganza Dynasty, **17th:** 425, 430, 960
Bragg, Braxton, **19th:** 613; **Notor:** 247
Bragg, Sir Lawrence, **20th:** 474-478
Bragg, William Henry, **20th:** 474
Braggart Warrior, The. See *Miles gloriosus*
Brahe, Sophie, **Ren:** 126-128
Brahe, Tycho, **Ren:** 126, 128-131, 774, 841; **17th:** 259, 372, 458
Brahmagupta, **MA:** 110, 195-197
Brahmans, **Anc:** 130, 925
Brahmasūtrabhāsya. See *Vedānta Sūtras of Bādarāyana with the Commentary of Samkara, The*
Brahmasphuṭasiddhānta, **MA:** 195
Brahmo Samaj, **19th:** 1868, 2368
Brahms, Johannes, **19th:** 296-299, 331, 712, 2030, 2190
Braille, Louis, **19th:** 299-302
Bramante, Donato, **Ren:** 29, 132-134, 520
Bramer, Leonaert, **17th:** 956
Branch Davidians, **20th:** 3417
Brancusi, Constantin, **20th:** 478-481
Brand (Ibsen), **19th:** 1165
Brandeis, Louis D., **20th:** 18, 482-486; **Notor:** 1057
Brandenburg Concertos (Bach), **18th:** 72
Brandenburgische Flugzeugwerke, **20th:** 1746
Brando, Marlon, **20th:** 486-489
Brandt, Willy, **20th:** 490-493
Brant, Joseph, **18th:** 159-162
Brant, Molly, **18th:** 159
Brantinghame Hall (Gilbert), **19th:** 919
Braque, Georges, **20th:** 493-497, 3238
Braschi, Giovanni Angelo. *See* Pius VI
Brasília, creation of, **20th:** 2968
Brattain, Walter, **20th:** 234
Brattle Square Church, **19th:** 1905
Bratton, Henry de. *See* Bracton, Henry de
Bratya Karamazovy. See *Brothers Karamazov, The*
Braudel, Fernand, **20th:** 497-500
Braun, Eva, **Notor:** 137-139, 421, 479
Braun, Wernher von, **20th:** 500-503, 1747, 3009
Brave Are My People (Waters), **17th:** 614
Brave New World (Huxley), **20th:** 1962
Bravo, The (Cooper), **19th:** 554

Brazen Age, The (Heywood), **17th:** 374
Brazil. *See* Geographical Index
Brazilian Social Democratic Party, **20th:** 651
Bread-Winners, The (Hay), **19th:** 1055
Breakfast at Tiffany's (Capote), **20th:** 645
Breakspear, Nicholas. *See* Adrian IV
Breasts of Tiresias, The (Apollinaire), **20th:** 106
Breathless (film), **20th:** 1503
Breauté, Fawkes de, **MA:** 212
Brecht, Bertolt, **20th:** 504-507, 1339, 4274
Breckinridge, John C., **19th:** 1383
Breda, Declaration of (1660), **17th:** 137, 148, 168, 651
Breda, Treaty of (1667), **17th:** 148, 892
Breeches role (acting), **18th:** 848, 1102
Breedlove, Sarah. *See* Walker, Madam C. J.
Breen, David. *See* Chambers, Whittaker
Breitenfeld, First Battle of (1631), **17th:** 338, 925
Breitenfeld, Second Battle of (1642), **17th:** 926
Brekespere, Nicholas. *See* Adrian IV
Bremer, Arthur, **Notor:** 139-141, 1088
Bremer, Edward, **Notor:** 556
Bremer Beiträger, **18th:** 562
Brennan, William J., **20th:** 507-509
Brennoralt (Suckling), **17th:** 894
Brent, Margaret, **17th:** 92-93
Brentano, Franz, **20th:** 1110
Bresci, Gaetano, **Notor:** 253
Brescia, Siege of (1238), **MA:** 391
Bresdin, Rodolphe, **19th:** 1875
Bresnaham, William. *See* Brocius, Curly Bill
Brest-Litovsk, Treaty of (1918), **20th:** 1181, 2462
Brethren of the Common Life, **MA:** 1022
Brétigny, Peace of (1360), **MA:** 351
Breton, André, **20th:** 510-513, 711, 1152; Salvador Dalí, 906; Max Ernst, 1177; René Magritte, 2548; Joan Miró, 2760
Breton Village Covered by Snow (Gauguin), **19th:** 881
Bretton, Henry de. *See* Bracton, Henry de
Breuer, Josef, **20th:** 514-517, 1323
Breuer, Lee, **20th:** 39
Breuil, Henri-Édouard-Prosper, **20th:** 517-520
Breviary of Blanche of France, The (Pucelle), **MA:** 866
Breviloquium (Bonaventure), **MA:** 180
Breviloquium (Ockham), **MA:** 780
Brevísima relación de la destruyción de las Indias. See *Tears of the Indians, The*
Brewster, William, **17th:** 84, 878
Breyer, Stephen G., **20th:** 520-522, 785
Brezhnev, Leonid, **20th:** 523-526, 1044, 1530, 2130
Brezhnev Doctrine, **20th:** 524
Briand, Aristide, **20th:** 599, 1777, 2011, 3897
Brick and Marble in the Middle Ages (Street), **19th:** 2192
Bridal of Triermain, The (Scott), **19th:** 2048
Bride, The (Klimt), **20th:** 2181
Bride of Abydos, The (Byron), **19th:** 380
Bride of Lammermoor, The (Scott), **19th:** 2048
Bride Stripped Bare by Her Bachelors, Even, The (Duchamp), **20th:** 1052
Bridge, The (Crane), **20th:** 859
Bridge for Passing, A (Buck), **20th:** 559
Bridges, **19th:** Brooklyn Bridge, 1929; Clifton Bridge, 335; engineering, 716, 735; England, 335; Europe, 735; Niagara Bridge, 1929; suspension, 1929, 2142, 2242; United States, 419, 716
Bridges at Toko-Ri, The (Michener), **20th:** 2728
Bridgewater Foundry, **19th:** 1646
Bridgewater House, **19th:** 144
Bridgman, Laura, **19th:** 1142
Bridgman, Percy Williams, **20th:** 526-529
Bridie, James, **Notor:** 154
Brief Account of the Devastation of the Indies. See *Tears of the Indians, The*
Brief Account of the Intended Bank of England, A (Paterson), **17th:** 717
Brief Account of the Province of Pennsylvania, A (Penn), **17th:** 726
Brief an den Vater. See *Letter to His Father*
Brief Encounter (Coward), **20th:** 856
Brief History of Epidemic and Pestilential Diseases, A (Webster), **19th:** 2404
Brief History of Time, A (Hawking), **20th:** 1714
Brief Narrative of the Case and Tryal of John Peter Zenger, A (Zenger), **18th:** 1118
Brief Summary of the Most Important Laws of England Concerning Women, A, **19th:** 263
Briefe, die neueste Literatur betreffend (literary journal), **18th:** 599
Briefe zu Beförderung der Humanität. See *Letters for the Advancement of Humanity*
Brigg Fair (Delius), **20th:** 955
Briggs, Henry, **Ren:** 712
Bright, John, **19th:** 302-306, 521, 1770

Bright Eyes (film), **20th:** 3973
Brightman, Sarah, **20th:** 2415
Brighton Rock (Greene), **20th:** 1578
Brigit, Saint, **MA:** 198-200, 689
Brindley, James, **18th:** 162-165
Bring Me a Unicorn (Lindbergh), **20th:** 2391
Bringing It All Back Home (Dylan), **20th:** 1073
Bringing up Baby (film), **20th:** 1572, 1770
Brinkley, John (astronomer), **19th:** 1015
Brinkley, John R. (medical fraudster), **Notor:** 141-142
Bristol, Battle of (1645), **17th:** 756, 805
Britain, **Anc:** Agricola and, 17; Celts and, 936; post-Roman, 394; Pytheas and, 730
Britain, Battle of (1940), **20th:** 277, 1547, 2118
Britain and the British Seas (Mackinder), **20th:** 2519
Britannicus, **Anc:** 561, 591
Britannicus (Racine), **17th:** 774
British-African trade, **18th:** 766
British-American conflicts, **18th:** 198, 206, 253, 257, 386, 507, 518, 1043, 1054
British-American diplomacy, **18th:** 12, 372, 540
British-American Indian conflicts, **18th:** 385, 802
British-American Indian relations, **18th:** 40, 144, 159, 626, 744
British-American Tobacco Company, **19th:** 693
British Atomic Scientists Association, **20th:** 3537
British Broadcasting Corporation, **20th:** 810, 3410
British-Burmese treaty, **18th:** 30
British Canada, **18th:** 38-42, 507, 694, 790, 919-921, 1104-1108
British-Chinese relations, **18th:** 817
British Chronicle, **19th:** 317
British Columbia, **18th:** 1007
British Commonwealth of Nations, **20th:** 424
British Constitution. *See* Constitution, British
British East India Company, **17th:** 137, 412, 465, 718; **18th:** 176, 410; and Bengalese attack on Calcutta, 260; Boston Tea Party, 18; Burma, 30; and charter amendment, 704; corruption, 739; and East India Act, 790; and fraud, 279; government regulation of, 469; Persia, 552
British Empire, **18th:** George III, 409; increased power, 1107
British-French conflicts, **18th:** 39, 246, 311, 384, 406, 510, 661, 693, 786, 790, 851, 881, 984; North American colonies, 801
British-French diplomacy, **18th:** 151, 939
British Imperial Expedition, **20th:** 4340
British India, **18th:** 259-262, 278-281, 311, 469, 522-523
British North America. *See* Canada
British North America Act (1867), **19th:** 710, 1453, 2316
British Novelists, The (Barbauld, ed.), **18th:** 88
British-Prussian alliance, **18th:** 939
British Royal Marines, **18th:** 50
British South Africa Company, **19th:** 1407, 1893
British Southern Indian Department, **18th:** 626
British-Spanish conflicts, **18th:** 626, 1036; West Indies, 986
Brittany, **Ren:** 48
Britten, Benjamin, **20th:** 529-534
Broadway Boogie Woogie (Mondrian), **20th:** 2788
Broadway Melody, The (film), **20th:** 2663
Broadway Melody of 1938 (film), **20th:** 1410
Broadwell, Dick, **Notor:** 257
Brocius, Curly Bill, **Notor:** 143-144
Brock, Sir Isaac, **19th:** 306-308
Brodie, William (Deacon Brodie), **Notor:** 145-146
Brodribb, John Henry. *See* Irving, Henry
Brodsky, Joseph, **20th:** 44
Broglie, Louis de, **20th:** 534-536
Broken Blossoms (film), **20th:** 1497, 1595
Broken Cord, The (Dorris), **20th:** 1169
Broken Glass (Miller), **20th:** 2744
Broken Jug, The (Kleist), **19th:** 1289
Broken Wing, The (Naidu), **20th:** 2900
Brome, Richard, **17th:** 374, 443
Brome, Viscount. *See* Cornwallis, Charles, first Marquess
Brömsebrö, Treaty of (1645), **17th:** 706
Bronco Buster, The (Remington), **19th:** 1882
Bronenosets Potyomkin. See *Potemkin*
Bronstein, Lev Davidovich. *See* Trotsky, Leon
Brontë, Anne, **19th:** 308-311
Brontë, Charlotte, **19th:** 308-311
Brontë, Emily, **19th:** 308-311
Brook Farm, **19th:** 842, 1736
Brooke, Sir Alan Francis. *See* Alanbrooke, First Viscount
Brooklyn Bridge, **19th:** 1929
Brooklyn Vampire. *See* Fish, Albert
Brooks, Gwendolyn, **20th:** 537-539
Brooks, James, **Notor:** 19
Brooks, Preston, **19th:** 2202
Brooks-Randolph, Angie, **20th:** 4103
Broome, Jack, **Notor:** 513
Broonzy, Big Bill, **20th:** 4240
Brother to Dragons (Warren), **20th:** 4238

Brotherhood of Sleeping Car Porters, **20th:** 3371
Brotherhood of the Blessed Virgin, **Ren:** 120
Brotherhood of the Kingdom, **20th:** 3383
Brothers, The. See *Adelphoe*
Brothers Club, England, **18th:** 137
Brothers Karamazov, The (Dostoevski), **19th:** 679
Brougham, Henry (first Baron Brougham), **19th:** 312-315, 709
Browder, Earl, **Notor:** 915
Brown, Carol. *See* Shakur, Assata Olugbala
Brown, Edmund G., **20th:** 2984
Brown, George, **19th:** 316-318, 1443, 1458
Brown, Helen Gurley, **20th:** 539-541
Brown, John, **19th:** 319-323, 484, 2275, 2314; Frederick Douglass, 686; Thomas Wentworth Higginson, 1097; Samuel Gridley Howe, 1142; Robert E. Lee, 320; Theodore Parker, 1737
Brown, Lancelot, **18th:** 165-168
Brown, Molly, **20th:** 542-544
Brown, Olympia, **19th:** 323-325
Brown, Peter, **19th:** 316
Brown, Ruth. *See* Snyder, Ruth
Brown, Three Fingers. *See* Lucchese, Tommy
Brown, Tommy. *See* Lucchese, Tommy
Brown on Resolution (Forester), **20th:** 1283
Brown-Trickey, Minnijean, **Notor:** 349
Brown v. Board of Education of Topeka, Kansas (1954), **20th:** 1310, 2634, 2891, 4234
Browne, Felicia Dorothea. *See* Hemans, Felicia Dorothea
Browne, Sir Richard, **17th:** 676
Browne, Sir Thomas, **17th:** 94-96
Browne's Vulgar Errors (Browne), **17th:** 95
Brownian motion, **20th:** 1119
Browning, Elizabeth Barrett, **19th:** 326-328
Browning, Robert, **19th:** 326
Brownlow, Kevin, **20th:** 1383
Broz, Josip. *See* Tito
Bruce, David. *See* David II
Bruce, James, **18th:** 168-171
Bruce, Robert, **MA:** 200-205, 307, 346-347, 1073
Bruce, Stanley M., **20th:** 1932
Brucellosis, **20th:** 3774
Bruck, David, **Notor:** 977
Brücke, Die, **20th:** 2164, 3661
Bruckner, Anton, **19th:** 329-332
Bruegel, Pieter, the Elder, **Ren:** 135-138
Brueghel, Jan, **Ren:** 137
Brueghel, Pieter, the Younger, **Ren:** 137
Brugha, Cathal, **20th:** 808
Brundtland, Gro Harlem, **20th:** 544-547
Brundtland Commission, **20th:** 545-546
Brunel, Isambard Kingdom, **19th:** 333-336, 339
Brunel, Marc Isambard, **19th:** 333, 337-340, 549
Brunelleschi, Filippo, **MA:** 84, 104, 205-208, 418, 700; **Ren:** 18
Brunfels, Otto, **Ren:** 357
Brunham, Margery. *See* Kempe, Margery
Brunhild, **MA:** 382
Bruni, Leonardo, **MA:** 208-210, 850
Brunner, Emil, **20th:** 547-550
Bruno, Giordano, **Ren:** 138-142, 427; **17th:** 630, 811
Bruno, Leonardo. *See* Bruni, Leonardo
Bruno of Egisheim. *See* Leo IX
Brunswick Manifesto, **18th:** 290
Brussels, Union of (1577), **Ren:** 995
Brussels Convention, **19th:** 1982
Brutinae quaestiones in Oratorem Ciceronis (Ramus), **Ren:** 817
Brutus, Lucius Junius, **Anc:** 166, 518, 846
Brutus, Marcus Junius, **Anc:** 74, 146, 166-168, 174, 185, 431; **Notor:** 146-148
Brutus Receiving the Bodies of His Sons (David), **19th:** 608
Bruyas, Jacques, **17th:** 909
Bryan, William Jennings, **19th:** 59, 510, 1018, 1461; **20th:** 550-554, 915; **Notor:** 253
Bryant, Louise, **20th:** 3052
Bryant, William Cullen, **19th:** 340-343
Bryggman, Erik, **20th:** 1
Bryn Mawr College, **19th:** 2040
Brynner, Yul, **20th:** 999
BSAC. *See* British South Africa Company
BSkyB, **20th:** 2876
Bstan-'dzin-rgya-mtsho. *See* Dalai Lama (fourteenth)
BTK Killer. *See* Rader, Dennis
Buade, Louis de. *See* Frontenac, comte de
Buber, Martin, **20th:** 549, 554-557
Bubonic plague. *See* Black Death
Bübschens Weihnachtstraum (Humperdinck), **19th:** 1155
Bucareli Agreements of 1923, **20th:** 3015
Bucentoro at the Molo on Ascension Day, The (Canaletto), **18th:** 191
Bucer, Martin, **Ren:** 142-145, 306, 403
Buch der Bilder, Das. See *Book of Images, The*
Buch der hängenden Gärten, Das (Schoenberg), **20th:** 3665
Buch der Lieder. See *Book of Songs*
Buch Paragranum, Das. See *Against the Grain*
Buchalter, Louis, **Notor:** 23, 148-149, 277
Buchanan, George, **Ren:** 146-148

Buchanan, James, **19th:** 343-346, 783, 833, 1792; **Notor:** 171, 1085
Büchlein, Das. See *Lament, The*
Buck, Pearl S., **20th:** 557-560
Buckey, Peggy McMartin, **Notor:** 676
Buckey, Raymond, **Notor:** 676
Buckhouse, Louis. *See* Buchalter, Louis
Buckingham, first duke of (George Villiers, 1592-1628), **17th:** 18, 96-99, 132, 143, 158, 166, 177, 364, 368, 414, 496, 552, 650, 767, 884; **Notor:** 352
Buckingham, second duke of (George Villiers, 1628-1687), **17th:** 149, 241, 506, 816, 839
Buckingham Palace, **19th:** 1644
Buckley, William F., Jr., **20th:** 561-563
Bucktails, **19th:** 514
Bucolics. See *Eclogues* (Vergil)
Bucolicum carmen. See *Eclogues* (Petrarch)
Buczacz, Peace of (1672), **17th:** 429
Budd, Grace, **Notor:** 355-356
Buddenbrooks (Mann), **20th:** 2595
Buddha, **Anc:** 49, 131, 160, 169-171, 345
Buddha Dainichi, **MA:** 1040
Buddhabhadra, **Anc:** 346
Buddhacarita (Aśvaghosa), **Anc:** 130
Buddhism, **Anc:** 355, 930, 933; Buddha as god, 160; China, 345, 975; Christianity and, 130; Daoism and, 502, 504; Empedocles and, 296; Hīnayāna, 931, 934; Hinduism and, 171; India, 131, 345; Kushūns and, 500; Mādhyamaka, 112; Mahāyāna, 111, 130; Menander and, 550; patriarchs, 160; philosophy of, 111; Sarvāstivāda, 500, 930; scriptures, 169; Skepticism and, 723; Theravāda, 898, 931, 934; Vaibhāśika, 930; Vijñānavāda, 931; Yogācāra, 111, 930; Zen, 130, 160, 504, 932; **MA:** 1136, 1159; China, 970, 996, 1085, 1128; India, 461, 926; Japan, 620, 623, 940, 975; Korea, 1083; Lotus sect, 758; Mongols, 627; Nichiren, 758; nuns, 772; Sŏn, 1083; Tendai sect, 581; **Ren:** 733; **17th:** Lamaism, 2; Zen, 868, 998; **18th:** 450-452; China, 1114; Thailand, 969; Zen, 450; **20th:**. artistic inspiration, 2637, 3610; Tibet, 903; Zen, 2981. *See also* Esoteric Buddhism; Hīnayāna Buddhism; Pure Land Buddhism; Shingon Buddhism; Tendai sect; Zen Buddhism
Buddhist Council, First (383 B.C.E.), **Anc:** 50
Buddhist Council, Fourth (first century C.E.), **Anc:** 500
Buddhist Records of the Western World (Xuanzang), **MA:** 1138
Budge, Don, 3217
Budh Singh. *See* Ranjit Singh
Budushchaia voina. See *Future of War, in Its Technical, Economic, and Political Relations, The*
Buel, James William, **Notor:** 1119
Buell, Sarah Josepha. *See* Hale, Sarah Josepha
Buen Retiro, **17th:** 954
Buena Vista, Battle of (1847), **19th:** 612, 1991, 2232
Bufera e altro, La. See *Storm, and Other Poems, The*
Buffalo Bill. *See* Cody, William
Buffalo Bill's Wild West Show, **19th:** 388, 524, 1692, 2110
Buffalo hunting, **19th:** 524
Buffett, Warren, **20th:** 563-565
Buffon, comte de, **18th:** 171-173
Buffoons, War of the, **18th:** 827
Bugaku Dancers (Sōtatsu), **17th:** 869
Bugeaud, Thomas Robert, **19th:** 2
Bugliosi, Vincent, **Notor:** 691
Buhari, Muhammadu, **Notor:** 1
Building a Character (Stanislavsky), **20th:** 3822
Buke hyakunin isshu (Moronobu), **17th:** 376
Bukhara, **MA:** 683
Bukharin, Nikolay Ivanovich, **20th:** 566-568; **Notor:** 314, 991, 1080
Bulfinch, Charles, **19th:** 346-349
Bulfinch, Thomas, **19th:** 346
Bulgakov, Alexis, **20th:** 985
Bulgar Slayer. *See* Basil II
Bulgaria, **MA:** 105, 189, 296, 550, 794, 957; Christianity, 189, 767; czars, 191. *See also* Geographical Index
Bulgarian massacres (1876), **19th:** 669
Bulgars, **MA:** 106, 1021, 1060; Volga, 87, 1068. *See also* Bulgaria
Bulkeley, Peter, **17th:** 386
Bull, John, **Ren:** 150; **17th:** 310
Bull Bear, **19th:** 1872
Bull Run, Battle of. *See* Manassas, First Battle of (1861)
Bullard, Margie. *See* Barfield, Velma Margie
Buller, Charles, **19th:** 709
Buller, Redvers, **20th:** 440
Bullinger, Heinrich, **Ren:** 1013
Bullock, Fanny. *See* Workman, Fanny Bullock
Bülow, Adam Heinrich Dietrich von, **19th:** 500
Bülow, Bernhard von, **19th:** 1121; **20th:** 569-572, 1181
Bülow, Hans von, **20th:** 3885
Bultmann, Rudolf, **20th:** 572-574
Bulwark, The (Dreiser), **20th:** 1035
Bulwer-Lytton, Edward, **19th:** 982; **Notor:** 31
Bunche, Ralph, **20th:** 180, 574-577
Bundy, Ted, **Notor:** 149-151, 879
Bung Karno, Bapak. *See* Sukarno

Bunker Hill, Battle of (1775), **18th:** 511, 1043
Bunner Sisters, The (Wharton), **20th:** 4302
Bunsen, Robert, **19th:** 996
Buntline, Ned, **19th:** 524
Buñuel, Luis, **20th:** 578-580, 905; **Notor:** 927
Bunyan, John, **17th:** 100-103; **19th:** 1282
Buonarroti, Michelangelo. *See* Michelangelo
Buoncompagni, Ugo. *See* Gregory XIII
Buono, Angelo, Jr., **Notor:** 95, 151-152
Burbage, Cuthbert, **17th:** 104
Burbage, James, **17th:** 104
Burbage, Richard, **17th:** 104-106, 279, 441
Burbank, Luther, **19th:** 350-353
Burbank plum, **19th:** 351
Burbank potato, **19th:** 350
Burbidge, Geoffrey, **20th:** 60
Burchard, Johannes, **Ren:** 117; **Notor:** 15, 130
Burckhardt, Jacob, **19th:** 354-356
Burdach, Karl Friedrich, **19th:** 114
Bureaucracy, **Anc:** Chinese, 958; Roman, 219
Burfield, Lana. *See* Hazzard, Linda Burfield
Burger, Warren E., **20th:** 382, 581-584
Burgers, Thomas, **19th:** 1299
Burgess, Guy, **Notor:** 109, 152-153, 164, 674, 836
Burgess, W. Starling, **20th:** 1366, 4406
Burgh, Hubert de, **MA:** 211-214
Burghley, first Baron. *See* Cecil, William
Burghley, Lord. *See* Cecil, William
Burgraves, The (Hugo), **19th:** 1148
Burgundians, **Anc:** 351
Burgundy, **MA:** 488; historiography, 1060; **Ren:** 217, 224, 574, 631; Habsburg control of, 646
Burgundy, Mary of. *See* Mary of Burgundy
Burial at Ornans, The (Courbet), **19th:** 559
Burial Mound (Ibsen), **19th:** 1165
Burial of the Count of Orgaz, The (El Greco), **Ren:** 391
Buridan, Jean, **MA:** 215-218, 761
Burke, Edmund, **18th:** 174-177, 425, 812, 1109; conservatism, 174; pamphlet wars, 621
Burke, Jimmy, **Notor:** 465
Burke, John, **19th:** 524
Burke, Martha Jane. *See* Calamity Jane
Burke, Thomas Henry, **Notor:** 509
Burke, William, **Notor:** 154-155
Burks, Charlotte, **Notor:** 655
Burks, Tommy, **Notor:** 654
Burlador de Sevilla, El. See *Love Rogue, The*
Burma, **18th:** 29, 817; conflicts with Siam, 968; **19th:** British rule, 596; **20th:** human rights, 176; independence of, 3986; World War II, 3759. *See also* Geographical Index
Burmese-British treaty, **18th:** 30
Burmese Days (Orwell), **20th:** 3081
Burmese War, Second (1851), **19th:** 596
Burnand, F. C., **19th:** 918
Burne-Jones, Edward, **19th:** 1606
Burnell, Jocelyn, **20th:** 584-586
Burnet, Sir Macfarlane, **20th:** 587-590
Burnet, Thomas, **17th:** 106-108
Burnett, Frances Hodgson, **19th:** 357-360
Burney, Charles, **18th:** 177-180
Burney, Fanny, **18th:** 177, 180-183, 235
Burnham, Daniel Hudson, **19th:** 360-363
Burns, Anthony, **19th:** 1737
Burns, Robert, **18th:** 183-187
Burns, William J., **Notor:** 713
Burnside, Ambrose, **19th:** 1199
Burnt-out Paper Rolls (Sutherland), **20th:** 3921
Burr, Aaron, **18th:** 530; duel with Alexander Hamilton, 455; **19th:** 363-367, 503, 512, 1794; duel with Alexander Hamilton, 365; trial of, 1500; **Notor:** 155-157, 1104
Burroughs, Edgar Rice, **20th:** 590-593
Burrus, Sextus Afranius, **Anc:** 591, 767
Burton, Dick, **Notor:** 1060
Burton, Richard (actor), **20th:** 3954
Burton, Sir Richard Francis (explorer), **19th:** 368-371, 2124; on Brigham Young, 2476
Burton, Robert, **17th:** 108-110
Bus Stop (film), **20th:** 2798
Buscón, El. See *Life and Adventures of Buscon, the Witty Spaniard, The*
Bush, George H. W., **20th:** 594-597, 784, 3322, 4434
Bush, George W., **20th:** 594, 596, 786, 1539, 1980, 3323, 3795; Florida recount, 3022, 3408; Texas governorship, 3437; **Notor:** 457, 619, 646, 759
Bush v. Gore (2000), **20th:** 3022, 3408
Bushidō, **17th:** 998
Bushnell, Ben, **Notor:** 411
Business. *See* Category Index
Busnoys, Antoine, **Ren:** 516
Busoni, Ferruccio, **20th:** 4273
Buss, Frances Mary, **19th:** 159
Bussy d'Ambois (Chapman), **Ren:** 215
Bustamante, Anastasio, **19th:** 1991
Bustamente y Rivero, José Luis, **20th:** 1718
Bustan. See *Orchard, The*
Busza, Treaty of (1617), **17th:** 855
Butcher, the. *See* Ta Mok

Butcher of Africa. *See* Amin, Idi
Butcher of Amritsar. *See* Dyer, Reginald
Butcher of Elmendorf. *See* Ball, Joe
Butcher of Lyon. *See* Barbie, Klaus
Butcher of Prague. *See* Heydrich, Reinhard
Buthos, **Anc:** 918
Butler, Benjamin, **19th:** 147; New Orleans, 764
Butler, Frances Anne. *See* Kemble, Fanny
Butler, Frank, **19th:** 1692
Butler, James. *See* Ormond, first duke of
Butler, Joseph, **18th:** 187-189; **19th:** 1576
Butler, Josephine, **19th:** 371-373, 767
Butler, Nicholas Murray, **20th:** 597-601
Butler, Pierce Mease, **19th:** 1268
Butler, R. A., **20th:** 602-605
Butler, Richard Girnt, **Notor:** 157-158
Butler, Samuel, **19th:** 374-376
Butt, Der. See *Flounder, The*
Buttafuoco, Joey, **Notor:** 159-160
Buttafuoco, Mary Jo, **Notor:** 159
Butte, Battle of (1877), **19th:** 568
Butter Battle Book, The (Seuss), **20th:** 3712
Butterfield 8 (film), **20th:** 3954
Butters, Mary, **Notor:** 160-162
Butzer, Martin. *See* Bucer, Martin
Buxton, Angela, **20th:** 1475
Buxton, Sir Thomas Fowell, **19th:** 376-379, 574, 840
Buxton Report, **19th:** 378
Buyids, **MA:** 21, 775
By Jupiter (Rodgers and Hart), **20th:** 1693
By the Light of My Father's Smile (Walker), **20th:** 4198
By the Shores of Silver Lake (Wilder), **20th:** 4338
By Way of Sainte-Beuve (Proust), **20th:** 3343
Byck, Samuel Joseph, **Notor:** 162-163
Bye and Main Plots, **Ren:** 845; **17th:** 253
Bygmester Solness. See *Master Builder, The*
Byloe i Dumy. See *My Past and Thoughts*
Byōdōin Hōōdō, **MA:** 582
Byrd, Richard, **20th:** 85, 606-608
Byrd, William, **Ren:** 148-151, 701, 918; **17th:** 310
Byrhtnoth, **MA:** 363
Byrne, Frank, **Notor:** 509
Byrne, Joe, **Notor:** 563
Byrne, John J., **20th:**4297
Byron, Augusta Ada. *See* Lovelace, countess of
Byron, Joanne. *See* Shakur, Assata Olugbala
Byron, Lady. *See* Lovelace, countess of
Byron, Lord, **19th:** 56, 379-382, 636, 1256, 1420, 1995, 2088, 2093; *Childe Harold's Pilgrimage*, 56
Byzantine Empire, **Anc:** 282; **MA:** 298, 467, 613, 711, 1069; architecture, 602; Bulgarians, 190; Christianity, 549, 600; emperors, 135, 507, 550, 600, 1011; historiography, 865, 1020; Hungarians and, 105; law, 600, 864; law codes, 134; medicine, 814; Norman invasion of, 176; philosophy, 863; Seljuk Turks and, 72; Serbian invasion of, 958; trade, 135, 913. *See also* Geographical Index
Byzantium, **Anc:** 242. *See also* Constantinople

C

C Major Symphony (Schumann), **19th:** 2033
Cab Calloway Orchestra, **20th:** 1481
Cabal, **17th:** 507, 839
Cabaret (film), **20th:** 1292
Cabbages and Kings (Henry), **19th:** 1082
Cabeza de Vaca, Álvar Núñez, **Ren:** 152-155, 245, 903
Cabinet government, **18th:** British, 401, 404, 740, 772, 1037; United States, 1045
Cable News Network. *See* CNN
Cabot, John, **Ren:** 155-158, 159, 440
Cabot, Sebastian, **Ren:** 157, 159-160
Caboto, Giovanni. *See* Cabot, John
Caboto, Sebastiano. *See* Cabot, Sebastian
Cabral, Pedro Álvars, **Ren:** 366, 605, 971
Cabrilho, João Rodrigues. *See* Cabrillo, Juan Rodríguez
Cabrillo, Juan Rodríguez, **Ren:** 161-162
Cabrini, Frances Xavier, **19th:** 383-386
Cabrinovic, Nedjelko, **Notor:** 862
Caccia di Diana, La (Boccaccio), **MA:** 170
Caccini, Francesca, **17th:** 111-112
Cachucha (Barre), **19th:** 744
Cadamosto, Alvise, **MA:** 479
Cadmus et Hermione (Lully and Quinault), **17th:** 570
Caduta degli Dei, La. See *Damned, The*
Cady, Elizabeth. *See* Stanton, Elizabeth Cady
Caecilius Statius, **Anc:** 850
Cædmon, **MA:** 219-221, 510
Caedwalla, **MA:** 938
Caenis, **Anc:** 943
Caepia Brutus, Quintus. *See* Brutus, Marcus Junius
Caepio, Quintus Servilius, **Notor:** 146
Caepionis, Servilia, **Notor:** 146
Caesalpinus, Andreas. *See* Cesalpino, Andrea
Caesar, Julius, **Anc:** 20, 73, 145, 166, 172-175, 185, 189, 198,

212, 230, 403, 682, 742, 815, 828, 927, 935; **Notor:** 146, 189
Caesar and Cleopatra (Shaw), **20th:** 3718
Caesarea, **Anc:** 405
Caesarea, Council of (314), **Anc:** 797
Caesarion, **Anc:** 230
Caesarism, **Anc:** 175
Caesaropapism, **MA:** 190, 244, 985
Caetani, Benedict. *See* Boniface VIII
Café de l'Europe, **18th:** 267
Cage, John, **20th:** 454, 886
Cagney, James, **Notor:** 804
Cagnolo, Niccolò, **Notor:** 130
Cahena, el-. *See* Kāhina, Damia al-
Cahier d'un retour au pays natal. See *Return to My Native Land*
Cahier noir, Le. See *Black Notebook, The*
Cahiers. See *Notebooks*
Cahiers, Les (Valéry), **20th:** 4137
Cahiers d'André Walter, Les. See *Notebooks of André Walter, The*
Cahiers de jeunesse (Renan), **19th:** 1885
Cai Ao, **20th:** 4465
Caillat, Guy de. *See* Guy de Chauliac
Cailliau, Robert, **20th:** 331
Câinele roșu. *See* Antonescu, Ion
Cairncross, John, **Notor:** 109, 164-165
Cairo Agreement (1969), **20th:** 111
Cajetan, Thomas, **Ren:** 582
Calais, Siege of (1346), **MA:** 308
Calais Pier (Turner), **19th:** 2323
Calamity Jane, **19th:** 386-389
Calculating machines, **17th:** France, 713; Germany, 514, 818, 819; Japan, 832; **19th:** 108
Calculus, **17th:** England, 679, 970; France, 271; Germany, 515; Italy, 922; Japan, 832; Scotland, 319; Switzerland, 48. *See also* Agnesi, Maria Gaetana; Alembert, Jean le Rond d'; Châtelet, marquise du; Euler, Leonhard; Lagrange, Joseph-Louis; Maclaurin, Colin; Monge, Gaspard
Calcutta, India, **18th:** 260, 469
Calder, Alexander, **20th:** 609-611
Calderón, Pedro, **Notor:** 130
Calderón Bridge, Battle of (1811), **19th:** 1095
Calderón de la Barca, Fanny, **19th:** 389-391
Calderón de la Barca, Pedro, **17th:** 113-116, 210, 740, 914, 950
Caldwell, Erskine, **20th:** 462
Caledonian Canal, **19th:** 2242
Calendar of 558 names, **19th:** 1046
Calendars, **Anc:** agricultural, 416, 816; astronomical, 579; Chinese, 783; Julian, 174, 816; Roman, 815; **MA:** Church, 313; Persian solar, 796; **Ren:** Gregorian, 394; Julian, 394; **18th:** 1039. *See also* Gregory XIII
Calgacus, **Anc:** 19
Calhoun, John C., **19th:** 392-396, 849
Caliari, Paolo. *See* Veronese, Paolo
Caliban (Renan), **19th:** 1887
Calichough. *See* Kalicho
Calico Act (1774), **18th:** 56
Calico Jack. *See* Rackham, John
California, **18th:** Spanish expeditions to, 394-396; Spanish possession, 228; **19th:** exploration of, 428, 832; gold rush, 429, 2100, 2132
California and Oregon Trail, The (Parkman), **19th:** 1743
California Institute of Technology, **20th:** 2751
Caligula, **Anc:** 17, 23, 72, 176-179, 217, 510, 591, 640, 766, 890; **Notor:** 165-167, 195, 458, 777
Caligula (Camus), **20th:** 628
Caliphs, **MA:** ʿAbbāsid, 469; Almohads, 7; Orthodox, 1038; Umayyad, 4, 10
Calixtus. *See* Callistus
Call Me Madam (Berlin), **20th:** 329
Call of the Snowy Hispar, The (Workman and Workman), **19th:** 2468
Call of the Toad, The (Grass), **20th:** 1575
Call of the Wild (film), **20th:** 1369
Call of the Wild, The (novel by London), **20th:** 2421
Callas, Maria, **20th:** 612-614
Calles, Plutarco Elías, **20th:** 615-618, 648, 3016
Calley, William, **Notor:** 168-170
Callicho. *See* Kalicho
Calligrammes (Apollinaire), **20th:** 106
Calligraphy, **Anc:** China, 956, 975; **MA:** China, 718; Japan, 621; **17th:** Japan, 696, 868
Callimachus, **Anc:** 158, 179-181, 196, 314
Callimachus (Hrosvitha), **MA:** 518
Calling of Saint Matthew, The (Caravaggio), **Ren:** 171
Calling Youth to Christ (Graham), **20th:** 1558
Callisthenes, **Anc:** 872
Callistratus, **Anc:** 264
Callistus, **Anc:** 425
Callistus III, **Notor:** 14
Callot, Jacques, **17th:** 116-119
Calloway, Cab, **20th:** 1481
Calm Down Mother (Terry), **20th:** 3983
Calmette, Albert, **20th:** 618-621
Cālukya Dynasty, **MA:** 461
Calumet Building, **19th:** 361
Calvert, Cecilius, **17th:** 92, 120
Calvert, George, **17th:** 92, 119-121
Calvetti, Olimpio, **Notor:** 192

Calvi, Roberto, **Notor:** 170-171
Calvin, John, **Ren:** 144, 163-166, 462, 529, 584, 618, 862. *See also* Calvinism; Luther, Martin; Menno Simons; Protestantism; Reformation; Zwingli, Huldrych
Calvin, Melvin, **20th:** 621-623
Calvin cycle, **20th:** 622
Calvini, Gian Roberto. *See* Calvi, Roberto
Calvinism, **Ren:** doctrines, 164; England, 762; France, 462, 817; Germany, 651; Netherlands, 60; Scotland, 529; **17th:** 327, 495; **18th:** 33, 75, 314, 382, 1074
Calzabigi, Raniero, **18th:** 419
Cam Cong, **Ren:** 547
Cambacérès, Jean-Jacques-Régis de, **19th:** 396-399
Cambiale di matrimonio, La (Rossini), **19th:** 1944
Cambio 90-Nueva Mayoría, **20th:** 1359
Cambodia. *See* Geographical Index
Cambrai, League of, **Ren:** 519, 613, 648
Cambrai, Treaty of (1529), **Ren:** 411, 614, 997
Cambrai, War of the League of (1508-1509), **Ren:** 84
Cambyses I, **Anc:** 248
Cambyses II, **Anc:** 136, 251
Cambyses III, **Notor:** 850
Camera, motion picture, **19th:** 732
Camera obscura, **19th:** 1676
Cameron, Richard, **17th:** 121-124
Cameron, Simon, **19th:** 1336; **Notor:** 171-173
Cameron, Vernon Lovett, **19th:** 2278
Cameron's Covenant, **17th:** 123
Camilla (Burney), **18th:** 182
Camille (film), **20th:** 1393
Camillus, Marcus Furius, **Anc:** 512, 833
Camino de perfección, El. See *Way of Perfection, The*
Camões, Luís de, **Ren:** 167-170
Camp David Accords (1979), **20th:** 668, 3359, 3588
Campagnes Océanographiques Françaises, **20th:** 851
Campaign, The (Addison), **18th:** 20
Campaldino, Battle of (1289), **MA:** 301
Campanella, Tommaso, **17th:** 65, 124-126, 629, 723
Campbell, Alexander, **19th:** 399-402; Mark Twain, 401
Campbell, Archibald, **17th:** 147, 655
Campbell, Colin, **19th:** 1719
Campbell, John. *See* Argyll, second duke of
Campbell, Judith. *See* Exner, Judith Campbell
Campbell, Kim, **20th:** 624-627, 762, 2868
Campbell, Robert. *See* Rob Roy
Campbell and Cowall, earl of. *See* Argyll, second duke of
Campbell-Bannerman, Sir Henry, **20th:** 149, 1588
Campbell's Soup Can (Warhol), **20th:** 4227
Campeggio, **Ren:** 189
Camperdown, Battle of (1797), **18th:** 128
Campi, Bernardino, **Ren:** 46
Campini, Giuseppe, **17th:** 134
Campion, Edmund, **Ren:** 149, 200
Campion, Thomas, **17th:** 127-129
Cámpora, Hector, **20th:** 3207
Camus, Albert, **20th:** 628-631, 3639
Can Such Things Be? (Bierce), **19th:** 230
Can You Forgive Her? (Trollope), **19th:** 2301
Canaan, **Anc:** Abraham and, 4; Jewish settlement, 258
Canada, **17th:** colonization, 141, 499; education, 500; **18th:** British colonialism, 196; British forces, 39; exploration of, 629; French colonialism, 196; French forces, 39; government, 197; Indians, 160, 974; **19th:** Dominion of, 1443, 2316; relations with Britain, 709; unification of, 317. *See also* Geographical Index
Canadian Crusoes (Traill), **19th:** 2292
Canadian Freeman, **19th:** 1456
Canadian Pacific Railway Company, **19th:** 2317
Canadian Space Agency, **20th:** 1413
Canadian Wildflowers (Traill), **19th:** 2292
Canaletto, **18th:** 190-193
Canali, Isabella. *See* Andreini, Isabella
Canals, **18th:** England, 162-165, 1058; United States, 706; **19th:** Caledonian Canal, 2242; Ellesmere Canal, 2241; engineering, 846; Erie Canal, 514; Gotha Canal, 2242; Panama Canal, 580, 1055, 1357; Suez Canal, 1357
Cancer, **20th:** radiation therapy, 3537; research, 1022, 3157, 3545, 4145
Cancer and Vitamin C (Pauling), **20th:** 3157
Cancer Ward (Solzhenitsyn), **20th:** 3784
Canciones, 1921-1924. See *Songs*
Candela, Felix, **20th:** 631-634
Candida (Shaw), **20th:** 3718
Candide (Bernstein et al.), **20th:** 339
Candide (Voltaire), **18th:** 1026
Candish, Thomas. *See* Cavendish, Thomas
Candolle, Alphonse de, **19th:** 861
Candra Gupta. *See* Chandragupta Maurya
Cannae, Battle of (216 B.C.E.), **Anc:** 190, 343, 383, 758

Cannary, Martha Jane. *See* Calamity Jane
Cannery Row (Steinbeck), **20th:** 3850
Cannibals and Christians (Mailer), **20th:** 2564
Cannibals and Missionaries (McCarthy), **20th:** 2502
Canning, Charles, **19th:** 1718
Canning, George, **19th:** 377, 403-405, 439, 892, 1398, 1534, 2409, 2446
Cannizzaro, Stanislao, **19th:** 103
Cannon, Annie Jump, **20th:** 635-638, 2317
Cannon, Billy, **Notor:** 173-174
Cannon manufacturing, **18th:** 1088
Cano, Alonso, **17th:** 1003
Cano, Juan Sebastián del. *See* Elcano, Juan Sebastián de
Canon (Polyclitus), **Anc:** 676
Canon in D (Pachelbel), **17th:** 709
Canon law, **Anc:** 796
Canon Masudicus (al-Bīrūnī), **MA:** 164
Canon of Medicine (Avicenna), **MA:** 124
Canonchet, **17th:** 634
Canonicus, **17th:** 129-131, 613
Canonization, **18th:** of Junípero Serra, 892; study of, 102
"Canonization, The" (Donne), **17th:** 231
Canova, Antonio, **19th:** 406-409
Cantar de mío Cid, El. See *Poem of the Cid, The*
Cantatas, **18th:** Johann Sebastian Bach, 73; George Frideric Handel, 463; Alessandro Scarlatti, 884
Cantate, ariette, e duetti (Strozzi), **17th:** 888
Cantatrice chauve, La. See *Bald Soprano, The*
Canterbury Tales, The (Chaucer), **MA:** 265
Cántico espiritual. See *Spiritual Canticle of the Soul, A*
Cantiere Internazionale d'Arte, **20th:** 1764
Cantiones, quae ab argumento sacrae vocantur (Byrd and Tallis), **Ren:** 149
Cantiones sacrae (Byrd and Tallis), **Ren:** 149, 918
Cantique des cantiques de Salomon, Le. See *Song of Songs of Solomon, The*
Cantiques spirituels (Racine), **17th:** 775
Canto a la Argentina, oda a Mitre, y otros poemas (Darío), **19th:** 602
Canto épico a las glorias de Chile (Darío), **19th:** 601
Canto errante, El (Darío), **19th:** 602
Canto general (Neruda), **20th:** 2938
Cantor, Georg, **19th:** 630
Cantos de vida y esperanza (Darío), **19th:** 602
Cantwell, Lloyd. *See* Chambers, Whittaker
Canudo, Ricciotto, **20th:** 1382
Canute I the Great, **MA:** 221-225, 337, 363, 457, 786
Canute VI, **MA:** 837, 1047
Canutt, Yakima, **20th:** 4250
Canyons of the Colorado (Powell), **19th:** 1829
Canzoni e sonate (Gabrieli), **Ren:** 363
Canzoniere. See *Rhymes*
Cão, Diogo, **Ren:** 286, 511
Cao Cao, **Anc:** 182-184
Cao Xueqin, **18th:** 194-196
Cao Zhan. *See* Cao Xueqin
Caonabo, **Ren:** 409
Cap de Bonne-Espérance, Le (Cocteau), **20th:** 794
Cape-and-sword plays, **17th:** 950
Cape Cod (Thoreau), **19th:** 2275
Cape Cod Evening (Hopper), **20th:** 1877
Čapek, Karel, **20th:** 638-640
Capel, Arthur "Boy," **20th:** 728
Capet, Louis. *See* Louis XVI
Capetian kings of France, **MA:** 168, 668, 840
Capetians, **MA:** 166, 837, 839
Capital. See *Kapital, Das*
Capital of Pain (Éluard), **20th:** 1152
Capital punishment, **Anc:** 294; **20th:** 914; legality of, 383, 508, 3326; New York State, 3480
Capitale de la douleur. See *Capital of Pain*
Capitalism, **18th:** 341; François Quesnay, 821; **19th:** 1897; **20th:** 335, 4155; Chile, 3258; collapse of, 2484; freedom, 1334; Vladimir Ilich Lenin, 2343; Protestant ethic, 4260; United States, 1375
Capitalism and Freedom (Friedman), **20th:** 1334
Capito, Wolfgang, **Ren:** 143
Capitol Building (U.S.), **19th:** 1326
Capitulation of Montreal (1760), **18th:** 40, 385, 694
Capo di Tutti Capi. *See* Gambino, Carlo; Maranzano, Salvatore
Capodistrias, John, **19th:** 2479
Capone, Al, **20th:** 641-644; **Notor:** 175-177, 752, 774, 804, 1096
Capote, Truman, **20th:** 644-647
Cappadocian Fathers, **Anc:** 365
Cappella del Sacramento, **MA:** 85
Capriccio (Brahms), **19th:** 298
Capriccio espagnol (Rimsky-Korsakov), **19th:** 1915
Caprices, The (Callot), **17th:** 117
Caprices, The (Goya), **18th:** 438
Captain, The (Beaumont and Fletcher), **Ren:** 94
Captain Dampier's Vindication of His Voyage to the South Seas in the Ship St. George (Campier), **17th:** 216
Captains Courageous (film), **20th:** 4066
Captains Courageous (novel by Kipling), **19th:** 1286

Captain's Daughter, The (Pushkin), **19th:** 1850
Captain's Verses, The (Neruda), **20th:** 2938
Captivity tales, **18th:** 975
Capuchins, **17th:** 720
Carabiniers, Les. See *Riflemen, The* (film)
Caracalla, **Anc:** 482, 484
Caractacus (Elgar), **20th:** 1134
Caractères, Les (La Bruyère), **17th:** 475
Caraffa, Gian Pietro, **Ren:** 769
Caraka, **Anc:** 501
Caratacus, **Anc:** 163
Caravaggio, **Ren:** 170-172
Caravans, trade and, **Anc:** 334
Carbon dioxide, **18th:** 116
Carbonaria, **19th:** 381, 1531
Carchemish, Battle of (605 B.C.E.), **Anc:** 582
Card Party, The (ballet), **20th:** 3890
Cardano, Gerolamo, **Ren:** 172-175, 920
Cárdenas, Lázaro, **20th:** 617, 647-650
Cardinal, The (Shirley), **17th:** 847
Cardinal Guido Bentivoglio (van Dyck), **17th:** 244
Cardinal Virtues, The (Andrea del Sarto), **Ren:** 39
Cardinal Virtues (Raphael), **Ren:** 820
Cardinals, College of, **MA:** 1044
Cardiology, **20th:** 3831
Cardoso, Fernando Henrique, **20th:** 651-653
Cardozo, Benjamin N., **20th:** 653-656
Cardsharps, The (Caravaggio), **Ren:** 170
Careless Husband, The (Oldfield), **18th:** 749
Carew, Thomas, **17th:** 503
Carey, Harry, Jr., **20th:** 4251
Carey, Harry, Sr., **20th:** 4251
Carey, James, **Notor:** 509
Carey, William, **19th:** 409-412
Cargill, Donald, **17th:** 122
Caribs, **Ren:** 408, 805. *See also* Guacanagarí; Ponce de León, Juan
Carissimi, Giacomo, **Ren:** 363
Caritat, Marie-Jean-Antoine-Nicolas. *See* Condorcet, marquis de
Carleton, Sir Guy, **18th:** 196-199
Carleton, James H., **19th:** 429
Carlist Wars (1833-1840, 1846-1848, 1872-1876), **19th:** 413, 414
Carlists, **19th:** 1183
Carloman, **MA:** 242
Carlos II. *See* Charles II (1661-1700; king of Spain)
Carlos VI, **19th:** 114
Carlos VII, **19th:** 414, 1183
Carlos, Don, **19th:** 412-415
Carlos Luis. *See* Carlos VI
Carlos the Jackal. *See* Ramírez Sánchez, Ilich
Carlotta of Aragon, **Notor:** 128
Carlowitz, Treaty of. *See* Karlowitz, Treaty of
Carlson, Chester F., **20th:** 657-659
Carlstadt, Andreas, **Ren:** 665
Carlyle, Jane, **Notor:** 976
Carlyle, Thomas, **19th:** 415-418, 746
Carmarthen, marquis of. *See* Leeds, first duke of
Carmelites, **MA:** 1053; **Ren:** 4, 507, 929; Calced, 507; Discalced, 507, 670, 929; Reformed, 4
Carmen (Bizet), **19th:** 242
Carmen (Mérimée), **19th:** 242
Carmen de vita sua (Gregory of Nazianzus), **Anc:** 361
Carmen Deo Nostro (Crashaw), **17th:** 203
Carmen Saeculare (Horace), **Anc:** 432
Carmontelle, Louis Carrogis de, **18th:** 296
Carnap, Rudolf, **20th:** 659-662
Carnatic Wars (1746-1754), **18th:** 259, 312
Carnation Revolution (1974), **20th:** 3607
Carnegie, Andrew, **19th:** 419-422, 651, 1601; **20th:** 598; **Notor:** 194
Carnegie Corporation, **19th:** 421
Carnegie Corporation Survey of the Negro in America, **20th:** 575
Carnegie Endowment for International Peace, **20th:** 598
Carnegie Foundation for the Advancement of Teaching, **19th:** 421
Carnegie Institution, **19th:** 421
Carnegie-Mellon University, **19th:** 421
Carnegie Steel Company, **19th:** 420
Carnival, The (Homer), **19th:** 1125
Carnival Evening (Rousseau), **19th:** 1953
Carnival of the Animals, The (Saint-Saëns), **20th:** 3600
Carnmoney witch. *See* Butters, Mary
Carnot, Lazare, **18th:** 200-202
Carnot, Marie-François Sadi, **Notor:** 180
Carnot, Sadi, **19th:** 663, 1339
Carnot cycle, **19th:** 663
Caro, Joseph. *See* Karo, Joseph ben Ephraim
Carol II, **Notor:** 25
Caroline (1683-1737; queen of Great Britain and Ireland), **18th:** 203-205, 360
Caroline (1768-1821; queen consort of King George IV of Great Britain), **19th:** 313, 404, 518, 892, 979, 1398
Caroline Mathilde (queen of Denmark), **Notor:** 208
Carolingian Empire, **MA:** 245, 252, 516, 662, 664, 871
Carolingian Renaissance, **MA:** 244
Carolla, Sam, **Notor:** 698
Carolus Magnus. *See* Charlemagne

Carolus Martellus. *See* Charles Martel
Caron, Pierre-Augustin. *See* Beaumarchais, Pierre-Augustin Caron de
Carousal, The. See *Symposion* (Lucian)
Carousel (Rodgers and Hammerstein), **20th:** 1659, 3487
Carpentier, Georges, **20th:** 966
Carpini, Giovanni da Pian del, **MA:** 226-229, 955
Carpio, Lope de Vega. *See* Vega Carpio, Lope de
Carr, George, **17th:** 221
Carr, Robert, **17th:** 16, 131-133, 414
Carracci, Agostino, **Ren:** 175-178
Carracci, Annibale, **Ren:** 171, 175-178
Carracci, Ludovico, **Ren:** 175-178, 338
Carranza, Venustiano, **20th:** 615, 647, 3014, 4161, 4365, 4449; **Notor:** 1070, 1130
Carré (Stockhausen), **20th:** 3874
Carrel, Alexis, **20th:** 2395
Carrera, José, **19th:** 1703
Carrie (film), **20th:** 3042
Carrie (novel by King), **20th:** 2152
Carried Away (Munro), **20th:** 2874
Carrillo, Alfonso, **Ren:** 328, 503
Carrillo, Joaquín. *See* Murieta, Joaquín
Carrington, Henry B., **19th:** 567
Carroll, Charles, **18th:** 205-208
Carroll, James, **19th:** 1878
Carroll, John, **18th:** 795
Carroll, Lewis, **19th:** 423-426
Carson, Kit, **19th:** 426-430, 831, 1092
Carson, Rachel, **20th:** 662-665
Carta al serenísimo Luis XIII (Quevedo y Villegas), **17th:** 771
Carta atenagórica (Cruz), **17th:** 209
Carta de Jamaica. See *Jamaica Letter, The*
Cartagena, Juan de, **Ren:** 592
Carte, Richard D'Oyly, **19th:** 919
Carter, Henry Rose, **19th:** 1879
Carter, Howard, **Anc:** 909
Carter, Jimmy, **20th:** 666-671, 783, 1016, 1277, 3057, 3592; Panama, 4049; **Notor:** 471, 608, 644, 1000
Carthage, **Anc:** destruction of, 756; Numidia and, 542; Rome and, 191, 342, 373, 382, 542, 738, 813; trade and, 385; Vandals and, 353
Carthage, Battle of (533), **MA:** 600
Carthaginian Peace, **Anc:** 384
Carthusians, **MA:** 1043
Cartier, George Étienne, **19th:** 1442
Cartier, Jacques, **Ren:** 178-181
Cartier-Bresson, Henri, **20th:** 671-674
Cartimandua, **Anc:** 163
Carto, Willis A., **Notor:** 177-178, 838
Cartography, **Anc:** Alexandrian, 315; astronomical, 418; Greek, 55; **Ren:** 160, 678, 827, 971; Flanders, 679; North America, 159, 180. *See also* Category Index
Cartoon Network, **20th:** 4120
Cartouche, **Notor:** 178-179
Cartwright, Thomas, **Ren:** 762
Cartwright, William, **17th:** 443, 503
Carus, **Anc:** 280
Caruso, Enrico, **20th:** 675-677, 4051
Carvalho e Mello, Sebastião José de. *See* Pombal, marquês de
Carver, Bill, **Notor:** 182
Carver, George Washington, **20th:** 678-680
Cary, Elizabeth Cabot. *See* Agassiz, Elizabeth Cabot
Cary, Mary Ann Shadd, **19th:** 431-433
Casa de Bernarda Alba, La. See *House of Bernarda Alba, The*
Casa Guidi Windows (Browning), **19th:** 326
Casablanca (film), **20th:** 322, 407
Casals, Pablo, **20th:** 681-684
Casals Festival, **20th:** 682
Casanova, **18th:** 208-211; arrest, 209
Casanova (film), **20th:** 1233
Casaubon, Isaac, **17th:** 281
Case-Book of Sherlock Holmes, The (Doyle), **19th:** 689
Case Is Altered, The (Jonson), **17th:** 440
Case of Sacco and Vanzetti, The (Frankfurter), **20th:** 1308
Case of the Velvet Claws, The (Gardner), **20th:** 1404
Casement, Roger, **Notor:** 633
Caserio, Sante Jeronimo, **Notor:** 180-181
Cases of Conscience Concerning Evil Spirits (Mather), **18th:** 673
Casimir I, **MA:** 637
Casimir III the Great, **MA:** 229-233, 1120
Cass Timberlane (Lewis), **20th:** 2366
Cassady, Neal, **20th:** 2114
Cassander, **Anc:** 63, 598, 720
Cassaria, La. See *Coffer, The*
Cassatt, Mary, **19th:** 433-436
Cassian, John, **Anc:** 947
Cassian, Saint, **MA:** 155
Cassiano del Pozzo, **17th:** 302, 307
Cassidy, Butch, **Notor:** 181-183, 651
Cassin, René, **20th:** 684-688
Cassini, Gian Domenico, **17th:** 134-136, 348
Cassiodorus, **Anc:** 139, 391; **MA:** 76, 233-235, 1015
Cassiodorus: Explanation of the Psalms (Cassiodorus), **MA:** 235
Cassirer, Ernst, **20th:** 688-690, 2264

Cassius, **Anc:** 146, 166, 174, 185-187, 568; **Notor:** 147
Cassius Dio. *See* Dio Cassius
Cassius Longinus. *See* Longinus, Cassius
Cassius Longinus, Gaius. *See* Cassius
Cassou, Louis. *See* Hory, Elmyr de
Castagno, Andrea del, **Ren:** 601
Caste system, Indian, **Anc:** 171, 204, 500
Castelfranco, Giorgio da. *See* Giorgione
Castelfranco, Zorzo de. *See* Giorgione
Castellano, Paul, **Notor:** 183-185, 397, 432, 435
Castelli, Benedetto, **17th:** 65, 921
Castelli, Francesco. *See* Borromini, Francesco
Castelnau, Michel de, **Ren:** 139
Castelnau, Noël de, **20th:** 2010
Castiglia, Francesco. *See* Costello, Frank
Castiglione, Baldassare, **Ren:** 181-183, 235, 383, 821
Castiglione, Giovanni, **17th:** 330
Castiglioni, Camillo, **20th:** 1746
Castigo sin venganza, El. See *Justice Without Revenge*
Castile, kings of, **MA:** 61
Castilian Days (Hay), **19th:** 1054
Castillo, Bernal Díaz de. *See* Díaz del Castillo, Bernal
Castillo, Ramón S., **20th:** 3205; **Notor:** 823
Castillo interior, El. See *Interior Castle, The*
Castle, The (Kafka), **20th:** 2068
Castle Dangerous (Scott), **19th:** 2049
Castle Howard, **18th:** 473, 1003
Castle in the Forest, The (Mailer), **20th:** 2565
Castle Rackrent (Edgeworth), **19th:** 729
Castlemaine, countess of, **17th:** 137
Castlereagh, Viscount, **19th:** 404, 437-441
Castner, Burton M., **20th:** 1466
Castro, Fidel, **20th:** 691-695, 1609; **Notor:** 73, 185-187, 308, 341, 406, 436, 605, 941-942, 1004
Castro, Thomas. *See* Orton, Arthur
Cat and Mouse (Grass), **20th:** 1574
Cat and Mouse Act of 1913, **20th:** 3104
Cat in the Hat, The (Seuss), **20th:** 3711
Cat on a Hot Tin Roof (film), **20th:** 3954
Catalan Anti-Artistic Manifesto, The. See *Manifest Groc*
Catalan Landscape (Miró), **20th:** 2760
Catalan uprising, **17th:** 425
Catalano, Marzio, **Notor:** 192
Catalaunian Plains, Battle of the (451), **Anc:** 140
Catalina. See *Catiline* (Ibsen)
Catalina of Aragon. *See* Catherine of Aragon
Catalogue de fleurs (Milhaud), **20th:** 2736
Catalogus Stellarum Australium (Halley), **17th:** 348
Catanei, Vannozza dei, **Notor:** 14
Catastrophe, The (Kerensky), **20th:** 2112
Catastrophism, **19th:** 587, 1424
Catch, Jack. *See* Ketch, Jack
Catcher in the Rye, The (Salinger), **20th:** 3609
Cateau-Cambrésis, Treaty of (1559), **Ren:** 32, 184, 228, 425, 654, 780, 993
Catechism of the Industrialists (Saint-Simon), **19th:** 1976
Categoriae (Aristotle), **Anc:** 688
Categorical imperative (Kant), **18th:** 550
Caterina Benincasa. *See* Catherine of Siena, Saint
Catesby, Robert, **Ren:** 326
Catharsis (Orozco), **20th:** 3070
Cathcart, Charles Murray, **19th:** 124
Cathedra Petri (Bernini), **17th:** 46
Cathedral of Pisa, **MA:** 848
Cathedral schools, **MA:** 400
Cather, Willa, **20th:** 696-700
Catherine II. *See* Catherine the Great
Catherine d'Angennes. *See* Rambouillet, marquise de
Catherine de Médicis, **Ren:** 184-187, 284, 423, 426, 429, 569, 627, 658, 663, 703, 729; **Notor:** 214, 800
Catherine of Aragon, **Ren:** 51, 111, 187-190, 230, 266, 270, 330, 335, 369, 439, 441, 639, 765, 868, 947
Catherine of Braganza, **17th:** 137-139, 148, 343, 654
Catherine of Cleves (Dumas), **19th:** 696
Catherine of Genoa, Saint, **Ren:** 191-192
Catherine of Siena, Saint, **MA:** 236-239; **Notor:** 1053
Catherine the Great, **18th:** 211-215, 778, 808, 814, 955, 1059; ascension, 755-758, 779; and Denis Diderot, 309; manifesto, 212; **Notor:** 516
Catherine Was Great (West), **20th:** 4298
Catherine Wheel, The (dance drama), **20th:** 3990
Cathode rays, study of, **20th:** 4007
Catholic Association, **19th:** 1696
Catholic Center Party (Germany), **20th:** 1180
Catholic Church. *See* Roman Catholic Church and Catholicism
Catholic Committee, Ireland, **18th:** 983
Catholic Concordance, The (Nicholas of Cusa), **Ren:** 725
Catholic emancipation, **18th:** 440-442; **19th:** 1697, 1769
Catholic Hour, The (radio program), **20th:** 3722

Catholic League, **Ren:** 426, 429; **17th:** 268, 293
Catholic missions. *See* Missions
Catholic Relief Act (1793), **18th:** 983
Catholic Revival. *See* Counter-Reformation
Catholic Social Studies Movement, **19th:** 1493
Catholic Telecommunications Network, **20th:** 91
Catholic Worker, The (newspaper), **20th:** 926
Catholic Worker movement, **20th:** 927
Catholicism. *See* Roman Catholic Church and Catholicism
Catholicon, **MA:** 443
Cathy of Heilbronn (Kleist), **19th:** 1290
Catilina, Lucius Sergius. *See* Catiline
Catiline, **Anc:** 188-190, 212, 233, 494, 742; **Notor:** 188-189
Catiline (Ibsen), **19th:** 1165
Catiline (Jonson), **17th:** 442
Catlin, George, **19th:** 232, 441-444
Cato maior de senectute (Cicero), **Anc:** 210
Cato Street Conspiracy, **19th:** 892
Cato the Censor, **Anc:** 190-194, 301, 759
Cato the Elder. *See* Cato the Censor
Cato the Younger, **Anc:** 194-196, 683, 743; **Notor:** 146, 189
Cato Uticensis. *See* Cato the Younger
Catriona (Stevenson), **19th:** 2175
Cats (Lloyd Webber and Eliot), **20th:** 1141, 2415
Cats, Jakob, **17th:** 824
Cat's Eye (Atwood), **20th:** 170
Catt, Carrie Chapman, **20th:** 23, 701-704
Catullus, **Anc:** 196-199, 233, 706, 835
Catulus, Quintus Lutatius, **Anc:** 534
Catus Decianus, **Anc:** 164
Caucasian Chalk Circle, The (Brecht), **20th:** 505
Cauchy, Augustin-Louis, **19th:** 11, 858
Cauldron, Battle of the (1942), **20th:** 3504
Cauliaco, Guy de. *See* Guy de Chauliac
Causa, La (farmworkers movement), **20th:** 739
Cause, Concept, and Prophylaxis of Childbed Fever, The (Semmelweis), **19th:** 2066
Cavalcade (Coward), **20th:** 855
Cavalcanti, Guido, **MA:** 239-241, 301
Cavalier poets, **17th:** 443, 563
Cavalieri, Bonaventura, **17th:** 922, 969
Cavalli, Francesco, **17th:** 888
Cavalry, **Anc:** Assyrian, 121; Greek, 306; Macedonian, 638; Roman, 759
Cave paintings, prehistoric, **20th:** 518
Cavelier, René-Robert. *See* La Salle, sieur de
Cavendish, Sir Charles, **17th:** 676
Cavendish, Frederick, **19th:** 926; **Notor:** 509
Cavendish, Georgiana, **18th:** 215-217
Cavendish, Henry, **18th:** 217-220, 683; chemistry of gases, 218; electricity, 219; hydrogen, 218; water, 219
Cavendish, Margaret. *See* Newcastle, duchess of
Cavendish, Spencer Compton, **19th:** 1749
Cavendish, Thomas, **Ren:** 193-195, 277
Cavendish, William (1505-1557; courtier of Henry VIII), **Ren:** 103
Cavendish, William (1592-1676; duke of Newcastle), **17th:** 262, 676
Cavendish Society, **18th:** 219
Caversham Entertainment, The (Campion), **17th:** 128
Caves du Vatican, Les. See *Lafcadio's Adventures*
Cavour, Count, **19th:** 444-447, 872, 1533, 1803
Caxton, William, **Ren:** 196-199, 598
Cayley, George, **19th:** 447-450
Cayor, **19th:** 757
Cayugas, **Ren:** 281, 448
CBS Evening News with Walter Cronkite (television news program), **20th:** 872
CCAR. *See* Central Conference of American Rabbis
CCXI Sociable Letters (Newcastle), **17th:** 677
Ceauşescu, Nicolae, **20th:** 704-706; **Notor:** 26, 190-191
Cecchina, La. *See* Caccini, Francesca
Cecil, John, **Notor:** 961
Cecil, Robert (1563-1612). *See* Salisbury, first earl of
Cecil, Robert (1830-1903). *See* Salisbury, third marquis of
Cecil, William, **Ren:** 199-202, 310, 762, 844; **17th:** 175
Cecilia (Burney), **18th:** 181
Cecora on the Pruth, Battle of (1620), **17th:** 855
Cédras, Raoul, **20th:** 126
Cela sans plus (Josquin), **Ren:** 516
Çelebî, Kâtib. *See* Kâtib Çelebî
Celeste, Maria. *See* Maria Celeste
Celestine I, **Anc:** 948
Celestine III, **MA:** 542
Celestine IV, **MA:** 545
Celestine V, **MA:** 187; **Notor:** 115
Celibacy, **Anc:** Christianity and, 600, 613; monasticism and, 862; **20th:** clerical, 3150
Cellini, Benvenuto, **Ren:** 202-206, 231, 654
Cellular Pathology as Based upon Physiological and Pathological Histology (Virchow), **19th:** 2366

Celsus, Aulus Cornelius, **Anc:** 199-202, 330
Celts, **Anc:** 99, 173, 756, 838, 935
Cem, **Ren:** 87, 660, 808
Cemal Paşa, Ahmed, **20th:** 1158, 1203
Cena de le Ceneri, La. See *Ash Wednesday Supper, The*
Cenabum, Battle of (52 B.C.E.), **Anc:** 936
Cenci, The (Shelley), **19th:** 2095
Cenci, Beatrice, **Notor:** 192-193
Cenci, Cristoforo, **Notor:** 192
Cenci, Francesco, **Notor:** 192
Cenerentola, La (Rossini), **19th:** 1945
Censorship, **18th:** China, 818; English theater, 347; France, 480; Japan, 980; Russia, 214; United States, 238; Voltaire, 1027; **20th:** 4231; Germany, 1515; Soviet Union, 1130; United States, 1033, 2690
120 journées de Sodome, Les. See *120 Days of Sodom, The*
Central African Republic. *See* Geographical Index
Central Committee to Convoke a General Congress of German Workers, **19th:** 1322
Central Conference of American Rabbis, **19th:** 2454
Central Design Bureau, **20th:** 4109
Central Hindu College, **19th:** 213
Central Hindu Girls' School, **19th:** 213
Central Intelligence Agency, **20th:** Cambodia, 3740; Chile, 73; Congo, 2477, 2774, 4093; covert activity, 1126; Cuba, 692, 2100; Dominican Republic, 4085; Egypt, 2914; Guatemala, 1609; Iran, 2780, 2846; Nicaragua, 3072; Vietnam, 2952
Central Pacific Railroad, **19th:** 2133
Central Park, **19th:** 1707
Centralists, **19th:** 99
Centre d'Études Marines Avancées, **20th:** 851
Centuries (Nostradamus), **Ren:** 729
Century (magazine), **19th:** 1332
Century of Dishonor (Jackson), **19th:** 1195
Cerco de Numancia, El. See *Siege of Numantia, The*
Cercylas, **Anc:** 750
Cerda, Ana de Mendoza y de la. *See* Mendoza y de la Cerda, Ana de
Cerdic, **Anc:** 396
Cerebellum as a Neuronal Machine, The (Eccles), **20th:** 1091
Cerebri anatome. See *Anatomy of the Brain, The*
Cérémonie des adieux, La. See *Adieux*
Ceremony of Carols (Britten), **20th:** 530
Cerf, Vinton Gray, **20th:** 707-709
Cermak, Anthony, **Notor:** 1128
Cervantes, Miguel de, **Ren:** 26, 206-211; **17th:** 738
Césaire, Aimé, **20th:** 709-713, 3703
Cesalpino, Andrea, **Ren:** 211-213
Cesari, Giuseppe, **Ren:** 170
Cespedes, Carlos Manuel, **19th:** 1503
Cet obscur objet du desir. See *That Obscure Object of Desire*
Cetshwayo, **19th:** 450-452, 1299
Cetywayo and His White Neighbours (Haggard), **19th:** 1006
Ceuta, capture of (1415), **MA:** 478
Cézanne (Fry), **20th:** 1353
Cézanne, Paul, **19th:** 453-456, 1800, 1889; **20th:** 493, 951, 2335
Chabrol, Charles, **Notor:** 604
Chacabuco, Battle of (1817), **19th:** 1704
Chaco War (1932-1935), **20th:** 3172
Chad, **20th:** 1077. *See also* Geographical Index
Chadwick, Cassie L., **Notor:** 193-194
Chadwick, Edwin, **19th:** 456-460
Chadwick, Sir James, **20th:** 443, 714-717, 1636, 2034, 3536
Chaerea, Cassius, **Notor:** 195-196
Chaeronea, Battle of (338 B.C.E.), **Anc:** 39, 266, 452, 523, 597, 639
Chagall, Marc, **20th:** 717-720
Chagatai, **MA:** 412
Chahár Maqála (Nizāmī ʿArūzī), **MA:** 796
Chaikin, Joseph, **20th:** 3982
Chain, Ernst B., **20th:** 1255, 1261, 4181
Chainbearer, The (Cooper), **19th:** 555
Chairs, The (Ionesco), **20th:** 1969
Chaka. *See* Shaka
Chalcedon, Council of (451), **Anc:** 864, 866
Chalcedonians, **MA:** 600
Chalcidian League, **Anc:** 638
Chaldea. *See* Babylonia
Challenge to Affluence (Myrdal), **20th:** 2892
Challenge to World Poverty, The (Myrdal), **20th:** 2892
Challenger (space shuttle) accident, **20th:** 137
Châlons, Battle of (451), **MA:** 290
Chamber music, **18th:** 73, 131, 713
Chamber Symphony (Zwilich), **20th:** 4476
Chamberlain, Houston Stewart, **Notor:** 196-198, 937, 1081
Chamberlain, Joseph, **19th:** 150, 460-464, 1749; **20th:** 210
Chamberlain, Neville, **20th:** 166, 207, 349, 720-725, 1101
Chamberlain, Wilt, **20th:** 725-727

Chambers, Sandra. *See* Kimes, Sante
Chambers, Whittaker, **20th:** 1822; **Notor:** 198-200, 476
Chambers v. Florida (1940), **20th:** 378
Chamorro, Emiliano, **Notor:** 984
Chamorro, Violeta Barrios de, **20th:** 3072
Champ Blanc, Battle of (1650), **17th:** 933
Champa, **MA:** Khmer invasion of, 982; **Ren:** 546
Champier, Symphorien, **Ren:** 862
Champlain, Samuel de, **17th:** 139-143, 433
Champs magnétiques, Les. See *Magnetic Fields, The*
Chan Buddhism. *See* Buddhism; Zen Buddhism
Chancas, **Ren:** 746
Chance (Conrad), **20th:** 826
Chancellor, Richard, **Ren:** 279, 493
Chancellorsville, Battle of (1863), **19th:** 1199, 1336
Chandler, John Davis, **Notor:** 222
Chandragupta II, **Anc:** 496
Chandragupta Maurya, **Anc:** 124, 202-204
Chandramas Nanda. *See* Dhanananda
Chanel, Coco, **20th:** 727-731, 2378; **Notor:** 998
Chang Chih-tung. *See* Zhang Zhidong
Chang Chiu-ling. *See* Zhang Jiuling
Change 90-New Majority. *See* Cambio 90-Nueva Mayoría
Changeling, The (Middleton and Rowley), **17th:** 637
Chang-sun Wu-chi. *See* Zhangsun Wuji
Channing, William Ellery, **19th:** 464-467, 1268, 1332, 1487, 1761, 1868
Chanson de Roland. See *Song of Roland*
Chansons de Bilitis (Debussy), **20th:** 938
Chantaburi, Battle of (1767), **18th:** 968
Chantelou, Paul Fréart de, **17th:** 750
Chants d'ombre (Senghor), **20th:** 3703
Chants for Socialists (Morris), **19th:** 1608
Chants pour Naëtt (Senghor), **20th:** 3704
Chanute, Octave, **20th:** 4404
Chao Tzu-yang. *See* Zhao Ziyang
Chaos theory, **20th:** 2589
Chapel of the Holy Shroud, **17th:** 331
Chapel Royal, **Ren:** 148, 918; **17th:** 502; **18th:** 464
Chapelain, Jean, **17th:** 833
Chaplin, Charles, **20th:** 731-734, 3245; **Notor:** 32, 604, 974
Chapman, Carrie. *See* Catt, Carrie Chapman
Chapman, George, **Ren:** 213-217
Chapman, J. Wilbur, **20th:** 3917
Chapman, John. *See* Appleseed, Johnny
Chapman, Mark David, **Notor:** 200-201
Chapone, Hester, **18th:** 221-223
Chapultepec Accords (1992), **20th:** 1041
Character of a Trimmer (Savile), **17th:** 817
Character of England, A (Evelyn), **17th:** 256
Charactēres ethikōi (Theophrastus), **Anc:** 547, 874
Characteristics of Women (Jameson), **19th:** 1218
Characters or Pourtaicts of the Present Court of France, The (Montpensier), **17th:** 662
Charbonneau, Toussaint, **19th:** 1962
Charcot, Jean-Martin, **20th:** 510
Chardin, Jean-Siméon, **18th:** 223-226, 367, 1052
Charge Delivered to the Clergy of the Diocese of Durham, A (Butler), **18th:** 188
Charge of the Rough Riders of San Juan Hill (Remington), **19th:** 1882
Charging Chasseur (Géricault), **19th:** 899
Charity (Andrea del Sarto), **Ren:** 40
Charity (Sirani), **17th:** 857
Charity Organization Society, **19th:** 1106
Charlemagne, **MA:** 49, 155, 242-247, 353, 550, 870, 902, 1094
Charles I of Anjou (1227-1285; king of Naples and Sicily), **MA:** 102, 669, 821
Charles I (1288-1342; king of Hungary), **MA:** 957
Charles I (1316-1378; king of Bohemia). *See* Charles IV (1316-1378; Holy Roman Emperor)
Charles I (1500-1558; king of Spain). *See* Charles V (1500-1558; Holy Roman Emperor)
Charles I (1600-1649; king of Great Britain and Ireland), **17th:** 143-146; and Richard Baxter, 33; and Aphra Behn, 42; and Thomas Betterton, 51; and Robert Blake, 55; and Jacques-Bénigne Bossuet, 72; and Anne Bradstreet, 89; and the first duke of Buckingham, 98; and George Calvert, 120; and Richard Cameron, 121; and Canonicus, 130; and Robert Carr, 133; and Catherine of Braganza, 137; and Charles II of England, 149; and the first earl of Clarendon, 166; and Sir Edward Coke, 177; and John Cotton, 198; and Abraham Cowley, 199; and Richard Crashaw, 202; and Oliver Cromwell, 204; and Lady Eleanor Davies, 221; and John Dryden, 240; and Sir Anthony

van Dyck, 245; and John Eliot, 247; and Elizabeth of Bohemia, 252; and Elizabeth Stuart, 254; and John Evelyn, 256; and third Baron Fairfax, 262; and Nicholas Ferrar, 275; and Frederick Henry, 288; and Artemisia Gentileschi, 308; and Orlando Gibbons, 311; and Nell Gwyn, 343; and Matthew Hale, 345; and William Harvey, 357; and Henrietta Maria, 364; and Robert Herrick, 369; and James I, 415; and James II, 416; and Inigo Jones, 436; and Ben Jonson, 443; and John Lambert, 483; and William Laud, 496; and Henry Lawes, 503; and John Lilburne, 535; and Louis XIII, 552; and Richard Lovelace, 562; and Roger Ludlow, 567; and Marie de Médicis, 599; and Andrew Marvell, 605; and Mary II, 610; and Thomas Middleton, 638; and John Milton, 640; and George Monck, 650; and Rory O'More, 699; and Opechancanough, 703; and Samuel Pepys, 728; and Thomas Pride, 756; and John Pym, 767; and Cardinal de Richelieu, 791; and Prince Rupert, 805; and Santorio Santorio, 811; and Sir George Savile, 815; and the first earl of Shaftesbury, 838; and James Shirley, 847; and the first earl of Strafford, 885; and Sir John Suckling, 893; and Maarten and Cornelis Tromp, 930; and Sir Henry Vane the Younger, 941; and John Wallis, 969; and William III, 979; and Gerrard Winstanley, 989; and John Winthrop, 991; and Sir Christopher Wren, 994

Charles I at the Hunt (van Dyck), **17th:** 246

Charles I on Horseback (van Dyck), **17th:** 246

Charles II the Bald (823-877; Holy Roman Emperor), **MA:** 254-256, 311, 662, 879

Charles II (1630-1685; king of Great Britain and Ireland), **17th:** 147-150; and Nathaniel Bacon, 29; and Richard Baxter, 34; and Aphra Behn, 42; and John Biddle, 54; and Robert Blake, 58; and Robert Boyle, 80; and Sir Thomas Browne, 94; and John Bunyan, 101; and Richard Cameron, 121; and Catherine of Braganza, 137; and the first earl of Clarendon, 168; and Abraham Cowley, 200; and Oliver Cromwell, 205; and John Davenport, 219; and John Dryden, 240; and Elizabeth Stuart, 254; and John Evelyn, 256; and the third Baron Fairfax, 264; and George Fox, 284; and James Gregory, 319; and Nell Gwyn, 342; and Matthew Hale, 346; and Edmond Halley, 348; and Henrietta Maria, 364; and Robert Herrick, 369; and Thomas Hobbes, 380; and James II, 416; and John IV, 431; and John Lambert, 485; and Henry Lawes, 503; and the first duke of Leeds, 506; and John Locke, 544; and Roger Ludlow, 568; and the Mancini sisters, 586; and Andrew Marvell, 606; and Mary II, 610; and Mary of Modena, 607; and John Milton, 640; and George Monck, 650; and the duke of Monmouth, 653; and the duchesse de Montpensier, 661; and the duchess of Newcastle, 677; and Titus Oates, 692; and William Penn, 725; and Samuel Pepys, 729; and Sir William Petty, 734; and Katherine Philips, 742; and Thomas Pride, 757; and Henry Purcell, 763; and Prince Rupert, 805; and Sir George Savile, 815; and Friedrich Hermann Schomberg, 821; and the first earl of Shaftesbury, 839; and Cornelis Tromp, 931; and Sir Henry Vane the Younger, 942; and John Wallis, 969; and Thomas Willis, 986; and Sir Christopher Wren, 994; **18th:** 672

Charles II (1661-1700; king of Spain), **17th:** 151-153, 426, 528, 555, 602, 739, 980; **18th:** 781; **Notor:** 201-202, 306, 802, 962

Charles III the Fat (839-888; Holy Roman Emperor), **MA:** 901

Charles III the Simple (879-929; king of France), **MA:** 902

Charles III (1685-1740; king of Hungary). *See* Charles VI (1685-1740; Holy Roman Emperor)

Charles III (1716-1788; king of Spain), **18th:** 227-229, 437; music patronage, 130

Charles IV (1316-1378; Holy Roman Emperor), **MA:** 257-260, 830, 899, 1088

Charles IV (1604-1675; duke of Lorraine), **17th:** 493, 528

Charles V (1337-1380; king of France), **MA:** 273; **Notor:** 203, 213

Charles V (1500-1558; Holy Roman Emperor), **Ren:** 8, 31, 50, 54, 58, 112, 144, 152, 204, 220-224, 266, 309, 330, 410, 422, 445, 505, 538, 549, 559, 583, 614, 648, 650, 778, 937, 967, 997; Americas and, 159, 247, 254, 592, 801, 978; Catholicism and, 639; England and, 189; France and, 229, 347, 423; Henry VIII and, 443; Italy and, 229, 347; Netherlands and, 615, 636; Ottoman Empire and, 915; Protestantism and, 769;

sack of Rome and, 182; **Notor:** 39, 801, 962
Charles VI (1368-1422; king of France), **MA:** 502, 895; **Notor:** 203-204
Charles VI (1685-1740; Holy Roman Emperor), **17th:** 152; **18th:** 229-231, 653, 1020; and Ottoman Empire, 27
Charles VII (1403-1461; king of France), **MA:** 277, 578; **Ren:** 124-226, 174; **Notor:** 204
Charles VIII (1470-1498; king of France), **Ren:** 28, 49, 84, 227-229, 365, 439, 498, 518, 575, 577, 587, 612, 852, 872; **Notor:** 15
Charles IX (1550-1574; king of France), **Ren:** 184, 426, 429, 541, 569, 703; **Notor:** 801
Charles IX (1550-1611; king of Sweden), **17th:** 336, 854, 945
Charles X Gustav (1622-1660; king of Sweden), **17th:** 153-155, 164, 527, 706
Charles X (1757-1836; king of France), **19th:** 477
Charles XI (1655-1697; king of Sweden), **17th:** 155
Charles XII (1682-1718; king of Sweden), **17th:** 625; **18th:** 232-234, 775
Charles XIII (1748-1818; king of Sweden), **19th:** 469
Charles XIV John (1763-1844; king of Sweden), **19th:** 468-470
Charles, Ray, **20th:** 735-738
Charles Albert (king of Sardinia-Piedmont), **19th:** 444, 872, 922, 1803
Charles de Valois. *See* Charles the Bold
Charles Dickens (Chesterton), **20th:** 744
Charles d'Orléans, **MA:** 247-250
Charles Edward (Bonnie Prince Charlie), **18th:** 406, 623
Charles-Louis de Secondat. *See* Montesquieu
Charles Martel, **MA:** 184, 242, 250-254
Charles of Luxembourg. *See* Charles IV (1316-1378; Holy Roman Emperor)
Charles of Navarre, **MA:** 1054
Charles, Prince of Wales, **20th:** 989, 1143
Charles River Bridge v. Warren Bridge, **19th:** 2181, 2227
Charles the Bold (duke of Burgundy), **Ren:** 217-220, 351, 574, 631
Charles the First (Shelley), **19th:** 2096
Charles the Great. *See* Charlemagne
Charles the Hammer. *See* Charles Martel
Charlesbourg, **Ren:** 179
Charleston, South Carolina, **18th:** 257, 279, 444, 1055
Charlestown Neck, Battle of. *See* Bunker Hill, Battle of
Charleton, Walter, **17th:** 240
Charlie Brown Christmas, A (television special), **20th:** 3673
Charlotte (queen of Great Britain and Ireland), **18th:** 181, 235-237, 1059
Charlottetown Accord, **20th:** 2868
Charm of Dynamite, The (film), **20th:** 1383
Charme discret de la bourgeoisie, Le. See *Discreet Charm of the Bourgeoisie, The*
Charmed Life, A (McCarthy), **20th:** 2501
Charmes, ou poèmes (Valéry), **20th:** 4137
Charmides, **Anc:** 801
Charrière, Henri, **Notor:** 204-205
Charter 77, **20th:** 1707
Charterhouse of Parma, The (Stendhal), **19th:** 2163
Chartier, Alain, **MA:** 260-263
Chartism (Carlyle), **19th:** 416
Chartist movement, **19th:** 1045
Chartres, cathedral school at, **MA:** 400
Charulata. See *Lonely Wife, The*
Chase, Salmon P., **19th:** 470-474, 545
Chase, Samuel, **18th:** 237-240; judicial partisanship, 239
Chasse d'Ossian, La (Bizet), **19th:** 241
Chasseur maudit, Le (Franck), **19th:** 823
Chaste Maid in Cheapside, A (Middleton), **17th:** 636
Château de Balleroy, **17th:** 588
Château de Berny, **17th:** 588
Château de Clagny, **17th:** 590
Château de Maisons, **17th:** 588
Château de Vaux-le-Vícomte, **17th:** 532
Châteaubriand, Edict of (1551), **Ren:** 424
Chateaubriand, François-René de, **19th:** 474-478
Châtelet, marquise du, **18th:** 240-243, 1027
Chatham, baron of. *See* Argyll, second duke of
Chatham, Battle of (1667), **17th:** 808
Chatham, first earl of. *See* Pitt, William, the Elder
Châtiments, Les (Hugo), **19th:** 1148
Chattanooga, Battle of (1863), **19th:** 960
Chatterton, Ruth, **20th:** 142
Chattopadhyay, Sarojini. *See* Naidu, Sarojini
Chaucer, Geoffrey, **MA:** 264-267
Chauliac, Guy de. *See* Guy de Chauliac
Chaumont, Treaty of (1814), **19th:** 439
Chauncey, Isaac, **19th:** 1779
Chautemps, Camille, **Notor:** 998
Chávez, César, **20th:** 738-740, 1915
Chávez, Federico, **Notor:** 1004
Chavez, Hugo, **20th:** 694

Chayka. See *Seagull, The*
Chazal, André, **19th:** 2297
Che Guevara on Guerrilla Warfare (Guevara), **20th:** 1610
"Cheap Repository Tracts" (More), **18th:** 703
Cheap Thrills (Joplin), **20th:** 2043
Cheat, The (film), **20th:** 960
Cheat with the Ace of Clubs (La Tour), **17th:** 494
Cheat with the Ace of Diamonds (La Tour), **17th:** 494
Chechen War, First (1994-1996), **20th:** 4433
Cheerful Yesterdays (Higginson), **19th:** 1099
Cheiroballistra (Hero of Alexandria), **Anc:** 401
Cheke, John, **Ren:** 199
Chekhov, Anton, **19th:** 478-481; **20th:** 3822
Cheltenham Ladies' College, **19th:** 159
Cheltenham Ladies' College Magazine, The, **19th:** 160
Chemical Analysis by X Rays and Its Applications (Hevesy), **20th:** 1793
Chemical History of a Candle, The (Faraday), **19th:** 760
Chemical nomenclature, **18th:** 116
Chemical Revolution, **18th:** Germany, 934; Scotland, 115-117, 858-862
Chemical weapons, **20th:** gas, 1630, 1636; Iraq, 1948
Chemins de la liberté, Les. See *Roads to Freedom, The*
Chemistry, **Ren:** 127; **17th:** Belgium, 362; England, 79; Germany, 40; **18th:** Joseph Black, 115-117; Henry Cavendish, 217-220; empirical, 935; iatrochemistry, 933; Antoine-Laurent Lavoisier, 579-582; Nicolas Leblanc, 587-590; Andreas Sigismund Marggraf, 651-653; modern foundations, 812; Gaspard Monge, 683; Joseph Priestley, 811-814; Russia, 613; Lazzaro Spallanzani, 927; Georg Ernst Stahl, 933-937; sugar extraction, 652; Alessandro Volta, 1023; **19th:** 617, 888; analytical, 1900; electrochemisty, 760; gases, 102; Germany, 2456; organic, 1367, 1545, 2456; periodic table, 1546. *See also* Category Index
Chemistry of Cooking and Cleaning, The (Richards), **19th:** 1900
Chemistry of the Sun, The (Lockyer), **19th:** 1414
Ch'en I. *See* Xuanzang
Ch'en Ch'ien-sheng. *See* Chen Duxiu
Chen Duxiu, **20th:** 741-743
Chen Duxiu zui hou dui yu min zhu zheng zhi di jian jie (Chen), **20th:** 743
Chen Liang, **MA:** 1160
Chen Qiansheng. *See* Chen Duxiu
Chen Shu, **17th:** 156-158
Ch'en Tu-hsiu. *See* Chen Duxiu
Chen Yi. *See* Xuanzang
Cheng. *See* Shi Huangdi
Cheng Ch'eng-kung. *See* Zheng Chenggong
Cheng Chih-lung. *See* Zheng Zhilong
Cheng Ho. *See* Zheng He
Cheng I Sao, **Notor:** 205-207
Cheng weishi lun (Xuanzang), **MA:** 1138
Cheng-te. *See* Zhengde
Chengzu. *See* Yonglo
Chenhao, **Ren:** 987
Cheops. *See* Khufu
Chéri (Colette), **20th:** 805
Chernyshevsky, Nikolay, **19th:** 50, 1086, 1627
Cherokees, **18th:** 143; **19th:** 831, 1130, 1937, 2053, 2067; removal of, 1191, 1501; treaties with U.S. government, 1410; **20th:** 2591
Cherokee Badman. *See* Starr, Henry
Cherokee Nation v. Georgia, **19th:** 2182
Cherry, Bobby Frank, **Notor:** 79
Cherry Orchard, The (Chekhov), **19th:** 480
Chesimard, Joanne Deborah Byron. *See* Shakur, Assata Olugbala
Chesimard, Pat. *See* Shakur, Assata Olugbala
Chesimard, Sister-Love. *See* Shakur, Assata Olugbala
Chesnoy, Madame de Guyon du. *See* Guyon, Madame
Chesnutt, Charles W., **19th:** 703
Chess Game, The (Anguissola), **Ren:** 46
Chessman, Caryl, **Notor:** 151
Chesterfield Act (1751), **18th:** 773
Chesterton, Arthur Kenneth, **Notor:** 1050
Chesterton, G. K., **20th:** 744-746
Chevalier, Maurice, **20th:** 1693
Chevalier de l'Ordre Royal de la Légion d'Honneur, **18th:** 585
Chevalier de Seingalt. *See* Casanova
Chevalier d'Harmental, Le (Dumas), **19th:** 696
Chevallon, Claude, **Ren:** 413
Chevallonii, vidua Claudii. *See* Guillard, Charlotte
Chevreuse, duchesse de, **17th:** 18, 158-160, 487
Cheyenne, **19th:** 568, 583
Cheyney, James, **Notor:** 898
Chhit Choeun. *See* Ta Mok
Chi. *See* Sonni ʿAlī
Chiang Ch'ing. *See* Jiang Qing
Chiang Kai-shek, **20th:** 742, 746-750, 2382, 2457, 4221; Guo Moruo, 1620; Ho Chi Minh, 1835; Zhou Enlai, 4462; **Notor:** 692
Chiang Tse-min. *See* Jiang Zemin
Chiara di Assisi, Santa. *See* Clare of Assisi, Saint

Chiaroscuro (John), **20th:** 2016
Chiat-Day Building, **20th:** 1439
Chicago (Kander and Ebb), **20th:** 1292
Chicago, Judy, **20th:** 750-752
Chicago, University of, **19th:** 1032, 1729
Chicago Bulls, **20th:** 2050
Chicago City Ballet, **20th:** 3942
Chicago Plan of 1909, **19th:** 362
Chicago Poems (Sandburg), **20th:** 3619
Chicago Race Riots, The (Sandburg), **20th:** 3620
Chicago School, **20th:** 3619
Chicherin, Georgi Vasilievich, **20th:** 2405
Chickahominys, **17th:** 752
Chickasaws, **Ren:** 904; **17th:** 402
Chien andalou, Un. See *Andalusian Dog, An*
Ch'ien-lung. *See* Qianlong
Chienne, La (film), **20th:** 3421
Chien-wen. *See* Jianwen
Chigi, Fabio. *See* Alexander VII (1599-1667; pope)
Chijin no ai. See *Naomi*
Chikamatsu Monzaemon, **18th:** 243-245
Chikatilo, Andrei, **Notor:** 207-208
Child, Lydia Maria, **19th:** 482-486
Child from Five to Ten, The (Gesell and Ilg), **20th:** 1466
Child Jesus Among the Doctors (Rouault), **20th:** 3543
Child Language, Aphasia, and Phonological Universals (Jakobson), **20th:** 1987
Child of War, Woman of Peace (Hayslip), **20th:** 1727
Child Who Never Grew, The (Buck), **20th:** 559
Childe Harold's Pilgrimage (Byron), **19th:** 56, 380, 1995
Childebert I, **MA:** 381
Childeric, **MA:** 381
Childhood (Tolstoy), **19th:** 2283
Children, **18th:** education, 732; **20th:** ballet, 196, 908; development of, 1465, 3815; education, 23, 603, 2804, 3232; entertainment, 1007; health care, 2696; literature, 2355, 3316, 3711, 4021, 4039; medicine, 3950; orphans, 559, 3977; poetry, 2754; psychology of, 34, 3231-3232; welfare of, 1097, 2272, 4185
Children of Gebelawi (Mahfouz), **20th:** 2555
Children of Herakles, The. See *Hērakleidai*
Children of the Age (Hamsun), **20th:** 1661
Children of the Chapel, **Ren:** 214
Children of the Game (Cocteau), **20th:** 795
Children of the Sea, The (Conrad), **20th:** 826
Children's Bureau, U.S., **20th:** 2273, 2696
Children's Corner Suite (Debussy), **20th:** 938
Children's Defense Fund, **20th:** 1097
Children's Games (Bruegel), **Ren:** 136
Children's Hour, The (Hellman), **20th:** 1752
Child's Conception of the World, The (Piaget), **20th:** 3232
Child's Garden of Verses, A (Stevenson), **19th:** 2174
Chile. *See* Geographical Index
Chilperic I, **MA:** 381
Chilton, Thomas, **19th:** 571
Chimalpopoca, **MA:** 559; **Ren:** 721
Chimene (Lipchitz), **20th:** 2399
Chimes, The (Dickens), **19th:** 655
Ch'in Kuei. *See* Qin Gui
Ch'in Shihn Huang-ti. *See* Shi Huangdi
China, **MA:** architecture, 1138; art, 677, 718, 1140; coinage, 1127; education, 1159; historiography, 945; influence on Japan, 941; influence on Vietnam, 756; law, 1079; Ming emperors, 1149; Mongol conquest of, 677; Northern Song rulers, 1080, 1146; painting, 677, 720, 970, 1140; philosophy, 809; poetry, 322, 653, 656, 808, 968, 1086; Tang emperors, 996; theology, 1137; trade, 627, 1127, 1134, 1157; Yuan emperors, 627; **Ren:** France, 86, 217; Portugal and, 792; Spain, 209, 223; **18th:** government reform, 1113; and Korean art, 248; literature, 194-196; philosophy, 287-289; Qing Dynasty, 817-819; and Zen Buddhism, 450; **19th:** examination system, 2487; Great Britain, 949; trade, 579; **20th:** Henry Kissinger, 2171; Richard Nixon, 2985; Soviet relations with, 2129. *See also* Geographical Index
Chinese Book of Etiquette and Conduct for Women and Girls, The. See *Nu jie* (Ban Zhao)
Chinese-British relations, **18th:** 817
Chinese Civil War (1946-1949), **20th:** 748, 1905, 2603, 3192, 4463, 4467; United States, 19
Chinese Exclusion Act of 1882, **19th:** 509
Chinese Revolution (1911-1912), **20th:** 3914
Chinese-Russian treaty, **18th:** 776, 1113
Chinese-Vietnamese conflicts, **18th:** 737
Chinese Wall, The (Frisch), **20th:** 1339
Ch'ing Dynasty. *See* Qing Dynasty
Ch'ing Kao-tsung. *See* Qianlong
Ching K'o. *See* Jing Ke
Ching Shih. *See* Cheng I Sao
Ch'ing T'ai-tsung. *See* Abahai
Chinggis Khan. *See* Genghis Khan
Chini, Eusebio Francesco. *See* Kino, Eusebio Francisco

Chinmoku. See *Silence* (Endō)
Chino, el. *See* Fujimori, Alberto
Ch'in-shan. *See* Ma Yuan
Chionites, **Anc:** 776
Chipewyans, **18th:** 974
Chiplunkar, Vishnu Krishna, **20th:** 4024
Chippewa, Battle of (1813), **19th:** 2052
Chippewas, **17th:** 423, 433, 603; **18th:** 801; **19th:** 244, 1604
Chirac, Jacques, **20th:** 2771; **Notor:** 325, 637
Chiricahuas, **19th:** 905
Chirico, Giorgio de, **20th:** 2548
Chirurgia magna. See *Cyrurgie of Guy de Chauliac, The*
Chirwa, Orton, **20th:** 220
Chisholm, Shirley, **20th:** 753-757
Chisholm v. Georgia (1793), **18th:** 525, 1093
Chishtī, **MA:** 41
Chissano, Joaquim, **20th:** 2516
Chitepo, Herbert, **Notor:** 761
Chivalry, **MA:** 392, 425, 464, 1075, 1123
Chlodomer, **MA:** 381
Chlodovech. *See* Clovis
Chlodovicus. *See* Clovis
Chlorine, **19th:** 888
Chlorofluorocarbons, ban on use of, **20th:** 3549
Chlotar I, **MA:** 381, 427
Chlotar II, **MA:** 383
Chlothilde. *See* Clotilda, Saint
Chmielnicki, Bohdan. *See* Khmelnytsky, Bohdan
Chmielnicki massacres (1648-1649), **17th:** 836
Chocolate, **18th:** 22
Choctaws, **Ren:** 904, 922
Chodkiewicz, Jan, **17th:** 854
Chōeiken. *See* Suzuki Harunobu
Choëphores, Les (Milhaud), **20th:** 2735
Choēphoroi (Aeschylus), **Anc:** 9
Choice Before Us, The (Thomas), **20th:** 4004
Choice Psalms Put into Music (Lawes), **17th:** 503
Choiseul, Étienne François de, **18th:** 246-247, 448, 798
Choix des élues (Giraudoux), **20th:** 1493
Cholera, **19th:** 1293
Cholesterol, study of, **20th:** 995
Chomedey, Paul de. *See* Maisonneuve, sieur de
Chomsky, Noam, **20th:** 757-760
Chŏng Sŏn, **18th:** 248-249
Chongde. *See* Abahai
Chongzhen, **17th:** 160-162, 235, 848, 912
Chopin, Frédéric, **19th:** 486-490
Chopin, Kate, **19th:** 490-493
Choral (Beethoven), **19th:** 178
Choreutics (Laban), **20th:** 2222
Choruses from the Iphigenia in Aulis (H. D.), **20th:** 1624
Chos-byung (Bu-ston), **Anc:** 111
Chou En-lai. *See* Zhou Enlai
Chou Shu-jên. *See* Lu Xun
Chouans, Les (Balzac), **19th:** 126
Chouart, Médard. *See* Groseilliers, sieur des
Chowdhury, Ajay, **Notor:** 980
Chremonidean War (266-261 B.C.E.), **Anc:** 108, 716
Chrétien, Jean, **20th:** 626, 761-764
Chrétien de Troyes, **MA:** 267-270, 407, 1124
Chrisálidas (Machado), **19th:** 1449
Christ. *See* Jesus Christ
Christ (Epstein), **20th:** 1166
Christ and Saint Thomas (Verrocchio), **Ren:** 963
Christ and the Woman of Samaria (Michelangelo), **Ren:** 236
Christ at the Pillar (Bramante), **Ren:** 132
Christ Carrying the Cross (Bosch), **Ren:** 120
Christ Carrying the Cross (van Hemessen), **Ren:** 421
Christ Conferring Authority on Saints Peter and Thomas Aquinas (Orcagna), **MA:** 798
Christ Healing the Blind (El Greco), **Ren:** 390
Christ Healing the Sick in the Temple (West), **18th:** 1069
Christ in the House of Martha and Mary (Vermeer), **17th:** 956
Christ Legends (Lagerlöf), **20th:** 2235
Christ of Velázquez, The (Unamuno), **20th:** 4130
Christ on the Cross (Zurbarán), **17th:** 1004
Christ on the Cross Adored by Saint Dominic (Fra Angelico), **MA:** 85
Christ Scorned (Fra Angelico), **MA:** 85
Christ Taking Leave of His Mother (Correggio), **Ren:** 249
Christ with Saint Joseph in the Carpenter's Shop (La Tour), **17th:** 494
Christabel (Coleridge), **19th:** 530
Christian I, **Ren:** 496
Christian IV, **Ren:** 130, 290
Christian VII, **Notor:** 208-209
Christian Association of Washington, **19th:** 399
Christian Baptism (Menno), **Ren:** 676
Christian Baptist (journal), **19th:** 400
Christian Democratic Party (El Salvador). *See* Partido Demócrata Cristiano
Christian Democratic Party (Italy), **20th:** 946
Christian Democratic Union, **20th:** 27
Christian Doctrine of Justification and Reconciliation, The (Ritschl), **19th:** 1919
Christian era, **MA:** 314
Christian Faith, The (Schleiermacher), **19th:** 2013
Christian Hero, The (Steele), **18th:** 941
Christian Life, The (Arnold), **19th:** 77
Christian Mission. *See* Salvation Army

Christian Morals (Browne), **17th:** 95
Christian Philosopher (Mather), **18th:** 669
Christian Realism, **20th:** 2963
Christian Science Monitor, The, **19th:** 727
Christian Science Publishing Society, **19th:** 726
Christian Science Sentinel, The, **19th:** 726
Christian Scientists. *See* Church of Christ, Scientist
Christian Socialism, **19th:** 1519
Christian Trade Union Movement, **20th:** 1180
Christian Union (newspaper), **19th:** 174
Christiana of Denmark, Duchess of Milan (Holbein the Younger), **Ren:** 455
Christianae religionis institutio. See *Institutes of the Christian Religion*
Christianismi restitutio (Servetus), **Ren:** 862
Christianity, **Anc:** Abraham in, 6; appeal of, 42; Buddhism and, 130; Catholicism, 353; church formation, 625; church organization, 225; classical scholarship and, 435; Constantine's conversion, 132; David in, 257; Diocletian and, 280; Epicurianism and, 309; Ethiopia and, 333; Ezekiel and, 337; Gnosticism and, 444; Hadrian and, 372; John and, 472; Judaism and, 330, 437, 472, 612, 822; martyrdom and, 205; Moses and, 574; Neoplatonism and, 688; paganism and, 268, 791, 798, 853, 869; persecution of, 437, 531, 592, 600, 776; Philo of Alexandria and, 642; Rome and, 240, 330, 905; **MA:** 1050; Bohemia, 670; Bulgaria, 189, 767; Byzantine Empire, 549, 600; education, 96, 180, 234; England, 49, 152, 219, 431, 938; Franks, 242, 290; Gaul, 288; Germany, 184, 226; Greenland, 642; Hungary, 638, 964; Ireland, 199, 811; Kievan Rus, 86, 793, 1068; Mongols, 547, 627; Moravia, 295; Muslims and, 1029; Saxony, 1096; Scandinavia, 767; Slavs, 296; Spain, 10, 555; spread of, 133, 244; theater, 517; Vikings, 222, 786, 790, 902; Visigoths, 784, 1014; women, 81, 144-145, 198, 236, 270, 284, 509, 513, 549, 596, 607, 629, 708, 856; **Ren:** Central America, 34; China, 1002; Ethiopia, 1006; faith, 584; Japan, 944, 1001; Kongo, 9; North America, 673; Russia, 387; South America, 6; **17th:** England, 94, 545; France, 71, 715; Germany, 60; Italy, 125; Russia, 27; science and, 106; Scotland, 121; **18th:** colonial America, 1062; Ethiopia, 678; Paul-Henri-Dietrich d'Holbach, 502; and Jewish conversion, 676; **20th:** Émile Durkheim, 1066; Germany, 2971, 4070; history of, 1682; Judaism, 187; in literature, 2354; missionaries, 2850-2851; New Testament scholarship, 572; peace activism, 2973; philosophy, 1489; social reform, 3383; socialism, 3383; Switzerland, 244, 548; unification of, 3782; United States, 2962. *See also* Adamites; Anglican Church; Arianism; Bible; Calvinism; Carmelites; Cistercians; Dissenters; Dominicans; Evangelism; Franciscans; Lutheran Church and Lutheranism; Monophysites; Nestorians; Orthodox Church; Presbyterian Church and Presbyterianism; Protestantism; Puritanism; Revivalism; Roman Catholic Church and Catholicism; Settlement, Act of; Taborites
Christianity and the New Idealism (Eucken), **20th:** 1186
Christianity and the Social Crisis (Rauschenbusch), **20th:** 3384
Christianizing the Social Order (Rauschenbusch), **20th:** 3384
Christians, **MA:** Celtic, 510; Roman, 510
Christie, Dame Agatha, **20th:** 765-768
Christie, John Reginald Halliday, **Notor:** 210-211
Christina (queen of Sweden), **17th:** 163-166; and Giovanni Alfonso Borelli, 66; and René Descartes, 164, 228; and Frederick William, 290; and Ninon de Lenclos, 521; and the duchesse de Montpensier, 661; music patronage, 190; and Blaise Pascal, 713; and António Vieira, 960; **18th:** 884
Christina of Markyate, **MA:** 270-273
Christina's World (Wyeth), **20th:** 4411
Christine (Dumas), **19th:** 696
Christine de Pizan, **MA:** 273-278
Christliche Dogmatik im Entwurf, Die. See *Dogmatics in Outline*
Christliche Glaube: Nach den Grundsätzen der evangelischen Kirche im Zusammenhange dargestellt, Der. See *Christian Faith, The*
Christliche Lehre von der Rechtfertigung und Versöhnuns, Die. See *Christian Doctrine of Justification and Reconciliation, The*
Christmas, date of, **Anc:** 458
Christmas Carol, A (Dickens), **19th:** 655
Christmas Eve (Rimsky-Korsakov), **19th:** 1916
Christmas Oratorio (Bach), **18th:** 74

Christoffel von Grimmelshausen, Hans Jakob. *See* Grimmelshausen, Hans Jakob Christoffel von
Christology, **Anc:** 863, 866; Valentinian, 920
Christoph und Else lesen in den abendstunden das Buch "Lienhard und Gertrud" (Pestalozzi), **19th:** 1783
Christophe, Henri, **19th:** 494-496
Christophe Colomb (Milhaud), **20th:** 2736
Christopher, Saint, **Anc:** 205-207
Christopher Isherwood and Don Bachardy (Hockney), **20th:** 1846
Christopher Strong (film), **20th:** 142
Christ's Passion (Grotius), **17th:** 327
Christ's Tears over Jerusalem (Nashe), **Ren:** 715
Christus (Liszt), **19th:** 1395
Christus (Longfellow), **19th:** 1419
Christus (Mendelssohn), **19th:** 1550
Christus patiens. See *Christ's Passion*
Christy, Edwin P., **19th:** 803
Christy Minstrels, **19th:** 803
Chrodechilde. *See* Clotilda, Saint
Chromosomes, **20th:** 2504
Chronica Hungarorum. See *Chronicle of the Hungarians*
Chronicle (Salimbene), **MA:** 921
Chronicle (Villani), **MA:** 1056
Chronicle of Geoffry de Villehardouin, Marshal of Champagne and Romania, Concerning the Conquest of Constantinople, by the French and Venetians, Anno MCCIV, The. See *Conquête de Constantinople, Le*
Chronicle of James I, King of Aragon, Surnamed the Conqueror, The (James I the Conqueror), **MA:** 573
Chronicle of Jean de Venette, The (Jean de Venette), **MA:** 1053
Chronicle of Salimbene de Adam, The. See *Chronicle* (Salimbene)
Chronicle of the Conquest of Granada, A (Irving), **19th:** 1181
Chronicle of the Hungarians, **MA:** 105
Chronicles (Froissart), **MA:** 392, 1033
Chronicles of Narnia (Lewis), **20th:** 2355
Chronicon (Eusebius), **Anc:** 330
Chroniques de France, d'Engleterre, d'Éscose, de Bretaigne, d'Espaigne, d'Italie, de Flandres et d'Alemaigne. See *Chronicles*
Chronochromie (Messiaen), **20th:** 2717
Chronographia (Psellus), **MA:** 864
Chronographia (Theophanes), **MA:** 1020
Chronographiai (Eratosthenes), **Anc:** 315
Chronologia (Mercator), **Ren:** 680
Chronology of Ancient Nations, The (al-Bīrūnī), **MA:** 163
Chronycles of Englande, Fraunce, Spayne . . . , The. See *Chronicles*
Chrotechildis. *See* Clotilda, Saint
Chrysanthemum and the Sword, The (Benedict), **20th:** 298
Chrysippus of Cnidus, **Anc:** 310, 320, 982
Chrysis (Pius II), **Ren:** 794
Chrysostom, Saint John, **Anc:** 208-209, 862
Chto delat'? See *What Is to Be Done?* (Chernyshevsky); *What Is to Be Done?* (Lenin)
Chto takoye iskusstvo? See *What Is Art?*
Chu Hou-chao. *See* Zhengde
Chu Hsi. *See* Zhu Xi
Chu Teh. *See* Zhu De
Chu Ti. *See* Yonglo
Chu Yuan, **Anc:** 844
Chu Yüan-chang. *See* Hongwu
Chu Yu-chiao. *See* Tianqi
Chu Yu-chien. *See* Chongzhen
Chu Yut'ang. *See* Xiaozong
Chūai, **Anc:** 465
Chuang Chou. *See* Zhuangzi
Chuang Lieh-ti. *See* Chongzhen
Chuang-tzu. *See* Zhuangzi
Chuanxi lu. See *Instructions for Practical Living*
Chumash, **Ren:** 161
Chun Doo Hwan, **20th:** 2136
Ch'ung-chen. *See* Chongzhen
Ch'ung-te. *See* Abahai
Chung-tsung. *See* Zhongzong
Chunqiu (Confucius), **Anc:** 149
Chuquicamata copper mine, **20th:** 1614
Chur-Brandenburgische Hoff-Wehe-Mutter, Die. See *Court Midwife of the Electorate of Brandenburg, The*
Church, **MA:** architecture, 971; criticism of, 1051; England, 93, 543; Jews and, 544; music, 741; political power of, 188; reform, 27, 50, 57, 399, 433, 544, 645, 769; relationship to state, 27, 188, 190, 437, 438, 542, 545, 645, 706, 768, 807; taxation of, 187; **17th:** separation from state, 984; **18th:** conflict with state, 545, 793; **20th:** separation from state, 521, 1211. *See also* Christianity; Category Index
Church, The (Hus), **MA:** 524
Church, Benjamin (1639-1718), **17th:** 634
Church, Benjamin (1734-1778), **Notor:** 211-212
Church Dogmatics (Barth), **20th:** 245
Church government. *See* Category Index

Church History. See *Historia ecclesiastica*
Church Missionary Society, **19th:** 574
Church of Christ (Bulfinch church), **19th:** 348
Church of Christ, Scientist, **19th:** 724
Church of England, **Ren:** 51, 113, 189, 231, 258, 267, 271, 458, 529, 699, 761, 947; **17th:** 15, 939. *See also* Protestantism
Church of Jesus Christ of Latter-day Saints, **19th:** 2117, 2475
Church of Saint Anne, **MA:** 717
Church of Saint Damiano, **MA:** 379
Church of Saint Francis, **MA:** 282
Church of San Andrea, **MA:** 848
Church of San Damiano, **MA:** 285
Church of San Domenico, **MA:** 102
Church of San Francesco, **MA:** 283
Church of San Frediano, Trenta chapel, **MA:** 567
Church of San Giovanni Laterano, **MA:** 102
Church of San Miniato al Monte, **MA:** 103
Church of San Petronio, main portal, **MA:** 567
Church of Santa Croce, **MA:** 103
Church of Santa Maria del Carmine, **MA:** 700
Church of Santa Maria Novella, **MA:** 103, 282
Church of Scientology, **20th:** 1910-1911
Church of Scotland, **17th:** 941. *See also* Presbyterian Church
Church of the Assumption, **Anc:** 392
Church of the Feillants, **17th:** 588
Church of the Holy Sepulchre, **MA:** 717
Church of the Nativity, **Anc:** 392
Church of the Spilt Blood, **19th:** 50
Church of the Val-de-Grâce, **17th:** 589
Church reform. *See* Category Index under Church Government and Reform
Churches of Christ, **19th:** 402
Churchill, John. *See* Marlborough, first duke of
Churchill, Lord Randolph, **19th:** 1979
Churchill, Sarah, **18th:** 45, 250-252; marriage to first duke of Marlborough, 660
Churchill, Sir Winston, **20th:** 150, 166, 206, 768-771, 3819; R. A. Butler, 603; Anthony Eden, 1101; France, 1427; George VI, 1456; İsmet Paşa, 1973; portrait, 3921; **Notor:** 152, 264, 512, 675, 756, 770
Churchman, John, **Ren:** 457
Ci (Chinese songs), **MA:** 808, 968
CIA. *See* Central Intelligence Agency
CIA Inspector General's Report on Plots to Assassinate Fidel Castro, **20th:** 693
Cibber, Colley, **18th:** 749
Cíbola, **Ren:** 245
Cicero, **Anc:** 145, 185, 188, 194, 210-213, 233, 267, 494, 512, 520, 692, 742, 757, 834, 838; **Notor:** 188, 834
Cicerone, The (Burckhardt), **19th:** 355
Cicognini, Jacopo, **17th:** 111
Cid, El, **MA:** 278-281
Cid, The (Corneille), **17th:** 193
Cien años de soledad. See *One Hundred Years of Solitude*
Cien sonetos de amor. See *One Hundred Love Sonnets*
Cigarrales de Toledo, Los (Tirso), **17th:** 913
Cilnius, Gaius Maecenas. *See* Maecenas, Gaius
Cimabue, **MA:** 282-283, 421
Cimarrón, El (Henze), **20th:** 1764
Cimbri, **Anc:** 533, 831
Cimento dell'armonia e dell'inventione, Il. See *Four Seasons, The*
Cimmerians, **Anc:** 244; Assyria and, 118
Cimon, **Anc:** 128, 213-217, 564, 616, 620, 678, 860
Cimon Koalemos, **Anc:** 213, 563
Cinadon, **Anc:** 15
Cincinnati Penny Post, **19th:** 2057
Cincinnati Reds, **20th:** 3467, 3526
Cinderella (animated film), **20th:** 1008
Cinématograph, **20th:** 2473
Cinna (Corneille), **17th:** 194
Cinna, Lucius Cornelius, **Anc:** 535, 832; **Notor:** 1010
Cinq Cents Millions de la Bégum, Les. See *Begum's Fortune, The*
Cinq Semaines en ballon. See *Five Weeks in a Balloon*
Cinque canti (Ariosto), **Ren:** 58
CIO. *See* Congress of Industrial Organizations
Cione, Andrea di. *See* Orcagna, Andrea
Cione, Andrea di Michele. *See* Verrocchio, Andrea del
Circle Game, The (Atwood), **20th:** 170
Circular Forms (Delaunay), **20th:** 952
Circulation of the Blood, The (Harvey), **17th:** 357
Circumcision, **Anc:** 5
Circumference of Earth, **Anc:** 315
Circumnavigation of the globe, **Ren:** 307, 591; **18th:** 151
Circus (Calder), **20th:** 609
Circus Maximus, **Anc:** 847
Cirencester, Battle of (1642), **17th:** 805
Cirque Fernando, Le (Toulouse-Lautrec), **19th:** 2288
Cisneros, Gonzalo Jiménez de. *See* Jiménez de Cisneros, Francisco
Cistercians, **MA:** 144, 160, 167, 399, 575, 709, 972, 1115

Citadelle, **19th:** 495
Cité Industrielle, Une (Garnier), **20th:** 1415
Cities (Delaunay), **20th:** 951
Citizen Kane (film), **20th:** 1737, 4284
Citizen of the World, The (Goldsmith), **18th:** 434
Citizenship, **Anc:** Athenian, 221; Roman, 210, 212, 359; Spartan, 228
Citoyenne, La, **19th:** 90
Citroën, André-Gustave, **20th:** 772-774
Citroën expeditions, **20th:** 773
Città che sale (Boccioni), **20th:** 403
Città del sole, La. See *City of the Sun*
Città delle donne, La. See *City of Women*
Cittamātra, **Anc:** 112
City of God, The. See *De civitate Dei*
City of Paris, The (Delaunay), **20th:** 951
City of the Saints (Burton), **19th:** 369
City of the Sun (Campanella), **17th:** 126
City of Tomorrow and Its Planning, The (Le Corbusier), **20th:** 2323
City of Women (film), **20th:** 1233
Civic Repertory Theatre, **20th:** 2332
Civil Constitution of the Clergy (1790), **18th:** 793
Civil engineering, **19th:** 1325
Civil liberties (U.S.), **18th:** 206; **20th:** Federal Bureau of Investigation, 1868, 4292; protection of, 4003; U.S. Supreme Court, 378, 484, 655, 1922
Civil List Act (1782), **18th:** 410
Civil rights, **18th:** England, 88, 425; European Jews, 676; France, 648, 844; Ireland, 965; Thomas Paine, 760; William Pitt the Elder, 788; United States, 664; women, 1109; **20th:** accused persons, 4234; legislation, 2100; NAACP, 4309; Soviet Union, 3604; U.S. Supreme Court, 485, 1030; World War I, 3879. *See also* Bill of Rights, U.S.; Civil liberties; Religious freedom; States' rights; Category Index
Civil Rights Act of 1866, **19th:** 1232
Civil Rights Act of 1875, **19th:** 686
Civil Rights Act of 1957, **20th:** 1127, 2030
Civil Rights Act of 1960, **20th:** 1127
Civil Rights Act of 1964, **20th:** 2030, 2149
Civil Rights Memorial, **20th:** 2386
Civil Rights movement, **20th:** James Baldwin, 203; Jesse Jackson, 1978; Malcolm X, 2571; memorial, 2386; Montgomery bus boycott, 12, 2148, 3120; U.S. Supreme Court, 382; voting rights, 1096, 1651
Civil service, Chinese, **Anc:** 960
Civil War, U.S. (1861-1865), **19th:** 613; Clara Barton, 145; John Bright, 304; George A. Custer, 582; David G. Farragut, 764; financing, 472, 544; James A. Garfield, 869; William Lloyd Garrison, 877; Ulysses S. Grant, 959; guns, 535; Benjamin Harrison, 1041; Rutherford B. Hayes, 1061; Wild Bill Hickok, 1093; Andrew Jackson, 1199; Andrew Johnson, 1230; Robert E. Lee, 1335; Abraham Lincoln, 1383; William McKinley, 1460; Thomas Nast, 1649; New Mexico, 429; photography, 294; Winfield Scott, 2054; William Tecumseh Sherman, 2099; Edwin M. Stanton, 2143
Civil Wars, The. See *Comentarii de bello civili*
Civil Wars, Roman (49-69), **Anc:** 18, 195, 508, 535
Civil Works Administration, **20th:** 1873
Civilian Conservation Corps, **20th:** 2493
Civilización y barbarie. See *Life in the Argentine Republic in the Days of the Tyrants*
Civilization and Capitalism, Fifteenth to Eighteenth Century (Braudel), **20th:** 499
Civilization of the Renaissance in Italy, The (Burckhardt), **19th:** 355
Civitate, Battle of (1053), **MA:** 646
Cixi, **19th:** 496-498, 1253, 1364, 2484, 2486; **20th:** 741; **Notor:** 1123
Claflin, Victoria. *See* Woodhull, Victoria
Claiborne, Billy, **19th:** 721
Claims of the Bible and of Science, The (Maurice), **19th:** 1520
Clairmont, Claire, **19th:** 2088, 2093
Clamor Validus. *See* Hrosvitha
Clan-na-Gael, **19th:** 1113
Clanton, Billy, **19th:** 721; **Notor:** 315
Clanton, Ike, **19th:** 721; **Notor:** 315
Clanton, Newman "Old Man," **Notor:** 144
Clapham sect, **18th:** 702, 704, 1080
Clapiers, Luc de. *See* Vauvenargues, marquis de
Clare of Assisi, Saint, **MA:** 284-286, 379, 438
Clarel (Melville), **19th:** 1540
Claremount, Arnesto, **20th:** 3500
Clarence Darrow (Rintels), **20th:** 1266

Clarendon, first earl of, **17th:** 147, 166-170, 240, 507, 816, 839
Clarendon Code (1661-1665), **17th:** 121, 148, 169, 347
Clarification of Questions, A (Khomeini), **20th:** 2124
Clarino Quartet (Zwilich), **20th:** 4476
Clarissa (Richardson), **18th:** 221, 577, 842
Clark, Arizona Donnie. *See* Barker, Ma
Clark, George Rogers, **18th:** 160, 253-256
Clark, Joe, **20th:** 2866, 3654, 4078
Clark, Marcia, **Notor:** 960
Clark, William, **19th:** 442, 1359-1363, 1962; journal, 1361
Clarke, Aileen. *See* Hernandez, Aileen Clarke
Clarke, Daniel, **Notor:** 30
Clarke, Edward Young, **Notor:** 957
Clarke, Judith, **Notor:** 978
Clarke, Samuel, **17th:** 516
Clarke-Butler correspondence, **18th:** 187
Clarke Institution, **19th:** 1143
Clarkson, Laurence, **17th:** 666
Class structure, **Anc:** Athens, 808; Hindu, 500; **18th:** China, 818; in drama, 599; England, 156, 167, 1109; France, 78, 821, 997; in literature, 98, 180-183, 210; Prussia, 379; **Ren:** Africa, 10; England, 302, 543; France, 424; Japan, 944; Russia, 490
Classes plantarum (Linnaeus), **18th:** 606
Classic of Filial Piety for Women. See *Nü xiao jing*
Classical music, **18th:** 281-284, 418-421; **20th:** Andalusian influence, 1207; Austria, 2559, 4263; Brazil, 4164; conducting, 339, 450, 4050; contemporary, 454, 3873, 4415, 4476; Czechoslovakia, 1989; Denmark, 2965; education, 450; England, 954, 1133, 4148, 4218; Finland, 3736; France, 937, 2716, 3318, 3386, 3600; Germany, 1763, 1812, 3885, 4274; Italy, 2703, 3346; Japan, 3923; Russia, 3339, 3361, 3728, 3888; Spain, 681, 1207; Spanish guitar, 3692; United States, 230, 838, 1553, 1886, 1975, 4143. *See also* Cantatas; Opera; Oratorios; Organ music
Classical symphony (Prokofiev), **20th:** 3339
Claude, Georges, **20th:** 775-777
Claude Lorrain, **17th:** 171-173
Claude Neon Company, **20th:** 776
Claudel, Paul, **20th:** 2735
Claude's Confession (Zola), **19th:** 2489
Claudian, **Anc:** 824
Claudine at School (Gauthier-Villars), **20th:** 804
Claudius I, **Anc:** 23, 72, 102, 178, 217-220, 511, 561, 591; **Notor:** 195, 777
Claudius, Appius, **Anc:** 359
Claudius Drusus Nero Germanicus, Tiberius. *See* Claudius I
Claudius Ptolemaeus. *See* Ptolemy (astronomer)
Clausewitz, Carl von, **19th:** 499-502, 929, 2006; on war, 501
Clausius, Rudolf, **20th:** 2934
Clay, Cassius Marcellus, Jr. *See* Ali, Muhammad
Clay, Henry, **19th:** 22, 502-507, 579, 782, 855, 1589, 1821
Claypoole, Betsy. *See* Ross, Betsy
Cleanthes of Assos, **Anc:** 690
Clear Mirror, The, **MA:** 773
Cleis, **Anc:** 750
Cleisthenes of Athens, **Anc:** 8, 214, 221-223, 226, 564
Clelia (Scudéry), **17th:** 829
Clemenceau, Georges, **20th:** 778-782, 3293
Clemens, Samuel Langhorne. *See* Twain, Mark
Clement I (bishop of Rome), **Anc:** 223-226, 270
Clement III (antipope), **MA:** 435, 707, 1043
Clement III (pope), **MA:** 541, 576
Clement IV (pope), **MA:** 128, 182, 853, 1106
Clement V (pope), **MA:** 897; **Notor:** 116
Clement VI (pope), **MA:** 763, 780; **Ren:** 143
Clement VII (antipope), **MA:** 237
Clement VII (pope), **Ren:** 44, 54, 112, 182, 184, 189, 203, 221, 229-232, 411, 423, 514, 559, 589, 622, 639, 658, 683, 768, 997; **Notor:** 212-214, 631, 1053
Clement VIII (pope), **Ren:** 430; **17th:** 720; **Notor:** 192
Clement IX (pope), **17th:** 406, 422
Clement X (pope), **17th:** 406, 607
Clément, Jacques, **Ren:** 428, 705; **Notor:** 214-215
Clement of Alexandria, **Anc:** 423
Clementina, La (Boccherini), **18th:** 130
Cleombrotus, **Anc:** 304
Cleomenes I, **Anc:** 221, 226-229, 505
Cleomenes II, **Anc:** 226-229
Cleomenes III, **Anc:** 226-229
Cleon, **Anc:** 90
Cleonice, **Anc:** 616
Cleopatra (sister of Alexander the Great), **Anc:** 597
Cleopatra (film), **20th:** 3954
Cleopatra (Haggard), **19th:** 1007
Cleopatra VII, **Anc:** 21, 71, 75, 108, 146, 174, 229-232, 404, 705, 814, 987; **Notor:** 384
Clephane, James O., **19th:** 1558
Clérel, Alexis-Henri-Charles-Maurice. *See* Tocqueville, Alexis de
Clergy, marriage and, **MA:** 434
Clerks Regular, **17th:** 330
Clermont, Council of (1095), **MA:** 1044-1045

Clerville, chevalier de, **17th:** 946
Clesson, Olivier de, **Notor:** 203
Cleveland, Grover, **19th:** 59, 252, 507-511, 1042, 1461; on Chinese immigrants, 509; conservation, 1624; Thomas Nast, 1650; **Notor:** 1031
Cleveland Indians, **20th:** 3468
Cleveland Penny Press, **19th:** 2056
Clifford of Chudleigh, first Baron (Thomas Clifford), **17th:** 507, 839
Cliffs at Étretat After the Storm (Courbet), **19th:** 560
Clifton Bridge, **19th:** 335
Cligés (Chrétien), **MA:** 267
Climate Near the Ground, The (Geiger), **20th:** 1443
Climate of Fear (Soyinka), **20th:** 3806
Clinton, Bill, **20th:** 465, 596, 783-789, 1016; Madeleine Albright, 55; impeachment of, 3408; Jesse Jackson, 1980; **Notor:** 472, 901, 1121
Clinton, DeWitt, **19th:** 512-516
Clinton, George, **19th:** 364
Clinton, Sir Henry, **18th:** 61, 256-259, 852
Clinton, Hillary Rodham, **20th:** 783, 788-790
Clintonianism, **19th:** 513
Clive, Kitty, **18th:** 1; rivalry with Peg Woffington, 1103
Clive, Robert, **18th:** 259-262, 312, 469
Cloaca Maxima, **Anc:** 847
Clock Without Hands (McCullers), **20th:** 2509
Clocks, **Anc:** medicine and, 411; water, 247; **19th:** electric, 550
Clodia, **Anc:** 197, 233-235, 706
Clodius Pulcher, Publius, **Anc:** 212, 233, 682
Clothbeating Block, The (Zeami), **MA:** 1154
Clothed Maja (Goya), **18th:** 438
Clotilda, Saint, **MA:** 287-289, 291, 381
Cloud in Pants, A (Mayakovsky), **20th:** 2659
Cloud Messenger, The. See *Meghadūta*
Cloudcuckooland, **Anc:** 92
Clouds, The. See *Nephelai*
Clough, Arthur Hugh, **19th:** 72
Clovis, **MA:** 242, 287, 290-294, 381, 427
Clovis et Clotilde (Bizet), **19th:** 241
Clown, The (Böll), **20th:** 412
Clownesse, Cha-U-Kao, La (Toulouse-Lautrec), **19th:** 2290
Cluniacs, **MA:** 161, 399
Clurman, Harold, **20th:** 862
Clutterbuck, Dorothy, **Notor:** 215-217
Clyfton, Richard, **17th:** 84
CMS. *See* Church Missionary Society
CNN, **20th:** 4119; Headline News, 4120
Coal, **18th:** 162, 294, 717, 734, 859, 1087; **20th:** miners' strikes, 2360, 2362
Coal Smoke Abatement Society, **19th:** 1106
Coat of Many Colors (Parton), **20th:** 3128
Cobb, Ty, **20th:** 791-793; **Notor:** 521
Cobbett, William, **19th:** 517-520, 642
Cobden, Richard, **19th:** 302, 520-523, 1770
Cobden-Chevalier Treaty (1860), **19th:** 522
Cobden Club, **19th:** 522
Cobdenism, **19th:** 521
COBOL (programming language), **20th:** 1881
Cobwebs from an Empty Skull (Bierce), **19th:** 229
Cochise, **19th:** 905
Cochise War (1861-1872), **19th:** 905
Cochran, Johnnie L., **Notor:** 959-960
Cochrane, Alexander Baillie, **19th:** 667
Cochrane, Robert, **Ren:** 496
Cochrane, Thomas, **19th:** 1704
Cock (Brancusi), **20th:** 480
Cock, Hieronymus, **Ren:** 135
Cockaigne Overture (Elgar), **20th:** 1134
Cockerell, Samuel Pepys, **19th:** 1325
Cocksure (Richler), **20th:** 3438
Cocktail Party, The (Eliot), **20th:**1141
Cocteau, Jean, **20th:** 794-796, 986, 2735, 3643
Coddington, William, **17th:** 130
Code breaking, **20th:** 4112
Code Henri, **Ren:** 428
Code Napoleon, **19th:** 2003
Code of 1650 (Connecticut), **17th:** 568
Code of Jewish Law (Karo), **Ren:** 525
Code of Maimonides, The (Maimonides), **MA:** 687, 747
Codex Argenteus (Ulfilas), **Anc:** 912
Codex Iustinianus. See *Justinian's Codification*
Cody, William, **19th:** 388, 524-527, 1692, 2110; George A. Custer, 526
Coe, Sebastian, **20th:** 797-801
Coecke van Aelst, Pieter, **Ren:** 135
Coeducation, **18th:** 90
Coele-Syria, **Anc:** 66
Coelebs in Search of a Wife (More), **18th:** 703
Coelestius, **Anc:** 948
Coercive Acts (1774), **18th:** 11, 460
Coeur, Jacques, **Ren:** 226
Coffeehouses, **18th:** 22
Coffer, The (Ariosto), **Ren:** 57
Coffin, Henry Sloane, **20th:** 2962
Coffin, Lucretia. *See* Mott, Lucretia
Coffman, Faye Robert. *See* Gilmore, Gary

Cognac, League of, **Ren:** 230, 411
Cogswell, Joseph, **19th:** 130
Cohen, Paul J., **20th:** 1512
Cohn, Ferdinand Julius, **19th:** 527-529, 1293
Cohn, Harry, **20th:** 1731
Cohn, Roy, **20th:** 2499; **Notor:** 217-219, 670
Cohnheim, Julius, **19th:** 1293
Coincidence counting technique, **20th:** 444
Coins and currency, **MA:** Arabic, 4; Chinese, 1127; Scandinavian, 692; **18th:** Benjamin Franklin, 371; Japanese, 981; manufacture of, 157; U.S., 207, 1045
COINTELPRO, **20th:** 1867
Coke, Sir Edward, **Ren:** 571; **17th:** 132, 174-179, 414, 767, 982
Cōlas, **MA:** 876
Colbert, Claudette, **20th:** 142
Colbert, Jean-Baptiste, **17th:** 135, 180-183, 398, 505, 554, 558, 570, 588, 590, 622, 731; **18th:** 362
Colbertisme, **18th:** 362, 821
Colborne, John, **19th:** 1457
Colburn, Zerah, **19th:** 1015
Colchester, Siege of (1648), **17th:** 263
Cold War, **20th:** 1823, 1832, 2100, 2376, 3819, 4088
Cold War, The (Lippmann), **20th:** 2402
Cole, Thomas, **19th:** 232
Colebrooke, Henry, **19th:** 1866
Coleman, Bessie, **20th:** 801-803
Colenso, John, **19th:** 1520
Coleridge, Samuel Taylor, **19th:** 529-533, 746, 997, 2462; **Notor:** 261
Coleridge, Stephen, **20th:** 260, 3831
Coleridge, William, **19th:** 617
Colet, John, **Ren:** 232-235, 333, 697
Colette, **20th:** 804-807, 1767; **Notor:** 933
Colfax, Schuyler, **Notor:** 19, 219-221
Coligny, Gaspard II de, **Ren:** 429, 703; **17th:** 896
Coliseo del Buen Retiro, El, **17th:** 113
Coll, Peter, **Notor:** 938
Coll, Vincent, **Notor:** 221-222, 695, 938
Collages, **20th:** 1177, 3380
Collationes in Hexaemeron. See *Collations on the Six Days*
Collations on the Six Days (Bonaventure), **MA:** 182
Colle, Giovanni, **17th:** 565
Collected Essays (Bradley), **19th:** 289
Collected Papers of Charles Sanders Peirce (Peirce), **19th:** 1773
Collected Poems (Cummings), **20th:** 881
Collected Poems (Frost), **20th:** 1350
Collected Poems of H. D. (H. D.), **20th:** 1624
Collected Works of Billy the Kid, The (Ondaatje), **20th:** 3048
Collection of English Words (Ray), **17th:** 782
Collection of Private Devotions, A (Cosin), **17th:** 202
Collectiones catholicae et canonicae scripturae (William of Saint-Amour), **MA:** 1112
Collections of the Maine Historical Society (Hakluyt), **Ren:** 419
College (film), **20th:** 2091
Collège des Quatre-Nations, **17th:** 533
Collichang. *See* Kalicho
Collin, Frank, **Notor:** 222-223
Collins, Joel, **Notor:** 68
Collins, Michael, **20th:** 136, 807-810, 843, 1592
Collins, Norman, **20th:** 810-813
Collip, James Bertram, **20th:** 226, 2526
Colloquia familiaria. See *Colloquies of Erasmus, The*
Colloquies of Erasmus, The (Erasmus), **Ren:** 316
Colloquy of _______. *See* _______, Colloquy of
Collor de Melo, Fernando, **20th:** 651
Colombe, La (Gounod), **19th:** 953
Colombia, **19th:** independence, 2195. *See also* Geographical Index
Colombian Congress of Angostura (1819), **19th:** 269
Colombières, Treaty of (1189), **MA:** 836
Colombo, Christopher, **Notor:** 224
Colombo, Joe, **Notor:** 224-225, 393, 396, 864
Colombo, Matteo Realdo, **Ren:** 862
Colón, Cristóbal. *See* Columbus, Christopher
Colonels (Irish military recruiters), **17th:** 700
Colonial Act of 1930, **20th:** 3607
Colonial Advocate (newspaper), **19th:** 1456
Colonialism, **18th:** British in Africa, 766; British in Australia, 783-785; British in Canada, 196; British in India, 469-472; British in North America, 802; British in West Indies, 855; French in North America, 802; French in West Indies, 153, 985; Spanish in the Americas, 394-396, 891, 993; **19th:** Britain in Africa, 1893; Britain in Australia, 2379; Britain in Burma, 596; Britain in New Zealand, 2379; **20th:** 3464; Africa, 1213; Algeria, 9; Vietnam, 1835, 4169
Colonization, **Anc:** Assyrian, 753; Carthaginian, 385; Phoenician, 273; Roman, 359; **Ren:** England of North America, 193, 397, 420, 771, 813; France

of North America, 179, 673; Portugal of China, 168, 1009; Portugal of India, 23, 167, 367, 1000; Portugal of South America, 513; Spain of Southeast Asia, 551; Spain of the Americas, 26, 35, 76, 220, 239, 245, 252, 273, 409, 512, 537-538, 621, 672, 800, 802, 804, 902; **17th:** Dutch of New Amsterdam, 393; Dutch of New England, 890; Dutch of New York, 644; England of New England, 768, 875, 878; England of North America, 864; England of Pennsylvania, 726; England of the Jerseys, 726; France of Canada, 141, 499; France of Louisiana, 402, 491; Portugal of Africa, 687; Sweden of North America, 645. *See also* Exploration
Colonna, Pompeo, **Ren:** 230
Colonna, Vittoria, **Ren:** 235-237; Fracastoro's treatment of, 345
Color and Democracy (Du Bois), **20th:** 1049
Color field movement, **20th:** 3540
Color of Money, The (film), **20th:** 3682
Color Purple, The (film), **20th:** 4373
Color Purple, The (novel by Walker), **20th:** 4197
Color Struck (Hurston), **20th:** 1944
Coloradeau of Medusa (Ernst), **20th:** 1178
Colorado mine strike (1913-1914), **20th:** 2041, 3477
Colored Women's Progressive Franchise Association, **19th:** 432
Colosimo, "Big Jim," **20th:** 641
Colossus, and Other Poems, The (Plath), **20th:** 3286
Colson, Charles W., **Notor:** 225-227, 443
Colt, Samuel, **19th:** 533-536
Coltrane (Coltrane), **20th:** 814
Coltrane, John, **20th:** 814-816
Columbia University, **20th:** 599
Columbus, Christopher, **Ren:** 156, 237-241, 252, 288, 330, 344, 408, 512, 537, 591, 789, 803, 970; personal log, 239; **Notor:** 14
Columbus, Diego, **Ren:** 805
Columbus, New Mexico, raid of, **20th:** 4161
Columbus Hospital, **19th:** 384
Column of Infamy, The (Manzoni), **19th:** 1497
Colville Indian Reservation, **19th:** 1240
Comanche, **19th:** 429, 1794, 2116
Combat avec l'ange (Giraudoux), **20th:** 1493
Combes, Émile, **20th:** 1777
Comedias de capa y espada. See Cape-and-sword plays
Comédie-Française, **18th:** 98, 597
Comédiens du Roy, **17th:** 774
Comédies-ballets, **17th:** 570
Comedy, **Anc:** Greek, 90, 548, 876; Plautus and, 663; Roman, 850; **20th:** comic strips, 3672; film, 876, 1871, 3697; Buster Keaton, 2091; Keystone Kops, 732; Martin and Lewis, 2357; musicals, 1460, 1691; slapstick, 3707; stand-up, 840, 3492; television, 213; theater, 854, 2754, 3720
Comedy of Human Life, The. See *Human Comedy, The*
Comedy of manners, **Anc:** 851
Comenius, Jan Amos. *See* Komenský, Jan
Comentarii de bello cinli (Caesar), **Anc:** 828
Comentarii de bello civili (Caesar), **Anc:** 172
Comentarii de bello Gallico (Caesar), **Anc:** 172, 828, 935
Comentarios de Don Bernardino de Mendoça de lo sucedido en las guerras de los Payses Baxos (Mendoza), **Ren:** 669
Comet Halley (Hoyle), **20th:** 1904
Cometographia (Hevelius), **17th:** 372
Comic acting, **18th:** 749
Comic opera, **18th:** 597, 713
Comic theater, **18th:** 905
Coming of Age, The (Beauvoir), **20th:** 273
Coming of Age in Samoa (Mead), **20th:** 2669
Coming of Quetzalcoatl, The (Orozco), **20th:** 3070
Coming up for Air (Orwell), **20th:** 3082
Comiskey, Charles A., **Notor:** 522
Commedia dell'arte, **Ren:** 42, 360
Commedia delle ninfe. See *Ninfale d'Ameto, Il*
Commentaire philosophique sur ces paroles de Jésus-Christ "Contrain-les d'entrer." See *Philosophical Commentary on These Words in the Gospel, Luke XIV, 23, A*
Commentaire sur Desportes (Malherbe), **17th:** 577
Commentari di C. Givlio Cesare, I (Palladio), **Ren:** 754
Commentaria in artem medicinalem Galeni (Santorio), **17th:** 811
Commentaria in primam fen primi libri canonis Avicennae (Santorio), **17th:** 811
Commentaria Oxoniensia ad IV libros magistri Sententiarum. See *Ordinatio*
Commentaries of Lorenzo Ghiberti, The (Ghiberti), **MA:** 282, 420
Commentaries of Pius II, The (Pius II), **Ren:** 795
Commentaries on American Law (Kent), **19th:** 1272
Commentaries on the Constitution of the United States (Story), **19th:** 2182
Commentaries on the Laws of England (Blackstone), **18th:** 118

Commentarii. See *Commentaries of Lorenzo Ghiberti, The*
Commentarii. See *Commentaries of Pius II, The*
Commentarii initiatorii in quartuor Evangelia (Lefèvre), **Ren:** 549
Commentariolus (Copernicus), **Ren:** 242
Commentariorum de religione Christiana libri quatuor (Ramus), **Ren:** 817
Commentary on Ecclesiastes (Neckam), **MA:** 752
Commentary on Martianus Capellus (Neckam), **MA:** 750
Commentary on Proverbs (Neckam), **MA:** 752
Commentary on the Effect of Electricity on Muscular Motion (Galvani), **18th:** 392
Commentary on the Law of Prize and Booty (Grotius), **17th:** 327
Commentary on the Song of Songs (Neckam), **MA:** 752
Commentary on True and False Religion (Zwingli), **Ren:** 1012
Commerce, **18th:** 341; Montesquieu, 697
Commerce clause (U.S. Constitution), **20th:** 521, 3408
Commerce of Algiers, The (Cervantes), **Ren:** 208
Committee for Peasant Unity, **20th:** 2686
Committee of Correspondence (U.S.); **18th:** John Adams, 18; American independence, 1041; Charles Carroll, 206; Elbridge Gerry, 412; John Jay, 524; Robert Morris, 707; Paul Revere, 833; John Witherspoon, 1100
Committee of Imperial Defense, **20th:** 210
Committee of Public Safety (France), **18th:** 291, 460, 649-650, 846, 878
Committee of Union and Progress, **19th:** 8; **20th:** 1157
Commodore, The (Forester), **20th:** 1284
Commodus, **Anc:** 350, 372, 425, 531; **Notor:** 227-229
Common law (England), **18th:** 118-121, 643-647
Common Law, The (Holmes), **20th:** 1857
Common Market, **20th:** 2795
Common Reader, The (Woolf), **20th:** 4398
Common Sense (Holbach), **18th:** 502
Common Sense (Paine), **18th:** 759
Common Sense About the War (Shaw), **20th:** 3720
Commoner, The (newspaper), **19th:** 2449
Commonitoria (Vincent of Lérins), **Anc:** 948
Commons Preservation Society, **19th:** 1105
Commonsense Book of Baby and Child Care, The (Spock), **20th:** 3814
Commonwealth (English, 1649-1660), **17th:** 33, 51, 54, 56, 137, 168, 256, 263, 345, 640, 757, 942, 989
Communal society, **18th:** 879
Commune des Arts, **19th:** 608
Communicating Vessels (Breton), **20th:** 512
Communications. *See* Category Index
Communism, **19th:** 1510; **20th:** Bertolt Brecht, 505; China, 2381, 2448, 2602; Francisco Franco, 1299; Germany, 2484; Hungary, 2468; Philippines, 2621; Soviet Union, 1922, 2342, 3733; United States, 1867, 2498
Communist League, **19th:** 750
Communist Manifesto, The (Marx and Engels), **19th:** 750, 1510
Communist parties, **20th:** Australia, 2707; China, 742, 2602, 4462; Czechoslovakia, 1043; Germany, 4125, 4457; Indonesia, 3906; Kampuchea, 3298; Kingdom of the Serbs, Croats, and Slovenes, 4034; North Korea, 2139; Romania, 704; Serbia, 2757; United States, 1867
Community and Society (Tönnies), **20th:** 4045
Community Service Organization, **20th:** 1915
Compagnia dei Comici Gelosi. *See* Gelosi
Company of Captain Frans Banning Cocq and Lieutenant Willem van Ruytenburch, The. See *Night Watch, The*
Company of Pastors, **Ren:** 164
Company She Keeps, The (McCarthy), **20th:** 2501
Comparative Physiology of Respiratory Mechanisms, The (Krogh), **20th:** 2206
Comparative Study of Religions, The (Wach), **20th:** 4178
Compasses, **MA:** 822
Compassion, Buddhist concept of, **Anc:** 112, 169
Compendium of Roman History. See *Annales* (Vellius)
Compleat Gentleman, The (Gracián), **17th:** 317
Complementarity, principle of, **20th:** 409
Complete Andersen, The (Andersen), **19th:** 62
Complete Collection of the Four Treasures (Dai Zhen, ed.), **18th:** 287
Complete Fairy Tales and Stories, The. See *Complete Andersen, The*
Complete Poems (Frost), **20th:** 1350
Complete Poems (Sandburg), **20th:** 3621
Complete Poems of Marianne Moore, The (Moore), **20th:** 2822
Complete Works (Martí), **19th:** 1504

Complutensian Polyglot Bible. *See* Polyglot Bible

Composers, **18th:** Johann Sebastian Bach, 71-74; Luigi Boccherini, 129-132; Joseph Boulogne, 153-155; François Couperin, 281-284; George Frideric Handel, 462-466; Joseph Haydn, 476-479; Wolfgang Amadeus Mozart, 711-715; Jean-Philippe Rameau, 826-829; Alessandro Scarlatti, 883-887; Georg Philipp Telemann, 970-973; Antonio Vivaldi, 1019-1022

Composition (Giacometti), **20th:** 1471

Composition VIII (Kandinsky), **20th:** 2075

Composition in Red, Yellow, and Blue (Mondrian), **20th:** 2788

Compositiones (Scribonius), **Anc:** 291

Comprehensive Test Ban Treaty (1963), **20th:** 56, 3970

Compromise of 1850, **19th:** 320, 506, 612, 681, 783, 2232

Compromise of 1867, **19th:** 819

Compton, Arthur Holly, **20th:** 443, 535, 817-820, 1237, 2751

Compton effect, **20th:** 818

Computed tomography, **20th:** 1893

Computer and the Brain, The (von Neumann), **20th:** 2946

Computer science. *See* Category Index

Computers, **20th:** development of, 1892, 4112; IBM, 4248; John von Neumann, 2945; personal, 2007; programming, 331, 707, 1421, 1880

Comstock, Anthony, **19th:** 2460; **20th:** 3626; **Notor:** 229-231, 893

Comte, Auguste, **19th:** 536-539, 865, 1045

Comte de Monte-Cristo, Le. See *Count of Monte-Cristo, The*

Comtesse de Tende, The (La Fayette), **17th:** 478

Comulgatorio, El. See *Sanctuary Meditations*

Comunero Revolt (1520-1522), **Ren:** 8, 220

Comus (Milton), **17th:** 502, 640

CONAKAT. *See* Confederation of Tribal Associations of Katanga

Conant, James Bryant, **20th:** 820-824

Conceptualism, **MA:** 13

Concerning Children (Gilman), **20th:** 1486

Concerning Famous Women (Boccaccio), **MA:** 171, 275

Concerning Modern Errors, Socialism, Communism, Nihilism (Leo XIII), **19th:** 1343

Concerning the Body and Blood of the Lord (Ratramnus), **MA:** 879

Concerning the Election of Grace (Böhme), **17th:** 61

Concerning the Spiritual in Art, and Painting in Particular (Kandinsky), **20th:** 2075

Concerning the Study of Literature (Bruni), **MA:** 209

Concerning the Three Principles of the Divine Essence (Böhme), **17th:** 61

Concerning Virginal Conception and Original Sin (Anselm), **MA:** 94

Concert champêtre (Giorgione/Titian), **Ren:** 385

Concert champêtre (Poulenc), **20th:** 3318

Concert de la Loge Olympique, Le, **18th:** 154

Concert des Amateurs, **18th:** 154

Concert Rondo in B Minor (Schubert), **19th:** 2027

Concert Spirituel, **18th:** 154

Concert Symphony in C Major (Wagner), **19th:** 2374

Concerti, **18th:** 1020

Concertino for French Horn (Weber), **19th:** 2395

Concerto for Cello and Orchestra (Schumann), **19th:** 2033

Concerto for Orchestra (Bartók), **20th:** 252

Concerto for Piano and Orchestra (Copland), **20th:** 838

Concerto for Violin and Wind Orchestra (Weill), **20th:** 4273

Concerto in G Minor (Poulenc), **20th:** 3319

Concerto No. 1 in D Minor, Op. 15 (Brahms), **19th:** 297

Conciliator differentiarum philosophorum et praecipue medicorum (Abano), **MA:** 1

Conciliator of R. Manasseh ben Israel, The (Manesseh ben Israel), **17th:** 583

Concini, Concino, **17th:** 551, 598, 791

Concluding Unscientific Postscript (Kierkegaard), **19th:** 1279

Concord, Battle of. *See* Lexington and Concord, Battle of

Concord Summer School of Philosophy and Literature, **19th:** 40

Concordat of Bologna. *See* Bologna, Concordat of

Concordia, Shrine of, **Anc:** 510

Concret PA (Xenakis), **20th:** 4415

Concrete, prestressed, **20th:** 1327

Condé, The Great (1621-1686; Louis II of Bourbon), **17th:** 159, 184-187, 549, 559, 621, 661, 821, 829, 896, 926, 933

Condé, third prince of (1588-1646; Henry II of Bourbon), **17th:** 548, 551

Condenado por desconfiado, El. See *Saint and the Sinner, The*

Condillac, Étienne Bonnot de, **18th:** 263-266

Condillac's Treatise on the Sensations (Condillac), **18th:** 264

Condition humaine, La. See *Man's Fate*

Condition humaine I, La (Magritte), **20th:** 2549
Condition of Labor, The (Leo XIII), **19th:** 1343
Condition of the Working Class in England in 1844, The (Engels), **19th:** 750, 1370
Condor Legion, **20th:** 2117
Condorcanqui, José Gabriel. *See* Tupac Amaru II
Condorcet, marquis de, **18th:** 267-269
Conducător. *See* Antonescu, Ion
Conduct of Life, The (Emerson), **19th:** 746
Conduct of the Allies, The (Swift), **18th:** 136
Conducting, Austro-German school, **20th:** 2082
Confederación de Trabajadores de México, **20th:** 649
Confederate States of America, **19th:** 612
Confédération Générale du Travail, **20th:** 780, 4053
Confederation of Tribal Associations of Katanga, **20th:** 4091
Confessing Church, **20th:** 419
Confession (Saint Patrick), **MA:** 811
Confession, A (Tolstoy), **19th:** 2285
Confession de Claude, La. See *Claude's Confession*
Confession of Faith Touching the Holy Trinity, According to Scripture, A (Biddle), **17th:** 53
Confession of the Four Cities. *See* Tetrapolitana
Confessiones (Augustine), **Anc:** 142
Confessions de J.-J. Rousseau, Les. See *Confessions of J.-J. Rousseau, The*
Confessions d'un révolutionnaire, Les (Proudhon), **19th:** 1836
Confessions of a Mask (Mishima), **20th:** 2763
Confessions of an Inquiring Spirit (Coleridge), **19th:** 532
Confessions of Felix Krull, Confidence Man (Mann), **20th:** 2596
Confessions of J.-J. Rousseau, The (Rousseau), **18th:** 870
Confessions of Lady Nijō, The (Nijō), **MA:** 771
Confidence Man, The (Melville), **19th:** 1539
Confieso que he vivido. See *Memoirs* (Neruda)
Confirming and Restoring of Ministers, Act for (1660), **17th:** 34
Confluence Project, **20th:** 2387
Confraternity of Charity, **17th:** 962
Confucianism, **Anc:** 554, 576, 779, 978; Ban Gu and, 149; Chinese government and, 960; Daoism and, 502; government and, 732; Legalism and, 380; persecution of, 780; poetry and, 184, 845; ritual and, 237; superstition and, 953; **MA:** 809, 1079, 1159; Japan, 940, 976; **18th:** 747, 817; **19th:** 1252, 2486. *See also* Neo-Confucianism
Confucius, **Anc:** 236-239, 502, 552, 783, 954
Congo, Democratic Republic of the, **20th:** independence of, 2476, 2773, 3810, 4092. *See also* Geographical Index
Congo and the Founding of Its Free State, The (Stanley), **19th:** 2140
Congo Crisis (1960-1965), **20th:** 576, 1655, 4091
Congo Free State, **19th:** 1350, 2140, 2450
Congolese National Movement. *See* Mouvement National Congolais
Congonhas do Campo (Brazil), **18th:** 608
Congrégation de Nôtre-Dame, **17th:** 75
Congregation of the Mission, **17th:** 962
Congregation of the Oratory, **Ren:** 718; **17th:** 721
Congregational Church, **18th:** 76, 668, 671
Congregationalism, **17th:** 197, 205; **19th:** New England, 465
Congregazione dei Virtuosi di Santa Cecilia, **17th:** 190
Congress Hall (Morse), **19th:** 1610
Congress of Berlin (1878), **19th:** 239
Congress of Industrial Organizations, **20th:** 2361, 2672, 3426. *See also* AFL-CIO
Congress of Paris (1856), **19th:** 445
Congress of Vienna (1815), **19th:** 47, 404
Congress Party (India), **20th:** 1385
Congressional government, United States, **18th:** 705, 910
Congressional Union. *See* National Woman's Party
Congreve, Richard, **19th:** 1045
Congreve, William, **17th:** 52, 82
Conic sections, **Anc:** 76
Cōnica (Apollonius of Perga), **Anc:** 77, 607
Coniectanea in M. Terentium Varronem de lingua latina (Scaliger), **Ren:** 856
Coningsby (Disraeli), **19th:** 667-668
Conjectures of a Guilty Bystander (Merton), **20th:** 2714
Conkling, Roscoe, **19th:** 80, 251, 1063
Conn, Billy, **20th:** 2439
Connecticut, **17th:** 567, 892; **18th:** 36, 59, 908
Connecticut Compromise. *See* Great Compromise
Connecticut Wits, **18th:** 988
Connecticut Yankee, A (Rodgers and Hart), **20th:** 1692

Connecticut Yankee in King Arthur's Court, A (Twain), **19th:** 2331
Connelly, Charles, **Notor:** 258
Connelly, John, **Notor:** 295
Conner, David, **19th:** 1777
Connolly, Owen, **17th:** 700
Connolly, Richard B., **19th:** 1650, 2334
Connor, Patrick E., **19th:** 567
Connors, Jimmy, **20th:** 428, 1193
Conon of Samos, **Anc:** 76, 80
Conquering Bear, **19th:** 566
Conquerors, The (Malraux), **20th:** 2577
Conquest. *See* Category Index under Warfare and Conquest
Conquest of Granada by the Spaniards, The (Dryden), **17th:** 241, 343
Conquest of Happiness, The (Russell), **20th:** 3563
Conquête de Constantinople, Le (Villehardouin), **MA:** 1060
Conrad I, **MA:** 805
Conrad II, **MA:** 966
Conrad III, **MA:** 162, 357, 384, 499
Conrad IV, **MA:** 390, 547
Conrad, Joseph, **19th:** 564; **20th:** 824-828; **Notor:** 633
Conrad Gesner: A Bio-Bibliography (Gesner), **Ren:** 375
Conscience (Dumas), **19th:** 697
Conscience, Council of, **17th:** 963
Conscious Lovers, The (Steele), **18th:** 942
Consciousness, **Anc:** Buddhism and, 932
Conscription, **19th:** Australia, 1493; **20th:** Muhammad Ali, 63; Australia, 892, 1932, 2489; Canada, 2158; New Zealand, 2644
Consequentie (Buridan), **MA:** 216
Conservation. *See* Category Index
Conservation of Youth and Defense of Age, The (Arnold of Villanova), **MA:** 100
Conservationists, **19th:** 1624, 1707
Conservatism, **18th:** John Adams, 13; England, 139, 174-177; Adam Smith, 922
Conservative Party (Canada), **19th:** 1453
Conservative Party (United Kingdom), **20th:** 209, 2292
Considerations on the Currency and Banking System of the United States, **19th:** 856
Considerations on the "Discourses" of Machiavelli (Guicciardini), **Ren:** 411
Considerations sur le pouvoir spirituel (Comte), **19th:** 538
Considerazioni sui "Discorsi" de Machiavelli. See *Considerations on the "Discourses" of Machiavelli*
Consolation à Monsieur du Périer sur la mort de sa fille (Malherbe), **17th:** 577
Consolation of Philosophy, The (Boethius), **MA:** 174, 265, 1015
Consolations in Travel (Davy), **19th:** 618
Consolatoria (Guicciardini), **Ren:** 411
Conspiracies, **Anc:** by Arsinoe I, 107; against Attila, 140; against Julius Caesar, 74, 146, 166, 174, 185; against Caligula, 178; by Catiline, 189, 194, 212, 742; by Cinadon of Sparta, 15; against Claudius, 102; against Nero, 593; against Tiberius, 72
Conspiracy and Tragedy of Charles, Duke of Byron, The (Chapman), **Ren:** 215
Conspiracy of Catiline, The. See *Bellum Catilinae*
Constable, John, **19th:** 540-543, 636; **20th:** 2790
Constance, Council of (1414-1418), **MA:** 209, 238, 524, 850, 1091, 1132
Constance, Treaty of (1153), **MA:** 385
Constant Prince, The (Calderón), **17th:** 114
Constantia and Philetus (Cowley), **17th:** 199
Constantine (saint). *See* Cyril, Saint
Constantine I the Great (c. 272/285-337), **Anc:** 132, 239-243, 330, 391, 775, 825
Constantine I of Ethiopia (1399-1468). *See* Zara Yaqob
Constantine I (1868-1923; king of Greece), **20th:** 4158; **Notor:** 724
Constantine II (b. 1940; king of Greece), **20th:** 3106
Constantine V Copronymus (719-775; Eastern Roman emperor), **MA:** 548, 1020
Constantine VI (771-797; Eastern Roman emperor), **MA:** 467, 549
Constantine VII Porphyrogenitus (905-959; Eastern Roman emperor), **MA:** 793
Constantine IX Monomachus (c. 980-1055; Byzantine emperor), **MA:** 863
Constantine X Ducas (1007?-1067; Byzantine emperor), **MA:** 865
Constantine XI Palaeologus (1404-1453; Byzantine emperor), **MA:** 711; **Ren:** 659, 749
Constantine, Donation of, **MA:** 646, 1051
Constantine, Learie, **20th:** 829-831
Constantinople, **Anc:** 242, 361, 751, 797, 825, 868, 911; Hunnic invasion of, 139; **MA:** 158; Siege of (626), 934; Siege of (717), 1020; Siege of (1453), 479, 712; **Ren:** fall of (1453), 659, 795; **18th:** 26, 416, 602, 639, 687, 719. *See also* Byzantium

Constantinople, Battle of (1203), **MA:** 299, 1059
Constantinople, Council of (381), **Anc:** 364, 796, 869
Constantinople, Council of (553), **Anc:** 862
Constantinople, Council of (786), **MA:** 549
Constantinople, Council of (861), **MA:** 766
Constantinople, Iconoclast Synod of (754), **MA:** 590
Constantinople, Second Battle of (1204), **MA:** 299, 1059
Constantinople, Synod of (382), **Anc:** 913
Constantius I (Chlorus), **Anc:** 239, 281, 391
Constantius II, **Anc:** 134, 242, 775
Constitution (newspaper), **19th:** 1458
Constitution a Pro-Slavery Compact, The (Phillips), **19th:** 1787
Constitution Act of 1842 (Australia), **19th:** 2414
Constitution Act of 1852 (New Zealand), **19th:** 1483
Constitution Act of 1982 (Canada), **20th:** 4078
Constitution, U.S., **18th:** 13; Sir William Blackstone, 118; John Dickinson, 306; analysis in *The Federalist*, 454; First Amendment, 76; Alexander Hamilton, 453; John Hancock, 460; Patrick Henry, 484; John Jay, 525; James Madison, 636-638; George Mason, 665; Gouverneur Morris, 705-707; Daniel Shays, 903; Roger Sherman, 910; James Wilson, 1092
Constitution of 1887 (Hawaii), **19th:** 1374
Constitutional Convention, U.S. (1787), **18th:** 705, 903, 910, 1045
Constitutional government, **18th:** France, 619, 648, 680, 845, 878, 918; Great Britain, 138, 400-412, 421-424, 739
Constitutional View of the Late War Between the States, A (Stephens), **19th:** 2166
Constitutions, **Anc:** Athenian, 214, 221, 293, 564, 807; Roman, 832, 848; Sparta, 228; **18th:** British, 119, 740; French, 845, 918; Haitian, 987; **19th:** Argentina, 2001; Australia, 150, 624, 1741; Bolivia, 269; Canada, 710; Cherokee, 1937; Chile, 1703; Confederate States of America, 2165; Germany, 239; Japan, 1186, 1631; Mexico, 1246; New South Wales, 2415; South African Republic, 1298; United States, 2400
Constitutions of Clarendon (1164), **MA:** 57, 148, 484
Constructeurs, Les (Léger), **20th:** 2336
Construction of a Marvelous Canon of Logarithms (Napier), **Ren:** 712
Consuelo (Sand), **19th:** 1988
Consul, The (Menotti), **20th:** 2705
Consultatio de causa matrimoniali (Ockham), **MA:** 780
Consumer movement, **20th:** 2898
Contact (Sagan), **20th:** 3592
Contagious Diseases Acts of 1864, **19th:** 1866, 1869, 372, 766
"Containing Some Microbial Observations, About Animals in the Scurf of the Teeth . . ." (Leeuwenhoek), **17th:** 511
Containment policy, U.S., **20th:** 4088
Conte di Carmagnola, Il (Manzoni), **19th:** 1496
"Contemplations" (Bradstreet), **17th:** 90
Contemplations, Les (Hugo), **19th:** 1148
Contemporary American History, 1877-1913 (Beard), **20th:** 263
Contempt (film), **20th:** 1504
Contes à Ninon. See *Stories for Ninon*
Contes de Jacques Tournebroche. See *Merrie Tales of Jacques Tournebroche, The*
Contes de ma mère l'oye. See *Tales of Mother Goose*
Contes des fées. See *Tales of Mother Goose*
Contes d'Hoffmann, Les (Offenbach), **19th:** 1701
Contes et nouvelles en vers. See *Tales and Short Stories in Verse*
Continens Medicinae. See *Kitāb al-hāwī fiʿl ṭibb, al-*
Continental army. *See* Army, U.S.
Continental Congress, **18th:** 528; John Adams, 11; Samuel Chase, 238; American flag, 866; Benjamin Franklin, 372; Alexander Hamilton, 453; John Hancock, 460; Patrick Henry, 483; John Jay, 524; James Madison, 636; Gouverneur Morris, 705; Robert Morris, 707; and religious freedom, 76; Roger Sherman, 909; George Washington, 1043; James Wilson, 1091; John Witherspoon, 1100
Continental drift, **20th:** 4266
Continental navy. *See* Navy, U.S.
Continental Shelf Station, **20th:** 851
Continuation War (1941-1944), **20th:** 2599
Contra Apionem (Josephus), **Anc:** 479
Contra Arianos (Athanasius), **Anc:** 134
Contra Celsum (Origen), **Anc:** 601
Contra Eunomium (Gregory of Nyssa), **Anc:** 364
Contra graecorum opposita (Ratramnus), **MA:** 880
Contra War (1970-1987), **20th:** 122

Contrabandistas, The (Sullivan and Burnand), **19th:** 918
Contrasts (Pugin), **19th:** 1839
Contrasts of Forms (Léger), **20th:** 2335
Contrat social, Du. See *Treatise on the Social Contract, A*
Contre Sainte-Beuve. See *By Way of Sainte-Beuve*
Contribution to a Critique of Political Economy, A (Marx), **19th:** 1511
Contribution to the Sanitary History of the British Army During the Late War with Russia, A (Nightingale), **19th:** 1687
Contributions to the Natural History of the United States (Agassiz), **19th:** 32
Conventicle Act (1664), **17th:** 34, 101, 122
Conventicle of God's Real Servants, **17th:** 59
Convention of 1832 (Texas), **19th:** 100
Convention of 1833 (Texas), **19th:** 100
Convention of Vergara (1839), **19th:** 414
Convention People's Party (Ghana), **20th:** 2989
Conventional Lies of Our Civilization, The (Nordau), **20th:** 2993
Conventuals, **MA:** 922
Conversations nouvelle sur divers sujets (Scudéry), **17th:** 829
Conversations sur divers sujets. See *Conversations upon Several Subjects*
Conversations upon Several Subjects (Scudéry), **17th:** 829
Conversations with Children on the Gospels (Alcott), **19th:** 40, 1761
Conversations with Stalin (Djilas), **20th:** 1012
Conversion of Saint Paul, **Anc:** 613
Conversion of Saint Paul, The (Caravaggio), **Ren:** 171
Conversion of Saint Paul, The (Michelangelo), **Ren:** 684
Conversos. *See* New Christians
Convivio, Il. See *Banquet, The*
Conway, Anne, **17th:** 187-189, 252
Cook, Frederick, **20th:** 3177
Cook, James, **18th:** 80, 270-274, 1006; **19th:** 1249; **Notor:** 261
Cooke, Janet, **Notor:** 231-233
Cooke, Jay, **19th:** 472, 544-547
Cooke, William Fothergill, **19th:** 547-551
Cookie (film), **20th:** 1163
Coolhaes, Caspar, **Ren:** 60
Coolidge, Calvin, **20th:** 832-836, 2767
Cooper, Anthony Ashley. *See* Shaftesbury, first earl of
Cooper, D. B., **Notor:** 233-235
Cooper, Dan. *See* Cooper, D. B.
Cooper, Gary, **20th:** 998
Cooper, James Fenimore, **19th:** 552-556
Cooper, Leon, **20th:** 235
Cooper, Terence, **Notor:** 283
Coote, Richard, **17th:** 464
Coowescoowe. *See* Ross, John (Native American leader)
Cope, John Lachlan, **20th:** 4340
Copeland, John, **19th:** 321
Copenhagen, Battle of (1801), **18th:** 128
Copenhagen, Treaty of (1660), **17th:** 155
Copernicus, Nicolaus, **Anc:** 78, 419; **Ren:** 130, 241-245, 823
Copland, Aaron, **20th:** 836-840, 958, 1976
Copland-Sessions Concerts, **20th:** 838
Copley, John Singleton, **18th:** 274-277
Copley Medal, **18th:** 492, 1024
Coppélia (Delibes), **19th:** 639
Coppoc, Edwin, **19th:** 321
Coppola, Francis Ford, **20th:** 2450
Coq d'Or, Le (Rimsky-Korsakov), **20th:** 986
Coquette (film), **20th:** 3245
Coquette (play by Abbott and Bridgers), **20th:** 1724
Coquette vangée, La (Lenclos), **17th:** 521
Coral Sea, Battle of (1942), **20th:** 1648
Coralli, Jean, **19th:** 744
Corbeil, Treaty of (1258), **MA:** 572
Corbett, Richard, **17th:** 443
Corbridge, First Battle of (914), **MA:** 32
Corbridge, Second Battle of (917), **MA:** 32
Corbusier, Le. *See* Le Corbusier
Corday, Charlotte, **18th:** 650; **Notor:** 235-237, 697
Córdoba, **MA:** 11; Umayyad caliphs, 10; University of, 11
Córdoba, Gonzalo Fernández de, **Ren:** 228, 330
Córdoba, Treaty of (1821), **19th:** 1991
Cordovero, Moses ben Jacob, **Ren:** 579
Cordus, Valerius, **Ren:** 376
Coreglia, Michelotto, **Ren:** 116, 118
Corelli, Arcangelo, **17th:** 190-192; **18th:** 282, 463
Corésus Sacrificing Himself to Save Callirhoé (Fragonard), **18th:** 367
Corey, Robert B., **20th:** 3156
Corinna of Tanagra, **Anc:** 646
Corinne (Staël), **18th:** 931
Corinth, League of, **Anc:** 639
Corinthian War (395-386 B.C.E.), **Anc:** 15, 304
Corinthians, **Anc:** 224
Coriolanus (Shakespeare), **Anc:** 672
Cork, first earl of. *See* Boyle, Richard
Cormac, Anne. *See* Bonny, Anne
Cormack, Allan, **20th:** 1893

Cormorants, The (Sōtatsu), **17th:** 869
Corn Laws, **19th:** critique of, 1897; of 1815, 1398; repeal of, 521, 643, 667
Cornaro Chapel, **17th:** 46
Cornaro Piscopia, Elena. *See* Piscopia, Elena Cornaro
Corneille, Pierre, **17th:** 193-196; and Jean de La Fontaine, 482; and the duchesse de Longueville, 550; and Jean-Baptiste Lully, 570; and Molière, 647; and Katherine Philips, 742; and Nicolas Poussin, 751; and Jean Racine, 774; and the French salons, 780; and Madame de Sévigné, 834
Cornell, George, **Notor:** 592, 594
Corner of the Moulin de la Galette, A (Toulouse-Lautrec), **19th:** 2289
Cornfeld, Bernie, **Notor:** 359
Cornhuskers (Sandburg), **20th:** 3620
Corning, Kyle. *See* Gardner, Erle Stanley
Cornwallis, Charles, first Marquess, **18th:** 258, 278-281, 444, 852; surrender at Yorktown, 152, 279, 853; **19th:** 438
Coronado, Carolina, **19th:** 556-558
Coronado, Francisco Vásquez de, **Ren:** 154, 245-248
Coronation of the Virgin (Bellini), **Ren:** 97
Corot, Camille, **19th:** 1799
Corpus Hippocraticum (Hippocrates), **Anc:** 420
Corpus inscriptionum Latinarum, **MA:** 852; **19th:** 1584
Corpus juris civilis, **MA:** 601
Corpus Tibullianum, **Anc:** 835
Corpuscular philosophy, **17th:** 80
Correggio, **Ren:** 175, 249-251, 486; **19th:** 434
Correntes, **17th:** 296
Correspondence of Samuel Richardson, The (Barbauld), **18th:** 88
Corrigan, Michael, **19th:** 384
Corrogationes Promethei (Neckam), **MA:** 751-752
Corsair, The (Byron), **19th:** 380
Corsaire, Le (ballet), **19th:** 639
Corsey, Eliza Hopewell, **Notor:** 135
Cortés, Fernando. *See* Cortés, Hernán
Cortés, Hernán, **Ren:** 34, 161, 220, 245, 252-255, 273, 621, 695, 801
Cortese, Paolo, **Ren:** 517
Cortéz, Hernán. *See* Cortés, Hernán
Cortigiana, La. See *Courtesan, The*
Cortisone, synthesis of, **20th:** 4394
Cortlandt, Stephanus van, **17th:** 519
Cortona, Pietro da, **17th:** 937
Corvin, Mátyás. *See* Matthias I Corvinus
Corvinus, Matthias I. *See* Matthias I Corvinus
Cosby, Bill (entertainer), **20th:** 840-842
Cosby, William (governor of New York), **18th:** 1116
Cosby Show, The (television program), **20th:** 841
Cose fiorentine (Guicciardini), **Ren:** 411
Cosgrave, William T., **20th:** 843-846
Così è (se vi pare). See *Right You Are (If You Think So)*
Cosimo I de Medici. *See* Medici, Cosimo I de'
Cosimo II. *See* Medici, Cosimo II de'
Cosimo the Great. *See* Medici, Cosimo I de'
Cosin, John, **17th:** 202
Cosmas, **MA:** 587
Cosmic Connection (Sagan), **20th:** 3590
Cosmic cycles, **Anc:** 295
Cosmic order, **Anc:** 407
Cosmic rays, **20th:** 2751, 3241
Cosmochemistry, **20th:** 4134
Cosmogony, **Anc:** Greek, 414
Cosmogony (Ehrenfels), **20th:** 1111
Cosmology, **Anc:** Chinese, 951; Greek, 52, 295; Heraclitus and, 399; **20th:** 140, 1712, 1913
Cosmopolitan (magazine), **20th:** 540
Cosmos (television program), **20th:** 3591
Cosmotheoros (Huygens), **17th:** 398
Cosner, Paul. *See* Lake, Leonard
Cossacks, **17th:** 12, 428, 452, 461, 624, 668, 784, 836, 855, 944; **18th:** 232, 776, 809, 814
Cossinius, **Anc:** 819
Cost of Discipleship, The (Bonhoeffer), **20th:** 419
Costa, Lorenzo, **Ren:** 486
Costa Rica. *See* Geographical Index
Costello, Frank, **Notor:** 23, 237-238, 389, 403, 407, 605, 660, 709, 954
Coster, Dirk, **20th:** 1793
Cot and Cradle Stories (Traill), **19th:** 2292
Cotán, Juan Sánchez, **17th:** 1005
Côte d'Ivoire. *See* Ivory Coast
Cotterell, Charles, **17th:** 742
"Cotter's Saturday Night, The" (Burns), **18th:** 184
Cotton, John, **17th:** 196-199, 218, 386, 394, 982
Cotton Club, **20th:** 1146
Cotton gin, **18th:** 1076
Cotton Kingdom, The (Olmsted), **19th:** 1706
Cotton manufacturing, **18th:** England, 56, 466; United States, 1077
Coubertin, Pierre de, **20th:** 846-849

Coughlin, Charles E., **20th:** 3722; **Notor:** 239-240, 973
Couleurs de la cité céleste (Messiaen), **20th:** 2717
Council of _______. *See* _______, Council of
Counselor Ayres' Memorial (Machado), **19th:** 1451
Count Federico da Montefeltro (Piero), **Ren:** 787
Count Frontenac and New France Under Louis XIV (Parkman), **19th:** 1744
Count Nulin (Pushkin), **19th:** 1849
Count of Monte-Cristo, The (Dumas), **19th:** 697
Count Robert of Paris (Scott), **19th:** 2049
Counterfeiters, The (Gide), **20th:** 1479
Countermannerism, **Ren:** 960. *See also* Mannerism
Counter-Reformation, **Ren:** 3, 717; art and, 391; Jesuits, 484, 769; Spain, 222, 446
Counter-Remonstrants, **17th:** 288
Countess of Pembroke's Arcadia, The. See *Arcadia*
Country Doctor, The (Jewett), **19th:** 1227
Country Girl, The (film), **20th:** 876
Country music, **20th:** 736, 1073, 2256, 3128
Country of the Pointed Firs, The (Jewett), **19th:** 1227
Coup d'etat permanent, Le (Mitterrand), **20th:** 2770
Coupe du roi de Thulé, La (Bizet), **19th:** 242
Couperin, François, **18th:** 281-284
Cour du roi Pétaud, La (Delibes), **19th:** 639
Courage, the Adventuress (Grimmelshausen), **17th:** 325
Courant, Le (Borodin), **19th:** 280
Courbet, Gustave, **19th:** 433, 559-562, 1889
Cours de philosophie positive (Comte), **19th:** 537
Course in General Linguistics (Saussure), **20th:** 3650
Court Midwife of the Electorate of Brandenburg, The (Siegemundin), **17th:** 851
Court of King's Bench, **18th:** condemnation of John Wilkes, 1084; first earl of Mansfield, 644
Court of Love, **MA:** 262
Court poetry, **Anc:** 844
Court ranks, system of, **MA:** 940
Court Secret, The (Shirley), **17th:** 846
Courtenay, Edward, **Ren:** 640
Courtesan, The (Aretino), **Ren:** 54
Courtiers Manual Oracle, The (Gracián), **17th:** 317
Courting of Dinah Shadd and Other Stories, The (Kipling), **19th:** 1285
Courtly love, **MA:** 274, 358, 423, 1075, 1123
Courtly poetry, **MA:** 465
Courtrai, Battle of (1302), **MA:** 840
Courtship of Miles Standish, The (Longfellow), **19th:** 1417
Cousens, Charles Hugh, **Notor:** 1036
Cousin Bette (Balzac), **19th:** 128
Cousteau, Jacques, **20th:** 849-852
Cousteau Society, **20th:** 851
Coûture, Guillaume, **17th:** 423
Covenant, Jewish, **Anc:** 573
Covenant of Grace Opened, The (Hooker), **17th:** 387
Covenanters, **17th:** 147, 700, 885
Covent Garden Theatre, **18th:** David Garrick, 397; Sarah Siddons, 912; Peg Woffington, 1102; **19th:** 1257, 1267, 1468
Cover Girl (film), **20th:** 1731, 2096
Coverdale, Miles, **Ren:** 255-259, 267
Covilhã, Pêro da, **Ren:** 259-262
Coward, Sir Noël, **20th:** 853-857
Cowart, Edward, **Notor:** 150
Cow-boys of Arizona (Remington), **19th:** 1881
Cowen, Joshua Lionel, **Notor:** 218
Cowley, Abraham, **17th:** 199-201, 203, 232, 742
Cowley, Hannah, **18th:** 284-286
Cowlings, Al, **Notor:** 959
Cowpox, **18th:** 532
Cow's Skull (O'Keeffe), **20th:** 3032
Cox and Box (Sullivan and Burnand), **19th:** 918
Coxcomb, The (Beaumont and Fletcher), **Ren:** 94
Coxe, Thomas, **17th:** 901
Coyne, James, **20th:** 994
Crabwalk (Grass), **20th:** 1576
Craft, Robert, **20th:** 3890
Craft of Musical Composition, The (Hindemith), **20th:** 1812
Craig, Gordon, **19th:** 2250
Craig v. Boren (1976), **20th:** 508
Crainquebille, Putois, Riquet and Other Profitable Tales (France), **19th:** 816
Cramm, Gottfried von, **20th:** 3217
Cranach, Hans, **Ren:** 263
Cranach, Lucas, the Elder, **Ren:** 262-265
Cranach, Lucas, the Younger, **Ren:** 263
Cranborne, Viscount. *See* Salisbury, third marquis of
Crane, Hart, **20th:** 858-860
Crane, Stephen, **19th:** 562-565
Cranfield, Lionel, **17th:** 275
Craniometry, **20th:** 2320
Cranmer, Thomas, **Ren:** 144, 256, 266-269, 305, 335, 369, 443, 468, 544, 639, 766, 834, 898
Crashaw, Richard, **17th:** 202-204, 232, 276, 562
Crassus, Marcus Licinius, **Anc:** 173, 189, 194, 212, 681, 820
Crater, The (Cooper), **19th:** 555
Crates of Thebes, **Anc:** 70, 285, 981

Cratinus, **Anc:** 127
Crawford, Cheryl, **20th:** 861-864, 2333
Crawford, Joan, **20th:** 143, 156
Crawford, William H., **19th:** 503, 1589
Craxi, Bettino, **Notor:** 241-242
Crayford, Battle of (c. 456), **Anc:** 395
Crayon, Geoffrey. *See* Irving, Washington
Crazy Horse, **19th:** 566-570
Crazy Joe. *See* Gallo, Joe
Crazy Salad (Ephron), **20th:** 1162
Creating a Role (Stanislavsky), **20th:** 3822
Creation, The (Haydn), **18th:** 477
Création du monde, La (ballet), **20th:** 2736
Creation of the World (Tasso), **Ren:** 926
Creation Society, **20th:** 1619
Creationism, **20th:** 552; arguments against, 1556
Creative Credo (Klee), **20th:** 2177
Creative Evolution (Bergson), **20th:** 324
Creatures of Prometheus (ballet), **20th:** 2378
Crécy, Battle of (1346), **MA:** 351, 680
Credi, Lorenzo di, **Ren:** 561
Cree, **18th:** 974
Creek War (1813-1814), **19th:** 1709
Creeks, **19th:** 1189, 1709, 2237
Crelaceous Formation of the Black Hills as Indicated by the Fossil Plants, The (Ward), **19th:** 2384
Crelle, August Leopold, **19th:** 10
"Cremation of Sam McGee, The" (Service), **20th:** 3709
Cremer, Gerard de. *See* Mercator, Gerardus
Cremona, **18th:** Antonio Stradivari, 944
Creoles, discrimination against, **19th:** 1984
Creoles in Peru, **18th:** 994
Crépy, Treaty of (1544), **Ren:** 31, 777
Cresson, Edith, **20th:** 2771
Crete, independence of, **20th:** 4157
Crevole *Madonna* (Duccio), **MA:** 326
Crick, Francis, **20th:** 477, 865-868, 1317, 3156, 3623, 4243, 4344
Cricket, **19th:** 956; **20th:** 471, 829
Cricket on the Hearth, The (Dickens), **19th:** 655
Cries and Whispers (film), **20th:** 318
Crime and criminals, **Anc:** and religion, 293; **18th:** 100-102; American colonies, 460; reform of punishment, 100. *See also* Category Index
Crime and Punishment (Dostoevski), **19th:** 678
Crime of Monsieur Lange, The (film), **20th:** 3421
Crime of Sylvestre Bonnard, The (France), **19th:** 815
Crimea, **18th:** 639, 720; annexation by Russia, 809
Crimean Khanate, **17th:** 866
Crimean War (1853-1856), **19th:** 49, 303, 368, 1672; John Bright on, 303; John Laird Mair Lawrence, 1328; Napoleon III, 1640; Florence Nightingale, 1685
Crimes de l'amour, Les. See *Crimes of Love, The*
Crimes of Love, The (Sade), **18th:** 876
Criminal, The (Ellis), **20th:** 1149
Criminal Law Amendment Act, **19th:** 373
Crimson Cloud Mansion, **17th:** 541
Cripples, The (Bruegel), **Ren:** 136
Cripps, Sir Richard Stafford, **20th:** 349, 357
Crisis in the German Social Democracy, The (Luxemburg), **20th:** 2484
Crisis papers (Paine), **18th:** 759
Crispi, Francesco, **Notor:** 180
Crispin, Rival of His Master (Lesage), **18th:** 597
Crispus, Gaius Sallustius. *See* Sallust
Cristero War (1926-1929), **20th:** 616
Cristiani, Alfredo, **20th:** 1041
Cristo de Velásquez, El. See *Christ of Velázquez, The*
Cristoforo, Colombo. *See* Columbus, Christopher
Critias of Athens, **Anc:** 801
Critica, La (journal), **20th:** 869
Critical and Exegetical Commentary on Amos and Hosea (Harper), **19th:** 1032
Critical and Historical Essays (Macaulay), **19th:** 1436
Critical and Historical Introduction to the Canonical Scriptures of the Old Testament, A (De Wette), **19th:** 1735
Critical Essays (Barthes), **20th:** 248
Critick, The (Gracián), **17th:** 317
Criticón, El. See *Critick, The*
Critique générale de l'histoire du calvinisme de M. Maimbourg (Bayle), **17th:** 36
Critique of Dialectical Reason I (Sartre), **20th:** 3639
Critique of Judgment, The (Kant), **18th:** 550
Critique of Practical Reason, The (Kant), **18th:** 549
Critique of Pure Reason, The (Kant), **18th:** 548
Critique of the Gotha Program (Marx), **19th:** 1371
Crixus, **Anc:** 819
Croatia, **MA:** 639. *See also* Geographical Index
Croatian-Hungarian Compromise, **19th:** 622
Croce, Benedetto, **20th:** 869-871, 1448
Crocker, Charles, **19th:** 2133

Crocker, Steve, **20th:** 707
Crockett, David, **19th:** 571-573; **Notor:** 616
Crocus Plain, Battle of the (352 B.C.E.), **Anc:** 638
Croesus, **Anc:** 11, 244-246, 249, 408, 654
Croisos. *See* Croesus
Croker, Richard, **Notor:** 1049
Crome, Edward, **Ren:** 544
Cromwell (Hugo), **19th:** 1147
Cromwell of Okeham, Baron. *See* Cromwell, Thomas
Cromwell, Oliver, **17th:** 204-207; and Richard Baxter, 33; and John Biddle, 54; and Robert Blake, 56; and John Bunyan, 100; and Richard Cameron, 121; and Catherine of Braganza, 137; and Charles I, 145; and Charles II of England, 147; and the first earl of Clarendon, 168; and the Great Condé, 186; and John Cotton, 198; and Abraham Cowley, 199; and John Dryden, 239; and the third Baron Fairfax, 262; and George Fox, 284; and Frederick Henry, 288; and Matthew Hale, 346; and Thomas Hobbes, 380; and Inigo Jones, 437; and John Lambert, 483; and Henry Lawes, 502; and Roger Ludlow, 568; and Manasseh ben Israel, 583; and Andrew Marvell, 606; and George Monck, 651; and Rory O'More, 701; and William Penn, 724; and Samuel Pepys, 728; and Sir William Petty, 734; and Katherine Philips, 741; and Thomas Pride, 756; and Henry Purcell, 763; and Prince Rupert, 805; and Sir George Savile, 815; and the first earl of Shaftesbury, 838; and James Shirley, 846; and Maarten and Cornelis Tromp, 931; and James Ussher, 940; and Sir Henry Vane the Younger, 941; and Mary Ward, 975; and Thomas Willis, 986; and Gerrard Winstanley, 989; and Sir Christopher Wren, 994; **Notor:** 961
Cromwell, Richard, **17th:** 485, 757, 942
Cromwell, Thomas, **Ren:** 51, 112, 256, 266, 269-273, 369, 443, 467, 544, 898, 947, 951
Cronica. See *Chronicle* (Salimbene)
Croniche fiorentine. See *Chronicle* (Villani)
Cronique de Pierre Belon, médecin (Belon), **Ren:** 101
Cronkite, Walter, **20th:** 872-874
Cronwright-Schreiner, Samuel Cron, **19th:** 2023
Crook, George, **19th:** 567, 584, 905
Crooke, Andrew, **17th:** 94
Crosby, Bing, **20th:** 132, 157, 874-877, 1871, 2358
Crosley, George. *See* Chambers, Whittaker
Cross Currents in Europe To-day (Beard), **20th:** 264
Cross Keys, Battle of (1862), **19th:** 834
Crossing Borders (Menchú), **20th:** 2687
Crossing the Water (Plath), **20th:** 3287
Crowd, The (Le Bon), **20th:** 2320
Crowley, Aleister, **Notor:** 242-244, 613
Crowning with Thorns, The (Bosch), **Ren:** 121
Crows, **19th:** 2115
Crowther, Samuel Ajayi, **19th:** 574-576
Crucible, The (Miller), **20th:** 2743
Crucified Christ with Saint Dominic and Saint Catherine of Siena, The (van Dyck), **17th:** 245
Crucifixion, The (Fra Angelico), **MA:** 85
Crucifixion (Cranach, the Elder), **Ren:** 262
Crucifixion (Grünewald), **Ren:** 405
Crucifixion (Michelangelo), **Ren:** 236
Crucifixion (Sutherland), **20th:** 3921
Crucifixion (Tintoretto), **Ren:** 933
Crucifixion (Zurbarán). See *Christ on the Cross*
Crucifixion of Saint Paul, The (Michelangelo), **Ren:** 684
Crucifixion of Saint Peter, The (Caravaggio), **Ren:** 171
Crucifixion with Angels (Le Brun), **17th:** 504
Cruickshank, Bobby, **20th:** 2037
Cruikshank, George, **Notor:** 944
Cruise of the Little Dipper, and Other Fairy Tales, The (Langer), **20th:** 2264
Cruise of the Snark, The (London), **20th:** 2422
Crusade in Europe (Eisenhower), **20th:** 1126
Crusader kings of Jerusalem, **MA:** 716
Crusades, **MA:** 34, 141, 178, 464, 1044; First, 90, 93, 177, 1003; Second, 162, 356, 717, 972; Third, 387, 584, 836, 891, 919; Fourth, 298, 543, 1017, 1059; Fifth, 389; Sixth, 436, 726; Seventh, 140, 166, 228, 668; Eighth, 43, 140, 669; Princes', 177; Spain, 572; time line, 1045
Crusading Order of Santiago, **Ren:** 329
Crusts and Crusades (Hughes), **20th:** 1933
Cruz, Celia, **20th:** 877-879
Cruz, Sor Juana Inés de la, **17th:** 208-210
Cry, the Beloved Country (film), **20th:** 3296
Cry, the Beloved Country (novel by Paton), **20th:** 3139

Crystallography, **19th:** 1751; **20th:** macromolecular, 1849
Ctesias of Cnidus, **Anc:** 744
Ctesibius of Alexandria, **Anc:** 247-248, 401
Ctesiphon, **Anc:** 266
Cuauhtémoc, **Ren:** 254, 273-275; capture of, 274
Cuba, **Ren:** 34, 252; **19th:** independence of, 1462, 1503; **20th:** Elián González, 3418; independence of, 3519; music, 878. *See also* Geographical Index
Cuban Missile Crisis (1962), **20th:** 692, 2101, 2104, 2130, 2541, 3987
Cuban Revolution (1953-1959), **20th:** 692, 1609
Cuban Revolutionary Party, **19th:** 1503
Cubism, **20th:** 1051, 2335, 2548, 3092; Georges Braque, 494; sculpture, 2397
Cubs (Kabbalist group), **Ren:** 579
Cuéllar, Javier Pérez de. *See* Pérez de Cuéllar, Javier
Cuffe, Paul, **19th:** 576-578
Cui, César Antonovich, **19th:** 1915
Cui Xiyi, **MA:** 1086
Cuitláhuac, **Ren:** 273, 695
Cujas, Jacques, **Ren:** 856
Cukor, George, **20th:** 1571
Culahatthipadopama Sutta, **Anc:** 899
Culloden, Battle of (1746), **18th:** 406
Culp, Oveta. *See* Hobby, Oveta Culp
Culpeper, Thomas, **Ren:** 467
Cultural Revolution (China), **20th:** 969, 1905, 2382, 2409, 2604, 3192, 4463, 4468
Culture and Anarchy (Arnold), **19th:** 74
Culture of Organs, The (Lindbergh and Carrel), **20th:** 2395
Cumann na nGaedheal, **20th:** 844, 1591
Cumans, **MA:** 637
Cumberland, duke of. *See* Rupert, Prince
Cummings, E. E., **20th:** 879-882
Cummings v. Missouri, **19th:** 778
Cuna y la sepultura, La (Quevedo y Villegas), **17th:** 771
Cunanan, Andrew, **Notor:** 245-246
Cunaxa, Battle of (401 B.C.E.), **Anc:** 968
Cunha, Tristão da, **Ren:** 22
Cunimund, **MA:** 47
Cunin, Adelard. *See* Moran, Bugs
Cunning Man, The (Davies), **20th:** 918
Cunningham, Imogen, **20th:** 883-885
Cunningham, Merce, **20th:** 886-888
CUP. *See* Young Turk Movement
Cupid, **Anc:** 696
Cupid and Psyche (Canova), **19th:** 407
Cupid and Psyche (David), **19th:** 609
Cupid and Psyche (van Dyck), **17th:** 246
Cupid's Revenge (Beaumont and Fletcher), **Ren:** 94
Cur Deus Homo (Anselm), **MA:** 93
Cure for a Cuckold, A (Webster and Rowley), **17th:** 977
Curial, The (Chartier), **MA:** 261
Curie, Marie, **19th:** 167; **20th:** 888-891, 2032; **Notor:** 810
Curie, Pierre, **20th:** 888-891, 2032; **Notor:** 810
Curiosa Mathematica (Carroll), **19th:** 425
Curium, **20th:** 3685
Curly Bill. *See* Brocius, Curly Bill
Curry, "Flat Nose George," **Notor:** 182
Cursus honorum, **Anc:** 166, 210, 832, 837
Curtain (Christie), **20th:** 766
Curtin, John, **20th:** 891-894, 1933
Curtis, Alex, **Notor:** 727
Curtiss, Glenn H., **19th:** 184; **20th:** 4405
Curzon, George Nathaniel, **20th:** 205, 222, 894-897
Cusanus, Nicolaus. *See* Nicholas of Cusa
Cushing, Caleb, **19th:** 578-581
Cushing, Harvey Williams, **20th:** 898-901
Cushing's syndrome, **20th:** 900
Cushman, Pauline, **Notor:** 246-247
Cushman, Robert E., Jr., **Notor:** 169
Cusi Inca Yupanqui. *See* Pachacuti
Cust, Henry, **19th:** 767
Custer, George A., **19th:** 567, 582-585, 2109; William Cody, 526; **Notor:** 248-250
Custom (Tönnies), **20th:** 4045
Custom of the Country, The (Fletcher and Massinger), **17th:** 279
Custom of the Country, The (Wharton), **20th:** 4302
Cutpurse, Moll, **Notor:** 250-251
Cutter of Coleman Street, The (Cowley), **17th:** 200
Cuvier, Georges, **19th:** 32, 115, 585-588
Cuyen, **17th:** 1
Cuzco (Inca Empire), **18th:** 994; Siege of (1781), 994
Cyanosis. *See* Blue baby syndrome
Cyaxares, **Anc:** 583
Cybele, **Anc:** 535
Cybernetics (Wiener), **20th:** 4322
Cyclotron, **20th:** 2300, 2533
Cylon, **Anc:** 293
Cynewulf, **Anc:** 392; **MA:** 219
Cynicism, **Anc:** 69, 88, 284, 314, 801, 981
Cynic's Word Book, The. See *Devil's Dictionary, The*

Cynthia (subject of Propertius's poetry), **Anc:** 704
Cynthia's Revels (Jonson), **17th:** 441
Cypselus of Corinth, **Notor:** 251-252
Cyrano de Bergerac, **17th:** 211-214
Cyrano de Bergerac (Rostand), **17th:** 211
Cyrenaics, **Anc:** 801
Cyril, Saint, **MA:** 294-297
Cyril of Alexandria, **Anc:** 435, 866
Cyropaedia. See *Kyrou paideia*
Cyrurgie of Guy de Chauliac, The (Guy de Chauliac), **MA:** 445
Cyrus II. *See* Cyrus the Great
Cyrus the Great, **Anc:** 136, 244, 248-251, 337-338, 408, 583, 969
Czar's Bride, The. See *Tsar's Bride, The*
Czech reform movement, **MA:** 522
Czech Republic. *See* Geographical Index
Czechoslovak Legion, **20th:** 300
Czechoslovak-Soviet Treaty of Friendship, Mutual Assistance, and Postwar Cooperation, **20th:** 301
Czechoslovakia, **20th:** establishment of, 300, 2641; Soviet invasion of (1968), 524, 1044, 1707. *See also* Geographical Index under Czech Republic
Czolgosz, Leon, **19th:** 1462; **Notor:** 252-254, 425

D

Da ren fu (Sima Xinagru), **Anc:** 787
Da Xue. See *Great Learning, The*
Dablon, Claude, **17th:** 433, 603
Dacko, David, **Notor:** 113
Dadaism, **20th:** 511, 1052, 1176, 2548, 2581
Daedalus and Icarus (Canova), **19th:** 406
Daemonologie (James I), **17th:** 413
Daemonum investigatio peripatetica (Cesalpino), **Ren:** 212
Dafne (Schütz), **17th:** 826
Dafydd, **MA:** 345
Dagbok, Mårbacka III. See *Diary of Selma Lagerlöf, The*
Daguerre, Jacques, **19th:** 589-592, 1611, 1678
Daguerreotype process, **19th:** 292, 591, 997
Dahmer, Jeffrey, **Notor:** 255-256
Dahmer, Vernon, **Notor:** 79
Dai Dongyuan. *See* Dai Zhen
Dai Viet su ky toan thu (Ngo), **Ren:** 547
Dai Zhen, **18th:** 287-289
Dáil Éireann, **20th:** 979, 1591
Daimler, Gottlieb, **19th:** 198, 592-595
Daimler Motor Company, **19th:** 594; **20th:** 2242
Daimons, **Anc:** 801
Daimyos, **18th:** 980
Dainichi. *See* Mahāvairocana
Daisan (Jin prince), **17th:** 1
Daisy Chain, The (Yonge), **19th:** 2472
Daisy Miller (James), **19th:** 1207
Daixuan Jing, **Anc:** 951
Daizong, **MA:** 80
Dakotas, **17th:** 603
D'Aladar, Maurice. *See* Beniowski, Maurycy
Dalai Lama (fourteenth), **20th:** 902-904, 2932
Dalālat al-ḥaʾirīn. See *Guide of the Perplexed, The*
Dale, Henry, **20th:** 1089
Dalhousie, first marquis of, **19th:** 595-597, 1718
Dalí, Salvador, **20th:** 578, 904-907, 1153
Daling He, Siege of (1631), **17th:** 2
Dalitz, Morris, **Notor:** 481
Dalton, Bill, **Notor:** 257
Dalton, Bob, **Notor:** 257-258, 296
Dalton, Emmett, **Notor:** 257-259, 296
Dalton, Frank, **Notor:** 257
Dalton, Grattan, **Notor:** 257
Dalton, John, **19th:** 102, 597-600, 887
Dalton, Robert Rennick. *See* Dalton, Bob
Dama boba, La. See *Lady Nit-Wit, The*
Dama duende, La. See *Phantom Lady, The*
Damascus, Battle of (1303), **MA:** 413
Damask Drum, The (Zeami), **MA:** 1154
Damasus I, **Anc:** 457
Damn Yankees (Adler and Ross), **20th:** 1292
Damnation de Faust, La (Berlioz), **19th:** 202
Damned, The (film), **20th:** 4168
Damned for Despair. See *Saint and the Sinner, The*
Damnés de la terre, Les. See *Wretched of the Earth, The*
Damo. *See* Bodhidharma
Damon, **Anc:** 620
Dampier, William, **17th:** 215-218; **Notor:** 260-262
Damya. *See* Kāhina, Damia al-
Dana, H. W. L., **Notor:** 1057
Dana, Richard Henry, **19th:** 1618
Danae (Klimt), **20th:** 2181
Danaids (Aeschylus), **Anc:** 9
Danby, first earl of. *See* Leeds, first duke of
Dance, **18th:** and classical music, 283, 713, 828; expressionism, 296; France, 295-297; **19th:** England, 1591. *See also* Ballet; Modern dance; Category Index
Dance and Music (Matisse), **20th:** 2651
Dance Class, The (Degas), **19th:** 633

Dance of Death I, The (Strindberg), **20th:** 3898
Dance of Death II, The (Strindberg), **20th:** 3898
Dance of Life, The (Ellis), **20th:** 1150
Dance of Salome. See *Feast of Herod, The*
Dance of the Forests, A (Soyinka), **20th:** 3804
Dance of the Happy Shades, and Other Stories (Munro), **20th:** 2874
Dance to Death, The (Lazarus), **19th:** 1332
Dancer (Lipchitz), **20th:** 2397
Dances of Haiti (Dunham), **20th:** 1062
Dancing at the Moulin de la Galette, Montmartre (Renoir), **19th:** 1889
Dancing Bees, The (Frisch), **20th:** 1337
Dancing Naked in the Mind Field (Mullis), **20th:** 2865
Dandolo, Enrico, **MA:** 298-300
Danes, **MA:** 223, 1094; raids on England, 31
Danforth, Thomas, **18th:** 894
Dangerous (film), **20th:** 920
Dangerous Liaisons (Laclos), **18th:** 753
Dangling Man (Bellow), **20th:** 288
Daniel, Samuel, **17th:** 128
Daniel Deronda (Eliot), **19th:** 741
Daniel the Prophet (Pusey), **19th:** 1845
Daniela Dormes (Suttner), **19th:** 2206
Daniell, John Frederic, **19th:** 549, 996
Daniels, Josephus, **Notor:** 230
Danilova, Alexandra, **20th:** 908-911
Danish kings of England, **MA:** 224, 339, 459
Danish-Prussian War (1864), **19th:** 819
Danjon, André-Louis, **20th:** 911-913
Danjon astrolabe, **20th:** 912
Dannoura, Battle of (1185), **MA:** 723, 992
Danse de La Goulue, La (Toulouse-Lautrec), **19th:** 2290
Danse macabre (Saint-Saëns), **20th:** 3601
Dansereau, Bruno. *See* Mesrine, Jacques
Dante, **MA:** 172, 239, 282, 300-304; **Notor:** 116, 147
Dante and Virgil Crossing the Styx (Delacroix), **19th:** 636
Danton, Georges, **18th:** 289-292, 918; **Notor:** 236, 907
Dao De Jing (Laozi), **Anc:** 502, 950, 989
Dao Zheng, **Anc:** 345
Daoguang, **19th:** 1378
Daoism, **Anc:** 502, 780, 977, 989; poetry and, 845; women and, 153; **MA:** 653, 1128
Daoud. *See* Askia Daud
Daoud, Abu, **20th:** 112
Dapper Don. *See* Gotti, John
Dar. See *Gift, The*
Dārā, **17th:** 23, 844
D'Arblay, Frances. *See* Burney, Fanny
Darby, Abraham, **18th:** 292-295
Dardanus, Treaty of (85 B.C.E.), **Anc:** 568
Darden, Christopher, **Notor:** 960
Daremberg, Jean-Baptiste. *See* Alembert, Jean le Rond d'
Dargomyzhski, Aleksandr, **19th:** 1627
Darien scheme, **17th:** 718
Darío, Rubén, **19th:** 601-603, 1503
Darius I (the Great), **Anc:** 36, 52, 109, 136, 226, 251-254, 408, 564, 971
Darius III, **Anc:** 40
Dark of the Moon (Teasdale), **20th:** 3961
Dark Victory (film), **20th:** 921
Darlan, François, **Notor:** 262-264
Darnand, Joseph, **Notor:** 263-265, 298
Darnley, earl of. *See* Stewart, Henry
Darré, Richard Walther, **Notor:** 266-267
Darrow, Clarence, **20th:** 552, 913-916; **Notor:** 451, 635, 648
Dart, Raymond, **20th:** 2313
Dartiguenave, Philippe Sudré, **Notor:** 307
Dartmouth, Battle of (1646), **17th:** 756
Dartmouth College v. Woodward, **19th:** 2181
Daruma. *See* Bodhidharma
Darvulia, Anna, **Ren:** 82
Darwin, Charles, **18th:** 764; **19th:** 33, 115, 174, 603-607, 860, 964, 1425; Samuel Butler, 375; Asa Gray on, 965; Thomas Henry Huxley, 1161; Herbert Spencer, 2128; **Notor:** 261, 415
Darwin, Erasmus, **18th:** 897
Darwinism, **19th:** 606, 2128; Louis Agassiz, 33; Samuel Butler, 374; Germany, 1003; Sir Charles Lyell, 1426; Victorian society and, 275
Das fliessende Licht der Gottheit. See *Flowing Light of the Godhead, The*
Dasgupta, Surendranath, **20th:** 1136
Dash for Timber, A (Remington), **19th:** 1882
Dassin, Joe, **Notor:** 121
Data. See *Dedomena, Ta*
Datang xiyouji. See *Buddhist Records of the Western World*
Datongshu (Kang), **19th:** 1253
Dauberval, Jean, **18th:** 295-297; ballet, 295-297
Daubié, Julie, **19th:** 89
Daud. *See* Askia Daud
Daudet, Alphonse, **19th:** 242

Daugherty, Harry M., **20th:** 1676; **Notor:** 713
Daughters of Charity, **17th:** 963
Daughters of Revolution (Wood), **20th:** 4389
Daulat Khan, **Ren:** 478
Daumont, Simon François. *See* Saint Lusson, sieur de
Dauversière, Jérôme Le Royer de la, **17th:** 575
Davaine, Casimir-Joseph, **19th:** 1292
Davenant, Sir William, **17th:** 51, 502
Davenport, John, **17th:** 218-220
David (king of Judah and Israel), **Anc:** 155, 255-258, 749, 803; house of, 447
David (Bernini), **17th:** 45
David (Donatello), **MA:** 320, 321
David (Michelangelo), **Ren:** 682
David (Milhaud), **20th:** 2737
David (Verrocchio), **Ren:** 962
David I (king of Scotland), **MA:** 304-307
David II (king of Scotland), **MA:** 204, 307-310, 843
David, Father. *See* Berg, David
David, Jacques-Louis, **18th:** portrait of Jean-Paul Marat, 650; portrait of Marie-Antoinette, 659; **19th:** 607-610, 635, 898, 1171
David Balfour. See *Catriona*
David Copperfield (Dickens), **19th:** 655
Davideis (Cowley), **17th:** 200
Davies, Lady Eleanor, **17th:** 220-222, 989
Davies, Emily, **19th:** 264
Davies, Sir John, **17th:** 221
Davies, Marion, **20th:** 1736
Davies, Robertson, **20th:** 917-919
Dávila, Don Pedro Arias. *See* Pedrarias
Davis, Bette, **20th:** 212, 919-922
Davis, Gordon. *See* Hunt, E. Howard
Davis, Howell, **Notor:** 905
Davis, Jefferson, 19th: 246, 610-616, 715, 850, 969, 2165; on Compromise of 1850, 613
Davis, John, **Ren:** 276-278
Davis, Miles, **20th:** 814, 3114
Davis, Richard Allen, **Notor:** 267-268
Davis, Varina, **19th:** 614
Davis, Volney, **Notor:** 556
Davis v. Monroe County Board of Education (1999), **20th:** 3023
Davison, Francis, **17th:** 127
Davout, Louis N., **19th:** 469
Davulia, Anna, **Notor:** 71
Davy, Sir Humphry, **19th:** 616-619, 759, 888, 2167, 2295
Davy lamp, **19th:** 617
Davys, John. *See* Davis, John
Dawes Act (1887), **19th:** 509
Dawidowicz, Lucy S., **20th:** 922-925
Dawit I, **Ren:** 1006
Dawlat al-atrak, **MA:** 140
Dawlat Khān Lodī, **Ren:** 70
Dawn (Haggard), **19th:** 1006
Dawn (Michelangelo), **Ren:** 683
Dawn (Nash), **20th:** 2911
Dawn of a Tomorrow, The (Burnett), **19th:** 359
Dawn of Astronomy, The (Lockyer), **19th:** 1415
Dawson, John William, **19th:** 1425
Dawud, Abu, **Notor:** 5
Day (Michelangelo), **Ren:** 683
Day, Dorothy, **20th:** 925-928
Day, Thomas, **17th:** 311
Day After, The (television movie), **20th:** 3592
Day for Night (film), **20th:** 4082
Day in the Country, A (film), **20th:** 3421
Day of the Dupes. *See* Dupes, Day of the (1630)
Day of Wrath (film), **20th:** 1038
Dayan, Moshe, **20th:** 294, 929-932
Days and Nights in the Forest (film), **20th:** 3395
Days of Hope (Malraux), **20th:** 2577
Days of My Life, The (Haggard), **19th:** 1007
Dazai Shundai, **18th:** 747
D.C. Sniper. *See* Malvo, Lee Boyd; Muhammad, John Allen
DDT. *See* Dichloro-diphenyl-trichloroethane
De Abrahamo (Philo), **Anc:** 641
De abstinentia. See *Peri apochēs empsychōn*
De admirabili operum antiquorum . . . praestantia (Belon), **Ren:** 102
De agricultura (Cato), **Anc:** 192
De anima (Aristotle), **Anc:** 94
De anima (Tertullian), **Anc:** 854
De anima brutorum. See *Two Discourses Concerning the Soul of Brutes Which Is That of the Vital and Sensitive of Man*
De animalibus (Albertus Magnus), **MA:** 44
De antiquissima Italorum sapientia (Vico), **18th:** 1013
De aquatilibus (Belon), **Ren:** 102
De arboribus coniferis, resiniferis, aliis quoque nonnullis sempiterna fronde virentibus (Belon), **Ren:** 102
De architectura (Vitruvius), **Anc:** 247
De artibus (Celsus), **Anc:** 199
De augmentis scientiarum. See *Advancement of Learning*
De avaritia (Poggio), **MA:** 851
De bombyce (Malpighi), **17th:** 580
De Buonaparte et des Bourbons. See *On Buonaparte and the Bourbons*
De caelo (Aristotle), **Anc:** 321
De casibus virorum illustrium. See *Fall of Princes, The*
De causis criticorum dierum libellus (Fracastoro), **Ren:** 344
De causis plantarum. See *Peri phytikōn aitiōn*

De causis proporietatum elementorum (Albertus Magnus), **MA:** 44
De cerebro (Malpighi), **17th:** 580
De Christiana religione (Ficino), **Ren:** 333
De circulatione sanguinis. See *Circulation of the Blood, The*
De Cive. See *Philosophical Rudiments Concerning Government and Society*
De civili dominio (Wyclif), **MA:** 1131
De civitate Dei (Augustine), **Anc:** 142, 518
De clementia. See *On Clemency*
De computo (Rabanus), **MA:** 871
De conceptu virginali et originali peccato. See *Concerning Virginal Conception and Original Sin*
De concordantia Catholica. See *Catholic Concordance, The*
De concordia praescientiae et praedestinationis et gratiae dei cum libero arbitrio. See *Harmony of the Foreknowledge, the Predestination, and the Grace of God with Free Choice, The*
De coniecturis (Nicholas of Cusa), **Ren:** 726
De conservatione juventutis et retardatione senectutis. See *Conservation of Youth and Defense of Age, The*
De consideratione. See *Treatise on Consideration*
De consolatione philosophiae. See *Consolation of Philosophy, The*
De contagione et contagiosis morbis et eorum curatione (Fracastoro), **Ren:** 344
De contagionibus et contagiosis morbis et eorum curatione libri tres. See *De contagione et contagiosis morbis et eorum curatione*
De contemplando Deo. See *On Contemplating God*
De contemptu mundi. See *On the Misery of the Human Condition*
De copia (Erasmus), **Ren:** 315
De corpore et sanguine Domini. See *Concerning the Body and Blood of the Lord*
De Corpore Politico (Hobbes), **17th:** 379
De correptione et gratia (Augustine), **Anc:** 947
De creatione problemata XXX (Manasseh ben Israel), **17th:** 583
De Decalogo (Philo), **Anc:** 641
De dimensione parabolae, solidique hyperbolici problemata duo. See *Opera geometrica*
De docta ignorantia. See *Of Learned Ignorance*
De doctrina Christiana (Augustine), **Anc:** 208
De doctrina Christiana (Milton), **17th:** 641
De duobus amantibus Eurialo et Lucresia. See *Tale of Two Lovers, The*
De duplici copia verborum ac rerum. See *De copia*
De ecclesia. See *Church, The*
De emendatione temporum (Scaliger), **Ren:** 856
De ente et uno. See *Of Being and the One*
De eruditione filiorum nobilium (Vincent of Beauvais), **MA:** 1063
De fabrica (Vesalius), **Ren:** 966, 967
De falso credita et ementita Constantini donatione declamatio. See *Treatise of Lorenzo Valla on the Donation of Constantine, The*
De' fenomeni della circolazione . . . . See *Experiments upon the Circulation of the Blood . . .*
De fide (Ambrose), **Anc:** 43
De fide et officiis Christianorum liber. See *Faith and Duties of Christians, The*
De figuris et nominibus numerorum, et de normis et ponderibus (Priscian), **MA:** 860
De fundamentis astrologiae certioribus (Kepler), **17th:** 458
De grammaticis et rhetoribus (Suetonius), **Anc:** 941
De historia plantarum. See *Peri phytikōn historiōn*
De historia stirpium. See *Herbal of Leonhart Fuchs, The*
De hominis dignitate oratio. See *Oration on the Dignity of Man*
De humani corporis fabrica libri septem. See *De fabrica*
De humani generis redemptione. See *Meditations Concerning the Redemption of Mankind*
De imperatorum et pontificum potestate (Ockham), **MA:** 780
De incarnatione Verbi Dei (Athanasius), **Anc:** 134
De institutione clericorum (Rabanus), **MA:** 870
De institutione feminae Christianae. See *Instruction of a Christian Woman, The*
De ira libri tres (Seneca), **Anc:** 767
De iure belli ac pacis libri tres. See *On the Law of War and Peace*
De iure belli libri tres. See *Three Books on the Law of War, The*
De iuris interpretibus dialogi sex (Gentili), **Ren:** 372
De Josepho (Philo), **Anc:** 641
De jure naturae et gentium libri octo. See *Of the Law of Nature and Nations*
De jure praede commentarius. See *Commentary on the Law of Prize and Booty*
De jure regni apud Scotos (Buchanan), **Ren:** 147

De la capacité politique des classes ouvrières (Proudhon), **19th:** 1836
De la défense des places fortes (Carnot), **18th:** 201
De la démocratie en Amérique. See *Democracy in America*
De la division du travail social. See *Division of Labor in Society, The*
De la educacion popular (Sarmiento), **19th:** 2001
De la fragilidad humana (Manasseh ben Israel), **17th:** 583
De la grammatologie. See *Of Grammatology*
De la justice dans la révolution et dans l'église (Proudhon), **19th:** 1836
De la nature et diversité des poissons. See *De aquatilibus*
De la réorganisation de la société européenne (Saint-Simon), **19th:** 1975
De la terre à la lune. See *From the Earth to the Moon*
De l'Allemagne. See *Germany* (Staël)
De l'amour. See *Maxims of Love*
De l'attaque et de la defense des places (Montalembert), **18th:** 691
De laude imperatoris Anastasii. See *Priscian of Caesarea's De Laude Anastasii Imperatoris*
De laudibus legum Angliæ. See *Learned Commendation of the Politique Lawes of Englande*
De laudibus sanctae crucis (Rabanus), **MA:** 870
De legationibus libri tres. See *Three Books on Embassies*
De legibus et consuetudinibus Angliae. See *Bracton on the Laws and Customs of England*
De l'Éloquence française (Vair), **17th:** 577
De l'esprit (Helvétius), **18th:** 480
De liber alter de consecratione ecclesiae Sancti Dionysii. See *Abbot Suger on the Abbey Church of St. Denis and Its Art Treasures*
De libero arbitrio. See *On Free Will*
De libris revolutionum Nicolai Copernici narratio prima. See *Narratio prima*
De l'infinito universo e mondi. See *On the Infinite Universe and Worlds*
De lingua Latina (Varro), **Anc:** 929
De l'institution, usage, et doctrine du saint sacrament de l'Eucharistie (Mornay), **Ren:** 705
De maculis in sole observatis (Johannes Fabricius), **17th:** 260
De magnete (Gilbert), **Ren:** 382
De magnetica vulnerum curatione (Helmont), **17th:** 362
De Maria Scotorum regina. See *Detection of the Actions of Mary Queen of Scots, Concerning the Murder of Her Husband, and Her Conspiracy, Adultery, and Pretended Marriage with the Earl Bothwel*
De materia medica (Dioscorides), **Anc:** 289
De medicina (Celsus), **Anc:** 114, 199
De metallicis libri tres (Cesalpino), **Ren:** 212
De militia (Bruni), **MA:** 209
De mineralibus et rebus metallicis. See *Book of Minerals*
De miseria conditionis humanae. See *On the Misery of the Human Condition*
De morali principis institutione (Vincent of Beauvais), **MA:** 1064
De motu animalium. See *On the Movement of Animals*
De motu corporum in gyrum (Newton), **17th:** 349
De motu gravium naturaliter descendentium et proiectorum libri duo. See *Opera geometrica*
De motu stellarum. See *De scientia stellarum*
De mulieribus claris. See *Concerning Famous Women*
De mundo nostro sublunari philosophia nova. See *New Philosophy of the Sublunary World*
De musculis et glandulis observationum specimen (Steno), **17th:** 881
De nativitate Christi (Ratramnus), **MA:** 880
De natura (Epicurus), **Anc:** 308
De natura deorum (Cicero), **Anc:** 794
De natura et dignitate amoris. See *On the Nature and Dignity of Love*
De natura fossilium (Agricola), **Ren:** 13
De natura legis naturæ (Fortescue), **Ren:** 341
De naturis rerum (Neckam), **MA:** 751
De nominibus utensilium (Neckam), **MA:** 750
De nova et nullius aevi memoria prius visa stella (Brahe), **Ren:** 129
De oblatione puerorum (Rabanus), **MA:** 871
De officio hominis et civis juxta legem naturalem libri duo. See *Whole Duty of Man According to the Law of Nature, The*
De operatione Dei. See *Book of Divine Works*
De opificis mundi (Philo), **Anc:** 641
De optimo reipublicae statu, deque nova insula utopia. See *Utopia*
De oratore (Cicero), **Anc:** 793

De orbe novo. See *History of the West-Indies, The*
De origine et situ Germanorum (Tacitus), **Anc:** 19, 99, 838
De orthographia (Cassiodorus), **MA:** 235
De ortu et causis subterraneorum (Agricola), **Ren:** 12
De otio religioso (Petrarch), **MA:** 830
De ovo incubato. See *Marcello Malpighi and the Evolution of Embryology*
De passionibus mulierum ante, in, et post partum (Trotula), **MA:** 1031
De perfectione vitae ad sorores. See *Holiness of Life*
De periculis novissimorum temporum (William of Saint-Amour), **MA:** 1112
De philosophia (Aristotle), **Anc:** 94
De pictura. See *Of Painting*
De plantis (Cesalpino), **Ren:** 212
De poetica (Aristotle), **Anc:** 9, 812, 877
De pontificibus et sanctis ecclesiae Eboracensis. See *Bishops, Kings, and Saints of York, The*
De praedestinatione (Ratramnus), **MA:** 880
De praemiis et poenis (Philo), **Anc:** 641
De principiis. See *Peri archōn*
De processione Spiritus Sancti. See *Theology of Saint Anselm Concerning the Procession of the Holy Spirit to Confute the Opposition of the Greeks, The*
De procuranda Indorum salute (Acosta), **Ren:** 6
De professione religiosorum (Valla), **MA:** 1051
De Profundis (Wilde), **19th:** 2434
De propria vita liber. See *Book of My Life, The*
De providentia (Seneca), **Anc:** 767
De pulmonibus observationes anatomicae (Borelli), **17th:** 580
De re aedificatoria. See *Architecture of Leon Battista Alberti in Ten Books, The*
De re metallica (Agricola), **Ren:** 12
De re militari (Cato), **Anc:** 192
De re rustica (Varro), **Anc:** 929
De rebus in administratione sua gestis (Suger), **MA:** 973
De regno Christi (Bucer), **Ren:** 144
De remediis utriusque fortunae. See *On Remedies for Good and Bad Fortunes*
De republica (Cicero), **Anc:** 757
De rerum fossilium, lapidum, et gemmarum maximè, figuris et similitudinibus liber (Gesner), **Ren:** 376
De rerum natura (Lucretius), **Anc:** 302, 309, 520
De rerum naturis (Rabanus), **MA:** 872
De rerum Scoticarum historia. See *History of Scotland, The*
De reverentia filiorum erga patres (Rabanus), **MA:** 871
De revolutionibus (Copernicus), **Ren:** 242, 243, 823; **17th:** 300
De sacerdotio (Chrysostom), **Anc:** 208
De sacramento altaris. See *On the Sacrament of the Altar*
De sacris ordinibus, sacramentis divinis, et vestimentis sacerdotalibus (Rabanus), **MA:** 872
De sacro alteris mysterio (Innocent III), **MA:** 542
De scientia stellarum (al-Battānī), **MA:** 138
De secreto conflictu curarum mearum. See *My Secret*
De sensu rerum et magia (Campanella), **17th:** 125
De servorum Dei beatificatione et beatorum canonizatione (Benedict XIV), **18th:** 102
De sex alis seraphim. See *Virtues of a Religious Superior, The*
De solido intra solidum naturaliter contento dissertationis prodromus. See *Prodromus*
De sphaera. See *Sphera of George Buchanan, The*
De sphaera et solidis sphaeralibus libri duo. See *Opera geometrica*
De spiritibus et corporibus. See *Kitāb al-asrār wa-sirr al asrra*
De statu imperii Germanici, ad Laelium fratrem, dominum Trezolani, liber unus. See *Present State of Germany, The*
De statu mortuorum et resurgentium liber. See *Treatise Concerning the State of Departed Souls, Before, and at, and After the Resurrection, A*
De statu primitivae ecclesiae (Hotman), **Ren:** 463
De statua. See *Of Sculpture*
De stella nova in pede serpentarii (Kepler), **17th:** 458
De studiis et litteris. See *Concerning the Study of Literature*
De sympathia et antipathia rerum (Fracastoro), **Ren:** 344
De synodo dioecesana (Benedict XIV), **18th:** 103
De termino vitae (Manasseh ben Israel), **17th:** 583
De trinitate (Augustine), **Anc:** 142
De trinitate (Boethius), **MA:** 173
De trinitatis erroribus libri septem (Servetus), **Ren:** 861
De triplici via. See *Enkindling of Love, Also Called the Triple Way*
De tulipa Turcarum (Gesner), **Ren:** 376
De universo. See *Universe of Creatures, The*
De usu partium corporis humani. See *Peri chreias morion*

De varietate fortunae (Poggio), **MA:** 850-851
De vegetabilibus et plantis (Albertus Magnus), **MA:** 44
De venarum ostiolis (Fabricius), **Ren:** 320; **17th:** 355
De venenis eorumque remediis (Abano), **MA:** 1
De vera et falsa religione commentarius. See *Commentary on True and False Religion*
De verborum significatu (Verrius), **Anc:** 942
De vero bono. See *On Pleasure*
De vi attractiva ignis electrici (Volta), **18th:** 1023
De vi percussionis (Borelli), **17th:** 66
De viribus electricitatis in motu musculari commentarius. See *Commentary on the Effect of Electricity on Muscular Motion*
De viris illustribus (Jerome), **Anc:** 853
De viris illustribus (Petrarch), **MA:** 828
De viris illustribus (Suetonius), **Anc:** 940
De virtutibus et vitiis (Rabanus), **MA:** 871
De virtutibus sancti Martini. See *Miracles of Saint Martin, The*
De viscerum structura exercitatio anatomica (Malpighi), **17th:** 580
De vita Caesarum (Suetonius), **Anc:** 18, 23, 508, 685
De vita curiali. See *Curial, The*
De vita et rebus gentis Guillielmi Duicis Novo-castrensis. See *Life of William Cavendish, Duke of Newcastle, The*
De vita Julii Agricolae (Tacitus), **Anc:** 17, 163, 838
De vita libri tres. See *Three Books of Life, The*
De vita Moysis (Philo), **Anc:** 641
De vita solitaria. See *Life of Solitude, The*
De voluptate. See *On Pleasure*
De vulgari eloquentia (Dante), **MA:** 302
Dead Sea Scrolls, **Anc:** 476
Dead Souls (Gogol), **19th:** 938
Dead Sparrow, The (Marc), **20th:** 2606
Deák, Antal, **19th:** 619
Deák, Ferenc, **19th:** 619-623
Deák Party Club, **19th:** 621
Deakin, Alfred, **19th:** 623-626
Dealtry, Frederick John, Baron Lugard of Abinger. *See* Lugard, Lord
Dean, James, **Notor:** 994
Dean, Jerry Lynn, **Notor:** 1044
Dean, John, **Notor:** 321, 443, 738
Deane, Richard, **17th:** 56, 651, 932
De Angelis, Tino, **Notor:** 268-269
Dean's December, The (Bellow), **20th:** 290
Dearborn, Henry, **19th:** 1779
Dearest Enemy (Rodgers and Hart), **20th:** 1692
Death (Kollwitz), **20th:** 2190
Death and Fire (Klee), **20th:** 2178
Death and Taxes (Parker), **20th:** 3117
Death and the King's Horseman (Soyinka), **20th:** 3805
Death and the Lover (Hesse), **20th:** 1790
Death Comes for the Archbishop (Cather), **20th:** 699
Death in Midsummer, and Other Stories (Mishima), **20th:** 2764
Death in the Afternoon (Hemingway), **20th:** 1757
Death in Venice (film), **20th:** 4168
Death in Venice (novel by Mann), **20th:** 2595
Death in Venice (opera by Britten), **20th:** 532
Death Kit (Sontag), **20th:** 3788
Death Notebooks, The (Sexton), **20th:** 3715
Death of a Salesman (Miller), **20th:** 2742
Death of Agrippina, The (Cyrano), **17th:** 211
Death of General Wolfe, The (Romney), **18th:** 862
Death of General Wolfe, The (West), **18th:** 1069
Death of Ivan Ilyich, The (Tolstoy), **19th:** 2285
Death of King Edmund, The (Romney), **18th:** 862
Death of Leonardo da Vinci in the Arms of Francis I, The (Ingres), **19th:** 1172
Death of Sardanapalus, The (Berlioz), **19th:** 201
Death of Sardanapalus, The (Delacroix), **Anc:** 119; **19th:** 636
Death of Socrates, The (David), **19th:** 608
Death of the Earl of Chatham, The (Copley), **18th:** 276
Death of the Miser, The (Bosch), **Ren:** 121
Death of the Saint, The (Andrea del Sarto), **Ren:** 39
Death of Tintagiles, The (Maeterlinck), **20th:** 2722
Death on a Pale Horse (Turner), **19th:** 2324
Death penalty. *See* Capital punishment
Death Row Granny. *See* Barfield, Velma Margie
Death Valley Days (television program), **20th:** 3401
Deathwatch (Genet), **20th:** 1446
Debauchee, The (Behn), **17th:** 43
De Beauvoir, Simone. *See* Beauvoir, Simone de
De Beers Mining Company, **19th:** 1893
De Bérulle, Pierre, **Ren:** 3
Deborah (Israeli prophet), **Anc:** 258-260
Debs, Eugene V., **20th:** 914, 932-936, 2040, 4003
Debussy, Claude, **20th:** 936-940, 3642
Decadence, **18th:** 28, 658, 875

Decameron (Boccaccio), **MA:** 170, 239
Decatur, Stephen, **19th:** 626-629
Decay of the Angel, The (Mishima), **20th:** 2764
Deccan, **17th:** 25
Deccan Education Society, **20th:** 4024
Decebalus, **Anc:** 906
Decembrist Revolt (1825), **19th:** 1670
Decisive Moment, The (Cartier-Bresson), **20th:** 673
Decius (Roman emperor), **Anc:** 269, 282
Declaration of Arboath. *See* Arboath, Declaration of (1320)
"Declaration of Conscience" speech (Smith), **20th:** 3770
Declaration of Independence, **18th:** 238, 409, 413, 460, 528, 909, 1092, 1100; foundation, 11
Declaration of Rights (1689), **17th:** 611
"Declaration of Rights" (Adams), **18th:** 11
Declaration of Sentiments, **19th:** 2147
Declaration of the People's Natural Right to a Share in the Legislature, A (Sharp), **18th:** 900
Declaration of Women's Rights, **19th:** 65
Decline and Fall of the Roman Empire. See *History of the Decline and Fall of the Roman Empire*
Deconstructionism, **20th:** 976
Decorative arts, **18th:** 4, 95-97, 132-135, 472-475, 494-497, 978
Decorative Figure (Matisse), **20th:** 2651
Decouverte de la terre, La. See *Discovery of the Earth, The*
Decretals of Gregory IX, **MA:** 882
Decretals of Siricius, **Anc:** 796
Dedekind, Richard, **19th:** 629-631
Dedomena, Ta (Euclid), **Anc:** 78, 318
Deductive logic, **Anc:** 261
Dee, John, **Ren:** 276, 278-280
Dee Lay. *See* Beckwith, Byron De La
Deep River (Endō), **20th:** 1156
Deephaven (Jewett), **19th:** 1226
Deer in the Woods I (Marc), **20th:** 2607
Deer Park, The (Mailer), **20th:** 2563
Deerbrook (Martineau), **19th:** 1506
Deerslayer, The (Cooper), **19th:** 553
Defence and Illustration of the French Language, The (du Bellay), **Ren:** 294, 425
Defence of Guenevere, The (Morris), **19th:** 1606
Defence of Poesie (Sidney), **Ren:** 881
Defenestration of Prague (1618), **17th:** 293, 470, 966
Defengting zhuji (Wang), **18th:** 1040
Defense, The (Nabokov), **20th:** 2894
Défense et illustration de la langue française, La. See *Defence and Illustration of the French Language, The*
Defense of Free-Thinking in Mathematics, A (Berkeley), **18th:** 112
Defense of Rhyme, A (Daniel), **17th:** 128
Defense of Saint Augustine, The. See *Pro Augustino responsiones ad capitula objectionum Vincentianarum*
Defense of the Constitutions of the United States of America, A (Adams), **18th:** 13
Defense of the Right of the People to Elect Representatives for Every Session of Parliament, A (Sharp), **18th:** 900
Defensoria (Guicciardini), **Ren:** 411
Defiance Campaign (South Africa), **20th:** 2479
Defiant Ones, The (film), **20th:** 3297
Deficit, Madame. *See* Marie-Antoinette
Defoe, Daniel, **17th:** 216; **18th:** 298-301, 568; **Notor:** 81, 261, 891, 1103
De Forest, Lee, **20th:** 127, 940-943
DeFreeze, Donald, **Notor:** 455
Degan, William, **Notor:** 1091
Deganawida, **Ren:** 281-283, 448
Degas, Edgar, **19th:** 434, 632-634, 880, 1800, 2288; **20th:** 422, 2791
De Gasperi, Alcide, **20th:** 944-947
Degen, Ferdinand, **19th:** 9
Degeneration (Nordau), **20th:** 2993
Degré zéro de l'écriture, Le. See *Writing Degree Zero*
Degrelle, Léon, **Notor:** 270-271
De Guzmán, Domingo. *See* Dominic, Saint
Dehumanization of Art and Notes on the Novel, The (Ortega), **20th:** 3079
Dehya. *See* Kāhina, Damia al-
Dei delitti e delle penne. See *Essay on Crimes and Punishments, An*
Deification of rulers, **Anc:** Egyptian, 588, 773; Japanese, 596; Mesopotamian, 366; Ptolemaic, 716; Roman, 178, 185, 268, 281, 521, 686, 945
Deighton, Len, **Notor:** 675
Deimier, Pierre de, **17th:** 578
Deir Yassin, massacre of (1948), **20th:** 286
Deism, **18th:** 314; **19th:** 2280
Dejazmach Wube, **19th:** 2255
Déjeuner sur l'herbe (Manet), **19th:** 1480
Dejoie, Louis, **Notor:** 308
Deken, Aagje, **18th:** 301-303

Dekker, Thomas, **17th:** 132, 223-225, 441, 636, 846, 977; **Notor:** 936
De Klerk, F. W., **20th:** 948-950, 2585
De Kock, Eugene, **Notor:** 271-272
Del primato morale e civile degli Italiani (Gioberti), **19th:** 922, 1802
Del romanzo storico (Manzoni), **19th:** 1497
Del único modo (Las Casas), **Ren:** 539
Delacroix, Eugène, **19th:** 635-638, 898, 1147, 1174
De la Faye, Antoine, **Ren:** 139
De la Gardie, Magnus Gabriel, **17th:** 153, 164
Delahaye, Ernest, **19th:** 1912
Delane, John Thaddeus, **19th:** 2382
Delano grape strike (1965-1970), **20th:** 739, 1916
DeLaughter, Bobby, **Notor:** 79
De l'Aulne, Baron. *See* Turgot, Anne-Robert-Jacques
Delaunay, Robert, **20th:** 950-953, 1176, 2177, 2607
Delaware Aqueduct, **19th:** 1928
Delaware prophet, **18th:** 803
Del Cano, Juan Sebastián. *See* Elcano, Juan Sebastián de
Delcassé, Théophile, **20th:** 780
D'elchingen, Duke. *See* Ney, Michel
Deleboe, Franz, **17th:** 361
Delehanty, Thomas, **Notor:** 471
Deleytar aprovechando (Tirso), **17th:** 914
Del Ferro, Scipione, **Ren:** 173, 920
Delgado, Humberto, **20th:** 3608
Delhi sultanate, **MA:** 888; **Ren:** 478
Delian League, **Anc:** 52, 214, 620-621, 633, 678, 810, 860
Delian problem, **Anc:** 321
Delibes, Léo, **19th:** 639-642
Delicate Delinquent, The (film), **20th:** 2358
Délices de la poésie française (Malherbe), **17th:** 578
De Littleton, Thomas. *See* Littleton, Sir Thomas
Delius, Frederick, **20th:** 953-956
Della-cruscans, **18th:** 849
Della famiglia. See *Family in Renaissance Florence, The*
Della Rovere, Giuliano. *See* Julius II
Della tranquillità dell' anima (Alberti), **Ren:** 19
Dellacroce, Aniello, **Notor:** 431, 659
Delle cagioni de le febbri maligna (Borelli), **17th:** 65
Dell'invenzione (Manzoni), **19th:** 1497
Dell'unita della lingua e dei mezzi di diffonderla (Manzoni), **19th:** 1497
DeLorean, John, **Notor:** 272-274
Delorme, Marion, **17th:** 521
Delorme, Philibert, **Ren:** 284, 566
Delos, Oracle at, **Anc:** 283, 321, 651
Delphi, **Anc:** omphalos at, 55; Oracle at, 11, 39, 221, 227, 244, 246, 265, 283, 293, 429, 505, 617, 639, 670, 695, 799, 807, 968; sanctuary at, 679
Delphine (Staël), **18th:** 931
Delvig, Anton, **19th:** 937
Demaratus, **Anc:** 227, 505, 846
Demarcation, Line of. *See* Line of Demarcation
Dementia Praecox (Bleuler), **20th:** 392
Demes, **Anc:** 221
Demeter, **Anc:** 7
Demetrio e Polibio (Rossini), **19th:** 1944
Demetrius of Phalerum, **Anc:** 317, 547, 628, 872
Demetrius Poliorcetes, **Anc:** 63, 106, 157
Demian (Hesse), **20th:** 1788
De Mille, Agnes, **20th:** 957-959
DeMille, Cecil B., **20th:** 957, 960-964, 1524, 2662
DeMille Foundation for Political Freedom, **20th:** 963
DeMio, Joe. *See* Adonis, Joe
Demiurge, **Anc:** 919
Democedes, **Notor:** 851
Democracy, **Anc:** 214, 221, 801; **18th:** John Adams, 12; and the arts, 768-771; Mary Astell, 64-67; Georges Danton, 289-292; France, 649, 680; Elbridge Gerry, 413; Ireland, 983; Thomas Jefferson, 528; James Madison, 637; Montesquieu, 697; opposition to, 175; Thomas Paine, 12; Poland, 566; radical, 426; Robespierre, 844; Jean-Jacques Rousseau, 868-872; Louis de Saint-Just, 878; James Wilson, 1092. *See also* Liberalism
Democracy (Adams), **19th:** 17
Democracy and Military Service (Jaurès), **19th:** 1221
Democracy and Social Ethics (Addams), **20th:** 24
Democracy in America (Tocqueville), **19th:** 2281
Democratic Convention of 1852, **19th:** 344
Democratic-Farm Labor Alliance, **20th:** 1938
Democratic Ideals and Reality (Mackinder), **20th:** 2519
Democratic Party, **19th:** 59, 508
Democratic Republican Party. *See* Anti-Federalist Party
Democratic Union of the Algerian Manifesto, **20th:** 9
Democratic Vistas (Whitman), **19th:** 2426
Democritus, **Anc:** 59, 115, 261-264, 307, 858
Democritus (Bramante), **Ren:** 132
Demoiselles d'Avignon, Les (Picasso), **20th:** 3238
Demon Barber of Fleet Street. *See* Todd, Sweeney
Demonax, **Anc:** 514
Demons, **Ren:** 122, 212

Demonstratio evangelica (Eusebius), **Anc:** 330
Demonstration of the Principle of Harmony (Rameau), **18th:** 827
Demophilus, **Anc:** 869
Demosthenes, **Anc:** 264-268, 275
Dempsey, Jack, **20th:** 964-968
Denbigh, Baron. *See* Leicester, earl of
Denby, Edward, **Notor:** 342
Deneuve, Catherine, **20th:** 579
Deng Xiaoping, **20th:** 968-971, 1906, 1908, 2000, 2368; Liu Shaoqi, 2409; Zhao Ziyang, 4459; **Notor:** 757
Denh Vuong, **19th:** 907
Denham, Sir John, **17th:** 994
Denikin, Anton, **20th:** 2520
De Niro, Robert, **20th:** 3682; **Notor:** 141
Denis, Jean Baptiste, **17th:** 565
Denis, Maurice, **20th:** 972-974, 4173
Denis, Saint, **Anc:** 268-271
Denis Duval (Thackeray), **19th:** 2259
Denis the Little. *See* Dionysius Exiguus
Denishawn, **20th:** 1563, 3595
Denison House, **20th:** 197
Denmark, **MA:** kings, 691, 1048. *See also* Geographical Index
Dennis v. United States (1951), **20th:** 378, 1030, 1309
Denny, Reginald, **Notor:** 586
Density 21:5 (Varèse), **20th:** 4143
Denslow, William Wallace, **19th:** 156
Dent, J. M., **19th:** 162
Dent, Lancelot, **19th:** 1378
Dentistry, **19th:** 1613
Denys. *See* Denis, Saint
Deoxyribonucleic acid, **20th:** decoding, 1380, 3623; fingerprints, 3623; structure of, 865, 1316, 3156, 4243, 4343
Departed, The (film), **20th:** 3683
Departmental Ditties (Kipling), **19th:** 1285
Dependency and Development in Latin America (Cardoso and Faletto), **20th:** 651
Dépit amoureux, Le. See *Love-Tiff, The*
Deposition, The (Correggio), **Ren:** 250
Depressions, economic. *See* Great Depression; Panic of _______
Deraismes, Maria, **19th:** 89
Derby, fourteenth earl of, **19th:** 642-645, 667
Dereham, Francis, **Ren:** 466
Derevlians, **MA:** 793
Dergue, **20th:** 2701
Derketo, **Anc:** 744
Dermer, Thomas, **17th:** 876
Dernier jour d'un condamné, Le. See *Last Day of a Condemned, The*
Dernier Recueil (Malherbe), **17th:** 578
Derniers Vers, Les (Ronsard), **Ren:** 839
Derrida, Jacques, **20th:** 974-979
Dershowitz, Alan, **Notor:** 959, 1076
Dersu Uzala (film), **20th:** 2219
Derwent River, **18th:** 56
Des canyons aux étoiles (Messiaen), **20th:** 2717
Des lettres de cachet et des prisons d'état (Mirabeau), **18th:** 680
DeSalvo, Albert, **Notor:** 274-275
Desargues, Girard, **17th:** 630
Desastres de la guerra, Los (Goya), **19th:** 1995
Descartes, René, **17th:** 226-229; and Jakob Bernoulli, 48; and Giovanni Alfonso Borelli, 67; and Queen Christina, 164; and Anne Conway, 188; on doubt, 228; and Elizabeth of Bohemia, 251; and Pierre de Fermat, 271; and Pierre Gassendi, 305; and William Harvey, 357; and Christiaan Huygens, 398; iatromechanism, 362; and Jean de La Fontaine, 482; and Gottfried Wilhelm Leibniz, 514; and Marin Mersenne, 628; and the duchess of Newcastle, 677; and Blaise Pascal, 713; and Anna Maria van Schurman, 824; on space and matter, 333; and Baruch Spinoza, 871; and Nicolaus Steno, 881; on thinking, 228; and John Wallis, 970; and Thomas Willis, 986; **18th:** 26, 241, 264
Descent from the Cross (Rubens), **17th:** 802
Descent from the Cross, The (Rogier van der Weyden), **MA:** 1092
Descent of Christ into Limbo (Tintoretto), **Ren:** 933
Descent of Man and Selection in Relation to Sex, The (Darwin), **19th:** 606
D'Escogne, Félix, **Notor:** 980
Description de l'Égypte (Fourier), **19th:** 810
Description of a Marvelous Canon of Logarithms (Napier), **Ren:** 712
Description of a New Blazing World, The (Newcastle), **17th:** 677
Description of Greece. See *Periegesis Hellados*
Description of New England, A (Smith), **17th:** 864
Descriptive Catalogue, A (Blake), **18th:** 123
Descriptive Sketches (Wordsworth), **19th:** 2462
Descrittione dell' Africa. See *History and Description of Africa and of the Notable Things Therein Contained, The*
Desegni d'architettura civile e ecclesiastica (Guarini), **17th:** 331
Desegregation, **20th:** American South, 11; United States, 508; U.S. military, 3372; U.S. Supreme Court, 1923, 3325;

George C. Wallace, 4204. *See also* Civil Rights movement
Deserted Village, The (Goldsmith), **18th:** 434
Deserts (Varèse), **20th:** 4143
Deshayes, Catherine. *See* Monvoisin, Madame
Design, industrial, **20th:** 1432
Design for Living (Coward), **20th:** 855
Designs for Gold and Silversmiths (Pugin), **19th:** 1839
De Silva, Andrew. *See* Cunanan, Andrew
DeSimone, Tommy, **Notor:** 465
Desire Under the Elms (O'Neill), **20th:** 3052
Desmichels, Louis Alexis, **19th:** 1
Desolation Angels (Kerouac), **20th:** 2116
Despenser, Hugh le, **MA:** 348
Despenser, Hugh le, the Younger, **MA:** 348, 552
Desperate Remedies (Hardy), **19th:** 1028
Desportes, Philippe, **17th:** 577
Despréaux, Nicolas Boileau-. *See* Boileau-Despréaux, Nicolas
Desprez, Josquin. *See* Josquin des Prez
Dessalines, Jean-Jacques, **19th:** 494
Destiny (film), **20th:** 2254
Destour Party (Tunisia), **20th:** 457
Destruction of Sennacherib, The (Mussorgsky), **19th:** 1627
Destry Rides Again (film), **20th:** 999, 3861
Desvallières, Georges, **20th:** 973
D'Étaples, Jacques Lefèvre. *See* Lefèvre d'Étaples, Jacques
Detection of the Actions of Mary Queen of Scots, Concerning the Murder of Her Husband, and Her Conspiracy, Adultery, and Pretended Marriage with the Earl Bothwel (Buchanan), **Ren:** 147
Detroit Evening News, **19th:** 2056
Detroit Tigers, **20th:** 791
Detstvo. See *Childhood*
Dettingen, Battle of (1743), **18th:** 405
Deuce Coupe (ballet), **20th:** 3990
Deulino, Treaty of (1618), **17th:** 855
Deuterium, discovery of, **20th:** 1793, 4133
Deutsche Gelehrtenrepublik, Die (Klopstock), **18th:** 562
Deutsche Geschichte im Zeitalter der Reformation. See *History of the Reformation in Germany*
Deutsche Gotteserkenntnis, **20th:** 2464
Deutsche Ideologie, Die. See *German Ideology, The*
Deutsches Wörterbuch (Grimm brothers), **19th:** 992
Deutschland. See *Germany* (Heine)
Deux Pêcheurs, Les (Offenbach), **19th:** 1700
Deux Sources de la morale et de la religion, Les. See *Two Sources of Morality and Religion, The*
Deux Sous de charbon (Delibes), **19th:** 639
Deux Vieilles Gardes (Delibes), **19th:** 639
Deuxième Sexe, Le. See *Second Sex, The*
Dev, Guru Nānak. *See* Nānak
Devadatta, **Anc:** 49
Devagupta, **MA:** 460
De Valera, Eamon, **19th:** 1493; **20th:** 808, 843, 979-981, 1591, 3035
De Valois, Ninette, **20th:** 1268
Devaraja, cult of the, **MA:** 981
Development of Modern Europe, The (Beard and Robinson), **20th:** 262
Devere, Madam Lydia. *See* Chadwick, Cassie L.
Devereux, Robert (1566-1601). *See* Essex, second earl of
Devereux, Robert (1591-1646). *See* Essex, third earl of
Devi. See *Goddess, The*
Devi, Phoolan, **Notor:** 275-276
Devi, Savitri. *See* Savitri Devi
Devil, **Anc:** 60, 205, 993
Devil Is an Ass, The (Jonson), **17th:** 442
Devil upon Two Sticks, The (Lesage), **18th:** 597
Devil's Dictionary, The (Bierce), **19th:** 229, 230
Devil's Law-Case, The (Webster), **17th:** 977
Devin, Sheila. *See* Barrows, Sydney
Devoir et l'inquiétude, Le (Éluard), **20th:** 1152
Devolution, War of (1667-1668), **17th:** 151, 186, 555, 558, 602, 934, 946
Devonshire, duchess of. *See* Cavendish, Georgiana
Devonshire, eighth duke of. *See* Cavendish, Spencer Compton
Devotio moderna, **MA:** 1022
Devotions upon Emergent Occasions (Donne), **17th:** 232
Devshirme, **18th:** 27
De Wette, W. M. L., **19th:** 1735
Dewey, George, **19th:** 645-648
Dewey, John, **20th:** 982-984
Dewey, Melvil, **19th:** 649-652; library classification system, 651
Dewey, Thomas E., **20th:** 1055, 4234; **Notor:** 661, 939, 955
Dewey decimal classification system, **19th:** 649
Dexter, Caroline H., **19th:** 1592
Dhanananda, **Anc:** 202
Dhanu. *See* Rajaratnam, Thenmuli
Dharanīndravarman I, **MA:** 980
Dharma, **Anc:** 124, 169, 497, 931
Dharma Bums, The (Kerouac), **20th:** 2116
D'Herbois, Collot, **Notor:** 908
Dhuoda, **MA:** 310-313
Diabetes, **20th:** 224, 1900, 2526
Diable boiteux, Le. See *Devil upon Two Sticks, The*
Diadochi, **Anc:** 64, 598

Diadumenos (Polyclitus), **Anc:** 676
Diaghilev, Sergei, **20th:** 985-989; George Balanchine, 194; Jean Cocteau, 794; Michel Fokine, 1263; Juan Gris, 1598; Serge Lifar, 2378; Dame Alicia Markova, 2627; Léonide Massine, 2647; Vaslav Nijinsky, 2975; Anna Pavlova, 3166; Sergei Prokofiev, 3339; Igor Stravinsky, 3888
Diaitētikon (Herophilus), **Anc:** 412
Dial, The (magazine), **19th:** 747
Dialecticae disputationes (Valla), **MA:** 1050
Dialecticae partitiones (Ramus), **Ren:** 817
Dialectical materialism, **19th:** 1509
Dialectics (Ramus), **Ren:** 818
Dialoghi ad Petrum Paulum historum (Bruni), **MA:** 209
Dialogic Imagination, The (Bakhtin), **20th:** 191
Dialogo. See *Spiritual Dialogue, The*
Dialogo da pintura. See *Four Dialogues on Painting*
Dialogo del reggimento di Firenze. See *Dialogue on the Government of Florence*
Dialogorum de trinitate libri duo, de justicia regni Christi capitual quatuor (Servetus), **Ren:** 861
Dialogue, The (Catherine of Siena), **MA:** 237
Dialogue Between Some Young Men Born in New England and Sundry Ancient Men That Came out of Holland (Bradford), **17th:** 86
Dialogue Concerning Oratory, A. See *Dialogus de oratoribus*
Dialogue Concerning the Two Chief World Systems, Ptolemaic and Copernican (Galileo), **17th:** 300, 594, 631, 936
Dialogue of a Philosopher with a Jew and a Christian (Abelard), **MA:** 16
Dialogue of the Seraphic Virgin, Catherine of Siena, The. See *Dialogue, The*
Dialogue on the Government of Florence (Guicciardini), **Ren:** 410
Dialogues, **Anc:** Aristotelian, 94; Confucian, 236; Platonic, 514, 660; Sima Xiangru, 785; Socratic, 799. See also *Eranistes seu Polymorphus*
Dialogues Concerning Eloquence in General, and Particularly That Kind Which Is Fit for the Pulpit (Fénelon), **17th:** 266
Dialogues Concerning Natural Religion (Hume), **18th:** 515
Dialogues des carmélites (Poulenc), **20th:** 3319
Dialogues des inutiles (Éluard), **20th:** 1152
Dialogues of the Courtesans. See *Hetairikoi dialogoi*
Dialogues of the Dead. See *Nekrikoi dialogoi*
Dialogues of the Gods. See *Theōn dialogoi*
Dialogus (Ockham), **MA:** 780
Dialogus de oratoribus (Tacitus), **Anc:** 838
Dialogus de vita S. Joannis Chrysostomi (Palladius), **Anc:** 208
Dialogus inter philosophum, Judaeum et Christianum. See *Dialogue of a Philosopher with a Jew and a Christian*
Diamond, Jack. *See* Diamond, Legs
Diamond, Legs, **Notor:** 277-278, 938
Diamond Jim. *See* Fisk, James
Diamond Jubilee, **19th:** 461
Diamond Lil (West), **20th:** 4298
Diamond necklace affair, **18th:** 657
Diamonds, South Africa, **19th:** 462, 1892
Diamorphoses (Xenakis), **20th:** 4415
Diana (Saint-Gaudens), **19th:** 1973
Diana and Her Companions (Vermeer), **17th:** 956
Diana, Princess of Wales, **20th:** 989-992, 1144
Diane Chassereuse (Renoir), **19th:** 1889
Diane de Poitiers, **Ren:** 184, 283-285, 423, 627
Dianetics (Hubbard), **20th:** 1910
Diard, Raymond. *See* Landru, Henri Désiré
Diarists, **18th:** James Boswell, 146; Samuel Sewall, 895
Diarium sive rerum urbanarum commentarii (Burchard), **Ren:** 117
Diary of a Mad Old Man (Tanizaki), **20th:** 3945
Diary of an Ennuyée (Jameson), **19th:** 1218
Diary of Anne Frank, The (Frank), **20th:** 1303
Diary of Samuel Pepys, The (Pepys), **17th:** 728
Diary of Selma Lagerlöf, The (Lagerlöf), **20th:** 2235
Dias, Bartolomeu, **Ren:** 237, 286-289, 511
Diatribae duae medico-philosophicae. See *Of Fermentation*
Diatribae Thomae Willisii de febribus vindicatio (Lower), **17th:** 564
Díaz, Melchior, **Ren:** 246
Díaz, Porfirio, **19th:** 652-654, 1247; **20th:** 647, 2544, 4160, 4448; **Notor:** 278-280, 1070, 1129
Díaz, Ruy. *See* Cid, El
Díaz de Vivar, Rodrigo. *See* Cid, El
Díaz del Castillo, Bernal, **Ren:** 621
Dibbs, Sir George Richard, **19th:** 150

Dichloro-diphenyl-trichloroethane, **20th:** 663
DiCiccio, Frank, **Notor:** 432, 435
Dickens, Charles, **19th:** 655-658; *Oliver Twist*, 140
Dickinson, Charles, **19th:** 1189
Dickinson, Emily, **19th:** 658-663, 1098, 1193
Dickinson, John, **18th:** 303-307, 1090
Dickinson, Roscoe G., **20th:** 3155
Dictatorship Versus Democracy (Trotsky), **20th:** 4074
Dictatus papae (Gregory VII), **MA:** 434, 706
Dictionariolum trilinguae (Ray), **17th:** 782
Dictionary of Music (Rousseau), **18th:** 178
Dictionary of the English Language, A (Johnson), **18th:** 536
Dictionnaire historique et critique. See *Historical and Critical Dictionary, An*
Didacticism, history and, **Anc:** 783
Diderot, Denis, **18th:** 32, 307-311, 502, 820, 868
Didier. *See* Bastien-Thiry, Jean-Marie
Dido, **Anc:** 271-274, 382, 987
Dido and Aeneas (Purcell), **Anc:** 273; **17th:** 764
Dido Building Carthage (Turner), **19th:** 2323
Dido, Queen of Carthage (Marlowe and Nashe), **Anc:** 273; **Ren:** 624
Didrikson, Babe. *See* Zaharias, Babe Didrikson
Didymus. *See* Thomas, Saint
Diefenbaker, John G., **20th:** 992-994, 3175
Diels, Otto Paul Hermann, **20th:** 995-997
Diels-Alder reaction, **20th:** 996
Diem, Ngo Dinh. *See* Ngo Dinh Diem
Diemen, Antony van, **17th:** 905
Dien Bien Phu, Battle of (1954), **20th:** 4171
Dieppe raid (1942), **20th:** 2855
Dies Irae (Liszt), **19th:** 1395
Diesel, Rudolf, **19th:** 663-666
Dieses Volk. See *This People Israel*
Diet, **Anc:** Greek, 278; theories of, 277
Dietrich, Marlene, **20th:** 997-1000, 3861
Dietrich, Robert. *See* Hunt, E. Howard
Dietwald und Amelinde (Grimmelshausen), **17th:** 325
Dieux ont soif, Les. See *Gods Are Athirst, The*
Difference Between Fichte's and Schelling's Philosophy, The (Hegel), **19th:** 1066
Difficulty of Being, The (Cocteau), **20th:** 796
Digby, Sir Everard, **Ren:** 326
Digest of Justinian, The, **MA:** 601
Digesta. See *Digest of Justinian, The*
Digestion, study of, **20th:** 3164
Diggers, **17th:** 989
Digters bazar, En. See *Poet's Bazaar, The*
Dihya. *See* Kāhina, Damia al-
Dikran. *See* Tigranes the Great
Dilas, Milovan. *See* Djilas, Milovan
Diletantizm v nauke (Herzen), **19th:** 1085
Dilke, Sir Charles, **19th:** 461
Dillinger, John, **Notor:** 281-282, 491, 775
DiMaggio, Joe, **20th:** 1001-1003, 1436, 2798
Dimetos (Fugard), **20th:** 1356
Dimock Community Health Center. *See* New England Hospital for Women and Children
Dīn, Jahāl-ud-. *See* Akbar
Ding-an-sich, **18th:** 343, 549
Dingane, **19th:** 1298, 2082
Dingiswayo, **19th:** 2081
Dingley Act (1897), **19th:** 1461
Dinh Bo Linh, **MA:** 757
Dinner Party, The (Chicago), **20th:** 751
Dinosaurs, extinction theory, **20th:** 75
Dio Cassius, **Anc:** 274-277, 484, 486; **Notor:** 291, 384
Dio Chrysostom, **Anc:** 274
Diocles of Carystus, **Anc:** 277-279
Dioclesian (Purcell), **17th:** 765
Diocletian, **Anc:** 43, 239, 280-282, 391, 775; **Notor:** 391
Diodore of Tarsus, **Anc:** 208, 863
Diodorus Cronus, **Anc:** 981
Diodorus Siculus, **Anc:** 556
Diogenes Laertius, **Anc:** 399, 608, 963, 965
Diogenes of Sinope, **Anc:** 69, 283-285
Dioklēs epistolē prophulaktikē (Diocles), **Anc:** 278
Dion Cassius. *See* Dio Cassius
Dionis. *See* Denis, Saint
Dionysia (festival), **Anc:** 8, 90, 621, 876
Dionysius. *See* Denis, Saint
Dionysius I, **Anc:** 87
Dionysius Exiguus, **MA:** 313-315
Dionysius of Paris. *See* Denis, Saint
Dionysius the Aeropagite, Saint, **Anc:** 270
Dionysus, **Anc:** 92, 512, 695, 793, 876
Diophanes of Mitylene, **Anc:** 357
Diophantus, **Anc:** 286-289, 435; **MA:** 22, 110, 195
Diopter, invention of, **Anc:** 418
Dioptra (Hero of Alexandria), **Anc:** 401
Dioptrice (Kepler), **17th:** 458
Dior, Christian, **20th:** 730; **Notor:** 283
Dior, Françoise, **Notor:** 283-284
Dior, Raymond, **Notor:** 283
Dioramas, **19th:** 589

Dioscorides, Pedanius, **Anc:** 289-292
Diphtheria, **19th:** 180; **20th:** 1116
Diplomacy, **18th:** first Viscount Bolingbroke, 135-140; Étienne François de Choiseul, 246-247; colonial America, 627; Benjamin Franklin, 373; Elbridge Gerry, 413; John Jay, 524; Thomas Jefferson, 529; Wenzel Anton von Kaunitz, 557; Increase Mather, 672; Gouverneur Morris, 706; Pontiac, 802; first Earl Stanhope, 937-940; Thanadelthur, 975; U.S. and Spain, 524; Charles Gravier de Vergennes, 1011-1013; Robert Walpole, 1036; West Africa, 915. *See also* Category Index
Dirac, Paul A. M., **20th:** 1004-1006
Dirac equation, **20th:** 1004
Dirac notation. *See* Bra-ket notation
Dirección Nacional de Inteligencia (Chile), **20th:** 3257
Directions on Health for Plistarchus. See *Hugieina pros Pleistarkhon*
"Dirge for Hui Yuan" (Xie Lingyun), **Anc:** 976
Dirichlet, Peter Gustav Lejeune, **19th:** 629
Dirksen, Everett, **20th:** 2455
Disabilities, attitudes toward, **Anc:** Egypt, 27; Rome, 217; Sparta, 14
"Disappointment, The" (Behn), **17th:** 44
Disasters of War (Goya), **18th:** 438
Disc (Delaunay), **20th:** 952
Discarded Image, The (Lewis), **20th:** 2355
Disciples of Christ, **19th:** 401
Discontented Colonel, The. See *Brennoralt*
Discorsi del poema eroico. See *Discourses on the Heroic Poem*
Discorsi sulla prima deca di Tito Livio. See *Discourses on the First Ten Books of Titus Livius*
Discours à Mme de La Sablière (La Fontaine), **17th:** 482
Discours de la cause de la pesanteur (Huygens), **17th:** 399
Discours de la méthode. See *Discourse on Method*
Discours des misères de ce temps (Ronsard), **Ren:** 838
Discours et conférences (Renan), **19th:** 1887
Discours politiques, 1560-1568 (L'Hospital), **Ren:**, 569
Discours préliminaire. See *Preliminary Discourse to the Encyclopedia of Diderot*
Discours sur le colonialisme. See *Discourse on Colonialism*
Discours sur les sciences et les arts. See *Discourse on the Arts and Sciences, A*
Discours sur l'histoire universelle. See *Discourse on the History of the Whole World, A*
Discours sur l'origine et les fondements de l'inégalité. See *Discourse upon the Origin and Foundation of the Inequality Among Mankind, A*
Discourse of a Discoverie for a New Passage to Cataia, A (Gilbert), **Ren:** 379
Discourse of the Religion Anciently Professed by the Irish and the British, A (Ussher), **17th:** 939
Discourse on Colonialism (Césaire), **20th:** 711
Discourse on Matters Pertaining to Religion, A (Parker), **19th:** 1736
Discourse on Method (Descartes), **17th:** 227
Discourse on Political Arithmetick (Petty), **17th:** 734
Discourse on the Arts and Sciences, A (Rousseau), **18th:** 868
Discourse on the Constitution of the United States, A (Calhoun), **19th:** 394
Discourse on the History of the Whole World, A (Bossuet), **17th:** 70
Discourse on the Nature and Offices of Friendship (Taylor), **17th:** 742
Discourse upon the Origin and Foundation of the Inequality Among Mankind, A (Rousseau), **18th:** 869
Discourses (Reynolds), **18th:** 838
Discourses in America (Arnold), **19th:** 74
Discourses in Verse on Man (Voltaire), **18th:** 1027
Discourses of the Muslims (al-Ashʿarī), **MA:** 112
Discourses on the First Ten Books of Titus Livius (Machiavelli), **Ren:** 588
Discourses on the Heroic Poem (Tasso), **Ren:** 926
Discovery of India, The (Nehru), **20th:** 2932
Discovery of the Earth, The (Verne), **19th:** 2355
Discovery of the Great West, The. See *France and England in North America*
Discovery of the Large, Rich, and Beautiful Empire of Guiana . . . , The (Ralegh), **Ren:** 814
Discovery of the Mammalian Egg, The (Baer), **19th:** 114
Discovery, Settlement, and Present State of Kentucke (Filson), **18th:** 145
Discreet Charm of the Bourgeoisie, The (film), **20th:** 579
Discreto, El. See *Compleat Gentleman, The*
Discrimination, **20th:** African Americans, 1046, 1773, 2147,

2891, 3296, 3464, 4201, 4291, 4307; African Americans in education, 802, 4309; African Americans in entertainment, 88, 1063, 1854, 3335; African Americans in medicine, 347; African Americans in sports, 5, 726, 1474, 3568; African Americans in the military, 3470; African Americans in theater, 1929; blacks in Jamaica, 1417; blacks in West Indies, 829; British toward Indians, 221; employment, 3372; reverse, 3326; South Africa, 3139; U.S. Supreme Court, 1310; women, 146, 508, 3938

Discurso pronunciado por el general Bolívar al congreso general de Venezuela en el aeto de su instalacion. See *Speech of His Excellency, General Bolívar at the Installation of the Congress of Venezuela*

Discussion sur l'évolution de l'univers (Lemaître), **20th:** 2339

Diseases, **Anc:** causes of, 421; classification of, 85; diagnosis of, 116, 200; gods and, 441; treatment of, 86; **18th:** and chemistry, 933; and slave trade, 325; **20th:** Africa, 1086; AIDS, 706; antibiotics, 1254, 1261; bacterial infections, 1021-1022; Cushing's syndrome, 900; diabetes, 1900, 2526; diagnostic tracers, 4420; diptheria, 1116; farm animals, 3773; Hodgkin's disease, 2696; infection and immunity, 587; malaria, 3533; mental, 34, 1108; pernicious anemia, 4305; polio, 2251, 3614; public health issues, 546; research, 4304; sickle-cell anemia, 3156; syphilis, 1117; tuberculosis, 619, 3773; venereal, 3626; Vietnam, 618; yellow fever, 1542. *See also* Medicine; Scurvy; Smallpox

Dishonored (film), **20th:** 999

Disinherited (group of nobles), **MA:** 307

Disney, Walt, **20th:** 1006-1011

Disney cartoonist strike (1941), **20th:** 1008

Disneyland, **20th:** 1008

Disorder and Early Sorrow (Mann), **20th:** 2596

Dispute over the Sacrament (Raphael), **Ren:** 820

Disques, Les (Léger), **20th:** 2336

"Disquieting Muses, The" (Plath), **20th:** 3287

Disquisition on Government, A (Calhoun), **19th:** 394

Disquisitiones arithmeticae. See *Arithmetical Inquisitions*

Disquisitiones generales circa superficies curvas. See *General Investigations of Curved Surfaces*

Disraeli, Benjamin, **19th:** 304, 643, 666-670, 925, 1770, 1949, 2361; Salisbury, 1978

Dissection, human, **Anc:** 410

Dissenters, **18th:** 298, 402, 424, 1109

Dissertatio. See *Learned Maid, The*

Dissertatio epistolica de formatione pulli in ovo. See *Marcello Malpighi and the Evolution of Embryology*

Dissertatiocum nuncio sidereo. See *Kepler's Conversation with Galileo's Sidereal Messenger*

Dissertation sur l'église visible (Mornay), **Ren:** 703

Dissertation upon Parties, A (Bolingbroke), **18th:** 139

Dissertations on Government, the Affairs of the Bank, and Paper Money (Paine), **18th:** 760

Dissertations on the English Language (Webster), **19th:** 2404

Dissertations Relative to the Natural History of Animals and Vegetables (Spallanzani), **18th:** 927

Distant Mirror, A (Tuchman), **20th:** 4106

Distant Thunder (film), **20th:** 3395

District of Columbia survey, **18th:** 85

Disturbing the Peace (Havel), **20th:** 1708

Dit de la rose, Le (Christine de Pizan), **MA:** 275

Ditch, Campaign of the (627), **MA:** 735

Dithyrambs, **Anc:** 877

Ditié de Jeanne d'Arc, Le. See *Tale of Joan of Arc, The*

Diuturnum illud. See *On Civil Government*

Divākarapandita, **MA:** 981

Divan, The (Hafiz), **MA:** 451

Dive Bomber (Orozco), **20th:** 3070

Divers jeux rustiques (du Bellay), **Ren:** 296

Divers portraits (La Fayette), **17th:** 477

Divers Voyages Touching the Discouerie of America (Hakluyt), **Ren:** 419

Diversity of Life, The (Wilson), **20th:** 4359

Divina commedia, La. See *Divine Comedy, The*

Divine, Father. *See* Father Divine

Divine Comedy, The (Dante), **Anc:** 168, 437; **MA:** 239, 275, 300, 710; **18th:** 124

Divine Faith, **Ren:** 17

Divine Imperative, The (Brunner), **20th:** 548

Divine Looking-Glass, A (Muggleton and Reeve), **17th:** 667

Divine Maxims of Government . . . (Quevedo y Villegas), **17th:** 770

Divine Milieu, The (Teilhard), **20th:** 3964

Divine Narcissus, The (Cruz), **17th:** 209

Divine Principle (Moon), **20th:** 2811
Divini, Eustachio, **17th:** 134
Divini Redemptoris (Pius XI), **20th:** 3276
Divino Narciso, El. See *Divine Narcissus, The*
Divisament dou monde. See *Travels of Marco Polo, The*
Division of Labor in Society, The (Durkheim), **20th:** 1067
Divisionism, **19th:** 2075
Divorce, **Ren:** Anne Boleyn and, 112; Catherine of Aragon and, 188; Henry VIII and, 51, 62, 112, 143, 184, 188, 231, 266, 335, 369, 443, 639, 699, 834, 947, 997
Dix, Dorothea, **19th:** 671-674, 1142
18 Brumaire, **18th:** 118, 131
Dixon, John. *See* Brodie, William
Dixon, Robert, **19th:** 244
Dixon, Thomas, Jr., **Notor:** 284, 286, 957
Djamileh (Bizet), **19th:** 242
Djilas, Milovan, **20th:** 1011-1014, 4035
Djinns, Les (Franck), **19th:** 823
Djoser. *See* Zoser
Dmitry (grandson of Ivan the Great), **Ren:** 750
Dmitry, False, **Ren:** 388; **17th:** 794, 854, 944
Dmitry, Second False, **17th:** 794, 944
Dmitry Ivanovich (prince of Russia), **Ren:** 387; **17th:** 943
Dmitri Roudine. See *Rudin*
DNA. *See* Deoxyribonucleic acid
DNA (Watson), **20th:** 4244
Do Everything (Willard), **19th:** 2443
Doan Trung, **19th:** 2310
Doberval, Jean. *See* Dauberval, Jean
Dockers' Union, **20th:** 356
Docteur Eugène. *See* Petiot, Marcel
Doctor Faustus (Mann), **20th:** 2596
Doctor Faustus (Marlowe), **Ren:** 624
Doctor Fludd's Answer (Fludd), **17th:** 282
Doctor in Spite of Himself, The (Molière), **17th:** 648; **19th:** operat by Gounod, 953
Dr. Johnson. *See* Johnson, Samuel
Dr. Livingstone, I Presume? (Stanley), **19th:** 2138
Dr. Mabuse the Gambler (film), **20th:** 2254
Dr. Montessori's Own Handbook (Montessori), **20th:** 2806
Dr. Rochecliffe Performing Divine Service in the Cottage of Joceline Jocliffe at Woodstock (Hunt), **19th:** 1157
Doctor Sax (Kerouac), **20th:** 2115
Dr. Seuss. *See* Seuss, Dr.
Dr. Strangelove (film), **20th:** 3696
Doctor Thorne (Trollope), **19th:** 2300
Dr. Willis's Practice of Physick (Willis), **17th:** 987
Doctor Zhivago (Pasternak), **20th:** 3132
Doctors. *See* Physicians
Doctor's Wife, The (Braddon), **19th:** 287
Doctrina Christiana, y catecismo para instrucción de los Indios (Acosta), **Ren:** 6
Doctrine and Discipline of Divorce, The (Milton), **17th:** 640
"Doctrine of Fascism, The" (Mussolini), **20th:** 2887
Doctrine of the Mean, The, **MA:** 1160
Doctrine of the Real Presence, The (Pusey), **19th:** 1846
Dodana. *See* Dhuoda
Dodd, William, **Notor:** 286-287
Dodesukaden (film), **20th:** 2219
Dodge, Joseph M., **20th:** 1965
Dodgson, Charles Lutwidge. *See* Carroll, Lewis
Dodsworth (Lewis), **20th:** 2365
Doe, Samuel K., **Notor:** 288-289, 1021
Doering, William, **20th:** 4394
Doesburg, Theo van, **20th:** 2788, 3092
Dog (Giacometti), **20th:** 1472
Dog Barking at the Moon (Miró), **20th:** 2761
Dog Beneath the Skin, The (Auden and Isherwood), **20th:** 172
Dog Shogun. *See* Tokugawa Tsunayoshi
Dog Years (Grass), **20th:** 1574
Dogma of Christ, The (Fromm), **20th:** 1345
Dogmatics (Brunner), **20th:** 549
Dogmatics in Outline (Barth), **20th:** 244
Dogmatism, **Anc:** 84, 279
Doheny, Edward L., **Notor:** 342
Dōkyō, **MA:** 624
Dolce stil nuovo, **MA:** 169, 240, 303, 697
Dolce vita, La (film), **20th:** 1232
Dole, Bob, **20th:** 786, 1014-1019
Dole, Elizabeth, **20th:** 1016, 1018-1020
Dolgoruky, Vasily Vladimirovich, **17th:** 12
Dolin, Anton, **20th:** 2628
Döllinger, Ignaz von, **19th:** 31, 114
Döllinger, Johann Joseph Ignaz von, **19th:** 12
Doll's House, A (Ibsen), **19th:** 1166
Dolphy, Eric, **20th:** 815
Dom Casmurro (Machado), **19th:** 1451
Dom João VI, **19th:** 1763
Domagk, Gerhard, **20th:** 1021-1023, 1255
Domaines for Clarinet Alone or with Twenty-one Other Instruments (Boulez), **20th:** 454
Dombey and Son (Dickens), **19th:** 655

Dome of Many-Colored Glass, A (Lowell), **20th:** 2445
Dome of the Rock, **MA:** 5
Domenichino, Il, **17th:** 749
Domenico Cassini, Gian. *See* Cassini, Gian Domenico
Domesday Book, **MA:** 1119
Domestic Affections, The (Hemans), **19th:** 1076
Domestic Manners of the Americans (Trollope), **19th:** 2303
Dominic, Saint, **MA:** 316-319
Dominican Republic. *See* Hispaniola; Geographical Index
Dominicans, **MA:** 85, 317, 819, 882, 1027, 1063, 1110; **Ren:** 138, 142, 582
Dominion Lands, **19th:** 1909
Dominique, Captain. *See* You, Dominique
Dominis, Mrs. John O. *See* Liliuokalani
Domino theory, **20th:** 2030
Dominus regnavit (Josquin), **Ren:** 516
Domitian, **Anc:** 104, 224, 370, 437, 493, 537, 838, 943; **Notor:** 289-291
Domitianus Augustus, Caesar. *See* Domitian
Don Carlo. *See* Gambino, Carlo
Don Carlos (Verdi), **19th:** 2352
Don Gil of the Green Breeches (Tirso), **17th:** 913
Don Giovanni (Mozart), **18th:** 712
Don Juan (Byron), **19th:** 381
Don Juan (Frisch), **20th:** 1339
Don Juan (Molière), **17th:** 648
Don Juan of Austria, **Ren:** 207, 321
Don Pasquale (Donizetti), **19th:** 676
Don Procopio (Bizet), **19th:** 241
Don Quixote de la Mancha (Cervantes), **Ren:** 207; **17th:** 738
Donald III (king of Scotland), **MA:** 304
Donatello, **MA:** 206, 319-322, 419, 567, 700, 949; **Ren:** 18, 601
Donation of Constantine, The (Raphael), **Anc:** 392
Donation of Pépin (754), **MA:** 243
Donatism, **Anc:** 241, 353
Donato di Niccolò di Betto Bardi. *See* Donatello
Donato di Pascuccio d'Antonio. *See* Bramante, Donato
Donatus, Aelius, **Anc:** 456; **MA:** 861
Donders, Franciscus Cornelius, **20th:** 1122
Dong, Pham Vam. *See* Pham Vam Dong
Dong shan chou he ji (Liu and Qian), **17th:** 541
Dong Zhongshu, **Anc:** 381, 960
Donglin faction, **17th:** 911
Dongzhen. *See* Kawashima, Yoshiko
Doni Madonna (Michelangelo), **Ren:** 682
Dönitz, Karl, **Notor:** 132, 292-293, 895, 988
Donizetti, Gaetano, **19th:** 674-676; **20th:** 676
Donna del lago, La (Rossini), **19th:** 1945
Donna Quixote (Richardson), **19th:** 1904
Donnacona, **Ren:** 178
Donne, John, **17th:** 16, 132, 200, 202, 230-234, 253, 366, 741
Donnellys, Black, **Notor:** 294-295
Donovan, Bill, **Notor:** 490
Doolin, Bill, **Notor:** 257, 259, 296-297
Doolittle, Hilda. *See* H. D.
Doolittle, Jimmy, **20th:** 1023-1026, 1648
Doors of Perception, The (Huxley), **20th:** 1963
Dorantes, Andrés, **Ren:** 152
Dorat, Jean, **Ren:** 837
Dorchester, first Baron. *See* Carleton, Sir Guy
Dorchester, Lord. *See* Carleton, Sir Guy
Dorgon, **17th:** 1, 234-237, 848
Doriot, Jacques, **Notor:** 264, 298-299
Dornröschen (Humperdinck), **19th:** 1155
Doroshenko, Petro, **17th:** 452, 624
Dorothy and the Wizard of Oz (Baum), **19th:** 157
Dorris, Michael, **20th:** 1169
Dorr's Rebellion, **19th:** 800
Dorsey, Tommy, **20th:** 3747
Dort, Synod of (1618), **17th:** 619
Dory, Joseph. *See* Hory, Elmyr de
Dory-Boutin, Elmyr. *See* Hory, Elmyr de
Dorylaeum, Battle of (1097), **MA:** 177
Doryphorus (Polyclitus), **Anc:** 523, 676
Dos Passos, John, **Notor:** 925
Dos Santos, Marcelino, **20th:** 2515
Dōshō, **MA:** 1138
Dost Mohammed, **19th:** 1718
Dostoevski, Fyodor, **19th:** 677-681, 2320
Dot and Tot of Merryland (Baum), **19th:** 157
Doto, Giuseppe Antonio. *See* Adonis, Joe
Dou Xian, **Anc:** 151
Double, The (Dostoevski), **19th:** 677
Double Helix, The (Watson), **20th:** 865, 1318, 4243
Double Oval Bronze (Moore), **20th:** 2820
Doughty, Thomas, **Notor:** 301
Douglas, Archibald, **Ren:** 497, 501
Douglas, Helen Gahagan, **20th:** 1026-1029
Douglas, Margaret, **Ren:** 104
Douglas, Stephen A., **19th:** 345, 506, 681-683, 782, 1382, 2202
Douglas, Thomas, **17th:** 122
Douglas, William O., **20th:** 1029-1032; **Notor:** 369

Douglass, Frederick, **19th:** 322, 684-687, 2460
Douhet, Giulio, **20th:** 2767
Doumergue, Gaston, **Notor:** 998
Douro, Baron. *See* Wellington, duke of
Douze Préludes (Debussy), **20th:** 938
Dover, Treaty of (1670), **17th:** 149, 693, 816, 839
Dover Castle, Siege of (1216), **MA:** 211
Doveri dell'uomo. See *Duties of Man, The*
Dowland, John, **Ren:** 289-291; **17th:** 127, 502
Down and Out in London and Paris (Orwell), **20th:** 3082
Down on Stovall's Plantation (Waters), **20th:** 4240
Down Survey, **17th:** 734
Downs, Battle of the (1638), **17th:** 288
Downs, Diane, **Notor:** 299-300
Downs, Hugh, **20th:** 4211
Doxa (Parmenides), **Anc:** 609
Doyle, Sir Arthur Conan, **19th:** 688-691; **Notor:** 633, 1069, 1107
Doyle, Michael J., **Notor:** 746
Dózsa, György, **Ren:** 984
Draco, **Anc:** 293-294
Dracula, Vlad. *See* Vlad III the Impaler
Draft of Shadows, and Other Poems, A (Paz), **20th:** 3171
Drag, The (West), **20th:** 4297
Dragasani, Battle of (1821), **19th:** 2479
Dragons of Eden, The (Sagan), **20th:** 3591
Drahomíra, **MA:** 671
Drake, Sir Francis, **Ren:** 193, 291-294, 354, 396, 419, 780, 883; **Notor:** 301-302
Drama, **18th:** and French politics, 97-99; historical, 889; **19th:** England, 1175, 1255, 1267, 1467, 2096; France, 696, 1147; Germany, 1289; Norway, 1165; Russia, 479, 1354, 1849; United States, 790
Draped Reclining Mother and Baby (Moore), **20th:** 2820
Draper, William, **19th:** 292
Drapier's Letters to the People of Ireland, The (Swift), **18th:** 966
Drayton, Michael, **17th:** 237-239
Dream, The (Rousseau), **19th:** 1953
Dream King. *See* Ludwig II
Dream of Christopher Columbus, The (Dalí), **20th:** 906
Dream of Gerontius, The (Elgar), **20th:** 1134
Dream of John Ball, A (Morris), **19th:** 1608
Dream of the Red Chamber (Cao Xueqin), **18th:** 194
Dream Play, A (Strindberg), **20th:** 3898
Dreamers (Hamsun), **20th:** 1661
Dreaming Emmett (Morrison), **20th:** 2836
Dreams, **Anc:** Herophilus on, 412; Jerome on, 456
Dreams (film), **20th:** 2219
Dreams for Sale (Davis), **20th:** 1026
Dreams of a Spirit-Seer, Illustrated by Dreams of Metaphysics (Kant), **18th:** 962
DreamWorks, **20th:** 3812
Dred Scott v. Sandford (1857), **19th:** 195, 341, 345, 471, 2043, 2227
Drei Abhandlungen zur Sexualtheorie. See *Three Essays on the Theory of Sexuality*
Drei Kameraden. See *Three Comrades*
Dreigroschenoper, Die. See *Threepenny Opera, The*
Dreisch, Hans, **20th:** 2826
Dreiser, Theodore, **20th:** 698, 1032-1036
Dreiser Looks at Russia (Dreiser), **20th:** 1035
Dresden insurrection, **19th:** 119
Dresden Maenad, The (Scopas), **Anc:** 762
Drew, Daniel, **Notor:** 357
Drexel, Morgan, and Company, **19th:** 1600
Drey, Alan. *See* Lake, Leonard
Dreyer, Carl Theodor, **20th:** 1037-1040
Dreyfus, Alfred, **19th:** 815, 1088, 2491; **20th:** 780, 2993, 3292; **Notor:** 334
Dreyfus affair, **19th:** 1220; **20th:** 780, 3792
Drift and Mastery (Lippmann), **20th:** 2400
Driftwood (Homer), **19th:** 1125
Drucci, Vincent, **Notor:** 751
Drugs, **Anc:** Celsus on, 200; classification of, 291; Diocles on, 278; Dioscorides on, 290; Ebers Papyrus, 441; Galen on, 350
Druidism, **Anc:** 219
Druids, **Anc:** 164, 935
Druilletes, Gabriel, **17th:** 603
Drum Taps (Whitman), **19th:** 2426
Drummer, The (Addison), **18th:** 22
Drummond, Edward (pirate). *See* Teach, Edward
Drummond, Edward (secretary to Sir Robert Peel), **Notor:** 678
Drummond, William, **17th:** 443
Drury Lane Theatre, **17th:** 51; **18th:** Fanny Abington, 1; David Garrick, 397; Mary de la Rivière Manley, 641; Anne Oldfield, 749; Richard Brinsley Sheridan, 906; Sarah Siddons, 912; Peg Woffington, 1102; **19th:** 1255, 1467
Drusus, Marcus Livius, **Anc:** 194, 508
Drusus, Nero Claudius, **Anc:** 217
Drusus Nero Germanicus, Tiberius Claudius. *See* Claudius I
Dryden, John, **17th:** 43, 52, 64, 201, 233, 239-243, 342, 394, 442, 765, 817

Du droit de propriété (Thiers), **19th:** 2265
Du Fu, **MA:** 322-326, 655
Du Mingshi, **Anc:** 975
Du Ruhui, **MA:** 995
Du suc gastrique et de son rôle dans la nutrition (Bernard), **19th:** 205
Du suc pancréatique, et de son rôle dans les phénomènes de la digestion (Bernard), **19th:** 206
Du système pénitentiaire aux États-Unis et de son application en France. See *On the Penitentiary System in the United States and Its Application in France*
Dual Mandate in British Tropical Africa, The (Lugard), **20th:** 2467
Dualism, **Anc:** Buddhist, 931; Platonic, 263
Duan Qirui, **20th:** 2448
Duane, William John, **Notor:** 1019
Duarte, José Napoleon, **20th:** 1040-1042
Duarte, María Eva. *See* Perón, Eva
Dubček, Alexander, **20th:** 524, 1042-1046
Du Bellay, Joachim, **Ren:** 285, 294-296
Dublin, Ireland, **18th:** and Irish independence, 357, 440, 983; Peg Woffington, 1102
Dubliners (Joyce), **20th:** 2056
Du Bois, W. E. B., **19th:** 703, 2393; **20th:** 1046-1050, 1419; **Notor:** 285
Du Camp, Maxime, **19th:** 785
Duccio di Buoninsegna, **MA:** 326-329, 660, 696, 867
Duchamp, Marcel, **20th:** 1051-1054, 2580
Duchess of Malfi, The (Webster), **17th:** 977
Duchess of Padua, The (Wilde), **19th:** 2433
Duclaux, Émile, **19th:** 1752
Ducretet, Eugène, **19th:** 1826
Dudevant, Baronne. *See* Sand, George
Dudley, Anne. *See* Bradstreet, Anne
Dudley, Lady Jane. *See* Grey, Lady Jane
Dudley, John, **Ren:** 199, 267, 305, 399, 553, 639, 899
Dudley, Robert. *See* Leicester, earl of
Dudley, Thomas, **17th:** 992
Due Foscari, I (Verdi), **19th:** 2351
Duel (Xenakis), **20th:** 4416
Duhig, James, **19th:** 1494
Dühring, Eugen, **19th:** 751
Duino Elegies (Rilke), **20th:** 3455
Duke, David, **Notor:** 177, 303-304, 726, 912
Duke, James Buchanan, **19th:** 692-695
Duke and Duchess of Osuna, The (Goya), **18th:** 437
Duke and Sons, W., **19th:** 692
Duke Bluebeard's Castle (Bartók), **20th:** 251
Duke Power Company, **19th:** 693
Duke University, **19th:** 694
Duke's Canal, **18th:** 163
Duke's Company, **17th:** 51
Dukkehjem, Et. See *Doll's House, A*
Dulcamara (Gilbert), **19th:** 917
Dulcimer Street (Collins), **20th:** 811
Dulcitius (Hrosvitha), **MA:** 517
Dulles, John Foster, **20th:** 1054-1058, 1102, 4005
Dumas, Alexandre, *père*, **19th:** 695-698, 872, 1557, 1591, 2354
Dumas, Frédéric, **20th:** 850
Dumas, Jean-Baptiste André, **19th:** 1368
Dumas, Léon, **20th:** 3703
Dumbo (animated film), **20th:** 1008
Dumont, Gabriel, **19th:** 1909
Dunant, Jean-Henri, **19th:** 699-701
Dunbar, Battle of (1296), **MA:** 202
Dunbar, Battle of (1650), **17th:** 205, 757
Dunbar, Paul Laurence, **19th:** 701-704
Dunbar, William, **Ren:** 499
Duncan, Isadora, **20th:** 985, 1058-1061, 1362, 2974; **Notor:** 933
Duncan, Veronica. *See* Lucan, Lady
Dunciad, The (Pope), **Anc:** 180; **18th:** 806, 989
Dundalk, Encampment of (1689), **17th:** 821
Dunes, Battle of the (1658), **17th:** 206, 417, 425, 933
Dungeness, Battle of (1652), **17th:** 57
Dunham, Katherine, **20th:** 1061-1065
Dunham School of Arts and Research, **20th:** 1063
Dunkerly, William, **19th:** 1113
Dunkirk, Siege of (1646), **17th:** 562
Dunlop Holding, **20th:** 3267
Dunn, Jacob P., Jr., **19th:** 1238
Dunn, Kaye. *See* Dunham, Katherine
Duns Scotus, John, **MA:** 329-333
Dunstable, John, **MA:** 333-336
Duong Dien Nghe, **MA:** 756
Duong Van Minh, **20th:** 2952
Duperron, Jacques Davy, **Ren:** 430
Dupes, Day of the (1630), **17th:** 19, 552, 599
Dupleix, Joseph-François, **18th:** 311-313
Du Pont, Eleuthère Irénée, **19th:** 705-707
Du Pont, John E., **Notor:** 305-306
Du Pont de Nemours and Company, E. I., **19th:** 706
Dupplin Moor, Battle of (1323), **MA:** 307

Durand, Asher B., **19th:** 232
Durant, Henry Fowle, **19th:** 1728
Durant, Thomas, **Notor:** 18, 220
Duranty, Edmund, **19th:** 632
Dürer, Albrecht, **Ren:** 100, 262, 297-300, 316, 453
Durham, first earl of, **19th:** 708-711
Durkheim, Émile, **20th:** 1065-1068
Duse, Eleonora, **20th:** 2331
Dusk (Michelangelo), **Ren:** 683
Dusk of Dawn (Du Bois), **20th:** 1049
Dust Tracks on a Road (Hurston), **20th:** 1944
Dustūr al-amal li islah al-khalal (Kâtib Çelebî), **17th:** 455
Dutch East India Company, **17th:** 288, 445, 618, 905
Dutch Interiors (Miró), **20th:** 2761
Dutch Reformed Church, **Ren:** 60. *See also* Protestantism
Dutch studies (Japan), **18th:** 504
Dutch Wars of Independence (1568-1648), **Ren:** 136, 200, 311, 322, 373, 397, 526, 616, 703, 740, 779, 798, 883, 994; **17th:** 287, 289, 618
Dutch West India Company, **17th:** 359, 518, 618, 643, 890
Duties of Man, The (Mazzini), **19th:** 1532
Duval, Claude, **Notor:** 306-307
Duval, Count. *See* Lustig, Victor
Duval, Jeanne, **19th:** 152
Duvalier, Duval, **Notor:** 307
Duvalier, François, **20th:** 124, 1069-1071; **Notor:** 307-309
Duvalier, Jean-Claude, **20th:** 124; **Notor:** 307, 309-311
Duvalier, Papa Doc. *See* Duvalier, François
Duvalierville, Haiti, **20th:** 1070
Duxborough. *See* Duxbury
Duxbury, **17th:** 8, 879
Dvenadtsat. See *Twelve, The*
Dvesti let vmeste (1795-1995) (Solzhenitsyn), **20th:** 3786
Dvořák, Antonín, **19th:** 711-714; **20th:** 1989
Dvoryanskoye gnezdo. See *House of Gentlefolk, A*
Dvoynik. See *Double, The*
Dwyer, Arthur. *See* Chambers, Whittaker
Dwyer, William Vincent, **Notor:** 237
Dyadics, **19th:** 914
Dyadya Vanya. See *Uncle Vanya*
Dyck, Sir Anthony van, **17th:** 244-246, 302, 671, 723
Dyer, Reginald, **Notor:** 311-312
Dyer's Hand, The (Auden), **20th:** 173
Dying Slave, The (Michelangelo), **Ren:** 683
Dylan, Bob, **20th:** 1072-1074
Dym. See *Smoke*
Dynamic equilibrium, **20th:** 4359
Dynamic Sociology (Ward), **19th:** 2385
Dynamite, **19th:** 1690
Dynamos, **19th:** 550, 2107
Dynasts, The (Hardy), **19th:** 1030
Dynasty of Raghu, The. See *Raghuvamśa*
Dyskolos, **Anc:** 548
Dyson, Arthur, **Notor:** 815
Dzerzhinsky, Felix, **Notor:** 312-314, 1112
Dzhugashvili, Joseph Vissarionovich. *See* Stalin, Joseph

E

E la nave va. See *And the Ship Sails On*
E.28/39 (airplane), **20th:** 4319
Eads, James Buchanan, **19th:** 715-717
Eadward. *See* Edward the Confessor; Edward the Elder
Eadweard. *See* Edward the Elder
Eakins, Thomas, **19th:** 717-720
Ealhwine. *See* Alcuin
Earhart, Amelia, **20th:** 1075-1078
Earl Hines Orchestra, **20th:** 1481
Earl Marshal's Court, **17th:** 167
Early Closing Act of 1904, **20th:** 415
Earp, Morgan, **19th:** 721; **Notor:** 144, 315, 899
Earp, Virgil, **19th:** 721; **Notor:** 144, 315
Earp, Wyatt, **19th:** 720-722; **Notor:** 144, 315-317, 485, 899
Earth in the Balance (Gore), **20th:** 1538
Earth sciences. *See* Category Index
Earth Trembles, The (film), **20th:** 4167
Earthly Paradise, The (Morris), **19th:** 1607
Earthquakes, **18th:** 796, 1027
East and West Association, **20th:** 559
East Germany, establishment of, **20th:** 4125
East India Act (1785), **18th:** 790
East India Association. *See* India Lobby
East India Company. *See* British East India Company; Dutch East India Company
East Indies, **18th:** 127, 829
East Meets West Foundation, **20th:** 1728
East of Eden (Steinbeck), **20th:** 3850
East Slope (Paz), **20th:** 3171
East Timor, **20th:** 3902
Easter, date of, **MA:** 313, 510, 741
Easter and the Totem (Pollock), **20th:** 3303
Easter Offensive. *See* Nguyen Hue Offensive
Easter Parade (film), **20th:** 1410
Easter Rising (1916), **20th:** 808, 843, 979, 3026, 3035
Eastern Grove Monastery, **Anc:** 975
Eastern Life (Martineau), **19th:** 1507

Eastern Orthodox Church, **Ren:** Catholic Church and, 394; Russia, 387, 490, 493, 957
Eastman, George, **20th:** 1078-1081
Eastman Kodak, **20th:** 1080
Eastman School of Music, **20th:** 1564
Eastward Ho! (Chapman, Jonson, and Marston), **Ren:** 215; **17th:** 442
Easy Virtue (Coward), **20th:** 854
Eaton, John Henry, **19th:** 2226
Eaton, Theophilus, **17th:** 218
Eau de jouvence, L' (Renan), **19th:** 1887
Eban, Abba, **20th:** 1082-1085
Ebb-Tide, The (Stevenson), **19th:** 2175
Ebbers, Bernard, **Notor:** 317-319
Eberhard, **MA:** 805
Ebers Papyrus, **Anc:** 441
Eberst, Jacob. *See* Offenbach, Jacques
Ebert, Friedrich, **Notor:** 319
Ebissa, **Anc:** 395
Ebner, Ferdinand, **20th:** 549
Eboli, princess of. *See* Mendoza y de la Cerda, Ana de
Éboué, Félix, **20th:** 1085-1089
Ecce beatam lucem (Striggio), **Ren:** 919
Ecce Homo (Nietzsche), **19th:** 1682
Eccles, Sir John Carew, **20th:** 1089-1092
Ecclesiastical Characteristics (Witherspoon), **18th:** 1099
Ecclesiastical History of the English People (Bede the Venerable), **Anc:** 394; **MA:** 151
Ecevit, Bülent, **20th:** 1973
Echdosis tēs orthodoxon pisteōs. See *Exposition of the Orthodox Faith*
Eck, Johann, **Ren:** 582, 665
Eckart, Dietrich, **Notor:** 319-320
Eckener, Hugo, **20th:** 1092-1096
Eckford, Elizabeth, **Notor:** 349
Eckstine, Billy, **20th:** 3114
Eclectic Readers (McGuffey), **19th:** 1447
Eclecticism, **Anc:** 84
Eclipses, solar and lunar, **Anc:** 53, 857; prediction of; **18th:** 1039
Eclogues (Petrarch), **MA:** 830
Eclogues (Vergil), **Anc:** 431, 528, 938
École de Fontainebleau, **20th:** 450
École des femmes, L'. See *School for Wives, The*
École des maris, L'. See *School for Husbands, The*
École Militaire, Paris, **18th:** 799
École Normale de Musique, **20th:** 449
École Polytechnique, **18th:** 200, 684
École Royale du Génie. *See* Mézières
Ecology, Greek, **Anc:** 874
Economic and Philosophic Manuscripts of 1844 (Marx), **19th:** 1509
Economic Consequences of the Peace, The (Keynes), **20th:** 2120
Economic development, **18th:** 922
Economic Interpretation of the Constitution of the United States, An (Beard), **20th:** 263
Economic reform, **18th:** Robert Morris, 708; New Spain, 395; Portugal, 796; Anne-Robert-Jacques Turgot, 997
Economical Table, The (Quesnay), **18th:** 820
Economics, **18th:** 341; American South, 1078; England, 175; free marketplace, 923; Honda Toshiaki, 504-506; Karīm Khān Zand, 552; self-interest and, 922. *See also* Category Index
Économistes. *See* Physiocracy
Economy, **17th:** China, 912; England, 717; France, 182, 554, 897; Ireland, 734; Massachusetts Bay Colony, 992; Powhatans, 753; **19th:** France, 1976; India, 1635; Mexico, 653, 1247; New Zealand, 2372; political, 1509, 1896; United States, 1662; **20th:** Canada, 763; France after World War II, 2794; Great Britain, 3993; John Maynard Keynes, 2120; market, 1721; social market theory, 1173-1174; Soviet Union, 1531; United States, 1582, 3402. *See also* Economics; Mercantilism
Economy and Society (Weber), **20th:** 4260
Écrits (Lacan), **20th:** 2225
Écrits de Londres et dernières lettres (Weil), **20th:** 4271
Écriture et la différence, L'. See *Writing and Difference*
Ecstasy of Saint Teresa (Bernini), **17th:** 46
Ecuador, **19th:** independence of, 2195. *See also* Geographical Index
Ecumenical Council, Second (381), **Anc:** 362, 913
Ecumenism, **18th:** Count von Zinzendorf, 1121; **20th:** 3782
Eddington, Arthur Stanley, **20th:** 2338
Eddy, Asa Gilbert, **19th:** 724
Eddy, Mary Baker, **19th:** 723-728
Edeco, **MA:** 782
Edelman, Marian Wright, **20th:** 1096-1099
Eden, Sir Anthony, **20th:** 604, 1099-1104
Eden, Charles, **Notor:** 1024
Edessa, Battle of (1144), **MA:** 356
Edessa, Siege of (544), **MA:** 614
Edgar (king of the English), **MA:** 362
Edgar (king of Scotland), **MA:** 304
Edge of the Sea, The (Carson), **20th:** 664

Edge of the Sword, The (de Gaulle), **20th:** 1427
Edgehill, Battle of (1642), **17th:** 204, 416, 805
Edgeworth, Maria, **19th:** 728-730
Edible Woman, The (Atwood), **20th:** 170
Edict of _______. *See* _______, Edict of
Edicts on Compassion for Living Things (Tsunayoshi), **17th:** 919
Edinburgh (Stevenson), **19th:** 2173
Edinburgh, Treaty of (1560), **Ren:** 199, 635
Edinburgh Review, **19th:** 312, 1223
Edington, Battle of (878), **MA:** 64
Edison, Thomas Alva, **19th:** 731-734, 2210, 2252, 2417; **20th:** 1280
Edison and Swan United Electric Company, **19th:** 2210
Edmonton Oilers, **20th:** 1585
Edmund II Ironside, **MA:** 223, 364
Edmund Tudor, **Ren:** 90
Édouard, Louis-René, **18th:** 657
Édouard-Alexandre. *See* Henry III (1551-1589; king of France)
Edrisi. *See* Idrīsī, al-
Education, **Anc:** Chinese, 238, 552; Greek, 450, 670, 751, 981; Roman, 929, 941; Sophism and, 707; women's, 434; **MA:** 49, 1063; China, 1159; classics, 851; England, 152; France, 400, 984; Jews, 409; monastic, 234; Muslim, 18, 370, 776; Poland, 232; religious, 96, 180; Spain, 11, 555; universities, 2, 318; women, 373; **Ren:** Catholic, 45, 394; England, 92, 109, 233; France, 817; Germany, 665, medicine, 320; **17th:** France, 266, 573, 622, 963; Japan, 998; medical, 355; Ottoman Empire, 456; Persian, 842; Sweden, 337; universal, 470; women, 265, 314, 364, 744, 823, 828, 865; **18th:** Abigail Adams, 7-11; and American Indians, 159; Hester Chapone, 221-223; equal, 7, 65, 90; Catherine Macaulay, 622; musical, 73; nonsectarian, 89; physical, 91, 869; secular, 267; sex, 90; **19th:** African Americans, 2391; Catholic, 2072; Egypt, 5; England, 76, 794, 1304, 1520; Germany, 836, 1307; Great Britain, 972; India, 2363; kindergarten, 837; libraries, 650; military, 2261; monitorial school, 1304; public, 1487; readers, 1447; slaves, 797; Switzerland, 1782; United States, 39, 135, 737, 1032; universal, 2385; Noah Webster, 2403; women, 160, 169, 1428, 2039, 2439, 2481; **20th:** African Americans, 347, 4309; Arkansas, 784; children, 2804, 3232; John Dewey, 983; England, 386, 603, 3993; France, 1778; Italy, 1449; measurement of, 4014; music, 3923; Turkey, 30; United States, 598, 822, 1257, 1958; Wal-Mart, 4215; women in art, 751. *See also* Category Index
Education Act of 1870, **19th:** 794, 926
Education Act of 1891, **19th:** 1490
Education Act of 1944, **20th:** 603
Education Acts of 1902-1903, **20th:** 209, 4254
Education and the Modern World (Russell), **20th:** 3563
Education of a Christian Prince, The (Erasmus), **Ren:** 316
Education of Henry Adams, The (Adams), **19th:** 16, 18
Education of Man, The (Froebel), **19th:** 837
Education of the Human Race, The (Lessing), **18th:** 601
Éducation sentimentale, La. See *Sentimental Education, A*
Educational reform, **18th:** Johann Bernhard Basedow, 89-92; Marquis de Condorcet, 267; Honda Toshiaki, 505; Marquês de Pombal, 796; Jean-Jacques Rousseau, 869
Edward I (1239-1307; king of England), **MA:** 187, 201, 343-347, 492, 840, 1072
Edward II (1284-1327; king of England), **MA:** 202, 347-350, 552, 842
Edward II (Marlowe), **Ren:** 624
Edward III (1312-1377; king of England), **MA:** 308, 348, 350-352, 493, 552, 842, 894, 1054
Edward IV (1442-1483; king of England), **Ren:** 301-303, 340, 436, 496, 571, 990; France and, 574; Lancastrians and, 438; Richard III and, 828; Wars of the Roses and, 90; **Notor:** 896
Edward IV (Heywood), **17th:** 373
Edward V (1470-1483; king of England), **Ren:** 830; **Notor:** 897
Edward VI (1537-1553; king of England), **Ren:** 144, 160, 199, 257, 267, 303-307, 310, 370, 399, 443, 528, 543, 634, 639, 835, 869, 898, 947
Edward VII (1841-1910; king of Great Britain), **19th:** 151, 1313; **20th:** 1104-1107
Edward VIII (1894-1972). *See* Windsor, duke of
Edward the Black Prince, **MA:** 351, 493
Edward the Confessor, **MA:** 224, 337-340, 457, 1117
Edward the Elder, **MA:** 30, 340-343
Edwards, Blake, **20th:** 3697
Edwards, Chet, **Notor:** 457
Edwards, Jonathan, **18th:** 75, 314-317, 1074

Edwards, Tracy, **Notor:** 255
EEOC. *See* Equal Employment Opportunity Commission
Effects of Slavery, on Morals and Industry (Webster), **19th:** 2404
Effort (Laban and Lawrence), **20th:** 2222
Égalité, Philippe. *See* Orléans, duc d'
Egas Moniz, António, **20th:** 1107-1110
Egbert (West Saxon king), **MA:** 353-355
Egerton, Sir Thomas, **17th:** 231
Egypt, **Anc:** Assyria and, 118, 710, 753; Cyrene and, 157; Hittites and, 736; Israel and, 803; Jews and, 572; Kadesh and, 886; Nubia and, 570, 655, 772; Palmyra and, 987; Rome and, 230; trade with Africa, 334; unification of, 556, 570; **MA:** French invasion of, 140; Mamlūk sultans, 141; Mongol invasion of, 140; Muslim invasion of, 507, 1038; Muslims, 674; Syrian invasion of, 918; **19th:** 1552; **20th:** British army in, 2174; Great Britain and, 68; independence of, 4439. *See also* Geographical Index
Egyptian Coptic church, **Anc:** 333; **MA:** 632
Egyptian Institute, **18th:** 684
Egyptians (Aeschylus), **Anc:** 9
Ehrenfels, Christian von, **20th:** 1110-1112
Ehrlich, Eugen, **20th:** 1113-1114, 1118
Ehrlich, Paul, **19th:** 180; **20th:** 1021, 1115-1117, 1254
Ehrlichman, John D., **Notor:** 226, 320-322, 442
Eichmann, Adolf, **20th:** 119, 188; trial of, 4329; **Notor:** 322-324, 463, 814
Eichmann in Jerusalem (Arendt), **20th:** 119
Eickemeyer, Rudolf, **19th:** 2157
Eielson, Carl Ben, **20th:** 4340
Eiffel, Gustave, **19th:** 734-736
Eiffel and Company, G., **19th:** 735
Eiffel Tower, **19th:** 735
Eiffel Tower (Delaunay), **20th:** 951
8½ (film), **20th:** 1232
Eight Cousins (Alcott), **19th:** 43
18 Brumaire, **18th:** 918, 931; **19th:** 396
Eighteen Hundred and Eleven (Barbauld), **18th:** 88
Eighteenth Dynasty (Egypt), **Anc:** 388, 585, 588, 885
Eightfold Path, **Anc:** 131, 170
Eighth Symphony (Mahler), **20th:** 2561
'89 Club, **18th:** 267
Eighty Years' War (1568-1648), **17th:** 618, 698, 739
Eikonoklastes (Milton), **17th:** 640
Eimi (Cummings), **20th:** 881
Einführung in die organische Chemie (Diels), **20th:** 996
Einführung in eine Philosophie des Geisteslebens. See *Life and the Spirit, The*
Einhard, **MA:** 242
Einhorn, Ira, **Notor:** 324-326
Einstein, Albert, **19th:** 1818; **20th:** 409, 818, 1118-1122, 2279, 3283; theory of relativity, 2433; uncertainty principle, 438
Einthoven, Willem, **20th:** 1122-1125
Eire Constitution of 1937, **20th:** 3035
Eirēnē (Aristophanes), **Anc:** 92
Eirenicon, An (Pusey), **19th:** 1846
Eis Loutra tēs Pallados (Callimachus), **Anc:** 180
Eisenhower, Dwight D., **20th:** 581, 1055, 1125-1129, 3858; **Notor:** 75, 217, 263, 348, 670, 794
Eisenhower Farm (Grandma Moses), **20th:** 2843
Eisenstein, Sergei, **20th:** 1129-1132
Eissner, Clara. *See* Zetkin, Clara
Ejercicios espirituales. See *Spiritual Exercises, The*
Ek Choeun. *See* Ta Mok
Ekalē (Callimachus), **Anc:** 180
Ekklesiazousai (Aristophanes), **Anc:** 92
El Alamein, Battle of (1942), **20th:** 2809
El Cid. *See* Cid, El
El-Rei Seleuco (Camões), **Ren:** 167
El Salvador. *See* Geographical Index
Elaboration on the Meaning of the Book of Documents (Wang), **17th:** 972
Elagabal, **Anc:** 480, 483, 487
Elagabalus, **Anc:** 483, 487; **Notor:** 326-327
Elam, **Anc:** 119
Elcano, Juan Sebastián de, **Ren:** 307-309
Elchingen, Battle of (1805), **19th:** 1667
Elder, Louisine, **19th:** 435
Eldredge, Niles, **20th:** 1555
Eleanor of Aquitaine, **MA:** 166, 355-359, 483, 584, 891; **Notor:** 534
Eleanor's Victory (Braddon), **19th:** 287
Eleatics, **Anc:** 261
Elections, U.S. presidential. *See* Presidency, U.S.
Elective Affinities (Goethe), **18th:** 430
Electoral Act of 1858, **19th:** 1740
Electoral college, U.S., **18th:** 1092
Electoral system reform (Great Britain), **19th:** 304
Electra (Giraudoux), **20th:** 1494
Electric batteries, **18th:** 393, 1023
Electric Boat Company, **19th:** 1115
Electric Telegraph Company, **19th:** 549

Electrical engineering, **19th:** 550, 2157, 2417
Electricity, **Ren:** William Gilbert, 381-382; **18th:** Henry Cavendish, 217-220; Benjamin Franklin, 372; Luigi Galvani, 391-394; Alessandro Volta, 1022-1026
Electrocardiography, **20th:** 259, 1123
Electrochemistry, **19th:** 617; **20th:** 1629
Electromagnetism, **19th:** 760, 914, 1529; **20th:** 2432
Electronic Data Systems Corporation, **20th:** 3209
Electronic music, **20th:** 455, 3873, 4415
Electronishe Studien I and II (Stockhausen), **20th:** 3874
Electrons, discovery of, **20th:** 4008
Electroweak theory, **20th:** 4277
Elegantiae linguae latinae (Valla), **MA:** 1050
Elegia di Madonna Fiammetta. See *Elegy of Lady Fiammetta, The*
Elegies, Roman, **Anc:** 835
Elegies series (Motherwell), **20th:** 2847
Elegy of Lady Fiammetta, The (Boccaccio), **MA:** 170
Elegy on Captain Cook (Seward), **18th:** 897
Elegy on the Death of Dudley, Lord Carlton (Cowley), **17th:** 199
Ēlektra (Euripides), **Anc:** 327, 811
Elektra (Strauss), **19th:** 1156; **20th:** 3886
Element Hafnium, Das (Hevesy), **20th:** 1793
Elemental Odes, The (Neruda), **20th:** 2938
Elemental Treatise on Electricity, An (Maxwell), **19th:** 1529
Elementarwerke (Basedow), **18th:** 90
Elementary Education Act of 1870, **19th:** 972
Elementary Forms of the Religious Life, The (Durkheim), **20th:** 1066
Elementary Principles in Statistical Mechanics Developed with Special Reference to the Rational Foundation of Thermodynamics (Gibbs), **19th:** 915
Elementary Treatise on Descriptive Geometry, An (Monge), **18th:** 685
Elemente der Psychophysik. See *Elements of Psychophysics*
Elementi di scienza politica. See *Ruling Class, The*
Elementorum jurisprudentiae universalis (Pufendorf), **17th:** 759
Elementorum myologiae specimen. See *Specimen of Elements of Myology*
Elements (fire, air, water, earth), **Anc:** 278, 349, 397, 984. See also *Stoicheia*
Éléments mécaniques (Léger), **20th:** 2336
Elements of Chemistry, in a New Systematic Order, Containing All the Modern Discoveries (Lavoisier), **18th:** 581
Elements of Geology (Lyell), **19th:** 1425
Elements of Law Natural and Politic, The (Hobbes), **17th:** 379
Elements of Politics (Sedgwick), **19th:** 2104
Elements of Psychophysics (Fechner), **19th:** 772
Elements of Quaternions, The (Hamilton), **19th:** 1017
Elements of Sir Isaac Newton's Philosophy (Voltaire), **18th:** 241
Elements of Theology, The. See *Stoikheiōsis theologikē*
Elenchou kai anatropes. See *Adversus haereses*
Elephant Célèbes, The (Ernst), **20th:** 1177
Elephants, **Anc:** Hannibal and, 382; use in warfare, 41, 121, 746
Eleusinian Mysteries. *See* Mystery religions
Eleutherius, **Anc:** 269, 443
Elevation of the Cross, The (Rubens), **17th:** 802
Eleventh Virgin, The (Day), **20th:** 926
Elgar, Sir Edward, **20th:** 1132-1136
Eli (priest at Shiloh), **Anc:** 747
Eli (Sachs), **20th:** 3585
Eliade, Mircea, **20th:** 1136-1139
Elie Wiesel Foundation, **20th:** 4326
Elijah, **Anc:** 474
Elijah (Mendelssohn), **19th:** 1550
Elijah ben Solomon, **18th:** 318-320
Elinvar, **20th:** 1618
Eliot, Charles William, **19th:** 17, 737-739
Eliot, George, **19th:** 263, 740-743; **Notor:** 976
Eliot, John, **17th:** 247-250
Eliot, T. S., **20th:** 1139-1142; **Notor:** 1107
Elisabeth of Thuringia. *See* Elizabeth of Hungary, Saint
Elisir d'amore, L' (Donizetti), **19th:** 675; **20th:** 676
Elizabeth I, **Ren:** 72, 104, 108, 113, 147, 149, 199, 271, 276, 279, 304, 310-314, 353, 378, 399, 403, 443, 553, 627, 639, 835, 844, 947; Catholicism and, 325, 668; Church of England and, 268, 761; church reform and, 530; English exploration and, 193; excommunication of, 798; Ireland and, 744; Netherlands and, 397; patronage and, 381,

813; plot to murder, 668; **17th:** 15, 104; **Notor:** 302, 350
Elizabeth II, **20th:** 47, 1143-1145
Elizabeth Nadasdy. *See* Báthory, Elizabeth
Elizabeth of Bohemia (1596-1662). *See* Elizabeth Stuart
Elizabeth of Bohemia (1618-1680), **17th:** 250-253, 254
Elizabeth of Hungary, Saint, **MA:** 359-362
Elizabeth of York, **Ren:** 91
Elizabeth Petrovna, **18th:** 321-323, 613, 755, 778; **Notor:** 515
Elizabeth Stuart, **17th:** 250, 253-255, 275, 293, 310, 805, 820
Ella Amida, **Anc:** 333
Elle et lui. See *She and He*
Ellen Terry as Lady Macbeth (Sargent), **19th:** 1998
Ellendun, Battle of (825), **MA:** 353
Ellēnika (Xenophon), **Anc:** 969
Ellesmere Canal, **19th:** 2241
Ellington, Duke, **20th:** 1145-1147
Elliot, John, **20th:** 1904
Elliott, Jesse Duncan, **19th:** 1780
Ellis, Charles D., **20th:** 714
Ellis, Havelock, **19th:** 2023; **20th:** 1148-1151
Ellis, John McTaggert, **20th:** 2814
Ellis, Ruth, **Notor:** 327-328
Elliston, Robert William, **19th:** 1257
Ellsberg, Daniel, **Notor:** 226, 321, 443, 500, 643
Ellsworth, Lincoln, **20th:** 606, 4341
Elm Tree on the Mall, The (France), **19th:** 816
Elmer Gantry (Lewis), **20th:** 2365
Eloisa to Abelard (Pope), **18th:** 805
Elphinstone, William, **Ren:** 498
Elpinice, **Anc:** 564, 678
Elsie Venner (Holmes), **19th:** 1118
Elssler, Fanny, **19th:** 743-745
Éluard, Gala, **20th:** 905
Éluard, Paul, **20th:** 905, 1151-1155, 1177
Elucidation of Islam's Foundation, The (al-Ashʿarī), **MA:** 112
Elwes, Sir Gervase, **17th:** 132
Elysee Agreement (1948), **20th:** 229
Elysium Britannicum (Evelyn), **17th:** 257
Emanation of the Giant Albion, The (Blake), **18th:** 123
Emanations, divine, **Anc:** 641
Emancipation Proclamation (1863), **19th:** 472, 877, 1383, 2308
Emancipists, **19th:** 2413
Emathla, Charley, **19th:** 1709
Embargo Act of 1807, **19th:** 2112
Embryology, **Anc:** 278; **19th:** 33, 1316; comparative, 115
Embryons desséchés (Satie), **20th:** 3643
Emerald City of Oz, The (Baum), **19th:** 157
Emerson, George, **19th:** 671
Emerson, John, **20th:** 2429
Emerson, Ralph Waldo, **19th:** 745-749; Louis Agassiz, 33; Bronson Alcott, 40; Louisa May Alcott, 42; William Ellery Channing, 466; Margaret Fuller, 842; Emma Lazarus, 1331; Theodore Parker, 1735; Elizabeth Palmer Peabody, 1762; Henry David Thoreau, 2274; Walt Whitman, 2425
EMIDEC 1100, **20th:** 1892
Émile. See *Emilius and Sophia*
Emilia Galotti (Lessing), **18th:** 601
Emilius and Sophia (Rousseau), **18th:** 869
Emin Pasha, **19th:** 2140
Emma (Austen), **19th:** 96
Emma (Cavendish), **18th:** 216
Emma Willard School, **19th:** 2440
Emmy Frisch with Red Flowers (Kirchner), **20th:** 2165
Emotions, Stoic concept of, **Anc:** 692
Empedocles, **Anc:** 59, 277, 295-298, 397, 521, 609, 610, 966
Empedocles on Etna (Arnold), **19th:** 73
Emperor and Galilean (Ibsen), **19th:** 1166
Emperor Jones, The (O'Neill), **20th:** 3052, 3463
Emperor of Portugallia, The (Lagerlöf), **20th:** 2235
Emperor of the Moon, The (Behn), **17th:** 43
Emperor Theodosius Is Forbidden by Saint Ambrose to Enter Milan Cathedral, The (van Dyck), **17th:** 244
Empire (newspaper), **19th:** 1739
Empiricism, **Anc:** 84, 199, 412, 724; **19th:** 289. *See also* Philosophy
Emptiness (Buddhist doctrine), **Anc:** 112, 160
En route pour la pêche (Sargent), **19th:** 1996
En weites Feld. See *Too Far Afield*
Enabling Act of 1933, **20th:** 1546
Enabling Act of 1956. *See* Loi-Cadre
Enahoro, Anthony, **Notor:** 2
Enchanted, The (Giraudoux), **20th:** 1494
Enchanted Lake, The (Sand), **19th:** 1988
Enchiridion militis Christiani. See *Manual of the Christian Knight, The*
Enciso, Martín Fernández de, **Ren:** 76
Encomium (poetic form), **Anc:** 793
Encounter (Lipchitz), **20th:** 2397
Encyclopedia (Diderot), **18th:** 32, 308, 479, 502, 820, 996
Encyclopedia of Philosophy (Hegel), **19th:** 1067
Encyclopedias, **Anc:** 929

Encyclopédie: Ou, Dictionnaire raisonné des sciences, des arts, et des métiers (Diderot), **18th:** 820
Encyclopedist of the Dark Ages, An (Isidore), **MA:** 556, 872
End of the Affair, The (Greene), **20th:** 1579
End to Torment (H. D.), **20th:** 1625
Endeavour, HMS, **18th:** 80, 270
Endgame (Beckett), **20th:** 282
Endicott, John, **17th:** 386
Endimion and Phoebe (Drayton), **17th:** 237
Endless Column (Brancusi), **20th:** 480
Endliches und ewiges Sein (Stein), **20th:** 3843
Endō, Shūsaku, **20th:** 1155-1157
Ends and Means (Huxley), **20th:** 1963
Endymion (Keats), **19th:** 1260
Energy, study of, **20th:** 342
Enfance du Christ, L' (Berlioz), **19th:** 203
Enfant chargé de chaînes, L'. See *Young Man in Chains*
Enfant sauvage, L'. See *Wild Child, The*
Enfantin, Prosper, **19th:** 1356
Enfantines (Ségalas), **19th:** 2062
Enfants terribles. See *Children of the Game*
Enfatriões (Camões), **Ren:** 167
Engel v. Vitale (1962), **20th:** 379
Engels, Friedrich, **19th:** 750-753, 1322, 1370, 1508; **Notor:** 600
Enghien, duc d', **19th:** 397, 476
Enghien, duke of. *See* Condé, The Great
Engines, **19th:** atmospheric, 1715; diesel, 664; gasoline, 593; internal combustion, 1338, 1676, 1715; steam, 2294
Engineering, **17th:** England, 814; France, 135, 712; Italy, 49; Switzerland, 49; **18th:** James Brindley, 162-165; Tadeusz Kościuszko, 565; military, 690; Gaspard Monge, 684; Marquis de Montalembert, 690-692; John Wilkinson, 1086-1089. *See also* Category Index
Engineers and the Price System, The (Veblen), **20th:** 4155
England, **MA:** Anglo-Saxon kings, 31, 65, 342, 354, 364; astrology, 128; Christianity, 49, 152, 219, 431, 938; Danish kings, 224, 339, 459; education, 65, 152, 573; feudalism, 344, 485; historiography, 151, 405; House of York, 496; Lancastrian kings, 495; law, 223, 344, 485; mathematics, 128; monasticism, 509; music, 334; mysticism, 271, 596, 607; Norman kings, 482, 1119; philosophy, 1130; Plantagenet kings, 345, 357, 485, 492, 892; poetry, 219, 264; science, 127; theology, 92, 817, 1130; Viking invasions of, 340, 790. *See also* Geographical Index
England and Spain (Hemans), **19th:** 1076
England, Ireland, and America (Cobden), **19th:** 521
England's Birth-Right (Lilburne), **17th:** 535
Englands Heroicall Epistles (Drayton), **17th:** 238
England's New Chains Discovered (Lilburne), **17th:** 535
England's Present Interest Discovered (Penn), **17th:** 725
Englehardt, Frederick. *See* Hubbard, L. Ron
Englische Geschichte, vornehmlich im 16 und 17 Jahrhundert. See *History of England Principally in the Seventeenth Century, A*
English Bards, and Scotch Reviewers (Byron), **19th:** 380
English Civil Wars (1642-1651), **17th:** 650, 756, 769, 805, 901, 988; First (1642-1646), 32, 55, 121, 137, 145, 147, 199, 205, 262, 379, 416, 483, 535, 838, 846, 941; Second (1647-1649), 205, 263, 484; Third (1650-1651), 757
English Governess at the Siamese Court, The (Leonowens), **19th:** 1347
English Humourists of the Eighteenth Century, The (Thackeray), **19th:** 2259
English-Irish conflicts, **18th:** 966, 983
English Literature in the Sixteenth Century, Excluding Drama (Lewis), **20th:** 2355
English Men of Science (Galton), **19th:** 861
English National Ballet, **20th:** 2628
English Opera Group, **20th:** 531
English Patient, The (Ondaatje), **20th:** 3049
English South African's View of the Situation, An (Schreiner), **19th:** 2024
English Traits (Emerson), **19th:** 748
English Traveler, The (Heywood), **17th:** 374
Englishwoman at the "Star," Le Havre, The (Toulouse-Lautrec), **19th:** 2290
Engraving, **18th:** 92, 95, 121, 497, 832
Enheduanna, **Anc:** 298-300
Enigma of Arrival, The (Naipaul), **20th:** 2904
Enigma of Faith, The (William of Saint-Thierry), **MA:** 1115
Enkindling of Love, Also Called the Triple Way (Bonaventure), **MA:** 181
Enlightenment (era), **18th:** Catholic Church, 102; colonial America, 673; Étienne Bonnot de Condillac, 263-266; Denis Diderot, 308; England, 65, 731, 813; France, 480, 617, 686, 799, 820, 829, 868, 929, 1009-

1010; Germany, 598-602, 653; Paul-Henri-Dietrich d'Holbach, 502; David Hume, 516; Thomas Jefferson, 530; Judaism, 676; Peter the Great, 775; Philip V, 782; Poland, 567-569; Portugal, 795-797; Russia, 613-615; Scotland, 338, 922, 1098; critique by Swedenborgians, 963; United States, 872; Voltaire, 1026-1029

Enlightenment (religious), **Anc:** 284, 925

Enneads (Plotinus), **Anc:** 669

Ennius, Quintus, **Anc:** 301-303, 520

Enormous Room, The (Cummings), **20th:** 880

Enough Rope (Parker), **20th:** 3117

ENQUIRE, **20th:** 331

Enquiries Concerning Human Understanding (Hume), **18th:** 514

Enquiry Concerning Political Justice, and Its Influence on General Virtue and Happiness, An (Godwin), **18th:** 425

Enquiry into the Obligations of Christians to Use Means for the Conversion of the Heathen, An (Carey), **19th:** 409

Enquiry into the Present State of Polite Learning in Europe, An (Goldsmith), **18th:** 433

Enracinement, L'. See *Need for Roots, The*

Enrique of Trastámara, **Notor:** 827

Enryakuji, **Ren:** 733

Enseignements psychologiques de la guerre européenne. See *Psychology of the Great War, The*

Ensinore, **Ren:** 771

Ensslin, Gudrun, **Notor:** 47, 684

Entartung. See *Degeneration*

Entertainer, The (Osborne), **20th:** 3042

Enthroned Madonna and Child (Bellini), **Ren:** 99

Entitlement theory, **20th:** 3000

Entombment (Tintoretto), **Ren:** 933

Entombment (Rogier van der Weyden), **MA:** 1093

Entomology, **17th:** England, 783; Italy, 581; Netherlands, 510, 898

Entrance to the Grand Canal (Canaletto), **18th:** 192

Entratta, Charles, **Notor:** 277

Entrepreneurship, **19th:** Horatio Alger, 52; John Jacob Astor, 86; P. T. Barnum, 139; Alexander Graham Bell, 183; James Gordon Bennett, 190; Carl Benz, 197; Sir Henry Bessemer, 220; Nicholas Biddle, 225; Marc Isambard Brunel, 338; Andrew Carnegie, 420; Samuel Colt, 534; Jay Cooke, 544, 550; Jacques Daguerre, 590, 1678; Gottlieb Daimler, 594; Rudolf Diesel, 664; James Buchanan Duke, 692; Eleuthère Irénée du Pont, 706; James Buchanan Eads, 715; Thomas Alva Edison, 731; Gustave Eiffel, 735; Robert Fulton, 847; Charles Goodyear, 947; Sir Robert Abbott Hadfield, 1000; James Jerome Hill, 1101; Elias Howe, 1135; Alfred Krupp, 1301; Eugen Langen, 1715; Cyrus Hall McCormick, 1438; Daniel and Alexander Macmillan, 1464; Ottmar Mergenthaler, 1559; J. P. Morgan, 1600; James Nasmyth, 1646; Nicéphore Niépce, 590, 1678; Alfred Nobel, 1689; Nikolaus August Otto, 1715; Robert Owen, 1720; Lydia E. Pinkham, 1798; John D. Rockefeller, 1922; Rothschild family, 1949; Siemens family, 2106; Samuel Slater, 2112; Leland Stanford, 2132; George Stephenson, 2168; Joseph Wilson Swan, 2210; Nikola Tesla, 2253; Cornelius Vanderbilt, 2349; Montgomery Ward, 2387; George Westinghouse, 2417; Sir Charles Wheatstone, 550; **20th:** automobiles, 772, 1240, 1280, 1860, 3267, 3496, 4063; cameras, 1079; computers, 361, 1421, 2007, 4247; cosmetics, 146, 2275, 4200; electronics, 2653, 2831; entertainment, 1007, 1524, 2663, 4374; finance, 564, 1613, 2683, 3210, 3795; media, 447, 1561, 1679, 1736, 2457, 2876, 4119; neon tubes, 776; restaurants, 2202; retail, 728, 4214

Entstehung der altkatholischen Kirche, Die (Ritschl), **19th:** 1919

Entstehung der Kontinente und Ozeane. See *Origin of Continents and Oceans*

Entwicklung der Dipteren, Die (Weismann), **19th:** 2406

Entwicklung des Christusdogmas, Die. See *Dogma of Christ, The*

Entwicklung des Sozialismus von der Utopie zur Wissenschaft. See *Socialism*

Enver Paşa, **20th:** 1157-1161, 1203

Environment, **20th:** activism, 1538, 4359; Canada, 2868; Lady Bird Johnson, 2026; Norway, 545; pollution of, 663-664; protection of, 2394, 2898, 3254, 3516-3517, 3549; Romania, 706. *See also* Category Index under Conservation and Environmentalism

Environmental Protection Agency, **20th:** 664, 2898

Environmentalism. *See* Category Index under Conservation and Environmentalism

Enzo, **MA:** 390

Enzymes, study of, **20th:** 3997
Éolides, Les (Franck), **19th:** 823
Eonta (Xenakis), **20th:** 4416
EPA. *See* Environmental Protection Agency
Epaminondas, **Anc:** 303-307
EPCOT, **20th:** 1009
Épernon, duc d'. *See* Nogaret de La Valette
Ephemerides, **Anc:** 579
Ephesus, **Anc:** Arsinoe II Philadelphus and, 106; Mary and, 540
Ephesus, Council of (431), **Anc:** 866
Ephetae, **Anc:** 294
Ephialtes, **Anc:** 215, 621
Ephorus of Cumae, **Anc:** 451
Ephron, Nora, **20th:** 1161-1164
Epicoene (Jonson), **17th:** 442
Epics, **Anc:** Babylonian, 378; Greek, 427, 633; history and, 827; Mesopotamian, 914; Sanskrit, 923
Epictetus Junior: Or, Maximes of Modern Morality. See *Maximes*
Epicureanism, **Anc:** 89, 520, 723, 938; **MA:** 1050; **18th:** 480
Epicurus, **Anc:** 89, 263, 307-310, 547
Epicycles, **Anc:** 418
Epidemiology, **17th:** Belgium, 362; England, 903, 987; Italy, 810; Netherlands, 511
Epigram (poetic form), **Anc:** 538, 793
Epigrammata (Callimachus), **Anc:** 180
Epigrammaton liber (Martial), **Anc:** 536
Epigrammatum Sacrorum Liber (Crashaw), **17th:** 202
Epimenides, **Anc:** 807
Epinikia (Pindar), **Anc:** 647
Epipledon isorropion (Archimedes), **Anc:** 82
Epipsychidion (Shelley), **19th:** 2096
Episcopacy, **17th:** 15, 33, 122, 496, 938
Episcopal Church, women's ordination in, **20th:** 1689
Episcopi de vera obedientia oratio (Gardiner), **Ren:** 369
Epistemology, **18th:** 113, 265, 343, 514-517, 548-549
Epistle of Diocles unto King Antigonus. See *Dioklēs epistolē prophulaktikē*
Epistle of Petrus Peregrinus de Maricourt, to Sygerus of Foucaucourt, Soldier, Concerning the Magnet (Peregrinus), **MA:** 820
Epistle to Dr. Arbuthnot, An (Pope), **18th:** 806
Epistle to Posterity (Petrarch), **MA:** 827
Epistle to the Romans, The (Barth), **20th:** 244
Epistle to William Wilberforce, Esq. on the Rejection of the Bill for Abolishing the Slave Trade (Barbauld), **18th:** 88
Epistles (Horace), **Anc:** 432
Epistles, Odes, and Other Poems (Moore), **19th:** 1224
Epistles of John, **Anc:** 472
Epistola ad fratres de Monte-Dei. See *Golden Epistle of Abbot William of St. Thierry, The*
Epistola ad milites Corotici. See *Letter to the Soldiers of Coroticus*
Epistola de ignoto cantu (Guido d'Arezzo), **MA:** 440
Epistola de Tolerantia. See *Letter Concerning Toleration, A*
Epistola, docens venam axillarem dextri cubiti in dolore laterali secandam. See *Bloodletting Letter of 1539, The*
Epistola, rationem modumque propinandi radicis Chynae. See *Vesalius on China-root*
Epistola Reverendissimi Domini Cardinalis Dertusensis ad facultatem theologiae Lovaniensem (Adrian VI), **Ren:** 8
Epistolae festales (Athanasius), **Anc:** 134
Epistolary literature. *See* Literature
Epístolas y poemas (Darío), **19th:** 601
Épistre du dieu d'amours, L'. See *Letter of Cupid, The*
Epistres et evangiles des cinquante-deux dimanches (Lefèvre), **Ren:** 549
Épistres sur "Le Roman de la rose," Les (Christine de Pizan), **MA:** 275
Epistulae morales ad Lucilium (Seneca), **Anc:** 767
Epitaph of a Small Winner (Machado), **19th:** 1450
Epithalamion (Spenser), **Ren:** 907
Epithalamium (Buchanan), **Ren:** 146
Epitoma magesti Ptolemaei (Peuerbach), **Ren:** 774
Epitome (Paul of Aegina), **MA:** 815
Epitome astronomiae Copernicanae (Kepler), **17th:** 459
Epitome of Some of the Chief Events and Transactions in the Life of Joseph Lancaster (Lancaster), **19th:** 1306
Épître à Huet (La Fontaine), **17th:** 482
Epitrepontes (Menander), **Anc:** 548
Épîtres (Boileau-Despréaux), **17th:** 63
Epodes (Horace), **Anc:** 432
Époques de la nature (Buffon), **18th:** 172
Epstein, Brian, **20th:** 267
Epstein, Sir Jacob, **20th:** 1165-1168
Epstein, Jean, **20th:** 578
Epyllion (poetic form), **Anc:** 180
Equal Employment Opportunity Commission, **20th:** 1774
Equal Rights Amendment, **20th:** 755, 1272, 3147, 3854

Equal Rights Association, **19th:** 66
Equal Rights Party, **19th:** 2460
"Equality of Men and Women, The" (Gourney), **17th:** 315
Equality of the Nationalities Act, **19th:** 622
Equestrian Monument of General Gattamelata (Donatello), **MA:** 321
Equestrian Statue of Colleoni (Verrocchio), **Ren:** 964
Equiano, Olaudah, **18th:** 324-326
Equinoxes, precession of the, **Anc:** 418
Equivocal Appearances (Scarlatti), **18th:** 884
Er jing ru (Bodhidharma), **Anc:** 161
ERA. *See* Equal Rights Amendment
Era of Good Feelings, **19th:** 22, 1587
Eranistes seu Polymorphus (Theodoret), **Anc:** 866
Erasistratus, **Anc:** 310-313, 410
Erasmus, Desiderius, **Ren:** 8, 11, 142, 188, 221, 233, 314-318, 453, 543, 549, 584, 609, 618, 637, 665, 697, 1011
Erasmus of Rotterdam (Dürer), **Ren:** 298
Eratosthenes of Cyrene, **Anc:** 80, 314-317, 419
Ercker, Lazarus, **Ren:** 13
Erdrich, Louise, **20th:** 1168-1172
Erec (Hartmann), **MA:** 463
Erec and Enide (Chrétien), **MA:** 267
Erewhon (Butler), **19th:** 374
Erewhon Revisited (Butler), **19th:** 375
Erga kai Emerai (Hesiod), **Anc:** 413, 939
Erhard, Ludwig, **20th:** 1173-1176
Erhard, Werner, **Notor:** 329-330
Eric Brighteyes (Haggard), **19th:** 1007
Erie Canal, **18th:** 706; **19th:** 514
Erik XIV, **Ren:** 417; **Notor:** 331-332
Erik of Pomerania, **MA:** 691
Erik the Red, **MA:** 640
Eritrea, Ethiopian annexation of, **20th:** 1641
Eritrean People's Liberation Front, **20th:** 2702
Erkennen und Leben. See *Knowledge and Life*
Erlebnislyrik, **18th:** 431
Erlebte Erdteile (Frobenius), **20th:** 1343
Ernani (Verdi), **19th:** 2351
Ernst, Max, **20th:** 1176-1179
Ernst Heinkel Flugzeugwerke, **20th:** 1746
Eroica (Beethoven), **19th:** 177
Eros, **Anc:** 696
Eros (Praxiteles), **Anc:** 696
Errata recentiorum medicorum (Fuchs), **Ren:** 356
Ershiwu yan (Ricci), **Ren:** 826
Erskine, first Baron (Thomas Erskine), **18th:** 326-330
Ertuğrul, **MA:** 800
Erwartung (Schoenberg), **20th:** 3665
Erzberger, Matthias, **20th:** 1180-1183
Erziehung des Menschengeschlechts, Die. See *Education of the Human Race, The*
Erzsébet Báthory. *See* Báthory, Elizabeth
Esarhaddon, **Anc:** 117, 710, 770
Esau and Jacob (Machado), **19th:** 1451
Escape from Freedom (Fromm), **20th:** 1346
Escaped Cock, The (Lawrence), **20th:** 2298
Escarmouche, L' (Toulouse-Lautrec), **19th:** 2289
Escher, M. C., **20th:** 1183-1185
Escobar, Pablo, **20th:** 1401; **Notor:** 332-334
Escobar, Roberto, **Notor:** 333
Escobedo, Juan de, **Ren:** 671
Escobedo v. Illinois (1964), **20th:** 4234
Esenin, Sergei Aleksandrovich, **20th:** 1059
Eşfahan, **17th:** 5
Esoteric Buddhism, **MA:** 620
España invertebrada. See *Invertebrate Spain*
Espartero, Baldomero, **19th:** 1183
Esperança de Israel. See *Hope of Israel, The*
Espinosa, Gonzalo Gómez de, **Ren:** 308
Espinosa, Pedro de, **17th:** 770
Espionage, **18th:** John André, 42-45; Benedict Arnold, 59-62
Espionage Act of 1917, **20th:** 935
Espoir, L'. See *Days of Hope*
Esprit de la philosophie médiévale, L'. See *Spirit of Medieval Philosophy, The*
Esprit de la révolution et de la constitution de France (Saint-Just), **18th:** 877
Esprit nouveau, L' (journal), **20th:** 2323
Espronceda, José de, **19th:** 557
Espurgatoire Saint Patriz (Marie de France), **MA:** 694
Esquipulas II accord (1987), **20th:** 122
Essai philosophique sur les probabilités. See *Philosophical Essay on Probabilities, A*
Essai sur le despotisme (Mirabeau), **18th:** 680
Essai sur les données immédiates de la conscience. See *Time and Free Will*
Essai sur les gens de lettres (Alembert), **18th:** 34
Essai sur les privilèges (Sieyès), **18th:** 917
Essai sur les révolutions. See *Historical, Political, Moral Essay on Revolutions, An*
Essai sur l'origine des connaissances humaines. See *Essay on the Origin of Human Understanding, An*

Essais critiques. See *Critical Essays*
Essais de théodicée sur la bonté de Dieu . . . . See *Theodicy*
Essay Concerning Human Understanding, An (Locke), **17th:** 545; **18th:** 263
Essay for the Recording of Illustrious Providences, An (Mather), **18th:** 673
Essay in Aid of a Grammar of Assent, An (Newman), **19th:** 1665
Essay of the Pathology of the Brain and Nervous Stock, An (Willis), **17th:** 986
Essay on Animal Reproductions, An (Spallanzani), **18th:** 926
Essay on Crimes and Punishments, An (Beccaria), **18th:** 100
Essay on Criticism, An (Pope), **18th:** 805
Essay on Man, An (Cassirer), **20th:** 689
Essay on Man, An (Pope), **18th:** 806
Essay on Pigs (Henze), **20th:** 1764
Essay on the First Principles of Government and on the Nature of Political, Civil, and Religious Liberty, An (Priestley), **18th:** 812
Essay on the History of Civil Society, An (Ferguson), **18th:** 338
Essay on the Influence of a Low Price of Corn on the Profits of Stock, An (Ricardo), **19th:** 1897
Essay on the Origin of Human Understanding, An (Condillac), **18th:** 263
Essay on the Principle of Population, An (Malthus), **19th:** 1476-1477, 1807
Essay on the Universal Plenitude of Being, An (Allen), **18th:** 37
Essay on Woman (anonymous), **18th:** 1084
Essay Towards a New Theory of Vision, An (Berkeley), **18th:** 111
Essay Towards the Present and Future Peace of Europe, An (Penn), **17th:** 726
Essayes (Bacon), **Ren:** 73
Essayes of a Prentise in the Divine Art of Poesie, The (James I), **17th:** 413
Essays (Emerson), **19th:** 747
Essays, The (Montaigne), **Ren:** 689
Essays and Lectures in Political Subjects (Fawcett and Fawcett), **19th:** 766
Essays and Reviews (Harrison), **19th:** 1046
Essays for Orchestra (Barber), **20th:** 231
Essays in Criticism (Arnold), **19th:** 74
Essays in the Liberal Interpretation of History (Acton), **19th:** 15
Essays in the Public Philosophy (Lippmann), **20th:** 2402
Essays on Church and State (Acton), **19th:** 15
Essays on Freedom and Power (Acton), **19th:** 15
Essays on Professional Education (Edgeworth), **19th:** 729
Essays on Truth and Reality (Bradley), **19th:** 289
Essays, Physical and Chemical (Lavoisier), **18th:** 580
Essays: Second Series (Emerson), **19th:** 747
Essays upon Heredity and Kindred Biological Problems (Weismann), **19th:** 2408
Essence of Judaism, The (Baeck), **20th:** 187
Essendon, Baron Cecil of. *See* Salisbury, third marquis of
Essenes, **Anc:** 459
Essex, earl of. *See* Cromwell, Thomas
Essex, second earl of, **Ren:** 312, 554, 814, 844; **17th:** 175, 230
Essex, third earl of, **17th:** 132, 756
Essex divorce case (1613), **17th:** 16
Esslinger, Friedrich Wilhelm, **19th:** 197
Est-il bon? Est-il méchant? (Diderot), **18th:** 310
Estado Novo, **20th:** 3607
Éstampes (Debussy), **20th:** 938
Estates-General (France), **18th:** 619, 681, 728, 844, 917
Este, Alfonso I d', **Ren:** 56, 118, 937
Este, Ippolito d', **Ren:** 56, 204
Este, Isabella d'. *See* Isabella d'Este
Este, Marie Beatrice Eleanor Anne Margaret Isabella d'. *See* Mary of Modena
Estée Lauder Companies, **20th:** 2276
Estella, marquis of. *See* Primo de Rivera, Miguel
Esterbrook, Tom. *See* Hubbard, L. Ron
Esterhazy, Ferdinand Walsin, **Notor:** 334-335
Esterházy, Miklós József, **18th:** 476
Estes, Billie Sol, **Notor:** 336-337
Estes, Lydia. *See* Pinkham, Lydia E.
Esteván, **Ren:** 152
Esther (Adams), **19th:** 17
Esther (Racine), **17th:** 775
Estigarribia, Marshal José Felix, **Notor:** 1004
Estilo culto, **17th:** 312
Estilo llano, **17th:** 312
Estimé, Dumarsais, **Notor:** 308
Estonia. *See* Geographical Index
Estrada, Joseph, **Notor:** 701
Estravagario. See *Extravagaria*
Estro armonico, L' (Vivaldi), **18th:** 1020
Et exspecto resurrectionem (Messiaen), **20th:** 2717
Étampes, Council of (1130), **MA:** 161

Étaples, Jacques Lefèvre d'. *See* Lefèvre d'Étaples, Jacques
Étaples, Treaty of (1492), **Ren:** 227
État mental des hystériques, L'. See *Mental State of Hystericals, The*
Etching, **17th:** Italy, 117; **18th:** William Blake, 122; Francisco de Goya, 438
Etelköz, **MA:** 105
Eternal Road, The (Werfel), **20th:** 4275
Eternal Word Television Network, **20th:** 90
Ethan Frome (Wharton), **20th:** 4301
Ethelfleda. *See* Æthelflæd
Ethelred II, the Unready, **MA:** 222, 337, 362-365, 457, 786, 790
Ethelwold, **MA:** 340
Ethelwulf, **MA:** 354
Ethica Eudemia (Aristotle), **Anc:** 95
Ethical Culture School, **19th:** 27
Ethical Studies (Bradley), **19th:** 289
Ethics, **Anc:** Greek, 69; Stoicism and, 691; Zoroastrian, 994; **18th:** altruism, 1009; Johann Gottlieb Fichte, 344; Paul-Henri-Dietrich d'Holbach, 502; David Hume, 514-517; Immanuel Kant, 549; Friedrich Schiller, 889; **20th:** 24, 926, 1346, 3392; existentialist, 273; medicine, 238; phenomenological theory of, 3657; Protestant, 4260. *See also* Aristotle; Hanfeizi; Plato; Plutarch
Ethics (Abelard), **MA:** 15
Ethics (Bonhoeffer), **20th:** 419
Ethics (Hartmann), **20th:** 1696
Ethics (Moore), **20th:** 2816
Ethics (Spinoza), **17th:** 873
Ethics (Wundt), **20th:** 4408
Ethics of Ambiguity, The (Beauvoir), **20th:** 273
Ethika (Plutarch), **Anc:** 550, 672
Ethiopia, **MA:** architecture, 633; trade, 632; **18th:** exploration of, 169; **20th:** Somali invasion of (1978), 3735. *See also* Geographical Index
Ethiopian Civil War (1974-1991), **20th:** 2701
Ethiopian Orthodox Church, **MA:** 632
Éthiopiques (Senghor), **20th:** 3704
Ethnography, **Anc:** Herodotus and, 408; travel and, 346; **19th:** 1603
Ethnology, historical approach, **20th:** 1342
Ethology, **20th:** 2435
Étioles, Jeanne-Antoinette Le Normant d'. *See* Pompadour, Madame de
Etō Shimpei, **19th:** 1970
Étoile Sans Lumière (film), **20th:** 3229
Étourdi, L'. See *Blunderer, The*
Étranger, L'. See *Stranger, The*
Être et le néant, L'. See *Being and Nothingness*
Être et l'essence, L'. See *Being and Some Philosophers*
Ett barns memoarner. See *Memories of My Childhood*
Ett drömspel. See *Dream Play, A*
Études (Debussy), **20th:** 938
Études sur les glaciers (Agassiz), **19th:** 32
Étui de nacre, L'. See *Tales from a Mother of Pearl Casket*
Etymologiae. See *Encyclopedist of the Dark Ages, An*
Eubulus, **Anc:** 265
Euchidas, **Anc:** 631
Eucken, Rudolf Christoph, **20th:** 1185-1187
Eucleria seu melioris partis electio (Schurman), **17th:** 824
Euclid, **Anc:** 77, 317-319, 401, 434; **MA:** 22
Euclid and His Modern Rivals (Carroll), **19th:** 424
Euclides adauctus et methodicus (Guarini), **17th:** 331
Eudemian Ethics. See *Ethica Eudemia*
Eudemos, **Anc:** 349
Eudes of Lagery. *See* Urban II
Eudoxia, **Anc:** 208
Eudoxus of Cnidus, **Anc:** 81, 320-323
Eugene of Savoy, **17th:** 528; **18th:** 142, 230, 330-332, 494, 661; and Ottoman Empire, 27
Eugene Onegin (Pushkin), **19th:** 1849
Eugenics Education Society, **19th:** 862
Eugenics movement, **19th:** 862; **20th:** 1111; opposition to, 2862
Eugénie (Beaumarchais), **18th:** 97
Eugénie Grandet (Balzac), **19th:** 128
Eugenius, **Anc:** 824, 870
Eugenius III, **MA:** 385, 512
Eugenius IV, **MA:** 85; **Ren:** 18, 350
Eukles, **Anc:** 631
Euler, Leonhard, **18th:** 333-335; **19th:** 9
Eulogia, **MA:** 1018
Eumenes, **Anc:** 720, 763
Eumenides (Aeschylus), **Anc:** 9
Euménides, Les (Milhaud), **20th:** 2735
Eunomians, **Anc:** 361, 364
Eunuchs, Chinese, **MA:** 1150, 1156
Eunuchus (Terence), **Anc:** 850
Eupalinos Tunnel, **Anc:** 324
Eupalinus of Megara, **Anc:** 323-325; **Notor:** 851
Eureka: A Prose Poem (Poe), **19th:** 1815
Euripides, **Anc:** 92, 326-329, 810
Europe (Blake), **18th:** 122
European Coal and Steel Community, **20th:** 2795, 3809
European Community, **20th:** 1174, 2795
European Economic Community, **20th:** 1740

European Recovery Act of 1948, **20th:** 2631
Europeans, The (James), **19th:** 1207
Euryanthe (Weber), **19th:** 2397
Eurydice, **Anc:** 637, 720
Eurymedon River, Battle of (466 B.C.E.), **Anc:** 214, 679
Euryphon, **Anc:** 420
Eusebius Hieronymus. *See* Jerome, Saint
Eusebius of Caesarea, **Anc:** 240, 330-332, 363, 391, 426, 442; **Notor:** 841
Eusebius of Nicomedia, **Anc:** 911
Eusebius Pamphili. *See* Eusebius of Caesarea
Eustace, **MA:** 963
Eustace Conway (Maurice), **19th:** 1518
Eustochium, **Anc:** 457
Eutaw Springs, Battle of (1781), **18th:** 445
Euterpe, **19th:** 985
Euthymenes, **Anc:** 387, 729
Euthyphrōn (Plato), **Anc:** 660, 799
Eutyches, **Anc:** 866
Evagoras (Isocrates), **Anc:** 451
Evangeline (Longfellow), **19th:** 1417
Evangelism, **18th:** colonial America, 75, 591, 1065, 1073-1075; Hannah More, 702; William Wilberforce, 1079-1082; Count von Zinzendorf, 1119-1122; **19th:** 1596; **20th:** 1210, 1558, 2851, 2971, 3917
Evangelium des Johannes, Das. See *Gospel of John, The*
Evangelium Marcions und das Kanonische Evangelium des Lucas, Das (Ritschl), **19th:** 1918
Evans, Sir Arthur, **19th:** 753-755, 2018
Evans, Hiram Wesley, **Notor:** 958
Evans, Mary Ann. *See* Eliot, George
Evans, Timothy, **Notor:** 210
Evatt, Herbert Vere, **20th:** 1188-1191
Evelina (Burney), **18th:** 181
Evelyn, John, **17th:** 95, 256-258, 677, 996
Evening Hours of a Hermit (Pestalozzi), **19th:** 1782
Evening Post, **19th:** 340
Evening Walk, An (Wordsworth), **19th:** 2462
Evenings on a Farm Near Dikanka (Gogol), **19th:** 937
Eventyr (Andersen), **19th:** 61
Eventyr (Delius), **20th:** 955
Eventyr og Historier. See *Complete Andersen, The*
Ever Since Darwin (Gould), **20th:** 1556
Everard, William, **17th:** 988
Everett, Edward, **19th:** 876
Everhard, Ed. *See* James, Jesse
Everlasting Man, The (Chesterton), **20th:** 745
Everleigh, Ada, **Notor:** 338-339
Evers, Medgar, **Notor:** 78
Evers, Myrlie, **Notor:** 78
Evert, Chris, **20th:** 1191-1194, 2144, 2923
Every Man a King (Long), **20th:** 2427
Every Man for Himself (film), **20th:** 1504
Every Man in His Humour (Jonson), **17th:** 440
Every Man Out of His Humour (Jonson), **17th:** 440
Everything That Rises Must Converge (O'Connor), **20th:** 3018
Evesham, Battle of (1265), **MA:** 492, 729
Evgeny Onegin. See *Eugene Onegin*
Evidence as to Man's Place in Nature (Huxley), **19th:** 1162
Evita. *See* Perón, Eva
Evita (Lloyd Webber and Rice), **20th:** 2415
Evodius, Saint, **Anc:** 437
Evola, Julius, **Notor:** 339-340
Evolution, **Anc:** 297; **18th:** comte de Buffon, 172; Carolus Linnaeus, 606; and religion, 763-765; **19th:** botany, 964; Charles Darwin, 604; embryology, 115; germ plasm continuity, 2407; Thomas Henry Huxley, 1162; opposition to, 587; Protestant acceptance of, 174; social, 1605; Herbert Spencer, 2128; **20th:** 552, 915, 1555
Evolution and Ethics (Huxley), **19th:** 1162
Évolution créatrice, L'. See *Creative Evolution*
Evolution of Man, The (Haeckel), **19th:** 1005
Evolution of Modern Medicine, The (Osler), **19th:** 1712
Evolution of Star and Galaxies (Baade), **20th:** 185
Evolution Old and New (Butler), **19th:** 375
Evolution Theory, The (Weismann), **19th:** 2408
Evolutionary Socialism (Bernstein), **20th:** 334, 2482
Ewing, Thomas, Jr., **Notor:** 1118
Ewostatewos, **Ren:** 1006
EWTN. *See* Eternal Word Television Network
Ex parte McCardle, **19th:** 473
Ex parte Milligan, **19th:** 473
Examen de la Genèse (Châtelet), **18th:** 241
Examen diatribae Thomae Willisii de febribus (Meara), **17th:** 564
Examination Board (Toulouse-Lautrec), **19th:** 2290
Examination of the Dred Scott Case (Benton), **19th:** 195
Examination system, Chinese, **MA:** 968; **19th:** 2487
Examinations (Askew), **Ren:** 62
Examined Life, The (Nozick), **20th:** 3000
Examiner, The (Swift), **18th:** 965
Examiner Defended, The (Williams), **17th:** 984

Excellent et moult utile Opuscule à touts necessaire qui desirent auoir cognoissance de plusiers exquises Receptes (Nostradamus), **Ren:** 728
Exclusion Crisis (1679-1681), **17th:** 608, 840
Exclusion principle, **20th:** 3153
Excommunication, **Anc:** 44
Excursion, The (Wordsworth), **19th:** 2463
Execestides, **Anc:** 807
Execration Texts, **Anc:** 772
Execution of Justice in England, The (Cecil), **Ren:** 200
Executioner's Song, The (Mailer), **20th:** 2565
Executions of May Second (Goya), **18th:** 438
Executions of May Third (Goya), **18th:** 438
Executive Order 8802, **20th:** 3372
Exemplary Novels (Cervantes), **Ren:** 209
Exercitatio anatomica de motu cordis et sanguinis in animalibus. See *Anatomical Exercises of Dr. William Harvey . . . Concerning the Motion of the Heart and Blood, The*
Exercitationes de generatione animalium. See *Anatomical Exercitations, Concerning the Generation of Living Creatures*
Exercitationes geometricae (Gregory), **17th:** 320
Exercitationes paradoxicæ adversus Aristoteleos (Gassendi), **17th:** 304
Exigit ordo. See *Universal Treatise of Nicholas of Autrecourt, The*
Exile, The (Buck), **20th:** 558
Exiles, **18th:** Lazare Carnot, 201; Thomas Hutchinson, 520; James II, 250; first duke of Marlborough, 662; Peter III, 755; Guillaume-Thomas Raynal, 830; Marquis de Sade, 875; Emmanuel-Joseph Sieyès, 918; Madame de Staël, 931; Toussaint-Louverture, 987; Voltaire, 1026; John Wilkes, 1084
Existential Background of Human Dignity, The (Marcel), **20th:** 2610
Existentialism, **19th:** 1279; **20th:** 630, 1471, 1744, 1997, 2611, 3640
Existenzphilosophie. See *Philosophy of Existence*
Exit the King (Ionesco), **20th:** 1970
Exits and Entrances (Fugard), **20th:** 1357
Exner, Judith Campbell, Notor: 340-341, 406
Exodus, **Anc:** 1, 573
Expansionism, **18th:** American, 627, 1056; British, 742; Canadian, 975; Chinese, 817-819; European, 829-831; Persian, 722; Russian, 776
Experientialism, **18th:** David Hume, 514; Immanuel Kant, 549
Experiment in Autobiography (Wells), **20th:** 4289
Experimental Novel, The (Zola), **19th:** 2489
Experiments and Considerations Touching Colours (Boyle), **17th:** 79
Experiments of Spiritual Life and Health (Williams), **17th:** 984
"Experiments upon Magnesia Alba, Quicklime, and Some Other Alcaline Substances" (Black), **18th:** 115
Experiments upon the Circulation of the Blood . . . (Spallanzani), **18th:** 926
Expiatory Church of the Sagrada Familia, **20th:** 1425
Explication des maximes des saints sur la vie intérieure, L'. See *Maxims of the Saints Explained, Concerning the Interiour Life, The*
Exploding Raphaelesque Head (Dalí), **20th:** 906
Exploration and conquest, **MA:** of Africa, 478; by China, 1156; by Europe, 853; of Greenland, 641; of Middle East, 703; **Ren:** England of Central America, 193; England of North America, 157, 159, 276, 279, 293, 353, 379, 522, 771; England of South America, 193, 397, 814; France of North America, 178; Italy of China, 825; literature, 419; Netherlands of Asia, 277, 367; Portugal of African coast, 286; Portugal of Asia, 286, 591; Portugal of China, 792; Portugal of India, 237, 259, 365, 511, 513, 605; Portugal of North America, 605; Portugal of South America, 288, 971; Spain of Asia, 308; Spain of North America, 923; Spain of South America, 307, 801, 902, 971; **17th:** Americas, 140; England of Australia, 216; England of New England, 875, 878; England of North America, 391; England of the South Seas, 215; Europeans of Japan, 446; France of North America, 433, 491; France of the Mississippi, 603; Netherlands of Australia, 905; Netherlands of New Guinea, 906; Netherlands of New Zealand, 907; Netherlands of Tasmania, 907; Netherlands of the Fiji Islands, 907; Netherlands of the Pacific Ocean, 905; **18th:** Africa, 168-171, 765-768; Daniel Boone, 143-146; Louis-Antoine de Bougainville, 150-153; British, 80, 151, 270-274; Danish, 108; Hawaiian Islands, 1006-1008; North America, 629-632, 1006-

1008; Northern Hemisphere, 108-111; Pacific, 270-274; Russian, 108, 776; Siberia, 108, 776; South Pacific, 126-129, 151. *See also* Category Index
Explorations of the Colorado River of the West and Its Tributaries. See *Canyons of the Colorado*
Expositio in Apocalypsim (Joachim), **MA:** 575
Expositio Psalmorum. See *Cassiodorus: Explanation of the Psalms*
Expositio super cantica canticorum. See *Exposition on the Song of Songs*
Exposition of the Orthodox Faith (John of Damascus), **MA:** 589
Exposition of Young Artists, **18th:** 224
Exposition on the Song of Songs (William of Saint-Thierry), **MA:** 1115
Expressionism, **18th:** 438; in music, 970; **20th:** 2165, 2185, 3542, 3662, 3665, 3899
Ex-Prodigy (Wiener), **20th:** 4321
Expulsion from Paradise, The (Masaccio), **MA:** 701
Expulsion of Attila (Raphael), **Ren:** 821
Expulsion of Heliodorus (Raphael), **Ren:** 821
Exquemelin, A. O., **Notor:** 261
Exterminating Angel, The (film), **20th:** 579
Extracts from the Virginia Charters (Mason), **18th:** 664
Extravagaria (Neruda), **20th:** 2939
Eyck, Hubert van, **MA:** 365-368
Eyck, Jan van, **MA:** 365-368, 833, 949, 1092; **Ren:** 99, 120
Eye Balloon, The (Redon), **19th:** 1876
Eye of Silence, The (Ernst), **20th:** 1178
Eyeless in Gaza (Huxley), **20th:** 1961
Eylau, Battle of (1807), **19th:** 1667
Eyquem de Montaigne, Michel. *See* Montaigne, Michel Eyquem de
Ezana, **Anc:** 333-335
Ezekiel, **Anc:** 335-338, 583
Ezhov, Nikolai Ivanovich. *See* Yezhov, Nikolay Ivanovich
Ezra, **Anc:** 338-341
Ezra Society, **20th:** 292

F

Fa Koli, **MA:** 978
Faber, David. *See* Fabricius, David
Faber, Frederick William, **19th:** 1664
Faber, Johannes, **Ren:** 473
Fabia, **Notor:** 189
Fabian Essays in Socialism, **19th:** 212
Fabian Society, **19th:** 212; **20th:** 1843, 4254, 4288
Fabius Maximus, Quintus, **Anc:** 342-345, 383
Fabius Maximus Rullianus, Quintus, **Anc:** 342
Fable of Polyphemus and Galatea (Góngora), **17th:** 312
Fables, **Anc:** Aesop's, 11, 628; Phaedrus, 628
Fables (Marie de France), **MA:** 694
Fables choisies, mises en vers. See *Fables Written in Verse*
Fables of Phaedrus, The. See *Phaedri augusti Liberti Fabularum Aesopiarum*
Fables of Poge the Florentyn, The (Poggio), **MA:** 851
Fables Written in Verse (La Fontaine), **17th:** 481
Fabri de Peiresc, Nicolas-Claude. *See* Peiresc, Nicolas-Claude Fabri de
Fabrici, Girolamo. *See* Fabricius ab Aquapendente, Hieronymus
Fabricius, David, **17th:** 259-261
Fabricius, Girolamo. *See* Fabricius ab Aquapendente, Hieronymus
Fabricius, Johannes, **17th:** 259-261
Fabricius ab Aquapendente, Hieronymus, **Ren:** 319-321; **17th:** 355
Fabristae, **Ren:** 549
Fabritius, Carel, **17th:** 956
Fabrizi, Aldo, **20th:** 1232
Fabrizio, Geronimo. *See* Fabricius ab Aquapendente, Hieronymus
Fábula de Polifemo y Galatea. See *Fable of Polyphemus and Galatea*
Façade (Walton and Sitwell), **20th:** 4217
Face au drapeau. See *For the Flag*
Face to Face (film), **20th:** 318
Face to Face (short-story collection by Gordimer), **20th:** 1535
Facetiae. See *Fables of Poge the Florentyn, The*
Facing Mount Kenya (Kenyatta), **20th:** 2107
Facing Reality (Eccles), **20th:** 1091
Fact and Fiction (Child), **19th:** 484
Factories, **18th:** development, 56; England, 156, 1060; lighting, 717; United States, 835. *See also* Manufacturing
Factories and Shop Act of 1885, **19th:** 625
Factory, The, **20th:** 4228
Factory Act of 1833, **19th:** 457, 979
Factory Act of 1874, **19th:** 372, 669
Factory Act of 1878, **19th:** 372, 669
Factory Report of 1833, **19th:** 457
Facts of Fiction, The (Collins), **20th:** 810
Facts Relating to the Punishment of Death in the Metropolis (Wakefield), **19th:** 2379

Fadren. See *Father, The*
Faerie Queene, The (Spenser), **Ren:** 907
Fahd (king of Saudi Arabia), **20th:** 1195-1198, 4424
Fahd Bin Abdallah Bin Khalid. *See* Mohammed, Khalid Shaikh
Fahd Plan (1981). *See* Fez Plan
Fahrenheit, Daniel Gabriel, **18th:** 336-338
Fahrenheit 451 (film), **20th:** 4081
Fa-hsien. *See* Faxian
Faidherbe, Louis, **19th:** 756-759
Faine, Simone Ovide, **Notor:** 309
Fair, A. A. *See* Gardner, Erle Stanley
Fair Deal, **20th:** 4087
Fair Employment Practices Commission, **20th:** 3372
Fair Haven, The (Butler), **19th:** 374
Fair Maid of Perth, The (Scott), **19th:** 242, 2049
Fair Maid of the Exchange, The (Heywood), **17th:** 374
Fairbanks, Douglas, Jr., **20th:** 999
Fairbanks, Douglas, Sr., **20th:** 732, 2429, 3245
Fairfax, Mary. *See* Somerville, Mary
Fairfax, third Baron (Thomas Fairfax), **17th:** 205, 261-265, 483, 605, 756, 986
Fairfax Resolves (Mason), **18th:** 664
Fairly Good Time, A (Gallant), **20th:** 1378
Fairy Tales. See *Complete Andersen, The*
Fairylogue and Radio-Plays (Baum), **19th:** 157
Faisal (king of Saudi Arabia), **20th:** 1195, 1198-1202, 4422
Faisal I (king of Iraq), **20th:** 1202-1206, 2304
Faisal II (king of Iraq), **20th:** 1952, 2916
Faisal bin Hussein. *See* Faisal I (king of Iraq)
Faisal ibn Abdul Aziz ibn Saud. *See* Faisal (king of Saudi Arabia)
Faith and Duties of Christians, The (Burnet), **17th:** 107
Faith of Graffiti, The (Mailer), **20th:** 2564
Faith of Our Fathers, The (Gibbons), **19th:** 910
Faithful Memoirs of the Life, Amours, and Performances of That Justly Celebrated, and Most Eminent Actress of Her Time, Mrs. Anne Oldfield (Egerton), **18th:** 750
Faithful Narrative of the Surprising Work of God, A (Edwards), **18th:** 315
Faithful Shepherdess, The (Fletcher), **Ren:** 93; **17th:** 279
Fakhr al-Dīn al-Rāzī, **MA:** 369-371
Fakhri, al- (al-Karaji), **Anc:** 286
Falco, Charles M., **20th:** 1847
Falco, Richard David. *See* Berkowitz, David
Falcon, the. *See* Boyce, Christopher John
Faletto, Enzo, **20th:** 651
Falkland Islands, **18th:** 151
Falklands War (1982), **20th:** 3196, 3994
Falkner (Shelley), **19th:** 2089
Falköping, Battle of (1388), **MA:** 691
Fall, Albert B., **20th:** 1676; **Notor:** 342-343
Fall of _______. *See* _______, fall of
Fall of Hyperion, The (Keats), **19th:** 1262
Fall of Princes, The (Boccaccio), **MA:** 171
Falla, Manuel de, **20th:** 1206-1209
Fallen Angels (Coward), **20th:** 854
Fallen Timbers, Battle of (1794), **18th:** 611, 1056; **19th:** 2238
Fallopius, Gabriel, **Ren:** 319
Falloux Law, **19th:** 2265
False Messiah, The (Grimmelshausen), **17th:** 325
Falstaff (Elgar), **20th:** 1135
Falstaff (Verdi), **19th:** 2353
Falun Gong, **20th:** 2001
Falwell, Jerry, **20th:** 1209-1212
Fame and Confession of the Fraternity of R:C:, The (Fludd), **17th:** 282
Fame and Glory of England Vindicated, The (Brown), **19th:** 317
Famensi, temple of, **MA:** 1128
Familiar Lessons in Astronomy (Fowler), **19th:** 812
Familiar Lessons on Phrenology (Fowler), **19th:** 812
Familiar Lessons on Physiology (Fowler), **19th:** 812
Familie Schroffenstein, Die. See *Schroffenstein Family, The*
Family in Renaissance Florence, The (Alberti), **Ren:** 19
Family Instructor, The (Defoe), **18th:** 299
Family Limitation (Sanger), **20th:** 3626
Family of Man, The (exhibition), **20th:** 3839
Family Reunion, The (Eliot), **20th:** 1141
Famine, **18th:** Japan, 505, 981; **19th:** Ireland, 1770, 1959
Famous Players-Lasky Company, **20th:** 1524
Fan Chung-yen. *See* Fan Zhongyan
Fan Zhongyan, **MA:** 809
Fanatics, The (Dunbar), **19th:** 703
Fanciulla del west, La (Puccini), **19th:** 1155; **20th:** 3347
Fanck, Arnold, **20th:** 3451
Fanfarlo, La (Baudelaire), **19th:** 153
Fang Hsuan-ling. *See* Fang Xuanling
Fang Xuanling, **MA:** 995
Fannia, **Anc:** 103

Fanny and Alexander (film), **20th:** 318
Fanon, Frantz, **20th:** 710, 1212-1214
Fanshawe (Hawthorne), **19th:** 1051
Fantasia (animated film), **20th:** 1008
Fantasia on a Theme by Tallis (Vaughan Williams), **20th:** 4148
Fantasies of Three Parts (Gibbons), **17th:** 309
Fantasy in F Minor (Schubert), **19th:** 2027
Fantôme de la Liberté, Le. See *Phantom of Liberty, The*
Far from the Madding Crowd (Hardy), **19th:** 1029
Fārābi, al-, **MA:** 120
Farabundo Martí National Liberation Front. *See* Frente Farabundo Martí para la Liberación Nacional
Faraday, Michael, **19th:** 548, 618, 759-762, 997, 1079, 1264
Fard, Wallace Dodd, **Notor:** 344-346, 764
Farel, Guillaume, **Ren:** 164
Farewell to Arms, A (film), **20th:** 1724
Farewell to Arms, A (novel by Hemingway), **20th:** 1756
Farm, The (Miró), **20th:** 2760
Farm Security Administration, **20th:** 2261
Farmer Boy (Wilder), **20th:** 4338
Farmer's Friend, The (Cobbett), **19th:** 518
Farmington (Darrow), **20th:** 914
Farmworkers' movement, **20th:** 738
Farnese, Alessandro (1468-1549; pope). *See* Paul III
Farnese, Alessandro (1545-1592; duke of Parma), **Ren:** 321-324, 616
Farnese, Isabella, **18th:** 782; marriage to Philip V, 781
Farnese Gallery, **Ren:** 176
Farnham, Battle of (893), **MA:** 340
Farouk I, **20th:** 1215-1216, 2554, 2914
Farragut, David G., **19th:** 762-765
Farrakhan, Louis, **20th:** 1217-1219
Farrand, Beatrix Jones, **20th:** 1219-1222
Faruk, al-. *See* ʿUmar I
Fascism, **20th:** 1449, 2887-2888, 3276
Fascist Party (Italy), **20th:** 2886
Fashionable Life (Trollope), **19th:** 2305
Fastow, Andrew, **Notor:** 618, 968
Fat Albert and the Cosby Kids (television program), **20th:** 841
Fatah, **20th:** 110
Fatal Galantry (La Fayette), **17th:** 478
Fatal Three, The (Braddon), **19th:** 287
Fate of Animals (Marc), **20th:** 2607
Father, The (Strindberg), **20th:** 3898
Father Coughlin. *See* Coughlin, Charles E.
Father David. *See* Berg, David
Father Divine, **Notor:** 346-348
Father Dowling Mysteries, The (television program), **20th:** 745
Father Goose, His Book (Baum), **19th:** 156
Father Goriot (Balzac), **19th:** 128
Father of the Blues (Handy), **20th:** 1667
Father of the Bride, The (film), **20th:** 3953
Fatherland Movement, **20th:** 162
Fathers and Sons (Turgenev), **19th:** 2320
Fatih, Mehmed. *See* Mehmed II
Fāṭimids, **MA:** 10, 71, 775, 918
Faubourg St.-Antoine, Battle of (1652), **17th:** 933
Faubus, Orval E., **Notor:** 100, 348-349
Faulkner, William, **20th:** 1222-1226
Fausse Industrie morcelée, répugnante, mensongère, et l'antidote, l'industrie naturelle, combinée, attrayante, veridique, donnant quadruple produit et perfection extrème en tous qualités, La (Fourier), **19th:** 806
Faust (Goethe). See *Tragedy of Faust, The*
Faust (Gounod), **19th:** 953
Faust Overture (Wagner), **19th:** 2374
Faust Symphony, A (Liszt), **19th:** 1394
Faustina, **Anc:** 530
Fauvism, **20th:** 493, 951, 2164, 2651, 3542
Faux-monnayeurs, Les. See *Counterfeiters, The*
Favola d'Orfeo, La (Monteverdi), **17th:** 658
Favorite, La (Donizetti), **19th:** 676
Fawcett, Henry, **19th:** 766
Fawcett, Dame Millicent Garrett, **19th:** 766-770
Fawkes, Guy, **Ren:** 324-327; **17th:** 16, 442; **Notor:** 350-351
Fawkes de Breauté. *See* Breauté, Fawkes de
Faxian, **Anc:** 345-347, 976
Faxian Zhuan (Faxian), **Anc:** 345
Fayed, Emad Mohamed "Dodi" al-, **20th:** 991
FBI. *See* Federal Bureau of Investigation
Fear of the Dead in Primitive Religion, The (Frazer), **20th:** 1320
Feast in the House of Levi, The (Veronese), **Ren:** 961
Feast of Herod, The (Donatello), **MA:** 320
Feast of Tabernacles, **Anc:** 340
Feast of the Gods (Bellini), **Ren:** 98-99

Feast of the Rose Garlands, The (Dürer), **Ren:** 297
Feather of the Dawn, The (Naidu), **20th:** 2900
February 28 Popular League, **20th:** 3500
Febvre, Lucien, **20th:** 497
Fechner, Gustav Theodor, **19th:** 770-773
Fécondité. See *Fruitfulness*
Federal Aid Highway Act of 1956, **20th:** 1127
Federal Bureau of Investigation, **20th:** 1867, 1911
Federal Emergency Relief Administration, **20th:** 1872
Federal Mine Safety Law of 1952, **20th:** 2362
Federalism, **18th:** John Adams, 13; Samuel Chase, 238; Elbridge Gerry, 413; Alexander Hamilton, 453; Patrick Henry, 484; Thomas Jefferson, 530; James Madison, 636; George Mason, 665; Gouverneur Morris, 705; Robert Morris, 709; Daniel Shays, 904; **20th:** 3022
Federalist, The (Hamilton, Madison, and Jay), **18th:** 454, 525, 636
Federalist Party, **18th:** Alien and Sedition Acts, 13; founding, 455; John Jay, 526; James Wilson, 1092; **19th:** 365
Federalist-Republican conflict, **18th:** 238
Federalists (Mexico), **19th:** 99
Fédération de l'unité en Italie, La (Proudhon), **19th:** 1836
Fédération Internationale d'Information et de Documentation, **20th:** 2231
Federation League, **19th:** 150
Fedorovich, Grand Duke Peter. *See* Peter III
Feeling and Form (Langer), **20th:** 2265
Feen, Die (Wagner), **19th:** 2374
Fehrbellin, Battle of (1675), **17th:** 291
Feinstein, Dianne, **20th:** 1227-1231
Feklisov, Alexander, **Notor:** 380, 915
Felician schism, **Anc:** 699, 797
Félicie, Jacqueline, **MA:** 372-374
Felipe III. *See* Philip III (1578-1621; king of Spain)
Felipe IV. *See* Philip IV (1605-1665; king of Spain)
Felix Holt, Radical (Eliot), **19th:** 741
Felix the Goodheart. *See* Dzerzhinsky, Felix
Fellini, Federico, **20th:** 1231-1234
Fellini Roma (film), **20th:** 1233
Fellini Satyricon (film), **20th:** 1233
Fellowship of the Ring, The (Tolkien), **20th:** 4039
Felsina Pittrice (Malvasia), **17th:** 856
Felt, Mark, **Notor:** 140, 491
Felton, John, **Notor:** 352-353
Female Anti-Slavery Society, **19th:** 483
Female Emigrant's Guide, The (Traill), **19th:** 2292
Female Quixote, The (Lennox), **18th:** 594
Female Tatler, The (Manley), **18th:** 642
Female Wits, The (anonymous), **18th:** 641
Feminine Mystique, The (Friedan), **20th:** 1329
Feminism, **18th:** Abigail Adams, 7-11; Sophie von La Roche, 578; Catherine Macaulay, 622; Mary de la Rivière Manley, 642; Mary Wortley Montagu, 688; Mary Robinson, 850; Mary Wollstonecraft, 1108-1112. *See also* Civil rights; Democracy; Education; Liberalism; Women; Women's rights
Feminist Art Program, **20th:** 751
Femme, La (Ségalas), **19th:** 2062
Femmes arabes en Algérie, Les (Auclert), **19th:** 90
Femmes au gouvernail, Les (Auclert), **19th:** 90
Femmes de bonne humeur, Les (ballet), **20th:** 2647
Femmes illustres, Les (Scudéry), **17th:** 829
Fénelon, François de Salignac de La Mothe-, **17th:** 265-267, 339, 573
Feng Guifen, **19th:** 2486
Feng Kuei-fen. *See* Feng Guifen
Feng Youxiang, **20th:** 968
Feng Yunshan, **19th:** 1128
Fenian Order, **19th:** 1113
Fenway Court, **20th:** 1407
Feo, Giacomo, **Ren:** 870
Ferdinand I (1016/1018-1065; king of Castile and León), **MA:** 278
Ferdinand I (1503-1564; Holy Roman Emperor), **Ren:** 31, 222, 473, 636, 650, 886
Ferdinand I (1793-1875; king of Hungary and Bohemia), **19th:** 620
Ferdinand II (1452-1516; king of Aragon and Castile), **Ren:** 2, 29, 76, 105, 116, 159, 187, 227, 237, 328-332, 433, 482, 504, 511, 575, 606, 804, 939; **Notor:** 15, 531
Ferdinand II (1578-1637; Holy Roman Emperor), **17th:** 267-270, 293, 317, 627, 820, 854-855, 967
Ferdinand II de' Medici (1610-1670; grand duke of Tuscany), **17th:** 297, 881, 921
Ferdinand III (1199-1252; king of León), **MA:** 59
Ferdinand III (1608-1657; Holy Roman Emperor), **17th:** 269, 526, 661, 705
Ferdinand VII (1784-1833; king of Spain), **19th:** 404, 412, 477, 1183, 1984, 1993

Ferdinand, Franz. *See* Francis Ferdinand
Ferdowsī. *See* Firdusi
Fergana, **Ren:** 69
Ferguson, Adam, **18th:** 338-342
Ferguson, Maynard, **20th:** 3226
Ferguson, Miriam, **Notor:** 812
Fermat, Pierre de, **Anc:** 288; **Ren:** 174; **17th:** 271-274, 630, 970
Fermi, Enrico, **20th:** 74, 341, 715, 1005, 1235-1239, 1636
Fermi-Dirac statistics, **20th:** 1005
Fermi mechanism, **20th:** 59
Fernández, Dolores. *See* Huerta, Dolores
Fernandez, Raymond, **Notor:** 1109
Fernando Po scandal, **20th:** 4102
Ferrabosco, Alfonso, the Elder, **Ren:** 149
Ferrar, Nicholas, **17th:** 202, 274-277, 367
Ferrara, duchess of. *See* Borgia, Lucrezia
Ferrara, dukes of, **Ren:** 56
Ferrari, Enzo, **20th:** 1239-1242
Ferraro, Geraldine, **20th:** 1242-1246
Ferrelo, Bartolome, **Ren:** 161
Ferrer, José, **Notor:** 974
Ferrer, Mel, **20th:** 1767
Ferrie, David, **Notor:** 942
Ferro, Don Vito, **Notor:** 709
Ferroconcrete, **20th:** 2941, 3213
Ferroelectricity, study of, **20th:** 2214
Ferromagnetism, study of, **20th:** 2926
Ferry, Jules, **20th:** 779
Fervor de Buenos Aires. See *Selected Poems, 1923-1967*
Festal Epistles, The. See *Epistolae festales*
Fetterman, William J., **19th:** 567, 1873
Fetterman Massacre, **19th:** 567, 1873
Feudalism, **Anc:** Central Asian, 500; Chinese, 237, 379; Sāsānian, 774; **MA:** England, 344, 485; feudalism, 200; Germany, 384, 423, 1123; Japan, 721; Norman, 1119; Scotland, 200; **18th:** France, 844; Prussia, 380; Vietnam, 736
Feuilles d'automne, Les (Hugo), **19th:** 1147
Few Days in Athens, A (Wright), **19th:** 2469
Feynman, Richard, **Notor:** 381
Fez Plan (1981), **20th:** 1195
Fianna Fáil, **20th:** 980
Fibonacci, Leonardo. *See* Leonardo of Pisa
Fibonacci sequence, **MA:** 649
Ficciones, 1935-1944 (Borges), **20th:** 432
Fichte, Johann Gottlieb, **18th:** 342-346; **19th:** 2152
Ficino, Marsilio, **Ren:** 332-334, 548, 557
Fiddler, The (Chagall), **20th:** 717
Fiddler on the Roof (Bock and Harnick), **20th:** 3461
Fidelio (Beethoven), **19th:** 177
Field, Cyrus, **19th:** 1523
Field, Kate, **19th:** 2301
Field, Marshall, **19th:** 773-776
Field, Nathan, **Ren:** 95
Field, Stephen J., **19th:** 777-781
Field Museum of Natural History, **19th:** 775
Field of Cloth of Gold (1520), **Ren:** 997
Fielden, Samuel, **19th:** 58
Fielding, Henry, **18th:** 346-350, 842; **Notor:** 1103
Fields, Annie, **19th:** 1226
Fields, Edward R., **Notor:** 1000
Fields, W. C., **20th:** 4298
Fieldston School, **19th:** 28
Fiend's Delight, The (Bierce), **19th:** 229
Fierro, Rodolfo, **Notor:** 1070
Fieschi, Caterina. *See* Catherine of Genoa, Saint
Fieschi, Giuseppe, **Notor:** 353-355
Fieschi, Sinibaldo. *See* Innocent IV
Fifteen Sermons Preached at the Rolls Chapel (Butler), **18th:** 188
Fifteen Years of a Dancer's Life (Fuller), **20th:** 1362
Fifteen Years' War (1591-1606), **Ren:** 82
Fifteenth Amendment (U.S. Constitution), **19th:** 801, 2178
Fifth Business (Davies), **20th:** 918
Fifth Extermination Campaign, **20th:** 4467
Fifth Plague of Egypt, The (Turner), **19th:** 2323
Fifty Poems (Cummings), **20th:** 881
Fight at Finnesburg, The, **Anc:** 394
"Fight for Birth Control, The" (Sanger), **20th:** 3627
Fight for Conservation, The (Pinchot), **20th:** 3255
Fight for the Water Hole, The (Remington), **19th:** 1882
Fighting Angel (Buck), **20th:** 558
Fighting Forms (Marc), **20th:** 2607
Fighting Irish, **20th:** 3481
Fighting Stags (Courbet), **19th:** 560
Fighting Temeraire Tugged to Her Last Berth to Be Broken Up, The (Turner), **19th:** 2324
Figure humaine (Poulenc), **20th:** 3319
Fiji Islands, **17th:** 907; **18th:** 128
Fil de l'épée, Le. See *Edge of the Sword, The*
Filioque doctrine, **MA:** 646, 1016
Filipepi, Alessandro di Mariano dei. *See* Botticelli, Sandro
Fille du régiment, La (Donizetti), **19th:** 676
Fille mal gardée, La (Dauberval), **18th:** 296
Fillmore, Millard, **19th:** 781-784, 833

Film. *See* Category Index under Radio, Film, and Television
Film Sense, The (Eisenstein), **20th:** 1131
Filmer, Robert, **17th:** 546
Filmmaking, **20th:** developmental research, 942; France, 1383, 3420, 4080; Germany, 2254; D. W. Griffith, 1594; Howard Hughes, 1926; India, 3394; Italy, 1232, 4166; Japan, 2218; MGM, 2663; New Wave, 1503; Soviet Union, 1130; Sweden, 317; United States, 142, 961, 2452, 3682, 3706, 3811, 4285, 4446; Andy Warhol, 4228. *See also* Category Index under Radio, Film, and Television
Filocolo, Il. See *Labor of Love*
Filodemo (Camões), **Ren:** 167
Filosofia come scienza dello spirito (Croce), **20th:** 869
Filostrato, The (Boccaccio), **MA:** 170, 265
Fin de partie. See *Endgame*
Final solution. *See* Holocaust
Financial reform, **18th:** Edmund Burke, 175; France, 726-729; Alexander Hamilton, 454; Robert Morris, 708; William Pitt the Younger, 790
Financier, The (Dreiser), **20th:** 1034
Finch, Anne. *See* Conway, Anne
Finch, Daniel. *See* Nottingham, second earl of
Finding of the Body of Saint Mark (Tintoretto), **Ren:** 932
Finding of the Saviour in the Temple, The (Hunt), **19th:** 1158
Findlay, Tom, **Notor:** 977
Fine Clothes to the Jew (Hughes), **20th:** 1928
Fine Gael, **20th:** 845
Finger-Prints (Galton), **19th:** 862
Fingida Arcadia, La (Tirso), **17th:** 913
Finishing Touches (John), **20th:** 2016
Finland, **20th:** independence of, 3738. *See also* Geographical Index
Finlandia (Sibelius), **20th:** 3737
Finlay, Carlos Juan, **19th:** 1878
Finnegans Wake (Joyce), **20th:** 2057
Finnish War of Independence (1918), **20th:** 2598
Finta pazza Licori, La (Monteverdi), **17th:** 659
Fiore, Antonio, **Ren:** 173, 920
Fiore, Order of, **MA:** 576
Fiori musicali di diverse compositioni (Frescobaldi), **17th:** 297
Firdusi, MA: 375-378, 685
Fire Next Time, The (Baldwin), **20th:** 203
Fire over England (film), **20th:** 3040
Fire Raisers, The (Frisch), **20th:** 1339
Firebird, The (ballet), **20th:** 986, 3889
Fireboard (Grandma Moses), **20th:** 2841
Fireworks (Stravinsky), **20th:** 3888
Fireworks Music (Handel), **18th:** 464
Firing Line (television talk show), **20th:** 562
Firpo, Luis Angel, **20th:** 966
First Account, The (Copernicus), **Ren:** 243
First Aero Squadron, **20th:** 2766
First Amendment (U.S. Constitution), **18th:** 76, 1118; **20th:** 379, 383, 508, 521, 1030, 1858
First Anniversary of the Government Under His Highness the Lord Protector, The (Marvell), **17th:** 606
First Artists Production Company, **20th:** 3297
First Blast of the Trumpet Against the Monstrous Regiment of Women, The (Knox), **Ren:** 530
First Book of Discipline, The (Knox), **Ren:** 530
First Book of Urizen, The (Blake), **18th:** 122
First Booke of Songs or Ayres, The (Dowland), **Ren:** 290
First Booke of Songs or Ayres (Morley), **Ren:** 702
First Chamber Symphony, Op. 9 (Schoenberg), **20th:** 3665
First Church (Boston), **17th:** 219
First Circle, The (Solzhenitsyn), **20th:** 3784
"First Citizen, The" (Carroll), **18th:** 206
First Clement. See *Klementos pros Korinthious epistola prōtē*
First Crossing of Greenland (Nansen), **20th:** 2908
First Dream (Cruz), **17th:** 209
First Dynasty (Egypt), **Anc:** 556
First Empire, creation of, **19th:** 1243
First Examinacyon of Anne Askewe, The. See *Examinations*
First Footsteps in Africa (Burton), **19th:** 368
First Four Voyages of Amerigo Vespucci, The (Vespucci), **Ren:** 970
First International, **19th:** 120
First Lesson in Natural History, A (Agassiz), **19th:** 30
First Love (Turgenev), **19th:** 2320
First Part of the Institutes of the Law of England, The (Coke), **Ren:** 571
First Part of the True and Honorable Historie of the Life of Sir John Old-Castle the Good Lord Cobham, The (Drayton), **17th:** 238
First Principle, **Anc:** 701, 918
First Salute, The (Tuchman), **20th:** 4105
First Set of Madrigals and Mottets, The (Gibbons), **17th:** 310
First Settlers of New England, The (Child), **19th:** 482

First Steps to the Study of History (Peabody), **19th:** 1761
First Symphony (Borodin), **19th:** 281
First Symphony (Schumann), **19th:** 2033
First Triumvirate, **Anc:** 173, 194, 212, 682. *See also* Second Triumvirate
First Year in Canterbury Settlement, A (Butler), **19th:** 374
Fischer von Erlach, Johann Bernhard, **18th:** 350-353, 494
Fischer von Erlach, Joseph Emanuel, **18th:** 352
Fish, Albert, **Notor:** 355-357
Fish-Wife of Mousehole. *See* Pentreath, Dolly
Fishdance Restaurant, **20th:** 1439
Fisher, Amy, **Notor:** 159
Fisher, Andrew, **20th:** 1931
Fisher, Eddie, **20th:** 3953
Fisher, George, **19th:** 1134
Fisher, John, **19th:** 541
Fisher, Saint John, **Ren:** 266, 270, 335-337
Fishermen at Sea (Turner), **19th:** 2322
Fisk, James, **19th:** 1601, 2335; **Notor:** 357-358
Fiske, Helen Maria. *See* Jackson, Helen Hunt
Fitch, John, **18th:** 353-356
Fitz-Boodle, George Savage. *See* Thackeray, William Makepeace
Fitzgerald, Lord Edward, **18th:** 356-358
Fitzgerald, Ella, **20th:** 1246-1249
Fitzgerald, F. Scott, **20th:** 1249-1253
Fitzgerald, Zelda, **20th:** 1251
Fitzherbert, Maria Anne, **18th:** 358-361
Fitzpatrick, Frank, **Notor:** 854
Fitzwilliam Virginal Book, The (Tregian), **Ren:** 150
Five Acts (1825-1826), **19th:** 1769
Five Ages of Man, **Anc:** 415
Five Canons on Latin Texts Op. 16 (Webern), **20th:** 4263
Five lords appellants, **MA:** 494
Five Men and Pompey (Benét), **20th:** 303
Five Modern Nō Plays (Mishima), **20th:** 2764
Five Orchestral Pieces Op. 16 (Schoenberg), **20th:** 4264
Five Piano Pieces Op. 23 (Schoenberg), **20th:** 3666
Five Pieces for Orchestra Op. 10 (Webern), **20th:** 4262
Five Songs with Orchestra (Berg), **20th:** 311
Five Weeks in a Balloon (Verne), **19th:** 2355
Five Women Who Loved Love (Saikaku), **17th:** 404
Five-Year Plan, First (1952), **20th:** 2603
Five-Year Plans, **20th:** 4463
Flaccus, Aulus Avilius, **Anc:** 640
Flagellation of Christ (Piero), **Ren:** 787
Flags in the Dust (Faulkner), **20th:** 1223
Flaiano, Ennio, **20th:** 1232
Flame and Shadow (Teasdale), **20th:** 3961
Flaminius, Gaius, **Anc:** 342, 383
Flamsteed, John, **17th:** 348, 371
Flanders, **MA:** art, 366; mysticism, 144; painting, 366
Flatiron Building, **19th:** 362
Flaubert, Gustave, **19th:** 785-788; **Notor:** 933
Flavia Domitilla, **Anc:** 943
Flavian, **Anc:** 863
Flavius Justinus. *See* Justin II
Flea Catcher, The (La Tour), **17th:** 494
Fledermaus, Die (Strauss), **19th:** 2189
Fleet, Biddy, **20th:** 3113
Flegenheimer, Arthur Simon. *See* Schultz, Dutch
Fleiss, Heidi, **Notor:** 359-360
Flémalle, Master of, **MA:** 1092
Fleming, Sir Alexander, **20th:** 1254-1256, 1260
Fleming, Williamina Paton Stevens, **19th:** 788-790; **20th:** 2317
Flesh and the Devil (film), **20th:** 1392
Fletcher, Giles, the Younger, **17th:** 278
Fletcher, John, **Ren:** 92-97, 879; **17th:** 105, 277-280, 636, 846, 977
Fletcher, Phineas, **17th:** 278
Fletcher v. Peck, **19th:** 2181
Fleurs du Mal, Les. See *Flowers of Evil*
Fleury, André-Hercule de, **18th:** 361-362; Louis XV, 616
Flexner, Abraham, **20th:** 1256-1259
Fliegende Holländer, Der (Wagner), **19th:** 2374
Flies, The (Sartre), **20th:** 3639
Fliess, Wilhelm, **20th:** 1324
Flight of Madeline and Porphyro (Hunt), **19th:** 1157
Flight of Swans, A (Tagore), **20th:** 3935
FLN. *See* National Liberation Front
Floating World art, Japan, **18th:** 958
Flodden Field, Battle of (1513), **Ren:** 188, 500-501
Flora of North America (Torrey), **19th:** 963
Florence, **MA:** 102, 209; as artistic center, 567, 699, 845; as cultural center, 206, 696; as financial center, 170, 1056; painting, 799; **Ren:** 587, 653, 655, 851
Florence, Council of (1431-1445), **Ren:** 1007
Florens Tertullianus, Quintus Septimius. *See* Tertullian
Florentine Codex (Sahagún), **Ren:** 621
Florentine History, The (Machiavelli), **Ren:** 588

Florentius, **MA:** 154
Flores de Oliva, Isabel. *See* Rose of Lima, Saint
Flores de poetas ilustres de España (Espinosa), **17th:** 770
Florey, Baron (Howard Walter Florey), **20th:** 1255, 1259-1262, 4181
Floriated Ornament (Pugin), **19th:** 1839
Florida, development of, **19th:** 850
Floridablanca, Count, **18th:** 524
Flos (Leonardo of Pisa), **MA:** 649
Flounder, The (Grass), **20th:** 1574
Flower Drum Song (Rodgers and Hammerstein), **20th:** 1659
Flower Fables (Alcott), **19th:** 42
Flowering Judas, and Other Stories (Porter), **20th:** 3312
Flowers and Grasses of the Four Seasons (Sōtatsu and Kōetsu), **17th:** 869
Flowers of Evil (Baudelaire), **19th:** 152
Flowing Light of the Godhead, The (Mechthild), **MA:** 709
FLOW-MATIC, **20th:** 1881
Floyd, Charles Arthur. *See* Floyd, Pretty Boy
Floyd, Pretty Boy, **Notor:** 360-362
Fludd, Robert, **17th:** 280-282, 629
Fluid mechanics, **20th:** 3327
Flying (Millett), **20th:** 2748
Flying Colours (Forester), **20th:** 1284
Flying Down to Rio (film), **20th:** 156
Flying the Arctic (Wilkins), **20th:** 4340
Flynn, Bill, **Notor:** 971
Flynn, Henry Francis, **19th:** 452
Flynt, Larry, **20th:** 1210
FMLN. *See* Frente Farabundo Martí para la Liberación Nacional
Foch, Ferdinand, **20th:** 781
Foerster, Werner, **Notor:** 940
Foix, Gaston de, **Ren:** 85
Fokine, Michel, **20th:** 194, 985, 1263-1265, 2647, 2974, 3166
Folger, Abigail, **Notor:** 690
Folger, Lydia. *See* Fowler, Lydia Folger
Folk music, **20th:** 1073; Brazil, 4163; Czechoslovakia, 1990; England, 4147; Finland, 3737; Hungary, 250; Spain, 3694
Folks from Dixie (Dunbar), **19th:** 703
Folle de Chaillot, La. See *Madwoman of Chaillot, The*
Folles-Avoines, **17th:** 433, 603
Following the Equator (Twain), **19th:** 2331
Following the Fleet (Bryne), **20th:** 4297
Folsom, Jim, **20th:** 4204; **Notor:** 362-363
Fonda, Henry, **20th:** 1265-1267
Fonda, Jane, **20th:** 1266, 4120
Fonda, Peter, **20th:** 1266
Foner, Samuel P. *See* Carto, Willis A.
Fons vitae (Ibn Gabirol), **MA:** 533
Fontaine, Jean de La. *See* La Fontaine, Jean de
Fontainebleau, Edict of (1685), **17th:** 821
Fontainebleau, Treaty of (1612), **17th:** 598
Fontana, Domenico, **17th:** 67
Fontana, Lavinia, **Ren:** 338-339
Fontana, Niccolò. *See* Tartaglia, Niccolò Fontana
Fontana, Prospero, **Ren:** 175, 338
Fonte Gaia, **MA:** 566
Fontei, Nicol, **17th:** 888
Fonteinne amoureuse, La. See *Fountain of Love, The*
Fonteyn, Dame Margot, **20th:** 1268-1271, 3002
Food Materials and Their Adulterations (Richards), **19th:** 1900
Food, synthetic, **20th:** 315
Food stamp program, **20th:** 4208
Football, Notre Dame University, **20th:** 3482
Football Players, The (Rousseau), **19th:** 1953
Foote, Henry S., **19th:** 612
For All Mankind (Blum), **20th:** 398
For God and the People (Rauschenbusch), **20th:** 3384
For Me and My Gal (film), **20th:** 1410, 2096
For Publius Quintius. See *Pro Quinctio*
For Self-Examination (Kierkegaard), **19th:** 1279
For Sertus Roscius of Ameria. See *Pro Roscio Amerino*
For the Flag (Verne), **19th:** 2356
For Thou Wilt Not Leave My Soul in Hell (Bach), **18th:** 71
For Whom the Bell Tolls (film), **20th:** 322
For Whom the Bell Tolls (novel by Hemingway), **20th:** 1757
Foraker, Joseph B., **19th:** 1018
Forbes, Charles, **20th:** 1676
Forbes, James D., **19th:** 1530
Forbidden books. See *Index of Prohibited Books*
Forbidden Forest, The (Eliade), **20th:** 1137
Force Act of 1833, **19th:** 2338
Force Acts of 1870-1871, **19th:** 961
Force and Freedom (Burckhardt), **19th:** 356
Forced Marriage, The (Behn), **17th:** 42
Ford, Betty, **20th:** 1272-1274
Ford, Charlie, **Notor:** 524
Ford, Gerald R., **20th:** 1016, 1272, 1274-1278, 2986, 3402; **Notor:** 76, 378, 1037
Ford, Harrison, **Notor:** 946
Ford, Henry, **19th:** 1340; **20th:** 1279-1282; **Notor:** 937, 973
Ford, John (film director), **20th:** 1525, 4066, 4250
Ford, John (playwright and poet), **17th:** 279, 976; **Notor:** 936

Ford, Larry C., **Notor:** 363-364
Ford, Philip, **17th:** 726
Ford, Robert, **19th:** 1212; **Notor:** 524
Ford Motor Company, **19th:** 1340; **20th:** 1280
Fordney-McCumber Tariff (1922), **20th:** 1675
Foreign Affair, A (film), **20th:** 999
Foreman, George, **20th:** 63
Forerunner, The (journal), **20th:** 1486
Forest Sanctuary, The (Hemans), **19th:** 1077
Forest Strip Killer. *See* Chikatilo, Andrei
Forester, C. S., **20th:** 1283-1285
Forestry, **20th:** 3254
Forêt interdite, La. See *Forbidden Forest, The*
Forgione, Francesco, **20th:** 1286-1287
Forgotten Ones, The (film), **20th:** 579
Forman, Milos, **20th:** 3990
Forman, Simon, **17th:** 132
Forme uniche della continuatà nello spazio (Boccioni), **20th:** 404
Formen des Wissens und die Bildung, Die (Scheler), **20th:** 3657
Formes élémentaires de la vie religieuse, Les. See *Elementary Forms of the Religious Life, The*
Formigny, Battle of (1450), **Ren:** 226
Forms, Platonic, **Anc:** 95, 660
Fornovo, Battle of (1495), **Ren:** 84, 228
Forrest, Edwin, **19th:** 271, 790-793, 1468
Forrest, Nathan Bedford, **Notor:** 365-367
Fors Clavigera (Ruskin), **19th:** 1956
Förster, Bernhard, **Notor:** 367
Forster, E. M., **20th:** 1288-1291
Forster, William Edward, **19th:** 793-796
Förster-Nietzsche, Elisabeth, **Notor:** 367-368
Forsyth, Frederick, **Notor:** 883
Fort Apache (film), **20th:** 4251
Fort Gibson, Treaty of (1833), **19th:** 1709
Fort Moultrie, Treaty of (1823), **19th:** 850
Fort Orange, **17th:** 643
Fort St. Louis, **17th:** 491
Fort Ticonderoga, **18th:** 565; Battle at (1775), 36, 60
Fort Wayne, Treaty of (1809), **19th:** 2238
Fortas, Abe, **Notor:** 369-370
Forten, Charlotte, **19th:** 796-799
Fortensky, Larry, **20th:** 3955
Fortescue, Sir John, **Ren:** 340-342, 571
Fortification perpendiculaire, La (Montalembert), **18th:** 691
Fortitude (Botticelli), **Ren:** 123
Fortuna disperata (Josquin), **Ren:** 516
Fortunatus, Venantius, **MA:** 428
Fortune (magazine), **20th:** 2457
Fortune in Her Wits (Quevedo y Villegas), **17th:** 771
Fortune Teller (La Tour), **17th:** 494
Fortunes of Nigel, The (Scott), **19th:** 2048
Fortunes of Perkin Warbeck, The (Shelley), **19th:** 2089
Fortuyn, Pim, **Notor:** 1055
Forty-five Guardsmen, The (Dumas), **19th:** 697
Forty Questions of the Soul (Böhme), **17th:** 61
Forty-two Articles of Religion, **Ren:** 268, 305
Forza del destino, La (Verdi), **19th:** 2352
Fosse, Bob, **20th:** 1291-1294
Fossey, Dian, **20th:** 2313
Foster, Abby Kelley, **19th:** 799-801, 1097
Foster, Lady Elizabeth, **18th:** 216
Foster, Jodie, **Notor:** 470
Foster, Marcus, **Notor:** 455
Foster, Stephen Collins, **19th:** 802-805
Fouché, Joseph, **Notor:** 908
Foulois, Benjamin D., **20th:** 2766
Foundation for Defense of Democracies, **20th:** 2169
Foundation of Plain Instruction, A (Menno), **Ren:** 676
Foundations of Arithmetic, The (Frege), **19th:** 828
Foundations of Sovereignty, and Other Essays, The (Laski), **20th:** 2269
Foundations of the Metaphysics of Morals (Kant), **18th:** 549
Founding Fathers, **18th:** John Adams, 11-15; Samuel Adams, 16-20; Charles Carroll, 205-208; Samuel Chase, 237-240; John Dickinson, 303-307; Benjamin Franklin, 370-375; Elbridge Gerry, 412-414; Alexander Hamilton, 452-456; John Hancock, 457-462; Patrick Henry, 482-485; John Jay, 524-527; Thomas Jefferson, 528-531; James Madison, 636-638; George Mason, 664-667; Gouverneur Morris, 705-707; Robert Morris, 707-711; Thomas Paine, 759-762; Benjamin Rush, 872-874; Roger Sherman, 908-911; George Washington, 1043-1047; James Wilson, 1090-1094; John Witherspoon, 1098-1102
Fountain (Duchamp), **20th:** 1052
Fountain, and Other Poems, The (Bryant), **19th:** 342
Fountain and the Tomb, The (Mahfouz), **20th:** 2556
Fountain of Age, The (Friedan), **20th:** 1331
Fountain of El Dorado (Whitney), **20th:** 4316
Fountain of Love, The (Machaut), **MA:** 680

Fountainhead, The (Rand), **20th:** 3367
Fouquet, Jean, **Anc:** 3
Fouquet, Nicolas, **17th:** 180, 481, 523, 532, 622
Four Apostles (Dürer), **Ren:** 299
Four Books (Confucian), **MA:** 1160
Four Books of Architecture, The (Palladio), **Ren:** 754, 755
Four Days' Battle (1666), **17th:** 806, 808
Four Dialogues on Painting (Holanda), **Ren:** 236
Four Georges, The (Thackeray), **19th:** 2259
Four Horsemen of the Apocalypse, The (Dürer), **Ren:** 298
Four Hundred, Council of, **Anc:** 808
Four Hundred Blows, The (film), **20th:** 4080
Four Loves, The (Lewis), **20th:** 2355
Four Monarchies, The (Bradstreet), **17th:** 89
Four Noble Truths, **Anc:** 131, 170, 899, 933
Four Prentices of London, The (Heywood), **17th:** 373
Four Psalms (Grieg), **19th:** 986
Four Quartets (Eliot), **20th:** 1141
Four Rivers Fountain, **17th:** 46
Four Seasons (Poussin), **17th:** 751
Four Seasons, The (Vivaldi), **18th:** 1020
Four Serious Songs, Op. 121 (Brahms), **19th:** 298
Four Souls (Erdrich), **20th:** 1171
Four Temperaments, The. *See* Symphony No. 2 (Nielsen)
Four Winds, **Ren:** 135
Fourier, Charles, **19th:** 805-808
Fourier, Joseph (Baron Fourier), **19th:** 809-811
Fourteenth Amendment (U.S. Constitution), **19th:** 778, 1232, 2043
Fourth Dynasty (Egypt), **Anc:** 558
Fourth of July (Ives), **20th:** 1975
Fourth Paper Presented by Major Butler, The (Williams), **17th:** 984
Fourth Symphony (Schumann), **19th:** 2033
Fowler, Katherine. *See* Philips, Katherine
Fowler, Lorenzo Niles, **19th:** 812
Fowler, Lydia Folger, **19th:** 812-814
Fowler, Raymond, **Notor:** 972
Fowler, William A., **20th:** 1902
Fox, Charles James, **18th:** 216, 363-367, 410, 740, 789; **19th:** 978
Fox, George, **17th:** 283-286, 726
Fox, Richard K., **Notor:** 995
Fox Broadcasting, **20th:** 2876
Fox Libel Act (1792), **18th:** 328
Foxe, Fanne, **Notor:** 734
Foxe, John, **Ren:** 63, 403
Foxe's Book of Martyrs (Foxe), **Ren:** 63, 403, 544, 835
Fra Grønland til Stillehavet. See *Across Arctic America*
Fracastoro, Girolamo, **Ren:** 343-346
Fractals, **20th:** 2589
Fragmens sur les institutions républicaines (Saint-Just), **18th:** 879
Fragment on Government, A (Bentham), **18th:** 105
Fragmenta Aurea (Suckling), **17th:** 895
Fragmente . . . aus den Papieren eines Ungenannten (Lessing), **18th:** 601
Fragments (Bolingbroke), **18th:** 138
Fragments d'un discours amoureux. See *Lover's Discourse, A*
"Fragments on the Fall of the Scopads" (Simonides), **Anc:** 793
Fragonard, Jean-Honoré, **18th:** 367-370; painting of Denis Diderot, 309
Frahm, Herbert Ernst Karl. *See* Brandt, Willy
Frailty and Hypocrisy (Beaumarchais), **18th:** 98
Framers. *See* Founding Fathers
Frames of Government of Pennsylvania, **17th:** 727
Framework Law of 1957, **20th:** 1897
Framley Parsonage (Trollope), **19th:** 2300
France, **MA:** 824; art, 866; astronomy, 742; Capetian kings, 168, 668, 840; Carolingian kings, 245, 252, 664; education, 400, 437, 942, 984; Gothic art, 326; historiography, 427, 1053, 1063; Islamic invasion of, 252; Jews, 101, 408; law, 293; mathematics, 742; medicine, 372; Merovingian kings, 291; monasticism, 160, 316-317, 1114; music, 24-25, 680, 741, 824, 1065; mysticism, 160, 181, 578; painting, 866; philosophy, 13, 180, 215, 761, 943, 1098, 1102; poetry, 248, 260, 268, 274, 356, 392, 693, 1065; theology, 942, 1114; **19th:** African colonies, 1982; war with Algeria, 2. *See also* Geographical Index
France, Anatole, **19th:** 815-818
France and England in North America (Parkman), **19th:** 1744
Francesca da Rimini (Tchaikovsky), **19th:** 2234
Francesco di Pietro di Bernardone. *See* Francis of Assisi, Saint
Franciabigio, **Ren:** 39
Franciade, La (Ronsard), **Ren:** 838
Francis (duke of Guise), **Ren:** 429
Francis I (1494-1547; king of France), **Ren:** 8, 40, 54, 85, 111, 178, 204, 221, 229, 346-350, 411, 423, 549, 558, 566,

578, 614, 617, 648, 915, 997; **Notor:** 213
Francis I (1708-1765; Holy Roman Emperor), **18th:** 655, 657
Francis I (1768-1835; emperor of Austria). *See* Francis II (1768-1835; Holy Roman Emperor)
Francis I (Kemble), **19th:** 1267
Francis II (1544-1560; king of France), **Ren:** 184, 311, 426, 429, 568, 627, 634
Francis II (1768-1835; Holy Roman Emperor), **19th:** 1561
Francis, Lydia Maria. *See* Child, Lydia Maria
Francis, Lord Russell, **17th:** 767
Francis d'Angoulême. *See* Francis I (1494-1547; king of France)
Francis de Sales, Saint, **Ren:** 192
Francis Ferdinand (archduke of Austria), **19th:** assassination of, 820; **20th:** 1294-1296; assassination of, 1589; **Notor:** 861-862
Francis Joseph I (emperor of Austria), **19th:** 223, 446, 621, 818-821, 1525
Francis of Assisi, Saint, **MA:** 81, 96, 180, 226, 284, 317, 378-381, 436, 545, 779, 922
Francis the Waif (Sand), **19th:** 1988
Franciscans, **MA:** 81, 95, 180, 226, 329, 379, 817, 899, 922, 1110; **Ren:** 44, 146; **18th:** 891
Franciscanus et fratres (Buchanan), **Ren:** 146
Francisco de Asis de Bourbon, Maria Fernando, **19th:** 1184
Franck, César, **19th:** 821-824
Franck, James, **20th:** 1780
Franckert, Hans, **Ren:** 136
Franco, Francisco, **20th:** 398, 579, 682, 1297-1300, 2060, 2286; **Notor:** 270, 298, 371-373, 512, 770, 836, 860, 928
Franco, Itamar, **20th:** 651
Franco-Austrian War (1477-1493), **Ren:** 228
Franco-Dutch Wars (1672-1678), **17th:** 291, 507, 559, 654, 821, 934, 946
Franco-Gallia (Hotman), **Ren:** 463
Franco-Prussian War (1870-1871), **19th:** 238, 757, 864, 1641; Friedrich von Holstein, 1120; **20th:** 778
Franco-Russian Alliance of 1893-1894, **19th:** 1120
Franco-Soviet Pact of Mutual Assistance (1935), **20th:** 2285
Franco-Spanish War of 1595-1598, **17th:** 897
Franco-Spanish Wars of 1635-1659, **17th:** 417, 425, 554, 933
Franco-Turkish Alliance (1544), **Ren:** 221
Franco-Turkish War (1529-1535), **Ren:** 221
François-Eugène. *See* Eugene of Savoy
François le champi. See *Francis the Waif*
Franconian kings of Germany, **MA:** 499
Frank, Andre Gunder, **Notor:** 847
Frank, Anne, **20th:** 1301-1304
Frank, Antoinette, **Notor:** 373-374
Frank, Hans Michael, **Notor:** 374-375
Frank Sinatra Sings for Only the Lonely (Sinatra), **20th:** 3748
Frankel, Martin, **Notor:** 376-377
Frankenstein (Shelley), **18th:** 1110; **19th:** 2088, 2090
Frankenthaler, Helen, **20th:** 1304-1307
Frankfurt, Council of (794), **MA:** 551
Frankfurt, Germany, **18th:** 971
Frankfurt Parliament, **19th:** 222
Frankfurter, Felix, **20th:** 18, 380, 1308-1311; **Notor:** 475, 925, 1058
Franklin, Aretha, **20th:** 1312-1315
Franklin, Benjamin, **18th:** 12, 370-375, 621; Richard Howe, 507; Thomas Hutchinson, 520; diplomacy with William Pitt the Elder, 787; appeal to Charles Gravier de Vergennes, 1011; George Whitefield, 1074; **19th:** 140; **Notor:** 86, 907, 1024
Franklin, Sir John, **19th:** 825-827; **20th:** 83
Franklin, Joseph Paul, **Notor:** 839
Franklin, Rosalind, **20th:** 1316-1318, 4244, 4343
Franklin Evans (Whitman), **19th:** 2424
Franks, **MA:** 183, 288, 381, 870, 1094; Capetian kings, 168, 668, 840; Carolingian kings, 245, 252, 664; Christianity, 242, 290; Merovingian kings, 291
Franks, Bobbie, **Notor:** 634, 647
Franny and Zooey (Salinger), **20th:** 3611
Franz Ferdinand. *See* Francis Ferdinand
Fraser, Simon, **19th:** 2272
Frauenromane, **18th:** 578
Frawley, William, **20th:** 213
Frazer, Sir James George, **20th:** 1319-1322
Frazer, Mark Petrovich. *See* Maclean, Donald Duart
Frazier, Audrey Marie. *See* Hilley, Marie
Frazier, Joe, **20th:** 63
Frazier-Lemke Act of 1934, **20th:** 3880
Fredegunde, **MA:** 381-384
Frederick I Barbarossa (c. 1123-1190; Holy Roman Emperor), **MA:** 28, 56, 384-388, 475, 1123
Frederick I (1657-1713; king of Prussia), **18th:** 375-377
Frederick II (1194-1250; Holy Roman Emperor), **MA:** 359, 389-392, 436, 542, 545, 648, 667, 821, 904, 1027, 1047, 1075

Frederick II, the Great (1712-1786; king of Prussia), **18th:** 378-381, 382; Jean le Rond d'Alembert, 32; Maria Theresa, 654; Siege of Silesia, 654, 881; patron of Voltaire, 1027
Frederick III (1415-1493; Holy Roman Emperor), **MA:** 520; **Ren:** 218, 350-352, 643, 646, 794
Frederick III (1463-1525; elector of Saxony), **Ren:** 262, 582
Frederick V (1415-1493; archduke of Austria). *See* Frederick III (1415-1493; Holy Roman Emperor)
Frederick V (1596-1632; elector of the Palatinate), **17th:** 97, 143, 250, 253, 268, 275, 293-295, 310, 415, 805, 820
Frederick VI (1768-1839; king of Denmark), **Notor:** 208
Frederick Henry, **17th:** 286-290, 619, 820, 933
Frederick the Younger. *See* Frederick III (1415-1493; Holy Roman Emperor)
Frederick William I (king of Prussia), **18th:** 381-383
Frederick William II (king of Prussia), **18th:** 130; **19th:** 1022
Frederick William III (king of Prussia), **19th:** 261, 929, 2006, 2151
Frederick William IV (king of Prussia), **19th:** 223, 238
Frederick William, the Great Elector, **17th:** 154, 290-293, 851
Fredericksburg, Battle of (1862), **19th:** 1199
Frederickson, Elizabeth Diane. *See* Downs, Diane
Fredigundis. *See* Fredegunde
Free Cultivator's Law (1803), **19th:** 45
Free Economic Society for the Encouragement of Agriculture and Husbandry (Russia), **18th:** 213
Free Enquirer (newspaper), **19th:** 2470
Free Joe and Other Georgian Sketches (Harris), **19th:** 1037
Free love, **19th:** 807; **20th:** 1521
Free Officers Society, **20th:** 2914
Free silver question, **19th:** 509; **20th:** 551
Free-Soil Party, **19th:** 471
Free Spirits, **MA:** 857
Free Synagogue, **20th:** 4377
Free to Choose (Friedmans), **20th:** 1334
Free trade, **19th:** 1770
Free Trader Party, **19th:** 624
Free Unionist Officers, **20th:** 3350
Free will, **Anc:** Ājīvika, 356; Christianity and, 143
Freedman, Alexander, **20th:** 2338
Freedmen's Book, The (Child), **19th:** 484
Freedmen's Bureau, **19th:** 1142, 1231
Freedom, **18th:** association, 366; children, 732; civic, 812; press, 328, 1083-1086, 1116-1119; religious, 76, 206, 636, 705, 983; speech, 14, 328, 366; United States, 592
Freedom Charter (1955), **20th:** 2479, 2584
Freedom, Education, and the Fund (Hutchins), **20th:** 1958
Freedom Farm Cooperative, **20th:** 1652
Freedom from Fear (Rockwell), **20th:** 3484
Freedom from Want (Rockwell), **20th:** 3484
Freedom League, **20th:** 2448
Freedom of Speech (Rockwell), **20th:** 3484
Freedom of the Seas, The (Grotius), **17th:** 327
Freedom of Will (Edwards), **18th:** 316
Freedom of Worship (Rockwell), **20th:** 3484
Freeh, Louis, **Notor:** 922
Freeholder, The (conservative periodical), **18th:** 22
Freeman, Alice Elvira. *See* Palmer, Alice Freeman
Freeman, Orville, **Notor:** 337
Freer, Charles, **19th:** 2422
Freethinker, The (Lessing), **18th:** 598
Freewheelin' Bob Dylan, The (Dylan), **20th:** 1073
Frege, Gottlob, **19th:** 828-831; **20th:** 659
Frei, Eduardo, **20th:** 71
Freigeist, Die. See *Freethinker, The*
Freire, Ramón, **19th:** 1705
Freischärler-Reminiscenzen (Aston), **19th:** 84
Freischütz, Der (Weber), **19th:** 2396
FRELIMO, **20th:** 2515
Fremin, Jacques, **17th:** 909
Frémont, John C., **19th:** 80, 195, 427, 507, 831-835
French, Kristen, **Notor:** 93
French-American diplomacy, **18th:** 373, 413, 706, 1011
French-American Indian relations, **18th:** 801
French-American Treaties (1778), **18th:** 12, 152, 253, 373, 507, 851, 1012
French and Indian War (1754-1763), **18th:** 196, 1091; Louis-Antoine de Bougainville, 151; George II, 406; Louis-Joseph de Montcalm, 694; William Pitt the Elder, 787; Pontiac, 802; James Wolfe, 1105
French-Austrian conflicts, **18th:** 330, 658, 881
French-British conflicts, **18th:** 39, 136, 246, 311, 384, 406, 510, 661, 693, 786, 790, 851, 881, 984; North American colonies, 801
French-British diplomacy, **18th:** 151, 939
French Canada, **18th:** 38-42, 507, 692-695, 1105

French-Canadians, **17th:** 76; **19th:** rights of, 124
French Constitution. *See* Constitution, French
French Equatorial Africa, **20th:** 1087
French India, **18th:** 311-313
French Indochina War (1858-1863), **19th:** 2311
French Indochina War (1946-1954). *See* Indochinese War, First
French-Irish conflicts, **18th:** 983
French-Ottoman relations, **18th:** 640
French-papal conflict, **18th:** 794
French Reformed Church. *See* Huguenots
French Republic, **18th:** 619, 918
French Resistance, **20th:** 1153, 1428, 2286, 2769
French Revolution (1789-1799), **18th:** Jean-Sylvain Bailly, 77-79; Edmund Burke, 176; Lazare Carnot, 200-202; Marquis de Condorcet, 267-269; Georges Danton, 289-292; George III, 410; William Godwin, 425; Paul-Henri-Dietrich d'Holbach, 503; Louis XVI, 618-620; Jean-Paul Marat, 648-651; Marie-Antoinette, 657-660; comte de Mirabeau, 679-682; Jacques Necker, 728; duc d'Orléans, 751-754; Thomas Paine, 760; William Pitt the Younger, 790; Joseph Priestley, 812; Robespierre, 844-847; Louis de Saint-Just, 877-880; Emmanuel-Joseph Sieyès, 916-919; Madame de Staël, 929; **19th:** 396, 475, 608, 705; Joséphine, 1241; William Wordsworth on, 2464
French Revolution, The (Blake), **18th:** 122
French Revolution, The (Carlyle), **19th:** 416
French-Russian conflicts, **18th:** 214, 570
French-Spanish alliance, **18th:** 227
French Sudan, **20th:** 1087
Frente Farabundo Martí para la Liberación Nacional, **20th:** 122, 1041
Frente Sandinista de Liberación Nacional. *See* Sandinista National Liberation Front
Frere, Henry Bartle, **19th:** 451
Frescobaldi, Girolamo, **Ren:** 364; **17th:** 295-297
Frescoes, **MA:** 421, 701
Fresnel, Augustin, **19th:** 1016
Freud, Sigmund, **20th:** 33, 392, 513, 515, 1323-1326, 1624, 2063
Frey, Amber, **Notor:** 829-830
Freydal (Maximilian), **Ren:** 648
Freyssinet, Eugène, **20th:** 1326-1328
Friars, Minor, Order of. *See* Franciscans
Frick, Henry Clay, **19th:** 420; **20th:** 1521; **Notor:** 425
Friedan, Betty, **20th:** 1329-1332
Friedjung, Heinrich, **20th:** 2641
Friedland, Battle of (1807), **19th:** 1667
Friedlander, Lee, **20th:** 116
Friedman, Alice "Litzi," **Notor:** 836
Friedman, Esther Pauline. *See* Landers, Ann
Friedman, Milton, **20th:** 1332-1335
Friedman, Pauline Esther. *See* Van Buren, Abigail
Friedman, Rose, **20th:** 1334
Friedrich III. *See* Frederick III (1415-1493; Holy Roman Emperor)
Friedrich Froebel's Pedagogics of the Kindergarten (Froebel), **19th:** 838
Friedrich Wilhelm von Hohenzollern, Kurfürst von Brandenburg. *See* Frederick William, the Great Elector
Friendly, Fred, **20th:** 2880
Friends, Society of. *See* Quakers and Quakerism
Friends of the Manifesto and of Liberty, **20th:** 8
Friendship Treaty (1939), **20th:** 3607
Frieze of Life, The (Munch), **20th:** 2871
Frigidus River, Battle of the (394), **Anc:** 824, 871
Frisch, Karl von, **20th:** 1335-1338
Frisch, Max, **20th:** 1338-1341
Frisch, Otto, **20th:** 1237
Frisians, **MA:** 184, 251
Frith, Mary. *See* Cutpurse, Moll
Fritigern, **Anc:** 911
Fritzius, Joachim, **17th:** 281
Froben, Johann, **Ren:** 453, 758
Frobenius, Leo, **20th:** 1341-1344
Frobenius Institute, **20th:** 1343
Frobisher, Sir Martin, **Ren:** 276, 279, 352-355, 522
Froebel, Friedrich, **19th:** 835-839, 1762
Frogs, The. See *Batrachoi*
Fröhliche Wissenschaft, Die. See *Joyful Wisdom, The*
Froissart (Elgar), **20th:** 1133
Froissart, Jean, **MA:** 392-396
Fröken Julie. See *Miss Julie*
From Man to Man (Schreiner), **19th:** 2024
From Memories of Childhood (Mussorgsky), **19th:** 1627
From That Place and Time (Dawidowicz), **20th:** 923
From the Bohemian Forest (Dvořák), **19th:** 713
From the Diary of a Snail (Grass), **20th:** 1574
From the Earth to the Moon (Verne), **19th:** 2357
From the House of the Dead (Janáček), **20th:** 1991
From the Life of the Marionettes (film), **20th:** 318

From the Other Shore (Herzen), **19th:** 1086
From U-Boat to Pulpit (Niemöller), **20th:** 2972
Fromm, Erich, **20th:** 1345-1348
Fromme, Lynette, **Notor:** 377-379
Fromme, Squeaky. *See* Fromme, Lynette
Fronde, Wars of the (1648-1653), **17th:** 19, 22, 159, 180, 185, 212, 477, 487, 521, 549, 554, 622, 661, 781, 821, 829, 933, 946
Front de Libération Nationale, **20th:** 1213
Front for National Salvation, **20th:** 2883
Frontenac, comte de, **17th:** 433, 490, 500, 603
Frontier in American History, The (Turner), **20th:** 4117
Frontier thesis, **20th:** 4117
Frontiero v. Richardson (1973), **20th:** 582
Frost, Elihu B., **19th:** 1114
Frost, F. S., **19th:** 232
Frost, Robert, **20th:** 1348-1351
Frottage, **20th:** 1177
Fruit Dish and Glass (Braque), **20th:** 495
Fruitfulness (Zola), **19th:** 2491
Fruitlands, **19th:** 40, 42
Fruits of Philosophy (Knowlton), **19th:** 212
Fruits of the Earth (Gide), **20th:** 1478
Frumentius, **Anc:** 333
Fry, Elizabeth, **19th:** 839-841
Fry, Roger, **20th:** 1351-1354, 2818
Fryer, Pauline C. *See* Cushman, Pauline
Frykowski, Wojciech, **Notor:** 690
FSLN. *See* Sandinista National Liberation Front
Fu (poetic form), **Anc:** 149, 785; **MA:** 324, 809
Fu Mattia Pascal, Il. See *Late Mattia Pascal, The*
"Fu of the Homeward Road" (Xie Lingyun), **Anc:** 977
Fuʾād I, **20th:** 1215, 4440
Fualaau, Vili, **Notor:** 640
Fuchs, Arved, **20th:** 2720
Fuchs, Klaus, **20th:** 3066; **Notor:** 379-380, 382
Fuchs, Leonhard, **Ren:** 356-358
Fuchs, Vivian, **20th:** 1805
Fuenteovejuna. See *Sheep-Well, The*
Fuentes de Oñoro, Battle of (1811), **19th:** 2410
Fuertes, Dolores Adios. *See* Menken, Adah Isaacs
Fugard, Athol, **20th:** 1354-1358
Fugate, Caril Ann, **Notor:** 993, 1109
Fugitive Slave Law (1850), **19th:** 80, 320, 471, 877, 2227
Fuglinn í fjörunni. See *Salka Valka*
Fuhrman, Mark, **Notor:** 960
Fujian, **17th:** 1001
Fujigawa, Battle of (1180), **MA:** 721
Fujimori, Alberto, **20th:** 1359-1361, 3196; **Notor:** 382-383
Fujisawa, Takeo, **20th:** 1860
Fujiwara clan, **MA:** 623, 758, 990
Fujiwara Kaneie, **MA:** 396
Fujiwara Kanezane, **MA:** 723
Fujiwara Korechika, **MA:** 396
Fujiwara Michinaga, **MA:** 396-399, 581, 738
Fujiwara Michitaka, **MA:** 931
Fujiwara Nakamaro, **MA:** 624
Fujiwara regents, **MA:** 398
Fujiwara Yasuhira, **MA:** 723
Fujiwara Yorimichi, **MA:** 397, 582
Fujiyama, Aiichiro, **20th:** 3646
Fukai kawa. See *Deep River*
Fukien. *See* Fujian
Fulbert of Chartres, Saint, **MA:** 399-401
Fulin. *See* Shunzhi
Fulk V, **MA:** 716
Full Employment Act of 1946, **20th:** 4208
Full Employment in a Free Society (Beveridge), **20th:** 354
Fuller, Alvan T., **Notor:** 925, 1057-1058
Fuller, Loie, **20th:** 1361-1364
Fuller, Margaret, **19th:** 841-845, 968, 1761
Fuller, R. Buckminster, **20th:** 1364-1367
Fulton, John, **20th:** 1108
Fulton, Robert, **18th:** 355; **19th:** 845-848
Fulton Sheen Program, The (television program), **20th:** 3723
Fulvia, **Notor:** 384-385
Fulvius, Gnaeus, **Anc:** 383
Fulvius Nobilior, **Anc:** 301
Fumifugium (Evelyn), **17th:** 257
Fun of It, The (Earhart), **20th:** 1076
Functionalism, **20th:** 297
Fund for the Republic, **20th:** 1960
Fundament des christelycken leers, Dat. See *Foundation of Plain Instruction, A*
Fundamenta astronomiae (Bessel), **19th:** 215
Fundamenta botanica (Linnaeus), **18th:** 606
Fundamenta chymiae dogmaticae et experimentalis (Stahl), **18th:** 935
Fundamental Concepts of Sociology. See *Community and Society*
Fundamental Orders of Connecticut, **17th:** 387, 568
Fundamental Principles of the Sociology of Law (Ehrlich), **20th:** 1114
Fundamental Problems of Philosophy (Nishida), **20th:** 2982
Funeral, The (Steele), **18th:** 941
Funeral of the Virgin (Carracci), **Ren:** 176
Funeral Oration for Henrietta of England (Bossuet), **17th:** 71

"Funeral Poem on the Death of C. E., an Infant of Twelve Months, A" (Wheatley), **18th:** 1072
Funeral Rites (Genet), **20th:** 1446
Funerall Poem, A (Tourneur), **17th:** 928
Funerary complexes, Egyptian, **Anc:** 571
Funny Girl (Styne and Merrill), **20th:** 3892
Fur trade, **18th:** 629, 974
Fur Traders Descending the Missouri (Bingham), **19th:** 235
Furetière, Antoine, **17th:** 480
Furman v. Georgia (1972), **20th:** 582
Furness, Frank, **19th:** 2198
Furniture, design of, **20th:** 2, 2732
Fürsorgliche Belagerung. See *Safety Net, The*
Further Account of the Province of Pennsylvania and Its Improvements, A (Penn), **17th:** 726
Further Adventures (Defoe), **18th:** 299
Further Adventures of Nils, The (Lagerlöf), **20th:** 2235
Further Range, A (Frost), **20th:** 1350
Fury (film), **20th:** 2254
Fūshikaden (Zeami), **MA:** 1153
Fuṣūs al-ḥikam. See *Bezels of Wisdom, The*
Futa-Toro, **19th:** 756
Fūten rōjin nikki. See *Diary of a Mad Old Man*
Futūhāt al-Makkīyah, al- (Ibn al-ʿArabī), **MA:** 526
Future of Germany, The (Jaspers), **20th:** 1998
Future of Mankind, The (Jaspers), **20th:** 1998
Future of Science, The (Renan), **19th:** 1885
Future of War, in Its Technical, Economic, and Political Relations, The (Bloch), **19th:** 2207
Futurism, **20th:** 403, 1051, 2548, 2659
Fyodor I, **Ren:** 387; **17th:** 683, 794, 943; **Notor:** 385-386
Fyodor II, **17th:** 865
Fyodor III, **Notor:** 514
Fyodor Ivanovich. *See* Fyodor I

G

Gabars, **Anc:** 995
Gabbard Shoal, Battle of the (1653), **17th:** 57, 931
Gable, Clark, **20th:** 1368-1370, 1724
Gabriel (Pushkin), **19th:** 1849
Gabriel, Ange-Jacques, **18th:** 799
Gabrieli, Andrea, **Ren:** 359-361, 362
Gabrieli, Giovanni, **Ren:** 362-364, 541; **17th:** 825
Gabrielle de Belle Isle (Dumas), **19th:** 696
Gacy, John Wayne, **Notor:** 387-388, 879
Gaddafi, Muʿammar al. *See* Qaddafi, Muammar al-
Gadsden, James, **19th:** 849-851
Gadsden Purchase, **19th:** 612, 850, 1991
Gaelic Nationalist Revival, **20th:** 3034
Gaffurio, Franchino, **Ren:** 517
Gagarin, Yuri, **20th:** 1370-1373, 2194, 3979
Gage, George. *See* Moran, Bugs
Gage, Matilda Joslyn, **19th:** 852-854
Gage, Thomas, **18th:** 16, 198, 384-387, 460, 511; **Notor:** 211
Gagliano, Marco da, **17th:** 297
Gagnan, Émile, **20th:** 850
Gaillardet, Frédéric, **19th:** 696
Gainsborough, Thomas, **18th:** 387-391, 857, 862
Gaiseric. *See* Genseric
Gaitskell, Hugh, **20th:** 350
Gakureki muyouron (Morita), **20th:** 2833
Galante, Carmine, **Notor:** 389-390
Galatea (Cervantes), **Ren:** 207
Galaxies, study of, **20th:** 1913, 3059
Galbraith, John Kenneth, **20th:** 1374-1376
Gale, Leonard Dunnell, **19th:** 1611
Gale, William Potter, **Notor:** 157
Galen, **Anc:** 116, 278, 289, 313, 348-351; **MA:** 67
Galerius, **Anc:** 239, 281; **Notor:** 390-392
Galgacus. *See* Calgacus
Galigai, Leonora, **17th:** 598
Galilei, Maria Celeste. *See* Maria Celeste
Galilei, Virginia. *See* Maria Celeste
Galileo, **Anc:** 83; **17th:** 298-301; and Giovanni Alfonso Borelli, 66; influence on Robert Boyle, 78; and Tommaso Campanella, 125; and René Descartes, 227; and Pierre Gassendi, 305; and Artemisia Gentileschi, 307; and William Harvey, 356; and Thomas Hobbes, 379; and Christiaan Huygens, 397; and Johannes Kepler, 459; tutor to Cosimo II de' Medici, 626; and Marin Mersenne, 630; and John Milton, 640; and Sir Isaac Newton, 680; censured by Pope Paul V, 721; and Nicolas-Claude Fabri de Peiresc, 722; and observations of planetary motion, 349; and Santorio Santorio, 811; and Nicolaus Steno, 881; observations of sunspots, 260; and telescopes, 539; and Evangelista Torricelli, 921; and Pope Urban VIII, 936
Gallagher, Michael, **Notor:** 239
Gallant, Mavis, **20th:** 1377-1378
Gallatin, Albert, **19th:** 854-857
Gallaudet, Thomas, **19th:** 135
Gallery of Illustrious Americans (Brady), **19th:** 293

Gallia (Gounod), **19th:** 954
Gallic Wars (58-52 B.C.E.), **Anc:** 173, 935
Gallic Wars, The. See *Comentarii de bello Gallico*
Gallican Liberties, Declaration of (1682), **17th:** 406
Gallicanus (Hrosvitha), **MA:** 517
Gallienne, Eva Le. *See* Le Gallienne, Eva
Gallo, Joe, **Notor:** 224, 392-393, 864
Gallo, Larry, **Notor:** 224
Gallopin' Gaucho (animated film), **20th:** 1007
Gallus, Didius, **Anc:** 163
Gallus, Gaius Aelius, **Anc:** 827
Galois, Évariste, **19th:** 857-859, 885
Galsworthy, John, **20th:** 826
Galt, Eric S. *See* Ray, James Earl
Galtieri, Leopoldo, **Notor:** 394-395
Galton, Francis, **19th:** 860-863
Galvani, Luigi, **18th:** 391-394
Galvanometers, **20th:** 1123
Gálvez, José de, **18th:** 394-396
Gama, Vasco da, **Ren:** 22, 168, 288, 365-368, 605
Gambetta, Léon, **19th:** 864-867, 2266
Gambino, Carlo, **Notor:** 23, 183, 224, 396-397, 408, 431, 659, 709
Gambling, baseball, **20th:** 3527
Game at Chess, A (Middleton), **17th:** 638
Game of Logic, The (Carroll), **19th:** 425
Game theory, **20th:** 2946
Gamow, George, **20th:** 1379-1381, 2339, 3969
Gance, Abel, **20th:** 1382-1384
Gandersheim, **MA:** 516
Gandhara School, **Anc:** 500
Gandhi, Indira, **20th:** 1385-1388, 2933; **Notor:** 962-963
Gandhi, Mohandas K. (Mahatma), **20th:** 222, 462, 1388-1392, 2003, 3099, 3135; Civil Rights movement, 2147; nonviolence campaign, 2901, 2930; **Notor:** 417
Gandhi, Rajiv, **20th:** 2932; **Notor:** 882, 963
Gandil, Chick, **Notor:** 522
Gang of Four, **20th:** 969, 1908, 2409
Gangsters, United States, **20th:** 1867. *See also* Category Index
Ganjōjuin, **MA:** 1040
Gannys, **Anc:** 488
Gao, Africa, **Ren:** 556, 597
Gao Xianzhi, **MA:** 79
Gaols Act of 1823, **19th:** 840
Gaon of Vilna. *See* Elijah ben Solomon
Gaozong (Southern Song emperor), **MA:** 677, 1146
Gaozong (Tang emperor), **MA:** 79, 1127, 1138, 1141
Gaozu (Tang emperor), **MA:** 993, 1127, 1140
Garbo, Greta, **20th:** 1368, 1392-1395
Garcia, Ramon. *See* Hanssen, Robert Philip
García Lorca, Federico, **20th:** 905, 1395-1397, 2937
García Márquez, Gabriel, **20th:** 1398-1402
Garden of Cyrus, The (Browne), **17th:** 95
Garden of Earthly Delights, The (Bosch), **Ren:** 120
Garden of Epicurus, The (France), **19th:** 816
Gardener's Dog, The (Lope de Vega), **17th:** 950
Gardens, **18th:** Austria, 495; botanical, 81, 171; England, 166
Gardiner, Stephen, **Ren:** 368-372, 898
Gardner, Alexander, **19th:** 294
Gardner, Erle Stanley, **20th:** 1403-1405
Gardner, Gerald Brosseau, **Notor:** 215-216
Gardner, Isabella Stewart, **20th:** 1406-1409
Gardoquí, Diego, **18th:** 525
Garfield, James A., **19th:** 79, 81, 252, 867-871; and Rutherford B. Hayes, 1063; **Notor:** 19, 439
Garfield, John, **Notor:** 974
Gargantua and Pantagruel (Rabelais), **Ren:** 810
Garibaldi, Giuseppe, **19th:** 284, 445, 696-697, 871-874, 1533, 1803
Garland, Judy, **20th:** 157, 1368, 1409-1412, 1464, 2096
Garneau, Marc, **20th:** 1412-1414
Garner, John Nance, **20th:** 3398
Garnered Sheaves from the Writings of A. D. Richardson (Richardson), **19th:** 1904
Garnier, Tony, **20th:** 1414-1417
Garrett, Danny, **Notor:** 1044
Garrett, Millicent. *See* Fawcett, Dame Millicent Garrett
Garrett, Thomas, **19th:** 2313
Garrick, David, **18th:** 1, 177, 397-400, 435, 912, 1102
Garrick Gaieties, The (Blitzstein et al.), **20th:** 1692
Garrison, Jim (district attorney), **Notor:** 942
Garrison, Jimmy (musician), **20th:** 815
Garrison, William Lloyd, **19th:** 471, 482, 685, 796, 874-878, 1617, 1786, 2327
Garter, Order of the, **MA:** 350
Garthauszien, Louis-Dominique. *See* Cartouche
Garvey, Marcus, **20th:** 180, 753, 1048, 1417-1420, 3371
Garzoni, Giovanna, **17th:** 302-304
Gascoyne-Cecil, Robert Arthur Talbot. *See* Salisbury, third marquis of
Gases, study of, **18th:** 580, 613
Gaslight (film), **20th:** 322
Gasmotorenfabrik Deutz, **19th:** 1715
Gassed (Sargent), **19th:** 1998
Gassendi, Pierre, **17th:** 211, 304-306, 389, 630, 723

Gasset, José Ortega y. *See* Ortega y Gasset, José
Gaston (brother of Louis XIII), **17th:** 551
Gaston de Blondeville (Radcliffe), **18th:** 823
Gate Fulford, Battle of (1066), **MA:** 458
Gate of the Kiss (Brancusi), **20th:** 480
Gates, The (Rukeyser), **20th:** 3557
Gates, Bill, **20th:** 1421-1423
Gates, Horatio, **Notor:** 1103
Gates of Hell, The (Rodin), **19th:** 1925
Gathas (Zoroaster), **Anc:** 993
Gather Together in My Name (Angelou), **20th:** 98
Gatti, Bernardino, **Ren:** 46
Gattopardo, Il. See *Leopard, The*
Gaude gloriosa Dei Mater (Tallis), **Ren:** 919
Gaudí, Antonio, **20th:** 1423-1426
Gaugamela, Battle of (331 B.C.E.), **Anc:** 40
Gauguin, Paul, **19th:** 879-882, 934, 2298; **20th:** 493, 954, 972
Gaul, **Anc:** 20, 99, 140, 163, 173, 189, 195, 268, 352, 443, 683, 699, 716, 819, 825, 869, 935, 947; **MA:** Christianity in, 288
Gaulard, Lucien, **19th:** 2417
Gaulle, Charles de, **20th:** 9, 1087, 1427-1430, 2578, 2699, 2769; June 18 Appeal, 1429; Georges Pompidou, 3305; **Notor:** 69, 263, 609
Gauls. *See* Celts
Gauss, Carl Friedrich, **Anc:** 83; **19th:** 883-886, 902, 1404
Gauthe, Gilbert, **Notor:** 397-398
Gauthier-Villars, Henri, **20th:** 804
Gautier, Théophile, **19th:** 153; **Notor:** 1068
Gaveston, Piers, **MA:** 347, 552
Gavriiliada. See *Gabriel*
Gay, John, **18th:** 1; **Notor:** 944, 1103
Gay Divorcee, The (film), **20th:** 156, 3309
Gay-Lussac, Joseph-Louis, **19th:** 102, 886-890
Gay-Lussac's law, **19th:** 887
Gaza, Battle of (312 B.C.E.), **Anc:** 63
Gdańsk Lenin Shipyard strike (1980), **20th:** 4191
Gebhard, Paul, **20th:** 2161
Gebot und die Ordnungen, Das. See *Divine Imperative, The*
Gebre Mesqal. *See* Lalibela
Geburt der Tragödie aus dem Geiste der Musik, Die. See *Birth of Tragedy Out of the Spirit of Music, The*
Gedaliah, **Anc:** 454
Gedanken über die Nachahmung der griechischen Werke . . . . See *Reflections on the Paintings and Sculpture of the Greeks*
Geddes, Norman Bel, **20th:** 1431-1434
Gehrig, Lou, **20th:** 1434-1437
Gehry, Frank, **20th:** 1438-1440
Geiger, Hans, **20th:** 442, 714, 1440-1442
Geiger, Rudolf, **20th:** 1443-1445
Geiger counter, **20th:** 1441
Geiger-Nuttall law, **20th:** 1441
Gein, Ed, **Notor:** 399-400
Geisel, Theodor Seuss. *See* Seuss, Dr.
Geist der Neuzeit (Tönnies), **20th:** 4046
Geistliche Chormusik (Schütz), **17th:** 827
Gellée, Claude. *See* Claude Lorrain
Gelli, Licio, **Notor:** 170
Gellius, Aulus, **Anc:** 939
Gelosi, **Ren:** 42
Gembloux, Battle of (1577), **Ren:** 322
Gemeinschaft und Gesellschaft. See *Community and Society*
Gemmei, **MA:** 623
Gempei War (1180-1185), **MA:** 721, 992
Gender reassignment, **20th:** 2054
Gendret, Father Antoine de, **17th:** 76
Gene theory, **20th:** 2861
Genealogia deorum gentilium (Boccaccio), **MA:** 171
Genealogy, **Anc:** epics and, 497; **Ren:** Danish noble houses, 127
General, The (film), **20th:** 2091
General Education Board, **20th:** 1257
General Electric Company, **19th:** 732, 2158
General Federation of Women's Clubs. *See* American Association for the Advancement of Women
General German Women's Association, **19th:** 1307
General German Workers' Association, **19th:** 1323, 1370
General History of Music, A (Burney), **18th:** 178
General History of the Things of New Spain. See *Florentine Codex*
General Idea of the Revolution in the Nineteenth Century, The (Proudhon), **19th:** 1836
General in His Labyrinth, The (García Márquez), **20th:** 1400
General Investigations of Curved Surfaces (Gauss), **19th:** 884
General Line, The (film), **20th:** 1130
General Motors, **20th:** 3210; sit-down strike (1937), 3425; strike (1945-1946), 3425; Toyota, 4064
General Psychopathology (Jasper), **20th:** 1997
General Regulations for the Army (Scott), **19th:** 2052
General strike, Great Britain (1926), **20th:** 206, 357, 416, 2270, 3411
General System of Nature, A (Linnaeus), **18th:** 605
General Theory of Employment, Interest, and Money, The (Keynes), **20th:** 1374, 2121

Generall Historie of Virginia, New-England, and the Summer Isles, The (Smith), **17th:** 863-864
Generation of 1837, **19th:** 2000
Generelle Morphologie der Organismen (Haeckel), **19th:** 1004
Genet, Jean, **20th:** 1445-1448
Genetics, **19th:** 1542. *See also* Category Index
Geneva, Treaty of (1864), **19th:** 146
Geneva Accords (1954), **20th:** 229, 1055, 1836, 2951, 2954
Geneva Accords (1962), **20th:** 1686
Geneva Conventions, **19th:** 699
Geneva Protocol, **20th:** 301
Geneva Tribunal of Arbitration on the Alabama Claims, **19th:** 580
Geneviève de Brabant (Offenbach), **19th:** 1701
Gengangere. See *Ghosts*
Genghis Khan, **MA:** 402-405, 626, 677, 954; **Notor:** 400-402
Génie du Christianisme, Le. See *Genius of Christianity, The*
"Genius," The (Dreiser), **20th:** 1034
Genius des Krieges und der deutsche Krieg, Der (Scheler), **20th:** 3656
Genius Loves Company (Charles), **20th:** 736
Genius of Christianity, The (Chateaubriand), **19th:** 475
Genius of Ray Charles, The (Charles), **20th:** 735
Genius of Universal Emancipation, **19th:** 875
Genius + Soul = Jazz (Charles), **20th:** 735
Genji. *See* Minamoto clan
Genji monogatari. See *Tale of Genji, The*
Genocide, **18th:** of American Indians, 803; **20th:** Armenian, 2352
Genomics, **20th:** 3623
Genovese, Vito, **Notor:** 7, 23, 237, 389, 396, 402-404, 407, 709
Genoveva (Schumann), **19th:** 2033
Genre painting, **18th:** 223-226, 390, 1051
Genroku Era (1688-1704), **17th:** 376
Genseric, **Anc:** 139, 351-354; **MA:** 783
Gensfleisch zur Laden, Johannes. *See* Gutenberg, Johann
Genshō, **MA:** 623
Gentile, Giovanni, **20th:** 1448-1451
Gentiles, conversions of, **Anc:** 626
Gentileschi, Artemisia, **17th:** 307-309
Gentili, Alberico, **Ren:** 372-374
Gentle Art of Making Enemies, The (Whistler), **19th:** 2420
Gentleman Jack. *See* Diamond, Legs; Sheppard, Jack
Gentleman Pirate. *See* Bonnet, Stede
Gentleman Usher, The (Chapman), **Ren:** 215
Gentleman's Agreement (film), **20th:** 3182
Gentlemen Prefer Blondes (film), **20th:** 2430, 2798
Genzinger, Maria Anna von, **18th:** 477
Geocentrism, **Anc:** 78, 418, 693, 712, 829
Geodesic domes, **20th:** 1365
Geodesy, **19th:** 884
Geoffrey of Anjou, **MA:** 961, 1117
Geoffrey of Monmouth, **MA:** 405-408
Geoffroy Saint-Hilaire, Étienne, **19th:** 586
Geographer, The (Vermeer), **17th:** 958
Geōgraphica (Strabo), **Anc:** 417, 550, 579, 827
Geographika (Eratosthenes), **Anc:** 315
Geōgraphikē hyphēgēsis (Ptolemy), **Anc:** 713
Geography, **Anc:** Alexandrian, 417; Hellenic, 713; Strabo and, 828; **MA:** Iraq, 618; Mediterranean, 158; Muslim, 164, 529, 704, 1143; Sicily, 539; **17th:** Japan, 447; Netherlands, 907; Ottoman Empire, 455; **19th:** 1152; England, 2122. *See also* Category Index
Geography and Plays (Stein), **20th:** 3847
Geological Evidences of the Antiquity of Man, The (Lyell), **19th:** 1426
Geological Studies (Agassiz), **19th:** 30
Geology, **17th:** England, 106; Italy, 882; **18th:** 172, 579; **19th:** 604; uniformitarianism, 1424
Geometria organica (Maclaurin), **18th:** 633
Geometriae Pars Universalis (Gregory), **17th:** 319
Geometrical Constructions with a Ruler, Given a Fixed Circle with Its Center (Steiner), **19th:** 2155
Géométrie descriptive. See *Elementary Treatise on Descriptive Geometry, An*
Geometriya (Lobachevsky), **19th:** 1404
Geometry, **Anc:** Euclid and, 317; Greek, 76, 81, 606; music and, 98; projective, 79; Pythagoras and, 725; Thales and, 858; **MA:** 864, 985; India, 109; **17th:** England, 970; France, 227, 272; Italy, 330, 921; Scotland, 319; Switzerland, 48; **19th:** algebraic, 1818; projective, 2154; Russia, 1404; **20th:** 1800. *See also* Agnesi, Maria Gaetana; Carnot, Lazare;

Lagrange, Joseph-Louis; Maclaurin, Colin; Monge, Gaspard
Geopolitics, **20th:** 2519
George (duke of Clarence), **Ren:** 828
George I (1660-1727; king of Great Britain), **17th:** 255; **18th:** 48, 400-403, 938
George I (1845-1913; king of Greece), **20th:** 4157
George II (1683-1760; king of Great Britain), **18th:** 401, 403-407, 772, 881; Burma, 30; marriage to Caroline, 203
George II (1890-1947; king of Greece), **20th:** 4158; **Notor:** 724
George III (1738-1820; king of Great Britain), **18th:** 235, 365, 408-412, 739, 789; Samuel Adams, 19; Edmund Burke, 174; land grants in early America, 36; Qianlong, 817; Benjamin West, 1069; William Wilberforce, 1080; John Wilkes, 1083; **19th:** 890, 978, 2446
George IV (1762-1830; king of Great Britain), **18th:** 359; **19th:** 313, 378, 404, 518, 890-894, 979, 1398
George V (1865-1936; king of Great Britain), **20th:** 1451-1454
George VI (1895-1952; king of Great Britain), **20th:** 207, 1454-1458, 4370
George, David Lloyd. *See* Lloyd George, David
George, Henry, **19th:** 894-897
George Chalmers of Pittencrieff (Raeburn), **19th:** 1852
George Fox Digg'd Out of His Burrows (Williams), **17th:** 984
George's Mother (Crane), **19th:** 563
Georgia (Caucasus), **MA:** 72, 998. *See also* Geographical Index
Georgia colony (North America), **18th:** 626, 742, 1064, 1074
Georgian Bowood, **19th:** 143
Georgian Rose Revolution of 2003, **20th:** 3796
Georgics (Vergil), **Anc:** 528, 929, 938
Georgius Florentius. *See* Gregory of Tours
Gepid-Lombard conflict, **MA:** 46
Gepids, **MA:** 45
Gerald of Windsor, **MA:** 753
Gérard, Balthasar, **Notor:** 404-405
Gerbert d'Aurillac. *See* Sylvester II
Gerhard, Wolfgang. *See* Mengele, Josef
Géricault, Théodore, **19th:** 635, 898-901
Germ-Plasm, The (Weismann), **19th:** 2408
Germain. *See* Bastien-Thiry, Jean-Marie
Germain, Sophie, **19th:** 901-904
Germaine de Staël. *See* Staël, Madame de
German Christian Movement, **20th:** 419
German Codification of 1900, **20th:** 1114
German Empire, **19th:** 223, 238
German Ideology, The (Marx), **19th:** 1509
German National Theater, **18th:** 600
German Popular Stories. See *Grimm's Fairy Tales*
German Requiem, Op. 45 (Brahms), **19th:** 297
German Socialist Workers Party, **20th:** 490
German Sociological Society, **20th:** 4046
German unification, **19th:** 222, 238, 751, 1641, 2152
Germania. See *De origine et situ Germanorum*
Germanic tribes, **MA:** 783
Germanicus Caesar, **Anc:** 23, 72, 100, 176, 217, 510
Germanicus, Gaius Caesar. *See* Caligula
Germans, **Anc:** 838; Britons and, 394; Rome and, 147, 351; Tacitus's description, 99
Germany, **MA:** anarchistic period in, 389; asceticism, 1022; chivalry, 1123; Christianity, 184, 226; feudalism, 384, 423, 1123; founding of, 665; Franconian/Salian kings, 499; Habsburg monarchy, 906; historiography, 516; Hohenstaufen kings, 387; Hohenstaufens, 390; Holy Roman Empire and, 1089; Jews, 408; monasticism, 1024; mysticism, 512, 708; philosophy, 778; poetry, 423, 463, 1075-1076, 1125; Saxon kings, 488, 807; Saxons, 497; science, 43; theater, 513; theology, 43; trade, 475; twelfth century, 384; unification of, 476, 487, 663, 805, 904; as universal empire, 243; **20th:** reunification of (1990), 2183. *See also* Geographical Index
Germany (Heine), **19th:** 1071
Germany (Staël), **18th:** 931
Germinal (Zola), **19th:** 2490
Geronimo, **19th:** 904-907; **Notor:** 27
Gerousia, the, **Anc:** 228
Geroy nashego vremeni. See *Hero of Our Time, A*
Gerpla. See *Happy Warriors, The*
Gerry, Elbridge, **18th:** 412-414
Gersaint's Shopsign (Watteau), **18th:** 1053
Gershom ben Judah, **MA:** 408-410
Gershwin, George, **20th:** 156, 1458-1462
Gershwin, Ira, **20th:** 156, 1458, 1462-1464, 4275
Gersonides. *See* Levi ben Gershom

Gertrud (film), **20th:** 1039
Gerusalemme conquistata. See *Jerusalem Conquered*
Gerusalemme liberata. See *Jerusalem Delivered*
Gesamtausgabe (Burckhardt), **19th:** 356
Gesang der Jånglinde (Stockhausen), **20th:** 3874
Geschichte der Kunst des Alterthums. See *History of Ancient Art*
Geschichte der romanischen und germanischen Völker von 1494 bis 1514. See *History of the Latin and Teutonic Nations from 1494 to 1514*
Geschichte der synoptischen Tradition, Die. See *History of the Synoptic Tradition, The*
Geschichte des Fräuleins von Sternheim. See *Sternheim*
Geschichte des Pietismus (Ritschl), **19th:** 1920
Geschichte des römischen Rechts im Mittelalter. See *History of Roman Law During the Middle Ages, The*
Geschichte und Klassenbewusstein. See *History and Class Consciousness*
Geschichte und Kritik der Grundbegriffe der Gegenwart (Eucken), **20th:** 1186
Gesell, Arnold, **20th:** 1465-1467
Gesner, Conrad, **Ren:** 13, 357, 375-378
Gesta Danorum. See *History of the Danes, The*
Gesta Ottonis. See *Hrosvithae Liber terius*
Gestalt theory, **20th:** 1110, 1112, 4293
Get a Life (Gordimer), **20th:** 1536
Getica. See *Gothic History Jordanes, The*
Getty, J. Paul (1892-1976), **Notor:** 1075
Getty, J. Paul, II. *See* Getty, Sir John Paul
Getty, Sir John Paul (1932-2003), **20th:** 1468-1470
Getty Oil, **20th:** 1469
Gettysburg Address (Lincoln), **19th:** 1382-1383
Géza, **MA:** 637
Gezeichneten, Die. See *Love One Another*
Ghalib, al-, **Ren:** 860
Ghana, **20th:** independence of, 2990. *See also* Geographical Index
Gharbi, Gamil Rodrigue. *See* Lépine, Marc
Ghare-Baire. See *Home and the World, The*
Gharib, al-. *See* Zarqawi, Abu Musab al-
Ghazali, al-. *See* Ghazzālī, al-
Ghazals, **MA:** 451, 909, 917
Ghāzān, Maḥmūd, **MA:** 411-414, 674
Ghaznavid Dynasty, **MA:** 164, 683-684, 774; art, 685
Ghazzālī, al-, **MA:** 113, 127, 415-417, 593, 673
Ghazzati, Nathan, **17th:** 836
Ghent, Pacification of (1576), **Ren:** 995
Ghent, Treaty of (1814), **19th:** 21, 392, 855, 1587
Ghent Altarpiece, The (van Eycks), **MA:** 367
Gheorghiu-Dej, Gheorghe, **20th:** 705; **Notor:** 190
Ghibellines, **MA:** 239, 301, 546
Ghiberti, Lorenzo, **MA:** 206, 282, 320, 418-420, 566, 845; **Ren:** 18
Ghislieri, Antonio. *See* Pius V
Ghiyās-ud-Dīn Balban, **MA:** 39
Ghost Dance (1889-1890), **19th:** 1873, 2110
Ghost of Lucrece, The (Middleton), **17th:** 636
Ghosts, **Anc:** 616
Ghosts (Ibsen), **19th:** 1166
Ghotbzadeh, Sadeq, **20th:** 2126
G.I. Bill (1944), **20th:** 3490
Gia Long, **19th:** 907-909
Giacometti, Alberto, **20th:** 1470-1473
Giancana, Sam, **Notor:** 340, 405-407
Gianni Schicchi (Puccini), **20th:** 3348
Giant Steps (Coltrane), **20th:** 814
Giaour, The (Byron), **19th:** 380
Giap, Vo Nguyen. *See* Vo Nguyen Giap
Gibbon, Edward, **18th:** 415-418
Gibbon, John, **19th:** 568, 584
Gibbons, Grinling, **17th:** 996
Gibbons, James, **19th:** 910-912
Gibbons, Orlando, **Ren:** 149; **17th:** 309-311
Gibbons v. Ogden, **19th:** 1500, 2181
Gibbs, John, **19th:** 2417
Gibbs, Josiah Willard, **19th:** 913-916
Gibbs' Vector Analysis (Wilson, ed.), **19th:** 914
Giberti, Gian Matteo, **Ren:** 54
Gibraltar, Battle of (1607), **17th:** 930
Gibraltar, Siege of (1779-1783), **18th:** 508
Gibson, Althea, **20th:** 1474-1477
Gibson, William, **20th:** 3908
Gide, André, **20th:** 973, 1477-1480
Gideon v. Wainwright (1963), **20th:** 379, 4234
Gierek, Edward, **Notor:** 526
Gifford, John, **17th:** 100
Gift (Man Ray), **20th:** 2581
Gift, The (Nabokov), **20th:** 2894
Gift from the Sea, A (Lindbergh), **20th:** 2391
Gigante, Vincent, **Notor:** 238, 403, 407-408
Giganti della montagna, I. See *Mountain Giants, The*
Gigi (Colette), **20th:** 806, 1767
Gil Blas (Lesage), **18th:** 597
Gilbert, Adrian, **Ren:** 276
Gilbert, Elizabeth Rosana. *See* Montez, Lola

Gilbert, Sir Humphrey, **Ren:** 378-380, 396, 813
Gilbert, Marie Dolores Eliza Rosanna. *See* Montez, Lola
Gilbert, W. S., **19th:** 916-921
Gilbert, William, **Ren:** 381-383; **17th:** 335
Gilda (film), **20th:** 1732
Gilded Age, The (Twain), **19th:** 2330
Gilgamesh, **Anc:** 378, 914
Gillain, Marie Anne Victorine Boivin. *See* Boivin, Marie Anne Victorine
Gillars, Mildred, **Notor:** 409-410
Gilles (Watteau), **18th:** 1053
Gillespie, Dizzy, **20th:** 132, 814, 1480-1483, 3113
Gillis, Lester Joseph. *See* Nelson, Baby Face
Gilman, Charlotte Perkins, **20th:** 1484-1487
Gilmore, Gary, **Notor:** 411-412
Gilson, Étienne, **20th:** 1488-1492
Gin Act (1751), **18th:** 773
Ginsberg, Allen, **20th:** 2114
Ginsburg, Ruth, **20th:** 785
Gioacchino da Fiore. *See* Joachim of Fiore
Gioberti, Vincenzo, **19th:** 921-924, 1802
Giorgi III, **MA:** 998
Giorgi IV Lasha, **MA:** 999
Giorgione, **Ren:** 100, 383-386, 936
Giorno di regno, Un (Verdi), **19th:** 2351
Giotto, **MA:** 103, 282, 326, 366, 421-423, 696, 700, 798, 846, 848
Giovanna d' Arco (Verdi), **19th:** 2351
Giovanni di Fidanza. *See* Bonaventure, Saint
Giovanni Leone. *See* Leo Africanus
Giovanni's Room (Baldwin), **20th:** 201
Gipp, George, **20th:** 3482
Giraudoux, Jean, **20th:** 1492-1495
Giri (obligation), **18th:** 244
Girl Crazy (Gershwin and Gershwin), **20th:** 1463
Girl Friend, The (Rodgers and Hart), **20th:** 1692
Girl from Samos, The. See *Samia*
Girl Guides, **19th:** 112; **20th:** 2442
Girl Like I, A (Loos), **20th:** 2430
Girl Scouts of the United States of America, **20th:** 2442
Girl Who Was Shorn, The. See *Perikeiromenē*
Girl with a Ball (Kupka), **20th:** 2211
Girl with Red Hair, The (Toulouse-Lautrec), **19th:** 2289
Girodias, Maurice, **Notor:** 983
Girondin-Jacobin conflict, **18th:** 649, 845
Girondins, **18th:** 267, 291, 649, 753, 760, 845, 878
Girton College, **19th:** 264
Giscard d'Estaing, Valéry, **Notor:** 114
Giselbert of Lotharingia, **MA:** 805
Giselle (ballet), **19th:** 639; **20th:** 1269, 3167
Gish, Lillian, **20th:** 1496-1498, 1594
Gist, George. *See* Sequoyah
Gitanjali (Song Offerings) (Tagore), **20th:** 3934
Giuliani, Rudolph, **Notor:** 732
Giuliano, Salvatore, **Notor:** 413-414
Giulietta degli spiriti. See *Juliet of the Spirits*
Giustiniani, Vincenzo, **Ren:** 171
Giusto, Paolo, **Ren:** 362
Givenchy, Hubert de, **20th:** 1767
Glaber, Clodius, **Anc:** 819
Gladiator, The (Bird), **19th:** 791
Gladiator, The (Sousa), **20th:** 3798
Gladiators, **Anc:** 818
Gladstone, William Ewart, **19th:** 14, 288, 304, 461, 667, 794, 924-928, 950, 1025, 1749, 2360; Sir Robert Peel, 1770; Salisbury, 1978; **20th:** 149, 209, 2267
Glagolitic Mass (Janáček), **20th:** 1991
Glanville, Ranulf de, **MA:** 193
Glasgow, James. *See* Farragut, David G.
Glasgow, Scotland, **18th:** 1048
Glashow, Sheldon, **20th:** 4277
Glasnost, **20th:** 1531
Glasperlenspiel, Das. See *Magister Ludi*
Glass, Philip, **20th:** 39
Glass Bead Game, The. See *Magister Ludi*
Glass Menagerie, The (Williams), **20th:** 4352
Glaucus Potnieus (Aeschylus), **Anc:** 8
Glazunov, Aleksandr, **19th:** 282
Gleanings from Westminster Abbey (Scott), **19th:** 2045
Glen Grey Act of 1894, **19th:** 1895
Glendower, Owen, **MA:** 495
Glenn, John, **20th:** 1499-1502
Glenn Gould's Solitude Trilogy (Gould), **20th:** 1554
Glessner House, J. J., **19th:** 1906
Gli Asolani (Bembo), **Ren:** 609
Glimpses of Fifty Years (Willard), **19th:** 2443
Glimpses of World History (Nehru), **20th:** 2931
Glinda of Oz (Baum), **19th:** 158
Glinskaya, Elena, **Ren:** 492; **Notor:** 517
Glinsky, Mikhail Lvovich, **Notor:** 517
Global Village Foundation, **20th:** 1729
Globe (newspaper), **19th:** 317
Globe Theatre, **17th:** 105, 279, 441-442, 928
Gloria (Poulenc), **20th:** 3320
Gloriana (Britten), **20th:** 531
Glorious First of June, Battle of the (1794), **18th:** 508

Glorious Revolution (1688-1689), **17th:** 123, 418, 464, 508, 518, 546, 609, 611, 694, 726, 730, 816, 821, 979; **18th:** 119, 621, 661
"Glorious Things of Thee Are Spoken" (Haydn), **18th:** 478
Gloss on the Psalter (Neckam), **MA:** 752
Glossary of Ecclesiastical Ornament and Costume (Pugin), **19th:** 1839
Gloster Meteor, **20th:** 4319
Gloucester, Richard, duke of. *See* Richard III
Gloyd, Charles, **19th:** 1652
Gluck, Christoph, **18th:** 178, 418-421
Glyn, Elinor, **19th:** 288
GM. *See* General Motors
Gneisenau, August von, **19th:** 261, 928-932, 2152
Gnosticism, **Anc:** 443, 600, 854, 918
Go-Daigo, **MA:** 115
Go-Fukakusa, **MA:** 771
Go-Nara, **Ren:** 735
Go-Shirakawa, **MA:** 721, 991
Go Tell It on the Mountain (Baldwin), **20th:** 201
Go-Toba, **MA:** 723
Go-Yōzei, **Ren:** 736
Goa, **Ren:** 23, 167, 1000; **20th:** annexation by India, 3607
Goat Amalthea with the Infant Jupiter and a Faun, The (Bernini), **17th:** 45
Gobbi and Other Bizarre Figures (Callot), **17th:** 118
Gobelin Manufactory, **17th:** 505
Gobineau, Arthur de, **Notor:** 197, 415-416
Goblin Market, and Other Poems (Rossetti), **19th:** 1941
Goblins, The (Suckling), **17th:** 895
God. *See* Yahweh
God and Intelligence (Sheen), **20th:** 3722
God and Man at Yale (Buckley), **20th:** 561
God and the Bible (Arnold), **19th:** 74
"God Bless America" (Berlin), **20th:** 329
God Is My King (Bach), **18th:** 71
Godard, Jean-Luc, **20th:** 1502-1506
Goddard, Robert H., **20th:** 500, 1507-1510, 1615
Goddess, The (film), **20th:** 3395
Gödel, Kurt, **20th:** 1510-1512, 1801
Godey, Alexis, **19th:** 428
Godey, Louis, **19th:** 1013
Godey's Lady's Book, **19th:** 1013
Godfather, The (film), **20th:** 488
Godfrey, Sir Edmund Berry, **17th:** 692
Godfrey of Strasbourg. *See* Gottfried von Strassburg
Godolphin, first earl of (Sidney Godolphin), **18th:** 421-424; and Queen Anne, 47
Gods, **Anc:** depictions in art, 635; Greek, 429, 966; human relationships to, 732; philosophy and, 856; rulers and, 556
Gods Are Athirst, The (France), **19th:** 817
Godse, Nathuram, **20th:** 1390; **Notor:** 416-418
Godunov, Boris, **Ren:** 387-390; **17th:** 794, 855, 943; **Notor:** 385
Godwin, **MA:** 337
Godwin, Edward William, **19th:** 2248
Godwin, Mary. *See* Shelley, Mary Wollstonecraft
Godwin, Mary Wollstonecraft. *See* Wollstonecraft, Mary
Godwin, William, **18th:** 424-428, 1110; **19th:** 365, 1260, 1477, 1807, 2088, 2093
Godwinson, Harold. *See* Harold II Godwinson
Goebbels, Joseph, **20th:** 1094, 1513-1517; **Notor:** 132, 418-421, 1002, 1098
Goebbels, Magda, **Notor:** 420-422
Goering, Hermann. *See* Göring, Hermann
Goethals, George Washington, **20th:** 1517-1519, 1543
Goethe, Johann Wolfgang von, **18th:** 428-432, 486; Friedrich Gottlieb Klopstock, 563; Friedrich Schiller, 888; Johann Joachim Winckelmann, 1095; **19th:** 1004, 1151, 2009
Goetz, Bernhard, **Notor:** 423-424
Gofukakusa-in no Nijō. *See* Nijō
Gogh, Vincent van, **19th:** 880, 932-936
Gogol, Nikolai, **19th:** 937-940; **20th:** 2723
Goh Chok Tong, **20th:** 2329
Going My Way (film), **20th:** 876
Gokhale, Gopal Krishna, **19th:** 1635, 1856
Golconda, **17th:** 859
Gold, Harry, **Notor:** 380, 915
Gold, Thomas, **20th:** 1902
Gold Rush, The (film), **20th:** 733
Gold rushes, **19th:** Black Hills, 567, 583, 1093, 1873, 2109; California, 429, 833, 2100, 2132; Orofino Creek, 1238; South Africa, 462, 1299, 1406; Transvaal, 1893
Gold Standard Act (1900), **19th:** 1461
Goldberg, Arthur J., **Notor:** 369
Goldberg v. Kelly (1970), **20th:** 508
Golden Age, The (film), **20th:** 578, 906
Golden Age, The (play by Heywood), **17th:** 374
Golden age, Ottoman. *See* Tulip Age
Golden Age, Spanish, **Ren:** 206, 222; **17th:** 113, 312, 317, 739, 913, 950, 953
Golden Ass, The. See *Metamorphoses* (Apuleius)

Golden Bough, The (Frazer), **20th:** 1320
Golden Bowl, The (James), **19th:** 1209
Golden Bull (1356), **MA:** 258
Golden Cockerel, The (Rimsky-Korsakov), **19th:** 1916
Golden Epistle of Abbot William of St. Thierry, The (William of Saint-Thierry), **MA:** 1114
Golden Fleece, Order of the, **MA:** 833
Golden Horde, **MA:** 53, 412, 1001
Golden Legend. See *Legenda aurea*
Golden Temple, Sikh occupation of, **20th:** 1386
Golden Threshold, The (Naidu), **20th:** 2900
Goldie, Sir George, **19th:** 940-942
Goldman, Emma, **20th:** 1519-1523, 1867; **Notor:** 230, 253, 424-426
Goldman, Ronald, **Notor:** 958
Goldsby, Crawford, **Notor:** 997
Goldsmid, Johann. *See* Fabricius, Johannes
Goldsmith, Oliver, **18th:** 432-436
Goldstein, Baruch, **Notor:** 427-428, 552
Goldwater, Barry, **Notor:** 50
Goldwyn, Samuel, **20th:** 143, 212, 920, 960, 1523-1526, 1753
Golenishchev-Kutuzov, Arseny, **19th:** 1628
Golf, **20th:** South Africa, 3288; United States, 2036, 2959, 4391, 4443
Goliath, **Anc:** 255
Golitsin, Anatoli, **Notor:** 837
Golitsyn, Vasily Vasilyevich, **17th:** 624, 866
Gomarists, **17th:** 619
Gomarus, Franciscus, **Ren:** 741
Gomez, Maximo, **19th:** 1504
Gómez de Silva, Ruy, **Ren:** 670
Gomorrah, **Anc:** 4
Gompers, Samuel, **19th:** 27, 943-945; **20th:** 832, 2360
Gomułka, Władysław, **20th:** 2129
Goncharov, Ivan, **19th:** 1353, 2320
Goncharova, Natalia, **20th:** 986
Gondar, Ethiopia, **18th:** 678
Gondi, Philippe-Emmanuel de, **17th:** 962
Gondola, Andrea di Pietro della. *See* Palladio, Andrea
Gondoliers, The (Gilbert and Sullivan), **19th:** 919
Gone with the Wind (film), **20th:** 1368
Gong. *See* Faxian
Gong, Prince, **19th:** 1364, 2484
Góngora y Argote, Luis de, **17th:** 312-314, 949, 953
Gongorismo, **17th:** 313
Gongylus, **Anc:** 616
Gonzaga, Ludovico, **Ren:** 602
Gonzales v. Carhart (2007), **20th:** 522, 3408
González, Elián, **20th:** 3418
González, José Victoriano. *See* Gris, Juan
González Prada, Manuel, **20th:** 1716
Good, Sandra, **Notor:** 378
Good, Sarah, **17th:** 690
Good and Bad Government (Lorenzetti), **MA:** 660
Good and Evil (Buber), **20th:** 556
Good Earth, The (Buck), **20th:** 558
Good Friday Agreement (1998), **20th:** 386
Good Glass of Beer, The (Manet), **19th:** 1481
Good Gray Poet, The (O'Connor), **19th:** 2426
Good Man Is Hard to Find, and Other Stories, A (O'Connor), **20th:** 3018
Good Mother, The (Fragonard), **18th:** 368
Good Neighbor Policy, **20th:** 1922, 1936
Good Night, Willie Lee, I'll See You in the Morning (Walker), **20th:** 4197
Good Society, The (Lippmann), **20th:** 2401
Good Woman of Setzuan, The (Brecht), **20th:** 505
Goodall, Jane, **20th:** 2313
Goodfellas (film), **20th:** 3682
Goodman, Benny, **20th:** 132, 1527-1530
Goodness Had Nothing to Do with It (West), **20th:** 4299
Goodrich, William B. *See* Arbuckle, Roscoe
Goodwill Games, **20th:** 4120
Goodwin, Thomas, **17th:** 198
Goody Two-Shoes (Goldsmith), **18th:** 434
Goodyear, Charles, **19th:** 946-949
Goodyear Rubber Company, **19th:** 948
Google, **20th:** 708
Gora (Tagore), **20th:** 3934
Gorbachev, Mikhail, **20th:** 567, 1045, 1530-1534, 1600, 3604, 4431
Gorchakov, Aleksandr Mikhailovich, **19th:** 49
Gordimer, Nadine, **20th:** 1534-1538
Gordon, Charles George, **19th:** 795, 926, 949-952, 1128, 1474, 2140
Gordon, George. *See* Byron, Lord
Gordon, Harry. *See* Holmes, H. H.
Gordon Riots (1780), **18th:** 645, 900
Gore, Al, **20th:** 784, 1538-1541; Florida recount, 3022
Gorenko, Anna Andreyevna. *See* Akhmatova, Anna
Gorgas, William Crawford, **20th:** 1541-1544
Gorges, Sir Ferdinando, **17th:** 875
Gorgias (Plato), **Anc:** 452, 660
Gorgo, **Anc:** 505
Gorham, Maurice, **20th:** 811
Gorillas, **Anc:** 386

Goring, George, **17th:** 894
Göring, Hermann, **20th:** 1545-1549, 2117; **Notor:** 132, 323, 428-430, 461-462, 468, 1002
Gorky, Maxim, **20th:** 1549-1552
Gośāla Maskarīputra, **Anc:** 355-357
Gosling, Raymond, **20th:** 1316, 4244, 4343
Gospel of John, **Anc:** 472
Gospel of John, The (Bultmann), **20th:** 573
Gosson, Stephen, **Ren:** 882; **17th:** 374
Gösta Berling's Saga. See *Story of Gösta Berling, The*
Gotha Canal, **19th:** 2242
Gotha Program, **19th:** 1371
Gothardt, Mathis. *See* Grünewald, Matthias
Gothic architecture, **18th:** 133, 473, 1004
Gothic art, **18th:** 121
Gothic History Jordanes, The (Jordanes), **MA:** 76
Gothic literature, **18th:** 823, 849, 1004
Gothic Revival, **19th:** 143
Goths, **Anc:** 825, 868, 911
Götterdämmerung (Wagner), **19th:** 2376
Gottfried von Strassburg, **MA:** 423-426, 465
Gotti, John, **Notor:** 24, 184, 218, 397, 431-432, 435
Gottschalk, **MA:** 871
Gottwald, Klement, **20th:** 301
Goujon, Jean, **Ren:** 566
Gould, Glenn, **20th:** 1553-1555
Gould, Gordon, **20th:** 4057
Gould, Jay, **19th:** 716, 1601, 2335; **Notor:** 357, 433-434
Gould, Stephen Jay, **20th:** 1555-1557
Goulue au Moulin Rouge, La (Toulouse-Lautrec), **19th:** 2289
Gounod, Charles, **19th:** 952-955
Goupil, René, **17th:** 423
Gournay, Marie le Jars de, **17th:** 314-316
Gouzenko, Igor, **Notor:** 837
Governance of England, The (Fortescue), **Ren:** 341
Government, **Anc:** Athenian, 221; Chinese, 554; Confucian, 236; Daoism and, 504, 990; law and, 294; Legalism and, 380, 780; philosophy and, 659; Roman Empire, 219, 280; **18th:** Montesquieu's three types, 696. *See also* Category Index
Government of India Act of 1935, **20th:** 2004
Government reform, **18th:** Austria, 655; China, 1113; England, 771-774; France, 648, 917; Great Britain, 789; Paul-Henri-Dietrich d'Holbach, 503; Honda Toshiaki, 505; Louis XVI, 619; Mahmud I, 640; New Spain, 395; Lord North, 739; Ottoman Empire, 719-721; Persia, 722-723; Peter the Great, 776; Marquês de Pombal, 795-797; Robespierre, 844; Spain, 781-783; Thailand, 969; Tokugawa Yoshimune, 980; Toussaint-Louverture, 987; Robert Walpole, 1037
Governor Bradford's Letter Book (Bradford), **17th:** 86
Govindapada, **MA:** 925
Gowen, Franklin P., **Notor:** 745
Goya, Francisco de, **18th:** 436-440; **19th:** 1995
Goyathlay. *See* Geronimo
Graaf, Regnier de, **17th:** 852, 898
Grabez, Trifko, **Notor:** 862
Gracchus, Gaius Sempronius, **Anc:** 357-360, 758
Gracchus, Tiberius Sempronius, **Anc:** 357-360, 757-758
Grace, William Gilbert, **19th:** 955-958
Grace Abounding to the Chief of Sinners (Bunyan), **17th:** 101
Gracián y Morales, Baltasar, **17th:** 316-318
Gradualia (Byrd), **Ren:** 150
Graf Nulin. See *Count Nulin*
Graham, Benjamin, **20th:** 563
Graham, Billy, **20th:** 1557-1560
Graham, Catherine Macaulay. *See* Macaulay, Catherine
Graham, John, **20th:** 2196
Graham, Katharine, **20th:** 1560-1563
Graham, Martha, **20th:** 610, 958, 1270, 1563-1566
Graham, William Brocius. *See* Brocius, Curly Bill
Grainne Mhaol. *See* O'Malley, Grace
Grammaire raisonée (Châtelet and Voltaire), **18th:** 241
Grammar, **MA:** Greek, 1105; Latin, 49, 750, 859
Grammar of Politics, A (Laski), **20th:** 2269
Grammatical Institute of the English Language, A (Webster), **19th:** 2403
Gramsci, Antonio, **20th:** 1566-1569
Gran teatro del mundo, El. See *Great Theater of the World*
Granada, **Ren:** 504; Cathedral of, 890; Muslims and, 105, 252, 330, 433, 504; Rebellion (1497), 537; Spain and, 105, 329
Grand Alliance, **17th:** 980; **18th:** 330, 661
Grand Alliance, War of the. *See* Augsburg, War of the League of
Grand Amour de Beethoven, Un. See *Life and Loves of Beethoven, The*
Grand Canal (China), **MA:** 1149
Grand Canal (Venice), **18th:** 191
Grand Canyon, **19th:** 1829; **20th:** 3516
Grand Déjeuner, Le (Léger), **20th:** 2336
Grand Duke, The (Gilbert and Sullivan), **19th:** 920
Grand Duo Concertant (Weber), **19th:** 2395

Grand Hotel (film), **20th:** 1393
Grand Illusion (film), **20th:** 3421
Grand National Consolidated Trades Union, **19th:** 1722, 1808
Grand Odalisque, The (Ingres), **19th:** 1173
Grand Remonstrance (1641), **17th:** 167, 204, 768
Grand Testament, Le. See *Great Testament, The*
Grand-Théâtre (Bordeaux), **18th:** 296
Grand Trunk Canal, England, **18th:** 164
Grande, Rutilio, **20th:** 3500
Grande Opéra. *See* Académie Royale de Musique
Grande Parade, La (Léger), **20th:** 2336
Grandes anales de quince días, Los (Quevedo y Villegas), **17th:** 770
Grandes Baigneuses, Les (Renoir), **19th:** 1890
Grandeur and Misery of Victory, The (Clemenceau), **20th:** 781
Grands Rhétoriqueurs, **MA:** 260
Grands Travaux de la ville de Lyon, Les (Garnier), **20th:** 1416
Granganimeo, **Ren:** 771
Grant, Cary, **20th:** 1570-1572, 1731, 1770, 4298
Grant, James Augustus, **19th:** 2125
Grant, John, **Ren:** 326
Grant, Ulysses S., **19th:** 80, 958-963, 1232, 1336, 1383, 2144; memoirs, 961; J. P. Morgan, 1601; Nez Perce, 1238; William Tecumseh Sherman, 2099; Charles Sumner, 2203; **Notor:** 219, 365
Grant Park, **19th:** 2389
Granuaile. *See* O'Malley, Grace
Granvelle, Antoine Perrenot de, **Ren:** 615, 993
Grapes of Wrath, The (film), **20th:** 1266, 4446
Grapes of Wrath, The (novel by Steinbeck), **20th:** 3851
Graphic arts, **20th:** 1183, 2190, 4174
Grass, Günter, **20th:** 1573-1577
Grass Harp, The (Capote), **20th:** 645
Grasse, comte de, **18th:** 852
Gratia-Hupp, Suzanne, **Notor:** 457
Gratian, **Anc:** 43, 364, 699, 868
Grattan, Henry, **18th:** 440-442
Gratton, J. L., **19th:** 566
Gratus, Valerius, **Anc:** 644
Grau y San Martín, Ramón, **Notor:** 73
Gravano, Sammy, **Notor:** 432, 434-436, 595
Gravissimo officii munere (Pius X), **20th:** 3273
Gray, Abby Durfee, **Notor:** 125
Gray, Asa, **19th:** 34, 963-966
Gray, Henry Judd, **Notor:** 979
Gray, Mark, **19th:** 273
Gray Cardinal. *See* Pobedonostsev, Konstantin Petrovich
Great and Small Things (Lankester), **19th:** 1316
Great Andean Rebellion, **18th:** 994
Great Art, The (Cardano), **Ren:** 174
Great Astronomy (Paracelsus), **Ren:** 759
Great Awakening, First **18th:** 75, 315, 872, 1062, 1074
Great Awakening, Second, **19th:** 168, 465, 868
Great Battles of the World (Crane), **19th:** 564
Great Bible, **Ren:** 257, 267, 369
Great Binding Law. *See* Great Peace and Power and Law
Great Books of the Western World (Hutchins, ed.), **20th:** 1959
Great Buddha, **MA:** 624
Great Compromise (1787), **18th:** 413, 910
Great Condé. *See* Condé, The Great
Great Contract (1610), **Ren:** 846
Great Depression, **20th:** 738, 1863, 1873; Canada, 2157
Great Dictator, The (film), **20th:** 733
Great Elector. *See* Frederick William, the Great Elector
Great Expectations (Dickens), **19th:** 656
Great Fire of London (1666), **17th:** 148, 346, 384, 729, 806, 995
Great Gatsby, The (Fitzgerald), **20th:** 1251
Great Highway, The (Strindberg), **20th:** 3899
Great Illusion, The (Angell), **20th:** 93
Great Instauration, The (Bacon), **Ren:** 73
Great Lakes region (North America), **18th:** 801
Great Leap Forward (1958-1960), **20th:** 968, 2382, 2409, 2604, 3192, 4463
Great Learning, The, **MA:** 1160
Great Lisbon earthquake (1755), **18th:** 796, 1027
Great Man, The. See *Da ren fu*
Great Ministry of 1848-1851, **19th:** 124
Great Mirror of Male Love, The (Saikaku), **17th:** 404
Great Moments in Ballet, **20th:** 910
Great Northern Expedition (1733-1742), **18th:** 109
Great Northern Hotel, **19th:** 361
Great Northern Railroad, **19th:** 1102, 1601
Great Northern War (1700-1721), **17th:** 625; **18th:** 108, 232, 382, 402, 775
Great Peace and Power and Law, **Ren:** 281
Great Persecution (303), **Anc:** 282
Great Philosophers, The (Jaspers), **20th:** 1998
Great Plague (1665), **17th:** 148, 342, 729

Great Privilege (1477), **Ren:** 631
Great Protestation (1621), **17th:** 177
Great Purge, **20th:** 2783
Great Reform Bill (1832), **19th:** 709
Great Renunciation (Jainism), **Anc:** 925
Great Salt Lake, **19th:** 832
Great Schism (1378-1417), **MA:** 57, 85, 238, 259, 395, 503, 522, 595, 1022, 1089, 1130
Great Service, **Ren:** 150
Great Society, **20th:** 2030
Great Solution, The (La Fontaine), **20th:** 2232
Great Surgery Book (Paracelsus), **Ren:** 759
Great Swamp Battle (1675), **17th:** 634
Great Swamp Fight (1637), **17th:** 567
Great Testament, The (Villon), **Ren:** 974
Great Theater of the World (Calderón), **17th:** 115
Great Trek of the Afrikaners, **19th:** 378
Great Wall of China, **Anc:** 780, 960; **Ren:** 1009
Great Western Railway, **19th:** 334
Great Western Steam Ship Company, **19th:** 333
Greater Inclination, The (Wharton), **20th:** 4301
Greatest Jazz Concert Ever, The (Gillespie and others), **20th:** 1482
Greatest Show on Earth, The (film), **20th:** 963
Greco, El, **Ren:** 390-393; **17th:** 738
Greece, **Anc:** India and, 551; Persia and, 137, 213, 252, 265, 408, 523, 564, 615, 630, 859, 969, 972; **MA:** mathematics, 110; **18th:** art, 1095; **19th:** independence of, 56, 381, 404, 2478. *See also* Geographical Index
Greek League, **Anc:** 39
Greeley, Horace, **19th:** 190, 843, 966-970, 2036
Green, Charles M. *See* Gardner, Erle Stanley
Green, Ernest, **Notor:** 349
Green, Shields, **19th:** 321
Green, Thomas, **17th:** 92
Green, Thomas Hill, **19th:** 971-973
Green Book, The (Qaddafi), **20th:** 3351
Green Hills of Africa (Hemingway), **20th:** 1757
Green March (1975), **20th:** 1700
Green Mountain Boys, **18th:** 36
Green Party (U.S.), **20th:** 2898
Green Revolution, **20th:** 435
Green Spring Faction, **17th:** 29
Green Water, Green Sky (Gallant), **20th:** 1378
Greene, Ann Terry, **19th:** 1786
Greene, Bob, **20th:** 4373
Greene, Graham, **20th:** 806, 1577-1580; **Notor:** 675
Greene, Nathanael, **18th:** 443-447
Greene, Robert, **Ren:** 876
Greene's Groatsworth of Wit (Greene), **Ren:** 876
Greenglass, David, **Notor:** 914-915
Greenglass, Ethel. *See* Rosenberg, Ethel
Greenhouse effect, **20th:** 3549
Greenland, **MA:** Christianity, 642; colonization of, 640; **Ren:** 276
Greenland by the Polar Sea (Rasmussen), **20th:** 3379
Greenspan, Alan, **20th:** 1581-1584
Greenville, Treaty of (1795), **18th:** 611, 1056; **19th:** 2238
Greenway, Francis, **19th:** 974-977
Greenwich, duke of. *See* Argyll, second duke of
Greenwich, earl of. *See* Argyll, second duke of
Greenwich House, **20th:** 198
Gregg v. Georgia (1976), **20th:** 508
Grégoire, Henri, **20th:** 1987
Gregorius (Hartmann), **MA:** 463
Gregory III, **MA:** 253
Gregory VII, **MA:** 433-435, 498, 639, 646, 706, 1043
Gregory VIII, **MA:** 387, 541
Gregory IX, **MA:** 97, 227, 285, 389, 436-438, 545, 882, 1098, 1102
Gregory X, **MA:** 182, 904, 1017
Gregory XI, **MA:** 1131; **Notor:** 1053
Gregory XII, **MA:** 524
Gregory XIII, **Ren:** 393-395, 541, 895, 930
Gregory, James, **17th:** 319-321
Gregory, Samuel, **19th:** 2481
Gregory of Nazianzus, **Anc:** 361-363, 869
Gregory of Nyssa, **Anc:** 363-365
Gregory of Tours, **Anc:** 270; **MA:** 290, 426-429
Gregory Palamas, Saint, **MA:** 1018
Gregory the Great, **MA:** 430-433
Greig, Mary. *See* Somerville, Mary
Grenouillière, La (Renoir), **19th:** 1889
Grenville, Sir Richard, **Ren:** 396-398, 771
Gretzky, Wayne, **20th:** 1585-1587
Grevy, Jules, **19th:** 865
Grey, Charles, second Earl, **18th:** 216; **19th:** 708, 977-980, 1534, 1732, 2446
Grey, Sir Edward, **20th:** 1587-1590
Grey, Sir George, **19th:** 981-984, 2059
Grey, Lady Jane, **Ren:** 305, 399-402, 553, 639, 761
Grey, Sarah, **Notor:** 816
Greynville, Sir Richard. *See* Grenville, Sir Richard

Gribeauval, Jean-Baptiste Vaquette de, **18th:** 447-449
Gribeauval system (artillery), **18th:** 448
Griechische Kulturgeschichte. See *History of Greek Culture*
Grief (Saint-Gaudens), **19th:** 1973
Grief Observed, A (Lewis), **20th:** 2355
Grieg, Edvard, **19th:** 984-988; **20th:** 954
Grierson, John, **20th:** 1038
Griffin, John, **17th:** 54
Griffin, Nick, **Notor:** 1050
Griffith, Arthur, **20th:** 843, 1591-1593, 3034
Griffith, D. W., **20th:** 732, 1382, 1496, 1593-1597, 3244, 3706; **Notor:** 286, 957
Griggs, William, **17th:** 690
Grimaldi, Francesco Maria, **17th:** 134, 321-323
Grimké, Angelina, **19th:** 798, 876, 988-991
Grimké, Charlotte Forten. *See* Forten, Charlotte
Grimké, Francis, **19th:** 798
Grimké, Sarah, **19th:** 876, 988-991
Grimm, Jacob, **19th:** 992-995
Grimm, Wilhelm, **19th:** 992-995
Grimmelshausen, Hans Jakob Christoffel von, **17th:** 324-326
Grimm's Fairy Tales (Grimm brothers), **19th:** 993
Grindal, Edmund, **Ren:** 402-404
Grindel, Eugène. *See* Éluard, Paul
Gris, Juan, **20th:** 1597-1599
Griscom, Elizabeth. *See* Ross, Betsy
Griswold v. Connecticut (1965), **20th:** 380, 1031
Gritz, Bo, **Notor:** 1092
Gromyko, Andrei, **20th:** 525, 1531, 1600-1602
Grønland Langs Polhavet. See *Greenland by the Polar Sea*
Groot, Huig de. *See* Grotius, Hugo
Groote, Gerhard, **MA:** 1022
Gropius, Walter, **20th:** 1602-1605, 2561, 2731
Grose, Francis, **19th:** 1431
Groseilliers, sieur des, **17th:** 777
Gross-Beeren, Battle of (1813), **19th:** 469
Grosse Wundarzney. See *Great Surgery Book*
Grossen Philosophen, Die. See *Great Philosophers, The*
Grosseteste, Robert, **MA:** 127
Grotius, Hugo, **Ren:** 741, 979; **17th:** 17, 326-329, 723, 759
Grouch, The. See *Dyskolos*
Grounds of Natural Philosophy (Newcastle), **17th:** 677
Group, The (McCarthy), **20th:** 2501
Group f.64, **20th:** 884
Group of Seven, **20th:** 4010
Group of United Officers, **20th:** 3205
Group Portrait with Lady (Böll), **20th:** 413
Group Theatre, **20th:** 862
Grove, Sir William Robert, **19th:** 996-999
Grove-Bunsen cell, **19th:** 996
Groves of Academe, The (McCarthy), **20th:** 2501
Growth of the Law, The (Cardozo), **20th:** 654
Growth of the Soil (Hamsun), **20th:** 1662
Grub Street, **18th:** William Hogarth, 497; Samuel Johnson, 536
Gruffydd ap Rhys, **MA:** 449
Grundgesetze der Arithmetik (Frege), **19th:** 829
Grundlagen der Arithmetik, Die. See *Foundations of Arithmetic, The*
Grundlegung der Soziologie des Rechts. See *Fundamental Principles of the Sociology of Law*
Grundlegung zur Metaphysik der Sitten. See *Foundations of the Metaphysics of Morals*
Grundlinien der Philosophie des Rechts. See *Philosophy of Right*
Grundriss der Psychologie. See *Outlines of Psychology*
Grundzüge der physiologischen Psychologie. See *Principles of Physiological Psychology*
Grünewald, Matthias, **Ren:** 405-407
Gruppen (Stockhausen), **20th:** 3874
Gruppenbild mit Dame. See *Group Portrait with Lady*
Grutter v. Bollinger (2003), **20th:** 3022
Guacanagarí, **Ren:** 408-410
Guadalcanal, Battle of (1942-1943), **20th:** 1648, 2979
Guadalete, Battle of (711), **MA:** 1006
Guadalupe Hidalgo, Treaty of (1848), **19th:** 850
Guam, annexation of, **19th:** 1462
Guami, Giuseppe, **Ren:** 362
Guan Zhong, **Anc:** 380
Guandu, Battle of (199), **Anc:** 183
Guangxu, **19th:** 496, 1252, 1364; **Notor:** 1123
Guanzi (Guan Zhong), **Anc:** 380
Guaranty Building, **19th:** 2199
Guardian (newspaper), **18th:** 22
Guardian Angel, The (Holmes), **19th:** 1118
Guarini, Giovanni Battista, **Ren:** 611
Guarini, Guarino, **17th:** 330-332
Guatemala. *See* Geographical Index
Guatémoc. *See* Cuauhtémoc
Guatemozín. *See* Cuauhtémoc
Gudden, Bernhard von, **Notor:** 663
Gudea, **Anc:** 366-369
Guderian, Heinz, **20th:** 1606-1609
Guðjónsson, Halldór Kiljan. *See* Laxness, Halldór
Guédridon, Le (Braque), **20th:** 495

Guelphs, **MA:** 239, 301, 546; Black, 827; White, 827
Guericke, Otto von, **17th:** 79, 333-336, 814
Guérin, Pierre-Narcisse, **19th:** 635, 898
Guernica (Picasso), **20th:** 3238
Guerra de guerrillas, La. See *Che Guevara on Guerrilla Warfare*
Guerre de Troie n'aura pas lieu, Le. See *Tiger at the Gates*
Guerre et la paix, La (Proudhon), **19th:** 1836
Guerrilla warfare, **Anc:** 384
Guerrillas (Naipaul), **20th:** 2904
Guesde, Jules, **19th:** 1221
Guess, George. *See* Sequoyah
Guess Who's Coming to Dinner (film), **20th:** 1770, 3297, 4067
Guest of Honor, A (Joplin), **19th:** 1236
Guest of Honour, A (Gordimer), **20th:** 1535
Gueux, Les, **Ren:** 616, 994
Guevara, Che, **20th:** 691, 1609-1612, 1764, 3173; **Notor:** 185, 436-438, 1071
Guevara de la Serna, Ernesto. *See* Guevara, Che
Guffey Act of 1935, **20th:** 2361
Guggenheim, Daniel, **20th:** 1613-1616
Guggenheim, Peggy, **20th:** 3302
Guggenheim Museum Bilbao, **20th:** 1439
Gugsa Wolie, Ras, **20th:** 1640
Guia Pratico (Villa-Lobos), **20th:** 4164
Guicciardini, Francesco, **Ren:** 410-413
Guide of the Perplexed, The (Maimonides), **MA:** 687, 730, 747; **Ren:** 1
Guide to the Flora of Washington, District of Columbia and Vicinity, A (Ward), **19th:** 2384
Guido d'Arezzo, **MA:** 439-441
Guido d'Arezzo's "Regule rithmice," "Prologue in antiphonarium," and "Epistola ad michahelem" (Guido d'Arezzo), **MA:** 440
Guido Ferranti. See *Duchess of Padua, The*
Guidonian Hand, **MA:** 440
Guidoriccio da Fogliano (Martini), **MA:** 698
Guild of St. Luke, **17th:** 352
Guilford, Baron. *See* North, Frederick
Guilford, second earl of. *See* North, Frederick
Guilford Courthouse, Battle of (1781), **18th:** 444
Guillard, Charlotte, **Ren:** 413-415
Guillaume, Charles-Édouard, **20th:** 1616-1619
Guillaume, Günter, **20th:** 492
Guillaume d'Angleterre. See *King William the Wanderer*
Guillaume de Moerbeke. *See* William of Moerbeke
Guillaume Tell (Rossini), **19th:** 1945
Guillemeau, Charles, **17th:** 74
Guillet, Lucien. *See* Landru, Henri Désiré
Guilty (Streisand), **20th:** 3893
Guinea, **20th:** independence of, 4054. *See also* Geographical Index
Guinizelli, Guideo, **MA:** 240
Guise, Marie de. *See* Mary of Guise
Guise family, **Ren:** 184, 429, 463, 569, 633
Guitar and Fruit Dish (Braque), **20th:** 494
Guitar Player, The (Vermeer), **17th:** 958
Guitarist, The (Courbet), **19th:** 559
Guiteau, Charles Julius, **19th:** 81, 870; **Notor:** 439-440
Guizot, François, **19th:** 2263
Gulag Archipelago, 1918-1956 (Solzhenitsyn), **20th:** 3784
Gulam Bogans. *See* Muhammad, Elijah
Gulf of Tonkin incident (1964), **20th:** 4172
Gulf Oil, **20th:** 2684
Gulf Stream, The (Homer), **19th:** 1126
Gulistan. See *Rose Garden, The*
Gullichsen, Harry, **20th:** 2
Gullichsen, Maire, **20th:** 2
Gulliver's Travels (Swift), **18th:** 966
Gumilyov, Nikolai, **20th:** 42
Gumm, Frances Ethel. *See* Garland, Judy
Gun-Free School Zones Act of 1990, **20th:** 3408
Gunby, David, **Notor:** 1102
Gundioc, **MA:** 287
Gundobad, **MA:** 287, 293
Gunnar, Charles. *See* Lake, Leonard
Gunness, Belle, **Notor:** 1109
Gunpowder Plot (1605), **Ren:** 324, 846; **17th:** 16, 175, 224, 414, 442, 720
Guns of August, The (Tuchman), **20th:** 4104
Gunslingers. *See* Category Index under Outlaws and Gunslingers
Guo Kaizhen. *See* Guo Moruo
Guo Moruo, **20th:** 1619-1622
Guo Xiang, **Anc:** 991
Guo Xingye. *See* Zheng Chenggong
Guomindang. *See* Kuomintang
Gupta Dynasty, **Anc:** 496
Gur Partap Surya (Bhai Santokh Singh), **19th:** 1859
Gurney, Elizabeth. *See* Fry, Elizabeth
Gurney, Joseph, **19th:** 840
Gurruchátegui, Miguel López de Legazpi y. *See* Legazpi, Miguel López de
Guru Nānak Dev. *See* Nānak
Gustafsson, Greta Lovisa. *See* Garbo, Greta
Gustav I Vasa, **Ren:** 415-418; **Notor:** 331
Gustav, Charles X. *See* Charles X Gustav

Gustavus II Adolphus, **17th:** 163, 184, 254, 262, 269, 294, 336-339, 527, 704, 791, 854, 894, 925, 967
Gustavus IV Adolphus, **19th:** 469
Gute Mensch von Sezuan, Der. See *Good Woman of Setzuan, The*
Gutenberg, Beno, **20th:** 3441
Gutenberg, Johann, **MA:** 441-445
Gutenberg Bible, **MA:** 442
Gutenberg Galaxy, The (McLuhan), **20th:** 2529
Gutermann, Sophie. *See* La Roche, Sophie von
Guthrie, Woody, **Notor:** 362
Guy de Chauliac, **MA:** 445-448
Guy Mannering (Scott), **19th:** 2048
Guy of Arezzo. *See* Guido d'Arezzo
Guyart, Marie. *See* Marie de l'Incarnation
Guyon, Madame, **17th:** 265, 339-341
Guyots, discovery of, **20th:** 1785
Güyük, **MA:** 227, 626, 954
Guzla de l'émir, La (Bizet), **19th:** 241
Guzman, Abimael, **20th:** 1359
Gúzman, Jacobo Arbenz, **Notor:** 899
Guzmán de Alfarache (Alemán), **Ren:** 25
Guzmán y Pimental, Gaspar de. *See* Olivares, count-duke of
Gwenllian verch Gruffydd, **MA:** 448-450
Gwyn, Nell, **17th:** 138, 240, 342-344
Gyges of Lydia, **Anc:** 118, 244, 710
Gylberte, Humfrey. *See* Gilbert, Sir Humphrey
Gynecology, **19th:** 266
Gypsies, The (Pushkin), **19th:** 1849
Gypsy (Styne and Sondheim), **20th:** 3461
Gypsy Ballads of García Lorca, The (García Lorca), **20th:** 1396
Gypsy Madonna, The (Titian), **Ren:** 937

H

H. D., **20th:** 1623-1626
Ha-Ari. *See* Luria, Isaac ben Solomon
Ha-gra. *See* Elijah ben Solomon
Haakon IV Haakonarson, **MA:** 951
Haakon VII, **Notor:** 873
Haakon Sigurdsson, **MA:** 790
Haarlem, Kenau Simonsdochter van. *See* Kenau Hasselaer
Haarlem, Siege of (1572-1573), **Ren:** 526, 740
Haarlem Academy, **17th:** 352
Habash, George, **20th:** 1626-1628
Habeler, Peter, **20th:** 2719
Haber, Fritz, **20th:** 313, 437, 1628-1631
Habermas, Jürgen, **20th:** 1632-1634
Habitat for Humanity International, **20th:** 669
Haboku Landscape (Sesshū), **Ren:** 866
Habsburg, Mary of. *See* Mary of Hungary
Habsburg, Maximilian von. *See* Maximilian I (1459-1519; Holy Roman Emperor)
Habsburg, Philip of. *See* Philip II (1527-1598; king of Spain)
Habsburg Dynasty, **MA:** 258, 904, 906; **Ren:** 220, 347, 350, 410, 425, 431, 612, 632, 636, 740, 778, 840, 888; **17th:** 526, 966; and Pope Alexander VII, 10; and King Charles II of Spain, 151, 739; financial burdens, 739; versus France, 431, 493, 554; and Frederick V, 293; and Frederick Henry, 286; and Gustavus II Adolphus, 337; conflict with Holy Roman Empire, 267; and John of Austria, 425; and Jan Komenský, 469; military, 337; in the Netherlands, 286, 618; and Philip III of Spain, 737; and Cardinal de Richelieu, 791; and Sigismund III Vasa, 854; Thirty Years' War, 621; and Pope Urban VIII, 937; **18th:** Charles VI, 229-231; Johann Bernhard Fischer von Erlach, 351; Wenzel Anton von Kaunitz, 557; versus Ottoman Empire, 230; Pragmatic Sanction, 230
Haçi Halife. *See* Kâtib Çelebî
Hackney, John, **Notor:** 376
Hackston, David, **17th:** 122
Hadden, Briton, **20th:** 2456
Haddington, Treaty of (1548), **Ren:** 634
Hadfield, Sir Robert Abbott, **19th:** 1000-1002
Ḥadīth, **MA:** 19, 36, 988; **18th:** 1000, 1030, 1032
Hadj, Messali, **20th:** 8
Hadleigh Castle (Constable), **19th:** 542
Hadrian, **Anc:** 31, 370-373, 493, 906
Hadrian IV. *See* Adrian IV
Hadrian VI. *See* Adrian VI
Hadrian's Temple, **Anc:** 371
Hadrian's Wall, **Anc:** 371
Haeckel, Ernst, **19th:** 115, 1002-1006
Hafiz, **MA:** 451-454, 909
Hafnium, discovery of, **20th:** 1793
Ḥafẓid Dynasty, **Ren:** 79
Haganah, **20th:** 284, 293, 929
Hagar, **Anc:** 5
Hageladas. *See* Ageladas
Haggard, H. Rider, **19th:** 1006-1008
Hagia Sophia, **MA:** 602, 1010
Hagiography, **Anc:** 205, 270; Ignatius, 438
Hague Peace Conference, First, **19th:** 2207
Hahl, August, **19th:** 1558

Hahn, Jessica, **Notor:** 51
Hahn, Otto, **20th:** 715, 1236, 1635-1638, 1750, 1781, 2679, 3970
Hahnemann, Samuel, **19th:** 1009-1012
Haider Ali Khan. *See* Hyder Ali
Haider Naik. *See* Hyder Ali
Haikai, **17th:** 617
Haiku, **17th:** 615
Hail Mary (film), **20th:** 1505
Haile Selassie I, **20th:** 1639-1642, 2701; **Notor:** 719
Hair (film), **20th:** 3990
Hairy Ape, The (O'Neill), **20th:** 3053
Haiti, **20th:** Rafael Trujillo, 4084; U.S. occupation of, 1069. *See also* Geographical Index
Haitian Revolution (1791-1803), **18th:** 985-988; **19th:** 494
Haiyue Waishi. *See* Mi Fei
Ḥājī Khalīfa. *See* Kâtib Çelebî
Ḥajjāj ibn Yūsuf, al-, **MA:** 4
Hakam II, al-, **MA:** 11
Ḥākim, al-, **MA:** 66; **Notor:** 441
Hakluyt, Richard, **Ren:** 419-421
Hakuchi. See *Idiot, The* (film)
Hakuin, **18th:** 450-452
Halberstam, David, **Notor:** 787
Halcyone (Glyn), **19th:** 288
Haldeman, H. R., **Notor:** 226, 320, 442-443
Hale, George Ellery, **20th:** 1643-1645
Hale, Matthew (jurist), **17th:** 345-348
Hale, Matthew F. (white supremacist), **Notor:** 444-445
Hale, Sarah Josepha, **19th:** 1012-1015
Hale Commission, **17th:** 346
Hale telescope, **20th:** 1644
Haley, Alex, **Notor:** 912
Haley, William, **20th:** 811
Half-Century of Conflict, A (Parkman), **19th:** 1744
Halicarnassus, **Anc:** 545
Halide Edib. *See* Adıvar, Halide Edib
Halidon Hill, Battle of (1333), **MA:** 308
Halifax, first marquis of. *See* Savile, Sir George
Halifax, Sir Thomas, **Notor:** 287
Hall, A. Oakey, **19th:** 1650, 2334
Ḥallāj, al-, **MA:** 454-456
Hallam, Arthur Henry, **19th:** 2244
Hallaren, Mary A., **20th:** 1645-1647
Halleck, Henry W., **19th:** 960
Halleck, Seymore, **Notor:** 978
"Hallelujah Chorus" (Handel), **18th:** 464
Hallett, Maria, **Notor:** 81
Halley, Edmond, **17th:** 348-351, 371, 680
Halley's comet, **17th:** 350; **18th:** 77; **19th:** 215
Hals, Frans, **17th:** 352-354
Halsey, William F., **20th:** 1647-1650, 2494, 2979
Hamaguchi, Osachi, **20th:** 1701
Hamburg Dramaturgy (Lessing), **18th:** 600
Hamburg Opera, **18th:** 972
Hamdi v. Rumsfeld (2004), **20th:** 4000
Hamen y León, Juan van der, **17th:** 1005
Hamer, Fannie Lou, **20th:** 1651-1653
Hamer, Frank, **Notor:** 812
Hamerton, Atikins, **19th:** 1967
Hamid bin Muhammed el Mujerbi. *See* Tippu Tib
Hamilcar Barca, **Anc:** 373-375, 382, 739
Hamilton, Alexander, **18th:** 452-456; John Adams, 13; duel with Aaron Burr, 455; Thomas Jefferson, 529; **19th:** 364; duel with Aaron Burr, 365; **Notor:** 155-156
Hamilton, Andrew, **18th:** 1117
Hamilton, Jack. *See* Floyd, Pretty Boy
Hamilton, James (second earl of Arran), **Ren:** 634
Hamilton, Lady. *See* Hart, Emma
Hamilton, Patrick, **Notor:** 636
Hamilton, Raymond, **Notor:** 812
Hamilton, Sir William Rowan, **19th:** 1015-1017, 1074
Hamlet (film), **20th:** 3041
Hamlet (Liszt), **19th:** 1394
Hamm, William, Jr., **Notor:** 556
Ḥammādid kingdom, **MA:** 7
Hammarskjöld, Dag, **20th:** 576, 1653-1656, 2376, 3987, 4092
Hammerlein, Thomas. *See* Thomas à Kempis
Hammerstein, Oscar, II, **20th:** 1657-1660, 1694, 3487
Hammett, Dashiell, **20th:** 1752
Hammurabi, **Anc:** 376-379, 915
Hammurabi, Code of, **Anc:** 253, 582
Hampden, John, **17th:** 144
Hampton, Lionel, **20th:** 1528
Hampton Court Conference, **17th:** 15
Hamsun, Knut, **20th:** 1660-1663
Ḥamzah ibn ʿAbd al-Muṭṭalib, **MA:** 735
Han d'Islande. See *Hans of Iceland*
Han Dynasty, **Anc:** 149, 182
Han Shu (Ban Gu), **Anc:** 149, 152, 785
Han state, **Anc:** 379
Han Wei, **MA:** 1079
Hana, **MA:** 1154
Hananiah, **Anc:** 454
Ḥanbalism, **18th:** 1030
Hanbalites, **MA:** 20, 38
Hancock, John, **18th:** 457-462
Hancock, Thomas, **19th:** 948
Hancock, Winfield S., **19th:** 583
Hand, Learned, **20th:** 1663-1666
Handbook for William (Dhuoda), **MA:** 310
Handbook of American Indian Languages (Boas), **20th:** 400
Handbook of the Women's Movement, **19th:** 1308
Handbuch der Physik (Pauli), **20th:** 3153

Handbuch der physiologischen Optik. See *Treatise on Physiological Optics*
Handel, George Frideric, **18th:** 462-466; influence on Joseph Haydn, 477
Handmaid's Tale, The (Atwood), **20th:** 170
Handy, W. C., **20th:** 1667-1669
Hanfeizi (Hanfeizi), **Anc:** 379
Hanfeizi, **Anc:** 379-381, 979
Hanging of the Crane, The (Longfellow), **19th:** 1419
Hanifites, **MA:** 20, 36
Hanjour, Hani Saleh, **Notor:** 44
Hankey, Lord Maurice, **Notor:** 164
Hanna, Marcus A., **19th:** 1018-1021
Hannibal, **Anc:** 67, 190, 273, 342, 375, 382-385, 512, 542, 758, 812
Hanno, **Anc:** 374, 385-388, 739, 759
Hannon, Lindsay Robbi. *See* Hilley, Marie
Hanover Dynasty, **18th:** 1034; George I, 401; George II, 404; first Earl Stanhope, 938
Hanoverian succession, **18th:** 137, 401
Hans of Iceland (Hugo), **19th:** 1147
Hansards Parliamentary Debates, **19th:** 517
Hansberry, Lorraine, **20th:** 1669-1674
Hänsel und Gretel (Humperdinck), **19th:** 1155
Hanssen, Robert Philip, **Notor:** 445-447
Hansteen, Christopher, **19th:** 9
Hanumān, **Anc:** 923
Haoge, **17th:** 234
Happenings, **20th:** 2374, 3037
Happiness Is a Warm Puppy (Schulz), **20th:** 3673
Happy Days (Beckett), **20th:** 282
Happy Days (Mencken), **20th:** 2690
Happy Dispatches (Paterson), **19th:** 1758
Happy Prince and Other Tales, The (Wilde), **19th:** 2433
Happy Return, The (Forester), **20th:** 1284
Happy Warriors, The (Laxness), **20th:** 2309
Hara no yuki. See *Spring Snow*
Harambee, **20th:** 2108
Harbach, Otto, **20th:** 1657
Harbor in Normandy (Braque), **20th:** 494
Harbor Scene, The (Claude Lorrain), **17th:** 172
Hard, Darlene, **20th:** 1475
Hard Day's Night, A (film), **20th:** 268
Hard Times (Dickens), **19th:** 655
Hardenberg, Karl von, **19th:** 1021-1024, 1674
Hardewick Marriage Act (1753), **18th:** 773
Hardie, Keir, **19th:** 1025-1028
Hardin, John Wesley, **Notor:** 447-448, 653
Harding, Chester, **18th:** 145
Harding, Florence, **Notor:** 714
Harding, Warren G., **20th:** 832, 1674-1678, 1921; **Notor:** 342, 713
Hardouin-Mansart, Jules. *See* Mansart, Jules Hardouin-
Hardwick, Elizabeth. *See* Bess of Hardwick
Hardy, Thomas, **19th:** 1028-1031
Hare, Julius Charles, **19th:** 1464
Hare, William, **Notor:** 154
Harewood House, **19th:** 143
Harfleur, Siege of (1415), **MA:** 503
Hargreaves, James, **18th:** 55, 466-468, 561
Harington, Lucy, **17th:** 238
Hariot, Thomas, **Ren:** 772
Hark! (Hunt), **19th:** 1157
Harland, Henry, **19th:** 163
Harlem Globetrotters, **20th:** 726
Harlem Railroad, **19th:** 2349
Harlem Renaissance, **20th:** 1944
Harlem Suitcase Theatre, **20th:** 1929
Harlequin Carnival, The (Miró), **20th:** 2761
Harlot's Progress, A (Hogarth), **18th:** 498
Harlow, Jean, **20th:** 2430
Harman, Charles. *See* Schultz, Dutch
Harmensen, Jacob. *See* Arminius, Jacobus
Harmonices mundi. See *Harmonies of the World*
Harmonie der Welt, Die (Hindemith), **20th:** 1813
Harmonie universelle (Mersenne), **17th:** 631
Harmonies of the World (Kepler), **17th:** 459, 818
Harmonika (Ptolemy), **Anc:** 714
Harmonika stoicheia (Aristoxenus), **Anc:** 97
Harmonists, **Anc:** 98
Harmony in Blue and Gold (Whistler), **19th:** 2421
Harmony in Red (Matisse), **20th:** 2651
Harmony of the Foreknowledge, the Predestination, and the Grace of God with Free Choice, The (Anselm), **MA:** 94
Harmsworth, Alfred, **20th:** 93, 276, 388, 1678-1681
Harmsworth, Harold, **20th:** 1678-1681
Harnack, Adolf von, **20th:** 187, 243, 418, 1681-1684
Harney, W. S., **19th:** 566
Haro, Luis de, **17th:** 739
Harold II Godwinson, **MA:** 339, 457-460, 1117
Harold Harefoot, **MA:** 224
Harold in Italy (Berlioz), **19th:** 202
Harold the Dauntless (Scott), **19th:** 2048
Harper, James, **Notor:** 940
Harper, William Rainey, **19th:** 1031-1035, 1729

Harpers Ferry, raid on, **19th:** 321, 484, 686, 1142, 1335
Harper's Weekly, **19th:** 1123, 1649
Harpo Productions, **20th:** 4374
Harpsichord, **18th:** François Couperin, 282; George Frideric Handel, 465; Jean-Philippe Rameau, 826
Harriman, William Averell, **20th:** 1684-1688
Harrington (Edgeworth), **19th:** 730
Harriot, Thomas, **17th:** 970
Harris, Barbara, **20th:** 1689-1691
Harris, Jean, **Notor:** 448-450
Harris, Joel Chandler, **19th:** 1036-1040
Harris, Kevin, **Notor:** 1091
Harris, Mary. *See* Jones, Mother
Harris, Townsend, **19th:** 1169, 1969
Harris v. Forklift Systems (1993), **20th:** 2523, 3023
Harrison, Benjamin, **19th:** 252, 509, 1040-1044; conservation, 1624
Harrison, Carter H., Jr., **Notor:** 338
Harrison, Frederic, **19th:** 1044-1047
Harrison, George, **20th:** 266
Harrison, Pat, **Notor:** 99
Harrison, Thomas, **17th:** 484
Harrison, William Henry, **19th:** 505, 1048-1050, 1780, 1821, 2238, 2338; Daniel Webster, 2400
Harrison Horror, **19th:** 1042
Harron, Mary, **Notor:** 983
Harṣa, **MA:** 460-462, 1137
Harshacharita of Banabhatta, The (Bāṇa), **MA:** 460
Hart, Charley. *See* Quantrill, William Clarke
Hart, Emma. *See* Willard, Emma
Hart, Emma (Lady Hamilton), **18th:** 863; **19th:** 1658
Hart, Lorenz, **20th:** 1691-1695, 3486
Hartford, Treaty of (1643), **17th:** 891
Hartford Wits. *See* Connecticut Wits
Harthacnut, **MA:** 224, 337
Hartington, Lord. *See* Cavendish, Spencer Compton
Hartmann, Eduard von, **19th:** 2021
Hartmann, Nicolai, **20th:** 1696-1698
Hartmann von Aue, **MA:** 407, 463-466
Hartzenbusch, Juan Eugenio, **19th:** 557
Hārūn al-Rashīd, **MA:** 244, 467-470
Harvard College, **18th:** 672
Harvard standard, **20th:** 2318
Harvard University, **19th:** 737
Harvey (film), **20th:** 3862
Harvey, Anne Gray. *See* Sexton, Anne
Harvey, Gabriel, **Ren:** 715
Harvey, William, **Ren:** 320; **17th:** 66, 280, 355-358, 543, 564, 579, 723, 811, 899, 986
Ḥasan, al-, **Ren:** 79
Ḥasan al-Baṣrī, al-, **MA:** 471-473, 874
Ḥasan ibn Muḥammad al-Wazzān al-Zaiyātī, al-. *See* Leo Africanus
Hasdrubal, **Anc:** 273, 382, 544, 740, 758, 812
Hasidism, **18th:** 69; Elijah ben Solomon, 318; founding, 69; and Orthodox Judaism, 69; **20th:** 555
Hasil wa al-mahsul, al- (Avicenna), **MA:** 123
Haskalah, **18th:** 319
Haskaybaynaynatyl. *See* Apache Kid
Hassan II, **20th:** 1699-1701
Hasselaer, Kenau Simonsdochter. *See* Kenau Hasselaer
Hassler, Hans Leo, **Ren:** 362
Hastings, Battle of (1066), **MA:** 459, 1118
Hastings, John, **MA:** 346
Hastings, Warren, **18th:** 176, 469-472, 906; Hyder Ali, 523
Hastings, William Lord, **Ren:** 830
Hata, Sukehachiro, **20th:** 1117
Hataraku mono kara miru mono e (Nishida), **20th:** 2982
Hatchepsut. *See* Hatshepsut
Hatemongers. *See* Category Index under Racists and Hatemongers
Hateship, Friendship, Courtship, Loveship, Marriage (Munro), **20th:** 2874
Hathor, **Anc:** 46, 559, 901
Hathorne, John, **Notor:** 540
Hathth ʿala al-bahth, al-. See *Incitement to Investigation*
Hatoyama, Ichirō, **20th:** 1701-1704
Hatshepsut, **Anc:** 388-391, 571, 885, 902
Hatsubi sanpō (Seki), **17th:** 832
Hatta, Mohammad, **20th:** 1704-1706, 3905
Hattin, Battle of (1187), **MA:** 891
Hattori Nankaku, **18th:** 748
Hattyú, A. See *Swan, The*
Haugtussa (Grieg), **19th:** 986
Hauptmann, Bruno Richard, **20th:** 2390, 2393
Hauptprobleme der Religionsphilosophie der Gegenwart. See *Christianity and the New Idealism*
Haushofer, Karl, **20th:** 2520; **Notor:** 461
Haute Surveillance. See *Deathwatch*
Haüy, Valentin, **19th:** 299
Havana, Siege of (1762), **18th:** 395, 510
Have with You to Saffron-Walden (Nashe), **Ren:** 715
Havel, Hippolyte, **Notor:** 425
Havel, Václav, **20th:** 1045, 1707-1709
Havelock, Henry, **19th:** 1719
Havemeyer, H. O., **19th:** 435
Haw Haw, Lord. *See* Joyce, William

Hawaii (Michener), **20th:** 2728
Hawaiian Islands, **18th:** 271, 1006; **19th:** annexation, 1374, 1462
Hawaii's Story by Hawaii's Queen (Liliuokalani), **19th:** 1374
Hawke, Robert, **20th:** 1710-1712
Hawkesbury of Hawkesbury, Baron. *See* Liverpool, second earl of
Hawking, Stephen, **20th:** 1712-1716
Hawking radiation, **20th:** 1713
Hawkins, Aubrey, **Notor:** 902
Hawkins, John, **Ren:** 292; **Notor:** 301
Hawks, Howard, **20th:** 1525, 1571
Hawksmoor, Nicholas, **18th:** 472-475, 1003
Hawley-Smoot Tariff, **20th:** 1863
Haworth's (Burnett), **19th:** 357
Hawthorne, Alice, **Notor:** 922
Hawthorne, Nathaniel, **19th:** 1051-1053, 1538, 1789, 1814
Hay, John, **19th:** 1054-1057
Hay Fever (Coward), **20th:** 854
Hay-Herrán Treaty (1903), **19th:** 1055
Hay-Pauncefote Treaty (1901), **19th:** 1055
Hay Wain, The (Constable), **19th:** 541
Haya de la Torre, Víctor Raúl, **20th:** 1716-1720
Hayʾat al-ʾalan. See *Ibn al-Haytham's On the Configuration of the World*
Hayden, Ferdinand Vandeveer, **19th:** 1058-1060
Hayden, Robert. *See* Fish, Albert
Hayden, Scott, **19th:** 1236
Haydn, Joseph, **18th:** 131, 476-479; Wolfgang Amadeus Mozart, 712; **19th:** 176
Haydon, Benjamin Robert, **19th:** 1260
Hayek, F. A., **20th:** 1720-1723
Hayer, Talmadge, **20th:** 2572
Hayes, Helen, **20th:** 1723-1726
Hayes, Rutherford B., **19th:** 81, 252, 869, 1041, 1061-1065, 1460
Hayley, William, **18th:** 897
Haymarket Opera House, **18th:** 398
Haymarket Riot, **19th:** 58, 509
Hayne, Robert Y., **19th:** 2399
Hays, Will, **Notor:** 33, 34
Hayslip, Le Ly, **20th:** 1727-1730
Haywain (Bosch), **Ren:** 120
Hayward, Nathaniel, **19th:** 947
Haywood, Bill, **20th:** 914; **Notor:** 450-452
Hayworth, Rita, **20th:** 1730-1734
Hazlitt, William, **19th:** 1255, 1260
Hazzard, Linda Burfield, **Notor:** 453-454
He, **Anc:** 153
He-70, **20th:** 1746
He-111, **20th:** 1747
He-176, **20th:** 1747
He-178, **20th:** 1747, 4320
He-280, **20th:** 1747
He Knew He Was Right (Trollope), **19th:** 2301
He Zhong. *See* Ma Yuan
He Zizhen, **Notor:** 692
Head (Lipchitz), **20th:** 2398
Head, Sir Francis Bond, **19th:** 123, 1458
Head of a Woman (Leonardo da Vinci), **Ren:** 562
Head of an Infant (Epstein), **20th:** 1165
Headbirths (Grass), **20th:** 1575
Headsman, The (Cooper), **19th:** 554
"Healing Question, A" (Vane), **17th:** 942
Health. *See* Medicine
Health, Education, and Welfare, U.S. Department of, **20th:** 1840
Hearst, Patty, **Notor:** 454-456
Hearst, William Randolph, **20th:** 1093, 1558, 1734-1738, 1920; **Notor:** 33, 454, 803
Heart Is a Lonely Hunter, The (McCullers), **20th:** 2507
Heart Melodies (Folger), **19th:** 813
Heart of Darkness (Conrad), **20th:** 827
Heart of Midlothian, The (Scott), **19th:** 2048
Heart of the Matter, The (Greene), **20th:** 1579
Heart transplants, **20th:** 237
Heartbreak House (Shaw), **20th:** 3720
Heartburn (Ephron), **20th:** 1162
Heartease (Yonge), **19th:** 2472
Heartland, **20th:** 2519
Heat theorem, **20th:** 2935
Heath, Sir Edward, **20th:** 1738-1742, 4362
Heath, John, **19th:** 1781
Heathen Days (Mencken), **20th:** 2690
Heautontimorumenos (Terence), **Anc:** 850
Heaven and Earth (film), **20th:** 1729
Heavenly Arcana, The (Swedenborg), **18th:** 961
Hebdomades. See *Imagines*
Hebe (Canova), **19th:** 407
Hebrew Union College, **19th:** 2454
Hebrews. *See* Jews
Hebrides, The (Mendelssohn), **19th:** 1550
Hecataeus, **Anc:** 407
Hecht, Ben, **Notor:** 804
Hector, **Anc:** 428
Hectoris lytra (Ennius), **Anc:** 301
Hecyra (Terence), **Anc:** 850
Hedda Gabler (Ibsen), **19th:** 1166
Hedong, Madame. *See* Liu Yin
Hedonism, **Anc:** 88
Hedvig. *See* Jadwiga
Heemskerck, Jacob van, **17th:** 930
Hegel, Georg Wilhelm Friedrich, **19th:** 538, 1065-1069, 1321, 1508, 2009; **Notor:** 769
Hegelianism, **19th:** 1279, 1321
Hegesias, **Anc:** 89
Hegesipyle, **Anc:** 564

Heian period, **MA:** 397, 738; art, 581; emperors, 739
Heiandō. *See* Chikamatsu Monzaemon
Heidegger, Martin, **20th:** 118, 573, 689, 1742-1745, 1956, 1997
Heidenmauer, The (Cooper), **19th:** 554
Heiji disturbance (1159), **MA:** 721, 991
Heike. *See* Taira clan
Heike monogatari. See *Tale of the Heike, The*
Heilige Johanna der Schlachthöfe, Die. See *Saint Joan of the Stockyards*
Heilige und das Profane, Das. See *Sacred and the Profane, The*
Heimskringla (Snorri), **MA:** 785, 951
Heimsljos. See *World Light*
Hein, Piet, **17th:** 288, 359-361, 698
Heine, Heinrich, **19th:** 1069-1072, 1321, 1332
Heinkel, Ernst, **20th:** 1746-1748
Heinkel Corporation, **20th:** 4319
Heinmot Tooyalakekt. *See* Joseph, Chief
Heinrich IV. *See* Henry IV (1050-1106; Holy Roman Emperor)
Heinrich der Heilige. *See* Henry II the Saint
Heinrich der Löwe. *See* Henry the Lion
Heinricus Sagittarius. *See* Schütz, Heinrich
Heinzen, Karl, **19th:** 2482
Heir of Redclyffe, The (Yonge), **19th:** 2473
Heirat wider Willen, Die (Humperdinck), **19th:** 1155
Heiria, Council of (754), **MA:** 549
Heisenberg, Werner, **20th:** 438, 1749-1752, 3669
Hekabē (Euripides), **Anc:** 327
Helen (Edgeworth), **19th:** 730
Helen (legendary figure), **Anc:** 428
Helen of Troy, and Other Poems (Teasdale), **20th:** 3960
Helen of Wales. *See* Nest verch Rhys ap Tewdwr
Helena, Saint, **Anc:** 239, 391-393
Helenē (Euripides), **Anc:** 328
Helfferich, Karl, **20th:** 1181
Helga. *See* Olga, Saint
Heliocentrism, **Anc:** 78, 418, 713
Heliogabalus. *See* Elagabalus
Heliography, **19th:** 1678
Helios (Nielsen), **20th:** 2965
Helium, liquefaction of, **20th:** 2072
Hell (Bosch), **Ren:** 120
Hellas (Shelley), **19th:** 2096
Hellenism, **Anc:** 39; Alexandria and, 721; Christianity and, 821, 918; ideology and, 450; Judaism and, 612; Rome and, 75
Hellenistic art, **Anc:** 524
Hellespont, crossing of, **Anc:** 972
Hellman, Lillian, **20th:** 1525, 1752-1755
Hello, Dolly! (film), **20th:** 3893
Hell's Angels (film), **20th:** 1925
Helm, Charles, **19th:** 1406
Helmasperger Instrument, **MA:** 442
Helmholtz, Hermann von, **19th:** 997, 1073-1076, 1530; **20th:** 2934
Helmont, Franciscus Mercurius van, **17th:** 188, 251, 362
Helmont, Jan Baptista van, **17th:** 361-363
Helms, Richard, **Notor:** 942
Héloïse, **MA:** 14
Helots, **Anc:** 15, 616, 621
Help! (film), **20th:** 268
Helpmann, Robert, **20th:** 1268
Helvering v. Davis (1937), **20th:** 655
Helvétius, Claude-Adrien, **18th:** 479-482
Helvia, **Anc:** 766
Helvidius Priscus, **Anc:** 104
Hemans, Felicia Dorothea, **19th:** 1076-1078
Hemerken, Thomas. *See* Thomas à Kempis
Hemessen, Catharina van, **Ren:** 421-423
Hemessen, Sanders van, **Ren:** 421
Hemingway, Ernest, **20th:** 1755-1759
Henderson, Fletcher, **20th:** 130
Henderson, Oran K., **Notor:** 169
Henderson the Rain King (Bellow), **20th:** 289
Henge ga maki (Moronobu), **17th:** 376
Hengist, **Anc:** 394-396
Henie, Sonja, **20th:** 1759-1762
Hennard, George, **Notor:** 456-457, 497
Henney, Nella Braddy, **20th:** 3909
Henri I. *See* Christophe, Henri
Henri II. *See* Henry II (1519-1559; king of France)
Henri III. *See* Henry III (1551-1589; king of France)
Henri III et sa cour. See *Catherine of Cleves*
Henri, Robert, **20th:** 1876
Henrician Articles (1574), **Ren:** 426
Henrietta Anne, **17th:** 72
Henrietta Maria, **17th:** 364-366; Catholicism of, 496; and King Charles I of England, 144; and son King Charles II of England, 147; and the first earl of Clarendon, 168; and Abraham Cowley, 199; and Richard Crashaw, 202; and Lady Eleanor Davies, 221; and Sir Anthony van Dyck, 246; and son King James II of England, 416; and Richard Lovelace, 562; daughter of Marie de Médicis, 598; and naming of Maryland, 120; and the duke of Monmouth, 653; and the duchesse de Montpensier, 661; and the Netherlands, 288; and the duchess of Newcastle, 676;

patronage, 846, 975; and Prince Rupert, 805; and the theater, 374; and Maarten Tromp, 931
Henrietta's Wish (Yonge), **19th:** 2472
Henriette Renan. See *My Sister Henrietta*
Henry (count of Schwerin), **MA:** 1048
Henry (duke of Orléans). *See* Henry III (1551-1589; king of France)
Henry (duke of Saxony). *See* Henry the Lion
Henry I (c. 876-936; king of Germany), **MA:** 805
Henry I (c. 920-955; duke of Bavaria), **MA:** 486, 805
Henry I (c. 1008-1060; king of France), **MA:** 1117
Henry I (1068-1135; king of England), **MA:** 94, 304, 481-483, 754, 960
Henry I of Lorraine (1550-1588; duke of Guise), **Ren:** 426, 429, 464, 669, 705
Henry II the Saint (973-1024; Holy Roman Emperor), **MA:** 408, 486-490, 965
Henry II (1133-1189; king of England), **MA:** 29, 57, 147, 272, 306, 357, 476, 483-486, 584, 693, 836, 891, 963
Henry II (1519-1559; king of France), **Ren:** 184, 222, 284, 295, 423-425, 426, 429, 463, 565, 568, 627, 634, 780, 838; **Notor:** 214, 534, 800
Henry II of Bourbon (1588-1646). *See* Condé, third prince of
Henry III (1017-1056; Holy Roman Emperor), **MA:** 644, 705
Henry III (1207-1277; king of England), **MA:** 211, 343, 490-493, 547, 668, 725
Henry III (1551-1589; king of France), **Ren:** 108, 139, 185, 323, 426-428, 429, 464, 668, 690, 705; **Notor:** 214
Henry III (1553-1610; king of Navarre). *See* Henry IV (1553-1610; king of France)
Henry IV (1050-1106; Holy Roman Emperor), **MA:** 384, 433, 497-501, 639, 646, 1043
Henry IV (1367-1413; king of England), **MA:** 266, 493-497, 501, 895
Henry IV (1425-1474; king of Castile), **Ren:** 328, 432-434
Henry IV (1553-1610; king of France), **Ren:** 42, 186, 200, 427, 429-432, 464, 619, 668, 705, 780; **17th:** 111, 141, 315, 364, 551, 577, 587, 598, 737, 779, 790, 896; **Notor:** 214, 888
Henry IV (Pirandello), **20th:** 3261
Henry V (1086-1125; Holy Roman Emperor), **MA:** 971
Henry V (1387-1422; king of England), **MA:** 261, 277, 496, 501-504, 578; **Ren:** 224; **Notor:** 203
Henry V (film), **20th:** 3041
Henry VI (1165-1197; Holy Roman Emperor), **MA:** 542
Henry VI (1421-1471; king of England), **Ren:** 90, 301, 340, 434-437, 438, 828, 989; **Notor:** 896
Henry VII (1275?-1313; Holy Roman Emperor), **MA:** 302
Henry VII (1457-1509; king of England), **Ren:** 51, 90, 156, 159, 187, 438-441, 499, 697, 830, 946
Henry VIII (1050-1106; duke of Bavaria). *See* Henry IV (1050-1106; Holy Roman Emperor)
Henry VIII (1491-1547; king of England), **Ren:** 8, 62, 85, 91, 111, 159, 188, 230, 266, 270, 303, 310, 335, 368, 399, 439, 441-445, 467, 627, 639, 764, 868, 898, 947, 996; art patronage and, 454; Church of England and, 231, 256, 270, 544, 834; excommunication of, 834; Scotland and, 502, 634; **Notor:** 212
Henry X the Proud (c. 1100-1139; duke of Bavaria), **MA:** 474
Henry XII (1129-1195; duke of Bavaria). *See* Henry the Lion
Henry, Andrew, **19th:** 2114
Henry, Bill. *See* Longley, Bill
Henry, Frederick. *See* Frederick Henry
Henry, Hubert Joseph, **Notor:** 335
Henry, John. *See* Carto, Willis A.
Henry, Joseph, **19th:** 1078-1081, 1611
Henry, O., **19th:** 1081-1084
Henry, Patrick, **18th:** 482-485
Henry, William, **19th:** 598
Henry Esmond, Esq. (Thackeray), **19th:** 2258-2259
Henry Ford Hospital (Kahlo), **20th:** 2070
Henry of Anjou. *See* Henry II (1133-1189; king of England)
Henry of Bourbon. *See* Henry IV (1553-1610; king of France)
Henry of Lancaster. *See* Henry IV (1367-1413; king of England)
Henry of Monmouth. *See* Henry V (1387-1422; king of England)
Henry of Navarre. *See* Henry IV (1553-1610; king of France)
Henry of Winchester. *See* Henry III (1207-1277; king of England)
Henry of Windsor. *See* Henry VI (1421-1471; king of England)
Henry Street Settlement, **20th:** 4185
Henry the Lion, **MA:** 473-477
Henry the Navigator (prince of Portugal), **MA:** 477-481; **Ren:** 286
Henryson, Robert, **Ren:** 499
Hensel, Fanny, **19th:** 952
Henslowe, Philip, **Ren:** 214; **17th:** 223, 440, 977
Henson, Matthew A., **20th:** 3178
Henze, Hans Werner, **20th:** 1762-1766

Hepburn, Audrey, **20th:** 1766-1768
Hepburn, James, **Ren:** 147, 629
Hepburn, Katharine, **20th:** 143, 862, 1571, 1769-1772, 4067
Hepburn Act of 1906, **20th:** 3517
Hepburn v. Griswold, **19th:** 473, 779
Hepta epi Thēbas (Aeschylus), **Anc:** 9
Heptameron, The (Marguerite de Navarre), **Ren:** 619
Heptaplus (Pico della Mirandola), **Ren:** 784
Hera of Argos (Polyclitus), **Anc:** 676
Heracles, **Anc:** 70, 374
Heráclito cristiano (Quevedo y Villegas), **17th:** 770
Heraclitus (Bramante), **Ren:** 132
Heraclitus (poet), **Anc:** 180
Heraclitus of Ephesus, **Anc:** 59, 397-400
Heraclius, **MA:** 505-508, 933
Hērakleidai (Euripides), **Anc:** 327
Herbal of Leonhart Fuchs, The (Fuchs), **Ren:** 357
Herbalists, **Anc:** 291
Herbert, George, **17th:** 17, 203, 232, 276, 366-368
Herbert, Stanley, **19th:** 1685
Herbst, Josephine, **20th:** 3313
Hercules, **Anc:** 73
Hercules and Omphale (Artemisia), **17th:** 308
Hercules Romanus. *See* Commodus
Herder, Johann Gottfried, **18th:** 486-489, 888
Here Begynneth the Life of the Gloryous Confessoure of Oure Lorde Ihesu Criste Seynt Francis. See *Life of Saint Francis of Assisi, The*
Hereditary Genius (Galton), **19th:** 861
Herencia (Matto), **19th:** 1513
Heresy, **Anc:** Arian, 43; Eusebius and, 331; Irenaeus and, 443; Priscillian and, 699; **MA:** against Pietro d'Abano, 2; Peter Abeland, 16; Arian, 242, 290; Saint Dominic and, 316; against Duns Scotus, 331; against al-Ḥallāj, 455; against Jan Hus, 524, 1091; iconoclasm, 549-550; against John Italus, 865; against William of Ockham, 778; persecution of heretics, 630; against Marguerite Porete, 856; against Michael Psellus, 864; against Lorenzo Valla, 1051; **Ren:** 29, 62, 144, 164, 284, 332, 370, 397, 424, 463, 467, 514, 544, 559, 640, 666, 677, 699, 779, 853, 862, 899, 940-941, 949, 994, 1000, 1013
Hering, Constantine, **19th:** 1010
Hering-Breuer reflex, **20th:** 514
Herland (Gilman), **20th:** 1486
Herman, Robert, **20th:** 1380
Herman, Woody, **20th:** 1528
Hermann I, **MA:** 359
Hermann, Jakob. *See* Arminius, Jacobus
Hermann, Wilhelm, **20th:** 572
Hermann Moritz. *See* Saxe, comte de
Hermansen, Jacob. *See* Arminius, Jacobus
Hermarchus, **Anc:** 308
Hermes, **Anc:** 695
Hermes (Praxiteles), **Anc:** 694
Hermes Carrying the Infant Dionysus (Kephisodotus), **Anc:** 694
Hermetic Definition (H. D.), **20th:** 1625
Hermeticists, **17th:** 629
Hermias, **Anc:** 65, 872
Hermippus, **Anc:** 128
Hermit Songs, The (Barber), **20th:** 232
Hermitage, **17th:** 499
Hermitages, Christian, **Anc:** 62
Hermits, **Anc:** Saint Anthony of Egypt, 60; Christian, 205
Hernandez, Aileen Clarke, **20th:** 1773-1776
Hernández Martínez, Maximiliano, **20th:** 1040
Hernani (Hugo), **19th:** 1147
Hero, The (Gracián), **17th:** 317
Hero and Leander (Marlowe), **Ren:** 625
Hero of Alexandria, **Anc:** 325, 401-403; **MA:** 195
Hero of Our Time, A (Lermontov), **19th:** 1354
Herod I. *See* Herod the Great
Herod Agrippa I, **Anc:** 626, 640
Herod Antipas, **Anc:** 475, 645; **Notor:** 458-459
Herod the Great, **Anc:** 75, 403-406, 458; **Notor:** 458-460
Herodes Magnus. *See* Herod the Great
Herodian of Syria, **Anc:** 486
Herodias, **Notor:** 458, 932
Herodotus, **Anc:** 244, 407-409, 556, 558, 884; **Notor:** 251, 851
Heroic epic, Germany, **MA:** 1123
Heroic Stanzas (Dryden), **17th:** 240
Heroism, **Anc:** Greek, 507; Roman, 518
Herold, David E., **Notor:** 124, 859, 1012
Herophilus, **Anc:** 311, 410-413
Herr, Lucien, **20th:** 396
Herr Eugen Dühring's Revolution in Science (Engels), **19th:** 751
Herrera, Antonio de, **Ren:** 805
Herrera, Francisco, the Younger, **17th:** 671
Herrera, Francisco de, the Elder, **17th:** 1004
Herrera, Juan de, **Ren:** 445-447
Herrera, Omar Torrijos. *See* Torrijos, Omar
Herrick, Robert, **17th:** 368-371, 443
Herring Net, The (Homer), **19th:** 1125
Herriot, Édouard, **20th:** 1777-1779, 3294
Herrmann, Wilhelm, **20th:** 243
Herrn Eugen Dührings Umwälzung der Wissenschaft.

See *Herr Eugen Dühring's Revolution in Science*
Herrnhut religious community, **18th:** 1120
Herschel, Caroline Lucretia, **18th:** 489-492
Herschel, William, **18th:** 490, 492-493
Hertford, earl of. *See* Somerset, first duke of
Hertwig, Richard von, **20th:** 1335
Hertz, Gustav, **20th:** 1780-1782
Hertz, Heinrich, **19th:** 1074; **20th:** 374
Hertzog, Jan, **20th:** 441
Hertzsprung, Ejnar, **20th:** 3571
Hertzsprung-Russell diagram, **20th:** 3571
Herut, **20th:** 286
Herz, Cornelius, **20th:** 779
Herzberg, Gerhard, **20th:** 1783-1785
Herzen, Aleksandr, **19th:** 119, 1085-1087, 1353
Herzl, Theodor, **19th:** 1088-1091; **20th:** 2993, 4280
Herzog (Bellow), **20th:** 289
Herzog, Baron. *See* Hory, Elmyr de
Hesiod, **Anc:** 413-417, 856, 966
Hesperides (Herrick), **17th:** 369
Hess, Harry Hammond, **20th:** 1785-1787
Hess, Rudolf, **Notor:** 131, 460-462, 478
Hess, Walter R., **20th:** 1109
Hesse, Hermann, **20th:** 1787-1791
Hesychasm, **MA:** 1017
Hetaeras, **Anc:** 127
Hetairikoi dialogoi (Lucian), **Anc:** 515
Hetch Hetchy Valley, **19th:** 1625; **20th:** controversy, 3254
Hetman state, **17th:** 461
Hetty's Strange History (Jackson), **19th:** 1195
Heures de Turin (van Eycks), **MA:** 366
Hevelius, Elisabetha, **17th:** 371-373
Hevelius, Johannes, **17th:** 348, 371-373
Hevesy, Georg von, **20th:** 1792-1795
Hewel, Johann. *See* Hevelius, Johannes
Hewish, Antony, **20th:** 584
Hewitt, James, **20th:** 991
Hexapla (Origen), **Anc:** 600
Heydrich, Reinhard, **20th:** 1547; **Notor:** 322, 430, 462-464, 469, 512
Heyerdahl, Thor, **20th:** 1795-1799
Heyne, Christian Gottlob, **19th:** 883
Heyward, DuBose, **20th:** 1459, 1463
Heywood, Thomas, **17th:** 373-375, 977
Hezbollah, **20th:** 154
Hezekiah, **Anc:** 448, 769
Hiawatha, **Ren:** 281, 448-450
Hiawatha (Saint-Gaudens), **19th:** 1972
Hickok, Wild Bill, **19th:** 387, 1091-1094; **Notor:** 447
Hicks, Stephen, **Notor:** 255
Hicks, William, **19th:** 1474
Hidalgo y Costilla, Miguel, **19th:** 1094-1096
Hidatsas, **19th:** 1962
Hideyoshi. *See* Toyotomi Hideyoshi
Hiero I, **Anc:** 8, 794
Hiero II, **Anc:** 80
Higginson, Thomas Wentworth, **19th:** 661, 797, 1097-1100, 1194
Higglety Pigglety Pop! (Sendak), **20th:** 3699
High, Nathaniel Rue, **Notor:** 137
High and Deep Searching Out of the Threefold Life of Man, The (Böhme), **17th:** 61
High and Low (film), **20th:** 2219
High Button Shoes (Styne and Cahn), **20th:** 3461
High Price of Bullion, The (Ricardo), **19th:** 1896
High Sierra (film), **20th:** 407
High society, **18th:** in art, 367-370; Casanova, 209; Georgiana Cavendish, 216; Madame de Pompadour, 798
High Society (film), **20th:** 3309
Highway Beautification Act of 1965, **20th:** 2026
Highway 61 Revisited (Dylan), **20th:** 1073
Higuchi, Susana, **Notor:** 382
Hijrah, **MA:** 734, 1037
Ḥikāyāt Ḥāratinā. See *Fountain and the Tomb, The*
Hiketides (Aeschylus), **Anc:** 9, 877
Hiketides (Euripides), **Anc:** 327
Hilalians, **MA:** 7
Hilarius, **Anc:** 947
Hilbert, David, **20th:** 1800-1802
Hilbert space, **20th:** 1801
Hilda of Whitby, Saint, **MA:** 509-511
Hildebrand. *See* Gregory VII
Hildebrandt, Johann Lucas von, **18th:** 494-497
Hildegard von Bingen (Saint Hildegard), **MA:** 512-515
Hilderic, **Anc:** 354
Hill, Anita, **20th:** 3999
Hill, Henry, **Notor:** 465-466
Hill, James Jerome, **19th:** 1100-1103
Hill, Mildred. *See* Hill, Susanna Mildred
Hill, Octavia, **19th:** 1103-1107
Hill, Percival, **Notor:** 917
Hill, Susanna Mildred, **Notor:** 466
Hill, Virginia, **Notor:** 955
Hillary, Sir Edmund, **20th:** 1802-1806
Hillel, Rabbi, **Anc:** 2, 29, 468
Hilley, Marie, **Notor:** 467-468
Hillquit, Morris, **20th:** 4003
Hillside Strangler. *See* Bianchi, Kenneth; Buono, Angelo, Jr.
Hilton, Conrad, Jr., **20th:** 3953

Hima-Súmac (Matto), **19th:** 1513
Himerius, **Anc:** 361
Himiko, **Anc:** 465
Himmler, Heinrich, **20th:** 501, 1807-1810; **Notor:** 132, 266, 323, 375, 420, 429, 462, 464, 468-470, 477, 512, 717, 1074
Hīnayāna Buddhism, **MA:** 1137
Hinchingbrooke, Viscount. *See* Sandwich, first earl of
Hinckley, John, Jr., **Notor:** 141, 470-473, 678
Hincmar of Reims, **MA:** 765
Hind and the Panther, The (Dryden), **17th:** 241
Hindemith, Paul, **20th:** 1811-1814
Hindenburg, Paul von, **20th:** 315, 1814-1817, 2462, 3110; **Notor:** 479
Hindenburg disaster, **20th:** 1094, 4455
Hindu Family Annuity Fund, **19th:** 2364
Hindu-Muslim conflicts, **18th:** 1032
Hindu Widow Remarriage Act (1856), **19th:** 2364
Hinduism, **Anc:** 501; Buddhism and, 171; Zoroastrianism and, 993; **MA:** 461, 877, 925; **Ren:** India, 16, 475; Mongol Dynasty, 16; Portugal and, 1001; Sikhism and, 707; **17th:** Mughal Empire, 24; Śivājī, 858; **19th:** India, 1867; monistic, 2368-2369
Hindustan, Mongol invasion of, **Ren:** 70
Hindustan Seva Dal, **20th:** 2930
Hines, Earl, **20th:** 131
Hines, Jimmy, **Notor:** 237, 939
Hingston Down, Battle of (837), **MA:** 354
Hints to the Colored People of the North (Cary), **19th:** 431
Hints Towards Forming the Character of a Young Princess (More), **18th:** 703
Hipparchikos (Xenophon), **Anc:** 969
Hipparchus (astronomer), **Anc:** 417-420, 712
Hipparchus of Athens, **Anc:** 651, 793
Hippēs (Aristophanes), **Anc:** 91
Hippias of Athens, **Anc:** 226, 651, 793, 859
Hippocrates, **Anc:** 84, 114, 199, 277, 349, 420-423
Hippocratic oath, **Anc:** 422
Hippolyte et Aricie (Rameau), **18th:** 826
Hippolytos (Euripides), **Anc:** 327
Hippolytus of Rome, **Anc:** 423-427
Hiram of Tyre, **Anc:** 804
Hiraoka, Kimitake. *See* Mishima, Yukio
Hirayama Tōgo. *See* Ihara Saikaku
Hireling Ministry None of Christs, The (Williams), **17th:** 984
Hirohito, **20th:** 46, 1818-1821; **Notor:** 473-475, 865
Hiroshige, **19th:** 1107-1110
Hiroshima, bombing of, **20th:** 822, 1237, 4087-4088
His Girl Friday (film), **20th:** 1572
His Last Bow (Doyle), **19th:** 689
His Maiesties Poeticall Exercises at Vacant Houres (James I), **17th:** 413
His Picture in the Papers (film), **20th:** 2429
Hishikawa Moronobu, **17th:** 375-377
Hispanicae advocationis libri duo. See *Two Books of the Pleas of a Spanish Advocate, The*
Hispaniola, **Ren:** 238, 408, 800, 804
Hiss, Alger, **20th:** 19, 1822-1825, 1867, 2984; **Notor:** 199, 217, 475-477, 793
Histoire comique des états et empires de la lune, L'. See *Other World, The*
Histoire comique des états et empires du soleil, L'. See *States and Empires of the Sun, The*
Histoire de Belgique (Pirenne), **20th:** 3270
Histoire de France. See *History of France, The*
Histoire de Geoffroy de Villehardouyn, mareschal de Champagne et de Roménie, L'. See *Conquête de Constantinople, Le*
Histoire de Gil Blas de Santillane. See *Gil Blas*
Histoire de la littérature anglaise. See *History of English Literature*
Histoire de la nature des oyseaux, L' (Belon), **Ren:** 102
Histoire de la peinture de Italie (Stendhal), **19th:** 2161
Histoire de la princesse de Paphlagonie (Montpensier), **17th:** 662
Histoire de la révolution française. See *History of the French Revolution*
Histoire de l'art religieux (Denis), **20th:** 973
Histoire de l'astronomie moderne (Bailly), **18th:** 78
Histoire de ma vie. See *History of My Life*
Histoire de Madame Henriette d'Angleterre. See *Fatal Galantry*
Histoire des croyances et des idées religieuses. See *History of Religious Ideas, A*
Histoire du consulat et de l'empire. See *History of the Consulate and the Empire of France Under Napoleon*
Histoire du XIXe siècle (Michelet), **19th:** 1564
Histoire du peuple d'Israël. See *History of the People of Israel*
Histoire naturelle des éstranges poissons marins, L' (Belon), **Ren:** 101

Histoire naturelle, générale et particulière. See *Natural History, General and Particular*
Histoire philosophique et politique, des établissemens et du commerce des Européens dans les deux Indes. See *Philosophical and Political History of the Settlements and Trade of the Europeans in the East and West Indies*
Histoire socialiste de la révolution française (Jaurès), **19th:** 1221
Histoires. See *Tales of Mother Goose*
Histoires naturelles (Ravel), **20th:** 3386
Historia (Krasicki), **18th:** 568
Historia Arianorum (Athanasius), **Anc:** 134
Historia Augusta, **Anc:** 486, 987
Historia Britonum (Nennius), **Anc:** 394
Historia calamitatum. See *Story of My Misfortunes, The*
Historia coelestis Britannica (Flamsteed), **18th:** 490
Historia Danica. See *History of the Danes, The*
Historia de las Indias. See *History of the Indies*
Historia de regibus Gothorum, Vandalorum, et Suevorum. See *History of the Kings of the Goths, Vandals, and Suevi*
Historia ecclesiastica (Eusebius), **Anc:** 330, 442
Historia ecclesiastica gentis Anglorum. See *Ecclesiastical History of the English People*
Historia ecclesiastica tripartita (Cassiodorus), **MA:** 235
Historia Francorum. See *History of the Franks, The*
Historia general de la orden de Nuestra Señora de las Mercedes (Tirso), **17th:** 914
Historia general de las cosas de Nueva España. See *Florentine Codex*
Historia general de las Indias (Oviedo), **Ren:** 804
Historia general de los hechos de los castellanos (Herrera), **Ren:** 805
Historia insectorum (Ray), **17th:** 783
Historia insectorum generalis (Swammerdam), **17th:** 899
Historia Mongalorum quos nos Tartaros appellamus (Carpini), **MA:** 228
Historia mundi (Mercator), **Ren:** 680
Historia natural y moral de las Indias. See *Natural and Moral History of the Indies, The*
Historia plantarum et vires ex Dioscoride, Paulo Aegineta, Theophrasto, Plinio, et recētioribus Graecis (Gesner), **Ren:** 375
Historia plantarum generalis (Ray), **17th:** 782
Historia regum Britanniae. See *History of the Kings of Britain*
Historia tou Peloponnesiacou polemou (Thucydides), **Anc:** 478, 882
Historia universal de la infamia. See *Universal History of Infamy, A*
Historia verdadera de la conquista de Nueva España. See *True History of the Conquest of New Spain, The*
Historiae (Sallust), **Anc:** 743
Historiae (Tacitus), **Anc:** 838
Historiae animalium (Gesner), **Ren:** 376
Historiae Florentini populi. See *History of the Florentine People*
Historiai Herodotou (Herodotus), **Anc:** 109, 136, 248, 251, 407, 618, 631, 807, 827
Histórias sem data (Machado), **19th:** 1451
Historical and Critical Dictionary, An (Bayle), **17th:** 37
Historical and Moral View of the Origin and Progress of the French Revolution (Wollstonecraft), **18th:** 1110
Historical Enquiry into the Probable Causes of the Rationalist Character Lately Predominant in the Theology of Germany, An (Pusey), **19th:** 1845
Historical Essays and Studies (Acton), **19th:** 15
Historical, Political, Moral Essay on Revolutions, An (Chateaubriand), **19th:** 475
Historical relativism, **20th:** 264
Historicism and Its Problems (Troeltsch), **20th:** 4070
Historie des origines du christianisme. See *History of the Origins of Christianity, The*
Historie van den Heer Willem Leevend, De (Deken and Wolff), **18th:** 302
Historie van Mejuffrouw Sara Burgerhart, De (Deken and Wolff), **18th:** 302
Histories, The (Polybius), **Anc:** 674
Historiography, **Anc:** Chinese, 149, 782; Christian, 330; Dio Cassius, 275; geography and, 828; Greek, 883, 970; Herodotus and, 407; Livy and, 511; Plutarch and, 671; Polybius and, 673; Posidonius and, 692; Roman, 743; Tacitus, 838; **MA:** Burgundy, 1060; Byzantine Empire, 865, 1020; China, 945; England, 151, 405; France, 427, 1053, 1063; Germany, 516; Iceland, 951; Italy, 576, 923, 1056; Muslim, 164, 376, 537, 704, 989, 1144; Persia, 41, 413; Renaissance, 1058; **Ren:** Americas, 6, 419;

Italy, 411, 588; North Africa, 555; Scotland, 147; Vietnam, 547; **18th:** 1095-1098; Edward Gibbon, 415-418; Catherine Macaulay, 621-623; Montesquieu, 696; **19th:** England, 415, 1435; France, 1565, 1885, 2218, 2264; Germany, 1582, 1674, 1860; Switzerland, 355; United States, 132, 1744, 1832, 2450; **20th:** 4105; frontier thesis, 4117. *See also* History; Category Index
Historische Fragmente. See *Gesamtausgabe*
Historismus und seine Probleme, Der. See *Historicism and Its Problems*
History, **Anc:** geography and, 828; rhetoric and, 451; Roman, 302; travel and, 619; **18th:** Vico's ages, 1014. *See also* Historiography
History, The. See *Historiai Herodotou*
History and Class Consciousness (Lukács), **20th:** 2468
History and Description of Africa and of the Notable Things Therein Contained, The (Leo Africanus), **Ren:** 555
History and Present State of Electricity, The (Priestley), **18th:** 811
History as the Story of Liberty (Croce), **20th:** 870
History of a Six Weeks' Tour Through a Part of France, Switzerland, Germany, and Holland (Shelley and Shelley), **19th:** 2089
History of al-Ṭabarī, The (al-Ṭabarī), **Anc:** 988; **MA:** 988
History of Ancient Art (Winckelmann), **18th:** 1095
History of British India (Mill), **19th:** 1572, 1575
History of Charles XII, The (Voltaire), **18th:** 1027
History of Christian Philosophy in the Middle Ages (Gilson), **20th:** 1490
History of Creation, The (Haeckel), **19th:** 1005
History of Dogma (Harnack), **20th:** 1682
History of England (Hume), **18th:** 515
History of England During the Thirty Years Peace (Martineau), **19th:** 1507
History of England from the Accession of James I to that of the Brunswick Line, The (Macaulay), **18th:** 621
History of England from the Accession of James the Second, The (Macaulay), **19th:** 1435-1436
History of England Principally in the Seventeenth Century, A (Ranke), **19th:** 1861
History of English Literature (Taine), **19th:** 2217
History of Europe in the Nineteenth Century (Croce), **20th:** 870
History of Florence, The (Guicciardini), **Ren:** 410
History of France, The (Michelet), **19th:** 1565
History of Freedom and Other Essays, The (Acton), **19th:** 15
History of Friedrich II of Prussia, Called Frederick the Great, The (Carlyle), **19th:** 417
History of Greek Culture (Burckhardt), **19th:** 356
History of Henrietta, The (Lennox), **18th:** 595
History of Italy, The (Guicciardini), **Ren:** 411
History of Italy, 1871-1915, A (Croce), **20th:** 870
History of Japan, The (Kämpfer), **17th:** 446-447
History of Jason (Caraccis), **Ren:** 176
History of Little Goody Two-Shoes, The (Newbery), **18th:** 731
History of Mary Prince, The (Traill), **19th:** 2292
History of Massachusetts Bay (Hutchinson), **18th:** 18
History of Mr. Polly, The (Wells), **20th:** 4288
History of My Life (Sand), **19th:** 1989
History of New York, A (Irving), **19th:** 1180
History of Our Country from Its Discovery by Columbus to the Celebration of the Centennial Anniversary of Its Declaration of Independence, The (Richardson), **19th:** 1904
History of Plymouth Plantation (Bradford), **17th:** 86, 130, 878
History of Religious Ideas, A (Eliade), **20th:** 1138
History of Richard III (More), **Ren:** 698
History of Roman Law During the Middle Ages, The (Savigny), **19th:** 2004
History of Rome (Arnold), **19th:** 78
History of Rome, The (Livy). See *Ab urbe condita libri*
History of Rome, The (Mommsen), **19th:** 1583
History of Scotland, The (Buchanan), **Ren:** 147
History of Spiritualism, The (Doyle), **19th:** 690
History of the Adventures of Joseph Andrews, and of His Friend Mr. Abraham Adams, The (Fielding), **18th:** 348
History of the Affairs of Greece. See *Ellēnika*
History of the Arians. See *Historia Arianorum*
History of the Cheltenham Ladies' College, 1853-1901 (Beale), **19th:** 160
History of the Colony and Province of Massachusetts Bay, The (Hutchinson), **18th:** 520
History of the Common Law (Hale), **17th:** 347

History of the Conquest of Mexico (Prescott), **19th:** 390, 1832
History of the Conquest of Peru (Prescott), **19th:** 390, 1832
History of the Conspiracy of Pontiac and the Indian War After the Conquest of Canada (Parkman), **19th:** 1743
History of the Consulate and the Empire of France Under Napoleon (Thiers), **19th:** 2265
History of the Danes, The (Saxo), **MA:** 928
History of the Decline and Fall of the Roman Empire (Gibbon), **Anc:** 139; **18th:** 416
History of the Earth, and Animated Nature, An (Goldsmith), **18th:** 432
History of the Florentine People (Bruni), **MA:** 209
History of the Formation of the Constitution of the United States of America (Bancroft), **19th:** 133
History of the Former Han Dynasty. See *Han Shu*
History of the Franks, The (Gregory of Tours), **MA:** 290, 427
History of the French Revolution (Michelet), **19th:** 1565
History of the French Revolution, The (Thiers), **19th:** 2263
History of the Fresh Water Fishes of Central Europe (Agassiz), **19th:** 32
History of the Future (Vieira), **17th:** 960
History of the Indies (Las Casas), **Ren:** 538
History of the Kings of Britain (Geoffrey of Monmouth), **Anc:** 394; **MA:** 405
History of the Kings of the Goths, Vandals, and Suevi (Isidore), **MA:** 556
History of the Latin and Teutonic Nations from 1494 to 1514 (Ranke), **19th:** 1860
History of the Life and Voyages of Christopher Columbus, A (Irving), **19th:** 1181
History of the Negro Race in America from 1619 to 1880 (Williams), **19th:** 2450-2451
History of the Negro Troops in the War of the Rebellion, 1861-1865 (Williams), **19th:** 2450
History of the Origins of Christianity, The (Renan), **19th:** 1885
History of the Peloponnesian War. See *Historia tou Peloponnesiacou polemou*
History of the People of Israel (Renan), **19th:** 1886
History of the Pleas of the Crown (Hale), **17th:** 347
History of the Popes During the Last Four Centuries, The (Ranke), **19th:** 1861
History of the Rebellion and Civil Wars in England, The (Clarendon), **17th:** 167
History of the Reformation in Germany (Ranke), **19th:** 1861
History of the Reformation of Religion Within the Realm of Scotland, The (Knox), **Ren:** 530
History of the Reign of Ferdinand and Isabella the Catholic (Prescott), **19th:** 1832
History of the Reign of Philip the Second, King of Spain (Prescott), **19th:** 1832
History of the Rise, Progress, and Termination of the American Revolution (Warren), **18th:** 1042
History of the Russian Revolution, The (Trotsky), **20th:** 4075
History of the Standard Oil Company, The (Tarbell), **19th:** 1923; **20th:** 3948
History of the Synoptic Tradition, The (Bultmann), **20th:** 573
History of the Thirty Years' War (Schiller), **18th:** 889
History of the Twelve Caesars. See *De vita Caesarum*
History of the United States (Bancroft), **19th:** 132
History of the Valorous and Wittie Knight-Errant, Don Quixote of the Mancha, The. See *Don Quixote de la Mancha*
History of the Wars of the Emperor Justinian, The (Procopius), **MA:** 76
History of the West-Indies, The (Hakluyt), **Ren:** 419
History of the World, The (Ralegh), **Ren:** 815
History of Trade Unionism, The (Webbs), **20th:** 4254
History of Western Philosophy (Russell), **20th:** 3563
History of Woman Suffrage (Stanton et al.), **19th:** 853, 2149
Histriomastix (Marston), **17th:** 223
Hitchcock, Alfred, **20th:** 1571, 1825-1828, 3863; **Notor:** 636
Hitchy-Koo (Porter), **20th:** 3308
Hitler, Adolf, **20th:** 1829-1833, 2321, 2463, 3110; Christianity, 2971; Czechoslovakia, 301, 1043; France, 2285; Joseph Goebbels, 1513; Hermann Göring, 1545; Heinz Guderian, 1606; Paul von Hindenburg, 1816; IBM, 4248; Italy, 2888; propaganda, 3451; rocket program, 501; Erwin Rommel, 3503; Gerd von Rundstedt, 3559; Soviet Union, 2784; *Time* magazine, 2457; United Kingdom, 723, 4370; **Notor:** 131, 137, 196-197, 265-266, 270, 292, 319, 323, 371, 374, 418, 421, 429, 461-462, 468, 477-480, 609, 717, 770, 801, 873, 894, 911, 934, 937, 969, 987, 992, 1001-1002, 1059, 1074, 1081
Hitori kangai. See *Solitary Thoughts*

Hittites, **Anc:** sacking of Babylon, 377; in Egypt, 47, 736
Hiyoshimaru. *See* Toyotomi Hideyoshi
H.M.S. Pinafore (Gilbert and Sullivan), **19th:** 919
Ho Chi Minh, **20th:** 228, 1834-1838, 2951, 4169
Ho Chung. *See* Ma Yuan
Ho Xuan Huong, **19th:** 1110-1112
Ho Yen, **Anc:** 950
Hoare, Samuel, **20th:** 2286
Hoare-Laval Agreement (1935), **20th:** 2286
Hobbes, Thomas, **17th:** 147, 188, 300, 306, 357, 378-382, 543, 630, 676, 733, 759, 970; **18th:** 621
Hobbit, The (Tolkien), **20th:** 4039
Hobby, Oveta Culp, **20th:** 1838-1841
Hobhouse, Leonard T., **20th:** 1841-1845
Hobomok, **17th:** 879
Hobomok (Child), **19th:** 482
Hochberg, Leonard, **Notor:** 54
Hochbichler, Peter. *See* Mengele, Josef
Hoche, Luise Hoche. *See* Aston, Luise
Hockey, **20th:** 1585
Hockney, David, **20th:** 1845-1848
Hodges, John, **20th:** 814
Hodges, Thomas J. *See* Bell, Tom
Hodgkin, Alan Lloyd, **20th:** 1090
Hodgkin, Dorothy Crowfoot, **20th:** 1849-1851
Hodgkin's disease, **20th:** 2696
Hodgson, Frances Eliza. *See* Burnett, Frances Hodgson
Hoff, Jacobus Henricus van't, **19th:** 103; **20th:** 139, 3089
Hoffa, Jimmy, **20th:** 2103, 2673; **Notor:** 76, 480-482
Hoffman, Abbie, **Notor:** 483-484
Hoffman, Elmyr. *See* Hory, Elmyr de
Hoffman, Friedrich, **18th:** 933
Hoffman, Gertrude, **Notor:** 933
Hoffman, Mark, **Notor:** 664
Hoffmann, Heinrich, **Notor:** 137
Hofmann, Hans, **20th:** 2196, 3303
Hofmannsthal, Hugo von, **20th:** 3886
Hofstadter, Robert, **20th:** 4436
Hogarth, William, **18th:** 497-501; **19th:** 235
Hōgen disturbance (1156), **MA:** 721, 991
Hogg, Thomas Jefferson, **19th:** 2092
Hohenheim, Philippus Aureolus Theophrastus Bombast von. *See* Paracelsus
Hohenstaufen Dynasty, **MA:** 387, 389-390, 474, 1077, 1123; Holy Roman Empire, 727
Hohenzollern, Friedrich Wilhelm von. *See* Frederick William, the Great Elector
Hojarasca, La. See *Leaf Storm, and Other Stories*
Hōjō family, **Ren:** 451
Hōjō no umi. See *Sea of Fertility, The*
Hōjō Tokimasa, **MA:** 721
Hōjō Ujimasa, **Ren:** 451-453; **17th:** 916
Hōjōji, **MA:** 397, 582
Hokumat-e-Eslami. See *Islamic Government*
Holanda, Francisco de, **Ren:** 236
Holbach, Paul-Henri-Dietrich d', **18th:** 501-504
Holbein, Hans, the Younger, **Ren:** 316, 453-456
Holbrooke, Richard, **20th:** 56
Holden, Charles, **20th:** 1165
Holderness, earl of. *See* Rupert, Prince
Holiday, Billie, **20th:** 1852-1855
Holiday, Grant. *See* Gardner, Erle Stanley
Holiday Inn (film), **20th:** 329
Holiness of Life (Bonaventure), **MA:** 181
Holland, John Philip, **19th:** 1113-1116
Hölldobler, Bert H., **20th:** 4359
Holleman, Jerry, **Notor:** 337
Holley, Major, **20th:** 1313
Holliday, Doc, **19th:** 721; **Notor:** 144, 315, 485-486, 899
Holliday, George, **Notor:** 585
Hollis Street Church (Boston), **19th:** 347
Hollmann, Fritz. *See* Mengele, Josef
Hollow Men series (Motherwell), **20th:** 2848
Hollywood League Against Nazism, **20th:** 1658
Hollywood Madam. *See* Fleiss, Heidi
Hollywood or Bust (film), **20th:** 2358
Holmboe, Bernt Michael, **19th:** 9
Holmes, H. H., **Notor:** 486-487
Holmes, Oliver Wendell (writer), **19th:** 1116-1119, 2065
Holmes, Oliver Wendell, Jr. (jurist), **19th:** 1773; **20th:** 1856-1859; **Notor:** 475, 1057
Holocaust, **20th:** 28, 924, 1302, 1547, 1809, 1831-1832, 2286, 4324, 4328; Roman Catholic Church, 3279; U.S. Congress, 3490
Holocaust and the Historians, The (Dawidowicz), **20th:** 924
Holocaust Museum at Yeshiva University, **20th:** 4330
Holocaust Project, The (Chicago and Woodman), **20th:** 752
Holocaust Reader, A (Dawidowicz), **20th:** 924
Holstein, Friedrich von, **19th:** 1119-1122
Holtzman v. Schlesinger (1973), **20th:** 1031
Holy Alliance, **19th:** 1023
Holy Brotherhood, **Ren:** 329
Holy City, The (Lagerlöf), **20th:** 2235
Holy Family (Garzoni), **17th:** 302
Holy Family of the Little Bird (Murillo), **17th:** 671

Holy Family with Angels, The (Rembrandt), **17th:** 787
Holy Family with the Butterfly (Dürer), **Ren:** 298
Holy Kinship Altarpiece (Cranach, the Elder), **Ren:** 262
Holy Land, **MA:** Muslims, 236, 542, 1003
Holy League (1495), **Ren:** 28, 228, 648, 853
Holy League (1511), **Ren:** 410, 499, 519, 588
Holy Roman Emperors, **18th:** Charles VI, 229-231, 653; Joseph II, 544-547, 558; Leopold I, 376
Holy Roman Empire, **MA:** 391, 488, 516, 542, 806, 906; Germany and, 1089; Hohenstaufen Dynasty, 727
Holy Trinity Church, **Ren:** 496
Holy Trinity with the Virgin and Saint John (Masaccio), **MA:** 701
Holy War, The (Bunyan), **17th:** 102
Holy wars. *See* Crusades; *Jihad*
"Holy Willie's Prayer" (Burns), **18th:** 184
Homage to Bach (Braque), **20th:** 495
Homage to Catalonia (Orwell), **20th:** 3082
Homan, Robbi. *See* Hilley, Marie
Homans, Eugene V., **20th:** 2037
Homba. See *Runaway Horses*
Home, The (Gilman), **20th:** 1486
Home and the World, The (film), **20th:** 3395
Home as Found (Cooper), **19th:** 554
Home at Grasmere (Wordsworth), **19th:** 2463
Home Ballads and Other Poems (Whittier), **19th:** 2431
Home Protection Party, **19th:** 2443
Home rule, **19th:** Ireland, 304, 461, 794, 1894; **20th:** India, 178, 222, 1388, 2003, 2855, 2901, 2931, 3100, 3135; Ireland, 808, 843, 979, 1452, 1588, 2292, 3025, 3034
Home Rule Confederation of Great Britain, **19th:** 1748
Home Rule for India League, **19th:** 213
Home Truths (Gallant), **20th:** 1377
Homeopathy, **19th:** 1009
Homer, **Anc:** 196, 407, 427-430, 633, 827, 856, 966
Homer, Winslow, **19th:** 1122-1127
Homestead Steel strike (1892), **19th:** 420, 1042; **20th:** 482, 1521
Homeward Bound (Cooper), **19th:** 554
Homicide, **Anc:** 294; pollution and, 293
Hommage à Cézanne (Denis), **20th:** 973
Hommage à Goya (Redon), **19th:** 1875
Homme armé super voces musicales, L' (Josquin), **Ren:** 516
Homme et son désir, L' (ballet), **20th:** 2735
Homme révolté, L'. See *Rebel, The*
Hommes contre l'humain, Les. See *Men Against Humanity*
Homo Faber (Frisch), **20th:** 1339
Homo habilis, **20th:** 2313, 2315
Homo sapiens, origin of, **20th:** 2312
Homo Viator (Marcel), **20th:** 2609
Homocentricorum sive de stellis (Fracastoro), **Ren:** 344
Homolka, Karla, **Notor:** 93, 488-489
Homosexuality, **Anc:** Greek, 14; Roman, 494; **20th:** early definitions of, 1149; Ireland, 3474; in literature, 202; Nation of Islam, 1218; in plays, 4297; Roman Catholic Church, 2023; study of, 1149, 2162; Zimbabwe, 2859
Homērika zētēmata (Porphyry), **Anc:** 689
Homs, Battle of (1299), **MA:** 412
Homutawake no Mikoto. *See* Ōjin Tennō
Honami Kōetsu, **17th:** 695, 868
Honda, Soichiro, **20th:** 1859-1862
Honda Motor Company, **20th:** 1859
Honda Toshiaki, **18th:** 504-506
Honest Whore, The (Dekker and Middleton), **17th:** 224, 636
Honey Sweeter than Blood (Dalí), **20th:** 905
Hong Bao, **19th:** 2310
Hong Huoxiu. *See* Hong Xiuquan
Hong Kong, retrocession of (1997), **20th:** 970
Hong Taiji. *See* Abahai
Hong Xiuquan, **19th:** 1127-1130, 2484
Honganji, **Ren:** 733
Honglou-meng. See *Dream of the Red Chamber*
Hongwen, Wang, **Notor:** 529
Hongwu, **MA:** 1147, 1156; **Ren:** 1004
Hongxue, **18th:** 195
Hongzhi. *See* Xiaozong
Honnōji Incident (1582), **Ren:** 733
Honoria, **Anc:** 140
Honorius III, **MA:** 389, 436, 1102
Honorius IV, **MA:** 187, 906
Honorius, Flavius, **Anc:** 352, 824, 870
Honthorst, Gerard, **17th:** 823
Hood, James, **20th:** 4205; **Notor:** 1088
Hood, John Bell, **19th:** 613, 2099
Hood, Robin. *See* Robin Hood
Hooft, Gerard 't, **20th:** 4277
Hook (film), **20th:** 3812
Hooke, Robert, **17th:** 48, 79, 349, 372, 383-385, 509, 564, 677, 680, 734, 986
Hooker, Joseph, **19th:** 605, 1199
Hooker, Richard, **Ren:** 457-459; **17th:** 15

Hooker, Thomas, **17th:** 196, 247, 386-388, 567
Hooker telescope, **20th:** 1644
Hooke's law, **17th:** 384
Hooper, Charles, **20th:** 4305
Hoorn, Johan van, **17th:** 852
Hoover, Herbert, **20th:** 655, 1677, 1862-1866, 3510, 3763; **Notor:** 240
Hoover, J. Edgar, **20th:** 1866-1869; **Notor:** 61, 217, 282, 361, 403, 406, 489-491, 556, 890
Hoover, Mrs. *See* Chadwick, Cassie L.
Hoover Moratorium (1931), **20th:** 1864
Hope, Bob, **20th:** 876, 1870-1872, 2358
Hope, Henry, **19th:** 667
Hope Fountain Mission, **19th:** 1406
Hope of Israel, The (Manasseh ben Israel), **17th:** 583
Hopes and Fears (Yonge), **19th:** 2472
Hopi, **Ren:** 246
Hôpital, Michel de L'. *See* L'Hospital, Michel de
Hopkins, Harry, **20th:** 1872-1876
Hopkins, Mark, **19th:** 2133
Hopper, Edward, **20th:** 1876-1879
Hopper, Grace Murray, **20th:** 1879-1882
Hora de todos y la fortuna con seso, La. See *Fortune in Her Wits*
Horace, **Anc:** 196, 430-434, 493, 528, 602, 939
Horace (Corneille), **17th:** 194
Horemheb, **Anc:** 27, 585, 587, 908
Horiuchi, Lon, **Notor:** 1093
Horizons (Geddes), **20th:** 1432
Horkheimer, Max, **20th:** 1632
Horn Trio in E-flat Major, Op. 40 (Brahms), **19th:** 297
Hornby, Ruth. *See* Ellis, Ruth
Horne, Johannes van, **17th:** 898
Horneman, C. F. E., **19th:** 985
Horney, Karen, **20th:** 1346, 1883-1885
Hornigold, Ben, **Notor:** 82, 1023
Hornsby, Rogers, **Notor:** 521
Horologium (Huygens), **17th:** 398
Horologium oscillatorium (Huygens), **17th:** 398
Horowitz, Vladimir, **20th:** 1886-1889
Horrocks, Jeremiah, **17th:** 388-390
Horror vacui (mechanical principle), **Anc:** 311
Horrox, Jeremiah. *See* Horrocks, Jeremiah
Horsa, **Anc:** 394
Horse-Hoing Husbandry (Tull), **18th:** 991
Horse in Landscape (Marc), **20th:** 2607
Horses, Central Asian, **Anc:** 960
Horthy, Elemér. *See* Hory, Elmyr de
Horthy, Miklós, **Notor:** 970
Horti Sallustiani, **Anc:** 742
Horticulture, **19th:** 351
Horus, **Anc:** 557, 705, 996
Horváthová, Margita. *See* Bangová, Margita
Hory, Baron de. *See* Hory, Elmyr de
Hory, Elmyr de, **Notor:** 492-493, 510
Hoshea, **Anc:** 893
Hosokawa Gracia, **Ren:** 459-461
Hosokawa Tadaoki, **Ren:** 459
Hosokawa Tamako. *See* Hosokawa Gracia
Hospital, Michel de L'. *See* L'Hospital, Michel de
Höss, Rudolf, **Notor:** 319, 323
Hossō, **MA:** 1138
Hosties noires (Senghor), **20th:** 3703
Hotchkiss, Hazel Virginia. *See* Wightman, Hazel
Hôtel de Bourgogne, **17th:** 774
Hôtel de Carnavalet, **17th:** 834
Hôtel de Noailles, **17th:** 591
Hôtel de Rambouillet, **17th:** 780, 829, 833
Hôtel des Invalides, **17th:** 590
Hotel Room (Hopper), **20th:** 1878
Hotman, François, **Ren:** 461-466
Hotta Masatoshi, **17th:** 919
Hotta Masayoshi, **19th:** 1170
Ho-tung, Madame. *See* Liu Yin
Hou Hsien. *See* Hou Xian
Hou Xian, **MA:** 1150
Houdini, Harry, **19th:** 690; **20th:** 1889-1891
Hound of the Baskervilles, The (Doyle), **19th:** 689
Hounsfield, Sir Godfrey Newbold, **20th:** 1892-1895
Hounsfield scale, **20th:** 1894
Houphouët-Boigny, Félix, **20th:** 1895-1899
Houphouët-Boigny Law (1946), **20th:** 1897
Hour of Decision, The (radio and television program), **20th:** 1558
Hours of Idleness (Byron), **19th:** 380
Hours of Jeanne of Savoy, The (Pucelle), **MA:** 866
House at Pooh Corner, The (Milne), **20th:** 2754
House by the Railroad (Hopper), **20th:** 1877
House Committee on Un-American Activities, **20th:** 1822, 2664; Charles Chaplin, 733; Arthur Miller, 2743; Ronald Reagan, 3401; Jerome Robbins, 3461; Jack Warner, 4231
House Divided, A (Buck), **20th:** 558
House for Mr. Biswas, A (Naipaul), **20th:** 2903
House Gun, The (Gordimer), **20th:** 1536
House of Bernarda Alba, The (García Lorca), **20th:** 1396
House of Fame, The (Chaucer), **MA:** 264

House of Gentlefolk, A (Turgenev), **19th:** 2319
House of Mirth, The (Wharton), **20th:** 4301
House of Savoy, **17th:** 331
House of Tears (Orozco), **20th:** 3069
House of the Seven Gables, The (Hawthorne), **19th:** 1052
Household Education (Martineau), **19th:** 1507
Householders (Cossacks), **17th:** 785
Houseman, Richard, **Notor:** 30
Houses and House-Life of the American Aborigines (Morgan), **19th:** 1605
Houses of Parliament (British), **19th:** 143, 1840
Houssay, Bernardo Alberto, **20th:** 1899-1902
Houston, Charles H., **20th:** 2633
Houston, Sam, **19th:** 100, 1130-1133, 1991
Hoveyda, Amir Abbas, **20th:** 2781
How Gertrude Teaches Her Children (Pestalozzi), **19th:** 1783
How Green Was My Valley (film), **20th:** 4446
How I Found Livingstone (Stanley), **19th:** 2139
How the Grinch Stole Christmas! (Seuss), **20th:** 3711
How to Marry a Millionaire (film), **20th:** 2798
How to Observe Morals and Manners (Martineau), **19th:** 1506
How to Pay for the War (Keynes), **20th:** 2121
How to Talk with Practically Anybody About Practically Anything (Walters), **20th:** 4211
How Wars Are Got Up in India (Cobden), **19th:** 522
Howard, Catherine, **Ren:** 52, 267, 271, 443, 466-469, 765, 947
Howard, Elizabeth, **Ren:** 111
Howard, Lady Frances, **17th:** 16, 132
Howard, Frank. *See* Fish, Albert
Howard, John Davis. *See* James, Jesse
Howard, Oliver Otis, **19th:** 905, 1231, 1238, 1240
Howard, Sir Robert, **17th:** 240, 765
Howard, Roy, **19th:** 2057
Howard, Thomas. *See* Norfolk, duke of
Howe, Elias, **19th:** 1133-1136
Howe, Elizabeth, **17th:** 690
Howe, Julia Ward, **19th:** 1098, 1137-1142, 1618
Howe, Richard, **18th:** 506-510
Howe, Samuel Gridley, **19th:** 671, 1137, 1141-1144, 1487
Howe, William, **18th:** 510-513
Howelcke, Jan. *See* Hevelius, Johannes
Howell, Vernon Wayne. *See* Koresh, David
Howells, William Dean, **19th:** 702, 2331
Howick, Viscount. *See* Grey, Charles
Howlth incident, **Ren:** 744
Hoxha, Enver, **Notor:** 493-494
Hoxha, Nexhmije, **Notor:** 493-494
Hoyle, Sir Fred, **20th:** 1902-1904
Hoyle, Geoffrey, **20th:** 1904
Hozumi Harunobu. *See* Suzuki Harunobu
Hrabanus. *See* Rabanus Maurus
Hrolfr. *See* Rollo
Hrorekr. *See* Rurik
Hrosvitha, **MA:** 516-518
Hrosvithae Liber terius (Hrosvitha), **MA:** 516
Hsi Kai. *See* Cheng I Sao
Hsia Kuei. *See* Xia Gui
Hsiang-yang. *See* Mi Fei
Hsiao-ch'in. *See* Cixi
Hsiao-tsung. *See* Xiaozong
Hsieh K'ang-lo. *See* Xie Lingyun
Hsieh Ling-yün. *See* Xie Lingyun
Hsien Huang-hau. *See* Cixi
Hsi-tsung. *See* Tianqi
Hsüan-tsang. *See* Xuanzang
Hsüan-t'ung. *See* Puyi
Hu Hanmin, **20th:** 4221
Hu Hao, **Anc:** 781
Hu Yaobang, **20th:** 970, 1905-1908, 2368, 4460
Hu Yao-pang. *See* Hu Yaobang
Hua Guofeng, **20th:** 969, 1906-1909; **Notor:** 529
Hua Kuo-feng. *See* Hua Guofeng
Huai Wang, **Anc:** 732
Huai-tsung. *See* Chongzhen
Huaizong. *See* Chongzhen
Huallpa, Inti Cusi. *See* Huáscar
Huang Yuan Jie, **17th:** 541
Huáscar, **Ren:** 66, 469-472
Huayna Capac, **Ren:** 66, 469
Hubbard, L. Ron, **20th:** 1909-1912; **Notor:** 244, 495-496
Hubble, Edwin Powell, **20th:** 1912-1914, 2338
Hubble constant, **20th:** 1913
Hubble time, **20th:** 1914
Hubble Tuning Fork Diagram, **20th:** 1913
Hubble's law, **20th:** 1913, 2339
Hubert, Robert, **Notor:** 565
Hubertsburg, Treaty of (1763), **18th:** 379
Huberty, Etna, **Notor:** 497
Huberty, James Oliver, **Notor:** 456, 497-498
Hubmaier, Balthasar, **Ren:** 472-474
Hudibras (Butler), **18th:** 989
Hudson, Henry, **17th:** 390-393
Hudson River, **18th:** and Erie Canal, 706; West Point, 565
Hudson River Railroad, **19th:** 2349
Hudson River school, **19th:** 232
Hudson's Bay Company, **17th:** 401, 777; **18th:** 974; **19th:** 2271
Huerta, Adolfo de la, **20th:** 615
Huerta, Dolores, **20th:** 739, 1915-1919

Huerta, Victoriano, **20th:** 2546, 3014, 4160, 4365, 4449; **Notor:** 1070, 1130
Huet, Pierre-Daniel, **17th:** 477, 661
Huffington, Michael, **20th:** 1229
Huggins, Margaret Lindsay, **19th:** 1144-1146
Huggins, William, **19th:** 1145
Hugh of LePuiset, **MA:** 715
Hughenden of Hughenden, Viscount. *See* Disraeli, Benjamin
Hughes, Charles Evans, **20th:** 1677, 1920-1924
Hughes, Howard, **20th:** 1925-1927; **Notor:** 510, 974
Hughes, Jermaine, **Notor:** 922
Hughes, Langston, **20th:** 1928-1931
Hughes, William Morris, **19th:** 1493; **20th:** 1931-1934, 2489
Hughes Aircraft Company, **20th:** 1926
Hugieina pros Pleistarkhon (Diocles), **Anc:** 278
Hugo, Victor, **19th:** 89, 208, 1146-1150; **Notor:** 1068
Huguenots, **Ren:** 164, 185, 424, 426, 429, 462, 568, 704, 856; **17th:** 98, 552, 598, 790, 821, 896; New York, 518; persecution of, 407, 555, 560
Huiguo, **MA:** 620
Huike Severing His Arm (Sesshū), **Ren:** 866
Huis clos. See *No Exit*
Huit Scènes de Faust (Berlioz), **19th:** 201
Huitzilhuitl, **MA:** 559
Hülegü, **MA:** 411
Huliganii (Eliade), **20th:** 1137
Hull, Cordell, **20th:** 1934-1937
Hull, Siege of (1643), **17th:** 262
Hull, William, **19th:** 307
Hull House, **20th:** 22, 2272, 3198
Hull-House Maps and Papers (Lathrop), **20th:** 2272
Hulst, Hendrik van de, **20th:** 3059
Human, All Too Human (Nietzsche), **19th:** 1682
Human Comedy, The (Balzac), **19th:** 128
Human Condition, The (Arendt), **20th:** 119
Human Cycle, The (Aurobindo), **20th:** 179
Human Factor, The (Greene), **20th:** 1579
Human figure, sculpture of, **Anc:** 676
Human Knowledge (Russell), **20th:** 3563
Human Liberty (Leo XIII), **19th:** 1343
Human Mystery, The (Eccles), **20th:** 1091
Human Nature (Hobbes), **17th:** 379
Human Physiology (Houssay), **20th:** 1901
Human rights, **20th:** Bosnia, 2524; Burma, 176; Cambodia, 1943, 3741; Canada, 994; Chile, 3258; China, 970, 2448, 2604; Congo, 2774; Cuba, 694; Dominican Republic, 4084; El Salvador, 3501; Ethiopia, 2702; Germany, 1809, 1831; Ghana, 3390; Haiti, 1070; India, 2930, 3099; Indonesia, 3901; Iran, 2780, 3429; Iraq, 1948; Italy, 2887; Kampuchea, 3299; Malawi, 220; Malaysia, 2552; Nigeria, 182; North Korea, 2140, 2142; Pakistan, 4473; Panama, 4048; Peru, 1360; Portugal, 3608; prisoners, 4000; Romania, 705; Saudi Arabia, 1197; South Africa, 4122; Soviet Union, 1533, 2785; Spain, 1153; Tibet, 903; Uganda, 81; United Nations, 686, 3475; United States, 2172; Yugoslavia, 2757; Zimbabwe, 2858
Human Use of Human Beings, The (Wiener), **20th:** 4323
Human Work (Gilman), **20th:** 1486
Humanae Vitae (Paul VI), **20th:** 3150
Humani Generis (Pius XII), **20th:** 3279
Humanism, **Anc:** Confucian, 237; paganism and, 363; **MA:** 209, 400, 831, 851, 1049; **Ren:** 142, 146, 317, 609; England, 197, 234, 699; France, 548, 618; Germany, 264, 648; Italy, 18, 782; Poland, 242; Portugal, 606
Humanism and Terror (Merleau-Ponty), **20th:** 2711
Humanisme intégral. See *Integral Humanism*
Humanitarian socialism, **19th:** 255
Humanität (Herder), **18th:** 488
Humāyūn, **Ren:** 15, 70, 475-477
Humbert, Cardinal, **MA:** 646
Humble Petition and Advice (1657), **17th:** 206, 485
Humboldt, Alexander von, **19th:** 32, 268, 603, 856, 885, 887, 1151-1154, 2122, 2152
Humboldt, Wilhelm von, **19th:** 1674, 2152
Humboldt's Gift (Bellow), **20th:** 290
Hume, David, **18th:** 113, 514-517
Hume, Joseph, **19th:** 1807, 1897
Humors, theory of the four, **Anc:** 84, 115, 278, 312, 349, 422
Humourous Day's Mirth, An (Chapman), **Ren:** 214
Humperdinck, Engelbert, **19th:** 1154-1157
Humphrey, Hubert H., **20th:** 755, 1938-1941, 2985
Humphreys, Laud, **Notor:** 498-499
Hun Bunall. *See* Hun Sen
Hun Samrach. *See* Hun Sen
Hun Sen, **20th:** 1942-1944, 3741
Hunchback of Notre-Dame, The (Hugo), **19th:** 1148
Hundejahre. See *Dog Years*
Hundred Associates, **17th:** 141

Hundred Days (France), **19th:** 397, 609
Hundred Days' Reform (China), **19th:** 497, 2487
Hundred Flowers Campaign, **20th:** 968
Hundred Schools period, **Anc:** 979
Hundred Slain, Battle of (1866). *See* Fetterman Massacre
Hundred Years' War (1337-1453), **MA:** 247, 257, 261, 264, 350, 393, 445, 491, 578, 1054; **Ren:** 226, 301, 434, 574
Hung Hsiu-ch'üan. *See* Hong Xiuquan
Hung Taiji. *See* Abahai
Hungarian Revolution (1848-1849), **19th:** 621
Hungarian Revolution (1956), **20th:** 1056, 1655, 2129
Hungarian Rhapsodies (Liszt), **19th:** 1394
Hungary, **Anc:** Huns in, 140; **MA:** 105; Christianity, 638, 964; kings, 107, 521, 638, 966; law, 638; Turkish invasion of, 521; **Ren:** Ottoman invasion of, 636; **17th:** 453, 528, 861; **19th:** 819. *See also* Geographical Index
Hungary, Mary of. *See* Mary of Hungary
Hung-chih. *See* Xiaozong
Hunger (Hamsun), **20th:** 1661
Hunger Artist, A (Kafka), **20th:** 2068
Hungry Lion, The (Rousseau), **19th:** 1953
Hung-wu. *See* Hongwu
Hunneric, **Anc:** 353
Huns, **Anc:** 138, 776, 868
Hunt, E. Howard, **Notor:** 443, 499-501, 643
Hunt, Helen Maria. *See* Jackson, Helen Hunt
Hunt, Leigh, **19th:** 381, 1260
Hunt, Richard Morris, **19th:** 775
Hunt, Thomas, **17th:** 875
Hunt, Walter, **19th:** 1135
Hunt, William Holman, **19th:** 1157-1160, 1755, 1940
Hunter, Robert, **19th:** 1105
Hunters in the Snow (Bruegel), **Ren:** 136
Hunting of the Snark, The (Carroll), **19th:** 424
Hunting Tigers Under Glass (Richler), **20th:** 3439
Huntington, Collis, **19th:** 2133
Hunyadi, János, **MA:** 519-522, 711; **Ren:** 642, 981; **Notor:** 1072
Hunyadi, Mátyás. *See* Matthias I Corvinus
Hurdes, Las. See *Land Without Bread*
Hurons, **Ren:** 448; **17th:** 141, 423, 499, 575, 603
Hurrians, **Anc:** 121
Hurston, Zora Neale, **20th:** 1944-1947
Hurtado de Mendoza, Ana. *See* Mendoza y de la Cerda, Ana de
Hus, Jan, **MA:** 522-525, 1023, 1090, 1162
Husamuddin Ḥasan, Chalabī, **MA:** 909
Ḥusayn ibn ʿAlī, **20th:** 1202
Hussein I, **20th:** 112, 153, 1102, 1950-1955
Hussein, Qusay Saddam, **Notor:** 501-502, 506
Hussein, Saddam, **20th:** 56, 1947-1950, 3323; **Notor:** 6, 101, 375, 501, 503-505
Hussein, Uday, **Notor:** 501, 505-507
Hussein ibn Talal. *See* Hussein I
Husserl, Edmund, **20th:** 1742, 1955-1957, 2611, 3841
Hussey, Obed, **19th:** 1438
Hussite Overture (Dvořák), **19th:** 713
Hussites, **MA:** 1090, 1162
Hustler Magazine and Flynt v. Falwell (1988), **20th:** 1210
Huston Plan (1970), **20th:** 1868
Hut, Hans, **Ren:** 473
Hutaosâ. *See* Atossa
Hutchins, Robert M., **20th:** 1958-1961
Hutchins, William. *See* Tyndale, William
Hutchinson, Anne, **17th:** 196-197, 247, 386, 394-396, 941, 992
Hutchinson, Thomas, **18th:** 17, 518-521
Hutten, Ulrich von, **Ren:** 775
Hutterites, **Ren:** 474
Huxley, Aldous, **20th:** 1961-1964
Huxley, Andrew Fielding, **20th:** 1090
Huxley, Thomas Henry, **19th:** 276, 605, 1161-1164
Huygens, Christiaan, **17th:** 135, 320, 323, 335, 371, 385, 397-400, 510, 514, 710
Huygens, Constantijn, **17th:** 250, 397, 823
Huysmans, Karl Joris, **Notor:** 933
Hvad Christus dømmer om officiel Christendom. See *What Christ's Judgment Is About Official Christianity*
Hydaspes, Battle of the (326 B.C.E.), **Anc:** 202
Hydatius of Emerita, **Anc:** 698
Hyde, Edward. *See* Clarendon, first earl of
Hyde Park (Shirley), **17th:** 847
Hyde Park Declaration (1941), **20th:** 2157
Hyder Ali, **18th:** 522-523
Hydraulic engineering, Greek, **Anc:** 323
Hydriotaphia Urne-Buriall (Browne), **17th:** 95
Hydrodynamics (Bernoulli), **17th:** 49
Hydrogen bomb, **20th:** development of, 343, 1380, 2945, 3970; Soviet Union, 2215, 3066, 3603; United States, 2215, 2302, 3356
Hygieia, **Anc:** 761
Hygiene, **Anc:** Greek, 278
Hyginus of Cordova, **Anc:** 698, 918

Hyksos, **Anc:** 389, 585
Hymn (Cædmon), **MA:** 220
Hymn of Praise (Mendelssohn), **19th:** 1550
"Hymn to Intellectual Beauty" (Shelley), **19th:** 2094
Hymn to St. Cecilia, A (Britten), **20th:** 530
Hymnen (Stockhausen), **20th:** 3875
Hymnes, Les (Ronsard), **Ren:** 838
Hymns, **Anc:** 298, 732
Hymns and Sacred Poems (Wesley), **18th:** 1063
Hymns for Childhood (Hemans), **19th:** 1077
Hymns in Prose for Children (Barbauld), **18th:** 87
Hymns of the Forty-ninth Parallel (Lang), **20th:** 2258
Hymns on the Works of Nature for the Use of Children (Hemans), **19th:** 1077
Hymnus Amoris (Nielsen), **20th:** 2965
Hypar shell, **20th:** 632
Hypatia, **Anc:** 79, 434-436
Hyperion (Longfellow), **19th:** 1417
Hyperprism (Varèse), **20th:** 4143
Hypertext, **20th:** 331
Hypothèse de l'atome primitif, L'. See *Primeval Atom, The*
Hypsicles of Alexandria, **Anc:** 317
Hypsilantis. *See* Ypsilantis
Hyrcanus, **Anc:** 403
Hysteresis, law of, **19th:** 2157
Hysteria, **20th:** 510, 515

I

I and the Village (Chagall), **20th:** 717
I and Thou (Buber), **20th:** 554
I Feel Bad About My Neck (Ephron), **20th:** 1163
I-4, **20th:** 4108
I, Governor of California—And How I Ended Poverty (Sinclair), **20th:** 3752
I Know Why the Caged Bird Sings (Angelou), **20th:** 98
I Live in Fear (film), **20th:** 2219
I Married an Angel (Rodgers and Hart), **20th:** 1693
I Never Loved a Man (the Way I Loved You) (Franklin), **20th:** 1313
I Remember (Flexner), **20th:** 1258
I Remember (Pasternak), **20th:** 3133
I, Rigoberta Menchú (Menchú), **20th:** 2686
I-Thou philosophy, **20th:** 549, 556
I Thought of Daisy (Wilson), **20th:** 4355
I vitelloni (film), **20th:** 1232
I Wonder as I Wander (Hughes), **20th:** 1929
Ia Orana Maria (Gauguin), **19th:** 880
Iaia Garcia (Machado), **19th:** 1450
Iambic senarii (poetic meter), **Anc:** 629
Iamblichus, **Anc:** 288, 701
Iamboi (Callimachus), **Anc:** 180
Iatrochemistry, **17th:** 361, 986
Iatromechanism, **17th:** 362
Ibanah ʿan usul al-diyanah, Al-. See *Elucidation of Islam's Foundation, The*
Ibáñez, Carlos, **20th:** 71
Iberian Peninsula, Muslim invasion of, **MA:** 33
Iberville, Pierre Le Moyne d', **17th:** 401-403
IBM, **20th:** 1421, 4247; System/360, 4248
Ibn Abī Bakr Ture, Muḥammad. *See* Mohammed I Askia
Ibn al-ʿArabī, **MA:** 526-529
Ibn al-Haytham. *See* Alhazen
Ibn al-Haytham's On the Configuration of the World (Alhazen), **MA:** 68
Ibn al-Zubayr, **MA:** 4
Ibn Baṭṭūṭah, **MA:** 529-532
Ibn Gabirol, **MA:** 532-535
Ibn Khaldūn, **MA:** 536-539, 704
Ibn Muḥammad al-Wazzān al-Zaiyātī, al-Ḥasan. *See* Leo Africanus
Ibn Rushd, Abū al-Walīd Muḥammad ibn Aḥmad ibn Muḥammad. *See* Averroës
Ibn Tufayl, **MA:** 119
Ibn Tūmart, **MA:** 6
Ibn Yadir, **Ren:** 595
Ibos, massacre of, **20th:** 182
İbrahim (Ottoman sultan), **17th:** 472, 670
Ibrahim (Scudéry), **17th:** 829
Ibrāhīm ibn Adham, **MA:** 875
Ibrāhīm Lodī, **Ren:** 70, 478-479
İbrahim Paşa (c. 1493-1536; Ottoman vizier), **Ren:** 480-482
Ibrāhīm Paşa (1789-1848; Egyptian viceroy), **19th:** 1621
Ibsen, Henrik, **19th:** 986, 1165-1168; **20th:** 2056
Ibuka, Masaru, **20th:** 2831
Ibycus, **Notor:** 851
Icare (ballet), **20th:** 2379
Ice-Bound Heights of the Mustagh (Workman and Workman), **19th:** 2468
Iceland, **MA:** historiography, 951; law, 951; **20th:** independence of, 2309. *See also* Geographical Index
Icelandic Collection (Banks), **18th:** 81
Iceman, the. *See* Kuklinski, Richard
Iceman Cometh, The (O'Neill), **20th:** 3053
Ich und Du. See *I and Thou*
Ichiban utsukushiku. See *Most Beautiful, The*
Ichijō, **MA:** 397, 739, 931
Ichinotani, Battle of (1194), **MA:** 722
Ichiyūsai Hiroshige. *See* Hiroshige
Ici et maintenant (Mitterrand), **20th:** 2771
Icones principum vivorum doctorum pictorum . . . . See *Iconography, The*
Iconoclasm, **MA:** 588

Iconoclastic Controversy, **MA:** 549, 588, 1020
Iconography, The (van Dyck), **17th:** 245
Ida of Nivelles, **MA:** 145
Idea of a Patriot King, The (Bolingbroke), **18th:** 138
Idea of a University Defined and Illustrated, The (Newman), **19th:** 1664
Idea of National Interest, The (Beard), **20th:** 264
Idea of the University, The (Jaspers), **20th:** 1998
Idea, the Shepheards Garland (Drayton), **17th:** 237
Ideal Husband, An (Wilde), **19th:** 2433
Idealism, **Anc:** in art, 635; **18th:** 344, 514, 548, 887-890; **19th:** 290, 972, 1065, 1774, 2009; **20th:** 1842, 2814
Ideals, Platonic, **Anc:** 88, 660
Ideas Mirrour (Drayton), **17th:** 237
Idée générale de la révolution au XIXe siècle. See *General Idea of the Revolution in the Nineteenth Century, The*
Ideen zu einer Philosophie der Nature. See *Introduction to the Philosophy of Nature*
Ideen zur Philosophie der Geschichte der Menschheit. See *Outlines of a Philosophy of the History of Man*
Idiot, The (film), **20th:** 2218
Idiot, The (novel by Dostoevski), **19th:** 679
Idol of Paris, The (Bernhardt), **19th:** 210
Idolatry, **Anc:** 1, 258, 574
Idris I, **20th:** 3351
Idrīsī, al-, **MA:** 539-541
Idylls of the King (Tennyson), **19th:** 2245
Iesu no shōgai. See *Life of Jesus, A*
If You Know Not Me, You Know Nobody (Heywood), **17th:** 374
Ifriqiya, Almohad capture of, **MA:** 8
Iggereth Hashemad (Maimonides), **MA:** 686
Iglesia de la Virgen Milagrosa, **20th:** 633
Ignatius, **MA:** 766
Ignatius His Conclave (Donne), **17th:** 232
Ignatius of Antioch, **Anc:** 437-439
Ignatius of Loyola, Saint, **Ren:** 482-485, 769, 1000
Ignoth, **Ren:** 522
Igor, **MA:** 792
Ihara Saikaku, **17th:** 403-405
Iḥyāʿ ʿulūm al-dīn. See *Revival of Religious Sciences, The*
Ii Naosuke, **19th:** 1168-1171, 1969
Ikeda, Hayato, **20th:** 1965-1967, 3646
Ikiru (film), **20th:** 2218
Ikkyū, **MA:** 1154
Il-Khanid Dynasty, **MA:** 411
Île des pingouins, L'. See *Penguin Island*
Île mystérieuse, L'. See *Mysterious Island, The*
Ilg, Frances L., **20th:** 1466
ILGWU. *See* International Ladies' Garment Workers Union
Iliad (Homer), **Anc:** 407, 427, 635
Ilios (Schliemann), **19th:** 2017
Ilipa, Battle of (206 B.C.E.), **Anc:** 758
Iliupersis (Polygnotus), **Anc:** 678
I'll Leave It to You (Coward), **20th:** 853
Illinois (tribe), **17th:** 434
Illness as Metaphor (Sontag), **20th:** 3790
Illumination, The (Maimonides), **MA:** 687
Illumination, manuscript, **MA:** 366, 866
Illuminations (Verlaine), **19th:** 1913
Illuminatus, Doctor. *See* Lull, Raymond
Illusion comique, L' (Corneille), **17th:** 193
Illusions du progrès, Les (Sorel), **20th:** 3792
Illustrated Account Given by Hevelius in His "Machina celestis" of the Method of Mounting His Telescopes and Erecting an Observatory, The. See *Machina coelestis*
Illustration, **19th:** England, 162; United States, 1881
Illustrations and Proofs of the Principle of Population (Place), **19th:** 1807
Illustrations of Political Economy (Martineau), **19th:** 1506
Illustrations of Taxation (Martineau), **19th:** 1506
Illyria, **Anc:** 638
ILP. *See* Independent Labour Party
Ilsŏn gun, Battle of (936), **MA:** 1082
Iltutmish, **MA:** 888
Ilyushin, Sergey, **20th:** 4109
Im Dickicht der Städte. See *In the Jungle of Cities*
Im Krebsgang. See *Crabwalk*
I'm No Angel (film), **20th:** 4298
I'm Not Stiller (Frisch), **20th:** 1339
Im Schatten des Kongostaates (Frobenius), **20th:** 1342
Im Westen nichts Neues. See *All Quiet on the Western Front*
iMac, introduction, **20th:** 2008
Imagawa family, **Ren:** 451
Imagawa Yoshimoto, **Ren:** 451, 732; **17th:** 915
Images (Debussy), **20th:** 938
Images à la sauvette. See *Decisive Moment, The*
Imaginary Invalid, The (Molière), **17th:** 648
Imaginary Portraits (Pater), **19th:** 1756
Imagines (Varro), **Anc:** 929
Imagism, **20th:** 1623, 2445
Imallye, Granny. *See* O'Malley, Grace

Imbangala, **17th:** 687
Imhotep, **Anc:** 439-442, 996
Imitating Tang Yin's "Dwelling in the Summer Mountains" (Chen), **17th:** 157
Imitation of Christ, The (Thomas à Kempis), **MA:** 1023
Imlay, Gilbert, **18th:** 1110
Immaculate Conception, **Anc:** 539; **MA:** 330
Immaculate Conception of the Escorial, The (Murillo), **17th:** 671
Immigration, **19th:** 911; Italy to United States, 383; laws governing, 779; opposition to, 944; **20th:** Jews to Israel, 2676; policies regarding, 2418; Slavs to United States, 198
Immoralist, The (Gide), **20th:** 1478
Immortal Swan, The (film), **20th:** 3167
Immortale Dei. See *On the Christian Constitution of States*
Immunogenicity, **20th:** 2251
Immunological Surveillance (Burnet), **20th:** 589
Immunology, **19th:** 1753; **20th:** 587, 2865
Impaler, Vlad the. *See* Vlad III the Impaler
Impeachments (U.S.), **18th:** Samuel Chase, 239; Warren Hastings, 176; **19th:** 1230; **20th:** Bill Clinton, 786, 790, 3419; Richard M. Nixon, 2047, 2986
Imperfect Indicative (Krasner), **20th:** 2197
Imperial Academy (China), **Anc:** 960
Imperial Ballet (Russia), **20th:** 1263
Imperial Germany and the Industrial Revolution (Veblen), **20th:** 4155
Imperial Hotel, Tokyo, **20th:** 4401
Imperial Rescript on Education (1890), **19th:** 1632
Imperial Rescript to Soldiers and Sailors (1882), **19th:** 1631
Imperial Theater, Vienna, **18th:** 129
Imperial War Council, **18th:** 331
Imperial Woman (Buck), **20th:** 559
Imperialism, **Anc:** Roman, 19; **19th:** Belgium, 1349; Britain, 461, 981, 1407; Britain in Africa, 941; Britain in India, 1203; Europe in Africa, 1981; France in Africa, 756; opposition to, 510; **20th:** 2343. *See also* Expansionism
Imperialism and World Economy (Bukharin), **20th:** 567
Imphal, Battle of (1945), **20th:** 3760
Impiété des déistes, athées, et libertins de ce temps, L' (Mersenne), **17th:** 629
Importance of Being Earnest, The (Wilde), **19th:** 2433
Importants, Les, **17th:** 159
Impresiones y paisajes. See *Impressions and Landscapes*
Impression, Sunrise (Monet), **20th:** 2791
Impressionen unter Wasser. See *Underwater Impressions*
Impressionism, **18th:** Jean-Siméon Chardin, 225; Francisco de Goya, 437; **19th:** 434, 453, 632, 879, 934, 1481, 1800, 1889; **20th:** 1876, 2164, 2335, 2650, 2790; music, 1207
Impressions and Landscapes (García Lorca), **20th:** 1395
Improvement of Moral Qualities, The (Ibn Gabirol), **MA:** 533
Improvisata over to norske folkeviser (Grieg), **19th:** 986
Improvisatore, The (Andersen), **19th:** 61
In a Free State (Naipaul), **20th:** 2903
In Advance of the Broken Arm (Duchamp), **20th:** 1052
In Cold Blood (Capote), **20th:** 646
In Connection with the De Willoughby Claim (Burnett), **19th:** 358
In Darkest England and the Way Out (Booth), **19th:** 275
In Delum (Callimachus), **Anc:** 180
In den Wohnungen des Todes (Sachs), **20th:** 3584
In laudem Basilii Magni (Gregory of Nazianzus), **Anc:** 361
In Love and Trouble (Walker), **20th:** 4197
In Male and Female (Mead), **20th:** 2669
In Memoriam (Sullivan), **19th:** 918
In Memoriam (Tennyson), **19th:** 2245
In Montgomery, and Other Poems (Brooks), **20th:** 538
In Our Time (Hemingway), **20th:** 1756
In Praise of Constantine. See *Oratio de laudibus Constantini*
In Praise of the Baʿal Shem Tov, **18th:** 69
In Retrospect (McNamara), **20th:** 2542
In Search of Lost Time. See *Remembrance of Things Past* (Proust)
In Search of Our Mothers' Gardens (Walker), **20th:** 4197
In the Clearing (Frost), **20th:** 1350
In the Court of Public Opinion (Hiss), **20th:** 1823
In the Heat of the Night (film), **20th:** 3297
In the Ice World of the Himálaya (Workman and Workman), **19th:** 2467
In the Jungle of Cities (Brecht), **20th:** 504
In the Midst of Life (Bierce), **19th:** 229
In the Night Kitchen (Sendak), **20th:** 3699
In the Skin of a Lion (Ondaatje), **20th:** 3049

In the South (Elgar), **20th:** 1134
In the Steppes of Central Asia (Borodin), **19th:** 282
In the Wee Small Hours (Sinatra), **20th:** 3748
In This Our World (Gilman), **20th:** 1485
Inanna, **Anc:** 298, 915
Inaugural addresses, U.S. presidents, **20th:** Calvin Coolidge, 834; Franklin D. Roosevelt, 3512
Inca, Topa. *See* Topa Inca
Inca, Viracocha. *See* Viracocha Inca
Inca Empire, **Ren:** 66, 469, 746, 801, 902; civil war, 68; **18th:** 993-995
Inca Urcon, **Ren:** 746
Inca Yupanqui, Pachacutec. *See* Pachacuti
Incest, **Anc:** 107; brother-sister, 213, 545, 716; father-daughter, 188, 588; sibling marriage, 136
Incitement to Investigation (al-Ashʿarī), **MA:** 112
Incoherence of the Incoherence (Averroës), **MA:** 121
Incoherence of the Philosophers (al-Ghazzālī), **MA:** 121, 416
Income Doubling Plan, **20th:** 1966
Income tax, Mexico, **20th:** 616
Incomparable Atuk, The (Richler), **20th:** 3438
Incompleteness theorem, **20th:** 1510
Inconvenient Truth, An (Gore), **20th:** 1540
Incoronazione di Poppea, L' (Monteverdi), **17th:** 659
Incredulity of St. Thomas, The (Caravaggio), **Ren:** 171
Indemnity, Act of (1660), **17th:** 169, 942
Independence, **19th:** Belgium, 1732; Bolivia, 2196; Brazil from Portugal, 1764; Chile, 1985; Colombia, 2195; Cuba, 1462, 1503; Ecuador, 2195; Greece, 56, 381, 404, 2478; Mexico, 1095, 1991; Peru, 1985, 2196; Texas, 1991; Venezuela, 2195; **20th:** Algeria, 8; Angola, 3607; Bangladesh, 369, 2005; Bosnia, 2758; Burma, 3986; Crete, 4157; Cuba, 3519; Democratic Republic of the Congo, 2476, 2773, 3810, 4092; Egypt, 4439; Finland, 3738; Ghana, 2990; Guinea, 4054; Iceland, 2309; Indonesia, 1705, 3904; Ivory Coast, 1897; Katanga, 4091; Kenya, 2107; Libya, 3351; Malawi, 219; Morocco, 1699; Mozambique, 2515, 3607; Nigeria, 181; Norway, 2909; Pakistan, 1389, 2004, 2856; Philippines, 2493, 2620; Poland, 3252; Rhodesia, 4361; Senegal, 3704; Tanzania, 3005; Trinidad and Tobago, 830; Tunisia, 458, 2699; Uganda, 80, 3011; Vietnam, 228, 1836, 2699, 4170. *See also* Home rule
Independence, Netherlands Wars of. *See* Dutch Wars of Independence
Independent (journal), **19th:** 174
Independent Commission on International Development Issues, **20th:** 492
Independent Labour Party, **19th:** 1026
Independent People (Laxness), **20th:** 2309
Indeterminate analysis, **Anc:** 82
Index librorum prohibitorum. See *Index of Prohibited Books*
Index of Forbidden Books. See *Index of Prohibited Books*
Index of Prohibited Books, **Ren:** 29, 394, 589, 689, 929; **17th:** 300; **18th:** 103; **20th:** 3273
India, **Anc:** Christianity and, 880; Greece and, 551; **MA:** architecture, 41; astronomy, 109, 195; geometry, 109; Ghaznavid invasion of, 684; Khaljī Dynasty, 41; mathematics, 109, 195; Muslim invasion of, 40; philosophy, 876, 926; poetry, 109, 195; theater, 461; **Ren:** Mughal Empire and, 71, 475; Portugal and, 22, 366; **18th:** British colonialism, 469-472; first Marquess Cornwallis, 279; Joseph-François Dupleix, 311-313; military, 522; nationalism, 523; **19th:** British rule of, 410, 596, 1328, 1434, 1718, 2409; home rule, 213; social reform, 213; **20th:** George Nathaniel Curzon, 895; home rule, 178, 222, 1388, 2003, 2855, 2901, 2931, 3100, 3135; Louis Mountbatten, 2854. *See also* Geographical Index
India Act of 1784, **18th:** 365, 470, 789
India Act of 1935, **20th:** 602
India Independence Act of 1947, **20th:** 2004
India Lobby, **19th:** 1634
India-Pakistan War (1965), **20th:** 368
India-Pakistan War (1971), **20th:** 369, 1386
Indian Association, **20th:** 221
Indian Currency and Finance (Keynes), **20th:** 2120
Indian Emperor, The (Dryden), **17th:** 240
Indian Grammar, The (Eliot), **17th:** 248
Indian National Congress, **19th:** 1635, 1856
Indian Queen, The (Dryden, Purcell, and Howard), **17th:** 240, 765
Indian Removal Bill (1830), **19th:** 571, 1937
Indian reservations, **19th:** Iroquois, 1603; Lakota, 568, 1873, 2109; Nez Perce, 1240
Indian Territory, **19th:** 2069
Indiana (Sand), **19th:** 1987

Indians of North-west America (Gallatin), **19th:** 856
"Indications of the Goals of the Three Teachings" (Kūkai), **MA:** 620
"Indictment of Nanna, The" (Enheduanna), **Anc:** 299
Indies, Council of the, **Ren:** 223, 538. *See also* New Laws
Indigenismo, **19th:** 1514; **20th:** 1716
Individualism and Economic Order (Hayek), **20th:** 1722
Indochinese War, First (1946-1954), **20th:** 1836, 4170
Índole (Matto), **19th:** 1513
Indonesia, **20th:** independence of, 1705, 3904. *See also* Geographical Index
Indulgence, Act of (1667), **17th:** 122
Indulgence, Declarations of (1672, 1687), **17th:** 101, 417
Industrial Charter (1947), **20th:** 603
Industrial Democracy (Webbs), **20th:** 4254
Industrial Revolution, **18th:** Sir Richard Arkwright, 55-59; Queen Caroline, 203; Abraham Darby, 292-295; England, 156-158, 162, 1058, 1087; John Kay, 559-561; mass production, 156; William Murdock, 717; Thomas Newcomen, 733-735; United States, 1077; James Watt, 1049; workers, 57, 560
Industrial Revolution (Beard), **20th:** 262
Industrial System (Saint-Simon), **19th:** 1976
Industrialism, **18th:** Sir Richard Arkwright, 55; Matthew Boulton, 157; James Brindley, 162; Abraham Darby, 293; England, 162, 715; France, 589; Scotland, 858-862; steam engine, 735; transportation, 162; **20th:** 3751, 3818, 3956
Industry. *See* Category Index under Business and Industry
Inés de la Cruz, Sor Juana. *See* Cruz, Sor Juana Inés de la
Infant and Child in the Culture of Today (Gesell and Ilg), **20th:** 1466
Infant Behavior (Gesell, Thompson, and Amatruda), **20th:** 1466
Infant Christ and St. John the Baptist Playing with a Lamb (van Hemessen), **Ren:** 421
Infant Life Protection Act of 1872, **19th:** 372
Infantry Tactics (Scott), **19th:** 2052
Infelicia (Menken), **19th:** 1557
Infernal Machine, The (Cocteau), **20th:** 795
Inferno, The (Hoyles), **20th:** 1904
Inferno (Strindberg), **20th:** 3898
Inflation, **20th:** Brazil, 652; Canada, 4078; economic theory, 1333; Poland, 4193; Tunisia, 459; United Kingdom, 3993; United States, 668, 1276, 1581; Zimbabwe, 2859
Infusoria, **18th:** 926
Ingalls, Laura Elizabeth. *See* Wilder, Laura Ingalls
Ingeborg, **MA:** 543
Ingenioso hidalgo don Quixote de la Mancha, El. See *Don Quixote de la Mancha*
Ingenue (Lang), **20th:** 2258
Ingersoll, Robert G., **19th:** 252
Ingle, Richard, **17th:** 92
Ingle's Rebellion (1644), **17th:** 92
Inglis, Frances Erskine. *See* Calderón de la Barca, Fanny
Ingoldsby, Richard, **17th:** 519
Ingres, Jean-Auguste-Dominique, **19th:** 1171-1175
Inherit the Wind (film), **20th:** 4067
Inhibitory Pathways of the Central Nervous System, The (Eccles), **20th:** 1091
Inklings (literary group), **20th:** 4039
Inland Voyage, An (Stevenson), **19th:** 2173
Inleidinge tot de Hollandsche Rechts-geleerdheyd. See *Introduction to Dutch Jurisprudence*
"In-min-me-hus-a" (Enheduanna), **Anc:** 299
Inner Commentary to the Book of Changes (Wang), **17th:** 972
Inni sacri. See *Sacred Hymns, The*
Innocent II, **MA:** 161, 272
Innocent III, **MA:** 226, 316, 379, 436, 541-545, 571, 585, 837, 1047, 1059, 1105
Innocent IV, **MA:** 286, 391, 545-548, 1053, 1111
Innocent VI, **MA:** 899
Innocent VII, **MA:** 209
Innocent VIII, **Ren:** 518, 603, 657, 783, 851, 940
Innocent X, **17th:** 9, 68, 422, 773
Innocent XI, **17th:** 405-407, 744, 882
Innocent XIII, **17th:** 265
Innocent Love (Martin), **20th:** 2638
Innocents Abroad, The (Twain), **19th:** 2330
Innommable, L'. See *Unnamable, The*
Inorganic Evolution as Studied by Spectrum Analysis (Lockyer), **19th:** 1414
Inquiries into the Human Faculty and Its Development (Galton), **19th:** 862
Inquiry Concerning the Principles of Political Justice, An (Godwin), **19th:** 2093
Inquiry into Cause and Effects of the Variolæ Vaccinæ, An (Jenner), **18th:** 534
Inquiry into Meaning and Truth (Russell), **20th:** 3563
Inquiry into the Colonial Policy of the European Powers, An (Brougham), **19th:** 312

Inquiry into the Good, An (Nishida), **20th:** 2981
Inquiry into the Nature and Causes of the Wealth of Nations, An. See *Wealth of Nations, The*
Inquiry into the Nature of Peace and the Terms of Its Perpetuation, An (Veblen), **20th:** 4155
Inquiry Whether Crime and Misery Are Produced or Prevented by Our Present System of Prison Discipline, An (Buxton), **19th:** 377
Inquisition, **MA:** 2, 318, 437, 763, 778, 858, 882; **Ren:** France, 619; Hungary, 842; Italy, 960; Jews and, 330, 606, 940; Portugal, 146, 514, 606; punishments, 940; Roman, 140, 174, 769, 797; Spain, 330, 928, 940; Switzerland, 863; women and, 235, 619, 929; **17th:** Bologna, 581; Campanella, 125; Ferdinand II's use of, 269; Galileo, 227, 300, 594, 936; Helmont, 362; Jewish conversions, 871; Netherlands, 288; Rose of Lima, 797; Sarpi, 720; Vieira, 960; **18th:** Charles III, 228; reform of, 796
Insanity defense, **18th:** 328
"Inscription on the Buddha-Shadow" (Xie Lingyun), **Anc:** 976
Inscriptions regni Neapolitani Latinae (Mommsen), **19th:** 1582
Insect Play, The (Čapeks), **20th:** 639
Insect Societies, The (Wilson), **20th:** 4359
Inspector General, The (Gogol), **19th:** 938; **20th:** 2723
Instantius, **Anc:** 698
Instauratio magna. See *Great Instauration, The*
Institut de France, **18th:** 219
Institut d'Égypte. *See* Egyptian Institute
Institute for Advanced Study, **20th:** 1258
Institute for Sex Research, **20th:** 2160
Institute for the Morphology of Culture. *See* Frobenius Institute
Institute of Plant Physiology, **19th:** 528
Institute of the Blessed Virgin Mary, **17th:** 974
Institutes (Coke), **Ren:** 572; **17th:** 178
Institutes of Gaius, **MA:** 601
Institutes of Natural and Revealed Religions (Priestley), **18th:** 811
Institutes of the Christian Religion (Calvin), **Ren:** 163, 165, 462, 619, 863
Institutio principis Christiani. See *Education of a Christian Prince, The*
Institutiones (Cassiodorus), **MA:** 235, 313
Institutiones (Gaius). See *Institutes of Gaius*
Institutiones anatomicae (Vesalius), **Ren:** 966
Institutiones calculi differentialis (Euler), **18th:** 335
Institutiones calculi integralis (Euler), **18th:** 335
Institutiones divinarum et humanarum lectionum. See *Institutiones* (Cassiodorus)
Institutiones grammaticae (Priscian), **MA:** 860
Institutions de physique (Châtelet), **18th:** 241
Instituzioni Analitiche ad Uso della Gioventù Italiana. See *Analytical Institutions*
Instruction of a Christian Woman, The (Vives), **Ren:** 188
Instructions for Practical Living (Wang), **Ren:** 987
Instructions for the Education of a Daughter (Fénelon), **17th:** 265
Instructionum. See *Memoriale*
Instrument of Government (1653), **17th:** 54, 206, 485
Instrumentalism, **20th:** 984
Insulin, **20th:** discovery of, 226, 2526; structure of, 1850, 3623
Integral Humanism (Maritain), 2625
Intelligent Individual and Society, The (Bridgman), **20th:** 528
Intelligent Universe, The (Hoyle), **20th:** 1904
Intentions (Wilde), **19th:** 2433
Interesting Narrative of the Life of Olaudah Equiano, The (Equiano), **18th:** 324
Interfaith marriage, **18th:** 103
Interior (Braque), **20th:** 495
Interior Castle, The (Teresa of Ávila), **Ren:** 929
Interior design, **18th:** Adam brothers, 5; England, 95; Johann Lucas von Hildebrandt, 496; Antônio Francisco Lisboa, 609
Intermarriage, Judaism on, **Anc:** 340
Interment Report (Chadwick), **19th:** 458
Intermezzo (film), **20th:** 321
Intermezzo (Brahms), **19th:** 298
Intermezzo (Giraudoux). See *Enchanted, The*
Intermezzo in modo classico (Mussorgsky), **19th:** 1627
International Brotherhood of Teamsters, **20th:** 2673
International Business Machines. *See* IBM
International Christian University (Tokyo), **20th:** 549
International Council of Women, **19th:** 2084
International Court of Justice, **20th:** 2758
International Federation for Information and Documentation. *See* Fédération Internationale d'Information et de Documentation

International Judicature (La Fontaine), **20th:** 2232
International Ladies' Garment Workers Union, **20th:** 1773
International Olympic Committee, **20th:** 847
International Peace Bureau, **20th:** 2231
International Psychoanalytical Association, **20th:** 1324
International Red Cross, **19th:** 699
International Style, **20th:** 2, 2694, 3092
International Typographical Union, **19th:** 1559
International Women's Congress for Peace and Freedom, **20th:** 198
Internet, **20th:** development of, 332, 708; online stores, 360
Internet Explorer, **20th:** 1422
Interpretation of Dreams, The (Freud), **20th:** 1324
Interpretation of History, The (Nordzu), **20th:** 2994
Interpreters, The (Soyinka), **20th:** 3805
Interstate Commerce Act (1887), **19th:** 509, 1923
Inti Cusi Huallpa. *See* Huáscar
Intifada (1987-1993), **20th:** 112, 1627, 1953, 3359
Intifada, Second (beg. 2000), **20th:** 113
Intimate Theater, **20th:** 3899
Intolerable Acts. *See* Coercive Acts
Intolerance (film), **20th:** 1496, 1595
Introductio in analysin infinitorum (Euler), **18th:** 335
Introduction à la métaphysique. See *Introduction to Metaphysics, An*
Introduction à l'étude de la médecine expérimentale. See *Introduction to the Study of Experimental Medicine, An*
Introduction à l'histoire universelle (Michelet), **19th:** 1565
Introduction of Porphyry, The. See *Isagoge*
Introduction to Divine and Human Readings, An. See *Institutiones* (Cassiodorus)
Introduction to Dutch Jurisprudence (Grotius), **17th:** 327
Introduction to Genetic Analysis, An (Mendel), **19th:** 1542
Introduction to Idealism (Schelling), **19th:** 2010
Introduction to Mathematics, An (Whitehead), **20th:** 4313
Introduction to Metaphysics, An (Bergson), **20th:** 324
Introduction to Semantics (Carnap), **20th:** 660
Introduction to Symbolic Logic, An (Langer), **20th:** 2264
Introduction to Symbolic Logic and Its Applications (Carnap), **20th:** 660
Introduction to the Philosophy of Nature (Schelling), **19th:** 2010
Introduction to the Principles of Morals and Legislation, An (Bentham), **18th:** 106, 763
Introduction to the Science of Mythology (Lévi-Strauss), **20th:** 2349
Introduction to the Study of Experimental Medicine, An (Bernard), **19th:** 206, 2489
Introduction to the Study of Indian Languages (Powell), **19th:** 1830
Introduction to Theoretical Physics (Planck), **20th:** 3284
Introductory Account of Certain Modern Ideas and Methods in Plane Analytical Geometry, An (Scott), **19th:** 2040
Introductory Chapters of Yaqut's "Muʿjam al-buldān," The. See *Kitāb muʿjam al-buldān*
Intuition and Reflection in Self-Consciousness (Nishida), **20th:** 2982
Intuitionism, **19th:** 2103
Inuit, **Ren:** 353, 522; Baffin Island, 354
Invar, **20th:** 1617
Invariances (Nozick), **20th:** 3000
Invectiva contra eum qui maledixit Italiae (Petrarch), **MA:** 829
Invective Quadrilogue, The (Chartier), **MA:** 262
Inventarium einer Seele (Suttner), **19th:** 2206
Invention, The (Soyinka), **20th:** 3804
Inventions, **18th:** John Fitch, 353-356; Benjamin Franklin, 372; James Hargreaves, 466-468; John Kay, 559-561; plaster of Paris, 579; urban lighting, 579, 715-718; James Watt, 1048-1051; Josiah Wedgwood, 1057-1061; Eli Whitney, 1076-1079; John Wilkinson, 1086-1089; **19th:** Charles Babbage, 108; Becquerel family, 166; Alexander Graham Bell, 183; Carl Benz, 197; Sir Henry Bessemer, 218; Louis Braille, 299; Marc Isambard Brunel, 337; George Cayley, 448; Samuel Colt, 534; William Fothergill Cooke, 549; Jacques Daguerre, 589; Gottlieb Daimler, 593; Sir Humphry Davy, 617; Rudolf Diesel, 663; James Buchanan Eads, 715; Thomas Alva Edison, 731; Michael Faraday, 760; Robert Fulton, 846; Carl Friedrich Gauss, 884; Charles Goodyear, 947; Sir William Robert Grove, 996; Hermann von Helmholtz, 1074; Joseph Henry, 1080; John Philip Holland, 1113; Elias Howe, 1134, 1141; Samuel Pierpont Langley, 1310; Étienne Lenoir, 1338; Cyrus Hall McCormick, 1438; Ottmar Mergenthaler, 1559; Samuel F. B. Morse, 1611; James Nasmyth, 1647; Nicéphore Niépce, 1676;

Alfred Nobel, 1689; Nikolaus August Otto, 1715; Aleksandr Stepanovich Popov, 1825; Siemens family, 2105; George Stephenson, 2167; Joseph Wilson Swan, 2209; Nikola Tesla, 2253; Richard Trevithick, 2295; George Westinghouse, 2416; Sir Charles Wheatstone, 549; **20th:** airplanes, 4404; color photography process, 2472; computed tomography, 1893; copy machine, 657; Danjon astrolabe, 912; FM, 128; Geiger counter, 1441; geodesic dome, 1365; Kodak camera, 1080; Frederick William Lanchester, 2241; lasers, 257; MS-DOS, 1421; neon tubes, 776; radio, 940; rocketry, 1507; telegraph, 2617; Wankel engine, 4224; World Wide Web, 332. *See also* Category Index
Invertebrate Spain (Ortega), **20th:** 3078
Investigation of the Meaning of the Four Books (Wang), **17th:** 972
Investigations into the Nature, Causation, and Prevention of Texas or Southern Cattle Fever (Smith), **20th:** 3773
Investiture Controversy, **MA:** 384, 500, 706, 971
Invincibilis, Doctor. *See* Ockham, William of
Invincibles, the. *See* Irish Invincibles
Invisible College, **17th:** 79
Invisible Man, The (Wells), **20th:** 4288
Invitation to a Beheading (Nabokov), **20th:** 2894
Invitée, L'. See *She Came to Stay*
Iolanthe (Gilbert and Sullivan), **19th:** 919
Iōn (Euripides), **Anc:** 328
Ionesco, Eugène, **20th:** 1968-1971
Ionescu, Nae, **20th:** 1137
Ionisation (Varèse), **20th:** 4143
Ionization theory, **20th:** 139, 3089
Iophon (son of Sophocles), **Anc:** 811
Iorga, Nicolae, **Notor:** 25
Iov (patriarch of Moscovy), **Ren:** 388
İpekçi, Abdi, **Notor:** 8
Iphigeneia ē en Aulidi (Euripides), **Anc:** 328
Iphigeneia ē en Taurois (Euripides), **Anc:** 328
Iphigenia in Aulis (Racine), **17th:** 775
Iphigenia in Taurus (Goethe), **18th:** 429
Iphigénie en Tauride (Gluck), **18th:** 420
iPod, introduction, **20th:** 2008
Ippolita Savignani at Twelve Months (Fontana), **Ren:** 338
Ipsilantis, Alexander. *See* Ypsilantis, Alexander
Ipsilantis, Demetrios. *See* Ypsilantis, Demetrios
Ipsus, Battle of (301 B.C.E.), **Anc:** 64, 203
Iran, **MA:** astronomy, 124, 796; medicine, 123; philosophy, 125; poetry, 375, 796; Sāsānian kings, 615. *See also* Persia; Geographical Index
Iran-Contra affair (1986-1989), **20th:** 3072, 3402
Iran hostage crisis (1979-1981), **20th:** 668, 2126
Iran-Iraq War (1980-1988), **20th:** 1948, 2126
Iraq, **MA:** astronomy, 68, 137, 617; mathematics, 617; optics, 66. *See also* Geographical Index
Iraq Liberation Act of 1998, **20th:** 1948
Iraq War (beg. 2003), **20th:** 373, 1949, 3324; United Kingdom, 386
Ireland, **MA:** Christianity, 199, 811; monasticism, 199; paganism, 811; **18th:** independence, 356-358, 440-442, 982-984; **19th:** home rule, 304, 461, 794, 926, 1490, 1748, 1894, 1979; Sir Robert Peel, 1768; potato famine, 925, 1959; **20th:** home rule, 151, 808, 843, 979, 1452, 1588, 1591, 2292, 3025, 3034. *See also* Geographical Index
Ireland, Megan Louise, **Notor:** 508
Irenaeus, Saint, **Anc:** 224, 423, 442-446
Irene, Saint, **MA:** 244, 467, 548-551, 590
Ireton, Henry, **17th:** 484, 756
Irgun Z'vai Leumi, **20th:** 284, 294
Iridium, **20th:** 75
Irina (sister of Fyodor I), **Notor:** 385
Iris and Roses (Chen), **17th:** 157
Irises (Kōrin), **17th:** 696
Irish Articles (1615), **17th:** 938
Irish Church Reform Act of 1833, **19th:** 979
Irish Civil War (1922-1923), **20th:** 1592, 3035
Irish Coercion Bill of 1881, **19th:** 794
Irish Dail. *See* Dáil Éireann
Irish-English conflicts, **18th:** 966, 983
Irish Free State, **20th:** 844
Irish-French conflicts, **18th:** 983
Irish Guards in the Great War, The (Kipling), **19th:** 1286
Irish Invincibles, **Notor:** 509-510
Irish Land Act of 1870, **19th:** 304
Irish Land Act of 1881, **19th:** 304
Irish Literary Renaissance, **20th:** 2055
Irish National Land League, **19th:** 1748
Irish Rebellion (1641-1650), **17th:** 700, 768, 885, 939
Irish Rebellion (1798), **18th:** 280, 357, 442, 791, 983
Irish Republican Army, **20th:** 844, 1592

Irish Republican Brotherhood, **20th:** 807, 979
Irish Republicanism, **18th:** 356-358, 982-984
Irish Volunteers, **20th:** 979
Irish War of Independence (1919-1921), **20th:** 1591
Iron, Ralph. *See* Schreiner, Olive
Iron Age, The (Heywood), **17th:** 374
Iron barges, **18th:** 1088
Iron Commissar. *See* Kaganovich, Lazar
Iron Duke. *See* Alva, duke of
Iron Felix. *See* Dzerzhinsky, Felix
Ironmaking, **18th:** England, 292-295, 1087; Scotland, 859
Ironsides (English regiment), **17th:** 205
Iroquois, **Ren:** 178, 281, 448; **17th:** 423, 499, 644, 908; in Quebec, 575; **19th:** 1603
Iroquois Confederacy, **Ren:** 449; constitution, 282
Iroquois Country, **18th:** 159
Irrende Ritter, Der (Kokoschka), **20th:** 2187
Irrigation, **Anc:** Assyrian, 769; Mesopotamian, 916
Irrigation Act (1886), **19th:** 625
Irrigation in Western America (Deakin), **19th:** 625
Irving, Clifford, **20th:** 1927; **Notor:** 492, 510-511
Irving, David, **Notor:** 512-514
Irving, Henry, **19th:** 1175-1179, 2248; Ellen Terry, 1177
Irving, Washington, **19th:** 88, 1180-1183
Irwin, Noel, **20th:** 3760
"Is," definition of, **Anc:** 609
Is 5 (Cummings), **20th:** 881
Is My Baby All Right? (Apgar), **20th:** 102
Is Sex Necessary? (Thurber and White), **20th:** 4020
Isaac, **Anc:** 6
Isaac II Angelus, **MA:** 1059
Isaac Comnenus, **MA:** 864
Isaak, Abraham, **Notor:** 253
Isabella I, **Ren:** 2, 105, 187, 237, 328-332, 433, 504, 511, 575, 606, 789, 939; **Notor:** 1038
Isabella II, **19th:** 414, 1183-1185
Isabella Brandt (van Dyck), **17th:** 244
Isabella d'Este, **Ren:** 99, 485-487
Isabella of Aragon, **Ren:** 872
Isabella of France, **MA:** 347-348, 350, 552-554, 842
Isabella the Fair. *See* Isabella of France
Isaeus, **Anc:** 264
Isagoge (Porphyry), **Anc:** 688
Isagoras, **Anc:** 221, 226
Isaiah, **Anc:** 446-449
Isandlwana, Battle of (1879), **19th:** 451
Isenheim altarpiece, **Ren:** 405
Iserin, Georg Joachim. *See* Rheticus
Ishaq Khan, Ghulam, **20th:** 366
Isherwood, Christopher, **20th:** 172, 530
Ishibashiyama, Battle of (1180), **MA:** 721
Ishida Mitsunari, **Ren:** 460
Ishmael, **Anc:** 5
Ishme-Dagan, **Anc:** 376
Ishtar, **Anc:** 582, 769
Isidore of Seville, Saint, **MA:** 555-558, 872
Isidro de Borbón, Carlos María. *See* Carlos, Don
Isis, **Anc:** 11, 107, 231
Iskender Paşa, **17th:** 855
Islam, **Anc:** Abraham in, 6; Aksum and, 334; Moses and, 574; **MA:** 471, 611, 734, 988, 1037; architecture, 5, 41; education, 18, 370, 745, 776, 884; fundamentalist, 113; historiography, 164, 376, 537, 704, 989, 1144; law, 18, 36, 415; medicine, 562; mysticism, 454; North Africa, 605; poetry, 875; Spain, 9; spread of, 745; women, 612, 873, 890; **Ren:** Christianity and, 105, 252, 330; India, 475; al-Maghīlī on, 596; Mongol Dynasty, 16; North Africa, 595; Songhai Empire, 686; Spain and, 504; **17th:** India, 859; Mughal Empire, 23, 843; Ottoman Empire, 454; Ṣafavid Dynasty, 4; Twelver Shia, 6; **18th:** Africa, 914-916; India, 1032-1033; law, 1030, 1032; reform movement, 1030; scholarship, 1000; **19th:** Algeria, 2; Egypt, 4; India, 36; Iran, 105, 117; **20th:** Egypt, 2915; Indonesia, 1705, 3904; Iran, 2124; Nation of Islam, 2570; Pakistan, 2005, 4473; Tunisia, 458; Turkey, 163. *See also* Asharism; Caliphs; Hanbalites; Hanifites; Ismāʿīlīs; Kharijites; Malikites; Muḥammad; Muslims; Mutazilites; Qurʾān; Shafites; Shīʿa Islam; Sunni Islam
Islam Giray III, **17th:** 462
Islamic Government (Khomeini), **20th:** 2125
Islamic Revolution of 1979, **20th:** 2781
Island Nights' Entertainments (Stevenson), **19th:** 2175
Island of Dr. Moreau, The (Wells), **20th:** 4288
Island Princess, The (Fletcher), **17th:** 279
Íslandsklukkan (Laxness), **20th:** 2309
Isle of Dogs, The (Nashe and Jonson), **Ren:** 715; **17th:** 440
Isle of the Dead, The (Rachmaninoff), **20th:** 3361
Isly, Battle of (1844), **19th:** 2
Ismaello (Martí), **19th:** 1504
Ismāʿīl, **MA:** 683
Ismāʿīl I, **Ren:** 69, 88
Ismāʿīl Pasha, **19th:** 1204, 1552
Ismāʿīlīs, **MA:** 416, 562, 684, 775
İsmet Paşa, **20th:** 68, 1971-1974
Isocrates, **Anc:** 128, 450-452
Isomura Yoshinori, **17th:** 831
Isozutai (Makuzu), **19th:** 2212
Ispoved. See *Confession, A*

Israel, **Anc:** division of, 2; Egypt and, 803; kingdom of, 447; state of, 5; **20th:** establishment of, 284, 293, 929, 2676, 3358, 4282. *See also* Judaea; Judah, kingdom of; Geographical Index
Israel, Manasseh ben. *See* Manasseh ben Israel
Israel Potter (Melville), **19th:** 1539
Israeli War of Independence. *See* Arab-Israeli War (1948)
Isserles, Moses ben Israel, **Ren:** 525
Istanbul. *See* Constantinople
Istanbul, Treaty of (1590), **17th:** 4
Istanbul, Treaty of (1736), **18th:** 639
Istnofret, **Anc:** 585
Istorie fiorentine. See *Florentine History, The*
Istoriya russkoy revolyutsii. See *History of the Russian Revolution, The*
István. *See* Stephen I
István Báthory. *See* Stephen Báthory
It Can't Happen Here (Lewis), **20th:** 2366
It Changed My Life (Friedan), **20th:** 1330
It Happened One Night (film), **20th:** 1368
Itagaki Taisuke, **19th:** 1970
Italian, The (Radcliffe), **18th:** 823
Italian Popular Party, **20th:** 945
Italian Symphony (Mendelssohn), **19th:** 1550
Italian Wars (1494-1559), **Ren:** 31, 227, 578
Italiani in Algeri, L' (Rossini), **19th:** 1945
Italo-Ethiopian War, Second (1935-1936), **20th:** 95, 1101, 2888
Italskii, Prince. *See* Suvorov, Aleksandr Vasilyevich
Italy, **MA:** architecture, 104, 206, 422, 769, 798; art, 83, 206, 282, 320, 326, 418, 421, 659, 700, 769, 798, 845, 847; barbarian kings, 784; education, 92; Gothic art, 103; historiography, 576, 923, 1056; Lombard conquest of, 47; Lombard kings, 47; medicine, 1, 1031; monasticism, 234; music, 439, 635; mysticism, 81, 97; painting, 83, 282, 326, 421, 659, 700, 798; philosophy, 174, 1028, 1050; poetry, 169, 239, 301-302, 827; sculpture, 102, 206, 320, 418, 566, 798, 845, 847; Sicilian and Neapolitan kings, 391; theology, 1029, 1050; women, 1031. *See also* Geographical Index
Itano, Harvey, **20th:** 3156
Ithacius, **Anc:** 699
I-ti. *See* Zhengde
Itinerarium Curiosum (Stukeley), **18th:** 952
Itinerarium mentis in Deum. See *Journey of the Soul to God, The*
Itinerary of Benjamin of Tudela (Benjamin of Tudela), **MA:** 157
Ito, Lance, **Notor:** 960
Itō Hirobumi, **19th:** 1185-1188
It's a Wonderful Life (film), **20th:** 3862
It's Too Late Now. See *Autobiography* (Milne)
I-tsung. *See* Tianqi
Iturbide, Agustín de, **19th:** 1991
Itzcóatl, **MA:** 558-561; **Ren:** 721
Iusupov, Feliks Feliksovich. *See* Yusupov, Felix
Ivan III (the Great), **Ren:** 487-492, 493, 749, 957; **Notor:** 385
Ivan IV (Bizet), **19th:** 242
Ivan IV (the Terrible), **Ren:** 387, 492-495, 750, 888, 957; **17th:** 943; **Notor:** 313, 385, 517-518
Ivan V, **17th:** 865; **Notor:** 514-515
Ivan VI, **Notor:** 515-516
Ivan Alekseyevich. *See* Ivan V
Ivan Alexander (emperor of Bulgaria), **MA:** 957
Ivan Antonovich. *See* Ivan VI
Ivan Molodoi, **Ren:** 750
Ivan the Ignorant. *See* Ivan V
Ivan the Terrible (film), **20th:** 1131
Ivanhoe (Scott), **19th:** 2048
Ivanovich, Fyodor I. *See* Fyodor I
Ives, Charles, **20th:** 195, 1974-1977
Ivory Coast, **20th:** independence of, 1897. *See also* Geographical Index
Iwakura Tomomi, **19th:** 1186
Iwasa Matabe, **17th:** 375
Iwein (Hartmann), **MA:** 463
Iwerks, Ub, **20th:** 1007
Ixtcóatl. *See* Itzcóatl
Ixtlilxóchitl, **Ren:** 720
Iyasu II, **18th:** 678
Izambard, Georges, **19th:** 1912
Izu Dancer, The (Kawabata), **20th:** 2084
Izumo no Okuni, **17th:** 408-409
Izutsu. See *Well-curb*

J

J. and W. Seligman and Company, **19th:** 26
Jābir ibn Ḥayyān, Abū Mūsā, **MA:** 562-565
Jabotinsky, Vladimir, **20th:** 284
J'Accuse! (film), **20th:** 1382
Jack the Lad. *See* Sheppard, Jack
Jack the Ripper, **Notor:** 519-520
Jackal, the. *See* Ramírez Sánchez, Ilich
Jacklight (Erdrich), **20th:** 1168
Jackson, A. Y., **20th:** 4011
Jackson, Andrew, **19th:** 1189-1193; Amalgamation Party, 343; Thomas Hart Benton, 193-194; Nicholas Biddle, 226; John C. Calhoun, 393; Henry Clay, 505; David Crockett, 571; election of 1824, 22, 503; James Gadsden, 849; Sam Houston, 1130; John Marshall,

1501; Native Americans and, 1937; James K. Polk, 1820; Winfield Scott, 2051; John Tyler, 2337; Martin Van Buren, 2345; **Notor:** 601, 615, 1018, 1117
Jackson, Bill. *See* Longley, Bill
Jackson, Charles T., **19th:** 1613
Jackson, David, **19th:** 2115
Jackson, Helen Hunt, **19th:** 1193-1197
Jackson, J. T. *See* James, Jesse
Jackson, Jesse, **20th:** 1978-1982; **Notor:** 890
Jackson, Shawn, **Notor:** 1044
Jackson, Shoeless Joe, **Notor:** 521-522
Jackson, Stonewall, **19th:** 834, 1197-1200
Jackson, Thomas Jonathan. *See* Jackson, Stonewall
Jackson, William Henry, **19th:** 233
Jacksonians, **19th:** 131, 504
Jacob, François, **20th:** 1982-1986
Jacob Two-Two Meets the Hooded Fang (Richler), **20th:** 3439
Jacobi, Carl Gustav, **19th:** 11, 885
Jacobi, Mary Putnam, **19th:** 1200-1202
Jacobin-Girondin conflict, **18th:** 649, 845
Jacobins, **18th:** 267, 290, 649, 703, 760, 845, 878; **19th:** 705
Jacobite Rebellion (1715-1716), **18th:** 54, 938
Jacobite Rebellion (1745-1746), **18th:** 634, 772
Jacobites, **17th:** 821; **18th:** 137, 661
Jacobs, Mike, **20th:** 2438
Jacobsen, Carlyle, **20th:** 1108
Jacopo della Quercia, **MA:** 566-568, 949
Jacquerie movement (1358), **MA:** 395
Jacques (Sand), **19th:** 1988
Jacques the Fatalist and His Master (Diderot), **18th:** 309
Jacson, Frank. *See* Mercader, Ramón
Jadarī wa al-Ḥasbah, al-. See *Treatise on the Small-Pox and Measles, A*
Jadhima, **Anc:** 988
Jadwiga, **MA:** 1120-1123
Jael, **Anc:** 259
Jagger, Mick, **Notor:** 564
Jagiełło, Vladislav. *See* Vladislav II
Jagiellonian Dynasty, **Ren:** 983
Jahāl-ud-Dīn. *See* Akbar
Jahan, Shah. *See* Shah Jahan
Jahāngīr, **Ren:** 17; **17th:** 410-412, 842
Jāḥiẓ, al-, **MA:** 568-571
Jai Singh, **17th:** 859
Jailhouse Rock (film), **20th:** 3331
Jainism, **Anc:** 355, 924; Chandragupta Maurya and, 204; Digambara, 925; Svetambara, 925
Jaipal, **MA:** 683
Jakarta, **17th:** 905
Jakobsleiter, Die (Schoenberg), **20th:** 3666
Jakobson, Roman, **20th:** 1986-1989
Jalāl al-Dīn Shāh Shujāʿ, **MA:** 451
Jalāl Khan, **Ren:** 478
Jalāl-ud-Dīn Fīrūz Khaljī, **MA:** 39
Jaleo, El (Sargent), **19th:** 1997
Jalsaghar. See *Music Room, The*
Jama Masjid, **17th:** 844
Jamaica. *See* Geographical Index
Jamaica Letter, The (Bolívar), **19th:** 269
Jamāl al-Dīn al-Afghānī, **19th:** 4, 1203-1206
James I the Conqueror (1208-1276; king of Aragon), **MA:** 571-575, 748, 882
James I (1394-1437; king of Scotland), **MA:** 261
James I (1566-1625; king of England), **Ren:** 73, 312, 325, 815, 845; **17th:** 413-416; and Lancelot Andrewes, 15; and William Bradford, 84; and the first duke of Buckingham, 96; and Richard Burbage, 105; and Robert Burton, 109; and George Calvert, 119; and Richard Cameron, 121; and Robert Carr, 131; and Charles I, 143; and Sir Edward Coke, 175; and Thomas Dekker, 223; and Sir Anthony van Dyck, 244; and John Eliot, 247; and Elizabeth of Bohemia, 250; and Elizabeth Stuart, 253; and Nicholas Ferrar, 274; and Frederick V, 293; and Orlando Gibbons, 309; and William Harvey, 355; and Jahāngīr, 412; and Inigo Jones, 436; and Ben Jonson, 442; and William Laud, 496; and Richard Lower, 565; and Thomas Middleton, 636; and Rory O'More, 699; and Paul V, 720; and Nicolas-Claude Fabri de Peiresc, 722; and Philip III, 737; and Pocahontas, 747; and Michael Romanov, 795; and Prince Rupert, 805; and Friedrich Hermann Schomberg, 820; and John Smith, 864; and Sir John Suckling, 893; and James Ussher, 939; and John Webster, 976; **Notor:** 350, 352, 936
James II (1430-1460; king of Scotland), **Ren:** 496
James II (1633-1701; king of England), **17th:** 416-419; and Richard Baxter, 34; and John Bunyan, 102; and Thomas Burnet, 106; and Richard Cameron, 123; and Catherine of Braganza, 138; and John Dryden, 241; and George Fox, 285; and Nell Gwyn, 343; and Henrietta Maria, 364; and Innocent XI, 407; and the first duke of Leeds, 508; and Jacob Leisler, 518; and Leopold I, 528; and Mary II, 610; and Mary of Modena, 607; and the duke of Monmouth, 655; and

Sir Isaac Newton, 681; and Titus Oates, 692; and William Paterson, 717; and William Penn, 725; and Samuel Pepys, 729; and Henry Purcell, 764; and Sir George Savile, 817; and Thomas Sydenham, 902; and Maarten and Cornelis Tromp, 931; and William III, 979; **18th:** 46, 250, 623, 660, 672; **Notor:** 802
James III (1451/1452-1458; king of Scotland), **Ren:** 496-498
James IV (1473-1513; king of Scotland), **Ren:** 188, 439, 498-500, 501
James V (1512-1542; king of Scotland), **Ren:** 146, 500, 501-503, 634
James VI (1566-1625; king of Scotland). *See* James I (1566-1625; king of England)
James, Alexander Franklin. *See* James, Frank
James, Beau. *See* Walker, James J.
James, Buck. *See* James, Frank
James, Dingus. *See* James, Jesse
James, Frank, **19th:** 1211-1213; **Notor:** 523-524, 871, 1118
James, Harry, **20th:** 1528
James, Henry, **19th:** 1206-1210; **20th:** 1406; **Notor:** 976
James, Jesse, **19th:** 1211-1213; **Notor:** 257, 523-525, 871, 994, 1118
James, Saint, **Anc:** 471, 624
James, William, **19th:** 289, 772, 1213-1217, 1773; **20th:** 4014
James J. Hill Company, **19th:** 1101
Jameson, Anna, **19th:** 1217-1219
Jameson, Leander Starr, **19th:** 462, 1299, 1408, 1894
Jameson Raid of 1895-1896, **19th:** 462, 1299
Jameson, Robert, **19th:** 1218
Jamestown, **17th:** 30, 702, 746, 752, 862
Jamison, Judith, **20th:** 37
Janab-i Táhirih. *See* Táhirih
Janáček, Leoš, **20th:** 1989-1992
Jane Avril at Divan Japonais (Toulouse-Lautrec), **19th:** 2289
Jane Avril at the Jardin de Paris (Toulouse-Lautrec), **19th:** 2289
Jane Avril Dancing at Moulin Rouge (Toulouse-Lautrec), **19th:** 2289
Jane Avril Entering Moulin Rouge (Toulouse-Lautrec), **19th:** 2289
Jane Avril Leaving Moulin Rouge (Toulouse-Lautrec), **19th:** 2289
Jane Eyre (Brontë), **19th:** 310
Janet, Pierre, **20th:** 510, 1993-1996
Janet Doncaster (Fawcett), **19th:** 766
Janissaries, **17th:** 668, 674
Janissary corps, **18th:** 27, 639, 719
Jankow, Battle of (1645), **17th:** 926
Jannings, Emil, **20th:** 998
Jansen, Cornelius Otto, **17th:** 419-422, 714, 773, 936
Jansenism, **17th:** 22, 265, 406, 421, 713, 773, 936, 964; **18th:** 103, 247, 362, 616
Jansenist-Jesuit conflict, **18th:** 616
Janssen, Pierre Jules César, **19th:** 1413
Janssen, Zacharias, **17th:** 537
Janůfa (Janáček), **20th:** 1990
Japan, **Anc:** China and, 595; Korea and, 594; **MA:** architecture, 583; art, 117, 581, 1040; Asuka emperors, 976; Confucianism, 940, 976; emperors, 116, 723; feudalism, 721; Fujiwara regents, 398; Heian emperors, 739; historic periods, 941; Kamakura shoguns, 724; law, 116; Mongol invasions of, 627, 724, 759; music, 773; Nara emperors, 624; relations with China, 1150; sculpture, 581, 1040; shoguns, 117; theater, 1152; trade, 990; women, 738, 771; **18th:** government administration, 746-748; lifting of foreign book ban, 980; modernization, 504-506; **19th:** opening of ports, 1169, 1777; **20th:** surrender of, 2494. *See also* Geographical Index
Japanese Family Storehouse, The (Saikaku), **17th:** 404
Jardin d'Épicure, Le. See *Garden of Epicurus, The*
Jarnac, Battle of (1569), **Ren:** 426, 798
Jarrah, Ziad Samir, **Notor:** 43
Jarry, Alfred, **19th:** 1952; **20th:** 104
Jaruzelski, Wojciech, **20th:** 4192; **Notor:** 525-527
Jason, **Anc:** 326
JASON Project, **20th:** 217
Jaspar, G. *See* De Gasperi, Alcide
Jaspers, Karl, **20th:** 118, 1996-1999
Jātakas, **Anc:** 345
Játiva, Battle of (1097), **MA:** 280
Játiva, Siege of (1239-1252), **MA:** 572
Jauréguiberry, Jean, **19th:** 757
Jaurès, Jean, **19th:** 1220-1222; **20th:** 397
Javier, Francisco. *See* Xavier, Saint Francis
Jawaharlal Nehru (Nehru), **20th:** 2931
Jaworów, Treaty of (1675), **17th:** 429
Jaws (film), **20th:** 3811
Jay, John, **18th:** 12, 524-527; portrait by Gilbert Stuart, 949; **19th:** 1272
Jayavarman VI, **MA:** 980
Jay's Treaty (1794), **18th:** 413, 526, 1046
Jazz, **20th:** 814, 1459; bands, 1146; bebop, 1481; Canada, 3227; New Orleans, 130; scat singing, 1247; singers, 1247, 1313, 1853; swing, 1527. *See also* Swing music
Jazz (Morrison), **20th:** 2836

Jazz at the Philharmonic, **20th:** 3226
Je t'aime series (Motherwell), **20th:** 2847
Je vous salue, Marie. See *Hail Mary*
Jean II, **MA:** 1065
Jean de Nivelle (Delibes), **19th:** 640
Jeanne d'Arc. *See* Joan of Arc
Jeanneret, Charles-Édouard. *See* Le Corbusier
Jebel Hamrin, **Anc:** 299
Jefferies, Dorothy. *See* Pentreath, Dolly
Jefferson, Thomas, **18th:** 86, 239, 528-531; **19th:** 365, 1471; Albert Gallatin, 855; James Monroe, 1586; Frances Trollope on, 2304; **Notor:** 155
Jeffersonian Republicans. *See* National Republicans
Jeffery, Dorothy. *See* Pentreath, Dolly
Jeffrey, Lord (Francis Jeffrey), **19th:** 1223-1226
Jehangir. *See* Jahāngīr
Jehoiachin, **Anc:** 336
Jehoiakim, **Anc:** 335, 453, 582
Jehovah. *See* Yahweh
Jehu, **Notor:** 527
Jekyll, Gertrude, **20th:** 1220
Jem. *See* Cem
Jena, Battle of (1806), **19th:** 929
Jenkin, Fleeming, **19th:** 606
Jenkins, Mary Elizabeth. *See* Surratt, Mary
Jenkinson, Robert Banks. *See* Liverpool, second earl of
Jenkins's Ear, War of (1739-1748), **18th:** 49, 744, 1036
Jenks, Amelia. *See* Bloomer, Amelia
Jenne, Siege of (1473-1480), **Ren:** 901
Jenner, Edward, **18th:** 532-535
Jennie Gerhardt (Dreiser), **20th:** 1034
Jennings, Sarah. *See* Churchill, Sarah
Jenseits von Gut und Böse. See *Beyond Good and Evil*
Jensen, Jens, **19th:** 362
Jensen, Max, **Notor:** 411
Jen-tsung. *See* Renzong
Jepthes. See *Tragedies*
Jeremiah, **Anc:** 336, 453-455, 582
Jeremiah Symphony (Bernstein), **20th:** 338
Jeroboam, **Anc:** 806
Jerome, Saint, **Anc:** 365, 426, 456-458, 520, 796
Jerome Clock Company, **19th:** 139
Jero's Metamorphosis (Soyinka), **20th:** 3805
Jerseys, colonization of, **17th:** 726
Jerusalem, **Anc:** as Christian metaphor, 143; David and, 255; Sennacherib and, 770; **MA:** architecture, 717; Battle of (1099), 1004, 1045; Crusader kings, 716
Jerusalem (Lagerlöf), **20th:** 2235
Jerusalem (Mendelssohn), **18th:** 676
Jerusalem Conquered (Tasso), **Ren:** 926
Jerusalem Delivered (Tasso), **Ren:** 925
Jervis, John, **19th:** 1657
Jesse L. Lasky Feature Play Company, **20th:** 960
Jessop, William, **19th:** 1325
Jesu, Joy of Man's Desiring (Bach), **18th:** 74
Jesuit-Jansenist conflict, **18th:** 616
Jesuit Relations, **17th:** 575, 596, 910
Jesuits, **Ren:** 5, 222, 231, 483, 514, 769, 825, 1000; Asia, 483; England, 149, 200; South America, 5; **17th:** 420, 714, 720, 773, 974; American Southwest, 467; Brazil, 960; Canada, 77, 423, 499, 575, 596, 603, 908; China, 161, 449, 849; **18th:** Étienne François de Choiseul, 247; Clement XIV, 793; expulsion from Spain and its colonies, 228, 395; France, 247; Pius VI, 793; Marquês de Pombal, 796; suppression of, 616. *See also* Carmelites; Dominicans; Franciscans; Monasticism; Ursuline order
Jesuits in North America in the Seventeenth Century, The. See *France and England in North America*
Jesup, Thomas S., **19th:** 1710, 2231
Jesus, Society of. *See* Jesuits
Jesus and the Word (Bultmann), **20th:** 573
Jesus bar-Abbas. *See* Barabbas
Jesus Christ, **Anc:** 3, 255, 458-462, 470, 539, 645, 879; **Notor:** 56, 458-459, 544, 840. *See also* Christianity
Jesus Christ Superstar (Lloyd Webber and Rice), **20th:** 2415
Jésus de Nazareth (Gounod), **19th:** 954
Jethro, **Anc:** 573
Jeu d'Adam (Adam de la Halle), **MA:** 25
Jeu de Robin et de Marion, Le. See *Play of Robin and Marion, The*
Jeune Algérien, Le (Abbas), **20th:** 7
Jeune Parque, La (Valéry), **20th:** 4137
Jeux (ballet), **20th:** 986
Jew of Malta, The (Marlowe), **Ren:** 624
Jewett, Sarah Orne, **19th:** 1226-1229
Jewish Colonial Trust, **19th:** 1090
Jewish National Committee, **20th:** 555
Jewish Naturalization Bill (1753), **18th:** 773
Jewish Presence, The (Dawidowicz), **20th:** 924
Jewish State, A (Herzl), **19th:** 1089

Jewish War (66-70), **Anc:** 469, 879

Jews, **Anc:** 1; Christianity and, 43; Cyrus the Great and, 249; deportations of, 893; Egypt and, 572; Hadrian and, 371; history of, 805; Philistines and, 747; Rome and, 219, 477; **MA:** Berber, 604; Christians and, 1099; Church and, 544; education, 409; France, 101, 408; Germany, 408; law, 410, 687; Majorca, 673; Mediterranean, 158; persecution of, 157, 1003; Provence, 650; Spain, 157, 533, 573, 591, 604, 686, 730, 747, 883; **Ren:** expulsion from Germany, 472; expulsion from Portugal, 524, 606; expulsion from Spain, 2, 330, 524, 579, 941; North Africa, 596; Spain, 1, 25, 928; Spanish Inquisition and, 940; **17th:** England, 206; Netherlands, 582; persecution of, 871; Poland, 462; Portugal, 961; return to England, 583; Turkey, 837; **18th:** integration of, 676; support of, 599; **19th:** anti-Semitism, 2207; discrimination against, 650, 666, 1950; England, 1949; Europe, 1089; homeland, 1332; United States, 2453; **20th:** African Americans, 1218, 1980; Germany, 119, 1301, 1514; Israel, 930; Judaism, 187; Palestine, 929; Poland, 284; settling in Israel, 2676; Soviet Union, 3786, 4328; United States, 922. *See also* Anti-Semitism; Holocaust; Judaism; Zionism

Jews, The (Lessing), **18th:** 598

Jezebel, **Notor:** 527-528

Jezebel (film), **20th:** 920

Jiajing (Ming emperor), **Ren:** 987

Jian An (literary period), **Anc:** 184

Jiang Bin, **Ren:** 1009

Jiang Jieshi. *See* Chiang Kai-shek

Jiang Qing, **20th:** 969, 1908, 2409, 2604, 4468; **Notor:** 528-529, 692

Jiang Zemin, **20th:** 971, 2000-2002

Jianwen, **MA:** 1148

Jiaoyou lun (Ricci), **Ren:** 826

Jidai-mono (historical plays), **18th:** 244

Jihad, **MA:** 41, 735, 919

Jihannuma (Kâtib Çelebî), **17th:** 455

Jihei. *See* Suzuki Harunobu

Jikaku ni okeru chokkan to hansei. See *Intuition and Reflection in Self-Consciousness*

Jiménez de Cisneros, Francisco, **Ren:** 330, 503-506, 537

Jimmu Tennō, **Anc:** 462-464; **MA:** 623

Jin Bihui. *See* Kawashima, Yoshiko

Jin Dynasty, **MA:** 1146

Jin Dynasty, Later, **17th:** 1

Jin si lü. See *Reflections on Things at Hand*

Jina. *See* Vardhamāna

Jing Ke, **Notor:** 530, 948

Jing Xiang, **Anc:** 733

Jinga. *See* Njinga

Jingū, **Anc:** 465-468, 594

Jinkōki. See *Book of Large and Small Numbers*

Jinnah, Mohammed Ali, **20th:** 1389, 2002-2006, 2856, 2901

Jiren Shipian (Ricci), **Ren:** 826

Jirgalang, **17th:** 234

Jirobei. *See* Suzuki Harunobu

Jisu jieyi (Wang Chong), **Anc:** 953

Jiu ge (Qu Yuan), **Anc:** 732

Jixia Academy, **Anc:** 978

Jiyū Minshutō. *See* Liberal Democratic Party (Japan)

Joachim, Joseph, **19th:** 297

Joachim of Fiore, **MA:** 575-577, 922

Joan I (queen of Castile and Aragon). *See* Joan the Mad

Joan of Arc, **MA:** 261, 277, 578-581; **Ren:** 225, 435

Joan the Mad, **Ren:** 50, 220, 330, 505, 614, 648; **Notor:** 531-532

Joannes Scotus. *See* Duns Scotus, John

João IV. *See* John IV

Jobs, Steve, **20th:** 2006-2009

Jocasta and the Famished Cat (France), **19th:** 815

Jōchō, **MA:** 581-584, 1040

Jockey, The (Toulouse-Lautrec), **19th:** 2290

Jockey perdu, Le (Magritte), **20th:** 2548

Jodl, Alfred, **Notor:** 533-534

Jōdo. *See* Pure Land Buddhism

Jodocus Pratensis. *See* Josquin des Prez

Joel, Billy, **20th:** 3990

Joffre, Joseph-Jacques-Césaire, **20th:** 2009-2012

Joffrey, Robert, **20th:** 2012-2014, 3989

Joffrey Ballet, **20th:** 2013

Jogaila. *See* Władysław II Jagiełło

Jogiches, Leo, **20th:** 2482

Jogues, Saint Isaac, **17th:** 423-424

Johanan ben Zakkai, **Anc:** 468-471

Johann Georg I, **17th:** 826

Johann Georg II, **17th:** 827

Johann Parricida. *See* John Parricida

Johannes Leo de Medicis. *See* Leo Africanus

Johannesson, Olof. *See* Alfvén, Hannes

John (1166-1216; king of England), **MA:** 211, 358, 491, 543, 584-587, 725, 837, 892, 1054; **Notor:** 534-536, 910

John I Tzimisces (925-976; Byzantine emperor), **MA:** 794

John I (1357-1433; king of Portugal), **MA:** 477

John I Albert (1459-1501; king of Poland), **Ren:** 885, 983

John I (1487-1540; king of Hungary), **Ren:** 636, 651, 886, 910, 915
John II Comnenus (1087-1143; Byzantine emperor), **MA:** 89
John II (1319-1364; king of France), **MA:** 308
John II (1397-1479; king of Aragon and Navarre), **Ren:** 328
John II (1405-1454; king of Castile and León), **Ren:** 328, 432
John II (1455-1495; king of Portugal), **Ren:** 237, 259, 286, 365, 511-513, 591, 605
John II Casimir Vasa (1609-1672; king of Poland), **17th:** 154, 186, 428, 462, 624
John III (1502-1557; king of Portugal), **Ren:** 513-515, 1000
John III Sobieski (1629-1696; king of Poland), **17th:** 406, 427-430, 453, 528, 744
John IV (1605-1656; king of Portugal), **17th:** 137, 425, 430-432, 960
John V Palaeologus (1332-1391; Byzantine emperor), **MA:** 959
John VI Cantacuzenus (1292?-1383; Byzantine emperor), **MA:** 958
John X (d. 928; pope), **Notor:** 706
John XI (c. 910-935/936; pope), **Notor:** 706
John XII (c. 937-964; pope), **MA:** 806; **Notor:** 707
John XXII (c. 1244-1334; pope), **MA:** 779, 843
John XXIII (1370-1419; antipope), **MA:** 524
John XXIII (1881-1963; pope), **20th:** 2017-2020, 3149
John, Augustus, **20th:** 2014-2017
John Barleycorn (London), **20th:** 2422
John Biglin in a Single Scull (Eakins), **19th:** 718
John Brown (Warren), **20th:** 4237
John Brown's Body (Benét), **20th:** 303
John Bull (newspaper), **20th:** 447
John Damascene. *See* John of Damascus
John Dee on Astronomy (Dee), **Ren:** 280
John Ermine of the Yellowstone (Remington), **19th:** 1882
John Frederick the Magnanimous (elector of Saxony), **Ren:** 262, 776
John Hancock Tower, **20th:** 3184
John Keble's Parishes (Yonge), **19th:** 2473
John Marr and Other Sailors (Melville), **19th:** 1540
John McClellan Committee, **20th:** 2103
John of Austria, **17th:** 151, 425-427
John of Brienne, **MA:** 389
John of Cappadocia, **MA:** 599, 1010
John of Damascus, **MA:** 587-591
John of Fidanza. *See* Bonaventure, Saint
John of Gaunt, **MA:** 493, 894, 1131
John of Luxembourg, **MA:** 230, 257, 679
John of Nepomuk, Saint, **MA:** 1090
John of Parma, **MA:** 180
John of Plano Carpini. *See* Carpini, Giovanni da Pian del
John of Ravenna, **MA:** 765
John of Rochester. *See* Fisher, Saint John
John of Spain, the Younger, Don. *See* John of Austria
John of Swabia. *See* John Parricida
John of the Cross, Saint, **Ren:** 4, 192, 507-510, 930
John P. Holland Torpedo Boat Company, **19th:** 1114
John Parricida, **Notor:** 536-537
John Paul II, **20th:** 2020-2024, 3844, 4189; **Notor:** 8, 700, 1121
John Randolph (Adams), **19th:** 17
John Sigismund (king of Hungary), **Ren:** 910
John the Apostle, **Anc:** 437, 471-473, 624
John the Baptist, Saint, **Anc:** 474-476, 539, 879; **Notor:** 458, 932
John the Steadfast, **Ren:** 262
John Wesley Harding (Dylan), **20th:** 1073
John Zápolya. *See* John I (1487-1540; king of Hungary)
Johnness. *See* You, Dominique
Johnny Holmes Orchestra, **20th:** 3226
Johns, Jasper, **20th:** 3381
Johnson, Andrew, **19th:** 960, 1229-1235; impeachment of, 2172, 2203; Edwin M. Stanton, 2144; state of the union address, 1232; Alexander H. Stephens, 2165; **Notor:** 859, 1013
Johnson, Aphra. *See* Behn, Aphra
Johnson, Charles S., **20th:** 1944
Johnson, Dr. *See* Johnson, Samuel
Johnson, Hinton, **20th:** 2571
Johnson, Jack, **20th:** 2438
Johnson, James Weldon, **Notor:** 285
Johnson, John. *See* Fawkes, Guy
Johnson, Lady Bird, **20th:** 2025-2027
Johnson, Lyndon B., **20th:** 1939, 2025, 2027-2032, 2100, 2634; Sam Rayburn, 3399; Vietnam War, 1686, 2542, 2954; war on poverty, 2029; **Notor:** 49, 337, 369, 491, 613
Johnson, Samuel, **18th:** 66, 111, 146, 169, 178, 221, 535-539, 594, 898; **Notor:** 287
Johnson, Yormie, **Notor:** 1021
Johnson v. Transportation Agency of Santa Clara County (1987), **20th:** 3022
Johnson Wax Company headquarters complex, **20th:** 4401

Johnston, Joseph E., **19th:** 613, 1335, 2099
Johnstown flood (1889), **19th:** 147
Joinville, Treaty of (1584), **Ren:** 780
Jolie Fille de Perth, La (Bizet), **19th:** 242
Joliot, Frédéric, **20th:** 715, 890, 2032-2035, 2214
Joliot-Curie, Irène, **20th:** 715, 890, 2032-2035
Jolliet, Louis, **17th:** 433-435, 490, 603
Jolly Flatboatmen, The (Bingham), **19th:** 235
Jomini, Antoine-Henri de, **19th:** 500
Jonah's Gourd Vine (Hurston), **20th:** 1945
Jones, Bobby, **20th:** 2036-2039
Jones, Della Mae, **Notor:** 1006
Jones, Elvin, **20th:** 815
Jones, Inigo, **17th:** 436-438, 442
Jones, Jim, **Notor:** 537-539
Jones, John Paul, **18th:** 539-543
Jones, Margaret, **Notor:** 540-541
Jones, Mary Harris. *See* Jones, Mother
Jones, Mother, **20th:** 2039-2042
Jones, Tom. *See* Longley, Bill
Jones, W. D., **Notor:** 812
Jones, William, **19th:** 1866
Jones v. Alfred H. Mayer Co. (1967), **20th:** 382
Jones v. Van Zandt, **19th:** 471
Jonghelinck, Niclaes, **Ren:** 136
Jonson, Ben, **Ren:** 93, 215, 536, 715, 878; **17th:** 52, 105, 167, 223, 232, 278-279, 368, 373, 436, 439-444, 649, 747, 846
Joplin, Janis, **20th:** 2043-2045, 3766
Joplin, Scott, **19th:** 1235-1237
Jōrakuji, **MA:** 1041
Jordan, **20th:** expulsion of Palestinian guerrillas (1970), 1627. *See also* Geographical Index
Jordan, Barbara, **20th:** 2046-2049
Jordan, Colin, **Notor:** 283, 1050
Jordan, Dorothea, **19th:** 2445
Jordan, Michael, **20th:** 2050-2052
Jordanes, **Anc:** 911; **MA:** 76
Jordanus Nemorarius, **MA:** 648
Jorgensen, Christine, **20th:** 2053-2055
Jōruri (puppet theater), **18th:** 243
Joseph (husband of Mary), **Anc:** 539
Joseph II, **18th:** 544-547, 558, 654, 657, 793; **Notor:** 86
Joseph, Chief, **19th:** 1238-1241
Joseph, Frank. *See* Collin, Frank
Joseph and His Brothers (Mann), **20th:** 2596
Joseph and the Amazing Technicolor Dreamcoat (Lloyd Webber and Rice), **20th:** 2414
Joseph ben Matthias. *See* Josephus, Flavius
Joseph Hone (John), **20th:** 2015
Joseph of Volokolamsk, **Ren:** 490, 958
Joseph the Younger. *See* Joseph, Chief
Joseph und seine Brüder. See *Joseph and His Brothers*
Joséphine, **19th:** 1241-1244
Josephism, **18th:** 793
Josephus, Flavius, **Anc:** 30, 249, 260, 338, 405, 459, 475, 477-480, 557, 645; **Notor:** 56, 458-459, 541-542, 840
Joshua Then and Now (Richler), **20th:** 3438
Josiah, **Anc:** 335, 453
Joskin des Prez. *See* Josquin des Prez
Joslyn, Matilda. *See* Gage, Matilda Joslyn
Josquin des Prez, **Ren:** 149, 515-517; **18th:** 179
Joubert, Petrus, **20th:** 440
Joule, James Prescott, **19th:** 1264
Journal (Kemble), **19th:** 1268
Journal du voleur. See *Thief's Journal, The*
Journal métaphysique. See *Metaphysical Journal*
Journal of a Residence on a Georgian Plantation in 1838-1839 (Kemble), **19th:** 1269
Journal of a Tour to the Hebrides, with Samuel Johnson, LL.D. (Boswell), **18th:** 147
Journal of Christian Science, The, **19th:** 725
Journal of George Fox, The (Fox), **17th:** 283
Journal of the Plague Year, A (Defoe), **18th:** 299
Journal to Stella (Swift), **18th:** 965
Journalism, **18th:** Daniel Defoe, 299; John Wilkes, 1083; **20th:** Great Britain, 93, 276, 446, 1679; radio, 2880; United States, 697, 3948; yellow, 1735. *See also* Category Index
Journey Continued (Paton), **20th:** 3140
Journey of the Soul to God, The (Bonaventure), **MA:** 181
Journey to a War (Auden and Isherwood), **20th:** 172
Journey to Accompong (Dunham), **20th:** 1062
Journey to the Centre of the Earth, A (Verne), **19th:** 2357
Journey to the East, The (Hesse), **20th:** 1790
Journey to the West (Wu), **MA:** 1138
Journey to the Western Islands of Scotland (Boswell), **18th:** 147
Journey Without Maps (Greene), **20th:** 1578
Jouvenel, Henri de, **20th:** 805
Jouvet, Louis, **20th:** 1493
Jovian, **Anc:** 776
Jovovic, Blagoje, **Notor:** 814
Joy of Life (Lipchitz), **20th:** 2398
Joyce, James, **20th:** 240, 279, 2055-2059
Joyce, William, **Notor:** 409, 542-543, 999

Joyful Wisdom, The (Nietzsche), **19th:** 1683
Juan Carlos I, **20th:** 1299, 2060-2062; **Notor:** 372
Juan de Austria, Don. *See* John of Austria
Juan de Yepes y Álvarez. *See* John of the Cross, Saint
Juana la Loca. *See* Joan the Mad
Juárez, Benito, **19th:** 1245-1248, 1526; and Porfirio Díaz, 653; **Notor:** 278
Juba II, **Anc:** 829
Jubbāʿī, Abū ʿAlī Muḥammad ibn ʿAbd al-Wahhāb al-, **MA:** 111
Jubilee Jim. *See* Fisk, James
Jud, Leo, **Ren:** 1012
Judaea, **Anc:** Herod and, 404; Rome and, 469, 682. *See also* Israel; Judah, kingdom of
Judah, kingdom of, **Anc:** 335, 338, 447, 453, 711, 770, 893; Nebuchadnezzar and, 582. *See also* Israel; Judaea
Judah, tribe of, **Anc:** 1
Judah ha-Levi, **MA:** 591-595
Judah Halevi's Kitab al Khazari. See *Book of the Kuzari*
Judaism, **Anc:** difficulties in Babylon, 337; return from Babylonian Exile, 339; Christianity and, 330, 372, 437, 612, 822, 879; Dio Cassius on, 276; Ezekiel and, 337; history of, 6, 478; Jesus Christ and, 459; paganism and, 453; Pharisees and, 468; priests, 1; reform of, 460; Rome and, 404, 644; scholarship in, 29; Talmudic, 470; Temple and, 469, 804; **MA:** 593; **Ren:** 1; **18th:** Baʿal Shem Tov, 68-70; Elijah ben Solomon, 318-320; Joseph II, 545; Moses Mendelssohn, 675-677; revival of, 68; Friedrich Schiller, 889; **20th:** 187. *See also* Jews
Judaizers, **Ren:** 490
Judas Iscariot, **Anc:** 460; **Notor:** 544-545
Judas Macabeo (Calderón), **17th:** 113
Jude the Obscure (Hardy), **19th:** 1029
Juden, Die. See *Jews, The*
Judenstaat. See *Jewish State, A*
Judge Louis. *See* Buchalter, Louis
Judges, The (Wiesel), **20th:** 4326
Judgment, The (Kafka), **20th:** 2066
Judgment of Paris, The (Cranach, the Elder), **Ren:** 263
Judgment of Paris (Renoir), **19th:** 1890
Judgment of the Archbishops and Bishops of Ireland (Ussher et al.), **17th:** 938
Judicial activism, **20th:** 508
Judicial reform, **18th:** 100, 328
Judicial restraint, **20th:** 521, 1310, 1666
Judiciary Act of 1903, **19th:** 624
Judith (Klimt), **20th:** 2180
Judith and Her Maid (Botticelli), **Ren:** 124
Judith and Her Maidservant (Artemisia), **17th:** 307
Judith Slaying Holofernes (Artemisia), **17th:** 307
Judith with the Head of Holofernes (Sirani), **17th:** 857
Judocus Pratensis. *See* Josquin des Prez
Judson, E. Z. C. *See* Buntline, Ned
Judson, Edward, **20th:** 1731
Judy Garland Show, The (television program), **20th:** 1411
Jugendstil, **20th:** 2074
Juges, Les. See *Judges, The*
Jugo, Miguel de Unamuno y. *See* Unamuno y Jugo, Miguel de
Jugurtha, **Anc:** 533, 743, 831; **Notor:** 1010
Jugurthine War, **Anc:** 533
Jui-tsung. *See* Ruizong
Jules and Jim (film), **20th:** 4081
Julia III, **Anc:** 489-492, 591
Julia Agrippina. *See* Agrippina the Younger
Julia Domna, **Anc:** 480-483, 487, 988
Julia Livilla, **Anc:** 766
Julia Maesa, **Anc:** 487; **Notor:** 326
Julia Mamaea, **Anc:** 483-486, 601
Julia Soaemias, **Anc:** 486-489
Julian and Maddalo (Shelley), **19th:** 2095
Julian calendar, **Anc:** 174, 816; **Ren:** 394
Julian of Norwich, **MA:** 595-598, 607
Julian the Apostate, **Anc:** 134, 242, 363, 776
Julianstown, Battle of (1641), **17th:** 700
Julie. See *New Héloïse, The*
Juliet and Her Nurse (Turner), **19th:** 2324
Juliet of the Spirits (film), **20th:** 1232
Juliette (Sade), **18th:** 876
Julius II, **Ren:** 29, 57, 84, 116, 133, 188, 410, 499, 518-521, 558, 578, 588, 613, 648, 683, 820; **Notor:** 15
Julius III, **Ren:** 393, 751
Julius Caesar (Shakespeare), **Anc:** 168
Julius Caesar, Gaius. *See* Caesar, Julius
Julius Phaeder, Gaius. *See* Phaedrus
July Days (1917), **20th:** 2112
July 14 Movement, **20th:** 4085
July Fourth (Grandma Moses), **20th:** 2842
July 26 Movement, **20th:** 691, 1609
Jumbo the Elephant, **19th:** 140
Junayd, al-, **MA:** 454
Jung, Carl, **20th:** 392, 513, 1324, 1790, 2062-2065, 3153
Jungfrukällan. See *Virgin Spring, The*
Jungle, The (Sinclair), **20th:** 3751
Jungle Book, The (Kipling), **19th:** 1286

Junius Pamphlet, The (Luxemburg), **20th:** 2483
Junnin, **MA:** 624
Juno, **Anc:** 272
Jurassic Park (film), **20th:** 3812
Jurchen, **MA:** 1145, 1149
Jurchen Jin Dynasty, **MA:** 678
Jurieu, Pierre, **17th:** 36
Juristische Methodenlehre, nach der Ausarbeitung des Jakob Grimm (Savigny), **19th:** 2004
Jurists, **18th:** Sir William Blackstone, 118-121; Samuel Chase, 237-240; John Jay, 524-527; first earl of Mansfield, 643-647; Samuel Sewall, 894; James Wilson, 1093
Jūrukosai no nikki (Kawabata), **20th:** 2084
Just So Stories (Kipling), **19th:** 1286
Justice, **Anc:** Athenian, 293; Mencius on, 555
Justice, U.S. Department of, **19th:** 580
Justice and Expediency (Whittier), **19th:** 2429
Justice as Fairness (Rawls), **20th:** 3392
Justice Without Revenge (Lope de Vega), **17th:** 950
Justin I, **MA:** 76, 598, 1014; **Notor:** 1028
Justin II, **MA:** 615; **Notor:** 546, 1029
Justine (Sade), **18th:** 876
Justinian I, **Anc:** 354; **MA:** 234, 598-603, 613, 1010; **Notor:** 1028
Justinian II, **MA:** 937
Justinian the Great. *See* Justinian I
Justinian's Codification, **MA:** 601
Justinus II. *See* Justin II
Juvenal, **Anc:** 493-495
Juvenalian satire, **Anc:** 493
Juvenile Miscellany, **19th:** 482
Juzjani, Abū ʿUbayd al-, **MA:** 123
Jūzjānī, Minhāj Sirāj, **MA:** 888

K

K-capture, **20th:** 4437
K teorii imperialisticheskogo gosudarstva (Bukharin), **20th:** 567
Kaaba, Covenant of the, **MA:** 468
Kabaka Yekka, **20th:** 3012
Kabbalah, **MA:** 730; **18th:** 68
Kabbalism, **Ren:** 524, 579, 783; Luria on, 580; **17th:** 835
Kabila, Laurent-Désiré, **20th:** 2772; **Notor:** 741
Kabuki theater, **17th:** 408; **18th:** 243
Kabyles, **Ren:** 79
Kaczynski, David, **Notor:** 548
Kaczynski, Theodore, **Notor:** 547-549, 978
Kadensho. See *Fūshikaden*
Kadesh (state), **Anc:** 886
Kadesh, Battle of (1274 B.C.E.), **Anc:** 737
Kadic v. Karadzic (1995), **20th:** 2524
Kaelin, Kato, **Notor:** 960
Kaffirs. *See* Ngunis
Kafka, Franz, **20th:** 2066-2069
Kāfū, **MA:** 40
Kaganovich, Lazar, **Notor:** 549-550
Kagemusha (film), **20th:** 2219
Kahane, Meir, **Notor:** 427, 551-552
Kahekili, **19th:** 1249
Kāhina, Damia al-, **MA:** 604-606
Kahlenberg, Battle of (1683), **17th:** 429, 528
Kahlo, Frida, **20th:** 2069-2071, 3458
Kahn, Robert, **20th:** 707-708
Kahnweiler, Daniel-Henry, **20th:** 1597
Kahr, Gustav Ritter von, **Notor:** 461
Kaianerekowa. *See* Great Peace and Power and Law
Kaihō Yūshō, **17th:** 868
Kaika, **Anc:** 465
Kaiser, Georg, **20th:** 4273
Kaiser Wilhelm Institute for Physical Chemistry and Electrochemistry, **20th:** 1630
Kaiserstil, **18th:** 352, 494
Kaiserwaltzer (Strauss), **19th:** 2190
Kalanikupule, **19th:** 1249
Kalanimoku, **19th:** 1250
Kalckstein, Christian Ludwig von, **17th:** 292
Kalendarium Hortense (Evelyn), **17th:** 257
Kalhu (Assyria), **Anc:** 122
Kalicho, **Ren:** 522-523
Kālidāsa, **Anc:** 496-498
Kalisz, Treaty of (1343), **MA:** 231, 1121
Kalisz, Treaty of (1813), **19th:** 1023
Kallir, Otto, **20th:** 2842
Kalmar Union (1397), **MA:** 691; **Ren:** 416
Kama Sutra of Vatsyayana, **19th:** 370
Kamakaeha, Lydia. *See* Liliuokalani
Kamakura Code (1232), **MA:** 116
Kamakura period, **MA:** 115, 759, 992, 1040
Kamakura shogunate, **MA:** 115, 723, 724
Kambun Kyōshi, **17th:** 375
Kamchatka Peninsula, **18th:** 109
Kamehameha I, **18th:** 1007; **19th:** 1249-1251
Kamen no kokuhaku. See *Confessions of a Mask*
Kamenev, Lev, **Notor:** 314, 990, 1080, 1138
Kamerlingh Onnes, Heike, **20th:** 2072-2074
Kameyama, **MA:** 772
Kamil Paşa, **20th:** 1158
Kaminaga Hime, **Anc:** 595
Kamisori. *See* Tojo, Hideki
Kammermusik (Hindemith), **20th:** 1812
Kammu, **MA:** 620
Kämpfer, Engelbert, **17th:** 445-448

Kan, Kikuchi, **20th:** 2084
Kan'ami, **MA:** 1152
Kanchenjungha (film), **20th:** 3395
Kandinsky, Wassily, **20th:** 2074-2077, 2606
Kaneie, Fujiwara. *See* Fujiwara Kaneie
Kanemi, al-, **19th:** 2343
Kang Sheng, **Notor:** 529
Kang Youwei, **19th:** 497, 1252-1254, 2487
Kangde. *See* Puyi
K'ang-hsi. *See* Kangxi
Kangxi, **17th:** 448-451, 850; **18th:** 1113
Kanishka, **Anc:** 130, 499-501
Kanizane, Fujiwara. *See* Fujiwara Kanezane
Kankan. *See* Mūsā, Mansa
Kannauj, Battle of (1540), **Ren:** 475
Kansas Jayhawks, **20th:** 725
Kansas-Nebraska Act (1854), **19th:** 195, 320, 344, 471, 681, 1132, 2202; Franklin Pierce, 1792
Kansas territory, **19th:** 720, 1092
Kant, Immanuel, **18th:** 548-551; Johann Gottlieb Fichte, 342; David Hume, 516; Friedrich Schiller, 888; critique of Emanuel Swedenborg, 962; **Notor:** 769
Kant's Life and Thought (Cassirer), **20th:** 689
Kanō school, **17th:** 695
Kanuni, Süleyman. *See* Süleyman the Magnificent
Kanze Motomasa, **MA:** 1153
Kao-tsung. *See* Gaozong (Southern Song emperor); Gaozong (Tang emperor)
Kapellmeisters, **18th:** Georg Frideric Handel, 463; Georg Philipp Telemann, 971
Kapici Bashi. *See* Shabbetai Tzevi
Kapital, Das (Marx), **19th:** 752, 1511
Kapitanskaya dochka. See *Captain's Daughter, The*
Kapitsa, Pyotr Leonidovich, **20th:** 2077-2080, 2245, 3578
Kaplan, Fanya, **Notor:** 313, 552-553
Kaplan, Nelly, **20th:** 1383
Kapp Putsch (1920), **20th:** 2463, 3689
Kaprow, Allan, **20th:** 2374
Kapteyn, Jacobus, **20th:** 3059
Kara Mustafa Paşa, Merzifonlu, **17th:** 451-454, 528
Karadžić, Radovan, **Notor:** 554-555, 735, 739
Karaites, **MA:** 593
Karajan, Herbert von, **20th:** 2081-2083, 3335
Karakazov, Dmitry V., **19th:** 50
Karamanlis, Constantine, **20th:** 3107
Karameh, Battle of (1968), **20th:** 111
Karbala, Iraq, **18th:** 1000
Kardelj, Edvard, **20th:** 1012
Kardis, Treaty of (1660), **17th:** 155
Kari O Komal (Tagore), **20th:** 3934
Karīm Khān Zand, **18th:** 552-553
Kariya Kiyoshi, **Notor:** 41
Karl (Wyeth), **20th:** 4411
Karl XII. *See* Charles XII
Karl der Grosse. *See* Charlemagne
Karlmark, Gloria Ray, **Notor:** 349
Karlowitz, Treaty of (1699), **17th:** 453, 528; **18th:** 331
Karlsbad Decrees, **19th:** 1023
Karlskirche, **18th:** 351
Karlstadt, Andreas Rudolf Bodenstein von, **Ren:** 582
Karma, **Anc:** 161; Jainism and, 925
Kármán, Theodore von, **20th:** 3328
Karnak, temples at, **Anc:** 26
Karno, Fred, **20th:** 732
Karo, Joseph ben Ephraim, **Ren:** 524-525
Karpis, Alvin, **Notor:** 61, 556-557
Kars, Treaty of (1921), **20th:** 1159
Karsavina, Tamara, **20th:** 909, 985, 2974
Kary, Charlie, **Notor:** 593
Kasabian, Linda, **Notor:** 690
Kasavubu, Joseph, **20th:** 2476, 2774, 4091
Käsebier, Gertrude, **20th:** 883
Kashchey the Immortal (Rimsky-Korsakov), **19th:** 1916
Kashf al-ẓunūnʿan asāmī al-kutub wa al-funūn (Kâtib Çelebî), **17th:** 455
Kashima kikō. See *Visit to the Kashima Shrine, A*
Kashmir, conflict over, **20th:** 2932
Kaskaskia, **19th:** 244
Kassa. *See* Tewodros II
Kassya (Delibes), **19th:** 640
Kastrioti, George. *See* Skanderbeg
Kasuri, Ahmed Khan, **20th:** 369
Kata Christanōn (Porphyry), **Anc:** 688
Kata Kelsou (Origen), **Anc:** 330
Kata pasōn haireseōn elenkhos (Hippolytus), **Anc:** 423
Kata Philippou (Demosthenes), **Anc:** 265
Kata tōn sophistōn (Isocrates), **Anc:** 450
Katanga, **20th:** independence of, 4091
Katharmoi (Empedocles), **Anc:** 295
Käthchen von Heilbronn, Das. See *Cathy of Heilbronn*
Kâtib Çelebî, **17th:** 454-456
Katoptron sive speculum artis medicae Hippocraticum (Cesalpino), **Ren:** 212
Katz, Bernard, **20th:** 1090
Katz und Maus. See *Cat and Mouse*
Kauffmann, Angelica, **18th:** 554-556
Kaufman, Irving R., **Notor:** 916
Kaufmann House, **20th:** 4401
Kaukasische Kreidekreis, Der. See *Caucasian Chalk Circle, The*
Kaumualii, **19th:** 1250

Kaunda, Kenneth, **20th:** 3012
Kaunitz, Wenzel Anton von, **18th:** 557-559
Kaunitz-Reitberg, prince of. *See* Kaunitz, Wenzel Anton von
Kautsky, Karl, **20th:** 334, 2482
Kavadh I, **MA:** 613
Kavanagh (Longfellow), **19th:** 1417
Kavkazskiy plennik. See *Prisoner of the Caucasus, The*
Kavya (poetic form), **Anc:** 131, 496
Kawabata, Yasunari, **20th:** 2084-2086, 2763
Kawara Jūrōbei, **17th:** 999
Kawashima, Kiyoshi, **20th:** 1861
Kawashima, Yoshiko, **Notor:** 558-559
Kay, John, **18th:** 55, 559-561
Kayendanegea. *See* Brant, Joseph
Kazakhstan. *See* Geographical Index
Kazan khanate, Russian annexation of, **Ren:** 493
Kazantzakis, Nikos, **20th:** 2087-2090
Kazdin, David, **Notor:** 584
Kazimierz Wielki. *See* Casimir III the Great
Ke, Madame, **17th:** 161, 911
Kean, Edmund, **19th:** 791, 1254-1259, 1467, 2248
Kearns, Jack, **20th:** 965
Kearny, Stephen Watts, **19th:** 428, 833
Keating, Tom, **Notor:** 559-560
Keating-Owen Act of 1916, **20th:** 2274
Keaton, Buster, **20th:** 2090-2092
Keats, John, **19th:** 1259-1263
Keble, John, **19th:** 77, 1663, 1845, 2472
Keenan, Joseph, **Notor:** 474
Keep America Beautiful, **20th:** 2026
Keeper of the Flame (film), **20th:** 4067
Kefauver, Estes, **Notor:** 605
Kei school, **MA:** 1040
Keian incident (1651), **17th:** 999
Keimplasma, Das. See *Germ-Plasm, The*
Keisei hisaku (Honda), **18th:** 505
Keitai, **Anc:** 462; **MA:** 975
Keizairoku shūi (Dazai), **18th:** 747
Kejeser og Galilæer. See *Emperor and Galilean*
Kejsaren av Portugallien. See *Emperor of Portugallia, The*
Kelawatsets, **19th:** 2116
Keller, Helen, **19th:** 184; **20th:** 2093-2095, 3908
Kelley, Abigail. *See* Foster, Abby Kelley
Kelley, Edward, **Ren:** 279
Kelley, Florence, **20th:** 4185
Kelley, Tom, **20th:** 2798
Kellogg-Briand Pact (1928), **20th:** 599, 2405, 3897
Kelly, Dan, **Notor:** 563
Kelly, Edward, **Notor:** 746
Kelly, Gene, **20th:** 157, 1410, 1731, 2096-2098
Kelly, George R. *See* Kelly, Machine Gun
Kelly, Jane, **Notor:** 560
Kelly, John, **19th:** 508
Kelly, Kathryn, **Notor:** 561
Kelly, Machine Gun, **Notor:** 561-562
Kelly, Ned, **Notor:** 562-564
Kelly, William, **19th:** 220
Kelly Pneumatic Process, **19th:** 220
Kelsey-Hayes sit-down strike (1936), **20th:** 3425
Kelvin, Baron, **19th:** 761, 1264-1267
Kelvin, Lord. *See* Kelvin, Baron
Kemal Pasha Zade, **Ren:** 88
Kemble, Fanny, **19th:** 1267-1270
Kemble, John Philip, **19th:** 1255
Kemble, Sarah. *See* Siddons, Sarah
Kemmu emperors, **MA:** 723
Kemmu Formulary (1336), **MA:** 116
Kemmu Restoration (1333-1336), **MA:** 115
Kempe, Margery, **MA:** 595, 607-609
Kempe, Will, **17th:** 104
Kempis, Thomas à. *See* Thomas à Kempis
Kenau Hasselaer, **Ren:** 526-527
Kendrake, Carleton. *See* Gardner, Erle Stanley
Kenilworth (Scott), **19th:** 2048
Kenilworth, Dictum of (1266), **MA:** 492
Kennedy, Aimee Elizabeth. *See* McPherson, Aimee Semple
Kennedy, Jacqueline. *See* Onassis, Jacqueline Kennedy
Kennedy, John F., **20th:** 2026, 2030, 2098-2102, 3045, 3858, 4234; election to presidency, 2984; shipwreck, 217; Soviet Union, 2130; **Notor:** 49, 186, 309, 337, 340, 406, 490, 698, 941, 965
Kennedy, Joseph P., **Notor:** 406, 965
Kennedy, Joseph W., **20th:** 3685
Kennedy, Ludovic, **Notor:** 210
Kennedy, Minnie Pearce, **Notor:** 680
Kennedy, Robert F., **20th:** 739, 2099, 2102-2106; **Notor:** 49, 75, 217, 406, 481, 698, 965
Kennedy, Khrushchev, and the Test Ban (Seaborg), **20th:** 3687
Kenny, Charles J. *See* Gardner, Erle Stanley
Kenny's Window (Sendak), **20th:** 3699
Kent, James, **19th:** 1271-1274
Kent, kingdom of, **Anc:** 395; **MA:** 354
Kentish Knock, Battle of (1652), **17th:** 57
Kentish Petition, **17th:** 562
Kentucky, **18th:** Daniel Boone expedition, 143; George Rogers Clark, 253
Kentucky Resolutions (1798-1799), **18th:** 530, 637

Kentucky v. Dennison, **19th:** 472
Kenya, **20th:** independence of, 2107. *See also* Geographical Index
Kenya African Union, **20th:** 2107
Kenyatta, Jomo, **20th:** 2106-2110, 2312
Kenzan. *See* Ogata Kenzan
Keokuk, **19th:** 245
Kephisodotos, **Anc:** 694
Kepler, Johannes, **Anc:** 78; **Ren:** 130, 712, 841; **17th:** 259, 281, 299, 305, 349, 357, 388, 457-461, 680, 818, 966
Kepler's Conversation with Galileo's Sidereal Messenger (Kepler), **17th:** 459
Kerboga of Mosul, **MA:** 178
Kereits, **MA:** 402, 954
Kerelöszentpál, Battle of (1575), **Ren:** 910
Kerensky, Aleksandr Fyodorovich, **20th:** 2110-2113
Kerensky Offensive (1917), **20th:** 2112
Kern, Jerome, **20th:** 156, 1657
Kerouac, Jack, **20th:** 2114-2117
Kerr, Frank, **20th:** 3060
Kerrigan, James, **Notor:** 746
Kesef mishneh (Karo), **Ren:** 525
Kesselring, Albert, **20th:** 2117-2119
Ketawayo. *See* Cetshwayo
Ketch, Jack, **Notor:** 565-566
Ketchum, Black Jack. *See* Ketchum, Tom
Ketchum, Jesse, **19th:** 123
Ketchum, Tom, **Notor:** 566-567
Ketchwayo. *See* Cetshwayo
Ketenes, study of, **20th:** 3833
Keter Malkhut. See *Kingly Crown, The*
Kett, Robert, **Ren:** 305
Kettle, Lady Alice. *See* Kyteler, Lady Alice
Kett's Rebellion (1549), **Ren:** 305, 899
Keusche Joseph, Der (Grimmelshausen), **17th:** 325
Kevorkian, Jack, **Notor:** 567-569
Key, Francis Scott, **19th:** 1274-1277, 2226; **Notor:** 616, 1018
Key, Philip B., **19th:** 2143
Keyes, Asa, **Notor:** 680
Keynes, John Maynard, **20th:** 357, 1374, 2120-2123
Keys of the Kingdom, The (film), **20th:** 3181
Keyser, Martin de, **Ren:** 256
Keystone Kops, **20th:** 732, 3707
Keystone Pictures Studio, **20th:** 3706
Khadafi, Muammar al-. *See* Qaddafi, Muammar al-
Khadīja, **MA:** 610-612, 734
Khafre, **Anc:** 558
Khair al-Dīn. *See* Barbarossa
Khakhuli Theotokos, **MA:** 999
Khalailah, Ahmad Fadil al-. *See* Zarqawi, Abu Musab al-
Khālid (king of Saudi Arabia), **20th:** 1195
Khalid (son of Saʿīd ibn Sulṭān), **19th:** 1967
Khalid Abdul Wadood. *See* Mohammed, Khalid Shaikh
Khalifa, **19th:** 2278
Khaljīs, **MA:** 39, 41
Khamerernebty II, **Anc:** 559
Khan, Sayyid Ahmad. *See* Ahmad Khan, Sir Sayyid
Khan Akhmed, **Ren:** 489
Kharijites, **MA:** 4, 1143
Khartoum, **18th:** 169; **19th:** defense of, 288, 794, 926, 950
Khatib Chelebi. *See* Kâtib Çelebî
Khauna, Battle of (1527), **Ren:** 475
Khayr al-Dīn. *See* Barbarossa
Khayronnesa Begum, **17th:** 4
Khazars, **Anc:** 141; **MA:** 912, 1068
Khentkawes, **Anc:** 560
Khiḍr. *See* Barbarossa
Khieu Samphan, **Notor:** 569-571
Khin Nyunt, **Notor:** 1026
Khitans, **MA:** 1083, 1145
Khmelnytsky, Bohdan, **17th:** 452, 461-463, 624
Khmelnytsky, Yurii, **17th:** 452
Khmer, **MA:** 981; law, 982; relations with China, 982
Khmer Rouge, **20th:** 1942, 3298, 3741
Khnum, **Anc:** 440
Khomeini, Ayatollah, **20th:** 2123-2127, 2781; **Notor:** 571-573, 742
Khosrow I, **MA:** 613-616
Khosrow II, **MA:** 505
Khotin, Battle of (1673), **17th:** 429
Khovanshchina, **17th:** 866
Khovanshchina (Mussorgsky), **19th:** 1628
Khovansky, Ivan, **17th:** 866
Khovansky Mischief. *See* Khovanshchina
Khrushchev, Nikita S., **20th:** 524, 2128-2131, 2784, 3979, 4471; **Notor:** 90, 186, 550, 574-576, 597, 722, 748, 1137
Khufu, **Anc:** 558
Khufu's Wisdom (Mahfouz), **20th:** 2554
Khurram. *See* Shah Jahan
Khusru, **17th:** 410, 842
Khwārizmī, al-, **MA:** 617-619; **Ren:** 173
Ki-di-nu, **Anc:** 580
Ki no Tsurayuki, **MA:** 1155
Kiakhta, Treaty of (1727), **18th:** 776, 1113
Kibi no Makibi, **MA:** 624
Kichibē. *See* Hishikawa Moronobu
Kichihōshi. *See* Oda Nobunaga
Kidd, Billy, **20th:** 2132
Kidd, Captain. *See* Kidd, William
Kidd, Thomas I., **20th:** 914
Kidd, William, **17th:** 464-467; **Notor:** 576-578
Kidnapped (Stevenson), **19th:** 2174
Kido Kōin, **19th:** 1186, 1970
Kierkegaard, Søren, **19th:** 1278-1281
Kievan Rus, **MA:** 86, 913; Christianity, 86, 793, 1068; Mongol invasion of, 627;

paganism, 87, 1068; rulers, 88, 794, 913, 1070
Kikuyu, **20th:** 2106, 2310
Kilajua, **17th:** 687
Kilkenny, Confederation of, **17th:** 701
Killiecrankie, Battle of (1689), **17th:** 611
Killigrew, Thomas, **17th:** 240, 342
Killy, Jean-Claude, **20th:** 2132-2135
Kilmainham Treaty of 1882, **19th:** 794
Kilmore, baron of. *See* Melbourne, second Viscount
Kilrush, Battle of (1642), **17th:** 700
Kilwardby, Robert, **MA:** 817, 861
Kim (Kipling), **19th:** 1286
Kim, Young Oon, **20th:** 2812
Kim Dae Jung, **20th:** 2136-2138
Kim Il Sung, **20th:** 2138-2141; **Notor:** 578-581
Kim Jong Il, **20th:** 2137, 2141-2143; **Notor:** 579, 581-583
Kim Jong-suk, **Notor:** 581
Kimba, Evariste, **20th:** 4093
Kimball, William W., **19th:** 1114
Kimes, Sante, **Notor:** 584-585
Kimmei, **MA:** 974
Kimmel, Husband E., **20th:** 2978
Kimoto, Mike. *See* Ng, Charles
Kinder- und Hausmärchen. See *Grimm's Fairy Tales*
Kindersprache, Aphasie und allgemeine Lautgesetze. See *Child Language, Aphasia, and Phonological Universals*
Kindertotenlieder (Mahler), **20th:** 2560
Kinetoscope, **20th:** 2473
King, Ada. *See* Lovelace, countess of
King, Billie Jean, **20th:** 1191, 2143-2146
King, Coretta Scott, **Notor:** 890
King, Dexter, **Notor:** 890
King, Edmund, **17th:** 565
King, Ernest J., **20th:** 2978
King, Martin Luther, Jr., **20th:** 11, 576, 1868, 1978, 2147-2151, 3121; **Notor:** 491, 698, 857, 889-890, 1000
King, Michael. *See* Kahane, Meir
King, Mike. *See* Frankel, Martin
King, Rodney, **Notor:** 585-587, 960
King, Stephen, **20th:** 2151-2154
King, William, **Notor:** 356
King, William Lyon Mackenzie, **20th:** 2155-2159, 3597
King Amuses Himself, The (Hugo), **19th:** 1148
King and Collier (Dvořák), **19th:** 712
King and I, The (Rodgers and Hammerstein), **20th:** 1659, 3461, 3488
King and No King, A (Beaumont and Fletcher), **Ren:** 94; **17th:** 279
King Arthur (Dryden and Purcell), **17th:** 765
King Coal (Sinclair), **20th:** 3752
King David Hotel, bombing of, **20th:** 285
King George's War. *See* French and Indian War
King in New York, A (film), **20th:** 733
King Leopold's Soliloquy (Twain), **19th:** 1351
King of Comedy, The (film), **20th:** 2358, 3682
King Philip's War. *See* Metacom's War
King Playing with the Queen, The (Ernst), **20th:** 1178
King Poděbrad of Bohemia (Mussorgsky), **19th:** 1628
King Solomon's Mines (Haggard), **19th:** 1007
King William the Wanderer (Chrétien), **MA:** 268
King William's War. *See* Augsburg, War of the League of
Kingdom of Christ, The (Maurice), **19th:** 1519
Kingdom of Man, The (Lankester), **19th:** 1316
Kingfish, the. *See* Long, Huey
Kingly Crown, The (Ibn Gabirol), **MA:** 533
King's Great Matter, **Ren:** 112, 189, 443
King's Men, **Ren:** 94, 878; **17th:** 105, 279, 342, 442, 636, 846, 977. *See also* Lord Chamberlain's Men
King's Private Musick, **17th:** 502
King's Row (film), **20th:** 3400
Kingsblood Royal (Lewis), **20th:** 2366
Kingsbury, Mary, **20th:** 198
Kingship, **Anc:** Chinese, 553; Egyptian, 887; Jewish, 747; religion and, 736
Kingsley, Charles, **19th:** 1465, 1519, 1665
Kingsley, Mary, **19th:** 1281-1284
Kingston, Council of (838), **MA:** 354
Kingston Russell, Russell of. *See* Russell, John
Kinkakuji, **MA:** 1153
Kinney, Abbot, **19th:** 1196
Kinney, John, **Notor:** 143
Kino, Eusebio Francisco, **17th:** 467-469
Kinsey, Alfred, **20th:** 2159-2163
Kinsky of Wchinitz and Wettau, Bertha Félicie Sophia, Countess. *See* Suttner, Bertha von
Kintōsho (Zeami), **MA:** 1154
Kintyre and Lorne, marquess of. *See* Argyll, second duke of
Kinuta. See *Clothbeating Block, The*
Kiowas, **19th:** 429
Kipling, Rudyard, **19th:** 1284-1288
Kippōshi. *See* Oda Nobunaga
Kipps (Wells), **20th:** 4288
Kirby-Smith, Edmund, **19th:** 583
Kirchliche Dogmatik, Die. See *Church Dogmatics*

Kirchner, Ernst Ludwig, **20th:** 2164-2166
Kirill, **MA:** 53
Kirk, Jackson Michael. *See* Swango, Michael
Kirkby, Christopher, **17th:** 692
Kirkholm, Battle of (1605), **17th:** 854
Kirkpatrick, Jeane, **20th:** 2167-2170
Kirov, Sergei, **Notor:** 991, 1080, 1112, 1137
Kirov Ballet, **20th:** 253
Kirstein, Lincoln, **20th:** 194
Kishi, Nobusuke, **20th:** 1703, 1965, 3645
Kiss, The (Klimt), **20th:** 2180
Kiss, The (Rodin), **19th:** 1926
Kiss for the Leper, A (Mauriac), **20th:** 2657
Kiss Hollywood Goodbye (Loos), **20th:** 2430
Kiss Me, Stupid (film), **20th:** 3697
Kissinger, Henry, **20th:** 1277, 2170-2173, 2985; **Notor:** 794
Kit-Kat Club, **18th:** 21
Kitab al-akhbar. See *Green Book, The*
Kitāb al-asrār wa-sirr al asrra (al-Rāzī), **MA:** 886
Kitāb al-Bayan wa-al-Tabyin (al-Jāḥiẓ), **MA:** 569
Kitāb al-bukhalāʾ (al-Jāḥiẓ), **MA:** 569
Kitāb al-ḥāwī fiʿl ṭibb, al- (al-Rāzī), **MA:** 886
Kītab al-Ḥujjah waal dalīl fi nasr al-dīn al dhalīl. See *Book of the Kuzari*
Kitab al-ijtihad waʿl-akhbar (Vaḥīd Bihbahānī), **18th:** 1001
Kitāb al-jabr wa al-muqābalah (al-Khwārizmī), **MA:** 617
Kitāb al-kamil (Abul Wefa), **MA:** 22
Kitāb al-luma. See *Book of Highlights*
Kitāb al-mawāzīn (Jābir), **MA:** 563
Kitāb al-qanūn al-Masʿūdī. See *Canon Masudicus*
Kitāb al-sabʿīn (Jābir), **MA:** 563
Kitāb al-tafsir al-kabir (al-Rāzī), **MA:** 370
Kitāb al-Tanbīh wa al-Ishrāf (al-Masʿūdī), **MA:** 703
Kitāb al-ṭibb al-Manṣūrī (al-Rāzī), **MA:** 884
Kitāb al-ṭibb al-rūḥānī. See *Book of Spiritual Physick, The*
Kitāb al-zij. See *De scientia stellarum*
Kitāb ar-Rujārī (al-Idrīsī), **MA:** 540
Kitāb fasl al-maqāl. See *On the Harmony of Religion and Philosophy*
Kitāb fi ma yahtaj ilayh al-kuttab wa l-ʾummal min ʿilm al-hisab (Abul Wefa), **MA:** 22
Kitāb iṣlāḥ al-akhlāq. See *Improvement of Moral Qualities, The*
Kitāb muḥaṣṣal afkār al-mutaqaddimīn wa-al-mutaʾakhkhirīn. See *Muḥaṣṣal*
Kitāb muʿjam al-buldān (Yaqut), **MA:** 1143
Kitāb nuzhat al-mushtāq fi ikhtirāq al-āfāq. See *Kitāb ar-Rujārī*
Kitāb-ul-Hind (al-Bīrūnī), **MA:** 685
Kitagawa Sōtatsu. *See* Sōtatsu
Kitaj, Ron, **20th:** 1845
Kitasato Shibasaburo, **19th:** 180
Kitchen Cabinet, **19th:** 193
Kitchener, Lord (Horatio Herbert Kitchener), **20th:** 151, 440, 896, 2173-2176
Kitzler, Otto, **19th:** 330
Kiwalao, **19th:** 1249
Kiya, **Anc:** 28, 588
Kiyohara no Motosuke, **MA:** 930
Kjœmpehøien. See *Burial Mound*
Klaas, Marc, **Notor:** 267
Klaas, Polly, **Notor:** 267
Klage, Die. See *Lament, The*
Klamath, **19th:** 428
Klassen, Ben, **Notor:** 444
Klee, Paul, **20th:** 2176-2179
Klein, Christian Felix, **19th:** 1818
Kleine geistliche Concerte (Schütz), **17th:** 827
Kleist, Heinrich von, **19th:** 1289-1291, 2152
Klement, Ricardo. *See* Eichmann, Adolf
Klementos pros Korinthious epistola prōtē (Clement), **Anc:** 224
Klima der bodennahen Luftschicht, Das. See *Climate Near the Ground, The*
Klimt, Gustav, **20th:** 2180-2182
Klinghoffer, Leon, **Notor:** 241
Klingsor's Last Summer (Hesse), **20th:** 1788
Kloher, John, **Notor:** 258
Klop. See *Bedbug, The*
Klopstock, Friedrich Gottlieb, **18th:** 428, 562-564
Klug, Aaron, **20th:** 1317
Klushino, Battle of (1610), **17th:** 855, 945
Knäred, Treaty of (1613), **17th:** 336, 704
Knickerbocker Holiday (Weill and Anderson), **20th:** 4275
Knight, Richard Payne, **19th:** 1643
Knight, Death, and Devil (Dürer), **Ren:** 299
Knight in the Panther's Skin, The (Rustaveli), **MA:** 999
Knight of the Burning Pestle, The (Beaumont), **Ren:** 93
Knight of the Revolution. *See* Dzerzhinsky, Felix
Knights, The. See *Hippēs*
Knights of Labor, **19th:** 910
Knights Templar, **MA:** 162
Know-Nothing Party, **19th:** 783, 911
Knowledge and Life (Eucken), **20th:** 1186
Knowlton, Charles, **19th:** 212
Knox, John, **Ren:** 528-531, 628, 634

Knoxville: Summer of 1915, Op. 24 (Barber), **20th:** 232
Knut. *See* Canute I the Great
Knute Rockne, All American (film), **20th:** 3400, 3482
Knyaginya Ligovskaya. See *Princess Ligovskaya*
Ko no Moronao, **MA:** 115
Ko no Moroyasu, **MA:** 115
Kober, Tobias, **17th:** 60
Kōbō Daishi, **MA:** 620-622
Koch, Robert, **19th:** 528, 1291-1295, 1753; **20th:** 1116
Kodak camera, **20th:** 1079
Kodály, Zoltán, **20th:** 250
Kōetsu. *See* Honami Kōetsu
Kofi, Francis Nwia. *See* Nkrumah, Kwame
Kōfukuji, **MA:** 582, 1040
Kofun tombs, **Anc:** 596
Kogdá razguliayetsa. See *When the Skies Clear*
Koguryŏ kingdom, **Anc:** 466; **MA:** 996
Koh-i-noor diamond, **Ren:** 476
Kohima, Battle of (1944), **20th:** 3760
Kohl, Helmut, **20th:** 2182-2184
Köhler, Wolfgang, **20th:** 1112
Koischwitz, Max Otto, **Notor:** 409
Koiso, Kuniaki, **Notor:** 587-588
Kojiki, **Anc:** 462, 465; **MA:** 623
Kōjō, **MA:** 581
Kōken, **MA:** 623-625
Kokin Wakashū, **MA:** 1155
Kokinshū. See *Kokin Wakashū*
Kokoschka, Oskar, **20th:** 2185-2188
Kokusenya kassen. See *Battles of Coxinga, The*
Kol Nidre (Schoenberg), **20th:** 3666
Kolhörster, Werner, **20th:** 443
Kollwitz, Käthe, **20th:** 2189-2191
Komarov, Vladimir, **20th:** 1372
Kōmei, **19th:** 1631
Komenský, Jan, **17th:** 469-471
Komyō, **MA:** 115
Kon-Tiki (Heyerdahl), **20th:** 1797
Kong Qiu. *See* Confucius
Kongfuzi. *See* Confucius
Kongi's Harvest (Soyinka), **20th:** 3805
Kongo, **Ren:** 9, 237, 511
Kongzi. *See* Confucius
König, Franz Niklaus, **19th:** 589
Koniggrätz, Battle of (1866), **19th:** 819
Königsberg, Treaty of (1656), **17th:** 154
Konigsberg v. State Bar of California (1957), **20th:** 379
Königskinder (Humperdinck), **19th:** 1155
Konparu Zenchiku, **MA:** 1153
Konrad von Marburg, **MA:** 360
Kontakte (Stockhausen), **20th:** 3874
Kontra-Punkte (Stockhausen), **20th:** 3873
Konzertmeisters, **18th:** Christoph Gluck, 419; Georg Philipp Telemann, 971
Konzertstück (Weber), **19th:** 2396
Kopernik, Mikołaj. *See* Copernicus, Nicolaus
Kopfgeburten. See *Headbirths*
Koppány, **MA:** 965
Köprülü Mehmed Paşa, **17th:** 451
Korea, **Anc:** 465, 594; **MA:** influence on Japan, 940; Koryŏ rulers, 1083; **Ren:** Japanese invasions of, 944; **18th:** art, 248-249; **19th:** Japanese takeover of, 1187. *See also* North Korea; Geographical Index
Korean Provisional Government, **20th:** 3431
Korean War (1950-1953), **20th:** 2139, 2495, 3431, 4089; China, 2382, 3192; end of war, 1126; Japanese industry, 4063; Taiwan, 749; U.S. involvement, 19
Korechika, Fujiwara. *See* Fujiwara Korechika
Korematsu v. United States (1944), **20th:** 378
Koresh, David, **20th:** 3417; **Notor:** 589-591
Kōrin, Ogata. *See* Ogata Kōrin
Kormchaia Kniga, **17th:** 684
Kornilov, Lavr, **20th:** 2112
Kornilov Revolt (1917), **20th:** 2112
Korolev, Sergei, **20th:** 2191-2195, 4096
Korvin-Krukovskaya, Sofya Vasilyevna. *See* Kovalevskaya, Sofya
Koryŏ Dynasty, **MA:** 1082; rulers, 1083
Korzeniowski, Jósef Teodor Konrad Nałęcz. *See* Conrad, Joseph
Kosakievicz, Olga, **20th:** 272
Kościuszko, Tadeusz, **18th:** 564-566
Köse Mihal, **MA:** 802
Kösem Mahpeyker. *See* Kösem Sultan
Kösem Sultan, **17th:** 472-474, 668
Kōshō. *See* Jōchō
Kōshoku gonin onna. See *Five Women Who Loved Love*
Kōshoku ichidai onna. See *Life of an Amorous Woman, The*
Kōshoku ichidai otoko. See *Life of an Amorous Man, The*
Koskotas, George, **20th:** 3108
Kosmogonie. See *Cosmogony*
Kosovo, Battle of (1389), **MA:** 959
Kosovo, Battle of (1448), **MA:** 711
Kossuth, Lajos, **19th:** 620, 819; **Notor:** 596
Kossuth Symphony (Bartók), **20th:** 250
Koster, Samuel W., **Notor:** 169
Koštunica, Vojislav, **Notor:** 736
Koussevitsky, Serge, **20th:** 338, 837
Kovalevskaya, Sofya, **19th:** 1295-1297
Kōwa, Seki. *See* Seki Kōwa
Koxinga. *See* Zheng Chenggong

Koya, **19th:** 1872
Kraanerg (ballet), **20th:** 4416
Krakatit (Čapek), **20th:** 639
Krapp's Last Tape (Beckett), **20th:** 282
Krasicki, Ignacy, **18th:** 567-569
Krasner, Lee, **20th:** 2195-2198, 3302
Krasnoe koleso. See *Red Wheel, The*
Kraus, Karl, **20th:** 2185
Kray, Charlie, **Notor:** 591
Kray, Reginald, **Notor:** 591-593
Kray, Ronald, **Notor:** 591, 593-594
Krebs, Sir Hans Adolf, **20th:** 2199-2201
Krebs, Nicholas. *See* Nicholas of Cusa
Krebs cycle, **20th:** 2199
Kreisky, Bruno, **20th:** 4330
Kremer, Gerhard. *See* Mercator, Gerardus
Krenwinkel, Patricia, **Notor:** 690
Kreutzer Sonata, The (Tolstoy), **19th:** 2285
Kreuzewissenschaft. See *Science of the Cross, The*
Krewo, Treaty of (1385), **MA:** 1120
Krieg und Aufbau (Scheler), **20th:** 3656
Krio, **Anc:** 227
Krise des Sozialdemokratie, Die. See *Crisis in the German Social Democracy, The*
Krishnadevaraya, **Ren:** 532-534
Krishnamurti, Jiddu, **19th:** 214
Kristina of Markyate. *See* Christina of Markyate
Kristuslegender. See *Christ Legends*
Kritik der praktischen Vernunft. See *Critique of Practical Reason, The*
Kritik der Urteilskraft. See *Critique of Judgment, The*
Krivitsky, Walter, **Notor:** 837
Kroc, Ray, **20th:** 2201-2204
Krogh, August, **20th:** 2204-2207
Kroisos. *See* Croesus
Krsnadev Rai. *See* Krishnadevaraya
Kruger, Paul, **19th:** 1298-1300, 1894; **20th:** 440
Krupa, Gene, **20th:** 1527
Krupp, Alfred, **19th:** 1301-1303
Kryfts, Nicholas. *See* Nicholas of Cusa
Ksar el Kebir, Battle of. *See* Three Kings, Battle of
Kto vinovat? See *Who Is to Blame?*
Ku Klux Klan, **19th:** 961, 2166; **20th:** 347, 378, 1595, 2386, 3925
Kublai Khan, **MA:** 404, 547, 626-628, 853, 955
Kübler-Ross, Elisabeth, **20th:** 2207-2210
Kubrick, Stanley, **20th:** 3696
Kudō Ayako. *See* Tadano Makuzu
Kuffler, Stephen, **20th:** 1090
Kugler, Franz, **19th:** 354
Kuhhorn, Martin. *See* Bucer, Martin
Kühn, Eusebio Francesco. *See* Kino, Eusebio Francisco
Kujūla Kadphises, **Anc:** 499
Kūkai. *See* Kōbō Daishi
Kuklinski, Richard, **Notor:** 435, 595-596
Kullervo (Sibelius), **20th:** 3736
Kultur der Renaissance in Italien, Die. See *Civilization of the Renaissance in Italy, The*
Kumārasambhava (Kālidāsa), **Anc:** 497
Kumawashi, Hashirō, **Anc:** 465
Kumin, Maxine, **20th:** 3714
Kumonosu-jo. See *Throne of Blood*
Kun, Béla, **Notor:** 596-597
Kun en Spillemand. See *Only a Fiddler*
Kunduri, al-, **MA:** 71, 774
K'ung Ch'iu. *See* Confucius
K'ung-Fu-Tzu. *See* Confucius
Kunta peoples, **18th:** 915
Kuntze, Otto, **Notor:** 196
Kunyu wanguo quantu (Ricci), **Ren:** 826
Kunze, Wilhelm, **Notor:** 1077
Kuo Hsing-yeh. *See* Zheng Chenggong
Kuo Mo-jo. *See* Guo Moruo
Kuomintang, **20th:** 741, 2448, 2603, 3914, 4462
Kupka, František, **20th:** 2211-2213
Kurchatov, Igor Vasilyevich, **20th:** 2214-2216; **Notor:** 380
Kurds, **20th:** 164, 1205, 1949
Kurosawa, Akira, **20th:** 2217-2220
Kurs grazhdanskago prava (Pobedonostsev), **19th:** 1811
Kush, **Anc:** 655; Aksum and, 334
Kushāns, **Anc:** 499, 775, 959
Küstrin-Spandau Officers' Putsch (1923), **20th:** 3689
Kusunoki Fuden, **17th:** 998
Kutná Hora, Battle of (1421), **MA:** 1163
Kutschmann, Walter, **20th:** 4329
Kutter, Hermann, **20th:** 547
Kutuzov, Mikhail Illarionovich, **18th:** 569-572
Kuwait, **20th:** Iraq invasion of (1990), 372. *See also* Geographical Index
Kvaternik, Dido, **Notor:** 813
Kwangjong, **MA:** 1084
Kyakuraika (Zeami), **MA:** 1154
Kyd, Thomas, **Ren:** 624
Kydd, Bill Shand, **Notor:** 657
Kykloy metresis (Archimedes), **Anc:** 82
Kyme, Anne. *See* Askew, Anne
Kynēgetikos (Xenophon), **Anc:** 969
Kyo-nam-myongs ngch' op (Chŏng Sŏn), **18th:** 248
Kyōgen, **MA:** 1154
Kyŏn-hwŏn, **MA:** 1082
Kypselos of Korinthos. *See* Cypselus of Corinth
Kyrle Society, **19th:** 1105
Kyrou anabasis (Xenophon), **Anc:** 968

Kyrou paideia (Xenophon), **Anc:** 248, 969
Kyteler, Lady Alice, **MA:** 629-631; **Notor:** 598-599
Kytice. See *Wreath, The*
Kyōgoku Takatsugu, **Ren:** 738

L

La Hogue, Battle of (1692), **17th:** 609
La Jolla Playhouse, **20th:** 3182
La Plata, Viceroyalty of (Buenos Aires), **18th:** 228
La Pléiade, **Ren:** 285, 294, 425, 542, 837
La Rochelle, siege of (1627-1628), **17th:** 552
La Rochelle Assembly, **17th:** 552
Labadie, Jean de, **17th:** 824
Laban, Rudolf, **20th:** 2221-2223
Labanotation, **20th:** 2222
Laberinto de la soledad, El. See *Labyrinth of Solitude, The*
LaBianca, Leon, **Notor:** 690
LaBianca, Rosemary, **Notor:** 690
Labor, **18th:** division of, 923; and the natural order, 340; South American silver mines, 994; **19th:** child, 457, 2304; coal strike, 1020; England, 518, 1535, 1769, 1808; Germany, 1302, 1322; mine strikes, 1043; Wendell Phillips, 1787; Scotland, 1025; unrest, 59, 509; working conditions, 1721
Labor of Love (Boccaccio), **MA:** 170
Labor Party (Australia), **19th:** 624; **20th:** 891, 1190, 1710
Labor Question, The (Phillips), **19th:** 1787
Labor unions, **19th:** 669, 895, 910, 943, 2057, 2298; coal strike, 1020; England, 669; France, 2298; Samuel Gompers, 943; Knights of Labor, 910; Alfred Krupp, 1302; mine strikes, 1043; newspaper, 2057; Scotland, 1025; technological innovation, 1559; United States, 895; women, 212; **20th:** 2040; African Americans, 3370; automobile industry, 3425; Canada, 2155; Calvin Coolidge, 832; Clarence Darrow, 914; Eugene V. Debs, 933; farmworkers, 1915; France, 780, 4270; Felix Frankfurter, 1308; governmental reforms, 3200; Great Britain, 4254; Guinea, 4053; Mexico, 649; New Zealand, 2644; Peru, 1717; Poland, 4191; United States, 2360, 2672
Labour Exchanges Act of 1909, **20th:** 352
Labour Movement, The (Hobhouse), **20th:** 1842
Labour Party (United Kingdom), **19th:** 1026; **20th:** 165, 205, 350, 2511, 4256
La Brède et de Montesquieu, Baron de. *See* Montesquieu
La Bruyère, Jean de, **17th:** 475-476
Labyrint světa a Ráj srdce. See *Labyrinth of the World and the Paradise of the Heart*
Labyrinth of Solitude, The (Paz), **20th:** 3170
Labyrinth of the World and the Paradise of the Heart (Komenský), **17th:** 470
Labyrinthine Ways, The. See *Power and the Glory, The*
Lacan, Jacques, **20th:** 2224-2227
LaCaze, Rogers, **Notor:** 373
La Chapelle, Ferdinand Bonnier de, **Notor:** 264
Lachēs (Plato), **Anc:** 799
Lachish, siege of, **Anc:** 769
Lachrimae (Dowland), **Ren:** 290
Lacombe, François, **17th:** 339
Lacordaire, Père, **19th:** 952
Lactantius, **Notor:** 391
Ladera este. See *East Slope*
Ladies' Almanack, A (Barnes), **20th:** 240
Ladies' Magazine, **19th:** 1012
Ladies' National Association, **19th:** 372
Ladies' Peace. *See* Cambrai, Treaty of
Ladislas I. *See* László I, Saint
Ladislas V, **Ren:** 642
Ladislaus II. *See* Władysław II Jagiełło
Lady Audley's Secret (Braddon), **19th:** 284
Lady Be Good (film), **20th:** 1658
Lady Be Good (Gershwin and Gershwin), **20th:** 1459, 1462
Lady Chatterley's Lover (Lawrence), **20th:** 2297
Lady Eleanor Her Appeal, The (Davies), **17th:** 221
Lady from Shanghai, The (film), **20th:** 1732
Lady in Satin (Holiday), **20th:** 1854
Lady in the Dark (Weill and Gershwin), **20th:** 1463, 4275
Lady Jane (Webster and Henslowe), **17th:** 977
Lady Macbeth of Mtsensk (Shostakovich), **20th:** 3728
Lady Nijō. *See* Nijō
Lady Nit-Wit, The (Lope de Vega), **17th:** 950
Lady of May, The (Sidney), **Ren:** 881
Lady of Pleasure, The (Shirley), **17th:** 847
Lady of the Lake, The (Scott), **19th:** 2047
Lady Sassoon (Sargent), **19th:** 1999
Lady Sings the Blues (Holiday), **20th:** 1852
Lady Windermere's Fan (Wilde), **19th:** 2433
Lady Worsley (Reynolds), **18th:** 838
Laelius, Gaius, **Anc:** 757, 813, 850
Laelius de amicitia (Cicero), **Anc:** 757

La Fayette, Madame de, **17th:** 72, 477-479, 487, 662, 833; *The Princess of Clèves*, 478
Lafayette, marquis de, **18th:** 79, 267, 529, 851; **Notor:** 697
Lafcadio's Adventures (Gide), **20th:** 1478
La Ferté-Sénectère, Henri, maréchal de, **17th:** 494
Laffite, Jean, **Notor:** 600-601, 1117
Laffite, Pierre, **Notor:** 600, 1117
La Flesche, Susan. *See* Picotte, Susan La Flesche
La Follette, Robert M., **20th:** 2227-2230, 4003
La Fontaine, Henri-Marie, **20th:** 2231-2233
La Fontaine, Jean de, **Anc:** 13; **17th:** 186, 480-483, 586, 773, 834
La Fontaine, Louis Hippolyte, **19th:** 124
La Force, Robert-Henri de Caumont, **Notor:** 283
La Fossalta, Battle of (1249), **MA:** 391
Lagash, **Anc:** 915
Lage der arbeitenden Klasse in England, Die. See *Condition of the Working Class in England in 1844, The*
Lagerkvist, Pär, **Notor:** 56
Lagerlöf, Selma, **20th:** 2234-2237, 3584
Lagrange, Joseph-Louis, **18th:** 573-576; **19th:** 9, 809
Lagrangia, Giuseppe Luigi. *See* Lagrange, Joseph-Louis
Lagrime di San Pietro (Lasso), **Ren:** 542
La Guardia, Fiorello Henry, **20th:** 2237-2240; **Notor:** 237
L'Ag'Ya (ballet), **20th:** 1062
Laíno, Domingo, **Notor:** 1004
Laird, Maggie, **Notor:** 154
Lais. See *Lays, The*
Lais, Le. See *Legacy, The*
Laissez-faire economics, **18th:** 820, 921-925, 996-999, 1081
Laius (Aeschylus), **Anc:** 9
Lake, Leonard, **Notor:** 602-603, 785
Lake Erie, Battle of (1813), **19th:** 1779
Lake Peipus, Battle of (1242), **MA:** 52
Lake Placid Club, **19th:** 650
Lake Regions of Central Africa (Burton), **19th:** 369
Lakmé (Delibes), **19th:** 640
Lakota. *See* Sioux peoples
Lalande, John, **17th:** 424
Lale devri. *See* Tulip Age
Lalemant, Charles, **17th:** 575
Lalemant, Jerôme, **17th:** 596
Lalibela, **MA:** 632-634
Lamar, Robert. *See* Lustig, Victor
Lamarck, Jean-Baptiste, **19th:** 115, 587; **Notor:** 668
Lamb, Lady Caroline, **19th:** 380, 1535
Lamb, Charles, **19th:** 1260
Lamb, William. *See* Melbourne, second Viscount
Lambert, Constant, **20th:** 4217
Lambert, John, **17th:** 483-486, 651, 942
Lambertini, Prospero Lorenzo. *See* Benedict XIV
Lamberville, Jacques de, **17th:** 909
Lambeth, Treaty of (1217), **MA:** 211
Lambeth articles (1604), **17th:** 939
Lambton, Viscount (John George Lambton). *See* Durham, first earl of
Lament, The (Hartmann), **MA:** 463
Lament for Ignacio Sánchez Mejás (García Lorca), **20th:** 1396
Lamentabili sane exitu (Holy Office), **20th:** 3273
Lamentation or Complaynt of a Sinner, A (Parr), **Ren:** 766
Lamentations of Jeremiah (Tallis), **Ren:** 919
Laments for the Living (Parker), **20th:** 3117
Lami Dozo, Basilio, **Notor:** 394
Lamian War (323-322 B.C.E.), **Anc:** 267
Lamiel (Stendhal), **19th:** 2163
Lamoricière, Christophe de, **19th:** 2
La Motte, Jeanne-Marie Bouvier de. *See* Guyon, Madame
Lamour, Dorothy, **20th:** 876
Lamprus, **Anc:** 809
Lan Ping. *See* Jiang Qing
Lancaster, Burt, **Notor:** 1007
Lancaster, Joseph, **19th:** 1304-1306
Lancaster House Agreement (1979), **20th:** 2858
Lancastrians, **MA:** 496; kings of England, 495; **Ren:** 340, 434, 828. *See also* Plantagenets; Yorkists
Lancelot (Chrétien), **MA:** 267
Lanchester, Frederick William, **20th:** 2240-2243
Lanchester Motor Company, **20th:** 2242
Land Act of 1800, **19th:** 1048
Land Acts of 1861, **19th:** 1740
Land and Freedom Party, **19th:** 1086
Land grants, Canada, **19th:** 2220
Land League, **19th:** 794
Land reform, **20th:** El Salvador, 3500; Mexico, 649; Zimbabwe, 2858
Land Without Bread (film), **20th:** 578
Land Without Justice (Djilas), **20th:** 1013
Landau, Lev Davidovich, **20th:** 2079, 2244-2247
Landauer, Gustav, **20th:** 555
Lander, Frederick W., **19th:** 232
Landers, Ann, **20th:** 2247-2249
Landini, Francesco, **MA:** 635-637
Landis, Kenesaw Mountain, **Notor:** 521
Landloper (Bosch), **Ren:** 121
Landru, Henri Désiré, **Notor:** 603-604
Landscape (Nash), **20th:** 2911

Landscape After Wang Meng (Zhang), **17th:** 157
Landscape architecture, **18th:** 165-168
Landscape of the Brown Fungus (Nash), **20th:** 2912
Landscape of the Puff Ball (Nash), **20th:** 2912
Landscape of the Red Fungus (Nash), **20th:** 2912
Landscape painting, **18th:** 166, 248, 390
Landscape with a Rainbow (Rubens), **17th:** 803
Landscape with a Sunset (Rubens), **17th:** 803
Landscape with Disc (Delaunay), **20th:** 951
Landscape with Sun (Ernst), **20th:** 1176
Landscape with the Gathering of the Ashes of Phocion (Poussin), **17th:** 750
Landscape with the Château De Steen (Rubens), **17th:** 803
Landscapes of the Four Seasons (Sesshū), **Ren:** 866
Landsteiner, Karl, **20th:** 2250-2253, 3156
Landstrykere. See *Vagabonds*
Lane, John, **19th:** 162
Lane, Rose Wilder, **20th:** 4337
Lanfranc of Bec, **MA:** 92, 400
Lang, Fritz, **20th:** 2253-2256
Lang, K. D., **20th:** 2256-2259
Langage et la pensée chez l'enfant, Le. See *Language and Thought of the Child, The*
Lange, Dorothea, **20th:** 2260-2263
Lange, Erik, **Ren:** 127
Lange, Helene, **19th:** 1307-1309
Lange, Sophie Brahe. *See* Brahe, Sophie
L'Angelier, Emile, **Notor:** 975
Langen, Eugen, **19th:** 1715
Langensalza, Battle of (1075), **MA:** 497
Langer, Susanne K., **20th:** 2263-2266
Langley, Samuel Pierpont, **19th:** 1309-1312; **20th:** 4406
Langley's law, **19th:** 1310
Langton, Stephen (archbishop of Canterbury), **MA:** 211, 543
Langtry, Lillie, **19th:** 1312-1314
Language. *See* Category Index
Language and Mind (Chomsky), **20th:** 758
Language and Myth (Cassirer), **20th:** 2264
Language and Thought of the Child, The (Piaget), **20th:** 3232
Lanier, Carlotta Walls, **Notor:** 349
Lankester, Sir Edwin Ray, **19th:** 1315-1317
Lansbury, George, **20th:** 357
Lansdowne, Lord (Henry Charles Keith Petty-Fitzmaurice), **20th:** 2266-2268
Lansdowne Heracles (Scopas), **Anc:** 762
Lansing Declaration (1918), **20th:** 2641
Lansky, Meyer, **Notor:** 23, 74, 237, 408, 604-605, 660, 695, 918, 954
Lanting xu (Wang Xizhi), **Anc:** 957
Lanuvinus, Luscius, **Anc:** 851
Lanyer, Aemilia, **Ren:** 535-537
Lanzmann, Claude, **20th:** 273
Lao Ai, **Anc:** 779
Lao Dan. *See* Laozi
Laocoön (Lessing), **18th:** 600
Laocoön statue, **18th:** 1095
Laodice, **Anc:** 567
Laon and Cynthia. See *Revolt of Islam, The*
Laos, **Ren:** 547. *See also* Geographical Index
Lao-tan. *See* Laozi
Lao-tzu. *See* Laozi
Laozi, **Anc:** 502-505
La Pasture, Roger de. *See* Weyden, Rogier van der
Laplace, Pierre-Simon, **19th:** 809, 1317-1321
Lara (Byron), **19th:** 380
La Ramée, Pierre de. *See* Ramus, Peter
Larionov, Mikhail, **20th:** 986
Larkin, Thomas O., **19th:** 832
Larmes, Les (Man Ray), **20th:** 2581
Larmes de Saint Pierre, Les (Malherbe), **17th:** 577
Lärobok I teoretisk elektrokemi. See *Text-book of Electrochemistry*
La Roche, Sophie von, **18th:** 577-579
La Rochefoucauld, François de, **17th:** 477, 487-489, 548, 662
LaRouche, Lyndon H., Jr., **Notor:** 606-608
Lars Porsenna, **Anc:** 846
Las Casas, Bartolomé de, **Ren:** 537-540, 979
Las Navas de Tolosa, Battle of (1212), **MA:** 59, 121, 557, 571
Las Salinas, Battle of (1538), **Ren:** 802
La Sablière, Madame de, **17th:** 482
La Salle, sieur de, **17th:** 401, 435, 490-493
La Salle and the Discovery of the Great West (Parkman), **19th:** 1745
Lascaux, cave paintings at, **20th:** 519
Lascelles, Caroline. *See* Braddon, Mary Elizabeth
Lascelles, John, **Ren:** 468
Lasco, John a', **Ren:** 676
La Serna y Hinojosa, José de, **19th:** 2196
Lasers, **20th:** 256-257, 4057
Lasker, Eduard, **19th:** 239
Laski, Harold J., **20th:** 2269-2271
Lasky, Jesse L., **20th:** 960
Lassalle, Ferdinand, **19th:** 1321-1324, 1370
Lassalle's Open Letter to the National Labor Association of Germany (Lassalle), **19th:** 1322

Lasso, Orlando di, **Ren:** 150, 359, 362, 540-542
Lassus, Roland de. *See* Lasso, Orlando di
Last Call for Blackford Oakes (Buckley), **20th:** 562
Last Communion of Saint Jerome, The (Carracci), **Ren:** 176
Last Constantine, The (Hemans), **19th:** 1077
Last Day of a Condemned, The (Hugo), **19th:** 1149
Last Essays on Church and Religion (Arnold), **19th:** 74
Last Fight of the Revenge, The (Ralegh), **Ren:** 814
Last Judgment, The (Giotto), **MA:** 422
Last Judgment, The (Michelangelo), **Ren:** 684
Last Judgment, The (Tintoretto), **Ren:** 932
Last Man, The (Shelley), **19th:** 2089
Last of the Mohicans, The (Cooper), **19th:** 554
Last Poems (Browning), **19th:** 328
Last Poems and Plays (Yeats), **20th:** 4430
Last Rambles Amongst the Indians of the Rocky Mountains and the Andes (Catlin), **19th:** 443
Last Remains of Sir John Suckling, The (Suckling), **17th:** 895
Last Report on the Miracles at Little No Horse, The (Erdrich), **20th:** 1170
Last Supper, The (Andrea del Sarto), **Ren:** 40
Last Supper, The (Leonardo da Vinci), **Ren:** 562
Last Supper, The (Tintoretto), **Ren:** 932
Last Temptation of Christ, The (film), **20th:** 3682
Last Temptation of Christ, The (novel by Kazantzakis), **20th:** 2088
Last Trek, The (de Klerk), **20th:** 949
Last Tycoon, The (Faulkner), **20th:** 1252
Last Waltz, The (film), **20th:** 3681
Last Words (Crane), **19th:** 564
Last Yankee, The (Miller), **20th:** 2744
Lasus of Hermione, **Anc:** 646, 793
László I, Saint, **MA:** 637-640, 966
László V, **Ren:** 350, 773
Lat Dior, **19th:** 757
Late Lancashire Witches, The (Heywood and Brome), **17th:** 374
Late Mattia Pascal, The (Pirandello), **20th:** 3260
Late Regulations Respecting the British Colonies on the Continent of America Considered, The (Dickinson), **18th:** 304
Later Jin Dynasty. *See* Jin Dynasty, Later
Later Koguryŏ (901-918), **MA:** 1082
Later Paekche, **MA:** 1082
Lateran Councils, **MA:** Fourth (1215), 523, 543, 880, 882; Third (1179), 58; **Ren:** Fifth (1512-1517), 519, 558
Lateran Pact of 1929, **20th:** 2888
Lathrop, Julia C., **20th:** 2272-2275
Latifundia, **Anc:** 358
Latimer, Hugh, **Ren:** 543-545, 835
Latimer, Lord. *See* Neville, John
Latin, **Anc:** Bible and, 457; philology, 217
Latium, **Anc:** 848
La Tour d'Auvergne, Henri de. *See* Turenne, Viscount de
La Tour, Georges de, **17th:** 493-495
Latrobe, Benjamin Henry, **19th:** 1325-1327
Latter-Day Pamphlets (Carlyle), **19th:** 416
Lattime, Vance "J. R.," **Notor:** 972
Lattre Examinacyon of Anne Askewe, The. See *Examinations*
Latvia. *See* Geographical Index
Lauchen, Georg Joachim von. *See* Rheticus
Laud, William, **17th:** 145, 167, 197, 218, 247, 275, 345, 386, 495-498, 768, 887, 938, 982, 991
Laudatio Florentinae urbis (Bruni), **MA:** 209
Lauder, Estée, **20th:** 2275-2278
Lauderdale, first duke of, **17th:** 507, 839
Laue, Max von, **20th:** 475, 2278-2280
Laugh and Lie Down (Tourneur), **17th:** 928
Laughing Cavalier, The (Hals), **17th:** 353
Laughing Girl Teaching an Older Woman to Read, A (Anguissola), **Ren:** 46
Laughter (Bergson), **20th:** 324
Laurens, John, **Notor:** 622
Laurentius Vallensis. *See* Valla, Lorenzo
Laurier, Sir Wilfrid, **19th:** 2317; **20th:** 424, 2155, 2281-2285
Laurrell, Ferdinand, **19th:** 943
Laus beatissime virginis (Neckam), **MA:** 752
Laus sapiente divine (Neckam), **MA:** 751
Lausanne, Treaty of (1923), **20th:** 163, 1972
Lautaro Lodge, **19th:** 1984
Lauzun, Antonin-Nompar de Caumont de, **17th:** 662
Laval, François, **17th:** 76, 498-501, 576
Laval, Pierre, **20th:** 2285-2288; **Notor:** 263, 609-610, 825
La Valette, Nogaret de. *See* Nogaret de La Valette
La Vallière, Françoise-Louise de la Baume Le Blanc de, **17th:** 586, 601

Laveau, Marie, **Notor:** 610-611
Laver, Rod, **20th:** 2288-2291
LaVey, Anton Szandor, **Notor:** 612-614
LaVey, Zeena Galatea, **Notor:** 612
Lavoisier, Antoine-Laurent, **18th:** 579-582, 683; Joseph Black, 116; Henry Cavendish, 219; Mikhail Vasilyevich Lomonosov, 613; **19th:** 705
La Voisin, Madame. *See* Monvoisin, Madame
Lavon, Pinḥas, **20th:** 294
Law, **Anc:** Babylonian, 582; Dao as, 503; Draco's code, 293; Greek, 293; Greek oratory and, 264; Hammurabi's code, 377; Jewish, 574, 611; Lucretius on, 521; Roman, 210, 371, 537, 766, 853; Solon and, 807; Ur-Nammu's code, 915; **MA:** Bohemia, 258; Byzantine Empire, 134, 600, 864; China, 1079; common, 193; ecclesiastical, 437; England, 223, 344, 485; French, 293; Hungary, 638; Iceland, 951; Japan, 116; Jewish, 410, 687; Khmer, 982; Mongol, 402; Muslim, 18, 36, 415; Ottoman Empire, 713; Poland, 231; Rome, 898; Saxony, 1096; Serbia, 958; Spain, 60, 556, 572; Visigoths, 1015; **Ren:** England, 341, 373, 572; France, 428, 430, 463; Germany, 648; Hungary, 644, 984; international, 373, 979; Iroquois Confederacy, 281, 450; Jewish, 524; Mongol Dynasty, 16; Moscow, 490, 493; Portugal, 605; Vietnam, 547; **17th:** Americas, 93; England, 174; natural, 543, 759; Netherlands, 327; Russia, 12; **18th:** Burma, 30; colonial America, 519, 646, 1090-1094; commercial, 646; England, 104-108; France, 844; history of, 696; individual rights, 328; Islam, 1000; judicial restraint, 239; judicial review, 239; Scotland, 326-330; substantive due process, 239; United States, 120, 239, 303, 524-527, 909; **19th:** England, 457; Germany, 2003; Russia, 46, 50, 2131; United States, 1273, 2143, 2182; Vietnam, 908; women as lawyers, 1410. *See also* Crime and criminals; Legal reform; Prisons and jails; Category Index
Law, Bonar, **20th:** 151, 205, 275, 2292-2294
Law, John, **Notor:** 614-615
Law Courts (London), **19th:** 2193
Law of Freedom on a Platform, The (Winstanley), **17th:** 989
Law of Population (Besant), **19th:** 212
Law of Twenty-Two Prairial, **18th:** 846, 878
Lawes, Henry, **17th:** 370, 502-503
Lawless Roads, The (Greene), **20th:** 1578
Lawrence, D. H., **20th:** 699, 2295-2300
Lawrence, Ernest Orlando, **20th:** 74, 2300-2303
Lawrence, F. C., **20th:** 2222
Lawrence, first Baron (John Laird Mair Lawrence), **19th:** 1328-1330
Lawrence, Richard, **Notor:** 615-616
Lawrence, T. E., **20th:** 67, 1204, 2303-2308
Lawrence, Thomas, **18th:** 583-586
Lawrence of Arabia. *See* Lawrence, T. E.
Laws. See *Nomoi*
Laws and Golden Calf (Tintoretto), **Ren:** 932
Laws and Ordinances of the Sea (1652), **17th:** 57
Laxism, **17th:** 406
Laxness, Halldór, **20th:** 2308-2310
Lay, Elzy, **Notor:** 182
Lay, Kenneth, **Notor:** 617-619, 967
Lay Down Your Arms (Suttner), **19th:** 2206
Lay investiture, **MA:** 434
Lay of the Last Minstrel, The (Scott), **19th:** 2047
Lays, The (Marie de France), **MA:** 693
Lays of Ancient Rome (Macaulay), **19th:** 1435
Lays of Many Lands, The (Hemans), **19th:** 1077
Lays of Marie de France and Other French Legends. See *Lays, The*
Lays of My Home and Other Poems (Whittier), **19th:** 2429
Lazarillo de Tormes (Alemán), **Ren:** 25
Lazarists. *See* Congregation of the Mission
Lazarus (Epstein), **20th:** 1167
Lazarus (Pirandello), **20th:** 3261
Lazarus, Emma, **19th:** 1331-1334
Lazear, Jesse, **19th:** 1879
Lazzari, Bramante. *See* Bramante, Donato
Le Duc Tho, **20th:** 2955
Le Dynasty, **Ren:** 546
Le Hien Tong, **Ren:** 546
Le Loi. *See* Le Thai To
Le Nghi Dan, **Ren:** 546
Le Nhan Tong, **Ren:** 546
Le Thai To, **Ren:** 546
Le Thanh Tong, **Ren:** 546-548
Le Tu Thanh. *See* Le Thanh Tong
Le Verger, Treaty of (1488), **Ren:** 48
Leach, Archibald Alexander. *See* Grant, Cary
Leaf Storm, and Other Stories (García Márquez), **20th:** 1398
League for/of _______. *See also* _______, League for/of

League of Augsburg, War of the. *See* Augsburg, War of the League of
League of Music, **20th:** 955
League of Nations, **20th:** 94, 210, 3870, 3897, 4366
League of the Cross, **19th:** 1490
League of the Gaels. *See* Cumann na nGaedheal
League of the Ho-dé-no-sau-nee, or Iroquois (Morgan), **19th:** 1603
League of Women Voters, **20th:** 3146
League of Youth, The (Ibsen), **19th:** 1165
Leakey, L. S. B., **20th:** 2310-2315
Leakey, Mary, **20th:** 2311, 2315-2317
Leakey, Richard, **20th:** 2311
Leaning Tower, and Other Stories, The (Porter), **20th:** 3312
Learned Commendation of the Politique Lawes of Englande (Fortescue), **Ren:** 341, 571
Learned Maid, The (Schurman), **17th:** 823
Leary, Timothy, **20th:** 1963; **Notor:** 619-621, 643
Leatherstocking Tales (Cooper), **19th:** 553
Leaven of Malice (Davies), **20th:** 918
Leaves from the Notebook of a Tamed Cynic (Niebuhr), **20th:** 2962
Leaves of Grass (Whitman), **19th:** 2424
Leavitt, Henrietta Swan, **20th:** 2317-2319
Lebanese Civil War (1975-1990), **20th:** 154, 3195
Lebanon. *See* Geographical Index
LeBaron, Ervil, **Notor:** 664
Lebediny stan (Tsvetayeva), **20th:** 4099
Leben des Galilei. See *Life of Galileo*
Lebensanschauungen der grossen Denker, Der. See *Problem of Human Life as Viewed by the Great Thinkers from Plato to the Present Time, The*
Lebensbeschreibung der Ertzbetrügerin und Landstörtzerin Courasche. See *Courage, the Adventuress*
Lebenserinnerungen (Eucken), **20th:** 1187
Lebenswunder, Die. See *Wonders of Life, The*
Leblanc, Nicolas, **18th:** 587-590
Le Bon, Gustave, **20th:** 2320-2322
Le Brun, Charles, **17th:** 504-506, 523, 532
Le Brun, Nicolas, **17th:** 504
Le Carré, John, **Notor:** 675
Lech, Battle of (1632), **17th:** 926
Lechfeld, Battle of (955), **MA:** 806
Leck, Bart van der, **20th:** 2788
Lecky, William Edward Hartpole, **19th:** 926
Leclerc, Charles, **19th:** 494
Leclerc, Georges-Louis. *See* Buffon, comte de
Leclerc, Marie-Andrée, **Notor:** 980
Leçon, La. See *Lesson, The*
Leçons sur les phénomènes de la vie communs aux animaux et aux végétaux (Bernard), **19th:** 207
Leçons sur les propriétés des tissus vivants (Bernard), **19th:** 207
Le Corbusier, **20th:** 2323-2326, 2731, 2967, 4414
Lectures on Ancient History (Niebuhr), **19th:** 1674
Lectures on Modern History (Acton), **19th:** 15
Lectures on Quaternions (Hamilton), **19th:** 1016
Lectures on Roman History (Niebuhr), **19th:** 1674
Lectures on the French Revolution (Acton), **19th:** 15
Lectures on the Philosophy of History (Hegel), **19th:** 1067
Lectures on the Religion of the Semites (Smith), **20th:** 1319
Lectures on the Rise and Development of Medieval Architecture (Scott), **19th:** 2045
Lederer, Eppie. *See* Landers, Ann
Ledger, Heath, **Notor:** 564
Ledrede, Richard de, **MA:** 629; **Notor:** 598
Lee, Andrew Daulton. *See* Lee, Daulton
Lee, Ann, **18th:** 591-594
Lee, Charles, **Notor:** 211, 621-622
Lee, Daulton, **Notor:** 133, 623-624
Lee, Harper, **20th:** 646
Lee, Harry. *See* Lee Kuan Yew
Lee, Robert E., **19th:** 613, 960, 1199, 1334-1338, 1383; and John Brown, 320
Lee, Spike, **Notor:** 92, 784
Lee Hsien Loong, **20th:** 2329
Lee Kuan Yew, **20th:** 2326-2330
Leeds, first duke of, **17th:** 149, 506-508, 693, 816, 840
Leeson, Nick, **Notor:** 624-626
Leeuwenhoek, Antoni van, **17th:** 399, 509-513, 898, 958
Le Favre, Robert. *See* Robin Hood
Lefebre-Desnoüettes, Charles, **19th:** 1994
Lefèvre d'Étaples, Jacques, **Ren:** 548-550, 618
Lefkow, Joan, **Notor:** 445
Legacy, The (Villon), **Ren:** 974
Legacy for Young Ladies, A (Barbauld), **18th:** 88
Legal reform, **18th:** England, 104-108; Ireland, 441; procedure, 645
Legal Tender Act (1777), **18th:** 206
Legal Tender cases, **19th:** 473, 779
Legalism, **Anc:** 379, 503, 578, 779, 979
Le Gallienne, Eva, **20th:** 863, 2330-2334

Legari, Farooq, **20th:** 366
Legate, Bartholomew, **17th:** 16
Legazpi, Miguel López de, **Ren:** 550-552
Legend of Good Women, The (Chaucer), **MA:** 265
Legend of Montrose, A (Scott), **19th:** 2048
Legend of the Centuries, The (Hugo), **19th:** 1148
Legend of the Invisible City of Kitezh and the Maid Fevronia, The (Rimsky-Korsakov), **19th:** 1916
Legend of the True Cross (Piero), **Ren:** 786
Legenda aurea (Jacobus de Voragine), **Anc:** 205
Legenda maior. See *Life of Catherine of Siena, The*; *Life of Saint Francis of Assisi, The*
Légende des siècles, La. See *Legend of the Centuries, The*
Legende von der heiligen Elisabeth, Die (Liszt), **19th:** 1395
Legendre, Adrien-Marie, **19th:** 11, 902
Legends, **Anc:** births of rulers, 248; foundation of Carthage, 272; Diogenes, 284; historiography and, 783; Japanese, 594; poetry and, 794; foundation of Rome, 273; Sammu-ramat and, 746; Zoroaster, 992
Legends (Lowell), **20th:** 2446
Legends of New-England (Whittier), **19th:** 2429
Legends of the Madonna (Jameson), **19th:** 1218
Léger, Fernand, **20th:** 2334-2337
Legion of the Archangel Michael, Iron Guard, **20th:** 1137
Legiony Polskie, **20th:** 3251
Legnano, Battle of (1176), **MA:** 58
Le Goulet, Treaty of (1200), **MA:** 585
Leguía, Augusto, **20th:** 1717
Lehi. *See* Lohamei Herut Yisrael
Lehrbuch der Dogmengeschichte. See *History of Dogma*
Lehrbuch der Radioaktivität. See *Manual of Radioactivity, A*
Lehre von den Tonempfindungen als physiologische Grundlage für die Theorie der Musik, Die. See *On the Sensations of Tone as a Physiological Basis for the Theory of Music*
Leibniz, Gottfried Wilhelm, **17th:** 513-517; and Pierre Bayle, 37; dispute over invention of calculus, 49, 681; and Anne Conway, 188; and Elizabeth of Bohemia, 252; and Pierre de Fermat, 271; and John Locke, 545; and Sir Isaac Newton, 681; and Seki Kōwa, 832; and Baruch Spinoza, 874; and John Wallis, 970; and Erhard Weigel, 759; **18th:** 25, 203, 241, 264, 351, 675
Leibniz-Clarke debate (1715), **18th:** 204
Leicester, earl of, **Ren:** 200, 311, 372, 553-555; **17th:** 618
Leicester's Men, **Ren:** 554
Leiden, University of, **18th:** 501
Leiden des jungen Werthers, Die. See *Sorrows of Young Werther, The*
Leif Eriksson, **MA:** 640-643, 790
Leigh, Vivien, **20th:** 3040
Leighton, William, **Ren:** 150
Leipzig, Battle of (1631), **17th:** 894
Leipzig, Battle of (1813), **19th:** 469, 930, 1023
Leipzig Disputation, **Ren:** 665
Leipzig Opera, **18th:** 970
Leisler, Jacob, **17th:** 518-520
Lélia (Sand), **19th:** 1987
Lélio (Berlioz), **19th:** 201
Lella. *See* Angela of Foligno, Blessed
Lemaître, Georges, **20th:** 2337-2340
LeMay, Curtis, **Notor:** 1087
Lemercier, Jacques, **17th:** 523, 532, 589
Lemke, William, **Notor:** 973
Lemoine, Henri, **Notor:** 627-628
Lemon v. Kurtzman (1971), **20th:** 582
Le Moyne, Pierre. *See* Iberville, Pierre Le Moyne d'
Lena (Ariosto), **Ren:** 58
Lena Goldfields massacre (1912), **20th:** 2111
Lenaea. *See* Dionysia
Lenclos, Ninon de, **17th:** 520-522
Lend-Lease Act of 1941, **20th:** 1685, 2157
L'Enfant plan, **19th:** 362
Lenin (Lukács), **20th:** 2469
Lenin, Vladimir Ilich, **20th:** 566, 1550, 2341-2344, 3793, 3817, 4073; **Notor:** 198, 312, 452, 553, 574, 596, 628-630, 746, 990, 1040, 1080, 1137-1138
Leninism, **20th:** 2342
Lennon, John, **20th:** 266
Lennox, Charlotte, **18th:** 594-596
Lennox, countess of. *See* Douglas, Margaret
Lenny (film), **20th:** 1292
Lenoir, Étienne, **19th:** 593, 1338-1341, 1714
Le Nôtre, André, **17th:** 523-526, 532, 590
Lens, Battle of (1648), **17th:** 549, 621
Lenten Synod (1075), **MA:** 498
Lenten Synod (1080), **MA:** 499
Lentulus, Publius Cornelius, **Anc:** 819
Leo I (c. 400-474; Eastern Roman emperor), **MA:** 1012
Leo II (d. 683; pope), **MA:** 936
Leo III (c. 680-741; Byzantine emperor), **MA:** 549, 588, 1020
Leo III (d. 816; pope), **MA:** 244
Leo IV (749-780; Byzantine emperor), **MA:** 549
Leo IV (d. 855; pope), **MA:** 63
Leo V (d. 820; Byzantine emperor), **MA:** 1021

Leo VI (866-912; Byzantine emperor), **MA:** 105
Leo IX (1002-1054; pope), **MA:** 433, 644-647
Leo X (1475-1521; pope), **Ren:** 53, 85, 184, 229, 316, 410, 513, 555, 557-560, 582, 658, 683, 871; **Notor:** 212, 630-632
Leo XI (1535-1605; pope), **17th:** 720
Leo XIII (1810-1903; pope), **19th:** 383, 1342-1345
Léo, André, **19th:** 89
Leo Africanus, **Ren:** 555-557
Leo de Bagnols, Maestro. *See* Levi ben Gershom
Leo Hebraeus, Maestro. *See* Levi ben Gershom
Leo the Great, **Anc:** 140, 353
León, Alonso de, **17th:** 491
León, Battle of (1915), **20th:** 3014
Leonard and Gertrude (Pestalozzi), **19th:** 1783
Leonardo da Vinci, **Ren:** 39, 125, 132, 348, 486, 561-565, 819, 964
Leonardo of Pisa, **MA:** 619, 648-650
Leonidas I, **Anc:** 505-508, 615, 973
Leonidas II, **Anc:** 228
Léonin, **MA:** 824
Leonov, Alexei, **20th:** 2194
Leonowens, Anna, **19th:** 1346-1349
Leontiades, **Anc:** 304
Leopard, The (film), **20th:** 4168
Leopardi, Giacomo, **19th:** 922
Leopold I (1640-1705; Holy Roman Emperor), **17th:** 40, 151, 406, 453, 526-529, 555; **18th:** 330, 376
Leopold I (1676-1747; prince of Anhalt-Dessau), **18th:** 90
Leopold I (1790-1865; king of Belgium), **19th:** 1732, 2360
Leopold II (1835-1909; king of Belgium), **19th:** 1349-1352, 2140, 2278, 2451; **Notor:** 632-634
Leopold III (1901-1983; king of Belgium), **20th:** 3809
Leopold, Nathan F., Jr., **20th:** 915; **Notor:** 634-636, 647
Leopold Ignatius. *See* Leopold I (1640-1705; Holy Roman Emperor)
Leopold Lodewijk Filips Maria Victor. *See* Leopold II
Leotychides, **Anc:** 227
Lepanto, Battle of (1571), **Ren:** 207, 322, 395, 798
Le Pen, Jean-Marie, **Notor:** 636-638
Lepidus, Marcus Aemilius, **Anc:** 145; **Notor:** 147
Lépine, Marc, **Notor:** 638-639
Lepke, Louis, **Notor:** 661
Leplée, Louis, **20th:** 3229
Leprosy, **Anc:** 86, 391
Lerdo de Tejada, Sebastián, **19th:** 1247; **Notor:** 279
Lerinensis, Vincentius. *See* Vincent of Lérins, Saint
Lerma, duke de, **17th:** 530-532, 697, 736, 913
Lermontov, Mikhail, **19th:** 1352-1355
Leroux, Pierre, **19th:** 1988
Les Gueux. *See* Gueux, Les
Lesage, Alain-René, **18th:** 596-598
Lesage, Jean, **20th:** 2345
Lesbia. *See* Clodia
Lesbianism, **Anc:** 751
Lescot, Pierre, **Ren:** 565-568
Leshy. See *Wood Demon, The*
Leslie, C. R., **19th:** 542
Leslie, Frank, **19th:** 1649
Lesseps, Ferdinand de, **19th:** 1356-1359
Lessing, Gotthold Ephraim, **18th:** 343, 428, 598-602, 675
Lesslie, James, **19th:** 1458
Lesson, The (Ionesco), **20th:** 1969
Lesson from Aloes, A (Fugard), **20th:** 1356
Lessons for Children (Barbauld), **18th:** 87
Lessons for Women. See *Nu jie* (Ban Zhao)
Lester, Ada. *See* Everleigh, Ada
Lester, Tony. *See* Boyce, Christopher John
Leszczyński, Stanisław I, **18th:** 232
Let It Be (Beatles), **20th:** 269
Le Tellier, François-Michel. *See* Louvois, marquis de
Le Tellier, Michel, **17th:** 72, 180, 266, 558
Le Tonnelier de Breuteil, Gabrielle-Émilie. *See* Châtelet, marquise du
Letourneau, Mary Kay, **Notor:** 640-641
Letourneau, Steve, **Notor:** 640
Letter Concerning Toleration, A (Locke), **17th:** 545
Letter from Birmingham City Jail (King), **20th:** 2149
Letter from Sydney, A (Wakefield), **19th:** 2379
Letter of Cupid, The (Christine de Pizan), **MA:** 275
Letter on Humanism (Heidegger), **20th:** 1744
Letter on the Spirit of Patriotism (Bolingbroke), **18th:** 138
Letter to a Friend, upon Occasion of the Death of His Intimate Friend, A (Browne), **17th:** 95
Letter to His Countrymen, A (Cooper), **19th:** 554
Letter to His Father (Kafka), **20th:** 2067
Letter to Sir William Wyndham, A (Bolingbroke), **18th:** 137
Letter to the Commonalty of Scotland (Knox), **Ren:** 530
Letter to the Soldiers of Coroticus (Saint Patrick), **MA:** 813
Letter to Working Mothers, A (Stopes), **20th:** 3883
"Letter XXII: No Characteristic Difference in Sex" (Macaulay), **18th:** 622
Lettera di Amerigo Vespucci delle isole nouvamente trovate in

quattro suoi viaggi. See *First Four Voyages of Amerigo Vespucci, The*
Lettere (Andreini), **Ren:** 42
Letters and Notes on the Manners, Customs, and Conditions of North American Indians (Catlin), **19th:** 443
Letters and Papers from Prison. See *Prisoner for God*
Letters and Social Aims (Emerson), **19th:** 748
Letters for Literary Ladies (Edgeworth), **19th:** 728
Letters for the Advancement of Humanity (Herder), **18th:** 487
Letters from New York (Child), **19th:** 483
Letters of a Traveller (Sand), **19th:** 1988
Letters of Marsilio Ficino, The (Ficino), **Ren:** 333
Letters of Old Age (Petrarch), **MA:** 830
Letters of the Living, **19th:** 2214
Letters on Education with Observations on Religious and Metaphysical Subjects (Macaulay), **18th:** 622
Letters on the Improvement of the Mind (Chapone), **18th:** 222
Letters to Father (Maria Celeste), **17th:** 594
Letters to Lucilius. See *Epistulae morales ad Lucilium*
Letters to Olga (Havel), **20th:** 1708
Letters Written During a Short Residence in Sweden, Norway, and Denmark (Wollstonecraft), **18th:** 1110
*Lettre à M. *** sur l'unité de temps et de lieu dans la tragédie* (Manzoni), **19th:** 1496
Lettre sur la comète. See *Miscellaneous Reflections Occasion'd by the Comet Which Appear'd in December, 1680*
Lettres (Cyrano), **17th:** 212
Lettres d'un habitant de Genève à ses contemporains (Saint-Simon), **19th:** 1975
Lettres d'un voyageur. See *Letters of a Traveller*
Lettres Persanes. See *Persian Letters*
Lettres provinciales. See *Provincial Letters, The*
Lettres sur l'Atalantide de Platon et sur l'ancienne histoire de l'Asie (Bailly), **18th:** 78
Leucippus, **Anc:** 261, 610
Leuctra, Battle of (371 B.C.E.), **Anc:** 16, 227, 304, 969
Levanevsky, Sigesmund, **20th:** 4341
Le Vau, Louis, **17th:** 523, 532-534, 590
Levellers, **17th:** 205, 263, 535
Levellers' Large Petition, **17th:** 535
Levers, **Anc:** 82
Leveson-Gower, Granville, **Notor:** 83
Lévesque, René, **20th:** 2345-2347, 3653, 4078
Levey, Howard Stanton. *See* LaVey, Anton Szandor
Levi ben Gershom, **MA:** 650-653
Lévi-Strauss, Claude, **20th:** 2347-2351
Leviathan (Hobbes), **17th:** 379, 543
Levin, Meyer, **Notor:** 636
Levine, Dennis, **Notor:** 111, 642
Levni, **18th:** 602-604
Levy, Lucien, **20th:** 128
Lewes, Battle of (1264), **MA:** 492, 728
Lewes, George Henry, **19th:** 740
Lewes, Marian. *See* Eliot, George
Lewinsky, Monica, **20th:** 786, 790
Lewis, Bernard, **20th:** 2351-2353
Lewis, C. S., **20th:** 2353-2356, 4039
Lewis, Gilbert Newton, **20th:** 621
Lewis, Jerry, **20th:** 2357-2359
Lewis, John L., **20th:** 2360-2363, 2672
Lewis, Leopold, **19th:** 1176
Lewis, Meriwether, **19th:** 1359-1363, 1962
Lewis, Sinclair, **20th:** 2363-2367
Lewis, Ted, **20th:** 1527
Lewiston, Lew, **Notor:** 299
Lexicography, **Anc:** Latin, 942; **19th:** 2404
Lexington and Concord, Battle of (1775), **18th:** 11, 60, 175, 386
Ley Lerdo, **19th:** 1246
Leyden jar, **18th:** 392, 1023
Leyte Gulf, Battle of (1944), **20th:** 1649, 2979
Lhamo Dhondrub. *See* Dalai Lama (fourteenth)
L'Hospital, Michel de, **Ren:** 568-570
Li, **Anc:** 979
Li Bai. *See* Li Bo
Li Bai yu Du Fu (Guo), **20th:** 1621
Li Bo, **MA:** 323, 653-656
Li Ch'ing-chao. *See* Li Qingzhao
Li Dazhao, **20th:** 742
Li Er. *See* Laozi
Li Fan Yuan, **17th:** 2
Li-Fournier Agreement (1884), **19th:** 2486
Li Guangli, **Anc:** 959
Li Hongzhang, **19th:** 1363-1366, 2484
Li Hung-chang. *See* Li Hongzhang
Li Linfu, **MA:** 79, 324, 1085
Li Ling, **Anc:** 783
Li Ma-tou. *See* Ricci, Matteo
Li Pai. *See* Li Bo
Li Peng, **20th:** 2367-2370
Li Po. *See* Li Bo
Li Qingzhao, **MA:** 656-658
Li Sao (Qu Yuan), **Anc:** 733
Li Shimin. *See* Taizong
Li Shumeng. *See* Jiang Qing
Li Si, **Anc:** 381, 780, 979
Li T'ai-po. *See* Li Bo
Li Tzu-Ch'eng. *See* Li Zicheng
Li Yunhe. *See* Jiang Qing
Li Zicheng, **17th:** 161, 235, 849
Li Zicheng's Revolt (1642), **17th:** 161, 235, 972

Liang Qichao, **19th:** 1252
Liao Dynasty, **MA:** 1145
Liaquat, Ali Khan, **Notor:** 10
Libanius, **Anc:** 862
Libation Bearers. See *Choēphoroi*
Libavius, Andreas, **17th:** 565
Libby, Willard F., **20th:** 2371-2373
Libel, **18th:** John Wilkes, 1083; John Peter Zenger, 1117
Liber abaci (Leonardo of Pisa), **MA:** 648
Liber de concordia Novi ac Veteris Testamenti (Joachim), **MA:** 575
Liber figurarum (Joachim), **MA:** 576
Liber Manualis. See *Handbook for William*
Liber Pontificalis, **Anc:** 796
Liber quadratorum. See *Book of Squares, The*
Liber regulae pastoralis. See *Pastoral Care*
Liber Studiorum (Turner), **19th:** 2324
Liber veritatis (Claude Lorrain), **17th:** 171
Liber vitae meritorum (Hildegard von Bingen), **MA:** 513
Liber vitae patrum. See *Life of the Fathers*
Liberal-Conservative Party (Canada), **19th:** 1442
Liberal Democratic Party (Japan), **20th:** 1702, 3646
Liberal Party (Canada), **19th:** 1453
Liberal Party (Mexico), **19th:** 652
Liberal-Protectionist Party (Australia), **19th:** 624
Liberal Republican Party (U.S.), **19th:** 2036
Liberal Triennium (1820-1823), **19th:** 412
Liberal Unionists, **19th:** 461
Liberalism, **18th:** first Baron Erskine, 329; William Godwin, 425; Montesquieu, 696; Robespierre, 844; Adam Smith, 922; Madame de Staël, 929; Wolfe Tone, 983; Mary Wollstonecraft, 1109; **19th:** 304. *See also* Democracy
Liberalism (Hobhouse), **20th:** 1844
Liberata. *See* Auclert, Hubertine
Liberation of Saint Peter from Prison (Raphael), **Ren:** 821
Liberation of the Prisoners of the Spanish Inquisition (Géricault), **19th:** 900
Liberation, War of (1813), **19th:** 1023
Liberator, The, **19th:** 685
Liberazione di Ruggiero dall'isola d'Alcina, La (Caccini), **17th:** 111
Liberia, **19th:** 1776. *See also* Geographical Index
Libertas praestantissimum. See *Human Liberty*
Liberty incident (1768), **18th:** 19, 458
Liberty Leading the People (Delacrois), **19th:** 637
Liberty University, **20th:** 1210
Liberty versus state authority, **Anc:** 839
Libraries, **Anc:** Roman, 927; **Ren:** England, 108, 188, 623, 763; France, 283, 348; Hungary, 644; India, 17; Italy, 657, 726, 848; Songhai Empire, 65; Spain, 240, 504; Vatican City, 520, 894
Library of Fathers of the Holy Catholic Church Anterior to the Division of East and West (Pusey and Newman), **19th:** 1846
Libre de contemplació. See *Book of Contemplation*
Libre dels feyts. See *Chronicle of James I, King of Aragon, Surnamed the Conqueror, The*
Libri Plantarum (Cowley), **17th:** 200
Libro de la vita mirabile e dottrina santa de la beta Caterinetta da Genoa. See *Spiritual Doctrine of Saint Catherine of Genoa, The*
Libro de su vida. See *Life of the Mother Teresa of Jesus, The*
Libro del cortegiano, Il. See *Book of the Courtier, The*
Libro della arte guerra. See *Art of War, The*
Libro della divina dottrina. See *Dialogue, The*
Libya, **20th:** independence of, 3351. *See also* Geographical Index
Licht (Stockhausen), 3875
Lichtenstein, Roy, **20th:** 2373-2375, 4227
Licinius, Valerius Licinianus, **Anc:** 240, 242
Liddell, Alice, **19th:** 424
Liddy, G. Gordon, **Notor:** 443, 500, 643-644
Lie, Trygve, **20th:** 1654, 2375-2377
Liebesmahl der Apostel, Das (Wagner), **19th:** 2375
Liebesverbot, Das (Wagner), **19th:** 2374
Liebig, Justus von, **19th:** 997, 1366-1369, 2456
Liebknecht, Karl, **20th:** 2484
Liebknecht, Wilhelm, **19th:** 1370-1372
Liechao shiji, **17th:** 541
Lied von der Erde, Das. See *Song of the Earth, The*
Lieder eines fahrenden Gesellen. See *Songs of a Wayfarer*
Liège, Jacques de, **MA:** 742
Liège, rebellion of (1468), **Ren:** 217
Liegnitz, Battle of (1241), **MA:** 227
Lienhard und Gertrud. See *Leonard and Gertrude*
Lienü zhuan (Ban Zhao), **Anc:** 154
Lifar, Serge, **20th:** 988, 2378-2381
Life (magazine), **20th:** 462, 2454

Life, origins of, **20th:** 622, 3062
Life Amongst the Indians (Catlin), **19th:** 443
Life and Adventures of Buscon, the Witty Spaniard, The (Quevedo y Villegas), **17th:** 770
Life and Adventures of Michael Armstrong, the Factory Boy, The (Trollope), **19th:** 2304
Life and Adventures of Jonathan Jefferson Whitlaw, The (Trollope), **19th:** 2304
Life and Death (Klimt), **20th:** 2180
Life and Death of Jason, The (Morris), **19th:** 1607
Life and Death of Mr. Badman, The (Bunyan), **17th:** 102
Life and Habit (Butler), **19th:** 374
Life and Loves of Beethoven, The (film), **20th:** 1383
Life and Strange Surprizing Adventures of Robinson Crusoe, of York, Mariner, Written by Himself, The. See *Robinson Crusoe*
Life and the Spirit, The (Eucken), **20th:** 1186
Life and Times of Frederick Douglass, 1881 (Douglass), **19th:** 685
Life and Travels in India (Leonowens), **19th:** 1348
Life Divine, The (Aurobindo), **20th:** 179
Life in a Jewish Family (Stein), **20th:** 3842
Life in Mexico During a Residence of Two Years in That Country (Calderón), **19th:** 389-390
Life in the Argentine Republic in the Days of the Tyrants (Sarmiento), **19th:** 2000
Life in the Clearings Versus the Bush (Moodie), **19th:** 1594
Life in the Sickroom (Martineau), **19th:** 1507
Life Is a Dream (Calderón), **17th:** 114
Life Is Worth Living (television program), **20th:** 3723
Life of Agricola, The. See *De vita Julii Agricolae*
Life of Albert Gallatin, The (Adams), **19th:** 17
Life of an Amorous Man, The (Saikaku), **17th:** 403
Life of an Amorous Woman, The (Saikaku), **17th:** 403
Life of Beatrice of Nazareth, The, **MA:** 144
Life of Benvenuto Cellini, The (Cellini), **Ren:** 204
Life of Catherine of Siena, The (Raymond of Capua), **MA:** 238
Life of Charlemagne (Einhard), **MA:** 242
Life of Christina of Markyate, **MA:** 270
Life of Constantine. See *Vita Constantini*
Life of Courage, The. See *Courage, the Adventuress*
Life of Dante (Boccaccio), **MA:** 172
Life of Don Quixote and Sancho, The (Unamuno), **20th:** 4129
Life of Edward, Earl of Clarendon, The (Clarendon), **17th:** 167
Life of Ferdinand de' Medici, The (Callot), **17th:** 117
Life of Franklin Pierce, The (Hawthorne), **19th:** 1052
Life of Galileo (Brecht), **20th:** 505
Life of George Washington, The (Irving), **19th:** 1181
Life of Henry Brulard, The (Stendhal), **19th:** 2160
Life of Jesus, A (Endō), **20th:** 1156
Life of Jesus, The (Renan), **19th:** 1885
Life of Lord Beaconsfield (O'Connor), **20th:** 3025
Life of Ma-ka-tai-me-she-kia-kiak (Black Hawk), **19th:** 244
Life of Martin Van Buren, The, **19th:** 572
Life of Merlin (Geoffrey of Monmouth), **MA:** 406
Life of Napoleon Buonaparte, The (Scott), **19th:** 2049
Life of Olive Schreiner, The (Cronwright-Schreiner), **19th:** 2023
Life of Reason, The (Santayana), **20th:** 3629
Life of Richard Nash, Esq., The (Goldsmith), **18th:** 434
Life of Saint Anthony, The. See *Vita S. Antonii*
Life of Saint Francis (Giotto), **MA:** 422
Life of Saint Francis of Assisi, The (Bonaventure), **MA:** 181
Life of St. Jerome (Zurbarán), **17th:** 1005
Life of Samuel Johnson (Hawkins), **18th:** 148
Life of Samuel Johnson, LL.D., The (Boswell), **18th:** 147, 538, 898
Life of Sir William Osler (Cushing), **20th:** 900
Life of Solitude, The (Petrarch), **MA:** 830
Life of the Archpriest Avvakum, by Himself, The (Avvakum), **17th:** 26
Life of the Fathers (Gregory of Tours), **MA:** 428
Life of the Most Holy Father Saint Francis, The. See *Life of Saint Francis of Assisi, The*
Life of the Mother Teresa of Jesus, The (Teresa of Ávila), **Ren:** 929
Life of the Universe as Conceived by Man from Earliest Ages to the Present Time, The (Arrhenius), **20th:** 140
Life of William Cavendish, Duke of Newcastle, The (Newcastle), **17th:** 677
Life on the Mississippi (Twain), **19th:** 2329

Life So Far (Friedan), **20th:** 1331
Lifecloud (Hoyle and Wickramasinghe), **20th:** 1904
Liggett and Myers, **19th:** 693
Light, study of, **20th:** 3365
Light in August (Faulkner), **20th:** 1224
Light of Life, The (Elgar), **20th:** 1134
Light of the World, The (Hunt), **19th:** 1158
Light That Failed, The (Kipling), **19th:** 1285
Lightfoot, James, **17th:** 940
Lighting, incandescent, **19th:** 732
Ligny, Battle of (1815), **19th:** 931
Lij Kassa Hailu. *See* Tewodros II
Lilburne, John, **17th:** 534-536
Liliecrona's Home (Lagerlöf), **20th:** 2235
Lilies of the Field (film), **20th:** 3297
Liliom (Molnár), **20th:** 2331
Liliuokalani, **19th:** 1373-1376
Liljecronas hem. See *Liliecrona's Home*
Lille, Battle of (1667), **17th:** 934
Lilo. *See* Galante, Carmine
Lily, The (newspaper), **19th:** 257
Lima, Almeida, **20th:** 1108
Limann, Hilla, **20th:** 3390
Li-ma-teou. *See* Ricci, Matteo
Limelight (film), **20th:** 733
Limousin, Claude, **20th:** 1327
Lin, Maya Ying, **20th:** 2385-2389
Lin Biao, **20th:** 1907, 2381-2384, 2604; **Notor:** 692
Lin Likuo, **20th:** 2383
Lin Piao. *See* Lin Biao
Lin Tse-hsü. *See* Lin Zexu
Lin Yurong. *See* Lin Biao
Lin Zexu, **19th:** 1376-1380
Lincoln, Abraham, **19th:** 272, 294, 472, 682, 1380-1385; election of, 612; John C. Frémont, 834; Gettysburg Address, 1382; John Hay, 1054; Andrew Johnson on, 1232; Robert E. Lee, 1336; Carl Schurz, 2036; William H. Seward, 2079; slavery, 345; Edwin M. Stanton, 2143; Walt Whitman, 2426; **Notor:** 123, 171, 220, 858, 1012, 1020
Lincoln, Battle of (1141), **MA:** 962
Lincoln, Mary Todd, **19th:** 1385-1387
Lincoln Center for Performing Arts, **20th:** 3477
Lincoln's Inn Fields Theatre, **17th:** 51
Lind, Jenny, **19th:** 62, 139, 1387-1390
Linda di Chamounix (Donizetti), **19th:** 676
Lindbergh, Anne Morrow, **20th:** 2389-2392
Lindbergh, Charles A., **20th:** 389, 1508, 2389, 2392-2396; **Notor:** 491
Lindgren, Armas, **20th:** 1
Lindh, Anna, **Notor:** 727
Lindh, John Walker, **Notor:** 645-646
Lindsay, Margaret. *See* Huggins, Margaret Lindsay
Lindsay, Vachel, **20th:** 1928, 3960
Line of Demarcation, **Ren:** 29, 307, 330
Linguistics, **18th:** Russia, 613; Giambattista Vico, 1013; **20th:** 758, 1986. *See also* Category Index under Language and Linguistics
Linh, Dinh Bo. *See* Dinh Bo Linh
Linnaeus, Carolus, **Anc:** 291; **18th:** 604-608; comte de Buffon, 172
Linnean Society, **18th:** 606
Linotype, **19th:** 1559
Linton, Thomas Byron. *See* Metzger, Tom
Linus Pauling Institute of Science and Medicine, **20th:** 3157
Lion and the Jewel, The (Soyinka), **20th:** 3804
Lion Hunt, The (Delacroix), **19th:** 637
Lion of Janina. *See* Ali Paşa Tepelenë
Lion, the Witch, and the Wardrobe, The (Lewis), **20th:** 2355
Lionne, Hugues de, **17th:** 622
Liouville, Joseph, **19th:** 859
Lipchitz, Jacques, **20th:** 2397-2399
Lipmann, Fritz, **20th:** 2200
Lippershey, Hans, **17th:** 537-540
Lippi, Filippo, **Ren:** 123, 601
Lippmann, Gabriel, **20th:** 2472
Lippmann, Walter, **20th:** 2400-2403
Lipsius, Justus, **17th:** 314
Lipstadt, Deborah, **Notor:** 513
Liquid Air, Oxygen, Nitrogen (Claude), **20th:** 775
Lisboa, Antônio Francisco, **18th:** 608-610
Lisbon, Siege of (1147), **MA:** 34
Lisbon, Treaty of (1668), **17th:** 426, 432
Lisbon earthquake. *See* Great Lisbon earthquake
Liṣṣ wa-al-kilāb, Al-. See *Thief and the Dogs, The*
Listen! The Wind (Lindbergh), **20th:** 2391
Lister, Joseph, **19th:** 1390-1393
Lister Institute of Preventive Medicine, **19th:** 1392
Liston, Sonny, **20th:** 62
Liszt, Franz, **19th:** 282, 297, 487, 822, 986, 1393-1396
Literacy, **Anc:** Japan, 595; Mesopotamia, 117
Literary criticism, **Anc:** Alexandrian, 316; **17th:** England, 128; France, 63; **18th:** England, 88; Johann Gottfried Herder, 486; Gotthold Ephraim Lessing, 599; **19th:** 1814
Literary patronage, **Anc:** Roman, 527; **18th:** Elizabeth Petrovna, 322

Literary Remains of Henry James, The (James), **19th:** 1214
Literature, **Ren:** England, 62, 93, 198, 312, 598, 625, 698, 714, 766, 876, 881, 906; Ethiopia, 1007; Europe, 609, 855; France, 414, 689, 728, 809, 837, 974; Italy, 42, 53, 56, 181, 925; Portugal, 167; Scotland, 146, 499; Spain, 5, 26, 208; travel, 101; **17th:** England, 729; France, 63, 475, 477, 481, 487, 732, 829; Germany, 325; Japan, 403; Spain, 317, 771, 913, 950; **18th:** American, 988-990; antislavery, 88; autobiography, 146-150, 870; characterization, 842; children's, 87-89, 433, 730-732; China, 194-196; England, 20-24, 64, 87, 181, 298-301, 841-843; epistolary, 689, 842, 965; erotic, 875-877; everyday life, 195, 434; female gothic, 823; France, 97-99, 1026-1029; gender bending in, 850; Germany, 428, 599; government suppression of, 875-877; Italy, 209; Japan, 243-245, 746-748; landscapes, 823; memoirs, 208-211; morality, 841; of the mundane, 148; neoclassical, 805; philology, 613; picturesque, 825; political, 424-428; psychological realism, 842; realism, 195, 600; Romanticism, 121-125, 850, 869, 898, 931, 953, 1010; Russia, 613; satire, 964-967, 988-990; Scotland, 183-187; sublime, 824, 869; tragedy, 599; treason, 88; women, 1041-1043; **19th:** Canada, 1594, 2292; Cuba, 1504; Denmark, 61; England, 74, 96, 310, 424, 532, 655, 688, 741, 1218; France, 126, 210, 476, 696, 815, 1835, 2161, 2297; Germany, 1071; Peru, 1513; Russia, 478, 678, 937, 1085; travel, 369, 860, 940, 1070, 2090, 2162, 2467; United States, 52, 357, 482, 491, 553, 798, 843, 1036, 1083, 1181, 1194; Urdu, 36. *See also* Category Index
Literature and Dogma (Arnold), **19th:** 74
Lithuania, **MA:** 52; conversion to Catholicism, 1120; **Ren:** Moscow and, 489. *See also* Geographical Index
Litigants, The (Racine), **17th:** 774
Little, Malcolm. *See* Malcolm X
Little Adam. *See* Worth, Adam
Little Bighorn, Battle of the (1876), **19th:** 568, 584, 2109
Little Caesar. *See* Maranzano, Salvatore
Little Caesar (film), **20th:** 4230, 4446
Little Colonel, The (film), **20th:** 3973
Little Dorrit (Dickens), **19th:** 655
Little Fadette (Sand), **19th:** 1988
Little Foxes, The (film), **20th:** 921, 1525
Little Foxes, The (play by Hellman), **20th:** 1753
Little Gidding, **17th:** 202, 275, 367
Little House on the Prairie (Wilder), **20th:** 4336
Little John, **Notor:** 909
Little Lord Fauntleroy (Burnett), **19th:** 358
Little Lyndon. *See* Baker, Bobby
Little Match Girl, The (film), **20th:** 3420
Little Men (Alcott), **19th:** 42
Little Miss Marker (film), **20th:** 3973
Little Pierre (France), **19th:** 815
Little Pretty Pocket-Book, A (Newbery), **18th:** 731
Little Princess (Burnett), **19th:** 358
Little Reader's Assistant, The (Webster), **19th:** 2403
Little Regiment and Other Episodes of the American Civil War, The (Crane), **19th:** 563
Little Soldier, The (film), **20th:** 1503
Little Steel Strike (1937), **20th:** 2361
Little Suite for Strings (Nielsen), **20th:** 2965
Little Sweep, The (Britten), **20th:** 531
Little Testament, The. See *Legacy, The*
"Little Tom Thumb" (Perrault), **17th:** 732
Little Town on the Prairie (Wilder), **20th:** 4338
Little Turtle, **18th:** 610-612, 1056
Little Turtle's War (1790-1794), **18th:** 610
Little Women (Alcott), **19th:** 42
Littleton, Sir Thomas, **Ren:** 570-573
Liturgy, **MA:** 432, 439
Litvinov, Maksim Maksimovich, **20th:** 2404-2407, 2783
Litvinov Protocol, **20th:** 2405
Liu Bang, **Anc:** 781, 958
Liu Ch'e. *See* Wudi
Liu Chin. *See* Liu Jin
Liu Hongcao, **MA:** 756
Liu Hung-ts'ao. *See* Liu Hongcao
Liu Jin, **Ren:** 986, 1009
Liu Kuni, **19th:** 2487
Liu Shao-ch'i. *See* Liu Shaoqi
Liu Shaoqi, **20th:** 969, 2408-2410, 4459; **Notor:** 692
Liu Shi. *See* Liu Yin
Liu Wu, **Anc:** 785
Liu Xiang, **Anc:** 979
Liu Yi, **Anc:** 975
Liu Yin, **17th:** 540-542
Live entertainment. *See* Category Index under Theater and Live Entertainment
Live or Die (Sexton), **20th:** 3714

Liverpool, second earl of, **19th:** 1397-1399
Liverpool and Manchester Railway, **19th:** 2169
Lives and Opinions of Eminent Philosophers. See *Peri biōn dogmatōn kai apophthegmatōn tōn en philosophia eudokimēsantōn*
Lives of Girls and Women (Munro), **20th:** 2874
Lives of the First Abbots of Wearmouth and Jarrow: Benedict, Ceolfrid, Eosterwine, Sigfrid, and Huetbert (Bede the Venerable), **MA:** 151
Lives of the Grammarians. See *De grammaticis et rhetoribus*
Lives of the Most Eminent Painters, Sculptors, and Architects (Vasari), **MA:** 282, 319; **Ren:** 422, 954
Lives of the Most Eminent Literary and Scientific Men of France (Shelley), **19th:** 2090
Lives of the Most Eminent Literary and Scientific Men of Italy, Spain, and Portugal (Shelley), **19th:** 2090
Livia Drusilla, **Anc:** 146, 489, 508-511, 842, 888
Living by the Word (Walker), **20th:** 4197
Living Flame of Love (John of the Cross), **Ren:** 509
Living It Up (film), **20th:** 2358
Living on the Third Planet (Alfvéns), **20th:** 60
Living Sea, The (Cousteau and Dumas), **20th:** 851
Livingood, Jack, **20th:** 2301, 3684
Livingston, Edward, **19th:** 364
Livingston, M. Stanley, **20th:** 2301, 2533
Livingston, Robert R., **19th:** 364, 846, 1587
Livingstone, Charles, **19th:** 1401
Livingstone, David, **19th:** 1400-1403, 2125, 2137, 2278; Henry Morton Stanley, 2138
Livius Andronicus, **Anc:** 301
Livonia, **17th:** 854
Livonian Order, **Ren:** 494
Livonian War (1558-1583), **Ren:** 494, 888, 911
Livre d'architecture (Boffrand), **18th:** 133
Livre de la cité des dames, Les. See *Book of the City of Ladies, The*
Livre de la mutacion de fortune, Le (Christine de Pizan), **MA:** 274
Livre de mon ami, Le. See *My Friend's Book*
Livre des fais et bonnes mœurs du sage roi Charles V, Le (Christine de Pizan), **MA:** 275
Livre des trois vertus, Le. See *Book of the Three Virtues, The*
Livre dou Voir-Dit, Le. See *Book of the True Poem, The*
Livre du chemin de long éstude, Le (Christine de Pizan), **MA:** 274-275
Livre ouvert I, 1938-1940, Le (Éluard), **20th:** 1153
Livre ouvert II, 1939-1941, Le (Éluard), **20th:** 1153
Livy, **Anc:** 382, 511-513, 813
Liz (Warhol), **20th:** 4228
Liza. See *House of Gentlefolk, A*
Llama de amor viva. See *Living Flame of Love*
Llangollen Vale (Seward), **18th:** 898
Llanto por Ignacio Sánchez Mejías. See *Lament for Ignacio Sánchez Mejás*
Llewelyn ap Gruffydd, **MA:** 345, 728
Lloyd, Chris Evert. *See* Evert, Chris
Lloyd, Edward, **Notor:** 94
Lloyd, Humphrey, **19th:** 1016
Lloyd, John, **20th:** 1193
Lloyd George, David, **19th:** 769, 1090; **20th:** 150, 160, 205, 210, 781, 2293, 2411-2414
Lloyd Webber, Sir Andrew, **20th:** 1141, 2414-2416; **Notor:** 822
Llull, Ramon. *See* Lull, Raymond
Loaisa, García Jofre de, **Ren:** 309
Lobachevsky, Nikolay Ivanovich, **19th:** 1403-1406
Lobengula, **19th:** 1406-1409, 1893
Lobotomy, **20th:** 1108
Local Anaesthetic (Grass), **20th:** 1574
Local Government Act of 1888, **19th:** 1979
Locarno, Treaty of (1925), **20th:** 206, 3897
Lochow and Glenyla, viscount of. *See* Argyll, second duke of
Loci Communes, The (Melanchthon), **Ren:** 665
Locke, John, **17th:** 37, 107, 306, 381, 516, 542-548, 564, 642, 761, 783, 840, 901; **18th:** 91, 113, 263, 315, 732
Lockerbie disaster, **20th:** 3353
Lockwood, Belva A., **19th:** 1409-1412
Lockwood Bill, **19th:** 1410
Lockyer, Sir Joseph Norman, **19th:** 1412-1416
Locomotives, **19th:** 2169
Lodewijk, Willem, **17th:** 618
Lodge, Henry Cabot, **20th:** 2417-2420
Lodger, The (film), **20th:** 1825
Lodī, Ibrāhīm Hussain. *See* Ibrāhīm Lodī
Lodī Dynasty, **Ren:** 478
Lodore (Shelley), **19th:** 2089
Loeb, Jacques, **20th:** 2826
Loeb, Richard A., **20th:** 915; **Notor:** 634-635, 647-649
Log Cabin, **19th:** 968
Log from the Sea of Cortez, The (Steinbeck and Ricketts), **20th:** 3850
Logan, Harvey "Kid Curry," **Notor:** 182
Loge de l'Opéra (Ségalas), **19th:** 2062

Loges, François des. *See* Villon, François
Logic, **Anc:** 261; music and, 98
Logic of Life, The (Jacob), **20th:** 1984
Logic of Modern Physics, The (Bridgman), **20th:** 527
Logical Foundations of Probability (Carnap), **20th:** 661
Logical Investigations (Husserl), **20th:** 1955
Logical positivism, **20th:** 660
Logical Structure of the World, The (Carnap), **20th:** 660
Logical Syntax of Language, The (Carnap), **20th:** 660
Logik (Wundt), **20th:** 4408
Logique du vivant, La. See *Logic of Life, The*
Logische Aufbau der Welt, Der. See *Logical Structure of the World, The*
Logische Syntax der Sprache. See *Logical Syntax of Language, The*
Logische Untersuchungen. See *Logical Investigations*
Logoi treis apologētikoi pros toms diabollontas tas agaias eikonas. See *On Holy Images*
Logos, **Anc:** 397; Yahweh and, 642
Logos eis Agēsilaon Basilea (Xenophon), **Anc:** 969
Lohamei Herut Yisrael, **20th:** 284
Lohman, Anna Caroline. *See* Restell, Madame
Loi-Cadre (1956), **20th:** 1897
Loie Fuller at the Folies Bergère (Toulouse-Lautrec), **19th:** 2289
Lois psychologiques de l'évolution des peuples, Les. See *Psychology of Peoples, The*
Lok, John, **Ren:** 352
Lokamanya. *See* Tilak, Bal Gangadhar
Lolita (Nabokov), **20th:** 2895
Lollards, **MA:** 502, 523, 608; **Ren:** 543
Lomax, Alan, **20th:** 4240
Lombard, Carole, **20th:** 1369
Lombard, Peter, **MA:** 180, 761, 1028, 1103
Lombard League, **MA:** 390
Lombardi alla prima crociata, I (Verdi), **19th:** 2351
Lombards, **MA:** 45, 47, 253, 430
Lombardy, **MA:** 386, 488; German invasion of, 437
Lombroso, Cesare, **Notor:** 996
Lomellini Family, The (van Dyck), **17th:** 245
Lomonosov, Mikhail Vasilyevich, **18th:** 613-615
Lon Nol, **20th:** 1942, 3298, 3741
London, **Anc:** sack of (60/61), 164; **18th:** American artists in, 769, 1068; classical music, 476; in literature, 123; publishing, 730; theater, 1102
London (Johnson), **18th:** 536
London, Jack, **20th:** 2420-2423; **Notor:** 613
London, Treaty of (1604), **17th:** 737
London, Treaty of (1827), **19th:** 405
London, Treaty of (1915), **20th:** 1589
London and Westminster Chartered Gas Light and Coke Company, **18th:** 717
London Conference of 1841, **19th:** 1733
London Corresponding Society, **19th:** 1806
London Dockers' Strike (1889), **19th:** 1490
London Metropolitan Police, **19th:** 1769
London School of Economics, **20th:** 353, 4255
London University, **19th:** 313
Londonderry, Robert Stewart, second marquis of. *See* Castlereagh, Viscount
Londonderry, Siege of (1689), **17th:** 609
Lonely Wife, The (film), **20th:** 3395
Long, Charlie, **Notor:** 1061
Long, Huey, **20th:** 2424-2428; **Notor:** 237, 649-651, 819, 973, 1095
Long, Stephen, **19th:** 232
Long Before Forty (Forester), **20th:** 1283
Long Day's Journey into Night (film), **20th:** 1771
Long Day's Journey into Night (play by O'Neill), **20th:** 1725, 3053
Long March (1934-1935), **20th:** 2381, 2602, 3191, 4463, 4467
Long Parliament (1640-1648), **17th:** 55, 145, 148, 497, 562, 651, 768, 838, 942
Long Vacation, The (Yonge), **19th:** 2472
Long Winter, The (Wilder), **20th:** 4336
Longabaugh, Harry, **Notor:** 182, 651-652
Longest Day, The (film), **20th:** 4447
Longfellow, Henry Wadsworth, **19th:** 748, 1137, 1416-1420
Longinus, Cassius (philosopher), **Anc:** 687, 751, 988
Longinus, Gaius Cassius. *See* Cassius
Longitude and navigation, **18th:** 152
Longley, Bill, **Notor:** 653-654
Longmen, **MA:** 1128
Longstreet, James, **19th:** 1199
Longueil, René de, **17th:** 588
Longueville, duchesse de, **17th:** 487, 548-550, 933
Lonigan, Thomas, **Notor:** 563
Look and Bow Down (Byrd), **Ren:** 149
Look Homeward, Angel (Wolfe), **20th:** 4384
Look Mickey (Lichtenstein), **20th:** 2374
Look Stranger! (Auden), **20th:** 172
Looking Glass, **19th:** 1239
Lookout—All's Well, The (Homer), **19th:** 1125

Loony-Bin Trip, The (Millett), **20th:** 2748
Looper, Byron, **Notor:** 654-655
Looper, Max, **Notor:** 654
Loos, Adolph, **20th:** 2185
Loos, Anita, **20th:** 2428-2431
Lopez, Roderigo, **Notor:** 655-656
López de Legazpi y Gurruchátegui, Miguel. *See* Legazpi, Miguel López de
López Pérez, Rigoberto, **Notor:** 985
Lorax, The (Seuss), **20th:** 3712
Lord, Otis Phillips, **19th:** 661
Lord Acton on Papal Power (Acton), **19th:** 15
Lord Admiral's Company, **Ren:** 624
Lord Admiral's Men, **17th:** 104, 373
Lord Burleigh. *See* Cecil, William
Lord Chamberlain's Men, **Ren:** 877; **17th:** 104, 440. *See also* King's Men
Lord Dunmore's War (1774), **18th:** 143, 253
Lord Haw Haw. *See* Joyce, William
Lord Hay's Masque (Campion), **17th:** 128
Lord Jim (Conrad), **20th:** 826
Lord of the Isles, The (Scott), **19th:** 2048
Lord of the Rings, The (Tolkien), **20th:** 4039
Lord Ribblesdale (Sargent), **19th:** 1998
Lord's Masque, The (Campion), **17th:** 128
Lords of the Congregation, **Ren:** 634
Lorelei (Mendelssohn), **19th:** 1550
Lorentz, Hendrik Antoon, **20th:** 2431-2434
Lorentz force, **20th:** 2432
Lorenz, Konrad, **20th:** 2434-2437
Lorenzetti, Ambrogio, **MA:** 659-661, 696
Lorenzetti, Pietro, **MA:** 320, 659-661, 696
Lorenzo, Nicola di. *See* Rienzo, Cola di
Lorenzo the Magnificent. *See* Medici, Lorenzo de' (1449-1492)
Lorrain, Claude. *See* Claude Lorrain
Lorraine, **MA:** 488; **Ren:** Burgundy and, 218
Lorraine, Mary of. *See* Mary of Guise
Lorris, Guillaume de, **MA:** 275
Los Angeles Kings, **20th:** 1585
Los Angeles Lakers, **20th:** 726
Los Angeles Rams, **20th:** 3553
Lost Generation, **20th:** 1142, 1756
Lost Honor of Katharina Blum, The (Böll), **20th:** 413
Lost in the Stars (Weill and Anderson), **20th:** 4275
Lost Prince, The (Burnett), **19th:** 359
Lost World, The (Doyle), **19th:** 688
Lot, **Anc:** 4
Lotario, Giovanni, comte de Segni. *See* Innocent III
Lothair I (795-855; Holy Roman Emperor), **MA:** 254, 662
Lothair II (835-869; king of Lotharingia), **MA:** 664, 765
Lothair III (1075?-1138; king of Germany and Holy Roman Emperor), **MA:** 473
Lotus Sutra, **MA:** 758
Louis I the Pious (778-840; Holy Roman Emperor), **MA:** 155, 254, 310, 662, 870
Louis I the Great (1326-1382; king of Hungary and Poland), **MA:** 231, 957, 1120
Louis I (1462-1515; duke of Orleans). *See* Louis XII
Louis II the German (c. 804-876; king of Germany), **MA:** 254, 662-666, 766, 872
Louis II (1506-1526; king of Hungary), **Ren:** 480, 636, 984
Louis II of Bourbon (1621-1686). *See* Condé, The Great
Louis IV (921-954; king of France), **MA:** 257, 386
Louis VI (1081-1137; king of France), **MA:** 356, 971
Louis VII (1121?-1180; king of France), **MA:** 160, 162, 356, 584, 717, 836, 972
Louis VIII (1187-1226; king of France), **MA:** 166, 211, 666
Louis IX (1214-1270; king of France), **MA:** 43, 140, 166, 228, 491, 586, 666-670, 1063, 1103, 1107, 1110
Louis XI (1423-1483; king of France), **Ren:** 217, 226, 574-576, 613, 631, 794
Louis XII (1462-1515; king of France), **Ren:** 28, 49, 84, 111, 115, 118, 227, 347, 499, 519, 577-578, 587, 648, 873; **Notor:** 14
Louis XIII (1601-1643; king of France), **Ren:** 705; **17th:** 18, 126, 141, 144, 158, 184, 193, 211, 493, 532, 551-553, 585, 627, 660, 897; and architecture, 587; arts patronage, 118, 523; and Louyse Bourgeois, 74; and Catalonia, 425; support of exiled Hugo Grotius, 327; and Henrietta Maria, 364; and the duchesse de Longueville, 548; and Louis XIV, 554; and François de Malherbe, 578; and mother Marie de Médicis, 598; and Jules Mazarin, 621; and Francisco Gómez de Quevedo y Villegas, 771; and Cardinal de Richelieu, 790; and Saint Vincent de Paul, 962; **Notor:** 889
Louis XIV (1638-1715; king of France), **17th:** 158, 487, 554-557; Anne of Austria as regent for, 19, 660; and architecture, 533, 590; arts patronage, 46, 750; ascension, 425, 585; and

Nicolas Boileau-Despréaux, 63; and Jacques-Bénigne Bossuet, 70; and Saint Marguerite Bourgeoys, 77; Canadian settlement, 499; and Catherine of Braganza, 137; and Queen Christina, 165; and Jean-Baptiste Colbert, 180; and the Great Condé, 185; and Cyrano de Bergerac, 212; and England, 149; financial crises, 475; France as world power, 464; and Frederick William, the Great Elector, 291; French Royal Academy of Sciences, 710; and the Fronde, 549; versus the Huguenots, 518; support of Christiaan Huygens, 398; opposition to Pope Innocent XI, 406; opposition to Jansenism, 22, 422; and John III Sobieski, 429; and Jean de La Fontaine, 481; and François Laval, 499; and the first duke of Leeds, 507; and Gottfried Wilhelm Leibniz, 514; and Ninon de Lenclos, 521; and André Le Nôtre, 523; and Leopold I, 527; and Louis XIII, 551; Louisiana colony, 402; and the marquis de Louvois, 558; marriage to Marie-Thérèse, 601; and Mary of Modena, 608; and Jules Mazarin, 621; and Molière, 647; and music at court, 764; opposition to mysticism, 340; attack on the Spanish Netherlands, 151; and the Papacy, 10; Partition Treaties, 547; and Charles Perrault, 731; and Philip IV, 738; and Elena Cornaro Piscopia, 744; and Jean Racine, 773; and Cardinal de Richelieu, 792; and Sir George Savile, 816; and Friedrich Hermann Schomberg, 821; and Madeleine de Scudéry, 829; and Spain, 151; Treaty of Dover (1670), 693; and Viscount de Turenne, 933; and Sébastien Le Prestre de Vauban, 946; and Diego Velázquez, 955; and William III, 979; **18th:** 661; arts patronage, 133; **Notor:** 707

Louis XV (1770-1774; king of France), **18th:** 246, 361, 615-618, 798

Louis XVI (1754-1793; king of France), **18th:** 290, 618-620, 649, 657, 752, 846, 878, 917; Brunswick Manifesto, 290; **19th:** 396, 705; execution of, 2464; **Notor:** 907

Louis XVIII (1755-1824; king of France), **19th:** 397, 476, 1668; **Notor:** 1068

Louis, Joe, **20th:** 2437-2441, 2614

Louis, Saint. *See* Louis IX

Louis Agassiz (Agassiz), **19th:** 30

Louis-Auguste. *See* Louis XVI

Louis of Battenberg, Prince. *See* Mountbatten, Louis

Louis of Valois (duke of Orléans), **Notor:** 203

Louis-Philippe (king of France), **19th:** 254, 477, 1639, 1732; **Notor:** 353, 632, 1068

Louis-Philippe-Joseph. *See* Orléans, duc d'

Louisa (Seward), **18th:** 898

Louisbourg, Siege of (1758), **18th:** 39, 196, 510, 694, 787, 1105

Louise of Savoy, **Ren:** 614, 617

Louisiana, **17th:** colonization, 402, 491; **19th:** 1361, 1587; business opportunities, 87; exploration of, 1793

Loukios e Onos (Lucian), **Anc:** 515

Lourdes (Zola), **19th:** 2491

Louvois, marquis de, **17th:** 182, 186, 555, 558-561, 622; **Notor:** 707

Louvre, **Ren:** 348, 424, 566; **17th:** 533; **20th:** 3185

Louvre, The (Morse), **19th:** 1610

Love (Morrison), **20th:** 2836

Love, Christopher, **17th:** 345

Love, Harry, **Notor:** 768

Love for Three Oranges (Prokofiev), **20th:** 3339

Love in the Time of Cholera (García Márquez), **20th:** 1400

Love Letter, The (Vermeer), **17th:** 957

Love Letters Between a Nobleman and His Sister (Behn), **17th:** 44

Love Me Tender (film), **20th:** 3331

Love Medicine (Erdrich), **20th:** 1169

Love of Landry, The (Dunbar), **19th:** 703

Love One Another (film), **20th:** 1037

Love Poems (Sexton), **20th:** 3715

Love poetry, **Anc:** 197, 704, 835

Love Rogue, The (Tirso), **17th:** 913

Love Songs (Teasdale), **20th:** 3961

Love Suicides at Amijima, The (Chikamatsu), **18th:** 244

Love Suicides at Sonezaki, The (Chikamatsu), **18th:** 243

Love Supreme, A (Coltrane), **20th:** 815

Love, the Greatest Enchantment (Calderón), **17th:** 114

Love-Tiff, The (Molière), **17th:** 647

Love Tricks. See *School of Compliment, The*

Lovecraft, H. P., **Notor:** 613

Lovejoy, Elijah, **19th:** 341, 876, 1786

Lovel the Widower (Thackeray), **19th:** 2259

Lovelace, countess of, **19th:** 1420-1422

Lovelace, Richard, **17th:** 443, 503, 562-564

Lovell, John, **19th:** 1594

Lover's Discourse, A (Barthes), **20th:** 248

Loves of Cupid and Psyche, The (La Fontaine), **17th:** 482
Loves of Jupiter (Correggio), **Ren:** 250
Loves Riddle (Cowley), **17th:** 199
Lovett, Margery (Sarah), **Notor:** 1033
Lovett, William, **19th:** 1808
Low, Juliette Gordon, **20th:** 2441-2444
Lowell, A. Lawrence, **Notor:** 925
Lowell, Amy, **20th:** 2444-2447
Lowell, James Russell, **19th:** 1118
Lowell, Percival, **20th:** 140, 4042
Lowell Fulson Band, **20th:** 735
Lower, Richard, **17th:** 564-566, 986
Lower Depths, The (Gorky), **20th:** 1550
Lowestoft, Battle of (1665), **17th:** 417
Loyalists, British, **18th:** 12, 61, 198, 305, 512, 518, 592
Loyola, Saint Ignatius of. *See* Ignatius of Loyola, Saint
LP-28. *See* February 28 Popular League
LSD. *See* Lysergic acid
Lu Buwei, **Anc:** 779
Lu Chiu-yüan. *See* Lu Jiuyuan
Lu Hsün. *See* Lu Xun
Lu Jiuyuan, **MA:** 1160
Lü Tsu-ch'ien. *See* Lü Zuqian
Lu Xun, **20th:** 2447-2449
Lü Zuqian, **MA:** 1160
Lublin, Union of (1569), **Ren:** 888, 910
Lucan, **Anc:** 593
Lucan, Lady, **Notor:** 657
Lucan, seventh earl of, **Notor:** 657-658
Lucas, George, **20th:** 2450-2453
Lucas, Margaret. *See* Newcastle, duchess of
Lucas, Victoria. *See* Plath, Sylvia
Lucasfilm, **20th:** 2452
Lucasta: Epodes, Odes, Sonnets, Songs, &c. to Which Is Added Aramantha, a Pastorall (Lovelace), **17th:** 563
Lucasta: Posthume Poems of Richard Lovelace, Esq. (Lovelace), **17th:** 562
Lucchese, Tommy, **Notor:** 658-660
Luce, Clare Boothe, **20th:** 2453-2456, 2458
Luce, Henry R., **20th:** 461, 2454, 2456-2459
Lucia di Lammermoor (Donizetti), **19th:** 675
Lucian (satirist), **Anc:** 513-516, 631; **Notor:** 834-835
Lucian of Antioch, **Anc:** 791
Luciano, Lucky, **Notor:** 6, 23, 148, 221, 237, 396, 402, 408, 604, 659-662, 695, 709, 918, 939, 954
Lucid, Shannon W., **20th:** 2460-2461
Lucien Leuwen (Stendhal), **19th:** 2163
Lucifer (Pollock), **20th:** 3303
Lucilla, **Notor:** 228
Lucius III, **MA:** 387
Lucius: Or, The Ass. See *Loukios e Onos*
Lucius Sergius Catilina. *See* Catiline
Luck and Pluck (Alger), **19th:** 52
Luck of Barry Lyndon, The. See *Barry Lyndon*
Luck or Cunning (Butler), **19th:** 375
Lucknow Pact (1916), **20th:** 2003
Lucky Chance, The (Behn), **17th:** 43
Lucky Lucan. *See* Lucan, seventh earl of
Lucretia, **Anc:** 512, 517-519, 846
Lucretius, **Anc:** 263, 520-522
Lucretius Tricipitinus, Spurius, **Anc:** 517
Lucrezia Borgia (Donizetti), **19th:** 675
Lucullus, Lucius Licinius, **Anc:** 568, 896
Luddite Riots, **19th:** 518
Ludendorff, Erich, **20th:** 2462-2465; **Notor:** 461
Ludendorff offensive (1918), **20th:** 2463
Ludlow, J. M., **19th:** 1519
Ludlow, Roger, **17th:** 567-569
Ludlow Massacre (1914), **20th:** 2041, 3476
Ludmilla, Saint, **MA:** 670-672
Ludus Tonalis (Hindemith), **20th:** 1813
Ludwig I, **19th:** 1591
Ludwig II, **Notor:** 662-663
Ludwig II der Deutsche. *See* Louis II the German
Ludwig IV, **MA:** 779
Ludwig Friedrich Wilhelm. *See* Ludwig II
Luftwaffe, **20th:** 1546, 2117
Lugard, Lord (Frederick John Dealtry Lugard), **19th:** 941; **20th:** 2465-2467
Luisa Miller (Verdi), **19th:** 2352
Luitpold (prince of Bavaria), **Notor:** 663
Lukács, György, **20th:** 2468-2471
Lull, Raymond, **MA:** 673-676; **Ren:** 174
Lully, Jean-Baptiste, **17th:** 482, 554, 569-571
Lulu (Berg), **20th:** 311
Lumière, Auguste, **20th:** 2471-2475
Lumière, Louis, **20th:** 2471-2475
Lumumba, Patrice, **20th:** 2471-2475; **Notor:** 740
Lun heng (Wang Chong), **Anc:** 953
Luna, Álvaro de, **Ren:** 432
Luna 2, **20th:** 2193
Lunar Asparagus (Ernst), **20th:** 1178
Lunar Society, **18th:** Matthew Boulton, 157; Joseph Priestley, 812; John Roebuck, 860; Josiah Wedgwood, 1059
Luncheon on the Grass (Manet), **19th:** 1800

Lundgren, Alice Keehler, **Notor:** 664
Lundgren, Jeffrey, **Notor:** 664-665
Lundy, Benjamin, **19th:** 875
Lundy's Lane, Battle of (1813), **19th:** 2052
Lunyu. See *Analects, The*
Luque, Hernando de, **Ren:** 801
Luria, Isaac ben Solomon, **Ren:** 579-581
Lusādas, Os. See *Lusiads, The*
Lushington, Stephen, **19th:** 377
Lusiads, The (Camões), **Ren:** 168
Lustig, Victor, **Notor:** 665-666
Lute Player, The (Hals), **17th:** 354
Luther, Martin, **Anc:** 89; **Ren:** 142, 231, 513, 559, 582-586, 650, 768, 797, 947; Anabaptists and, 472; art and, 264; confessional, 666; Desiderius Erasmus and, 316; Diet of Worms and, 220; England and, 834; on faith, 584; Germany and, 775; Henry VIII and, 442; Huldrych Zwingli and, 1012; John Calvin and, 163; Lutheranism and, 651; Mary of Hungary and, 637; opposition to, 335; Philipp Melanchthon and, 665; **Notor:** 212, 631
Luther, Robert, **20th:** 883
Luther Burbank Company, **19th:** 352
Luther Burbank Press, **19th:** 352
Luther Burbank Society, **19th:** 352
Lutheran Church and Lutheranism, **Ren:** 8, 164, 231, 255, 442, 559; Germany, 356, 651, 666, 776; Italy, 797; **17th:** 267; **18th:** colonial Georgia, 743; Count von Zinzendorf, 1121. *See also* Calvinism; Counter-Reformation; Protestantism; Reformation; Roman Catholic Church and Catholicism
Luther's and Zwingli's Propositions for Debate (Zwingli), **Ren:** 1012
Luttelton, Thomas. *See* Littleton, Sir Thomas
Lutterell, John, **MA:** 778
Lutuli, Albert, **20th:** 2478-2481
Lützen, Battle of (1632), **17th:** 163, 338, 705, 926, 967
Luweros, **20th:** 3012
Lux, Adam, **Notor:** 236
Luxe, Calm, et Volupté (Matisse), **20th:** 2650
Luxembourg, House of, **MA:** 259
Luxembourg Commission, **19th:** 256
Luxembourg Palace, **17th:** 599
Luxemburg, Rosa, **20th:** 335, 2482-2485, 4457; **Notor:** 312
Luxor, temples at, **Anc:** 46
Lwoff, André, **20th:** 1983
Lyadov, Anatoly, **19th:** 282
Lyceum, **Anc:** 95, 277, 872, 981
Lyceum Theatre, **19th:** 1176
Lycurgus of Athens, **Anc:** 649
Lycurgus of Babylon, **Anc:** 11
Lydia (Aston), **19th:** 84
Lydia E. Pinkham Medicine Company, **19th:** 1797
Lyell, Sir Charles, **19th:** 587, 603, 1423-1427, 2122
Lynch, B. Suárez. *See* Borges, Jorge Luis
Lynchings, **20th:** 4290, 4308
Lyne, Sir William, **19th:** 151
Lyon (Liszt), **19th:** 1394
Lyon, Elizabeth, **Notor:** 943
Lyon, First Council of (1245), **MA:** 546
Lyon, Mary, **19th:** 1428-1430
Lyon, Nathaniel, **19th:** 834
Lyon, Second Council of (1274), **MA:** 182, 572, 1017, 1106
Lyons, Emily, **Notor:** 922
Lyons, Dame Enid Muriel, **20th:** 2486-2489
Lyons, Joseph Aloysius, **20th:** 1933, 2486, 2489-2491, 2707
Lyons, Sophie, **Notor:** 688
Lyric and Dramatic Poetry, 1946-1982 (Césaire), **20th:** 710
Lyric Poems (Quevedo y Villegas), **17th:** 771
Lyric Suite (Berg), **20th:** 311
Lyrical Ballads (Wordsworth and Coleridge), **19th:** 530, 2462
Lyrical Tales (Robinson), **18th:** 850
Lyrics of Lowly Life (Dunbar), **19th:** 703
Lyrics of the Hearthside (Dunbar), **19th:** 703
Lyrides, The (Camões), **Ren:** 168
Lyrische Stücke (Grieg), **19th:** 986
Lyriske smaastykker (Grieg), **19th:** 986
Lys rouge, Le. See *Red Lily, The*
Lysander of Sparta, **Anc:** 14, 34
Lysandra, **Anc:** 106, 716
Lysanias, **Anc:** 314
Lysenko, Trofim D., **20th:** 2862, 4152; **Notor:** 667-668
Lysergic acid, **20th:** 4395
Lysicles, **Anc:** 128
Lysimachus, **Anc:** 63, 105, 716, 721, 763
Lysippus, **Anc:** 523-526
Lysis of Tarentum, **Anc:** 303
Lysistratē (Aristophanes), **Anc:** 92
Lysozyme, **20th:** 1254, 1260
Lyttelton, Thomas. *See* Littleton, Sir Thomas
LZ-1, **20th:** 4454

M

M (film), **20th:** 2254
Ma double vie. See *My Double Life*
Ma Jolie (Picasso), **20th:** 494
Ma Part de vérité, de rupture à l'unité (Mitterrand), **20th:** 2771
Ma Rong, **Anc:** 153
Ma Sanbao. *See* Zheng He
Ma Sœur Henriette. See *My Sister Henrietta*
Ma Vie (Lifar), **20th:** 2378

Ma-Xia school of painting, **MA:** 678, 1135
Ma Yuan, **MA:** 677-679, 1134
Ma Zu, **Anc:** 149
Maastricht, Battle of (1673), **17th:** 821
Maastricht, Battle of (1748), **18th:** 882
Maastricht Treaty (1992), **20th:** 2182
Ma'at, **Anc:** 735, 902
Maatkare. *See* Hatshepsut
Mabel's Strange Predicament (film), **20th:** 732
Mabila, Battle of (1540), **Ren:** 922
Mabinogion, **MA:** 450
Mabou Mines, **20th:** 39
Mac Flecknoe (Dryden), **17th:** 241
McAfee, Lee Roy, **Notor:** 284
Macapagal, Diosadado, **20th:** 2621
Macaroni Parson. *See* Dodd, William
MacArthur, Charles, **20th:** 1724
MacArthur, Douglas, **20th:** 1126, 1648, 2492-2497, 2631, 2978, 4089; Australia, 892; Hirohito, 1819; Korean War, 470; **Notor:** 474
Macarthur, James, **19th:** 2414
MacArthur, John, **19th:** 1431-1433
MacArthur, Mary, **20th:** 415
MacArthur, Robert H., **20th:** 4359
Macaulay, Catherine, **18th:** 621-623
Macaulay, Thomas Babington (Lord Macaulay), **19th:** 1433-1437
Macaulay, Zachary, **19th:** 377, 1572
Macbeth (Verdi), **19th:** 2351
Maccabaeus, Judas, **Anc:** 403
McCafferty, James, **Notor:** 509
McCall, Jack, **19th:** 387
McCarey, Leo, **20th:** 1571
McCarthy, Eugene, **20th:** 1939, 2104
McCarthy, Joseph, **20th:** 822, 1127, 1960, 2497-2500, 3927, 4088; opposition to, 2881, 3770; **Notor:** 199, 217, 490, 669-671, 914, 916, 965
McCarthy, Mary, **20th:** 120, 1754, 2501-2503
McCarthy, Timothy, **Notor:** 471
McCartney, Paul, **20th:** 266
McCarty, Henry. *See* Bonney, William H.
McClellan, George B., **19th:** 1199, 1335, 1383, 2143
McClintock, Barbara, **20th:** 2504-2507
McCord, Adelaide. *See* Menken, Adah Isaacs
McCord, James W., Jr., **Notor:** 671-672
McCormick, Cyrus Hall, **19th:** 1438-1440
McCormick Seminary, **19th:** 1439
McCoy, Richard, **Notor:** 234
McCreary County v. ACLU of Kentucky (2005), **20th:** 521
McCullers, Carson, **20th:** 2507-2510
McCulloch v. Maryland, **19th:** 2181
Macdermots of Ballycloran, The (Trollope), **19th:** 2300
McDonald, Andrew. *See* Pierce, William Luther, III
MacDonald, Colette, **Notor:** 673
MacDonald, Flora, **18th:** 623-625
MacDonald, Jeffrey, **Notor:** 673-674
Macdonald, Sir John Alexander, **19th:** 317, 1441-1445, 1453, 2317; **20th:** 2282
Macdonald, John Sandfield, **19th:** 1443
MacDonald, Kimberley, **Notor:** 673
MacDonald, Kristen, **Notor:** 673
McDonald, Maurice, **20th:** 2202
MacDonald, Ramsay, **20th:** 94, 205, 349, 1453, 2510-2514; Horatio W. Bottomley, 448; Egypt, 4440; Great Depression, 357
McDonald, Ronald, **20th:** 2202
McDougal, Nell, **Notor:** 154
McDougall, William, **19th:** 1909
McDowell, Irvin, **19th:** 1198
Macedonia, **Anc:** Athens and, 638; Illyria and, 638; Sparta and, 637; Thebes and, 637
Macedonius, **Anc:** 865
Maćek, Vlatko, **Notor:** 813, 876
McEnroe, John, **20th:** 428
Maceo, Antonio, **19th:** 1504
McFarland, Abby Sage. *See* Richardson, Abby Sage
McFarland, Daniel, **19th:** 1902
M'Fingal (Trumbull), **18th:** 989
McGillivray, Alexander, **18th:** 626-629
MacGillivray, William, **19th:** 93
McGovern, George, **20th:** 755, 2168, 2986
McGraw, Phil, **Notor:** 85
MacGregor, Robert Roy. *See* Rob Roy
McGuffey, William Holmes, **19th:** 1445-1449
McGuinness, Jim, **Notor:** 974
McGurn, Jack, **Notor:** 176, 752
Machado de Assis, Joaquim Maria, **19th:** 1449-1452
Machado y Morales, Gustavo, **Notor:** 73
Machaut, Guillaume de, **MA:** 335, 635, 679-682, 826
Machaut's Mass (Machaut), **MA:** 680
Machel, Samora, **20th:** 2515-2518
Machiavelli, Niccolò, **Ren:** 116, 269, 316, 373, 411, 587-591; **Notor:** 128, 228
Machina coelestis (Hevelius), **17th:** 372
Machine infernale. See *Infernal Machine, The*
Machines agricoles (Milhaud), **20th:** 2736
Macintosh, **20th:** 2007

Mack, Connie, **Notor:** 521
Macke, August, **20th:** 1176
Mackenzie, Sir Alexander (explorer), **18th:** 629-632
Mackenzie, Alexander (prime minister of Canada), **19th:** 1452-1454; **20th:** 2281
Mackenzie, Duncan, **19th:** 754
Mackenzie, William Lyon, **19th:** 123, 1454-1459
Mackenzie Rebellion (1837), **19th:** 124
Mackenzie River expeditions, **18th:** 630
McKim, Charles, **19th:** 362
Mackinder, Sir Halford John, **20th:** 2518-2521
McKinley, William, **19th:** 510, 1018, 1055, 1460-1463; **20th:** 552, 3516, 3519; **Notor:** 253
McKinley Act (1890), **19th:** 252, 1460
MacKinnon, Catharine A., **20th:** 2522-2525
McLaughlin, James, **19th:** 2110
McLaughlin, John, **Notor:** 776
Maclaurin, Colin, **18th:** 632-635
McLaurin, John L., **Notor:** 1031
McLaury, Billy, **19th:** 721
McLaury, Frank, **19th:** 721; **Notor:** 315
McLaury, Tom, **Notor:** 315
Maclean, Donald Duart, **Notor:** 109, 152, 164, 674-676, 837
McLean, Evalyn Walsh, **Notor:** 714
Macleod, John J. R., **20th:** 225, 2526-2528
MacLeod, Margaretha Geertruida. *See* Mata Hari
McLeod, Mary Jane. *See* Bethune, Mary McLeod
McLuhan, Marshall, **20th:** 2529-2532
MacMahon, Marshal, **19th:** 865
McManus, George, **Notor:** 918
McMartin, Virginia, **Notor:** 676-677
Macmillan, Alexander, **19th:** 1464-1466
Macmillan, Daniel, **19th:** 1464-1466
McMillan, Edwin Mattison, **20th:** 2301, 2532-2536, 3684
Macmillan, Harold, **20th:** 603, 1740, 2536-2540
Macmillan Publishing Company, **19th:** 1465
Macmillan's Magazine, **19th:** 1465
MacNab, The (Raeburn), **19th:** 1854
McNabb, Allan, **19th:** 1442
M'Naghten, Daniel, **Notor:** 677-678
McNall, Belva. *See* Lockwood, Belva A.
McNamara, James B., **20th:** 914
McNamara, John J., **20th:** 914
McNamara, Robert, **20th:** 492, 2541-2543, 4172
Macodu, **19th:** 757
McPherson, Aimee Semple, **Notor:** 679-681
MacPherson v. Buick Motor Company (1916), **20th:** 654
Macquarie, Luchlan, **19th:** 975
Macquarie Tower and Light House, **19th:** 975
McRae, Milton, **19th:** 2057
Macready, William Charles, **19th:** 792, 1256, 1467-1470
Macrinus, **Anc:** 482, 487
Macro, Naevius Cordus Sutorius, **Anc:** 177
Macrobius, **Anc:** 489
Macromolecular theory, **20th:** 3834
McShann, Jay, **20th:** 3113
McSon Trio, **20th:** 735
McVeigh, Timothy, **Notor:** 549, 591, 681-683, 790, 838, 1092
McVitie, Jack, **Notor:** 592, 594
Mad Anthony. *See* Wayne, Anthony
Mad Caliph. *See* Ḥākim, al-
Mad Dog Coll. *See* Coll, Vincent
Mad Love (Breton), **20th:** 512
Mad Lover, The (Fletcher), **17th:** 279
Mad World, My Masters, A (Middleton), **17th:** 636
Madagascar. *See* Geographical Index
Madam C. J. Walker Company, **20th:** 4200
Madama Butterfly (Puccini), **20th:** 3347
Madame Bovary (film), **20th:** 3421
Madame Bovary (novel by Flaubert), **19th:** 785
Madame Charpentier and Her Children (Renoir), **19th:** 1889
Madame de Treymes (Wharton), **20th:** 4301
Madame Gautreau (Sargent), **19th:** 1997
Madame Secretary (Albright), **20th:** 56
Madden, Owney, **Notor:** 237
Maddox, Lester, **Notor:** 100, 1000
Maddux, Holly, **Notor:** 324
Madeiras, Portuguese occupation of, **MA:** 479
Madeleine de Scudéry. *See* Scudéry, Madeleine de
Madeleine Férat (Zola), **19th:** 2489
Mademoiselle de Belle-Isle. See *Gabrielle de Belle Isle*
Mademoiselle Eglantine's Troupe (Toulouse-Lautrec), **19th:** 2290
Mlle Fiocre in the Ballet "La Source" (Degas), **19th:** 632
Maderno, Carlo, **17th:** 67
Madero, Francisco, **19th:** 654; **20th:** 647, 2544-2547, 3014, 4160, 4449; **Notor:** 280, 1070, 1129
Madgearu, Virgil, **Notor:** 25
Madhyāntavibhāga, **Anc:** 113
Madikizela, Nkosikazi Nobandle Nomzamo. *See* Mandela, Winnie
Madinat az-Zahra, **MA:** 11
Madiodio, **19th:** 757
Madison, Dolley, **19th:** 1470-1473

Madison, James, **18th:** 636-638; Elbridge Gerry, 413; Thomas Jefferson, 529; **19th:** 1470, 1587
Madiun Affair (1946), **20th:** 1705
Madmen and Specialists (Soyinka), **20th:** 3805
Madonna, **Notor:** 822
Madonna (Duccio), **MA:** 282, 326
Madonna and Child (Dürer), **Ren:** 298
Madonna and Child (Jacopo), **MA:** 567
Madonna and Child (Moore), **20th:** 2820
Madonna and Child with Saint Anne and Angels (Masaccio), **MA:** 700
Madonna and Child with Saints (Andrea del Sarto), **Ren:** 40
Madonna Benois (Leonardo da Vinci), **Ren:** 562
Madonna del Sacco (Andrea del Sarto), **Ren:** 40
Madonna Enthroned (Cimabue), **MA:** 283
Madonna Enthroned with Saints (Mantegna), **Ren:** 602
Madonna Enthroned with Saints John the Baptist and Donatus (Verrocchio), **Ren:** 963
Madonna Linaivoli Altarpiece (Fra Angelico), **MA:** 83
Madonna of Saint Francis (Correggio), **Ren:** 249
Madonna of the Bargellini Family (Carracci), **Ren:** 176
Madonna of the Harpies (Andrea del Sarto), **Ren:** 39
Madonna of the Meadows (Raphael), **Ren:** 820
Madonna of the Pesaro Family, The (Titian), **Ren:** 937
Madonna of the Rocks (Leonardo da Vinci), **Ren:** 562
Madonna of the Rosary (van Dyck), **17th:** 244
Madonna of the Steps, The (Michelangelo), **Ren:** 682
Madonna of the Victory (Mantegna), **Ren:** 603
Madonna with Chancellor Rolin (van Eyck), **MA:** 367
Madonna with Four Saints (Rogier van der Weyden), **MA:** 1093
Madonna with Saint John Evangelist and Saint Catherine (Carracci), **Ren:** 176
Madrasas, **MA:** 776
Madrassah-i-Rahimiyah, **18th:** 1033
Madrid Riot (1766), **18th:** 227
Madrigalls to Foure Voyces (Morley), **Ren:** 701
Madrigals, **Ren:** 149, 359, 611, 701; **17th:** 656
Madwoman of Chaillot, The (Giraudoux), **20th:** 1494
Maecenas, Gaius, **Anc:** 21, 431, 527-529, 602, 704, 939
Maes, Battle of (1136), **MA:** 448
Maestà (Duccio), **MA:** 326
Maestà (Lorenzetti), **MA:** 660
Maestà (Martini), **MA:** 696
Maeterlinck, Maurice, **20th:** 938
Mafeking, Siege of (1899-1900), **19th:** 111
Mafia incident, **19th:** 1042
Magaddino, Stefano, **Notor:** 224
Magallanes, Fernando de. *See* Magellan, Ferdinand
Magas, **Anc:** 716
Mage, Eugène, **19th:** 757
Magellan, Ferdinand, **Ren:** 307, 551, 591-595
Magendie, François, **19th:** 205
Maggie (Crane), **19th:** 563
Maggie Cassidy (Kerouac), **20th:** 2115
Maghīlī, Muḥammad ibn ʿAbd al-Karīm, al-, **Ren:** 595-597
Magic, **Anc:** Egyptian, 440; religion and, 424
Magic Flute, The (Mozart), **18th:** 712
Magic Motorways (Geddes), **20th:** 1433
Magic Mountain, The (Mann), **20th:** 2595
Magic Skin, The (Balzac), **19th:** 126
Magical Mystery Tour (film), **20th:** 269
Magical realism, **20th:** 1401
Mágico prodigioso, El. See *Wonder-Working Magician, The*
Maginot line, **20th:** 3223
Magister Ludi (Hesse), **20th:** 1788
Magisterium divinale sive sapientale (William of Auxerre), **MA:** 1099
Magliocco, Joe, **Notor:** 224, 864
Magloire, Paul Eugène, **Notor:** 308
Magna Carta (1215), **MA:** 211, 586; reissue of (1225), 490
Magna Graecia, **Anc:** 36
Magna Societas, **MA:** 130
Magnalia Christi Americana (Mather), **18th:** 668
Magnalia Naturæ (Becher), **17th:** 40
Magnesia, Battle of (190 B.C.E.), **Anc:** 895
Magnetic Fields, The (Breton and Soupault), **20th:** 510
Magnetic Lady, The (Jonson), **17th:** 443
Magnetism, **MA:** 821; **Ren:** Gilbert's studies of, 381
Magnetohydrodynamics, **20th:** 59
Magnetrons, **20th:** 3356
Magnificent Ambersons, The (film), **20th:** 4284
Magnificent Entertainment Given to King James, The (Dekker), **17th:** 224
Magnolia Blossom (Tower of Jewels) (Cunningham), **20th:** 884
Magnum Bonum (Yonge), **19th:** 2472
Magnum Photos, **20th:** 672
Magnus liber organi (Léonin), **MA:** 824

Magritte, René, **20th:** 2547-2551; **Notor:** 927
Magsaysay, Ramon, **20th:** 107
Maguire, Conor, **17th:** 700
Magyars, **MA:** 105, 806; **17th:** 528
Mahabat Khan, **17th:** 411
Mahābhārata, **Anc:** 922
Mahaffy, Leslie, **Notor:** 93
Mahagonny Songspiel (Weill), **20th:** 4274
Mahākassapa, **Anc:** 50
Mahanagar. See *Big City, The*
Mahāpajāpatī, **Anc:** 50
Mahāparinirvāṇa Sūtra, **Anc:** 346
Mahara's Minstrels, **20th:** 1667
Maharashtra, **17th:** 25
Mahathir bin Mohamad, Datuk Seri, **20th:** 2551-2553
Mahāvairocana (a Buddha), **MA:** 621
Mahāvairocana Sūtra, **MA:** 622
Mahāvamsa, **Anc:** 898
Mahāvīra. *See* Vardhamāna
Mahāvīra (mathematician), **MA:** 196
Mahāvīra Monastery, **Anc:** 899
Mahāyāna Buddhism, **Anc:** 931, 934; Chinese, 950; **MA:** 1136. *See also* Buddhism
Mahāyānasaṁgraha (Asanga), **Anc:** 112, 930
Mahāyānasūtralankāra (Asanga), **Anc:** 113
Mahdi, the (Sudanese revolutionary), **19th:** 1473-1475
Mahdi, Sadiq al- (prime minister of Sudan), **Notor:** 66
Mahfouz, Naguib, **20th:** 2553-2557
Mahinda Thera, **Anc:** 898, 934
Mahler, Alma, **20th:** 2186
Mahler, Gustav, **20th:** 2186, 2558-2562
Mahler, Horst, **Notor:** 47, 684-685
Mahmud I, **18th:** 28, 639-641
Mahmud II, **19th:** 55, 1620
Maḥmūd of Ghazna, **MA:** 164, 375, 683-686
Mahomet et Charlemagne. See *Mohammed and Charlemagne*
Mahrem, **Anc:** 334
Maid of Arran, The (Baum), **19th:** 156
Maid of Pskov, The (Rimsky-Korsakov), **19th:** 1915
Maids, The (Genet), **20th:** 1446
Maid's Tragedy, The (Beaumont and Fletcher), **Ren:** 94; **17th:** 279
Mailer, Norman, **20th:** 2563-2566
Maiman, Theodore H., **20th:** 4058
Maimonides, Moses, **MA:** 651, 686-689, 730, 747; **Ren:** 1
Main Currents in American Thought (Parrington), **20th:** 3124
Main Plot, **17th:** 253
Main Street (Lewis), **20th:** 2364
Maine, USS, **19th:** 1462
Maine Woods, The (Thoreau), **19th:** 2275
Mains jointes, Les (Mauriac), **20th:** 2657
Maintenon, Madame de, **17th:** 266, 340, 572-574, 602, 775
Maiōtikon (Herophilus), **Anc:** 411
Maipu, Battle of (1818), **19th:** 1704
Maisonneuve, sieur de, **17th:** 76, 574-576
Maitland, John. *See* Lauderdale, first duke of
Maitland, Sir Peregrine, **19th:** 123, 1456
Maître du monde. See *Master of the World*
Maitreya, **Anc:** 112, 345. *See also* Buddha
Maitreyanātha, **Anc:** 111, 113
Majali, Hazza al-, **20th:** 1952
Majestas Carolina, **MA:** 258
Majid, **19th:** 1967
Majid, Ali Hassan al-, **20th:** 1949; **Notor:** 504
Majmu, al- (Avicenna), **MA:** 123
Major, John (philosopher and teacher), **Ren:** 146, 528
Major, John (prime minister of the United Kingdom), **20th:** 2567-2569
Majorca, **MA:** 673; Jewish community at, 673; mysticism, 673
Majorcan Landscape (Rivera), **20th:** 3457
Majors and Minors (Dunbar), **19th:** 702
Majuba Hill, Battle of (1881), **19th:** 1299
Makarova, Natalia, **20th:** 253
Ma-ka-tai-me-she-kia-kiak. *See* Black Hawk
Make the Connection (Winfrey and Greene), **20th:** 4373
Makhpíya-Lúta. *See* Red Cloud
Making of a Marchioness, The (Burnett), **19th:** 358
Making of a Missionary, The (Yonge), **19th:** 2472
Making of Americans, The (Stein), **20th:** 3847
Making War to Keep Peace (Kirkpatrick), **20th:** 2169
Makioka Sisters, The (Tanizaki), **20th:** 3945
Makonnen, Tafari. *See* Haile Selassie I
Maktab al-Khidmat, **20th:** 372
Makura no sōshi. See *Pillow Book of Sei Shōnagon, The*
Makuzu. *See* Tadano Makuzu
Malade imaginaire, La. See *Imaginary Invalid, The*
Málaga, Battle of (1483), **Ren:** 106
Malamir, **MA:** 190
Malan, Daniel François, **Notor:** 1064
Malaprop, Mrs., **18th:** 907
Malaria, **19th:** 1879; **20th:** 3533
Mālavikāgnimitra (Kālidāsa), **Anc:** 496
Malawi, **20th:** independence of, 219. *See also* Geographical Index

Malawi Congress Party, **20th:** 219
Malay Dilemma, The (Mahathir), **20th:** 2551
Malaysia, **20th:** establishment of, 2327. *See also* Geographical Index
Malchus. *See* Porphyry
Malcolm IV, **MA:** 306
Malcolm X, **20th:** 2570-2573
Maldonaldo, Alonso del Castillo, **Ren:** 152
Malebranche, Nicolas de, **17th:** 252, 514
Maleczech, Ruth, **20th:** 39
Malenkov, Georgi M., **20th:** 2128, 2573-2576, 4471; **Notor:** 90, 550, 574, 748, 1137
Maler, Lucas. *See* Cranach, Lucas, the Elder
Malesov, Battle of (1423), **MA:** 1163
Malevich, Kasimir, **20th:** 718
Malherbe, François de, **17th:** 315, 480, 577-579, 779
Malheurs d'Orphée, Les (Milhaud), **20th:** 2736
Mali, **MA:** 744, 978; architecture, 745; trade, 744; **Ren:** Songhai invasions of, 65. *See also* Geographical Index
Malibran, Maria Felicia Garcia, **19th:** 952
Malik al-Nāṣir Ṣalāḥ al-Dīn Yūsuf ibn Ayyūb ibn Shadi, al-. *See* Saladin
Mālik ibn Anas, **MA:** 36
Malik-Shāh, **MA:** 72, 775, 795
Malikites, **MA:** 10, 20, 36
Malinche, La. *See* Marina, Doña
Malinowski, Bronislaw, **20th:** 297
Malintzin. *See* Marina, Doña
Mallarmé, Stéphane, **19th:** 880; **20th:** 454, 1478, 2791
Malleus maleficarum (Krämer and Sprenger), **Ren:** 121
Mallock, William Hurrell, **19th:** 1756
Mallon, Mary, **Notor:** 685-686
Mallory, Richard, **Notor:** 1109
Mallowan, Agatha Mary Clarissa. *See* Christie, Dame Agatha
Malone, Vivian, **20th:** 4205; **Notor:** 1088
Malone Dies (Beckett), **20th:** 281
Malory, Thomas, **MA:** 407; **Ren:** 197, 598-600
Malouine Islands. *See* Falkland Islands
Malpighi, Marcello, **17th:** 66, 510, 579-582, 899
Malplaquet, Battle of (1709), **18th:** 53, 331, 662
Malraux, André, **20th:** 2576-2579
Maltese Falcon, The (film), **20th:** 407
Malthus, Thomas Robert, **19th:** 1475-1479, 1807, 1897
Malvasia, Carlo Cesare, **17th:** 856
Malvo, Lee Boyd, **Notor:** 765-766
Maly, Teodor, **Notor:** 109, 836
Mamanatowick. *See* Powhatan
Mamelles de Tirésias (Apollinaire). See *Breasts of Tiresias, The*
Mamelles de Tirésias, Les (Poulenc), **20th:** 3319
Mamlūks and Mamlūk Dynasty, **MA:** 140, 411, 412; Baḥrī Line, 141; **Ren:** 87, 807
Man (Calder), **20th:** 610
Man, Henri de, **20th:** 3808
Man Against Himself (Menninger), **20th:** 1346
Man and Superman (Shaw), **20th:** 3719
Man Died, The (Soyinka), **20th:** 3805
Man for Himself (Fromm), **20th:** 1346
Man from Snowy River, and Other Verses, The (Paterson), **19th:** 1758
Man in Revolt (Brunner), **20th:** 548
Man in the Holocene (Frisch), **20th:** 1340
Man into Space (Oberth), **20th:** 3010
Man of Fire (Orozco), **20th:** 3070
Man of the People, A (Achebe), **20th:** 15
Man Ray, **20th:** 2580-2582; **Notor:** 927
Man Who Died, The. See *Escaped Cock, The*
Man Who Knew Coolidge, The (Lewis), **20th:** 2365
Man Who Knew Too Much, The (film), **20th:** 1826, 3863
Man Who Shot Liberty Valance, The (film), **20th:** 4252
Man Who Was Thursday, The (Chesterton), **20th:** 744
Man with Seven Toes, The (Ondaatje), **20th:** 3048
Man Within, The (Greene), **20th:** 1578
Manantiales, Los, **20th:** 633
Manassas (Sinclair), **20th:** 3751
Manassas, First Battle of (1861), **19th:** 1198
Manassas, Second Battle of (1862), **19th:** 1199
Manasseh, **Anc:** 448
Manasseh ben Israel, **17th:** 582-584
Manasses of Hierges, **MA:** 717
Mance, Jeanne, **17th:** 76, 575
Manchukuo, **20th:** 4222, 4463
Manchus, **17th:** 1, 160, 234, 448, 848, 911, 1001; **18th:** 1114
Mancini sisters, **17th:** 585-587
Manco Capac II, **Ren:** 68, 802
Mandan, **19th:** 442
Mandanamisra, **MA:** 925
Mandarins, The (Beauvoir), **20th:** 273
Mandate of heaven, **Anc:** 553; **MA:** 1083
Mandela, Nelson, **20th:** 949, 2479, 2583-2587, 4122; **Notor:** 2, 271, 686, 1065
Mandela, Winnie, **Notor:** 686-688

Mandelbaum, Frederika, **Notor:** 688-689, 1107
Mandelbrot, Benoit B., **20th:** 2588-2590
Mandelstam, Osip, **20th:** 44, 3132
Mander, Karel van, **17th:** 352
Mandingo, **MA:** 977
Mandrake, The (Machiavelli), **Ren:** 588
Manet, Édouard, **19th:** 433, 453, 632, 1479-1483, 1800
Manetho, **Anc:** 556
Manfred (Byron), **19th:** 381
Manfred (Tchaikovsky), **19th:** 2235
Mangakahia, Meri Te Tai, **19th:** 1483-1485
Mangano, Vincent, **Notor:** 23, 396
Manggultai, **17th:** 1
Mangopeomen. *See* Opechancanough
Mangu, **MA:** 626, 955, 1108
Manhattan Cocktail (film), **20th:** 142
Manhattan Project, **20th:** 74, 528, 1237, 2944, 3537, 3685, 3969; Arthur Holly Compton, 819; James Bryant Conant, 822; fission explosion development, 343; J. Robert Oppenheimer, 3066; plutonium research, 2534; Soviet awareness of, 2215; uranium isotope, 2371
Manichaeanism, **Anc:** 142, 698
Manifest der Kommunistischen Partei. See *Communist Manifesto, The*
Manifest destiny, **19th:** 27
Manifest Groc, **20th:** 905
Manifeste du choregraphe, Le (Lifar), **20th:** 2379
Manifesto for the New South Africa (de Klerk), **20th:** 949
Manifesto of Surrealism (Breton), **20th:** 511, 1152
Manifesto of the Algerian People, **20th:** 8
Manifesto of 343, **20th:** 273
Manifesto tecnico della scultura futurista (Boccioni), **20th:** 403-404
Manila, Battle for the Liberation of (1945), **20th:** 2494
Manila Bay, Battle of (1898), **19th:** 646
Manitoba Act (1870), **19th:** 1909
Mankiller, Wilma, **20th:** 2591-2594
Manley, Mary de la Rivière, **18th:** 641-643
Manlius, Gaius, **Notor:** 189
Manly, Charles, **19th:** 1311
Mann, Horace, **19th:** 672, 1142, 1486-1489, 1618, 1761
Mann, Thomas, **20th:** 2594-2597
Mannequin d'osier, Le. See *Wicker Work Woman, The*
Mannerheim, Carl Gustaf, **20th:** 2598-2601
Mannerism, **Ren:** 40, 177, 390, 932; **17th:** 504. *See also* Countermannerism
Manners, John, **19th:** 667
Mannheim Gas Engine Manufacturing Company, **19th:** 197
Manning, Henry Edward, **19th:** 1489-1492
Människan inför världsgåtan. See *Life of the Universe as Conceived by Man from Earliest Ages to the Present Time, The*
Mannix, Daniel, **19th:** 1492-1495
Mannucci, Aldo. *See* Manutius, Aldus
Manoel Dias Soeiro. *See* Manasseh ben Israel
Manon Lescaut (Puccini), **20th:** 3347
Manox, Henry, **Ren:** 466
Man's Fate (Malraux), **20th:** l2577
Man's Hope. See *Days of Hope*
Mansart, François, **17th:** 523, 573, 587-590
Mansart, Jules Hardouin-, **17th:** 533, 589-593
Mansfeld, Peter Ernst, **17th:** 98
Mansfield, first earl of, **18th:** 643-647
Mansfield, Josie, **Notor:** 358
Mansfield, William Murray, **Notor:** 287
Mansfield Park (Austen), **19th:** 96
Manson, Charles, **Notor:** 377, 689-691, 980
Manṣūr, Abū Yūsuf Yaʿqūb al-, **MA:** 8, 120
Mansur, Hasan ʿAlī, **20th:** 2125, 2781
Mantegna, Andrea, **Ren:** 97, 132, 298, 486, 601-604
Manticore, The (Davies), **20th:** 918
Mantinea, Battle of (361 B.C.E.), **Anc:** 306
Mantra (Stockhausen), **20th:** 3875
Mantua, marquise of. *See* Isabella d'Este
Mantua, succession of (1629), **17th:** 552
Manual of American Principles, **19th:** 2470
Manual of Private Devotions, The (Andrewes), **17th:** 16
Manual of Radioactivity, A (Hevesy), **20th:** 1793
Manual of the Botany of the Northern United States (Fray), **19th:** 964
Manual of the Christian Knight, The (Erasmus), **Ren:** 315, 549
Manual of the Mother Church (Eddy), **19th:** 726
Manuel I Comnenus (1120?-1180; Eastern Roman emperor), **MA:** 28, 356
Manuel I (1469-1521; king of Portugal), **Ren:** 22, 259, 330, 366, 513, 591, 605-608, 792
Manufacturing, **18th:** copper, 834; England, 95, 156, 466, 560, 859; France, 587-590, 821; United States, 455, 834, 1077; Wedgwood ceramics, 1058

Manugye (Burmese legal treatise), **18th:** 30
Manuscript illumination. *See* Illumination, manuscript
Manutius, Aldus, **Ren:** 11, 315, 608-610
Manuzio, Aldo. *See* Manutius, Aldus
Manville, Edward, **20th:** 2242
Manzikert, Battle of (1071), **MA:** 73, 865
Manzoni, Alessandro, **19th:** 922, 1495-1498
Mao, Madame. *See* Jiang Qing
Mao Tse-tung. *See* Mao Zedong
Mao Zedong, **20th:** 742, 1905, 1907, 2381, 2408, 2601-2605, 4463; Great Leap Forward, 4459; Hundred Flowers Campaign, 968; Peng Dehuai, 3191; Red Army, 4467; **Notor:** 528, 579, 691-694, 757, 866
Maori Representation Act (1867), **19th:** 1484
Maoris, **17th:** 907; **19th:** 1483, 2371; Great Britain, 981
Map of Virginia, with a Description of the Country, A (Smith), **17th:** 864
Mapah (Isserles), **Ren:** 525
Maplewood Theatre, **20th:** 863
Mapmaking. *See* Cartography
Maqalat al-Islamiyin wa-ikhtilaf al-musallin. See *Discourses of the Muslims*
Maqdisi, Mohammed al-, **Notor:** 1133
Marabotto, Don Cattaneo, **Ren:** 191
Maranzano, Salvatore, **Notor:** 7, 23, 221, 659-660, 694-695, 708
Marat, Jean-Paul, **18th:** 648-651; **Notor:** 235, 696-697, 907
Marāthā Empire, **17th:** 25, 858; **18th:** 522
Marathon, Battle of (490 B.C.E.), **Anc:** 8, 52, 92, 109, 253, 408, 505, 565, 630, 651, 678, 794, 859
Marathon Man, The (film), **20th:** 3044
Marathons, **Anc:** 632
Mårbacka (Lagerlöf), **20th:** 2235
Marble Faun, The (Faulkner), **20th:** 1223
Marble Faun, The (Hawthorne), **19th:** 1052
Marburg Colloquy (1529), **Ren:** 143
Marbury, Anne. *See* Hutchinson, Anne
Marbury v. Madison, **19th:** 1500
Marc. *See* Bohemond I
Marc, Franz, **20th:** 2606-2608
Marcel, Gabriel, **20th:** 2609-2612
Marcella, **Anc:** 457
Marcelle Lender Dancing the Boléro in "Chilperic" (Toulouse-Lautrec), **19th:** 2290
Marcellina, **Anc:** 42
Marcello, Carlos, **Notor:** 698-699
Marcello Malpighi and the Evolution of Embryology (Malpighi), **17th:** 580
Marcellus, Marcus Claudius (268?-208 B.C.E.), **Anc:** 83, 343, 383
Marcellus, Marcus Claudius (42-23 B.C.E.), **Anc:** 490
Marcellus, Varius, **Anc:** 487
March, Fredric, **20th:** 142
March Commission, **17th:** 567
March of Folly, The (Tuchman), **20th:** 4106
March of the Ten Thousand, **Anc:** 968
March on Washington (1941), **20th:** 3372
March to the Sea (1864), **19th:** 2099
March to the Sea (1930), **20th:** 2931
Marchenko, V. *See* Petlyura, Symon
Märchenoper, **19th:** 1155
Marciano, Rocky, **20th:** 2440, 2612-2615
Marcincus, Paul C., **Notor:** 170
Marcion, **Anc:** 600
Marcionism, **Anc:** 854
Marconi, Guglielmo, **19th:** 1825; **20th:** 2615-2619
Marconi scandal (1912), **20th:** 2412
Marcos, Ferdinand, **20th:** 108, 2619-2623; **Notor:** 699-702
Marcos, Imelda, **20th:** 108; **Notor:** 699, 702-704
Marcus, Lyn. *See* LaRouche, Lyndon H., Jr.
Marcus, Siegfried, **19th:** 197
Marcus Aurelius, **Anc:** 372, 443, 530-532; **Notor:** 227
Mardi and a Voyage Thither (Melville), **19th:** 1538
Mardonius, **Anc:** 110, 615
Marduk, **Anc:** 337, 582, 971
Mare liberum. See *Freedom of the Seas, The*
Marenzio, Luca, **Ren:** 610-612
Marescalco, The (Aretino), **Ren:** 54
Margaret I of Denmark, Norway, and Sweden, **MA:** 689-693
Margaret, Maid of Norway (queen of Scotland), **MA:** 201
Margaret of Angoulême. *See* Marguerite de Navarre
Margaret of Anjou, **Ren:** 435, 828, 990
Margaret of Austria, **Ren:** 227, 321, 612-615, 632, 636, 648; **17th:** 18, 737
Margaret of Burgundy, **Ren:** 439, 498
Margaret of Navarre. *See* Marguerite de Navarre
Margaret of Parma, **Ren:** 615-617, 703, 993
Margaret of Valois, **Ren:** 430
Margaret of York. *See* Margaret of Burgundy
Margaret Stuart (wife of Louis XI), **MA:** 261
Margaret Theresa. *See* Marie-Thérèse

Margaret Tudor, **Ren:** 499, 501
Margarita de Parma. *See* Margaret of Parma
Marggraf, Andreas Sigismund, **18th:** 651-653
Marguerite de Navarre, **Ren:** 549, 617-620, 810
Marguerite of Hainaut. *See* Porete, Marguerite
Margus, Treaty of (434), **Anc:** 139
Mārī Diāṭa. *See* Sundiata
Maria (Wollstonecraft), **18th:** 1110
Maria I, **18th:** 796
Maria II, **19th:** 1764, 1766
Maria Agustina. *See* Saragossa, La
Maria Anna of Bavaria-Neuburg, **17th:** 152
Maria Celeste, **17th:** 593-595
María Cristina of Bourbon-Two Sicilies, **19th:** 413, 1183
Maria di Rohan (Donizetti), **19th:** 676
Maria Louisa de Tassis (van Dyck), **17th:** 245
Maria Magdalena of Austria, **17th:** 627
María Teresa de Austria. *See* Marie-Thérèse
Maria Theresa (archduchess of Austria), **18th:** 378, 557, 653-657, 881; Joseph II, 544; **Notor:** 705
Maria Theresa of Spain. *See* Marie-Thérèse
Maria van Hongarije. *See* Mary of Hungary
Mariage sous Louis XV, Un. See *Marriage of Convenience, A*
Mariamne, **Anc:** 404
Marian period (1553-1558), **Ren:** 199, 529
Mariana de Austria, **17th:** 151, 426
Marie-Antoinette, **18th:** 657-660; Louis XVI, 618; Maria Theresa, 655; Mary Robinson, 849; portraits by Élisabeth Vigée-Lebrun, 1016; **Notor:** 704-706, 908
Marie Antoinette and Her Children (Vigée-Lebrun), **18th:** 1017
Marie Casimire de la Grange d'Arquien. *See* Marysieńka
Marie d'Autriche. *See* Mary of Hungary
Marie de France, **MA:** 407, 693-695
Marie de l'Incarnation, **17th:** 595-597
Marie de Médicis, **17th:** 598-600; and Anne of Austria, 18; and Louyse Bourgeois, 74; and Francesca Caccini, 111; and daughter Henrietta Maria, 364; marriage to Henry IV, 551; and François de Malherbe, 578; and Nicolas Poussin, 749; and Cardinal de Richelieu, 790; **Notor:** 889
Marie-Henriette, **Notor:** 632
Marie Louise Gonzaga de Nevers, **17th:** 428
Marie Louise of Orléans, **17th:** 151
Marie-Thérèse, **17th:** 19, 72, 151, 572, 585, 600-602, 622, 662
Marignano, Battle of (1515), **Ren:** 85, 347, 558
Marillac, Louise de, **17th:** 963
Marilyn (Mailer), **20th:** 2564
Marilyn Monroe (Warhol), **20th:** 4228
Marina, Doña, **Ren:** 621-623
Marinetti, Filippo Tommaso, **20th:** 403
Marini, Giambattista, **17th:** 202, 749
Marīnid Abū Salim, **MA:** 536
Marinism, **17th:** 202
Marino Faliero (Donizetti), **19th:** 675
Marinus, **Anc:** 701
Mariology, **Anc:** 540
Maritain, Jacques, **20th:** 2624-2627
Mariuccia. *See* Marozia
Marius, Gaius, **Anc:** 172, 359, 533-536, 681, 691, 743, 831
Marius the Epicurean (Pater), **19th:** 1756
Mariyah the Copt, **MA:** 735
Marjorova, Erzsi, **Ren:** 82; **Notor:** 71
Mark I, **20th:** 1880
Markens grøde. See *Growth of the Soil*
Markham, Mrs. Mary. *See* Cutpurse, Moll
Markova, Dame Alicia, **20th:** 2627-2629
Markova-Dolin Ballet, **20th:** 2628
Marković, Mirjana, **Notor:** 735
Marksizm I natsional'nyi vopros. See *Marxism and the National and Colonial Question*
Marlborough, duchess of. *See* Churchill, Sarah
Marlborough, first duke of, **18th:** 331, 660-663; Joseph Addison, 20; first earl of Godolphin, 423; marriage to Sarah Churchill, 250
Marlborough Family, The (Reynolds), **18th:** 838
Marling, Melinda, **Notor:** 675
Marlones, García de. *See* Gracián y Morales, Baltasar
Marlowe, Christopher, **Ren:** 623-626, 876
Marmion (Scott), **19th:** 2047
Marne, First Battle of the (1914), **20th:** 2010
Maro, Publius Vergilius. *See* Vergil
Maroons, **18th:** 724; and retaining African tradition, 725
Marot, Clément, **Ren:** 618, 975
Marozia, **Notor:** 706-707
Marquette, Jacques, **17th:** 433, 603-605
Marquise, The (Coward), **20th:** 855
Marquise of O . . . , The (Kleist), **19th:** 1289
Marranos, **17th:** 582. *See also* Moriscos' expulsion from Spain

Marriage, **Anc:** in comedy, 548; Egyptian customs, 107; **MA:** Byzantine Empire, 1009; China, 1081; England, 30, 148, 200, 483, 780, 843, 960; France, 166, 176, 356, 383, 543, 707, 837, 839, 963, 1047; Franks, 46, 287, 765; Hungary, 360; Japan, 397, 738; Mongols, 954; Normans, 305; Roman Empire, 133, 244; Scandinavia, 692; Sweden, 791; Wales, 753; **18th:** interfaith, 103
Marriage and Morals (Russell), **20th:** 3563
Marriage Cycle, A (Palmer), **19th:** 1729
Marriage of Convenience, A (Dumas), **19th:** 696
Marriage of Figaro, The (Beaumarchais), **18th:** 98
Marriage of Heaven and Earth, The (Ernst), **20th:** 1178
Marriage of Heaven and Hell, The (Blake), **18th:** 122
Marriage of Isaac and Rebecca, The (Claude Lorrain), **17th:** 172
Marriage of Saint Catherine (Correggio), **Ren:** 249
Marriage of the Virgin (Raphael), **Ren:** 819
Married Love (Stopes), **20th:** 3882
Mars, **Anc:** 758
Mars gallicus (Jansen), **17th:** 420
Marshall, Arthur, **19th:** 1236
Marshall, George C., **20th:** 469, 1126, 2629-2632, 3221
Marshall, John, **19th:** 1498-1502, 2181, 2227; **Notor:** 156, 1019
Marshall, Thurgood, **20th:** 2633-2636
Marshall Field and Company, **19th:** 774, 2387
Marshall Field Wholesale Store, **19th:** 1906
Marshall Plan, **20th:** 358, 1686, 2631
Marshman, Joshua, **19th:** 411
Marsillac, Prince de. *See* La Rochefoucauld, François de
Marston, John, **Ren:** 215; **17th:** 105, 223, 441, 976
Marston Moor, Battle of (1644), **17th:** 199, 205, 262, 484, 805
Marteau sans maître, Le (Boulez), **20th:** 453
Martha Graham School of Contemporary Dance, **20th:** 1564
Martí, Farabundo, **20th:** 3499
Martí, José, **19th:** 1503-1505
Martial, **Anc:** 102, 493, 536-538
Martial arts, Bodhidharma and, **Anc:** 161
Martin IV, **MA:** 186
Martin V, **MA:** 209
Martin, Agnes, **20th:** 2636-2639
Martin, Clyde, **20th:** 2161
Martin, Dean, **20th:** 2357
Martin, James, **19th:** 1740
Martin, Pierre-Émile, **19th:** 2106
Martin, Susannah, **17th:** 690
Martin, Teri. *See* Hilley, Marie
Martin Chuzzlewit (Dickens), **19th:** 655
Martin Eden (London), **20th:** 2422
Martin v. Hunter's Lessee, **19th:** 2181
Martin Van Buren to the End of His Political Career (Bancroft), **19th:** 133
Martineau, Harriet, **19th:** 1505-1508
Martinet, Jean, **Notor:** 707-708
Martínez de Perón, Isabel. *See* Perón, Isabel
Martini, Simone, **MA:** 328, 660, 696-699
Martinique, **20th:** 1087. *See also* Geographical Index
Martiro di S Agata, Il (Cicognini), **17th:** 111
Martyrdom, **Anc:** Christianity and, 205, 268, 600, 613, 626, 853; Ignatius, 438; pagans, 435; saints and, 821; torture and, 206; **MA:** Christian, 95; Constantinople, 588; England, 149, 729; Joan of Arc, 580; Muslim, 455; theater, 518; **Ren:** Austria, 473; England, 62-63, 268, 306, 371, 403, 544, 629, 640, 699, 815, 835, 951; Italy, 140, 853; Japan, 460; Netherlands, 742; Scotland, 528; Switzerland, 863, 1013; **17th:** French in North America, 424; Quakers, 284
Martyrdom of Four Saints, The (Correggio), **Ren:** 250
Martyrdom of Saint Erasmus (Poussin), **17th:** 749
Martyrdom of Saint James (Mantegna), **Ren:** 602
Martyrdom of Saint Justina (Veronese), **Ren:** 960
Martyrdom of Saint Matthew, The (Caravaggio), **Ren:** 171
Martyrdom of Saint Maurice, The (El Greco), **Ren:** 391
Martyrdom of Saint Stephen (Fontana), **Ren:** 339
Martyrologium (Rabanus), **MA:** 872
Martyrs, The (Chateaubriand), **19th:** 476
Marubashi Chūya, **17th:** 999
Marvell, Andrew, **17th:** 232, 563, 605-607
Marvelous Land of Oz, The (Baum), **19th:** 157
Marwān, **MA:** 4
Marwanid Dynasty, **MA:** 5
Marx, Karl, **19th:** 119, 750, 1322, 1371, 1508-1512, 1835; **Notor:** 596, 600, 769
Marxism and the National and Colonial Question (Stalin), **20th:** 3817
Mary (mother of Jesus), **Anc:** 539-541
Mary (Braddon), **19th:** 287
Mary I (queen of England), **Ren:** 108, 111, 199, 304, 370, 399, 402, 544, 553, 627, 639-642, 778, 868, 898, 947; Act of

Succession and, 336; Catherine of Aragon and, 189; Elizabeth I and, 310; Henry VIII and, 443; rejection of Protestantism, 257, 268, 278, 761, 835; Scotland and, 529; Spain and, 779; **18th:** 45
Mary II (queen of England), **17th:** 138, 169, 284, 508, 608, 610-612, 817, 821, 979; American colonists' reaction to enthronement, 518; **18th:** 53, 250, 422, 660-661, 673
Mary, a Fiction (Wollstonecraft), **18th:** 1109
Mary Kay Cosmetics, **20th:** 146
Mary McCarthy's Theatre Chronicles, 1937-1962 (McCarthy), **20th:** 2502
Mary Magdalen (Donatello), **MA:** 321
Mary of Burgundy, **Ren:** 575, 631-633, 646
Mary of Gueldres, **Ren:** 496
Mary of Guise, **Ren:** 501, 529, 627, 633-635
Mary of Hungary, **Ren:** 422, 636-638
Mary of Lorraine. *See* Mary of Guise
Mary of Modena, **17th:** 138, 417, 607-610, 839
Mary of Scotland (Anderson), **20th:** 1725
Mary Poppins (film), **20th:** 1009
Mary, Queen of Scots, **Ren:** 104, 146, 184, 200, 305, 310, 501, 528, 553, 627-630, 634, 899, 948
Maryinsky Theater, **20th:** 3166
Maryland Colony, **17th:** 92, 120
Marylebone Park, **19th:** 1644
Marysieńka, **17th:** 429
Masaccio, **MA:** 699-702
Masada, **Anc:** 477
Masaniello, **17th:** 425
Masaryk, Tomáš, **20th:** 299, 638, 2639-2642
Mascherata delle ninfe di Senna, La (Rinuccini), **17th:** 111
Maschinenzeitalter, Das (Suttner), **19th:** 2206
Mascoutens, **17th:** 433, 603
Masculine-Feminine (film), **20th:** 1504
Masinissa, **Anc:** 542-544, 759, 813
Maskarad. See *Masquerade*
Maskaya noch. See *May Night*
Maske Presented at Ludlow Castle, A (Milton and Lawes), **17th:** 502
Maʾmūn, al-, **MA:** 468-469, 568, 617
Masnadieri, I (Verdi), **19th:** 2352
Mason, George, **18th:** 664-667
Masonic Temple, **19th:** 361
Masque of Anarchy, The (Shelley), **19th:** 2095
Masque of Blackness, The (Jonson), **17th:** 436, 442
Masque of Proteus and the Adamantine Rock, The (Campion and Davison), **17th:** 127
Masque of the Inner Temple and Grayes Inn, The (Beaumont), **Ren:** 94
Masque Presented at Ludlow Castle 1634 on Michaelmas Night, A (Milton), **17th:** 640
Masquerade (Lermontov), **19th:** 1353; **20th:** 2965
Masques, **17th:** 436, 442, 502, 764
Mass in D Minor (Bruckner), **19th:** 330
Mass in E-flat Major (Schubert), **19th:** 2027
Mass in F Major (Schubert), **19th:** 2026
Mass media, **20th:** 1679, 2529, 2876
Mass of Bolsena (Raphael), **Ren:** 821
Mass of Life, A (Delius), **20th:** 955
Mass of Saint Gregory, The (Bosch), **Ren:** 121
Mass production, **18th:** and aesthetics, 95; Abraham Darby, 293; England, 95, 156, 293, 1060; **20th:** automobiles, 1281. *See also* Factories; Industrial Revolution; Industrialism; Manufacturing
Mass Puer natus est nobis (Tallis), **Ren:** 919
Mass Strike, The (Luxemburg), **20th:** 2483
Massachusetts, **18th:** 7, 11, 16; charter, 17, 672, 894; John Hancock, 460; Thomas Hutchinson, 518-521
Massachusetts Anti-Slavery Society, **19th:** 877
Massachusetts Bay Colony, **17th:** 8, 88, 130, 197, 218, 247, 386, 394, 567, 982, 991
Massachusetts Bay Government Act (1774), **18th:** 460
Massachusetts General Court, **18th:** 458
Massachusetts General Hospital, **19th:** 348
Massachusetts Indians, **17th:** 248, 879
Massachusetts State Kansas Committee, **19th:** 320
Massachusetts statehouse, **19th:** 348
Massacre at Chios, The (Delacroix), **19th:** 636
Massacre at Paris, The (Marlowe), **Ren:** 625
Massacre of the Innocents, The (Bruegel), **Ren:** 136
Massacres, **Anc:** Pontius Pilate and, 645; Thessalonica, 44
Massacres in the Mountains (Dunn), **19th:** 1238
Massagetae, **Anc:** 249
Massaʿot. See *Itinerary of Benjamin of Tudela*
Massasoit, **17th:** 86, 129, 249, 612-614, 633, 876, 878
Massatamohtnock. *See* Opechancanough
Masseria, Joe, **Notor:** 7, 23, 402, 659-660, 694, 708-709, 864
Massey, William Ferguson, **20th:** 2643-2646

Massie, Robert, **Notor:** 886
Massie, Thomas, **20th:** 915
Massine, Léonide, **20th:** 909, 986, 1269, 2646-2649
Massinger, Philip, **Ren:** 94; **17th:** 279, 846
Masson, André, **20th:** 1471
Massylians, **Anc:** 542
Massys, Quentin, **Ren:** 316
Mastai-Ferretti, Giovanni Maria. *See* Pius IX
Master Builder, The (Ibsen), **19th:** 1167
Master Butchers Singing Club, The (Erdrich), **20th:** 1171
"MASTER HAROLD" . . . and the Boys (Fugard), **20th:** 1356
Master of Ballantrae, The (Stevenson), **19th:** 2174
Master of Go, The (Kawabata), **20th:** 2085
Master of the Law. *See* Xuanzang
Master of the World (Verne), **19th:** 2357
Masterman, C. F. G., **20th:** 447
Masterson, Bat, **19th:** 721; **Notor:** 315
Mastery of Movement on the Stage, The (Laban), **20th:** 2222
Masʿūd ibn Maḥmūd, **MA:** 164
Masʿūdī, al-, **MA:** 703-705
Masukagami. See *Clear Mirror, The*
Masurian Lakes, Battle of the (1914), **20th:** 1815
Mat. See *Mother, The* (Gorky)
Mata Hari, **Notor:** 710-712, 933
Matchmaker's Union, **19th:** 212
Matelots, Les (ballet), **20th:** 2648
Material culture. *See* Bateman, Hester; Boulton, Matthew; Revere, Paul; Ross, Betsy; Wedgwood, Josiah
Materialis, **Anc:** 263
Mathematical Foundations of Quantum Mechanics, The (von Neumann), **20th:** 2944
Mathematical Principles of Natural Philosophy. See *Principia*
Mathematicall Praeface to the Elements of Geometrie of Euclid of Megara, The (Dee), **Ren:** 279
Mathematics, **Anc:** Alexandrian, 402, 434; Arabic, 288; astronomy and, 78, 579; and concept of beauty, 677; Eratosthenes and, 316; Eudoxus and, 320; geography and, 828; Greek, 76, 81, 286, 606; human proportions and, 676; sculpture and, 523; **MA:** 650; England, 128; France, 742; Greece, 110; India, 109, 195; Iraq, 617; Muslim, 164, 648; Persia, 21; **Ren:** Austria, 774, 824; England, 279; Italy, 173, 920; Netherlands, 913; Scotland, 711; **17th:** England, 679, 969; France, 226, 271, 631; Germany, 514; Italy, 66, 921; Japan, 831; Netherlands, 397; Scotland, 319; Switzerland, 48; **18th:** China, 1039; England, 204; France, 31-35, 200, 240-243, 573-576, 682-687; Italy, 24; Scotland, 632-635; Switzerland, 333-335; United States, 84-87; **19th:** algebraic geometry, 2039; automorphic functions, 1817; Bessel's functions, 216; dyadics, 914; England, 108, 424, 1421; France, 857, 902, 1317; definition of functions, 810; Germany, 884, 1296; irrational numbers, 630; logic, 828; Norway, 9; probability, 1318; quaternions, 1016; Switzerland, 2154. *See also* Algebra; Trigonometry; Category Index
Mathēmatikē syntaxis (Ptolemy), **Anc:** 78, 417, 435, 580, 606, 713
Mather, Cotton, **18th:** 667-672
Mather, Increase, **18th:** 667, 671-675
Mathews, Elkin, **19th:** 162
Mathews, Robert Jay, **Notor:** 712-713, 838
Mathilda (Shelley), **19th:** 2088
Mathilde. *See* Matilda of Canossa
Mathis der Maler (Hindemith), **20th:** 1812
Mathnawi, The (Rūmī), **MA:** 909
Matho, **Anc:** 374
Matière et mémoire. See *Matter and Memory*
Matignon Agreements (1936), **20th:** 397
Mati'-ilu, **Anc:** 892
Matilda (Drayton), **17th:** 237
Matilda (queen of England), **MA:** 305, 482-483, 960
Matilda of Canossa, **MA:** 705-708, 1044
Matilda of Tuscany. *See* Matilda of Canossa
Matisse, Henri, **20th:** 2649-2652
Matnefrure, **Anc:** 737
Mato, Grimanesa Martina. *See* Matto de Turner, Clorinda
Matoaka. *See* Pocahontas
Matralia, Festival of, **Anc:** 510
Matrimonial Causes Act (1857), **19th:** 314
Mats, Chapter of the (1221), **MA:** 96
Matsudaira Hirotada, **17th:** 915
Matsudaira Nobutsuna, **17th:** 999
Matsudaira Takechiyo. *See* Tokugawa Ieyasu
Matsukaze. See *Wind in the Pines, The*
Matsumoto, Chizuo. *See* Asahara, Shoko
Matsuo Bashō, **17th:** 403, 615-617
Matsuo Kinsaku. *See* Matsuo Bashō
Matsushita, Konosuke, **20th:** 2653-2656
Matsushita Electric Company, **20th:** 2653
Matteotti, Giacomo, **20th:** 2887
Matter, concepts of, **Anc:** 58
Matter and Memory (Bergson), **20th:** 323

Matter and Motion (Maxwell), **19th:** 1529
Matthews, Robert, **Notor:** 158
Matthiae, John, **17th:** 163
Matthias (Holy Roman Emperor), **Ren:** 82, 842; **17th:** 737, 966
Matthias I Corvinus (king of Hungary), **MA:** 519; **Ren:** 351, 642-646, 983; **Notor:** 1073
Matthias, Joseph ben. *See* Josephus, Flavius
Matthison-Hansen, Gottfred, **19th:** 985
Matto de Turner, Clorinda, **19th:** 1512-1514
Matveyev, Artamon Sergeyevich, **17th:** 13
Mátyás. *See* Matthias I Corvinus
Mau Mau Uprising (1952-1960), **20th:** 80, 2107, 2312
Maucroix, François, **17th:** 480
Maud and Other Poems (Tennyson), **19th:** 2245
Maud Martha (Brooks), **20th:** 537
Maudslay, Henry, **19th:** 1646
Maulānā. *See* Rūmī, Jalāl al-Dīn
Maulawiyah, **MA:** 909
Maupassant, Guy de, **19th:** 786, 1515-1517
Mauprat (Sand), **19th:** 1988
Mauriac, François, **20th:** 2657-2659
Maurice (Byzantine emperor), **MA:** 505, 615
Maurice, Frederick Denison, **19th:** 1518-1521
Maurice of Nassau, **Ren:** 913; **17th:** 286, 326, 337, 538, 618-620, 924, 933
Maurice of Saxony. *See* Saxe, comte de
Maurin, Peter, **20th:** 926
Maurits van Nassau. *See* Maurice of Nassau
Maurras, Charles, **20th:** 2624
Maury, Matthew Fontaine, **19th:** 1522-1525
Maurya. *See* Chandragupta Maurya
Mauryan Dynasty, **Anc:** 203, 898
Mausalous. *See* Mausolus
Mausoleum of Halicarnassus, **Anc:** 761
Mausolus, **Anc:** 545-547, 761
Mawlānā. *See* Rūmī, Jalāl al-Dīn
Mawlawis. *See* Maulawiyah
Mawson, John, **19th:** 2209
Max Schmitt in a Single Scull (Eakins), **19th:** 718
Maxentius, **Anc:** 282
Maxim Gorky, **20th:** 4108
Maximes (La Rochefoucauld), **17th:** 487, 488
Maximian, **Anc:** 239, 281, 391, 645
Maximilian (1832-1867; emperor of Mexico), **19th:** 1247, 1525-1527, 1641, 1991; death of, 820; **Notor:** 279
Maximilian I (1459-1519; Holy Roman Emperor), **Ren:** 49, 85, 219, 227, 299, 350, 498, 519, 575, 587, 612, 631, 636, 646-650, 872, 984; **Notor:** 537
Maximilian I (1573-1651; elector of Bavaria), **17th:** 268, 293
Maximilian II (1527-1576; Holy Roman Emperor), **Ren:** 541, 650-652, 798, 824, 840, 911
Maximilien (Milhaud), **20th:** 2737
Maximinus, **Anc:** 426
Maxims (genre), **17th:** 487
Maxims of Love (Stendhal), **19th:** 2162
Maxims of the Saints Explained, Concerning the Interiour Life, The (Fénelon), **17th:** 265, 340
Maximus, Magnus, **Anc:** 43, 699, 797
Maximus of Isaurian Seleucia, **Anc:** 862
Maxtla, **MA:** 559; **Ren:** 721
Maxwell, James Clerk, **19th:** 1074, 1265, 1528-1531, 1931; **20th:** 2431, 2472
Maxwell, John, **19th:** 284
Maxwell, Lowe. *See* Cassidy, Butch
Maxwell, Mary Elizabeth. *See* Braddon, Mary Elizabeth
May, Samuel Joseph, **19th:** 876
May Fourth Movement, **20th:** 742, 2447, 2602
May Night (Rimsky-Korsakov), **19th:** 1915
Māyā (Buddha's mother), **Anc:** 169
Mayakovsky, Vladimir, **20th:** 2659-2662, 2723
Maybach, Wilhelm, **19th:** 593
Mayer, Ernst, **20th:** 1997
Mayer, Joseph, **20th:** 4132
Mayer, Louis B., **20th:** 1392, 1409, 2096, 2662-2665
Mayer, Maria, **20th:** 4132
Mayflower (ship), **17th:** 7
Mayflower Compact, **17th:** 7, 85
Mayflower Madam. *See* Barrows, Sydney
Maynard, François, **17th:** 578
Maynooth endowment, **19th:** 1959
Mayo, Charles H., **20th:** 2665-2667
Mayo, William J., **20th:** 2665-2667
Mayo Clinic, **20th:** 2666
Mayor encanto, amor, El. See *Love, the Greatest Enchantment*
Mayor of Casterbridge, The (Hardy), **19th:** 1029
Mayor of Zalamea, The (Calderón), **17th:** 114
Maypeyker Sultan. *See* Kösem Sultan
Mazarin, Jules, **17th:** 9, 620-624; and Anne of Austria, 19; architecture, 532; arts patronage, 504; and the duchesse de Chevreuse, 158; and Queen Christina, 165; and Jean-Baptiste Colbert, 180; and the Great Condé, 185; Council of Conscience, 963; and Cyrano de Bergerac, 212; and the Fronde, 549; and Guarino Guarini, 331; opposition to Jansenism, 421; and François de La

Rochefoucauld, 487; and the duchesse de Longueville, 549; and Louis XIV, 554; and the Mancini sisters, 585; and Marie-Thérèse, 601; and the duchesse de Montpensier, 660; and music, 570; and Peiresc's letters, 723; and Cardinal de Richelieu, 792; and Sweden, 706; and Viscount de Turenne, 933
Mazda rotary-engine automobiles, **20th:** 4225
Mazdak, **MA:** 613
Mazepa, Ivan Stepanovich, **17th:** 624-626; **18th:** 232
Mazeppa (Milner), **19th:** 1555
Mazrui, **19th:** 1966
Mazzini, Giuseppe, **19th:** 445, 871, 922, 1531-1534, 1802
Mbamba, **17th:** 687
Mbande, **17th:** 687
Mbeki, Thabo, **20th:** 949, 2586
Mbemba, Nzinga. *See* Afonso I (c. 1455-1543; king of Kongo)
Mbulazi, **19th:** 450
Mbundus, **17th:** 687
Me llamo Rigoberta Menchú y así me nació la conciencia. See *I, Rigoberta Menchú*
Mead, Margaret, **20th:** 297, 2668-2671
Mead, William, **17th:** 725
Meade, George G., **19th:** 960, 1336
Meadows of Gold and Mines of Gems (al-Mas^cūdī), **MA:** 703
Mean Streets (film), **20th:** 3682
Meaning and Value of Life, The (Eucken), **20th:** 1186
Means, Gaston Bullock, **Notor:** 713-714
Meany, George, **20th:** 2672-2674, 3426; **Notor:** 75
Meara, Edmund, **17th:** 564
Measure of a Man, The (Poitier), **20th:** 3297
Meaux, Siege of (1421-1422), **MA:** 503
Mécanique analytique (Lagrange), **18th:** 573
Mechanical Bride, The (McLuhan), **20th:** 2529
Mechanics, **18th:** 24, 32, 335, 573, 1039
Mechanikē syntaxis (Philon of Byzantium), **Anc:** 247
Mechanism of Mendelian Heredity, The (Morgan et al.), **20th:** 2826
Mechanism of the Heavens, The (Somerville), **19th:** 2122
Mechthild von Magdeburg, **MA:** 708-710
Meckel, Johann, **19th:** 115
Medawar, Peter, **20th:** 587
Medea, **Anc:** 326
Médecin malgré lui, Le. See *Doctor in Spite of Himself, The*
Mēdeia (Euripides), **Anc:** 326, 810
Mediator, The (Brunner), **20th:** 548
Mediator Dei (Pius XII), **20th:** 3279
Medical diagnosis, **Anc:** 86, 278
Medical Education in Europe (Flexner), **20th:** 1257
Medical Education in the United States and Canada (Flexner), **20th:** 1257
Medical Essays, 1842-1882 (Holmes), **19th:** 1117
Medical Inquiries and Observations upon the Diseases of the Mind (Rush), **18th:** 873
Medici, Alessandro de' (1510-1537), **Ren:** 615, 653
Medici, Cosimo de' (1389-1464), **MA:** 84, 207
Medici, Cosimo I de' (1519-1574), **Ren:** 18, 204, 211, 332, 411, 653-655, 798, 871
Medici, Cosimo II de' (1590-1621), **17th:** 112, 118, 307, 593, 626-628
Medici, Cosimo III de' (1642-1723), **17th:** 857, 882
Medici, Ferdinando I de' (1549-1609), **Ren:** 42
Medici, Giovanni de' (1475-1521). *See* Leo X
Medici, Giuliano de' (1453-1478), **Notor:** 212
Medici, Giulio de' (1478-1534). *See* Clement VII (pope)
Medici, Lorenzino de' (1514-1548), **Ren:** 653
Medici, Lorenzo de' (1449-1492), **Ren:** 410, 587, 655-659, 682, 851, 870; **Notor:** 147, 212, 630
Medici, Lorenzo de' (1492-1519), **Ren:** 184
Medici, Marie de' (1575-1642), **Ren:** 431
Medici family, **Ren:** 39, 123, 184, 410, 557, 588, 653, 655, 962; Catholic Church and, 717
Medici Madonna (Michelangelo), **Ren:** 683
Medicina Catholica (Fludd), **17th:** 281
Medicina Statica (Santorio), **17th:** 811
Medicine, **Anc:** Alcmaeon's philosophy of, 36; Egyptian, 440; Greek, 36, 84, 114, 277; Hippocratic, 420; Roman, 199, 290; **MA:** Bologna, 445; Byzantine Empire, 814; Europe, 100; France, 372; Iran, 123; Italy, 1, 1031; Muslim, 562; Persia, 884; Spain, 99; women, 1031; **Ren:** France, 809, 862, 965; Germany, 12, 357; Italy, 211, 319, 343; Switzerland, 758; **17th:** Amsterdam, 898; England, 902, 987; France, 74; Germany, 851; Italy, 66, 355, 810; **18th:** Luigi Galvani, 391-394; homeopathy, 69; immunology, 532; physiology, 391, 925-928, 934, 961; surgery, 820; **19th:** antiseptics, 1391; education, 1201, 2481; Germany, 2064, 2367;

homeopathy, 1009; infectious diseases, 180; midwifery, 266; patient-physician relationship, 1712; women in, 248, 813. *See also* Anatomy; Disease; Physicians; Science; Category Index

Médicis, Catherine de. *See* Catherine de Médicis

Médicis, Marie de. *See* Marie de Médicis

Médico de su honra, El. See *Surgeon of His Honor, The*

Medieval Cities (Pirenne), **20th:** 3270

Medina, Ernest, **Notor:** 168-169

Medina del Campo, Treaty of (1489), **Ren:** 187

Méditation sur le prélude de S. Bach (Gounod), **19th:** 954

Meditationes de prima philosophia. See *Meditations on First Philosophy*

Meditations. See *Tōn eis heauton*

Meditations, The (William of Saint-Thierry), **MA:** 1115

Meditations Concerning the Redemption of Mankind (Anselm), **MA:** 94

Meditations Divine and Moral (Bradstreet), **17th:** 90

Meditations on First Philosophy (Descartes), **17th:** 227, 251, 305

Meditations on Quixote (Ortega), **20th:** 3078

Meditativae orationes. See *Meditations, The*

Mediterranean and the Mediterranean World in the Age of Philip II, The (Braudel), **20th:** 498

Medium, The (Menotti), **20th:** 2704

Medvedev, Pavel Nikolayevich, **20th:** 191

Medzhibozh, Poland, **18th:** Hasidism, 69

Meech Lake Accord (1987), **20th:** 2867

Meeresstille und glückliche Fahrt (Mendelssohn), **19th:** 1550

Meerssen, Treaty of (870), **MA:** 664

Meeting at Telgte, The (Grass), **20th:** 1574

Megacles, **Anc:** 293, 649

Megalópolis, Arcadia, **Anc:** 305

Megarics, **Anc:** 801

Megasthenes, **Anc:** 204

Meghadūta (Kālidāsa), **Anc:** 496

Megiddo (city), **Anc:** 804

Megiddo, Battle of (c. 1482 B.C.E.), **Anc:** 259, 887

Megyery, Imre, **Ren:** 82

Mehmed II, **MA:** 521, 711-715; **Ren:** 87, 659-661, 662; **Notor:** 1072

Mehmed III, **Ren:** 661-664

Mehmed IV, **17th:** 451, 472

Mehmed Fatih (Mehmed the Conqueror). *See* Mehmed II

Mehmet Ali. *See* Muḥammad ʿAlī Pasha

Mei Yaoqian, **MA:** 810

Meier, Bernhard, **Notor:** 642

Meighen, Arthur, **20th:** 2156

Meiji era (1868-1912), **19th:** 1186, 1631

Meiji Restoration, **19th:** 1970

Meiji Tennō. *See* Mutsuhito

Meijin. See *Master of Go, The*

Mein Kampf (Hitler), **20th:** 1830

Mein Leben. See *My Life* (Wagner)

Mein Name sei Gantenbein. See *Wilderness of Mirrors, A*

Meine Emancipation, Verweisung, und Rechtfertigung (Aston), **19th:** 84

Meinhof, Ulrike, **Notor:** 47, 684, 715-716

Meinong, Alexius, **20th:** 1110

Meir, Golda, **20th:** 292, 931, 2674-2678, 3359

Meir, Rabbi, **Anc:** 30

Meir, Simcha. *See* Nordau, Max

Meisho Edo Hyakkei (Hiroshige), **19th:** 1109

Meistersinger von Nürnberg, Die (Wagner), **19th:** 2376

Meitner, Lise, **20th:** 1237, 1636, 1781, 2679-2682, 3970

Mejia Victores, Oscar Humberto, **Notor:** 900

Melanchros, **Anc:** 653

Melanchthon, Philipp, **Ren:** 143, 164, 543, 584, 664-667, 823

Melbourne, second Viscount, **19th:** 709, 1534-1536, 2447

Melchizadek, **Anc:** 5

Meleager, **Anc:** 761

Melencolia I (Dürer), **Ren:** 298

Melfi, Council of (1089), **MA:** 1043, 1045

Melisende, **MA:** 715-718

Melissus, **Anc:** 610

Mélite (Corneille), **17th:** 193

Mélito, countess of. *See* Mendoza y de la Cerda, Ana de

Mellon, Andrew, **20th:** 642, 833, 2683-2685

Mellon Institute, **20th:** 2684

Mellon Plan, **20th:** 2684

Melqart, **Anc:** 271, 373

Melville, Herman, **19th:** 1052, 1537-1541

Member of the Wedding, The (McCullers), **20th:** 2508

Memling, Hans, **Ren:** 120

Memmius, Gaius, **Anc:** 520

Memoir (Davis), **19th:** 614

Mémoire sur le système primitif des voyelles dans les langues indo-européennes (Saussure), **20th:** 3649

Mémoire sur une propriété générale d'une classe très-étendue de fonctions transcendantes (Abel), **19th:** 11

Mémoires (Beaumarchais), **18th:** 98

Mémoires de la cour de France pour les années 1688 et 1689. See *Memoirs of the Court of France for the Years 1688-1689*

Memoires de ma vie. See *Memoirs of My Life*
Mémoires de mademoiselle de Montpensier (Montpensier), **17th:** 661
Mémoires d'une jeune fille rangée. See *Memoirs of a Dutiful Daughter*
Mémoires sur différens sujets de mathématiques (Diderot), **18th:** 33
Mémoires sur la régence d'Anne d'Autriche. See *Memoirs of the Duke de La Rochefoucault, The*
Mémoires sur la respiration. See *Memoirs on Respiration*
Memoirs (Neruda), **20th:** 2939
Memoirs (Robinson), **18th:** 850
Memoirs of a Dutiful Daughter (Beauvoir), **20th:** 271
Memoirs of a Tourist (Stendhal), **19th:** 2163
Memoirs of an Egotist (Stendhal), **19th:** 2160
Memoirs of Dr. Charles Burney (Burney), **18th:** 182
Memoirs of Field-Marshal the Viscount Montgomery of Alamein, The (Montgomery), **20th:** 2810
Memoirs of Halide Edib (Adıvar), **20th:** 31
Memoirs of Hecate County (Wilson), **20th:** 4355
Memoirs of Jacques Casanova de Seingalt, The (Casanova), **18th:** 210
Memoirs of My Life (Perrault), **17th:** 732
Memoirs of Rossini (Stendhal), **19th:** 2162
Memoirs of Sherlock Holmes, The (Doyle), **19th:** 689
Memoirs of the Author of a Vindication of the Rights of Woman (Godwin), **18th:** 426
Memoirs of the Court of France for the Years 1688-1689 (La Fayette), **17th:** 478
Memoirs of the Crusades. See *Conquête de Constantinople, Le*
Memoirs of the Duke de La Rochefoucault, The (La Rochefoucauld), **17th:** 487
Memoirs on Respiration (Spallanzani), **18th:** 927
Memorabilia of Socrates. See *Apomnēmoneumata*
Memorandum of My Martinique. See *Return to My Native Land*
Memoriae Matris Sacrum (Herbert), **17th:** 167
"Memorial and Remonstrance Against Religious Assessments" (Madison), **18th:** 636
Memorial de Ayres. See *Counselor Ayres' Memorial*
Memorial de l'art d'accouchements (Boivin), **19th:** 266
Memorial to W. H. Hudson (Epstein), **20th:** 1166
Memoriale (Blessed Angela of Foligno), **MA:** 81
Memórias póstumas de Bráz Cubas. See *Epitaph of a Small Winner*
Memories of a Catholic Girlhood (McCarthy), **20th:** 2501
Memories of My Childhood (Lagerlöf), **20th:** 2235
Memories of My Life (Galton), **19th:** 860
Memory of Solferino, A (Dunant), **19th:** 699
Memory of Two Mondays, A (Miller), **20th:** 2742
Men Against Humanity (Marcel), **20th:** 2611
Men in Dark Times (Arendt), **20th:** 120
Men livet lever. See *Road Leads On, The*
Menaechmi (Plautus), **Anc:** 662
Ménage, Gilles, **17th:** 833
Menander (dramatist), **Anc:** 307, 547-550, 663, 850
Menander (Greco-Bactrian king), **Anc:** 550-552
Ménard, Anne-Caroline. *See* Ségalas, Anaïs
Menchú, Rigoberta, **20th:** 2686-2688
Mencius, **Anc:** 238, 380, 552-555, 577, 954, 979, 989
Mencken, H. L., **20th:** 2688-2691; **Notor:** 613
Mendel, Gregor, **19th:** 1541-1544
Mendeleyev, Dmitry Ivanovich, **19th:** 1544-1549
Mendelsohn, Erich, **20th:** 2692-2695
Mendelssohn, Felix, **19th:** 952, 1549-1551, 2033
Mendelssohn, Moses, **18th:** 599, 675-677
Mendenhall, Dorothy Reed, **20th:** 2695-2698
Menderes, Adnan, **20th:** 1973
Mendès-France, Pierre, **20th:** 458, 2698-2701, 2770
Mendiant de Jérusalem, Le. See *Beggar in Jerusalem, A*
Mendicants, **MA:** 180, 817
Mendoza, Antonio de, **Ren:** 161, 245
Mendoza, Bernardino de, **Ren:** 668-669
Mendoza, Pedro de, **Ren:** 504
Mendoza y de la Cerda, Ana de, **Ren:** 670-671
Meneghini, Giovanni Battista, **20th:** 612
Menelaus of Alexandria, **Anc:** 419
Menelik II, **19th:** 1552-1554, 2256
Menem, Carlos Saúl, **Notor:** 824, 1067
Menéndez de Avilés, Pedro, **Ren:** 672-675
Menes, **Anc:** 556-558
Menexenos (Plato), **Anc:** 128
Meng Haoran, **Anc:** 844
Mengde. *See* Cao Cao

Mengele, Josef, **20th:** 4329; **Notor:** 717-719, 1004, 1136
Mengistu Haile Mariam, **20th:** 2701-2703; **Notor:** 719-721
Mengke. *See* Mencius
Mengk'o. *See* Mencius
Meng-te. *See* Cao Cao
Meng-tzu. *See* Mencius
Mengzi (Mencius), **Anc:** 552; **MA:** 1160
Meninas, Las (Velázquez), **17th:** 955
Menippean Satires. See *Saturae Menippiae*
Menippus, **Anc:** 514
Menkaure, **Anc:** 558-560
Menken, Adah Isaacs, **19th:** 1555-1557
Menkheperre' Thutmose. *See* Thutmose III
Menninger, Karl, **20th:** 1346
Menno Simons, **Ren:** 675-678
Mennonites, **Ren:** 677
Menōn (Plato), **Anc:** 660
Menotti, Gian Carlo, **20th:** 231, 2703-2706
Mensch erscheint im Holozän, Der. See *Man in the Holocene*
Mensch im Widerspruch, Der. See *Man in Revolt*
Menschen im Weltraum. See *Man into Space*
Menschenerziehung, Die. See *Education of Man, The*
Menschenkenntnis. See *Understanding Human Nature*
Menschliches, Allzumenschliches. See *Human, All Too Human*
Menshikov, Aleksander, **17th:** 625
Mental illness, **Anc:** Asclepiades on, 116; Caligula, 178; Herod, 404; **19th:** treatment of, 671, 1486
Mental State of Hystericals, The (Janet), **20th:** 1994
Mentewab, **18th:** 677-679
Menti Nostrae (Pius XII), **20th:** 3279
Mentuemhat, **Anc:** 710
Mentuhotep II. *See* Montuhotep II
Menzies, Sir Robert Gordon, **20th:** 1189, 1933, 2490, 2707-2709
Méphis (Tristan), **19th:** 2298
Mépris, Le. See *Contempt*
Mer, La (Debussy), **20th:** 938
Mercader, Ramón, **Notor:** 721-722, 1041
Mercantilism, **17th:** England, 808; France, 181, 554; **18th:** 727
Mercator, Gerardus, **Ren:** 678-681
Merce Cunningham Dance Company, **20th:** 886
Mercedarians, **MA:** 882
Mercedes automobile, **19th:** 594
Mercenaries, **18th:** 140-142
Merchant Shipping Act of 1876, **19th:** 669
Mercia, **MA:** 64, 341, 353
Mercier, François, **20th:** 1327
Merciless Parliament (1388), **MA:** 895
Mercurius in sole visus (Gassendi), **17th:** 305
Mercury Theater, **20th:** 4284
Mercy Philbrick's Choice (Jackson), **19th:** 1195
Mere Christianity (Lewis), **20th:** 2355
Merekli (John), **20th:** 2015
Merenptah, **Anc:** 585, 737
Mergenthaler, Ottmar, **19th:** 1558-1560
Mergenthaler Linotype Company, **19th:** 1559
Meridian (Walker), **20th:** 4197
Mérimée, Prosper, **19th:** 242
Merisi, Michelangelo. *See* Caravaggio
Meritaton, **Anc:** 28
Meritor Savings Bank v. Vinson (1986), **20th:** 2523
Merleau-Ponty, Maurice, **20th:** 2710-2712
Mermaid Tavern, **17th:** 278
Merman, Ethel, **20th:** 329
Merodachbaladan, **Anc:** 753, 769, 894
Merovech, **MA:** 290, 381
Merovingians, **MA:** 242, 250, 290, 381, 427; kings, 291
Merriam, Charles, **19th:** 2404
Merriam, George, **19th:** 2404
Merrie Tales of Jacques Tournebroche, The (France), **19th:** 816
Merry Men and Other Tales and Fables, The (Stevenson), **19th:** 2176
Merry Moll. *See* Cutpurse, Moll
Merry Widow, The (film), **20th:** 1693
Merryman, John, **19th:** 2228
Merrymount, **17th:** 879
Mersenne, Marin, **17th:** 281, 305, 628-632, 722
Mertola, count of. *See* Schomberg, Friedrich Hermann
Merton, Thomas, **20th:** 2713-2715
Meryetamen, **Anc:** 586
Mes Mémoires. See *My Memoirs*
Mes rêveries (Saxe), **18th:** 882
Meshafa Berhan (Zara Yaqob), **Ren:** 1007
Mesothorium, discovery of, **20th:** 1636
Mesrine, Jacques, **Notor:** 723-724
Messa da requiem (Verdi), **19th:** 2353
Message (newspaper), **19th:** 1459
Message from the People, A (Charles), **20th:** 736
Messalla, **Anc:** 834
Messallina, Statilia, **Anc:** 593
Messallina, Valeria, **Anc:** 24, 102, 219, 235, 561-563, 766; **Notor:** 1030
Messe de morts. See *Requiem* (Berlioz)
Messe de Nostre Dame, La. See *Machaut's Mass*
Messe solennelle de Sainte Cécile (Gounod), **19th:** 953
Messenger (magazine), **20th:** 3370

Messenia, foundation of, **Anc:** 305
Messerschmitt, Willy, **20th:** 1747
Messiaen, Olivier, **20th:** 452, 2715-2718, 3873, 4414
Messiah, **Anc:** Jesus Christ as, 255, 539; in Judaism, 31, 879
Messiah (Handel), **18th:** 464
Messiah, The (Klopstock), **18th:** 562
Messina, Treaty of (1191), **MA:** 837
Messner, Reinhold, **20th:** 2718-2722
Metabolism, study of, **20th:** 2199
Metacom, **17th:** 249, 612, 633-635, 876
Metacom's War (1675-1676), **17th:** 249, 614, 635, 798, 876
Metallurgy, **Ren:** 212; **19th:** England, 218; Germany, 1301; United States, 1000
Metamora (Stone), **19th:** 792
Metamorphoses (Apuleius), **Anc:** 515
Metamorphoses (Ovid), **Anc:** 180, 521, 603
Metamorphosis, The (Kafka), **20th:** 2066
Metaphysica (Aristotle), **Anc:** 95, 322, 609, 725
Metaphysical Club, **19th:** 1773
Metaphysical Journal (Marcel), **20th:** 2609
Metaphysical Theory of the State, The (Hobhouse), **20th:** 1844
Metaphysics, **18th:** 201, 241, 264, 343, 517, 548, 675
Metaphysics. See *Tōn meta ta physika*
Métastasis (Xenakis), **20th:** 4414
Metaxas, Ioannis, **20th:** 4159; **Notor:** 724-725
Metcalfe, Sir Charles, **19th:** 124, 1858
Metellus, Quintus Caecilius, **Anc:** 533
Metempsychosis. *See* Transmigration of souls
Meteoritic Hypothesis, The (Lockyer), **19th:** 1414
Meteorology, **17th:** England, 384; Italy, 922; **18th:** 336, 1039; **20th:** microclimates, 1443; Norway, 376
Methane, discovery of, **18th:** 1023
Method acting, **20th:** 487, 863
Method of Chemical Nomenclature (Lavoisier), **18th:** 580
Method of Reaching Extreme Altitudes, A (Goddard), **20th:** 1508
Methodenbuchs für Väter und Mütter der Familien und Völker, Des. See *Elementarwerke*
Méthodes nouvelles de la mécanique céleste, Les (Poincaré), **19th:** 1817
Methodi vitandorum errorum omnium qui in arte medica contingunt (Santorio), **17th:** 810
Methodical Realism (Gilson), **20th:** 1489
Methodism (medical school of thought), **Anc:** 84, 115, 199
Methodism (religious movement), **18th:** Francis Asbury, 62-64; George Whitefield, 1073; Count von Zinzendorf, 1121
Methodist Church, **18th:** 1064-1067
Methodius, Saint, **MA:** 191, 294-297, 670
Methods of Ethics, The (Sidgwick), **19th:** 2103
Methods of Study in Natural History (Agassiz), **19th:** 34
Methodus Curandi Febres (Sydenham), **17th:** 902
Methodus plantarum nova (Ray), **17th:** 782
Methvin, Henry, **Notor:** 812
Metilius, **Anc:** 343
Metis, **19th:** 1909
Metius, Jacob, **17th:** 537
Metodo della pedagogia scientifica applicato all' educazione infantile nelle case dei bambini, Il. See *Montessori Method, The*
Metric system, **18th:** 575
Metro-Goldwyn-Mayer. *See* MGM
Metrodorus the Younger, **Anc:** 308
Metropolis (film), **20th:** 2254
Metropolitan Opera, **20th:** 676
Metternich, **19th:** 222, 404, 440, 818, 1023, 1561-1564
Metzger, John, **Notor:** 726
Metzger, Tom, **Notor:** 726-727
Meung, Jean de, **MA:** 275
Meunier d'Angibault, Le. See *Miller of Angibault, The*
Meurs, John of. *See* Muris, Johannes de
Mexica, **MA:** 558
Mexican-American War. *See* Mexican War
Mexican Confederation of Workers. *See* Confederación de Trabajadores de México
Mexican Revolution (1910-1920), **19th:** 654; **20th:** 2545, 4160, 4365; Emiliano Zapata, 4449
Mexican War (1846-1848), **19th:** 25, 194, 1821-1822, 1991; Kit Carson, 428; Jefferson Davis, 611; David G. Farragut, 764; Ulysses S. Grant, 958; guns, 535; Matthew C. Perry, 1777; Franklin Pierce, 1790; Winfield Scott, 2053; Zachary Taylor, 2231
Mexico, **19th:** 820; French intervention in, 1246; independence of, 1095, 1991. *See also* Geographical Index
Mexico City Blues (Kerouac), **20th:** 2116
Mey, Lev, **19th:** 1915
Meyer, Lothar, **19th:** 103, 1547
Meyerhold, Vsevolod Yemilyevich, **20th:** 2660, 2722-2725
Meyers, Alton B., **Notor:** 996
Meyers, Tom. *See* Lake, Leonard

Mézières, France (military school), **18th:** 682
Mézy, chevalier de, **17th:** 500
MGM, **20th:** 1409, 1525, 2663, 3860, 4120
Mhlangane, **19th:** 2082
Mi Fei, **MA:** 718-720
Miamis, **18th:** 610, 801
Miantonomo, **17th:** 129
Miaos, **17th:** 911
Michael (film), **20th:** 1037
Michael (Wordsworth), **19th:** 2463
Michael I, **MA:** 244
Michael III, **MA:** 133, 190, 295, 766
Michael VI Stratioticus, **MA:** 864
Michael VII Ducas, **MA:** 865
Michael VIII Palaeologus, **MA:** 1017
Michael Kohlhaas (Kleist), **19th:** 1290
Michael of Cesena, **MA:** 779
Michael Robartes and the Dancer (Yeats), **20th:** 4429
Michaelmas Term (Middleton), **17th:** 636
Michal, **Anc:** 255
Michal Wiśniowiecki, **17th:** 429
Michelangelo, **Ren:** 29, 46, 133, 175, 231, 236, 390, 486, 520, 564, 682-685, 819, 931, 938, 953; Vasari on, 954; **Notor:** 213
Michelet (Barthes), **20th:** 247
Michelet, Jules, **19th:** 1564-1566
Michelin, André, **20th:** 2725-2727
Michelin, Édouard, **20th:** 2725-2727
Michelin Tire Company, **20th:** 773
Michelozzo, **Ren:** 18
Michelson, Albert A., **19th:** 1567-1571; **20th:** 2432
Michelson interferometer, **19th:** 1568
Michener, James A., **20th:** 2728-2730
Michi no Omi, **Anc:** 463
Michiel, Marcantonio, **Ren:** 384
Michihito. *See* Ōgimachi
Michikinikwa. *See* Little Turtle
Michinaga, Fujiwara. *See* Fujiwara Michinaga
Michinomiya Hirohito. *See* Hirohito
Mickey Mouse, **20th:** 1007
Mickey Mouse Club (television program), **20th:** 1008
Mickiewicz, Adam, **19th:** 487
Microbiology, **19th:** 1752, 2407
Microclimates, **20th:** 1443
Micro-cynicon (Middleton), **17th:** 636
Micrographia (Hooke), **17th:** 383, 509, 677
Micrologus de disciplina artis musicae (Guido d'Arezzo), **MA:** 439
Microsoft Corporation, **20th:** 1421
Microsoft Disk Operating System. *See* MS-DOS
Midaq Alley (Mahfouz), **20th:** 2554
Midas (Shelley), **19th:** 2088
Midday on the Moor (Schmidt-Rottluff), **20th:** 3662
Middle-Aged Man on the Flying Trapeze, The (Thurber), **20th:** 4021
Middle Kingdom (Egypt), **Anc:** 887
Middle Passage, The (Naipaul), **20th:** 2903
Middle Way, **Anc:** 131, 169
Middle Way, The (Macmillan), **20th:** 2537
Middlemarch (Eliot), **19th:** 741
Middlesex, first earl of. *See* Cranfield, Lionel
Middleton, Frederick D., **19th:** 1911
Middleton, Thomas, **17th:** 224, 279, 636-638, 846, 928, 977
Midhat Paşa, **20th:** 1157
Midian. *See* Mi Fei
Midnight Frolic (musical revue), **20th:** 3492
Midnight Ride of Paul Revere (Wood), **20th:** 4389
Midsummer Night's Dream, A (Mendelssohn), **19th:** 1549
Midway, Battle of (1942), **20th:** 1648, 2979; shipwrecks, 217
Midwifery, **17th:** 74
Midwifery. See *Maiōtikon*
Mies van der Rohe, Ludwig, **20th:** 2731-2734
Mifune, Toshiro, **20th:** 2218
Mighty and the Almighty, The (Albright), **20th:** 56
Mighty Handful, **19th:** 1915
Mignard, Pierre, **17th:** 505
Migration, Germanic, **Anc:** 351
Miguel, Dom, **19th:** 413, 1764
Mihajlović, Draža, **20th:** 4034
Mihnah, **MA:** 37
Miho Museum, **20th:** 3158
Mijailovic, Mijailo, **Notor:** 727-728
Mikado, The (Gilbert and Sullivan), **19th:** 919
Mikhailovich, Aleksei. *See* Alexis
Mikrokosmos (Bartók), **20th:** 251
Milan Commission, **19th:** 892
Milborne, Jacob, **17th:** 519
MILCON. *See* Military Construction, Veterans Affairs, and Related Agencies
Miles, Nelson, **19th:** 525, 568, 906, 1240
Miles Davis Quintet, **20th:** 814
Miles gloriosus (Plautus), **Anc:** 663
Miletus, scientists from, **Anc:** 58
Milgram, Stanley, **Notor:** 729-731
Milhaud, Darius, **20th:** 2735-2738, 4164
Milieu divin, Le. See *Divine Milieu, The*
Milindapañha (Menander), **Anc:** 550
Milione, Il. See *Travels of Marco Polo, The*
Military, **Ren:** China, 1004, 1009; Hungary, 643; India, 532; Italy, 654; Japan, 733; Netherlands,

913; Ottoman Empire, 660, 916; Russia, 493; Scotland, 499; Songhai Empire, 900; Vietnam, 546; women and, 526; **17th:** England, 205; France, 184, 559, 946; Japan, 998; Netherlands, 619; Russia, 12; Sweden, 925; **19th:** Prussia, 930; United States, 962. *See also* Armies; Artillery; Navies; Category Index
Military Academy, U.S., **19th:** 2261
Military affairs. *See* Category Index
Military Construction, Veterans Affairs, and Related Agencies, **20th:** 1230
Military leaders, **18th:** Eugene of Savoy, 330-332; Richard Howe, 506-513; Hyder Ali, 522-523; John Paul Jones, 539-543; Tadeusz Kościuszko, 564-566; Mikhail Illarionovich Kutuzov, 569-572; Little Turtle, 610-612; Alexander McGillivray, 626-629; first duke of Marlborough, 660-663; Louis-Joseph de Montcalm, 692-695; James Edward Oglethorpe, 742-746; Aleksey Grigoryevich Orlov, 755-758; Arthur Phillip, 783-785; Pontiac, 801-805; Grigori Aleksandrovich Potemkin, 808-810; comte de Rochambeau, 851-854; George Rodney, 854-858; Louis de Saint-Just, 878; comte de Saxe, 881-883; John Graves Simcoe, 919-921; Aleksandr Vasilyevich Suvorov, 954-958; Anthony Wayne, 1054-1057; James Wolfe, 1104-1108
Military reform, **18th:** first Marquess Cornwallis, 280; France, 200; Frederick William I, 381-383; Jean-Baptiste Vaquette de Gribeauval, 447-449; Hyder Ali, 522; Mahmud I, 640; Marquis de Montalembert, 690-692; Robert Morris, 708; Ottoman Empire, 720; Peter III, 779; Peter the Great, 775; Grigori Aleksandrovich Potemkin, 809; Russia, 954-958
Military Reorganization Commission, **19th:** 929
Militia Act (1792), **18th:** 1046
Milk, Harvey, **Notor:** 1099
Milken, Michael, **Notor:** 112, 731-733
Milkmaid of Bordeaux, The (Goya), **18th:** 439
Mill, The (Claude Lorrain), **17th:** 171
Mill, James, **19th:** 1571-1574, 1576, 1807
Mill, John Stuart, **18th:** 105, 516; **19th:** 264, 1572, 1574-1579, 2103; and Dame Millicent Garrett Fawcett, 768
Mill on the Floss, The (Eliot), **19th:** 741
Millais, John Everett, **Anc:** 3; **19th:** 1755, 1940
Millay, Edna St. Vincent, **20th:** 2738-2741
Mille regretz (Josquin), **Ren:** 517
Millennial Harbinger, **19th:** 400
Millennium Fantasy for Piano and Orchestra (Zwilich), **20th:** 4477
Miller, Alfred Jacob, **19th:** 232
Miller, Arthur, **20th:** 2742-2745, 2799; **Notor:** 540
Miller, Phineas, **18th:** 1076
Miller, Robert. *See* Lustig, Victor
Miller, S. L., **20th:** 3063
Miller, Stanley, **20th:** 4134
Miller, William Allen, **19th:** 1145
Miller of Angibault, The (Sand), **19th:** 1988
Miller v. California (1973), **20th:** 583, 1030
Millett, Kate, **20th:** 2746-2749
Millikan, Robert Andrews, **20th:** 2750-2753, 3441
Milliner, Mary, **Notor:** 1102
Million Man March (1995), **20th:** 1218
Mills, Wilbur, **Notor:** 733-734
Milne, A. A., **20th:** 2753-2756
Milner, Alfred, **20th:** 440, 4440
Milner, Henry M., **19th:** 1555
Milošević, Slobodan, **20th:** 2756-2759; **Notor:** 375, 735-737, 739
Miloslavsky, Ilya, **17th:** 664
Miltiades the Younger, **Anc:** 213, 563-566, 631, 649, 794, 859
Milton (Blake), **18th:** 123
Milton, Frances. *See* Trollope, Frances
Milton, John, **17th:** 109, 201, 300, 502, 605, 639-643, 942
Milvian Bridge, Battle of the (312), **Anc:** 240
Milwaukee Braves, **20th:** 5
Minacore, Calogero. *See* Marcello, Carlos
Minamoto clan, **MA:** 398, 721, 991, 1040
Minamoto Noriyori, **MA:** 722
Minamoto Yorimasa, **MA:** 721, 992, 1152
Minamoto Yoritomo, **MA:** 721-724, 992, 1040
Minamoto Yoshinaka, **MA:** 721
Minamoto Yoshitomo, **MA:** 721
Minamoto Yoshitsune, **MA:** 722
Minamoto Yukiie, **MA:** 721
Minas Gerais, Brazil, **18th:** 609
Mind (Langer), **20th:** 2265
Mind and Matter (Schrödinger), **20th:** 3670
Mind in Evolution (Hobhouse), **20th:** 1843
Mind of Primitive Man, The (Boas), **20th:** 401
Mind's Road to God. See *Journey of the Soul to God, The*
Mind's Wit and Art, The (Gracián), **17th:** 317
Ming (emperor), **Anc:** 149
Ming Dynasty, **MA:** 1147; emperors, 1149; **Ren:** 826,

1003; **17th:** 1, 160, 448, 848, 912, 972, 1001
Mingo and Other Sketches in Black and White (Harris), **19th:** 1036
Mingus, Charles, **20th:** 1482
Mingus Dances (ballet), **20th:** 2013
Minh Mang, **19th:** 908
Minhag America (Wise, comp.), **19th:** 2454
Minimalism, **20th:** 2637
Minin, Nikita. *See* Nikon
Mining, **18th:** 734, 1049; **19th:** England, 2167; ore-crushing machines, 733
Minister's Wooing, The (Stowe), **19th:** 2185
Minkus, Ludwig, **19th:** 639
Minna von Barnhelm (Lessing), **18th:** 600
Minneconjous, **19th:** 569
Minnelli, Liza, **20th:** 1410
Minnewit, Peter. *See* Minuit, Peter
Minor Commentary to the Book of Changes (Wang), **17th:** 972
Minor Prophets with a Commentary Explanatory and Practical, The (Pusey), **19th:** 1845
Minority Report of the Poor Law Commission, The (Webb), **20th:** 4255
Minot, George Richards, **20th:** 4305
Minstrel shows, **19th:** 802
Minstrelsy of the Scottish Border, The (Scott), **19th:** 2047
Mint, The (Lawrence), **20th:** 2306
Minto, Lord Gilbert, **20th:** 222
Minucia, **Anc:** 512
Minucius, Lucius, **Anc:** 343
Minuit, Peter, **17th:** 643-646, 706
Minute Men of Louisiana, **20th:** 2426
Mir space station, **20th:** 2461
Mirabeau, comte de, **18th:** 679-682; Marie-Antoinette, 658; François Quesnay, 821
Miracle of the Loaves and Fishes (Tintoretto), **Ren:** 932
Miracle of the Rose (Genet), **20th:** 1446
Miracle plays, **Anc:** 270
Miracle Worker, The (Gibson), **20th:** 3908
Miracles, **Anc:** Apostles and, 626; Saint Christopher and, 205; Jesus and, 460; True Cross and, 392
Miracles of Antichrist, The (Lagerlöf), **20th:** 2234
Miracles of Saint Martin, The (Gregory of Tours), **MA:** 426
Miracles Performed by the Relics of the Saint (Andrea del Sarto), **Ren:** 39
Miraculous Mandarin, The (Bartók), **20th:** 251
Mirakel, Das (Humperdinck), **19th:** 1156
Miranda, Francisco de, **19th:** 268
Miranda Prosus (Pius XII), **20th:** 3279
Miranda v. Arizona (1966), **20th:** 4234
Mireille (Gounod), **19th:** 953
Miriam, **Anc:** 2
Mirifici logarithmorum canonis constructio. See *Construction of a Marvelous Canon of Logarithms*
Mirifici logarithmorum canonis descriptio. See *Description of a Marvelous Canon of Logarithms*
Mirleau, Hubert de, **Notor:** 283
Miró, Joan, **20th:** 905, 2759-2763
Miroir des âmes simples, Le. See *Mirror of Simple Souls, The*
Mirovich, Vasily, **Notor:** 516
Mirovoe khoziaistvo i imperializm. See *Imperialism and World Economy*
Mirror for Princes, A (Skelton), **Ren:** 441
Mirror Has Two Faces, The (film), **20th:** 3893
Mirror of Faith, The (William of Saint-Thierry), **MA:** 1115
Mirror of Mans Lyfe, The. See *On the Misery of the Human Condition*
Mirror of Simple Souls, The (Porete), **MA:** 857
Mirsky, Alfred, **20th:** 3156
Mirtilla, La (Andreini), **Ren:** 42
Mīrzā ʿalī. *See* Bāb, the
Mīrzā Ḥoseynʿalī Nūrī. *See* Bahāʾullāh
Mīrzā Rezā Kermānī, **19th:** 1205
Misăheun, **Anc:** 466
Misanthrope, The (Molière), **17th:** 648
Miscellaneous Poems (Marvell), **17th:** 606
Miscellaneous Reflections Occasion'd by the Comet Which Appear'd in December, 1680 (Bayle), **17th:** 36
Miscellanies. See *Saturae* (Ennius)
Miscellany Tracts (Browne), **17th:** 95
Mise of Amiens (1264). *See* Amiens, Mise of (1264)
Miser, The (Molière), **17th:** 648
Misérables, Les (Hugo), **19th:** 1148
Miserere (Rouault), **20th:** 3543
Miseries of War (Callot), **17th:** 118
Misfits, The (film), **20th:** 1369
Mishima, Yukio, **20th:** 2763-2765
Mishnah, **Anc:** 29
Mishneh Torah. See *Code of Maimonides, The*
Mismeasure of Man, The (Gould), **20th:** 1556
Miss Julie (Strindberg), **20th:** 3898
Miss Liberty (Berlin), **20th:** 329
Miss Sadie Thompson (film), **20th:** 1732
Miss Sara Sampson (Lessing), **18th:** 599

Missa ad fugam (Josquin), **Ren:** 516
Missa Choralis (Liszt), **19th:** 1395
Missa L'Homme armé sexti toni (Josquin), **Ren:** 516
Missa Papae Marcelli (Palestrina), **Ren:** 751
Missa sine nomine (Josquin), **Ren:** 516
Missa Solemnis (Beethoven), **19th:** 178
Missarum Josquin liber secundus (Josquin), **Ren:** 516
Missarum Josquin liber tertius (Josquin), **Ren:** 516
Misse Josquin (Josquin), **Ren:** 516
Missionaries, **Anc:** Apostles as, 626; Buddhist, 898; Christianity and, 613; Saint Thomas, 880; **17th:** French in North America, 433; Jesuits in Brazil, 960; Jesuits in Canada, 499; Jesuits in China, 161, 449, 849; Jesuits in North America, 423, 603, 908; Jesuits in the American Southwest, 467; Massachusetts, 247; **18th:** in China, 1114; **20th:** 2850, 3678
Missionaries of Charity, **20th:** 3976
Missionary Offering, A (Lyon), **19th:** 1429
Missionary Sisters of the Sacred Heart, **19th:** 385
Missionary Travels and Researches in South Africa (Livingstone), **19th:** 1400
Missions, **Ren:** Catholic Church, 6, 29, 162, 483, 514, 538, 673, 825, 1000; Jesuits, 394; **18th:** California, 891-893; Moravian, 1121; **19th:** Africa, 1401; Anglicans in Africa, 574; William Carey on, 410; Christians in Vietnam, 2310; Protestants to India, 410
Mississippi Freedom Democratic Party, **20th:** 1652
Mississippi River, **Ren:** European discovery of, 904; **17th:** exploration, 433, 491, 603
Missouri, **19th:** 1362; slavery, 194
Missouri Compromise (1820), **19th:** 22, 503
Mister Roberts (film), **20th:** 1266
Misteriya-buff. See *Mystery-Bouffe*
Mistress, The (Cowley), **17th:** 199
Mistress of the Theologians. *See* Angela of Foligno, Blessed
Mit brennender Sorge (Pius XI), **20th:** 3276
Mit Livs Eventyr. See *Story of My Life, The* (Andersen)
Mitanni, **Anc:** 887
Mitate (visual likening), **18th:** 958
Mitchell, John, Notor: 226, 643, 737-738
Mitchell, Maria, 19th: 812, 1580-1582
Mitchell, William, 20th: 2765-2769
Mithra, **Anc:** 994
Mithradates V Euergetes, **Anc:** 567
Mithradates VI Eupator, Anc: 535, 567-569, 682, 827, 831, 895, 927
Mithradates Chrestus, **Anc:** 567
Mithradatic Wars, **Anc:** 568
Mithridates (Racine), **17th:** 775
Mithrism, **Anc:** 994
Mitre, Bartolomé, **19th:** 2001
Mitridate Eupatore, Il (Scarlatti), **18th:** 885
Mitropolskaia. *See* Kaplan, Fanya
Mitropoulos, Dmitri, **20th:** 339
Mitsou (Colette), **20th:** 805
Mitterrand, François, 20th: 2769-2772; **Notor:** 801
Mittler, Der. See *Mediator, The*
Mixture of Frailties, A (Davies), **20th:** 918
Mizan al-ḥaqq fi lkhtijārī al-ahaqq. See *Balance of Truth, The*
Mlada (Rimsky-Korsakov), **19th:** 1916
Mladić, Ratko, Notor: 739
Mniszech, Jerzy, **17th:** 855
Mobile Bay, Battle of (1864), **19th:** 764
Mobile Indians. *See* Choctaws
Mobutu, Joseph Désiré. *See* Mobutu Sese Seko
Mobutu Sese Seko, 20th: 2477, 2773-2776, 4091; **Notor:** 633, 740-741
Moby Dick (Melville), **19th:** 1539
Mocenigo, Zuane, **Ren:** 140
Mochihito, **MA:** 721, 992
Mocking of Christ, The (Grünewald), **Ren:** 405
Moctezuma II. *See* Montezuma II
Mode de valeurs et d'intensités (Messiaen), **20th:** 2717
Model, Lisette, **20th:** 115
Model of Moses His Judicials (Cotton), **17th:** 219
Model T, **20th:** 1280
Modern art, **20th:** 1846, 2636, 3539
Modern Broods (Yonge), **19th:** 2472
Modern dance, **20th:** Europe, 2222, 3594; United States, 36, 887, 958, 1058, 1062, 1362, 1564, 3989
Modern Educational Dance (Laban), **20th:** 2222
Modern Greece (Hemans), **19th:** 1076
Modern Mephistopheles, A (Alcott), **19th:** 43
Modern Painters (Ruskin), **19th:** 1954
Modern Sounds in Country and Western Music (Charles), **20th:** 736
Modern Theme, The (Ortega), **20th:** 3078
Modern Times (film), **20th:** 733
Modernism, **20th:** 453, 2580, 2731, 3386
Modernismo, **19th:** 601; **20th:** 1424

Modes of Thought (Whitehead), **20th:** 4314
Modest Proposal for Preventing the Children of Poor People of Ireland from Being a Burden to Their Parents, A (Swift), **18th:** 966
Modigliani, Amedeo, **20th:** 2776-2778
Modiste, La (Toulouse-Lautrec), **19th:** 2290
Moffat, John Smith, **19th:** 1407
Moffat, Robert, **19th:** 1402
Moffat, W. B., **19th:** 2044
Moffat Treaty (1888), **19th:** 1407
Möglichkeit und Wirklichkeit (Hartmann), **20th:** 1697
Mohács, Battle of (1526), **Ren:** 480, 636, 645, 886, 910, 915, 984
Mohammad Reza Shah Pahlavi, **20th:** 2124, 2779-2782, 2845, 3428; **Notor:** 47, 572, 742-743, 798
Mohammed I Askia, **Ren:** 64, 596-597, 686-689, 901
Mohammed V (king of Morocco), **20th:** 1699
Mohammed, Khalid Shaikh, **Notor:** 744-745, 760
Mohammed Ahmed, **19th:** 950, 1553
Mohammed-Ali, F. *See* Fard, Wallace Dodd
Mohammed and Charlemagne (Pirenne), **20th:** 3270
Mohawks, **Ren:** 281, 448; **17th:** 141, 424, 634, 643, 777, 909; **18th:** American Revolution, 159; sanctuary in Canada, 160
Mohegans, **17th:** 130
Mohism, **Anc:** 576
Moi, Daniel arap, **20th:** 2109
Moissan, Henri, **Notor:** 627
Molakai. *See* Veerappan
Molander, Gustav, **20th:** 321
Moldavia, **17th:** 463
Molière, **17th:** 19, 186, 212, 305, 482, 487, 521, 524, 554, 570, 646-649, 662, 774
Molina, Arturo, **20th:** 1041, 3500
Molina, Mario J., **20th:** 3548
Molina, Tirso de. *See* Tirso de Molina
Molinet, Jean, **Ren:** 517
Molinos, Miguel de, **17th:** 340, 406
Moll, Gerrit, **19th:** 1079
Moll Flanders (Defoe), **18th:** 299
Moller, Margarethe, **18th:** 562
Moller, Martin, **17th:** 59
Mollie Bailey's Traveling Family Circus (Terry), **20th:** 3984
Molloy (Beckett), **20th:** 281
Molly Maguires, **Notor:** 745-746
Molnár, Ferenc, **20th:** 2331
Moloch, **Anc:** 805
Molodoi, Ivan. *See* Ivan Molodoi
Molon, **Anc:** 65
Molotov, Vyacheslav Mikhailovich, **20th:** 359, 2129, 2406, 2783-2786; **Notor:** 550, 746-749, 895, 1080
Molotov-Ribbentrop Pact (1939), **20th:** 2784
Moltke, Helmuth von, **19th:** 501
Moluccas. *See* Spice Islands
Momente (Stockhausen), **20th:** 3874
Mommsen, Theodor, **19th:** 1582-1585
Mommu, **MA:** 623
Mon Faust. See *My Faust*
Mona Lisa (Leonardo da Vinci), **Ren:** 563
Monachomachia (Krasicki), **18th:** 567
Monadnock Building, **19th:** 361
Monaldeschi, Gian Rinaldo, **17th:** 165
Monarchy, **Anc:** empire versus, 281; Roman, 517, 846; **MA:** 387; **Ren:** France, 347, 578; Jewish view of, 1; limited, 341. *See also* Category Index
Monasteries, **Anc:** Buddhist, 112; Christian, 61
Monastery, The (Scott), **19th:** 2048
Monasticism, **Anc:** Athanasius and, 134; Buddhist, 50, 345, 899, 934; Christian, 208, 456, 789, 862, 865, 947; Pythagorean brotherhood and, 725; **MA:** England, 509; France, 160, 316-317, 1114; Germany, 1024; Ireland, 199; Italy, 234; Rome, 154; Saxony, 516; Tours, 870; Turkey, 295; women, 438, 509; **Ren:** France, 4; Italy, 44; Spain, 508, 930
Monck, George, **17th:** 57, 137, 148, 206, 485, 650-653, 758, 806, 838, 931, 942
Mondale, Walter, **20th:** 1016, 1243, 3402, 3435
Monday Night Football (television sports program), **20th:** 3555
Monde, Le (Descartes), **17th:** 227
Monde san soleil, Le. See *World Without Sun*
Mondino dei Liucci, **MA:** 445
Mondlane, Eduardo C., **20th:** 2515
Mondrian, Piet, **20th:** 609, 2075, 2786-2789, 2957, 3092
Monet, Claude, **19th:** 453, 632, 1800, 1888; **20th:** 422, 2790-2793
Monetarism, **20th:** 1333
Monetary History of the United States, 1867-1960, A (Friedman and Schwartz), **20th:** 1333
Monge, Gaspard, **18th:** 682-687; **19th:** 809
Mongkut, **19th:** 1346; invitation to Anna Leonowens, 1347
Mongol Empire, **Ren:** 488-489, 493
Mongolia. *See* Geographical Index
Mongols, **MA:** 626, 853; Christianity, 547, 627; conquest of China, 677; conversion to Islam, 412; expulsion from China, 1147; French alliance with, 1108; invasions of Europe, 227; Kereits and, 954; law codes, 402; Muslims, 403; Nestorians

and, 627; rulers, 404; trade, 403, 853; as warriors, 402
Monikins, The (Cooper), **19th:** 554
Monism, **Anc:** 58, 609; **17th:** 188; **19th:** 1004; **20th:** 3090
Monitor, The (Krasicki), **18th:** 567
Moniz, António Egas. *See* Egas Moniz, António
Monjo, Robert. *See* Abagnale, Frank W., Jr.
Monk, George. *See* Monck, George
Monk, Thelonious, **20th:** 814, 1481
Monkey's Raincoat (Bashō), **17th:** 616
Monmartre-sur-Seine (film), **20th:** 3229
Monmouth, Battle of (1778), **18th:** 258
Monmouth, duke of, **17th:** 122, 149, 241, 417, 545, 653-656, 693, 816; **Notor:** 565
Monmouth, Humphrey, **Ren:** 950
Monnet, Jean, **20th:** 2793-2796
Monod, Jacques, **20th:** 1983
Monody, **17th:** 112
Monody on the Death of Major André (Seward), **18th:** 897
Monogram (Rauschenberg), **20th:** 3381
Monograph on the Fossil Fishes of the Old Red or Devonian of the British Isles and Russia (Agassiz), **19th:** 32
Monologen. See *Schleiermacher's Soliloquies*
Monologion (Anselm), **MA:** 92
Mononobe clan, **MA:** 940
Monophysites, **MA:** 507, 600, 934, 1009
Monopolies, **19th:** 88, 1923
Monotheism, **Anc:** Egyptian, 28, 588, 902, 908; Greek, 70, 966; Judaism and, 4; paganism and, 604; Zoroastrian, 993; **18th:** Islamic, 1030
Monothelism, **MA:** 935
Monroe, James, **19th:** 21, 348, 404, 1586-1590
Monroe, Marilyn, **20th:** 1002, 1369, 2743, 2797-2800, 3042
Monroe Doctrine (1823), **19th:** 22, 404, 503, 1587-1588
Monroe-Pinkney Treaty (1806), **19th:** 1587
Mons Graupius, Battle of (83), **Anc:** 18
Monsieur Bergeret in Paris (France), **19th:** 816
Monsieur Pascal's Thoughts, Meditations, and Prayers. See *Pensées*
Monsieur Verdoux (film), **20th:** 733
Monster and Other Stories, The (Crane), **19th:** 564
Monsters, origin of, **Anc:** 295
Mont Blanc (Shelley), **19th:** 2093
Mont-Saint-Michel and Chartres (Adams), **19th:** 17
Montage of a Dream Deferred (Hughes), **20th:** 1929
Montage technique (film), **20th:** 1131
Montagnais, **17th:** 141
Montagu, Charles, **17th:** 717
Montagu, Edward. *See* Sandwich, first earl of
Montagu, Elizabeth, **18th:** 221
Montagu, Mary Wortley, **18th:** 687-690
Montaigne, Michel Eyquem de, **Ren:** 689-692
Montale, Eugenio, **20th:** 2801-2803
Montalembert, marquis de, **18th:** 690-692
Montalto, Felice Peretti di. *See* Sixtus V
Montanism, **Anc:** 443, 854
Montauk (Frisch), **20th:** 1340
Montauk Building, **19th:** 361
Montcalm and Wolfe (Parkman), **19th:** 1744
Montcalm, Louis-Joseph de, **18th:** 151, 692-695
Montcorbier, François de. *See* Villon, François
Monteagle, Lord, **Notor:** 350
Montecuccoli, Raimundo, **17th:** 527, 934
Montefeltro, Guidobaldo da, **Ren:** 181
Montemurlo, Battle of (1537), **Ren:** 653
Montenegro. *See* Geographical Index under Serbia and Montenegro
Monterey Pop Festival, **20th:** 2043
Montes Claros, Battle of (1665), **17th:** 426, 821
Montesinos Torres, Vladimiro, **Notor:** 382
Montespan, Madame de, **17th:** 572, 590, 601
Montesquieu, **18th:** 479, 648, 695-698; **Notor:** 907
Montessori, Maria, **20th:** 2804-2807
Montessori Method, The (Montessori), **20th:** 2806
Monteverdi, Claudio, **Ren:** 363; **17th:** 296, 656-660, 826
Montez, Lola, **19th:** 1590-1592
Montezuma I, **Ren:** 693, 722
Montezuma II, **Ren:** 35, 253, 273, 622, 693-696
Montfort, Simon de, **MA:** 343, 491, 571, 725-730
Montgolfier, Jacques-Étienne, **18th:** 698-701
Montgolfier, Joseph-Michel, **18th:** 698-701
Montgomery, Bernard Law, **20th:** 470, 2808-2811, 3504
Montgomery, Richard, **Notor:** 36
Montgomery bus boycott, **20th:** 11, 2148, 3122
Montgomery convention, **19th:** 612
Montgomery Ward and Company, **19th:** 2387
Montijo, Battle of (1644), **17th:** 432

Montini, Giovanni Battista. *See* Paul VI
Montlhéry, Battle of (1465), **Ren:** 574
Montojo, Patricio, **19th:** 646
Montpensier, duchesse de, **17th:** 477, 569, 660-663
Montreal, Siege of (1760), **18th:** 40, 385
Montroig Landscape (Miró), **20th:** 2760
Montrose, James Graham, marquess of, **17th:** 147
Montu, **Anc:** 570
Montuhotep II, **Anc:** 570-572
Monvoisin, Madame, **17th:** 586
"Mood Indigo" (Ellington), **20th:** 1146
Moodie, Susanna, **19th:** 1593-1595, 2292
Moody, Dwight L., **19th:** 1596-1599; **20th:** 2850
Moody Bible Institute, **19th:** 1597
Moody Memorial Church, **19th:** 1596
Moon, Hak Ja Han, **Notor:** 750
Moon, Sun Myung, **20th:** 2811-2813; **Notor:** 749-751
Moon, Yong Myung. *See* Moon, Sun Myung
Mooney, Tom, **20th:** 1308
Moonlight Battle (1780), **18th:** 856
Moonlight, Early Evening (Thomson), **20th:** 4011
Moonwalk, **20th:** 3726
Moor. *See* Sforza, Ludovico
Moore, Ben. *See* Einhorn, Ira
Moore, Carry Amelia. *See* Nation, Carry
Moore, Fred H., **20th:** 3581
Moore, G. E., **20th:** 2814-2817, 3562
Moore, Henry, **20th:** 2818-2821
Moore, Marianne, **20th:** 2821-2824
Moore, Rory. *See* O'More, Rory
Moore, Thomas, **19th:** 1224
Moore, Tyria, **Notor:** 1109
Moore, William, **Notor:** 577
Moorish architecture, **Ren:** 890
Moorish Rhapsody (Humperdinck), **19th:** 1156
Moors, **MA:** 882; **Ren:** 79, 105, 252, 433, 537, 803; **17th:** expulsion from Spain (1603), 530. *See also* Islam; Muslims
Mor, Anthonis, **Ren:** 422
Moral and Metaphysical Philosophy (Maurice), **19th:** 1520
Moral Culture of Infancy and Kindergarten Guide (Peabody), **19th:** 1762
Moral Majority, **20th:** 1210-1211
Moral virtue, **18th:** 188, 1080
Morales, Baltasar Gracián y. *See* Gracián y Morales, Baltasar
Moralia (Gregory the Great), **MA:** 430
Morals, **Anc:** Confucianism and, 236; fables and, 629; pleasure and, 88; virtue and, 88
Morals and Evolution of Man (Nordau), **20th:** 2994
Morals in Evolution (Hobhouse), **20th:** 1843
Morals on the Book of Job. See *Moralia*
Moran, Bugs, **20th:** 642; **Notor:** 176, 751-752, 804, 1096
Moran, Jack. *See* Diamond, Legs
Moran, Thomas, **19th:** 233
Moravia, **MA:** 107; Christianity, 295
Moravia, Alberto, **Notor:** 193
Moravian Duets (Dvořák), **19th:** 712
Moravian missions, **18th:** 1121
Moravians in colonial Georgia, **18th:** 743, 1062, 1064
Moray, Sir Andrew de, **MA:** 308, 1073
Morceaux de Fantaisie (Rachmaninof), **20th:** 3361
Mörder Hoffnung der Frauen (Kokoschka), **20th:** 2185
More, Hannah, **18th:** 702-704
More, Henry, **17th:** 187, 252
More, Rory. *See* O'More, Rory
More, Sir Thomas, **Ren:** 11, 113, 188, 266, 270, 301, 315, 336, 442, 454, 697-701, 951, 997
More Die of Heartbreak (Bellow), **20th:** 290
More Pricks than Kicks (Beckett), **20th:** 280
More Reasons for the Christian Religion (Baxter), **17th:** 35
More than Lore (Talbot), **20th:** 3937
Moreau, Gustave, **20th:** 2650; **Notor:** 933
Moreau, Jean-Jacques. *See* Mesrine, Jacques
Morel, Edmund Dene, **20th:** 94; **Notor:** 633
Morelli, Felice, **19th:** 384
Morelli, Mario, **20th:** 675
Morello, Peter, **Notor:** 709
Morelos, José María, **19th:** 1096
Moresby Treaty (1822), **19th:** 1967
Morey, Pierre, **Notor:** 354
Morgan, Sir Henry, **Notor:** 260, 753-754
Morgan, J. P., **19th:** 421, 510, 1102, 1599-1603, 2253; **20th:** 1614
Morgan, Lewis Henry, **19th:** 1603-1606
Morgan, Thomas Hunt, **20th:** 2825-2828
Morganfield, McKinley. *See* Waters, Muddy
Morgenstern, Oskar, **20th:** 2946
Morgenstunden (Mendelssohn), **18th:** 676
Morgenthau, Hans Joachim, **20th:** 2828-2831
Morgenthau, Henry, Jr., **20th:** 1936
Morgenthau, Henry, Sr., **19th:** 27
Morgenthau Plan (1944), **20th:** 1936
Mōri Shigeyoshi, **17th:** 831
Moriae encomium. See *Praise of Folly, The*
Morien, Chrétien de, **Ren:** 422

Moriscos' expulsion from Spain, **17th:** 737. *See also* Marranos
Morisot, Berthe, **19th:** 1800
Morita, Akio, **20th:** 2831-2834
Morituri Salutamus (Longfellow), **19th:** 1419
Moritz, Hermann. *See* Saxe, comte de
Moritz of Hessen-Kassel, **17th:** 825
Morley, Edward Williams, **19th:** 1568; **20th:** 2432
Morley, Thomas, **Ren:** 150, 701-703
Mormons. *See* Church of Jesus Christ of Latter-day Saints
Mornard, Jacques. *See* Mercader, Ramón
Mornay, Philippe de, **Ren:** 703-706
Morning Courier and New York Enquirer, **19th:** 190
Morning Glory (film), **20th:** 1770
Moro, Il. *See* Sforza, Ludovico
Morocco, **MA:** Almohad conquest of, 7; architecture, 8; **Ren:** 556; Portuguese invasion of, 859; sultanate of, 916; **20th:** independence of, 1699. *See also* Geographical Index
Morocco (film), **20th:** 998
Moronao, Ko no. *See* Ko no Moronao
Morones, Luis, **20th:** 615
Moronobu, Hishikawa. *See* Hishikawa Moronobu
Moroyasu, Ko no. *See* Ko no Moroyasu
Morozov, Boris Ivanovich, **17th:** 11, 663-665
Morris, Charles A., **19th:** 1114
Morris, Gouverneur, **18th:** 705-707, 1118
Morris, Mark, **20th:** 254
Morris, Robert, **18th:** 707-711, 1092
Morris, William, **19th:** 1606-1609
Morris and Company, **19th:** 1607
Morrison, Marion Michael. *See* Wayne, John
Morrison, Toni, **20th:** 2834-2838
Morrissey, George. *See* Moran, Bugs
Morrow, Dwight D., **20th:** 616
Morse, Samuel F. B., **19th:** 292, 535, 557, 1080, 1610-1613
Morse code, **19th:** 1611, 1826
Mort d'Agrippine, La. See *Death of Agrippina, The*
Mort dans l'âme, La. See *Troubled Sleep*
Mort de Tintagiles, La. See *Death of Tintagiles, The*
Mortal Antipathy, A (Holmes), **19th:** 1118
Morte a Venezia. See *Death in Venice* (film)
Morte d'Arthur, Le (Malory), **MA:** 407; **Ren:** 197, 598
Mortemart, Françoise-Athénaïs, Rochechouart de. *See* Montespan, Madame de
Mortemer, Battle of (1054), **MA:** 1117
Mortification of the flesh, **Anc:** 789
Mortimer, Roger, **MA:** 348, 350, 553, 842
Mortimeriados (Drayton), **17th:** 237
Mortimer's Cross, Battle of (1461), **Ren:** 301, 438, 990
Morton, Samuel, **Notor:** 804
Morton, Thomas, **17th:** 232, 879
Morton, William Thomas Green, **19th:** 1613-1616
Morui wenji (Guo), **20th:** 1621
Mosaddeq, Mohammad. *See* Mossadegh, Mohammad
Mosaicall Philosophy (Fludd), **17th:** 281
Mosby, John, **Notor:** 858
Mosca, Gaetano, **20th:** 2838-2841
Moscone, George, **Notor:** 1099
Moscow, Russia, **18th:** 571
Moscow, Treaty of (1686), **17th:** 429, 866
Moscow, University of, **18th:** 322, 613
Moscow Art Theatre, **20th:** 2722, 3822
Moscow-Berlin Pact of 1939, **20th:** 4004
Moscow Linguistic Circle, **20th:** 1986
Moscozo, Flore-Célestine-Thérèse-Henriette Tristan y. *See* Tristan, Flora
Mosè in Egitto (Rossini), **19th:** 1945
Moses, **Anc:** 1, 539, 572-575
Moses (Michelangelo), **Ren:** 683
Moses, Grandma, **20th:** 2841-2844
Moses, Phoebe Anne. *See* Oakley, Annie
Moses ben Maimon. *See* Maimonides, Moses
Moses ben Naḥman. *See* Naḥmanides
Moses ben Shem Tov de León. *See* Moses de León
Moses David. *See* Berg, David
Moses de León, **MA:** 730-733
Moses Gerondi, Rabbenu ("Our" Rabbi Moses of Gerona). *See* Naḥmanides
Moses, Man of the Mountain (Hurston), **20th:** 1945
Moses und Aron (Schoenberg), **20th:** 3666
Mosharrif al-Dīn ibn Moṣliḥ al-Dīn. *See* Saʿdi
Moskovskii sbornik. See *Reflections of a Russian Statesman*
Moskowa, Prince de la. *See* Ney, Michel
Mosley, Sir Oswald, **Notor:** 542, 755-756
Mossadegh, Mohammad, **20th:** 2124, 2779, 2844-2847; **Notor:** 742
Mosses from an Old Manse (Hawthorne), **19th:** 1051
Mossi, Songhai invasions of, **Ren:** 65

Most, Johann, **20th:** 1520; **Notor:** 425
Most Beautiful, The (film), **20th:** 2218
Motets, **MA:** 25, 334, 681, 825, 1066
Mothe-Fénelon, François de La. *See* Fénelon, François de Salignac de La Mothe-
Mother, The (Brecht), **20th:** 504
Mother, The (Gorky), **20th:** 1551
Mother and Child (Moore), **20th:** 2819
Mother Angelica's Answers, Not Promises (Mother Angelica), **20th:** 90
Mother Ann. *See* Lee, Ann
Mother Courage and Her Children (Brecht), **20th:** 504
Mother Earth (journal), **20th:** 1521
Mother Goose in Prose (Baum), **19th:** 156
Mother-in-Law, The. See *Hecyra*
Mother Millett (Millett), **20th:** 2748
Mother-Play and Nursery Songs (Froebel), **19th:** 838
Mother Sawyer. *See* Sawyer, Elizabeth
Mothering Heart, The (film), **20th:** 1496
Mothershed-Wair, Thelma, **Notor:** 349
Motherwell, Robert, **20th:** 2847-2849, 3539
Motion pictures, **19th:** 732; **20th:** development of, 2472
Motley, John Lothrop, **Ren:** 780
Motomasa, Kanze. *See* Kanze Motomasa
Motors, electric, **19th:** 760
Mott, John R., **20th:** 199, 549, 2849-2853
Mott, Lucretia, **19th:** 257, 1616-1619
Motteville, Françoise Bertaut de, **17th:** 662
Mou Qizhong, **Notor:** 757-758
Mouches, Les. See *Flies, The*
Moulin, Jean, **Notor:** 58
Moulton, Elizabeth Barrett. *See* Browning, Elizabeth Barrett
Mounseer Nongtongpaw (Shelley), **19th:** 2089
Mount, William Sidney, **19th:** 235
Mount Everest, summiting, **20th:** 1804, 2720
Mount Hiei, **MA:** 621
Mount Holyoke Female Seminary, **19th:** 1429
Mount Kōya, **MA:** 621
Mount Rainier, **18th:** 1007
Mount Sinai, **Anc:** 1
Mount Vesuvius, **Anc:** 666
Mountain Giants, The (Pirandello), **20th:** 3261
Mountain Interval (Frost), **20th:** 1349
Mountain Symphony (Liszt), **19th:** 1394
Mountaineering, **19th:** 2466; **20th:** 1803, 2718
Mountains and Sea (Frankenthaler), **20th:** 1304
Mountains of California, The (Muir), **19th:** 1625
Mountbatten, Louis (first Earl Mountbatten of Burma), **20th:** 989, 2853-2857
Mountfort, William, **17th:** 82
Mourning Becomes Electra (O'Neill), **20th:** 3053
Mourning of Christ (Carracci), **Ren:** 177
Mourning Parents (Kollwitz), **20th:** 2190
Mourt's Relation (Bradford and Winslow), **17th:** 86
Mouse That Roared, The (film), **20th:** 3696
Mousetrap, The (Christie), **20th:** 766
Moussaoui, Zacarias, **Notor:** 744, 758-760
Mouvement de la Libération des Femmes, **20th:** 273
Mouvement National Congolais, **20th:** 2476, 2773
Mouvement Souveraineté-Association, **20th:** 2345
Moveable Feast, A (Hemingway), **20th:** 1758
Movement, the. *See* Catholic Social Studies Movement
Movement for the Triumph of Democratic Liberties, **20th:** 9
Movements in European History (Lawrence), **20th:** 2297
Movimento Popular Brasileiro, **20th:** 651
Movimiento Nacionalista Revoluciononario. *See* National Revolutionary Movement
Movin' Out (Joel), **20th:** 3990
Mowat, Oliver, **Notor:** 295
Mowbray, Thomas, **MA:** 895
Moya zhizn. See *My Life* (Trotsky)
Moyen court et très facile de faire oraison. See *Worship of God in Spirit and in Truth, The*
Moynier, Gustave, **19th:** 699
Mozaffarids, **MA:** 451
Mozambique, **20th:** civil war (1975-1992), 2516; conflict with Angola, 3196; independence of, 2515, 3607. *See also* Geographical Index
Mozambique Liberation Front. *See* FRELIMO
Mozambique National Resistance. *See* RENAMO
Mozart, Wolfgang Amadeus, **18th:** 99, 131, 711-715
Mozart and Salieri (Rimsky-Korsakov), **19th:** 1915
Mozi, **Anc:** 576-578
Mpande, **19th:** 450
Mr. and Mrs. Clark with Percy (Hockney), **20th:** 1846
Mr. Britling Sees It Through (Wells), **20th:** 4288
Mr. Brouček's Excursion to the Fifteenth Century (Janáček), **20th:** 1991

Mr. Cottons Letter Lately Printed, Examined, and Answered (Williams), **17th:** 983
Mr. Peters' Connections (Miller), **20th:** 2744
Mr. Pim Passes By (Milne), **20th:** 2753
Mr. Sammler's Planet (Bellow), **20th:** 289
Mr. Smith Goes to Washington (film), **20th:** 3861
Mrs. Abington as the Comic Muse (Reynolds), **18th:** 2
Mrs. Dalloway (Woolf), **20th:** 4398
Mrs. Warren's Profession (Shaw), **20th:** 3718
Ms. (magazine), **20th:** 3853
MS-DOS, **20th:** 1421
MTB-1, **20th:** 4108
Mu Qizhong. *See* Mou Qizhong
Mu'āwiyah I, **MA:** 3, 605
Mu'āwiyah II, **MA:** 3
Mubārak. *See* Quṭb-ud-Dīn Mubārak Shāh
Mubarak, Suzanne, **Notor:** 506
Mubāriz al-Dīn Muḥammad, **MA:** 451
Mudd, Samuel A., **Notor:** 124, 1013
Müde Tod, Der. See *Destiny*
Mudgett, Herman Webster. *See* Holmes, H. H.
Mueller, Johannes von. *See* Müller, Johannes von
Mugabe, Robert, **20th:** 2516, 2702, 2858-2860; **Notor:** 720, 761-762
Muggleton, Lodowick, **17th:** 665-667
Muggletonians, **17th:** 666
Mughal Empire, **Ren:** 15, 69, 475; **17th:** 23, 410, 842, 859; **18th:** and Muslims, 1032
Muhajir, Abu Hamza al-Muhajir, **Notor:** 1134
Muḥammad (Prophet), **Anc:** 6; **MA:** 471, 507, 610, 733-737, 873, 1037
Muḥammad II. *See* Mehmed II
Muḥammad XI. *See* Boabdil
Muḥammad XII. *See* Boabdil
Muḥammad XIII, **Ren:** 106. *See also* Muḥammad al-Zaghall
Muhammad, Abu. *See* Zarqawi, Abu Musab al-
Muḥammad, Askia. *See* Mohammed I Askia
Muhammad, Elijah, **20th:** 1217, 2570; **Notor:** 345, 763, 765
Muhammad, John Allen, **Notor:** 765-766
Muhammad, Wallace Fard. *See* Fard, Wallace Dodd
Muḥammad ʿAbduh, **19th:** 1204
Muḥammad Aḥmad ibn as-Sayyid ʿAbd-Allāh. *See* Mahdi, the
Muḥammad al-Wazzān al-Zaiyātī, al-Ḥasan ibn. *See* Leo Africanus
Muḥammad al-Zaghall, **Ren:** 106
Muḥammad ʿAlī Pasha, **19th:** 1620-1623, 1733, 2265
Muhammad Ballo. *See* Bello, Muḥammad
Muḥammad Bello ibn Uthman. *See* Bello, Muḥammad
Muḥammad ibn Tughluq, **MA:** 530
Muhammad Ibrahim. *See* Zawahiri, Ayman al-
Muḥammad Karīm Beg. *See* Karīm Khān Zand
Muḥammad Özbeg, **MA:** 530
Muḥammad R'uf Pasha, **19th:** 1474
Muhammad Shah, **Notor:** 772
Muḥammad Shaybānī Khān, **Ren:** 69
Muḥammad Tawfīq Pasha, **19th:** 1204
Muhammad Ture. *See* Mohammed I Askia
Muḥammad ʿUthmān Abu Qarja, **19th:** 1474
Muhammadan Anglo-Oriental College, **19th:** 37
Muhammed Ahmed, **19th:** 2140
Muhammed Bin Hamid. *See* Tippu Tib
Muḥaṣṣal (al-Rāzī), **MA:** 370
Mühlberg, Battle of (1547), **Ren:** 31, 222, 650, 777
Muir, John, **19th:** 748, 1623-1626; **20th:** 3255
Mujahid Shaykh. *See* Bin Laden, Osama
Muʿjam al-udaba'. See *Yaqut's Dictionary of Learned Men*
Mujibur Rahman, **20th:** 369
Mujtahid, **18th:** 1000
Mukai Kyorai, **17th:** 616
Mukashibanashi (Makuzu), **19th:** 2212
Mukhabarat, **20th:** 154
Mukherji, Savitri Devi. *See* Savitri Devi
Mukhtar, Omnar, **20th:** 3350
Mulatto (Hughes), **20th:** 1929
Mulattoes, **18th:** Joseph Boulogne, 154; West Indies, 985
Mulberry Grove, **18th:** 445, 1076
Mules and Men (Hurston), **20th:** 1945
Mullā Ḥūsayn, **19th:** 105
Müller, Heinrich, **20th:** 4329
Muller, Hermann Joseph, **20th:** 2861-2864
Müller, Johannes, **19th:** 1003
Müller, Johannes von, **Notor:** 536
Müller, Lucas. *See* Cranach, Lucas, the Elder
Müller, Ludwig, **20th:** 2971
Müller, Walther, **20th:** 1441
Muller v. Oregon (1908), **20th:** 483
Mulligan Letters, **19th:** 252
Mullins, Priscilla, **17th:** 7
Mullis, Kary B., **20th:** 2864-2866
Mulroney, Brian, **20th:** 625, 762, 2866-2870, 3654
Mulso, Hester. *See* Chapone, Hester
Muluzi, Elson Bakili, **20th:** 220
Mu'minin, Amir al-. *See* ʿAbd al-Mu'min
Mummification, **Anc:** 909; anatomy and, 410
Mummy's curse, **Anc:** 909

Mumtaz Mahal, **17th:** 842
Munāẓarāt jarat fī bilād mā warā ʿa al-nahr. See *Transoxianian Controversies*
Munch, Edvard, **20th:** 2870-2873
Muncke, Georg Wilhelm, **19th:** 547
Mundus novus (Vespucci), **Ren:** 971
Munera Pulveris (Ruskin), **19th:** 1956
Munger, Charles T., **20th:** 564
Munich Accords (1938), **20th:** 301, 639, 723, 769, 1101
Munich Putsch (1923), **20th:** 1830, 2463, 3689
Municipal Corporations Bill of 1835, **19th:** 2447
Municipal Franchise Act (1869), **19th:** 767
Munificentissimus Deus (Pius XII), **20th:** 3279
Munitions of War Act of 1915, **20th:** 353
Munro, Alice, **20th:** 2873-2875
Münster, Treaty of (1648), **17th:** 619
Münzer, Thomas, **Ren:** 775
Muqaddimah, The (Ibn Khaldūn), **MA:** 537
Muqtadir, al-, **MA:** 280, 884
Mur, Le. See *Wall, and Other Stories, The*
Murad (son of Shah Jahan), **17th:** 24, 844
Murad II, **MA:** 520, 711; **Notor:** 1072
Murad III, **Ren:** 661, 911
Murad IV, **17th:** 451, 454, 472, 668-670, 674
Murad V, **19th:** 7
Murad, Abdul Hakim, **Notor:** 1121
Murad Oglu Ahmed I. *See* Murad IV
Mural movement, **20th:** 3068, 3457
Murasaki Shikibu, **MA:** 738-740, 930
Murat, Joachim, **19th:** 2224; **Notor:** 353
Murchison, Sir Roderick Impey, **19th:** 369, 1423, 2125
Murder at the Vicarage (Christie), **20th:** 766
Murder in the Cathedral (Eliot), **20th:** 1140
Murder of Roger Ackroyd, The (Christie), **20th:** 766
Murder on the Orient Express (film), **20th:** 322
Murderers. *See* Assassins; Category Index under Assassins and Murderers
Murderer's Row, **20th:** 1435
Murdoch, Rupert, **20th:** 2876-2879
Murdock, William, **18th:** 715-718
Muret, Battle of (1213), **MA:** 571
Murieta, Joaquín, **Notor:** 80, 767-768
Murillo, Bartolomé Esteban, **17th:** 670-672, 1005
Murillo, Gerardo, **20th:** 3068
Muris, Johannes de, **MA:** 741-743
Muromachi emperors, **MA:** 116
Murphy (Beckett), **20th:** 280
Murphy, Anna Brownell. *See* Jameson, Anna
Murphy, Charles, **Notor:** 1049
Murphy, Jim, **Notor:** 68
Murphy, William P., **20th:** 4305
Murray, Margaret Lindsay. *See* Huggins, Margaret Lindsay
Murray, William. *See* Mansfield, first earl of
Murrow, Edward R., **20th:** 2879-2882
Murs, Jehan des. *See* Muris, Johannes de
Murther and Walking Spirits (Davies), **20th:** 918
Murūj al-dhahab wa maʿādin al-jawāhir. *See* Masʿūdī, al-
Mūsā, Mansa, **MA:** 744-746, 979
Mūsa ibn Maymūn ibn ʿUbayd Allāh, Abū ʿImrān. *See* Maimonides, Moses
Mūsā ibn Nuṣayr, 1005
Musʿab, **MA:** 4
Muscovy, **17th:** 784
Muscular Dystrophy Association, **20th:** 2358
Muses, **Anc:** 11, 413
Muses Elizium, The (Drayton), **17th:** 238
Museum of Alexandria, **Anc:** mathematics, 317
Museum of Comparative Zoology, **19th:** 33
Museum of Modern Art (New York), **20th:** 3477
Museveni, Yoweri Kaguta, **20th:** 2883-2885, 3012
Music, **Anc:** Confucianism on, 237; poetry and, 647; **MA:** education, 440; England, 334; France, 24-25, 680, 741, 824, 1065; Italy, 439, 635; Japan, 773; **Ren:** England, 290, 701, 918; English church, 148; Flanders, 540; France, 515; Italy, 359, 362, 610, 751; Netherlands, 913; Venice, 363; **17th:** England, 127, 309, 502, 763; France, 569, 630; Germany, 708, 826; Italy, 111, 190, 295, 656, 825, 888; **18th:** Baroque, 1019-1022; chamber, 73, 131, 713; church, 464; classical, 281-284, 418-421; criticism, 178; England, 177; France, 154, 281-284; French versus Italian, 827; Germany, 71; history, 178; Italy, 129; Neapolitan school, 886; orchestration, 1020; patronage, 130; popularization, 972; preclassical versus Baroque, 970-973; reform of Christoph Gluck, 420; rococo, 131; Scotland, 185; string quartet, 129; theory, 72, 826-827, 972; violin making, 944-947; **19th:** Austria, 329, 2026, 2188; Czech nation, 711; England, 918; France, 201, 241, 487, 822, 952, 1699; Germany, 297,

1154, 1549, 2029, 2033, 2374, 2395; Hungary, 1393; Italy, 674, 1724, 1944, 2351; Norway, 985; ragtime, 1235; Russia, 281, 1627, 1915, 2234; United States, 802, 1235, 2268; Vienna, 176. *See also* Ballet; Blues music; Chamber music; Classical music; Country music; Electronic music; Folk music; Jazz; Opera; Popular music; Rock and roll; Swing music; Theater; Category Index

Music for Chameleons (Capote), **20th:** 646

Music for Strings, Percussion, and Celesta (Bartók), **20th:** 251

Music for the Theater (Copland), **20th:** 838

Music Ho! (Lambert), **20th:** 4218

Music Room, The (film), **20th:** 3394

Musica speculativa secundum Boetium (Muris), **MA:** 741-742

Musical intervals, **Anc:** 726

Musical orphanages, **18th:** 1019

Musician, The (Braque), **20th:** 495

Muskie, Edmund, **20th:** 54

Muslim League, **20th:** 1389, 2003

Muslims, **MA:** 1020; Christianity and, 1029; capture of Edessa, 162; Egypt, 674; Holy Land, 236, 542, 1003; Mongols, 403; North Africa, 478; Spain, 33, 380; Tunis, 674; Valencia, 572; **17th:** expulsion from Spain (1603), 530; **18th:** versus Hindus, 1032; Mughal Empire, 1032. *See also* Islam; Moors

Musnad (Ibn Ḥanbal), **MA:** 38

Musset, Alfred de, **19th:** 1988

Mussolini, Benito, **20th:** 870, 1100, 1449, 2885-2889, 3793; denunciation of, 945; invasion of Ethiopia, 1640; *Time* magazine, 2457; **Notor:** 240, 339, 368, 371, 769-771, 796, 813, 823, 928, 969

Mussorgsky, Modest, **19th:** 281, 1626-1630, 1915

Mustafa I, **17th:** 472, 668, 673-675

Mustafa III, **18th:** 719-721

Muşţafa ibn ʿabd Allāh. *See* Kâtib Çelebî

Mustafa Kemal. *See* Atatürk

Muʿtamin, al-, **MA:** 280

Muʿtaṣim, al-, **MA:** 37, 468, 617

Mutawakkil, al-, **MA:** 37

Mutazilites, **MA:** 37, 111, 369, 569, 703

Müteferrika, İbrahim, **18th:** 28

Mutesa, Edward II, **20th:** 81, 3012

Mutina, Battle of (43 B.C.E.), **Anc:** 145

Mutina, Battle of (73 B.C.E.), **Anc:** 819

Mutiny of 1857, **19th:** 36, 596, 1329, 1718

Mutiny on the *Bounty*. See *Bounty*, HMS

Mutiny on the Bounty (film), **20th:** 1368

Mutsuhito, **19th:** 1631-1633

Mutter, Die. See *Mother, The* (Brecht)

Mutter des Legionärs, Die (Ehrenfels), **20th:** 1111

Mutter- und Kose-lieder. See *Mother-Play and Nursery Songs*

Muʿzzī slave kings of India, **MA:** 889

Mutual Welfare League, **20th:** 3086

Muybridge, Eadweard, **20th:** 2472

My Adventures as a Spy (Baden-Powell), **19th:** 112

My American Journey (Powell), **20th:** 3323

My Ántonia (Cather), **20th:** 699

My Apprenticeship (Webb), **20th:** 4255

My Autobiography (Chaplin), **20th:** 733

My Birth (Kahlo), **20th:** 2070

My Blue Heaven (film), **20th:** 1163

My Bondage and My Freedom (Douglass), **19th:** 685

My Children! My Africa (Fugard), **20th:** 1357

My Double Life (Bernhardt), **19th:** 210

My Fair Lady (film), **20th:** 4231

My Faust (Valéry), **20th:** 4138

My First Summer in the Sierra (Muir), **19th:** 1625

My Four Years in Germany (film), **20th:** 4230

My Friend from Limousin (Giraudoux), **20th:** 1493

My Friend's Book (France), **19th:** 815

My Kalulu (Stanley), **19th:** 2139

My Ladye Nevells Booke (Byrd), **Ren:** 150

My Life (Duncan), **20th:** 1058

My Life (Ellis), **20th:** 1148

My Life (Fugard), **20th:** 1357

My Life (Trotsky), **20th:** 4075

My Life (Wagner), **19th:** 2377

My Life in Art (Stanislavsky), **20th:** 3821

My Life in Sculpture (Lipchitz), **20th:** 2399

My Little Chickadee (film), **20th:** 4298

My Memoirs (Dumas), **19th:** 698

My Past and Thoughts (Herzen), **19th:** 1086

My Quest for the Yeti (Messner), **20th:** 2720

My Religion (Keller), **20th:** 2094

My Robin (Burnett), **19th:** 359

My Secret (Petrarch), **MA:** 829

My Several Lives (Conant), **20th:** 823

My Sister Henrietta (Renan), **19th:** 1884

My Sister, Life (Pasternak), **20th:** 3132

My Story (Monroe), **20th:** 2799

My Tennessee Mountain Home (Parton), **20th:** 3128

My Wife and I (Stowe), **19th:** 2460

Myanmar. *See* Burma

Mycenæ (Schliemann), **19th:** 2017

Mycenaean era, **Anc:** 427

Myngs, Christopher, **Notor:** 753
Mynydd Carn, Battle of (1081), **MA:** 753
Myortvye dushi. See *Dead Souls*
Myra Breckinridge (film), **20th:** 4299
Myrdal, Gunnar, **20th:** 575, 2890-2893
Myron, **Anc:** 633
Myrsilus, **Anc:** 653
Myrtle, Marmaduke. *See* Addison, Joseph
Myself and My Heroes (Hockney), **20th:** 1845
Mysore, India, **18th:** 470, 522
Mystère de l'être, Le. See *Mystery of Being, The*
Mysteries (Hamsun), **20th:** 1661
Mysteries of Samothrace. *See* Mystery religions
Mysteries of Udolpho, The (Radcliffe), **18th:** 823
Mysterious Affair at Styles, The (Christie), **20th:** 765
Mysterious Island, The (Verne), **19th:** 2357
Mysterious Stranger, The (Twain), **19th:** 2332
Mysterium cosmographicum. See *Secret of the Universe, The*
Mysterium Magnum (Böhme), **17th:** 61
Mystery and detective fiction, **20th:** 766, 1404
Mystery and Manners (O'Connor), **20th:** 3018
Mystery-Bouffe (Mayakovsky), **20th:** 2660
Mystery of Being, The (Marcel), **20th:** 2610
Mystery of Edwin Drood, The (Dickens), **19th:** 656
Mystery of the Blue Train, The (Christie), **20th:** 766
Mystery of the Leaping Fish, The (film), **20th:** 2429
Mystery religions, **Anc:** 423, 597; Eleusinian, 7; Judaism and, 642; Orphic, 70; Samothrace, 597
Mystical Marriage of Saint Catherine, The (Murillo), **17th:** 672
Mystici Corporis Christi (Pius XII), **20th:** 3279
Mysticism, **Anc:** Daoism and, 503; Jewish, 336; nature and, 397; **MA:** 857, 1105; England, 271, 596, 607; Flanders, 144; France, 160, 181, 578; Germany, 512, 708; Italy, 81, 97; Majorca, 673; Muslim, 454, 874; Rome, 236; **Ren:** France, 4; Italy, 191, 928; Jewish, 524, 581; Spain, 509; **17th:** Belgium, 362; England, 284; France, 339-340, 499; Germany, 62; Peru, 797; Spain, 265
Mystik und das Wort, Die (Brunner), **20th:** 548
Myszeis (Krasicki), **18th:** 567
"Myth of Inanna and Ebih, The." *See* "In-min-me-hus-a"
Myth of Sisyphus, and Other Stories, The (Camus), **20th:** 628
Myth of the State, The (Cassirer), **20th:** 689
Mythologies (Barthes), **20th:** 247
Mythology, **Anc:** Buddhist, 161; Chinese, 553, 732; civilization and, 415; classical, 603; Greek, 414; Greek drama, 326; history and, 408; philosophy and, 307, 856; poetry and, 646, 704, 795; Roman drama, 301; science and, 58; travel and, 619
Mzali, Muhammad, **20th:** 459
Mzilikazi, **19th:** 1406

N

Na (Ionesco), **20th:** 1968
NAACP. *See* National Association for the Advancement of Colored People
Nabis, **20th:** 972, 4173
Nabokov, Vladimir, **20th:** 2894-2897
Nabonidus, **Anc:** 249, 298, 583
Nabopolassar, **Anc:** 335, 582, 711
Nabū-kudurri-uṣur. *See* Nebuchadnezzar II
Nabu-nasir, **Anc:** 892
Nabu-rimanni, **Anc:** 579-581
Nabucco (Verdi), **19th:** 2351
Nabulsi, Suleyman an-, **20th:** 1952
Nachfolge. See *Cost of Discipleship, The*
Nachmanides. *See* Naḥmanides
Nada the Lily (Haggard), **19th:** 1007
Nádasdy, Elizabeth. *See* Báthory, Elizabeth
Nadasdy, Ferenc, **Ren:** 81
Nader, Ralph, **20th:** 2897-2900
Nādir Khan Afshar. *See* Nādir Shāh
Nādir Shāh, **17th:** 4; **18th:** 552, 640, 722-723; **Notor:** 772-773
Nadja (Breton), **20th:** 511
Nadr Kuli. *See* Nādir Shāh
Naevius, Gnaeus, **Anc:** 301
Nafata, **19th:** 2342
NAFTA. *See* North American Free Trade Agreement
Nag Hammadi works, **Anc:** 918
Nagama Nayaka, **Ren:** 532
Nágánanda (Harṣa), **MA:** 461
Nagano Shuzen, **19th:** 1168
Nāgārjuna, **Anc:** 112
Nagasaki, Japan, bombing of, **20th:** 3685, 4087
Nagashino, Battle of (1575), **Ren:** 452, 733
Nagasune Hiko, **Anc:** 463
Nägeli, Karl Wilhelm von, **19th:** 1543
Naguib Mahfouz at Sidi Gaber (Mahfouz), **20th:** 2556
Nagy, Imre, **20th:** 2469
Naha, Treaty of (1854), **19th:** 1778
Nahāvand, Battle of (642), **MA:** 1038
Naḥmanides, **MA:** 747-749
Naidu, Sarojini, **20th:** 2900-2902

Naipaul, Sir V. S., **20th:** 2903-2905
Naismith, James, **20th:** 2905-2907
Nakamaro, Fujiwara. *See* Fujiwara Nakamaro
Nakanoin Masatada no Musume. *See* Nijō
Nakanune. See *On the Eve*
Nakatsuhime, **Anc:** 594
Naked and the Dead, The (Mailer), **20th:** 2563
Naked Maja, The (Goya), **18th:** 438
Nālānda, **Anc:** 113; **MA:** 1137
Namaskets, **17th:** 876
Namcheck, Jim. *See* Boyce, Christopher John
Namibia, **20th:** 3195
Namik Kemal, **20th:** 1157
Namphy, Henri, **20th:** 125
Nana (film), **20th:** 3420
Nana (novel by Zola), **19th:** 2490
Nānak, **Ren:** 478, 707-710
Nanak Parkash (Bhai Santokh Singh), **19th:** 1859
Nanboku-cho. *See* Northern and Southern Courts
Nancy, Battle of (1477), **Ren:** 218
Nanda (half brother of Buddha), **Anc:** 130
Nanda Dynasty, **Anc:** 203
Nanjing, Treaty of (1842), **19th:** 1379
Nanna, **Anc:** 298, 915
Nanna (Fechner), **19th:** 771
Nanny, **18th:** 724-726
Nansen, Fridtjof, **20th:** 83, 2907-2910; **Notor:** 873
Nanshoku ōkagami. See *Great Mirror of Male Love, The*
Nanshū. *See* Saigō Takamori
Nantes, Edict of (1598), **Ren:** 430, 465, 570
Naomi (Tanizaki), **20th:** 3944
Naoroji, Dadabhai, **19th:** 1634-1635
Napier, Charles James, **19th:** 368, 1718
Napier, John, **Ren:** 710-713; **17th:** 818
Napier, Robert, **19th:** 2256
Napier, William, **19th:** 1378
Naples, **MA:** kings, 391; **Ren:** 657; conquest of, 330; France and, 577
Napoléon (film), **20th:** 1383
Napoleon I, **18th:** Lazare Carnot, 200; Mikhail Illarionovich Kutuzov, 570; Gaspard Monge, 684; Pius VI, 794; Emmanuel-Joseph Sieyès, 918; John Graves Simcoe, 920; Madame de Staël, 931; Toussaint-Louverture, 987; Alessandro Volta, 1024; **19th:** 21, 177, 260, 397, 407, 468, 1241, 1561, 1636-1639, 1667, 1993, 2223; art patronage, 609, 898; François-René de Chateaubriand, 476; Joseph Fourier, 809; Russia, 46; Freiherr vom Stein, 2151; duke of Wellington, 2409; **Notor:** 353, 801, 1117
Napoleon III, **19th:** 2, 49, 238, 445, 864, 1246, 1526, 1639-1642, 1804, 1949, 2265; art patronage, 1480; Lord Palmerston, 1733; Rothschild family, 1949; Vietnam, 2311; writers and, 1836; **Notor:** 279
Napoleonic code, **19th:** 397
Napoleonic Wars (1803-1815), **19th:** 260, 439, 468, 499, 891, 929, 1636; Metternich, 1562; Michel Ney, 1667; Prussia, 1022; duke of Wellington, 2409
Nara period, **MA:** 623; art, 582; emperors, 624
NARAL Pro-Choice America, **20th:** 1330
Naram-Sin, **Anc:** 299, 366, 916
Narcissus, **Anc:** 219, 561
Narcissus (Shirley), **17th:** 846
Narcissus and Goldmund. See *Death and the Lover*
Narconon, **20th:** 1910
Narendranath Datta. *See* Vivekananda
Narita International Airport, **20th:** 3647
Narmer, **Anc:** 557
Narragansetts, **17th:** 129, 612, 633, 879
Narratio prima (Rheticus), **Ren:** 823
Narratio prima de libris revolutionum. See *First Account, The*
Narratio Prima of Rheticus, The. See *Narratio prima*
Narrative of a Journey to the Shores of the Polar Sea, in the Years 1819, 20, 21, and 22 (Franklin), **19th:** 825
Narrative of an Expedition to the Zambezi and Its Tributaries (Livingstone and Livingstone), **19th:** 1401
Narrative of Arthur Gordon Pym, The (Poe), **19th:** 1814
Narrative of Colonel Ethan Allen's Captivity, A (Allen), **18th:** 37
Narrative of Sojourner Truth (Truth), **19th:** 2308
Narrative of the Life of Frederick Douglass (Douglass), **19th:** 685
Narrative of the Life of David Crockett of the State of Tennessee (Crockett), **19th:** 572
Narrative of the United States Exploring Expedition (Wilkes), **19th:** 2436
Narrow Road to the Deep North, The (Bashō), **17th:** 616
Narses, **MA:** 600
Naruhito, **20th:** 49
Narutowicz, Gabriel, **20th:** 3252; **Notor:** 792
Narváez, Pánfilo de, **Ren:** 152, 161
Narvaez, Zoilamérica, **20th:** 3073
Naryshkina, Natalya Kirillovna, **17th:** 13

Narziss und Goldmund. See *Death and the Lover*
NASA. *See* National Aeronautics and Space Administration
Nascimento, Edson Arantes do. *See* Pelé
Naseby, Battle of (1645), **17th:** 205, 263, 756
Nāser od-Dīn, **19th:** 1204
Nash, Frank, **Notor:** 361
Nash, John, **19th:** 1642-1645
Nash, Paul, **20th:** 2910-2913
Nash, Thomas, **Notor:** 1048
Nashe, Thomas, **Ren:** 714-717; **17th:** 440
Nashe's Lenten Stuffe (Nashe), **Ren:** 715
Nashoba, **19th:** 2470
Nashville Skyline (Dylan), **20th:** 1073
Nasier, Alcofribas. *See* Rabelais, François
Nāṣin-ud-Dīn Muḥammad. *See* Humāyūn
Nāṣir al-Dīn Shāh, **19th:** 2215
Nasmyth, James, **19th:** 1646-1648
Naso, Publius Ovidius. *See* Ovid
Nassau, count of. *See* Frederick Henry
Nassau, Maurice of. *See* Maurice of Nassau
Nassauer Denkschrift (Stein), **19th:** 2151
Nasser, Gamal Abdel, **20th:** 111, 1056, 1102, 2555, 2914-2918, 3350, 3587; Israel, 930; Jordan, 1951; Saudi Arabia, 1200; **Notor:** 867
Nast, Thomas, **19th:** 1649-1651, 2335
Natchez, The (Chateaubriand), **19th:** 477
Nathan, **Anc:** 155, 256, 803
Nathan, George Jean, **20th:** 2689
Nathan the Wise (Lessing), **18th:** 601, 676
Nation, Carry, **19th:** 1652-1655
Nation, David, **19th:** 1652
Nation of Islam, **20th:** 63, 1217, 2570, 2572
National Aeronautics and Space Administration, **20th:** 135, 502, 1127
National African Company, **19th:** 941
National American Woman Suffrage Association, **19th:** 67, 2085; **20th:** 701
National Anti-Corn Law League, **19th:** 521
National Apostasy, Considered in a Sermon Preached in St. Mary's (Keble), **19th:** 1845
National Assembly of France, **18th:** 648, 681, 728, 844, 878, 917, 985. *See also* Third Estate (France)
National Association for the Advancement of Colored People, **19th:** 2393; **20th:** 1048, 2633, 4292, 4308
National Association for the Repeal of Abortion Laws. *See* NARAL Pro-Choice America
National Association for the Repeal of the Contagious Diseases Acts, **19th:** 372
National Cancer Act of 1971, **20th:** 2248
National Citizen and Ballot Box, The, **19th:** 853
National Colonization Society, **19th:** 2379
National Congolese Movement, **20th:** 4091
National Congress (India), **20th:** 222
National Conservation Commission, **20th:** 3254
National Convention (France), **18th:** 267, 649
National Convention of Nigeria and the Cameroons, **20th:** 181
National Defense Education Act, **20th:** 1127
National Economic Development Council, **20th:** 2539
National Equal Rights Party, **19th:** 1411
National Federation of Women Workers, **20th:** 415
National Football League, **20th:** 3553
National Gallery of Art, East Building, **20th:** 3185
National Geographic Society, **19th:** 184
National Health Services, Great Britain, **20th:** 350
National Industrial Recovery Act of 1933, **20th:** 3880
National Institute for the Blind, **19th:** 299
National Insurance Act of 1911, **20th:** 352, 2411
National Intelligence Directorate (Chile). *See* Dirección Nacional de Inteligencia
National Labor Relations Act of 1935, **20th:** 1922, 2361
National League for Democracy, **20th:** 175
National League of Cities v. Usery (1975), **20th:** 3407
National Legion of the South (France), **18th:** 154
National Liberal Federation, **19th:** 461
National Liberation Army, **20th:** 9
National Liberation Front, **20th:** 9
National Lyrics and Songs for Music (Hemans), **19th:** 1077
National Negro Business League, **19th:** 2393
National Organization for Women, **20th:** 1330, 1774
National Organization of the Jews of Germany, **20th:** 188
National Policy (Canada), **19th:** 1444
National Recovery Act of 1933, **20th:** 1922
National Reformer (newspaper), **19th:** 211
National Republicans (U.S. political party), **18th:** 13; Elbridge Gerry, 413; Thomas

Jefferson, 529; Paul Revere, 835
National Resistance Movement, **20th:** 2883
National Review (magazine), **20th:** 561
National Revolutionary Movement, **20th:** 3172
National Revolutionary Party (Mexico). *See* Partido Nacional Revolucionario
National Secular Society, **19th:** 211
National Socialism, **20th:** 1807, 1816, 1830
National Space Institute, **20th:** 502
National Trust, **19th:** 1105
National Unification Policy (Liberia), **20th:** 4102
National Union of General and Municipal Workers, **20th:** 416
National Union of Women's Suffrage Societies, **19th:** 768; **20th:** 3103
National Velvet (film), **20th:** 3953
National Woman Suffrage Association, **19th:** 66, 852, 1618, 2085, 2149
National Woman's Party (U.S.), **20th:** 702
National Woman's Rights Convention (1850), **19th:** 800, 2177, 2307
Nationalism, **Anc:** Germany, 101; **18th:** Austria, 653-656; Germany, 380, 383; India, 523; Ireland, 441, 983; Russia, 614; Saudi Arabia, 1030-1031; United States, 304, 452, 636, 1046; **20th:** 1485
Nationalist Party (China). *See* Kuomintang
Nationalist Party (India), **20th:** 178
Nationalist Party of Indonesia, **20th:** 3904
Nationalization of resources, Mexico, **20th:** 616, 649
Nations, Les (Couperin), **18th:** 281
Nations, Battle of (1813), **19th:** 47
Native America. *See* Geographical Index
Native Americans, **17th:** treaties with Europeans, 8, 130, 567, 613, 644, 876, 878, 891; **19th:** attitudes toward, 553, 1195, 1604, 1746; conflicts with, 566, 1239, 2110; Florida, 1190; Harrison, 1048; languages, 856; paintings of, 442; relations with European settlers, 427, 1361, 1873, 1938, 2237; removal of, 2052, 2068; study of, 1830; treaties, 567; **20th:** alcoholism, 1171, 3248; Cherokees, 2592; education, 4016; health issues, 3248; in literature, 1169, 1171; ocean travel, 1797. *See also* American Indian leaders; American Indians; Canada, Indians; *specific nations*; Category Index
Native Land Act (1865), **19th:** 1484
Nativity (Correggio), **Ren:** 249
Nativity (Piero), **Ren:** 787
NATO. *See* North Atlantic Treaty Organization
Natta, Giulio, **20th:** 2919-2922
Natural and Moral History of the Indies, The (Acosta), **Ren:** 6
Natural history, **Ren:** England, 74; France, 101; Switzerland, 375; **18th:** 171-173, 533, 605, 926; **19th:** 604; United States, 92. *See also* Category Index
Natural History. See *Naturalis historia*
Natural History, General and Particular (Buffon), **18th:** 171
Natural Inheritance (Galton), **19th:** 862
Natural law, **Anc:** doctrine of, 692; **18th:** Paul-Henri-Dietrich d'Holbach, 503; William Paley, 763
Natural Questions. See *Quaestiones naturales*
Natural science, **Anc:** Greek, 295; **18th:** 172, 532, 548, 696
Natural selection, **19th:** 604, 2407
Natural Theology (Paley), **18th:** 763
Naturalis historia (Pliny the Elder), **Anc:** 23, 665, 677, 817
Naturalism, **19th:** 1450, 2490
Nature, **Anc:** concepts of, 55; culture and, 283; cycles and, 56; **18th:** landscape architecture and painting, 166; study of, 68
Nature (Anaxagoras), **Anc:** 52
Nature (Emerson), **19th:** 746
Nature (scientific journal), **19th:** 1413
Nature and Destiny of Man, The (Niebuhr), **20th:** 2963
Nature and the Greeks (Schrödinger), **20th:** 3670
Nature of Enzyme Action, The (Bayliss), **20th:** 260
Nature of Rationality, The (Nozick), **20th:** 3000
Nature of the Chemical Bond and the Structure of Molecules and Crystals, The (Pauling), **20th:** 3156
Nature of the Judicial Process, The (Cardozo), **20th:** 654
Nature poetry, **Anc:** Chinese, 977
Natureklärung und Psyche (Pauli and Jung), **20th:** 3153
Nature's Pictures (Newcastle), **17th:** 676
Natürliche Schöpfungsgeschichte. See *History of Creation, The*
Naufragios, Los. See *Relación, La*
Naufragium Joculare (Cowley), **17th:** 199
Naugerius sive de poetica dialogus (Fracastoro), **Ren:** 345
Nauka Pobezhdat (Suvorov), **18th:** 956
Nausea (Sartre), **20th:** 3638
Nautilus, **20th:** 3445

Nautilus Submarine Boat Company, **19th:** 1114
Nauvoo, **19th:** 2118, 2476
Navajos, **19th:** 429
Naval warfare, **Anc:** 109; Punic Wars, 373
Navarino, Battle of (1827), **19th:** 405, 2480
Navarre, Marguerite of. *See* Marguerite de Navarre
Navies, **Anc:** Greece, 859; **17th:** England, 57-58; Netherlands, 932; **18th:** Great Britain, 50, 126, 506, 508, 1006; Russia, 108, 542; United States, 540; **19th:** United States, 1777
Navigation Act (1651), **17th:** 57, 808
Navigation and longitude, **18th:** 152
Navigator, The (film), **20th:** 2091
Navratilova, Martina, **20th:** 1192, 2922-2925
Navy, British, **18th:** William Bligh, 126; Richard Howe, 506; George Vancouver, 1006. *See also* Admiralty (Royal Navy)
Navy, U.S., **18th:** 540; **19th:** 1777
Nawrūz, **MA:** 411
Nazarín (film), **20th:** 579
Nazism, **20th:** German Christians, 419; German Jews, 187, 3828; Germany, 26, 1743; Joseph Goebbels, 1513; Hermann Göring, 1546; Heinrich Himmler, 1807; Adolf Hitler, 1830; Iran, 3429; John Paul II, 2021; in literature, 629, 639; Norway, 1662; opposition to, 245, 4324, 4328; Roman Catholic Church, 3276-3277, 3279. *See also* Hitler, Adolf; Holocaust
Ndebele kingdom, **19th:** 1406
Ndongo, **17th:** 687
Ne irascaris (Byrd), **Ren:** 149
Ne Win, **Notor:** 773-774
Nebhepetra. *See* Montuhotep II
Nebuchadnezzar II, **Anc:** 335, 338, 453, 582-584
Nécessité de faire bon accueil aux femmes étrangères (Tristan), **19th:** 2298
Nécessités de la vie et les conséquences des rêves, Les (Éluard), **20th:** 1152
Necessity of Atheism, The, **19th:** 2092
Nechayannaya radost (Blok), **20th:** 394
Nechayev, Sergey Gennadiyevich, **19th:** 120, 1086
Necho I, **Anc:** 118, 710
Necho II, **Anc:** 387, 582
Neck of the Quakers Broken, The (Muggleton), **17th:** 667
Neckam, Alexander, **MA:** 750-753
Necker, Anne Louise Germaine. *See* Staël, Madame de
Necker, Jacques, **18th:** 726-729, 929
Necotawance, **17th:** 703
Necromancer, The (Ariosto), **Ren:** 57
Necropolises, **Anc:** 997
Nectanabo, **Anc:** 11
Neden, Hester. *See* Bateman, Hester
Neebe, Oscar, **19th:** 58
Need for Roots, The (Weil), **20th:** 4272
Needham, Hester. *See* Bateman, Hester
Néel, Louis-Eugène-Félix, **20th:**2926-2929
Néel temperature, **20th:** 2927
Néel walls, **20th:** 2928
Néel's spikes, **20th:** 2928
Nefertari, **Anc:** 585-587, 737, 902
Nefertiti, **Anc:** 27, 46, 587-590, 902
Neferure, **Anc:** 389
Negotiating with the Dead (Atwood), **20th:** 171
Nègres, Les. See *Blacks, The*
Negritude, **20th:** 710, 1212, 3703
Negro Factories Corporation, **20th:** 1418
Negro Silent Protest parade (1917), **20th:** 4201
Negro World (newspaper), **20th:** 1418
Negromante, Il. See *Necromancer, The*
Neguib, Muhammad, **20th:** 2914
Nehemiah, **Anc:** 339
Nehru, Jawaharlal, **20th:** 902, 1385, 2856, 2929-2933, 3099, 3136
Nehru, Swarup Kumari. *See* Pandit, Vijaya Lakshmi
Neilson, Ruth. *See* Ellis, Ruth
Neithhotep, **Anc:** 557
Nekrikoi dialogoi (Lucian), **Anc:** 514
Nekyia (Polygnotus), **Anc:** 679
Nelson, Baby Face, **Notor:** 281, 774-775
Nelson, George. *See* Nelson, Baby Face
Nelson, Glen. *See* Nelson, Leslie
Nelson, Lord Horatio, **19th:** 1656-1660; **Notor:** 261
Nelson, Leslie, **Notor:** 776-777
Nelson, Theodore. *See* Bundy, Ted
Nemerov, Howard, **20th:** 116
Nemirovich-Danchenko, Vladimir, **20th:** 3822
Nenemattanaw, **17th:** 702
Neo-Assyrian Empire, **Anc:** 753, 769, 894
Neoclassicism, **18th:** architecture and design, 6; art, 554, 1068, 1097; Chinese literature, 746; literature, 538; **19th:** 1172
Neo-Confucianism, **Ren:** 987; **17th:** 919, 973; **18th:** 287. *See also* Confucianism
Neo-Dadaism, **20th:** 3381
Neo-Daoism, **Anc:** 950, 955
Neo-Destour Party (Tunisia), **20th:** 457
Neo-idealism, **20th:** 1448
Neo-Impressionism, **19th:** 1801, 2075; **20th:** 951

Neolin, **18th:** 803
Neo-Malthusianism, **19th:** 1478
Neomycin, **20th:** 4182
Neon tubes, **20th:** 776
Neoorthodoxy, **20th:** 418
Neoplasticism, **20th:** 2788, 3092
Neoplatonism, **Anc:** 263, 668, 688; Augustine and, 142; Christianity and, 361; Hypatia and, 435; mathematics and, 607; religion and, 702; Valentinians and, 921; **MA:** 400, 415, 534, 864, 1029, 1105; **Ren:** 138, 232, 315, 332, 620, 724, 759, 906, 1007. *See also* Platonism
Neorealism, **20th:** 1232, 4166
Neosalvarsan, **20th:** 1117
Neoterics, **Anc:** 198
Neper, John. *See* Napier, John
Nephelai (Aristophanes), **Anc:** 91, 708
Nepos, Cornelius, **Anc:** 197
Nepos, Julius, **MA:** 782
Neptune, **Anc:** 178
Neptunium, discovery of, **20th:** 2301, 2533, 3685
Neptuno alegórico, El (Cruz), **17th:** 209
Nerchinsk, Treaty of (1689), **17th:** 449, 866; **18th:** 1113
Neri, Saint Philip, **Ren:** 717-720; **17th:** 721
Nernst, Walther Hermann, **20th:** 313, 2934-2936
Nero (Roman emperor), **Anc:** 23, 71, 104, 176, 219, 591-593, 685, 767, 944; **Notor:** 777-779
Nero Caesar Augustus, Tiberius Claudius. *See* Tiberius
Nero Claudius Caesar Augustus Germanicus. *See* Nero
Nero Germanicus, Tiberius Claudius Drusus. *See* Claudius I
Neruda, Pablo, **20th:** 2937-2940, 3170
Nerva, Marcus Cocceius, **Anc:** 904
Nerve impulses, transmission of, **20th:** 1090
Nervi, Pier Luigi, **20th:** 2940-2943
Nesbit, Evelyn, **Notor:** 1027
Ness, Eliot, **20th:** 643
Nest of Deheubarth. *See* Nest verch Rhys ap Tewdwr
Nest of Pembroke. *See* Nest verch Rhys ap Tewdwr
Nest verch Rhys ap Tewdwr, **MA:** 753- 755
Nesta. *See* Nest verch Rhys ap Tewdwr
Nestorianism, **Anc:** 864
Nestorians, **MA:** 402, 955, 1108; Mongols and, 627
Nestorius, **Anc:** 540, 864, 948
Netanyahu, Benjamin, **20th:** 113
Netherlands, **MA:** art, 947, 1092; painting, 1092; philosophy in, 1105; sculpture, 947; **Ren:** military, 913; painting, 135; Protestantism, 60, 526, 994; Spain and, 32; **18th:** art, 225, 1051; literature, 302; Peter the Great, 775; Sir Joshua Reynolds, 839; comte de Saxe, 881. *See also* United Provinces of the Netherlands; Geographical Index
Netherlands Wars of Independence. *See* Dutch Wars of Independence
Netjerikhet. *See* Zoser
Nettles, Bonnie, **Notor:** 28, 779-780
Neue Gedichte. See *New Poems*
Neue Gemeinschaft. *See* New Community
Neue Rheinische Zeitung, **19th:** 750
Neue Sachlichkeit, **20th:** 3092
Neue Wege der Ontologie. See *New Ways of Ontology*
Neuf-Brisach, **17th:** 947
Neumann, John von. *See* Von Neumann, John
Neun Bücher preussischer Geschichte (Ranke), **19th:** 1861
Neurology, **20th:** 1108
Neurosis and Human Growth (Horney), **20th:** 1884
Neurosurgery, **20th:** 899
Neurotic Constitution, The (Adler), **20th:** 33
Neurotic Personality of Our Time, The (Horney), **20th:** 1884
Neustrians, **MA:** 251
Neutrino hypothesis, **20th:** 3153
Neutrons, discovery of, **20th:** 714, 1636, 1783, 2034
Neva River, **18th:** 775
Neva River, Battle of (1240), **MA:** 52
Nevelson, Louise, **20th:** 2947-2951
Never-Ending Wrong, The (Porter), **20th:** 3312
Nevertheless (Moore), **20th:** 2823
Neville, John, **Ren:** 764
Neville, Richard. *See* Warwick, earl of
Neville's Cross, Battle of (1333), **MA:** 844
Neville's Cross, Battle of (1346), **MA:** 308
New Amsterdam, **17th:** 393, 518, 644, 892. *See also* New York City
New and Accurate Account of the Provinces of South Carolina and Georgia, A (Oglethorpe), **18th:** 743
New Arabian Nights, The (Stevenson), **19th:** 2176
New Art of Writing Plays, The (Lope de Vega), **17th:** 949
New Astronomy (Kepler), **17th:** 459
New Astronomy, The (Langley), **19th:** 1311
New Atlantis (Bacon), **Ren:** 74
New-born, The (La Tour), **17th:** 494
New Christians, **Ren:** 25, 606; **17th:** 960
New Class, The (Djilas), **20th:** 1012

New Colony, The (Pirandello), **20th:** 3261
"New Colossus, The" (Lazarus), **19th:** 1333
New Comedy, **Anc:** 93, 547, 663, 850
New Community, **20th:** 555
New Creations in Fruits and Flowers (Burbank), **19th:** 351
New Criticism, **20th:** 4239
New Deal, **20th:** 3398, 3511; constitutionality, 3880; opposition to, 3926; U.S. Supreme Court, 655
New Democracy Party (Greece), **20th:** 3107
New Echota, Treaty of (1835), **19th:** 1938
New England, **17th:** colonization, 768, 875, 878, 890; **18th:** 43, 60, 315, 512, 668, 671, 894
New England Anti-Slavery Society, **19th:** 800, 876
New England Confederation, **17th:** 568
New England Courant, The (newspaper), **18th:** 370
New England Female Medical College, **19th:** 2481
New England Hospital for Women and Children, **19th:** 2482
New England Nonresistance Society, **19th:** 877
New England Primer, The (Webster), **19th:** 2403
New England Woman Suffrage Association, **19th:** 800, 1098
New Englands Trials (Smith), **17th:** 864
New English School, **20th:** 4024
New Essays Concerning Human Understanding (Leibniz), **17th:** 516
New Experiments and Observations Touching Cold (Boyle), **17th:** 79
New Experiments Physio-Mechanicall, Touching the Spring of the Air and Its Effects (Boyle), **17th:** 79
New Fourth Army, **20th:** 2408
New France, **17th:** 141, 500, 603; **18th:** 693
New Guinea, **17th:** 906
New Hampshire (Frost), **20th:** 1350
New Hampshire Grants, **18th:** 35
New Harmony, Indiana, **19th:** 1722
New Haven Colony, **17th:** 219
New Haven's Case Stated (Davenport), **17th:** 219
New Héloïse, The (Rousseau), **18th:** 869
New Holland, **17th:** 907
New Industrial State, The (Galbraith), **20th:** 1376
New Inn, The (Jonson), **17th:** 443
New Jersey Woman Suffrage Association, **19th:** 2178
New Kids in the Neighborhood (Rockwell), **20th:** 3484
New Kingdom (Egypt), **Anc:** 26, 388, 441, 735, 886, 902
New Lanark, Scotland, **19th:** 1721
New Law of Righteousness, The (Winstanley), **17th:** 989
New Laws of Spain (1542-1543), **Ren:** 223, 538
New Liberalism, **20th:** 1844
New Life, The (Dante), **MA:** 240, 301
New Mexico, **19th:** 429
New Model Army, **17th:** 205, 262, 756
New Moon, The (Romberg and Hammerstein), **20th:** 1658
New Natural Philosophy of the Magnet, Magnetic Bodies, and the Great Terrestrial Magnet, A. See *De magnete*
New Negro Theatre, **20th:** 1929
New Netherland, **17th:** 643, 890
New Novel movement, **20th:** 3636
New Order program, **20th:** 3901
New Orleans, Battle of (1815), **19th:** 1189
New Philosophy of the Sublunary World (Gilbert), **Ren:** 382
New Poems (Rilke), **20th:** 3455
New Policies (China), **MA:** 1079
New Poor Law of 1834, **19th:** 457, 518, 667, 979, 1507
New Presidential Elite, The (Kirkpatrick), **20th:** 2168
New Republic, The (Mallock), **19th:** 1756
New Science, The (Planck), **20th:** 3284
New Science, The (Vico), **18th:** 1013
New Seeds of Contemplation (Merton), **20th:** 2714
New South Church (Boston), **19th:** 348
New Spain, **18th:** 228, 395
New Spirit, The (Ellis), **20th:** 1149
New Statesman (journal), **20th:** 4255
New Structure of the Muscles and Heart (Steno), **17th:** 881
New Sweden, **17th:** 706, 891; colonization of, 645
New System of Chemical Philosophy (Dalton), **19th:** 599
New System of Music Theory (Rameau), **18th:** 826
New Testament, **Anc:** 135, 445
New Theoretical and Practical Treatise on Navigation, A (Maury), **19th:** 1522
New View of Society, A (Owen), **19th:** 1721
New Voyage Round the World, A (Dampier), **17th:** 215
New Way of Making Fowre Parts in Counter-point, A (Campion), **17th:** 128
New Ways in Psychoanalysis (Horney), **20th:** 1884
New Ways of Ontology (Hartmann), **20th:** 1697
New World Symphony (Dvořák), **19th:** 713
New Yeers Gift for the Parliament and Armie, A (Winstanley), **17th:** 989
New York (Man Ray), **20th:** 2581

New York Central Railroad, **19th:** 2350
New York City, **17th:** 518, 892; colonization of, 644; **18th:** 529, 949, 1043. *See also* New Amsterdam
New York City Ballet, **20th:** 194, 254
New York City Opera, **20th:** 3744
New York Herald, **19th:** 190, 967
New York Infirmary for Women and Children, **19th:** 249, 2481
New York Philharmonic, **20th:** 339
New York Shakespeare Festival, **20th:** 40
New York Society for Ethical Culture, **19th:** 26
New York State, **18th:** 524
New York Times v. Sullivan (1964), **20th:** 379, 508
New York Times v. United States (1971), **20th:** 380, 582
New York Tribune, **19th:** 968
New York v. United States (1992), **20th:** 3408
New York Weekly Journal (newspaper), **18th:** 1116
New York World (newspaper), **19th:** 1842
New York Yankees, **20th:** 1001, 1435, 3573
New Zealand, **17th:** 907; **18th:** 271; **19th:** 981; British colonization of, 2379. *See also* Geographical Index
New Zealand Association, **19th:** 2379
New Zealand Company, **19th:** 708, 2379
Newbery, John, **18th:** 433, 730-732
Newbury, Donald, **Notor:** 901
Newcastle, duchess of, **17th:** 676-678
Newcomb, George, **Notor:** 257
Newcomb, Simon, **19th:** 1660-1663; on life on the Moon, 1661
Newcomen, Thomas, **17th:** 814; **18th:** 733-735, 1048
Newcomen steam engine, **18th:** 715, 734, 860, 1048, 1087
Newcomes, The (Thackeray), **19th:** 2258
Newfoundland, **Ren:** 379; **17th:** 120
Newgate Prison, **19th:** 839
Newman, John Henry, **19th:** 77, 1663-1666, 1846
Newport, Christopher, **17th:** 754
Newport, Treaty of (1648), **17th:** 941
News Corporation, **20th:** 2876
News from Nowhere (Morris), **19th:** 1608
News of a Kidnaping (García Márquez), **20th:** 1401
Newspaper Days (Mencken), **20th:** 2690
Newton, Benjamin, **19th:** 660
Newton, Florence, **Notor:** 781-782
Newton, Goody. *See* Newton, Florence
Newton, Huey, **Notor:** 782-784
Newton, Sir Isaac, **Anc:** 83; **17th:** 37, 49, 66, 79, 107, 271, 306, 319, 323, 349, 385, 390, 398, 459, 515, 547, 679-682, 734, 832, 970, 994; **18th:** 112, 220, 241, 632; **19th:** 1530
Newton's Discs (Kupka), **20th:** 2212
NeXT, **20th:** 2007
Nextstep, **20th:** 2007
Ney, Michel, **19th:** 261, 1667-1670
Nez Perce, **19th:** 1238
Nez Perce War (1877), **19th:** 1239
Nezahualcóyotl, **MA:** 559; **Ren:** 720-724
Nezib, Battle of (1839), **19th:** 1621
NFL. *See* National Football League
Ng, Charles, **Notor:** 602, 784-785
Ngengi, Kamau. *See* Kenyatta, Jomo
Nghe, Duong Dien. *See* Duong Dien Nghe
Nghe-Tinh Revolt (1930-1931), **20th:** 1835
Ngo Dinh Diem, **20th:** 228, 1836, 2951-2954, 4171; **Notor:** 786
Ngo Dinh Nhu, **Notor:** 786
Ngo Dinh Nhu, Madame. *See* Nhu, Madame
Ngo Quyen, **MA:** 756-757
Ngo Si Lien, **Ren:** 547
Ngunis, **19th:** 982
Nguyen Anh. *See* Gia Long
Nguyen Cao Ky, **20th:** 2954
Nguyen Chi Thanh, **20th:** 4171
Nguyen Hue, **18th:** 736-738; **19th:** 908, 1110
Nguyen Hue Offensive (1972), **20th:** 4171
Nguyen Phuc Anh. *See* Gia Long
Nguyen Phuc Cenh, **19th:** 908
Nguyen Phuc Dem. *See* Minh Mang
Nguyen Phuoc Hoang Nham. *See* Tu Duc
Nguyen That Thanh. *See* Ho Chi Minh
Nguyen Tri Phuong, **19th:** 2310
Nguyen Van Thieu, **20th:** 2954-2956
Nguyen Vinh Thuy. *See* Bao Dai
Nguyen Vuong. *See* Gia Long
Nguza Karl-I-Bond, **20th:** 2774
Nhu, Madame, **Notor:** 786-787
Nhuon Kang. *See* Ta Mok
Ní Mháille, Gráinne. *See* O'Malley, Grace
Ni Ni Roku incident (1936), **20th:** 1819
Niagara Bridge, **19th:** 1929
Niagara Movement, **20th:** 1048
Nian rebellion (1865-1868), **19th:** 2484
Nicaea, Council of (325), **Anc:** 133, 331, 364, 392, 444, 540, 797, 912; **MA:** 292
Nicaea, Council of (787), **MA:** 550, 590
Nicaragua. *See* Geographical Index

Niccoli, Niccolò, **MA:** 850
Nicene Creed, **Anc:** 44, 242, 363, 392, 854, 869; Athanasius and, 133
Nicephorus I, **MA:** 467, 551
Nichiren, **MA:** 758-760
Nicholas I the Great (c. 819-867; pope), **MA:** 190, 764-767, 880
Nicholas I (1796-1855; czar of Russia), **19th:** 48, 819, 1670-1673; **Notor:** 788-789
Nicholas II (c. 980-1061; pope), **MA:** 706
Nicholas II (1868-1918; czar of Russia), **19th:** 1863, 2207; **20th:** 566, 2111; **Notor:** 845, 886, 1040, 1126, 1138
Nicholas III (c. 1225-1280; pope), **MA:** 906
Nicholas IV (1227-1292; pope), **MA:** 187, 906
Nicholas V (1397-1455; pope), **MA:** 85, 768-771; **Ren:** 18, 134
Nicholas Nickleby (Dickens), **19th:** 655
Nicholas of Autrecourt, **MA:** 215, 761- 764
Nicholas of Cusa, **Ren:** 724-728
Nichols, Terry, **Notor:** 591, 682, 790- 791
Nichols, William R., **19th:** 1899
Nicholson, Ben, **20th:** 2956-2959
Nicholson, Francis, **17th:** 518
Nicias, **Notor:** 11
Nicklaus, Jack, **20th:** 2959-2961
Nicodemo el fariseo (Unamuno), **20th:** 4129
Nicolaism, **MA:** 644
Nicolaus de Autricuria. *See* Nicholas of Autrecourt
Nicolay, John, **19th:** 1055
Nicole, Pierre, **17th:** 774
Nicolet, Jean, **17th:** 433
Nicollet, Joseph Nicolas, **19th:** 831
Nicolls, Richard, **17th:** 892
Nicomède (Corneille), **17th:** 195
Nicomedes III, **Anc:** 895
Nicomedes IV, **Anc:** 895
Nicopolis, Battle of (1396), **MA:** 494
Nicuesa, Diego de, **Ren:** 76
Nidal, Abu. *See* Abu Nidal
Niebelungen, Die (film), **20th:** 2254
Niebuhr, Barthold Georg, **19th:** 1673-1676
Niebuhr, Reinhold, **20th:** 2962-2964
Nielsen, Carl, **20th:** 2965-2967
Nieman, Fred C. *See* Czolgosz, Leon
Niemeyer, Oscar, **20th:** 2967-2970
Niemöller, Martin, **20th:** 2971-2974
Nien rebellions, **19th:** 1364
Niépce, Nicéphore, **19th:** 590, 1676-1680
Nietzsche, Friedrich, **19th:** 1680-1684; **Notor:** 367, 613, 769
Nietzsche, Therese Elisabeth Alexandra. *See* Förster-Nietzsche, Elisabeth
Niewiadomski, Eligiusz, **Notor:** 792- 793
Nigantha Nātaputra. *See* Vardhamāna
Niger River exploration, **18th:** 765
Nigeria, **Ren:** 37; **19th:** 940; **20th:** as British colony, 2466; independence of, 181. *See also* Geographical Index.
Night (Michelangelo), **Ren:** 683
Night (Wiesel), **20th:** 4324
Night After Night (film), **20th:** 4298
Night and Day (film), **20th:** 3309
Night in Acadie, A (Chopin), **19th:** 492
Night of the Iguana, The (Williams), **20th:** 921
Night on Bare Mountain (Mussorgsky), **19th:** 1627
Night on the El Train (Hopper), **20th:** 1878
Night Rider (Warren), **20th:** 4237
Night Watch, The (Rembrandt), **17th:** 787
Nighthawks (Hopper), **20th:** 1878
Nightingale, Florence, **19th:** 1684-1688; Australia, 1740
Nightingale Training School for Nurses, **19th:** 1687
Nights of Cabiria, The (film), **20th:** 1232
Nights with Uncle Remus (Harris), **19th:** 1036
Nightwood (Barnes), **20th:** 241
Nihilism, **19th:** 1295
Nihon shoki, **Anc:** 462, 465; **MA:** 623, 940, 974
Nihongi. See *Nihon shoki*
Nijinska, Bronisława, **20th:** 987
Nijinsky, Vaslav, **20th:** 985, 2647, 2974-2977
Nijmegen, Treaty of (1678), **17th:** 426, 507, 560, 979
Nijō, **MA:** 771-774
Nika Riots (532), **MA:** 600, 1010
Nikolaev, Leonid, **Notor:** 1112
Nikolayev, Andrian G., **20th:** 3979
Nikon, **17th:** 13, 27, 683-686
Nile, Battle of the (1798), **19th:** 1658
Nile River, **19th:** 2124
Nils Holgerssons underbara resa genom Sverige. See *Wonderful Adventures of Nils, The*
Nimitz, Chester W., **20th:** 1648, 2494, 2977-2980
Ninan Cuyochi, **Ren:** 469
9/11. *See* September 11, 2001, attacks on U.S.
Nine Hundred Days (1941-1944), **20th:** 2599
Nine Songs, The. See *Jiu ge*
Nine to Five (film), **20th:** 3129
Nine Years' War (1688-1697). *See* Augsburg, War of the League of
Nineteen Eighty-Four (Orwell), **20th:** 3083
1960 Masks, **20th:** 3804
1933 (Nicholson), **20th:** 2957

Nineteenth Amendment (U.S. Constitution), **20th:** 703, 3146
Nineteenth Dynasty (Egypt), **Anc:** 585, 735
Ninety-five Poems (Cummings), **20th:** 881
Ninety-five Theses, **Ren:** 582
Ninety-Three (Hugo), **19th:** 1149
Nineveh, **Anc:** architecture, 769; library at, 119
Nineveh, Battle of (627), **MA:** 507
Ninfale d'Ameto, Il (Boccaccio), **MA:** 170
Ningirsu, **Anc:** 366
Ning-tsung. *See* Ningzong
Ningzong, **MA:** 677
Ninjō (human feeling), **18th:** 244
Ninotchka (film), **20th:** 1393
Ninsun, **Anc:** 914
Ninth Symphony (Bruckner), **19th:** 331
Nintoku, **Anc:** 594
Ninurta, **Anc:** 122
Ninus, **Anc:** 745
Nippon eitaigura. See *Japanese Family Storehouse, The*
Nishida, Kitarō, 20th: 2981-2984
Nishiki-e (multicolor prints), **18th:** 958
Nisibis, Peace of (298 B.C.E.), **Anc:** 775
Nissim ben Jacob ben Nissim ibn Shahim, **MA:** 533
Nitocris, **Anc:** 710
Nixon, Edward, **20th:** 12
Nixon, Richard M., 20th: 1940, 2984-2988; Bob Dole, 1016; Helen Gahagan Douglas, 1028; Gerald R. Ford, 1272, 1276; Barbara Jordan, 2047; John F. Kennedy, 2100; presidential pardon of, 1276; Vietnam War, 1687, 2954; Watergate affair, 595; **Notor:** 140, 162, 169, 226, 320, 442-443, 476, 480, 490, 500, 529, 643, 672, 734, 737, 793-795, 966
Niyata, **Anc:** 356
Niyazi Bey, **20th:** 1158
Niyazov, Saparmurat, Notor: 796-797
Niza, Marcos de, **Ren:** 154, 245
Niẓām al-Mulk, MA: 415, 774-777, 795
Niẓām-ud-Dīn Awliyā, Shaykh, **MA:** 41
Nizāmī ʿArūzī, **MA:** 796
Nizamiyas. *See* Madrasas
Njegoš (Djilas), **20th:** 1013
Njinga, 17th: 687-689
Nkomati Accord (1984), **20th:** 2516
Nkomo, Joshua, **20th:** 2858; **Notor:** 761
Nkrumah, Kwame, 20th: 2988-2992, 4055
Nkuwa, Nzinga. *See* Nzinga Nkuwa
No and Yes (Eddy), **19th:** 725
No Cross, No Crown (Penn), **17th:** 725
No Direction Home (film), **20th:** 1073
Nō drama, **MA:** 1153
No Exit (Sartre), **20th:** 3639
No Longer at Ease (Achebe), **20th:** 14
No Man of Her Own (film), **20th:** 1369
No Way Out (film), **20th:** 3296
Noa Noa (Gauguin), **19th:** 881
Noah, Mordecai, **19th:** 189
Nobel, Alfred, 19th: 1689-1691, 2205; **Notor:** 193
Nobel Prizes, **19th:** 1691
Nobile, Umberto, **20th:** 85
Nobility, **18th:** French, 917; Russian, 778
Noble, R. G., **20th:** 1236
Nobleman, The (Tourneur), **17th:** 929
Nobody Knows My Name (Baldwin), **20th:** 202
Nobunaga, Oda. *See* Oda Nobunaga
Noces corinthiennes, Les (France), **19th:** 815
Noche del sábado, La. See *Saturday Night*
Noche Triste, La, **Ren:** 35, 254
Noches en los jardines de España (Falla), **20th:** 1207
Noctes Atticae (Gellius), **Anc:** 939
Nocturne (Miró), **20th:** 2761
Nocturnes (Debussy), **20th:** 938
Nodier, Charles, **19th:** 696
Noe, Joey, **Notor:** 938
Nofretete. *See* Nefertiti
Nōgaku koten: Zeami jūrokubushū. See "Zeami's Sixteen Treatises"
Nogaret de La Valette, **17th:** 598
Nogi, Marusuke, **Notor:** 473
Noire et Blanche (Man Ray), **20th:** 2581
Nolan, Sydney, **Notor:** 564
Noland, John Thomas. *See* Diamond, Legs
Noli me tangere (Fontana), **Ren:** 338
Nomenclature chimique (Lavoisier), **18th:** 219
Nominalism, **Anc:** 88, 688; **MA:** 215, 761
Nomoi (Plato), **Anc:** 660
Non Abbiamo Bisogno (Pius XI), **20th:** 3276
Nonconformists, **17th:** 34, 54, 100, 122, 386, 414
Nonconformity, Presbyterian, **Ren:** 404, 762
Noncontradiction, **MA:** 761
Non-Intercourse Act of 1809, **19th:** 2112
Nonne sanglante, La (Gounod), **19th:** 953
Nonomura Sōtatsu. *See* Sōtatsu
Nonrecognition Doctrine of 1932, **20th:** 3870
Nonsense of Common Sense, The (Montagu), **18th:** 688
Nonviolent resistance, **20th:** 1389, 2149
Noonan, Fred, **20th:** 1077
Nootka Sound Convention (1790), **18th:** 790, 1007
Nora (Fowler), **19th:** 813
Norcross, John, **Notor:** 776
Norcross, Richard, **Notor:** 776

Nord, Le. *See* Colbert, Jean-Baptiste
Nordau, Max, **20th:** 2992-2995
Nördlingen, Battle of (1634), **17th:** 705
Nordraak, Rikard, **19th:** 985
Norfolk, duke of, **Ren:** 113, 200, 271, 311, 368
Noriega, Luis Carlos Hurtado, **Notor:** 797
Noriega, Manuel, **20th:** 3322; **Notor:** 797-799
Noriyori, Minamoto. *See* Minamoto Noriyori
Norman, Geraldine, **Notor:** 560
Norman, Jessye, **20th:** 2995-2999
Norman Conquest (1066), **MA:** 339, 458, 1117
Norman Controversy, **MA:** 914
Norman Rockwell Art Museum, **20th:** 3485
Normand, Mabel, **Notor:** 32
Normandy Invasion (1944), **20th:** 3504
Normanist Russia, **18th:** 614
Normans, **MA:** 176, 338, 406, 902; kings of England, 482, 1119; in Africa, 8; feudalism, 1119
Norris, Sir John, **Notor:** 301
Norske folkeviser (Grieg), **19th:** 986
North, Frederick (Lord North), **18th:** 174, 364, 409, 738-741, 789
North Africa, **MA:** Muslim invasion of, 604; Muslims, 478
North African campaign (1940-1943), **20th:** 3503
North America, **18th:** coast, 272; Spanish settlement, 228
North American Free Trade Agreement (1994), **20th:** 2867, 3210
North Atlantic Treaty Organization, **20th:** 19, 359
North Briton controversy, **18th:** 1083
North by Northwest (film), **20th:** 1572, 1827
North Country Sketches (Delius), **20th:** 955
North Korea, **20th:** establishment of, 2139. *See also* Korea; Geographical Index under Korea
North of Boston (Frost), **20th:** 1349
North of the Danube (Caldwell and Bourke-White), **20th:** 462
North Pacific exploration, **18th:** James Cook, 271; George Vancouver, 1006
North Pole, **20th:** 606, 3179
North Star, The (newspaper), **19th:** 685
North to the Orient (Lindbergh), **20th:** 2391
North Vietnam, **20th:** establishment of, 229, 2951. *See also* Geographical Index under Vietnam
North West Company, **18th:** 630
North Wind (Moore), **20th:** 2819
Northampton, Treaty of (1328), **MA:** 204
Northanger Abbey (Austen), **19th:** 96
Northcliffe, Lord. *See* Harmsworth, Alfred
Northern and Southern Courts, **MA:** 115
Northern California Costal Wild Heritage Wilderness Act of 2006, **20th:** 1230
Northern Confederate Indians (Canada), **18th:** 160
Northern Earls, Rebellion of the (1569), **Ren:** 629
Northern Expedition (1926-1927), **20th:** 747, 2381, 4462, 4466
Northern Ireland, **20th:** violence in, 1740. *See also* Geographical Index under Ireland and Northern Ireland
Northern Pacific Railroad, **19th:** 545, 567, 583, 1102, 1601
Northern Peoples Congress, **20th:** 181
Northern Securities Company, **19th:** 1601
Northern War, First (1655-1660), **17th:** 12, 154, 290, 428, 527
Northumberland, duke of. *See* Dudley, John
Northumbria, **MA:** 509; fall of, 354
Northward Ho! (Webster and Dekker), **17th:** 977
Northwest campaign (Clark), **18th:** 253
Northwest Company, **19th:** 2271
Northwest Passage, **Ren:** 276, 279, 353, 522; **17th:** 391; **18th:** 108, 271, 975, 1007; **19th:** 825; **20th:** navigation of, 83
Northwest Rebellion. *See* Riel Rebellion, Second (1885)
Northwest Territory, **18th:** 1056; George Rogers Clark, 253-256; Sir Alexander Mackenzie, 630
Northwood (Hale), **19th:** 1012
Norway, **MA:** kings, 789; **20th:** independence of, 2909. *See also* Geographical Index
Norwegian North Polar Expedition, The (Nansen, ed.), **20th:** 2909
Nostradamus, **Ren:** 728-731; **Notor:** 799-801
Nostromo (Conrad), **20th:** 826
Not Without Laughter (Hughes), **20th:** 1928
Notable History Containing Four Voyages Made by Certain French Captains Unto Florida, A (Hakluyt), **Ren:** 419
Note-Books of Samuel Butler, The (Butler), **19th:** 375
Notebooks (Weil), **20th:** 4271
Notebooks of André Walter, The (Gide), **20th:** 1478
Notebooks of Malte Laurids Brigge, The (Rilke), **20th:** 3455
Notes from the Field (Taylor and Lange), **20th:** 2261

Notes from the Underground (Dostoevski), **19th:** 678
Notes of a Native Son (Baldwin), **20th:** 202
Notes of Canada West (Cary), **19th:** 431
Notes on a Visit to Some of the Prisons in Scotland and the North of England in Company with Elizabeth Fry (Gurney), **19th:** 840
Notes on Hospitals (Nightingale), **19th:** 1687
Notes on Matters Affecting the Health, Efficiency, and Hospital Administration of the British Army (Nightingale), **19th:** 1687
Notes on Nursing (Nightingale), **19th:** 1686-1687
Notes on Sport and Travel (Kingsley), **19th:** 1283
Notes on the Semi-Civilized Nations of Mexico, Yucatan, and Central America (Gallatin), **19th:** 856
Noticia de un secuestro. See *News of a Kidnaping*
Notions of the Americans (Cooper), **19th:** 554
Notizia d'opere di disegno (Michiel), **Ren:** 384
Notorious (film), **20th:** 322, 1827
Notradame, Michel de. *See* Nostradamus
Nôtre, André Le. *See* Le Nôtre, André
Notre-Dame de Paris. See *Hunchback of Notre-Dame, The*
Notre Dame de Paris (cathedral), **MA:** 824; **18th:** 134
Nôtre-Dame de Recouvrance, **17th:** 596
Notre-Dame des Fleurs. See *Our Lady of the Flowers*
Notre Dame University, football, **20th:** 3481
Notredame, Michel de. *See* Nostradamus
Notti di Cabiria, Le. See *Nights of Cabiria, The*
Nottingham, second earl of, **17th:** 508
Nourritures terrestres, Les. See *Fruits of the Earth*
Nous, **Anc:** 918
Nouveau Christianisme (Saint-Simon), **19th:** 1976
Nouveau Monde amoureux, La (Fourier), **19th:** 806
Nouveau Monde industriel et sociétaire, Le (Fourier), **19th:** 805
Nouveau Système de musique théorique. See *New System of Music Theory*
Nouveau traité des hemmoragies de l'uterus (Boivin), **19th:** 266
Nouveaux essais sur l'entendement humain. See *New Essays Concerning Human Understanding*
Nouvelle continuation des amours (Ronsard), **Ren:** 838
Nouvelle Revue française, La (journal), **20th:** 1478
Nouvelles, **17th:** 477, 829
Nouvelles Catholiques, **17th:** 265
Nouvelles françaises, Les (Segrais), **17th:** 477
Nouvelles Théories sur l'art moderne, sur l'art sacré, 1914-1921 (Denis), **20th:** 973
Nov. See *Virgin Soil*
Nova musculorum et cordis fabrica. See *New Structure of the Muscles and Heart*
Novatianism, **Anc:** 796
Novelas ejemplares. See *Exemplary Novels*
Novelists, **18th:** Fanny Burney, 180- 183; Daniel Defoe, 298-301; Aagje Deken, 301-303; Henry Fielding, 346-350; Johann Wolfgang von Goethe, 428- 432; Ignacy Krasicki, 567-569; Sophie von La Roche, 577-579; Charlotte Lennox, 594-596; Alain-René Lesage, 596-598; Ann Radcliffe, 823-825; Samuel Richardson, 841-843; Anna Seward, 897-899; Madame de Staël, 929-932; Betje Wolff, 301-303
Novels, **17th:** England, 42, 102; France, 266, 314, 477, 662, 829; Germany, 325; Japan, 403; Spain, 317, 770, 913, 949; **19th:** adventure, 1538; Australia, 1758; Austria, 2206; Brazil, 1450; Denmark, 61; England, 96, 284, 310, 655, 1006, 1030, 2258, 2300; France, 696, 786, 816, 1148, 1988, 2162, 2298, 2356, 2489; Germany, 84, 1290; Ireland, 729; Italy, 1496; mystery, 688; New Zealand, 2372; Peru, 1513; popular, 52, 2472; realistic, 741; romantic, 1331; Russia, 678, 1354, 1850, 2285, 2320; science fiction, 2356; Scotland, 2048, 2174; South Africa, 2023; Switzerland, 1783; United States, 483, 491, 553, 1051, 1207, 1227, 1417, 2185; utopian, 374
Novels and Tales of Henry James, The (James), **19th:** 1209
Novgorod, **MA:** 52; **Ren:** annexation to Moscow, 488; **17th:** uprising in (1650), 684
Novotný, Antonín, **20th:** 1044
Novum organum (Bacon), **Ren:** 73
Novus avianus (Neckam), **MA:** 750
Novus Esopus (Neckam), **MA:** 750
Novykh, Grigori Yefimovich. *See* Rasputin, Grigori Yefimovich
NOW. *See* National Organization for Women
Now and Then (Warren), **20th:** 4238
Now Is the Time to Open Your Heart (Walker), **20th:** 4198
Now We Are Six (Milne), **20th:** 2754
Noy, William, **17th:** 345

Noyes, Arthur A., **20th:** 3155
Nozarashi kikō. See *Records of a Weather-Exposed Skeleton, The*
Nozawa Bonchō, **17th:** 616
Nozick, Robert, **20th:** 2999-3001, 3392
Nozze di Figaro, Le (Mozart), **18th:** 712
Nu jie (Ban Gu), **Anc:** 149
Nu jie (Ban Zhao), **Anc:** 153
Nü xiao jing, **Anc:** 153
Nubia, **Anc:** 46, 48, 570, 655, 772
Nuclear chemistry, **20th:** 2301
Nuclear energy, **20th:** fission, 1237, 1637, 1781, 2034, 2681; fusion, 2079; policies, 716, 822, 3066, 3356, 3686; production of, 1236-1237, 1781; Soviet Union, 2215; submarines, 3445
Nuclear medicine, **20th:** 2301, 3687
Nuclear Test Ban Treaty (1963), **20th:** 2130, 2216, 3686
Nuclear weapons, **20th:** 3647, 3969
Nude Descending a Staircase, No. 2 (Duchamp), **20th:** 1051
Nude with Violin (Coward), **20th:** 856
Nueva comedia, **17th:** 914
Nuggets and Dust Panned in California (Bierce), **19th:** 229
Nūh ibn Manṣūr, **MA:** 123
Nuit, La. See *Night* (Wiesel)
Nuit américaine, La. See *Day for Night*
Nullification Controversy, **19th:** 24, 393, 504, 2337, 2400
Numantine Wars, **Anc:** 358
Numantinus, Publius Cornelius Scipio Aemilianus Africanus. *See* Scipio Aemilianus
Number 5 (Pollock), **20th:** 3303
Number theory, **18th:** 574
Numbers, **Anc:** and music, 98; polygonal, 288
Numeral systems, **MA:** 648
Numerology, **Anc:** Chinese, 464; Greek, 424
Numidia, **Anc:** Carthage and, 542, 813; Rome and, 533, 743, 813
Numidians, **Anc:** 542
Numisianos, **Anc:** 348
Nuns, Buddhist, **Anc:** 899
Nuova colonia, La. See *New Colony, The*
Nupe, **19th:** 941
Nūr Jahān, **17th:** 411, 842
Nureddin, **MA:** 918
Nuremberg trials, **20th:** 4329
Nureyev, Rudolf, **20th:** 1269, 3001-3004
Nurhaci, **17th:** 1, 234, 848, 911
Nurse, Rebecca, **17th:** 689-691
Nursery, The (Mussorgsky), **19th:** 1628
Nursing, **19th:** 1685
Nus dans la forêt, Les (Léger), **20th:** 2335
Nushen. See *Selected Poems from "The Goddesses"*
Nussbaum, Martha, **20th:** 3392
Nutcracker, The (Tchaikovsky), **19th:** 2235; **20th:** 195
Nutiok, **Ren:** 522
Nuttall, John Mitchell, **20th:** 1441
Nuwar, Ali Abu, **20th:** 1952
NUWSS. *See* National Union of Women's Suffrage Societies
Nyasaland. *See* Malawi
Nye, Philip, **17th:** 198
Nye mennesker. See *People of the Polar North, The*
Nyerere, Julius, **20th:** 81, 2517, 2883, 3004-3007, 3012
Nymph of Fontainebleau (Cellini), **Ren:** 204
Nymphes des bois (Josquin), **Ren:** 517
Nymphes des bois (Molinet), **Ren:** 517
Nystadt, Treaty of (1721), **18th:** 233, 776
Nyström, Gustaf, **20th:** 1
Nzinga. *See* Njinga
Nzinga Mbemba. *See* Afonso I (c. 1455-1543; king of Kongo)
Nzinga Nkuwa, **Ren:** 9

O

O Pioneers! (Cather), **20th:** 698
Ō Sadaharu. *See* Oh, Sadaharu
O. T. (Andersen), **19th:** 61
O the Chimneys (Sachs), **20th:** 3585
Oak and Ivy (Dunbar), **19th:** 702
Oakley, Annie, **19th:** 525, 1692-1695
Oasis, The (McCarthy), **20th:** 2501
Oates, Titus, **17th:** 138, 149, 692-695, 816, 839; **Notor:** 802-803
Oath of the Horatii, The (David), **19th:** 608
Oath of the Tennis Court (1789), **18th:** 619
Oath of the Tennis Court, The (David), **19th:** 609
OAU. *See* Organization of African Unity
O'Banion, Dion, **20th:** 642; **Notor:** 751, 803-805, 1096
Obasanjo, Olusegun, **Notor:** 1022
Obedience of a Christian Man, and How Christian Rulers Ought to Govern, The (Tyndale), **Ren:** 951
Oberon (Weber), **19th:** 2397
Oberon, Merle, **20th:** 143, 3040
Oberth, Hermann, **20th:** 1508, 3008-3011, 4096
Oberto, conte di San Bonifacio (Verdi), **19th:** 2351
Obertyn, Battle of (1531), **Ren:** 886
Object in Five Planes (Peace) (Calder), **20th:** 610
Object poétique (Miró), **20th:** 2761
Object to Be Destroyed (Man Ray), **20th:** 2581
Objections of the Hon. George Mason to the Proposed Federal Constitution, The (Mason), **18th:** 665
Objections to the Enfranchisement of Women Considered (Bodichon), **19th:** 264
Objectivism, **20th:** 1581, 3368

"Objects of Human Knowledge" (Berkeley), **18th:** 113
Oblako v shtanakh. See *Cloud in Pants, A*
Oblation, **MA:** 871
Obligationenrecht, Das (Savigny), **19th:** 2004
Oblivion, Act of (1652), **17th:** 54
Oblivion of Genius and Other Original Poems, The (Hale), **19th:** 1012
Oboi, **17th:** 448
Obote, Milton, **20th:** 80, 2883, 3011-3013; **Notor:** 20
Obregón, Álvaro, **20th:** 615, 3013-3017, 4161, 4449
O'Brien, Charles, **Notor:** 482
O'Brien, Kitty, **Notor:** 1005
O'Brien, Larry, **Notor:** 443
Observationes Medicae (Sydenham), **17th:** 902
Observations (Moore), **20th:** 2822
Observations de plusieurs singularitez et choses memorables trouvées en Grèce, Asie, Judée, Egypte, Arabie, et autres pays étranges (Belon), **Ren:** 102
Observations diverses (Bourgeois), **17th:** 74
Observations in the Art of English Poesie (Campion), **17th:** 128
Observations on the Natural History of the Cuckoo (Jenner), **18th:** 533
Observations on the New Constitution, and on the Federal and State Conventions (Warren), **18th:** 1042
Observations on the Visiting, Superintendence, and Government, of Female Prisoners (Fry), **19th:** 840
Observations upon Experimental Philosophy (Newcastle), **17th:** 677
Observations upon the Cities of London and Rome (Petty), **17th:** 735
Obwandiyag. *See* Pontiac
Occam, William of. *See* Ockham, William of
Occasional Conformity Bill (1711), **18th:** 47
Occasioni, Le (Montale), **20th:** 2802
Occidental Literary Club, **20th:** 933
Occom, Samson, **18th:** 1071
Occultism, **Ren:** 278, 730, 757, 841
Occultists. *See* Category Index under Witches and Occultists
Oceanography, **19th:** 1522; **20th:** 850, 3242
Ocherki I rasskazy. See *Selected Short Stories*
Ochino, Bernardino, **Ren:** 235
Ocho comedias y ocho entremeses nuevos (Cervantes), **Ren:** 209
Ockeghem, Jean d', **Ren:** 516
Ockham, William of, **MA:** 215, 761, 778-781
Ockham's Theory of Propositions (Ockham), **MA:** 778
Ockham's Theory of Terms (Ockham), **MA:** 778
Ocomorenia, Joaquín. *See* Murieta, Joaquín
O'Connell, Daniel, **19th:** 642, 1534, 1695-1699, 1769
O'Connor, Daniel Basil, **20th:** 3613
O'Connor, Flannery, **20th:** 3017-3020
O'Connor, Rory, **20th:** 844
O'Connor, Sandra Day, **20th:** 3020-3024, 3406
O'Connor, Thomas Power, **20th:** 3024-3026
O'Connor, William, **19th:** 2426
Octavia, **Anc:** 71, 75, 561, 591, 685
Octavian. *See* Augustus
Octavius, Gnaeus, **Anc:** 832
Octavius, Marcus, **Anc:** 358
Octha. *See* Oisc
Octo quaestiones de potestate papae (Ockham), **MA:** 780
October (film), **20th:** 1130
October Crisis (1970), **20th:** 4077
Oda Nobuhide, **17th:** 915
Oda Nobunaga, **Ren:** 451, 459, 732-735, 736, 737, 738, 943; **17th:** 915
Odaenathus, Septimus, **Anc:** 986
Odalisque with the Slave (Ingres), **19th:** 1173
Odani no Kata. *See* Oichi
Odas elementales. See *Elemental Odes, The*
Ode (Wordsworth), **19th:** 2463
"Ode to Aphrodite" (Sappho), **Anc:** 751
Ode to Charles Fourier (Breton), **20th:** 512
Ode to Napoleon (Schoenberg), **20th:** 3666
Odes. See *Epinikia*
Odes (Horace), **Anc:** 432, 528, 604
Odes (Ronsard), **Ren:** 837
Odes et ballades (Hugo), **19th:** 1147
Odescalchi, Benedetto. *See* Innocent XI
Odets, Clifford, **20th:** 863
Odin den' Ivana Denisovicha. See *One Day in the Life of Ivan Denisovich*
Odo of Lagery. *See* Urban II
Odoacer, **MA:** 782-785, 1012
Odoms, Barbara. *See* Shakur, Assata Olugbala
O'Donovan Rossa, Jeremiah, **Notor:** 509
Odria, Manuel A., **20th:** 1718
Odysseus, **Anc:** 428
Odyssey (Homer), **Anc:** 315, 427, 432, 610, 689
Odyssey, The (Kazantzakis), **20th:** 2088
Oecolampadius, Johannes, **Ren:** 861
Oedipus (Aeschylus), **Anc:** 9
Oedipus (Ernst), **20th:** 1178
Oedipus (Voltaire), **18th:** 1026
Oedipus at Colonus. See *Oidipous epi Kolōnōi*

Oedipus complex, **20th:** 1324
Oedipus in Athens (Mussorgsky), **19th:** 1627
Oedipus Rex (Ernst), **20th:** 1177
Oedipus Rex (Stravinsky), **20th:** 3890
Oedipus Solving the Riddle of the Sphinx (Ingres), **19th:** 1173
Oedipus Tyrannus (Shelley), **19th:** 2095
Oeiras, count of. *See* Pombal, marquês de
Oenomaus, **Anc:** 819
Oeung Choeun. *See* Ta Mok
Œuvres diverses (Boileau-Despréaux), **17th:** 63
Of Being and the One (Pico della Mirandola), **Ren:** 784
Of Dramatic Poesie (Dryden), **17th:** 241
Of Education (Milton), **17th:** 640
Of Feavours (Willis), **17th:** 986
Of Fermentation (Willis), **17th:** 986
Of Flies, Mice, and Men (Jacob), **20th:** 1984
Of Flight and Life (Lindbergh), **20th:** 2394
Of Grammatology (Derrida), **20th:** 975
Of Human Freedom (Schelling), **19th:** 2011
Of Learned Ignorance (Nicholas of Cusa), **Ren:** 725, 726
Of Men and Women (Buck), **20th:** 558
Of Molecules and Men (Crick), **20th:** 867
Of Myself (Cowley), **17th:** 200
Of Painting (Alberti), **Ren:** 18, 602
"Of Poets and Poesie" (Drayton), **17th:** 238
Of Reformation Touching Church Discipline in England (Milton), **17th:** 640
Of Sculpture (Alberti), **Ren:** 18
Of Seven Manners of Holy Loving (Beatrice of Nazareth), **MA:** 144
Of the Law of Nature and Nations (Pufendorf), **17th:** 760
Of the Lawes of Ecclesiasticall Politie (Hooker), **Ren:** 457, 458
"Of the Mixed Tree of Evil and Good" (Böhme), **17th:** 61
Of the Progress of the Soule (Donne), **17th:** 232
Of the Vocation of Our Age for Legislation and Jurisprudence (Savigny), **19th:** 2003
Of Thee I Sing (Gershwin and Gershwin), **20th:** 1459, 1463
Of Time and the River (Wolfe), **20th:** 4385
Offa, **MA:** 50, 244, 353
Offenbach, Jacques, **19th:** 640, 1699-1702
Official Languages Act of 1969, **20th:** 4077
Offnes Antwortschreiben an das Central-Comité zur Berufung eines Allgemeinen Deutschen Arbeitercongresses zu Leipzig. See *Lassalle's Open Letter to the National Labor Association of Germany*
Offrandes (Varèse), **20th:** 4143
O'Flaherty, Donal, **Ren:** 743; **Notor:** 805
O'Flaherty, Katherine. *See* Chopin, Kate
Ogaryov, Nikolay, **19th:** 1085
Ogata Kenzan, **17th:** 377, 695, 868
Ogata Kōrin, **17th:** 377, 695-697, 868
Ogatai, **MA:** 227, 404, 626, 954; **Notor:** 401
Ogawa, Hideki. *See* Yukawa, Hideki
Ogdensburg Agreement (1940), **20th:** 2157
Oghul Qaimish, **MA:** 955
Ogilby, John, **17th:** 846
Ōgimachi, **Ren:** 735-737
Oglala. *See* Sioux peoples
Ogle, Chaloner, **Notor:** 906
Oglethorpe, James Edward, **18th:** 742-746, 1062, 1064
Ognibene de Adam. *See* Salimbene
Ogre of Bereng. *See* Bokassa, Jean-Bédel
Ogyū Sorai, **18th:** 504, 746-748
Oh, Sadaharu, **20th:** 3027-3030
Oh, the Places You'll Go! (Seuss), **20th:** 3712
Ohain, Hans Pabst von, **20th:** 4319
O'Hara, Maureen, **20th:** 4251
O'Higgins, Bernardo, **19th:** 1703-1705
Ohio Company, **18th:** 253
Ohio Country, **18th:** 160, 611
Ohnesorg, Benno, **Notor:** 47
Ohosazaki. *See* Nintoku
Oi no kobumi. See *Records of a Travel-Worn Satchel, The*
Oichi, **Ren:** 737-739
Oidipous epi Kolōnōi (Sophocles), **Anc:** 809
Oidipous tyrannos (Sophocles), **Anc:** 9, 810
Oil! (Sinclair), **20th:** 3752
Oil embargo (1973), **20th:** 1201
Oil market, Saudi Arabia, **20th:** 1196
Oisc, **Anc:** 395
Oiseaux de passage, Les (Ségalas), **19th:** 2063
Ojeda, Alonzo de, **Ren:** 76
Ojibwes. *See* Chippewas
Ōjin Tennō, **Anc:** 466, 594-596
O'Keeffe, Georgia, **20th:** 3031-3034, 3867
Okehazama, Battle of (1560), **Ren:** 732, 736
Okello, Tito, **20th:** 2883
O'Kelly, Seán T., **20th:** 3034-3036
Okewas, First Day of (1622), **17th:** 703
Okewas, Second Day of (1644), **17th:** 703
Okhrannaya gramota. See *Safe Conduct*

Okinaga Tarashi Hime no Mikoto. *See* Jingū
Oklahoma! (Rodgers and Hammerstein), **20th:** 958, 1659, 3487
Ökonomische und philosophische Manuskripte. See *Economic and Philosophic Manuscripts of 1844*
Oktyabr'. See *October*
Oku no hosomichi. See *Narrow Road to the Deep North, The*
Ōkubo Toshimichi, **19th:** 1186, 1969
Ōkuma Shigenobu, **19th:** 1970
Okuni. *See* Izumo no Okuni
Olaf I (c. 968-1000; king of Norway), **MA:** 642, 786, 789-792
Olaf II, Saint (c. 995-1030; king of Norway), **MA:** 222, 785-788, 791, 952
Olaf II (1370-1387; king of Denmark), **MA:** 689
Olaf IV (1370-1387; king of Norway). *See* Olaf II (1370-1387; king of Denmark)
O'Laughlin, Michael, **Notor:** 1013
Olbers, Wilhelm, **19th:** 215
Olcott, Henry, **19th:** 212
Old Age Pensions Act (1898), **19th:** 2060
Old Believers, **17th:** 13, 27, 685, 865
Old Bush Songs (Paterson), **19th:** 1758
Old Comedy, **Anc:** 92, 850
Old Curiosity Shop, The (Dickens), **19th:** 655
Old-Fashioned Girl, An (Alcott), **19th:** 42
Old Hall, East Bergholt (Constable), **19th:** 540
Old House of Representatives, The. See *Congress Hall*
Old Kingdom (Egypt), **Anc:** 559
Old Love-Letters (Richardson), **19th:** 1904
Old Man and the Sea, The (film), **20th:** 4067
Old Man and the Sea, The (novella by Hemingway), **20th:** 1757
Old Man Seated in an Armchair, An (Rembrandt), **17th:** 788
Old Mortality (Scott), **19th:** 2048
Old-New Land (Herzl), **19th:** 1090
Old Northwest, **19th:** 2237
Old Oaken Bucket, The (Grandma Moses), **20th:** 2842
Old Possum's Book of Practical Cats (Eliot), **20th:** 1141
Old Régime and the Revolution, The (Tocqueville), **19th:** 2281
Old Régime in Canada, The (Parkman), **19th:** 1744
Old Ritualists. *See* Old Believers
Old Settlers, **19th:** 2068
Old Smoke, **19th:** 1872
Old Testament, **Anc:** composition of, 135; David and, 255; **18th:** and racial equality, 1071
Old Time Gospel Hour (television program), **20th:** 1210
Old Times at Otterbourne (Yonge), **19th:** 2473
Old Walton Bridge (Canaletto), **18th:** 192
Old Whig, The (pamphlet), **18th:** 22
Old Woman's Outlook, An (Yonge), **19th:** 2473
Oldcastle, Sir John, **MA:** 502
Oldenbarnevelt, Johan van, **Ren:** 740-743; **17th:** 288, 326, 618
Oldenburg, Claes, **20th:** 3037-3039
Oldendorf, William, **20th:** 1893
Oldfield, Anne, **18th:** 749-751
Oldham, John, **17th:** 130
Oldstyle, Jonathan. *See* Irving, Washington
Oldtown Folks (Stowe), **19th:** 2185
Olduvai Gorge (Leakey), **20th:** 2316
Olga, Saint, **MA:** 86, 792-795
Oligarchy, Athenian, **Anc:** 221
Oliva, Treaty of (1660), **17th:** 155, 290, 428, 527
Olivares, count-duke of, **17th:** 317, 431, 697-699, 739, 770, 914, 953
Olive, L' (du Bellay), **Ren:** 295
Olive Grove, The (Miró), **20th:** 2760
Olive Oil King. *See* Profaci, Joseph
Oliveira Salazar, António de. *See* Salazar, António de Oliveira
Oliver, Joe "King," **20th:** 130
Oliver Twist (Dickens), **19th:** 655
Olivier, Sir Laurence, **20th:** 1525, 3039-3045
Öljeitü, **MA:** 412
Ollokot, **19th:** 1239
Olmstead v. United States (1928), **20th:** 485
Olmsted, Frederick Law, **19th:** 361, 1706-1709
Olod Mongols, **17th:** 449
Olomouc, Peace of (1478), **Ren:** 644
Olor Iscanus (Vaughan), **17th:** 741
Olunthiakos (Demosthenes), **Anc:** 265
Olvidados, Los. See *Forgotten Ones, The*
Olympia (film), **20th:** 3452
Olympia (painting by Manet), **19th:** 1481
Olympia, shrine at, **Anc:** 676
Olympiads, **Anc:** 316
Olympias, **Anc:** 39, 108, 364, 597-599, 639
Olympic Park Bomber. *See* Rudolph, Eric
Olympionikai (Eratosthenes), **Anc:** 315
Omaha Magic Theatre, **20th:** 3983
O'Malley, Grace, **Ren:** 743-745; **Notor:** 805-806
Oman. *See* Geographical Index
Omar Khayyám, **MA:** 795-798, 909

Omari, Abdulaziz al-, **Notor:** 44
Omdurman, Battle of (1898), **20th:** 2174
Omega Workshops, **20th:** 1352
Omens, **Anc:** 244; dreams, 240, 245, 275; interpretation of, 11; Tanaquil and, 841; Tarquin and, 840
Omer, Treaty of (1469), **Ren:** 218
Omoo (Melville), **19th:** 1538
O'More, Rory, **17th:** 699-701
On Abraham. See *De Abrahamo*
On Admonition and Grace. See *De correptione et gratia*
On Aggression (Lorenz), **20th:** 2436
On Agriculture. See *De agricultura*; *De re rustica*
On Ancient Medicine. See *Peri archaies ietrikes*
On Architecture. See *De architectura*
On Balance. See *Lun heng*
On Bandages. See *Peri epideomōn*
On Buonaparte and the Bourbons (Chateaubriand), **19th:** 476
On Christian Doctrine. See *De doctrina Christiana* (Augustine)
On Christian Marriage (Leo XIII), **19th:** 1343
On Civil Government (Leo XIII), **19th:** 1343
On Clemency (Calvin), **Ren:** 163
On Comparative Longevity in Man and the Lower Animals (Lankester), **19th:** 1316
On Conoids and Spheroids. See *Peri konoeideon kai sphaireodeon*
On Contemplating God (William of Saint-Thierry), **MA:** 1114
On Death and Dying (Kübler-Ross), **20th:** 2209
"On Desire" (Behn), **17th:** 43
On Digestion. See *Peri pepeseōs*
"On Distinguishing What Is Essential." *See* "Bienzong Lun"
On Divisions of Figures. See *Peri diaireseon biblion*
On Duelling (Sharp), **18th:** 901
On Fevers. See *Peri puretōn*
On Fire and Air. See *Peri puros kai aeros*
On First Principles. See *Peri archōn*
On Floating Bodies. See *Peri ochoymenon*
On Free Will (Valla), **MA:** 1050
On Friendship. See *Laelius de amicitia*
On Germinal Selection as a Source of Definite Variation (Weismann), **19th:** 2408
On Golden Pond (film), **20th:** 1266
On Hearing the First Cuckoo in Spring (Delius), **20th:** 955
On His Life. See *Carmen de vita sua*
On Holy Images (John of Damascus), **MA:** 589
On Human Nature (Wilson), **20th:** 4359
On Hunting. See *Kynēgetikos*
On Illustrious Men. See *De viris illustribus* (Jerome)
On Joseph. See *De Josepho*
"On Leaving My District" (Xie Lingyun), **Anc:** 977
On Lethal Drugs. See *Peri thanasimōn pharmakōn*
On Liberty (Mill), **19th:** 1577
On Molecular and Microscopic Science (Somerville), **19th:** 2122
On Nature. See *De natura*; *Peri physeōs*
On Old Age. See *Cato maior de senectute*
On Overgrown Paths (Hamsun), **20th:** 1662
On Philosophy. See *De philosophia*
On Photography (Sontag), **20th:** 3789
On Pleasure (Valla), **MA:** 1049
On Prayer. See *Peri eykhēs*
On Providence. See *De providentia*
On Pulses. See *Peri sphygmōn*
On Racine (Barthes), **20th:** 247
On Religion (Schleiermacher), **19th:** 2013
On Remedies for Good and Bad Fortunes (Petrarch), **MA:** 830
On Rewards and Punishments. See *De praemiis et poenis*
On St. Basil the Great. See *In laudem Basilii Magni*
On Spirals. See *Peri helikon*
On the Art of War. See *Sunzi Bingfa*
On the Banks of Plum Creek (Wilder), **20th:** 4336
On the Cavalry General. See *Hipparchikos*
"On the Chersonese." *See* "Peri tōn en Cherronesoi"
On the Christian Constitution of States (Leo XIII), **19th:** 1343
On the Circulation of the Blood (Leeuwenhoek), **17th:** 510
On the Connexion of the Physical Sciences (Somerville), **19th:** 2122
On the Constitution of the Church and State, According to the Idea of Each (Coleridge), **19th:** 532
On the Correlation of Physical Forces (Grove), **19th:** 997
On the Creation. See *De opificis mundi*
"On the Crown." *See* "Peri tou Stephanou"
"On the Death of a Young Lady of Five Years of Age" (Wheatley), **18th:** 1072
On the Death of Mr. William Hervey (Cowley), **17th:** 199
On the Death of Mr. Crashaw (Cowley), **17th:** 199
On the Decalogue. See *De Decalogo*
"On the Dictatorship of the People's Democracy" (Mao), **20th:** 2603

On the Dynamics of the Circular Vortex with Applications to the Atmosphere and Atmospheric Vortex and Wave Motion (Bjerknes), **20th:** 376
"On the Electricity Excited by the Mere Contact of Conducting Substances of Different Kinds" (Volta), **18th:** 1024
On the Equilibrium of Planes. See *Epipledon isorropion*
On the Equipment of a Surgery. See *Peri tōn kat iētreion*
On the Establishment of the Orthodox Teaching and the Peace of the Nation (Nichiren), **MA:** 759
On the Eve (Turgenev), **19th:** 2319
On the Fabric of the Human Body. See *De fabrica*
On the Fourfold Root of the Principle of Sufficient Reason (Schopenhauer), **19th:** 2020
On the Genealogy of Morals (Nietzsche), **19th:** 1682
On the Harmony of Religion and Philosophy (Averroës), **MA:** 121
On the Heavens. See *De caelo*
On the Incarnation (Theodore of Mopsuestia), **Anc:** 863
On the Incarnation of the Word of God. See *De incarnatione Verbi Dei*
On the Infinite Universe and Worlds (Bruno), **Ren:** 139
On the Latin Language. See *De lingua Latina*
On the Law of War and Peace (Grotius), **17th:** 328
On the Life of Moses. See *De vita Moysis*
On the Measurement of the Circle. See *Kykloy metresis*
On the Method of Mechanical Theorems. See *Peri tōn mechanikon theorematon*
On the Misery of the Human Condition (Innocent III), **MA:** 541
On the Movement of Animals (Borelli), **17th:** 66
On the Nature and Dignity of Love (William of Saint-Thierry), **MA:** 1114
On the Nature of Things. See *De rerum natura*
On the Origin of Species by Means of Natural Selection (Darwin), **19th:** 33, 605, 860, 964, 1003, 1161
On the Penitentiary System in the United States and Its Application in France (Tocqueville and Beaumont), **19th:** 2280
On the Priesthood. See *De sacerdotio*
On the Principles of Political Economy and Taxation (Ricardo), **19th:** 1897
On the Quadrature of the Parabola. See *Tetragonismos ten tou orthogonion konoy tomes*
On the Revolutions of the Heavenly Spheres. See *De revolutionibus*
On the Road (Kerouac), **20th:** 2114
On the Sacrament of the Altar (William of Saint-Thierry), **MA:** 1114
On the Sensations of Tone as a Physiological Basis for the Theory of Music (Helmholtz), **19th:** 1074
On the Soul. See *De anima* (Tertullian)
On the Spectacles. See *Epigrammaton liber*
On the Sphere and the Cylinder. See *Peri sphairas kai kylindron*
On the Study Methods of Our Times (Vico), **18th:** 1013
On the Study of the Scriptures (Leo XIII), **19th:** 1343
On the Subjection of Women (Mill), **19th:** 264
On the Sublime. See *Peri hypsous*
On the Town (film), **20th:** 2097
On the Town (musical by Bernstein, Comden, and Green), **20th:** 338, 3461
On the Trinity. See *De trinitate* (Augustine)
On the Twelve Prophets (Theodore of Mopsuestia), **Anc:** 864
On the Twofold Abundance of Words and Things. See *De copia*
On the Unchangeableness of God. See *Quod Deus sit immutabilis*
On the Usefulness of the Parts of the Body. See *Peri chreias morion*
On the Waterfront (film), **20th:** 339, 487
On the Way Home (Wilder), **20th:** 4336
On the Will in Nature (Schopenhauer), **19th:** 2021
On This Island. See *Look Stranger!*
On Translating Homer (Arnold), **19th:** 74
On Treatment. See *Peri therapeiōn*
On Vegetables. See *Rhizotomika, Peri lakhanōn*
On War (Clausewitz), **19th:** 500, 931
On Ways and Means. See *Poroi*
On Women's Diseases. See *Peri gunaikeiōn*
On Your Toes (Rodgers and Hart), **20th:** 1693, 3487
On'ami, **MA:** 1153
Onassis, Aristotle, **20th:** 613, 3047
Onassis, Jacqueline Kennedy, **20th:** 2099, 3045-3048; **Notor:** 787
Oñaz y Loyola, Iñigo de. *See* Ignatius of Loyola, Saint

Once Emerged from the Gray of Night . . . (Klee), **20th:** 2177
Oncogenes, **20th:** 4145
Ondaatje, Michael, **20th:** 3048-3050
Ondine (ballet), **20th:** 1269
Ondine (Giraudoux), **20th:** 1494
One-Cornered Ma. *See* Ma Yuan
One Day in the Life of Ivan Denisovich (Solzhenitsyn), **20th:** 3785
150,000,000 (Mayakovsky), **20th:** 2660
One Hundred Love Sonnets (Neruda), **20th:** 2939
120 Days of Sodom, The (Sade), **18th:** 876
One Hundred Years of Solitude (García Márquez), **20th:** 1399
One, None, and a Hundred Thousand (Pirandello), **20th:** 3260
One of Ours (Cather), **20th:** 699
1 × 1 (Cummings), **20th:** 881
One Touch of Venus (Weill and Nash), **20th:** 4275
Oneidas, **Ren:** 281, 448
O'Neill, Eugene, **20th:** 3051-3055
O'Neill, Oona, **20th:** 3052
O'Neill, Owen Roe, **17th:** 700
O'Neill, Sir Phelim, **17th:** 700
O'Neill, Tip, **20th:** 3055-3058
Ōnin Wars (1467-1477), **Ren:** 865
Oninga. *See* Radisson, Pierre Esprit
Only a Fiddler (Andersen), **19th:** 61
Only Angels Have Wings (film), **20th:** 1731
Only Words (MacKinnon), **20th:** 2523
Onnes, **Anc:** 745
Onnes, Heike Kamerlingh, **20th:** 2078
Onnes effect, **20th:** 2072
Ono, Yoko, **20th:** 269
Ono no Komachi, **18th:** 958
Onondagas, **Ren:** 281, 448
Ontology, **20th:** 1697, 1742
O'odhams, **17th:** 467
Oort, Jan Hendrik, **20th:** 3059-3061
Oort cloud, **20th:** 3059
Opachisco, **17th:** 747
Oparin, Aleksandr Ivanovich, **20th:** 3062-3064
OPEC. *See* Organization of Petroleum Exporting Countries
Opechancanough, **17th:** 702-704, 752
Open Boat and Other Tales of Adventure, The (Crane), **19th:** 564
Open Door at Home, The (Beard), **20th:** 264
Open Door notes, **19th:** 1055
Open Door Policy (Liberia), **20th:** 4102
Open Heart to the World, **20th:** 3265
Open Letter to His Serene Majesty, Leopold II, King of the Belgians, An (Williams), **19th:** 2451
Open Secrets (Munro), **20th:** 2874
Open Sore of a Continent, The (Soyinka), **20th:** 3806
Open Theatre, **20th:** 3982
Opens series (Motherwell), **20th:** 2848
Opera, **17th:** England, 52, 764; France, 570; Italy, 111, 658, 888; **18th:** 99, 178, 295, 884; Christoph Gluck, 418-421; George Frideric Handel, 463; Jean-Philippe Rameau, 826; Alessandro Scarlatti, 883-887; Georg Philipp Telemann, 970; **19th:** Austria, 2189; Czech nation, 712; France, 639, 953, 1700; Germany, 1155, 2374, 2396; Italy, 674, 1944, 2351; light, 918; Russia, 1915; singers, 1388; **20th:** conductors, 2560, 4051; Czech Republic, 1990; England, 531, 954; France, 938, 2735, 3319, 3387, 3600; Germany, 311, 1763, 1812, 3886, 4274; Italy, 2703, 3346; production, 985; Russia, 3339, 3728; singers, 88, 612, 676, 2996, 3159, 3335, 3744; Spain, 1207; United States, 231, 1459, 3666
Opera and Drama (Wagner), **19th:** 2375
Opera botanica (Gesner), **Ren:** 376
Opera geometrica (Torricelli), **17th:** 921
Opera nova (Aretino), **Ren:** 53
Opera posthuma (Horrocks), **17th:** 389
Operant conditioning, **20th:** 3756
Operation Ajax, **20th:** 2846
Operation Breadbasket, **20th:** 1978
Operation Desert Storm, **20th:** 596, 1196, 3323
Operation Mongoose, **20th:** 693
Operation Murambatsvina, **20th:** 2859
Operation People United to Save Humanity, **20th:** 1979
Operation Petticoat (film), **20th:** 1571
Operationalism, **20th:** 528
Operons, **20th:** 1984
Ophthalmoscope, invention of, **19th:** 1074
Opinions of Jerome Coignard, The (France), **19th:** 816
Opitchapan, **17th:** 702, 752
Opium, **19th:** 1127
Opium War, First (1839-1842), **19th:** 496, 1128, 1378
Oppenheimer, Franz, **20th:** 1173
Oppenheimer, J. Robert, **20th:** 343, 438, 1237, 2945, 3065-3068, 3356, 3969
Oprah Winfrey Show, The (television talk show), **20th:** 4373
Oprichnina, **Ren:** 494
Optica Promota (Gregory), **17th:** 319

Opticae thesaurus Alhazeni libri vii. See *Optics* (Alhazen)
Optics, **MA:** Iraq, 66; **17th:** England, 679; France, 272; Germany, 458; Italy, 322, 923; Netherlands, 399, 509, 537; Poland, 372; Scotland, 319; **20th:** 3659
Optics (Alhazen), **MA:** 67
Optics (Kepler), **17th:** 458
Optics of Ibn al-Haytham, The. See *Optics* (Alhazen)
Optika (Euclid), **Anc:** 318
Opus majus (Bacon), **MA:** 128
Opus minus (Bacon), **MA:** 128
Opus nonaginta dierum (Ockham), **MA:** 780
Opus Oxoniense. See *Ordinatio*
Opus palatinum de triangulis (Otto), **Ren:** 824
Opus paramirum (Paracelsus), **Ren:** 759
Opus quadripartitum numerorum (Muris), **MA:** 741
Opus tertium (Bacon), **MA:** 128
Opuscoli di fisica animale e vegetabile. See *Tracts on Animals and Vegetables*
Opuscula hebraea, graeca, latina, gallica (Schurman), **17th:** 823
Opuscula medica inaudita. See *Unheard of Little Works on Medicine*
Oquendo, Antonio de, **17th:** 288
Oquendo, Juan Lechín, **20th:** 3173
Or San Michele, **MA:** 320, 799
Oracles, **Anc:** Hypatia, 434; prophecy and, 259. *See also* Delos; Delphi
Oráculo manual y arte de prudencia. See *Courtiers Manual Oracle, The*
Oraison funèbre d'Henriette Anne d'Angleterre. See *Funeral Oration for Henrietta of England*
Oral tradition, **Anc:** Aśoka, 124; Buddhism, 50, 345; Homer, 427; Polybius's use of, 674; Roman, 848
Oran, **Ren:** 505; conquest of, 330
Oran, Battle of (1832), **19th:** 1
Orange Free State, **19th:** 1298
Orange, Synod of (529), **MA:** 155
Orange, William of. *See* William III
Orangist faction, **17th:** 519
Oratio apologetica de fuga sua (Gregory of Nazianzus), **Anc:** 361
Oratio de laudibus Constantini (Eusebius), **Anc:** 331
Oration on the Dignity of Man (Pico della Mirandola), **Ren:** 782, 783
Orationae (Gregory of Nazianzus), **Anc:** 361
Orations of Divers Sorts (Newcastle), **17th:** 677
Oratorios, **18th:** 73, 463, 476, 886, 972
Oratory, **Anc:** Cato the Censor, 192; Cicero, 210; Greek, 33, 128, 209, 264, 450, 622; politics and, 172; Roman, 194, 210, 513; **17th:** 71
Orbis sensualium pictus. See *Visible World*
Orbital symmetry, conservation of, **20th:** 4395
Orcagna, Andrea, **MA:** 798-800
Orchard, The (Saʿdi), **MA:** 915
Orchestra of the Opera, The (Degas), **19th:** 633
Order 11 (Bingham), **19th:** 236
Order of Our Lady of Mount Carmel. *See* Carmelites
Ordet (film), **20th:** 1038
Ordinatio (Duns Scotus), **MA:** 330
Ordinatio Imperii (817), **MA:** 662
Ordóñez, Bartholome, **Ren:** 890
Ordovices, **Anc:** 17
Oregon, **19th:** annexation of, 194, 1822; exploration of, 831
Oregon Trail, **19th:** 2115
Oresteia (Aeschylus), **Anc:** 9, 633, 810
Orestēs (Euripides), **Anc:** 328
Orestes (prefect of Alexandria), **Anc:** 435
Orestes (Roman politician), **MA:** 782
Orfeo ed Euridice (Gluck and Calzabigi), **18th:** 419
Organ music, **18th:** Johann Sebastian Bach, 72; François Couperin, 281; George Frideric Handel, 465
Organic Act of 1902, **20th:** 3520
Organic Chemistry in Its Applications to Agriculture and Physiology (Liebig), **19th:** 1368
Organic synthesis, **20th:** 4394
Organisation Africaine et Malgache de Coopération Économique, **20th:** 1897
Organization for European Economic Co-operation, **20th:** 358
Organization of African Unity, **20th:** 2990
Organization of Petroleum Exporting Countries, **20th:** 1200, 4423
Organized crime, **20th:** 641
Organizer, The (Saint-Simon), **19th:** 1976
Organon of the Healing Art (Hahnemann), **19th:** 1010
Orgen, Jacob "Little Augie," **Notor:** 277
Orient Express. See *Stamboul Train*
Orientales, Les (Hugo), **19th:** 1147
Orientalism (Said), **20th:** 2352
Origen, **Anc:** 209, 330, 363, 423, 485, 599-602, 668; **MA:** 1115
Origenism, **Anc:** 699
Origin and Goal of History, The (Jaspers), **20th:** 1998
Origin myths, **Anc:** Japanese, 462; Roman, 939
Origin of African Civilizations, The (Frobenius), **20th:** 1342
Origin of Continents and Oceans (Wegener), **20th:** 4267

Origin of Life, The (Oparin), **20th:** 3063
Origin of the Family, Private Property, and the State, The (Engels), **19th:** 752
Original Dixieland Jazz Band, **20th:** 1527
Original intent theory, **20th:** 4000
Original Sin, **Anc:** doctrine of, 854; Saint Augustine on, 143
Original Sonnets on Various Subjects, and Odes Paraphrased from Horace (Seward), **18th:** 898
Original Stories from Real Life (Wollstonecraft), **18th:** 122
Originalism, **20th:** 521
Origines (Cato), **Anc:** 192
Origins of Ismailism, The (Lewis), **20th:** 2352
Origins of Totalitarianism, The (Arendt), **20th:** 119
Orinda. *See* Philips, Katherine
Orlando furioso (Ariosto), **Ren:** 57
Orlav, Count. *See* Orlov, Grigori Grigoryevich
Orléans, Anne-Marie-Louise d'. *See* Montpensier, duchesse de
Orléans, duc d', **18th:** 751-754
Orléans, Gaston d', **17th:** 598, 660
Orléans, Louis d', **MA:** 277
Orleanskaya Dyeva (Tchaikovsky), **19th:** 2234
Orlov, Aleksey Grigoryevich, **18th:** 755-756, 809, 814
Orlov, Count. *See* Orlov, Aleksey Grigoryevich
Orlov, Grigori Grigoryevich, **18th:** 757-758, 779, 809; and Catherine the Great, 212
Orme du mail, L'. See *Elm Tree on the Mall, The*
Ormiston, Kenneth G., **Notor:** 680
Ormond (Edgeworth), **19th:** 730
Ormond, first duke of, **17th:** 507
Ornithes (Aristophanes), **Anc:** 90
Ornithological Biography (Audubon), **19th:** 93
Oroetes, **Notor:** 851
Oroonoko (Behn), **17th:** 44
Orosius, Paulus, **Anc:** 699
Orozco, José Clemente, **20th:** 3068-3071
Orozco, Pascual, **20th:** 3014; **Notor:** 280
Orphans, Asia, **20th:** 559, 3977
Orphans Fund of the City of London, **17th:** 718
Orphée aux enfers (Offenbach), **19th:** 1700
Orpheus (Cocteau), **20th:** 794
Orpheus (Liszt), **19th:** 1394
Orphic Mysteries. *See* Mystery religions
Orsini, Cardinal Giordano, **Ren:** 725
Ortega, Daniel, **20th:** 3072-3074
Ortega, Katherine Davalos, **20th:** 3074-3077
Ortega y Gasset, José, **20th:** 3077-3080
Orthez, Battle of (1814), **19th:** 2410
Orthodox caliphs, **MA:** 1038
Orthodox Church, **MA:** 53, 190, 1070; **Ren:** Ethiopian, 1006; **18th:** Ethiopian, 678; Russian, 776, 779
Orthodoxy, Christian, **Anc:** 948
Ortiz Rubio, Pascual, **20th:** 617
Örtlich betäubt. See *Local Anaesthetic*
Ortografía castellana (Alemán), **Ren:** 25
Orton, Arthur, **Notor:** 806-807
Ortus medicinae. See *Ternary of Paradoxes, A*
O'Ruddy, The (Crane), **19th:** 564
Orus Apollo, fils de Osiris, roi de Ægipte niliacque (Nostradamus), **Ren:** 728
Orwell, George, **20th:** 349, 3080-3085
Oryx and Crake (Atwood), **20th:** 171
Osage, **19th:** 244, 1794
Osborne, John, **20th:** 3042
Osborne, Thomas. *See* Leeds, first duke of
Osborne, Thomas Mott (prison reformer), **20th:** 3085-3088
Osburn, Sarah, **17th:** 690
Oscar I, **19th:** 469
Osceola, **19th:** 1709-1711, 2052, 2231
Osen, **18th:** 959
O'Shaughnessy Dam, **20th:** 3254
Ōshūbanashi (Makuzu), **19th:** 2212
Osiander, Andreas, **Ren:** 243
Osiris, **Anc:** 107, 996
Osler, Sir William, **19th:** 1711-1714; **20th:** 900
Oslo Peace Accords (1993), **20th:** 113, 3359
Osman I, **MA:** 800-804
Osman II, **17th:** 472, 674, 855
Osman Gazi. *See* Osman I
Osnovy khimii. See *Principles of Chemistry, The*
Ospedale degli Innocenti, **MA:** 207
Osservazioni sulla morale cattolica. See *Vindication of Catholic Morality, A*
Ossessione (film), **20th:** 4166
Ossi di seppia. See *Bones of the Cuttlefish*
Ossoli, Giovanni Angelo, **19th:** 843
Ossoli, Marchesa. *See* Fuller, Margaret
Ostend, Siege of (1601-1604), **17th:** 928
Ostpolitik, **20th:** 491
Ostracism, **Anc:** 215, 222; Themistocles, 861
Ostrogoths, **Anc:** 353; **MA:** 75, 233, 293, 600, 782, 1012; kings, 76, 1014
Ostrov Sakhalin (Chekhov), **19th:** 479
Ostwald, Wilhelm, **20th:** 139, 3088-3091
Osuna, duke of, **17th:** 770
Oswald, Lee Harvey, **Notor:** 698, 807-809, 942
Otago Daily Times, **19th:** 2371

Otakar II, **MA:** 905
Otello (Rossini), **19th:** 1945
Otello (Verdi), **19th:** 2353
Othello (film), **20th:** 3043, 4285
Other People's Money and How the Bankers Use It (Brandeis), **20th:** 483
Other Voices, Other Rooms (Capote), **20th:** 645
Other World, The (Cyrano), **17th:** 211
Otho, Marcus Salvius, **Anc:** 685
Otho of Lagery. *See* Urban II
Otis, James, **18th:** 519
Otis, Mercy. *See* Warren, Mercy Otis
Otluk Beli, Battle of (1483), **Ren:** 87
Ottaniack. *See* Powhatan
Ottawas, **17th:** 603
Otto I, **MA:** 243, 516, 794, 805-808, 983
Otto II, **MA:** 516, 806
Otto III, **MA:** 487, 985
Otto IV, **MA:** 359, 389, 476, 543, 586, 837, 1047
Otto, Nikolaus August, **19th:** 1714-1717
Otto, Valentin, **Ren:** 824
Otto and Langen, **19th:** 593
Otto the Great. *See* Otto I
Ottoboni, Pietro, **17th:** 190
Ottoman-Austrian conflicts, **18th:** 330, 639
Ottoman Empire, **MA:** 519, 711, 803; law, 713; sultans, 713, 802; **Ren:** 87, 221, 480, 659, 661, 914, 915; invasion of Baghdad, 481; invasion of Hungary, 480, 799; Jews and, 524; Mamlūks and, 807; North Africa and, 81; Papacy and, 798; **17th:** 4, 406, 668, 866; **18th:** art, 602-604; Charles VI, 230; Westernization, 28; **19th:** 2479; Greece, 55; **20th:** World War I, 2304. *See also* Geographical Index
Ottoman-French relations, **18th:** 640
Ottoman-Persian conflicts, **18th:** 639, 723
Ottoman-Polish Wars (1672-1676), **17th:** 429
Ottoman-Russian-Austrian War (1736-1739), **18th:** 639
Ottoman-Russian conflicts, **18th:** 570, 720, 775, 955; Ottoman-Russian Wars (1768-1792), 720
Ottoman sultans, **18th:** Ahmed III, 26-29; Mahmud I, 639-641
Ottoman-Swedish alliance, **18th:** 232
Ottosøn, Tyge Brahe. *See* Brahe, Tycho
Ottsy i deti. See *Fathers and Sons*
Oud, J. J. P., **20th:** 2692, 3092-3094
Oudh, British annexation of, **19th:** 1718
Oulot, Berta. *See* Suttner, Bertha von
Our Asiatic Cousins (Leonowens), **19th:** 1348
Our Common Future (Brundtland Commission), **20th:** 546
Our Corner, **19th:** 211
Our Hospitality (film), **20th:** 2091
Our Hunting Fathers (Britten), **20th:** 530
Our Inner Conflicts (Horney), **20th:** 1884
Our Knowledge of the External World (Russell), **20th:** 3563
Our Lady of Mount Carmel, Order of. *See* Carmelites
Our Lady of Ransom, Order of, **MA:** 882
Our Lady of the Angels Monastery, **20th:** 90
Our Lady of the Flowers (Genet), **20th:** 1446
Our Lady of the Immaculate Conception (Murillo), **17th:** 672
Our Land and Land Policy, National and State (George), **19th:** 895
Our Mr. Wrenn (Lewis), **20th:** 2364
Our Mutual Friend (Dickens), **19th:** 656
Our National Parks (Muir), **19th:** 1625
Our Partnership (Webb), **20th:** 4255
Our Penal Machinery and Its Victims (Altgeld), **19th:** 58
Our Slavic Fellow Citizens (Balch), **20th:** 198
Ourique, Battle of (1139), **MA:** 33
Ousamequin. *See* Massasoit
Out of My Life (Hindenburg), **20th:** 1816
Out of the Dark (Keller), **20th:** 2093
Out of the Silent Planet (Lewis), **20th:** 2354
Outback Marriage, An (Paterson), **19th:** 1758
Outer Commentary to the Book of Changes (Wang), **17th:** 972
Outlaw, The (film), **20th:** 1926
Outlaw Doc. *See* Bell, Tom
Outlaws. *See* Category Index
Outline of History, The (Wells), **20th:** 4289
Outline of the History of Ethics (Sedgwick), **19th:** 2104
Outlines of a Philosophy of the History of Man (Herder), **18th:** 487
Outlines of Psychology (Wundt), **20th:** 4408
Outrageous Acts and Everyday Rebellions (Steinem), **20th:** 3854
Outram, Sir James, **19th:** 1717-1720
Outre-Mer (Longfellow), **19th:** 1417
Outside Over There (Sendak), **20th:** 3700
Ouyang Xiu, **MA:** 808-810, 1079, 1088
Oval Composition with Bright Colors (Mondrian), **20th:** 2788
Ovando, Nicolás de, **Ren:** 240, 804

Over Strand and Field (Flaubert and Du Camp), **19th:** 785
Over the Teacups (Holmes), **19th:** 1118
Over the Town (Chagall), **20th:** 717
Overbury, Sir Thomas, **17th:** 132
Overseas Library Program, **20th:** 2499
Overton, Richard, **17th:** 535
Ovi mammalium et hominis genesis epistola, De. See *Discovery of the Mammalian Egg, The*
Ovid, **Anc:** 180, 491, 521, 602-605, 834
Ovid's Banquet of Sense (Chapman), **Ren:** 214
Oviedo, Fernández de, **Ren:** 804
Owain ap Cadwgan, **MA:** 754
Owen, Anne, **17th:** 742
Owen, David, **Notor:** 735
Owen, Robert, **19th:** 400, 1720-1723, 2470
Owens, Jesse, **20th:** 3095-3098
Oxenbridge, John, **Ren:** 404
Oxenstierna, Axel, **17th:** 153, 163, 328, 337, 704-707
Oxeon kai chronion nouson therapeutikon biblion (Aretaeus), **Anc:** 85
Oxford, Provisions of (1258), **MA:** 491, 727
Oxford and Cambridge Magazine, **19th:** 1606
Oxford Group, **20th:** 549
Oxford Movement, **19th:** 77, 1490, 1519, 1663, 1845
Oxley, Michael, **Notor:** 619, 968
Oxygen (television network), **20th:** 4374
Oxygen, discovery of, **18th:** 116, 812
Oxygen-15, **20th:** 2533
Oyster Gatherers of Cancale, The. See *En route pour la pêche*
Ozawa, Jisaburō, **20th:** 1649
Őzbay, Mehmet. *See* Ağca, Mehmet Ali
Ozgun, Faruk. *See* Ağca, Mehmet Ali
Ozma of Oz (Baum), **19th:** 157
Ozone layer, depletion of, **20th:** 3548
Ozu, Yasujiro, **20th:** 2217
"Ozymandias" (Shelley), **Anc:** 737

P

På gjengrodde stier. See *On Overgrown Paths*
Paasikivi, Juho Kusti, **20th:** 2600
Pablo Christiani, **MA:** 748
Pacelli, Eugenio Maria Giuseppe Giovanni. *See* Pius XII
Pacem in terris (John XXIII), **20th:** 2019
Pachacutec Inca Yupanqui. *See* Pachacuti
Pachacuti, **Ren:** 746-748
Pacheco, Francisco, **17th:** 953, 1003
Pacheco, Johnny, **20th:** 878
Pacheco, Juan, **Ren:** 432
Pachelbel, Johann, **17th:** 708-710
Pacific, War of the (1879-1884), **19th:** 1513
Pacific Northwest, mapping of, **18th:** 1006
Pacific Ocean, European discovery of, **Ren:** 593
Pacific Railway, **19th:** 1444; building of, 1453
Pacific Scandal of 1873, **19th:** 1444
Paço de Ribera, **Ren:** 445
Pact of Steel (1939), **20th:** 2888
Pacte de Famille, **18th:** 246
Pädagogik des Kindergartens, Die. See *Friedrich Froebel's Pedagogics of the Kindergarten*
Pädagogisches Skizzenbuch. See *Pedagogical Sketchbook*
Paderhorn, Diet of (777), **MA:** 1094
Padilla, Maria de, **Notor:** 827
Paekche, **Anc:** 466
Paetus, Aulus Caecina, **Anc:** 102
Páez, José Antonio, **19th:** 268
Paganini, Niccolò, **19th:** 1724-1726
Paganism, **Anc:** 331; Christianity and, 268, 437, 791, 798, 853, 869; decline of, 42; Dio Cassius on, 276; Gothic, 911; Saint Helena and, 392; Judaism and, 4, 340, 453; Neoplatonism and, 701; philosophy and, 702; revival of, 363; **MA:** Anglo-Saxons, 183; Ireland, 811; Kievan Rus, 87, 1068; Saxony, 1095; Vikings, 222
Paganism Immortal (Whitney), **20th:** 4315
Page, William, **19th:** 292
Pagerie, Marie-Joséphe-Rose Tascher de la. *See* Joséphine
Paget, Eusebius, **Ren:** 403
Pago Pago, **19th:** 1462
Pahlavi, Mohammad Reza Shah. *See* Mohammad Reza Shah Pahlavi
Pailles rompues, Les (Verne), **19th:** 2355
Paine, Lewis. *See* Powell, Lewis
Paine, Thomas, **18th:** 328, 759-762
Painted Desert, The (film), **20th:** 1368
Painted Drum, The (Erdrich), **20th:** 1171
Painted Veil, The (film), **20th:** 1393
Painter and His Pug, The (Hogarth), **18th:** 498
Painters, **18th:** Canaletto, 190-193; Jean-Siméon Chardin, 223-226; Chŏng Sŏn, 248-249; John Singleton Copley, 274-277; Jean-Honoré Fragonard, 367-370; Thomas Gainsborough, 387-391; Francisco de Goya, 436-440; William Hogarth, 497-501; Angelica Kauffman, 554-556; Thomas Lawrence, 583-586; Levni, 602-604; Charles

Willson Peale, 768-771; Sir Joshua Reynolds, 836-840; George Romney, 862-865; Gilbert Stuart, 947-951; Giovanni Battista Tiepolo, 976-979; Élisabeth Vigée-Lebrun, 1016-1019; Antoine Watteau, 1051-1054; Benjamin West, 1068-1070
Painter's Studio, The (Courbet), **19th:** 560
Painting, **MA:** China, 677, 720, 970, 1140; Flanders, 366; Florence, 799; France, 866; Gothic, 697; Italy, 83, 282, 326, 421, 659, 700, 798; Netherlands, 1092; **Ren:** China, 865; England, 454; Flanders, 421; Florence, 39, 123; Germany, 262, 297, 406, 453; Italy, 46, 132, 170, 175, 249, 338, 383, 390, 561, 601, 785, 819, 931, 935-936, 953, 959, 963; Japan, 865; Netherlands, 120, 135; Venice, 98; **17th:** Baroque, 955; Belgium, 244; China, 156, 540; France, 171, 493; Italy, 45, 171, 302, 307, 749, 856; Japan, 695, 868; Netherlands, 352, 786, 802, 956; Spain, 953, 1003; **18th:** domestic themes, 368; erotic themes, 367, 1052; everyday life, 191, 225, 368, 1051-1052; *fête galante*, 1051; illusionism, 977; landscape, 248; manuscript, 603; neoclassicism, 838; Ottoman Empire, 603; Roman school, 555; Spain, 436-440; **19th:** American West, 232; England, 264, 540, 1158, 1606, 1997, 2322, 2421; France, 559, 607, 632, 635, 879, 898, 1171, 1480, 1799, 1951, 1997, 2287; Impressionism, 453, 1889, 2074; Japan, 1107; Missouri, 235; Netherlands, 933; Scotland, 1852; Symbolism, 1875; United States, 92, 235, 433, 441, 718, 1123, 1610, 1882; **20th:** abstract, 1846, 2196, 2212, 2606, 2636, 2788, 2847, 2957, 3303, 3539; Canada, 4010; France, 105, 421, 493, 973, 1051, 2777, 4173; Futurism, 403; Germany, 2177, 2185; Great Britain, 3920; Impressionism, 2335, 2790; Italy, 1472; landscape, 2911; murals, 2762; Norway, 2871; portraits, 2015, 2777; Russia, 717, 2075; Spain, 905, 1597; Surrealism, 1178, 2761; United States, 1304, 2847, 4410. *See also* Landscape painting; Portraiture
Painting and Reality (Gilson), **20th:** 1490
Paiutes, **19th:** 2110
Paiva, Afonso de, **Ren:** 259
Pajama Game, The (Adler and Ross), **20th:** 1291, 3461
Paki, Lydia Kamekaeha. *See* Liliuokalani
Pakistan, **20th:** independence of, 1389, 2004, 2856. *See also* Geographical Index
Pakistan People's Party, **20th:** 369
Pal Joey (Rodgers and Hart), **20th:** 1693, 2096, 3487
Palace at 4 A.M., The (Giacometti), **20th:** 1471
Palace of Desire (Mahfouz), **20th:** 2554
Palace of Luxembourg, **17th:** 587
Palace of Minos, The (Evans), **19th:** 754
Palace Walk (Mahfouz), **20th:** 2554
Palaeologus, Andronicus II. *See* Andronicus II Palaeologus
Palaeologus, Andronicus III. *See* Andronicus III Palaeologus
Palaeologus, Sophia, **Ren:** 490, 749-750, 957
Palafox, José de, **19th:** 1993
Palais Royal (Paris), **18th:** 752
Palatine of the Rhine, count. *See* Rupert, Prince
Palazzo Carignano, **17th:** 331
Palazzo Clerici (Milan), **18th:** 977
Palazzo di Parte Guelfa, **MA:** 207
Palazzo Vecchio, **MA:** 102
Pale Fire (Nabokov), **20th:** 2896
Pale Horse, Pale Rider (Porter), **20th:** 3312
Paleontology, **Ren:** Gesner's work in, 376; **17th:** 882; **19th:** 586; **20th:** China, 3965
Palestine, **20th:** 358, 576. *See also* Israel; Judaea; Judah, kingdom of; Geographical Index under Israel/Palestine
Palestine Liberation Organization, **20th:** 110, 930, 1200, 1952, 2917
Palestrina, Giovanni Pierluigi da, **Ren:** 150, 540, 751-753; **18th:** 179
Paley, William, **18th:** 763-765
Pāli Canon, **Anc:** 169
Pāli Tipiṭaka, **Anc:** 934
Palimpsest (H. D.), **20th:** 1624
Palko v. Connecticut (1937), **20th:** 655
Palladino, Eusapia, **Notor:** 810-811
Palladio, Andrea, **Ren:** 753-757, 848; **18th:** 5, 133
Pallas, **Anc:** 219
Pallas Athene (Klimt), **20th:** 2180
Palmer, Alice Freeman, **19th:** 1727-1730
Palmer, Arnold, **20th:** 2960, 3289
Palmer, Barbara Villiers. *See* Castlemaine, countess of
Palmer, George Herbert, **19th:** 1728
Palmer, John. *See* Turpin, Dick
Palmer, William, **19th:** 998
Palmerston, Lord, **19th:** 439, 522, 644, 668, 925, 1379, 1731-1734, 1959, 2361
Palmyrene Empire, **Anc:** 988
Palsgraf v. Long Island R.R. (1928), **20th:** 654
Pamela (Richardson), **18th:** 841
Pamphilus, **Anc:** 330

Pamphleteering, **18th:** Granville Sharp, 900; Emmanuel-Joseph Sieyès, 916-919; Richard Steele, 942
Pamunkeys, **17th:** 702, 752
Pan, **Anc:** 631
Pan (Hamsun), **20th:** 1661
Pan Ku. *See* Ban Gu
Pan Meng-chien. *See* Ban Gu
Pan Podstoli (Krasicki), **18th:** 568
Pan Voyevoda (Rimsky-Korsakov), **19th:** 1915
Panaenus, **Anc:** 635
Panaetius of Rhodes, **Anc:** 690, 757
Pan Africanist Congress, **20th:** 2479
Panama. *See* Geographical Index
Panama Canal, **19th:** 580; **20th:** 1517, 1543, 3517; end of U.S. control, 668, 4048; scandal in France, 779
Panama Congress (1826), **19th:** 269
Pan-American Conference (1889), **19th:** 252
Panathenaea, Greater, **Anc:** 651
Panda's Thumb, The (Gould), **20th:** 1556
Pandectae. See *Digest of Justinian, The*
Pander, Christian Heinrich, **19th:** 114
Pandit, Vijaya Lakshmi, **20th:** 3099-3102
Pandora, **Anc:** 415
Panegyricus (Isocrates), **Anc:** 450
Pangenesis, **20th:** 868
Pangéométrie (Lobachevsky), **19th:** 1405
Pangolin and Other Verse, The (Moore), **20th:** 2823
Panhellenic League, **Anc:** 505
Panhellenic Socialist Movement, **20th:** 3106
Panhellenism, **Anc:** 41
Paniagua Corazao, Valentín, **Notor:** 383
Panic of 1837, **19th:** 88, 227
Panic of 1873, **19th:** 546, 1601
Panic of 1893, **19th:** 510, 1601
Panipat, Battle of (1526), **Ren:** 475, 478
Pan-Islamism, **19th:** 1204
Pankhurst, Emmeline, **19th:** 1026; **20th:** 3102-3105, 3145
Panopticon, **18th:** 106
Pan-sensism, **17th:** 125
Pansophy, **17th:** 470
Panspermia, **20th:** 140, 1904
Pantagruel. See *Gargantua and Pantagruel*
Pantagruéline prognostication (Rabelais), **Ren:** 810
Pantheism, **18th:** 69
Pantheon (Roman), **Anc:** 20, 371
Pantheon Opera House (London), **18th:** 296
Panther and the Lash, The (Hughes), **20th:** 1930
Pantophile. *See* Diderot, Denis
Pap (Armenian king), **Anc:** 776
Papa Doc. *See* Duvalier, François
Papacy, **Anc:** evolution of, 796; foundation of, 225; infallibility of popes, 425; Saint Peter and, 626; **MA:** power of, 435
Papadopoulos, George, **20th:** 3106
Papaioannou, Kostas, **20th:** 3170
Papal States, **Ren:** consolidation of, 520; reconquest of, 115
Papandreou, Andreas, **20th:** 3106-3109
Papandreou, George, **20th:** 3106
Papen, Franz von, **20th:** 3109-3112, 3559
Paper Against Gold (Cobbett), **19th:** 518
Paper Constitution (1244), **MA:** 491
Papers of Samuel Marchbanks, The (Davies), **20th:** 917
Papers on Literature and Art (Fuller), **19th:** 843
Paphnutius (Hrosvitha), **MA:** 518
Papillon. *See* Charrière, Henri
Papillon, Le (Offenbach), **19th:** 1701
Papin, Denis, **17th:** 710-713, 814
Papp, Joseph, **20th:** 40
Pappus, **Anc:** 78, 606-608
Pappus problem, **Anc:** 607
Par les champs et par les grèves. See *Over Strand and Field*
Parable of the Blind (Bruegel), **Ren:** 136
Parable of the Wicked Mammon, The (Tyndale), **Ren:** 951
Paracelsus, **Ren:** 757-760
Parade (ballet), **20th:** 3643
Parade, La (Seurat), **19th:** 2076
Paradis artificiels, Les. See *Artificial Paradises*
Paradise (Morrison), **20th:** 2836
Paradise (Tintoretto), **Ren:** 933
Paradise Lost (ballet), **20th:** 1270
Paradise Lost (Milton), **17th:** 640; **18th:** 123
Paradise Regained (Milton), **17th:** 642
Paradox of Acting, The (Diderot), **18th:** 309
Paradoxes (Nordau), **20th:** 2993
Paradoxes of Legal Science, The (Cardozo), **20th:** 654
Paraguay. *See* Geographical Index
Parallel Lives. See *Bioi paralleloi*
Parallele des anciens et des modernes (Perrault), **17th:** 732
Paramārtha, **Anc:** 111, 930
Pāramitās, **Anc:** 112
Paramount Studios, **20th:** 141, 961
Paraphrase Upon the Seaven Penitentiall Psalmes of the Kingly Prophet (Aretino), **Ren:** 54
Parasitism and Disease (Smith), **20th:** 3774
Parasol, The (Goya), **18th:** 437
Paravents, Les. See *Screens, The*
Parent, Steven, **Notor:** 690
Parente, Giuseppe, **Notor:** 775
Parent's Assistant, The (Edgeworth), **19th:** 728
Parentucelli, Tommaso. *See* Nicholas V
Parerga and Paralipomena (Schopenhauer), **19th:** 2021

Paria (Vincent), **17th:** 894
Parigi, Giulio, **17th:** 627
Paris (legendary figure), **Anc:** 428
Paris (city), **Anc:** Christianity and, 268; **18th:** first mayor of, 78; French Revolution, 78, 290, 619; Montesquieu, 695; opera, 154, 295-296; Jean-Philippe Rameau, 826; Robespierre, 844; Mary Robinson, 849; Jean-Jacques Rousseau, 868; Marquis de Sade, 875; sewer system, 996, waterworks, 1088
Paris (Zola), **19th:** 2491
Paris, Siege of (1590), **Ren:** 323
Paris, Treaty of (1259), **MA:** 491, 668
Paris, Treaty of (1303), **MA:** 1074
Paris, Treaty of (1763), **18th:** 40, 151, 227, 246, 558, 787
Paris, Treaty of (1783), **18th:** 14, 228, 254, 525, 1056
Paris, Treaty of (1814), **19th:** 439, 1562, 2224
Paris, Treaty of (1856), **19th:** 49, 949
Paris, Treaty of (1898), **19th:** 1462; **20th:** 552
Paris Commune, **18th:** 753, 845; **19th:** 120; **20th:** 778
Paris Normal School of Music, **20th:** 682
Paris Peace Accords (1973), **20th:** 2955
Paris Peace Conference of 1919, **20th:** 1055
Paris Spleen (Baudelaire), **19th:** 153
Parisina (Donizetti), **19th:** 675
Park, Mungo, **Anc:** 386; **18th:** 765-768
Park Chung Hee, **20th:** 2136
Parker, Bonnie, **Notor:** 62, 811-813
Parker, Charlie, **20th:** 1481, 3112-3115
Parker, Colonel Tom, **20th:** 3331
Parker, Dorothy, **20th:** 3116-3119
Parker, George. *See* Cassidy, Butch
Parker, Hyde, **19th:** 1658
Parker, Isaac C., **Notor:** 257, 995
Parker, Matthew, **Ren:** 403, 761-764
Parker, Robert LeRoy. *See* Cassidy, Butch
Parker, Steven J., **20th:** 3816
Parker, Theodore, **19th:** 1735-1738
Parker-Bowles, Camilla, **20th:** 991
Parkes, Sir Henry, **19th:** 150, 624, 1739-1742
Parkhouse, Hannah. *See* Cowley, Hannah
Parkman, Francis, **19th:** 1742-1747
Parks, Rosa, **20th:** 2148, 3119-3123
Parlement of Foules, The (Chaucer), **MA:** 265
Parliament, British, **MA:** 344; **18th:** 138, 175, 364, 402, 406, 408, 441; and American colonies, 519, 646, 1091; and Canada, 197; Lord North, 739; sovereignty, 118; Robert Walpole, 1034; **19th:** 143, 1840
Parliament, Irish, **18th:** 441
Parliament Act of 1911, **20th:** 151
Parliamentarians, **17th:** 484, 535, 805
Parliamentary History of England (Cobbett), **19th:** 518
Parliamentary Liberal Party, **19th:** 622
Parliamentary reform, **18th:** 364; Henry Grattan, 441; Granville Sharp, 900; Robert Walpole, 1034-1038; Wilkites, 1085
Parma, Battle of (1521), **Ren:** 410
Parma, Siege of (1247-1248), **MA:** 391
Parmenides, **Anc:** 261, 608-611, 984
Parmenter, F. A., **Notor:** 924, 1057
Parmigianino, **Ren:** 175
Parnasso español, El (Quevedo y Villegas), **17th:** 771
Parnell, Charles Stewart, **19th:** 794, 926, 1747-1750; **20th:** 3025; **Notor:** 509
Paroles catholiques. See *Words of Faith*
Parr, Catherine, **Ren:** 62, 303, 310, 443, 764-767, 947
Parr, Robert. *See* Gardner, Erle Stanley
Parr, Thomas, **17th:** 357
Parrington, Vernon Louis, **20th:** 3124-3127
Parris, Elizabeth, **17th:** 690
Parris, Samuel, **17th:** 689
Parrish, Maxfield, **19th:** 156
Parry, William Edward, **19th:** 1934
Parsees, **Anc:** 995
Parsifal (Wagner), **19th:** 2377
Parson Weems' Fable (Wood), **20th:** 4389
Parson's Cause (1763), **18th:** 482
Parson's Widow, The (film), **20th:** 1037
Parsva, **Anc:** 925
Part of King James, His Royall and Magnificent Entertainment (Jonson), **17th:** 442
Parthenia, **17th:** 310
Parthenia (Byrd, Bull, and Gibbons), **Ren:** 150
Parthenon, **Anc:** 634
Parthia, **Anc:** Antiochus and, 66; Rome and, 75, 530
Parti Démocratique de la Côte d'Ivoire, **20th:** 1896
Parti Québécois, **20th:** 2345, 4078
Parti Socialiste Français, **19th:** 1221
Particle accelerators, **20th:** 2302, 2534
Particular Open Communion Baptist, **17th:** 100
Partido Aprista Peruano, **20th:** 1717

Partido de Social Democracia Brasileira. *See* Brazilian Social Democratic Party
Partido Demócrata Cristiano, **20th:** 1041
Partido Nacional Revolucionario, **20th:** 616
Partie de campagne, Une. See *Day in the Country, A*
Parting of Hector and Andromache, The (Kauffman), **18th:** 555
Partisan politics (U.S.), **18th:** 413, 1046
Partition, First Treaty of (1698), **17th:** 152, 547, 980
Partition, Second Treaty of (1700), **17th:** 152, 547, 980
Partition of Poland, **18th:** 379, 567, 655
Parton, Dolly, **20th:** 3127-3131
Party of Socialist-Revolutionaries, **20th:** 2110
Parviz, **17th:** 842
Parzival (Wolfram), **MA:** 425, 1124
Pas d'acier, Les (ballet), **20th:** 2648
Paşa, Merzifonlu Kara Mustafa. *See* Kara Mustafa Paşa, Merzifonlu
Pasadena Lifesavers (Chicago), **20th:** 750
Pasado en claro. See *Draft of Shadows, and Other Poems, A*
Pascal, Blaise, **Ren:** 174; **17th:** 37, 271, 422, 487, 514, 632, 713-716, 819, 923
Pascal et Chambord (Offenbach), **19th:** 1699
Pascendi Dominici gregis (Pius X), **20th:** 3273
Paschal (d. 692; antipope), **MA:** 937
Paschal II (d. 1118; pope), **MA:** 94
Paschal III (d. 1168; antipope), **MA:** 57, 386
Paschasius Radbertus, Saint, **MA:** 879
PASOK. *See* Panhellenic Socialist Movement
Passacaglia (Walton), **20th:** 4219
Passacaglia, Op. 1 (Webern), **20th:** 4262
Passage to India, A (Forster), **20th:** 1289
Passage to India (Whitman), **19th:** 2426
Passagen-Werk, Das. See *Arcades Project, The*
Passarowitz, Treaty of (1718), **18th:** 28, 331
Passau, Truce of (1552), **Ren:** 777
Passignano, Domenico, **Ren:** 175
Passion Flowers (Howe), **19th:** 1138
Passion of Joan of Arc, The (Dreyer), **20th:** 1037
Passione di Gesù, La (Aretino), **Ren:** 54
Passions de l'âme, Les. See *Passions of the Soul, The*
Passions of the Soul, The (Descartes), **17th:** 228
Past and Present (Carlyle), **19th:** 416
Past Conditional (Krasner), **20th:** 2197
Pastemaster General. *See* Bilbo, Theodore G.
Pasternak, Boris, **20th:** 3131-3134, 4099
Pasteur, Louis, **19th:** 1316, 1391, 1751-1754
Pasteurization, **19th:** 1753
Pastoral (Beethoven), **19th:** 177
Pastoral Care (Gregory the Great), **MA:** 431
Pastoral poetry, Chinese, **Anc:** 843
Pastoral Symphony (Vaughan Williams), **20th:** 4149
Pastoralism, **19th:** 2413
Pastorals (Pope), **18th:** 805
Pastrana, duchess of. *See* Mendoza y de la Cerda, Ana de
Pastry Wars (1838-1839), **19th:** 1991
Pat and Mike (film), **20th:** 4067
Patchwork Girl of Oz, The (Baum), **19th:** 157
Patel, Vallabhbhai Jhaverbhai, **20th:** 3135-3138
Patent Arms Manufacturing Company, **19th:** 534
Pater, Walter, **Ren:** 385; **19th:** 1755-1757, 2432
Paterson, A. B., **19th:** 1758-1760
Paterson, William, **17th:** 716-719
Pathé, **20th:** 3707
Pather Panchali (film), **20th:** 3394
Pathétique (Tchaikovsky), **19th:** 2235
Pathfinder, The (Cooper), **19th:** 555
Pathologiae cerebri et nervosi generis specimen. See *Essay of the Pathology of the Brain and Nervous Stock, An*
Pathology, **19th:** 2365
Pathos aitia therapeia (Diocles), **Anc:** 278
Patience (Gilbert and Sullivan), **19th:** 919
Patler, John, **Notor:** 912
Paton, Alan, **20th:** 3138-3141
Patriarcha (Filmer), **17th:** 546
Patriarchate, Moscow, **Ren:** 387
Patriarchs, Buddhist, **Anc:** 130
Patriarchy, mythology and, **Anc:** 415
Patricius. *See* Patrick, Saint
Patrick, Mason M., **20th:** 2766
Patrick, Saint, **MA:** 811-814
Patriotic Gore (Wilson), **20th:** 4357
Patriotism Under Three Flags (Angell), **20th:** 93
Patron saints, **Anc:** 206
Patrona Halil Revolt (1730), **18th:** 28, 639
Patronage (Edgeworth), **19th:** 730
Patrons of the arts. *See* Category Index under Philanthropy and Patrons of the Arts
Patterns of Culture (Benedict), **20th:** 297

Patterson, Floyd, **20th:** 63
Patterson, Jim. *See* Longley, Bill
Patton, George S., **20th:** 469, 3142-3145; **Notor:** 348
Pau Casals Orchestra, **20th:** 682
Paul I, **18th:** 956; **19th:** 45
Paul III, **Ren:** 221, 393, 483, 538, 767-770, 1000
Paul IV, **Ren:** 393, 425; **17th:** 330
Paul V, **Ren:** 339; **17th:** 45, 67, 719-721, 810, 936, 962
Paul VI, **20th:** 3148-3151
Paul, Alice, **20th:** 702, 3145-3148
Paul, Oom. *See* Kruger, Paul
Paul, Saint, **Anc:** 6, 437, 458, 611-614, 823
Paul, Saint Vincent de. *See* Vincent de Paul, Saint
Paul Bunyan (Britten), **20th:** 530
Paul of Aegina, **MA:** 814-816
Paul of Tarsus. *See* Paul, Saint
Paul Prescott's Charge (Alger), **19th:** 52
"Paul Revere's Ride" (Longfellow), **18th:** 833
Paul the Apostle. *See* Paul, Saint
Paula, **Anc:** 457
Pauli, Max, **Notor:** 77
Pauli, Wolfgang, **20th:** 438, 3152-3154
Pauline Borghese as Venus Victorious (Canova), **19th:** 407
Pauling, Linus, **20th:** 476, 3155-3158, 4243, 4344
Paulinus (secretary to Saint Ambrose), **Anc:** 43
Paulinus, Suetonius, **Anc:** 163
Paulus, Lucius Aemilius, **Anc:** 343, 383, 755
Paulus Aegineta. *See* Paul of Aegina
Pausanias of Sparta, **Anc:** 15, 214, 615-617
Pausanias the Traveler, **Anc:** 618-620, 680, 761
Pavane pour une infante défunte (Ravel), **20th:** 3386
Pavarotti, Luciano, **20th:** 3159-3162
Pavelić, Ante, **Notor:** 813-815
Pavia, Battle of (1525), **Ren:** 221, 229, 347, 411, 423, 618
Pavia, Council of (1160), **MA:** 56
Pavia, Synod of (1022), **MA:** 489
Pavilon d'Armide, Le (ballet), **20th:** 985
Pavlov, Ivan Petrovich, **20th:** 3162-3165
Pavlova, Anna, **20th:** 985, 1263, 2974, 3166-3169
Pavlovich, Aleksandr. *See* Alexander I (1777-1825; czar of Russia)
Pavlovich, Dmitri, **Notor:** 1126
Pawnees, **19th:** 1794
Pawtuxets, **17th:** 86, 612, 875
Pax Hispanica, **17th:** 737
Pax Sinica, **Anc:** 960
Paya Sai Tiakapat, **Ren:** 547
Payment Deferred (Forester), **20th:** 1284
Payment of Dues (La Tour), **17th:** 494
Payne, Cecilia, **20th:** 3571
Payne, Lewis. *See* Powell, Lewis
Payne-Aldrich Tariff Act of 1909, **20th:** 3931
Payne's Landing, Treaty of (1832), **19th:** 1709
Paysan de la Garonne, Le. See *Peasant of the Garonne, The*
Payytanim, **MA:** 533
Paz, Octavio, **20th:** 3169-3171
Paz en la guerra. See *Peace in War*
Paz Estenssoro, Víctor, **20th:** 3172-3174
Pazzi Chapel, **MA:** 207
Pazzis, **Ren:** 657
Peabody, Elizabeth Palmer, **19th:** 1761-1763
Peace. See *Eirēnē*
Peace (Turner), **19th:** 2324
Peace, Charles, **Notor:** 815-816
Peace and Wealth (Kephisodotos), **Anc:** 694
Peace in War (Unamuno), **20th:** 4129
Peace of _______. *See* _______, Peace of
Peace with Honour (Milne), **20th:** 2754
Peacemaker. *See* Deganawida
Peacham, Edmund, **17th:** 176
Peacock Throne, **17th:** 843
Peaks and Glaciers of Nun Kun (Workman and Workman), **19th:** 2468
Peale, Charles Willson, **18th:** 768-771; portrait of John Paul Jones, 541; painting of American flag, 866
Peale, Titian Ramsay, **19th:** 232
Peanuts (crop), **20th:** 679
Peanuts (Schulz), **20th:** 3672
Peanuts Gallery (Zwilich), **20th:** 4477
Pearl (Joplin), **20th:** 2044
Pearl Harbor, bombing of, **20th:** 3513
Pearl of Orr's Island, The (Stowe), **19th:** 2185
Pearl S. Buck Memorial Fund, **20th:** 559
Pearls and Pebbles (Traill), **19th:** 2292
Pears, Peter, **20th:** 530
Pearse, Patrick, **20th:** 3035
Pearson, Drew, **Notor:** 217
Pearson, Lester B., **20th:** 761, 2376, 3174-3176, 3598
Peary, Robert Edwin, **20th:** 84, 3177-3181
Peasant Dance (Bruegel), **Ren:** 136
Peasant of the Garonne, The (Maritain), **20th:** 2626
Peasant Wedding (Bruegel), **Ren:** 136
Peasantry, **18th:** Austria, 544; French Revolution, 78, 844, 877; in literature, 597; Marie-Antoinette, 659; in painting, 390; Pugachev's Revolt, 816; Russia, 213. *See also* Poverty and the poor; Social reform
Peasants' Revolt (1381), **MA:** 130, 395, 493, 894, 1033

Peasants' War (1524-1526), **Ren:** 405, 584, 758
Peasants' War, The (Kollwitz), **20th:** 2190
Peau de chagrin, La. See *Magic Skin, The*
Peau noire, masques blancs. See *Black Skin, White Masks*
Pebbles and Sunshine (Richardson), **19th:** 1902
Pecci, Vincenzo Gioacchino. *See* Leo XIII
Pecham, John, **MA:** 817-820
Péchés de vieillesse (Rossini), **19th:** 1946
Pêcheurs de perles, Les (Bizet), **19th:** 241
Peck, Darlie Lynn. *See* Routier, Darlie
Peck, Gregory, **20th:** 3181-3183
Peculiar Doctrines of the Gospel, Explained and Defended (Webster), **19th:** 2404
Pedagogical Sketchbook (Klee), **20th:** 2178
Pedant Imitated, The. See *Ridiculous Pedant, The*
Pédant joué, Le. See *Ridiculous Pedant, The*
Pedersen, Knut. *See* Hamsun, Knut
Pedrarias, **Ren:** 77, 902
Pedraz, Santiago, **Notor:** 900
Pedro I, **19th:** 1763-1766
Pedro I of Castile. *See* Peter the Cruel
Pedro II, **19th:** 1766-1768, 1870
Peel, Sir Robert, **19th:** 303, 521, 643, 667, 840, 924, 1696, 1768-1771, 2122; **Notor:** 677
Peeling the Onion (Grass), **20th:** 1576
Peer Gynt (Grieg), **19th:** 986
Peer Gynt (Ibsen), **19th:** 1165
Peggy-Ann (Rodgers and Hart), **20th:** 1692
Pegnitz Junction, The (Gallant), **20th:** 1377
Pei, I. M., **20th:** 3183-3186
Pei Di, **MA:** 1086
P'ei Ti. *See* Pei Di
P'ei Yao-ch'ing. *See* Pei Yaoqing
Pei Yaoqing, **MA:** 1085
Peirce, Charles Sanders, **19th:** 1215, 1772-1775
Peiresc, Nicolas-Claude Fabri de, **17th:** 304, 577, 722-724
Pelagianism, **Anc:** 143, 864, 947. *See also* Semi-Pelagianism
Pelagius, **Anc:** 864
Pelé, **20th:** 3187-3190
Pélerin de Maricourt, Pierre le. *See* Peregrinus de Maricourt, Petrus
Pelham, Henry, **18th:** 405, 771-774
Pelléas et Mélisande (Debussy), **20th:** 938
Pellisson, Paul, **17th:** 480
Pelopidas, **Anc:** 303
Peloponnesian League, **Anc:** 622, 859
Peloponnesian War (431-404 B.C.E.), **Anc:** 14, 33, 68, 90, 127, 216, 304, 327, 622, 659, 882, 968
Pelops, **Anc:** 348
Peltrie, Madame de la, **17th:** 575, 596
Pelvis with Moon (O'Keeffe), **20th:** 3032
Pembroke's Men, **Ren:** 625
Pemisapan, **Ren:** 771-772
Pendennis (Thackeray), **19th:** 2258
Pendergast, James, **Notor:** 817
Pendergast, Thomas Joseph, **Notor:** 817-818
Pendleton Act of 1883, **19th:** 82, 870
Penei rabbah (Manasseh ben Israel), **17th:** 583
Penelope, **Anc:** 429
Peng Dehuai, **20th:** 2381, 3191-3193
P'eng Te-huai. *See* Peng Dehuai
Penguin Island (France), **19th:** 816-817
Penicillin, **20th:** 1255, 1260, 1850, 4181
Peninsular War (1808-1814), **19th:** 1993, 2410; Michel Ney, 1667
Penitent Magdalen, The (Caravaggio), **Ren:** 170
Penitent Magdalene (Artemisia), **17th:** 307
Penn, William, **17th:** 57, 252, 724-728; **Notor:** 753
Pennsylvania Academy of the Fine Arts, **18th:** 770; **19th:** 441
Pennsylvania colony, **17th:** 726
Pennsylvania Gazette, The (Franklin), **18th:** 371
Pennsylvania Railroad, **19th:** 419
Penruddock's Uprising (1655), **17th:** 206
Pensacola, Siege of (1780), **18th:** 626
Pensacola, Treaty of (1784), **18th:** 627
Pensacolas, **19th:** 1190
Pensée sauvage. See *Savage Mind, The*
Pensées (Pascal), **17th:** 715
Pensées philosophiques (Diderot), **18th:** 308
Pentagon Papers, publication of, **20th:** 1561
Pentateuch and Book of Joshua Critically Examined, The (Colenso), **19th:** 1520
Penthesilea (Kleist), **19th:** 1289
Penthilus, **Anc:** 653
Pentimento (Hellman), **20th:** 1753
Pentreath, Dolly, **Notor:** 818-819, 1110
Penzias, Arno A., **20th:** 1903
People, The (Michelet), **19th:** 1565
People of the Abyss, The (London), **20th:** 2422
People of the Polar North, The (Rasmussen), **20th:** 3379
People, Yes, The (Sandburg), **20th:** 3621
People's Charter (England), **19th:** 1808
People's Liberation Army, **20th:** 2381, 4467

People's National Movement, **20th:** 830
People's Party (U.S.), **20th:** 3815
Pépin I, **MA:** 254, 662
Pépin II, **MA:** 254
Pépin II of Herstal, **MA:** 250
Pépin III the Short, **MA:** 242, 253
Pepin, Pierre-Théodore-Florentine, **Notor:** 354
Pépin the Hunchback, **MA:** 242
Pepsodent Radio Show Starring Bob Hope, The (radio program), **20th:** 1870
Pepys, Samuel, **17th:** 51, 342, 349, 677, 728-731, 971
Pequots, **17th:** 130, 567
Perception, **Anc:** 88; **18th:** 111, 113, 264, 481, 514, 548
Perceval (Chrétien), **MA:** 267
Perceval, Spencer, **Notor:** 83
Percy (More), **18th:** 702
Percy, Henry, **MA:** 495
Percy, Thomas, **Ren:** 325
Percy conspiracy, **MA:** 495, 501
Percy's Year of Rhymes (Richardson), **19th:** 1902
Perdiccas, **Anc:** 63, 598, 720, 763
Perdiccas III, **Anc:** 420, 637
Père Goriot, La. See *Father Goriot*
Peregrinations of a Pariah (Tristan), **19th:** 2297
Peregrinus. *See* Vincent of Lérins, Saint
Peregrinus de Maricourt, Petrus, **MA:** 820-824
Perelandra (Lewis), **20th:** 2354
Perestroika, **20th:** 1531
Peretti, Felice. *See* Sixtus V
Pereyaslavl, Treaty of (1654), **17th:** 463, 624
Pérez, Antonio, **Ren:** 671, 780
Pérez, José Julían Martí y. *See* Martí, José
Perez, Leander, **Notor:** 819-820
Pérez de Cuéllar, Javier, **20th:** 3194-3197, 4188
Perfect Wagnerite, The (Shaw), **20th:** 3717
Perfume, **20th:** 729
Perfumed Garden of the Cheikh Nefzaoui, The, **19th:** 370
Pergamum, Library of, **Anc:** 315
Peri, Jacopo, **17th:** 658
Peri aition kai semeion oxeon kai chronion pathon (Aretaeus), **Anc:** 85
Peri apochēs empsychōn (Porphyry), **Anc:** 688
Peri archaias komoidias (Eratosthenes), **Anc:** 316
Peri archaies ietrikes (Hippocrates), **Anc:** 37, 421
Peri archōn (Origen), **Anc:** 601
Peri automatopoietikes (Hero of Alexandria), **Anc:** 401
Peri biōn dogmatōn kai apophthegmatōn tōn en philosophia eudokimēsantōn (Diogenes Laertius), **Anc:** 654, 723
Peri chreias morion (Galen), **Anc:** 349
Peri diaireseon biblion (Euclid), **Anc:** 318
Peri diaites oxeon (Hippocratic writers), **Anc:** 421
Peri epideomōn (Diocles), **Anc:** 278
Peri eykhēs (Origen), **Anc:** 601
Peri gunaikeiōn (Diocles), **Anc:** 278
Peri helikon (Archimedes), **Anc:** 82
Peri hippikēs (Xenophon), **Anc:** 969
Peri hypsous (Longinus), **Anc:** 751
Peri konoeideon kai sphaireodeon (Archimedes), **Anc:** 82
Peri ochoymenon (Archimedes), **Anc:** 82
Peri pepeseōs (Diocles), **Anc:** 278
Peri physeōs (Empedocles), **Anc:** 295, 397, 521, 609, 966
Peri phytikōn aitiōn (Theophrastus), **Anc:** 873
Peri phytikōn historiōn (Theophrastus), **Anc:** 873
Peri puretōn (Diocles), **Anc:** 278
Peri puros kai aeros (Diocles), **Anc:** 278
Peri sphairas kai kylindron (Archimedes), **Anc:** 81
Peri sphygmōn (Herophilus), **Anc:** 411
Peri thanasimōn pharmakōn (Diocles), **Anc:** 278
Peri therapeiōn (Diocles), **Anc:** 278
"Peri tōn en Cherronesoi" (Demosthenes), **Anc:** 265
Peri tōn kat iētreion (Diocles), **Anc:** 278
Peri tōn mechanikon theorematon (Archimedes), **Anc:** 82
Peri tou Ioudaikou polemou. See *Bellum Judaium*
"Peri tou Stephanou" (Demosthenes), **Anc:** 267
Periander, **Notor:** 251
Pericles, **Anc:** 33, 52, 127, 215, 564, 620-624, 707, 810
Pericles the Younger, **Anc:** 128
Periegesis Hellados (Pausanias the Traveler), **Anc:** 618
Perikeiromenē (Menander), **Anc:** 548
Perilaus, **Notor:** 834
Period-luminosity scale, **20th:** 2318
Periodic table of elements, **19th:** 1546
Peripateticarum quæstionum libri quinque (Cesalpino), **Ren:** 211
Peripatetics, **Anc:** 94, 277, 872
Periploi (travel guides), **Anc:** 618
Periplus (Hanno), **Anc:** 385
Perkins, Frances, **20th:** 1840, 3198-3201
Perkins, Maxwell, **20th:** 4385
Perkins Institute for the Blind, **19th:** 1141, 1487
Perón, Eva, **20th:** 3201-3204, 3206; **Notor:** 821-823
Perón, Isabel, **Notor:** 824, 1066
Perón, Juan, **20th:** 432, 1900, 3201, 3205-3208; **Notor:** 821, 823-824, 1066

Peronne Conference (1468), **Ren:** 574
Perot, H. Ross, **20th:** 3208-3212
Pérotin, **MA:** 824-826
Perotinus. *See* Pérotin
Perpetual Peace (Kant), **18th:** 550
Perpetual Peace, Treaty of (1502), **Ren:** 499
Perpignan, Battle of (1542), **Ren:** 31
Perpignan, Siege of (1642), **17th:** 933
Perrault, Charles, **17th:** 64, 533, 731-733; **19th:** 1155
Perret, Auguste, **20th:** 2323, 3213-3215
Perrier, François, **17th:** 504
Perro del hortelano, El. See *Gardener's Dog, The*
Perry, Carolina Coronado. *See* Coronado, Carolina
Perry, Fred, **20th:** 3216-3218
Perry, Horatio Justus, **19th:** 557
Perry, Linda. *See* Hazzard, Linda Burfield
Perry, Matthew C., **18th:** 505; **19th:** 1109, 1169, 1776-1779, 1969
Perry, Oliver Hazard, **19th:** 1776, 1779-1781
Persaeus of Citium, **Anc:** 983
Persai (Aeschylus), **Anc:** 8, 137, 633
Persecution, religious, **Ren:** Christians in Egypt, 1007; Christians in England, 149, 325, 668; Christians in Japan, 460; Jews in Spain, 580; Protestants in England, 370, 639; Protestants in France, 463, 817; **17th:** England, 34, 84, 92, 101, 218, 284, 877, 982; France, 36, 182, 407, 555, 560; Germany, 61; Jansenists, 422, 773; Japan, 917, 919; Jews, 582, 837, 871, 960-961; New Amsterdam, 891; Quakers, 284, 725; Scotland, 122; Virginia, 120; **18th:** Moravians, 1120; Shakers, 591
Perseus (Cellini), **Ren:** 204
Pershing, John J., **20th:** 2630, 3142, 3219-3222, 4161; **Notor:** 1071
Persia, **Anc:** Alcibiades and, 34; Alexander the Great and, 39; Caria and, 545; development of empire, 251; Greece and, 8, 137, 213, 252, 265, 408, 523, 564, 615, 630, 859, 969, 972; India and, 202; Rome and, 485; Xerxes' rule, 972; **MA:** architecture, 413; astronomy, 21; Eastern Roman Empire's invasion of, 507; historiography, 41, 413; mathematics, 21; medicine, 884; Mongol invasion of, 908, 915; philosophy, 884; physicians, 884; poetry, 41, 451, 908, 916. *See also* Iran; Geographical Index under Iran
Persian-Afghan Wars (1709-1747), **18th:** 722
Persian Gulf War (1990-1991), **20th:** 596, 1196, 1948, 1953, 3195, 3323; Syria, 154
Persian Letters (Montesquieu), **18th:** 695
Persian-Ottoman conflicts, **18th:** 639, 723
Persian Wars (499-479 B.C.E.), **Anc:** 109, 137, 407, 505, 630, 794
Persians, The. See *Persai*
Persika (Ctesias), **Anc:** 744
Person to Person (television program), **20th:** 2881
Persona (film), **20th:** 318
Personal Memoirs of U. S. Grant, The (Twain), **19th:** 2330
Personal Narrative of a Pilgrimage to El-Medinah and Meccah (Burton), **19th:** 368
Personal Narrative of Travels to the Equinoctial Regions of the New Continent During the Years 1799-1804 (Humboldt), **19th:** 603
Personal Recollections of Joan of Arc (Twain), **19th:** 2331
Personal Rule (1629-1640), **17th:** 768
Personality tests, **20th:** 3523
Persons and Places (Santayana), **20th:** 3630
Persuasion (Austen), **19th:** 96
Perth, Siege of (1312-1313), **MA:** 203
Pertharite, roi des Lombards (Corneille), **17th:** 195
Pertini, Sandro, **Notor:** 241
Peru, **18th:** independence of, 994; **19th:** independence of, 1985, 2196. *See also* Geographical Index
Perú (Matto), **19th:** 1513
Perugino, Pietro, **Ren:** 486, 561, 819
Perutz, Max, **20th:** 476
Peruzzi, Baldassare, **Ren:** 175
Pervaya lyubov. See *First Love*
Peshkov, Aleksey Maksimovich. *See* Gorky, Maxim
Pestalozzi, Johann Heinrich, **19th:** 1782-1785
Peste, La. See *Plague, The*
Pesticides, effect on farmworkers, **20th:** 739
Pestsaule, Vienna, **18th:** 350
Pet of the Household and How to Save It, The (Folger), **19th:** 813
Pétain, Philippe, **20th:** 398, 780, 1427, 2286, 3222-3225; **Notor:** 262-264, 298, 609, 825-827
Petchenegs, **MA:** 105-106, 794, 1069
Peter I the Great, **17th:** 13, 445, 625, 685, 795, 865; **18th:** 232, 774-777; Catherine the Great, 213; and Ottoman Empire, 27; Elizabeth Petrovna, 321; **Notor:** 514
Peter II, **17th:** 821
Peter III, **18th:** 212, 755, 778-780, 814; abdication, 755-758; Catherine the Great, 757; death of, 756; Grigori Grigoryevich Orlov, 757; Grigori

Aleksandrovich Potemkin, 808; **Notor:** 516
Peter, Saint, **Anc:** 223, 437, 472, 624-627
Peter and the Wolf (Prokofiev), **20th:** 3340
Peter Bell the Third (Shelley), **19th:** 2095
Peter des Roches, **MA:** 212, 490
Peter Grimes (Britten), **20th:** 531
Peter Halket of Mashonaland (Schreiner), **19th:** 2024
Peter of Galatia, **Anc:** 865
Peter of Maricourt. *See* Peregrinus de Maricourt, Petrus
Peter Pan (Leigh and Charlap), **20th:** 3461
Peter Porcupine. *See* Cobbett, William
Peter Schmoll und seine Nachbarn (Weber), **19th:** 2395
Peter the Cruel, **Notor:** 827-828
Peterloo Massacre, **19th:** 892
Peterson, Conner, **Notor:** 829
Peterson, Laci, **Notor:** 828
Peterson, Oscar, **20th:** 3226-3228
Peterson, Scott, **Notor:** 828-831
Peterwardein, Treaty of (1718), **18th:** 230
Pétion, Alexandre, **19th:** 268, 495
Petiot, Marcel, **Notor:** 831-832
Petit, Roland, **20th:** 1270
Petit Pierre, Le. See *Little Pierre*
Petit Soldat, Le. See *Little Soldier, The*
Petit Testament, Le. See *Legacy, The*
Petite Fadette, La. See *Little Fadette*
Petite Marchande d'allumettes, La. See *Little Match Girl, The*
Petite messe solennelle (Rossini), **19th:** 1946
Petite Suite (Borodin), **19th:** 282
Petition of Right (1628), **17th:** 98, 144, 178, 767, 884
Petition, Party of, **19th:** 621
Petlyura, Symon, **Notor:** 832-834
Petőfi, Sándor, **Notor:** 596
Petrarch, **MA:** 170, 264, 697, 827-831, 850, 897
Petrified Forest, The (Sherwood), **20th:** 406
Petrine Theory, **MA:** 646
Petrocelli, Daniel, **Notor:** 968
Petronilla of Meath, **Notor:** 598
Petrov affair, **20th:** 1190
Petrović, Karadjordje, **19th:** 2479
Petrovich, Avvakum. *See* Avvakum Petrovich
Petrovna, Elizabeth. *See* Elizabeth Petrovna
Petrucci, Ottaviano dei, **Ren:** 516
Petrushka (ballet), **20th:** 986
Pettigrew, Richard F., **19th:** 1019
Petty, Sir William, **17th:** 564, 733-735
Petty-Fitzmaurice, Henry Charles Keith. *See* Lansdowne, Lord
Peucestas, **Anc:** 763
Peuerbach, Georg von, **Ren:** 773- 775
Peuple, Le. See *People, The*
Peveril of the Peak (Scott), **19th:** 2048
Pflanze, Die (Cohn), **19th:** 528
Phaedon (Mendelssohn), **18th:** 675
Phaedōn (Plato), **Anc:** 12, 94, 963
Phaedra, **Anc:** 327
Phaedra (Henze), **20th:** 1765
Phaedra (Racine), **17th:** 774
Phaedri augusti Liberti Fabularum Aesopiarum (Phaedrus), **Anc:** 628
Phaedros (Plato), **Anc:** 450
Phaedrus, **Anc:** 13, 628-630
Phaenomena quondam Apolcalyptica (Sewall), **18th:** 894
Phaethon (Dekker), **17th:** 223
Phainomena (Euclid), **Anc:** 318
Phalanstère, Le, **19th:** 807
Phalaris, **Notor:** 834-835
Pham Vam Dong, **20th:** 1836
Phänomenologie des Geistes, Die. See *Phenomenology of Spirit, The*
Phantasmagoria (Carroll), **19th:** 424
Phantasy Quartet (Britten), **20th:** 530
Phantom Lady, The (Calderón), **17th:** 114
Phantom of Liberty, The (film), **20th:** 579
Phantom of the Opera, The (Lloyd Webber and Hart), **20th:** 2415
Phantom Public, The (Lippmann), **20th:** 2401
Pharaohs, **Anc:** Amenhotep III, 45; Menes, 556; Menkaure, 558; Montuhotep II, 570; Psamtik I, 710; Ramses II, 735; Sesostris III, 771; Thutmose III, 885; Tutankhamen, 908; women as, 388; Zoser, 996
Pharisees, **Anc:** 459, 468; and Saint Paul, 611
Pharisees, The (Schmidt-Rottluff), **20th:** 3662
Pharmaceutice rationalis (Willis), **17th:** 987
Pharmacology, **Anc:** Greek, 278; Roman, 289
Pharsalus, Battle of (48 B.C.E.), **Anc:** 166, 174, 185, 683, 927
Phasa Mikeun, **Anc:** 466
Phase stability, **20th:** 2534
Phèdre. See *Phaedra*
Pheidippides, **Anc:** 630-633
Phénix, Le (Éluard), **20th:** 1154
Phénomène humain, Le. See *Phenomenon of Man, The*
Phénoménologie de la perception. See *Phenomenology of Perception*
Phenomenology, **20th:** 1742, 1955, 2611, 2710, 3656, 3841
Phenomenology of Perception (Merleau-Ponty), **20th:** 2710
Phenomenology of Spirit, The (Hegel), **19th:** 1066
Phenomenon of Man, The (Teilhard), **20th:** 3965
Pheromones, **20th:** 4358
Phidias, **Anc:** 633-636, 675

Philadelphia, **18th:** 865, 873, 1090
Philadelphia Anti-Slavery Society, **19th:** 989
Philadelphia Convention, **18th:** 373, 413, 453, 636, 1092
Philadelphia Functionalists, **19th:** 2198
Philadelphia Museum, **18th:** 769
Philadelphia Negro, The (Du Bois), **20th:** 1047
Philadelphia Phillies, **20th:** 3527
Philadelphia 76ers, **20th:** 726
Philadelphia Story, The (film), **20th:** 1770, 3862
Philanthropy, **18th:** Hannah More, 702-704; **19th:** Andrew Carnegie, 421; James Buchanan Duke, 694; Marshall Field, 775; J. P. Morgan, 1602; Alfred Nobel, 1691; Robert Owen, 1721; Joseph Pulitzer, 1843; Cecil Rhodes, 1894; John D. Rockefeller, 1924; Leland Stanford, 2134; Montgomery Ward, 2389. *See also* Category Index
Philanthropinum, **18th:** 90
Philanthropist (newspaper), **19th:** 471
Philaret, **17th:** 663, 794, 944
Philaster (Beaumont and Fletcher), **Ren:** 94; **17th:** 279
Philby, Kim, **Notor:** 109, 152, 164, 674, 836-838
Philēbos (Plato), **Anc:** 660
Philémon et Baucis (Gounod), **19th:** 953
Philharmonic Society, **19th:** 2268
Philiki Hetairia, **19th:** 2478
Philinus of Cos, **Anc:** 412
Philip I (1478-1506; king of Spain), **Ren:** 50, 220, 330, 505, 614, 636; **Notor:** 531
Philip II of Macedonia (382-336 B.C.E.), **Anc:** 39, 265, 597, 637-640, 719, 872
Philip II (1165-1223; king of France), **MA:** 387, 389, 543, 584, 666, 725, 835-838, 891
Philip II the Bold (1342-1404; duke of Burgundy), **MA:** 832, 948; **Notor:** 203, 404
Philip II (1527-1598; king of Spain), **Ren:** 6, 208, 310, 321, 394, 425, 615, 637, 670, 672, 778-781, 967; Americas and, 551, 672; architecture and, 445; art patronage and, 391, 445, 937; Catholic League and, 428; Charles V and, 222; duke of Alva and, 31; Dutch Wars of Independence and, 668; France and, 184; Habsburg Dynasty and, 648; marriage to Mary I, 370, 401, 639; Netherlands and, 615; Pius V and, 798; Protestantism and, 629; Sofonisba Anguissola and, 46; William the Silent and, 993; **17th:** 431
Philip III Arrhidaeus (d. 317 B.C.E.), **Anc:** 719
Philip III the Bold (1245-1285; king of France), **MA:** 839
Philip III the Good (1396-1467; duke of Burgundy), **MA:** 366, 503, 832-835
Philip III (1578-1621; king of Spain), **Ren:** 208, 373; **17th:** 736-738, 959; and daughter Anne of Austria, 18; decline of Habsburg Spain, 425; and the duke de Lerma, 530; and count-duke of Olivares, 697; and son Philip IV, 738, 770; and Tirso de Molina, 913
Philip IV the Fair (1268-1314; king of France), **MA:** 187, 329, 347, 552, 839-842, 858, 1074; **Notor:** 115
Philip IV (1605-1665; king of Spain), **17th:** 138, 551, 738-741; and Anne of Austria, 19; arts patronage, 307; ascension, 770; and Pedro Calderón de la Barca, 113; and son Charles II (of Spain), 151; Queen Christina's conversion to Catholicism, 165; and Elizabeth de Médicis, 598; and John IV, 431; and son John of Austria, 425; and Marie-Thérèse, 585, 600; and Jules Mazarin, 622; and Cosimo II de' Medici, 627; and the duchesse de Montpensier, 661; and the count-duke of Olivares, 697; opposition to intellectuals, 913; and father Philip III, 738; and Diego Velázquez, 953; and Francisco de Zurbarán, 1005; **Notor:** 201
Philip V (238-179 B.C.E.; king of Macedonia), **Anc:** 67, 383
Philip V (1683-1746; king of Spain), **17th:** 152; **18th:** 136, 781-783; **Notor:** 202
Philip, King. *See* Metacom
Philip Augustus. *See* Philip II (1165-1223; king of France)
Philip of Anjou. *See* Philip V (1683-1746; king of Spain)
Philip of Hesse. *See* Philip the Magnanimous
Philip of Poakanoket. *See* Metacom
Philip of Swabia, **MA:** 389
Philip the Magnanimous, **Ren:** 143, 775-778
Philip the Pious. *See* Philip III (1578-1621; king of Spain)
Philipp der Grossmütige. *See* Philip the Magnanimous
Philippa of Hainaut, **MA:** 842-844
Philippe, duc d'Orléans. *See* Orléans, duc d'
Philippe le Roy (van Dyck), **17th:** 245
Philippi, Battle of (42 B.C.E.), **Anc:** 74, 146, 167, 186, 431, 527
Philippicae (Cicero), **Anc:** 73
Philippics. See *Kata Philippou*
Philippides, **Anc:** 631
Philippine-American War (1899-1902), **20th:** 3520
Philippines, **Ren:** 551; Spain and, 194, 593; **19th:** 647, 1462;

20th: independence of, 2493, 2620; William Howard Taft, 3929. *See also* Geographical Index
Philippos (Isocrates), **Anc:** 451
Philips, Frederick, **17th:** 519
Philips, Katherine, **17th:** 741-743
Philips, Peter, **Ren:** 151
Philips Pavilion, **20th:** 4415
Philistines, **Anc:** 747
Philistion of Locri, **Anc:** 278
Phillip, Arthur, **18th:** 783-785
Phillips, Albert. *See* Lustig, Victor
Phillips, Harold. *See* Chambers, Whittaker
Phillips, Sam, **20th:** 3330
Phillips, Wendell, **19th:** 1231, 1785-1788
Philo of Alexandria, **Anc:** 640-643; **Notor:** 840
Philoktētēs (Sophocles), **Anc:** 811
Philosophaster (Burton), **17th:** 109
Philosopher or Dog? (Machado), **19th:** 1451
Philosopher's stone, **MA:** 563
Philosopher's Way of Life, The (al-Rāzī), **MA:** 886
Philosophes, **18th:** Étienne Bonnot de Condillac, 265; *Encylopedia* project, 33; Claude-Adrien Helvétius, 479-482; Paul-Henri-Dietrich d'Holbach, 501-504
Philosophia Moysaica. See *Mosaicall Philosophy*
Philosophia sensibus demonstrata (Campanella), **17th:** 125
Philosophiae Naturalis Principia Mathematica. See *Principia*
Philosophical and Physical Opinions (Newcastle), **17th:** 676
Philosophical and Political History of the Settlements and Trade of the Europeans in the East and West Indies (Raynal), **18th:** 829
Philosophical Commentary on These Words in the Gospel, Luke XIV, 23, A (Bayle), **17th:** 37
Philosophical Essay on Probabilities, A (Laplace), **19th:** 1318
Philosophical Explanations (Nozick), **20th:** 3000
Philosophical Faith and Revelation (Jaspers), **20th:** 1998
Philosophical Fragments (Kierkegaard), **19th:** 1280
Philosophical Inquiry into the Origin of Our Ideas of the Sublime and Beautiful, A (Burke), **18th:** 174
Philosophical Investigations (Wittgenstein), **20th:** 4380
Philosophical Letters (Newcastle), **17th:** 677
Philosophical Radicalism, **19th:** 456, 1576
Philosophical Radicals. *See* Utilitarianism
Philosophical Rudiments Concerning Government and Society (Hobbes), **17th:** 379
Philosophical Society of Edinburgh, **18th:** 1050
Philosophical Studies (Moore), **20th:** 2816
Philosophicall Fancies. See *Philosophical and Physical Opinions*
Philosophie. See *Philosophy* (Jaspers)
Philosophie bergsonienne, La. See *Bergsonian Philosophy and Thomism*
Philosophie der Aufklärung, Die. See *Philosophy of the Enlightenment, The*
Philosophie der Mythologie (Schelling), **19th:** 2011
Philosophie der symbolischen Formen, Die. See *Philosophy of Symbolic Forms, The*
Philosophie des Unbewussten. See *Philosophy of the Unconscious*
Philosophie rurale, La (Quesnay and Mirabeau), **18th:** 821
Philosophies for Sale. See *Bion Prasis*
Philosophische Glaube angesichts der Offenbarung, Der. See *Philosophical Faith and Revelation*
Philosophische Untersuchungen über das Wesen der menschlichen Freiheit. See *Of Human Freedom*
Philosophiske Smuler. See *Philosophical Fragments*
Philosophy, **Anc:** Buddhist, 931; Chinese, 379, 502, 553, 577, 979; Christian, 142, 866; cosmology and, 295; culture and, 451; divisions of, 982; Eleatic, 610; Judaism and, 641; knowledge and, 724; medicine and, 36, 84, 421; music and, 97; nature and, 397; paganism and, 668; poetry and, 610; Pre-Socratic, 856, 965, 985; religion and, 54, 702; rulers and, 659; science and, 263; Sophism and, 707; theology and, 854; women and, 129; **MA:** Belgium, 1105; Byzantine Empire, 863-864; China, 809; England, 1130; France, 13, 180, 215, 761, 943, 1098, 1102; Germany, 778; India, 876, 926; Iran, 125; Italy, 174, 1028, 1050; Jewish, 687, 730; Muslim, 119, 121, 370, 526; Netherlands, 1105; Persia, 884; Scotland, 330; Spain, 533; **Ren:** China, 986; England, 73; Italy, 138, 345, 588, 782; **17th:** China, 972; England, 95, 188, 379, 543, 677; France, 227, 252, 305, 630, 715; Germany, 60, 514, 760; Italy, 125; Netherlands, 872; **18th:** China, 287-289; empiricism, 111-115, 264, 309; England, 104, 187-189; France, 31, 263-269, 307-311; Germany, 342-346, 548-

551, 598-602, 675-677; idealism, 111; materialism, 111; mechanical, 934; moralism, 922, 1009; Neo-Confucianism, 287; religion, 601; Scotland, 338-342; sensationalist theory, 264; **19th:** Denmark, 1278; England, 289, 1045, 1572, 1574, 2103, 2127; France, 255, 806, 1836, 1976; Germany, 837, 1066, 1682, 2009, 2020; Great Britain, 971; Japan, 2213; Russia, 120, 1811; United States, 746, 1215, 1773; **20th:** Christian, 1489; Germany, 688; Gestalt theory, 1111; Italy, 869; Japan, 2981; legal, 1114; political, 2829, 2999, 3391; speculative, 3629. *See also* Category Index
Philosophy (Jaspers), **20th:** 1997
Philosophy (Klimt), **20th:** 2180
Philosophy in a New Key (Lnager), **20th:** 2264
Philosophy of Earthquakes, Natural and Religious, The (Stukeley), **18th:** 953
Philosophy of Existence (Jaspers), **20th:** 1998
Philosophy of Friedrich Nietzsche, The (Mencken), **20th:** 2689
Philosophy of Physics, The (Planck), **20th:** 3284
Philosophy of Right (Hegel), **19th:** 1067
Philosophy of St. Thomas Aquinas (Gilson), **20th:** 1489
Philosophy of Symbolic Forms, The (Cassirer), **20th:** 689
Philosophy of the Enlightenment, The (Cassirer), **20th:** 689
Philosophy of the Revolution (Nasser), **20th:** 2915
Philosophy of the Unconscious (Hartmann), **19th:** 2021
Philostratus, **Anc:** 482
Philothea (Child), **19th:** 483
Phineas Redux (Trollope), **19th:** 2302
Phineus (Aeschylus), **Anc:** 8
Phipps, Sir William, **18th:** 673
Phlogiston theory, **18th:** 218, 580, 683, 933-937
Pho Sma Ton Camp, Battle of (1768), **18th:** 968
Phocas, **MA:** 432, 505, 933
Phoenicians, **Anc:** 271
Phoenix, The (Middleton), **17th:** 636
Phoenix Coyotes, **20th:** 1586
Phoenix Park murders, **19th:** 1749
Phonograph, **19th:** 731
Phonology, **20th:** 1987
Phormio (Terence), **Anc:** 850
Photius, **MA:** 766
Photo-Secession movement, **20th:** 3838, 3866
Photoelectric effect, **20th:** 2750
Photography, **19th:** 590; American West, 1058; development of, 1678; England, 423; United States, 293; **20th:** color, 1080, 2472; film, 1079; France, 672; United States, 115, 3865. *See also* Category Index
Photometric Researches (Peirce), **19th:** 1772
Photoplay (magazine), **20th:** 3246
Photosynthesis, study of, **20th:** 621
Phraya Taksin. *See* Taksin
Phrenology, **19th:** 812, 1143
Phryne, **Anc:** 695
Phrynichus, **Anc:** 877
Phrynon, **Anc:** 653
Phtochoules tou Theou, Ho. See *Saint Francis*
Phumiphon Adunlayadet. *See* Bhumibol Adulyadej
Phung Thi Le Ly. *See* Hayslip, Le Ly
Phya Tak. *See* Taksin
Physica (Aristotle), **Anc:** 95
Physica subterranea (Becher), **17th:** 40
Physical Geography (Somerville), **19th:** 2122
Physical Geography of the Sea (Maury), **19th:** 1523
Physicians, **MA:** Byzantine Empire, 815; education, 373, 446, 650; France, 372; Morocco, 120; Persia, 884; Spain, 592; women, 372, 1031; **18th:** Edward Jenner, 532-535; Benjamin Rush, 873. *See also* Medicine
Physician's Prayer, A (Maimonides), **MA:** 688
Physicke Against Fortune. See *On Remedies for Good and Bad Fortunes*
Physico-mathesis de lumine, coloribus, et iride (Grimaldi), **17th:** 322
Physics, **MA:** 216; **Ren:** Italy, 921; Netherlands, 913; **17th:** England, 710; Germany, 333, 458; Italy, 322, 922; Netherlands, 399; **18th:** Marquise du Châtelet, 241; Leonhard Euler, 333-335; Gaspard Monge, 683; theory of heat, 683; **19th:** atomic theory, 599, 887; celestial mechanics, 1817; conical refraction, 1016; conservation of energy, 997; dynamos, 760; electric cell, 996; electrodynamics, 1074; electromagnetism, 1079, 1529, 1825; England, 2122; France, 166; gases, 598, 617, 886; Germany, 1931; heat diffusion, 810; optics, 1074; radioactivity, 166; relativity theory, 1818; thermodynamics, 914, 1265; velocity of light, 1568; X rays, 1932; **20th:** Compton effect, 818; high-pressure, 527; low-temperature, 2079; mathematical, 1801; neutron, 715; operationalism, 528; radioactivity, 443; X-ray crystallography, 475. *See also* Category Index
Physikalische gesetzlichkeit im lichte neuer forschung. See *Universe in the Light of Modern Physics, The*

Physiocracy, **18th:** 267, 545, 727, 820-822, 830, 996
Physiocratie (Quesnay), **18th:** 821
Physiologie als Erfahrungswissenschaft, Die (Burdach), **19th:** 114
Physiologie humaine. See *Human Physiology*
Physiology, **Anc:** 36, 85; Galen on, 349; Greek, 278, 311; **19th:** France, 206; Germany, 1073; **20th:** Australia, 1090; Great Britain, 259; Hering-Breuer reflex, 514. *See also* Medicine; Category Index
Physiology of Food and Economy of Diet, The (Bayliss), **20th:** 261
Physiology of Synapses, The (Eccles), **20th:** 1091
Physiology of Vision, The (Raman), **20th:** 3366
Pi, value of, **Anc:** 82
Piaf, Edith, **20th:** 3228-3230
Piaget, Jean, **20th:** 3231-3234
Piankhi. *See* Piye
Piano Concerto in A Minor (Grieg), **19th:** 986
Piano Concerto in A Minor (Schumann), **19th:** 2033-2034
Piano Concerto No. 2 in B-flat, Op. 83 (Brahms), **19th:** 298
Piano Concerto No. 2 in C Minor (Rachmaninof), **20th:** 3361
Piano Concerto No. 3 (Bartók), **20th:** 252
Piano Concerto, Op. 7 (Schumann), **19th:** 2029
Piano Quintet in A Major (Schubert), **19th:** 2026
Piano Quintet in F Minor, Op. 34 (Brahms), **19th:** 297
Piano Trio in A Minor (Tchaikovsky), **19th:** 2234
Piano Trio in B Major, Op. 8 (Brahms), **19th:** 297
Piast Dynasty, **MA:** 229, 231
Piazzi, Giuseppi, **19th:** 884
Piazza San Marco, **Ren:** 848
Piazza Tales, The (Melville), **19th:** 1539
Picard, Émile, **20th:** 3234-3236
Picard's theorem, **20th:** 3234
Picaresque genre, **Ren:** 25; **18th:** 597
Picasso, Pablo, **20th:** 104, 494, 986, 2397, 2760, 3237-3240
Piccard, Auguste, **20th:** 3240-3243
Piccard, Jean-Felix, **20th:** 3240-3243
Piccolomini, Aeneas Silvius. *See* Pius II
Piccolomini, Francesco. *See* Pius III
Pickering, Edward, **20th:** 2318
Pickering-Fleming system, **19th:** 789
Pickett's charge (1863), **19th:** 1336
Pickford, Mary, **20th:** 732, 1496, 1594, 3244-3247
Pickup, The (Gordimer), **20th:** 1536
Pickwick Papers (Dickens), **19th:** 655
Pico della Mirandola, Giovanni, **Ren:** 333, 548, 557, 608, 782-784, 851
Picotte, Susan La Flesche, **20th:** 3247-3250
Picquart, Georges, **Notor:** 335
Picquigny, Peace of (1475), **Ren:** 574
Pictorialism, **20th:** 883
Picts, **Anc:** 394
Picture of Dorian Gray, The (Wilde), **19th:** 2433
Pictures from an Exhibition (Mussorgsky), **19th:** 1628
Pictures of Travel (Heine), **19th:** 1070
Picturesque movement, **18th:** 166; in literature, 825
Piedra del sol. See *Sun Stone*
Piedra gloriosa, o de la Estatua de Nebuchadnessar (Manasseh ben Israel), **17th:** 583
Pièges et charlatanisme des deux sectes Saint-Simon et Owen, qui promettent l'association et le progrès (Fourier), **19th:** 805
Pierce, Cecilia, **Notor:** 972
Pierce, Edward L., **19th:** 472
Pierce, Franklin, **19th:** 344, 612, 682, 1789-1793; **Notor:** 1084
Pierce, William Luther, III, **Notor:** 177, 838-839, 912
Pierce Penniless, His Supplication to the Divell (Nashe), **Ren:** 714
Piero della Francesca, **Ren:** 99, 132, 785-788
Piérola, Nicolás, **19th:** 1513
Pierpont, Harry, **Notor:** 281
Pierre (Melville), **19th:** 1539
Pierre and Jean (Maupassant), **19th:** 1516
Pierre Nozière (France), **19th:** 815
Pierrepont, Mary. *See* Montagu, Mary Wortley
Pierron, Jean, **17th:** 909
Pierrot Lunaire (Schoenberg), **20th:** 3665
Pietà (Michelangelo), **Anc:** 540; **Ren:** 236, 682
Pietà (Siloé), **Ren:** 890
Pietà with Virgin and Saint John (Bellini), **Ren:** 98
Pietism, **18th:** Hannah More, 704; Prussia, 376; Georg Ernst Stahl, 933; Count von Zinzendorf, 1119
Pigneau de Béhaine, Pierre Joseph Georges, **19th:** 908
Pijade, Moša, **20th:** 4034
Pike County Ballads and Other Pieces (Hay), **19th:** 1054
Pike, Zebulon, **19th:** 1793-1796
Pikes Peak, **19th:** 1794
Pikovaya dama. See *Queen of Spades, The* (Pushkin); *Queen of Spades, The* (Tchaikovsky)
Pilate, Pontius, **Anc:** 460, 475, 643-646; **Notor:** 56, 458, 840-842
Pilgrim, The (Fletcher), **17th:** 279
Pilgrim (Lipchitz), **20th:** 2399

Pilgrimage of Grace (1536-1537), **Ren:** 267, 271
Pilgrimage sites, **18th:** 609
Pilgrimage to Cythera (Watteau), **18th:** 1052
Pilgrims, **17th:** 84-85, 613, 876-877
Pilgrims of Hope, The (Morris), **19th:** 1608
Pilgrim's Progress, The (Bunyan), **17th:** 101; **18th:** 123
Pillars of the House, The (Yonge), **19th:** 2472
Pillow Book of Sei Shōnagon, The (Sei Shōnagon), **MA:** 930
Pilot, The (Cooper), **19th:** 553
Piłsudski, Józef, **20th:** 3250-3253
Pima Uprising. *See* Tubutama Revolt (1695)
Pimas. *See* O'odhams
Pimería Alta, **17th:** 467
Pinchot, Gifford, **20th:** 1614, 3253-3257, 3931
Pinchot-Ballinger affair, **20th:** 3255
Pindar, **Anc:** 646-649, 793
Pindaric Odes (Cowley), **17th:** 200
Pinelli, Jean-Vincent, **17th:** 722
Pinelli, Tullio, **20th:** 1232
Pink and White Tyranny (Stowe), **19th:** 2185
Pink Panther, The (film), **20th:** 3696
Pinkham, Lydia E., **19th:** 1796-1799
Pinkham's Vegetable Compound, **19th:** 1797
Pinkie, Battle of (1547), **Ren:** 899
Pinkney, William, **19th:** 1587
Pinochet Ugarte, Augusto, **20th:** 72, 3257-3259, 3995; **Notor:** 372, 842-844
Pinsker, Leo, **20th:** 2994
Pinturicchio, **Ren:** 29
Pinzón, Martín Alonso, **Ren:** 238, 789-791
Pinzón, Vicente Yáñez, **Ren:** 789- 791
Pio of Pietrelcina, Saint. *See* Forgione, Francesco
Pio Ospedale della Pietà, **18th:** 1019
Pioche de la Vergne, Marie-Madeleine. *See* La Fayette, Madame de
Pioneer Column, **19th:** 1408
Pioneer program, **20th:** 3591
Pioneers, The (Cooper), **19th:** 552
Pioneers of France in the New World. See *France and England in North America*
Piotrków, Diet of (1562-1563), **Ren:** 888
Piracy, **Ren:** Christians, 555; England, 193, 352; France, 513; Ireland, 744; Japan, 277; North Africa, 505; Spain, 397; **17th:** China, 1001; England, 464; South Seas, 215. *See also* Privateering
Pirandello, Luigi, **20th:** 3260-3263
Piranesi, Giovanni Battista, **18th:** 4
Pirate, The (film), **20th:** 2097
Pirate, The (novel by Scott), **19th:** 2048
Pirate Prince. *See* Bellamy, Samuel
Pirates. *See* Privateering; Category Index
Pirates of Penzance, The (Gilbert and Sullivan), **19th:** 916
Pire, Dominique, **20th:** 3264-3266
Pirelli, Alberto, **20th:** 3266-3268
Pirelli, Giovanni Battista, **20th:** 3266-3268
Pirelli, Piero, **20th:** 3266-3268
Pirenne, Henri, **20th:** 3269-3271
Pires, Tomé, **Ren:** 792-793, 1009
Pirkheimer, Willibald, **Ren:** 297
Pirro e Demetrio, Il, **18th:** 884
Pisa, Council of (1410), **MA:** 1090
Pisa Madonna (Masaccio), **Ren:** 954
Pisano, Andrea, **MA:** 418, 798, 845-847
Pisano, Giovanni, **MA:** 847-849, 867
Pisano, Nicola, **MA:** 102, 696, 845, 847-849
Pisciotta, Gaspare, **Notor:** 414
Piscopia, Elena Cornaro, **17th:** 743-745
Pisistratus, **Anc:** 221, 649-652, 859
Pisma iz Frantsii i Italii (Herzen), **19th:** 1085
Pisma ob izuchenii prirody (Herzen), **19th:** 1085
Piso, Gnaeus, **Anc:** 510
Pissarro, Camille, **19th:** 453, 879, 934, 1799-1802; **20th:** 2790
Pitchfork Ben. *See* Tillman, Benjamin
Pithon, **Anc:** 763
Pithoprakta (Xenakis), **20th:** 4415
Pitt, William, the Elder, **18th:** 406, 518, 786-789
Pitt, William, the Younger, **18th:** 327, 365, 410, 740, 789-792; **19th:** 437, 1397
Pittacus of Mytilene, **Anc:** 652-655, 750
Pitti Palace, **17th:** 627
Pittman, Aileen Carol. *See* Wuornos, Aileen Carol
Pittsburgh Pact (1918), **20th:** 2641
Pittura scultura futuriste (dinamismo plastico) (Boccioni), **20th:** 404
Pius II, **Ren:** 19, 27, 726, 794-797; **18th:** 794
Pius III, **Ren:** 518; **Notor:** 15
Pius IV, **Ren:** 394, 653
Pius V, **Ren:** 797-800, 895
Pius VI, **18th:** 545, 793-795
Pius IX, **19th:** 13, 872, 922, 1532, 1802-1805
Pius X, **20th:** 2017, 2624, 3272-3274
Pius XI, **20th:** 3275-3278
Pius XII, **20th:** 2018, 3149, 3278-3281

Pixar, **20th:** 2007
Pixodarus, **Anc:** 719
Piye, **Anc:** 655-658
Piyyutim, **MA:** 592
Pizarro, Francisco, **Ren:** 67, 76, 220, 471, 747, 800-803, 902
Pizzolo, Niccolò, **Ren:** 601
Place, Etta, **Notor:** 652
Place, Francis, **19th:** 1769, 1806-1809
Place royale, La (Corneille), **17th:** 193
Place Vendôme, **17th:** 591
Places in the Sun (Eden), **20th:** 1100
Placita philosophica (Guarini), **17th:** 331
Plăeşu, Ion. *See* Eliade, Mircea
Plague, The (Camus), **20th:** 629
Plagues, **Anc:** Athens, 622; biblical, 1; Egypt, 28, 573; Rome, 530; **18th:** Vienna, 351. *See also* Black Death
Plaideurs, Les. See *Litigants, The*
Plaine and Easie Introduction to Practicall Musicke, A (Morley), **Ren:** 702
Plaine Discovery of the Whole Revelation of St. John, A (Napier), **Ren:** 711
Plains of Abraham, Battle of the (1759), **18th:** 694, 802; William Howe, 510; Louis-Joseph de Montcalm, 1106; James Wolfe, 694, 1106
Plaisir du texte. See *Pleasure of the Text, The*
Plaisirs et les jours, Les. See *Pleasures and Regrets*
Plan de Agua Prieta, **20th:** 615
Plan de San Luis Potosí, **19th:** 654
Plan of 1809, **19th:** 2130
Plan of Ayala, **20th:** 4450
Plan of Civil and Historical Architecture . . . (Fischer von Erlach), **18th:** 351
Plan Seventeen, **20th:** 2010
Plancina, **Anc:** 510
Planck, Max, **19th:** 1818; **20th:** 535, 2679, 3282-3285
Plane Crazy (animated film), **20th:** 1007
Planetarium, The (Sarraute), **20th:** 3636
Planetary motion, theories of, **Anc:** 321
Planets, The (Urey), **20th:** 4134
Planned Parenthood of Southeastern Pennsylvania v. Casey (1992), **20th:** 3022
Plano Real, **20th:** 652
Plantagenet, Edward. *See* Edward III
Plantagenet, George, **Notor:** 896
Plantagenet, Richard. *See* Richard III
Plantagenets, **MA:** 345, 357, 485, 492, 892, 963. *See also* Edward I; Edward II; Edward III; Geoffrey of Anjou; Henry II (1133-1189; king of England); Henry III (1207-1277; king of England); John (1166-1216; king of England); Matilda (queen of England); Richard I
Plants, classification of, **Anc:** 290
Plassey, Battle of (1757), **18th:** 261, 469, 522
Plassey, first Baron Clive of. *See* Clive, Robert
Plastic Interludes (Calder), **20th:** 610
Plastics, development of, **20th:** 2921
Plataea, Battle of (479 B.C.E.), **Anc:** 615, 794, 882
Plataea, Oath of, **Anc:** 633
Plataicus (Isocrates), **Anc:** 450
Plate tectonics theory, **20th:** 216, 1786
Plath, Sylvia, **20th:** 3285-3288, 3714
Plato, **Anc:** 12, 94, 127, 263, 285, 321, 420, 450, 609, 659-662, 708, 799, 963, 968, 985; **MA:** 886
Plato and Platonism (Pater), **19th:** 1756
Platonic Academy, **Ren:** 232, 332
Platonic philosophy, **Ren:** 232, 332-333, 782
Platonic Theology (Ficino), **Ren:** 333
Platonism, **Anc:** 314; Christianity and, 600; Judaism and, 641; Pythagoras and, 725; **MA:** 1029. *See also* Neoplatonism
Platonists, **Anc:** 263; **17th:** Cambridge, 782
Platyn, John, **MA:** 937
Plautianus, Fulvius, **Anc:** 481
Plautius, Aulus, **Anc:** 163
Plautus, **Anc:** 549, 662-664, 928
Play of Giants, A (Soyinka), **20th:** 3806
Play of Robin and Marion, The (Adam de la Halle), **MA:** 25
Player, Gary, **20th:** 3288-3292
Players, The, **19th:** 273
Plays. *See* Drama; Miracle plays; Opera; Theater; Nō drama
Plays (Newcastle), **17th:** 677
Plays of William Shakespeare, The (Johnson), **18th:** 537
Playwrights, **Anc:** 877; **18th:** Chikamatsu Monzaemon, 243; Hannah Cowley, 284-286; Alain-René Lesage, 596-598; Gotthold Ephraim Lessing, 600; Mary de la Rivière Manley, 641; Hannah More, 702; Friedrich Schiller, 887; Richard Brinsley Sheridan, 905-907; Richard Steele, 941; Sir John Vanbrugh, 1002-1005
Please, Please Me (Beatles), **20th:** 268
Pleasure, philosophy of, **Anc:** 69, 88, 309
Pleasure Man, The (West), **20th:** 4297
Pleasure of the Text, The (Barthes), **20th:** 248
Pleasures and Regrets (Proust), **20th:** 3342
Plectrude, **MA:** 250
Pléiade, La. *See* La Pléiade
Plekhanov, Georgy, **20th:** 2341; **Notor:** 1138

Pleroma, **Anc:** 918
Plessis, Armand-Jean du. *See* Richelieu, Cardinal de
Plessis-Marly, Seigneur du. *See* Mornay, Philippe de
Pli selon pli (Boulez), **20th:** 454
Pliny the Elder, **Anc:** 385, 523, 665-667
Pliny the Younger, **Anc:** 102-103, 665, 837, 905
PLO. *See* Palestine Liberation Organization
Plombières, Pact of (1858), **19th:** 445
Plongeurs, Les (Léger), **20th:** 2336
Plonoye sobraniye zakanov Rossiyskoy imperii (Speransky), **19th:** 2131
Plotina, **Anc:** 370
Plotinus, **Anc:** 142, 435, 642, 668-670, 687, 701
Ploutos (Aristophanes), **Anc:** 93
Plutarch, **Anc:** 12, 64, 127, 231, 616, 631, 670-673, 794, 807, 811, 818; **Notor:** 384, 1011
Pluto, discovery of, **20th:** 4041
Pluto and Persephone (Bernini), **17th:** 45
Plutonium, discovery of, **20th:** 2301, 2534, 3685
Plyaenus, **Anc:** 308
Plymouth Colony, **17th:** 7, 85, 129, 876, 878
Pneumatica (Hero of Alexandria), **Anc:** 247, 401
Pneumatics, **Anc:** 247
Pneumatists, **Anc:** 84
Pnin (Nabokov), **20th:** 2896
Po-an. *See* Wang Yangming
Pobedonostsev, Konstantin Petrovich, **19th:** 1810-1813; **Notor:** 845-846
Pocahontas, **17th:** 702, 745-748, 753, 862-863
Pocahontas, Peace of, **17th:** 754
Podhajce, Battle of (1667), **17th:** 429
Podorozhnik (Akhmatova), **20th:** 44
Poe, Edgar Allan, **19th:** 153, 1813-1816; **Notor:** 1069
Poem of the Cid, The, **MA:** 279
Poem on the Lisbon Earthquake (Voltaire), **18th:** 1028
Poem Traveled Down My Arm, A (Walker), **20th:** 4198
Poem Without a Hero, A (Akhmatova), **20th:** 44
Poema de mío Cid. See *Poem of the Cid, The*
Poema gory (Tsvetayeva), **20th:** 4099
Poema konca (Tsvetayeva), **20th:** 4099
Poemata (Campion), **17th:** 127
Poemata (du Bellay), **Ren:** 296
Poemata Latina (Cowley), **17th:** 200
Poème électronique (Varèse), **20th:** 4143
Poèmes pour la paix (Éluard), **20th:** 1152
Poems (Auden), **20th:** 172
Poems (Barbauld), **18th:** 87
Poems (Browning), **19th:** 326
Poems (Bryant), **19th:** 340
Poems (Cowley), **17th:** 200
Poems (Drayton), **17th:** 238
Poems (Emerson), **19th:** 747
Poems (Hemans), **19th:** 1076
Poems (Holmes), **19th:** 1117
Poems (Moore), **20th:** 2822
Poems (Tennyson), **19th:** 2244
Poems (Wilde), **19th:** 2432
Poems and Essay (Very), **19th:** 1762
Poems and Fancies (Newcastle), **17th:** 676
Poems and Translations by Emma Lazarus (Lazarus), **19th:** 1331
Poems Before Congress (Browning), **19th:** 327
Poems by Currer, Ellis, and Acton Bell (Brontës), **19th:** 310
Poems by Edgar A. Poe (Poe), **19th:** 1813
Poems by the Incomparable, Mrs. K. P. (Philips), **17th:** 742
Poems by the Most Deservedly Admired Mrs. Katherine Philips, the Matchless Orinda (Philips), **17th:** 742
Poems, Chiefly in the Scottish Dialect (Burns), **18th:** 184
Poems, Chiefly Lyrical (Tennyson), **19th:** 2244
Poems &c. by James Shirley (Shirley), **17th:** 846
Poems for Our Children (Hale), **19th:** 1013
Poems of Emily Dickinson, The (Dickinson), **19th:** 1098
Poems of Shakespeare's Dark Lady, The. See *Salve deus rex Judæorum*
Poems on Slavery (Longfellow), **19th:** 1417
Poems on Various Subjects, Religious and Moral (Wheatley), **18th:** 1070
Poésie et vérité. See *Poetry and Truth, 1942*
Poet Assassinated, The (Apollinaire), **20th:** 106
Poet in New York (García Lorca), **20th:** 1396
Poet of the Breakfast-Table, The (Holmes), **19th:** 1118
Poeta en Nueva York. See *Poet in New York*
Poetaster (Jonson), **17th:** 223, 441
Poète assassiné, Le. See *Poet Assassinated, The*
Poetic meters, **Anc:** Greek, 415; Latin, 197
Poeticall Blossomes (Cowley), **17th:** 199
Poetics. See *De poetica*
Poetry, **Anc:** Chinese, 732, 785; epic, 427; genres of, 705; Greek, 750, 965; Latin, 210, 301, 431, 536, 603; music and, 647; philosophy and, 610; politics and, 807; Sanskrit, 130; women and, 298; **MA:** China, 322, 653, 656, 808, 968, 1086; England, 219, 264; France, 248, 260, 268, 274, 356, 392,

693, 1065; Germany, 423, 463, 1076, 1125; Hebrew, 410; India, 109, 195; Iran, 375, 796; Italy, 169, 239, 301-302, 827; Muslim, 875; Persia, 41, 451, 908, 916; Provençal, 1076; Spain, 532, 591; **Ren:** England, 214, 535, 623, 813, 877, 881, 906; France, 285, 294, 619, 837, 974; India, 532; Italy, 42, 53, 56, 182, 235, 343, 925; Michelangelo, 684; Nezahualcóytl, 721; Portugal, 167; Spain, 209; **17th:** Americas, 88; China, 157, 540; England, 43, 127, 199, 202, 232, 237, 240, 366, 368, 443, 503, 562, 606, 639, 676, 731, 741, 846, 894, 928; France, 315, 481, 577, 829; Góngora, 312; Japan, 403, 615; Metaphysical, 202-203, 231, 367; Mexico, 209; Netherlands, 327; Spain, 770; **18th:** China, 1039; Hannah Cowley, 284-286; England, 122; Johann Wolfgang von Goethe, 428-432; Oliver Goldsmith, 432-436; Samuel Johnson, 535-539; Friedrich Gottlieb Klopstock, 562-564; nostalgia, 434; Alexander Pope, 805-808; Romantic, 850; Anna Seward, 897-899; social criticism, 1039; **19th:** African Americans, 701; Australia, 1758; Brazil, 1449; Canada, 1593; Cuba, 1504; England, 326, 380, 1030, 1260, 1285, 1940, 2092, 2432, 2462; France, 153, 1147, 1912, 2062; Germany, 84, 1070; light verse, 1117; lyrical, 530; nature, 342; Nicaragua, 601; Norway, 1165; poet laureate of England, 2245; Russia, 1353, 1848; Scotland, 2174; Spain, 557; United States, 660, 797, 1098, 1331, 1417, 1557, 1607, 1813, 1902, 2425, 2429; Vietnam, 1111; **20th:** 2445; Argentina, 431; Canada, 170; children's, 2754; Chile, 2938; England, 1140; France, 105, 4136; Germany, 3455; Great Britain, 172; Italy, 2801; linguistic analysis of, 1987; Mexico, 3169; Russia, 43, 395, 2660, 3132, 4098; Spain, 1396; Surrealism, 512; United States, 303, 858, 880, 1928, 2740, 2822, 3714

Poetry and Truth, 1942 (Éluard), **20th:** 1153

Poet's Bazaar, The (Andersen), **19th:** 62

Poets laureate, **17th:** 240, 442

"Poet's Welcome to His Love-Begotten Daughter, A" (Burns), **18th:** 184

Poganuc People (Stowe), **19th:** 2186

Poggio, MA: 850-852

Poincaré, Henri, **19th:** 1816-1819

Poincaré, Raymond, **20th:** 781, 3292-3295

Poinsett, Joel, **19th:** 831

Point and Line to Plane (Kandinsky), **20th:** 2075

Pointillism, **19th:** 2075

Poiret, Marguerite de. *See* Porete, Marguerite

Poisonings, **Anc:** 510

Poisson, Jeanne-Antoinette. *See* Pompadour, Madame de

Poisson, Siméon-Denis, **19th:** 858, 903

Poissy, Colloquy of (1561), **Ren:** 185, 569

Poitier, Sidney, **20th:** 3296-3298

Poitiers, Battle of (1356), **MA:** 308, 351, 395, 1054

Poitiers, Diane de. *See* Diane de Poitiers

Pokanokets, **17th:** 876

Pol, Talitha, **20th:** 1468

Pol Pot, **20th:** 3298-3301, 3741; **Notor:** 569, 846-849, 1017

Poland, **MA:** 487; architecture, 232; education, 232; kings, 231, 1121; law, 231; **20th:** independence of, 3252; postwar government of, 1874. *See also* Geographical Index

Poland (Michener), **20th:** 2729

Polanski, Roman, **Notor:** 690

Polanyi, Michael, **20th:** 621

Pole, William de la. *See* Suffolk, duke of

Polemon. See *History of the Wars of the Emperor Justinian, The*

Policies and Potentates (Hughes), **20th:** 1933

Polignac, Jules de, **19th:** 477

Polikarpov, Nikolai, **20th:** 4109

Polio, **20th:** 2251, 3614

Polisario Front, **20th:** 1700

Polish Fables (Krasicki), **18th:** 567

Polish Legions. *See* Legiony Polskie

Polish-Lithuanian Commonwealth, **Ren:** 888, 910; **17th:** 462

Polish Military Force. *See* Polska Organizacja Wojskowa

Polish-Ottoman War (1618-1621), **17th:** 461

Polish-Russian conflicts, **18th:** 566, 956

Polish-Soviet War (1919-1921), **20th:** 3275

Polish Succession, War of the (1733-1735), **18th:** 230, 616, 881

Polish-Swedish alliance, **18th:** 232

Polish Ukraine, **18th:** 68

Politeia (Plato), **Anc:** 659-660, 708, 963

Politeia (Zeno of Citium), **Anc:** 981

Politica (Aristotle), **Anc:** 95

Política de Dios, gobierno de Christo, tirania de Satanas. See *Divine Maxims of Government . . .*

Political Anatomy of Ireland (Petty), **17th:** 734

Political Dialogue on the General Principles of Government, A (Priestly), **18th:** 812
Political economy, **19th:** 1509, 1896
Political Economy for Beginners (Fawcett), **19th:** 766
Political justice, **18th:** 425
Political Liberalism (Rawls), **20th:** 3392
Political parties, **18th:** 637. See also *specific parties*
Political philosophy, **18th:** 759-762; Paul-Henri-Dietrich d'Holbach, 502; Mary de la Rivière Manley, 641-643; Montesquieu, 695-698; Jean-Jacques Rousseau, 869
Political realism, **20th:** 2829
Political Register (Cobbett), **19th:** 517
Political Treatise, A (Spinoza), **17th:** 873
Political Woman (Kirkpatrick), **20th:** 2168
Politicians, **18th:** first Viscount Bolingbroke, 135-140; comte de Mirabeau, 679-682
Político Don Fernando el Católico, El (Gracián), **17th:** 317
Politics, **Anc:** geography and, 828; history and, 674; poetry and, 733, 807; **18th:** antiauthoritarianism, 871; colonial America, 1116; popularization, 1085; Mary Wollstonecraft, 1108-1112. *See also* Political parties; *specific political parties*; Category Index under Government and Politics
Politics Among Nations (Morgenthau), **20th:** 2830
Politics of Cruelty, The (Millett), **20th:** 2748
Politique Party, **Ren:** 185
Poliziano, Angelo, **Ren:** 557, 782
Polk, James K., **19th:** 132, 194, 344, 505, 1819-1824
Polka in D Minor (Borodin), **19th:** 280
Pollack, Ben, **20th:** 1527
Pollaiuolo, Antonio, **Ren:** 298
Pollard, Anne Henderson, **Notor:** 849
Pollard, Jonathan, **Notor:** 849-850
Pollenza, Battle of (402), **Anc:** 825
Pollock, Jackson, **20th:** 1304, 2196, 3301-3304
Pollution, **20th:** 664, 3549
Polo, Maffeo, **MA:** 627, 853
Polo, Marco, **MA:** 1, 627, 853-856
Polo, Niccolò, **MA:** 627, 853
Polonaise in D for Piano (Wagner), **19th:** 2374
Polonaise in G Minor (Chopin), **19th:** 486
Polonium, isolation of, **20th:** 889
Polska Organizacja Wojskowa, **20th:** 3252
Poltava (Pushkin), **19th:** 1849
Poltava, Battle of (1709), **17th:** 625; **18th:** 232, 776
Pólya, George, **20th:** 1184
Polyanov, Peace of (1634), **17th:** 795
Polybius, **Anc:** 384, 673-675, 756, 827
Polycarp, **Anc:** 443
Polyclitus, **Anc:** 523, 633, 675-678
Polycrates of Samos, **Anc:** 324, 725; **Notor:** 850-851
Polyeucte (Corneille), **17th:** 194
Polyeucte (Gounod), **19th:** 953
Polygamy, **Anc:** Egyptian, 585; **19th:** 2118, 2476
Polyglot Bible, **Ren:** 504
Polygnotus, **Anc:** 678-680
Polymerase chain reaction, **20th:** 2864
Polymers, **20th:** 2920
Polynesian Mythology and Ancient Traditional History of the New Zealanders, as Furnished by Their Priests and Chiefs (Grey), **19th:** 983
Poly-Olbion (Drayton), **17th:** 238
Polyperchon, **Anc:** 598
Polypropylene, **20th:** 2920
Polytheism, **Anc:** paganism and, 4; Persian, 993
Pombal, marquês de, **18th:** 795-797
Pomeroy, Wardell, **20th:** 2160
Pomona für Teutschlands Tochter (La Roche), **18th:** 578
Pomp and Circumstance (Elgar), **20th:** 1134
Pompadour, Madame de, **18th:** 798-800; Étienne François de Choiseul, 247; Louis XV, 616
Pompeia Paulina, **Anc:** 767
Pompeius Magnus, Gnaeus. *See* Pompey the Great
Pompeius Strabo, Gnaeus, **Anc:** 188
Pompes funèbres. See *Funeral Rites*
Pompey the Great, **Anc:** 74, 145, 166, 173, 185, 188, 194, 212, 403, 527, 569, 681-684, 692, 742, 827, 833, 896, 927; **Notor:** 146
Pompey the Younger, **Anc:** 74
Pompidou, Georges, **20th:** 3305-3307
Pomponazzi, Pietro, **Ren:** 343
Ponce de León, Hernán, **Ren:** 902
Ponce de León, Juan, **Ren:** 803-806
Ponei, Charles. *See* Ponzi, Charles
Ponet, John, **Ren:** 147
Pont Aven School, **20th:** 973
Pontedera, Andrea da. *See* Pisano, Andrea
Pontiac, **18th:** 801-805
Pontiac's Resistance (1763-1766), **18th:** 40, 385, 802. *See also* French and Indian War
Pontius Pilate. *See* Pilate, Pontius
Pontus, kingdom of, **Anc:** 567
Pony Tracks (Remington), **19th:** 1882
Ponzi, Charles, **Notor:** 852-854

Poole, Elijah. *See* Muhammad, Elijah
Poona Sarvajanik Sabha, **20th:** 4023
Poor and the Land, The (Haggard), **19th:** 1007
Poor Clares, **MA:** 284, 379, 438
Poor Folk (Dostoevski), **19th:** 677
Poor Ladies of Assisi. *See* Poor Clares
Poor Law Amendment Act. *See* New Poor Law of 1834
Poor Law Commission, **19th:** 458
Poor Laws and Paupers (Martineau), **19th:** 1506
Poor Little Rich Girl (film), **20th:** 3245
Poor Man's Friend, The (Cobbett), **19th:** 518
Poor People's Campaign, **20th:** 12
Poor Richard's Almanack (Franklin), **18th:** 371
Pop art, **20th:** 2374, 3037, 3381, 4227
Pope, Alexander, **18th:** 688, 805-808
Pope, John, **19th:** 1199
Pope, Thomas, **Notor:** 978
Pope Leo X with Cardinals (Raphael), **Ren:** 821
Popes, **18th:** Benedict XIV, 102-104; Pius II, 793; Pius VI, 793-795
Popham, Edward, **17th:** 56
Popish Plot (1678), **17th:** 138, 149, 417, 508, 692, 816, 839
Popov, Aleksandr Stepanovich, **19th:** 1824-1827
Poppaea Sabina, **Anc:** 235, 477, 592, 685-687; **Notor:** 778
Popper, Karl, **20th:** 1090
Poppies, The (Sōtatsu), **17th:** 869
Popular Front (France), **20th:** 397
Popular Front for the Liberation of Palestine, **20th:** 111, 1626
Popular music, **20th:** blues, 1668, 3765; concert bands, 3798; country, 2258, 3128; Cuba, 878; France, 3229; rhythm and blues, 735; rock and roll, 267, 2043, 3331; United States, 875, 1072, 1692, 3308, 3747, 4275
Population decline in Sparta, **Anc:** 14
Populorum Progressio (Paul VI), **20th:** 3150
Poquelin, Jean-Baptiste. *See* Molière
Porcupine, Peter. *See* Cobbett, William
Porete, Marguerite, **MA:** 856-859
Porgy (Heyward), **20th:** 1459, 1463
Porgy and Bess (Gershwin, Heyward, and Gershwin), **20th:** 1459, 1463
Pornography, **20th:** 2523
Poroi (Xenophon), **Anc:** 970
Porphyry, **Anc:** 668, 687-690
Porret, Marguerite de. *See* Porete, Marguerite
Porris, Georg Joachim de. *See* Rheticus
Port-Royal abbey, **17th:** 21
Port Royal colony, **17th:** 141
Port-Royal des Champs, Convent of, **17th:** 773
Portable Dorothy Parker, The (Parker), **20th:** 3118
Portas, Maximiani. *See* Savitri Devi
Porte-Enseigne Polka (Mussorgsky), **19th:** 1627
Porter, Cole, **20th:** 156, 3308-3310
Porter, David, **19th:** 762, 764
Porter, Edwin S., **20th:** 1594
Porter, Endymion, **17th:** 563
Porter, James, **Notor:** 854-855
Porter, John, **19th:** 763
Porter, Katherine Anne, **20th:** 3310-3314
Porter, William Sydney. *See* Henry, O.
Porter Wagoner Show, The (television program), **20th:** 3128
Portia Wounding Her Thigh (Sirani), **17th:** 857
Portico of a Palace (Canaletto), **18th:** 192
Portolá, Gaspar de, **18th:** 891
Portrait of a Girl (Schmidt-Rottluff), **20th:** 3662
Portrait of a Lady, The (James), **19th:** 1207
Portrait of a Man (van Hemessen), **Ren:** 422
Portrait of a Man Unknown (Sarraute), **20th:** 3636
Portrait of a Nun (Anguissola), **Ren:** 46
Portrait of a Woman (van Hemessen), **Ren:** 422
Portrait of a Woman (Verrocchio), **Ren:** 963
Portrait of a Woman (Rogier van der Weyden), **MA:** 1093
Portrait of an Actress (Lawrence), **18th:** 584
Portrait of Doge Leonardo Loredan (Bellini), **Ren:** 99
Portrait of Don Manuel Orsorio (Goya), **18th:** 437
Portrait of His Wife and Two Elder Children (Holbein the Younger), **Ren:** 454
Portrait of Pedro (Modigliani), **20th:** 2777
Portrait of Picasso (Gris), **20th:** 1598
Portrait of the Artist as a Young Man, A (Joyce), **20th:** 2056
Portrait of the Artist's Mother Reading (Toulouse-Lautrec), **19th:** 2288
Portrait of the Count of Floridablanca (Goya), **18th:** 437
Portrait of the Family of King Charles IV (Goya), **18th:** 438
Portrait of the Marchesa Brigida Spinola-Doria (Rubens), **17th:** 802
Portrait of Two Men (Tintoretto), **Ren:** 935
Portraits d'oyseaux, animaux, serpens, herbes, arbres,

hommes et femmes d'Arabie et Egypte (Belon), **Ren:** 102
Portraiture, **Anc:** Assyrian, 123; **18th:** John Singleton Copley, 274-277; Francisco de Goya, 437; Thomas Lawrence, 583; Sir Joshua Reynolds, 836; George Romney, 862-865; Gilbert Stuart, 948; Élisabeth Vigée-Lebrun, 1016; **20th:** Austria, 2185; England, 1353, 3921; France, 2651, 4175; photography, 884, 3838; sculpture, 1166; Spain, 3238; United States, 1460, 4228; Wales, 2015
Portugal, **MA:** kings, 34; theology, 95; trade, 478; **Ren:** India and, 22; Kongo alliance with, 10; North Africa and, 511, 605, 859; Spain and, 32; **17th:** 821. *See also* Geographical Index
Portuguese, The (Braque), **20th:** 494
Portuguese Mars. *See* Albuquerque, Afonso de
Porus, **Anc:** 202
Posidonius, **Anc:** 690-694
Positivism, **19th:** 537, 1045, 1774; **20th:** 869
Possessed, The (Dostoevski), **19th:** 679
Possessing the Secret of Joy (Walker), **20th:** 4197
Possevino, Antonio, **17th:** 855
Post, Wiley, **20th:** 3494
Post-Dispatch (newspaper), **19th:** 1842
Posteritati. See *Epistle to Posterity*
Posthumous Memoirs of Brás Cubas, The. See *Epitaph of a Small Winner*
Posthumous Poems of Percy Bysshe Shelley (Shelley), **19th:** 2096
Posthumous Works of Mrs. Chapone, The (Chapone), **18th:** 222
Postillon de Longjumeau, Le (Adam), **19th:** 639
Post-Impressionism, **19th:** 2288
Potato Eaters, The (van Gogh), **19th:** 933
Potato famine, **19th:** 521, 667
Potawatomis, **17th:** 433
Potemkin (film), **20th:** 1130
Potemkin, Grigori Aleksandrovich, **18th:** 808-810, 955; and Catherine the Great, 758
Potemkin village, **18th:** 810
Pothinus, **Anc:** 443
Potomacs, **17th:** 746, 752
Potsdam, Edict of (1686), **17th:** 821
Potter, Beatrix, **20th:** 3314-3317
Pottery, Japan, **17th:** 695
Pottinger, Henry, **19th:** 1379
Poulenc, Francis, **20th:** 3318-3321
Pound, Ezra, **20th:** 1140, 1349, 1623, 2056, 4429
Pour la révolution africaine. See *Toward the African Revolution*
Pour le piano (Debussy), **20th:** 938
Pour une morale de l'ambiguïté. See *Ethics of Ambiguity, The*
Poussin, Nicolas, **17th:** 171, 303, 749-752
Poverkh bari erov. See *Above the Barriers*
Poverty and the poor, **18th:** 340; Maria Gaetana Agnesi, 25; Jean-Paul Marat, 648; Hannah More, 703; Shakers, 592; John Wesley on, 1067; **19th:** attitudes toward, 53, 255, 275, 457; education and, 313; housing, 1105
Poverty and Un-British Rule in India (Naoroji), **19th:** 1635
Povesti Belkina. See *Tales of Belkin, The*
Powell, Adam Clayton, Jr., **Notor:** 856-857
Powell, Cecil Frank, **20th:** 4436
Powell, Colin, **20th:** 3321-3325
Powell, John Wesley, **19th:** 1827-1831
Powell, Lewis (attempted assassin), **Notor:** 858-859, 1012
Powell, Lewis F., Jr. (jurist), **20th:** 3325-3327
Power, Harry, **Notor:** 563
Power, Tyrone, **20th:** 1760
Power and the Glory, The (Greene), **20th:** 1578
Power Jets, **20th:** 4319
Power of Darkness, The (Tolstoy), **19th:** 2285
Power of the Powerless, The (Havel), **20th:** 1708
Powers, Bill, **Notor:** 257
Powers, Francis Gary, **20th:** 2130
Powhatan, **17th:** 702, 745, 752-756, 862-863
Powhatan Confederacy, **17th:** 702, 752
Powhatan Wars (1622-1646), **17th:** 703
Powick Bridge, Battle of (1642), **17th:** 805
Poyning's Law, **18th:** 441
Pozzo, Cassiano del, **17th:** 749
Prabhat Sangit (Tagore), **20th:** 3933
Practica geometriae (Leonardo of Pisa), **MA:** 649
Practica secundum Trotam (Trotula), **MA:** 1031
Practical Education (Edgeworth), **19th:** 728
Practical Treatise on the Diseases of the Uterus and Its Appendages, A, **19th:** 266
Practice and Theory of Bolshevism, The (Russell), **20th:** 3563
Practice of Philosophy, The (Langer), **20th:** 2264
Practice of Prelates, The (Tyndale), **Ren:** 951
Prades Festival, **20th:** 682
Pradilla, Francisco, **Notor:** 532
Prado y Ugarteche, Manuel, **20th:** 1718

Praeparatio evangelica (Eusebius), **Anc:** 330
Praesidenten. See *President, The*
Praeterita (Ruskin), **19th:** 1957
Praetorian Guard, **Anc:** 218
Pragmatic Sanction (1438), **Ren:** 794
Pragmatic Sanction (1713), **18th:** 230, 653
Pragmatic Sanction (1789), **19th:** 413
Pragmaticism, **19th:** 1773
Pragmatism, **19th:** 1215
Prague, Four Articles of, **MA:** 1162
Prague, Peace of (1635), **17th:** 269, 705
Prague, Siege of (1741), **18th:** 881
Prague Spring, **20th:** 1044
Praguerie (1440), **Ren:** 574
Prairie, The (Cooper), **19th:** 553
Praise of Folly, The (Erasmus), **Ren:** 315
"Praise Poem of Ur-Nammu, A" (Ur-Nammu), **Anc:** 914
Praise poetry, **Anc:** 648
Pralle, Arlene, **Notor:** 1109
Prandtl, Ludwig, **20th:** 3327-3330
Prandtl-Glaubert rule, **20th:** 3329
Prarthana Samaj, **19th:** 1855
Prästänkan. See *Parson's Widow, The*
Prasutagus, **Anc:** 163
Pratensis, Josquinus. *See* Josquin des Prez
Pratinas, **Anc:** 877
Pratt, David, **Notor:** 1065
Pratt, O. C. *See* Holmes, H. H.
Praxagoras, **Anc:** 410
Praxis universae artis medicae (Cesalpino), **Ren:** 212
Praxiteles, **Anc:** 676, 694-697
Prayer (Brancusi), **20th:** 480
Prayer Book of the Anglican Church in Mohawk, **18th:** 161
Prayer Society. *See* Prarthana Samaj
Prayers and Meditations (Parr), **Ren:** 766
Praying Jew, The (Chagall), **20th:** 717
PRB. *See* Pre-Raphaelite Brotherhood
Preachers, Order of, **MA:** 1027
Preaching. *See* Edwards, Jonathan; Wesley, Charles; Wesley, John; Whitefield, George
Precaution (Cooper), **19th:** 552
Precession of the equinoxes, **Anc:** 418
Précieuses ridicules, Les. See *Affected Young Ladies, The*
Predestination, **Anc:** 947; **Ren:** 60, 163
Predictions for the Ensuing Year, by Isaac Bickerstaff (Swift), **18th:** 964
Pre-emption Act, **19th:** 2340
Préface de Cromwell, La (Hugo), **19th:** 1147
Preface to Morals, A (Lippmann), **20th:** 2401
Preface to Politics, A (Lippmann), **20th:** 2400
Prejudice Reproved (Traill), **19th:** 2292
Preliminaries to Speech Analysis (Jakobson), **20th:** 1987
Preliminary Discourse to the Encyclopedia of Diderot (Alembert), **18th:** 33
Prelude, The (Wordsworth), **19th:** 2462
Prélude à l'aprés-midi d'un faune (Debussy), **20th:** 937
Préludes, Les (Liszt), **19th:** 1394
Premiers poèmes (Éluard), **20th:** 1152
Přemyslid Dynasty, **MA:** 257, 670
Preobrazhnesky, Evgeny, **20th:** 567
Preparation for the Gospel. See *Praeparatio evangelica*
Pre-Raphaelite Brotherhood, **19th:** 1157, 1940
Prerevolutionary politics, **18th:** colonial America, 1041, 1116; France, 997
Presbyterian Church and Presbyterianism, **Ren:** 530, 762; **17th:** 122, 145, 206, 941; **18th:** 1099; colonial Georgia, 743; **19th:** 173. *See also* Calvinism; Lutheran Church and Lutheranism; Reformation
Presbytery, **17th:** 15, 33
Prescott, William Hickling, **19th:** 390, 1831-1834
Present State of Germany, The (Pufendorf), **17th:** 759
Present State of Music in France and Italy, The (Burney), **18th:** 178
Present State of Music in Germany, the Netherlands, and the United Provinces, The (Burney), **18th:** 178
Presentation (Siloé), **Ren:** 890
Presentation in the Temple, The (Fra Angelico), **MA:** 84
Presentation in the Temple (Lorenzetti), **MA:** 661
Presentation of Jesus in the Temple, The (Rembrandt), **17th:** 787
Presentation of the Virgin in the Temple (Tintoretto), **Ren:** 932
Presidency, U.S., **18th:** term, 1046; George Washington, 1045; **19th:** Grover Cleveland, 509; election of 1824, 22, 1190, 2345; election of 1840, 505, 579, 2346; election of 1844, 505, 579; election of 1856, 783; election of 1860, 612; election of 1872, 67, 969, 2460; election of 1876, 869; election of 1880, 81, 870; election of 1884, 252; election of 1888, 509; election of 1892, 509, 1042; election of 1896, 110, 1461; election of 1900, 647; Millard Fillmore, 783; James A. Garfield, 870; Rutherford B. Hayes, 869; Abraham Lincoln, 612; William McKinley, 1461; Martin Van Buren, 2346
President, The (film), **20th:** 1037

President Roosevelt and the Coming of the War 1941 (Beard), **20th:** 265
Presidential Papers, The (Mailer), **20th:** 2564
Presidential Succession in 1910, The (Madero), **20th:** 2544
Presley, Elvis, **20th:** 3330-3333
Pre-Socratic philosophy, **Anc:** 37
Press Act (1848), **19th:** 621
Prester John (legendary figure), **MA:** 402, 627, 633; **Ren:** 259, 286, 511, 1007
Prester John of the Indies, The (Alvares), **Ren:** 261
Preston, Battle of (1648), **17th:** 205, 484, 756
Prestupleniye i nakazaniye. See *Crime and Punishment*
Pretender, The (Service), **20th:** 3709
Pretenders, The (Ariosto), **Ren:** 57
Pretenders to the throne, **18th:** England, 634; Russia, 214, 815
Pretorius, Andries, **19th:** 1298
Pretorius, Marthinus, **19th:** 1299
Prêtre de Némi, Le (Renan), **19th:** 1887
"Pretty Girl Is Like a Melody, A" (Berlin), **20th:** 328
Pretty Sister of José, The (Burnett), **19th:** 358
Prevention of Malaria, The (Ross), **20th:** 3535
Preveza, Battle of (1538), **Ren:** 80
Prez, Josquin des. *See* Josquin des Prez
Prezan, Constantin, **Notor:** 25
Price, Leontyne, **20th:** 232, 3334-3337
Price, Stephen, **19th:** 1257
Price, Uvedale, **19th:** 1643
Prices and Wages in England from the Twelfth to Nineteenth Century (Beveridge), **20th:** 354
Pride, Thomas, **17th:** 205, 651, 692, 756-758
Pride and Prejudice (Austen), **19th:** 95
Pride of Jennico (Richardson), **19th:** 1904
Pride's Purge (1648), **17th:** 263, 651, 757, 942
Priestesses, **Anc:** 298
Priestley, Joseph, **18th:** 116, 218, 580, 811-814, 1023
Priestly Element in the Old Testament, The (Harper), **19th:** 1032
Prigg v. Pennsylvania, **19th:** 2181, 2227
Priglashenie na kazn'. See *Invitation to a Beheading*
Prignano, Bartolomeo. *See* Urban VI
Primauté du spirituel. See *Things That Are Not Caesar's, The*
Primavera (Botticelli), **Ren:** 125
Prime Minister, The (Trollope), **19th:** 2302
Prime ministers, **18th:** George II, 404; George III, 408; first earl of Godolphin, 421-424; Lord North, 738-741; William Pitt the Elder, 786-789; William Pitt the Younger, 789-792; Robert Walpole, 1034-1038
Primero sueño. See *First Dream*
Primeval Atom, The (Lemaître), **20th:** 2339
Primi de stirpium historia commentariorum tomi vivae imagines (Fuchs), **Ren:** 357
Primo de Rivera, Miguel, **20th:** 4130; **Notor:** 860-861
Primo libro de' madrigali, Il (Frescobaldi), **17th:** 295
Primo libro de madrigali, Il (Strozzi), **17th:** 888
Primo libro delle canzoni, accomodate per sonare con ogni sorte de stromenti, Il (Frescobaldi), **17th:** 297
Primo libro delle fantasie, Il (Frescobaldi), **17th:** 296
Primo libro delle musiche, Il (Caccini), **17th:** 112
Primo libro di capricci, Il (Frescobaldi), **17th:** 296
Primordia coenobii Gandershemensis. See *Hrosvithae Liber terius*
Prince, The (Machiavelli), **Ren:** 116, 373, 511, 588
Prince and the Pauper, The (Twain), **19th:** 2330, 2473
Prince and the Showgirl, The (film), **20th:** 3042
Prince Igor (Borodin), **19th:** 282
Prince of Homburg, The (Henze), **20th:** 1763
Prince of Homburg, The (Kleist), **19th:** 1290
Prince of Tides, The (film), **20th:** 3893
Princeps pro suo succursu, An (Ockham), **MA:** 780
Princes, Era of, **19th:** 2255
Prince's Progress, and Other Poems, The (Rossetti), **19th:** 1941
Princess (Tennyson), **19th:** 2245
Princess Abe. *See* Kōken
Princess Casamassima, The (James), **19th:** 1207
Princess de Broglie (Ingres), **19th:** 1173
Princess Ida (Gilbert and Sullivan), **19th:** 919
Princess Ligovskaya (Lermontov), **19th:** 1354
Princess of Clèves, The (La Fayette), **17th:** 478
Princess of Mars, A (Burroughs), **20th:** 591
Princess of Monpensier, The (La Fayette), **17th:** 477
Princeton University, **18th:** 1100
Princip, Gavrilo, **Notor:** 861-863
Principall Navigations, Voiages, and Discoveries of the English Nation (Hakluyt), **Ren:** 419
Principate, Roman, **Anc:** 21, 281
Principe, Il. See *Prince, The*
Príncipe constante, El. See *Constant Prince, The*
Principes mathematiques de la philosophie naturelle (Châtelet), **18th:** 242

Principia (Newton), **17th:** 349, 385, 390, 680
Principia Ethica (Moore), **20th:** 2815
Principia Mathematica (Whitehead and Russell), **20th:** 660, 3562, 4312
Principia philosophiae. See *Principles of Philosophy*
Principia philosophiae antiquissima et recentissimae. See *Principles of the Most Ancient and Modern Philosophy, The*
Principles and Practice of Medicine (Osler), **19th:** 1713
Principles de la nature et de la grâce, fondés en raison. See *Principles of Nature and of Grace, The*
Principles of Biology, The (Spencer), **19th:** 2128
Principles of Chemistry, The (Mendeleyev), **19th:** 1546
Principles of Descartes' Philosophy, The (Spinoza), **17th:** 872
Principles of Ethics, The (Spencer), **19th:** 2128
Principles of General Physiology (Bayliss), **20th:** 260
Principles of Geology (Lyell), **19th:** 604, 1424
Principles of Logic, The (Bradley), **19th:** 289
Principles of Mathematics, The (Russell), **20th:** 3562
Principles of Moral and Political Philosophy, The (Paley), **18th:** 763
Principles of Moral and Political Science (Ferguson), **18th:** 338
Principles of Nature and of Grace, The (Leibniz), **17th:** 516
Principles of Philosophy (Descartes), **17th:** 251
Principles of Physiological Psychology (Wundt), **20th:** 4408
Principles of Political Economy (Mill), **19th:** 1575
Principles of Political Economy (Newcomb), **19th:** 1662
Principles of Political Economy (Sedgwick), **19th:** 2104
Principles of Psychology, The (James), **19th:** 1215; **20th:** 4014
Principles of Psychology, The (Spencer), **19th:** 2127
Principles of Quantum Mechanics (Dirac), **20th:** 1004
Principles of Scientific Management, The (Taylor), **20th:** 3956
Principles of Social Reconstruction (Russell), **20th:** 3563
Principles of Sociology, The (Spencer), **19th:** 2128
Principles of Soil Microbiology (Waksman), **20th:** 4181
Principles of the Most Ancient and Modern Philosophy, The (Conway), **17th:** 188
Principles of Zoology (Agassiz), **19th:** 32
Printing, **MA:** 442; **Ren:** England, 196; France, 413, 575; Italy, 608; music, 149; Scotland, 499; **18th:** John Baskerville, 92-94; Benjamin Franklin, 371; Ottoman Empire, 28; Samuel Richardson, 841; John Peter Zenger, 1116-1119
Printmaking, France, **20th:** 718
Printz v. United States (1997), **20th:** 3408
Prinz Friedrich von Homburg. See *Prince of Homburg, The* (Kleist)
Priscian, **MA:** 859-862
Priscian of Caesarea's De Laude Anastasii Imperatoris (Priscian), **MA:** 859
Priscianus Caesariensis. *See* Priscian
Priscillian, **Anc:** 698-700, 797
Priscillianism, **Anc:** 797
Priscus, Marius, **Anc:** 838
Prisoner for God (Bonhoeffer), **20th:** 419
Prisoner of Chillon, The (Byron), **19th:** 381
Prisoner of Sex, The (Mailer), **20th:** 2564
Prisoner of the Caucasus, The (Pushkin), **19th:** 1849
Prisoners from the Front (Homer), **19th:** 1123
Prisons, Les (Marguerite de Navarre), **Ren:** 620
Prisons and jails, **18th:** 100-102, 106; British convict colony, 784; James Edward Oglethorpe, 742; Voltaire, 1026; **20th:** reforms, 926, 3085, 3139
Pritchett, Henry S., **20th:** 1257
Privacy rights, **20th:** 482, 1031
Private Lives (Coward), **20th:** 855
Privateering, **Ren:** 397; England, 193, 292, 352, 779; Spain, 672. *See also* Piracy
Privileges, Charter of (1264), **MA:** 232
Privilegium Ottonianum (962), **MA:** 806
Prix de Rome, **18th:** 367
Priyadarśikā (Harṣa), **MA:** 461
Pro Augustino responsiones ad capitula objectionum Vincentianarum (Prosper of Aquitaine), **Anc:** 948
Pro Caelio (Cicero), **Anc:** 233
Pro eto. See *About That*
Pro Populo Anglicano Defensio (Milton), **17th:** 640
Pro Quinctio (Cicero), **Anc:** 210
Pro Roscio Amerino (Cicero), **Anc:** 211
Proaptin, **20th:** 3998
Proarche, **Anc:** 918
Probability, **19th:** 1318; **Ren:** Cardano's studies of, 174
Problem des Todes in der Philosophie unserer Zeit, Das (Wach), **20th:** 4178

Problem of Christianity, The (Royce), **20th:** 3551
Problem of Human Life as Viewed by the Great Thinkers from Plato to the Present Time, The (Eucken), **20th:** 1186
Problem of Pain, The (Lewis), **20th:** 2355
Problem We All Live With, The (Rockwell), **20th:** 3484
Problems of Art (Langer), **20th:** 2265
Problems of Dostoevsky's Poetics (Bakhtin), **20th:** 191
Problems of Philosophy, The (Russell), **20th:** 3562
Problemy poetiki Dostoevskogo. See *Problems of Dostoevsky's Poetics*
Process and Reality (Whitehead), **20th:** 4314
Proclus, **Anc:** 701-703, 727
Proconsul africanus, **20th:** 2315
Procopius, **MA:** 76; **Notor:** 1028-1029
Procuress, The (Vermeer), **17th:** 956
Prodigal Parents, The (Lewis), **20th:** 2365
Prodigal Son, The (ballet), **20th:** 194, 909, 988, 2378
Prodigal Son, The (Sullivan), **19th:** 918
Prodigy, The (Hesse), **20th:** 1789
Prodromo di un opera da imprimersi sopra le riproduzioni animali. See *Essay on Animal Reproductions, An*
Prodromus (Steno), **17th:** 882
Prodromus astronomiae. See *Star Atlas, The*
Profaci, Joseph, **Notor:** 393, 863-864
Professor, The (Brontë), **19th:** 310
Professor of Public Speaking, A. See *Rhētorōn didaskalos*
Professor of the Breakfast-Table, The (Holmes), **19th:** 1118
Professor's House, The (Cather), **20th:** 699
Profiles in Courage (Kennedy), **20th:** 2099
Profumo, John, **20th:** 2539
Prognōstikon (Diocles), **Anc:** 278
Progress and Poverty (George), **19th:** 896
Progress of Dulness, The (Trumbull), **18th:** 989
Progress of Love, The (Munro), **20th:** 2874
Progress of Religious Ideas, The (Child), **19th:** 484
Progressive Party (U.S.), **20th:** 2228, 4209
Prohaeresius, **Anc:** 361
Prohibition, **20th:** 641, 703
Project Apollo, **20th:** 136, 3726
Project 571, **20th:** 2383
Project Gemini, **20th:** 136
Project Mercury, **20th:** 1499
Project Mohole, **20th:** 1786
Project Plowshare, **20th:** 3970
Projective geometry, **Anc:** 79
Prokhorov, Aleksandr, **20th:** 256
Prokofiev, Sergei, **20th:** 194, 2648, 3338-3341
Proletarian art, **20th:** 1130
Proletariat (Kollwitz), **20th:** 2190
Proletkult Theater, **20th:** 1130
Promenade, The (Gournay), **17th:** 314
Promenades dans Londres (Tristan), **19th:** 2298
Promenades dans Rome. See *Roman Journal, A*
Promessi sposi, I. See *Betrothed, The*
Prometheus, **Anc:** 415
Prometheus (Orozco), **20th:** 3070
Prometheus Bound. See *Prometheus desmōtēs*
Prometheus desmōtēs (Aeschylus), **Anc:** 9
Prometheus Unbound (Shelley), **19th:** 2095
Promises (Warren), **20th:** 4238
Proof for the Unicity of God. See *Ordinatio*
Proof of the Gospel. See *Demonstratio evangelica*
Propaedeumata aphoristica. See *John Dee on Astronomy*
Propaganda, **Anc:** Roman, 527; **18th:** Anna Barbauld, 88; Georgiana Cavendish, 216; Daniel Defoe, 298; Mary de la Rivière Manley, 642; Thomas Paine, 759; Paul Revere, 832; Jonathan Swift, 965; John Wilkes, 1083
Propator, **Anc:** 918
Propertius, Sextus, **Anc:** 432, 528, 704-706
Prophecies, **Anc:** battles and, 615; Christ, 474; Christianity and, 698; disaster and punishment, 453; Egyptian, 559; Ezekiel, 336; foreign policy and, 448; Hebrew, 446; horoscopes and, 481; Japanese, 465; Jeremiah, 336, 453; Jewish, 459, 582; oracular, 283; Sammu-ramat and, 746; Samuel, 747; Saul, 748; schizophrenia and, 336
Prophecies of Merlin, The (Geoffrey of Monmouth), **MA:** 405
Prophesie of the Last Day to Be Revealed in the Last Times, and Then of the Cutting Off the Church and of the Redemption Out of Hell, A (Davies), **17th:** 221
Prophesyings, **Ren:** 404
Prophetess, The (Fletcher and Massinger), **17th:** 279
Prophetess, The (Purcell). See *Dioclesian*
Prophetiae Merlini. See *Prophecies of Merlin, The*
Prophetiae Sibyllarum (Lasso), **Ren:** 541
Prophetic Element in the Old Testament, The (Harper), **19th:** 1032
Prophéties de M. Michel Nostradamus, Les. See *Centuries*

Prophets, **Anc:** Abraham, 6; Deborah, 259; Isaiah, 446; playwrights and, 877
Proposal for Putting Reform to the Vote Throughout the Kingdom, A (Shelley), **19th:** 2093
Proposition for the Advancement of Experimental Philosophy, A (Cowley), **17th:** 200
Propositiones Philosophicae (Agnesi), **18th:** 24
Pros tas koinas doxas (Herophilus), **Anc:** 412
Prosas Profanas, and Other Poems (Darío), **19th:** 602
Prose, shift from poetry to, **Anc:** 58
Prose Edda, The (Snorri), **MA:** 951
Proserpine (Shelley), **19th:** 2088
Proslogion (Anselm), **MA:** 92
Prosper of Aquitane, **Anc:** 947
Prosvitianyn, S. *See* Petlyura, Symon
Protactinium, discovery of, **20th:** 1636, 2680
Protagonist, Der (Weill), **20th:** 4273
Protagoras, **Anc:** 326, 633, 707-709
Prōtagoras (Plato), **Anc:** 654, 708, 793
Protective Tariff of 1816, **19th:** 2112
Protectorate of England, **17th:** 168, 346, 417, 485, 838
Protein synthesis, **20th:** 867
Protestant-Catholic marriage, **18th:** 103
Protestant Ethic and the Spirit of Capitalism, The (Weber), **20th:** 4260
Protestant Reformation. *See* Reformation
Protestant Union, **17th:** 268, 293, 338
Protestantische Ethik und der Geist des Kapitalismus, Die. See *Protestant Ethic and the Spirit of Capitalism, The*
Protestantism, **Ren:** 163; Catholic Church and, 394; Catholicism and, 222, 235, 897; England, 62, 112, 199, 231, 255, 267, 271, 291, 305, 369, 399, 403, 443, 528, 543, 640, 761, 766, 834, 883, 899; France, 348, 424, 426, 429, 463, 569, 618, 703; Germany, 31, 51, 405, 582, 666; Holy Roman Empire, 842; Low Countries, 32; Moravia, 473; Netherlands, 60, 526, 616, 676, 994; Poland, 243; Scotland, 528, 634, 711; Switzerland, 473, 861; **17th:** Bohemia, 966; England, 33, 145, 275, 507, 767; France, 36, 265; Germany, 338; Ireland, 938; **18th:** Queen Caroline, 203; and English throne, 46; Great Britain, 402; Habsburg Dynasty, 544; Ireland, 357, 441, 983; Joseph II, 545; first duke of Marlborough, 660; missionary movement, 1121; George Whitefield, 1074; **19th:** Germany, 1919, 2013; United States, 399, 2117. *See also* Anabaptism; Bible; Calvinism; Counter-Reformation; Lutheran Church and Lutheranism; Presbyterian Church and Presbyterianism; Puritanism; Reformation; Unitarianism
Proteus (Aeschylus), **Anc:** 9
Proton, discovery of, **20th:** 4008
Proud Tower, The (Tuchman), **20th:** 4106
Proudhon, Pierre-Joseph, **19th:** 119, 1321, 1834-1837
Proumenoir de Monsieur de Montaigne, Le. See *Promenade, The*
Proust (Beckett), **20th:** 279
Proust, Antonin, **19th:** 1479
Proust, Marcel, **20th:** 3342-3345; **Notor:** 627
Provençal poetry, **MA:** 1076
Provence, Jewish community at, **MA:** 650
Proverbs, The (Goya), **18th:** 438
Providence, **17th:** 982
Providentissimus Deus. See *On the Study of the Scriptures*
Provinces of the Roman Empire from Caesar to Diocletian, The (Mommsen), **19th:** 1584
Provincial Congress, **18th:** Massachusetts, 412, 460; New Jersey, 1100
Provincial Freeman, **19th:** 432
Provincial Letters, The (Pascal), **17th:** 714
Provok'd Wife, The (Vanbrugh), **18th:** 1003
Proximus und Lympida (Grimmelshausen), **17th:** 325
Prozess. See *Trial, The* (Kafka)
Prudence in Woman (Tirso), **17th:** 913
Prufrock and Other Observations (Eliot), **20th:** 1140
Prussia, **18th:** War of the Austrian Succession, 378; Frederick I, 376; Frederick the Great, 378-381; Joseph II, 545; Wenzel Anton von Kaunitz, 558; military, 381-383; Seven Years' War, 378
Prussian Academy of Sciences, **18th:** 486
Prussian Academy of Arts, **18th:** 376
Prussian-Austrian relations, **18th:** 378, 557, 654
Prussian-British alliance, **18th:** 939
Prussian Reform movement, **19th:** 2152
Prussian-Russian relations, **18th:** 322, 779
Pruth, Treaty of the (1711), **18th:** 27
Prynne, William, **17th:** 497
Psalmen Davids (Schütz), **17th:** 826
Psalmes, Sonets, and Songs of Sadness and Pietie (Byrd), **Ren:** 149, 150

Psalmi Davidici (Gabrieli), **Ren:** 360
Psalms, composition of, **Anc:** 255
Psalterium decem chordarum (Joachim), **MA:** 575
Psamtik I, **Anc:** 118, 710-712
Psellus, Michael, **MA:** 91, 863-866
Pseudo-Dionysius, **Anc:** 270, 702
Pseudodoxia Epidemica. See *Browne's Vulgar Errors*
Pseudolus (Plautus), **Anc:** 663
Pseudo-Martyr (Donne), **17th:** 232
Psiammites (Archimedes), **Anc:** 82, 607
Pskovityanka. See *Maid of Pskov, The*
Psyché (Lully and Corneille), **17th:** 570
Psyché (Ségalas), **19th:** 2062
Psychiatry, **20th:** 391, 1997. *See also* Category Index under Psychology and Psychiatry
Psychic Factors of Civilization, The (Ward), **19th:** 2385
Psycho (film), **20th:** 1827
Psychoanalysis and psychotherapy, **20th:** 515, 1323, 1883, 1995, 2225
Psychoanalysis and the Unconscious (Lawrence), **20th:** 2297
Psychodiagnostics (Rorschach), **20th:** 3523
Psychologie der Weltanschauungen (Jaspers), **20th:** 1997
Psychologie des foules. See *Crowd, The*
Psychology, **Anc:** biography and, 671; history and, 512; sculpture and, 696; **19th:** 771, 863; United States, 1215; **20th:** Alfred Adler, 34; behaviorism, 3755, 4014; children, 3231-3232; of crowds, 2321; experimental, 4408; France, 1994; Erich Fromm, 1347; Germany, 4294; Gestalt, 1112; language, 759; study of, 3164; Switzerland, 2062. *See also* Psychiatry; Category Index
Psychology (Dewey), **20th:** 982
Psychology of Peoples, The (Le Bon), **20th:** 2320
Psychology of the Great War, The (Le Bon), **20th:** 2321
Psychology of the Unconscious (Jung), **20th:** 2063
Psychopathia sexualis (Krafft-Ebing), **18th:** 876
Psychophysics, **19th:** 771
Ptah, **Anc:** 556
Ptolemies, **Anc:** 229
Ptolemy (astronomer), **Anc:** 78, 417, 435, 580, 606, 712-715; **MA:** 22, 67, 137, 195
Ptolemy I Soter, **Anc:** 63, 105-106, 317, 716, 719-722, 763
Ptolemy II Philadelphus, **Anc:** 106, 157, 247, 715-718, 721
Ptolemy III Euergetes, **Anc:** 157, 315, 717
Ptolemy IV Philopator, **Anc:** 159
Ptolemy XII Neos Dionysos (Auletes), **Anc:** 230
Ptolemy XIII, **Anc:** 230
Ptolemy Ceraunus (king of Macedonia), **Anc:** 106, 715
Ptolemy Philadelphus (son of Antony and Cleopatra), **Anc:** 75
Þu vinviðour hreini. See *Salka Valka*
Pu Yi. *See* Puyi
Public Advertiser (newspaper), **18th:** 17
Public Citizen, **20th:** 2898
Public Enemy, The (film), **20th:** 4446
Public Good, The (Paine), **18th:** 760
Public Health Act of 1848, **19th:** 458
Public Health Act of 1875, **19th:** 669
Public land use, **19th:** 193
Public Opinion (Lippmann), **20th:** 2401
Public Sale (Wyeth), **20th:** 4411
Public Schools Act of 1866, **19th:** 1740
Public Theater, **20th:** 39
Public Weal, The League of the (1465), **Ren:** 574
Publicola, L. Gellius, **Anc:** 819
Puccini, Giacomo, **19th:** 1155; **20th:** 676, 3346-3349, 4051
Pucelle, Jean, **MA:** 328, 866-869
Puck of Pook's Hill (Kipling), **19th:** 1286
Puebla, Battle of (1862), **19th:** 653
Pueblo Revolt (1680), **17th:** 467
Puente, Dorothea, **Notor:** 1109
Puerperal fever, **19th:** 1116, 2064
Puerto Rico, **Ren:** 804; **19th:** annexation of, 1462
Pueyrredón, Juan Martín, **19th:** 1985
Pufendorf, Samuel von, **17th:** 545, 759-762
Pugachev, Yemelyan Ivanovich, **18th:** 814-816
Pugachev's Revolt (1773-1774), **18th:** 214, 809, 814-816
Pugin, Augustus Welby Northmore, **19th:** 143, 1838-1841, 2044
Pugno, Raoul, **20th:** 449
Pugwash Conferences on Science and World Affairs, **20th:** 60, 1850, 3537, 4345
P'u-I. *See* Puyi
Puits de Sainte-Claire, Le. See *Well of Santa Clara, The*
Pujo Committee, **19th:** 1601
Pulakeśin II, **MA:** 461
Pulitzer, Joseph, **19th:** 1841-1844, 2056
Pulitzer Prizes, **19th:** 1843
Pullman Company, **19th:** 59; **20th:** 3371
Pullman workers' strike (1894), **19th:** 510; **20th:** 914, 934
Pulsar, discovery of, **20th:** 584
Pumayatton, **Anc:** 271
Pumpiansky, Lev Vasilyevich, **20th:** 191

Pumpkin Papers, **20th:** 1823
P'ung-akdo (Chŏng Sŏn), **18th:** 248
Punic War, First (264-241 B.C.E.), **Anc:** 273, 373, 738, 758
Punic War, Second (218-202 B.C.E.), **Anc:** 82, 190, 273, 301, 342, 382, 542, 812
Punic War, Third (149-146 B.C.E.), **Anc:** 357, 673, 756, 760
Punishment for Intoxication (Homer), **19th:** 1123
Punitive Expedition (1915-1917), **20th:** 3220, 4161
Punjab, Ghaznavid invasion of, **MA:** 683
Punjab annexation, **19th:** 1328
Punkt und Linie zu Fläche. See *Point and Line to Plane*
Puppet Show, The (Blok), **20th:** 394
Purbach, Georg von. *See* Peuerbach, Georg von
Purcell, Henry, **17th:** 311, 763-766
Pure Food and Drug Act of 1906, **20th:** 3517
Pure Land Buddhism, **MA:** 397, 582, 758
Purgation and Purgatory (Catherine of Genoa), **Ren:** 192
Purgatorio. See *Purgation and Purgatory*
Purification of the Temple (El Greco), **Ren:** 390
Purifications. See *Katharmoi*
Purishkevich, Vladimir, **Notor:** 1126
Puritan, The (Saint-Gaudens), **19th:** 1973
Puritan and the Papist, The (Cowley), **17th:** 199
Puritan Revolution, **17th:** 256
Puritan Widow, The (Middleton), **17th:** 636
Puritanism, **Ren:** 403, 457, 554, 762; **17th:** 386, 768, 798; Americas, 196; conversion of Native Americans, 633; England, 101, 145, 202, 218, 247, 414, 496, 534, 991; Massachusetts, 941; New England, 387, 394; **18th:** colonial America, 314-317, 671-675; Cotton Mather, 667-671; Samuel Sewall, 893. *See also* Protestantism
Puritan's Lecture (Cowley), **17th:** 199
Purvis, Melvin, **Notor:** 361
Pusey, E. B., **19th:** 77, 1844-1848
Push Comes to Shove (ballet), **20th:** 3990
Pushkin, Alexander, **19th:** 937, 1848-1851; **20th:** 253
Putidamo. *See* Bodhidharma
Putin, Vladimir, **20th:** 1532, 4434
Putnam, Ann, **17th:** 690
Putnam, Mary Corinna. *See* Jacobi, Mary Putnam
Putto with a Dolphin (Verrocchio), **Ren:** 963
Puyi, **19th:** 498; **Notor:** 864-866, 1123
Pydna, Battle of (168 B.C.E.), **Anc:** 756
Pygmalion (Shaw), **20th:** 3719
Pygmalion and Galatea (Gilbert), **19th:** 918
Pyliavtsi, Battle of (1648), **17th:** 462
Pym, John, **17th:** 167, 767-769, 886, 941
Pyotr Alekseyevich. *See* Peter the Great
Pyramids, **Anc:** Egyptian, 558; Step, 440, 996
Pyramids in the Sea (Nash), **20th:** 2911
Pyrenees, Treaty of the (1659), **17th:** 10, 186, 425, 549, 586, 600, 622, 698, 933
Pyrrhon of Elis, **Anc:** 722-724
Pystrye rasskazy (Chekhov), **19th:** 479
Pythagoras (Greek philosopher), **Anc:** 36, 98, 399, 609, 725-728
Pythagoras of Rhegion (sculptor), **Anc:** 675
Pythagorean brotherhood, **Anc:** 36, 296
Pythagorean theorem, **Anc:** 318, 727
Pytheas, **Anc:** 729-731
Pythius, **Anc:** 546

Q

Qaddafi, Muammar al-, **20th:** 3350-3354; **Notor:** 867-869
Qaitbay. *See* Qāytbāy
Qājār Dynasty, **20th:** 2779, 3428
Qandahār, **17th:** 843
Qanun fi al-tibb, al-. See *Canon of Medicine*
Qaro, Joseph. *See* Karo, Joseph ben Ephraim
Qasidas, **MA:** 917
Qaṣr al-shawq. See *Palace of Desire*
Qassim, Abdul Karim, **Notor:** 503
Qavam, Ahmad, **20th:** 2779
Qavurt, **MA:** 71
Qāytbāy, **Ren:** 87, 807-808
Qazwini, Fāṭima Khanum Baragani. *See* Táhirih
Qi, **17th:** 972
Qian Chen Qun, **17th:** 156
Qian Feng, **17th:** 156
Qian Han Shu. See *Han Shu*
Qian Jie, **17th:** 156
Qian Long Guang, **17th:** 156
Qian Qian Yi, **17th:** 540
Qian Rui Cheng, **17th:** 156
Qian Zeng, **17th:** 541
Qianlong, **17th:** 236; **18th:** 817-819, 1114
Qin Dynasty, **Anc:** 150
Qin Gui, **MA:** 1146
Qin Shi Huangdi. *See* Shi Huangdi
Qin state, **Anc:** 379
Qing Dynasty, **17th:** 1, 162, 234, 448, 848, 972, 1001; **18th:** 817-819, 1113-1115; **19th:** 496, 1127, 1363, 1376, 2485-2486; **20th:** fall of, 747
Qing Gaozong. *See* Qianlong

Qing Taizong. *See* Abahai
Qingliu, **19th:** 2486
Qinshan. *See* Ma Yuan
Qu Yuan, **Anc:** 732-734
Qu Yuan (Guo), **20th:** 1621
Quadequina, **17th:** 876
Quaderni del carcere. See *Selections from the Prison Notebooks of Antonio Gramsci*
Quadrature, **Anc:** 82
Quadrilogue invectif, Le. See *Invective Quadrilogue, The*
Quadrivium, **Anc:** 929
Quadruple Alliance, **19th:** 413, 440
Quaestiones celeberrimæ in Genesim (Mersenne), **17th:** 629
Quaestiones in quartum Sententiarum praesertim circa sacramenta (Adrian VI), **Ren:** 8
Quaestiones naturales (Seneca), **Anc:** 767
Quaestiones quodlibetales. See *Quodlibetal Questions, The* (Duns Scotus)
Quaestiones quotlibeticae XII (Adrian VI), **Ren:** 7
Quakerism (Penn), **17th:** 725
Quakerism a-la-Mode (Bossuet), **17th:** 341
Quakers and Quakerism, **17th:** American colonies, 984; Anne Conway, 188; England, 206, 284; William Penn, 724; **18th:** Benjamin Banneker, 85; Abraham Darby, 292; Ann Lee, 591; Betsy Ross, 867; **19th:** 39, 41
Quan xue pian (Zhang), **19th:** 2487
Quand les cathédrales étaient blanches. See *When the Cathedrals Were White*
Quang Trung. *See* Nguyen Hue
Quanta Cura (Pius IX), **19th:** 13, 1803
Quantrill, William Clarke, **19th:** 1211; **Notor:** 523, 869-871, 994, 1118
Quantulumcunque Concerning Money (Petty), **17th:** 734
Quantum electrodynamics, **20th:** 343
Quantum Fund, **20th:** 3795
Quantum mechanics, **20th:** 409, 1004, 1236, 1379, 1441; liquids, 2245; photoelectric effect, 1119; uncertainty principle, 1750; wave mechanics, 3668
Quantum theory, **20th:** 438, 535, 2944, 3283, 3827
Quapaw, **17th:** 434, 604
Quaragesimo Anno (Pius XI), **20th:** 3276
Quarante-cinq, Les. See *Forty-five Guardsmen, The*
Quartering Act (1774), **18th:** 460
Quarterly Journal of Microscopical Science, **19th:** 1316
Quarterly Review, **19th:** 1224
Quasi War (1798-1800), **18th:** 1046
Quaternions, **19th:** 1016
Quatre-Bras, Battle of (1815), **19th:** 1668
Quatre Cents Coups. See *Four Hundred Blows, The*
Quatre Évangiles, Les (Zola), **19th:** 2491
Quatre-vingt-treize. See *Ninety-three*
Quattro libri dell'architettura, I. See *Four Books of Architecture, The*
Quatuor pour la fin du temps (Messiaen), **20th:** 2716
Quauhtémoc. *See* Cuauhtémoc
Qué Valor (Goya), **19th:** 1995
Quebec, Battle of (1759), **18th:** 151, 510, 694, 1105
Quebec, Battle of (1775), **18th:** 60
Quebec Act (1774), **18th:** 197
Quebec sovereignist movement, **20th:** 625, 762, 2345, 3175, 3654, 4078
Québécois Party. *See* Parti Québécois
Queen Anne's War. *See* Spanish Succession, War of the (1701-1714)
Queen Christina (film), **20th:** 1393
Queen Mab (Shelley), **19th:** 2093
Queen of Fences. *See* Mandelbaum, Frederika
Queen of Spades, The (Pushkin), **19th:** 1850
Queen of Spades, The (Tchaikovsky), **19th:** 2235
Queens of Persia at the Feet of Alexander (Le Brun), **17th:** 505
Queen's Theatre, **17th:** 52
Queen's Twin and Other Stories, The (Jewett), **19th:** 1227
Queen's Ware, **18th:** 1059
Queensferry Paper. *See* Cameron's Covenant
Queenstown, Battle of (1812), **19th:** 2051
Quelch, John, **Notor:** 871-872
Quentin Durward (Scott), **19th:** 2048
Querelle des femmes, la, **MA:** 275
Querelle of Brest (Genet), **20th:** 1446
Queries of Highest Consideration (Williams), **17th:** 983
Querists, The (Whitefield), **18th:** 1074
Quesnay, François, **18th:** 820-822
Qu'est-ce que la littérature? See *What Is Literature?*
Qu'est-ce que la propriété? See *What Is Property?*
Question of German Guilt, The (Jaspers), **20th:** 1998
Question of Rest for Women During Menstruation, The (Jacobi), **19th:** 1202
Quetzalcóatl, **Ren:** 253
Quevedo y Villegas, Francisco Gómez de, **17th:** 312, 770-772
Quiet American, The (Greene), **20th:** 1579
Quietism, **17th:** 265, 339, 406

Quimby, Phineas P., **19th:** 723
Quinault, Philippe, **17th:** 570
Quincas Borba. See *Philosopher or Dog?*
Quincy, Massachusetts. *See* Merrymount
Quinine, synthesis of, **20th:** 4394
Quinisext Council. *See* Trullan Synod, Second
Quintanilla-Perez, Selena, **Notor:** 930-931
Quintessence of Ibsenism, The (Shaw), **20th:** 3718
Quintet in F Minor (Borodin), **19th:** 281
Quintet in F Minor for Piano and Strings (Franck), **19th:** 823
Quintetto Boccherini, **18th:** 131
Quintilian, **Anc:** 838
Quintus Caepia Brutus. *See* Brutus, Marcus Junius
Quiroga, Juan Facundo, **19th:** 2000
Quisling, Vidkun, **Notor:** 873-875
Quivira, **Ren:** 247
Quizquiz, **Ren:** 68
Qumran community, **Anc:** 476
Quoc Âm Thi Tuyen (Ho), **19th:** 1112
Quod apostolici muneris. See *Concerning Modern Errors, Socialism, Communism, Nihilism*
Quod Deus sit immutabilis (Philo), **Anc:** 641
Quodlibeta septem. See *Quodlibetal Questions* (Ockham)
Quodlibetal Questions, The (Duns Scotus), **MA:** 330
Quodlibetal Questions (Ockham), **MA:** 778
Quorundam virorum illustrium epithoma. See *De viris illustribus* (Petrarch)
Qur'ān, **Anc:** 6; **MA:** 19, 36, 611, 734; commentaries, 988; **18th:** 1000, 1030, 1032-1033
Qurrat al-ʿAyn. *See* Táhirih
Qusṭā ibn Lūqā al-Baʿlabakkī, **Anc:** 286
Quṭ al-Dīn Ḥasan ibn ʿAlī, **MA:** 889
Qutb al-Din Ahmad ibn ʿAbd al-Raḥīm. *See* Walī Allāh, Shāh
Quṭb Mīnār, **MA:** 41
Qutb, Sayyid, **Notor:** 1135
Quṭb-ud-Dīn Mubārak Shāh, **MA:** 41
Qutlugh-Shāh, **MA:** 413
Qutlumush ibn Arslan Isrāʾīl, **MA:** 71
Quṭuz, **MA:** 140
Quwwāt al-Islām, **MA:** 41
Qwastantinos I. *See* Zara Yaqob

R

Ra (god), **Anc:** 901
Ra Expeditions, The (Heyerdahl), **20th:** 1798
Rabanus Maurus, **MA:** 861, 870-873
Rabat Conference (1974), **20th:** 111
Rabbi of Bacherach, The (Heine), **19th:** 1071
Rabbi of Vitebsk (Chagall), **20th:** 717
Rabbinic assembly, **Anc:** 29
Rabdologiae, seu numerationis per virgulas libri duo. See *Study of Divining Rods*
Rabelais, François, **Ren:** 619, 809-812
Rabelais and His World (Bakhtin), **20th:** 191
Rabi, Isidor Isaac, **20th:** 3355-3358, 4133
Rābiʿah al-ʿAdawiyah, **MA:** 873-876
Rabin, Yitzhak, **20th:** 113, 3358-3360
Rabindranath Tagore (film), **20th:** 3395
Rabinovitch, Emanuel. *See* Man Ray
Rabutin-Chantal, Marie de. *See* Sévigné, Madame de
Rācandra, **MA:** 40
Race (Benedict), **20th:** 297
Race riots, New Orleans and Memphis, **19th:** 1232
Rachmaninoff, Sergei, **20th:** 1886, 3361-3364
Račić, Puniša, **Notor:** 876-877
Racine, Jean, **17th:** 64, 72, 186, 194-195, 482, 554, 573, 773-776
Racine and Shakespeare (Stendhal), **19th:** 2162
Racism, **20th:** 2321, 2463. *See also* Discrimination
Racists. *See* Category Index
Racketty Packetty House (Burnett), **19th:** 359
Rackham, John, **Notor:** 122, 877-878, 891
Radagaisus, **Anc:** 825
Radcliffe, Ann, **18th:** 823-825
Radcliffe-Browne, A. R., **20th:** 297
Radcliffe College, **19th:** 30
Rader, Dennis, **Notor:** 879-880
Radewyns, Florentius, **MA:** 1022
Radha (dance drama), **20th:** 3594
Radiation therapy, **20th:** 3537
Radiative equilibrium, **20th:** 3675
Radić, Stjepan, **Notor:** 876
Radical Republicans, **20th:** 779
Radical-Socialist Party (France), **20th:** 1777
Radiguet, Raymond, **20th:** 794
Radimichi, **MA:** 1068
Radio, **19th:** 1825; **20th:** 128, 811, 941, 2832, 2880, 3411. *See also* Category Index
Radio Corporation of America, **20th:** 2618, 4480
Radioactinium, discovery of, **20th:** 1635
Radioactive Indicators (Hevesy), **20th:** 1794
Radioactive isotopes, **20th:** 621, 1794, 4419; identification of, 1637, 3684, 3779; as tracers, 1793, 4306, 4420
Radioactivity, **20th:** 2034, 3576, 3779

Radiocarbon dating, **20th:** 2371
Radiolarien, Die. See *Report on the Radiolaria*
Radiologie et la guerre, La (Curie), **20th:** 890
Radiotelegraphy, **20th:** 2617
Radisson, Pierre Esprit, **17th:** 777-779
Radium, isolation of, **20th:** 889
Radiyya. *See* Raziya
Radnitsky, Emmanuel. *See* Man Ray
Radomyslsky, Ovel Gershon Aronov. *See* Zinovyev, Grigory Yevseyevich
Radu II, **Notor:** 1072
Radu the Handsome, **Ren:** 982
Radziwill, Mikołaj, **Ren:** 911
Raeburn, Sir Henry, **19th:** 1852-1855
Raeder, Erich, **Notor:** 292
Raffaelli, Francesca. *See* Caccini, Francesca
Raffaelli, Tomaso, **17th:** 112
Rafsanjani, Hashemi, **20th:** 2126
Raft of the Medusa, The (Géricault), **19th:** 635, 899
Raft of the Medusa, The (Henze), **20th:** 1764
Ragaz, Leonhard, **20th:** 547
Ragged Dick (Alger), **19th:** 52
Raghuvamśa (Kālidāsa), **Anc:** 497
Raging Bull (film), **20th:** 3682
Ragionamenti, The (Aretino), **Ren:** 54
Ragionamento della Nanna et della Antonia. See *Ragionamenti, The*
Ragtime (film), **20th:** 3990
Ragtime Dance (Joplin), **19th:** 1236
Ragtime music, **19th:** 1236; **20th:** 328
Ragua Ocllo, **Ren:** 469
Rahman, Tunku Abdul, **20th:** 2327
Raibert Ruadh. *See* Rob Roy
Raiders of the Lost Ark (film), **20th:** 2451
Railways, **19th:** Canada, 1101, 1444, 2317; engineering, 2168, 2295; England, 334, 2169; laws governing, 779; locomotives, 2169, 2295; Ottoman Empire, 7; steel rails, 220; transcontinental, 1600, 2133; **20th:** Canada, 2283
Rain, Steam, and Speed (Turner), **19th:** 2324
Rainald of Dassel, **MA:** 385
Rainbow, The (Lawrence), **20th:** 2296
Rainey, Gertrude "Ma," **20th:** 3765
Raintree County (film), **20th:** 3954
Rais, Gilles de, **Notor:** 604, 880-882
Raisin in the Sun, A (Hansberry), **20th:** 1671
Raising of Drusiana, The (Giotto), **MA:** 422
Rajaratnam, Thenmuli, **Notor:** 882-883
Rajkumar, **Notor:** 1062
Rajputs, Mughals and, **Ren:** 15
Rājyasrī, **MA:** 460
Rājyavardhana, **MA:** 460
Rake's Progress, A (Hockney), **20th:** 1846
Rake's Progress, The (Hogarth), **18th:** 498
Rake's Progress, The (Stravinsky), **20th:** 173
Rakovy Korpus. See *Cancer Ward*
Ralbag. *See* Levi ben Gershom
Ralegh, Sir Walter, **Ren:** 193, 378, 396, 771, 813-816; **17th:** 132, 175, 230, 414
Rāma, **Anc:** 922
Rama IX of Thailand. *See* Bhumibol Adulyadej
Ramakrishna Paramhansa, **19th:** 2369
Raman, Sir Chandrasekhara Venkata, **20th:** 3364-3366
Raman effect, **20th:** 3365
Rāmānuja, **MA:** 876-878
Rāmāyaṇa (Vālmīki), **Anc:** 922
Ramban. *See* Naḥmanides
Rambler, The (journal), **18th:** 537
Rambles in Germany and Italy (Shelley), **19th:** 2090
Rambouillet, Julie-Lucine de, **17th:** 780
Rambouillet, marquise de, **17th:** 779-781
Rameau, Jean-Philippe, **18th:** 826-829
Ramée, Pierre de la. *See* Ramus, Peter
Rameses II. *See* Ramses II
Ramírez de Santillana, Juana Inés de Asbaje y. *See* Cruz, Sor Juana Inés de la
Ramírez Reina, José León. *See* Degrelle, Léon
Ramírez Sánchez, Ilich, **Notor:** 883-885
Ramona (Jackson), **19th:** 1194
Ram's Head with Hollyhock (O'Keeffe), **20th:** 3032
Ramsay, Charlotte. *See* Lennox, Charlotte
Ramsay, James Andrew Broun. *See* Dalhousie, first marquis of
Ramsay, William, **20th:** 139, 1635, 3779
Ramses I, **Anc:** 735
Ramses II, **Anc:** 585, 735-738, 773
Ramus, Peter, **Ren:** 817-819
Ran (film), **20th:** 2219
Ranade, Mahadev Govind, **19th:** 1855-1857
Ranariddh, Norodom, **20th:** 1943
Rancho Notorious (film), **20th:** 2254
Ranchos Church (O'Keeffe), **20th:** 3032
Rand, Ayn, **20th:** 1581, 3367-3369; **Notor:** 613
Rand, Walter Charles, **20th:** 4025
Rand-McNally Building, **19th:** 361
Randall, Patrick "Pete," **Notor:** 972

Randglossen zum Gothaer Partei Programm. See *Critique of the Gotha Program*
Randolph, A. Philip, **20th:** 3369-3374
Randolph, Edward, **18th:** 672
Randolph, Robert. *See* Rudolph, Eric
Randolph, Thomas, **17th:** 443
Rangaku (Dutch studies), **18th:** 504
Rangoni, Claudio, **17th:** 855
Ranjit Singh, **19th:** 1857-1859
Ranke, Leopold von, **19th:** 354, 1860-1862
Rankin, Jeannette, **20th:** 3374-3377
Ranković, Alexander, **20th:** 1012
Ransom of Hector, The. See *Hectoris lytra*
Ranson, Paul, **20th:** 972
Ranters, **17th:** 666
Ranuzzi, Annibale, **17th:** 857
Rape of Europa, The (Titian), **Ren:** 938
Rape of Lucretia, The (Britten), **20th:** 531
Rape of the Lock, The (Pope), **Anc:** 180; **18th:** 805
Raphael, **Ren:** 39, 134, 181, 390, 520, 558, 819-823
Rappe, Virginia, **Notor:** 32
Rapport sur les progrès et la marche de la physiologie générale en France (Bernard), **19th:** 206
Rapsodie nègre (Poulenc), **20th:** 3318
Rashid Bey Ayman, **19th:** 1474
Rashomon (film), **20th:** 2218
Raskol, **17th:** 13
Rasmussen, Knud Johan Victor, **20th:** 3377-3380
Raspe, Jan-Carl, **Notor:** 47
Rasputin, Grigori Yefimovich, **19th:** 1863-1866; **Notor:** 885-887, 1126
Rasselas (Johnson), **18th:** 537
Rastatt and Baden, Treaties of (1714), **18th:** 230, 331, 781
Rat, The (Grass), **20th:** 1575
Rathstübel Plutonis (Grimmelshausen), **17th:** 325
Rationalism, **Anc:** 407; **18th:** Paul-Henri-Dietrich d'Holbach, 503; David Hume, 514; Immanuel Kant, 548
Ratisbon, Diet of (1630), **17th:** 552
Ratnāvāli. See *Retnavali*
Ratramnus, **MA:** 879-881
Rattazzi, Urbando, **19th:** 446
Ratti, Ambrogio Damiano Achille. *See* Pius XI
Rättin, Die. See *Rat, The*
Ra'uf Pasha, **19th:** 1474
Rauschenberg, Robert, **20th:** 886, 3380-3382
Rauschenbusch, Walter, **20th:** 3382-3385, 4002
Ravachol, **Notor:** 180
Ravaillac, François, **Ren:** 431; **17th:** 598; **Notor:** 214, 888-889
Rāvaṇa, **Anc:** 923
Ravel, Maurice, **20th:** 195, 954, 3386-3389
Ravelstein (Bellow), **20th:** 290
Ravenna, Battle of (1512), **Ren:** 57, 85, 152, 519
Ravenna, fall of (493), **MA:** 784
Rawlings, Jerry John, **20th:** 3389-3391
Rawls, John, **20th:** 2999, 3391-3393
Rawnsley, Canon Hardwicke, **19th:** 1105
Ray, James Earl, **20th:** 2149; **Notor:** 889-891, 1000
Ray, John, **17th:** 29, 782-784
Ray, Man. *See* Man Ray
Ray, Rammohan, **19th:** 1866-1869
Ray, Satyajit, **20th:** 3394-3397
Ray Charles Robinson Foundation, **20th:** 736
Rayburn, Sam, **20th:** 2028, 3397-3399
Raymbault, Charles, **17th:** 423
Raymond IV, **MA:** 177
Raymond, Henry James. *See* Worth, Adam
Raymond of Peñafort, **MA:** 437, 881-883
Raymond of Poitiers, **MA:** 356, 716
Raymundian Code, **MA:** 882
Raynal, Guillaume-Thomas, **18th:** 829-831, 985
Raynal, L. E. *See* Hory, Elmyr de
Rāzī, al-, **MA:** 884-887
Razin, Stenka, **17th:** 12, 784-786
Raziya, **MA:** 888-890
Razmara, Ali, **20th:** 2779
Razvitiia kapitalizm v Rossii (Lenin), **20th:** 2341
RCA. *See* Radio Corporation of America
Reaching for the Moon (film), **20th:** 2429
Reaction propulsion, **20th:** 4095
Read, Mary, **Notor:** 122, 877, 891-892
Reade, Charles, **19th:** 2250
Reading, Council of (1279), **MA:** 818
Reading Mercury (newspaper), **18th:** 730
Ready and Easy Way to Establish a Free Commonwealth, The (Milton), **17th:** 640
Reagan, Ronald, **20th:** 595, 669, 1243, 3057, 3400-3405, 3435, 3732, 3994; EPCOT, 1009; **Notor:** 141, 199, 241, 394, 470
Reaganomics, **20th:** 3402
Real Life of Sebastian Knight, The (Nabokov), **20th:** 2895
Real Presence, The (Pusey), **19th:** 1846
Realism, **Anc:** Augustine, 142; four elements, 295; versus nominalism, 688; Parmenides, 610; in sculpture, 524; **20th:** 2056, 4412. *See also* Art; Literature
Réalisme méthodique. See *Methodical Realism*

Réalisme thomiste et critique de la connaissance. See *Thomist Realism and the Critique of Knowledge*
Realm of the Nebulae, The (Hubble), **20th:** 1913
Realms of Being (Santayana), **20th:** 3630
Realpolitik, **20th:** 2171
Reaper, The (Miró), **20th:** 2761
Rear Window (film), **20th:** 1827, 3863
Reason, **Anc:** Buddhism, 161; Christian thinkers, 863; versus common sense, 985; versus faith, 143; nature of, 261; Plato, 661; Porphyry, 689; Pyrrhon, 724; versus senses, 295; **18th:** Vauvenargues on, 1010
Reason and Existenz (Jaspers), **20th:** 1998
Reason of Church-Government Urg'd Against Prelaty, The (Milton), **17th:** 640
Reason the Only Oracle of Man (Allen), **18th:** 35, 37
Reasonableness of Christianity as Delivered in the Scriptures, The (Locke), **17th:** 546
Reasoner, Harry, **20th:** 4211
Reasons for and Against the Enfranchisement of Women (Bodichon), **19th:** 264
Reasons of the Christian Religion, The (Baxter), **17th:** 35
Rebecca (film), **20th:** 1826, 3041
Rebecca (oratorio by Franck), **19th:** 823
Rebecca and Rowena (Thackeray), **19th:** 2259
Rebecca of Sunnybrook Farm (film), **20th:** 3245
Rebekah, **Anc:** 6
Rebel, The (Camus), **20th:** 630
Rebel leaders, **18th:** Nanny, 724-726; Yemelyan Ivanovich Pugachev, 814-816; Daniel Shays, 902-905; Wolfe Tone, 982-984; Tupac Amaru II, 993-995
Rebelión de las masas, La. See *Revolt of the Masses, The*
Rebellion of the Northern Earls. *See* Northern Earls, Rebellion of the
Rebellions, **Anc:** against Alexander Severus, 485; against Ashurbanipal, 118; against Cambyses II, 136; against Carthage, 374; Catiline, 189; Cinna, 832; against Darius the Great, 251; Jewish, 944; against Nero, 593; against Rome, 163, 937; against Sargon of Akkad, 299; against Sparta, 304; against Tigranes the Great, 897; against Xerxes I, 971
Rebellious Slave, The (Michelangelo), **Ren:** 683
Rebels, The (Child), **19th:** 482
Rebirth, **Anc:** Christian, 474; Egyptian beliefs in, 559; Jainism and, 925
Rebouças, André, **19th:** 1869-1871
Recessions, U.S., **20th:** 1582-1583
Recherches anatomiques et physiologiques sur la corde du tympan, pour servir à l'histoire de l'hémiplegie faciale (Bernard), **19th:** 205
Recht des Besitzes, Das. See *Treatise on Possession*
Reciprocal Trade Agreements Act of 1934, **20th:** 1936
Récits des Antilles (Ségalas), **19th:** 2063
Reclamation Act (1902), **19th:** 1830
Reclining Figure (Moore), **20th:** 2820
Reclining River Nymph at the Fountain (Cranach, the Elder), **Ren:** 264
Recluse, The (Wordsworth), **19th:** 2463
Recollections of a Life (Hiss), **20th:** 1823
Recollections of Alexis de Tocqueville, The (Tocqueville), **19th:** 2281
Recollections of My Youth (Renan), **19th:** 1887
Reconquista, **MA:** 157, 536; **Ren:** 105, 252, 330
Reconstruction (American South), **19th:** 960, 1230; support for, 1061; Supreme Court, 472
Reconstruction (Macmillan), **20th:** 2537
Reconstruction Acts, **19th:** 1232
Reconstruction Finance Corporation, **20th:** 1864
Reconstruction of the Spiritual Ideal, The (Adler), **19th:** 27
Record of a Living Being. See *I Live in Fear*
Record of a School (Peabody), **19th:** 1761
Record of a School, Exemplifying the General Principles of Spiritual Culture, The (Alcott), **19th:** 40
Record of Family Faculties (Galton), **19th:** 862
Records of a Travel-Worn Satchel, The (Bashō), **17th:** 616
Records of a Weather-Exposed Skeleton, The (Bashō), **17th:** 615
Records of Ancient Matters. See *Kojiki*
Records of the Grand Historian of China. See *Shiji*
Records of Women (Hemans), **19th:** 1077
Rectification movement, **20th:** 2408
Rectification of Names, **Anc:** 237
Recueil de poésie (du Bellay), **Ren:** 295
Recueil des pieces nouveles et galantes (Montpensier), **17th:** 662
Recueil des plus beaux vers (Malherbe), **17th:** 578
Recueil des secrets (Bourgeois), **17th:** 74

Recusants, **Ren:** 200, 324; **17th:** 414
Red and the Black, The (Stendhal), **19th:** 2162
Red and White Plum Blossoms (Kōrin), **17th:** 696
Red Army, **20th:** 4467
Red Badge of Courage, The (Crane), **19th:** 563
Red Beard (film), **20th:** 2219
Red Cloud, **19th:** 567, 1871-1874
Red Cloud's War (1866-1868), **19th:** 567, 1873
Red Dust (film), **20th:** 1369
Red-Headed Woman (film), **20th:** 2430
Red Lily, The (France), **19th:** 816
Red Pill Case, **17th:** 911
Red River (film), **20th:** 4251
Red River Rebellion (1869-1870), **19th:** 1443, 1909
Red Scare (1919-1920), **20th:** 1866, 2612, 3879, 4003
Red Studio, The (Matisse), **20th:** 2651
Red Terror (Ethiopia), **20th:** 2702
Red Wheel, The (Solzhenitsyn), **20th:** 3785
Redbeard. *See* Barbarossa
Redburn (Melville), **19th:** 1537-1538
Rédemption (Franck), **19th:** 823
Rédemption, La (Gounod), **19th:** 954
Reden an die deutsche Nation. See *Addresses to the German Nation*
Redgauntlet (Scott), **19th:** 2048
Redon, Odilon, **19th:** 1875-1877
Redskins, The (Cooper), **19th:** 555
Rée, Paul, **19th:** 1682
Reece, Carroll, **20th:** 2162
Reed, Belle. *See* Starr, Belle
Reed, Dorothy. *See* Mendenhall, Dorothy Reed
Reed, Jim, **Notor:** 994
Reed, John, **20th:** 3052; **Notor:** 1071
Reed, Walter, **19th:** 1877-1880; **20th:** 1542
Reed Cutter, The (Zeami), **MA:** 1154
Reef, The (Wharton), **20th:** 4301
Reese, Marilyn, **Notor:** 945
Reeve, John, **17th:** 666
Reeve, William, **17th:** 665
Reeves, William Pember, **19th:** 982, 2059
Reflections in a Golden Eye (McCullers), **20th:** 2508
Reflections of a Russian Statesman (Pobedonostsev), **19th:** 1811
Reflections on the Causes of the Grandeur and Declension of the Romans (Montesquieu), **18th:** 696
Reflections on the Decline of Science in England and on Some of Its Causes (Babbage), **19th:** 108
Reflections on the Formation and Distribution of Wealth (Turgot), **18th:** 997
Reflections on the Paintings and Sculpture of the Greeks (Winckelmann), **18th:** 1095
Reflections on the Revolution in France (Burke), **18th:** 176, 760, 1109
Reflections on Things at Hand (Zhu Xi and Lü Zuqian), **MA:** 1160
Reflections on Violence (Sorel), **20th:** 3792
Reflections upon Marriage (Astell), **18th:** 66
Reflexes, study of, **20th:** 3164
Réflexions critiques sur Longin (Boileau-Despréaux), **17th:** 64
Reflexions on the Metaphysical Principles of the Infinitesimal Analysis (Carnot), **18th:** 201
Réflexions: Ou, Sentences et maximes morales. See *Maximes*
Réflexions sur la formation et la distribution des richesses. See *Reflections on the Formation and Distribution of Wealth*
Réflexions sur la métaphysique du calcul infinitesimal. See *Reflexions on the Metaphysical Principles of the Infinitesimal Analysis*
Réflexions sur la violence. See *Reflections on Violence*
Reform, War of the (1858-1861), **19th:** 1246, 1526
Reform Act of 1867, **19th:** 767
Reform Act of 1884, **19th:** 767
Reform Bill of 1832, **19th:** 77, 378, 667, 924, 979, 1434, 1572, 1732, 1808, 2447
Reform Club, **19th:** 143
Reform or Revolution? (Luxemburg), **20th:** 2482
Reform Party, **19th:** 1453
Reforma, La, **19th:** 1246
Reformation, **Ren:** 142, 163, 231; England, 189, 267, 467, 543, 947; France, 424, 462, 550; Germany, 650, 665, 775; Martin Luther and, 584; Papacy and, 798; Scotland, 502, 628; Spain, 779; Switzerland, 472, 1011. *See also* Counter-Reformation; Lutheran Church and Lutheranism; Protestantism; Roman Catholic Church and Catholicism
Reformed Carmelites. *See* Carmelites
Reformed Church, Dutch. *See* Dutch Reformed Church
Reformed Church, French. *See* Huguenots
Refraction Tables (Bessel), **19th:** 215
Refugee in America, The (Trollope), **19th:** 2303
Refutation of All Heresies, The. See *Kata pasōn haireseōn elenkhos*
Regarding the Pain of Others (Sontag), **20th:** 3790
Regatta on the Grand Canal, A (Canaletto), **18th:** 191
Regency Crisis (1788-1789), **18th:** 216, 365, 790

Regensburg, Diet of (1541), **Ren:** 144
Regensburg, Diet of (1546), **Ren:** 777
Regensburg Book, **Ren:** 144
Regent faction, **17th:** 519
Regent Street, **19th:** 1644
Regents of the University of California v. Bakke (1978), **20th:** 583
Regent's Park, **19th:** 1644
Regimen. See *Diaitētikon*
Regimen sanitatis Salerni (Arnold of Villanova), **MA:** 100
Regionalism, **20th:** 4389
Règle du jeu, La. See *Rules of the Game, The*
Regrets, The (du Bellay), **Ren:** 296
Regulae ad directionem ingenii. See *Rules for the Direction of the Mind*
Regulae rhythmicae in antiphonarii sui prologum prolate. See *Guido D'Arezzo's "Regule rithmice," "Prologue in antiphonarium," and "Epistola ad michahelem"*
Regulus, Anc: 738-741
Rehearsal, The (Buckingham), **17th:** 241
Rehearsal Transpros'd, The (Marvell), **17th:** 606
Rehnquist, William H., 20th: 3020, 3405-3409
Rei Encuberto, **Ren:** 860
Reichenbach, Hans, **20th:** 660
Reichenbach, Harry, **Notor:** 230
Reid, Sir George, **19th:** 624
Reign of Terror (1793-1794), **18th:** 268, 291, 650, 659, 846, 878, 930
Reina, Gaetano "Tom," **Notor:** 659
Reinhardt, Walther, **20th:** 3689
Reinwen, **Anc:** 395
Reisebilder. See *Pictures of Travel*
Reith of Stonehaven, first Baron (John Charles Walsham Reith), **20th:** 3410-3413
Reitman, Ben, **20th:** 1521
Reivers, The (Faulkner), **20th:** 1225
Rekviem. See *Requiem* (Akhmatova)
Relâche (ballet), **20th:** 3644
Relación, La (Cabeza de Vaca), **Ren:** 154
Relapse, The (Vanbrugh), **18th:** 1003
Relation d'un voyage en Limousin (La Fontaine), **17th:** 481
Relation écrite par la Mère Angélique sur Port-Royal (Arnauld), **17th:** 22
Relation sur le quiétisme. See *Quakerism a-la-Mode*
Relativism, **Anc:** 88
Relativity theory, **19th:** 1818; **20th:** 1119, 3675
Relaxati, **MA:** 181
Relectiones theologicae (Vitoria), **Ren:** 979
Reles, Abe, **Notor:** 238
Reliance Building, **19th:** 361
Relics, **Anc:** Buddhist, 900; Saint Helena, 392
Religio Laici (Dryden), **17th:** 241
Religio Medici (Browne), **17th:** 94
Religion, **Anc:** Assyrian, 753; community and, 721; Cyrus the Great and, 250; drama and, 877; Egyptian, 736; Greco-Roman sycretism, 108; law and, 293; Livy on, 512; medicine and, 421, 440; philosophy and, 702; Roman, 219, 240, 282, 889; science and, 726; Sumerian, 915; superstition and, 520; Vandals and, 353; **MA:** Aztecs, 560; Bulgaria, 190; Egypt, 142; Khmer, 981; Mali, 744; Mediterranean, 158; Ottoman Empire, 712; Turkey, 802; West Africa, 978; **Ren:** Aztec Empire, 253, 694; India, 478, 709; Ottoman Empire, 660; **17th:** England, 221; France, 211; Japan, 917; **18th:** America, 62-64; Joseph Butler, 187-189; Jonathan Edwards, 314-317; and emotion, 316, 1120; and evolution-creation, 763-765; David Hume, 515; theory of intelligent design, 763; Judaism, 68-70; Gotthold Ephraim Lessing, 598-602; Ukraine, 68; **19th:** England, 74; United States, 70, 465; **20th:** comparative study of, 1137, 4069, 4178, 4260; freedom of, 1310; fundamentalism, 915; India, 178; versus science, 3965. *See also* Christianity; Islam; Judaism; Theology; *specific denominations, sects, gods*; Category Index
Religion, French Wars of (1562-1629), **Ren:** 102, 164, 185, 285, 426, 429, 463, 569, 704; **17th:** 896
Religion innerhalb der Grenzen der blossen Vernunft, Die. See *Religion Within the Boundaries of Pure Reason*
Religion of Man (Tagore), **20th:** 3935
Religion Within the Boundaries of Pure Reason (Kant), **18th:** 550
Religionswissenschaft (Wach), **20th:** 4177
Religious Aspect of Philosophy, The (Royce), **20th:** 3551
Religious conversion, **18th:** Catholicism in the New World, 891; of indigenous peoples, 159; of Jews, 676; Shakers, 592
Religious criticism, **18th:** Paul-Henri-Dietrich d'Holbach, 501-504; Gotthold Ephraim Lessing, 601; Joseph Priestley, 811-814
Religious education, **18th:** colonial America, 1099; Hannah More, 702
Religious freedom, **18th:** American independence and, 206; colonial America, 76;

Continental Congress, 76; English law, 645; Ireland, 983; Irish Catholics, 442. *See also* Constitution, U.S.; First Amendment; Virginia Statute of Religious Liberty
Religious leaders, **18th:** Cotton Mather, 667-671; Increase Mather, 671-675; Charles Wesley, 1061-1063; John Wesley, 1064-1067; George Whitefield, 1073-1075; John Witherspoon, 1098-1102; Count von Zinzendorf, 1119-1122
Religious Liberty, Statute of (1786), **18th:** 636
Religious persecution. *See* Persecution, religious
Religious reform, **18th:** Holy Roman Empire, 793; Islam, 1030-1032; Joseph II, 545; Mustafa III, 722; Pius VI, 793; Robespierre, 846; Emanuel Swedenborg, 961
Religious Situation, The (Tillich), **20th:** 4028
Religious Socialist Movement, **20th:** 547
Religious Society of Friends. *See* Quakers and Quakerism
Remarks on American Literature (Channing), **19th:** 467
Remarks on the Uses of the Definitive Article in the Greek Text of the New Testament (Sharp), **18th:** 901
Remarque, Erich Maria, **20th:** 999, 3413-3416
Rembolt, Berthold, **Ren:** 413
Rembolt, vidua Bertholdi. *See* Guillard, Charlotte
Rembrandt, **17th:** 117, 353, 583, 786-789, 956
Remède de Fortune (Machaut), **MA:** 680
Remedy, The (Buxton), **19th:** 378, 574
"Remember the Ladies" (Adams), **18th:** 9
Remembrance of Things Past (Proust), **20th:** 3343
Reményi, Eduard, **19th:** 296
Remington, Frederic, **19th:** 1881-1884
Remington, William, **Notor:** 217
Reminiscences (Carlyle), **19th:** 417
Réminiscences de Don Juan (Liszt), **19th:** 1394
Remonstrance au peuple de France (Ronsard), **Ren:** 838
Remonstrances sur le default du labour et culture des plantes (Belon), **Ren:** 102
Remonstrants, **17th:** 288, 619
Removal of Jewish Disabilities (1858), **19th:** 668
Renaixença, **20th:** 1423
RENAMO, **20th:** 2516
Renan, Ernest, **19th:** 1204, 1884-1888
Renard, Simon, **Ren:** 640
Renascence, and Other Poems (Millay), **20th:** 2739
Renati Des Cartes principiorum philosophiae. See *Principles of Descartes' Philosophy, The*
Renaud, **Notor:** 604
René (Chateaubriand), **19th:** 476
Renga, **MA:** 1152
Rengae, **17th:** 403
Reni, Guido, **Notor:** 193
Reno, Janet, **20th:** 784, 3416-3419
Reno, Marcus, **Notor:** 249
Renoir, Jean, **20th:** 672, 3420-3424
Renoir, Pierre-Auguste, **19th:** 453, 632, 1800, 1888-1891; **20th:** 2790, 3420
Rensselaer, Nicholas van, **17th:** 518
Renzong, **MA:** 1079
Reorganized Church of Jesus Christ of Latter-day Saints, **19th:** 2476
Repeal movement, **19th:** 1697
Repentance of Mary Magdalene (La Tour), **17th:** 494
Repertorium (Browne), **17th:** 95
Reply to Mr. Bosanquet's Practical Observation on the Report of the Bullion Committee, A (Ricardo), **19th:** 1896
Reply to Sor Filotea de la Cruz (Cruz), **17th:** 209
Répons (Boulez), **20th:** 455
Report from Part One (Brooks), **20th:** 538
Report from Part Two (Brooks), **20th:** 538
Report of the Truth of the Fight About the Isles of Açores This Last Summer, A. See *Last Fight of the Revenge, The*
"Report on Manufactures" (Hamilton), **18th:** 455
Report on the Affairs of British North America (Durham), **19th:** 710
Report on the Deep-Sea Medusae (Haeckel), **19th:** 1004
Report on the Lands of the Arid Region of the United States, A (Powell), **19th:** 1829
Report on the Radiolaria (Haeckel), **19th:** 1003
Report on the Sanitary Condition of the Labouring Population, The (Chadwick), **19th:** 458
Report on Weights and Measures (Adams), **19th:** 24
Report Relative to a Provision for the Support of Public Credit (Hamilton), **18th:** 454
Report to the County of Lanark (Owen), **19th:** 1722
Reports (Coke), **17th:** 174
Reports on the Education of Girls, with Extracts from the Evidence (Beale), **19th:** 160
Reprehensio duodecim capitum seu anathema anathematismorum Cyrilli (Theodoret), **Anc:** 866
Représentation du monde chez l'enfant, La. See *Child's Conception of the World, The*

Representation of the Injustice and Dangerous Tendency of Tolerating Slavery, A (Sharp), **18th:** 900
Representative Men (Emerson), **19th:** 746
Reprieve, The (Sartre), **20th:** 3639
Repton, Humphrey, **18th:** 167
Republic. See *Politeia* (Plato)
Republic, The (Beard), **20th:** 265
Republican-Federalist conflict, **18th:** 238
Republican government, **18th:** Montesquieu, 696
"Republican motherhood," **18th:** 9
Republican National Convention (1880), **19th:** 81
Republican Party (U.S.), **19th:** 80, 253, 869, 1042; founding of, 471; Ohio, 1061
Republican People's Party (Turkey), **20th:** 164
Requiem (Akhmatova), **20th:** 44
Requiem (Berlioz), **19th:** 202
Requiem for a Futurologist (Soyinka), **20th:** 3806
Requiem Mass, Op. 89 (Dvořák), **19th:** 713
Rerum familiarium libri. See *Books on Personal Matters*
Rerum memoria dignarum (Verrius), **Anc:** 941
Rerum novarum. See *Condition of Labor, The*
Rerum suo tempore gestarum commentarius (Bruni), **MA:** 209
Rerum vulgarium fragmenta. See *Rhymes*
Resale Prices Act of 1964, **20th:** 1740
Reserpine, synthesis of, **20th:** 4395
Reservations. *See* Indian reservations
Residence on Earth, and Other Poems (Neruda), **20th:** 2937
Resistance of Air and Aviation Experiments Conducted at the Champs-de-Mars Laboratory, The (Eiffel), **19th:** 736
Resnais, Alain, **Notor:** 998
Resolution, HMS, **18th:** 271
Resolution, Party of, **19th:** 621
"Respect" (Franklin), **20th:** 1313
Responsa Nicolai ad Consulta Bulgarorum (Nicholas the Great), **MA:** 767
Responsibilities (Yeats), **20th:** 4429
Responsio Matthaei Torti (Bellarmine), **17th:** 16
Respuesta de la poetisa a la muy ilustre Sor Filotea de la Cruz. See *Reply to Sor Filotea de la Cruz*
Ressam Levni. *See* Levni
Ressentiment (Scheler), **20th:** 3656
Restell, Madame, **Notor:** 892-893
Restitution, Edict of (1629), **17th:** 269
Restoration, War of (1641-1668), **17th:** 432
Restoration Movement, **19th:** 402
Restoration of Charles II, **17th:** 506, 677; and Anglo-Catholicism, 497; and Robert Blake, 58; and John Bunyan, 101; and the first earl of Clarendon, 169; and Elizabeth Stuart, 254; execution of regicides, 757; and the third Baron Fairfax, 264; Fundamental Orders of Connecticut, 568; and Matthew Hale, 346; and Henrietta Maria, 365; and Thomas Hobbes, 381; and John Lambert, 485; and John Milton, 641; and George Monck, 652; Nonconformists, 54, 101; and William Penn, 724; and Sir William Petty, 734; Presbyterians, 121; and the Quakers, 284; and Prince Rupert, 805
Restoration of Works of Art to Italy, The (Hemans), **19th:** 1076
Resurrection (Piero), **Ren:** 786
Resurrection (Tintoretto), **Ren:** 933
Resurrection (Tolstoy), **19th:** 2285
Resurrection of Hungary, The (Griffith), **20th:** 1591
Resurreicão (Machado), **19th:** 1450
Retaliation (Goldsmith), **18th:** 435
Retnavali (Harṣa), **MA:** 461
Retour, Le (film), **20th:** 672
Retour à la vie, Le. See *Lélio*
Retour de l'U.R.S.S. See *Return from the U.S.S.R.*
Retrospect of Western Travel (Martineau), **19th:** 1506
Retrovirology, **20th:** 3546
Return from the U.S.S.R. (Gide), **20th:** 1479
Return of Frank James, The (film), **20th:** 2254
Return of Quetzalcoatl, The (Orozco), **20th:** 3070
Return of Sherlock Holmes, The (Doyle), **19th:** 689
Return of the King, The (Tolkien), **20th:** 4039
Return of the Native, The (Hardy), **19th:** 1029
Return to My Native Land (Césaire), **20th:** 710
Return to Paradise (Michener), **20th:** 2728
Reuther, Walter P., **20th:** 2673, 3424-3428
Revelation, Book of, **Anc:** 472
Revelations (ballet), **20th:** 37
Revelations of Divine Love. See *Showings of Julian of Norwich, The*
Revelations of Mechthild of Magdeburg, The. See *Flowing Light of the Godhead, The*
Revenge of Bussy d'Ambois, The (Chapman), **Ren:** 215

Revenger's Tragedy, The (Middleton), **17th:** 637
Revenger's Tragedy, The (Tourneur), **17th:** 928
Revenue Act of 1921, **20th:** 1675
Revere, Paul, **18th:** 276, 832-836
Rêverie (Mussorgsky), **19th:** 1627
Revival of Religious Sciences, The (al-Ghazzālī), **MA:** 415
Revivalism, **18th:** in colonial America, 1074; in Great Britain, 1074; Jewish, 68
Revizor. See *Inspector General, The*
Revolt of Islam, The (Shelley), **19th:** 2093
Revolt of the Angels, The (France), **19th:** 817
Revolt of the Balama. *See* Balama, Revolt of the
Revolt of the Masses, The (Ortega), **20th:** 3078
Révolte des anges, La. See *Revolt of the Angels, The*
Revolution Betrayed, The (Trotsky), **20th:** 4075
Revolution from Within (Steinem), **20th:** 3854
Revolution of 1800, **19th:** 512
Revolution of 1830, **19th:** 637, 696, 858, 1531; Rothschild family, 1948
Revolution of 1895, **19th:** 1513
Revolution of 1930 (Argentina), **20th:** 3205
Révolution sociale démontrée par le coup d'état du 2 décembre, La (Proudhon), **19th:** 1836
Revolution und Conterrevolution (Aston), **19th:** 84
Revolutionary Committee for Unity and Action, **20th:** 9
Revolutionary Petunias (Walker), **20th:** 4197
Revolutionary politics, **18th:** Georges Danton, 289-292; William Godwin, 424-428; John Hancock, 457-462; Patrick Henry, 482-485; Ireland, 357; Thomas Jefferson, 528-531; Louis XVI, 619; Flora MacDonald, 623-625; Jean-Paul Marat, 648-651; duc d'Orléans, 751-754; Paul Revere, 832; Robespierre, 844-847; Louis de Saint-Just, 877-880; Wolfe Tone, 983; Toussaint-Louverture, 985-988
Revolutionary Tribunal (France), **18th:** 291, 846, 878
Revolutionary War, American. *See* American Revolution
Revolutions of 1848, **19th:** 222, 255, 559, 819, 843, 872, 1322, 1533, 1835; Metternich, 1563
Revolver (Beatles), **20th:** 268
Revue Blanche (Toulouse-Lautrec), **19th:** 2289
Revue de progrès politique, social et litéraire, **19th:** 254
Rewane, Alfred, **Notor:** 2
Reyes, Bernardo, **20th:** 2545
Reynolds, John Hamilton, **19th:** 1260
Reynolds, Sir Joshua, **18th:** 275, 389, 554, 584, 836-840, 862, 1069; portrait of Fanny Abington, 2; portrait of George Rodney, 855; portrait of Sarah Siddons, 913
Reynolds, R. J., **19th:** 693
Reynolds v. Sims (1964), **20th:** 4234
Reza Khan. *See* Reza Shah Pahlavi
Reza Shah Pahlavi, **20th:** 2124, 2779, 2845, 3428-3430
Rgya gar chos 'byun (Tāranātha), **Anc:**, 111
Rh factor, **20th:** 2251
Rhabanus Magnentius. *See* Rabanus Maurus
Rhapsody in Blue (Gershwin), **20th:** 1459
Rhapsody on a Theme by Paganini (Rachmaninoff), **20th:** 3362
Rhäticus. *See* Rheticus
Rhazes. *See* Rāzī, al-
Rhee, Syngman, **20th:** 2136, 3430-3433
Rheingold, Das (Wagner), **19th:** 2375
Rhenish Symphony (Schumann), **19th:** 2033
Rheticus, **Ren:** 243, 823-825
Rhetoric, **Anc:** Greek, 451; Roman, 665; **Ren:** France, 817, 818. *See also* Philosophy; *Technē rhetorikēs*
Rhetorica (Ramus and Taleon), **Ren:** 818
Rhetoricae distinctiones in Quintilianum. See *Arguments in Rhetoric Against Quintilian*
Rhētorōn didaskalos (Lucian), **Anc:** 515
Rhett, William, **Notor:** 117
Rhineland Campaign (1674-1675), **17th:** 934
Rhinoceros (Ionesco), **20th:** 1970
Rhizotomika, Peri lakhanōn (Diocles), **Anc:** 278
Rhode Island, **17th:** 941, 983
Rhodes, Cecil, **19th:** 462, 1286, 1299, 1406, 1891-1895; **20th:** 3775
Rhodes, John, **17th:** 51
Rhodes, Marcus, **20th:** 2504
Rhodes scholarships, **19th:** 1894
Rhodesia, **20th:** independence of, 4361
Rhodesian Bush War (1964-1979), **20th:** 2858
Rhyme? and Reason? (Carroll), **19th:** 424
Rhymes (Petrarch), **MA:** 827
Rhymes of a Red Cross Man, The (Service), **20th:** 3709
Rhys ap Tewdwr, **MA:** 753
Rhythm and blues, **20th:** 735
Rhythms (Delaunay), **20th:** 952
Rians, Claude Fabri de, **17th:** 723
Riario, Gerolamo, **Ren:** 870
Ribbentrop, Joachim von, **20th:** 2784; **Notor:** 747, 894-895
Ribera, Jusepe, **17th:** 1005
Ricardo, David, **19th:** 1896-1898
Ricardo, John Lewis, **19th:** 549
Ricci, Matteo, **Ren:** 394, 825-827
Riccioli, Giambattista, **17th:** 322

Rice, Elmer, **20th:** 4275
Rice, Thomas "Daddy," **19th:** 802
Rice, Tim, **20th:** 2414; **Notor:** 822
Rich, Christopher, **17th:** 52, 83
Rich Lands and Poor (Myrdal), **20th:** 2891
Richard (duke of Gloucester). *See* Richard III
Richard (third duke of York), **Notor:** 896
Richard I (king of England), **MA:** 358, 387, 476, 584, 836, 891-893, 919; **Notor:** 534, 910
Richard II (king of England), **MA:** 266, 493, 501, 893-896, 1034
Richard II (Shakespeare), **Ren:** 877
Richard III (film), **20th:** 3042
Richard III (king of England), **Ren:** 91, 438, 441, 571, 828-833, 946; **Notor:** 896-898
Richard, Mira, **20th:** 179
Richard of Bordeaux. *See* Richard II
Richard the Lion-Hearted. *See* Richard I
Richards, Ann, **20th:** 3434-3438; **Notor:** 457
Richards, Ellen Swallow, **19th:** 1899-1901
Richardson, Abby Sage, **19th:** 1902-1905
Richardson, Albert Deane, **19th:** 1902
Richardson, Henry Hobson, **19th:** 1905-1908
Richardson, Samuel, **18th:** 221, 347, 577, 841-843
Richelieu, Cardinal de, **17th:** 141, 184, 315, 470, 487, 521, 660, 780, 790-793; and regency of Anne of Austria, 18; arts patronage, 193, 750; and Tommaso Campanella, 126; and the duchesse de Chevreuse, 158; and Frederick Henry, 287; and Cornelius Otto Jansen, 420; and reign of Louis XIII, 552; and Marie de Médicis, 599; and Jules Mazarin, 620; and alliance with Protestant forces, 937; and Friedrich Hermann Schomberg, 820; science patronage, 305; and reforms of the duke de Sully, 897; and Sweden, 706
Richemont, Arthur de, **Ren:** 225
Richer, Léon, **19th:** 89
Richetti, Adam "Eddie," **Notor:** 361
Richler, Mordecai, **20th:** 3438-3440
Richmond, earl of. *See* Henry VII (1457-1509; king of England)
Richmond and Derby, countess of. *See* Beaufort, Lady Margaret
Richter, Charles, **20th:** 3440-3442
Richter, Gregorius, **17th:** 60
Richter scale, **20th:** 3442
Ricimer, **MA:** 782
Rickard, George L. "Tex," **20th:** 965
Ricketts, Edward F., **20th:** 3849
Rickey, Branch, **20th:** 3470
Rickover, Hyman G., **20th:** 3443-3447
Ricordi (Guicciardini), **Ren:** 411
Riddle, Nelson, **20th:** 3748
Riddle of the Universe at the Close of the Nineteenth Century, The (Haeckel), **19th:** 1005
Ride, Sally, **20th:** 3447-3450
Ride Down Mt. Morgan, The (Miller), **20th:** 2744
Ridge, John, **19th:** 1938
Ridiculous Pedant, The (Cyrano), **17th:** 211
Ridley, Nicholas, **Ren:** 305, 402, 544, 833-836
Ridley, Robert, **Ren:** 833
Riefenstahl, Leni, **20th:** 3451-3453; **Notor:** 988
Riel, Louis, **19th:** 1443, 1908-1911; **20th:** 2282
Riel Rebellion, Second (1885), **19th:** 1909
Rienzi (Wagner), **19th:** 2374
Rienzo, Cola di, **MA:** 897-900
Rietschel, Magda. *See* Goebbels, Magda
Riflemen, The (film), **20th:** 1504
Riga, Treaty of (1920), **20th:** 3252
Riga Memorandum, **19th:** 1022
Riggs, Bobby, **20th:** 2145, 3218
Right, Petition of (1628). *See* Petition of Right
Right Excellent Nanny of the Maroons. *See* Nanny
Right Stuff, The (Wolfe), **20th:** 1500
Right You Are (If You Think So) (Pirandello), **20th:** 3261
Rights of Man, The (Paine), **18th:** 760, 1109
"Rights of Woman, The" (Barbauld), **18th:** 88
Rigley, Dane. *See* Gardner, Erle Stanley
Rigoberta Menchú Foundation, **20th:** 2686
Rigoletto (Verdi), **19th:** 2352; **20th:** 676
Riḥlah (Ibn Baṭṭūṭah), **MA:** 530
Rijn, Rembrandt van. *See* Rembrandt
Rijswijk, Treaty of (1697), **17th:** 152, 980
Riley, James Patrick, **Notor:** 364
Rilke, Rainer Maria, **20th:** 3454-3456
Rim-Sin, **Anc:** 376
Rimas (Camões). See *Lyrides, The*
Rimas (Darío), **19th:** 601
Rimbaud, Arthur, **19th:** 1912-1914
Rime (Andreini), **Ren:** 42
Rime della divina Vettoria Colonna, marchesana di Pescara (Colonna), **Ren:** 236
Rime of the Ancient Mariner, The (Coleridge), **19th:** 530
Rime . . . Parte seconda (Andreini), **Ren:** 43
Rimniksky, Count. *See* Suvorov, Aleksandr Vasilyevich
Rimpa (school of painting), **17th:** 696, 868

Rimsky-Korsakov, Nikolay, **19th:** 282, 1628, 1915-1917; **20th:** 985, 2647, 3888
Rin Tin Tin, **20th:** 4445
Rinaldo (Tasso), **Ren:** 925
Ring des Nibelungen, Der (Wagner), **19th:** 2375
Ringo, Johnny, **Notor:** 144, 898-899
Ringrose, Basil, **Notor:** 261
Rinnovamento civile d'Italia, Il (Gioberti), **19th:** 923
Rinuccini, Ottavio, **17th:** 111, 658
Rio Grande (film), **20th:** 4251
Rio Grande do Sul, **19th:** 871
Rio Grande's Last Race, and Other Verses (Paterson), **19th:** 1758
Ríos Montt, Efraín, **Notor:** 899-901
Ripley, George, **19th:** 1736
Riquelme, Bernardo. *See* O'Higgins, Bernardo
Riqueti, Honoré-Gabriel. *See* Mirabeau, comte de
Rire, Le. See *Laughter*
Risalat isthsan al-khawd fi ilm al-kalam. See *Incitement to Investigation*
Rise and Fall of the City of Mahagonny, The (Weill and Brecht), **20th:** 4274
Rise and Fall of the Confederate Government (Davis), **19th:** 614
Rise of American Civilization, The (Beard and Beard), **20th:** 263
Rising Green (Krasner), **20th:** 2197
Risorgimento, **19th:** 921, 1498, 1531, 1802
Risorgimento, Il (newspaper), **19th:** 444
Risposta di Hieronimo Veneroso nobile Genovese alla querela sotto nome di Difesa intorno allo sputo di Sangue (Cesalpino et al.), **Ren:** 212
Risshō ankoku ron. See *On the Establishment of the Orthodox Teaching and the Peace of the Nation*
Ritchings, Edna Rose, **Notor:** 347
Rite of Spring, The (ballet), **20th:** 986, 2647, 2975, 3889
Ritorno d'Ulisse in patria, Il (Monteverdi), **17th:** 659
Ritschl, Albrecht, **19th:** 1918-1921; **20th:** 1681
Ritschl, Friedrich Wilhelm, **19th:** 1681
Ritschlian School, **20th:** 1681
Ritthi Sen. *See* Hun Sen
Riva, Giovanni Guglielmo, **17th:** 565
Rivals, The (Sheridan), **18th:** 905
Rivas, George, **Notor:** 901-902
Rivaux, Peter des, **MA:** 490
River, The (film), **20th:** 3422
River Duddon, The (Wordsworth), **19th:** 2464
River of No Return (film), **20th:** 2798
River Slaak, Battle of the (1631), **17th:** 287
Rivera, Diego, **20th:** 2069, 3069, 3457-3459
Rivers to the Sea (Teasdale), **20th:** 3960
Riverside Church, **20th:** 3477
Rivet, André, **17th:** 824
Rivett, Sandra, **Notor:** 657
Rivinus, **17th:** 783
Rivlin, David, **Notor:** 568
Rizzo, Rita Antoinette. *See* Angelica, Mother
Road Back, The (Remarque), **20th:** 3414
Road Leads On, The (Hamsun), **20th:** 1662
Road to Calvary, The (Bruegel), **Ren:** 136
Road to Mecca, The (Fugard), **20th:** 1357
Road to Oz, The (Baum), **19th:** 157
Road to Serfdom, The (Hayek), **20th:** 1722
Road to Singapore (film), **20th:** 1871
Road to Wigan Pier, The (Orwell), **20th:** 3080
Roads, Roman, **Anc:** 219
Roads to Freedom, The (Sartre), **20th:** 3638
Roanocs, **Ren:** 771
Roaring Girl, The (Middleton and Dekker), **17th:** 637
Rob Roy, **Notor:** 902-903, 905
Rob Roy (Scott), **19th:** 2048
Robbers, The (Schiller), **18th:** 887
Robbins, Jerome, **20th:** 3459-3462
Robe, The (film), **20th:** 4446
Robe prétexte, La. See *Stuff of Youth, The*
Robert I. *See* Bruce, Robert
Robert VIII de Bruce. *See* Bruce, Robert
Robert, John. *See* Roberts, Bartholomew
Robert Guiscard, **MA:** 91, 176
Robert Guiskard (Kleist), **19th:** 1289
Robert Joffrey Ballet, **20th:** 2013
Robert of Anjou, **MA:** 697
Robert of Gloucester, **MA:** 961
Robert of Normandy, **MA:** 482
Robert of Wishart, **MA:** 346
Robert Stephenson and Company, **19th:** 2168
Robert the Bruce. *See* Bruce, Robert
Robert the Steward, **MA:** 308
Roberto Devereux (Donizetti), **19th:** 675
Roberts, Bartholomew, **Notor:** 905-906
Roberts, Great Pirate. *See* Roberts, Bartholomew
Roberts, Issachar J., **19th:** 1128
Roberts, Oral, **Notor:** 50
Roberts, Terrence, **Notor:** 349
Robertson, Anna Mary. *See* Moses, Grandma
Robertson, John, **19th:** 1740
Robertson, Pat, **Notor:** 50
Roberval, Gilles Personne de, **17th:** 922

Roberval, Jean-François de La Rocque de, **Ren:** 179
Robeson, Paul, **20th:** 1670, 3334, 3462-3467
Robespierre, **18th:** 267, 290, 844-847, 877, 918; **19th:** 254, 608, 705, 809; **Notor:** 236, 313, 697, 705, 907-909
Robie House, **20th:** 4400
Robin Hood, **Notor:** 121, 909-910
Robins, John, **17th:** 666
Robinson, Bill "Bojangles," **20th:** 3973
Robinson, Daniel N., **20th:** 1091
Robinson, Edward G., **Notor:** 974
Robinson, Frank, **20th:** 3467-3469
Robinson, Jackie, **20th:** 3470-3473
Robinson, James Harvey, **20th:** 262
Robinson, John, **17th:** 84
Robinson, Mary (actor and writer), **18th:** 848-850
Robinson, Mary (president of Ireland), **20th:** 3474-3476
Robinson Crusoe (Defoe), **17th:** 216; **18th:** 299
Robusti, Jacopo. *See* Tintoretto (Jacopo Robusti)
Robusti, Marietta. *See* Tintoretto, Marietta Robusti
Robyn of Locksley. *See* Robin Hood
Rocard, Michel, **20th:** 2771
Rocco and His Brothers (film), **20th:** 4167
Rochambeau, comte de, **18th:** 851-854
Rochas, Alphonse-Eugène Beau de, **19th:** 1716
Roches, Peter des. *See* Peter des Roches
Roches, William des, **MA:** 585
Rochester, John of. *See* Fisher, Saint John
Rochester, Viscount. *See* Carr, Robert
Rock and roll, **20th:** 267, 1073, 2043, 3331
Rock Edicts, **Anc:** 124
Rockefeller, John D. (1839-1937), **19th:** 1032, 1921-1925; **Notor:** 285
Rockefeller, John D., Jr. (1874-1960), **20th:** 3476-3478
Rockefeller, Nelson A., **20th:** 1276, 3476, 3478-3481, 3971, 4048
Rockefeller, Winthrop, **Notor:** 348
Rockefeller Center, **20th:** 3477
Rockefeller Foundation, **19th:** 1924; **20th:** 3477
Rocket Development (Goddard), **20th:** 1508
Rocketry, **20th:** 1507, 2192, 3008, 4096
Rockingham, Lord, **18th:** 740
Rockne, Knute, **20th:** 3481-3483
Rockwell, George Lincoln, **Notor:** 222, 838, 911-913
Rockwell, Norman, **20th:** 3483-3486
Rocky Mountain Fur Company, **19th:** 2114
Rocky Mountain school, **19th:** 233
Rococo art and design, **18th:** 133, 617, 978, 1052
Rocroi, Battle of (1643), **17th:** 184, 553, 926
Rodeo (ballet), **20th:** 838, 958
Roderick, **MA:** 1006
Roderick Hudson (James), **19th:** 1207
Rodgers, Richard, **20th:** 1657, 1691, 3486-3489
Rodin, Auguste, **19th:** 1925-1928; **20th:** 479, 3454
Rodney, George, **18th:** 854-858
Rodrigo (Handel), **18th:** 463
Rodriguez, Abelardo, **20th:** 617
Rodriguez, Michael, **Notor:** 901
Rodríguez Pedotti, Andrés, **Notor:** 1004
Rodzinski, Arthur, **20th:** 338
Roe v. Wade (1973), **20th:** 382, 583
Roebling, John Augustus, **19th:** 1928-1930
Roebuck, John, **18th:** 858-862, 1049
Roestraten, Pieter, **17th:** 352
Roger II (king of Sicily), **MA:** 385, 539
Roger Freeing Angelica (Ingres), **19th:** 1172
Roger Fry (Woolf), **20th:** 1353
Roger of Salisbury, **MA:** 482, 962
Rogers, Buddy, **20th:** 3245
Rogers, Edith Nourse, **20th:** 3489-3491
Rogers, Ginger, **20th:** 142, 156, 1463
Rogers, Jimmy, **20th:** 4240
Rogers, Will, **20th:** 3491-3495
Rogers, Woodes, **Notor:** 122, 1023
Roget, Peter Mark, **19th:** 548, 617
Rogni, Giacomo, **17th:** 302
Rogue, The. See *Guzmán de Alfarache*
Rogue Trader. *See* Leeson, Nick
Rohan, Marie de. *See* Chevreuse, duchesse de
Rohilla War (1772-1773), **18th:** 470
Röhm, Ernst, **Notor:** 461, 469
Roi l'a dit, Le (Delibes), **19th:** 640
Roi s'amuse, Le (Delibes), **19th:** 640
Roi s'amuse, Le (Hugo). See *King Amuses Himself, The*
Roi se meurt, Le. See *Exit the King*
Roitman, Faiga Khaimovna. *See* Kaplan, Fanya
Rokeby (Scott), **19th:** 2048
Rokewood, Ambrose, **Ren:** 326
Rokytny, I. *See* Petlyura, Symon
Roland Barthes by Roland Barthes (Barthes), **20th:** 248
Roland de Lassus. *See* Lasso, Orlando di

Rolf. *See* Rollo

Rolfe, John, **17th:** 702, 746, 754, 863

Rollo, MA: 900-903

Rolls, Charles Stewart, 20th: 3496-3499

Rolls-Royce Limited, **20th:** 3496

Rolph, John, **19th:** 122

Romagna, duke of. *See* Borgia, Cesare

Romaika (Dio Cassius), **Anc:** 23, 163, 508

Roman Academy of St. Luke, **18th:** 554

Roman Catholic Church and Catholicism, **Anc:** 869; **MA:** 381; **Ren:** 3, 8; Americas, 36, 179; church reform, 233, 235; England, 189, 200, 270, 311, 324, 335, 371, 399, 403, 544, 639, 668, 699; France, 185, 284, 424, 426, 429-430, 465, 549, 569, 838; Germany, 583, 650, 666; Holy Roman Empire, 842; Inquisition, 940; Italy, 851; Japan, 460; Kongo, 9; Low Countries, 32; Portugal, 513; Protestantism and, 142, 164, 222, 768; Scotland, 502, 530, 634; Spain, 330, 509; Switzerland, 1011; **17th:** Austria, 268; Bohemia, 966; England, 120, 132, 417, 608, 692, 721, 974, 979; France, 265, 573, 593, 598, 629, 962; Germany, 882; Ireland, 700, 938; Italy, 406, 720, 936; North America, 909; Peru, 797; Sweden, 165; **18th:** Benedict XIV, 102-104; Brazil, 609; clerical reform, 793; and the *Encyclopedia*, 33; France, 361-362; Habsburg Dynasty, 545; Josephism, 793; and natural history, 172; New World, 891-893; Pius VI, 793-795; Poland, 567; regional control of, 102; and Spanish monarchy, 228; United States, 795; **19th:** Lord Acton, 13; Australia, 1493; England, 1397, 1490, 1664, 1959; Europe, 1342; Ireland, 439, 1696; Italy, 922, 1803; Mexico, 1246; Pierre-Joseph Proudhon, 1836; United States, 383, 910, 2071; **20th:** 3149, 3275, 3278; Argentina, 3207; Canada, 2281; Dorothy Day, 926; El Salvador, 3500; Germany, 3842; Italy, 2888; John Paul II, 2022; in literature, 1578; Jacques Maritain, 2624; Mexico, 616; Pius X, 3272; radio and television, 3722; stigmata, 1286; television network, 91. *See also* Counter-Reformation; Inquisition; Protestantism; Reformation

Roman Catholic Methods of Birth Control (Stopes), **20th:** 3883

Roman Catholic Relief Act of 1829, **19th:** 893

Roman de la rose. See *Romance of the Rose, The*

Roman Elegies (Goethe), **18th:** 429

Roman Empire, **MA:** fall of (476), 782. *See also* Geographical Index

Roman expérimental. See *Experimental Novel, The*

Roman History. See *Romaika*

Roman History, The (Niebuhr), **19th:** 1674

Roman Holiday (film), **20th:** 1767

Roman Journal, A (Stendhal), **19th:** 2162

Roman Republic. *See* Geographical Index

Romance genre, **Anc:** 515; **MA:** 268, 463

Romance of Siamese Harem Life, The (Leonowens), **19th:** 1347

Romance of the Forest, The (Radcliffe), **18th:** 823

Romance of the Rose, The (Lorris and Meung), **MA:** 275

Romancero gitano. See *Gypsy Ballads of García Lorca, The*

Romania. *See* Geographical Index

Romanization, **Anc:** 19, 99, 219

Romanov, Aleksandr Nikolayevich. *See* Alexander II (1818-1881; czar of Russia)

Romanov, Aleksei Mikhailovich. *See* Alexis

Romanov, Anastasia, **Notor:** 385

Romanov, Fyodor Nikitich, **17th:** 794. *See also* Philaret

Romanov, Michael, 17th: 11, 337, 663, 794-796, 945

Romanov Dynasty, **Ren:** 388; **17th:** 11, 663, 794

Romans à clef, **18th:** 642, 849

Romanticism, **18th:** art, 437, 1053, 1069; literature, 121-125, 850, 869, 898, 931, 953, 1010; **19th:** Brazil, 1450; England, 1078, 2465; France, 635, 1147, 2162; Germany, 1156, 1550, 1565, 2009; Italy, 1496

Romanus IV Diogenes, **MA:** 72

Romanzero (Heine), **19th:** 1071

Rome, **Anc:** administration, 371, 485; Armenia and, 870, 895, 906; Carthage and, 191, 342, 373, 382, 542, 738, 813; Celts and, 756; Christianity and, 42, 143, 268, 330, 392, 905; consolidation of Empire, 372; Constantine and, 242; daily life, 537; division of Empire, 76; Egypt and, 230; Etruscans and, 840; extent of Empire, 99; fall of Empire, 457; fall of Republic, 212; foundation of Empire, 173; Germans and, 147, 351; Goths and, 825; government, 21, 281; Greek influence, 671, 755; Hunnic invasion, 139; Jews and, 477, 644; Judaea and, 404; land tenure, 358; military, 280; Numidia and, 533; Parthia and, 530; Persia and, 485; Pontus and, 568; religion, 241, 488, 643; Republic, 67, 187, 195; Republic versus Empire, 146, 167, 172, 683; rise of, 172; sack of, 352; satire and, 494;

social disruptions, 987; **MA:** 430, 897; invasion of, 782; law, 898; monasticism, 154; mysticism, 236; **Ren:** sack of (1527), 221, 230, 411, 486, 589; **18th:** and ancient history, 415; and archaeology, 1096; and the arts, 1068, 1096; and opera, 884
Rome (Zola), **19th:** 2491
Rome, Council of (863), **MA:** 766
Rome, Naples, and Florence in 1817 (Stendhal), **19th:** 2161
Rome, Siege of (1240), **MA:** 391
Romeo and Juliet (ballet), **20th:** 254, 3340
Romeo and Juliet (Shakespeare), **Ren:** 877
Romeo and Juliet (Tchaikovsky), **19th:** 2234
Roméo et Juliette (Berlioz), **19th:** 202
Roméo et Juliette (Gounod), **19th:** 953
Rømer, Olaus, **17th:** 135
Rømer, Ole, **18th:** 336
Römerbrief, Der. See *Epistle to the Romans, The*
Romero, Carlos Humberto, **20th:** 3500
Romero, Oscar, **20th:** 3499-3502
Römische Elegien. See *Roman Elegies*
Römische Geschichte (Mommsen). See *History of Rome, The* (Mommsen)
Römische Geschichte (Niebuhr). See *Roman History, The*
Römischen Päpste in den letzten 4 Jahrhunderten, Die. See *History of the Popes During the Last Four Centuries, The*
Römisches Staatsrecht (Mommsen), **19th:** 1584
Römisches Strafrecht (Mommsen), **19th:** 1584
Rommel, Erwin, **20th:** 2118, 2809, 3502-3505, 3560; **Notor:** 132
Romney, George, **18th:** 862-865
Romola (Eliot), **19th:** 741
Romorantin, Edicts of (1560), **Ren:** 569
Romualdez, Imelda. *See* Marcos, Imelda
Romulus Augustulus, **MA:** 782
Ronald McDonald House Charities, **20th:** 2203
Roncalli, Angelo Giuseppe. *See* John XXIII (1881-1963; pope)
Rong'an Jung'an. *See* Yuan Shikai
Ronsard, Pierre de, **Ren:** 285, 294, 425, 837-840
Röntgen, Wilhelm Conrad, **19th:** 1826, 1931-1933
Rookery, **19th:** 361
Room of One's Own, A (Woolf), **20th:** 4398
Room with a View, A (Forster), **20th:** 1288
Rooney, Mickey, **20th:** 1410, 2663
Roosevelt, Eleanor, **20th:** 3506-3509
Roosevelt, Franklin D., **20th:** 2361, 3506, 3509-3515, 3764, 4207; election of, 1864; France, 1427; New Deal, 264, 484; **Notor:** 75, 99, 237, 240, 491, 675, 755, 985, 1083, 1095, 1128
Roosevelt, Kermit, Jr., **20th:** 2846
Roosevelt, Theodore, **19th:** 646, 1019; John Hay, 1055; **20th:** 3254, 3515-3519, 3929; **Notor:** 254, 1031
Rooster Cogburn (film), **20th:** 4252
Root, Elihu, **20th:** 3519-3522
Root, Elisha, **19th:** 534
Root, John Wellborn, **19th:** 360
Root and Branch Bill (1641), **17th:** 167, 204
Root-Takahira Agreement (1908), **20th:** 3520
Rope and Faggot (White), **20th:** 4308
Rorik. *See* Rurik
Rorschach, Hermann, **20th:** 3522-3525
Rorschach test, **20th:** 3523
Rosa de Santa Maria. *See* Rose of Lima, Saint
Rosalind and Helen (Shelley), **19th:** 2095
Rosalinda (film), **20th:** 4167
Rosas, Juan Manuel de, **19th:** 2000
Rose, The (Yeats), **20th:** 4428
Rose, Max Caspar, **19th:** 197
Rose, Pete, **20th:** 3525-3529
Rose Garden, The (Saʿdi), **MA:** 916
Rose in Bloom (Alcott), **19th:** 43
Rose Marie (Friml et al.), **20th:** 1657
Rose of Lima, Saint, **17th:** 796-798
Rose of Testimony, The (Moses de León), **MA:** 731
Rosebud, Battle of (1876), **19th:** 568
Rosecrans, William S., **19th:** 869; **Notor:** 247
Roselli, Johnny, **Notor:** 340
Rosenberg, Alfred, **20th:** 1515
Rosenberg, Arthur, **Notor:** 319
Rosenberg, Ethel, **20th:** 1867; **Notor:** 217, 381, 913-916
Rosenberg, John Paul. *See* Erhard, Werner
Rosenberg, Julius, **20th:** 1867; **Notor:** 217, 381, 914-916
Rosenberg, Robert, **Notor:** 914
Rosenfeld, Paul, **20th:** 837
Rosenkavalier, Der (Strauss), **19th:** 1156; **20th:** 3886
Roses, Wars of the (1455-1485), **MA:** 496; **Ren:** 90, 301, 340, 434-435, 438, 571, 828, 946, 989
Rosicrucians, **17th:** 281
Roskilde, Treaty of (1658), **17th:** 154
Rosmersholm (Ibsen), **19th:** 1166
Rosny, marquis de. *See* Sully, duke de
Ross, Araminta. *See* Tubman, Harriet

Ross, Betsy, **18th:** 865-867
Ross, Sir James Clark, **19th:** 1934-1936
Ross, John (explorer), **19th:** 1934
Ross, John (Native American leader), **19th:** 1937-1939
Ross, Nellie Tayloe, **20th:** 3529-3532
Ross, Sir Ronald, **20th:** 3532-3536
Rosse, David. *See* Frankel, Martin
Rossellini, Roberto, **20th:** 322, 1232
Rosseter, Philip, **17th:** 127
Rossetti, Christina, **19th:** 1940-1943
Rossetti, Dante Gabriel, **19th:** 1157, 1606, 1755, 1940
Rossi, Pellegrino, **19th:** 1803
Rossini, Gioacchino, **18th:** 99; **19th:** 1701, 1944-1946
Rossiyskaya grammatika (Lomonosov), **18th:** 613
Rostand, Edmond, **17th:** 211
Rostislav, **MA:** 295
Rostov Ripper. *See* Chikatilo, Andrei
Roswitha. *See* Hrosvitha
Rota, Nino, **20th:** 1232
Rotblat, Sir Joseph, **20th:** 3536-3538
Roth, Hieronymus, **17th:** 292
Roth v. U.S. (1957), **20th:** 508
Rothenberg, Michael B., **20th:** 3816
Rothermere, first Viscount. *See* Harmsworth, Harold
Rothesay, duke of. *See* James IV
Rothko, Mark, **20th:** 3539-3541
Rothko Chapel, **20th:** 3540
Rothschild, Amschel Mayer, **19th:** 1947-1951
Rothschild, Carl Mayer, **19th:** 1947-1951
Rothschild, James Mayer, **19th:** 1947-1951
Rothschild, Mayer Amschel, **19th:** 1947-1951
Rothschild, Nathan Mayer, **19th:** 1947-1951
Rothschild, Salomon Mayer, **19th:** 1947-1951
Rothstein, Arnold, **Notor:** 237, 604, 917-918, 954, 1083
Rothstein, William, **20th:** 3934
Rôtisserie de la Reine Pédauque, La. See *At the Sign of the Reine Pédauque*
Rou. *See* Rollo
Rouault, Georges, **20th:** 3541-3544
Roue, La (film), **20th:** 1382
Rouen, Siege of (1417-1419), **MA:** 503
Rouge et le noir, Le. See *Red and the Black, The*
Rough Riders, **20th:** 3516
Roughing It (Twain), **19th:** 2330
Roughing It in the Bush (Moodie), **19th:** 1594, 2292
Rougon-Macquart Novels, The (Zola), **19th:** 2489
Rougoor, G. W., **20th:** 3060
Round Hill School for Boys, **19th:** 130
Rous, Peyton, **20th:** 3545-3547
Rous sarcoma virus, **20th:** 3546
Rous-Turner solution, **20th:** 3546
Rousseau, Captain. *See* Vidocq, Eugène François
Rousseau, Henri, **19th:** 1951-1954
Rousseau, Jean-Jacques, **18th:** 90, 147, 845, 868-872, 877, 1028, 1109; **Notor:** 907
Roussel, Gérard, **Ren:** 549
Routier, Darlie, **Notor:** 918-919
Rouvroy, Claude-Henri de. *See* Saint-Simon, Henri de
Rover, The (Behn), **17th:** 43
Rovere, Francesco della. *See* Sixtus IV
Rovere, Giuliano della. *See* Julius II
Rowett, John Quiller, **20th:** 4340
Rowland, F. Sherwood, **20th:** 3547-3550
Rowlands, John. *See* Stanley, Henry Morton
Rowlandson, Mary White, **17th:** 798-801
Rowley, William, **Ren:** 95; **17th:** 636, 977; **Notor:** 936
Roxana, **Anc:** 720
Roxana (Defoe), **18th:** 299
Roy, Rob. *See* Rob Roy
Royal Academy of Arts (Great Britain), **18th:** 388, 555, 584, 837, 948
Royal Academy of Music (Great Britain), **18th:** 464
Royal Academy of Painting and Sculpture (France), **17th:** 504; **18th:** 224, 1017, 1052; **19th:** 607
Royal Academy of San Fernando (Spain), **18th:** 437
Royal Academy of Sciences (France), **17th:** 710
Royal Astronomical Society (Great Britain), **18th:** 490
Royal Ballet (Great Britain), **20th:** 1269
Royal Gardens (France), **18th:** 171
Royal Geographical Society (Great Britain), **18th:** 82; **19th:** 368, 2139
Royal Guard (France), **18th:** 154
Royal Horticultural Society (Great Britain), **18th:** 82
Royal Irish Academy, **18th:** 490
Royal King and the Loyal Subject, The (Heywood), **17th:** 374
Royal Master, The (Shirley), **17th:** 846
Royal Mischief, The (Manley), **18th:** 641
Royal Niger Company, **19th:** 940
Royal Society (Great Britain), **17th:** 80, 256, 348, 383, 470, 510, 514, 681, 734, 806, 814, 987, 994; **18th:** 150, 217, 334, 490, 492, 533, 633, 811, 1050, 1059, 1069; sponsorship of Cook's voyage, 270
Royal Society of Arts (Great Britain), **18th:** 178

Royal Society of Edinburgh. *See* Philosophical Society of Edinburgh
Royal Society of Physicians (Great Britain), **17th:** 280
Royalists, **17th:** England, 345, 484; support from Henrietta Maria, 365; and Prince Rupert, 805; and the first earl of Shaftesbury, 838
Royce, Sir Frederick Henry, **20th:** 3496-3499
Royce, Josiah, **20th:** 3550-3552
Royo, Arístides, **20th:** 4049
Rozelle, Pete, **20th:** 3553-3556
Rtusamhāra (Kālidāsa), **Anc:** 496
Rubáiyát of Omar Khayyám, The (FitzGerald), **MA:** 796
Rubber, production of synthetic, **20th:** 2919
Rubber Soul (Beatles), **20th:** 268
Ruben, Samuel, **20th:** 2533
Rubens, Peter Paul, **Ren:** 137; **17th:** 244, 302, 352, 438, 599, 657, 671, 723, 802-804, 955, 1005
Rubinstein, Arthur, **20th:** 4164
Rubinstein, Ida, **Notor:** 933
Ruby, Jack, **Notor:** 919-921, 942
Ruby Bridges Goes to School. See *Problem We All Live With, The*
Ruby Ridge standoff, **20th:** 3419
Rucellai, Giovanni, **Ren:** 19
Rudbeck, Olaf, **17th:** 445
Rudd, Charles, **19th:** 1407
Rudd Concession (1888), **19th:** 1407
Ruddigore (Gilbert and Sullivan), **19th:** 919
Rudepoema (Villa-Lobos), **20th:** 4164
Rudimenta (Buchanan), **Ren:** 146
Rudin (Turgenev), **19th:** 2319
Rudolf (crown prince of Austria), **Notor:** 633
Rudolf (king of Germany and duke of Swabia), **MA:** 434, 499, 639
Rudolf I (Holy Roman Emperor), **MA:** 904-907
Rudolf II (Holy Roman Emperor), **Ren:** 130, 279, 652, 840-843; **17th:** 459; **Notor:** 536
Rudolf III (king of Burgundy), **MA:** 488
Rudolf of Habsburg. *See* Rudolf I
Rudolph, Eric, **Notor:** 921-923
Rue Mosnier with Pavers, The (Manet), **19th:** 1481
Rue Transnonain, Massacre in the (1834), **19th:** 2264
Rueil, Treaty of (1649), **17th:** 549
Ruete, Emily, **19th:** 1967
Rufinus, Tyrranius, **Anc:** 456
Rufius Crispinus, **Anc:** 685
Rufus, Marcus Caelius, **Anc:** 234
Rugby School, **19th:** 76
Rugeley poisoner. *See* Palmer, William
Rugians, **MA:** 783
Ruhr Valley, occupation of, **20th:** 3293
Ruines of Rome (du Bellay), **Ren:** 296
Ruins, **18th:** Edward Gibbon, 416; Ann Radcliffe, 823; William Stukeley, 953. *See also* Archaeology; Avebury; Stonehenge
Ruizong, **MA:** 1128
Rukeyser, Muriel, **20th:** 3556-3558
Ruknuddin Firūz Shāh, **MA:** 888
Rules for the Direction of the Mind (Descartes), **17th:** 227
Rules of the Game, The (film), **20th:** 3421
Ruling Class, The (Mosca), **20th:** 2840
Rum Rebellion, **19th:** 1432
Rūmī, Jalāl al-Dīn, **MA:** 908-911
Rump Parliament (1648-1653), **17th:** 484, 651, 757, 838
Rumsfeld, Donald, **Notor:** 646
Runaway, The (Cowley), **18th:** 284
Runaway Horses (Mishima), **20th:** 2764
Rundstedt, Gerd von, **20th:** 2119, 3559-3561
Rupert, Prince, **17th:** 56, 255, 262, 777, 805-807, 815
R.U.R. (Čapeks), **20th:** 639
Rural Constabulary Act (1839), **19th:** 458
Rural electrification program, **20th:** 4208
Rural England (Haggard), **19th:** 1007
Rural Rides (Cobbett), **19th:** 519
Rurik, **MA:** 911-914; **Notor:** 385
Rurik Dynasty, **17th:** 943
Rusalka. See *Water-Nymph, The*
Rush, Benjamin, **18th:** 872-874
Rushdie, Salman, **20th:** 2126; **Notor:** 572
Ruskin, John, **18th:** 839, 1069; **19th:** 1104, 1954-1958, 2421; Pre-Raphaelites, 1158; J. M. W. Turner, 2324; Oscar Wilde, 2432
Ruslan i Lyudmila (Pushkin), **19th:** 1848
Russell, Bertrand, **19th:** 289, 829; **20th:** 326, 659, 2814, 3562-3565, 4312, 4379
Russell, Beverly, **Notor:** 977
Russell, Bill, **20th:** 726, 3565-3570
Russell, Henry Norris, **20th:** 3570-3572
Russell, John, **19th:** 643, 668, 925, 1958-1961, 2360
Russell, Lucy. *See* Harington, Lucy
Russell, Rosalind, **20th:** 143
Russell-Einstein Manifesto, **20th:** 1121
Russell Paradox, **19th:** 829
Russia, **18th:** codification of laws, 213; coup against Czar Peter III, 756, 758; government centralization, 213; religious history, 756, 758; Slavophilism, 614; Westernization, 211-215, 614, 774-777. *See also* Kievan Rus; Geographical Index

Russia and History's Turning Point (Kerensky), **20th:** 2112
Russia and the Eastern Question (Cobden), **19th:** 521
Russian-Austrian alliance, **18th:** 570
Russian-Chinese treaty, **18th:** 776, 1113
Russian Civil War (1918-1921), **20th:** 4075
Russian Easter Festival Overture (Rimsky-Korsakov), **19th:** 1915
Russian-French conflicts, **18th:** 214, 570
Russian Life in the Interior. See *Sportsman's Sketches, A*
Russian Orthodox Church, **17th:** 13, 27, 684, 865; and Old Believers, 27; schism in, 13
Russian-Ottoman conflicts, **18th:** 570, 720, 775, 955
Russian-Polish conflicts, **18th:** 566, 956
Russian-Prussian relations, **18th:** 322, 779
Russian Revolution (1905), **20th:** 2482
Russian Revolution (1917), **20th:** 566, 1129, 2112, 2342, 4074
Russian Social Democratic Workers' Party, **20th:** 2342
Russian-Swedish conflicts, **18th:** 232, 776
Russland, Europa, Amerika (Mendelsohn), **20th:** 2693
Russland und Europa. See *Spirit of Russia, The*
Russo, Perry, **Notor:** 942
Russo-Japanese War (1904-1905), **19th:** 1632; **20th:** 2267, 3251
Russo-Turkish wars, **19th:** 7, 669, 2480
Rustaveli, Shota, **MA:** 999
Rustichello, **MA:** 855
Rusticus, **Anc:** 269
Ruth (Franck), **19th:** 822
Ruth, Babe, **20th:** 1435, 3572-3575; **Notor:** 521
Ruthenia, **MA:** 231
Rutherford, Ernest, **20th:** 408, 1379, 1440, 1792, 2077, 3576-3579, 3778, 4008
Rutherglen Declaration (1679), **17th:** 122
Ruy Blas (Hugo), **19th:** 1148
Ruyter, Michiel Adriaanszoon de, **17th:** 57, 807-809, 931
Ruyven, Claes van, **Ren:** 526
Ryan, James. *See* Cassidy, Butch
Ryan, Leo, **Notor:** 538
Ryder (Barnes), **20th:** 240
Rye House Plot (1683), **17th:** 149, 609, 655, 817
Rykov, Aleksey Ivanovich, **Notor:** 991, 1080
Ryle, Martin, **20th:** 1903
Rymnikskii, Count. *See* Suvorov, Aleksandr Vasilyevich
Ryswick, Treaty of (1697), **17th:** 401
Ryti, Risto Heikki, **20th:** 2660
Ryukyu Islands, reversion to Japan (1972), **20th:** 3647
Ryurik. *See* Rurik
Ryusai. *See* Hiroshige

S

S/Z (Barthes), **20th:** 247
Saavedra, José Daniel Ortega. *See* Ortega, Daniel
Saavedra, Miguel de Cervantes. *See* Cervantes, Miguel de
Sabbatai Sevi. *See* Shabbetai Tzevi
Sabin, Albert, **20th:** 3615
Sablé, marquise de, **17th:** 487
Sabotage (film), **20th:** 1826
Sabri, Ali, **20th:** 3588
Sabri Khalil Abd Al Qadir. *See* Abu Nidal
Sabri Khalil al-Banna. *See* Abu Nidal
Sabrina (film), **20th:** 1767
Saburō. *See* Oda Nobunaga
Saburouemon. *See* Honda Toshiaki
Sacagawea, **19th:** 1962-1965
Sacasa, Juan Batista, **Notor:** 985
Sacco, Nicola, **20th:** 1308, 3312, 3580-3583, 3752; **Notor:** 924-925, 1057
Sacerdos ad altare (Neckam), **MA:** 750
Sacerdotalis Caelibatus (Paul VI), **20th:** 3150
Sachi no Miya. *See* Mutsuhito
Sachs, Nelly, **20th:** 3583-3586
Sachsen, graf von. *See* Saxe, comte de
Sacrae symphoniae (Gabrieli), **Ren:** 363
Sacre du printemps, Le. See *Rite of Spring, The*
Sacred and Legendary Art (Jameson), **19th:** 1218
Sacred and the Profane, The (Eliade), **20th:** 1137
Sacred Edict (China), **18th:** 1114
Sacred Heart Orphan Asylum, **19th:** 384
Sacred Hymns, The (Manzoni), **19th:** 1496
Sacred marriages, **Anc:** 915
Sacred Theory of the Earth, The (Burnet), **17th:** 106
Sacred War, First (595-586 B.C.E.), **Anc:** 807
Sacred War, Third (356-346 B.C.E.), **Anc:** 639
Sacri musicali affetti (Strozzi), **17th:** 889
Sacrifice of Isaac, The (Tiepolo), **18th:** 976
Sacrifices, **Anc:** human, 6, 246, 273, 384, 805; Jewish, 748
Sacs, **19th:** 2052
Sadako, **MA:** 931
Sadat, Anwar el-, **20th:** 112, 154, 286, 464, 1200, 3587-3589; **Notor:** 868, 1135
Sadat Peace Initiative (1977), **20th:** 112
Saddam, Hussein. *See* Hussein, Saddam
Sadducees, **Anc:** 459
Sade, marquis de, **18th:** 875-877; **Notor:** 926-928
Saʿdī, **MA:** 909, 915-917

Saʿdī Dynasty, **Ren:** 860
Sadko (Rimsky-Korsakov), **19th:** 1916
Sadr, Abal Hassan Bani, **20th:** 2126
Ṣafavid Dynasty, **Ren:** 475, 915; **17th:** 4, 411, 844; **18th:** 552, 722-723, 1000
Safe Conduct (Pasternak), **20th:** 3132
Safety Net, The (Böll), **20th:** 413
Saffray, Augustin de. *See* Mézy, chevalier de
Safiye Sultan, **Ren:** 661
Saga (emperor of Japan), **MA:** 621
Saga nikki (Bashō), **17th:** 616
Sagami no Kami. *See* Hōjō Ujimasa
Sagan, Carl, **20th:** 3590-3593
Sage, Abby. *See* Richardson, Abby Sage
Sage, Anna, **Notor:** 282
Saggiatore (Galileo), **17th:** 300
Saggio di osservazioni microsopiche concernenti il sistema della generazione de' signori di Needham e Buffon (Spallanzani), **18th:** 926
Sahagún, Bernardino de, **Ren:** 621
Sahara Desert, **18th:** 914
Sahle Mariam. *See* Menelik II
Sahrawi, Abu Khalid al-. *See* Moussaoui, Zacarias
Saichō, **MA:** 620
Said, Edward, **20th:** 2352
Said, Mohammed, **19th:** 1356
Saʿīd ibn Sulṭān, **19th:** 1965-1968
Saʿīd Sayyid. *See* Saʿīd ibn Sulṭān
Saif al-Islam al-Qaddafi, **20th:** 3353
Saigō Takamori, **19th:** 1968-1972
Saigon, Treaty of (1862), **19th:** 2311
Saigyō, **MA:** 771
Saikaku, Ihara. *See* Ihara Saikaku
St. Albans, First Battle of (1455), **Ren:** 435, 828, 990
St. Albans, Second Battle of (1461), **Ren:** 990
Saint and the Sinner, The (Tirso), **17th:** 913
Saint Andrew (Garzoni), **17th:** 302
St. Anne-la-Royale, **17th:** 331
Saint-Aubin-du-Cormier, Battle of (1484), **Ren:** 227
Saint Augustine in His Cell (Botticelli), **Ren:** 124
Saint Augustine in Ecstasy (van Dyck), **17th:** 245
Saint Bartholomew's Day Massacre (1572), **Ren:** 185, 200, 395, 426, 429, 463, 569, 651, 703, 817, 881
Saint Bernard of Clairvaux (William of Saint-Thierry), **MA:** 1114
Saint Brice's Day Massacre (1002), **MA:** 222-223, 364
St. Clair, Arthur, **18th:** 611
St.-Clair-sur-Epte, Treaty of (911), **MA:** 902
Saint Curing the Possessed Woman (Andrea del Sarto), **Ren:** 39
Saint-Denis, **MA:** 971
Saint-Denis, Charles de Marguetel de, **17th:** 521
St. Denis, Ruth, **20th:** 1563, 3593-3596; **Notor:** 933
Saint-Étienne, sieur de, **17th:** 520
Saint-Evremond. *See* Saint-Denis, Charles de Marguetel de
Saint Francis (Kazantzakis), **20th:** 2089
Saint Francis in Ecstasy (Bellini), **Ren:** 99
St. Francis in Meditation (Zurbarán), **17th:** 1005
Saint Francis Xavier, Mission of, **17th:** 433
Saint François d'Assie (Messiaen), **20th:** 2717
Saint-Gaudens, Augustus, **19th:** 1972-1974
Saint Genet (Sartre), **20th:** 3639
Saint-George, Chevalier de. *See* Boulogne, Joseph
Saint George and the Dragon (Donatello), **MA:** 320
Saint George and the Dragon (Raphael), **Ren:** 819
Saint George Slaying the Dragon (Siloé), **Ren:** 890
Saint-Germain, Peace of (1570), **Ren:** 185, 426, 569
Saint-Germain, Treaty of (1139), **MA:** 539
Saint-Germain, Treaty of (1919), **20th:** 300
Saint-Germain-en-Laye, Treaty of (1632), **17th:** 142
Saint Irvyne (Shelley), **19th:** 2092
Saint James Baptizing Hermogenes (Mantegna), **Ren:** 602
Saint James Before Herod Agrippa (Mantegna), **Ren:** 602
Saint James Led to Execution (Mantegna), **Ren:** 602
St. James the Less (church), **19th:** 2192
Saint Jerome (van Dyck), **17th:** 244
Saint Jerome in His Study (Dürer), **Ren:** 299
Saint Jerome in Penitence (Cranach, the Elder), **Ren:** 262
Saint Joan of the Stockyards (Brecht), **20th:** 505
St. John, Baron. *See* Bolingbroke, first Viscount
Saint John the Baptist (Bosch), **Ren:** 121
Saint John the Baptist (Giotto), **MA:** 422
Saint John the Baptist (Leonardo da Vinci), **Ren:** 563
Saint John the Baptist Preaching (Rodin), **19th:** 1925
Saint John the Evangelist (Donatello), **MA:** 320
Saint-Just, Louis de, **18th:** 877-880; **Notor:** 908
St. Laurent, Louis, **20th:** 3174, 3597-3599
St. Lawrence River, **Ren:** 180

St. Leger, Harriet, **19th:** 1267
St. Leon (Godwin), **18th:** 426
St. Louis Chronicle (newspaper), **19th:** 2056
St. Louis Enquirer (newspaper), **19th:** 193
Saint Louis of Toulouse (Martini), **MA:** 697
Saint Lusson, sieur de, **17th:** 433
Saint Manuel Bueno, Martyr (Unamuno), **20th:** 4130
Saint Mark Rescuing a Slave (Tintoretto), **Ren:** 932
Saint Mark's Convent, **MA:** 84
Saint Mary Magdalene, Order of, **MA:** 438
Saint-Mihiel, Battle of (1918), **20th:** 2766
St. Pancras Station, **19th:** 2045
Saint Paul (Renan), **19th:** 1886
St. Paul and Protestantism (Arnold), **19th:** 74
St. Paul, Minneapolis, and Manitoba Railroad, **19th:** 1101
St. Paul's Cathedral, **17th:** 995
St. Peter's Basilica, **17th:** 45, 68, 721
St. Peter's Cathedral, **Ren:** 133
St. Peter's Square, **17th:** 10
St. Petersburg, Russia, **18th:** 613, 775
St. Petersburg, Treaty of (1881), **19th:** 2486
St. Petersburg Academy of Sciences, **18th:** 333
St. Quintin Fordham, Dorothy. *See* Clutterbuck, Dorothy
Saint Roche in Prison (Tintoretto), **Ren:** 933
St. Ronan's Well (Scott), **19th:** 2048
Saint-Saëns, Camille, **20th:** 3600-3602
Saint Sebastian Tended by Saint Irene (La Tour), **17th:** 494
St. Serapion (Zurbarán), **17th:** 1005
Saint-Simon, Henri de, **19th:** 537, 1975-1977
Saint-Simonians, **19th:** 1356
Saint Theresa in Ecstasy (Bernini), **17th:** 330
St. Urbain's Horseman (Richler), **20th:** 3438
Saint Ursula and Her Virgins (Tintoretto), **Ren:** 932
St. Valentine's Day Massacre, **20th:** 642
Saint-Vallier, Jean-Baptiste de, **17th:** 77
Saint Vitus's Cathedral, **MA:** 259
Saint Werburgh Street, **17th:** 846
Sainte-Beuve, Charles-Augustin, **19th:** 1147
Saints. See *specific saints' names*
Saints' lives (vitae), **Anc:** 205
Saionji, Kimmochi, **20th:** 1819
Saionji Sanekane, **MA:** 772
Saison au Congo, Une. See *Season in the Congo, A*
Saison en enfer, Une. See *Season in Hell, A*
Saite Renaissance, **Anc:** 711
Saitō Dōsan, **Ren:** 732
Saitō Tatsuoki, **Ren:** 732, 943
Sakamoto Ryōma, **19th:** 1969
Sakamoto Tsutsumi, **Notor:** 41
Sakas, **Anc:** 499, 776
Sakharov, Andrei, **20th:** 524, 3602-3606
Sakondo sip'um (Chŏng Sŏn), **18th:** 249
Sakonnets, **17th:** 634
Śakuntalā. See *Abhijñāānaśākuntala*
Śākya tribe, **Anc:** 49, 169, 933
Sākyamuni, **Anc:** 899
Saladin, **MA:** 141, 387, 891, 918-921
Sālah al-Dīn Zarkub, **MA:** 909
Salam, Abdus, **20th:** 4277
Salamandra (Paz), **20th:** 3170
Salameh, Mohammed, **Notor:** 1121
Salamis, Battle of (480 B.C.E.), **Anc:** 8, 109, 137, 214, 326, 860, 973
Salammbô (Flaubert), **19th:** 786
Salamon (Saint László's brother), **MA:** 637
Salazar, António de Oliveira, **20th:** 1107, 1137, 3606-3609; **Notor:** 928-929, 1059
Salazar şi revoluţia în Portugalia (Eliade), **20th:** 1137
Saldívar, Yolanda, **Notor:** 930-931
Salem Ali. *See* Mohammed, Khalid Shaikh
Salem witchcraft trials, **17th:** 689; **18th:** 667, 673, 893-896
Salerno, Tony, **Notor:** 218, 408
Salevsky, V. *See* Petlyura, Symon
Salian kings of Germany, **MA:** 499
Salignac de La Mothe-Fénelon, François de. *See* Fénelon, François de Salignac de La Mothe-
Ṣāliḥ, al-, **MA:** 919
Salīm. *See* Jahāngīr
Salimbene, **MA:** 921-924
Salinas, Battle of Las. *See* Las Salinas, Battle of
Salinger, J. D., **20th:** 3609-3613
Salisbury (Constable), **19th:** 541
Salisbury, first earl of (1563-1612; Robert Cecil), **Ren:** 844-847; **17th:** 132, 414
Salisbury, second earl of. *See* Warwick, earl of
Salisbury, third marquis of (1830-1903; Robert Cecil), **19th:** 462, 1977-1981; **20th:** 895
Salk, Jonas, **20th:** 3613-3616
Salk Institute for Biological Studies, **20th:** 3615
Salka Valka (Laxness), **20th:** 2309
Sallust, **Anc:** 188, 742-744
Salmagundi, **19th:** 1180
Salmon, Daniel, **20th:** 3772
Salmonia (Davy), **19th:** 618
Salome, **Anc:** 404, 475; **Notor:** 932-933
Salome (Strauss), **19th:** 1156; **20th:** 3886
Salomé, Lou von, **19th:** 1682; **Notor:** 367
Salon, The (Heine), **19th:** 1071

Salon des Indépendants, **19th:** 1952
Salon des Moulins, The (Toulouse-Lautrec), **19th:** 2289
Salon des Refusés, **19th:** 1800
Salón México, El (Copland), **20th:** 838
Salons (literary and artistic), **17th:** 487, 521, 779, 829, 833; **18th:** Café de l'Europe, 267; Queen Caroline, 203; England, 897; Paul-Henri-Dietrich d'Holbach, 502; rue Ste-Anne salon, 480; Madame de Staël, 929
Saloth Sar. *See* Pol Pot
Salsa music, **20th:** 878
Salsbury, Nate, **19th:** 524
Salt Lake City, Mormon march to, **19th:** 2477
Saltbush Bill, J. P., and Other Verses (Paterson), **19th:** 1758
Salutatio (ritual), **Anc:** 24
Salvadoran Civil War (1980-1992), **20th:** 122, 1041
Salvarsan, **20th:** 1117, 1254
Salvation Army, **19th:** 275
Salvatores Dei. See *Saviors of God, The*
Salve Deus Rex Judæorum (Lanyer), **Ren:** 535, 536
Salvianus, **Anc:** 698
Sam Mīrzā. *See* Shāh Safi I
Sāmānid Dynasty, **MA:** 683
Samaññaphala Sutta (Buddhaghosa), **Anc:** 355
Samaritans, **Anc:** 821
Samarqand, Mughal invasions of, **Ren:** 69
Sambhājī, **17th:** 25
Samdech Hun Sen. *See* Hun Sen
Same River Twice, The (Walker), **20th:** 4198
Samedi, **17th:** 829
Samia (Menander), **Anc:** 548
Samkara. *See* Śaṅkara
Sammu-ramat, **Anc:** 744-747
Sammy the Bull. *See* Gravano, Sammy
Samoilovych, Ivan, **17th:** 624
Samory Touré, **19th:** 1981-1983
Samoset, **17th:** 86, 612, 876
Samothrace, mysteries of, **Anc:** 597
Sampras, Pete, **20th:** 3616-3618
Sampson, William T., **19th:** 647
Samsāra, **Anc:** 112, 931
Samskrta Jantra and Book Depository, **19th:** 2363
Samson et Dalila (Saint-Saëns), **20th:** 3600
Samsuiluna, **Anc:** 378
Sämtliche Werke. See *Lectures on the Philosophy of History*
Samuel (Israeli religious leader), **Anc:** 747-749
Samuel ha-Nagid, **MA:** 532
Samugarh, Battle of (1658), **17th:** 24
Samurai, **MA:** 721, 992, 1155; **19th:** 1631
Samurai, The (Endō), **20th:** 1156
San Andrea al Quirinale, **17th:** 46
San Antonio de Padua (Alemán), **Ren:** 26
San Carlo alle Quattro Fontane, **17th:** 68
San Carlos Agency, **19th:** 905
San Francisco (film), **20th:** 4066
San Germano, Treaty of (1230), **MA:** 437
San guo zhi, **Anc:** 183, 950
San Ivo della Sapienza, **17th:** 68
San Jacinto, Battle of (1836), **19th:** 1131
San Lorenzo, **17th:** 331
San Manuel Bueno, mártir. See *Saint Manuel Bueno, Martyr*
San Martín, José de, **19th:** 269, 1703, 1984-1987
San Mateo v. Southern Pacific, **19th:** 779
San Paolo Fuori le Mura, **MA:** 102
San Stefano, Order of, **17th:** 627
San Stefano Treaty (1878), **19th:** 7
San Xia project. *See* Three Gorges Dam
Sánchez Cerro, Luis M., **20th:** 1718
Sanchez de Lozada, Gonzalo, **20th:** 3173
Sancho, **MA:** 279
Sancta Susanna (Hindemith), **20th:** 1812
Sanctorius, Sanctorius. *See* Santorio, Santorio
Sanctuary (Faulkner), **20th:** 1224
Sanctuary Meditations (Gracián), **17th:** 317
Sand, George, **19th:** 487, 1987-1990
Sand-Reckoner, The. See *Psiammites*
Sand River Convention (1852), **19th:** 1298
Sandburg, Carl, **20th:** 3619-3622
Sandeau, Jules, **19th:** 1987
Sanders, George. *See* Floyd, Pretty Boy
Sandhya Sangit (Tagore), **20th:** 3933
Sandinista National Liberation Front, **20th:** 3072
Sandino, Augusto César, **Notor:** 984
Sandoval y Rojas, Francisco Gómez de. *See* Lerma, duke de
Sandrocottus. *See* Chandragupta Maurya
Sands of Iwo Jima (film), **20th:** 4251
Sandwich, first earl of, **17th:** 57, 728
Sandwich Islands, **18th:** 272
Sane Society, The (Fromm), **20th:** 1347
Sanekane, Saionji. *See* Saionji Sanekane
Sanford, Henry Shelton, **Notor:** 632
Sang des autres, Le. See *Blood of Others, The*
Sang d'un poète, Le. See *Blood of a Poet, The*
Sanger, Frederick, **20th:** 3622-3624
Sanger, Margaret, **20th:** 558, 1150, 3625-3629; **Notor:** 230-231

Sängerweihe (Ehrenfels), **20th:** 1111
Sanghamitta, **Anc:** 899
"Sangō shiiki." *See* "Indications of the Goals of the Three Teachings"
Sanhedrin, **Anc:** 460, 821
Sanin, Joseph. *See* Joseph of Volokolamsk
Sanjō (emperor of Japan), **MA:** 397
Sanjō (writer). *See* Nijō
Sanjuro (film), **20th:** 2219
Śaṅkara, **MA:** 924-927
Sankey, Ira, **19th:** 1596
Sankhibtawy. *See* Montuhotep II
Sanmati. *See* Vardhamāna
Sanquhar Declaration (1680), **17th:** 123
Sanshiro Sugata (film), **20th:** 2217
Sanskrit literature, **Anc:** 496
Sansovino, Jacopo, **Ren:** 39, 54, 847-850
Santa, Battle of (1697), **17th:** 528
Santa Anna, Antonio López de, **19th:** 572, 612, 850, 1131, 1245, 1990-1993, 2053; Porfirio Díaz, 652
Santa Croce, **MA:** 103
Santa Juana, La (Tirso), **17th:** 913
Santa Maria del Fiore, **MA:** 103, 206, 283, 799
Santa Maria Novella, **Ren:** 19
Santamaria, Bartholomew Augustine, **19th:** 1493
Santander, Francisco, **19th:** 270
Santayana, George, **20th:** 3629-3631
Santillana, Juana Inés de Asbaje y Ramírez de. *See* Cruz, Sor Juana Inés de la
Santorio, Santorio, **17th:** 810-813
Santos-Dumont, Alberto, **20th:** 3632-3635
Sanusiya, **20th:** 3350
Sanzio, Raffaello. *See* Raphael
São Francisco de Assis (church), **18th:** 608
São Mamede, Battle of (1128), **MA:** 33
Saphead, The (film), **20th:** 2090
Sapho (Gounod), **19th:** 953
Sapientia (Hrosvitha), **MA:** 517
Sapor II. *See* Shāpūr II
Sappho, **Anc:** 11, 750-752
Sappho and Phaon (Robinson), **18th:** 850
Saracens, **MA:** 356
Sarachina Kikō. See *Visit to Sarashina Village, A*
Saragossa, La, **19th:** 1993-1996
Saragossa, Battle of (778), **MA:** 243
Saragossa, First Siege of (1808), **19th:** 1993
Saragossa, Second Siege of (1808-1809), **19th:** 1994
Saragossa y Domenech, Maria Agustina. *See* Saragossa, La
Sarah, **Anc:** 4
Sarah and Son (film), **20th:** 142
Sarah Siddons as the Tragic Muse (Reynolds), **18th:** 913
Saratoga, Battles of (1777), **18th:** 41, 61, 565
Sarauniya Aminatu. *See* Amina Sarauniya Zazzua
Sarbanes, Paul, **Notor:** 619, 968
Sardanapalus (Byron), **Anc:** 119
Sarduri III, **Anc:** 892
Sarekat Islam, **20th:** 3904
Sargent, John Singer, **19th:** 1996-2000
Sargon II, **Anc:** 123, 752-755, 769
Sargon of Akkad, **Anc:** 298, 753, 914
Sarit Dhanarajata, **20th:** 363
Šárka (Janáček), **20th:** 1990
Sarkin Zazzua Nohir, **Ren:** 37
Sarmiento, Domingo Faustino, **19th:** 2000-2002
Sarmiento, Félix Rubén García. *See* Darío, Rubén
Sarnoff, David, **20th:** 4480
Saro-Wiwa, Ken, **20th:** 3806; **Notor:** 1
Sarotti, Ambrose, **17th:** 711
Sarpi, Paolo, **17th:** 720, 810
Sarraute, Nathalie, **20th:** 3635-3637
Sarto, Giuseppe Melchiorre. *See* Pius X
Sartor Resartus (Carlyle), **19th:** 415, 746
Sartre, Jean-Paul, **20th:** 247, 272, 628, 1471, 1744, 2711, 3635, 3638-3641
Sarugaku, **MA:** 1153
Sarumino. See *Monkey's Raincoat*
Sasameyuki. See *Makioka Sisters, The*
Sāsānian Empire, **Anc:** 774; **MA:** 613; kings, 615
Ṣaṣāṇka, **MA:** 460
Såsom i en spegel. See *Through a Glass Darkly*
Sassamon, John, **17th:** 634
Satan Summoning up His Legions (Lawrence), **18th:** 584
Satanstoe (Cooper), **19th:** 555
Sataspes, **Anc:** 387
Satellites, information-gathering, **20th:** 4139
Satie, Erik, **20th:** 2647, 3641-3645
Satire, **Anc:** Horatian, 431; Roman, 513; social, 663; **17th:** 63
Satires, Les (Boileau-Despréaux), **17th:** 63
Satires (Horace), **Anc:** 430
Satires (Juvenal). See *Saturae* (Juvenal)
Satiromastix (Dekker), **17th:** 223, 441
Satō, Eisaku, **20th:** 3645-3648
Satori (enlightenment), **18th:** 450
Satraps, **Anc:** function of, 253; government by, 972
Satsuma Revolt (1877), **19th:** 1971
Satura (Montale), **20th:** 2803
Saturae (Ennius), **Anc:** 302

Saturae (Juvenal), **Anc:** 493
Saturae Menippiae (Varro), **Anc:** 928
Saturday Night (Benavente y Martínez), **20th:** 2332
Satyr (Praxiteles), **Anc:** 695
Satyricon (Petronius), **Anc:** 592
Satyrische Pilgram, Der (Grimmelshausen), **17th:** 325
Satyros, **Anc:** 348
Sauchieburn, Battle of (1488), **Ren:** 497-498
Saud (king of Saudi Arabia), **20th:** 1200
Saud, Fahd ibn Abd al-Aziz al-. *See* Fahd
Saʿūd, Muḥammad ibn, **18th:** 1030
Saudi Arabia, **20th:** creation of, 1199. *See also* Geographical Index
Saul (king of Israel), **Anc:** 255, 748
Saul of Tarsus. *See* Paul, Saint
Saumur, Assembly of (1612), **Ren:** 705
Saundarśnanda (Aśvaghosa), **Anc:** 130
Saunderson, Mary, **17th:** 51, 82
Saussure, Ferdinand de, **20th:** 1987, 3649-3652
Sauvé, Jeanne, **20th:** 3652-3655
Sauvé, Maurice, **20th:** 3652
Sauve qui peut (la vie). See *Every Man for Himself*
Savage, Richard, **18th:** 536
Savage Mind, The (Lévi-Strauss), **20th:** 2349
Savannah, Georgia, **18th:** 1055
Savarkar, Veer, **Notor:** 416
Savelli, Giulia, **17th:** 780
Savery, Thomas, **17th:** 712, 813-815; **18th:** 734
Savigny, Friedrich Karl von, **19th:** 2003-2005
Savile, Sir George, **17th:** 815-817
Saville, John, **18th:** 898
Saving Private Ryan (film), **20th:** 3812
Saving the Queen (Buckley), **20th:** 562
Saviors of God, The (Kazantzakis), **20th:** 2088
Savitri Devi, **Notor:** 340, 934-935
Savonarola, Girolamo, **Ren:** 29, 587, 657, 682, 850-855
Savoy, The (magazine), **19th:** 163
Saw Maung, **Notor:** 1026
Sawbridge, Catherine. *See* Macaulay, Catherine
Sawyer, Diane, **20th:** 4212
Sawyer, Elizabeth, **Notor:** 935-936
Saxe, comte de, **18th:** 881-883
Saxo Grammaticus, **MA:** 927-930
Saxons, **MA:** 1094; kings of Germany, 488, 807
Saxony, **MA:** Christianity, 1096; Franks invasion of, 243; law, 1096; monasticism, 516; paganism, 1095; rebellion against Germany, 497
Saxony, Maurice of. *See* Saxe, comte de
Say, Is This the U.S.A.? (Caldwell and Bourke-White), **20th:** 462
Sayad, Muhammad Muhammad Al-Amir Awad Al. *See* Atta al-Sayed, Mohammed
Sayed, Mohamed El. *See* Atta al-Sayed, Mohammed
Saying Grace (Rockwell), **20th:** 3485
Sayonara (Michener), **20th:** 2728
Sayyid ʿAlī Muḥammad Shīrāzi. *See* Bāb, the
Sayyid Kāẓīm Rashtī, **19th:** 105, 2214
Sayyid Saʿīd. *See* Saʿīd ibn Sulṭān
Scaevola, Quintus Mucius, **Anc:** 210
Scaff, Nicolas. *See* Mesrine, Jacques
Scalabrini, Giovanni Battista, **19th:** 383
Scalia, Antonin, **20th:** 521
Scaliger, Joseph Justus, **Ren:** 855-858
Scandinavia, **MA:** Christianity, 767; coinage, 692; trade, 913. *See also* Geographical Index
Scanlan, Michael, **Notor:** 563
Scapegoat, The (Hunt), **19th:** 1158
Scapula, Publius Ostorius, **Anc:** 163
Scarborough Rapist. *See* Bernardo, Paul
Scarecrow of Oz, The (Baum), **19th:** 158
Scarface. *See* Capone, Al
Scarlatti, Alessandro, **18th:** 190, 463, 883-887
Scarlet Letter, The (Hawthorne), **19th:** 1051
Scarron, Françoise. *See* Maintenon, Madame de
Scarron, Paul, **17th:** 521, 780
Scene of War in the Middle Ages (Degas), **19th:** 632
Scener ur ett äktenskap. See *Scenes from a Marriage*
Scenes and Hymns of Life, with Other Religious Poems (Hemans), **19th:** 1077
Scenes from a Marriage (film), **20th:** 318
Scenes from the Saga of King Olaf (Elgar), **20th:** 1134
Scenes in the Life of Harriet Tubman (Bradford), **19th:** 2315
Scenes of Clerical Life (Eliot), **19th:** 741
Scent (Pollock), **20th:** 3303
Sceptical Chymist, The (Boyle), **17th:** 79
Scepticism and Animal Faith (Santayana), **20th:** 3630
Schäffer, Anton, **19th:** 1250
Schall, Adam, **17th:** 448
Schall von Bell, Johann Adam, **17th:** 849
Scharnhorst, Gerhard Johann David von, **19th:** 499, 929, 2006-2008
Schary, Dore, **Notor:** 974
Schawlow, Arthur L., **20th:** 4057

Scheck, Barry, **Notor:** 959
Schedula Monitoria de Novae Febris Ingressu (Sydenham), **17th:** 902
Scheherazade (Rimsky-Korsakov), **19th:** 1915
Scheiner, Christoph, **17th:** 260
Scheler, Max, **20th:** 3655-3658
Schelling, Friedrich Wilhelm Joseph von, **19th:** 1065, 2009-2012
Schenck, Joseph, **20th:** 2090
Scherzo et marche funèbre (Bizet), **19th:** 241
Scherzo in B-flat major (Mussorgsky), **19th:** 1627
Scherzo in E Major (Borodin), **19th:** 281
Schickard, Wilhelm, **17th:** 818-820; on calculators, 819
Schiff, Jacob, **20th:** 1614
Schiller, Friedrich, **18th:** 887-890, 1095; **19th:** 2009; **Notor:** 536
Schindler's List (film), **20th:** 3812
Schionatulander and Sigune (Wolfram), **MA:** 1125
Schirach, Baldur von, **Notor:** 937-938
Schism, **MA:** Aquileia, 938; Roman and Eastern Orthodox church, 646, 1017; schism of 1130, 161. *See also* Great Schism (1378-1417)
Schizophrenia, **20th:** 392, 2062, 3911
Schlatter, Adolf, **20th:** 243
Schlegel, August Wilhelm, **19th:** 2009
Schlegel, Friedrich, **19th:** 2013
Schleicher, Kurt von, **20th:** 3110
Schleiermacher, Friedrich, **19th:** 2013-2016; **20th:** 548
Schleiermacher's Soliloquies (Schleiermacher), **19th:** 2014
Schleswig, Second War of. *See* Danish-Prussian War (1864)
Schley, Winifield S., **19th:** 647
Schlick, Moritz, **20th:** 660
Schlieffen, Alfred von, **20th:** 1815, 4347
Schlieffen Plan, **20th:** 2462
Schliemann, Heinrich, **19th:** 753, 2016-2019
Schloss, Das. See *Castle, The*
Schmalkaldic League, **Ren:** 144, 222, 776
Schmalkaldic War (1546-1547), **Ren:** 222, 650, 777
Schmeling, Max, **20th:** 2438
Schmidman, Jo Ann, **20th:** 3983
Schmidt, Bernhard Voldemar, **20th:** 3659-3661
Schmidt, Helmut, **20th:** 492
Schmidt, Maria, **20th:** 1823
Schmidt, Rachel. *See* Wall, Rachel
Schmidt-Rottluff, Karl, **20th:** 3661-3663
Schmidt telescope, **20th:** 3659
Schmitz, John G., **Notor:** 640
Schmitz, Mary Katherine. *See* Letourneau, Mary Kay
Schmitzev, Eduard Carl. *See* Emin Pasha
Schneider, René, **20th:** 72
Schoenberg, Arnold, **19th:** 1155; **20th:** 195, 310, 452, 3664-3668, 4262
Scholae in liberales artes (Ramus), **Ren:** 817
Scholar-officials, Confucian, **MA:** 1080
Scholar(s), The (Lovelace), **17th:** 562
Scholarship, **Anc:** Alexandrian, 434; Buddhist, 130; Chinese, 149; Roman, 217; Sri Lankan, 900; **17th:** China, 972; England, 80, 939; France, 722; Italy, 743; Jewish, 583; Netherlands, 824; Ottoman Empire, 455; **18th:** secular, 102; theological, 102. *See also* Category Index
Scholastic Philosophy (Leo XIII), **19th:** 1344
Scholasticism, **MA:** 16, 112, 180, 215, 332, 750, 761, 1028, 1064, 1102; Augustinian, 534; Muslim, 120
Schomberg, Friedrich Hermann, **17th:** 426, 820-822
Schönborn, Friedrich Carl von, **18th:** 495
Schöne Müllerin, Die (Schubert), **19th:** 2026
School and Society, The (Dewey), **20th:** 982
School for Husbands, The (Molière), **17th:** 647
School for Scandal, The (Sheridan), **18th:** 2, 905
School for Wives, The (Molière), **17th:** 648
School of American Ballet, **20th:** 194, 910
School of Athens (Raphael), **Ren:** 820
School of Compliment, The (Shirley), **17th:** 846
School of Love (Correggio), **Ren:** 250
School of Ragtime (Joplin), **19th:** 1236
Schoole of Abuse, The (Gosson), **Ren:** 882; **17th:** 374
Schopenhauer, Arthur, **19th:** 2019-2022
Schöpferische Konfession. See *Creative Credo*
Schrader, Justus, **17th:** 899
Schrader, Paul, **20th:** 3682
Schreiner, Olive, **19th:** 2023-2025
Schrieffer, Bob, **20th:** 235
Schriften zur Soziologie und Weltanschauungslehre (Scheler), **20th:** 3657
Schrödinger, Erwin, **20th:** 438, 1004, 3668-3671
Schroffenstein Family, The (Kleist), **19th:** 1289
Schroth, Claude, **19th:** 542
Schubert, Franz, **19th:** 2026-2029
Schuldfrage, Die. See *Question of German Guilt, The*
Schultz, Christine, **Notor:** 84

Schultz, David, **Notor:** 305
Schultz, Dutch, **Notor:** 148, 221, 277, 660-661, 918, 938-940, 955
Schultz, Elfred, Jr., **Notor:** 84
Schultz, Nancy, **Notor:** 305
Schulz, Charles M., **20th:** 3672-3674, 4477
Schuman, Robert, **20th:** 2795
Schumann, Clara, **19th:** 296, 2029-2031
Schumann, Robert, **19th:** 296, 2029, 2031-2035
Schurman, Anna Maria van, **17th:** 823-825
Schurz, Carl, **19th:** 2035-2038
Schütz, Heinrich, **Ren:** 362; **17th:** 825-828
Schutzstaffel (SS), **20th:** 1808
Schuyler, Philip, **19th:** 364
Schwab, Charles, **19th:** 421
Schwab, Michael, **19th:** 58
Schwanengesang (Schubert), **19th:** 2027
Schwann, Theodor, **19th:** 2366
Schwartz, Anna Jacobson, **20th:** 1333
Schwartzbard, Sholom, **Notor:** 833
Schwartzerd, Philipp. *See* Melanchthon, Philipp
Schwarze Dekameron. See *Black Decameron, The*
Schwarzenberg, Adam von, **17th:** 290
Schwarzkopf, H. Norman, **20th:** 3323
Schwarzschild, Karl, **20th:** 3674-3677
Schweitzer, Albert, **20th:** 3678-3681
Science, **Anc:** Alexandrian, 410; Hellenistic, 579; philosophy and, 263, 856; religion and, 726; Stoicism and, 691; **MA:** England, 127; experimental, 128; Germany, 43; **17th:** England, 200, 280, 357, 383, 734; France, 227, 306, 630; Italy, 322; **18th:** animal reproduction, 928; archaeology, 952-954, 1096; invention of balloon, 699; biology, 925-928, 961; blood circulation, 926; botany, 80-83, 171, 604-608; calendars, 1039; eclipses, 1039; fertilization, 927; geology, 172, 579; meteorology, 336, 1039; natural history, 171-173, 533, 605, 926; spontaneous generation, 926; temperature scales, 336-338; thermometers, 336-338; water, 219; zoology, 927. *See also* Anatomy; Astronomy; Biology; Botany; Calculus; Chemistry; Entomology; Epidemiology; Geography; Geology; Geometry; Iatrochemistry; Mathematics; Medicine; Meteorology; Natural history; Optics; Paleontology; Physics; Zoology; Category Index
Science (magazine), **19th:** 184
Science and Health (Eddy), **19th:** 724
Science and Humanism (Schrödinger), **20th:** 3670
Science and Method (Poincaré), **19th:** 1818
Science and the Modern World (Whitehead), **20th:** 4313
Science of Logic (Hegel), **19th:** 1067
Science of the Cross, The (Stein), **20th:** 3843
Scientific Foundations of Analytical Chemistry Treated in an Elementary Manner, The (Ostwald), **20th:** 3090
Scientific Man and Power Politics (Morgenthau), **20th:** 2829
Scientific Papers (Huggins and Huggins), **19th:** 1145
Scientology, **20th:** 1910-1911
Scipio Aemilianus, **Anc:** 357, 673, 755-757
Scipio Africanus, **Anc:** 191, 301, 344, 357, 382, 542, 755, 758-760, 813, 850
Scipio the Younger. *See* Scipio Aemilianus
Scipionic Circle, **Anc:** 756, 849
Scivias (Hildegard von Bingen), **MA:** 512
SCLC. *See* Southern Christian Leadership Conference
Scopas, **Anc:** 546, 761-763, 793
Scopes, John T., **20th:** 552, 915; **Notor:** 648
Scornful Lady, The (Beaumont and Fletcher), **Ren:** 94
Scorpion (Egyptian king), **Anc:** 557
Scorsese, Martin, **20th:** 3681-3683
Scotism, **MA:** 330, 332
Scotland, **MA:** English invasion of, 346; kings, 203, 306; philosophy, 330; theology, 330; **Ren:** English invasion of, 899. *See also* Geographical Index
Scotland Yard, **18th:** 346-350
Scots Highland regiment, **18th:** 53
Scots Musical Museum, The (Johnson), **18th:** 185
Scott, Charlotte Angas, **19th:** 2039-2041
Scott, David R., **20th:** 136
Scott, Dred, **19th:** 2041-2043, 2227; **Notor:** 1019
Scott, Sir George Gilbert, **19th:** 2044-2046, 2192
Scott, James. *See* Monmouth, duke of
Scott, Lydia. *See* Chadwick, Cassie L.
Scott, Robert Falcon, **20th:** 84
Scott, Thomas, **19th:** 1909
Scott, Sir Walter, **19th:** 1224, 2047-2051
Scott, Winfield, **19th:** 344, 764, 1790, 2051-2055
Scott and Moffat, **19th:** 2044
Scottish Labour Party, **19th:** 1026
Scottish Symphony (Mendelssohn), **19th:** 1550
Scottish War for Independence, **MA:** 202

Scoundrel Time (Hellman), **20th:** 1754
Scouting for Boys (Baden-Powell), **19th:** 112
Scouts of the Plains, The (Buntline), **19th:** 524
Scream, The (Munch), **20th:** 2872
Screens, The (Genet), **20th:** 1447
Screwtape Letters, The (Lewis), **20th:** 2354
Scribble Scribble (Ephron), **20th:** 1162
Scribes, **Anc:** Jewish, 339; women as, 298
Scribonius Largus, **Anc:** 291
Scripps, Edward Wyllis, **19th:** 2055-2058
Scripps-Howard newspaper conglomerate, **19th:** 2057
Scripps-McRae League, **19th:** 2057
Scripta Minoa (Evans), **19th:** 754
Scripts, Chinese, **Anc:** 956
Scriptural Views of Holy Baptism (Pusey), **19th:** 1846
Scriptures, Christian, **Anc:** 134
Scroll of the Emperors (Yan), **MA:** 1140
Scuba gear, development, **20th:** 850
Scudéry, Madeleine de, **17th:** 477, 487, 662, 828-830
Sculley, John, **20th:** 2007
Scullin, James H., **20th:** 2489
Sculpture, **Anc:** architecture and, 634; Greek, 523; Hellenistic, 762; nudity in, 696; psychology and, 696; Sumerian, 366; **MA:** Italy, 102, 206, 320, 418, 566, 798, 845, 847; Japan, 581, 1040; Netherlands, 947; **Ren:** Italy, 203, 682, 963; Spain, 890; **18th:** and interior design, 132; Antônio Francisco Lisboa, 608; Johann Joachim Winckelmann, 1095; **19th:** France, 1890, 1925; Italy, 406; United States, 1882, 1973; **20th:** cubism, 2397, 2948; England, 2818; France, 479, 1165, 2777; Futurism, 404; mobiles and stabiles, 609; Surrealism, 1471, 2948; United States, 4316
Sculpture (Lipchitz), **20th:** 2398
Scultetus, Johannes, **17th:** 566
Scuola di S. Rocco, **Ren:** 933
Scurvy, **18th:** 110, 273
Scythians, **Anc:** 252, 564
"Scythians, The" (Blok), **20th:** 395
Sea and Poison, The (Endō), **20th:** 1156
Sea Around Us, The (Carson), **20th:** 663
Sea Battle in the Straits of Messina (Bruegel), **Ren:** 135
Sea Drift (Delius), **20th:** 955
Sea Garden (H. D.), **20th:** 1624
Sea of Fertility, The (Mishima), **20th:** 2764
Sea Symphony, A (Vaughan Williams), **20th:** 4149
Sea-Wolf, The (London), **20th:** 2421
Seaborg, Glenn Theodore, **20th:** 2301, 2534, 3684-3688
Seaborgium, **20th:** 3687
Seagram Building, **20th:** 2733
Seagull, The (Chekhov), **19th:** 479; **20th:** 3822
Seale, Bobby, **Notor:** 782
Seaman's Secrets (Davis), **Ren:** 277
Search warrants (British law), **18th:** 518
Searchers, The (film), **20th:** 4251
Season in Hell, A (Verlaine), **19th:** 1913
Season in the Congo, A (Césaire), **20th:** 712
Season of Anomy (Soyinka), **20th:** 3805
Seasons, The (ballet), **20th:** 886
Seasons, The (Haydn), **18th:** 477
Seasons and calendars, **Anc:** 815
Seated Man Holding a Branch (Hals), **17th:** 354
Seaton Delaval (Vanbrugh), **18th:** 1004
Seattle SuperSonics, **20th:** 3568
Sebastian (king of Portugal), **Ren:** 859-860
Sebastopol (Tolstoy), **19th:** 2283
Sébillet, Thomas, **Ren:** 294
Sebring, Jay, **Notor:** 690
Secession (southern U.S. states), **19th:** 612, 2165; opposition to, 1230; Texas, 1132
Sechter, Simon, **19th:** 330
Second Birth (Pasternak), **20th:** 3132
Second Booke of Songs or Ayres, The (Dowland), **Ren:** 290
Second Empire, **19th:** 1640, 1700
Second Hurricane, The (Copland), **20th:** 838
Second International, **19th:** 1026
Second Jungle Book, The (Kipling), **19th:** 1286
Second Keeper of the Robes, **18th:** 181
Second Manifesto of Surrealism (Breton), **20th:** 512
Second Republic, **19th:** 255, 1639, 2265
Second Sex, The (Beauvoir), **20th:** 273
Second Sonata (Boulez), **20th:** 453
Second Stage, The (Friedan), **20th:** 1330
Second Symphony (Borodin), **19th:** 282
Second Symphony in B flat major (Dvořák), **19th:** 712
Second Triumvirate, **Anc:** 74, 145, 166, 212, 231, 888, 928. *See also* First Triumvirate
Second Vatican Council. *See* Vatican Council, Second
Second Viennese School, **20th:** 4149
Second Visit to the United States of North America (Lyell), **19th:** 1425
Seconda pratica (musical style), **17th:** 296
Secondat, Charles-Louis de. *See* Montesquieu

Secondo libro di toccate . . . , Il (Frescobaldi), **17th:** 297
Secotans. *See* Roanocs
Secret Adversary, The (Christie), **20th:** 766
Secret Agent, The (Conrad), **20th:** 826
Secret Doctrine, The (Blavatsky), **19th:** 212
Secret Garden, The (Burnett), **19th:** 359
Secret History of Queen Zarah and the Zarazians, The (Manley), **18th:** 642
Secret History of the Court of the Emperor Justinian (Procopius), **MA:** 77
Secret Life of Salvador Dalí, The (Dalí), **20th:** 906
"Secret Life of Walter Mitty, The" (Thurber), **20th:** 4021
Secret Love (Dryden), **17th:** 343
Secret Memoirs and Manners . . . (Manley), **18th:** 642
Secret of the Universe, The (Kepler), **17th:** 458
Secret Vengeance for Secret Insult (Calderón), **17th:** 114
Secretin, **20th:** 259
Secretum meum. See *My Secret*
Section Française de L'Internationale Ouvrière, **19th:** 1221
Secular Hymn, The. See *Carmen Saeculare*
Secularism, **18th:** colonial America, 669; Europe, 103; Prussia, 379
Seddon, Richard John, **19th:** 983, 2058-2061
Sedgemoor, Battle of (1685), **17th:** 655
Sedges, John. *See* Buck, Pearl S.
See It Now (television program), **20th:** 2880
Seeckt, Hans von, **20th:** 3688-3691
Seele und die Formen, Die. See *Soul and Form*
Sefer ha-Ge'ulah. See *Book of Redemption, The*
Sefirot, Luria on, **Ren:** 580
Ségalas, Anaïs, **19th:** 2062-2063
Segelfoss Town (Hamsun), **20th:** 1661
Segovia, Andrés, **20th:** 3691-3695
Segrais. *See* La Fayette, Madame de
Segrais, Jean Regnault de, **17th:** 477, 661
Segregation, **19th:** 2393
Segregation (Warren), **20th:** 4238
Séguie, Pierre, **17th:** 504
Segura, Juan Bautista de, **17th:** 702
Sei personaggi in cerca d'autore. See *Six Characters in Search of an Author*
Sei Shōnagon, **MA:** 930-933
Sein und Zeit. See *Being and Time*
Seingalt, chevalier de. *See* Casanova
Seipei, Stompie, **Notor:** 687
Seismicity of Earth (Richter and Gutenberg), **20th:** 3442
Seismology, **20th:** 3441
Seiyukai Party, **19th:** 1187
Seize the Day (Bellow), **20th:** 289
"Seizure" (Sappho), **Anc:** 751
Sejanus (Jonson), **17th:** 441
Sejanus, Lucius Aelius, **Anc:** 176, 628, 643, 890
Seki Kōwa, **17th:** 831-833
Sekigahara, Battle of (1600), **Ren:** 460; **17th:** 916
Selbstmord als sociale Massenerscheinung der modernen Civilisation, Der. See *Suicide and the Meaning of Civilization*
Selden, George Baldwin, **19th:** 1340
Selden patent case, **19th:** 1340
Selected Poems (Atwood), **20th:** 170
Selected Poems (Moore), **20th:** 2822
Selected Poems from the Dīwani Shamsi Tabriz (Rūmī), **MA:** 908
Selected Poems from "The Goddesses" (Guo), **20th:** 1620
Selected Poems, 1923-1967 (Borges), **20th:** 430
Selected Short Stories (Gorky), **20th:** 1550
Selected Stories (Munro), **20th:** 2874
Selected Writings (Jakobson), **20th:** 1988
Selections from the Prison Notebooks of Antonio Gramsci (Gramsci), **20th:** 1567
Selena. *See* Quintanilla-Perez, Selena
Selenium dehydrogenation, **20th:** 995
Selenographia (Hevelius), **17th:** 372
Seleucids, **Anc:** 65, 157, 896
Seleucus I Nicator, **Anc:** 63, 106, 203, 310, 716, 721, 763-765
Self-Analysis (Horney), **20th:** 1884
Self and Its Brain, The (Eccles and Popper), **20th:** 1091
Self-Denying Ordinance (1644), **17th:** 205, 941
Self-Examination (Beale), **19th:** 159
Self-immolation, Buddhist monks, **20th:** 2952
Self-Portrait (Degas), **19th:** 632
Self-Portrait (Dürer), **Ren:** 297
Self-Portrait (van Dyck), **17th:** 244
Self-Portrait (van Gogh), **19th:** 935
Self-Portrait (van Hemessen), **Ren:** 422
Self-Portrait (Miró), **20th:** 2760
Self-Portrait (Murillo), **17th:** 670
Self-Portrait (Poussin), **17th:** 750
Self-Portrait (Sirani), **17th:** 857
Self-Portrait (Tintoretto), **Ren:** 935

Self-Portrait as a Soldier (Kirchner), **20th:** 2165
Self-Portrait as Bacchus (Caravaggio), **Ren:** 170
Self-Portrait in the Studiolo (Fontana), **Ren:** 338
Self-Portrait of a Degenerate Artist (Kokoschka), **20th:** 2187
Self-Portrait of the Artist (Bingham), **19th:** 235
Self-Portrait with a Black Dog (Courbet), **19th:** 559
Self Portrait with Seven Fingers (Chagall), **20th:** 717
Self-Tormentor, The. See *Heautontimorumenos*
Seligman, Joseph, **19th:** 26
Selim I, **Ren:** 80, 88, 480, 914; **Notor:** 39
Selim III, **19th:** 1620
Selim Giray I, **17th:** 152
Seljuk Turks, **MA:** 70, 774, 795, 800, 918; Great Sultans, 72
Selkirk, Alexander, **17th:** 216
Sellers, Arthur Mann. *See* Gardner, Erle Stanley
Sellers, Peter, **20th:** 3695-3697
Selling of Joseph, The (Sewall), **18th:** 895
Selma-to-Montgomery march (1965), **20th:** 576, 2149
Selous, Frederick Courteney, **19th:** 1407
Seltsame Springinsfeld, Der. See *Singular Life Story of Heedless Hopalong, The*
Selva confusa, La (Calderón), **17th:** 113
Selznick, David O., **20th:** 143, 321, 2096
Semantics, **20th:** 661
Sembazuru. See *Thousand Cranes*
Semimaru (Zeami), **MA:** 1154
Seminole War, First (1817-1818), **19th:** 849, 1709
Seminole War, Second (1835-1842), **19th:** 535, 850, 1710, 2052, 2231
Seminoles, **19th:** 535, 849, 1709, 2052
Semiotics, **20th:** 3651
Semi-Pelagianism, **MA:** 155. *See also* Pelagianism
Semiramide (Rossini), **19th:** 1945
Semiramide riconosciuta (Gluck), **18th:** 418
Semmelweis, Ignaz Philipp, **19th:** 2064-2067
Semper Fidelis (Sousa), **20th:** 3798
Sempronius Longus, Tiberius, **Anc:** 382
Sen, Amartya, **20th:** 3392
Senate, Roman, **Anc:** 218, 275, 847
Sendak, Maurice, **20th:** 3698-3702
Sendero Luminoso, **20th:** 1359
Seneca the Elder, **Anc:** 766
Seneca the Younger, **Anc:** 25, 591, 766-768; **Notor:** 777
Senecas, **Ren:** 281, 448; **19th:** 1603
Senegal, **19th:** 756; **20th:** independence of, 3704. *See also* Geographical Index
Senegal River, **Anc:** 386
Senghor, Léopold, **20th:** 3702-3705
Sengoku Jidai. *See* Warring States period (1467-1600, Japan)
Senherib. *See* Sennacherib
Senilium rerum libri. See *Letters of Old Age*
Senlis, Treaty of (1493), **Ren:** 227, 613, 632
Senmut, **Anc:** 388
Sennacherib, **Anc:** 117, 448, 754, 769-771
Sennett, Mack, **20th:** 732, 3706-3708; **Notor:** 32
Sens, Council of (1140), **MA:** 16, 161
Sensationalists, **19th:** 2160
Sense and NonSense (Merleau-Ponty), **20th:** 2711
Sense and Sensibility (Austen), **19th:** 95
Sense of Beauty, The (Santayana), **20th:** 3629
Senso. See *Wanton Contessa, The*
Sent by Earth (Walker), **20th:** 4198
Sentence, The. See *Judgment, The*
Sentences (Lombard), **MA:** 180, 330, 522, 761, 778, 817, 1028
Sententiae. See *Aphormai pros ta noēta*
Sententiarum libri IV. See *Sentences*
Sentimental Education, A (Flaubert), **19th:** 786
Sentimiento trágico de la vida en los hombres y en los pueblos, Del. See *Tragic Sense of Life in Men and Peoples, The*
Separate Amenities Act of 1953, **20th:** 4122
Separatists, **17th:** England, 84; Holland, 122
Sepher ha-Rimmon. See *Book of the Pomegranate, The*
Sepher ha-Zohar. See *Zohar*
Sepoy Mutiny. *See* Mutiny of 1857
Sept Femmes de la Barbe-Bleue et autres contes merveilleux, Les. See *Seven Wives of Bluebeard and Other Marvellous Tales, The*
September 11, 2001, attacks on U.S., **20th:** 372-373, 1948, 3324; economic fallout, 1583; Saudi Arabia, 1197
Septimius Florens Tertullianus, Quintus. *See* Tertullian
Septuagint, **Anc:** 599
Sequoyah, **19th:** 2067-2070
Serampore College, **19th:** 411
Seraph on the Suwanee (Hurston), **20th:** 1945
Seraphim and Other Poems, The (Browning), **19th:** 326
Serapis, **Anc:** 721
Seraw, Mulugeta, **Notor:** 726
Serbia, **MA:** 957; law, 958; princes and czars, 958; **20th:** war with Austria, 1295. *See also* Geographical Index

Serena (niece of Theodosius I the Great), **Anc:** 824
Serenade (ballet), **20th:** 194
Serenity prayer, **20th:** 2963
Serfdom, **Ren:** Hungary, 984; Russia, 387, 490; **17th:** Russia, 12, 664, 784, 944; **18th:** abolition by Joseph II, 545; Russia, 213; **19th:** 45, 50
Serge, Victor, **Notor:** 121
Sgt. Pepper's Lonely Hearts Club Band (Beatles), **20th:** 269
Sergius I (d. 638; patriarch of Constantinople), **MA:** 506, 933-936
Sergius I, Saint (635-701; pope), **MA:** 936-939, 1010
Sergius III (d. 911; pope), **Notor:** 706
Serialism, **20th:** 453, 3873
Serious Proposal to the Ladies, A (Astell), **18th:** 65
Sermon on Death (Bossuet), **17th:** 71
Sermon on Providence (Bossuet), **17th:** 71
Serpent, the. *See* Sobraj, Charles
Serpent Players, **20th:** 1356
Serra, Junípero, **18th:** 891-893. *See also* Gálvez, José de
Serrano, Miguel, **Notor:** 340, 934
Serrano y Dominguez, Francisco, **19th:** 1184
Sert, Misia, **20th:** 2378
Sérusier, Paul, **20th:** 972, 4173
Servetus, Michael, **Ren:** 164, 861-864
Servian Constitution, **Anc:** 848
Service, Robert W., **20th:** 3708-3710
Servile War, Third (73-71 B.C.E.), **Anc:** 194, 681, 818
Servilia (Rimsky-Korsakov), **19th:** 1915
Servius Tullius, **Anc:** 841, 846
Sesostris III, **Anc:** 771-774
Sesshū, **Ren:** 865-867
Sesson Shūkei, **Ren:** 866
Sestra moia zhizn'. See *My Sister, Life*
Set theory, **20th:** 1511
Seth, **Notor:** 545
Seti I, **Anc:** 585, 735
Seton, Saint Elizabeth, **19th:** 2071-2074
Sette giornate del mondo creato, Le. See *Creation of the World*
Sette salmi de la penitenzia di David, I. See *Paraphrase Upon the Seaven Penitentiall Psalmes of the Kingly Prophet*
Settlement, Act of (1652), **17th:** 701
Settlement, Act of (1701), **17th:** 694; **18th:** 47, 137, 359, 400
Seurat, Georges, **19th:** 1800, 2074-2077
Seuss, Dr., **20th:** 3710-3713
Seven Against Thebes. See *Hepta epi Thēbas*
Seven Books of Paulus Aegineta, The. See *Epitome*
Seven Cities of Cíbola, **Ren:** 154
Seven Deadly Sins (Bruegel), **Ren:** 136
Seven Lamps of Architecture, The (Ruskin), **19th:** 1955
Seven Lectures to Young Men (Beecher), **19th:** 173
Seven Pillars of Wisdom (Lawrence), **20th:** 2306
Seven Sacraments (Poussin), **17th:** 750
Seven Sages, **Anc:** 653, 808, 858
Seven Samurai, The (film), **20th:** 2218
Seven Sinners (film), **20th:** 999
Seven Storey Mountain, The (Merton), **20th:** 2714
Seven Summits, **20th:** 2720
Seven Wives of Bluebeard and Other Marvellous Tales, The (France), **19th:** 817
Seven Year Itch, The (film), **20th:** 2798
Seven Years' War (1756-1763), **18th:** 38, 246, 851; Charles III, 227; Frederick the Great, 378; George II, 406; Richard Howe, 507; Louis XV, 616; Maria Theresa, 655; Louis-Joseph de Montcalm, 693; Peter III, 779; William Pitt the Elder, 786; Pontiac, 802; Russia, 322; James Wolfe, 1105
Seven Years' War (Spain, 1833-1840). *See* Carlist Wars
Seventeen Article Constitution (604), **MA:** 940, 976
1793 and 1853, in Three Letters (Cobden), **19th:** 522
Seventh Grade, The (Messner), **20th:** 2719
Seventh Seal, The (film), **20th:** 317
Sever Hall, **19th:** 1906
Severini, Gino, **20th:** 403
Severn River, England, **18th:** commercial waterway, 293; first iron bridge, 1088
Severus, Flavius Valerius, **Anc:** 282
Severus, Lucius Septimius, **Anc:** 424, 481, 483
Sévigné, Madame de, **17th:** 183, 477, 487, 521, 661-662, 829, 833-835
Seviye Talip (Adıvar), **20th:** 30
Şevket Paşa, Mahmud, **20th:** 1157
Sevres, Treaty of (1920), **20th:** 163
Sewa-mono, **18th:** 244
Sewall, Samuel (jurist and theologian), **18th:** 893-896
Sewall, Samuel E. (abolitionist), **19th:** 876
Seward, Anna, **18th:** 897-899
Seward, William H., **19th:** 968, 2077-2080, 2202; **Notor:** 124
Sewing machines, **19th:** 1134
Sex (West), **20th:** 4297
Sex and Temperament in Three Primitive Societies (Mead), **20th:** 2669
Sex and the Single Girl (Brown), **20th:** 540
Sex determination, **20th:** 2825
Sex digte (Grieg), **19th:** 986
Sexby, Edward, **Notor:** 961

Sextet in D Minor (Borodin), **19th:** 281
Sexton, Anne, **20th:** 3713-3716
Sextus Empiricus, **Anc:** 724
Sexual Behavior in the Human Female (Kinsey), **20th:** 2161
Sexual Behavior in the Human Male (Kinsey), **20th:** 2161
Sexual harassment, **20th:** 2522
Sexual Harassment of Working Women (MacKinnon), **20th:** 2522
Sexual Inversion (Ellis), **20th:** 1149
Sexual Politics (Millett), **20th:** 2746
Sexuality, **Anc:** in Greek drama, 92; politics and, 235; **18th:** in art, 1052; in education, 90; Marquis de Sade, 210; same-gender, 251, 301, 1097; **20th:** research, 1149, 2160
Seymour, Sir Edward. *See* Somerset, first duke of
Seymour, Jane, **Ren:** 51, 113, 266, 271, 303, 310, 443, 467, 765, 868-870, 898, 947
Seymour, John, **20th:** 1229
Seymour, Samuel, **19th:** 232
Seymour, Thomas, **Ren:** 304, 310, 765, 899
Seyton, Mary. *See* Braddon, Mary Elizabeth
Seyyid Saʿīd. *See* Saʿīd ibn Sulṭān
SFIO. *See* Section Française de L'Internationale Ouvrière
Sforza, Asanio, **Ren:** 132
Sforza, Bona, **Ren:** 886-887
Sforza, Caterina, **Ren:** 870-871
Sforza, Francesco, **Ren:** 230
Sforza, Gian Galeazzo, **Ren:** 872
Sforza, Giovanni, **Ren:** 118; **Notor:** 129
Sforza, Ludovico, **Ren:** 28, 132, 181, 228, 562, 648, 870, 872-875
Sganarelle (Molière), **17th:** 647
Shabaka, **Anc:** 657
Shabazz, El-Hajj Malik el-. *See* Malcolm X
Shabbetai Tzevi, **17th:** 835-837
Shabbetian movement, **17th:** 837
Shackleton, Ernest, **20th:** 4340
Shadd, Mary Ann. *See* Cary, Mary Ann Shadd
Shadow of a Doubt (film), **20th:** 1827
Shadow of Death, The (Hunt), **19th:** 1158
Shadow of the Night, The (Chapman), **Ren:** 214
Shadowland (Lang), **20th:** 2257
Shadwell, Thomas, **17th:** 384
Shāfiʿī, Abū ʿAbd Allāh ash-, **MA:** 37
Shafites, **MA:** 20
Shaftesbury, first earl of, **17th:** 149, 507, 544, 654, 693, 806, 816, 838-841
Shah Jahan, **17th:** 23, 411, 842-845
Shāh, Nādir. *See* Nādir Shāh
Shah Pahlavi, Mohammad Reza. *See* Mohammad Reza Shah Pahlavi
Shāh Safi I, **17th:** 5
Shāh Sur, **Ren:** 476
Shāh Walī Allāh of Delhi. *See* Walī Allāh, Shāh
Shah Zaman, **19th:** 1858
Shahnamah (Firdusi), **MA:** 375, 685
Shahryar, **17th:** 411, 842
Shaihu ʿUthman dan Fodio. *See* ʿUthman dan Fodio
Shaista Khan, **17th:** 859
Shaka, **19th:** 450, 2081-2083
Shakers, **18th:** 591-594
Shakespear Illustrated (Lennox), **18th:** 595
Shakespeare, William, **Anc:** 663; **Ren:** 93, 535, 876-880; **17th:** 104, 278, 440, 637, 639; **18th:** 399; **Notor:** 147
Shakespeare's Heroines (Jameson), **19th:** 1218
Shakespeare's Sonnets Reconsidered and in Part Rearranged (Butler), **19th:** 375
Shakespearian Equations (Man Ray), **20th:** 2581
Shaklovity, Fyodor, **17th:** 866
Shakur, Assata Olugbala, **Notor:** 940-941
Shall We Dance (film), **20th:** 1463
Shamanism, **Anc:** Chinese, 732; Japanese, 465
Shamela Andrews. See *Apology for the Life of Mrs. Shamela Andrews, An*
Shamkhor, Battle of (1195), **MA:** 998
Shams al-Dīn Muḥammed. *See* Hafiz
Shams al-Dīn of Tabrīz, **MA:** 908
Shams al-Mulk Nasʿr, **MA:** 73
Shang Yang, **Anc:** 380
Shangjun shu (Shang Yang), **Anc:** 380
Shanglin fu (Sima Xinagru), **Anc:** 786
Shangzi. See *Shangjun shu*
Śhaṅkara. *See* Śaṅkara
Shapiro, Jacob Gurrah, **Notor:** 277
Shapiro, Robert, **Notor:** 959
Shāpūr I, **Anc:** 774, 987
Shāpūr II, **Anc:** 774-778
Shaqil. *See* Moussaoui, Zacarias
Sharia (Islamic law), **18th:** 1030
Shariʿa in Songhay (al-Maghīlī), **Ren:** 597
Sharif, Nawaz, **20th:** 366
Sharon, Ariel, **20th:** 113
Sharp, Granville, **18th:** 899-902
Sharp, James, **17th:** 122
Sharp Resolution (1617), **Ren:** 741
Sharpshooter, The (Homer), **19th:** 1123
Shasta daisies, development of, **19th:** 351
Shaw, Anna Howard, **19th:** 2084-2087
Shaw, Artie, **20th:** 1528
Shaw, Clay, **Notor:** 941-943
Shaw, George Bernard, **19th:** 212, 1177-1178; **20th:** 160, 1166, 3716-3721

Shaw, Robert Gould, **19th:** 797
Shawn, Ted, **20th:** 1563, 3595
Shawnees, **19th:** 1048, 2237
Shaybānī Khān. *See* Muḥammad Shaybānī Khān
Shaykhīʿism, **19th:** 105, 2214
Shaykh. *See* Saʿdi
Shays, Daniel, **18th:** 902-905
Shays's Rebellion (1786-1787), **18th:** 413, 902-905, 910
Shchelkunchik. See *Nutcracker, The*
She (Haggard), **19th:** 1007
She and He (Sand), **19th:** 1988
She Came to Stay (Beauvoir), **20th:** 272
She Done Him Wrong (film), **20th:** 4298
She Stoops to Conquer (Goldsmith), **18th:** 432
She-Wolf, The (Pollock), **20th:** 3302
Shea, Frances, **Notor:** 592
Sheaffe, Roger, **19th:** 307
Shearer's Colt, The (Paterson), **19th:** 1758
Sheba, queen of, **Anc:** 805
Shebu ʿUthman dan Fodio. *See* ʿUthman dan Fodio
Sheen, Fulton J., **20th:** 3722-3724
Sheep May Safely Graze (Bach), **18th:** 74
Sheep-Well, The (Lope de Vega), **17th:** 950
Sheeran, Frank, **Notor:** 482
Sheffer, Henry, **20th:** 2264
Shehhi, Marwan Yousef al-, **Notor:** 43
Shehu, Mehmet, **Notor:** 494
Sheikh ʿUmar, **19th:** 187
Shekinah (Holy Spirit), **Anc:** 3
Shela, Battle of (1812), **19th:** 1966
Shelburne, Lord, **18th:** 740
Sheldon, Gilbert, **17th:** 986
Sheldonian Theater, **17th:** 994
Shelley, Mary Wollstonecraft, **18th:** 1110; **19th:** 2088-2091
Shelley, Percy Bysshe, 18th: 426, 1110; **19th:** 381, 1260, 2088, 2092-2097; **Notor:** 193
Shelton, Thomas, **17th:** 729
Shelton with Sunspots, The (O'Keeffe), **20th:** 3032
Shen Buhai, **Anc:** 380
Shen Dao, **Anc:** 380
Shen Yue, **Anc:** 844
Shenandoah (film), **20th:** 3862
Shen-tsung. *See* Shenzong
Shenzong, **MA:** 1079
Shepard, Alan, **20th:** 3725-3728
Shepard, Thomas, **17th:** 395
Shepheardes Calender, The (Spenser), **Ren:** 906
Sheppard, Jack, **Notor:** 943-944, 1103
Sheppard, Sam, **Notor:** 945-947
Sheppard-Towner Maternity and Infancy Act of 1921, **20th:** 2274
Shepsekhaf, **Anc:** 560
Shepstone, Theophilus, **19th:** 450
Shēr Khan Sur, **Ren:** 475
Shēr Shāh. *See* Shēr Khan Sur
Sheridan, Philip, **19th:** 567, 582, 1233
Sheridan, Richard Brinsley, **18th:** 2, 285, 905-907
Sherlock, Jr. (film), **20th:** 2091
Sherman, John, **19th:** 1019
Sherman, Roger, **18th:** 908-911
Sherman, William Tecumseh, **19th:** 960, 2097-2101; Edwin M. Stanton, 2144; **Notor:** 366
Sherman Antitrust Act of 1890, **19th:** 1923
Shermarke, Abdirashid Ali, **20th:** 3734
Sherrington, Charles S., **20th:** 1089
Sherrington, Scott, **20th:** 1260
Sherritt, Aaron, **Notor:** 563
Sheshbazzar, **Anc:** 339
Shevardnadze, Eduard, **20th:** 1601
Shi. *See* Sonni ʿAlī
Shi Huangdi, **Anc:** 779-782; **Notor:** 530, 947-948
Shi Suming, **MA:** 80
Shīʿa Islam, **MA:** 18, 454; **18th:** 640, 722, 1000, 1032; Usuli-Akhbari conflict, 1000. *See also* Sunni Islam
Shibata Katsuie, **Ren:** 738
Shichinin no samurai. See *Seven Samurai, The*
Shield, The. See *Aspis*
Shield of Achilles, The (Auden), **20th:** 173
Shield of the Revolution. *See* Dzerzhinsky, Felix
Shield Society. *See* Tate no Kai
Shigemori, Taira. *See* Taira Shigemori
Shigenobu, Fusako, **Notor:** 949-950
Shih Huang-ti. *See* Shi Huangdi
Shih Ssu-ming. *See* Shi Suming
Shih-tsung. *See* Yongzheng
Shiji (Sima Qian), **Anc:** 149, 379, 552, 782, 785, 960, 978
Shikibu, Murasaki. *See* Murasaki Shikibu
Shikojin. *See* Suzuki Harunobu
Shilāditya. *See* Harṣa
Shiloh, Battle of (1862), **19th:** 960, 2099
Shimazu Nariakira, **19th:** 1969
Shimonoseki, Treaty of (1895), **19th:** 497, 1187, 1252
Shingon Buddhism, **MA:** 620-621
Shining Path. *See* Sendero Luminoso
Shinjū ten no Amijima. See *Love Suicides at Amijima, The*
Shinkankaku-ha, **20th:** 2084
Shintō, **MA:** 623; **19th:** 1187
Ship Money Case, **17th:** 144
Ship of Fools, The (Bosch), **Ren:** 120
Ship of Fools (Porter), **20th:** 3312
Ship of the Line, A (Forester), **20th:** 1284
Shipbuilding, **19th:** 334
Shipman, Harold, **Notor:** 950-951
Shippen, Margaret, **18th:** 42
Shipton, Mother, **Notor:** 952-953
Shirakawa, **MA:** 990

Shiri, Perence, **20th:** 2858
Shirley (Brontë), **19th:** 310
Shirley, James, **17th:** 279, 846-848
Shirley, Jenny, **20th:** 626
Shirley, Myra Maybelle. *See* Starr, Belle
Shiroi hito (Endō), **20th:** 1155
Shirt of Flame, The (Adıvar), **20th:** 31
Shisetsu, **Anc:** 596
Shishigatani affair (1177), **MA:** 991
Shivaji. *See* Śivājī
Shivhei ha-Besht. See *In Praise of the Baʿal Shem Tov*
Shizong. *See* Yongzheng
Shizugatake, Battle of (1583), **Ren:** 738
Shmu'el. *See* Samuel
Shockley, William, **20th:** 234
Shoemaker's Holiday, The (Dekker), **17th:** 223
Shogi. See *Nihon shoki*
Shoin-ji temple, **18th:** 451
Shōjo, **MA:** 772
Shoju Rojin, **18th:** 451
Shokunin zukushi emaki (Moronobu), **17th:** 376
Shōmu, **MA:** 623
Shoot! The Notebooks of Serafino Gubbio, Cinematograph Operator (Pirandello), **20th:** 3260
Shooting of Dan McGrew, The (film), **20th:** 3709
"Shooting of Dan McGrew, The" (poem by Service), **20th:** 3709
Shooting the Russian War (Bourke-White), **20th:** 462
Shootist, The (film), **20th:** 4252
Shop Assistants' Union, **20th:** 415
Shop Hours Act of 1906, **20th:** 415
Short Parliament (1640), **17th:** 55, 145, 768, 838, 886
Short stories, **19th:** Brazil, 1451; England, 1285; France, 1515, 2489; Germany, 1289; Russia, 479, 937; United States, 1083, 1539, 1813
Short View of the Immorality and Profaneness of the English Stage, A (Collier), **18th:** 1003
Shōsetsu, Yui. *See* Yui Shōsetsu
Shoshan Edoth. See *Rose of Testimony, The*
Shoshones, **19th:** 1962
Shostakovich, Dmitri, **20th:** 3728-3731
Shōtoku Taishi, **MA:** 940-942, 975
Shōtoku Tennō. *See* Kōken
Shou-jen. *See* Wang Yangming
Shouren. *See* Wang Yangming
Show Boat (Kern and Hammerstein), **20th:** 1657
Show Your Tongue (Grass), **20th:** 1575
Shōwa Tennō. *See* Hirohito
Showings of Julian of Norwich, The (Julian of Norwich), **MA:** 595
Shrewsbury, Elizabeth. *See* Bess of Hardwick
Shrewsbury, sixth earl of. *See* Talbot, George
Shu Maung. *See* Ne Win
Shu su tie (Mi Fei), **MA:** 719
Shubb, William B., **Notor:** 1093
Shūbun, **Ren:** 865
Shuiskys, **Ren:** 492
Shujah, **17th:** 23, 844
Shukairy, Ahmed, **20th:** 110
Shulgi, **Anc:** 376, 915
Shulḥan arukh. See *Code of Jewish Law*
Shultz, George P., **20th:** 3731-3734
Shumway, Norman E., **20th:** 237
Shun-chih. *See* Shunzhi
Shunga (erotic prints), **18th:** 959
Shunrin Shuto, **Ren:** 865
Shunzhi, **17th:** 3, 234, 448, 848-850
Shusse Kagekiyo (Chikamatsu), **18th:** 245
Shusuan jiancun (Wang), **18th:** 1040
Shuttle, The (Burnett), **19th:** 358
Shuysky, Prince Vasily. *See* Vasily Shuysky
Shwebo, **18th:** 30
Si gira . . . . See *Shoot! The Notebooks of Serafino Gubbio, Cinematograph Operator*
Siad Barre, Muhammad, **20th:** 3734-3736; **Notor:** 953-954
Siam. *See* Thailand
Sibelius, Jean, **20th:** 3736-3739
Siberia, exploration of, **18th:** 108, 776
Sic et Non (Abelard), **MA:** 15
Sicily, **MA:** 390, 391. *See also* Geographical Index
Sick Child, The (Munch), **20th:** 2871
Sickingen, Franz von, **Ren:** 775
Sickle-cell anemia, **20th:** 3156
Sickles, Daniel E., **19th:** 2143
Sickness, Causes, and Treatment. See *Pathos aitia therapeia*
Siddhartha (Hesse), **20th:** 1789
Siddhārtha Gautama. *See* Buddha
Siddons, Sarah, **18th:** 284, 912-914
Sidereal Messenger, The (Galileo), **17th:** 299, 627
Sidereus nuncius. See *Sidereal Messenger, The*
Sidgwick, Henry, **19th:** 2102-2105
Sīdī al-Mukḥtār al-Kuntī, **18th:** 914-916
Sidney, Sir Philip, **Ren:** 881-885
Sieben Geisslein, Die (Humperdinck), **19th:** 1155
Sieber, Al, **Notor:** 27
Sieff, Joseph Edward, **Notor:** 884
Siege of _______. *See* _______, Siege of
Siege of Gibraltar, The (Copley), **18th:** 276
Siege of Numantia, The (Cervantes), **Ren:** 208
Siege of Valencia, The (Hemans), **19th:** 1077
Siegel, Bugsy, **Notor:** 7, 237, 604, 660-661, 709, 954-956

Siegemundin, Justine, **17th:** 851-853
Siegfried (Giraudoux), **20th:** 1493
Siegfried (Wagner), **19th:** 2376
Siegfried et le Limousin. See *My Friend from Limousin*
Siemens, Charles William. *See* Siemens, William
Siemens, Ernest Werner von. *See* Siemens, Werner
Siemens, Friedrich, **19th:** 2105-2108
Siemens, Karl, **19th:** 2105-2108
Siemens, Karl Wilhelm. *See* Siemens, William
Siemens, Werner, **19th:** 2105-2108
Siemens, William, **19th:** 2105-2108
Siemens and Halske, **19th:** 2106
Siemens-Martin process, **19th:** 1301, 2106
Siena, **MA:** 696; art, 326, 567, 696
Sierra Club, **19th:** 1625
Sierra Leone, **18th:** resettlement plan, 900; **19th:** 577
Siete Partidas, Las, **MA:** 60
Sieyès, Emmanuel-Joseph, **18th:** 916-919
Siger of Brabant, **MA:** 43, 942-945, 1028
Sigismund (1368-1437; king of Hungary and Holy Roman Emperor), **MA:** 503, 519, 524, 1089, 1163; **Notor:** 1072
Sigismund (1427-1496; archduke of Austria), **Ren:** 218, 725
Sigismund I, the Old (1467-1548; king of Poland), **Ren:** 885-887, 983
Sigismund II Augustus (1520-1572; king of Poland), **Ren:** 798, 824, 886, 887-889, 910
Sigismund III Vasa (1566-1632; king of Poland), **Ren:** 388, 611; **17th:** 336, 853-856, 945
Siglo del Oro. *See* Golden Age, Spanish
Sign in Sidney Brustein's Window, The (Hansberry), **20th:** 1672
Sign of Four, The (Doyle), **19th:** 688
Sign of Jonas, The (Merton), **20th:** 2714
Sign of the Cross, The (film), **20th:** 961
Signatura Rerum (Böhme), **17th:** 61
Significance of Sections in American History (Turner), **20th:** 4117
Signorini, Francesca. *See* Caccini, Francesca
Signorini, Giovanni Battista, **17th:** 112
Signorini-Malaspina, Francesca. *See* Caccini, Francesca
Signs (Merleau-Ponty), **20th:** 2711
Siguquanshu, **18th:** 818
Sigurd the Volsung (Morris), **19th:** 1607
Sihanouk, Norodom, **20th:** 1942, 3298, 3740-3743; **Notor:** 569, 846
Sikandar Lodī, **Ren:** 478
Sikh Wars (1845-1846, 1848-1849), **19th:** 596, 1328
Sikhism, **Ren:** 478, 707
Sikkak, Battle of (1836), **19th:** 2
Sikwaji. *See* Sequoyah
Silabhadra, **MA:** 1137
Silas Marner (Eliot), **19th:** 741
Silence (Endō), **20th:** 1156
Silence (Saint-Gaudens), **19th:** 1972
Silent Spring (Carson), **20th:** 664
Silent World, The (Cousteau and Dumas), **20th:** 851
Siles Zuazo, Hernán, **20th:** 3172
Silesian invasion (1740), **18th:** 103, 378, 881
Silings, **Anc:** 351
Silius, Gaius, **Anc:** 561
Silk Road, **Anc:** 500, 960; **MA:** 853, 995, 1127, 1137
Silk Stockings (Porter), **20th:** 3309
Silkwood (film), **20th:** 1162
Silla, **Anc:** 466; **MA:** 941, 1081
Sills, Beverly, **20th:** 3744-3746
Silmarillion, The (Tolkien), **20th:** 4039
Siloé, Diego de, **Ren:** 890-892
Silures, **Anc:** 163
Silva, Ana de. *See* Mendoza y de la Cerda, Ana de
Silvana (Weber), **19th:** 2395
Silver Age, The (Heywood), **17th:** 374
Silver Ghost, **20th:** 3496
Silver mining, **18th:** Bolivia, 994; Spain, 228
Silverman, Irene, **Notor:** 584
Silversmiths, **18th:** Hester Bateman, 95-97; Paul Revere, 832
Silvester, Saint, **Anc:** 392
Silvestri Madonna (Jacopo), **MA:** 566
Silvie and Bruno (Carroll), **19th:** 424
Silvie and Bruno Concluded (Carroll), **19th:** 424
Sima Guang, **MA:** 810, 945-947, 1079
Sima Qian, **Anc:** 149, 502, 779, 782-784, 960
Sima Tan, **Anc:** 782, 960
Sima Xiangru, **Anc:** 785-788
Simcoe, John Graves, **18th:** 919-921
Simeon Stylites, Saint, **Anc:** 789-792
Simeon the Elder. *See* Simeon Stylites, Saint
Simeon the Great, **MA:** 106, 191
Simla Agreement (1972), **20th:** 369
Simmons, William Joseph, **Notor:** 957-958
Simnel, Lambert, **Ren:** 439
Simon, George. *See* Lustig, Victor
Simon Wiesenthal Center for Holocaust Studies, **20th:** 4330
Simone Boccanegra (Verdi), **19th:** 2352

Simonides, **Anc:** 793-795
Simons, Menno. *See* Menno Simons
Simonsdochter, Kenau Hasselaer. *See* Kenau Hasselaer
Simony, **MA:** 434, 644
Simple Speaks His Mind (Hughes), **20th:** 1929
Simple Symphony (Britten), **20th:** 530
Simplicianischer zweyköpffiger Ratio Status (Grimmelshausen), **17th:** 325
Simplicissimus (Grimmelshausen), **17th:** 324
Simply Heaven (Hughes), **20th:** 1929
Simpson, James, **19th:** 1392
Simpson, Nicole Brown, **Notor:** 958
Simpson, O. J., **Notor:** 305, 958-961
Simpson, Wallis Warfield, **20th:** 4369
Sin. *See* Taksin
Sin and law, **Anc:** 854
Sin of Madelon Claudet, The (film), **20th:** 1724
Sinai, David. *See* Kahane, Meir
Sinatra, Frank, **20th:** 999, 3747-3749; **Notor:** 340, 661
Sinclair, Harry F., **Notor:** 342
Sinclair, Upton, **20th:** 1130, 3750-3753
Sind (Pakistan), **19th:** 1718
Sindercombe, Miles, **Notor:** 961-962
Sine nomine. See *Book Without a Name*
Sinfonia Espansiva. *See* Symphony No. 3 (Nielsen)
Sinfonietta (Britten), **20th:** 529
Singapore. *See* Geographical Index
Singer, Fred, **20th:** 59
Singer, Isaac M., **19th:** 1135
Singh, Beant, **Notor:** 962-964
Singh, Kehar, **Notor:** 962, 964
Singh, Raja Rampal, **19th:** 213
Singh, Satwant, **Notor:** 962-964
Singin' and Swingin' and Gettin' Merry Like Christmas (Angelou), **20th:** 98
Singin' in the Rain (film), **20th:** 2097
Singular Life Story of Heedless Hopalong, The (Grimmelshausen), **17th:** 325
Sinn der Geschichte, Der. See *Interpretation of History, The*
Sinn Féin, **20th:** 808, 843, 979, 1591, 3026, 3034
Sinn und Wert des Lebens, Der. See *Meaning and Value of Life, The*
"Sinners in the Hands of an Angry God" (Edwards), **18th:** 314
Sinngedichte (Strauss), **19th:** 2188
Sino-French War (1883-1885), **19th:** 1365, 2486
Sino-Japanese War (1894-1895), **19th:** 497, 1187, 1365, 1632, 2487
Sino-Japanese War (1937-1945), **20th:** 748, 2381, 2602, 3191, 4221, 4463
Sino-Pakistan Boundary Agreement (1963), **20th:** 368
Sins of Government, Sins of the Nation (Barbauld), **18th:** 88
Sinsã, **Anc:** 595
Sioux peoples, **19th:** Lakota, 442, 566, 583, 1794, 1871, 2108; Oglala, 567
Sioux War (1876-1877), **19th:** 1873
Siqueiros, David, **20th:** 3069, 3457
Sir Charles Grandison (Richardson), **18th:** 842
Sir Christopher Sykes and Lady Sykes (Romney), **18th:** 864
Sir Courtly Nice (Oldfield), **18th:** 749
Sir Fantasy. See *Zixu fu*
Sir Matthew Smith (John), **20th:** 2016
Siraj. See *Illumination, The*
Sirani, Elisabetta, **17th:** 856-858
Sīrat al-faylasūf. See *Philosopher's Way of Life, The*
Sirhan, Sirhan, **Notor:** 965-967
Sirica, John, **Notor:** 672, 738
Siricius, Saint, **Anc:** 796-798
Sirk, Douglas, **Notor:** 1069
Sirtori, Girolamo, **17th:** 537
Sirturus, Hieronymus. *See* Sirtori, Girolamo
Sisera, **Anc:** 259
Sisk, Mildred Elizabeth. *See* Gillars, Mildred
Sisley, Alfred, **19th:** 1800, 1888
Sister Aimee. *See* McPherson, Aimee Semple
Sister Carrie (Dreiser), **20th:** 1033
Sisters of Charity (Jameson), **19th:** 1218
Sisters of Charity of St. Joseph, **19th:** 2072
Sisters of the Common Life, **MA:** 1023
Sistine Chapel, **Ren:** 520, 683; Michelangelo on, 684
Sistine Madonna (Raphael), **Ren:** 821
Sītā, **Anc:** 923
Sita (Millett), **20th:** 2748
Sithole, Ndabaningi, **20th:** 2858; **Notor:** 761
Sitio de Breda, El (Calderón), **17th:** 113
Sitte, Die. See *Custom*
Sitter, Willem de, **20th:** 2338
Sitting Bull, **19th:** 525, 1692, 2108-2111; **Notor:** 249
Situations (Sartre), **20th:** 3640
Sitwell, Edith, **20th:** 4217
Sitwell, Osbert, **20th:** 4217
Śiva, **Anc:** 496
Śivājī, **17th:** 25, 858-861
Sivocci, Ugo, **20th:** 1239
Siwayi. *See* Sequoyah
Six, Les, **20th:** 2736, 3318, 3643
Six Anatomical Tables (Vesalius), **Ren:** 966
Six Articles, Act of (1539), **Ren:** 62, 257, 267, 369, 443, 544, 835

Six Characters in Search of an Author (Pirandello), **20th:** 3261
Six-Day War (1967), **20th:** 153, 931, 1083, 1952, 2677, 2916, 3359; Palestine Liberation Organization, 110
Six Edicts (France), **18th:** 997
Six Perfections. *See* Pāramitās
Six Pièces (Franck), **19th:** 822
Six Years Later (Dumas), **19th:** 697
Sixteenth Street Baptist Church bombing (1963), **20th:** 2149
Sixtus IV, **Ren:** 518, 657, 893-895, 940
Sixtus V, **Ren:** 895-897; **Notor:** 214
Sixty Million Jobs (Wallace), **20th:** 4208
Siyaad Barre, Maxamed. *See* Siad Barre, Muhammad
Siyāsat-nāma. See *Book of Government, The*
Sizwe Bansi Is Dead (Fugard), **20th:** 1355
Sjálfstœtt folk. See *Independent People*
Sjunde inseglet, Det. See *Seventh Seal, The*
Skanderbeg, **Ren:** 659
Skater, The (Stuart), **18th:** 948
Skazaniye o nevidimom grade kitezhe i deve Fevroniy. See *Legend of the Invisible City of Kitezh and the Maid Fevronia, The*
Skazka (Rimsky-Korsakov), **19th:** 1915
Skazka o tsare Saltane. See *Tale of Tsar Saltan, The*
Skazka o zolotom petushke. See *Tale of the Golden Cockerel, The*
Skazki Melpomeny. See *Tales of Melpomene*
Skelton, John, **Ren:** 441
Skepticism, **Anc:** 349, 723
Sketch Book of Geoffrey Crayon, Gent., The (Irving), **19th:** 1180
Sketch for a Historical Picture of the Progress of the Human Mind (Condorcet), **18th:** 268
Sketchbook 1966-1971 (Frisch), **20th:** 1339
Sketches and Eccentricities of Colonel David Crockett of West Tennessee, **19th:** 573
Sketches Awheel in Modern Iberia (Workman and Workman), **19th:** 2467
Sketches by Boz (Dickens), **19th:** 655
Sketches from Life (Chen), **17th:** 156
Sketches of American Character (Hale), **19th:** 1013
Sketches of American Policy (Webster), **19th:** 2403
Sketches of Canada and the United States (Mackenzie), **19th:** 1457
Ski-be-nan-ted. *See* Apache Kid
Skiing, **20th:** 2132
Skilling, Jeffrey, **Notor:** 618, 967-969
Skinner, B. F., **20th:** 3754-3758
Skinner, John S., **19th:** 1275
Skinner v. Oklahoma (Douglas), **20th:** 1031
Skirmish in the Wilderness, A (Homer), **19th:** 1123
Skopin-Shuysky, Mikhail, **17th:** 944
Skorzeny, Otto, **Notor:** 969-970
Skryabin, Vyacheslav Mikhailovich. *See* Molotov, Vyacheslav Mikhailovich
Sky Above Clouds II (O'Keeffe), **20th:** 3033
Sky Cathedral (Nevelson), **20th:** 2949
Skyloft Players, **20th:** 1929
Skyscrapers, **19th:** 2199
Skywalker Ranch, **20th:** 2452
Slater, Samuel, **19th:** 2111-2114
Slåtter (Grieg), **19th:** 986
Slaughter of the Innocents, The (Marini), **17th:** 202
Slaughterhouse cases, **19th:** 473
Slave rebellions, **18th:** 724, 855, 985; **19th:** 876
Slave trade, **18th:** abolition of, 900, 1079; of children, 279; Charles James Fox, 366; **19th:** Africa, 577, 1400, 1474, 1967, 2140, 2277; Britain, 979; Sir Thomas Fowell Buxton, 378; Stephen A. Douglas, 2164; Supreme Court, 2181; Martin van Buren on, 2345. *See also* Slavery
Slavers Throwing Overboard the Dead and Dying (Turner), **19th:** 2324
Slavery, **Anc:** Babylonian, 582; Chinese, 959; Germanic, 351; Greek, 11, 15, 70, 284, 308, 616, 808; Roman, 358, 485, 628, 664, 818, 849, 942; **MA:** 479; Africa, 978; Arabs, 587; Aztecs, 559; Central Asia, 139; Mongols, 1108; Slavs and Finns, 912; **Ren:** Algiers, 207; Brazil, 514; Caribbean, 804; Kongo, 10; of Native Americans, 538; slaving voyages, 292; Spain, 239; **17th:** Native Americans, 468, 635; Portugal, 687, 960; Spanish colonies, 152; Ukraine, 428; Virginia, 31; **18th:** abolition of, 920; economics, 830; English law, 645, 900; enslavers as non-Christians, 1071; Georgia, 744; Jamaica, 724; and poetry, 1070-1073; and U.S. Constitution, 706; West Indies, 126; **19th:** abolition in England, 2447; John Quincy Adams, 24; American Colonization Society, 1501; Henry Ward Beecher, 173; Brazilian opposition to, 1766, 1870; British opposition to, 312, 574, 643, 979; Aaron Burr, 364; Christianity and, 401; Henry Clay, 503; Colombia, 269; Jefferson Davis, 611;

expansion into U.S. territories, 194, 682, 782, 2078, 2164, 2181; John C. Frémont, 833; French opposition to, 2063; James A. Garfield, 869; Horace Greeley, 968; lawsuits regarding, 2042; Abraham Lincoln, 1382; literary depictions of, 702, 2184; personal experience of, 684, 2306, 2313; revolts, 2326; support for, 394, 580, 850, 1790; U.S. Civil War, 2172; U.S. opposition to, 66, 341, 577, 796, 1268, 2201, 2226, 2470; U.S. Supreme Court, 2227; Zanzibar, 1966, 2278; **20th:** Ethiopia, 1639; Saudi Arabia, 1200
Slavery (Channing), **19th:** 1268
Slavery Abolition Act (1833), **18th:** 1081
Slavonic Dances (Dvořák), **19th:** 712
Slavs, **MA:** 474, 806; Christianity, 296
Sleeping Beauty, The (ballet), **20th:** 1268
Sleeping Gypsy, The (Rousseau), **19th:** 1953
Sleeping Murder (Christie), **20th:** 766
Sleepless in Seattle (film), **20th:** 1163
Sleuth (film), **20th:** 3043
Slim, first Viscount, **20th:** 3758-3761
Sloan, David, **20th:** 2301
Sloane, Sir Hans, **17th:** 447
Slocum, Cuffe. *See* Cuffe, Paul
Sloughter, Henry, **17th:** 519
Slovakia. *See* Geographical Index under Czech Republic and Slovakia
Slovenia. *See* Geographical Index
Slums and Suburbs (Conant), **20th:** 823
Sluter, Claus, **MA:** 947-950
Sluys, Battle of (1340), **MA:** 351
Small, Albion, **20th:** 23
Smallpox, **Ren:** Americas and, 66, 254, 471, 771; **17th:** and Native Americans, 130, 423, 876, 908; **18th:** Edward Jenner, 533; Mary Wortley Montagu, 688
Smart, Gregory William, **Notor:** 971
Smart, Pamela Ann, **Notor:** 971-972
Smeaton, John, **19th:** 1325
Smenkhare, **Anc:** 28, 588, 902, 908
Smerdis, **Anc:** 136, 251
Smert' Ivana Il'icha. See *Death of Ivan Ilyich, The*
Smith, Adam, **18th:** 921-925
Smith, Alfred E., **20th:** 3762-3765; **Notor:** 99
Smith, Barbara Leigh. *See* Bodichon, Barbara Leigh Smith
Smith, Benjamin, **Notor:** 444
Smith, Bessie, **20th:** 131, 3765-3768
Smith, Clyde H., **20th:** 3768
Smith, David, **Notor:** 977
Smith, Emma, **19th:** 2476
Smith, F. O. J. "Fog," **19th:** 1611
Smith, Gerald L. K., **Notor:** 973-975
Smith, Gerrit, **19th:** 319, 2146
Smith, Horace, **19th:** 1260
Smith, Ian, **20th:** 2858; **Notor:** 761
Smith, Jedediah, **19th:** 2114-2117
Smith, John, **17th:** 391, 702, 745, 753, 861-865, 875
Smith, Joseph, **19th:** 2117-2121, 2475; **Notor:** 664
Smith, Madeleine, **Notor:** 975-976
Smith, Margaret Chase, **20th:** 3768-3772
Smith, Roger, **20th:** 3210, 4064
Smith, Susan, **Notor:** 977-978
Smith, Theobald, **20th:** 3772-3775
Smith, William Robertson, **20th:** 1319
Smith Act of 1940, **20th:** 1867
Smithers, Leonard, **19th:** 163
Smithsonian Astrophysical Observatory, **19th:** 1310
Smithsonian Institution, **19th:** 1080; natural history, 32
Smock Alley Theatre, **18th:** 397, 1102
Smoke (Turgenev), **19th:** 2320
Smoke Abatement Exhibition, **19th:** 1105
Smoke People. *See* Bad Faces
Smulltronstället. See *Wild Strawberries*
Smutnoe Vremya. *See* Time of Troubles
Smuts, Jan Christian, **20th:** 440, 3775-3778
Smythe, George, **19th:** 667
Smythe, Maria Anne. *See* Fitzherbert, Maria Anne
SNCC. *See* Student Nonviolent Coordinating Committee
Snegurochka. See *Snow Maiden, The*
Snodgrass, W. D., **20th:** 3714
Snorra Edda. See *Prose Edda, The*
Snorri Sturluson, **MA:** 950-954
Snow-Bound (Whittier), **19th:** 2431
Snow Country (Kawabata), **20th:** 2085
Snow Maiden, The (Rimsky-Korsakov), **19th:** 1915
Snow Storm (Turner), **19th:** 2323
Snow White and the Seven Dwarfs (animated film), **20th:** 1008
Snowman, the. *See* Lee, Daulton
Snyder, Albert, **Notor:** 979
Snyder, Gary, **20th:** 2114
Snyder, Ruth, **Notor:** 979-980
Soares Filho, Oscar Niemeyer. *See* Niemeyer, Oscar
Sobell, Morton, **Notor:** 915
Sobieski, Jan. *See* John III Sobieski
Sobornoye Ulozheniye (1649), **17th:** 12, 664
Sobraj, Charles, **Notor:** 980-981
Soccer, **20th:** 3187-3188

Social classes. *See* Class structure
Social criticism, **18th:** Claude-Adrien Helvétius, 481; Jean-Jacques Rousseau, 869; Samuel Sewall, 893-896; Jonathan Swift, 964-967; Voltaire, 1026-1029; Mary Wollstonecraft, 1109
Social Darwinism, **19th:** 1478, 2128
Social Democratic Federation, **19th:** 212
Social Democratic Party (Germany), **19th:** 1323, 1370; **20th:** 334, 490, 4456
Social Destiny of Man, The (Fourier), **19th:** 805
Social evolution, **18th:** 338
Social Insurance and Allied Services (Beveridge), **20th:** 354
Social realism, **20th:** 1551, 2660, 3302
Social reform, **18th:** China, 1114; England, 703; Paul-Henri-Dietrich d'Holbach, 503; Joseph II, 544; Jean-Paul Marat, 648; Russia, 776; Louis de Saint-Just, 877; Granville Sharp, 899-902; William Wilberforce, 1079-1082; John Wilkes, 1083-1086. *See also* Peasantry; Poverty and the poor; Category Index
Social Science (Fourier), **19th:** 805
Social Security Act of 1935, **20th:** 655, 3200, 3511
Social Statics (Spencer), **19th:** 2127
Social Teaching of the Christian Churches, The (Troeltsch), **20th:** 4070
Social War (356 B.C.E.), **Anc:** 546
Social War (91-87 B.C.E.), **Anc:** 535, 681, 896
Socialism, **18th:** William Godwin, 425; Jean-Paul Marat, 650; Françoise Quesnay, 821; **19th:** 1608; France, 1976, 2298; Germany, 1323, 1370; international, 1026; labor, 944; Russia, 1086; syndicalism, 1220; United States, 2158; **20th:** Africa, 4055; Chile, 70; Christian, 3383; France, 3792; Germany, 490; guild, 2269; reformist, 335, 397, 2482; Russia, 1551; Somalia, 3734; United States, 3750; women, 4456
Socialism (Engels), **19th:** 751
Socialisme du possible, Un (Mitterrand), **20th:** 2771
Socialist League, **19th:** 1608
Socialist parties, **20th:** Belgium, 3808; France, 2770; United States, 934, 4003
Société Anonyme des Engrenages Citroën, **20th:** 772
Société de 1789, **19th:** 705
Société des Amis de la Constitution et de l'Égalité, **19th:** 396
Society and Solitude (Emerson), **19th:** 748
Society for Free Psychoanalysis, **20th:** 33
Society for Psychical Research, **19th:** 2103
Society for the Abolition of Slavery (England), **18th:** 325, 900
Society for the Concession of Women's Rights, **19th:** 89
Society for the Extinction of the Slave Trade and the Civilisation of Africa, **19th:** 378
Society for the Propagation of the Gospel in New England and Parts Adjacent in North America, **17th:** 248
Society for the Protection of Ancient Buildings, **19th:** 2046
Society for the Reformation of Prison Discipline, **19th:** 377
Society for the Supporters of the Bill of Rights (England), **18th:** 1084
Society for the Suppression of Vice (England), **18th:** 1080
Society in America (Martineau), **19th:** 1506
Society of American Artists, **19th:** 1973
Society of Antiquaries (London), **18th:** 952
Society of Arcueil, **19th:** 886
Society of Artists (London), **18th:** 388, 862, 1068
Society of Arts and Manufactures (England), **18th:** 560
Society of Believers in Christ's Second Coming, United. *See* United Society of Believers in Christ's Second Coming
Society of Friends. *See* Quakers and Quakerism
Society of Friendship, **17th:** 741
Society of Gentlemen and Ladies of Nôtre-Dame of Montreal, **17th:** 575
Society of God Worshipers, **19th:** 1128
Society of Jesus. *See* Jesuits
Society of Roman Knights, **18th:** 952
Society of the Gaels. *See* Cumann na nGaedheal
Society of United Irishmen, **18th:** 357, 983
Socinus, Faustus, **17th:** 54
Sociobiology (Wilson), **20th:** 4359
Sociology, **19th:** England, 1506; founding of discipline, 2385; **20th:** establishment of discipline, 1066; Germany, 3657, 4045; Great Britain, 1843. *See also* Condorcet, marquis de; Ferguson, Adam; Smith, Adam; Vico, Giambattista; Category Index under Anthropology and Sociology
Socrate (Satie), **20th:** 3643
Socrates, Anc: 12, 33, 53, 69, 87, 91, 128, 238, 262, 524, 609, 659, 799-802, 962, 968, 981; **Notor:** 11, 13

Socrates Scholasticus, **Anc:** 434
Socratic method, **Anc:** 801
Soda production, **18th:** 587
Soddy, Frederick, **20th:** 3778-3780
Söderblom, Nathan, **20th:** 3781-3783
Soderini, Piero, **Ren:** 587
Sodom, **Anc:** 4
Soeharto, Haji Mohammad. *See* Suharto
Sofya Alekseyevna. *See* Sophia
Soga clan, **MA:** 940, 975
Soga Umako, **MA:** 940, 975
Sogwili. *See* Sequoyah
Soirées de Médan, Les, **19th:** 2490
Soissons, Battle of (719), **MA:** 251
Soissons, Council of (1201), **MA:** 1059
Sōjun. *See* Ikkyū
Soka Gakkai, **MA:** 760
Sokoto caliphate, **19th:** 2343
Sokoto sultanate, **19th:** 187
Sol Invictus, **Anc:** 240
Solanas, Valerie, **Notor:** 982-983
Solatium fidelis animae (Neckam), **MA:** 752
Soldier Saddling His Horse (Toulouse-Lautrec), **19th:** 2287
Soldier's Friend, The (Cobbett), **19th:** 517
Soldier's Legacy, A (Böll), **20th:** 413
Soldier's Tale, The (Stravinsky), **20th:** 3889
Soldiers Three (Kipling), **19th:** 1285
Soledades. See *Solitudes of Don Luis de Góngora, The*
Soleil des eaux, Les (Boulez), **20th:** 453
Soleil d'Or, **Ren:** 413
Solemn League and Covenant (1643), **17th:** 205, 941, 988
Solferino, Battle of (1859), **19th:** 699, 819
Solidarity, **20th:** 4191
Solitary Thoughts (Makuzu), **19th:** 2213
Solitudes of Don Luis de Góngora, The (Góngora), **17th:** 312
Sollertinsky, Ivan Ivanovich, **20th:** 191
Solmization, **MA:** 440
Solomon, **Anc:** 155, 256, 803-806
Solomon, Betty Jeanne, **Notor:** 1090
Solomon, Kristan, **Notor:** 1090
Solomon, Paul, **Notor:** 1090
Solomon Gursky Was Here (Richler), **20th:** 3438
Solomon Luria, Isaac ben. *See* Luria, Isaac ben Solomon
Solomon R. Guggenheim Museum, **20th:** 4402
Solomons, Ikey, Jr. *See* Thackeray, William Makepeace
Solon, **Anc:** 221, 245, 294, 649, 807-809, 876
Soltān Moḥammad Shāh, **17th:** 4
Solway Moss, Battle of (1542), **Ren:** 502, 627, 634
Solzhenitsyn, Aleksandr, **20th:** 524, 2469, 3783-3788
Somalia, **20th:** establishment of, 3734; revolution (1986-1992), 3735. *See also* Geographical Index
Somaliland, exploration of, **19th:** 2124
Some Account of Gothic Architecture in Spain (Street), **19th:** 2193
Some Considerations of the Consequences of Lowering of Interest, and Raising the Value of Money (Locke), **17th:** 546
Some Like It Hot (film), **20th:** 2799
Some Main Problems of Philosophy (Moore), **20th:** 2816
Some Prefer Nettles (Tanizaki), **20th:** 3944
Some Thoughts Concerning Education (Locke), **17th:** 546; **18th:** 732
Somerset, earl of. *See* Carr, Robert
Somerset, first duke of (Edward Seymour), **Ren:** 304, 399, 639, 898-900
Somerset Masque, The (Campion), **17th:** 128
Somersett, James, **18th:** 900
Somersett case (1771), **18th:** 645, 900
Somerville, Mary, **19th:** 1421, 2121-2123
Something of Myself (Kipling), **19th:** 1287
Something's Got to Give (film), **20th:** 2799
Sommer, Edith, **Notor:** 510
Sommerfeld, Arnold, **20th:** 3152
Sommers, Ann. *See* Restell, Madame
Sommershausen, Battle of (1648), **17th:** 933
Somnium (Buchanan), **Ren:** 146
Somoza Debayle, Anastasio, **20th:** 3072; **Notor:** 985
Somoza Debayle, Luis, **Notor:** 985
Somoza García, Anastasio, **Notor:** 984-985
Sŏn Buddhism, **MA:** 1083
Son-Jara. *See* Sundiata
Son of Sam. *See* Berkowitz, David
Son Sen, **20th:** 3300
Sonata for Violin and Piano (Poulenc), **20th:** 3319
Sonata for Violoncello and Piano (Barber), **20th:** 231
Sonata in A Major for Violin and Piano (Franck), **19th:** 823
Sonata in B Minor (Liszt), **19th:** 1395
Sonata in C Minor (Borodin), **19th:** 281
Sonata in F Minor, Op. 5 (Brahms), **19th:** 296
Sonata in Three Movements for Violin and Piano (Zwilich), **20th:** 4476

Sonatina (Ravel), **20th:** 3386
Sonette an Orpheus, Die. See *Sonnets to Orpheus*
Sonetti lussuriosi. See *Sonnets, The*
Sonezaki shinjū. See *Love Suicides at Sonezaki, The*
Song Dynasty, **MA:** 403, 718, 808, 968, 990, 1079; Mongol invasion of, 626, 956; rulers, 1080, 1146; **18th:** 248
Song of Hiawatha, The (Longfellow), **19th:** 1417
Song of Los, The (Blake), **18th:** 123
Song of Love, The (Chirico), **20th:** 2548
Song of Roland, **MA:** 243, 395, 1061
Song of Solomon (Morrison), **20th:** 2836
Song of Songs of Solomon, The (Guyon), **17th:** 340
Song of the Earth, The (Mahler), **20th:** 2561
Song of the High Hills, A (Delius), **20th:** 955
Song of the Lark, The (Cather), **20th:** 698
Song of the South (film), **20th:** 1008
Song of the Stone Wall, The (Keller), **20th:** 2093
Songe. See *Visions of Bellay*
Songe de Vaux, Le (La Fontaine), **17th:** 481
Songennante Böse, Das. See *On Aggression*
Songhai Empire, **MA:** 745; **Ren:** 64, 556, 597, 686, 900
Songs (García Lorca), **20th:** 1396
Songs and Dances of Death (Mussorgsky), **19th:** 1628
Songs and Sonnets in *Poems, by J. D.* (Donne), **17th:** 231
Songs for Young Lovers (Sinatra), **20th:** 3748
Songs of a Semite (Lazarus), **19th:** 1332
Songs of a Sourdough (Service), **20th:** 3709
Songs of a Wayfarer (Mahler), **20th:** 2559
Songs of Innocence and Experience (Blake), **18th:** 122
Songs of Sundrie Natures (Byrd), **Ren:** 149
Songs of Sunset (Delius), **20th:** 955
Songs of the Affections (Hemans), **19th:** 1077
Soninke dispersion, **MA:** 978
Sonnets, The (Aretino), **Ren:** 54
Sonnets for Helen (Ronsard), **Ren:** 838
Sonnets from the Portuguese (Browning), **19th:** 326
Sonnets to Duse, and Other Poems (Teasdale), **20th:** 3960
Sonnets to Orpheus (Rilke), **20th:** 3455
Sonni ʿAlī, **Ren:** 597, 686, 900-902
Sonntag, William. *See* Sunday, Billy
Sonora, marqués de la. *See* Gálvez, José de
Sons (Buck), **20th:** 558
Sons and Lovers (Lawrence), **20th:** 2296
Sons of Ben, **17th:** 846. *See also* Tribe of Ben
Sons of Liberty, **18th:** 237, 458, 520, 832
Sontag, Susan, **20th:** 3452, 3788-3791
Sony Corporation, **20th:** 2832
Soper, George, **Notor:** 685
Sophia (regent of Russia), **17th:** 445, 624, 865-867
Sophie of Bavaria, **19th:** 818
Sophism, **Anc:** 68, 88, 262, 274, 326, 633; Chinese, 577; Plato versus, 661; Protagoras and, 707
Sophismata (Buridan), **MA:** 216
Sophistēs (Plato), **Anc:** 985
Sophistic, Second, **Anc:** 514
"Sophisticated Lady" (Ellington), **20th:** 1146
Sophocles, **Anc:** 9, 326, 809-812, 877
Sophonisba of Numidia, **Anc:** 542, 812-815
Sophronius (c. 347-420). *See* Jerome, Saint
Sophronius (560-638; patriarch of Jerusalem), **MA:** 935
Sopron, Treaty of (1463), **Ren:** 351
Sor Juana. *See* Cruz, Sor Juana Inés de la
Sorel, Agnès, **Ren:** 226
Sorel, Georges, **20th:** 3792-3794; **Notor:** 769
Sörgemarsch over Rikard Nordraak (Grieg), **19th:** 986
Sorghaghtani Beki, **MA:** 954-956
Sōrinshi. *See* Chikamatsu Monzaemon
Sorkaktani. *See* Sorghaghtani Beki
Soros, George, **20th:** 3795-3797
Sorrows. See *Tristia*
Sorrows and Rejoicings (Fugard), **20th:** 1357
Sorrows of War (Orozco), **20th:** 3069
Sorrows of Young Werther, The (Goethe), **18th:** 429, 577
Sorsky, Nil, **Ren:** 490
Sort of Life, A (Greene), **20th:** 1577
Sortes Vergilianae, **Anc:** 940
Sosigenes, **Anc:** 174, 815-818
Sospetto d'Herode. See *Suspicion of Herod, The*
Sōtatsu, **17th:** 695, 868-870
Sotelo, Calvo, **20th:** 1297
Soto, Hernando de, **Ren:** 245, 902-905, 922
Soto-Mayor, Alonzo de, **Ren:** 84
Sotomayor, Cristóbal de, **Ren:** 804
Soul, **Anc:** body and, 688; Logos and, 398; philosophy and, 800
Soul and Form (Lukács), **20th:** 2468

Soul of a Butterfly, The (Ali), **20th:** 64
Soules Humiliation, The (Hooker), **17th:** 387
Soules Possession of Christ, The (Hooker), **17th:** 387
Soules Preparation for Christ, The (Hooker), **17th:** 386
Souls of Black Folk, The (Du Bois), **20th:** 1047
Sound and the Fury, The (Faulkner), **20th:** 1223
Sound of Music, The (Rodgers and Hammerstein), **20th:** 1659
Soundiata. *See* Sundiata
Soupault, Philippe, **20th:** 510
Source, La (Delibes), **19th:** 639
Source, The (Michener), **20th:** 2729
Souris, la mouche et l'homme, La. See *Of Flies, Mice, and Men*
Sousa, John Philip, **20th:** 3798-3801
Sousa, Tomé de, **Ren:** 514
Sousa's Grand Concert Band, **20th:** 3798
Souter, David H., **20th:** 3802-3803
South Africa, **19th:** British Empire, 462; diamonds, 462, 1892; Great Britain, 982. *See also* Geographical Index
South African Council of Churches, **20th:** 4122
South African Republic, **19th:** 1298
South African War (1899-1902). *See* Boer Wars
South Australia Association, **19th:** 2379
South Carolina Railroad Company, **19th:** 850
South Korea. *See* Korea; Geographical Index under Korea
South Pacific (Rodgers, Hammerstein, and Logan), **20th:** 1658, 3487
South Pacific exploration, **18th:** 151
South Pole, **20th:** expeditions to, 1805, 2720; flight over, 607
South Sea Bubble, **18th:** 939, 1035
South Sea Company, **18th:** slave trade monopoly, 136; Tories, 137
South Vietnam, **20th:** establishment of, 229, 2951. *See also* Geographical Index under Vietnam
Southeil, Ursula. *See* Shipton, Mother
Southern Christian Leadership Conference, **20th:** 12, 2148
Southern Justice (Rockwell), **20th:** 3484
Southern Pacific Corporation, **19th:** 2134
Southern Song Dynasty, **MA:** 1134, 1145; Mongol invasion of, 677. *See also* Song Dynasty
Southey, Robert, **18th:** 898; **19th:** 381, 617, 2242, 2462
Southwold Bay, Battle of (1672), **17th:** 417
Souvenir de Solferino, Un. See *Memory of Solferino, A*
Souvenirs de Alexis de Tocqueville. See *Recollections of Alexis de Tocqueville, The*
Souvenirs d'égotisme. See *Memoirs of an Egotist*
Souvenirs d'enfance et de jeunesse. See *Recollections of My Youth*
Souvré, Madeleine de. *See* Sablé, marquise de
Soveraignty and Goodness of God, The (Rowlandson), **17th:** 799-800
Soviet-Afghan War (1979-1989), **20th:** 4474
Soviet Communism (Webbs), **20th:** 4256
Soviet Union, **20th:** breakup of, 1532, 4433; U.S. relations with, 667, 1922. *See also* Geographical Index
Soyinka, Wole, **20th:** 3804-3807
Soyuz program, **20th:** 1372
Sozialdemokratische Partei Deutschlands. *See* Social Democratic Party (Germany)
Sozialismus und seine Lebensgestaltung, Der (Eucken), **20th:** 1187
Soziallehren der christlichen Kirchen und Gruppen, Die. See *Social Teaching of the Christian Churches, The*
Sozialreform oder Revolution? See *Reform or Revolution?*
Sozzini, Fausto Paolo. *See* Socinus, Faustus
Spaak, Paul-Henri, **20th:** 3808-3811
Space exploration, **20th:** Canada, 1412; *Challenger* explosion, 137; Germany, 3009; piloted flights, 1500; Soviet Union, 1371, 2193, 3979; United States, 4140. *See also* Aviation; Category Index under Aviation and Space Exploration
Spadafora, Hugo, **Notor:** 798
Spain, **Anc:** 374; **MA:** Almoravid invasion of, 280; art, 60; Castilian kings, 61; Christianity, 10, 555; education, 11, 555; Jews, 157, 533, 573, 591, 604, 686, 730, 747, 883; kings of Aragon, 573; law, 60, 556, 572; medicine, 99; Muslims, 33, 119, 380, 1006; North African invasion of, 60; philosophy, 533; poetry, 532, 591; theology, 882; trade, 11, 60; Umayyad caliphs, 10; **18th:** Charles III's reform, 227; Italian ministers, 227; in North America, 228; in South America, 228; trade reform, 228; **20th:** Andalusian music, 1207. *See also* Geographical Index
Spain (Auden), **20th:** 172
Spallanzani, Lazzaro, **18th:** 925-928

Spangler, Edward, **Notor:** 1013
Spanish-American Indian alliance, **18th:** 627
Spanish-American relations, **18th:** 227, 524, 627
Spanish-American War (1898), **19th:** 147; George Dewey, 646; John Hay, 1055; William McKinley, 1462; **20th:** 1736, 2419
Spanish Armada (1587-1588), **Ren:** 201, 293, 311, 322, 354, 397, 420, 554, 669, 780, 813, 844, 897, 942
Spanish-British conflicts, **18th:** 626, 1036; West Indies, 986
Spanish Civil War (1936-1939), **20th:** 1297, 2578, 4004, 4270; France, 398; Great Britain, 1101
Spanish-French alliance, **18th:** 227
Spanish Gypsy, The (Eliot), **19th:** 741
Spanish Navarre, conquest of, **Ren:** 330
Spanish Revolution of 1820-1823, **19th:** 404, 412
Spanish Revolution of 1868, **19th:** 557, 1184
Spanish Singer, The (Manet), **19th:** 1480
Spanish Succession, War of the (1701-1714), **17th:** 152, 265, 402, 555, 602, 946, 980; **18th:** 135, 141, 230, 331, 376, 661, 781
Spann, Otis, **20th:** 4240
Sparks, Chauncey, **20th:** 4203
Sparre, Ebba, **17th:** 164
Sparta, **Anc:** Alexander the Great and, 39; Antisthenes' admiration of, 69; Argos and, 227; Athens and, 33, 215, 226, 621, 631, 859, 882, 969; Macedonia and, 637; Persia and, 507; Thebes and, 227, 304
Spartacus, **Anc:** 194, 681, 818-821
Spartacus League, **20th:** 2484
SPD. *See* Social Democratic Party (Germany)
Speak, Memory (Nabokov), **20th:** 2895
Speaker, Tris, **20th:** 792
Spear, A. T., **Notor:** 194
Spear Bearer. See *Doryphorus*
Specie Circular, **19th:** 193
Species plantarum (Linnaeus), **18th:** 606
Specificity of Serological Reactions, The (Landsteiner), **20th:** 2251
Specimen Days and Collect (Whitman), **19th:** 2426
Specimen of Elements of Myology (Steno), **17th:** 881
Specimen of Some Observations Made by a Microscope, A (Leeuwenhoek), **17th:** 510
Speck, Richard, **Notor:** 986-987
Spectator, The (Addison and Steele), **18th:** 21, 942
Specter, Arlen, **Notor:** 325
Specter of a Rose (ballet), **20th:** 2975
Spectre's Bride, The (Dvořák), **19th:** 713
Spectroscopy, **20th:** 1784
Speculum fidei. See *Mirror of Faith, The*
Speculum majus (Vincent of Beauvais), **MA:** 1063
Speculum principis. See *Mirror for Princes, A*
Speculum speculationum (Neckam), **MA:** 752
Speech and Phenomena (Derrida), **20th:** 976
Speech of His Excellency, General Bolívar at the Installation of the Congress of Venezuela (Bolívar), **19th:** 269
Speech to the Electors of Bristol (Burke), **18th:** 175
Speeches, **Anc:** Livy's use of, 512; Sima Qian's use of, 783
Speeches on Questions of Public Policy (Bright), **19th:** 303
Speer, Albert, **Notor:** 938, 987-989
Speke, John Hanning, **19th:** 368, 2123-2126
Spell of the Yukon and Other Verses, The. See *Songs of a Sourdough*
Spem in Alium (Tallis), **Ren:** 919
Spencer, Georgiana. *See* Cavendish, Georgiana
Spencer, Herbert, **19th:** 2126-2129
Spendios, **Anc:** 374
Spenser, Edmund, **Ren:** 882, 906-909
Speransky, Mikhail Mikhaylovich, **19th:** 2129-2131
Spero, Tommy, **Notor:** 435
Spessivtseva, Olga, **20th:** 909, 2378
Speyer, First Diet of (1526), **Ren:** 221, 666, 775
Speyer, Second Diet of (1529), **Ren:** 666
Spezifizität der serologischen Reaktionen, Die. See *Specificity of Serological Reactions, The*
Sphēkes (Aristophanes), **Anc:** 12, 91
Sphera of George Buchanan, The (Buchanan), **Ren:** 146
Sphinx des glaces, Le. See *Antarctic Mystery, An*
Spice Islands, **Ren:** 23, 307, 514, 591. *See also* Trade
Spielberg, Steven, **20th:** 2451, 3811-3814
Spies. *See* Espionage; Category Index under Traitors and Spies
Spilbergen, Joris van, **17th:** 797
Spinning jenny, **18th:** 466
Spinning mule, **18th:** 561
Spínola, Ambrosio de, **17th:** 294, 619
Spinoza, Baruch, **17th:** 37, 188, 515, 871-875
Spiridion (Sand), **19th:** 1988

Spirit of Flight, The (Whitney), **20th:** 4317
Spirit of Liberty, The (Hand), **20th:** 1665
Spirit of Medieval Philosophy, The (Gilson), **20th:** 1489
Spirit of Modern Philosophy, The (Royce), **20th:** 3551
Spirit of Russia, The (Masaryk), **20th:** 2640
Spirit of St. Louis, The (Lindbergh), **20th:** 2395
Spirit of the Laws, The (Montesquieu), **18th:** 696
Spirit of Youth and the City Streets, The (Addams), **20th:** 24
Spiritual Canticle of the Soul, A (John of the Cross), **Ren:** 508
Spiritual democracy, **19th:** 27
Spiritual Dialogue, The (Catherine of Genoa), **Ren:** 192
Spiritual Doctrine of Saint Catherine of Genoa, The (Catherine of Genoa), **Ren:** 191
Spiritual Exercises, The (Saint Ignatius), **Ren:** 482
Spiritual Franciscans, **MA:** 779
Spiritual Torrents (Guyon), **17th:** 340
Spiritualist movement, **19th:** 690; **20th:** 1890
Spirituals (monastic movement), **MA:** 100, 181, 922
Spitignev, **MA:** 671
Spits, Werner. *See* Erhard, Werner
Spleen de Paris, Le. See *Paris Spleen*
Spock, Benjamin, **20th:** 3814-3817
Spock on Spock (Spock), **20th:** 3816
Sport of Gods, The (Dunbar), **19th:** 704
Sports. See *specific athletes and sports*; Category Index
Sports et divertissements (Satie), **20th:** 3643
Sportsman's Sketches, A (Turgenev), **19th:** 2319
Spotswood, Alexander, **Notor:** 1025
Spotted Tail, **19th:** 568
Sprache und Mythos. See *Language and Myth*
Spranger, Bartholomaus, **Ren:** 841
Sprechstimme (Schoenberg), **20th:** 3665
Spring and Summer Annals. See *Chunqiu*
Spring Floods. See *Torrents of Spring, The*
Spring Freshet (Wyeth), **20th:** 4411
Spring Snow (Mishima), **20th:** 2764
Spring Symphony (Britten), **20th:** 531
Spring Symphony (Schumann), **19th:** 2033
Springsteen, Bruce, **Notor:** 994
Spruce Goose, **20th:** 1926
Spurs, Battle of (1513), **Ren:** 996
Sputnik program, **20th:** 2193
Spy, The (Cooper), **19th:** 552
"Squabble of the Sea Nymphs, The" (Warren), **18th:** 1041
Squanto, **17th:** 86, 612, 875-877, 879
Squarcialupi Codex (Landini), **MA:** 635
Squarcione, Francesco, **Ren:** 601
Square Root of Wonderful, The (McCullers), **20th:** 2509
Squaw Man, The (film), **20th:** 960, 1524
Sri Harṣcarita. See *Harshacharita of Banabhatta, The*
Sri Lanka. *See* Geographical Index under India and Sri Lanka
Śrī Vaiṣṇavas, **MA:** 876
Śrībhāṣya (Rāmānuja), **MA:** 877
Ssu-ma Ch'ien. *See* Sima Qian
Ssu-ma Kuang. *See* Sima Guang
Ssu-tsung. *See* Chongzhen
ST/Four (Xenakis), **20th:** 4416
Stabat mater (Dvořák), **19th:** 712
Stabat mater (Rossini), **19th:** 1946
Stabat mater (Verdi), **19th:** 2353
Stables (O'Keeffe), **20th:** 3033
Stachka. See *Strike*
Stack, Lee, **20th:** 4440
Stadacona, **Ren:** 179
Stadtholder, **17th:** 618
Staël, Madame de, **18th:** 929-932
Stafford, George, **Ren:** 543
Stage design, **20th:** 1431
Stagecoach (film), **20th:** 4251
Stagl, Franz, **20th:** 4329
Stahl, Georg Ernst, **18th:** 218, 933-937
Ståhlberg, Kaarlo Juho, **20th:** 2599
Stalin, Joseph, **20th:** 2343, 2405, 3817-3821; de-Stalinization, 2129; Germany, 4125; Great Britain, 770; Vyacheslav Mikhailovich Molotov, 2783; music, 3728; Slovakia, 1043; Leon Trotstky, 4075; United States, 1685, 4088; **Notor:** 89, 207, 314, 493, 549, 574, 579, 597, 629, 675, 721, 747, 796, 990-992, 1040, 1052, 1074, 1079, 1112, 1115, 1137-1138
Stalky & Co. (Kipling), **19th:** 1284
Stalwarts (1869-1880), **19th:** 81
Stamboul Train (Greene), **20th:** 1578
Stamford Bridge, Battle of (1066), **MA:** 459, 1118
Stamp Act Crisis (1765-1766), **18th:** 17, 787
Stamp Act of 1765, **18th:** 11, 304, 457, 483, 519, 707; repeal, 174
Stand Up and Cheer (film), **20th:** 3973
Standard, Battle of the (1138), **MA:** 306
Standard Oil Company, **19th:** 1923; **20th:** 3476
Standish, Miles, **17th:** 7, 86, 614, 877-880
Stanford, Leland, **19th:** 2132-2136
Stanford University, **19th:** 2135

Stângebro, Battle of (1598), **17th:** 854
Stanhope, first Earl (James Stanhope), **18th:** 937-940, 1035
Stanislavski's Legacy (Stanislavsky), **20th:** 3822
Stanislavsky, Konstantin, **19th:** 1178; **20th:** 487, 2722, 3821-3824
Stanisław II August Poniatowski, **18th:** 567
Stankevich, Nikolai, **19th:** 1353
Stanley, Edward George Geoffrey Smith. *See* Derby, fourteenth earl of
Stanley, Henry Morton, **19th:** 369, 1350, 1401, 2125, 2136-2141, 2278; *In Darkest Africa*, 275; **Notor:** 632
Stanley, Thomas Lord, **Ren:** 91
Stanley, Wendell, **20th:** 3824-3826
Stanley, William, **19th:** 2417
Stanley and Livingston (film), **20th:** 4066
Stanley Home Products, **20th:** 146
Stanton, Charles M. *See* Gardner, Erle Stanley
Stanton, Edwin M., **19th:** 1233, 2142-2145; **Notor:** 124, 173, 859
Stanton, Elizabeth Cady, **19th:** 65, 257, 800, 852, 1617, 1904, 2146-2150
Stanton, Henry, **19th:** 2146
Staple of News, The (Jonson), **17th:** 443
Stapulensis, Jacobus Faber. *See* Lefèvre d'Étaples, Jacques
Star Atlas, The (Hevelius and Hevelius), **17th:** 372
Star catalogs, **Anc:** 418
Star Is Born, A (films), **20th:** 1410, 1464, 3118, 3893
Star Path Moon Stop (Terry), **20th:** 3984
"Star-Spangled Banner, The," **19th:** 1275
Star Wars (film), **20th:** 2450
Star Wars program. *See* Strategic Defense Initiative
Stark, Johannes, **20th:** 3827-3830
Starkweather, Charles, **Notor:** 993-994
Starling, Ernest Henry, **20th:** 259, 3830-3833
Staroobriadtsy. *See* Old Believers
Starovery. *See* Old Believers
Starr, Belle, **Notor:** 994-996
Starr, Henry, **Notor:** 996-997
Starr, Kenneth, **20th:** 786
Starr, Ringo, **20th:** 266
Starr, Sam, **Notor:** 995
Starr, Tom, **Notor:** 994
Starry Night, The (van Gogh), **19th:** 935
Stars, period luminosity of, **20th:** 2318
Stars and Stripes Forever, The (Sousa), **20th:** 3799
Stary, Zygmunt I. *See* Sigismund I, the Old
State and law, **Anc:** 293
State Fair (Rodgers and Hammerstein), **20th:** 1659
State in Its Relations with the Church, The (Gladstone), **19th:** 925
State Law and Order Restoration Council, **20th:** 175
State Lunatic Hospital, **19th:** 1486
State of France, The (Evelyn), **17th:** 256
State of the Finances of France (Necker), **18th:** 727
Statement of the Improvement and Progress of the Breed of Fine Woolled Sheep in New South Wales (MacArthur), **19th:** 1432
Staten Island Railroad, **19th:** 2349
States and Empires of the Sun, The (Cyrano), **17th:** 211
States' rights (U.S.), **18th:** 637, 665, 910; **20th:** 3406
Statesman's Manual, The (Coleridge), **19th:** 532
Stati d'animo (Boccioni), **20th:** 404
Statistical, Historical, and Political Description of the Colony of New South Wales and Its Dependent Settlements in Van Dieman's Land, A (Wentworth), **19th:** 2413
Statue of Liberty, **19th:** 735, 1332
Status of the Mesozoic Floras of the United States (Ward), **19th:** 2384
Statutes of Ohio, The (Chase), **19th:** 471
Statutory Authorities for Special Purposes (Webbs), **20th:** 4254
Staudinger, Hermann, **20th:** 2919, 3833-3836
Staudinger's law, **20th:** 3835
Stauffenberg, Claus Schenck von, **Notor:** 420
Stavisky, Alexandre, **Notor:** 998-999
Stayner, Sir Richard, **17th:** 57
Steady state theory, **20th:** 1902
Steam engines, **Anc:** 402; **17th:** 711, 814; **18th:** 116, 157, 715, 733-735, 860, 1048-1051, 1087, 1088
Steam hammers, **19th:** 1646
Steam-powered looms, **18th:** 561
Steam rolling mills, **18th:** 1088
Steamboat Willie (animated film), **20th:** 1007
Steamboats, **18th:** 353, 355; **19th:** 846
Steber, Eleanor, **20th:** 232
Steel alloys, **19th:** 1000
Steele, Richard, **18th:** 941-943; *The Tatler*, 21
Steelmaking, **19th:** 1301
Steensen, Niels. *See* Steno, Nicolaus
Steeplechase, The (Degas), **19th:** 632
Stefan Batory. *See* Stephen Báthory
Stefan Dušan, **MA:** 957-960
Stefan Uroš II Milutin, **MA:** 957
Stefan Uroš III Dečanski, **MA:** 957
Stefan Uroš IV. *See* Stefan Dušan

Stefan Uroš V, **MA:** 959
Stefanik, Milan, **20th:** 2641
Steichen, Edward, **20th:** 3837-3840
Stein, Edith, **20th:** 3840-3845
Stein, Freiherr vom, **19th:** 1022, 1674, 2151-2153
Stein, Gertrude, **20th:** 3845-3848
Steinbeck, John, **20th:** 3849-3852
Steinem, Gloria, **20th:** 3852-3856
Steiner, Jakob, **19th:** 2154-2156
Steinmetz, Charles Proteus, **19th:** 2156-2159
Stemming the Tide (Seaborg), **20th:** 3687
Sten, Anna, **20th:** 143
Sten Sture the Younger, **Ren:** 415
Stenberg v. Carhart (2000), **20th:** 522, 3022, 3408
Stenby, Treaty of (1238), **MA:** 1048
Stendhal, **19th:** 2160-2163
Steno, Nicolaus, **17th:** 881-883
Steno's law, **17th:** 882
Stephen (king of England), **MA:** 305, 357, 482-483, 960-964
Stephen I (king of Hungary), **MA:** 637, 964-967
Stephen, Saint, **Anc:** 613, 821-824
Stephen Báthory, **Ren:** 652, 910-912, 982; **Notor:** 517
Stephen Dushan. *See* Stefan Dušan
Stephen of Blois. *See* Stephen (king of England)
Stephen Uroš. *See* Stefan Dušan
Stephens, Alexander H., **19th:** 2164-2167
Stephenson, George, **19th:** 2167-2170
Stephenson, Robert, **19th:** 2169
Stepinac, Alojzije, **Notor:** 814
Steppenwolf (Hesse), **20th:** 1789
Steps to the Temple (Crashaw), **17th:** 203
Stereoscopes, **19th:** 549
Stern, Otto, **20th:** 2533
Sternberg, Josef von, **20th:** 998
Sternenbraut, Die (Ehrenfels), **20th:** 1111
Sternheim (La Roche), **18th:** 577
Sternverdunkelung (Sachs), **20th:** 3585
Stetigkeit und Irrationale Zahlen (Dedekind), **19th:** 630
Steunenberg, Frank, **Notor:** 451
Stevens, Aaron, **19th:** 321
Stevens, Eric. *See* Frankel, Martin
Stevens, Robert, **Notor:** 217
Stevens, Thaddeus, **19th:** 1231, 2171-2173
Stevens, Williamina Paton. *See* Fleming, Williamina Paton Stevens
Stevenson, Adlai E., **20th:** 1127, 3856-3860; **Notor:** 670
Stevenson, Coke, **20th:** 2029
Stevenson, Robert Louis, **19th:** 2173-2176; **Notor:** 145, 154
Stevin, Simon, **Ren:** 912-914; **17th:** 619
Stewart, Henry, **Ren:** 146, 311, 629
Stewart, Isabella. *See* Gardner, Isabella Stewart
Stewart, James (actor), **20th:** 999, 3860-3863
Stewart, James B. (journalist), **Notor:** 731
Stewart, Mary. *See* Mary, Queen of Scots
Stewart, Robert. *See* Castlereagh, Viscount
Stiava, La (Caccini), **17th:** 111
Stichus (Plautus), **Anc:** 663
Stickeen (Muir), **19th:** 1625
Stieglitz, Alfred, **20th:** 883, 3031, 3837, 3864-3868
Stiglets, John, **Notor:** 173
Stigmata, **20th:** 1286
Stigmatization of St. Francis (Fontana), **Ren:** 338
Stijl, De, **20th:** 2692, 2788, 3092
Stikhi k Bloku (Tsvetayeva), **20th:** 4099
Stile antico, **17th:** 296
Stilicho, Flavius, **Anc:** 352, 824-826
Still Life with an Old Shoe (Miró), **20th:** 2761
Still Life with Musical Instruments (Braque), **20th:** 494
Still-Life with Oranges (Zurbarán), **17th:** 1005
Still Life with Playing Cards (Braque), **20th:** 495
Still Life with Toy Horse (Miró), **20th:** 2760
Stiller, Moritz, **20th:** 1392
Stilo Praeconinus, **Anc:** 927
Stilpo, **Anc:** 981
Stilwell and the American Experience in China (Tuchman), **20th:** 4105
Stimmung (Stockhausen), **20th:** 3875
Stimson, Henry L., **20th:** 3869-3872
Stimson Doctrine (1932), **20th:** 1864
Stirling Bridge, Battle of (1297), **MA:** 202, 346, 1073
Stoa Poecile, **Anc:** 982
Stochastic method, **20th:** 4415
Stock market crash (1929), **20th:** 1863
Stock market crash (1987), **20th:** 1582
Stockhausen, Karlheinz, **20th:** 3872-3877
Stockholm Bloodbath, **Ren:** 415
Stockmar, Ernest, **19th:** 2360
Stockton, Robert F., **19th:** 833
Stockton and Darlington Railway, **19th:** 2168
Stoic, The (Dreiser), **20th:** 1034
Stoicheia (Euclid), **Anc:** 78, 317, 320, 606, 727
Stoicism, **Anc:** Arria the Elder and, 102; Arria the Younger and, 103; Cato the Younger and, 194; Christianity and, 44, 854; Cynicism and, 981; Eratosthenes and, 314; Judaism and, 641; Livy and, 511; Marcus Aurelius and, 530;

Pneumatism and, 84; Posidonius and, 690; Pyrrhon and, 723; Seneca the Younger and, 766; Strabo and, 827; Zeno of Citium and, 70; **MA:** 1050

Stoikheiōsis theologikē (Proclus), **Anc:** 701

Stoke, Battle of (1487), **Ren:** 439

Stokes, Edward S., **Notor:** 358

Stokes, George Gabriel, **20th:** 75

Stolbovo, Treaty of (1617), **17th:** 337, 704, 795

Stolen Kisses (film), **20th:** 4081

Stolen Moments (Parkes), **19th:** 1739

Stolypin, Pyotr, **Notor:** 886

Stone, Harlan Fiske, **20th:** 3878-3881; **Notor:** 1057

Stone, John A., **19th:** 792

Stone, Lucy, **19th:** 1097, 1618, 2177-2180

Stone, Oliver, **20th:** 1728

Stone, Samuel, **17th:** 386

Stone, William, **19th:** 340

Stone City, Iowa (Wood), **20th:** 4388

Stone of Scone, **MA:** 346

Stonebreakers, The (Courbet), **19th:** 559

Stonehenge, **18th:** 952-954

Stonehenge (Stukeley), **18th:** 953

Stonehenge and Other British Monuments Astronomically Considered (Lockyer), **19th:** 1415

Stonemason's Yard, The (Canaletto), **18th:** 190

Stoner, Edmund, **20th:** 3152

Stoner, J. B., **Notor:** 999-1000

Stones of Venice, The (Ruskin), **19th:** 1955

Stoney End (Streisand), **20th:** 3893

Stoning of Saint Stephen (Rembrandt), **17th:** 786

Stopes, Marie, **20th:** 3882-3884

Stora landsvägen. See *Great Highway, The*

Store (Oldenburg), **20th:** 3037

Store 2 (Oldenburg), **20th:** 3037

Storia come pensiero e come azione, La. See *History as the Story of Liberty*

Storia delle dottrine politiche (Mosca), **20th:** 2840

Storia d'Europa nel secolo decimonono. See *History of Europe in the Nineteenth Century*

Storia d'Italia. See *History of Italy, The*

Storia d'Italia, 1871-1915. See *History of Italy, 1871-1915, A*

Storie fiorentine. See *History of Florence, The*

Stories for Ninon (Zola), **19th:** 2489

Storm, and Other Poems, The (Montale), **20th:** 2802

Storm in Shanghai. See *Man's Fate*

Stormy Sea, The (Courbet), **19th:** 560

Story, Joseph, **19th:** 2180-2183, 2227

Story of an African Farm, The (Schreiner), **19th:** 2023-2024

Story of Gösta Berling, The (Lagerlöf), **20th:** 2234

Story of My Boyhood and Youth, The (Muir), **19th:** 1625

Story of My Life, The (Andersen), **19th:** 62

Story of My Life, The (Keller), **20th:** 2093, 3908

Story of My Life, The (Terry), **19th:** 2250

Story of My Misfortunes, The (Abelard), **MA:** 16

Story of Sapho, The (Scudéry), **17th:** 829

Story of the Glittering Plain, The (Morris), **19th:** 1608

Story of the Stone (Cao Xueqin), **18th:** 194

Stout, Robert, **19th:** 2059

Stowe, Harriet Beecher, **19th:** 171-172, 990, 2184-2187, 2460; *The American Woman's Home*, 170

Strabo (geographer), **Anc:** 827-830

Strabo, Gnaeus Pompeius. *See* Pompeius Strabo, Gnaeus

Strachan, John, **19th:** 1456

Strada, La (film), **20th:** 1232

Stradivari, Antonio, **18th:** 944-947

Strafford, first earl of, **17th:** 145, 167, 345, 768, 884-887, 895, 941

Strage degli innocenti, La. See *Slaughter of the Innocents, The*

Straight from the Heart (Chrétien), **20th:** 762

Strait of Magellan, **Ren:** 308, 593

Strange Case of Dr. Jekyll and Mr. Hyde, The (Stevenson), **19th:** 2173

Strange Newes of the Intercepting of Certain Letters (Nashe), **Ren:** 715

Strange Victory (Teasdale), **20th:** 3961

Stranger, The (Camus), **20th:** 628

Strasberg, Lee, **20th:** 862, 2798

Strasser, Adolph, **19th:** 943

Strasser, Gregor, **20th:** 1513; **Notor:** 418, 468

Strasser, Otto, **20th:** 1513

Strassmann, Fritz, **20th:** 715, 1236, 1637, 2681

Strategic Bombing Survey (Galbraith), **20th:** 1375

Strategic Defense Initiative, **20th:** 343, 3403, 3971

Strategy of Deception, The (Kirkpatrick), **20th:** 2167

Strato of Lampsacus, **Anc:** 277, 317, 716, 872

Stratton, Charles Sherwood, **19th:** 139

Strauss, Johann, **19th:** 2188-2191

Strauss, Richard, **19th:** 1156; **20th:** 250, 3885-3888; **Notor:** 933

Stravinsky, Igor, **20th:** 194, 794, 986, 2647, 3888-3892
Straw, The (O'Neill), **20th:** 3051
Strawberry Blonde, The (film), **20th:** 1731
Strayed Reveller, and Other Poems, The (Arnold), **19th:** 72
Street, Berlin (Kirchner), **20th:** 2165
Street, George Edmund, **19th:** 1606, 2191-2194
Street in Bronzeville, A (Brooks), **20th:** 537
Street Scene (Weill), **20th:** 4275
Streetcar Named Desire, A (film), **20th:** 4231
Streetcar Named Desire, A (play by Williams), **20th:** 487, 4352
Streicher, Julius, **Notor:** 461, 1001-1003
Streisand, Barbra, **20th:** 3892-3894
Streltsy, **18th:** 755, 757, 774
Strength of Gideon, and Other Stories, The (Dunbar), **19th:** 703
Streptomycin, **20th:** 4182
Stresemann, Gustav, **20th:** 3895-3897
Strickland, Catharine Parr. *See* Traill, Catharine Parr
Strickland, Susanna. *See* Moodie, Susanna
Stride Toward Freedom (King), **20th:** 2148
Striggio, Alessandro (c. 1540-1592), **Ren:** 919
Striggio, Alessandro, the Younger (1573?-1630), **17th:** 658
Strijdom, Johannes Gerhardus, **Notor:** 1065
Strik-Strikfeldt, Wilfried, **Notor:** 1074
Strike (film), **20th:** 1130
Strike Up the Band (Gershwin and Gershwin), **20th:** 1459, 1463
Strikes, **20th:** air traffic controllers (1981), 3402; Asturian miners (1934), 1297; Bisbee mine (1917), 1308; Boston police (1919), 832; coal miners, 2360, 2362; Colorado mines (1913-1914), 2041, 3477; Delano grape (1965-1970), 739, 1916; Disney cartoonists (1941), 1008; France, 398; Gdańsk Lenin Shipyard (1980), 4191; General Motors, 3425; general strike, Great Britain (1926), 206, 357, 416, 2270, 3411; Homestead Steel (1892), 482, 1521; Kelsey-Hayes sit-down (1936), 3425; Little Steel (1937), 2361; Pullman (1894), 914, 934; Turtle Creek mine (1897), 2040; Waihi gold mine (1912), 2644; West Virginia mines (1921), 2041. *See also* Labor
Strindberg, August, **19th:** 881, 1296; **20th:** 954, 3051, 3898-3901
String Quartet (Zwilich), **20th:** 4476
String Quartet in A Major (Borodin), **19th:** 282
String Quartet in D Major (Franck), **19th:** 823
String Quartet in D Minor (Sullivan), **19th:** 917
String Quartet in E Major (Boccherini), **18th:** 131
String Quartet in F Minor, Op. 9 (Dvořák), **19th:** 712
String Quartet in G Major (Schubert), **19th:** 2027
String Quartet in G Minor, Op. 27 (Grieg), **19th:** 986
String Quartet No. 2 in D Major (Borodin), **19th:** 282
String Quartet, Op. 10, No. 2 (Schoenberg), **20th:** 3665
String Quintet in C Major (Schubert), **19th:** 2027
String Trio, Op. 20 (Webern), **20th:** 4263
String Trio, Op. 45 (Schoenberg), **20th:** 3666
Strobel, Mike, **Notor:** 54
Stroessner, Alfredo, **Notor:** 1004-1005
Stromboli (film), **20th:** 322
Strong, Henry, **20th:** 1079
Strong, Jonathan, **18th:** 899
Strong Breed, The (Soyinka), **20th:** 3805
Stroud, Robert Franklin, **Notor:** 1005-1007
Strozzi, Barbara, **17th:** 888-890
Strozzi, Giulio, **17th:** 888
Strozzi, Piero, **Ren:** 653
Strozzi-Benucci, Alessandra, **Ren:** 57
Structural Transformation of the Public Sphere (Habermas), **20th:** 1632
Structuralism, **20th:** 248, 975
Structure of Behavior, The (Merleau-Ponty), **20th:** 2710
Struensee, Johann Friedrich, **Notor:** 209
Strukturwandel der Öffentlichkeit. See *Structural Transformation of the Public Sphere*
Struven, Jean. *See* Harris, Jean
Strychnine, synthesis of, **20th:** 4394
Stryker, Roy, **20th:** 2261
Stuart, Arbella, **Ren:** 104
Stuart, Elizabeth. *See* Elizabeth Stuart
Stuart, Gilbert, **18th:** 947-951
Stuart, James. *See* James I (1566-1625; king of England); James IV; James V
Stuart, Mary. *See* Mary II; Mary, Queen of Scots
Studd, J. E. K., **20th:** 2850
Student Nonviolent Coordinating Committee, **20th:** 2148
Student Volunteer Movement for Foreign Missions, **20th:** 2850
Student's Text-Book of English and General History from B.C. 100 to the Present Time, The (Beale), **19th:** 159
Studie über Minderwertigkeit von Organen. See *Study of Organ*

Inferiority and Its Psychical Compensation
Studien über Hysterie. See *Studies in Hysteria*
Studien zur Descendenztheorie. See *Studies in the Theory of Descent*
Studies in Hysteria (Breuer and Freud), **20th:** 515, 1323
Studies in Logical Theory (Dewey), **20th:** 983
Studies in Optics (Michelson), **19th:** 1569
Studies in the History of the Renaissance (Pater), **19th:** 1755, 2432
Studies in the Problem of Sovereignty (Laski), **20th:** 2269
Studies in the Psychology of Sex (Ellis), **20th:** 1149
Studies in the Theory of Descent (Weismann), **19th:** 2408
Studies of Plant Life in Canada (Traill), **19th:** 2292
Studio of Sacred Art, **20th:** 973
Study in Dying Colonialism, A (Fanon), **20th:** 1213
Study in Scarlet, A (Doyle), **19th:** 688, 690
Study of Divining Rods (Napier), **Ren:** 712
Study of History, A (Toynbee), **20th:** 4060, 4106
Study of Organ Inferiority and Its Psychical Compensation (Adler), **20th:** 33
Stuff of Youth, The (Mauriac), **20th:** 2657
Stukeley, William, **18th:** 952-954
Stummdorf, Treaty of (1635), **17th:** 854
Stundenbuch, Das. See *Book of Hours, The*
Sturgis, Frank, **Notor:** 500
Sturlung Age, **MA:** 951
Sturluson, Snorri. *See* Snorri Sturluson
Sturm und Drang, **18th:** 428, 486, 562, 887
Sturmer, Boris, **Notor:** 887
Sturzo, Don Luigi, **20th:** 945
Stuyvesant, Peter, **17th:** 518, 645, 890-893
Stylites. *See* Simeon Stylites, Saint
Su Dongpo, **MA:** 719, 809, 968-970, 1088
Su Shi. *See* Su Dongpo
Su Tung-p'o. *See* Su Dongpo
Su Zhu. *See* Hua Guofeng
Suárez, Adolfo, **20th:** 2061
Subh-i Azal, **19th:** 106, 117
Subida del Monte Carmelo, La. See *Ascent of Mount Carmel, The*
Subjection of Women, The (Mill), **19th:** 1578
Subjectivism, **Anc:** 708
Subjects of the Artist, **20th:** 3539
Sublette, William, **19th:** 2115
Submarines, **19th:** 846, 1113; **20th:** Arctic exploration, 4341; nuclear-powered, 3444; World War I, 1181
Subscription No Bondage (Maurice), **19th:** 1518
Substance and Function (Cassirer), **20th:** 688
Subterraneans, The (Kerouac), **20th:** 2115
Subüktigin, **MA:** 683
Subway Vigilante. *See* Goetz, Bernhard
Succat, Maewyn. *See* Patrick, Saint
Succession, Act of (1534), **Ren:** 270, 336, 443
Succession Pact (1560), **Ren:** 417
Suceava, Battle of (1653), **17th:** 463
Sucesion presidencial en 1910, La. See *Presidential Succession in 1910, The*
Sucesos, The (Alemán), **Ren:** 26
Suckling, Sir John, **17th:** 503, 893-895
Sucre, Antonio José de, **19th:** 2195-2197
Sudan, **Ren:** 556, 900; **18th:** exploration of, 169; **19th:** 926; Great Britain, 950. *See also* Geographical Index
Suddenly Last Summer (film), **20th:** 3954
Suddenly Last Summer (play by Williams), **20th:** 4352
Śuddhodana, **Anc:** 169
Sudeten Crisis (1938), **20th:** 3559
Südfeld, Simon Maximilian. *See* Nordau, Max
Sudley, Lord. *See* Seymour, Thomas
Suebi, **Anc:** 394
Sueños y discursos de verdades encubridoras de engaños. See *Visions: Or, Hel's Kingdome and the World's Follies and Abuses*
Suetonius, **Anc:** 18, 23, 72, 145, 168, 172, 176, 489, 508, 522, 591, 685, 904, 940, 941; **Notor:** 166, 290-291, 778
Suevi, **Anc:** 351
Suez Canal, **19th:** 1357; opening of, 1552
Suez Crisis (1956), **20th:** 930, 1056, 1102, 1655, 2129, 2538, 2915, 3174; Canada, 3598
Suffield, third Baron, **19th:** 377
Suffolk, duke of, **Ren:** 435
Suffolk County Court House, **19th:** 348
Suffrage Act of 1918, **20th:** 416
Suffrage des Femmes, **19th:** 90
Sufism, **MA:** 41, 415, 454, 472, 526, 562, 874, 908, 915; **18th:** Africa, 914-916; India, 1032; Persia, 1001
Sugar, **18th:** 652, 987
Sugar Act (1764), **18th:** 304, 457, 519
Sugar Street (Mahfouz), **20th:** 2554
Sugata Sanshirō. See *Sanshiro Sugata*
Suger, **MA:** 161, 971-974
Suharto, **20th:** 1705, 3901-3903; **Notor:** 1007-1009
Suharto, Tommy, **Notor:** 1009

Sui Dynasty, **MA:** 941, 976, 1136
Suicide (Durkheim), **20th:** 1067
Suicide and the Meaning of Civilization (Masaryk), **20th:** 2640
Suicides, **Anc:** Antonia Minor, 72; Marc Antony, 71, 75, 146; Arbogast, 871; Arria the Elder, 102, 104; Artemesia I, 110; Brutus, 168; Cambyses, 136; Cassius, 167, 186; Cleomenes I, 227; Cleopatra VII, 231; Demosthenes, 267; Dido, 272; Empedocles, 297; Eratosthenes, 316; Hanfeizi, 381; Hannibal, 384; Hu Hao, 781; Isocrates, 451; Jews at Masada, 478; Julia Domna, 482; Lu Buwei, 780; Lucretia, 517, 846; Macro, 178; Mithridates VI Eupator, 569; Nero, 593; Pontius Pilate, 645; Porcia, 167; Posthumus, 165; Ptolemy of Cyprus, 195; Qu Yuan, 733; Rāma, 923; Saul, 255; Seneca the Younger, 767; Sophonisba, 814; Themistocles, 861; Valentinian II, 870; Varus, 100; Zeno of Citium, 982
Suiko, **MA:** 940, 974-977
Suite bergamasque (Debussy), **20th:** 938
Suite by Chance (dance), **20th:** 887
Suite for Five (dance), **20th:** 887
Suite for Piano, Op. 25 (Schoenberg), **20th:** 3666
Suite in Three Keys (Coward), **20th:** 856
Suivante, La (Corneille), **17th:** 193
Sujin, **Anc:** 462
Sukarno, **20th:** 1705, 2327, 3901, 3904-3907; **Notor:** 1008
Sukkariya, Al-. See *Sugar Street*
Sukulung Kulukang, **MA:** 978
Sula (Morrison), **20th:** 2835
Sulaymān, **MA:** 71, 774, 1007
Suleiman I. *See* Süleyman the Magnificent
Süleyman II, **17th:** 472
Suleyman al-Faris. *See* Lindh, John Walker
Süleyman the Magnificent, **Ren:** 80, 88, 221, 480, 636, 651, 914-917
Sulfonamide, **20th:** 1022
Sulla, Lucius Cornelius, **Anc:** 172, 188, 210, 359, 533, 568, 681, 830-834, 895; **Notor:** 188, 392, 1010-1011
Sullivan, Anne, **20th:** 2093, 3908-3910
Sullivan, Arthur, **19th:** 916-921
Sullivan, Harry Stack, **20th:** 1346, 3910-3912
Sullivan, Louis, **19th:** 2198-2200
Sully, duke de, **17th:** 896-898
Sulpicia, **Anc:** 834-836
Sulpicians, **17th:** 76, 265, 401, 490, 499, 576, 596
Sulpicius Rufus, Publius, **Anc:** 831; **Notor:** 1010
Sult. See *Hunger*
Sultan, Kösem. *See* Kösem Sultan
Sultan ibn Aḥmad, **19th:** 1965
Sultan of Algiers. *See* ʿArūj
Suma Oriental (Pires), **Ren:** 792
Sumana Samanara, **Anc:** 898
Sumanguru Kanté, **MA:** 978
Sumeria, **Anc:** 368, 376
Summa aurea (William of Auxerre), **MA:** 1103
Summa contra gentiles (Thomas Aquinas), **MA:** 1028
Summa de casibus poenitentiae (Raymond of Peñafort), **MA:** 882
Summa logicae. See *Ockham's Theory of Propositions*; *Ockham's Theory of Terms*
Summa super quattuor libros sententiarum. See *Summa aurea*
Summa Theologica (Thomas Aquinas), **MA:** 318, 1028, 1064, 1106
Summary of the Great Vehicle, The. See *Mahāyānasaṁgraha*
Summer (Wharton), **20th:** 4302
Summer, Ann. *See* Restell, Madame
Summer Evening (Hopper), **20th:** 1877
Summer Night on the River (Delius), **20th:** 955
Summer on the Lake (Fuller), **19th:** 842
Summer School of Applied Ethics, **19th:** 28
Summer's Last Will and Testament (Nashe), **Ren:** 715
Summula de dialectica (Buridan), **MA:** 215
Summum Bonum, quod est verum magiae, cabalae, alchymae verae, Fratrum Roseae Crucis verorum subjectum (Fritzius), **17th:** 281
Sumner, Charles, **19th:** 671, 1231, 1737, 2201-2205
Sun Also Rises, The (Hemingway), **20th:** 1756
Sun and Steel (Mishima), **20th:** 2763
Sun Chung-shan. *See* Sun Yat-sen
Sun I-hsien. *See* Sun Yat-sen
Sun-Jata. *See* Sundiata
Sun King. *See* Louis XIV
Sun Records, **20th:** 3330
Sun Rising Through Vapour (Turner), **19th:** 2323
Sun Stone (Paz), **20th:** 3170
Sun Valley Serenade (film), **20th:** 1760
Sun Wen. *See* Sun Yat-sen
Sun Yat-sen, **20th:** 741, 747, 3913-3915, 4220, 4462; **Notor:** 1123
Sun Yixian. *See* Sun Yat-sen
Sun Zhongshan. *See* Sun Yat-sen
Sund Chiao-jen, **Notor:** 1123
Sundance Kid. *See* Longabaugh, Harry
Sunday, Billy, **20th:** 2365, 3916-3920
Sunday on the Grand Jatte, A (Seurat), **19th:** 2075
Sunday school movement, **18th:** 1081

Sunder, Lucas. *See* Cranach, Lucas, the Elder
Sunderland, third earl of, **18th:** 1035
Sundiata, **MA:** 744, 977-980
Sunless (Mussorgsky), **19th:** 1628
Sunni Ali. *See* Sonni ʿAlī
Sunni Islam, **MA:** 18, 70, 415, 454, 775; **18th:** 722, 1000, 1032. *See also* Shīʿa Islam
Sunrise (Nash), **20th:** 2911
Sun's Place in Nature, The (Lockyer), **19th:** 1414
Sunset Gun (Parker), **20th:** 3117
Sunzi Bingfa (Sunzi), **Anc:** 183
Sunzi Luejie (Cao Cao), **Anc:** 183
Suor Angelica (Puccini), **20th:** 3348
Super Bowl, first, **20th:** 3555
Super Size Me (film), **20th:** 2203
Superconductivity, **20th:** 235, 2073, 2078
Supper at Emmaus (Caravaggio), **Ren:** 171
Supper Controversy, **Ren:** 143
Suppliant Women, The. See *Hiketides* (Aeschylus)
Suppliants, The. See *Hiketides* (Aeschylus)
Suppositi, I. See *Pretenders, The*
Supralapsarianism, **Ren:** 60
Supremacy, Act of (1534), **Ren:** 113, 270, 336, 443
Supreme Court and the Constitution, The (Beard), **20th:** 263
Supreme Court of Canada, **19th:** 1453
Supreme Court of the United States, **18th:** 238, 525, 1093; **19th:** 1500; **20th:** Hugo L. Black, 378; Harry A. Blackmun, 383; Louis D. Brandeis, 484; William J. Brennan, 507; Stephen G. Breyer, 520; Warren E. Burger, 383, 581; Benjamin N. Cardozo, 655; William O. Douglas, 1029; Felix Frankfurter, 1309; Oliver Wendell Holmes, Jr., 1857; Charles Evans Hughes, 1920; Thurgood Marshall, 2634; Sandra Day O'Connor, 3021; Lewis F. Powell, Jr., 3326; William H. Rehnquist, 3406; David H. Souter, 3802; Harlan Fiske Stone, 3879; William Howard Taft, 3931; Clarence Thomas, 3999; Earl Warren, 4234
Sur Incises (Boulez), **20th:** 455
Sur la destruction des Jésuites en France. See *Account of the Destruction of the Jesuits in France, An*
Sur le pierre blanche. See *White Stone, The*
Sur Racine. See *On Racine*
Suréna (Corneille), **17th:** 195
Surgeon of His Honor, The (Calderón), **17th:** 114
Surgery, **Anc:** Greece, 86; Rome, 200; **MA:** Byzantine Empire, 815; **19th:** 1391
Surly Tim, and Other Stories (Burnett), **19th:** 357
Surman, Iswar Chandra. *See* Vidyasagar, Iswar Chandra
Surname-i Vehbi, **18th:** 603
Surprised by Joy (Lewis), **20th:** 2354
Surratt, John, **Notor:** 858
Surratt, Mary, **Notor:** 123, 859, 1012-1013
Surrealism, **18th:** 438; **20th:** 905, 2581, 2760, 2912; Belgium, 2548; André Breton, 510; literature, 578, 711, 1152, 1177, 1396, 3170; sculpture, 1471
Surrender of Breda, The (Velázquez), **17th:** 954
Sursis, Le. See *Reprieve, The*
Survey of International Affairs (Toynbee), **20th:** 4060
Survey of the Summe of Church-Discipline, A (Hooker), **17th:** 387
Survivance, Acte of (1631), **17th:** 289
Survivor from Warsaw, A (Schoenberg), **20th:** 3666
Suryavarman II, **MA:** 980-983
Susanna and the Elders (Artemisia), **17th:** 307
Susanna and the Elders (Tintoretto), **Ren:** 932
Sushun, **MA:** 975
Suskind, Richard, **Notor:** 510
Suslov, Mikhail, **Notor:** 1137
Suspended Ball (Giacometti), **20th:** 1471
Suspicion of Herod, The (Marini), **17th:** 202
Susquehannocks, **17th:** 30
Sutherland, Graham Vivian, **20th:** 3920-3922
Sutherland, Halliday, **20th:** 3883
Sutoku, **MA:** 991
Sutras, **Anc:** 50, 170
Su-tsung. *See* Suzong
Sutter, John Augustus, **19th:** 777
Suttner, Bertha von, **19th:** 2205-2208
Sutton, Willie, **Notor:** 1014-1015
Suvarna Banlang, **Ren:** 547
Suvorin, Aleksey S., **19th:** 479
Suvorov, Aleksandr Vasilyevich, **18th:** 954-958
Suwayd, Sakr Abu. *See* Zarqawi, Abu Musab al-
Suzong, **MA:** 80, 1086
Suzuki, D. T., **20th:** 1884
Suzuki Harunobu, **18th:** 958-960
Suzuki, Shinichi, **20th:** 3922-3924
Sværmere. See *Dreamers*
Svatební košile. See *Spectre's Bride, The*
Sverdlov, Yakov, **Notor:** 1112
Svoboda, Ludvik, **20th:** 1044
Svod Zakanov (Speransky), **19th:** 2131
Svolder, Battle of (1000), **MA:** 786, 791
Svyatoslav I, **MA:** 86, 794, 1068
Swabian War (1499), **Ren:** 648
Swaggart, Jimmy, **Notor:** 51
Swain, James W. *See* Hardin, John Wesley

Swallow, Ellen Henrietta. *See* Richards, Ellen Swallow
Swami Vivekananda. *See* Vivekananda
Swammerdam, Jan, **17th:** 362, 510, 898-900
Swamp Dwellers, The (Soyinka), **20th:** 3804
Swan, The (Molnár), **20th:** 2331
Swan, Joseph Wilson, **19th:** 2209-2211
Swan King. *See* Ludwig II
Swan Lake (ballet), **20th:** 254
Swan Lake (Tchaikovsky), **19th:** 2234
"Swanee" (Gershwin), **20th:** 1458
Swango, Michael, **Notor:** 1015-1016
Swann v. Charlotte-Mecklenburg Board of Education (1971), **20th:** 582
Sweden. *See* Geographical Index
Swedenborg, Emanuel, **18th:** 961-963; **19th:** 70
Swedish-Ottoman alliance, **18th:** 232
Swedish-Polish alliance, **18th:** 232
Swedish-Russian conflicts, **18th:** 232, 776
Sweeny, Peter Barr, **19th:** 1650, 2334
Sweet, Ossian, **20th:** 915
Sweet Charity (Coleman and Fields), **20th:** 1292
Sweyn (son of Godwin), **MA:** 338, 457
Sweyn I (king of Denmark), **MA:** 364
Sweyn Forkbeard, **MA:** 221, 790
Swift, Jonathan, **18th:** 136, 688, 942, 964-967; **Notor:** 261
Swinburne, Algernon Charles, **19th:** 1755
Swing, The (Fragonard), **18th:** 367
Swing music, **20th:** 1527
Swing Time (film), **20th:** 156
Switzerland. *See* Geographical Index
Sword Blades and Poppy Seeds (Lowell), **20th:** 2445
Sybil (Disraeli), **19th:** 667
Sybil of the Rhine. *See* Hildegard von Bingen
Sydenham, Thomas, **17th:** 901-904
Sydney, Australia, **18th:** 784
Sykes-Picot Agreement (1916), **20th:** 4281
Syllabus of Errors (Pius IX), **19th:** 1804
Sylph, The (Cavendish), **18th:** 216
Sylphides, Les (ballet), **20th:** 1263
Sylva (Evelyn), **17th:** 257
Sylvester II, **MA:** 399, 965, 983-987
Sylvia (Delibes), **19th:** 640
Sylvia Scarlett (film), **20th:** 1570
Sylvius, Franciscus. *See* Deleboe, Franz
Symbolic Logic (Carroll), **19th:** 425
Symbolist movement, **19th:** 1875; **20th:** 394, 2791
Syme, James, **19th:** 1391
Symmachus, **MA:** 1014
Symons, Arthur, **19th:** 163
Sympathy, universal, **Anc:** 702
Symphonia harmonia caelestium revelationum (Hildegard von Bingen), **MA:** 513
Symphoniae sacrae (Schütz), **17th:** 827
Symphonic Dances (Rachmaninoff), **20th:** 3363
Symphonic Metamorphosis of Themes by Carl Maria von Weber (Hindemith), **20th:** 1813
Symphonic Variations for Orchestra (Dvořák), **19th:** 713
Symphonie fantastique (Berlioz), **19th:** 201
Symphonies concertantes, **18th:** 154
Symphony in C (Bizet), **19th:** 241
Symphony in C Major (Schubert), **19th:** 2027
Symphony in D Minor (Franck), **19th:** 823
Symphony in D Minor, Op. 13 (Dvořák), **19th:** 712
Symphony in E Minor, Op. 95. See *New World* Symphony
Symphony in F, Op. 24 (Dvořák), **19th:** 712
Symphony in G, Op. 88 (Dvořák), **19th:** 713
Symphony No. 1 (Barber), **20th:** 231
Symphony No. 1 (Nielsen), **20th:** 2965
Symphony No. 1 (Walton), **20th:** 4218
Symphony No. 1 (Zwilich), **20th:** 4477
Symphony No. 1 in A-flat Major, Op. 55 (Elgar), **20th:** 1135
Symphony No. 1 in C Minor (Bruckner), **19th:** 330
Symphony No. 1 in C Minor, Op. 68 (Brahms), **19th:** 298
Symphony No. 1 in F Minor (Shostakovich), **20th:** 3728
Symphony No. 2 (Nielsen), **20th:** 2965
Symphony No. 2 in B Minor (Borodin), **19th:** 282
Symphony No. 2 in C Minor (Bruckner), **19th:** 330
Symphony No. 2 in E-flat Major, Op. 63 (Elgar), **20th:** 1135
Symphony No. 2 in E Minor (Rachmaninoff), **20th:** 3361
Symphony No. 3 (Copland), **20th:** 838
Symphony No. 3 (Ives), **20th:** 1975
Symphony No. 3 (Nielsen), **20th:** 2965
Symphony No. 3 (Zwilich), **20th:** 4477
Symphony No. 4 (Ives), **20th:** 1976
Symphony No. 4 (Sibelius), **20th:** 3737
Symphony No. 4 in E-flat Major (Bruckner), **19th:** 330
Symphony No. 5 (Nielsen), **20th:** 2966

Symphony No. 5 (Prokofiev), **20th:** 3340
Symphony No. 5 (Shostakovich), **20th:** 3730
Symphony No. 5 (Sibelius), **20th:** 3738
Symphony No. 6 (Sibelius), **20th:** 3738
Symphony No. 6 (Vaughan Williams), **20th:** 4149
Symphony No. 7 (Sibelius), **20th:** 3738
Symphony No. 7 (Villa-Lobos), **20th:** 4165
Symphony No. 8 (Bruckner), **19th:** 330
Symphony No. 9 (Henze), **20th:** 1764
Symphony No. 10 (Shostakovich), **20th:** 3729
Symphony No. 13 (Shostakovich), **20th:** 3730
Symphony of Psalms (Stravinsky), **20th:** 3890
Symphony Op. 21 (Webern), **20th:** 4263
Symphony to Dante's "Divina Commedia," A (Liszt), **19th:** 1394
Symphosius of Astorga, **Anc:** 698
Symposion (Lucian), **Anc:** 514
Symposion (Plato), **Anc:** 129, 514, 660
Symposion (Xenophon), **Anc:** 968
Symposium for Orchestra (Zwilich), **20th:** 4476
Symptomatology, **Anc:** 86
Syndicalism, revolutionary, **20th:** 3792
Syndics of the Drapers' Guild, The (Rembrandt), **17th:** 788
Synesius, **Anc:** 435
Synod of _______. *See* _______, Synod of
Synopsis Animalium Quadrupedum et Serpentini Generis (Ray), **17th:** 783
Synopsis of the Indian Tribes Within the United States East of the Rocky Mountains and in the British and Russian Possessions in North America, A (Gallatin), **19th:** 856
Syntagma philosophicum (Gassendi), **17th:** 305
Synthesis of Yoga, The (Aurobindo), **20th:** 179
Synthetic Philosophy, The (Spencer), **19th:** 2127
Syphax, **Anc:** 542, 813
Syphilis, **20th:** 1117, 2251
Syphilis (Fracastoro), **Ren:** 343
Syracuse, **Anc:** 33
Syria, **MA:** 141; **20th:** Faisal I (king of Iraq), 1204. *See also* Geographical Index
Syria-Palestine, Muslim invasion of, **MA:** 507, 934
Syrian Wars (c. 276-271 B.C.E., c. 260-253 B.C.E., 202-200 B.C.E.), **Anc:** 67, 716, 717
Syro-Ephramitic War (735-732 B.C.E.), **Anc:** 893
System, the, **20th:** 3822
System der Medusen, Das. See *Report on the Deep-Sea Medusae*
System der Philosophie (Wundt), **20th:** 4408
System des heutigen römischen Rechts (Savigny), **19th:** 2004
System des transzendentalen Idealismus. See *Introduction to Idealism*
System of Economic Contradictions (Proudhon), **19th:** 1835
System of Logic, A (Mill), **19th:** 1576
System of Nature, The. See *Common Sense* (Holbach)
System of Positive Polity (Comte), **19th:** 538
Systema naturae. See *General System of Nature, A*
Systematische Entwicklung der Abhängigkeit Geometrischer Gestalten (Steiner), **19th:** 2154
Système de politique positive. See *System of Positive Polity*
Système des contradictions économiques. See *System of Economic Contradictions*
Systèmes glaciaires (Agassiz), **19th:** 32
Systems of Consanguinity and Affinity of the Human Family (Morgan), **19th:** 1604
Syzygies, **Anc:** 918
Szabolcs, Synod of (1092), **MA:** 638
Szentgotthárd, Battle of (1664), **17th:** 527

T

Ta Mok, **Notor:** 1017-1018
Taaffe, Ellen. *See* Zwilich, Ellen Taaffe
Ṭabarī, al-, **MA:** 988-990
Tabarro, Il (Puccini), **20th:** 3348
Table of Silence (Brancusi), **20th:** 480
Table with Rabbit (Miró), **20th:** 2760
Tableau économique. See *Economical Table, The*
Taborites, **MA:** 1162
Tabulae anatomicae sex. See *Six Anatomical Tables*
Tabulae eclipsium super meridiano Viennensi (Peuerbach), **Ren:** 774
Tabulae regiomontanae. See *Refraction Tables*
Tabulae Rudolphinae (Kepler), **17th:** 460
Tacco, Ghino di. *See* Craxi, Bettino
Tach, Edward. *See* Teach, Edward
Tachibana no Norimitsu, **MA:** 930
Tacho I. *See* Somoza García, Anastasio
Tacitus, Cornelius, **Anc:** 17, 19, 23, 99, 102-104, 163, 351, 508, 561, 685, 837-840, 890, 904; **Notor:** 195, 290
Tadamori, Taira. *See* Taira Tadamori

Tadano Makuzu, **19th:** 2212-2214
Tadayoshi, Ashikaga. *See* Ashikaga Tadayoshi
Tade kuu mushi. See *Some Prefer Nettles*
T'aejo. *See* Wang Kŏn
Tafari, Ras. *See* Haile Selassie I
Tafari Benti, **20th:** 2702
Tafawa Balewa, Abubakar, **20th:** 181
Tafna, Treaty of (1837), **19th:** 2
Taft, Robert A., **20th:** 3925-3928
Taft, William Howard, **19th:** 362; **20th:** 598, 3929-3933; Philippines, 3520
Taft-Hartley Act of 1947, **20th:** 2672, 3927
Tagaskouita, Catherine. *See* Tekakwitha, Kateri
Tagebuch 1966-1971. See *Sketchbook 1966-1971*
Tagen Sufu, **17th:** 915
Taginae, Battle of (552), **MA:** 600
Tagore, Rabindranath, **20th:** 3933-3936
Tahāfut al-falāsifah. See *Incoherence of the Philosophers*
Tahāfut at-tahāfut. See *Incoherence of the Incoherence*
Taharqa, **Anc:** 118
Táhirih, **19th:** 105, 2214-2216
Tahiti, **18th:** 126, 271
Ṭahmāsap Qolī Khan. *See* Nādir Shāh
Ṭahmāsp I, **Ren:** 475
Ṭahmāsp II, **Notor:** 772
Tai Chen. *See* Dai Zhen
T'ai Ch'iang. *See* Taichang
Tai Tung-Yüan. *See* Dai Zhen
Taichang, **17th:** 911
Taika reforms (645), **MA:** 941, 976
Taine, Hippolyte, **19th:** 2216-2219
Tainos, **Ren:** 408
Taiping Rebellion (1851-1864), **19th:** 496, 949, 1128, 1363, 2484
Taira clan, **MA:** 721, 991
Taira Kiyomori, **MA:** 721, 990-993
Taira Shigemori, **MA:** 991
Taira Tadamori, **MA:** 991
Taisei sankei (Seki et al.), **17th:** 832
Taishō (emperor of Japan), **20th:** 1818; **Notor:** 473
Taitazak, Joseph, **Ren:** 524
Tai-tsung. *See* Daizong
T'ai-tsung. *See* Taizong
Taiwan. *See* Geographical Index
Taiyō to tetsu. See *Sun and Steel*
Taizong, **MA:** 79, 993-997, 1127, 1137, 1140
Taj Mahal, **17th:** 843
Takauji, Ashikaga. *See* Ashikaga Takauji
Takayama Ukon, **Ren:** 460
Takebe Katahiro, **17th:** 832
Takebe Katakira, **17th:** 832
Takechi no Sukune, **Anc:** 595
Takeda Katsuyori, **Ren:** 733
Takeda Shingen, **Ren:** 451, 733
Takigawa, Yukitoki, **20th:** 1702
Takizawa Bakin, **19th:** 2213
Taksin, **18th:** 968-969
Talas River, Battle of (751), **MA:** 79
Talât Paşa, Mehmed, **20th:** 1158
Talavera, Battle of (1809), **19th:** 2410
Talbot, Elizabeth. *See* Bess of Hardwick
Talbot, George, **Ren:** 104
Talbot, Marion, **20th:** 3937-3939
Talbot, Richard, **17th:** 821
Talbot, Thomas, **19th:** 2219-2221
Talcott, Mary White Rowlandson. *See* Rowlandson, Mary White
Tale of a Tub, A (Swift), **18th:** 964
Tale of Genji, The (Murasaki Shikibu), **MA:** 739, 931
Tale of Joan of Arc, The (Christine de Pizan), **MA:** 277
Tale of Peter Rabbit, The (Potter), **20th:** 3315
Tale of Possessors Self-Dispossessed, A (O'Neill), **20th:** 3053
Tale of the Golden Cockerel, The (Pushkin), **19th:** 1850
Tale of the Heike, The, **MA:** 992
Tale of the Love and Death of Cornet Christopher Rilke, The (Rilke), **20th:** 3455
Tale of Tsar Saltan, The (Rimsky-Korsakov), **19th:** 1916
Tale of Two Cities, A (Dickens), **19th:** 656
Tale of Two Lovers, The (Pius II), **Ren:** 794
Talented Tenth, **20th:** 1047
Talenti, Francesco, **MA:** 103
Tales and Heroic Scenes (Hemans), **19th:** 1076
Tales and Short Stories in Verse (La Fontaine), **17th:** 481
Tales from a Mother of Pearl Casket (France), **19th:** 816
Tales from the Vienna Woods (Strauss), **19th:** 2189
Tales of a Grandfather (Scott), **19th:** 2049
Tales of a Traveller (Irving), **19th:** 1181
Tales of a Wayside Inn (Longfellow), **19th:** 1419
Tales of Belkin, The (Pushkin), **19th:** 1849
Tales of Fashionable Life (Edgeworth), **19th:** 729
Tales of Melpomene (Chekhov), **19th:** 478
Tales of Mother Goose (Perrault), **17th:** 732
Tales of Soldiers and Civilians. See *In the Midst of Life*
Tales of the Crusaders (Scott), **19th:** 2048
Tales of the Grotesque and Arabesque (Poe), **19th:** 1814
Tales of the South Pacific (Michener), **20th:** 2728
Taliaferro, William B., **19th:** 320
Taliban, **20th:** 373
Taliesin, **20th:** 4401

Taliesin West, **20th:** 4401
Talikot, Battle of (1565), **Ren:** 532
Ta-ling Ho, Siege of (1631). *See* Daling He, Siege of (1631)
Talisman, The (Scott), **19th:** 2048
Tallchief, Maria, **20th:** 195, 3940-3943
Talleyrand, **19th:** 2221-2225
Tallis, Thomas, **Ren:** 148, 701, 918-919
Talmud, **Anc:** 31, 468; **MA:** commentaries, 409, 748
Talmudic scholarship, **18th:** 318
Talon, Jean-Baptiste, **17th:** 433
Talon, Omer, **Ren:** 817
"Tam o'Shanter" (Burns), **18th:** 185
Tamara, Queen, **MA:** 998-1000
Tamayo y Baus, Manuel, **Notor:** 532
Tamberlaine. *See* Tamerlane
Tambo, Oliver, **20th:** 2479
Tamburlaine the Great (Marlowe), **Ren:** 624
Tamerlane, **MA:** 452, 1000-1003, 1149
Tamerlane, and Other Poems (Poe), **19th:** 1813
Tamil Bandit. *See* Veerappan
Tamils, **Anc:** 934
Tamm, Igor, **20th:** 3602
Tammany Hall, **19th:** 508, 1650, 2334
Tammen, Harry, **19th:** 525
Tammuz, **Anc:** 915
Ta-mo. *See* Bodhidharma
Tan Malaka, **20th:** 1705
Tanabe, Hajime, **20th:** 2982
Tanagra, Battle of (457 B.C.E.), **Anc:** 621
Tanaka, Giichi, **20th:** 1701
Tanaquil, **Anc:** 840-843, 846
Tancred, **MA:** 178, 1003-1005
Tancredi (Rossini), **19th:** 1944
Taney, Roger Brooke, **19th:** 472, 2181, 2225-2229; **Notor:** 1018-1020
Tang Dynasty, **MA:** 79, 1127, 1137, 1140; emperors, 996
T'ang San-tsang. *See* Xuanzang
T'ang T'ai-tsung. *See* Taizong
Tanganyika African National Union, **20th:** 3005
Tangier expedition (1437), **MA:** 479
Tangled Tale, A (Carroll), **19th:** 424
Tanguy, Julien, **19th:** 934
Tanizaki, Jun'ichirō, **20th:** 3944-3946
Tanlin, **Anc:** 160
Tannenberg, Battle of (1410), **MA:** 1121
Tannenberg, Battle of (1914), **20th:** 1815
Tannhäuser (Wagner), **19th:** 2375
Tanzania, **20th:** independence of, 3005. *See also* Geographical Index
Tanzimat, **19th:** 7
Tao Qian, **Anc:** 843-845
Tapestry (Man Ray), **20th:** 2580
Tapiola (Sibelius), **20th:** 3738
Tappan, Lewis, **19th:** 800
Tar Baby (Morrison), **20th:** 2836
Taras Bulba (Janáček), **20th:** 1991
Tarascans, **Ren:** 253
Tarashikomi, **17th:** 869
Tarbell, Ida, **19th:** 1923; **20th:** 3947-3949
Tarchna. *See* Tarquinius Priscus, Lucius; Tarquinius Superbus, Lucius
Tardieu, André, **20th:** 2285
Tarentino, Quentin, **Notor:** 994
Tarentule, La (Coralli), **19th:** 744
Tarentum, Battle of (209 B.C.E.), **Anc:** 344
Tariff of 1828, **19th:** 23
Tariff of 1832, **19th:** 393
Tariff of 1897, **20th:** 2282
Tariff Reform League, **19th:** 462
Tarik ibn Zeyad. *See* Ṭāriq ibn-Ziyād
Tārʾīkh al-Hind. See *Al-Beruni's India*
Taʾrīkh al-rusul wa al-mulūk. See *History of al-Ṭabarī, The*
Ṭāriq ibn-Ziyād, **MA:** 1005-1008
Tarnower, Herman, **Notor:** 448
Tarquinius, Sextus, **Anc:** 517, 846
Tarquinius Collatinus, Lucius, **Anc:** 517, 846
Tarquinius Priscus, Lucius, **Anc:** 840, 846-849
Tarquinius Superbus, Lucius, **Anc:** 517, 841, 846-849
Tarquins. *See* Tarquinius Priscus, Lucius; Tarquinius Superbus, Lucius
Tartaglia, Niccolò Fontana, **Ren:** 173, 920-922
Tartuffe (Molière), **17th:** 19, 521, 648
Tarzan of the Apes (Burroughs), **20th:** 591
Tascalusa, **Ren:** 922-924
Tash, Edward. *See* Teach, Edward
Tashkent Declaration (1966), **20th:** 368
Tashunca-uitko. *See* Crazy Horse
Tasman, Abel Janszoon, **17th:** 905-908
Tasmania, **17th:** 907
Tassilo III, **MA:** 244
Tasso (Liszt), **19th:** 1394
Tasso, Torquato, **Ren:** 924-928
Tastaluca. *See* Tascalusa
Tatanka Iyotanka. *See* Sitting Bull
Tatars, **MA:** 53; **17th:** 428, 624, 784
Tatatara, **Anc:** 464
Tatch, Edward. *See* Teach, Edward
Tate, Sharon, **Notor:** 690
Tate no Kai, **20th:** 2764
Tatler, The (Addison and Steele), **18th:** 21, 942
Tattered Tom (Alger), **19th:** 52
Tatti, Jacopo. *See* Sansovino, Jacopo
Tatum, Art, **20th:** 3113
Taubman, George Dashwood Goldie. *See* Goldie, Sir George

Taunton, Siege of (1644), **17th:** 56
Taussig, Helen Brooke, **20th:** 3950-3952
Tavrichesky, Prince. *See* Potemkin, Grigori Aleksandrovich
Tawaraya Sōtatsu. *See* Sōtatsu
Tawfiq, **19th:** 4
Tawzīh al-masāʾil. See *Clarification of Questions, A*
Taxation, **Anc:** Caligula and, 178; Cao Cao and, 182; Cato and, 192; of Christians, 241; Cleopatra VII and, 230; Confucius on, 237; Cyrus the Great and, 250; Darius and, 136; Diocletian and, 281; Huns and, 140; Persia, 252; Roman, 682; **MA:** Byzantine Empire, 550, 599; China, 969, 995, 1079-1080; Church and, 187, 841; England, 130, 364, 894; France, 840; Japan, 723; Khmer, 982; Morocco, 8; Rome, 899; Sāsānian Empire, 613; **Ren:** France, 225, 348, 575, 577; Hungary, 644; Mongol Dynasty, 16; Sweden, 417; **17th:** Americas, 568; China, 449, 912; Ireland, 734; Japan, 916, 919; Russia, 12; Virginia, 29; **18th:** American colonies, 17, 304, 458, 483, 759; China, 1113; France, 844; Great Britain, 791, 1036; Habsburg Dynasty, 545; Massachusetts, 903; New Spain, 395
Taxi Driver (film), **20th:** 3682
Taxonomy, **18th:** comte de Buffon, 172; Carolus Linnaeus, 604-608
Tay Son Rebellion (1773-1802), **18th:** 736; **19th:** 907, 1110
Tayloe, Nellie Davis. *See* Ross, Nellie Tayloe
Taylor, Charles, **Notor:** 289, 1021-1022
Taylor, Dame Elizabeth, **20th:** 3953-3955
Taylor, Frederick Winslow, **20th:** 3955-3959
Taylor, Graham, **20th:** 2272
Taylor, Harriet, **19th:** 264
Taylor, Jeremy, **17th:** 741
Taylor, Paul Schuster, **20th:** 2261
Taylor, Zachary, **19th:** 506, 611, 782, 958, 1822, 2053, 2230-2233
Taylor Society, **20th:** 3957
TB-1, **20th:** 4108
TBS. *See* Turner Broadcasting Service
Tchaikovsky, Peter Ilich, **19th:** 2233-2237; **20th:** 937
Tchekhov, Anton. *See* Chekhov, Anton
Tcherepnin, Nikolai, **20th:** 985
Tcherniak, Nathalie Ilyanova. *See* Sarraute, Nathalie
Te Deum (Bruckner), **19th:** 330
Te Deum (Verdi), **19th:** 2353
Te Kotahitanga, **19th:** 1484
Te Rauparaha, **19th:** 981
Tea Act (1773), **18th:** 18, 459
Tea trade, **18th:** 82; British monopoly on, 18
Teach, Edward, **Notor:** 117, 1023-1025
Teacher (Keller), **20th:** 3909
Teacher's Word Book, The (Thorndike), **20th:** 4015
Teale, Karla Leanne. *See* Homolka, Karla
Teapot Dome Scandal, **20th:** 1676
Teares or Lamentacions of a Sorrowfull Soule (Leighton), **Ren:** 150
Tears of the Indians, The (Las Casas), **Ren:** 538
Teasdale, Sara, **20th:** 3959-3962
Technē rhetorikēs (Aristotle), **Anc:** 452
Technology. *See* Category Index under Invention and Technology
Tecumseh, **18th:** 612; **19th:** 307, 1048, 2237-2240
Teeter, Lawrence, **Notor:** 966
Tefnakht, **Anc:** 656, 710
Tegakwith. *See* Tekakwitha, Kateri
Teilhard de Chardin, Pierre, **20th:** 3963-3968
Tein, Battle of (1618), **17th:** 966
Tejada, Sebastian Lerdo de, **19th:** 653
Tejas, **Ren:** 247
Tejerazo, El, **20th:** 2061
Tejero, Antonio, **20th:** 2061
Tekakwitha, Kateri, **17th:** 908-910
Telegraphy, **19th:** Cooke-Wheatstone, 549; development of lines, 2106; electromagnetic, 1080; invention of, 1611; transatlantic cable, 1523; **20th:** development of, 2617
Teleki, László, **19th:** 621
Telemachus and Eucharis (David), **19th:** 609
Telemann, Georg Philipp, **18th:** 970-973
Telephones, **19th:** improvement of, 731; invention of, 183
Telescopes, **17th:** 135, 259, 299, 319, 372, 388, 397, 537; **18th:** 490, 492
Telescopium (Sirtori), **17th:** 537
Teleutaios peirasmos, Ho. See *Last Temptation of Christ, The*
Television, **20th:** cable, 4119; development of, 2832, 4479; Great Britain, 811; National Football League, 3554; news, 872, 4120. *See also* Category Index under Radio, Film, and Television
Telford, Thomas, **19th:** 2240-2243
Tell el-Amārna, **Anc:** 28
Tell Tale, The (Traill), **19th:** 2292
Teller, Edward, **20th:** 342, 1237, 3968-3972; **Notor:** 381
Téllez, Gabriel. *See* Tirso de Molina
Telluris theoria sacra. See *Sacred Theory of the Earth, The*
Tema de nuestro tiempo, El. See *Modern Theme, The*

Temin, Howard, **20th:** 4145
Temperance movement, **19th:** 257, 305, 813, 1652, 2084, 2148, 2442; **20th:** 701
Temperature scales, **18th:** 336
Tempest, The (Césaire), **20th:** 712
Tempest, The (Giorgione), **Ren:** 385
Tempest, The (Sullivan), **19th:** 917
Tempest-Tost (Davies), **20th:** 918
Tempesta, Antonio, **17th:** 116
Tempête, Une. See *Tempest, The* (Césaire)
Tempietto (Bramante), **Ren:** 133
Temple, The (Herbert), **17th:** 203, 367
Temple, Henry John. *See* Palmerston, Lord
Temple, Shirley, **20th:** 3973-3975
Temple, Sir William, **17th:** 507
Temple of Artemis at Ephesus, **Anc:** 761
Temple of Athena Alea at Tegea, **Anc:** 761
Temple of Athena the Maiden, **Anc:** 634
Temple of Dawn, The (Mishima), **20th:** 2764
Temple of Jerusalem, **Anc:** 31, 256, 339, 405, 468, 478, 803
Temple of Jupiter Optimus Maximus, **Anc:** 847
Temple of Mount Temple, Baron. *See* Palmerston, Lord
Temple of My Familiar, The (Walker), **20th:** 4197
Temple School, **19th:** 40
Temps déborde, Le (Éluard), **20th:** 1153
Temps des déracinés, Le. See *Time of the Uprooted, The*
Temptation of Saint Anthony, The (Bruegel), **Ren:** 136
Temptation of Saint Anthony, The (Callot), **17th:** 117
Temptation of Saint Anthony, The (Flaubert), **19th:** 785
Temptress, The (film), **20th:** 1392
Temüjin. *See* Genghis Khan
Ten Articles of Religion (1536), **Ren:** 266, 443
Ten Commandments, **Anc:** 1, 256, 574
Ten Commandments, The (film), **20th:** 961
Ten Dollar Bill, The (Lichtenstein), **20th:** 2374
Ten Hours' Act (1847), **19th:** 303
Ten Thousand, March of the. *See* March of the Ten Thousand
Tenant of Wildfell Hall, The (Brontë), **19th:** 310
Tendai sect, **MA:** 581, 620, 758
Tender Buttons (Stein), **20th:** 3847
Tender Husband, The (Steele), **18th:** 942
Tender Is the Night (Fitzgerald), **20th:** 1251
Teng Hsiao-p'ing. *See* Deng Xiaoping
Tengoku to jigoku. See *High and Low*
Tenney, Jack B., **Notor:** 974
Tennin gosui. See *Decay of the Angel, The*
Tennis, **20th:** Australia, 2288; England, 3216; Sweden, 426; United States, 1191, 1474, 2143, 2923, 3616, 4334
Tennyson, Alfred, Lord, **19th:** 1176, 2244-2247; on Charles George Gordon, 951
Tenochtitlán, **MA:** 558; **Ren:** 254, 273, 621
Tenshō Shūbun. *See* Shūbun
Tenskwatawa, **19th:** 2238
Tenth Muse Lately Sprung up in America, The (Bradstreet), **17th:** 89
Tenure of Kings and Magistrates, The (Milton), **17th:** 640
Tenure of Office Act, **19th:** 1233
Tenures (Littleton), **Ren:** 572
Tenzin Gyatso. *See* Dalai Lama (fourteenth)
Tenzing Norgay, **20th:** 1804
Tepanecans, **Ren:** 720
Tepesch, Vlad. *See* Vlad III the Impaler
Terence, **Anc:** 549, 757, 849-852
Teresa (queen of Portugal), **MA:** 33
Teresa, Mother, **20th:** 3975-3978
Teresa Benedicta of the Cross, Saint. *See* Stein, Edith
Teresa de Cepeda y Ahumada. *See* Teresa of Ávila, Saint
Teresa of Ávila, Saint, **Ren:** 4, 507, 670, 928-931
Tereshkova, Valentina, **20th:** 1372, 2194, 3978-3981
Terkhen-Khatun, **MA:** 776
Ternary of Paradoxes, A (Helmont), **17th:** 362
Terra Australis Incognito, **18th:** 270
Terra Trema, La. See *Earth Trembles, The*
Terrail, Pierre. *See* Bayard, Chevalier de
Terrorism, **20th:** Al-Qaeda, 373, 1197, 1948, 3324; Black September, 111; Germany, 413; hijackings, 81, 1626; India, 1386; Ireland, 844; Israel, 285, 3359; Italy, 1468; Libya, 3352; Peru, 1359; Quebec, 4077
Terrorists. *See* Category Index
Terrors of the Night, The (Nashe), **Ren:** 715
Terry, Alfred, **19th:** 568, 584, 2109
Terry, Ellen, **19th:** 1176, 2248-2252; and Henry Irving, 1177
Terry, Megan, **20th:** 3982-3985
Terry v. Ohio (1968), **20th:** 1030
Tertullian, **Anc:** 853-855
Teseida. See *Book of Theseus, The*
Tesla, Nikola, **19th:** 2252-2255, 2417
Tesla Electric Company, **19th:** 2253
Tess of the D'Urbervilles (Hardy), **19th:** 1029
Test Act (1673), **17th:** 148, 507, 693, 816, 839
Test oaths, **19th:** 778

Testimonies Concerning That One God, and the Persons of the Holy Trinity, The (Biddle), **17th:** 53
Tet Offensive (1968), **20th:** 4171
Tetanus, **19th:** 181
Tetrabiblos. See *Apotelesmatika*
Tetragonismos ten tou orthogonion konoy tomes (Archimedes), **Anc:** 82
Tetrapla (Origen), **Anc:** 600
Tetrapolitana, **Ren:** 143
Tetrarchy, Diocletian, **Anc:** 239, 281, 391
Tetsugaku no kompon mondai. See *Fundamental Problems of Philosophy*
Tettenhall, Battle of (910), **MA:** 31, 342
Tetzel, Johann, **Ren:** 582
Teustsche Michel, Der (Grimmelshausen), **17th:** 325
Teutoburg Forest, Battle of (9 C.E.), **Anc:** 100
Teutonic Knights, **MA:** 52, 230, 1120; **Ren:** 242, 885
Teutons, **Anc:** 533, 831
Tewkesbury, Battle of (1471), **Ren:** 91, 340, 830
Tewodros, **Ren:** 1006
Tewodros II, **19th:** 2255-2257
Texas, **19th:** annexation of, 194, 394, 1131, 1821, 2231; colonization, 98; independence of, 1991; Republic of, 100
Texas cattle fever, **20th:** 3773
Texas Revolution, **19th:** 99, 572, 583, 1131
Texas v. White, **19th:** 473
Texel, Battle of the (1653), **17th:** 57
Text-book of Electrochemistry (Arrhenius), **20th:** 139
Textile industry, **18th:** 466, 560
Tezozómoc, **Ren:** 720
Thābit ibn Qurrah, **MA:** 137
Thackeray, William Makepeace, **19th:** 741, 1956, 2257-2260
Thai-Burmese conflicts, **18th:** 968
Thailand, **18th:** 736, 968-969. *See also* Geographical Index
Thaïs (France), **19th:** 815
Thaksin Shinawatra, **20th:** 363
Thakur, Rabindranath. *See* Tagore, Rabindranath
Thales of Miletus, **Anc:** 55, 57-58, 244, 407, 725, 856-859, 965
Thalidomide, **20th:** 3951
Thames, Battle of the (1813), **19th:** 1049, 1780, 2239
Thames and the City of London from Richmond House, The (Canaletto), **18th:** 192
Thames Tunnel, **19th:** 333, 338
Than Shwe, **Notor:** 1026-1027
Thanadelthur, **18th:** 974-976
Thanatology, **20th:** 2209
Thanchvil. *See* Tanaquil
Thankmar, **MA:** 805
Thant, U, **20th:** 3986-3988
Tharp, Twyla, **20th:** 2013, 3989-3991
That Hamilton Woman (film), **20th:** 3041
That Hideous Strength (Lewis), **20th:** 2354
That Lass o' Lowrie's (Burnett), **19th:** 357
That Obscure Object of Desire (film), **20th:** 579
Thatch, Edward. *See* Teach, Edward
Thatcher, Margaret, **20th:** 1740, 2567, 3992-3996; **Notor:** 395
Thaw, Harry Kendall, **Notor:** 1027-1028
Thayendanegea. *See* Brant, Joseph
Thayer, Sylvanus, **19th:** 2260-2263
Thayer, Webster, **Notor:** 924, 1058
Theaetētos (Plato), **Anc:** 660, 799
Theaetetus, **Anc:** 321
Theagenes, **Anc:** 293
Theater, **MA:** Christian, 517; Germany, 513; India, 461; Japan, 1152; **Ren:** England, 93, 214, 554, 624, 715, 876, 882; France, 619; Italy, 42, 54, 57, 181, 588; Portugal, 167; Spain, 208; **17th:** England, 42, 51, 82, 104, 109, 223, 238, 240, 373, 436, 440, 502, 636, 729, 765, 846, 894, 928; France, 193, 212, 646, 774; Japan, 408; Spain, 113, 740, 913, 949; **18th:** Chikamatsu Monzaemon, 243-245; comedic, 907; David Garrick, 397-400; puppet play, 243; Restoration comedy, 1002; **19th:** England, 1313, 1590, 2248, 2433; France, 208, 2062, 2355; India, 2364; United States, 271, 1555, 1902, 1904; **20th:** Canada, 917; England, 3039, 3717; Germany, 504; Russia, 2723, 3822; Spain, 1396; stage design, 1431; United States, 862. *See also* Category Index
Theaters, War of the, **17th:** 223
Theatines, **17th:** 330, 720
Theatre, The (playhouse), **17th:** 104
Théâtre de la Foire, **18th:** 597
Théâtre de la Foire, Le (Lesage), **18th:** 597
Théâtre-Française, **19th:** 696, 1700
Theatre Guild Company, **20th:** 862
Theatrical Licensing Act (1737), **18th:** 347
Thébaïde, La. See *Theban Brothers, The*
Theban Brothers, The (Racine), **17th:** 774
Thebes, Egypt, **Anc:** capital, 26, 570
Thebes, Greece, **Anc:** Delian League and, 621; Macedonia and, 637; revolt against Alexander the Great, 39; Sparta and, 14, 16, 227
Theft, A (Bellow), **20th:** 290
Their Eyes Were Watching God (Hurston), **20th:** 1945

Theist's Confession of Faith, A (Ranade), **19th:** 1856
Theme System, **MA:** 508
Themistocles, **Anc:** 110, 214, 506, 794, 859-862, 973
Thenard, Louis Jacques, **19th:** 887
Theocritus, **Anc:** 939
Theodahad, **MA:** 77
Theodicy (Leibniz), **17th:** 516
Theodora (Byzantine empress), **MA:** 294, 599, 863, 1008-1011; **Notor:** 546, 1028-1030
Theodora (English ascetic). *See* Christina of Markyate
Theodora, Adel. *See* Menken, Adah Isaacs
Theodora the Elder (wife of Theophylact), **Notor:** 706
Theodore (ruler of Gonder), **19th:** 1552
Theodore II (emperor of Ethiopia). *See* Tewodros II
Theodore, Ada Bertha. *See* Menken, Adah Isaacs
Theodore of Mopsuestia, **Anc:** 862-865
Theodore Thomas Orchestra, **19th:** 2269
Theodoret of Cyrrhus, **Anc:** 789, 865-867
Theodoric the Great, **MA:** 75, 173, 233, 293, 783, 1012-1016
Theodorus, **Anc:** 89
Theodosius I the Great, **Anc:** 43, 352, 361, 364, 798, 824, 863, 868-872, 913
Theodosius II, **Anc:** 139, 825; **Notor:** 45
Theodosius, Flavius, **Anc:** 868
Theogenius (Alberti), **Ren:** 19
Theogonia (Hesiod), **Anc:** 413
Theoleptus of Philadelphia, **MA:** 1016-1019
Theologia platonica. See *Platonic Theology*
Theological Essays (Maurice), **19th:** 1520
Theological Orations. See *Orationae*
Theological Repository (Priestley), **18th:** 811
Theologico-Political Treatise, A (Spinoza), **17th:** 873
Theologie des Neuen Testaments. See *Theology of the New Testament*
Theologische Existenz heute (journal), **20th:** 245
Theology, **Anc:** Catholic, 361; Christian, 425, 456; Egyptian, 588; Mesopotamian, 299; Saint Paul, 613; **MA:** China, 1137; England, 92, 817, 1130; France, 942, 1114; Germany, 43; Italy, 1029, 1050; Jewish, 687; Muslim, 20, 37, 111, 370, 416, 455; Portugal, 95; Scotland, 330; Spain, 882; **18th:** Johann Gottfried Herder, 486; Ann Lee, 591-594; Samuel Sewall, 894; Granville Sharp, 901; Emanuel Swedenborg, 961-963; **20th:** 4028. *See also* Philosophy; Religion; Category Index under Religion and Theology
Theology for the Social Gospel, A (Rauschenbusch), **20th:** 3384
Theology of Saint Anselm Concerning the Procession of the Holy Spirit to Confute the Opposition of the Greeks, The (Anselm), **MA:** 94
Theology of the New Testament (Bultmann), **20th:** 573
Theōn dialogoi (Lucian), **Anc:** 514
Theophanes the Confessor, **MA:** 1020-1022
Theophano (Harrison), **19th:** 1046
Theophrastus, **Anc:** 94, 97, 277, 310, 872-875
Theophylact of Tusculum, **Notor:** 706
Theopompus of Chios, **Anc:** 451
Theorell, Hugo, **20th:** 3997-3999
Theoretical Chemistry from the Standpoint of Avogadro's Rule and Thermodynamics (Nernst), **20th:** 2935
Theoria medica vera (Stahl), **18th:** 934
Theorica y practica de guerra. See *Theorique and Practise of Warre*
Theoricae Mediceorum planetarum ex causis physicis deductae (Borelli), **17th:** 66
Theoricae novae planetarum (Peuerbach), **Ren:** 774
Théorie analytique de la chaleur. See *Analytical Theory of Heat, The*
Théorie analytique des probabilités (Laplace), **19th:** 1318
Théorie de la maneuvre des vaisseaux (Bernoulli), **17th:** 49
Théorie de l'unité universelle. See *Social Science*
Theorie des kommunikativen Handelns. See *Theory of Communicative Action, The*
Théorie des quatre mouvements and des destinées générales. See *Social Destiny of Man, The*
Theorie des Romans, Die. See *Theory of the Novel, The*
Theorie und Konstruktion eines rationellen Wärmemotors zum Ersatz der Dampfmaschinen und der heute bekannten Verbrennungsmotoren. See *Theory and Construction of a Rational Heat Motor*
Theorie und Praxis. See *Theory and Practice*
Theorique and Practise of Warre (Mendoza), **Ren:** 669
Theory and Calculation of Alternating Current Phenomena (Steinmetz), **19th:** 2158
Theory and Construction of a Rational Heat Motor (Diesel), **19th:** 664
Theory and Practice (Habermas), **20th:** 1633

Theory of Business Enterprise, The (Veblen), **20th:** 4155
Theory of Colors (Goethe), **18th:** 429
Theory of Communicative Action, The (Habermas), **20th:** 1633
Theory of Flight (Rukeyser), **20th:** 3556
Theory of Games and Economic Behavior (von Neumann and Morgenstern), **20th:** 2946
Theory of Heat (Maxwell), **19th:** 1529
Theory of Island Biogeography, The (Wilson and MacArthur), **20th:** 4359
Theory of Justice, A (Rawls), **20th:** 2999, 3392
Theory of Knowledge, The (Hobhouse), **20th:** 1842
Theory of Moral Sentiments, The (Smith), **18th:** 921
Theory of the Consumption Function, The (Friedman), **20th:** 1333
Theory of the Leisure Class, The (Veblen), **20th:** 4155
Theory of the Novel, The (Lukács), **20th:** 2468
Theory of Vision, The (Berkeley), **18th:** 112
Theosebeia, **Anc:** 363
Theosophic Questions (Böhme), **17th:** 61
Theosophical Society, **19th:** 212
Theosophy, **Anc:** 920
Theotokópoulos, Doménikos. *See* Greco, El
Therapeutae, **Anc:** 642
Therapeutica (Theodoret), **Anc:** 866
Therapeutika (Herophilus), **Anc:** 412
Theravāda Buddhism, **Anc:** 898, 931, 934
There's a Trick with a Knife I'm Learning to Do (Ondaatje), **20th:** 3049
There's No Business Like Show Business (film), **20th:** 2798
Thérèse (Mauriac), **20th:** 2657
Thérèse Raquin (Zola), **19th:** 2489
Theresienstadt concentration camp, **20th:** 188
Thermodynamics, **19th:** 914, 1265
Thermometers, **18th:** 336
Thermopylae, Battle of (480 B.C.E.), **Anc:** 506, 615, 794, 860, 973
Thersippus of Erchia, **Anc:** 631
Thesaurus temporum (Scaliger), **Ren:** 857
These Happy Golden Years (Wilder), **20th:** 4336
These Three (film), **20th:** 1525
Theseum, **Anc:** 678
Theseus, **Anc:** 214, 327, 678
Theseus and the Minotaur (Canova), **19th:** 406
Thesmophoriazousai (Aristophanes), **Anc:** 92
Thespis, **Anc:** 876-878
Thespis (Gilbert and Sullivan), **19th:** 918
Thessalian League, **Anc:** 638
Theuderic (son of Clovis), **MA:** 381
Theuerdank of 1517, The (Maximilian), **Ren:** 631, 648
Theurgy, **Anc:** 689, 701
Thévenot, Melchisedec, **17th:** 898
They Called It Purple Heart Valley (Bourke-White), **20th:** 462
They Came to Cordura (film), **20th:** 1733
They Had to See Paris (film), **20th:** 3494
Thibault, Jacques-Anatole-François. *See* France, Anatole
Thibaut III, **MA:** 1059
Thich Quang Duc, **Notor:** 786-787
Thief and the Dogs, The (Mahfouz), **20th:** 2555
Thief-Taker General of Great Britain and Ireland. *See* Wild, Jonathan
Thief's Journal, The (Genet), **20th:** 1446
Thier-Chemie, Die. See *Animal Chemistry*
Thiers, Adolphe, **19th:** 2263-2267
Thieu, Nguyen Van. *See* Nguyen Van Thieu
Things as They Are (Godwin), **18th:** 425
Things Fall Apart (Achebe), **20th:** 14
Things That Are Not Caesar's, The (Maritain), **20th:** 2625
Thinker, The (Rodin), **19th:** 1926
Third and Fourth Booke of Ayres, The (Campion), **17th:** 127
Third and Last Booke of Songs or Ayres, The (Dowland), **Ren:** 290
Third Book (Rabelais), **Ren:** 619
Third Dynasty (Egypt), **Anc:** 439, 996
Third Estate (France), **18th:** 78, 619, 648, 680, 728, 753, 844, 917. *See also* National Assembly of France
Third Letter for Toleration, A (Locke), **17th:** 37, 546
Third Life of Grange Copeland, The (Walker), **20th:** 4196
Third Piano Sonata (Boulez), **20th:** 454
Third Republic, **19th:** 256, 2266
Third Symphony (Borodin), **19th:** 282
Third Violet, The (Crane), **19th:** 562
Thirteen Years' War (1454-1466), **MA:** 1121
Thirteenth Amendment (U.S. Constitution), **19th:** 877, 1787, 2172
Thirty Lithographs (Toulouse-Lautrec), **19th:** 2290
Thirty-nine Steps, The (film), **20th:** 1826
Thirty Poems (Bryant), **19th:** 342
Thirty Tyrants, **Anc:** 659
Thirty Years' Peace, **Anc:** 622

Thirty Years' War (1618-1648), **17th:** 250, 268, 470, 705, 805, 820; and Pope Alexander VII, 9; and Charles X Gustav, 153; and the Great Condé, 184; Dutch participation, 619; English participation, 97, 261, 415, 495, 767; English refugees to North America, 218; and Frederick William, the Great Elector, 290; French participation, 554, 933; generals, 966; Grimmelshausen on, 324; in literature, 325; peace talks, 621; political writings, 761; and Portugal, 431; and Cardinal de Richelieu, 791; in Spanish literature, 115; Spanish participation, 737; Swedish participation, 163, 337, 925; and high taxes in France, 549; and Pope Urban VIII, 936
This Is My Life (film), **20th:** 1163
This Is the Army (Berlin), **20th:** 329
This Life (Poitier), **20th:** 3297
This Misery of Boots (Wells), **20th:** 4288
This People Israel (Baeck), **20th:** 188
This Side of Paradise (Fitzgerald), **20th:** 1250
This Was a Man (Coward), **20th:** 854
This Year of Grace! (Coward), **20th:** 855
Thistles (Sutherland), **20th:** 3921
Thököly, Imre, **17th:** 453
Thomas, Captain. *See* Bonnet, Stede
Thomas, Clarence, **20th:** 596, 3999-4002
Thomas, earl of Lancaster, **MA:** 347
Thomas, George, **19th:** 1858
Thomas, Jefferson, **Notor:** 349
Thomas, Norman, **20th:** 4002-4006
Thomas, Saint, **Anc:** 878-882
Thomas, Theodore, **19th:** 2267-2271
Thomas, William, **19th:** 1134
Thomas à Kempis, **MA:** 1022-1026
Thomas Aquinas, **MA:** 43, 180, 318, 944, 1027-1030, 1106, 1111
Thomas Howard, Second Earl of Arundel (van Dyck), **17th:** 244
Thomas l'imposteur. See *Thomas the Impostor*
Thomas of London. *See* Becket, Saint Thomas
Thomas of Strassburg, **MA:** 761
Thomas Road Baptist Church, **20th:** 1210
Thomas the Impostor (Cocteau), **20th:** 794
Thomassin, Philippe, **17th:** 116
Thomism, **20th:** 2625
Thomisme, Le. See *Philosophy of St. Thomas Aquinas*
Thomist Realism and the Critique of Knowledge (Gilson), **20th:** 1489
Thompson, David, **19th:** 2271-2273
Thompson, Helen, **20th:** 1466
Thompson, Ruth Plumly, **19th:** 158
Thompson, Wiley, **19th:** 1709
Thomson, Sir Joseph John, **20th:** 2432, 4007-4009
Thomson, Tom, **20th:** 4010-4013
Thomson, William. *See* Kelvin, Baron
Thoreau, Henry David, **19th:** 33, 42, 747, 1762, 2274-2277
Thorez, Maurice, **Notor:** 298
Thorndike, Edward L., **20th:** 4013-4016
Thorns (Sutherland), **20th:** 3921
Thornton, Deborah Ruth, **Notor:** 1044
Thorpe, George, **17th:** 702
Thorpe, Jim, **20th:** 4016-4019
Thott, Sophie Brahe. *See* Brahe, Sophie
Thoughts on African Colonization (Garrison), **19th:** 876
"Thoughts on American Liberty" (Witherspoon), **18th:** 1100
Thoughts on the Cause of the Present Discontents (Burke), **18th:** 174
Thousand and One Nights, The. See *Arabian Nights' Entertainments, The*
Thousand Cranes (Kawabata), **20th:** 2085
Thousand Nights and a Night, The. See *Arabian Nights' Entertainments, The*
Thousand Teachings, A (Śaṅkara), **MA:** 926
Thrale, Henry, **18th:** 537
Thrale, Hester, **18th:** 537
Thrasea Paetus, Publius Clodius, **Anc:** 103
Three Ages, The (film), **20th:** 2090
Three Ages, The (Klimt), **20th:** 2180
Three Books of Life, The (Ficino), **Ren:** 333
Three Books on Embassies (Gentili), **Ren:** 372
Three Books on the Law of War, The (Gentili), **Ren:** 373
Three Brides, The (Yonge), **19th:** 2472
Three Cities, The (Zola), **19th:** 2491
Three Comrades (Remarque), **20th:** 3415
Three Cornered Hat, The (Falla), **20th:** 1207
Three Days' Battle (1653), **17th:** 57
Three Dialogues Between Hylas and Philonous (Berkeley), **18th:** 111
Three Elephant Power, and Other Stories (Paterson), **19th:** 1758
Three Emperors' League, **19th:** 49
Three Essays on Anger. See *De ira libri tres*

Three Essays on the Theory of Sexuality (Freud), **20th:** 1324
Three Feudatories, **17th:** 449
Three Figures Outdoors (Giacometti), **20th:** 1471
Three Gorges Dam, **20th:** 2369
Three Graces, The (Rubens), **17th:** 803
Three Henrys, War of the (1587-1588), **Ren:** 200, 428-429, 464, 705
Three Kingdoms (China), **Anc:** 183
Three Kings, Battle of (1578), **Ren:** 860
Three Lectures on Architecture (Mendelsohn), **20th:** 2693
Three Little Pigs (animated film), **20th:** 1008
Three Lives (Stein), **20th:** 3846
Three Marys at the Sepulcher, The (van Eyck), **MA:** 366
Three Musketeers, The (Dumas), **19th:** 697
Three Philosophers, The (Giorgione), **Ren:** 385
Three Places in New England (Ives), **20th:** 1975
Three Principles of the People, **20th:** 3914
Three Reformers (Maritain), **20th:** 2625
Three Sisters (Chekhov), **19th:** 480
Three Sunsets and Other Poems (Carroll), **19th:** 424
Three Tales (Flaubert), **19th:** 786
Three Tenors Concert in Rome (Carreras, Domingo, and Pavarotti), **20th:** 3160
Three Times Dead (Braddon), **19th:** 284
Three Traditional Rhymes Op. 17 (Webern), **20th:** 4263
Threepenny Opera, The (Weill and Brecht), **20th:** 4274
Threshers (Pollock), **20th:** 3301
Thrift, Mary. *See* Cutpurse, Moll
Throckmorton, Elizabeth, **Ren:** 814
Throckmorton, Francis, **Ren:** 668
Throckmorton plot (1583), **Ren:** 201, 668
Throne of Blood (film), **20th:** 2219
Through a Glass Darkly (film), **20th:** 317
Through One Administration (Burnett), **19th:** 358
Through the Looking-Glass and What Alice Found There (Carroll), **19th:** 424
Through Town and Jungle (Workman and Workman), **19th:** 2467
Thuan Hoang De. *See* Le Thanh Tong
Thucydides, **Anc:** 275, 512, 743, 882-885, 969
Thule, island of, **Anc:** 730
Thule expeditions, **20th:** 3378
Thunder Over Mexico (film), **20th:** 1130
Thurber, James, **20th:** 4020-4023
Thurber Album, The (Thurber), **20th:** 4021
Thurber Carnival, The (Thurber), **20th:** 4021
Thuróczy, **MA:** 519
Thurzo, György, **Ren:** 82; **Notor:** 71
Thus Spake Zarathustra (Nietzsche), **19th:** 1682
Thutmes (sculptor), **Anc:** 589
Thutmose I, **Anc:** 388
Thutmose II, **Anc:** 388
Thutmose III, **Anc:** 388, 556, 885-888
Thuwain, **19th:** 1967
Tiananmen Square protests (1989), **20th:** 970, 2368, 4460
Tiancong. *See* Abahai
Tianjin incident (1870), **19th:** 1364, 2484
Tianqi, **17th:** 160, 911-912
Tianzhu shiyi. See *True Meaning of the Lord in Heaven, The*
Tibaldi, Domenico, **Ren:** 175
Tiberius, **Anc:** 72, 147, 176, 217, 490, 510, 604, 644, 766, 888-891; **Notor:** 166, 458, 841
Tiberius Claudius Nero (husband of Livia Drusilla), **Anc:** 508
Tibet, **17th:** 2; **20th:** British military expedition to, 896; Chinese invasion of, 2932. *See also* Geographical Index
Tibullus, **Anc:** 834
Tichborne, Roger, **Notor:** 806
Tichborne claimant. *See* Orton, Arthur
Tiech, Ludwig, **19th:** 2009
T'ien-ch'i. *See* Tianqi
T'ien-ts'ung. *See* Abahai
Tiepolo, Giovanni Battista, **18th:** 436, 976-979
Tiers livre. See *Third Book*
Tigellinus, Ofonius, **Anc:** 591
Tiger, The (Marc), **20th:** 2607
Tiger at the Gates (Giraudoux), **20th:** 1493
Tiger of Korea. *See* Koiso, Kuniaki
Tiger of Romagna. *See* Sforza, Caterina
Tiger Woman. *See* Snyder, Ruth
Tigers and Lions Hunt (Rubens), **17th:** 803
Tiglath-pileser III, **Anc:** 753, 892-895
Tigoni Primate Research Center, **20th:** 2313
Tigranes II, the Great, **Anc:** 895-897
Tigranes V, **Anc:** 776
Tigray People's Liberation Front, **20th:** 2702
Tiguex War (1540-1541), **Ren:** 247
Tik-Tok Man, The (Baum), **19th:** 158
Tikriti, Saddam Hussein al-. *See* Hussein, Saddam
Til Selvprøvelse. See *For Self-Examination*
Tilak, Bal Gangadhar, **19th:** 1635, 1856; **20th:** 178, 4023-4026

Tilden, Samuel J., **19th:** 1062; **Notor:** 1049
Till Damaskus. See *To Damascus*
Till We Have Faces (Lewis), **20th:** 2354
Tilled Field, The (Miró), **20th:** 2760
Tillich, Paul, **20th:** 1137, 4027-4029
Tillman, Benjamin, **Notor:** 1030-1032
Tillray, Les. *See* Gardner, Erle Stanley
Tilly, count of (Johan Tserclaes), **17th:** 294, 333, 337, 894, 966
Tilsit, Treaty of (1807), **19th:** 46, 1022, 2007, 2151, 2223
Timaeos (Plato), **Anc:** 641
Timbuktu, **Ren:** 556; Songhai conquest of, 901
Time, measurement of, **MA:** 109
Time and Free Will (Bergson), **20th:** 323
Time-and-motion studies, **20th:** 3956
Time Machine, The (Wells), **20th:** 4287
Time magazine, **20th:** 2456
Time of the Uprooted, The (Wiesel), **20th:** 4326
Time of Troubles (Russia), **Ren:** 388; **17th:** 11, 683, 794, 855, 945
Time Out of Mind (Dylan), **20th:** 1073
Times, The (London), **19th:** 2381
Times of Struggle (Lange), **19th:** 1308
Times They Are a-Changin', The (Dylan), **20th:** 1073, 3990
Timofey, Yermak, **Ren:** 494
Timoleon (Melville), **19th:** 1540
Timon of Athens (Middleton and Shakespeare), **17th:** 637
Timour. *See* Tamerlane
Timur, Amir, **Notor:** 772
Timurid Dynasty, **MA:** 1002
Timurlenk. *See* Tamerlane
Tin Drum (Grass), **20th:** 1573
Tindale, William. *See* Tyndale, William
Tintoretto (Jacopo Robusti), **Ren:** 175, 931-934, 935
Tintoretto, Marietta Robusti, **Ren:** 935-936
Tipiṭaka, **Anc:** 50, 934
Tipiṭaka Master. *See* Xuanzang
Tippecanoe, Battle of (1811), **19th:** 1048, 2238
Tippu Tib, **19th:** 2277-2279; **Notor:** 632
Tirana, La (Boccherini), **18th:** 130
Tirpitz, Alfred von, **19th:** 1121; **20th:** 1181, 4030-4033
Tirsi (Castiglione), **Ren:** 181
Tirso de Molina, **17th:** 114, 913-915, 952
Tīrthaṅkara, **Anc:** 925
Tiryns (Schliemann), **19th:** 2018
Tisquantum. *See* Squanto
Tissa, Dīvānaṃpiya, **Anc:** 898-900
Tisza, Kálmán, **19th:** 622
Titan, The (Dreiser), **20th:** 1034
Titanic, **20th:** discovery of sunken ship, 216; sinking of, 543
Titian, **Ren:** 54, 100, 175, 385, 390, 487, 932, 936-939
Tito, **20th:** 1012, 4034-4037; **Notor:** 493, 554, 735, 814, 876, 970, 1032-1033
Tituba, **17th:** 690
Titurel. See *Schionatulander and Sigune*
Titus, **Anc:** 478, 943; **Notor:** 289, 541
Titus Livius. *See* Livy
Titus Maccius Plautus. *See* Plautus
Tiy (Egyptian queen), **Anc:** 27, 46, 901-903
Tlaxcalans, **Ren:** 34, 253
TNT. *See* Turner Network Television
To BE or Not to BOP (Gillespie), **20th:** 1482
To Be Young, Gifted, and Black (Hansberry), **20th:** 1673
To Bedlam and Part Way Back (Sexton), **20th:** 3714
To Catch a Thief (film), **20th:** 1572
To Damascus (Strindberg), **20th:** 3898
To Delos. See *In Delum*
To Have and Have Not (film), **20th:** 407
To Jerusalem and Back (Bellow), **20th:** 290
To Kill a Mockingbird (film), **20th:** 3182
"To My Dear and Loving Husband" (Bradstreet), **17th:** 88
To My Mother Helvia, on Consolation. See *Ad Helviam matrem de consolatione*
To Philip. See *Philippos*
Tō Shikibu. *See* Murasaki Shikibu
To Sir, with Love (film), **20th:** 3297
To the Castle and Back (Havel), **20th:** 1708
To the Finland Station (Wilson), **20th:** 4356
To the Lighthouse (Woolf), **20th:** 4398
To the Nations. See *Ad nationes*
Toad of Toad Hall (Milne), **20th:** 2754
Toba-Fushimi, Battle of (1868), **19th:** 1970
Tobacco, **Ren:** discovery of, 239; **18th:** 395, 482
Tobacco mosaic virus, **20th:** 3825
Toccate e partite d'intavolatura di cimbalo (Frescobaldi), **17th:** 296
Tocqueville, Alexis de, **19th:** 2280-2283; **Notor:** 415
Tōdaiji, **MA:** 621, 624
Tod in Venedig, Der. See *Death in Venice* (Mann)
Today Show, The (television news program), **20th:** 4211
Todd, George, **Notor:** 870
Todd, Michael, **20th:** 3953

Todd, Sweeney, **Notor:** 1033-1034
Tofukumon-in, **17th:** 695
Toghrïl Beg, **MA:** 70, 774, 795
Toghrïl Khan, **MA:** 402, 954
Toguri, Ikuko. *See* Tokyo Rose
Tōhō, **20th:** 2217
Toilet of Venus (Bellini), **Ren:** 384
Toilette, La (Toulouse-Lautrec), **19th:** 2290
Tojo, Hideki, **Notor:** 587, 1034-1036
Tōkaidō Gojūsantsugi (Hiroshige), **19th:** 1108
Tokimasa, Hōjō. *See* Hōjō Tokimasa
Toklas, Alice B., **20th:** 3845
Toktamish Khan, **MA:** 1001
Tokugawa Hidetada, **17th:** 917, 998
Tokugawa Iemitsu, **17th:** 917, 919, 998
Tokugawa Ienobu, **17th:** 831, 920
Tokugawa Ietsuna, **17th:** 831, 919, 999
Tokugawa Ieyasu, **Ren:** 451, 460, 733, 943; **17th:** 408, 915-918, 998
Tokugawa Nariaki, **19th:** 1169
Tokugawa shogunate, **19th:** 1169, 1631
Tokugawa Tsunashige, **17th:** 831
Tokugawa Tsunayoshi, **17th:** 831, 919-920
Tokugawa Yorinobu, **17th:** 999
Tokugawa Yoshimune, **17th:** 920; **18th:** 980-982
Tokugawa Yoshinobu, **19th:** 1970
Tokyo Rose, **Notor:** 1036-1038
Tokyo Tsushin Kogyo, **20th:** 2831
Tolbert, William R., Jr., **Notor:** 1021
Tolbiacum, Battle of (496), **MA:** 288, 291
Toledo, Fourth Council of (633), **MA:** 555
Toledo, Juan Bautista de, **Ren:** 445
Toledo Manrique, Alejandro, **Notor:** 382
Toleration, Edict of (1562), **Ren:** 185
Toleration, Edict of (1764), **18th:** 545
Toleration Act of 1649, **17th:** 93
Toleration Act of 1689, **17th:** 34, 284
Tolkien, J. R. R., **20th:** 4038-4041
Tolman, Richard C., **20th:** 3155
Tolpuddle Martyrs, **19th:** 1535
Tolson, Clyde, **Notor:** 491
Tolstoy, Dmitry Andreyevich, **19th:** 50
Tolstoy, Leo, **19th:** 2283-2287, 2320
Toltecs, **Ren:** 694
Tolui, **MA:** 402, 954
Tom Sawyer Abroad (Twain), **19th:** 2331
Tom Sawyer, Detective (Twain), **19th:** 2331
Tom Telescope (Newbery), **18th:** 731
Tom Thumb (Fielding), **18th:** 347
Tom Thumb, General. *See* Stratton, Charles Sherwood
Tomb of Archduchess Maria Christina (Canova), **19th:** 407
Tomb of Pope Clement XIV (Canova), **19th:** 406
Tombaugh, Clyde William, **20th:** 4041-4044
Tombeau de Couperin, Le (Ravel), **20th:** 3386
Tomkins, Thomas, **Ren:** 149
Tomline, F. *See* Gilbert, W. S.
Tommaso d'Aquino. *See* Thomas Aquinas
Tommaso di Giovanni di Simone Guidi. *See* Masaccio
Tomoana, Akenehi, **19th:** 1484
Tompkins, Daniel D., **19th:** 513
Tompkins, Frank. *See* Carto, Willis A.
Tomsky, Mikhail, **Notor:** 991
Tomyris, **Anc:** 249
Tōn eis heauton (Marcus Aurelius), **Anc:** 531
Tōn meta ta physika (Theophrastus), **Anc:** 874
Tone, Wolfe, **18th:** 982-984
Tonge, Israel, **17th:** 692; **Notor:** 802
Tongmenghui, **20th:** 747, 3913, 4466
Tongzhi, **19th:** 496, 1364, 2484; **Notor:** 1123
Tonight or Never (Hatvany), **20th:** 1027
Tonio Kröger (Mann), **20th:** 2595
Tönnies, Ferdinand Julius, **20th:** 4044-4047
Tono-Bungay (Wells), **20th:** 4288
Tontine Crescent, **19th:** 347
Tonton Macoutes, **20th:** 124, 1070
Tonty, Henry de, **17th:** 490
Too Far Afield (Grass), **20th:** 1575
Too Late the Phalarope (Paton), **20th:** 3139
Toohoolhoolzote, **19th:** 1239
Toope, John, **Notor:** 961
Toorop, Jan, **20th:** 2787
Top Hat (film), **20th:** 156
Topa Inca, **Ren:** 747
Topkapi Sarayi, **18th:** 26
Toppan, Jane, **Notor:** 1109
Topper (film), **20th:** 1571
Tora! Tora! Tora! (film), **20th:** 2219
Torah, **Anc:** 2, 468
Toral, José de León, **20th:** 3016
Tordesillas, Treaty of (1494), **Ren:** 307, 330, 512, 514. *See also* Line of Demarcation
Tories, **17th:** 149, 464, 840; **19th:** 312, 643, 667, 891, 925; Sir Robert Peel, 1770. *See also* Tory Party
Torpedo War and Submarine Explosions (Fulton), **19th:** 847
Torpedoes, **19th:** 1523
Torquemada, Tomás de, **Ren:** 939-942; **Notor:** 1038-1039
Torre de la Parada, **17th:** 954

Torrent, The (film), **20th:** 1392
Torrents of Spring, The (Turgenev), **19th:** 2320
Torrents spirituels, Les. See *Spiritual Torrents*
Torres Strait, **18th:** 128
Torresani, Andrea, **Ren:** 608
Torrey, John, **19th:** 963
Torricelli, Evangelista, **17th:** 65, 333, 921-924
Torricelli's principle, **17th:** 921
Torricelli's theorem, **17th:** 922
Torrijos, Omar, **20th:** 4048-4050; **Notor:** 797
Torrington, earl of. *See* Monck, George
Torrio, Johnny, **20th:** 641; **Notor:** 175, 752, 804, 1096
Torstenson, Lennart, **17th:** 153, 924-927
Tortilla Flat (Steinbeck), **20th:** 3849
Tortura Torti (Andrewes), **17th:** 16
Tory Lover, The (Jewett), **19th:** 1227
Tory Party, **18th:** Daniel Defoe, 298; Mary de la Rivière Manley, 642; South Sea Company, 137; opposition of first Earl Stanhope, 938; Jonathan Swift, 942, 965; Whig Party conflicts, 47, 441, 772, 941, 1034. *See also* Tories
Tosca (Puccini), **20th:** 3347
Toscanini, Arturo, **20th:** 231, 1886, 3347, 4050-4053
Totalitarianism, **20th:** 1722, 2142
Totemism and Exogamy (Frazer), **20th:** 1320
Totentanz (Liszt), **19th:** 1395
Totes Meer (Nash), **20th:** 2912
Touch of Evil (film), **20th:** 4285
Touch of Innocence (Dunham), **20th:** 1063
Touchet, Eleanor. *See* Davies, Lady Eleanor
Toulouse-Lautrec, Henri de, **19th:** 934, 2287-2291
Toumi, Steven, **Notor:** 255
Tour, Georges de La. *See* La Tour, Georges de
Tour de France, Le (Tristan), **19th:** 2299
Tour de Nesle, La (Dumas), **19th:** 696
Tour du monde en quatre-vingts jours, Le. See *Around the World in Eighty Days*
Tour of the Prairies, A (Irving), **19th:** 1181
Touré, Ahmed Sékou, **20th:** 2991, 4053-4056
Tournefort, Joseph Pitton de, **17th:** 783
Tourneur, Cyril, **17th:** 928-930
Tours, Battle of (732), **MA:** 5, 252
Tours, Council of (1163), **MA:** 57
Tours, monasticism at, **MA:** 870
Toussaint Bréda, François Dominique. *See* Toussaint-Louverture
Toussaint-Louverture, **18th:** 985-988; **19th:** 494
Toussaint Louverture (Césaire), **20th:** 711
Tovar, Pedro de, **Ren:** 246
Toward the African Revolution (Fanon), **20th:** 1213
Towards a New Architecture (Le Corbusier), **20th:** 2324
Towards the Mountain (Paton), **20th:** 3140
Towazugatari. See *Confessions of Lady Nijō, The*
Tower, The (Yeats), **20th:** 4430
Tower of Blue Horses (Marc), **20th:** 2607
Town Beyond the Wall, The (Wiesel), **20th:** 4325
Town Fop, The (Behn), **17th:** 43
Towne, Rebecca. *See* Nurse, Rebecca
Townes, Charles Hard, **20th:** 256, 4057-4059
Towns Improvement Company, **19th:** 458
Townsend, Francis, **Notor:** 973
Townshend, Charles, **18th:** 1035
Townshend Acts (1767), **18th:** 18, 458
Toy, Crawford Howell, **19th:** 28
Toy Story (animated film), **20th:** 2008
Toynbee, Arnold, **20th:** 4059-4062, 4106
Tōyō. *See* Sesshū
Toyoda, Eiji, **20th:** 4062-4066
Toyota Motor Company, **20th:** 4063
Toyotomi Hideyori, **Ren:** 739
Toyotomi Hideyoshi, **Ren:** 451, 460, 732, 738, 943-946; **17th:** 916
Trabajos de Persiles y Sigismunda, Los. See *Travels of Persiles and Sigismunda, The*
Trachinai (Sophocles), **Anc:** 810
Track and field, **20th:** England, 797; United States, 3095, 4443
Tracks (Erdrich), **20th:** 1169
Tract Ninety (Newman), **19th:** 1663
Tractarians, **19th:** 1663
Tractatus apologeticus integritatem societatis de Rosea Cruce defendens (Fludd), **17th:** 281
Tractatus de anima (Rabanus), **MA:** 872
Tractatus de corde. See *Treatise on the Heart, A*
Tractatus de legibus et consuetudinibus regni Angliae (Glanville), **MA:** 193
Tractatus de Podagra et Hydrope (Sydenham), **17th:** 902
Tractatus de unitate et trinitate divina (Abelard), **MA:** 15
Tractatus Logico-Philosophicus (Wittgenstein), **20th:** 4379
Tractatus politicus. See *Political Treatise, A*
Tractatus super mulierem fortem (Neckam), **MA:** 752
Tractatus theologico-politicus. See *Theologico-Political Treatise, A*

Tracts for the Times (Newman), **19th:** 1663, 1846
Tracts on Animals and Vegetables (Spallanzani), **18th:** 926
Tracy, Spencer, **20th:** 1770, 4066-4068
Trade, **Anc:** routes, 367, 500, 564; **MA:** Aztecs, 559; Byzantine Empire, 135, 913; Central Asia, 703; China, 627, 1127, 1134, 1157; Ethiopia, 632; Europe and Asia, 854; Germany, 475; Islamic Empire, 469; Japan, 990; Mali, 744; Mediterranean, 573, 673; Mongols, 403, 853; Portugal, 478; Russia, 912; Scandinavia, 913; Spain, 11, 60; **Ren:** Asia, 792; between Europe and the Americas, 162, 180, 513, 522; between Europe and the East, 22, 157, 276, 286, 366, 511, 533, 605, 792; Kongo, 10; between Russia and England, 493, 641; slaves, 286; Sudan, 38; **17th:** Brazil, 960; China, 912; Dutch and Native Americans, 644; England and Native Americans, 633, 746, 754; France and North America, 401, 490, 644; French and Native Americans, 499; Japan and China, 161; Japan and Europe, 917; Portugal and Africa, 687; spices, 905; Sweden and Native Americans, 645; **18th:** American Indians and Europeans, 627, 743; China, 817; conflict, 458; and global economics, 923; Japan and Europe, 504; reform, 228, 796; Russia and China, 776, 1113; Russia and Japan, 109; Thailand and China, 969; Thailand and Europe, 969; trans-Saharan, 915. *See also* Spice Islands
Trades Union Congress, **19th:** 1025; **20th:** 356, 415
Trafalgar, Battle of (1805), **19th:** 1658
Traffic Safety Act of 1966, **20th:** 2897
Tragédie du Roi Christophe, La. See *Tragedy of King Christopher, The*
Tragedies (Buchanan), **Ren:** 146
Tragedy, Greek, **Anc:** 326, 811
Tragedy of Chabot, Admiral of France, The (Chapman), **Ren:** 215
Tragedy of Faust, The (Goethe), **18th:** 430
Tragedy of King Christopher, The (Césaire), **20th:** 711
Tragic Muse, The (James), **19th:** 1207
Tragic Sense of Life in Men and Peoples, The (Unamuno), **20th:** 4130
Tragicall History of D. Faustus, The. See *Doctor Faustus*
Tragicall History of Piramus and Thisbe, The (Cowley), **17th:** 199
Tragicomedy, **17th:** 279, 950
Trail of Tears, **19th:** 1938, 2053, 2069
Traill, Catharine Parr, **19th:** 1595, 2291-2293
Train, George Francis, **19th:** 67
Train Was on Time, The (Böll), **20th:** 411
Traité de dynamique (Alembert), **18th:** 32
Traité de l'association domestique-agricole. See *Social Science*
Traité de l'education des filles. See *Instructions for the Education of a Daughter*
Traité de législation civile et pénale (Bentham), **19th:** 1575
Traité de l'harmonie. See *Treatise on Harmony*
Traité des maladies de l'uterus et des annexes. See *Practical Treatise on the Diseases of the Uterus and Its Appendages, A*
Traité des sensations. See *Condillac's Treatise on the Sensations*
Traité des systèmes (Condillac), **18th:** 263
Traité élémentaire de chimie (Lavoisier), **18th:** 219
Traités élémentaires de calculus (Agnesi), **18th:** 25
Traitors. *See* Category Index
Traits of American Life (Hale), **19th:** 1013
Trajan, **Anc:** 370, 437, 903-907
Tramp Abroad, A (Twain), **19th:** 2330
Tran Le Xuan. *See* Nhu, Madame
Transatlantic flight, **20th:** 606, 2393
Transcaucasian architecture, **MA:** 999
Transcendent Spiritual Treatise, A (Reeve and Muggleton), **17th:** 666
Transcendentalism, **19th:** 39, 41, 466, 746, 842, 1735, 1761, 2274
Transcontinental railroad, **19th:** Canada, 1101; United States, 850
Transfiguration, The (Fra Angelico), **MA:** 85
Transfiguration de Notre Seigneur Jesus-Christ, La (Messiaen), **20th:** 2717
Transfiguration of Christ (Raphael), **Ren:** 821
Transformational drama, **20th:** 3983
Transformations (Fry), **20th:** 1353
Transformations (Sexton), **20th:** 3715
Transformed Metamorphosis, The (Tourneur), **17th:** 928
Transistors, development of, **20th:** 234
Transit of Venus over the Sun, The (Horrocks), **17th:** 389
Translation of an Abridgment of the "Vedant" (Ray), **19th:** 1867

Translation of the Body of Saint Mark (Tintoretto), **Ren:** 932
Translations, **MA:** Arabic to Latin, 100, 445, 1098, 1102, 1106; Bible, 219, 523, 1051, 1131; Greek to Arabic, 22; Greek to Latin, 1, 175, 209, 313, 769, 860, 1027, 1102, 1105; Latin to English, 65, 220; Sanskrit to Chinese, 1138; **Ren:** Bible into English, 256; Bible into German, 583; French into English, 196; Greek into English, 216; Greek into Latin, 332; Latin into French, 295
Translations from Camões and Other Poets (Hemans), **19th:** 1076
Transmigration of souls, **Anc:** 296, 356, 725
Transoxiana, **MA:** 1000
Transoxianian Controversies (al-Rāzī), **MA:** 369
Transport and General Workers' Union, **20th:** 356
Transportation, **18th:** 162, 1058
Transubstantiation, **MA:** 523, 544, 608, 880, 1132; **Ren:** 834, 1013
Transuranium elements, **20th:** 3685
Trans-Volga Elders, **Ren:** 490, 958
Transylvania, **Ren:** 910, 981; **17th:** 463
Trappists, **20th:** 2713
Trarza, **19th:** 756
Trastámara, Henry. *See* Henry IV (1425-1474; king of Castile)
Trato de Argel, El. See *Commerce of Algiers, The*
Trattatello in laude di Dante. See *Life of Dante*
Trattati dell'oreficeria e della scultura. See *Treatises of Benvenuto Cellini on Goldsmithing and Sculpture, The*
Traumdeutung, Die. See *Interpretation of Dreams, The*
Träume eines Geistersehers erläutert durch Träume der Metaphysik. See *Dreams of a Spirit-Seer, Illustrated by Dreams of Metaphysics*
Travail. See *Work*
Travel writing, **Anc:** Chinese, 345; Greek, 618, 729; **17th:** Germany, 445; Japan, 615; **18th:** 687
Traveling Wilburys, **20th:** 1073
Traveller, The (Goldsmith), **18th:** 434
Travellers' Club, **19th:** 142
Travels and Discoveries in North and Central Africa (Barth), **19th:** 940
Travels in North America with Geological Observations on the United States, Canada, and Nova Scotia (Lyell), **19th:** 1425
Travels in the Interior of Africa (Park), **18th:** 766
Travels in Two Democracies (Wilson), **20th:** 4355
Travels in West Africa (Kingsley), **19th:** 1282-1283
Travels of Fa-hsien, The. See *Faxian Zhuan*
Travels of Ibn Battuta. See *Riḥlah*
Travels of Marco Polo, The (Polo), **MA:** 627, 855
Travels of Persiles and Sigismunda, The (Cervantes), **Ren:** 209
Travels to Discover the Source of the Nile . . . (Bruce), **18th:** 170
Travels with a Donkey in the Cévennes (Stevenson), **19th:** 2173
Travels with Charley (Steinbeck), **20th:** 3850
Travers, Walter, **Ren:** 457
Traversari, Ambrogio, **MA:** 850
Traviata, La (Verdi), **19th:** 2352
Treasonable Practices Act and Seditious Meetings Act of 1795, **19th:** 1806
Treasure Island (Stevenson), **19th:** 2173
Treatise Against the Error of Transubstantiation (Ridley), **Ren:** 834
Treatise Concerning Religious Affections, A (Edwards), **18th:** 315
Treatise Concerning the Principles of Human Knowledge, A (Berkeley), **18th:** 111
Treatise Concerning the State of Departed Souls, Before, and at, and After the Resurrection, A (Burnet), **17th:** 107
Treatise of Fluxions, A (Maclaurin), **18th:** 634
Treatise of Human Nature, A (Hume), **18th:** 514
Treatise of Ireland, A (Petty), **17th:** 735
Treatise of Laws, A. See *Therapeutica*
Treatise of Lorenzo Valla on the Donation of Constantine, The (Valla), **MA:** 1050
Treatise on Consideration (Bernard of Clairvaux), **MA:** 161
Treatise on Domestic Economy (Beecher), **19th:** 170
Treatise on Harmony (Rameau), **18th:** 826
Treatise on Man, A (Helvetius), **18th:** 480
Treatise on Money, A (Keynes), **20th:** 2121
Treatise on Physiological Optics (Helmholtz), **19th:** 1074
Treatise on Possession (Savigny), **19th:** 2003
Treatise on Taxes and Contributions, A (Petty), **17th:** 734
Treatise on the Conics of Apollonius (Hypatia), **Anc:** 435
Treatise on the Good. See *Arthaśāstra*

Treatise on the Heart, A (Lower), **17th:** 566
Treatise on the Immutability of Moral Truth (Macaulay), **18th:** 622
Treatise on the Improvement of Canal Navigation (Fulton), **19th:** 846
Treatise on the Motive Powers Which Produce the Circulation of the Blood, A (Willard), **19th:** 2440
Treatise on the Small-Pox and Measles, A (al-Rāzī), **MA:** 885
Treatise on the Social Contract, A (Rousseau), **18th:** 869
Treatise on the Worship of Images, A (Ridley), **Ren:** 835
Treatise on Universal Algebra, A (Whitehead), **20th:** 4312
Treatise upon the Origin of Language (Herder), **18th:** 486
Treatises of Benvenuto Cellini on Goldsmithing and Sculpture, The (Cellini), **Ren:** 205
Treaty of _______. *See* _______, Treaty of
Treaty of 1818, **19th:** 22
Treaty of 1868, **19th:** 568, 2109
Tree of Night, and Other Stories, A (Capote), **20th:** 645
Treemonisha (Joplin), **19th:** 1236
Trees Near Hampstead Church (Constable), **19th:** 542
Treffen in Telgte, Das. See *Meeting at Telgte, The*
Tregian, Francis, **Ren:** 150
Trelawny, John, **19th:** 381
Trembleur (Ségalas), **19th:** 2062
Trench, The (Orozco), **20th:** 3069
Trenchard, Hugh, **20th:** 2767
Trenet, Charles, **Notor:** 604
Trenker, Luis, **Notor:** 138
Trent affair (1861), **19th:** 2202, 2437
Trent, Council of (1545-1563), **MA:** 880; **Ren:** 45, 222, 360, 390, 393, 430, 568-569, 717, 752, 769, 777, 798
Tresham, Francis, **Ren:** 326
Trevithick, Richard, **19th:** 2294-2297
Tri sestry. See *Three Sisters*
Trial, The (film), **20th:** 4285
Trial, The (novel by Kafka), **20th:** 2067
Trial by Jury (Gilbert and Sullivan), **19th:** 919
Trials, **Anc:** Roman, 211; **19th:** Susan B. Anthony for voting, 67; Annie Besant and Charles Bradlaugh for publishing obscenity, 212; Lizzie Borden for murder, 278; John Brown for treason, 321; Aaron Burr for treason, 365, 1500; André Chazal for attempted murder, 2298; Alfred Dreyfus for treason, 1089; divorce of James Buchanan Duke, 693; Wyatt Earp and Doc Holliday, 721; O. Henry for embezzlement, 1083; impeachment of Andrew Johnson, 1230; Louis XVI, 396; Daniel McFarland for murder, 1903; Mafia, 1042; Rugeley poisoner, 998; Nat Turner, 2327; Oscar Wilde, 2290, 2434
Triangle Pictures Corporation, **20th:** 3707
Triangle Shirtwaist Factory fire, **20th:** 3198
Triangulation, **Anc:** 325
Tribe of Ben, **17th:** 368, 443. *See also* Sons of Ben
Tribonian, **MA:** 599
Tribute Money, The (Masaccio), **MA:** 701
Tribute to Freud (H. D.), **20th:** 1624
Tric, Monsieur. *See* Landru, Henri Désiré
Trick to Catch the Old One, A (Middleton), **17th:** 636
Tricorne, Le (ballet), **20th:** 2647
Trigonometry, **Anc:** 419, 713; **MA:** Iraq, 137
Triṃśikā (Vasubandhu), **Anc:** 932
Trinidad and Tobago, **20th:** independence of, 830. *See also* Geographical Index
Trinitarian controversy, **Anc:** 912
Trinitarianism, **Ren:** 861; **19th:** 465
Trinity (Christian), **Anc:** 854; **MA:** 15, 161, 173, 575, 597, 857, 922, 1066, 1103, 1115; **17th:** denial of, 53
Trinity, The (El Greco), **Ren:** 392
Trinity Church, **19th:** 1905
Trio in G Major (Borodin), **19th:** 280
Trio, Op. 17 (Schumann), **19th:** 2030
Trionfi. See *Triumphs*
Tripartitum (1514), **Ren:** 984
Triple Alliance of 1668, **17th:** 559
Triple Intervention (1895), **19th:** 1121, 1365
Triplicinodo triplex cuneus (King James), **17th:** 16
Triremes, **Anc:** 214
Trissino, Gian Giorgio, **Ren:** 486, 753
Tristan, Flora, **19th:** 2297-2299
Tristan and Isolde (Gottfried), **MA:** 424
Tristan und Isolde (Wagner), **19th:** 2375
Tristan y Moscozo, Flore-Célestine-Thérèse-Henriette. *See* Tristan, Flora
Tristes tropiques (Lévi-Strauss), **20th:** 2348
Tristessa (Kerouac), **20th:** 2115
Tristia (Ovid), **Anc:** 491, 604
Tritium, discovery of, **20th:** 74
Triumph des Willens. See *Triumph of the Will*
Triumph of Caesar (Mantegna), **Ren:** 603
Triumph of Health and Prosperity, The (Middleton), **17th:** 637
Triumph of Life, The (Shelley), **19th:** 2096
Triumph of Mordecai, The (Veronese), **Ren:** 960

Triumph of the Will (film), **20th:** 3451
Triumphs (Petrarch), **MA:** 827
Triumphs of the Prince d'Amour, The (Davenant), **17th:** 502
Triumvirates. *See* First Triumvirate; Second Triumvirate
Trivia senatoria (Alberti), **Ren:** 19
Trivialliteratur, **18th:** 578
Trivium, **Anc:** 929
Troeltsch, Ernst, **20th:** 418, 4069-4072
Troia Britannica (Heywood), **17th:** 374
Trōiades (Euripides), **Anc:** 327
Troilus and Cressida (Walton), **20th:** 4219
Troilus and Criseyde (Chaucer), **MA:** 265
Trois Contes. See *Three Tales*
Trois-Frères, cave paintings at, **20th:** 518
Trois Gymnopédies (Satie), **20th:** 3642
Trois Morceaux en forme de poire (Satie), **20th:** 3643
Trois Mousquetaires, Les. See *Three Musketeers, The*
Trois Musiciens, Les (Léger), **20th:** 2336
Trois Petites Liturgies (Messiaen), **20th:** 2716
Trois réformateurs. See *Three Reformers*
Trois Villes, Les. See *Three Cities, The*
Troja (Schliemann), **19th:** 2018
Trojan War, **Anc:** 427; drama and, 327; Roman views on, 301
Trojan Women, The. See *Trōiades*
Trollope, Anthony, **19th:** 2299-2302, 2305
Trollope, Frances, **19th:** 2299, 2303-2305
Tromp, Cornelis, **17th:** 930-932
Tromp, Maarten, **17th:** 57, 288, 619, 808, 930-932
Tropical South Africa (Galton), **19th:** 860
Tropisms (Sarraute), **20th:** 3635
Trostnik (Akhmatova), **20th:** 44
Trota. *See* Trotula
Trotsky, Leon, **20th:** 566, 1551, 2070, 4072-4076; **Notor:** 89, 629, 697, 721, 990, 1040-1042, 1052, 1112, 1138
Trotting Horseman (Toulouse-Lautrec), **19th:** 2287
Trotula, **MA:** 1031-1033
Troubled Sleep (Sartre), **20th:** 3639
Troubles, Council of, **Ren:** 994
Trouille, Clovis, **Notor:** 927
Trovatore, Il (Verdi), **19th:** 2352
Trow, Ann. *See* Restell, Madame
Troy and Its Remains (Schliemann), **19th:** 2017
Troy Female Seminary. *See* Emma Willard School
Troyens, Les (Berlioz), **19th:** 203
Troyes, Council of (1128), **MA:** 162
Troyes, Treaty of (1420), **MA:** 262, 503; **Ren:** 224
Trudeau, Pierre, **20th:** 761, 2346, 3176, 3652, 4076-4079
True-Born Englishman, The (Defoe), **18th:** 298
True Christian Faith, The (Menno), **Ren:** 676
True Christian Religion (Swedenborg), **18th:** 962
True Constitution of a Particular Visible Church, The (Cotton), **17th:** 197
True Cross, **Anc:** 392
True Grit (film), **20th:** 4251
True History, A. See *Alēthon Diēgēmaton*
True History of the Conquest of New Spain, The (Díaz del Castillo), **Ren:** 621
True Interpretation of the Eleventh Chapter of the Revelations of Saint John, A (Muggleton), **17th:** 667
True Law of Free Monarchies, The (James I), **17th:** 413
True Levellers. *See* Diggers
True Meaning of the Lord in Heaven, The (Ricci), **Ren:** 827
True Principles of Pointed or Christian Architecture, The (Pugin), **19th:** 1839
True Relation of Such Occurrences and Accidents of Noate as Hath Hapned in Virginia Since the First Planting of That Collony, A (Smith), **17th:** 864
Truffaut, François, **20th:** 1383, 4080-4083
Trujillo, Rafael, **20th:** 4084-4086; **Notor:** 1042-1043
Trujillo, Ramfis, **20th:** 4085
Trullan Synod, Second (692), **MA:** 937
Truman, Harry S., **20th:** 166, 2495, 4086-4090, 4209; **Notor:** 75, 474, 491, 675, 817
Truman Doctrine, **20th:** 358, 1686
Trumbull, John, **18th:** 988-990; painting of American flag, 866
Trump, Donald, **Notor:** 218
Truth (Zola), **19th:** 2491
Truth and Reconciliation Commission (South Africa), **20th:** 4123
Truth Exalted (Penn), **17th:** 725
Truth of Religion, The (Eucken), **20th:** 1186
Truth, Sojourner, **19th:** 2306-2309
Trymphs. See *Triumphs*
Tsafendas, Dimitri, **Notor:** 1065
Tsander, Friedrich A., **20th:** 2192, 4097
Ts'ao Chan. *See* Cao Xueqin
Ts'ao Hsüeh-ch'in. *See* Cao Xueqin
Ts'ao Ts'ao. *See* Cao Cao
Tsar's Bride, The (Rimsky-Korsakov), **19th:** 1916
Tserclaes, Johan. *See* Tilly, count of (Johan Tserclaes)
Tshaka. *See* Shaka
Tshisekedi, Etienne, **20th:** 2775

Tshombe, Moïse, **20th:** 576, 2477, 2774, 4091-4094
Tsiolkovsky, Konstantin, **20th:** 2192, 4095-4098
Ts'u Hsi. *See* Cixi
Ts'ui Hsi-i. *See* Cui Xiyi
Tsunayoshi, Tokugawa. *See* Tokugawa Tsunayoshi
Tsvangirai, Morgan, **20th:** 2859; **Notor:** 762
Tsvetayeva, Marina, **20th:** 44, 4098-4101
Tsygany. See *Gypsies, The*
Tu Duc, **19th:** 2310-2312
Tu Fu. *See* Du Fu
Tu Ju-hui. *See* Du Ruhui
TU-144 (supersonic aircraft), **20th:** 4110
Tu solus, qui facis mirabilia (Josquin), **Ren:** 516
Tu Thanh. *See* Le Thanh Tong
Tuareg, **Ren:** 901
Tuberculosis, **19th:** 1293; **20th:** 619, 1022, 1116, 3773
Tübingen school, **19th:** 1918
Tubman, Harriet, **19th:** 2312-2316
Tubman, William V. S., **20th:** 4101-4104
Tubutama Revolt (1695), **17th:** 468
TUC. *See* Trades Union Congress
Tuc d'Audoubert, cave paintings at, **20th:** 518
Tuchman, Barbara W., **20th:** 4104-4107
Tucker, Karla Faye, **Notor:** 1044-1045
Tudor, Henry. *See* Henry VII (1457-1509; king of England)
Tudor, Mary. *See* Mary I
Tudor, Owen ap Meredith ap, **Ren:** 946. *See also* Tudor family
Tudor family, **Ren:** 91, 187, 438, 946-949. *See also* Edward VI; Elizabeth I; Grey, Lady Jane; Henry VII (1457-1509; king of England); Henry VIII (1491-1547; king of England); Lancastrians; Mary I
Tuhfat al-Kibar fi Asfar il-Bihar (Kâtib Çelebî), **17th:** 455
Tuḥfat al-nuẓẓār fi gharaʿib al-amsar wa-ʿajaʿib al-asfar. See *Riḥlah*
Tuileries, **17th:** 523, 533
Tukhachevsky, Mikhail, **Notor:** 1052
Tulip Age (Ottoman Empire), **18th:** 28, 639
Tulipe Noire, La. See *Black Tulip, The*
Tull, Jethro, **18th:** 990-993
Tullia, **Anc:** 841, 846
Tullius Cicero, Marcus. *See* Cicero
Tuluva Dynasty, **Ren:** 532
Tunisia, **MA:** Muslims in, 674; **20th:** independence of, 458, 2699. *See also* Geographical Index
Tunney, Gene, **20th:** 966
Tunstall, Cuthbert, **Ren:** 950
Tunstall, John, **Notor:** 119
Tupac Amaru II, **18th:** 993-995
Túpac Amaru Revolutionary Movement, **20th:** 1360
Tupac Cusi Huallpa. *See* Huáscar
Tupolev, Andrei Nikolayevich, **20th:** 2192, 4108-4111
Tupper, Sir Charles (first Baronet Tupper), **19th:** 2316-2318
Ṭur (Karo), **Ren:** 524
Turabi, Hassan al-, **Notor:** 67
Turandot (Puccini), **20th:** 3348
Turangalîla (Messiaen), **20th:** 2717
Turcaret (Lesage), **18th:** 597
Ture, Muḥammad. *See* Mohammed I Askia
Turenne, Viscount de, **17th:** 184, 416, 425, 549, 558, 820, 933-935
Turgenev, Ivan, **19th:** 2319-2321
Turgot, Anne-Robert-Jacques, **18th:** 619, 727, 821, 996-999
Turhan, **17th:** 472
Turing, Alan Mathison, **20th:** 1801, 4112-4114
Turing machine, **20th:** 4112
Turing Test, **20th:** 4113
Turkan Khatun, **MA:** 888
Turkey, **MA:** monasticism, 295; **19th:** 1732; **20th:** Armenians, 2352; Roman Catholic Church, 2018. *See also* Ottoman Empire; Geographical Index
Turkey blackhead, **20th:** 3774
Turkheim, Battle of (1675), **17th:** 934
Turkish Bath, The (Ingres), **19th:** 1173
Turkish Embassy Letters (Montagu), **18th:** 687
Turkish National Movement, **20th:** 163
Turkish Ordeal, The (Adıvar), **20th:** 31
Turkish War of Independence (1919-1922), **20th:** 68, 163, 1971
Turkmenbashi. *See* Niyazov, Saparmurat
Turkmenistan. *See* Geographical Index
Turn of the Screw, The (Britten), **20th:** 532
Turn of the Screw, The (James), **19th:** 1207
Turner, Anne, **17th:** 132
Turner, Clorinda Matto de. *See* Matto de Turner, Clorinda
Turner, Frederick Jackson, **20th:** 4115-4118
Turner, J. M. W., **18th:** 193; **19th:** 1954, 2322-2325; **20th:** 2790
Turner, Joseph, **20th:** 3546
Turner, Nat, **19th:** 876, 2326-2329
Turner, Ted, **20th:** 4118-4121
Turner Broadcasting Service, **20th:** 4119
Turner Network Television, **20th:** 4120
Turning Point, The (film), **20th:** 254
Turpin, Dick, **Notor:** 1045-1047

Turpin, John, **19th:** 1236
Turpio, Lucius Ambivius, **Anc:** 850
Turtle Creek mine strike (1897), **20th:** 2040
Turton, Thomas, **19th:** 709
Tuscaloosa. *See* Tascalusa
Tushmal Karīm. *See* Karīm Khān Zand
Tushratta, **Anc:** 902
Tuskaloosa. *See* Tascalusa
Tuskegee Institute, **19th:** 2391
Tutankhamen, **Anc:** 28, 908-910
Tutu, Desmond, **20th:** 4121-4124; **Notor:** 271
Tver', annexation to Moscow, **Ren:** 488
Tvorchestvo Fransua Rable I narodnaya kul'tura srednevekov'ya I Renessansa. See *Rabelais and His World*
Twain, Mark, **19th:** 961, 1039, 2329-2333; on Alexander Campbell, 401; on Leopold II, 1351; on Adah Isaacs Menken, 1556; Charlotte Mary Yonge, 2473; **Notor:** 633
Tweed, William Marcy, **19th:** 1650, 2333-2336; **Notor:** 357, 1047-1049
Tweed Ring, **19th:** 1650
Twelve, The (Blok), **20th:** 395
Twelve Arguments Drawn Out of Scripture (Biddle), **17th:** 53
Twelve Years' Truce (1609-1621), **Ren:** 741; **17th:** 359, 530, 619, 737
Twentieth Century-Fox, **20th:** 4446
Twenty-eighth Congregational Society, **19th:** 1736
Twenty-fifth Dynasty (Egypt), **Anc:** 658
Twenty Hours Forty Minutes (Earhart), **20th:** 1076
Twenty Love Poems and a Song of Despair (Neruda), **20th:** 2937
Twenty Thousand Leagues Under the Sea (Verne), **19th:** 2357
20/20 (television newsmagazine), **20th:** 4212
Twenty Years After (Dumas), **19th:** 697
Twenty Years at Hull House (Addams), **20th:** 23
Twice-Told Tales (Hawthorne), **19th:** 1051, 1814
Twin Menaechmi, The. See *Menaechmi*
Twittering Machine (Klee), **20th:** 2178
Two Admirals, The (Cooper), **19th:** 555
Two Bookes of Ayres (Campion), **17th:** 127
Two Books of the Pleas of a Spanish Advocate, The (Gentili), **Ren:** 373
Two Children Are Menaced by a Nightingale (Ernst), **20th:** 1177
Two Comedians (Hopper), **20th:** 1878
Two Days' Battle (1666), **17th:** 808
Two Discourses Concerning the Soul of Brutes Which Is That of the Vital and Sensitive of Man (Willis), **17th:** 986
Two Guardians, The (Yonge), **19th:** 2472
Two Kings, War of the (1689-1691), **17th:** 609
Two Sacred Songs for Voice and Piano (Frescobaldi), **17th:** 297
Two Scholars Disputing (Rembrandt), **17th:** 786
Two Sisters (Ernst), **20th:** 1177
Two Sources of Morality and Religion, The (Bergson), **20th:** 325
Two Summers in the Ice-Wilds of Eastern Karakoram (Workman and Workman), **19th:** 2468
Two Towers, The (Tolkien), **20th:** 4039
Two Treatises of Government (Locke), **17th:** 381, 544, 546
Two Ways of Entrance, The. See *Er jing ru*
Two Years Before the Mast (Melville), **19th:** 1538
Twofold Catechism, A (Biddle), **17th:** 54
Twoo Bookes of Francis Bacon of the Proficience and Advancement of Learning Divine and Humane, The. See *Advancement of Learning*
Twyla Tharp Dance (dance), **20th:** 3990
Twyla Tharp Dance Foundation, **20th:** 3989
Tyler, John, **19th:** 505, 579, 2337-2341
Tyler, Wat, **MA:** 130, 894, 1033-1036
Tyler's Revolt. *See* Peasants' Revolt (1381)
Tymish, **17th:** 463
Tynan, Kenneth, **20th:** 1969
Tyndale, William, **Ren:** 256, 267, 544, 949-952
Tyndall, John, **Notor:** 283, 1050-1051
Tyner, McCoy, **20th:** 815
Typee (Melville), **19th:** 1537
Typhoid Mary. *See* Mallon, Mary
Tyrannic Love (Dryden), **17th:** 343
Tyrannical-Government Anatomized (Buchanan), **Ren:** 146
Tyrannio, **Anc:** 827
Tyranny, **Anc:** 649, 653
Tyranny of the Status Quo (Friedmans), **20th:** 1334
Tyrconnel, duke of. *See* Talbot, Richard
Tyre, **Anc:** Alexander the Great and, 40; maritime empire, 373
Tyre, Synod of (335), **Anc:** 331
Tzara, Tristan, **20th:** 511
Tzepes, Vlad. *See* Vlad III the Impaler
Tzevi, Shabbetai. *See* Shabbetai Tzevi
Tz'u-hsi. *See* Cixi

U

U-boats, **20th:** 4032
U Nu, **Notor:** 773
U-2 incident, **20th:** 1127, 2130
UAR. *See* United Arab Republic
UAW. *See* United Auto Workers
Über Bacterien. See *Bacteria*
Über das Geistige in der Kunst, insbesondere in der Malerei. See *Concerning the Spiritual in Art, and Painting in Particular*
Über den Humanismus. See *Letter on Humanism*
Über den nervösen Charakter. See *Neurotic Constitution, The*
Über den Willen in der Natur. See *On the Will in Nature*
Über die Möglichkeit einer Form der Philosophie überhaupt (Schelling), **19th:** 2009
Über die Religion. See *On Religion*
Über die vierfache Wurzel des Satzes vom zureichende Grunde. See *On the Fourfold Root of the Principle of Sufficient Reason*
Über Entwickelungsgeschichte der Thiere (Baer), **19th:** 114
Übermensch, **19th:** 1682
Ubi Arcano Dei (Pius XI), **20th:** 3275
Ubu Imperator (Ernst), **20th:** 1177
Uccello, Paolo, **Ren:** 601
Uccialli, Treaty of (1889), **19th:** 1553
Uchenye zapiski, **19th:** 1404
Ueno hanami zu oshiebari byōbu (Moronobu), **17th:** 376
Uesugi Kagekatsu, **Ren:** 452
Uesugi Kenshin, **Ren:** 451
Uganda, **20th:** annexation by Great Britain, 2465; independence of, 80, 3011. *See also* Geographical Index
Uganda National Congress, **20th:** 3011
Uganda National Liberation Front, **20th:** 2883
Uganda People's Congress, **20th:** 3011
Uganda-Tanzania War (1977-1978), **20th:** 3006
Ugo of Segni. *See* Gregory IX
Uhud, Battle of (625), **MA:** 735
Uighurs, **17th:** 2
Ujamaa, **20th:** 3006
Ukiyo-e woodblock printing, **17th:** 375; **18th:** 958; **19th:** 1107
Ukiyozoshi, **17th:** 403
Ukraine. *See* Geographical Index
Ulászló II. *See* Vladislav II
Ulbricht, Walter, **20th:** 4125-4128
Ulfilas, **Anc:** 911-914
Uli, Mansa, **MA:** 979
Ulozheniye. *See* Sobornoye Ulozheniye (1649)
Ulpian, **Anc:** 484
Ulpius Trajanus, Marcus. *See* Trajan
Ulrich, Karl Peter. *See* Peter III
Ulrich Zwingli. *See* Zwingli, Huldrych
Ulrika Eleonora (queen of Sweden), **18th:** 233
Ulrikh, Vasili Vasilievich, **Notor:** 1052-1053, 1116
Ulster Protestants, massacre of (1642), **17th:** 700
Ulster rebellion (1798), **19th:** 438
Ulster Resistance, **20th:** 3035
Ulster Volunteer Force, **20th:** 979
Ultramontanism, **19th:** 13
Ulyanov, Vladimir Ilich. *See* Lenin, Vladimir Ilich
Ulysses (Joyce), **20th:** 2056
ʿUmar I, **MA:** 1037-1039
ʿUmar II, **MA:** 472, 1007
ʿUmar al-Farouq. *See* ʿUmar I
ʿUmar ibn Khaṭṭāb. *See* ʿUmar I
Umar Tal, al-Hājj, **19th:** 756
Umayado no Miko. *See* Shōtoku Taishi
Umayyads, **MA:** 20; caliphs, 4, 10
Umberto I, **Notor:** 180
Umi to dokuyaku. See *Sea and Poison, The*
Umkhonto we Sizwe, **20th:** 2480, 2585
U.N. *See* United Nations
Unabomber. *See* Kaczynski, Theodore
Unam sanctam, **MA:** 188, 857
Unamuno y Jugo, Miguel de, **20th:** 4128-4131
Uncalled, The (Dunbar), **19th:** 703
Uncas, **17th:** 130
Uncertainty principle, **20th:** 438
Uncle Remus (Harris), **19th:** 1036
Uncle Tom's Cabin (Stowe), **19th:** 990, 2184, 2186
Uncle Vanya (Chekhov), **19th:** 480
Unconscious Memory (Butler), **19th:** 375
Und niemand weiss weiter (Sachs), **20th:** 3585
Und sagte kein einziges Wort. See *Acquainted with the Night*
Under nordenvindens svobe. See *People of the Polar North, The*
Under the Greenwood Tree (Hardy), **19th:** 1028
Under the Sea-Wind (Carson), **20th:** 663
Under Western Eyes (Conrad), **20th:** 826
Underground Railroad, **19th:** 2313
Underhill, John, **17th:** 892
Understanding Human Nature (Adler), **20th:** 33
Understanding Media (McLuhan), **20th:** 2530
Understanding Poetry (Warren), **20th:** 4237
Undertakers (group of American colonists), **17th:** 86, 879
Underwater Impressions (film), **20th:** 3452
Undine (Schreiner), **19th:** 2024
Undiscovered Australia (Wilkins), **20th:** 4340
Unemployment (Beveridge), **20th:** 352
Unfinished Woman, An (Hellman), **20th:** 1753

Unfortunate Traveller (Nashe), **Ren:** 715
Ung aultre amer, D' (Josquin), **Ren:** 516
Ung choeun. *See* Ta Mok
Unges forbund. See *League of Youth, The*
Unheard of Little Works on Medicine (Helmont), **17th:** 362
Unification Church, **20th:** 2811
Uniform Dress Law (1928), **20th:** 3429
Uniformitarianism, **19th:** 1424
Uniformity, Act of (1549), **Ren:** 305, 899
Uniformity, Act of (1552), **Ren:** 305
Uniformity, Act of (1559), **Ren:** 403
Uniformity, Act of (1662), **17th:** 34, 121
Unigenitus (Clement XI), **18th:** 103, 362
Union, Act of (1707), **MA:** 204; **18th:** 53, 423
Union, Act of (1800), **18th:** 280, 411, 442, 791
Union, Act of (1801, Ireland), **19th:** 439
Union, Act of (1839, Oklahoma), **19th:** 1938
Union, Act of (1840, Canada), **19th:** 317, 1441, 1452
Union Africaine et Malgache, **20th:** 1897
Union for Armed Struggle. *See* Związek Walki Czynnej
Union of American Hebrew Congregations, **19th:** 2454
Union of Arms, **17th:** 698, 739
Union of Democratic Control, **20th:** 94
Union of International Associations, **20th:** 2232
Union of South Africa, **19th:** 1299
Union or Death. *See* Black Hand
Union ouvrière, L'. See *Worker's Union, The*
Union Pacific Railroad, **19th:** 2134
Union Steel, **20th:** 2683
Union Switch and Signal Company, **19th:** 2417
Union to Combat Anti-Semitism, **19th:** 2207
Union Trust, **20th:** 2683
Unions. *See* Labor unions
Unitarian Controversy, **19th:** 464
Unitarianism, **Ren:** 861; **17th:** 54; **18th:** 87-89, 812, 901; **19th:** 465, 1735, 1868
United African Company, **19th:** 941
United Arab Emirates, **20th:** 1200
United Arab Republic, **20th:** 1952, 2915
United Artists, **20th:** 732, 1595, 3245
United Australia Party, **20th:** 2486, 2490
United Auto Workers, **20th:** 3425
United Brethren Church, **18th:** 1120
United Colonies of New England, **17th:** 86
United Company, **17th:** 51
United Farm Workers, **20th:** 738, 1916
United Ireland Party. *See* Fine Gael
United Irishman (newspaper), **20th:** 1591
United Irishmen, **19th:** 438
United Mine Workers of America, **20th:** 914, 2040, 2360, 2672
United Nations, **20th:** 1654, 3548; Boutros Boutros-Ghali, 465; René Cassin, 686; India, 2931; Israel, 1082; leadership of, 2376; Palestine Liberation Organization, 112; Javier Pérez de Cuéllar, 3194; John D. Rockefeller, Jr., 3477; United States, 2169; Kurt Waldheim, 4188
United Nations, The (Evatt), **20th:** 1189
United Press, **19th:** 2057
United Provinces of the Netherlands, **Ren:** 740; **17th:** 618
United Service Organizations. *See* USO
United Society of Believers in Christ's Second Coming, **18th:** 593
United States. *See also* U.S.; *specific departments and agencies*; Geographical Index
United States Bank, **19th:** 225, 365, 503
United States, 1830-1850, The (Turner), **20th:** 4117
United States-Japan Security Treaty (1951), **20th:** 1965
United States v. Lopez (1995), **20th:** 3408
United States v. Morrison (2000), **20th:** 3408
United States v. Nixon (1974), **20th:** 583
United Steelworkers v. Weber (1979), **20th:** 3406
United We Stand America, **20th:** 3210
Unity Block, **19th:** 58
Unity of Philosophical Experience, The (Gilson), **20th:** 1490
UNIVAC I, **20th:** 1881
Universal Automatic Computer. *See* UNIVAC I
Universal Christian Conference on Life and Work, **20th:** 3781
Universal Declaration of Human Rights, **20th:** 686
Universal History (Ranke), **19th:** 1861
Universal History of Infamy, A (Borges), **20th:** 431
Universal Negro Improvement Association, **20th:** 1417
Universal Peace (Willard), **19th:** 2440
Universal Peace Union, **19th:** 1411
Universal Private Telegraph Company, **19th:** 550

Universal Treatise of Nicholas of Autrecourt, The (Nicholas), **MA:** 761
Universalism, **19th:** 324, 466
Universe (Calder), **20th:** 609
Universe, age of, **20th:** 185
Universe in the Light of Modern Physics, The (Planck), **20th:** 3284
Universe of Creatures, The (William of Auxerre), **MA:** 1100
Universities, **MA:** 2, 318. See also *specific college and university names*
University Hall at Harvard, **19th:** 348
University of California Regents v. Bakke (1978), **20th:** 3326
University of Peace, **20th:** 3265
University Wits, **Ren:** 876
Unkei, **MA:** 1040-1042
Unkenrufe. See *Call of the Toad, The*
Unmaking of a Mayor, The (Buckley), **20th:** 562
Unnamable, The (Beckett), **20th:** 281
Uno, nessuno centomila. See *One, None, and a Hundred Thousand*
Unordnung und frühes Leid. See *Disorder and Early Sorrow*
Unperfect Society, The (Djilas), **20th:** 1012
Unreasonableness of Infidelity, The (Baxter), **17th:** 35
Unsafe at Any Speed (Nader), **20th:** 2897
Unterm Rad. See *Prodigy, The*
Untermeyer, Louis, **20th:** 1349
Unterricht der Visitatorn (Melanchthon), **Ren:** 666
Unterweisung im Tonsatz. See *Craft of Musical Composition, The*
Unto This Last (Ruskin), **19th:** 1956
Unvanquished, The (film), **20th:** 3394
Up from Slavery (Washington), **19th:** 2392
Upadesasāhasrī. See *Thousand Teachings, A*
Upper Creeks, **18th:** 626
Upupa und der Triumph der Shonesliebe, L' (Henze), **20th:** 1765
Ur, **Anc:** Abraham and, 4; Enheduanna, 299
Ur-Nammu, **Anc:** 368, 914-917
Urania Titani (Brahe), **Ren:** 127
Uranium, **20th:** 3685, 4133
Uranographia (Hevelius), **17th:** 372
Urartu, **Anc:** 892
Urban II, **MA:** 93, 177, 499, 707, 1003, 1043-1046
Urban III, **MA:** 387, 576
Urban IV, **MA:** 181, 727
Urban V, **MA:** 236
Urban VI, **MA:** 237, 259; **Notor:** 1053-1054
Urban VIII, **17th:** 9, 45, 68, 126, 405, 421, 424, 620, 722, 792, 936-938
Urban development, **20th:** 2323
Urban functionalism, **20th:** 1416
Urban League, **19th:** 2393
Urban planning in Assyria, **Anc:** 122
Urbanisme. See *City of Tomorrow and Its Planning, The*
Urbino, duke of. *See* Montefeltro, Guidobaldo da
Urey, Harold C., **20th:** 2371, 3063, 4132-4135
Uriah, **Anc:** 155, 256
Urien's Voyage (Gide), **20th:** 973
Uritskii, Moisei, **Notor:** 313
Urriolagoitia, Mamerto, **20th:** 3172
Ursinus, **Anc:** 796
Ursprung der afrikanischen Kulturen, Der. See *Origin of African Civilizations, The*
Ursprung der Familie, des Privateigentums und des Staats, Der. See *Origin of the Family, Private Property, and the State, The*
Ursuline order, **Ren:** 4, 44, 231; **17th:** 77, 595
Urteil, Das. See *Judgment, The*
Uruguay, **19th:** and Argentina, 871; and Guiseppi Garibaldi, 871
ʿUrwat al-Wuthqā, al- (journal), **19th:** 1204
U.S. Capitol, **19th:** 348
U.S. Constitution. *See* Constitution, U.S.
U.S. Foreign Policy (Lippmann), **20th:** 2402
U.S. Geological Survey of Territories, **19th:** 1058
U.S. Sanitary Commission, **19th:** 1138, 1142
U.S. Steel Corporation, **19th:** 421, 1601; **20th:** 2683
U.S. War Aims (Lippmann), **20th:** 2402
Use and Need of the Life of Carry A. Nation, The (Nation), **19th:** 1653-1654
Usman dan Fodio. *See* ʿUthman dan Fodio
USO, **20th:** 1871
Ussher, James, **17th:** 35, 53, 938-940
Utagawa Hiroshige. *See* Hiroshige
Utagawa Kunisada, **19th:** 1109
Utagawa Kuniyoshi, **19th:** 1109
Utes, **19th:** 429
ʿUthman dan Fodio, **19th:** 186, 2342-2343
ʿUthmān ibn ʿAffān, **MA:** 3, 471, 1039
ʿUthman ibn Fūdī. *See* ʿUthman dan Fodio
Uthman, Muḥammad Bello ibn. *See* Bello, Muḥammad
Utilitarianism, **18th:** 100, 106, 763; **19th:** 289, 1572, 1574, 1721, 2103
Utilitarianism (Mill), **19th:** 1578
Utnapishtim, **Anc:** 914
Utopia (More), **Ren:** 442, 698

Utopia, Limited (Gilbert and Sullivan), **19th:** 920
Utopian socialism, **19th:** 806, 1722; **20th:** 1415
Utraquist revolt, **MA:** 1162
Utrecht, Treaty of (1713), **18th:** 48, 136, 141, 230, 331, 781
Utrecht, Union of (1579), **Ren:** 740
Utriusque cosmi maioris scilicet et minoris metaphysica, physica atque technica historia (Fludd), **17th:** 281
Uttiya, **Anc:** 900
Utus, Battle of (447), **Anc:** 140
Uzbekistan. *See* Geographical Index
Uzbeks, **Ren:** 69; **17th:** 4
Uzun Ḥasan, **MA:** 712; **Ren:** 87
Uzziah, **Anc:** 447

V

V kruge pervom. See *First Circle, The*
V sumerkakh (Chekhov), **19th:** 479
Vaccination, **18th:** 532-535
Vaché, Jacques, **20th:** 510
Václav. *See* Wenceslaus
Vadim (Lermontov), **19th:** 1354
Vagabond, The (Collette), **20th:** 805
Vagabonds (Hamsun), **20th:** 1662
Vaḥīd Bihbahānī, **18th:** 1000-1001
Vaik. *See* Stephen I
Vail, Alfred, **19th:** 1611
Vaillant, Auguste, **Notor:** 180
Vaillant, Édouard, **19th:** 1221
Vair, Guillaume du, **17th:** 577
Vajk. *See* Stephen I
Val-ès-Dunes, Battle of (1047), **MA:** 1117
Valdemar II, **MA:** 1047-1049
"Valediction" (Donne), **17th:** 231
Valence, Palamede de Fabri de, **17th:** 723
Valencia, **MA:** Muslims, 572; Spanish invasion of, 571
Valencia, duke of. *See* Borgia, Cesare
Valencia, Siege of (1093-1094), **MA:** 280
Valencia, Siege of (1102), **MA:** 280
Valens, **Anc:** 363, 776, 825, 868, 911
Valenti, Jack, **20th:** 4231
Valentine (Sand), **19th:** 1987
Valentine Rescuing Sylvia from Proteus (Hunt), **19th:** 1158
Valentinian I, **Anc:** 868
Valentinian II, **Anc:** 869
Valentinian III, **Anc:** 140, 353; **Notor:** 45
Valentinois, duchess of. *See* Diane de Poitiers
Valentinois, duke of. *See* Borgia, Cesare
Valentinus, **Anc:** 918-921
Valenzuela, Joaquín. *See* Murieta, Joaquín
Valerian, **Anc:** 269, 774, 987
Valerius Martialis, Marcus. *See* Martial
Valéry, Henri. *See* Petiot, Marcel
Valéry, Paul, **20th:** 4136-4138
Valeurs personelles (Magritte), **20th:** 2549
Válka s mloky. See *War with the Newts, The*
Valla, Lorenzo, **MA:** 1049-1052
Valladolid Cathedral, **Ren:** 446
Valle, Barbara. *See* Strozzi, Barbara
Valley Forge, **18th:** 512, 1043
Valley of Decision, The (Wharton), **20th:** 4301
Valley of Fear, The (Doyle), **19th:** 689
Valley of the Kings, **Anc:** 26, 48, 389
Valley of the Moon, The (London), **20th:** 2422
Valley Song (Fugard), **20th:** 1357
Vālmīki, **Anc:** 922-924
Valmy, Battle of (1792), **19th:** 260
Valois Dynasty, **MA:** 1054; **Ren:** 410, 428
Valperga (Shelley), **19th:** 2088
Valpincon Bather, The (Ingrew), **19th:** 1173
Valse (Delibes), **19th:** 639
Valse, Le (Ravel), **20th:** 3387
Valse triste (Sibelius), **20th:** 3738
Valses noble et sentimental (Ravel), **20th:** 3386
Vampyr (film), **20th:** 1038
Van dat rechte christen ghelooue. See *True Christian Faith, The*
Van seun manieren van heiliger minnin. See *Of Seven Manners of Holy Loving*
Van Tien Dung, **20th:** 4171
Van Aelst, Pieter Coecke. *See* Coecke van Aelst, Pieter
Van Allen, James, **20th:** 4139-4141
Van Allen radiation belts, **20th:** 59, 4140
Vanbrugh, Sir John, **17th:** 52; **18th:** 472, 1002-1005
Van Buren, Abigail, **20th:** 2248
Van Buren, Martin, **19th:** 344, 504, 514, 1049, 2344-2348; **Notor:** 616
Vance, Cyrus, **Notor:** 735
Vance, Vivian, **20th:** 213
Vancouver, George, **18th:** 1006-1008; **19th:** 1250
Vandals, **Anc:** 351, 824; **MA:** 233, 600
Van de Kamp, John, **20th:** 1228
Van Delft, Jan. *See* Vermeer, Jan
Vanderbilt, Cornelius, **19th:** 1601, 2348-2351, 2459; **Notor:** 357, 433, 1084
Vanderbilt, Gertrude. *See* Whitney, Gertrude Vanderbilt
Vanderbilt, Gloria, **20th:** 4317
Van der Graaf, Volkert, **Notor:** 1055-1056
Van der Meer, Jan. *See* Vermeer, Jan
Van Dijck, Anthonie. *See* Dyck, Sir Anthony van

Van Dyne, Edith. *See* Baum, L. Frank
Vane, Charles, **Notor:** 877
Vane, Sir Henry, the Younger, **17th:** 57, 395, 941-943
Vanessa (Barber), **20th:** 232
Van Gogh, Vincent. *See* Gogh, Vincent van
Van Haarlem, Kenau Simonsdochter. *See* Kenau Hasselaer
Van Hemessen, Catherina. *See* Hemessen, Catharina van
Van Houton, Leslie, **Notor:** 690
Vanity Fair (Thackeray), **19th:** 2258
Vanity of Human Wishes, The (Johnson), **18th:** 536
Van Meter, Homer, **Notor:** 281
Van Orden v. Perry (2005), **20th:** 521
Van Rensselaer, Stephen, **19th:** 307
Van Rijn, Rembrandt. *See* Rembrandt
Van Schurman, Anna Maria. *See* Schurman, Anna Maria van
Van Wagener, Isabella. *See* Truth, Sojourner
Vanzetti, Bartolomeo, **20th:** 1308, 3312, 3580, 3752; **Notor:** 924, 1056-1058
Varanasi, Battle of (1539), **Ren:** 475
Varangian incursion (859-862), **MA:** 912
Varaville, Battle of (1058), **MA:** 1117
Varazdat, **Anc:** 777
Varchi, Benedetto, **Ren:** 654
Vardhamāna, **Anc:** 355, 924-926
Varèse, Edgard, **20th:** 4142-4144
Vargas, Getúlio, **Notor:** 1059-1060
Variae (Cassiodorus), **MA:** 76, 234
Várias histórias (Machado), **19th:** 1451
Variations (Lloyd Webber), **20th:** 2415
Variations on a Theme by Haydn, Op. 56a (Brahms), **19th:** 297
Variations on a Theme of Frank Bridge (Britten), **20th:** 530
Variations on an Original Theme ("Enigma") (Elgar), **20th:** 1134
Variations symphoniques (Franck), **19th:** 823
Variations V (film), **20th:** 887
Varieties of Religious Experience, The (James), **19th:** 1214-1215
Varinius, Publius, **Anc:** 819
Vario, Paul, **Notor:** 465
Various Forces of Nature, The (Faraday), **19th:** 760
Världarnas utveckling. See *Worlds in the Making*
Varley, Samuel Alfred, **19th:** 2107
Varmus, Harold E., **20th:** 4145-4147
Varna, Battle of (1444), **MA:** 520, 711
Varro, Gaius Terentius, **Anc:** 343, 383
Varro, Marcus Terentius, **Anc:** 663, 927-930
Varus, Publius Quinctilius, **Anc:** 100, 147
Vasa, Gustav Eriksson. *See* Gustav I Vasa
Vasa Dynasty, **18th:** 232-234
Vasari, Giorgio, **MA:** 319, 566, 798; **Ren:** 40, 46, 98, 249, 383, 422, 561, 755, 848, 932, 936, 953-956, 962
Vasco da Gama. *See* Gama, Vasco da
Vasco da Gama (Bizet), **19th:** 241
Vases communicants, Les. See *Communicating Vessels*
Vasile, **17th:** 463
Vasili III Ivanovich. *See* Vasily III
Vasily II, **Ren:** 487
Vasily III, **Ren:** 488, 492, 750, 957-959
Vasily Ivanovich. *See* Vasily Shuysky
Vasily Shuysky, **17th:** 855, 943-945
Vasilyevich, Ivan III. *See* Ivan III (the Great)
Vasilyevich, Ivan IV. *See* Ivan IV (the Terrible)
Vásquez Lajara, Horacio, **20th:** 4084
Vassa, Gustavas. *See* Equiano, Olaudah
Vassall Morton (Parkman), **19th:** 1744
Vassar College, **19th:** 1580
Vasubandhu, **Anc:** 111, 930-933
Vasvár, Treaty of (1664), **17th:** 527
Vatican City. *See* Geographical Index
Vatican Council, First, **19th:** 1665, 1804
Vatican Council, Second, **20th:** 2018, 3149
Vatican Radio, **20th:** 3275
Vatican Swindle, The. See *Lafcadio's Adventures*
Vatican Virgil (Claude Lorrain), **17th:** 172
Vattagamani, **Anc:** 169, 933-935
Vauban, Sébastien Le Prestre de, **17th:** 559, 946-948; **18th:** 691
Vaugelas, seigneur de, **17th:** 780
Vaughan, Hank, **Notor:** 1060-1062
Vaughan, Henry, **17th:** 741
Vaughan, Sarah, **20th:** 3114
Vaughan Williams, Ralph, **20th:** 4147-4150
Vauvenargues, Luc de Clapiers, **18th:** 1010
Vauvenargues, marquis de, **18th:** 1009-1010
Vaux-le-Vicomte, **17th:** 523
Vavilov, Nikolai Ivanovich, **20th:** 4151-4153; **Notor:** 668
Vāyū Purāna, **Anc:** 551
Veblen, Thorstein, **20th:** 4154-4156
Vecellio, Tiziano. *See* Titian
Vecher (Akhmatova), **20th:** 43

Vechera na khutore bliz Dikanki. See *Evenings on a Farm Near Dikanka*
Vecherny albom (Tsvetayeva), **20th:** 4098
Vedānta Sūtras of Bādarāyana with the Commentary of Samkara, The (Śaṅkara), **MA:** 926
Vedāntas, **MA:** 877
Vedāntasāra (Rāmānuja), **MA:** 877
Vedārthasaṃgraha (Rāmānuja), **MA:** 877
Vedātadīpa (Rāmānuja), **MA:** 877
Vedic legends, **Anc:** 497
Veen, Otto van, **17th:** 802
Veerappan, **Notor:** 1062-1063
Vefarinn mikli frá Kasmír (Laxness), **20th:** 2308
Vega Carpio, Lope de, **17th:** 113, 279, 312, 738, 914, 949-952
Vegetables, Fruit, and Asters (Chen), **17th:** 157
Veglie dei Signori Unisoni, **17th:** 888
Veinte poemas de amor y una canción desesperada. See *Twenty Love Poems and a Song of Despair*
Velázquez, Diego, **Ren:** 35, 252; **17th:** 160, 671, 739, 953-956, 1003; **18th:** 437
Velbužd, Battle of (1330), **MA:** 957
Velikaya, Yekaterina. *See* Catherine the Great
Velvet Revolution (1989), **20th:** 1708
Venables, Robert, **Notor:** 753
Vendée, War in the (1793), **18th:** 846
Vendôme Column, **19th:** 561
Venerabilis Inceptor. *See* Ockham, William of
Venerable Bede. *See* Bede the Venerable, Saint
Venetian Academy, **18th:** 192
Venette, Jean de, **MA:** 1053-1055
Veneziano, Domenico, **Ren:** 785
Venezuela, **19th:** independence of, 2195. *See also* Geographical Index
Venice, **MA:** 298; **Ren:** 155, 613; Ottoman Empire and, 88; Papal States and, 519; **17th:** 720; **18th:** 192, 1019; painting, 978
Venice, League of. *See* Holy League (1495)
Venice, Treaty of (1201), **MA:** 299
Venizélos, Eleuthérios, **20th:** 4157-4159
Venn, Henry, **19th:** 574
Venus, **Anc:** 172, 272, 521
Venus (Epstein), **20th:** 1166
Venus and Cupid (Cranach, the Elder), **Ren:** 263
Venus and Cupid (Fontana), **Ren:** 339
Venus, Cupid, and Satyr (Correggio), **Ren:** 250
Venus in sole visa. See *Transit of Venus over the Sun, The*
Venus with Cupid the Honey-Thief (Cranach, the Elder), **Ren:** 264
Vepkhistkaosani. See *Knight in the Panther's Skin, The*
Vêpres siciliennes, Les (Verdi), **19th:** 2352
Ver, Fabian, **Notor:** 701
Vera Christiana religio. See *True Christian Religion*
Vera Circuli et Hyperbolae Quadratura (Gregory), **17th:** 319
Verbum sapienti (Petty), **17th:** 734
Vercingetorix, **Anc:** 173, 935-938
Verclaringhe des Christelycken doopsels. See *Christian Baptism*
Verdadeira informação das terras do Preste João das Indias. See *Prester John of the Indies, The*
Verdi, Giuseppe, **19th:** 2351-2354; **20th:** 676
Verdun, Treaty of (843), **MA:** 245, 663, 832, 911
Vere, Sir Francis, **17th:** 928
Vere, Sir Horace, **17th:** 261
Vereeniging, Peace of (1902), **20th:** 2174
Vergangenheitsbewältigung, **20th:** 1574
Vergennes, Charles Gravier de, **18th:** 1011-1013
Verger, Treaty of Le. *See* Le Verger, Treaty of
Vergil, **Anc:** 196, 273, 301, 302, 431, 521, 528, 602, 604, 929, 938-941
Vergine, Gugielmo, **20th:** 675
Vergne, Marie-Madeleine Pioche de la. *See* La Fayette, Madame de
Vergonzoso en palacio, El. See *Bashful Man at Court, The*
Vérité. See *Truth*
Vérité des sciences, contre les sceptiques ou Pyrrhoniens, La (Mersenne), **17th:** 630
Verkade, Jan, **20th:** 973
Verklärte Nacht (Schoenberg), **20th:** 3664
Verlaine, Paul, **19th:** 1912
Verlorene Ehre der Katharina Blum, Der. See *Lost Honor of Katharina Blum, The*
Vermächtnis, Das. See *Soldier's Legacy, A*
Vermeer, Jan, **17th:** 353, 511, 956-959; **18th:** 224; **20th:** 905
Vermischte Schriften (Savigny), **19th:** 2004
Vernaculars and Christianity, **Anc:** 912
Vernazza, Ettore, **Ren:** 191
Verne, Jules, **19th:** 2354-2358
Vernet, Horace, **19th:** 899
Vernuft und Existenz. See *Reason and Existenz*
Veronese, Paolo, **Ren:** 175, 959-962
Verrius Flaccus, Marcus, **Anc:** 941-943

Verrocchio, Andrea del, **Ren:** 561, 962-965
Vers l'armée de métier. See *Army of the Future, The*
Vers Lyriques (du Bellay), **Ren:** 295
Vers une architecture. See *Towards a New Architecture*
Versace, Gianni, **Notor:** 245
Versailles, **17th:** 505, 524, 533, 554, 590; **18th:** gardens, 166
Versailles, Treaty of (1919), **20th:** 781, 1181
Verschuer, Otmar von, **Notor:** 717
Verses (Rossetti), **19th:** 1940
Verses Lately Written upon Several Occasions (Cowley), **17th:** 200
Vershofen, Wilhelm, **20th:** 1173
Versions de quelques pièces de Virgile, Tacite et Saluste . . . (Gournay), **17th:** 315
Versos del Capitán, Los. See *Captain's Verses, The*
Versos libres (Martí), **19th:** 1504
Versos sencillos (Martí), **19th:** 1504
Verstehen, Das (Wach), **20th:** 4178
Versuch einer Kritik aller Offenbarung. See *Attempt at a Critique of All Revelation*
Vertical city, **20th:** 2324
Vertical Seconds (Nicholson), **20th:** 2958
Vertigo (film), **20th:** 1827, 3863
Vertsty I (Tsvetayev), **20th:** 4099
Verulam, baron of. *See* Bacon, Francis
Verus, Lucius Aurelius, **Anc:** 530
Verwandlung, Die. See *Metamorphosis, The*
Verwoerd, Hendrik Frensch, **Notor:** 1064-1065
Very, Jones, **19th:** 1762
Vesalius, Andreas, **MA:** 447; **Ren:** 319, 345, 965-969
Vesalius on China-root (Vesalius), **Ren:** 967
Veshniye vody. See *Torrents of Spring, The*
Vespasian, **Anc:** 470, 477, 943-946; **Notor:** 289, 541
Vespers of Palermo, The (Hemans), **19th:** 1076
Vespers of 1610 (Monteverdi), **17th:** 658
Vespucci, Amerigo, **Ren:** 969-973
Vessels of Magic (Rothko), **20th:** 3539
Vestal Virgins, **Anc:** 188
Vestris (ballet), **20th:** 253
Veuve, La (Corneille), **17th:** 193
Vexler, Vladimir I., **20th:** 2534
Via Crucis (Liszt), **19th:** 1395
Viaje del Parnaso, El. See *Voyage of Parnassus, The*
Viardot, Louis, **19th:** 952
Viardot, Pauline, **19th:** 952
Viatichi, **MA:** 1068
Vicar of Wakefield, The (Goldsmith), **18th:** 434
Vicar of Wrexhill, The (Trollope), **19th:** 2304
Vichy France, **20th:** 2286
Vico, Giambattista, **18th:** 1013-1016
Vicomte de Bragelonne, Le (Dumas), **19th:** 697
Vicomtesse d'Haussonville (Ingres), **19th:** 1173
Victor (Fugard), **20th:** 1357
Victor I, **Anc:** 425, 444
Victor III, **MA:** 1043
Victor IV, **MA:** 56, 386
Victor Emmanuel II, **19th:** 445, 872, 1803
Victor Emmanuel III, **20th:** 2886; **Notor:** 769
Victoria (Hamsun), **20th:** 1661
Victoria (queen of Great Britain and Ireland), **19th:** 140, 1535, 2359-2362; Lord Palmerston, 1733; **Notor:** 632
Victoria, Tómas Luis de, **Ren:** 150
Victoria Falls, **19th:** 1402
Victoria Luise, **20th:** 4454
Victoria Regina (Houseman), **20th:** 1725
Victorius of Aquitaine, **MA:** 314
Victory (Conrad), **20th:** 826
Victory (Saint-Gaudens), **19th:** 1973
Victory Boogie-Woogie (Mondrian), **20th:** 2788
Vida breve, La (Falla), **20th:** 1207
Vida de Don Quijote y Sancho, La. See *Life of Don Quixote and Sancho, The*
Vida de Lazarillo de Tormes y de sus fortunas y adversidades, La. See *Lazarillo de Tormes*
Vida del Buscón llamado Pablos . . . , La. See *Life and Adventures of Buscon, the Witty Spaniard, The*
Vida es sueño, La. See *Life Is a Dream*
Vida y hechos del pícaro Guzmán de Alfarache, La. See *Guzmán de Alfarache*
Videla, Jorge Rafael, **Notor:** 394, 1066-1067
Vidocq, Eugène François, **Notor:** 1067-1069
Vidyasagar, Iswar Chandra, **19th:** 2363-2365
Vie, Une. See *Woman's Life, A*
Vie de Henry Brulard. See *Life of Henry Brulard, The*
Vie de Jésus. See *Life of Jesus, The*
Vie de Rossini. See *Memoirs of Rossini*
Vie de saint Paul, La. See *Saint Paul*
Vie en fleur, Le. See *Bloom of Life, The*
Vie en Rose, La (film), **20th:** 3230
Vieira, António, **17th:** 959-961
Viellese, La. See *Coming of Age, The*
Vien, Joseph, **19th:** 607
Vienna, Austria, **18th:** Johann Bernhard Fischer von Erlach, 351; garden palaces, 495;

Christoph Gluck, 419; Johann Lucas von Hildebrandt, 495; Mikhail Illarionovich Kutuzov, 570; Wolfgang Amadeus Mozart, 711
Vienna, Concordat of (1448), **MA:** 768
Vienna, Congress of (1515), **Ren:** 886
Vienna, Congress of (1814-1815), **19th:** 1562, 2152
Vienna, Council of (1311), **MA:** 708
Vienna, Peace of (1606), **Ren:** 842
Vienna, Siege of (1683), **17th:** 453, 528
Vienna and the Austrians (Trollope), **19th:** 2304
Vienna Circle, **20th:** 660
Vienna Court Opera, **20th:** 2560
Vienna Psychoanalytical Association, **20th:** 1324
Vienna Secession movement, **20th:** 2180
Vier letzte Lieder (Strauss), **20th:** 3887
Viertzig Fragen von der Seele. See *Forty Questions of the Soul*
Viet Cong, **20th:** 1836, 2952, 4171
Viet Minh, **20th:** 228, 1836, 2951, 4170
Viet Rock (Terry), **20th:** 3983
Vietnam, **MA:** 756, 757, 982; Mongol invasion of, 626; **Ren:** 546; **18th:** conflicts with China, 737; **20th:** independence of (1945), 228, 1836, 2699, 4170; reunification, 4171. *See also* North Vietnam; South Vietnam; Geographical Index
Vietnam Veterans Memorial, **20th:** 2385
Vietnam War (1959-1975), **20th:** 1836, 2954, 4171; Cambodia, 3741; China, 1908; Gerald R. Ford, 1277; William Averell Harriman, 1687; Herbert H. Humphrey, 1940; Lyndon B. Johnson, 2030; Robert F. Kennedy, 2104; Henry Kissinger, 2171; memoirs, 1727; memorial, 2385; Richard Nixon, 2985; Tip O'Neill, 3056; opposition to, 759; U.S. strategy, 2542
Vietnamese civil war. *See* Tay Son Rebellion
View, The (television talk show), **20th:** 4212
View from Castle Rock, The (Munro), **20th:** 2874
View from the Bridge, A (Miller), **20th:** 2743
View of Basel and the Rhine (Kirchner), **20th:** 2165
View of Delft (Vermeer), **17th:** 958
View of the Conduct of the Executive, in the Foreign Affairs of the United States, A (Monroe), **19th:** 1587
View of the Evidences of Christianity, A (Paley), **18th:** 763
View on Hampstead Heath (Constable), **19th:** 541
View on the Stour near Dedham (Constable), **19th:** 541
Views of an Ex-President (Harrison), **19th:** 1043
Views of Saint-Séverin (Delaunay), **20th:** 951
Views of Society and Manners in America (Wright), **19th:** 2469
Vigée-Lebrun, Élisabeth, **18th:** 1016-1019
Vigilance Society, **19th:** 767
Vigilius, **MA:** 1010
Vijayanagar Empire, **Ren:** 532
Vikings, **MA:** 63, 221, 340, 363, 785, 789, 900, 911; Christianity, 222, 786, 790, 902; paganism, 222
Vikramāditya I, **Anc:** 496
Vikramorvaśiya (Kālidāsa), **Anc:** 497
Vildanden. See *Wild Duck, The*
Vilhjalmur Stefansson Arctic Expedition, **20th:** 4339
Villa, Pancho, **19th:** 229; **20th:** 2040, 3014, 3220, 4160-4163, 4449-4450; **Notor:** 280, 1069-1071, 1130-1131
Villa-Lobos, Heitor, **20th:** 4163-4166
Villafranca, Armistice of (1859), **19th:** 446
Village Romeo and Juliet, A (Delius), **20th:** 955
Villain, Raoul, **19th:** 1221
Villamena, Francesco, **17th:** 116
Villana de La Sagra, La (Tirso), **17th:** 913
Villana de Vallecas, La (Tirso), **17th:** 914
Villani, Giovanni, **MA:** 1056-1058
Villanueva, Pedro Díaz de, **17th:** 1003
Villarroel, Gualberto, **20th:** 3172
Ville de la chance, La. See *Town Beyond the Wall, The*
Ville-Marie de Montreal, **17th:** 575
Villegas, Francisco Gómez de Quevedo y. *See* Quevedo y Villegas, Francisco Gómez de
Villehardouin, Geoffroi de, **MA:** 1059-1062
Villeneuve, Pierre de, **19th:** 1658
Villes du moyen age, Les. See *Medieval Cities*
Villette (Brontë), **19th:** 310
Villi, Le (Puccini), **20th:** 3346
Villiers, George (1592-1628). *See* Buckingham, first duke of
Villiers, George (1628-1687). *See* Buckingham, second duke of
Villon, François, **Ren:** 973-977
Vima Kadphises I, **Anc:** 499
Vimeur, Jean-Baptiste Donatien de. *See* Rochambeau, comte de
Vincent, Thomas, **17th:** 894
Vincent de Paul, Saint, **17th:** 962-965
Vincent of Beauvais, **MA:** 228, 1063-1065

Vincent of Lérins, Saint, **Anc:** 947-949
Vincentian canon, **Anc:** 948
Vincentians. *See* Congregation of the Mission
Vincy, Battle of (717), **MA:** 251
Vindication of Catholic Morality, A (Manzoni), **19th:** 1496
Vindication of the Rights of Man, A (Wollstonecraft), **18th:** 1109
Vindication of the Rights of Woman, A (Wollstonecraft), **18th:** 1109
Vindiciae contra tyrannos (Mornay), **Ren:** 704
Vindiciae judaeorum (Manasseh ben Israel), **17th:** 583
Vinegar Hill, Battle of (1798), **19th:** 438
Vines, Ellsworth, **20th:** 3216
Vingt Ans après. See *Twenty Years After*
Vingt mille lieues sous les mers. See *Twenty Thousand Leagues Under the Sea*
Vinh Thuy. *See* Bao Dai
Vining, Elizabeth Gray, **20th:** 46
Viola, Roberto, **Notor:** 394
Viola Concerto (Walton), **20th:** 4218
Violence Against Women Act of 1994, **20th:** 3408
Violent Bear It Away, The (O'Connor), **20th:** 3018
Violin and Palette (Braque), **20th:** 494
Violin and Pitcher (Braque), **20th:** 494
Violin Concerto (Berg), **20th:** 312
Violin Concerto in B Minor, Op. 61 (Elgar), **20th:** 1135
Violin Concerto in D, Op. 77 (Brahms), **19th:** 298
Violin Concerto, Op. 14 (Barber), **20th:** 232
Viollet-le-Duc, Eugène, **20th:** 1424
Vios Kai politela tou Alexe Zormpa. See *Zorba the Greek*
Viracocha Inca, **Ren:** 746
Vīrappan. *See* Veerappan
Virchow, Rudolf, **19th:** 2365-2368
Virgil. *See* Vergil
Virgin and Child (Siloé), **Ren:** 890
Virgin and Child (Sirani), **17th:** 857
Virgin and Child with Saint Anne and the Infant Saint John (Leonardo da Vinci), **Ren:** 563
Virgin Queen. *See* Elizabeth I
Virgin Soil (Turgenev), **19th:** 2320
Virgin Spring, The (film), **20th:** 317
Virginia, **Ren:** settlement of, 193, 397, 771, 813; **17th:** 29, 120, 275
Virginia Resolution (1798-1799), **18th:** 637
Virginia Richly Valued (Hakluyt), **Ren:** 420
Virginia State Penitentiary, **19th:** 1326
Virginia Statute of Religious Liberty (1786), **18th:** 529, 664
Virginians, The (Thackeray), **19th:** 2259
Viridiana (film), **20th:** 579
Virtue, **Anc:** Confucianism on, 236; knowledge and, 800; Neoplatonism and, 688; philosophy and, 283; pleasure and, 88
Virtues of a Religious Superior, The (Bonaventure), **MA:** 181
Virtuoso, The (Shadwell), **17th:** 384
Viruses, study of, **20th:** 3825
Visconti, Luchino, **20th:** 4166-4168
Vishnyovy sad. See *Cherry Orchard, The*
Visible World (Komenský), **17th:** 470
Visigoths, **Anc:** 352, 868, 911; **MA:** 293, 556, 1006; Christianity, 784, 1014; education, 76; law, 1015; women, 76
Vision, A (Yeats), **20th:** 4429
Vision After the Sermon, The (Gauguin), **19th:** 879
Vision and Design (Fry), **20th:** 1353, 2818
Vision at Evening (Nash), **20th:** 2911
Vision of Alameda Central (Rivera), **20th:** 3458
Vision of Judgment, The (Byron), **19th:** 381
Vision of St. Hyacinth (Fontana), **Ren:** 339
Vision of the Blessed Herman Joseph (van Dyck), **17th:** 245
Visions, Christian, **Anc:** 240, 789
Visions of Bellay (du Bellay), **Ren:** 296
Visions of Cody (Kerouac), **20th:** 2115
Visions of Gerard (Kerouac), **20th:** 2116
Visions of the Daughters of Albion (Blake), **18th:** 122
Visions: Or, Hel's Kingdome and the World's Follies and Abuses (Quevedo y Villegas), **17th:** 770
Visit to Sarashina Village, A (Bashō), **17th:** 616
Visit to the Kashima Shrine, A (Bashō), **17th:** 616
Visita y anatomía de la cabeza del cardenal Richelieu (Quevedo y Villegas), **17th:** 771
Viskningar och rop. See *Cries and Whispers*
Visscher, Ann Roemers, **17th:** 824
Visscher, Frans Jacobsz, **17th:** 906
Vita Beatricis. See *Life of Beatrice of Nazareth, The*
Vita Constantini (Eusebius), **Anc:** 240, 331, 391
Vita di Benvenuto Cellini, La. See *Life of Benvenuto Cellini, The*
Vita Karoli magni imperatoris. See *Life of Charlemagne*

Vita Merlini. See *Life of Merlin*
Vita nuova, La. See *New Life, The*
Vita S. Antonii (Athanasius), **Anc:** 62, 134
Vita sanctorum abbatum monasterii in Wiramutha et Girvam, Benedicti, Ceolfridi, Easteruini, Sigfridi, atque Huaetbereti. See *Lives of the First Abbots of Wearmouth and Jarrow: Benedict, Ceolfrid, Eosterwine, Sigfrid, and Huetbert*
Vital, Ḥayyim, **Ren:** 579
Vitalism, **17th:** 188; **19th:** 2457
Vitamin B_{12}, **20th:** 1850, 4306, 4395
Vitamin C, **20th:** 3157
Vitamin C and the Common Cold (Pauling), **20th:** 3157
Vite de' più eccellenti architetti, pittori, et scultori italiani, da cimabue insino a' tempi nostri, Le. See *Lives of the Most Eminent Painters, Sculptors, and Architects*
Vite prima Bernardi abbatis. See *Saint Bernard of Clairvaux*
Vitellius, **Anc:** 645; **Notor:** 289
Vitkov, Battle of (1420), **MA:** 1163
Vitoria, Battle of (1813), **19th:** 2410
Vitoria, Francisco de, **Ren:** 978-980
Vitriaco, Philippus de. *See* Vitry, Philippe de
Vitruvius, **Anc:** 81, 247
Vitry, Philippe de, **MA:** 741, 1065-1067
Vittoria d'amore, La (Monteverdi), **17th:** 659
Vivaldi, Antonio, **18th:** 463, 1019-1022
Vivekananda, **19th:** 2368-2371
Vives, Juan, **Ren:** 188
Vivian Grey (Disraeli), **19th:** 666
Viviani, Vicenzo, **17th:** 921
Vividishananda. *See* Vivekananda
Viviparous Quadrupeds of North America (Audubon), **19th:** 93
Vivonne-Savelli, Catherine de. *See* Rambouillet, marquise de
Vizcaíno, Sebastián, **Ren:** 161
Vlad II, **Ren:** 981
Vlad III the Impaler, **MA:** 712; **Ren:** 981-983; **Notor:** 1072-1073. *See also* Báthory, Elizabeth
Vladimir I, **MA:** 87, 191, 794, 1068-1071
Vladimir, princes of, **MA:** 54
Vladimir, Saint. *See* Vladimir I
Vladimir Illich Lenin (Mayakovsky), **20th:** 2660
Vladimir Mayakovsky (Mayakovsky), **20th:** 2659
Vladimir Svyatoslavich. *See* Vladimir I
Vladimir the Great. *See* Vladimir I
Vladimir Veliky. *See* Vladimir I
Vladislav II, **Ren:** 636, 885, 983-985
Vlasov, Andrey Andreyevich, **Notor:** 1074-1075
Vlast tmy. See *Power of Darkness, The*
Vo Nguyen Giap, **20th:** 1836, 4169-4173
Vo ves golos. See *At the Top of My Voice*
Voet, Gijsbert. *See* Voetius, Gisbertus
Voetius, Gisbertus, **17th:** 824
Vogel, Sir Julius, **19th:** 2371-2373
Voice from the Other World (Mahfouz), **20th:** 2556
Voice of America, **20th:** 2499
Voice of India, **19th:** 1634
Voices of the Night (Longfellow), **19th:** 1417
Void, the, **Anc:** 261
Voitout, Jeanne. *See* Auclert, Hubertine
Voiture, Vincent, **17th:** 780
Voix du peuple, Le, **19th:** 1836
Voix et le phénomène, La. See *Speech and Phenomena*
Volcanoes, **Anc:** 828
Volcanology, **18th:** 927
Volk, Het, **20th:** 440
Völkerpsychologie (Wundt), **20th:** 4408
Volkhov, Andrey. *See* Vlasov, Andrey Andreyevich
Volkogonov, Dimitri, **20th:** 1823
Vollard, Ambroise, **20th:** 718, 3543
Volodymyr. *See* Vladimir I
Voloshinov, V. N. *See* Bakhtin, Mikhail
Volpini Exhibit, **19th:** 880
Volpone (Jonson), **Ren:** 93; **17th:** 442
Volshebny fonar (Tsvetayeva), **20th:** 4099
Volta, Alessandro, **18th:** 393, 1022-1026; **19th:** 996
Volta Laboratory, **19th:** 183
Voltaire, **17th:** 521; **18th:** 33, 147, 241, 1026- 1029
Voluntary Action (Beveridge), **20th:** 355
Voluntary Militia for National Security. *See* Tonton Macoutes
Volunteer Corps (Ireland), **18th:** 441
Vom andern Ufer. See *From the Other Shore*
Vom Beruf unserer Zeit für Gesetzgebung und Rechtswissenschaft. See *Of the Vocation of Our Age for Legislation and Jurisprudence*
Vom dreyfachen Leben des Menschen. See *High and Deep Searching Out of the Threefold Life of Man, The*
Vom Ich als Prinzip der Philosophie (Schelling), **19th:** 2009
Vom Kriege. See *On War*
Vom Stein, Freiherr. *See* Stein, Freiherr vom
Vom U-Boot zur Kanzel. See *From U-Boat to Pulpit*

Vom Ursprung and Zeit der Geschichte. See *Origin and Goal of History, The*
Von den drei Principien göttlichen Wesens. See *Concerning the Three Principles of the Divine Essence*
Von der Geburt und Bezeichnung aller Wesen. See *Signatura Rerum*
Von der Gnadenwahl. See *Concerning the Election of Grace*
Von der Weltseele, eine Hypothese der höheren Physik zur Erklärung des allgemeinen Organismus (Schelling), **19th:** 2010
Von 177 theosophischen Fragen. See *Theosophic Questions*
Von Anhalt-Zerbst, Sophie Friederike Auguste. *See* Catherine the Great
Von Braun, Wernher. *See* Braun, Wernher von
Von Bülow, Bernhard. *See* Bülow, Bernhard von
Von Bülow, Claus, **20th:** 1468; **Notor:** 1075-1077
Von Bülow, Cosima, **Notor:** 1076
Von Bülow, Sunny, **Notor:** 1075
Von Clausewitz, Carl. *See* Clausewitz, Carl von
Von Ehrenfels, Christian. *See* Ehrenfels, Christian von
Von Gneisenau, August. *See* Gneisenau, August von
Von Hardenburg, Karl. *See* Hardenberg, Karl von
Von Hevesy, George. *See* Hevesy, George von
Von Hindenburg, Paul. *See* Hindenburg, Paul von
Von Humboldt, Alexander. *See* Humboldt, Alexander von
Vonifatiev, Stephen, **17th:** 27, 683
Von Kleist, Heinrich. *See* Kleist, Heinrich von
Von Liebig, Justus. *See* Liebig, Justus von
Von Metternich, Clemens Wenzel Nepomuk Lothar. *See* Metternich
Von Neumann, John, **20th:** 2943-2946
Vonsiatsky, Anastase, **Notor:** 1077-1078
Von Sternberg, Josef. *See* Sternberg, Josef von
Von Tirpitz, Alfred. *See* Tirpitz, Alfred von
Von Zeppelin, Frederick. *See* Zeppelin, Frederick von
Voodoo, **20th:** 1070
Voodoo Queen of New Orleans. *See* Laveau, Marie
Voortrekkers, **19th:** 1298
Voprosy literatury I estetiki. See *Dialogic Imagination, The*
Voraussetzungen des Sozialismus und die Aufgaben de Sozialdemokratie, Die. See *Evolutionary Socialism*
Vorschule der Aesthetik (Fechner), **19th:** 772
Vorstellung an Menschenfreunde und vermögende Männer . . . (Basedow), **18th:** 90
Vortex, The (Coward), **20th:** 854
Vortigern, **Anc:** 394
Vortimer, **Anc:** 395
Vorträge über altbekannt Geschichte. See *Lectures on Ancient History*
Vorträge über Descendenztheorie. See *Evolution Theory, The*
Vorträge über die römische Geschichte. See *Lectures on Roman History*
Vorwärts, **19th:** 1371
Voskhod 1, **20th:** 2194
Voskreseniye. See *Resurrection* (Tolstoy)
Vostok 1, **20th:** 1371-1372, 2194
Vote des femmes, Le (Auclert), **19th:** 90
Voting rights, **20th:** 575, 1651. *See also* Woman suffrage
Voting Rights Act of 1965, **20th:** 2030, 2149
Vouet, Simon, **17th:** 523
Vow of Louis XIII, The (Ingres), **19th:** 1172
Vox Angelica (Ernst), **20th:** 1178
Voyage au centre de la terre. See *Journey to the Centre of the Earth, A*
Voyage aux régions équinoxiales du Nouveau Continent, fait en 1799, 1800, 1801, 1802, 1803, et 1804 (Humboldt and Bonpland), **19th:** 1152
Voyage d'Urien, Le. See *Urien's Voyage*
Voyage musical en Allemagne et en Italie (Berlioz), **19th:** 203
Voyage of Discovery to the North Pacific Ocean and Round the World (Vancouver), **18th:** 1007
Voyage of Parnassus, The (Cervantes), **Ren:** 209
"Voyage to the Island of Love" (Behn), **17th:** 43
Voyager Golden Record, **20th:** 3592
Voyages (Mackenzie), **18th:** 631
Voyages and Descriptions (Dampier), **17th:** 215
Voyages and Discoveries of the Companions of Columbus (Irving), **19th:** 1181
Voyna i mir. See *War and Peace*
Vozniknovenie zhizni na zemle. See *Origin of Life, The*
Vramshapuh, **Anc:** 777
Vredens dag. See *Day of Wrath*
Vtoroye rozhdeniye. See *Second Birth*
Vu, Chau, **Notor:** 373
Vuillard, Édouard, **20th:** 421, 972, 4173-4176
Vulcanization, **19th:** 948
Vulgate, **Anc:** 457
Vulso Longus, L. Malius, **Anc:** 739
Vyatka, annexation to Moscow, **Ren:** 488

Vyazma, annexation to Moscow, **Ren:** 489
Vyshinsky, Andrey, **Notor:** 1052, 1079-1080, 1116
Vytautas, **MA:** 1120

W

Wa-Tho-Huk. *See* Thorpe, Jim
Waban, **17th:** 248
Wach, Joachim, **20th:** 4177-4180
Wad el-Mekhazen, Battle of. *See* Three Kings, Battle of
Wadi Bakka, Battle of. *See* Guadalete, Battle of
Wadsworth, Charles, **19th:** 660
Wafd, **20th:** 4439
Waffen nieder!, Die. See *Lay Down Your Arms*
Wagadu, **MA:** 978
Wagner, Honus, **20th:** 792
Wagner, Richard, **19th:** 222, 297, 330, 1154, 1681, 2374-2378; **20th:** 937; **Notor:** 197, 367, 1081
Wagner, Robert F., **20th:** 3490
Wagner, Siegfried, **Notor:** 1081
Wagner, Winifred, **Notor:** 1081-1082
Wagner Act. *See* National Labor Relations Act of 1935
Wagner-Rogers Bill, **20th:** 3490
Wagoner, Porter, **20th:** 3128
Wagram, Battle of (1809), **19th:** 469, 1562
Wahhāb, Muḥammad ibn ʿAbd al-, **18th:** 1030-1031
Wahhābīs and Wahhābīism, **18th:** 1030-1031; **19th:** 1966
Waḥīd Bihbahānī. *See* Vaḥīd Bihbahānī
Wahl, Arthur C., **20th:** 3685
Wahlitits, **19th:** 1239
Wahlstatt, Battle of (1813), **19th:** 261
Wahlverwandtschaften, Die. See *Elective Affinities*
Wahrheitsgehalt der Religion, Der. See *Truth of Religion, The*
Wahunsenacawh. *See* Powhatan
Waihi gold mine strike (1912), **20th:** 2644
Wainwright Building, **19th:** 2198
Waitangi, Treaty of (1840), **19th:** 378, 1483
Waiting for Godot (Beckett), **20th:** 281
Wakarusa War (1855), **19th:** 320
Wakefield, Battle of (1460), **Ren:** 828
Wakefield, Edward Gibbon, **19th:** 708, 2378-2380
Waksman, Selman Abraham, **20th:** 4180-4183
Walachia, **Ren:** 981; **17th:** 463
Walatta Giyorgis. *See* Mentewab
Walays, William. *See* Wallace, William
Walcott, Jersey Joe, **20th:** 2439
Walcott, Louis Eugene. *See* Farrakhan, Louis
Wald, Lillian D., **20th:** 4184-4187
Waldemar I. *See* Valdemar II
Walden (Thoreau), **19th:** 2274
Walden Two (Skinner), **20th:** 3756
Waldensians, **MA:** 316
Waldheim, Kurt, **20th:** 3194, 4187-4190, 4330
Wales, **Anc:** 17; **MA:** Norman invasion of, 448; war with England, 345. *See also* Geographical Index
Wales, Statute of (1284), **MA:** 345
Wałęsa, Lech, **20th:** 4191-4195
Walī Allāh, Shāh, **18th:** 1032-1033
Walīdī I, al-, **MA:** 1007
Waliullah. *See* Walī Allāh, Shāh
Walker, Aida, **Notor:** 933
Walker, Alice, **20th:** 4196-4199
Walker, Andrew, **Notor:** 870
Walker, David, **19th:** 2327
Walker, James J., **20th:** 2238; **Notor:** 1082-1083
Walker, John. *See* Lindh, John Walker
Walker, Joseph R., **19th:** 428
Walker, Madam C. J., **20th:** 4199-4202
Walker, Samuel H., **19th:** 535
Walker, Sarah Breedlove McWilliams. *See* Walker, Madam C. J.
Walker, William (president of Nicaragua), **Notor:** 1084-1085
Walker, William Hall (camera maker), **20th:** 1079
Walking Man (Rodin), **19th:** 1926
Walks and Talks of an American Farmer in England (Olmsted), **19th:** 1706
Walküre, Die (Wagner), **19th:** 2375
Wall, Rachel, **Notor:** 1086-1087
Wall, and Other Stories, The (Sartre), **20th:** 3638
Wallace, Alfred Russel, **19th:** 604, 1282, 1426
Wallace, George C., **20th:** 1940, 4203-4206; **Notor:** 100, 140, 177, 363, 1087-1089
Wallace, Henry A., **20th:** 4005, 4207-4210
Wallace, Henry C., **20th:** 1677
Wallace, Jim, **Notor:** 143
Wallace, Lewis, **Notor:** 1105
Wallace, William, **MA:** 202, 346, 1072-1075
Wallace's Farmer (journal), **20th:** 4207
Wallach, Meier Moiseevich. *See* Litvinov, Maksim Maksimovich
Wallachia. *See* Walachia
Wallensis, William. *See* Wallace, William
Wallenstein, Albrecht Wenzel von, **17th:** 269, 290, 337, 460, 966-969
Waller, Fats, **20th:** 132
Wallflower at the Orgy (Ephron), **20th:** 1162
Wallis, Hal, **20th:** 4230
Wallis, John, **17th:** 564, 969-971
Walloons, **17th:** 643
Walls Do Not Fall, The (H. D.), **20th:** 1625

Wal-Mart, **20th:** 4214
Walo, **19th:** 756
Walpole, Robert, **18th:** 54, 138, 203, 401, 405, 786, 938, 1034-1038; **Notor:** 1103
Walt Disney Concert Hall, **20th:** 1439
Walt Disney World, **20th:** 1008
Walter, John, II, **19th:** 2380-2383
Walters, Barbara, **20th:** 4211-4213
Walther, Balthasar, **17th:** 60
Walther, Johann Gottfried, **18th:** 72
Walther von der Vogelweide, **MA:** 465, 1075-1078
Walton, Sam, **20th:** 4213-4216
Walton, Sir William, **20th:** 4216-4220
Waltz, **19th:** 2189
"Waltzing Matilda" (Paterson), **19th:** 1759
Walworth, Sir Thomas, **MA:** 1035
Walwyn, William, **17th:** 535
Wampanoags, **17th:** 86, 130, 612, 633, 876, 878
Wamsutta, **17th:** 614, 633
Wanda (Dvořák), **19th:** 712
Wanderer, The (Burney), **18th:** 182
Wanderlingen door Bourgogne (Deken and Wolff), **18th:** 302
Wandlungen und Symbole der Libido. See *Psychology of the Unconscious*
Wang Anshi, **MA:** 810, 945, 968, 1079-1081, 1088
Wang Bi, **Anc:** 950-952
Wang Chao-ming. *See* Wang Jingwei
Wang Chenchih. *See* Oh, Sadaharu
Wang Chin. *See* Wang Jin
Wang Ching-wei. *See* Wang Jingwei
Wang Chong, **Anc:** 950, 953-955
Wang Ch'ung. *See* Wang Chong
Wang Fu-chih. *See* Wang Fuzhi
Wang Fuzhi, **17th:** 972-974
Wang Geon. *See* Wang Kŏn
Wang Guangmei, **20th:** 2409
Wang Jin, **MA:** 1087
Wang Jingwei, **20th:** 747, 4220-4223
Wang Kŏn, **MA:** 1081-1084
Wang Wei, **Anc:** 844; **MA:** 1085-1088
Wang Xizhi, **Anc:** 955-958, 975
Wang Yangming, **Ren:** 986-989
Wang Zhaoming. *See* Wang Jingwei
Wang Zhenyi, **18th:** 1038-1040
Wang Zhenzhi. *See* Oh, Sadaharu
Wang Zhongren. *See* Wang Chong
Wanghia, Treaty of (1844), **19th:** 579
Wani, **Anc:** 595
Wankel, Felix, **20th:** 4224-4226
Wankel engine, **20th:** 4224
Wanli, **Ren:** 826
Wanton Contessa, The (film), **20th:** 4167
War (Kollwitz), **20th:** 2190
War Against the Jews, 1933-1945, The (Dawidowicz), **20th:** 924
War and Peace (film), **20th:** 1767
War and Peace (novel by Tolstoy), **19th:** 2283
War Between the States. *See* Civil War, U.S.
War criminals, Nazi, **20th:** 4328
War Emergency Workers' National Committee, **20th:** 416
War Hawks, **19th:** 392
War in South Africa, The (Doyle), **19th:** 689
War Is Kind (Crane), **19th:** 564
War machines, engineering of, **Anc:** 83
War of _______. *See* _______, War of
War of Attrition (1969-1970), **20th:** 2917
War of Beauty, The (Callot), **17th:** 117
War of 1812 (1812-1814), **19th:** 21, 627; business, 87; John C. Calhoun, 392; Henry Clay, 503; David G. Farragut, 762; Albert Gallatin, 855; William Henry Harrison, 1049; Andrew Jackson, 1190; Francis Scott Key, 1275; James Monroe, 1587; Oliver Hazard Perry, 1779; Winfield Scott, 2051; Zachary Taylor, 2230; Tecumseh, 2239; White House burning, 1472
War of Independence, American. *See* American Revolution
War of Jugurtha, The. See *Bellum Iugurthinum*
War of Love, The (Callot), **17th:** 117
War of the Grandfathers, **19th:** 133
War of the Worlds, The (novel by Wells), **20th:** 4288
War of the Worlds (radio drama), **20th:** 4284
War on Drugs, **20th:** 3402
War Relocation Authority, **20th:** 2262
War Requiem (Britten), **20th:** 532
War with the Newts, The (Čapek), **20th:** 639
Warbeck, Perkin, **Ren:** 439, 498
Ward, Aaron Montgomery. *See* Ward, Montgomery
Ward, Ann. *See* Radcliffe, Ann
Ward, Frederick Townsend, **19th:** 1128
Ward, Hannah, **Notor:** 815
Ward, John. *See* Peace, Charles
Ward, Julia. *See* Howe, Julia Ward
Ward, Lester Frank, **19th:** 2384-2386
Ward, Mary, **17th:** 974-976
Ward, Montgomery, **19th:** 2386-2390
Ward, William, **19th:** 411
Warden, The (Trollope), **19th:** 2300
Wardle, Lena. *See* Smith, Madeleine
Warfare, **Anc:** Aristophanes on, 90; Mozi on, 577. See also *specific wars, battles, and sieges*; Category Index

Warhol, Andy, **20th:** 2374, 4226-4229; **Notor:** 983
Warizansho (Mōri), **17th:** 832
Warmus, Carolyn, **Notor:** 1090-1091
Warner, Jack, **20th:** 4230-4232
Warner, John, **20th:** 3954
Warner Bros. Studios, **20th:** 4230
Warning to the Dragon and All His Angels (Davies), **17th:** 221
Warren, Earl, **20th:** 379, 1127, 4232-4236; **Notor:** 370
Warren, James. *See* Floyd, Pretty Boy
Warren, Mercy Otis, **18th:** 1041-1043
Warren, Robert Penn, **20th:** 4236-4239; **Notor:** 1095
Warren Association (Baptists), **18th:** 76
Warring States period (475-221 B.C.E.), **Anc:** 182, 379, 504, 577, 732, 779, 989
Warring States period (1467-1600, Japan), **Ren:** 452, 732, 735, 943
Wars of Caesar and Pompey, The (Chapman), **Ren:** 215
Warsaw, Battle of (1656), **17th:** 154
Warsaw Uprising (1944), **20th:** 1685
Wartime Journals (Lindbergh), **20th:** 2395
Warwick, earl of, **Ren:** 301, 340, 435, 828, 989-992; **Notor:** 896
Warwick, earl of (false, first). *See* Simnel, Lambert
Warwick, earl of (false, second). *See* Warbeck, Perkin
Was sind und was sollen die Zahlen? (Dedekind), **19th:** 630
Wasan, **17th:** 832
Washerwoman, The (Goya), **18th:** 437
Washington, Booker T., **19th:** 703, 2390-2394; **20th:** 1047; **Notor:** 633
Washington, George, **18th:** 852, 1043-1047; negotiations with Alexander McGillivray, 627; portrait by Charles Willson Peale, 769; portrait by Gilbert Stuart, 949; Betsy Ross, 865; **Notor:** 155, 621, 1103
Washington, March on (1963), **20th:** 2149
Washington, Treaty of (1871), **19th:** 961
Washington Conference on Naval Disarmament (1921), **20th:** 1921
Washington Post, The (newspaper), **20th:** 1560
Washington State, **18th:** 1006
Washingtonians (band), **20th:** 1146
Wasps, The. See *Sphēkes*
Wassulu Empire, **19th:** 1982
Waste Land, The (Eliot), **20th:** 1140
Wat Tyler's Revolt. *See* Peasants' Revolt (1381)
Watch on the Rhine (Hellman), **20th:** 1753
Water-frame, **18th:** 55
Water-Nymph, The (Dvořák), **19th:** 713
Water pumps, **18th:** 734
Waterford Academy for Young Ladies, **19th:** 2439
Watergate scandal, **20th:** 1561, 2986, 3326
Waterloo, Battle of (1815), **19th:** 261, 892, 931, 1637, 1668, 2411
Watermeadows at Salisbury (Constable), **19th:** 542
Waters, Frank, **17th:** 614
Waters, Muddy, **20th:** 4240-4242
Wathīq, al-, **MA:** 37
Wathiqat ahl al-Sudan (ʿUthman), **19th:** 2343
Watkin, Absalom, **19th:** 303
Watson, Charles, **Notor:** 690
Watson, James D., **20th:** 477, 865, 1317, 3156, 4242-4246, 4344
Watson, John C., **19th:** 624
Watson, Thomas A., **19th:** 183
Watson, Thomas J., Jr., **20th:** 4246-4249
Watson, Thomas J., Sr., **20th:** 4246-4249
Watson and the Shark (Copley), **18th:** 276
Watsons, The (Austen), **19th:** 96
Watt (Beckett), **20th:** 281
Watt, James, **18th:** 116, 157, 219, 715, 860, 1048-1051, 1087; **19th:** 2294
Watt, William, **Notor:** 666
Watteau, Antoine, **18th:** 1051-1054
Watts, George Frederick, **19th:** 2248
Wave Field, The (Lin), **20th:** 2387
Wave mechanics, **20th:** 3669
Wave of the Future, The (Lindbergh), **20th:** 2391
Wave-particle duality, **20th:** 535
Waverley (Scott), **19th:** 2047
Way Forward Is with a Broken Heart, The (Walker), **20th:** 4198
Way in the World, A (Naipaul), **20th:** 2904
Way of All Flesh, The (Butler), **19th:** 374
Way of Perfection, The (Teresa of Ávila), **Ren:** 929
Way of the Churches of Christ in New England, The (Cotton), **17th:** 198
Way of the Congregational Churches Cleared, The (Cotton), **17th:** 198
Way to Christ, The (Böhme), **17th:** 61
Way We Live Now, The (Trollope), **19th:** 2301
Way We Were, The (film), **20th:** 3893
Wayne, Anthony, **18th:** 611, 1054-1057; **19th:** 2238; **Notor:** 1104
Wayne, John, **20th:** 999, 4250-4253

Ways of White Folks, The (Hughes), **20th:** 1929
Ways to Spaceflight (Oberth), **20th:** 3008
Wazir, Khalil al-, **20th:** 110
WCTU. *See* Woman's Christian Temperance Union
We (Lindbergh), **20th:** 2395
We and Our Neighbors (Stowe), **19th:** 2185
We the Living (Rand), **20th:** 3367
Wealth of Nations, The (Smith), **18th:** 922
Weary Blues, The (Hughes), **20th:** 1928
Weaver, Randy, **Notor:** 591, 1091-1093
Weaver, Samuel, **Notor:** 1091
Weaver, Vicki, **Notor:** 1091
Weavers' Revolt, A (Kollwitz), **20th:** 2190
Weaving the Web (Berners-Lee), **20th:** 332
Web and the Rock, The (Wolfe), **20th:** 4384
Webb, Beatrice, **19th:** 1106; **20th:** 352, 4253-4257
Webb, Chick, **20th:** 1246
Webb, Jim. *See* Longley, Bill
Webb, Philip, **19th:** 1606
Webb, Sidney, **20th:** 352, 4253-4257
Webber, Andrew Lloyd. *See* Lloyd Webber, Andrew
Weber, Carl Maria von, **19th:** 2395-2398
Weber, Ernst Heinrich, **19th:** 771
Weber, Max, **20th:** 4258-4261
Weber-Fechner law, **19th:** 771
Webern, Anton von, **20th:** 452, 3666, 4262-4265
Webster, Daniel, **19th:** 2398-2402; on U.S. Constitution, 2400
Webster, John, **17th:** 132, 279, 636, 846, 976-978
Webster, Margaret, **20th:** 863, 2333
Webster, Martin, **Notor:** 283
Webster, Noah, **19th:** 2402-2405
Webster-Ashburton Treaty of 1842, **19th:** 2400
Wedding, The (Shirley), **17th:** 847
Wedekind, Frank, **20th:** 504
Wedgwood, Josiah, **18th:** 1057-1061
Weed, Thurlow, **19th:** 781, 968, 2077
Weeding Machine, The (Braque), **20th:** 496
Week on the Concord and Merrimack Rivers, A (Thoreau), **19th:** 2274
Weg der Verheissung, Der. See *Eternal Road, The*
Weg zu Christo, Der. See *Way to Christ, The*
Weg zurück, Der. See *Road Back, The*
Wege zur Physikalischen Erkenntnis. See *Philosophy of Physics, The*
Wege zur Raumschiffahrt. See *Ways to Spaceflight*
Wegener, Alfred, **20th:** 1786, 4266-4269
Wei Cheng. *See* Wei Zheng
Wei Chong-hsien. *See* Wei Zhongxian
Wei Jingsheng, **20th:** 970
Wei Zheng, **MA:** 995
Wei Zhongxian, **17th:** 161, 911
Weichmann, Louis, **Notor:** 1012
Weierstrass, Karl, **19th:** 1296
Weigel, Helene, **20th:** 504
Weil, Joseph, **Notor:** 1094-1095
Weil, Simone, **20th:** 4269-4272
Weill, Al, **20th:** 2614
Weill, Kurt, **20th:** 4273-4276
Weinberg, Steven, **20th:** 4277-4279
Weir of Hermiston (Stevenson), **19th:** 2175
Weise von Liebe und Tod des Cornets Christof Rilke, Die. See *Tale of the Love and Death of Cornet Christopher Rilke, The*
Weishi, **MA:** 1138
Weismann, August, **19th:** 2406-2409
Weiss, Carl, **20th:** 2427; **Notor:** 650, 1095-1096
Weiss, Ehrich. *See* Houdini, Harry
Weiss, Hymie, **Notor:** 751, 804, 1096-1097
Weiss, Johannes, **20th:** 572
Weiss, Mendy, **Notor:** 661
Weisskunig (Maximilian), **Ren:** 631, 648
Weiting. *See* Yuan Shikai
Weizmann, Chaim, **20th:** 293, 2994, 4279-4283
Welch, Joseph, **20th:** 2499; **Notor:** 218, 670
Welcome House, **20th:** 559
Weld, Angelina Grimké. *See* Grimké, Angelina
Weld, Maria Anne. *See* Fitzherbert, Maria Anne
Weld, Theodore Dwight, **19th:** 990
Welf V, **MA:** 1044
Welfs, **MA:** 474
Well-curb (Zeami), **MA:** 1154
Well of Santa Clara, The (France), **19th:** 816
Well-Tempered Clavier, The (Bach), **18th:** 72
Welles, Orson, **20th:** 1732, 1737, 4283-4286
Welles, Sumner, **20th:** 1922, 1936
Wellesley, Arthur. *See* Wellington, duke of
Wellesley College, **19th:** 1728
Wellington, duke of, **19th:** 261, 893, 979, 1696, 1731, 1769, 2409-2412, 2447
Wells, H. G., **20th:** 4287-4290
Wells, Horace, **19th:** 1613
Wells-Barnett, Ida B., **20th:** 4290-4293
Welsh Melodies (Hemans), **19th:** 1076
Welt, Die, **19th:** 1089
Welt als Wille und Vorstellung, Die. See *World as Will and Idea, The*

Welt des Tänzers, Die (Laban), **20th:** 2222
Weltalter, Die. See *Ages of the World, The*
Weltbild der neuen Physik, Das. See *Universe in the Light of Modern Physics, The*
Weltgeschichte. See *Universal History*
Weltgeschichtliche Betrachtungen. See *Force and Freedom*
Weltpolitik, **20th:** 570
Weltratsel, Die. See *Riddle of the Universe at the Close of the Nineteenth Century, The*
Weltreich der Caesaren, Das. See *Provinces of the Roman Empire from Caesar to Diocletian, The*
Wen Di. *See* Yonglo
Wen Ti. *See* Yonglo
Wenceslas I, **Notor:** 536
Wenceslas IV. *See* Wenceslaus
Wenceslas, Saint, **MA:** 671
Wenceslaus (king of Bohemia), **MA:** 259, 1088-1091, 1162
Wentworth, Thomas. *See* Strafford, first earl of
Wentworth, W. C., **19th:** 2412-2415
Wenzel von Wallenstein, Albrecht. *See* Wallenstein, Albrecht Wenzel von
Werfel, Franz, **20th:** 4275
Werk, Siege of (1523), **Ren:** 146
Wernher, Julius Charles, **Notor:** 627
Wertheimer, Max, **20th:** 1112, 4293-4296
Wertheimer, Pierre, **20th:** 730
Wesen des Christentums, Das. See *What Is Christianity?*
Wesen des Judentums, Das. See *Essence of Judaism, The*
Wesendonck Lieder (Wagner), **19th:** 2375
Wesley, Arthur. *See* Wellington, duke of
Wesley, Charles, **18th:** 743, 1061-1064, 1073
Wesley, John, **18th:** 62, 743, 1064-1067, 1073, 1121
Wessel, Horst, **Notor:** 1097-1099
Wesselényi, Miklós, **19th:** 620
Wessex, **MA:** 341, 353; Viking invasion of, 63
West, Benjamin, **18th:** 1068-1070; John Singleton Copley, 275; teacher of Gilbert Stuart, 948
West, Mae, **20th:** 4297-4300
West African Studies (Kingsley), **19th:** 1283
West Bank, **20th:** 1951
West from Home (Wilder), **20th:** 4337
West Indies, **18th:** 59, 126, 829, 854-858; and missionaries, 1121; slave rebellion, 724-726; slavery, 325
West Indies and the Spanish Main, The (Trollope), **19th:** 2300
West Point, New York, **18th:** 43, 61, 565
West-Running Brook (Frost), **20th:** 1350
West Side Story (Bernstein and Sondheim), **20th:** 339, 3461
Western American settlement, **18th:** California, 892; Kentucky, 143; negotiations over, 525; Northwest Territory, 1056; Ohio Valley, 611. *See also* American frontier; Expansionism
Western army, U.S., **18th:** 1056
Western Boatmen Ashore (Bingham), **19th:** 235
Western Female Institute, **19th:** 169
Western Reserve Eclectic Institute, **19th:** 867
Western Sahara, **20th:** 1700
Western Star (Benét), **20th:** 304
Western Union (film), **20th:** 2254
Westinghouse, George, **19th:** 2253, 2416-2419
Westinghouse Air Brake Company, **19th:** 2418
Westinghouse Electric Company, **19th:** 2417
Westmacott, Mary. *See* Christie, Dame Agatha
Westminster, Statute of (1931), **20th:** 2156
Westminster Abbey, **18th:** 474
Westminster Confession, **17th:** 33
Westminster Review, **19th:** 740
Westmoreland, William, **20th:** 2542; **Notor:** 169
Westmorland Seekers, **17th:** 284
Weston, Edward, **20th:** 884
Westphalia, **MA:** 1094
Westphalia, Treaty of (1648), **Ren:** 648; **17th:** 9, 153, 164, 185, 254, 290, 359, 470, 555, 619, 621, 706
Westward Ho! (Kingsley), **19th:** 1465
Westward Ho! (Webster and Dekker), **17th:** 977
Wethered, Roger, **20th:** 2037
Weyden, Rogier van der, **MA:** 833, 949, 1092-1094; **Ren:** 120
Weymouth, George, **17th:** 875
Wharton, Edith, **20th:** 4300-4304
What Are Years? (Moore), **20th:** 2823
What Are You Going to Do About It? (Huxley), **20th:** 1963
What Christ's Judgment Is About Official Christianity (Kierkegaard), **19th:** 1280
What Ever Happened to Baby Jane? (film), **20th:** 921
What I Saw in America (Chesterton), **20th:** 745
What Is Art? (Tolstoy), **19th:** 2285
What Is Christianity? (Harnack), **20th:** 187, 1683
What Is Life? (Schrödinger), **20th:** 3670
What Is Literature? (Sartre), **20th:** 3640
What Is Man? (Twain), **19th:** 2331

What Is Property? (Proudhon), **19th:** 1835
What Is Revelation? (Maurice), **19th:** 1520
What Is the Third Estate? (Sieyès), **18th:** 917
What Is to Be Done? (Chernyshevsky), **19th:** 1627
What Is to Be Done? (Lenin), **20th:** 2342
What Maisie Knew (James), **19th:** 1207
What Next? and Next? (Cobden), **19th:** 522
What Use Are Flowers? (Hansberry), **20th:** 1672
What You Will (Marston), **17th:** 441
Wheat and the Chaff, The (Mitterrand), **20th:** 2771
Wheatley, Phillis, **18th:** 1070-1073
Wheatstone, Charles, **19th:** 547-551, 1421, 2107
Wheel of Fortune, The (Piaf), **20th:** 3229
Wheelock, John Hall, **20th:** 3960
Wheelwright, John, **17th:** 386, 395
When Harry Met Sally (film), **20th:** 1163
When Heaven and Earth Changed Places (Hayslip), **20th:** 1727
When the Cathedrals Were White (Le Corbusier), **20th:** 2323
When the Skies Clear (Pasternak), **20th:** 3133
When We Were Very Young (Milne), **20th:** 2754
Where Do We Come From? What Are We? Where Are We Going? (Gauguin), **19th:** 881
Where Is Science Going? (Planck), **20th:** 3284
Where the Wild Things Are (Sendak), **20th:** 3699
Whewell, William, **19th:** 760
Whig Party (American), **19th:** 504, 579, 967, 1049, 2078
Whig Party (British), **17th:** 149, 464, 507, 693, 840; **18th:** 20, 216, 365, 642, 906, 937, 942, 964, 1003, 1034; conflicts with Tories, 47, 441, 772, 941, 1034; **19th:** 312, 667, 891, 1434, 1535, 1959; Foxite, 978
While the City Sleeps (film), **20th:** 2255
Whilomville Stories (Crane), **19th:** 562
Whipple, George Hoyt, **20th:** 4304-4307
Whiskey Rebellion (1794), **18th:** 455, 530, 1045
Whiskey Ring Scandal, **19th:** 961
Whistler, James McNeill, **19th:** 2420-2423
Whistler v. Ruskin (Whistler), **19th:** 2421
Whitaker, Alexander, **17th:** 746
Whitby, Synod of (664), **MA:** 510
White, Babbington. *See* Braddon, Mary Elizabeth
White, Dan, **Notor:** 1099-1100
White, E. B., **20th:** 4020
White, Fred, **Notor:** 144
White, Mary. *See* Rowlandson, Mary White
White, Stanford, **19th:** 1973; **Notor:** 1027
White, Walter, **20th:** 4307-4310
White Bird, **19th:** 1239
White Buildings (Crane), **20th:** 858
"White Christmas" (Berlin), **20th:** 329
White Crucifixion (Chagall), **20th:** 718
White Deer Hollow Academy, **MA:** 1159
White Devil, The (Webster), **17th:** 977
White Fang (London), **20th:** 2421
White-Footed Deer, The (Bryant), **19th:** 342
White Heron, and Other Stories, A (Jewett), **19th:** 1227
White Horse, The (Constable), **19th:** 541
White Horse Gazelle (Toulouse-Lautrec), **19th:** 2287
White-Jacket (Melville), **19th:** 1538
White Light (Pollock), **20th:** 3303
White Lotus Society, **17th:** 911
White Mill, **19th:** 2112
White Mountain, Battle of (1620), **17th:** 254, 294, 470, 721
White Nights (film), **20th:** 3990
White Nile River exploration, **18th:** 169
White Oak Dance Project, **20th:** 254
White Sister, The (film), **20th:** 1724
White Stone, The (France), **19th:** 816
White Terror, **20th:** 742
Whitechapel Murderer. *See* Jack the Ripper
Whitefield, George, **18th:** 75, 315, 743, 1062, 1064, 1073-1075
Whitehall and the Privy Gardens (Canaletto), **18th:** 192
Whitehead, Alfred North, **20th:** 660, 2264, 3562, 4311-4315
Whitewater real estate investment controversy, **20th:** 786, 3419
Whitgift, John, **Ren:** 404, 457; **17th:** 939
Whitman, Charles, **Notor:** 1101-1102
Whitman, Walt, **19th:** 748, 2423-2428
Whitney, Eli, **18th:** 1076-1079
Whitney, Eli, Jr., **19th:** 535
Whitney, Gertrude Vanderbilt, **20th:** 4315-4317
Whitney Museum of American Art, **20th:** 4316
Whitney v. California (1927), **20th:** 484-485
Whittaker, Charles. *See* Chambers, Whittaker
Whittaker, James, **18th:** 592
Whittier, John Greenleaf, **19th:** 875, 2428-2432

Whittle, Sir Frank, **20th:** 4318-4320
Who Do You Think You Are? See *Beggar Maid, The*
Who Is to Blame? (Herzen), **19th:** 1085
Who Speaks for the Negro? (Warren), **20th:** 4238
Whole Duty of Man According to the Law of Nature, The (Pufendorf), **17th:** 760
Whore of Babylon, The (Dekker), **17th:** 224
Whoroscope (Beckett), **20th:** 279
Who's Afraid of Virginia Woolf? (film), **20th:** 3954, 4231
Who's That Knocking at My Door (film), **20th:** 3681
Who's the Dupe? (Cowley), **18th:** 284
Why Are We in Vietnam? (Mailer), **20th:** 2564
Wichitas, **Ren:** 247
Wickedest Man in the World. *See* Crowley, Aleister
Wicker Work Woman, The (France), **19th:** 816
Wickersham Commission on Crime and Prohibition, **20th:** 1863
Wickramasinghe, Chandra, **20th:** 1904
Wiclif, John. *See* Wyclif, John
Widerstand und Ergebung. See *Prisoner for God*
Widow Capet. *See* Marie-Antoinette
Widow Ranter, The (Behn), **17th:** 43
Widow's Tears, The (Chapman), **Ren:** 215
Widukind, **MA:** 243, 1094-1097
Wie Gertrud ihre Kinder lehrt. See *How Gertrude Teaches Her Children*
Wieck, Clara Josephine. *See* Schumann, Clara
Wiener, Norbert, **20th:** 4321-4324
Wiener Werkstatte, **20th:** 2180
Wiesel, Elie, **20th:** 4324-4327
Wiesenthal, Simon, **20th:** 4189, 4328-4332
Wife, The (Overbury), **17th:** 132
Wightman, Hazel, **20th:** 4333-4336
Wiglaf, **MA:** 354
Wilberforce, Samuel, **19th:** 605, 1162
Wilberforce, William, **18th:** 702, 1079-1082; **19th:** 312, 377
Wild, Jonathan, **Notor:** 943, 1102-1103
Wild Child, The (film), **20th:** 4082
Wild Duck, The (film), **20th:** 318
Wild Gallant, The (Dryden), **17th:** 240
Wild Goose Chase, The (Fletcher), **17th:** 279
Wild Goose Pagoda, **MA:** 1138
Wild One, The (film), **20th:** 488
Wild Strawberries (film), **20th:** 317
Wild Swans at Coole, The (Yeats), **20th:** 4429
Wilde, Oscar, **19th:** 162, 209, 2290, 2432-2435; **20th:** 1478; **Notor:** 933
Wilde Rosen (Aston), **19th:** 84
Wilder, Billy, **20th:** 999
Wilder, Laura Ingalls, **20th:** 4336-4339
Wilderness, Battle of the (1864), **19th:** 960, 1336
Wilderness of Mirrors, A (Frisch), **20th:** 1339
Wilderness Road, **18th:** 143
Wildes, Sarah, **17th:** 690
Wilding, Michael, **20th:** 3953
Wilhelm II. *See* William II (1859-1941; emperor of Germany)
Wilhelm Heinrich. *See* William IV
Wilhelm Meister's Apprenticeship (Goethe), **18th:** 429
Wilhelmus Rubruquis. *See* William of Rubrouck
Wilkerson, Billy, **Notor:** 955
Wilkes, Charles, **19th:** 2435-2438
Wilkes, John, **18th:** 787, 1083-1086
Wilkes Expedition, **19th:** 2436
Wilkins, Sir George Hubert, **20th:** 4339-4342
Wilkins, Maurice, **20th:** 1316, 4342-4346
Wilkins-Hearst Expedition, **20th:** 4340
Wilkinson, James, **19th:** 365, 1793; **Notor:** 156, 1103-1104
Wilkinson, John, **18th:** 1086-1089
Wilkite movement, **18th:** 1085
Will to Believe, and Other Essays in Popular Philosophy, The (James), **19th:** 1215
Will to Power, The (Nietzsche), **19th:** 1682
Willard, Emma, **19th:** 2438-2441
Willard, Frances, **19th:** 2084, 2442-2445
Willard, Jess, **20th:** 965
Willard Association for Mutual Improvement of Female Teachers, **19th:** 2440
Wille zur Macht, Der. See *Will to Power, The*
Willehalm (Wolfram), **MA:** 1125
Willem van Ruysbroeck. *See* William of Rubrouck
William I (c. 1028-1087; king of England). *See* William the Conqueror
William I (1120-1166; king of Sicily). *See* William the Bad
William I (1533-1584; prince of Orange). *See* William the Silent
William I (1797-1888; king of Prussia), **19th:** 238; **Notor:** 662
William II (c. 1056-1100; king of England), **MA:** 92
William II (1859-1941; emperor of Germany), **19th:** 239, 1120; **20th:** 570, 4030, 4346-4350; **Notor:** 196
William III (1650-1702; king of England), **17th:** 138, 149, 608, 610, 718, 808, 816, 821, 979-982; American colonists'

reaction to enthronement, 518; and chaplain Thomas Burnet, 106; and English theater, 83; and Holy Roman Empire, 526; and Innocent XI, 407; and James II, 418; and the first duke of Leeds, 507; First Treaty of Partition (1698), 152; and Quakers, 284; **18th:** 53, 250, 422, 660-661, 673
William IV (1765-1837; king of Great Britain and Hanover), **19th:** 979, 2359, 2445-2448
William IX (1071-1126; duke of Aquitaine), **MA:** 355
William X (1099-1137; duke of Aquitaine), **MA:** 355
William, Lord Russell, **Notor:** 565
William Henry. *See* William IV
William Long-Sword, **MA:** 902
William of Auvergne, **MA:** 1097-1101
William of Auxerre, **MA:** 1101-1105
William of Champeaux, **MA:** 13
William of Cleves, **Ren:** 51
William of Conches, **MA:** 1115
William of Moerbeke, **MA:** 1028, 1105-1107
William of Nassau. *See* William the Silent
William of Orange. *See* William III; William the Silent
William of Paris. *See* William of Auvergne
William of Rubrouck, **MA:** 1107-1110
William of Saint-Amour, **MA:** 180, 1110-1113
William of Saint-Thierry, **MA:** 161, 1114-1116
William Penn's Treaty with the Indians . . . (West), **18th:** 1069
William the Bad, **MA:** 28
William the Conqueror, **MA:** 56, 92, 338, 457, 481, 753, 1117-1120
William the Silent, **Ren:** 32, 200, 311, 615, 740, 779, 993-996; **17th:** 286, 618, 933; **Notor:** 404
William Watts Sherman House, **19th:** 1906
Williams, Abigail, **17th:** 690
Williams, Frank. *See* Abagnale, Frank W., Jr.
Williams, George Washington, **19th:** 2449-2452; **Notor:** 633
Williams, John, **17th:** 275
Williams, Paulsgrave, **Notor:** 81
Williams, Roger, **17th:** 130, 197, 612, 941, 982-985, 992
Williams, Ronald, **Notor:** 373
Williams, Sunita, **20th:** 2460
Williams, Tennessee, **20th:** 863, 4350-4354
Williams, William, **18th:** teacher of Benjamin West, 1068
Williams, Winifred. *See* Wagner, Winifred
Williamson, Claire, **Notor:** 453
Willibrord, Saint, **MA:** 938
Willis, Thomas, **17th:** 362, 564, 985-988
Willoughby, Anne, **17th:** 894
Willughby, Francis, **17th:** 782
Willy, Colette. *See* Colette
Wilmot, David, **19th:** 1822
Wilmot Proviso, **19th:** 1822
Wilson, Edmund, **20th:** 1249, 4354-4358
Wilson, Edward O., **20th:** 4358-4360
Wilson, Sir Harold, **20th:** 4360-4363
Wilson, James, **18th:** 1090-1094
Wilson, Joseph T., **19th:** 2450
Wilson, Pete, **20th:** 1228
Wilson, Robert W., **20th:** 1903
Wilson, Teddy, **20th:** 1528
Wilson, Woodrow, **20th:** 484, 552, 781, 2419, 2829, 4364-4368
Wilson Observatory, **20th:** 1644
Winceby, Battle of (1643), **17th:** 262
Winchester, Treaty of (1153), **MA:** 483, 963
Winckelmann, Johann Joachim, **18th:** 554, 1068, 1095-1098; **19th:** 406
Wind and Current Chart of the North Atlantic (Maury), **19th:** 1523
Wind and Thunder Gods, The (Sōtatsu), **17th:** 869
Wind in the Pines, The (Zeami), **MA:** 1154
Winding Stair, and Other Poems, The (Yeats), **20th:** 4430
Windows (Delaunay), **20th:** 951
Windows (operating system), **20th:** 1422
Windsbraut, Die (Kokoschka), **20th:** 2186
Windsor, duke of, **20th:** 207, 1455, 2854, 4368-4371
Windy Day (Schmidt-Rottluff), **20th:** 3662
Wine, medicinal use, **Anc:** 116
Winfrey, Oprah, **20th:** 4372-4375
Wing-and-Wing, The (Cooper), **19th:** 555
Wingina. *See* Pemisapan
Wings of the Dove, The (James), **19th:** 1209
Winkler, Clemens, **19th:** 1546
Winnebagos, **17th:** 433
Winnie-the-Pooh (Milne), **20th:** 2754
Winogrand, Garry, **20th:** 116
Winslow, Edward, **17th:** 86
Winstanley, Gerrard, **17th:** 988-990
Winter (Wyeth), **20th:** 4411
Winter, Robert, **Ren:** 326
Winter, Thomas, **Ren:** 326
Winter of Our Discontent, The (Steinbeck), **20th:** 3850
Winter Offensive of 1975, **20th:** 3299
Winter Studies and Summer Rambles in Canada (Jameson), **19th:** 1218
Winter War (1939-1940), **20th:** 2599
Winter Words (Hardy), **19th:** 1030

Winterreise (Schubert), **19th:** 2027
Winthrop, John (cofounder of Massachusetts Bay Colony), **17th:** 386, 395, 470, 941, 982, 990-993
Winthrop, John, Jr. (governor of Connecticut), **17th:** 219, 892
Wirth, Adam. *See* Worth, Adam
Wirtschaft und Gesellschaft. See *Economy and Society*
Wirz, Henry, **Notor:** 1105-1106
Wisdom literature, Hebrew, **Anc:** 446
Wisdom of God Manifested in the Works of Creation, The (Ray), **17th:** 783
Wisdom of Solomon, Paraphrased, The (Middleton), **17th:** 636
Wise, Isaac Mayer, **19th:** 2453-2455
Wise, Stephen Samuel, **20th:** 4376-4378
Wise Blood (O'Connor), **20th:** 3017
Wise Parenthood (Stopes), **20th:** 3882
Wise Woman of Hogsdon, The (Heywood), **17th:** 374
Wishart, George, **Ren:** 528
Wisniewski, Stephen, **Notor:** 1096
Wissenschaft der Logik. See *Science of Logic*
Wissenschaftlichen Grundlagen der analytischen Chemie, Die. See *Scientific Foundations of Analytical Chemistry Treated in an Elementary Manner, The*
Wit at Several Weapons (Middleton and Rowley), **17th:** 636
"Witch of Agnesi," **18th:** 25
Witch of Atlas, The (Shelley), **19th:** 2095
Witchcraft, **Anc:** 749; **MA:** 629; **Ren:** 121, 212. *See also* Women; Category Index
Witchcraft trials. *See* Salem witchcraft trials
Witches. *See* Category Index
Witch's Head, The (Haggard), **19th:** 1006
Witherspoon, John, **18th:** 1098-1102
Withlacoochee, First Battle of the (1835), **19th:** 1710
Witness Tree, A (Frost), **20th:** 1350
Witt, Johan de, **17th:** 57, 808, 979
Wittekind. *See* Widukind
Wittelsbach Dynasty, **MA:** 258
Wittenberg Concord (1536), **Ren:** 143
Wittenmyer, Annie, **19th:** 2442
Wittgenstein, Ludwig, **20th:** 2816, 4378-4381
Wizard of Oz, The (film), **20th:** 1410
Władisław II. *See* Vladislav II
Władysław I, **MA:** 229
Władysław II Jagiełło, **MA:** 1120-1123
Władysław III, **MA:** 519
Władysław IV Vasa, **17th:** 111, 250, 290, 462, 795, 945
Wo warst du, Adam? See *Adam, Where Art Thou?*
Woden, **Anc:** 396
Woffington, Peg, **18th:** 397, 1102-1104
Wofford, Chloe Anthony. *See* Morrison, Toni
Woggle-Bug, The (Baum), **19th:** 157
Wohin treibt die Bundersrepublik? See *Future of Germany, The*
Wöhler, Friedrich, **19th:** 2456-2458
Wojas, Pamela Ann. *See* Smart, Pamela Ann
Wojciechowski, Earl. *See* Weiss, Hymie
Wojtyła, Karol Józef. *See* John Paul II
Wolf, Max, **20th:** 4382-4383
Wolfe, James, **18th:** 151, 694, 1104-1108
Wolfe, Thomas (1900-1938), **20th:** 4383-4386
Wolfe, Tom (b. 1931), **20th:** 1500
Wolff, Caspar Friedrich, **19th:** 114
Wolfram von Eschenbach, **MA:** 407, 425, 465, 1123-1126
Wollman, Elie, **20th:** 1983
Wollstonecraft, Mary, **18th:** 66, 88, 426, 622, 850, 1108-1112
Wolsey, Cardinal Thomas, **Ren:** 111, 188, 256, 269, 335, 368, 442, 544, 698, 996-999; **Notor:** 952
Woman and Gazelles (Lipchitz), **20th:** 2397
Woman and Labour (Schreiner), **19th:** 2024
Woman Bathing (Rembrandt), **17th:** 787
Woman Bathing in a Shallow Tub (Degas), **19th:** 633
Woman Called Golda, A (television miniseries), **20th:** 322
Woman, Church, and State (Gage), **19th:** 853
Woman Hater, The (Beaumont), **Ren:** 93
Woman Killed with Kindness, A (Heywood), **17th:** 374
Woman of No Importance, A (Wilde), **19th:** 2433
Woman of Paris, A (film), **20th:** 732
Woman of the Year (film), **20th:** 1770, 4067
Woman suffrage, **19th:** 258, 324, 800, 2084, 2149, 2178, 2443, 2459; African Americans, 432; France, 90; Great Britain, 264; New Zealand, 1484; **20th:** Jane Addams, 24; Australia, 2487; Great Britain, 415, 3102; Montana, 3375; United States, 701, 3145
Woman with a Parrot (Courbet), **19th:** 560
Woman with Black Boa (Toulouse-Lautrec), **19th:** 2289
Woman with Plants (Wood), **20th:** 4388

Woman with Serpent (Lipchitz), **20th:** 2397
Woman with the Hat (Matisse), **20th:** 2651
Woman's Bible, The (Stanton and Gage), **19th:** 853, 2149
Woman's Christian Temperance Union, **19th:** 1652, 2084, 2442; **20th:** 701
Woman's Journal, **19th:** 2178
Woman's Life, A (Maupassant), **19th:** 1515
Woman's Medical College, **19th:** 249
Woman's Record (Hale), **19th:** 1014
Woman's Rights Convention (1848), **19th:** 65, 686, 853, 1618, 2147
Woman's State Suffrage Society, Iowa, **19th:** 259
Woman's State Temperance Society of New York, **19th:** 65
Women, **Anc:** Assyria, 745; Babylonia, 378; China, 153; Christianity, 393, 822; Egypt, 390, 586, 589, 902; Etruscan, 841; Greece, 70, 110, 127, 308, 415, 597, 751, 962; India, 111; Japan, 594; Jews, 258; Palmyra, 987; Persia, 137; Phoenicia, 271; Rome, 25, 72, 103, 105, 233-234, 481, 488, 490, 494, 508, 517, 561, 687, 834; **MA:** asceticism, 236; Ashkenazi Jews, 409; Christianity, 81, 144-145, 198, 236, 270, 284, 509, 513, 549, 596, 607, 629, 708, 856; education, 30, 89, 209, 273, 356, 373, 597, 856; Italy, 1031; Japan, 738, 771; in literature, 171, 275; medicine, 1031; monasticism, 438, 509; Muslim, 612, 873, 890; Visigoths, 76; **Ren:** art and, 421; Christianity and, 3, 44, 62; Vietnam, 547; war and, 37, 527; witchcraft, 82, 113; writings about, 530, 535; **17th:** childbirth, 851; education, 265, 314, 364, 744, 823, 828, 865; England, 677; France, 662; Mexico, 209; **18th:** Anglican education, 65; art and artists, 554-556, 1016-1019; astronomy, 489-491, 1038-1040; British society, 182; business, 95, 865-867; freedom from marriage, 65, 1110; government and politics, 211-217, 358-361, 621-625, 641-643, 653-656, 677-679, 798-800, 929-932, 1042; leadership, 321-323; letter writing, 8; literature, 180-183, 301-303, 577-579, 594-596, 687-690, 702-704, 823-825, 848-850, 929-932, 1070-1073, 1108-1112; mathematics, 24-26, 240-243, 489-491, 1038-1040; physics, 241; and reason, 65; rebel leaders, 724-726; royal succession, 230; sexuality, 1110; theater, 912-914, 1102-1104; theologians, 591-594; **19th:** discrimination against, 67, 324-325, 1616, 2147; education, 170; portrayal in literature, 492; **20th:** health movement, 1272
Women and Economics (Gilman), **20th:** 1485
Women and Work (Bodichon), **19th:** 263
Women Beware Women (Middleton), **17th:** 637
Women in Love (Lawrence), **20th:** 2297
Women in the Garden (Monet), **20th:** 2790
Women in the Nineteenth Century (Fuller), **19th:** 843
Women of Trachis, The. See *Trachinai*
Women's Action Alliance, **20th:** 3853
Women's Armed Services Integration Act of 1948, **20th:** 1646, 3769
Women's Army Corps, **20th:** 1646, 1839, 3490
Women's International League for Peace and Freedom, **20th:** 24, 199
Women's Loyal National League, **19th:** 66, 800
Women's movement, **19th:** 65, 686, 843, 877, 1098, 1139, 1410, 1618, 2307; England, 766
Women's rights, **18th:** 7, 64-67, 221-223; American revolutionary period, 9; **19th:** 257, 324, 990, 1903, 2084, 2147, 2177, 2442; England, 263, 372; France, 89-90, 2298; Germany, 84; India, 2364; New Zealand, 1484, 2060; South Africa, 2024; **20th:** 558, 1521; aviation, 1076; France, 274; India, 2901; Iran, 3429; Ireland, 3474; legal issues, 3023; ordination, 1690; political arena, 755, 2168; Tunisia, 458; United States, 1329, 1485, 1774, 2746, 3147, 3853; worldwide, 56. *See also* Category Index
Women's Social and Political Union, **19th:** 769, 1026; **20th:** 3103, 3145
Women's State Temperance Society, **19th:** 2148
Women's Suffrage Society, Manchester, **19th:** 767
Women's Trade Union League, **20th:** 415
Wonder of Being Human, The (Eccles and Robinson), **20th:** 1091
Wonder-Working Magician, The (Calderón), **17th:** 114
Wonderful Adventures of Nils, The (Lagerlöf), **20th:** 2235
Wonderful Life (Gould), **20th:** 1556
Wonderful Visit, The (Wells), **20th:** 4288
Wonderful Wizard of Oz, The (Baum), **19th:** 156

Wonders of Life, The (Haeckel), **19th:** 1005
Wood, Annie. *See* Besant, Annie
Wood, Audrey, **20th:** 4352
Wood, Grant, **20th:** 4387-4390
Wood, Harriet. *See* Cushman, Pauline
Wood, Kimba, **Notor:** 732
Wood Demon, The (Chekhov), **19th:** 479
Woodblock printing, **17th:** 375; **18th:** 958; **19th:** 1107
Woodcuts, German, **Ren:** 262, 298, 455
Wooden Prince, The (Bartók), **20th:** 251
Woodhull, Victoria, **19th:** 1411, 2459-2461
Woodhull & Claflin's Weekly, **19th:** 2459
Woodlanders, The (Hardy), **19th:** 1029
Woodman, David, **20th:** 752
Woodrow Wilson (Sargent), **19th:** 1998
Woods, Frank, **20th:** 2429
Woods, Tiger, **20th:** 4390-4393
Woods Hole Biological Institute. *See* Anderson School of Natural History
Woodson, Ben. *See* James, Frank
Woodson, Tim. *See* James, Jesse
Woodstock (film), **20th:** 3681
Woodstock Music and Art Fair, **20th:** 2044
Woodville, Elizabeth, **Ren:** 829, 991
Woodward, Bob (journalist), **20th:** 1562; **Notor:** 672, 738
Woodward, Robert Burns (chemist), **20th:** 4393-4396
Wool industry, **19th:** 1432
Woolf, Virginia, **20th:** 1288, 1353, 4397-4399
Wootton, Noall, **Notor:** 411
Worcester, Battle of (1651), **17th:** 168, 757, 901
Worchester v. Georgia, **19th:** 2182
Worde, Wynken de, **Ren:** 198
Words of Faith (Mauriac), **20th:** 2658
Wordsworth, William, **19th:** 72, 530, 746, 1260, 2462-2465; **Notor:** 903
Work (Zola), **19th:** 2491
"Work of Many People, The" (Teller), **20th:** 3970
Worker's Union, The (Tristan), **19th:** 2298
Working Men's Association, **19th:** 1808
Working Men's College, **19th:** 1520
Working Woman's Association, **19th:** 66
Working Women and the Contemporary Woman Question (Zetkin), **20th:** 4456
Workingmen's Concert Association, **20th:** 682
Workman, Charlie "The Bug," **Notor:** 661
Workman, Fanny Bullock, **19th:** 2466-2469
Works and Days. See *Erga kai Emerai*
Works in Architecture, The (Adam brothers), **18th:** 6
Works of Hannah Cowley, The (Cowley), **18th:** 284
Works of Monsieur Boileau, Made English by Several Hands, The (Boileau-Despréaux), **17th:** 64
Works Progress Administration, **20th:** 1873, 3511
World and the Individual, The (Royce), **20th:** 3551
World as Will and Idea, The (Schopenhauer), **19th:** 2020
World Bank, **20th:** 2542
World Before Them, The (Moodie), **19th:** 1595
World Commission on Environment and Development. *See* Brundtland Commission
World Congress for Labor Palestine, **20th:** 293
World Court, **20th:** 3521
World I Live In, The (Keller), **20th:** 2093
World Light (Laxness), **20th:** 2309
World of Apu, The (film), **20th:** 3394
World of Jacques Cousteau, The (film), **20th:** 851
World of Wonders (Davies), **20th:** 918
World Runs on Wheels, The. See *All Fools*
World War I, **20th:** aviation, 389; Canada, 424; Anthony Eden, 1099; France, 780; Francis Ferdinand, 1296; Germany, 3896; Great Britain, 66, 151, 769, 2412; Paul von Hindenburg, 1815; Joseph-Jacques-Césaire Joffre, 2010; Lord Kitchener, 2175; Douglas MacArthur, 2492; Ramsay MacDonald, 2511; Bernard Law Montgomery, 2808; New Zealand, 2644; Ottoman Empire, 162; John J. Pershing, 3220; Philippe Pétain, 3223; propaganda, 448; Erwin Rommel, 3502; William II, 4348; Woodrow Wilson, 4366
World War II, **20th:** Nancy Astor, 160; Australia, 893, 1189, 2707; Canada, 2157; Bob Dole, 1014; Egypt, 1215; Dwight D. Eisenhower, 1126; fighter pilots, 1025, 4426; Germany, 2118; Heinz Guderian, 1607; Hirohito, 1819; Adolf Hitler, 1831; journalism, 462; Libya, 3351; Charles A. Lindbergh, 2394; George C. Marshall, 2630; Bernard Law Montgomery, 2809; Louis Mountbatten, 2855; Chester W. Nimitz, 2978; George S. Patton, 3143; Philippe Pétain, 3223; propaganda, 1515; refugees, 3264; Erwin Rommel, 3503; Franklin D. Roosevelt, 3513; Gerd von Rundstedt, 3560; first Viscount

Slim, 3759; South Africa, 3777; Soviet Union, 3819; Henry L. Stimson, 3870; Harry S. Truman, 4087; Tunisia, 458; Turkey, 1973; underground photographic unit, 672; United Kingdom, 51, 207, 277, 770, 1456; United States, 1874; Georgy Zhukov, 4470
World Wide Pictures, **20th:** 1558
World Wide Web, **20th:** 331, 709
World Without Sun (film), **20th:** 851
World Zionist Organization, **20th:** 293, 484, 4280
World's Columbian Exposition (1893), **19th:** 361, 2179
World's Hydrographical Description (Davis), **Ren:** 277
Worlds in the Making (Arrhenius), **20th:** 140
World's Olio, The (Newcastle), **17th:** 676
Worms, Colloquy of (1540), **Ren:** 144
Worms, Concordat of (1107), **MA:** 384
Worms, Concordat of (1122), **MA:** 94, 707, 971
Worms, Diet of (1521), **Ren:** 220, 316, 583, 647, 775
Worms, Synod of (1076), **MA:** 434
Worship of God in Spirit and in Truth, The (Guyon), **17th:** 340
Worship of Nature, The (Frazer), **20th:** 1321
Worship of Venus, The (Titian), **Ren:** 937
Worth, Adam, **Notor:** 688, 1107-1108
Would-Be Gentleman, The (Molière), **17th:** 570, 648
Wound and the Bow, The (Wilson), **20th:** 4356
Wounded Cuirassier (Géricault), **19th:** 899
Wounded Knee Massacre (1890), **19th:** 2110
Wounds in the Rain (Crane), **19th:** 564
Wovoka, **19th:** 2110
Wozniak, Steve, **20th:** 2006
Wozzeck (Berg), **20th:** 311
WPA. *See* Works Progress Administration
Wrangel, Karl Gustav, **17th:** 154, 926
Wratislaw, **MA:** 671
Wray, John. *See* Ray, John
Wreath, The (Dvořák), **19th:** 713
Wreck, The (Homer), **19th:** 1126
Wrecker, The (Stevenson), **19th:** 2175
Wren, Sir Christopher, **17th:** 80, 349, 383, 547, 564, 589, 986, 994-997; **18th:** 472
Wretched of the Earth, The (Fanon), **20th:** 1214
Wright, Almroth, **20th:** 1254
Wright, Chauncey, **19th:** 1773
Wright, Christopher, **Ren:** 326
Wright, Frances, **19th:** 2469-2471
Wright, Frank Lloyd, **19th:** 2199; **20th:** 2693, 4400-4403
Wright, Henry C., **19th:** 877
Wright, John, **Ren:** 326
Wright, Marian. *See* Edelman, Marian Wright
Wright, Orville, **20th:** 388, 4403-4407
Wright, Richard, **20th:** 201
Wright, Wilbur, **20th:** 388, 4403-4407
Wright Company, **20th:** 4405
Writing, **Anc:** Japanese, 462, 595; **MA:** Chinese, 719; Glagolitic, 295; Humanist, 850; Japan, 622, 738; Mongol, 627, 955; Slavic, 133, 295
Writing and Difference (Derrida), **20th:** 976
Writing Degree Zero (Barthes), **20th:** 246
WSPU. *See* Women's Social and Political Union
Wu Chao. *See* Wu Hou
Wu Hou, **MA:** 79, 1085, 1127-1129, 1142
Wu Sangui, **17th:** 235
Wu School, **17th:** 156
Wu Tse-t'ien. *See* Wu Hou
Wu Zetian. *See* Wu Hou
Wu Zhao. *See* Wu Hou
Wudi, **Anc:** 150, 160, 782, 958-961, 976
Wulfila. *See* Ulfilas
Wunderbarliche Vogelsnest, Das. See *False Messiah, The*
Wundt, Wilhelm, **20th:** 4294, 4407-4410
Wuornos, Aileen Carol, **Notor:** 1108-1110
Wusun (Asian tribe), **Anc:** 959
Wuthering Heights (film), **20th:** 3040
Wuthering Heights (novel by Brontë), **19th:** 310
Wu-ti. *See* Wudi
Wu-tsung. *See* Zhengde
Wuwei (Daoist doctrine), **Anc:** 990
Wuzong. *See* Zhengde
Wyandotte Iron Works, **19th:** 220
Wyatt, Sir Francis, **17th:** 703
Wyatt, Thomas, **Ren:** 306, 310
Wyatt's Rebellion (1554), **Ren:** 306, 401, 640
Wyclif, John, **MA:** 522, 608, 1023, 1090, 1112, 1130-1133, 1162; **Ren:** 543, 950
Wye River Agreement (1998), **20th:** 113
Wyeth, Andrew, **20th:** 4410-4413
Wyler, William, **20th:** 1525
Wyndham Sisters, The (Sargent), **19th:** 1999
Wynfrid. *See* Boniface, Saint
Wynne, Esmé, **20th:** 853
Wytte, Joan, **Notor:** 1110-1111
Wyttenbach, Thomas, **Ren:** 1010

X

X rays, **19th:** 1932; **20th:** 818, 889, 2279
Xaipe (Cummings), **20th:** 881
Xandramas. *See* Dhanananda
Xanthippe, **Anc:** 962-964

Xanthippus of Athens, **Anc:** 128
Xanthippus of Sparta, **Anc:** 740
Xavier, Saint Francis, **Ren:** 483, 514, 1000-1003
Xenakis, Iannis, **20th:** 4414-4418
Xenarchus, **Anc:** 827
Xenocrates, **Anc:** 94
Xenophanes, **Anc:** 608, 965-967
Xenophilus, **Anc:** 97
Xenophon, **Anc:** 87, 248, 451, 962, 968-971
Xerox Corporation, **20th:** 658
Xerxes I, **Anc:** 109, 137, 213, 253, 387, 505, 616, 860, 971-975
Xhosa peoples, **19th:** 982
Xia Gui, **MA:** 678, 1134-1136
Xi'an Incident, **20th:** 748
Xianfeng, **19th:** 496, 2484
Xiang Xiu, **Anc:** 991
Xiangyang. *See* Mi Fei
Xiao Chen, **19th:** 496
Xiaozong, **Ren:** 1003-1005, 1008
Xie Fuzhi, **Notor:** 529
Xie Hun, **Anc:** 975
Xie Kanglo. *See* Xie Lingyun
Xie Lingyun, **Anc:** 975-978
Xin Dynasty, **Anc:** 150
Xin qingnian (magazine), **20th:** 742
Xin Tang shu (Ouyang), **MA:** 809
Xin wudai shi (Ouyang), **MA:** 809
Xingzhonghui, **20th:** 3913
Xiongnu, **Anc:** 151, 499, 780, 958
Xiyouji. See *Journey to the West*
Xizong. *See* Chongzhen; Tianqi
Xoxe, Koçi, **Notor:** 494
Xuantong. *See* Puyi
Xuanxue, **Anc:** 951
Xuanzang (Buddhist monk), **Anc:** 124; **MA:** 460, 1128, 1136-1139
Xuanzong (Tang emperor), **MA:** 78, 324, 654, 1085
Xunzi, **Anc:** 238, 380, 978-980
XYZ affair (1797-1800), **18th:** 13, 413, 637

Y

Yagoda, Genrikh, **Notor:** 1112-1113, 1116
Yahweh, **Anc:** 1, 4, 255, 258, 337, 641
Yaḥyā the Barmakid, **MA:** 467
Yakub, Zara. *See* Zara Yaqob
Yakubun sentei (Ogyū Sorai), **18th:** 746
Yakut. *See* Yaqut
Yakut, Jamāl al-Dīn, **MA:** 889
Yale, Frankie, **20th:** 641; **Notor:** 7, 175
Yale Lectures on Preaching (Beecher), **19th:** 174
Yalow, Rosalyn, **20th:** 4419-4422
Yamagata Aritomo, **19th:** 1970
Yamamoto, Isoroku, **20th:** 1648
Yamani, Ahmad Zaki, **20th:** 4422-4425
Yamato clan, **MA:** 940
Yamato-e, **17th:** 868
Yamazaki, Battle of (1582), **Ren:** 460, 733
Yāmuna, **MA:** 876
Yan Liben, **MA:** 1140-1142
Yan Lide, **MA:** 1140
Yan Wu, **MA:** 325
Yanaihara, Isaku, **20th:** 1472
Yanayev, Gennady, **20th:** 4432
Yang Ai. *See* Liu Yin
Yang Guifei, **MA:** 78-79, 654, 1086
Yang Guozhong, **MA:** 79, 1086
Yang Kuei-fei. *See* Yang Guifei
Yang Kuo-chung. *See* Yang Guozhong
Yang Sen, **20th:** 4466
Yang Ying. *See* Liu Yin
Yangzhu, **Anc:** 578
Yanqui, el. *See* Somoza García, Anastasio
Yao Wenyuan, **Notor:** 529
Yaqut, **MA:** 165, 1143-1145
Yaqut's Dictionary of Learned Men (Yaqut), **MA:** 1143
Yarmūk, Battle of (636), **MA:** 1038
Yashima, Battle of (1185), **MA:** 723
Yaśodharā, **Anc:** 169
Yasu y Javier, Francisco de. *See* Xavier, Saint Francis
Yasuhira, Fujiwara. *See* Fujiwara Yasuhira
Yates, Andrea, **Notor:** 1113-1115
Yates, Russell, **Notor:** 1113
Yavneh, rabbinic assembly at, **Anc:** 29
Yayá Garcia. See *Iaia Garcia*
Yayoi period, **Anc:** 462
Yazdegerd III, **MA:** 1038
Yazīd, **MA:** 3
Yeager, Chuck, **20th:** 4425-4428
Yearling, The (film), **20th:** 3182
Yeats, William Butler, **20th:** 2055, 4428-4431
Yehime, **Anc:** 595
Yehuda, Enoch. *See* Yagoda, Genrikh
Yehuda ben Shemuel ha-Levi. *See* Judah ha-Levi
Yelizaveta Petrovna. *See* Elizabeth Petrovna
Yellow Book, The, **19th:** 163
Yellow Cow (Marc), **20th:** 2607
Yellow Feather. *See* Massasoit
Yellow fever, **19th:** 1878; **20th:** 1542
Yellow Kid. *See* Weil, Joseph
Yellow Manifesto. See *Manifest Groc*
Yellow Submarine (Beatles), **20th:** 269
Yellow Turbans Uprising (184), **Anc:** 182
Yellowstone Park Bill (1972), **19th:** 1059
Yeltsin, Boris, **20th:** 1532, 4431-4435
Yemen, Saudi-Egyptian conflict over (1962-1970), **20th:** 1200
Yen Li-pen. *See* Yan Liben
Yen Li-te. *See* Yan Lide
Yeni Turan (Adıvar), **20th:** 30
Yentl (film), **20th:** 3893
Yeoman of the Guard, The (Gilbert and Sullivan), **19th:** 919
Yepes y Álvarez, Juan de. *See* John of the Cross, Saint

Yerkes Observatory, **20th:** 1643
Yerma (García Lorca), **20th:** 1396
Yerushalmi, Hayim. *See* Kahane, Meir
Yeshua. *See* Barabbas
Yevgeny Onyegin (Tchaikovsky), **19th:** 2234
Yezhov, Nikolay Ivanovich, **20th:** 2574; **Notor:** 89, 1115-1116, 1137
Yidi. *See* Zhengde
Yijing, **Anc:** 950, 989
Yin and yang, **18th:** 288
Yinzhen. *See* Yongzheng
Yip, Yip, Yaphank (Berlin), **20th:** 328
Yizong. *See* Tianqi
YMCA. *See* Young Men's Christian Association
Yo Fei, **MA:** 1145-1147
Yockey, Francis, **Notor:** 177, 340
Yogācāra, **MA:** 1138
Yogācāra-bhūmi-shāstra, **Anc:** 113
Yohannes IV, **19th:** 1552, 2256
Yojimbo (film), **20th:** 2219
Yokomitsu, Riichi, **20th:** 2084
Yom Kippur War (1973), **20th:** 154, 931, 1084, 2171, 2677, 3359, 3588
Yōmei, **MA:** 940, 975
Yomiuri Giants, **20th:** 3027
Yonge, Charlotte Mary, **19th:** 2472-2474
Yonglo, **MA:** 1147-1151, 1156; **Ren:** 1004
Yongzheng, **18th:** 1113-1115
Yorimasa, Minamoto. *See* Minamoto Yorimasa
Yorimichi, Fujiwara. *See* Fujiwara Yorimichi
Yoritomo, Minamoto. *See* Minamoto Yoritomo
York, House of, **MA:** 496
Yorke, Harriot, **19th:** 1105
Yorkists, **Ren:** 340, 434, 828. *See also* Lancastrians
Yorkshire Tragedy, A (Middleton), **17th:** 637
Yorktown, Siege of (1781), **18th:** 279, 852, 1044, 1055
Yorozu no fumihōgu (Saikaku), **17th:** 404
Yoruba culture, **20th:** 1343
Yosemite, The (Muir), **19th:** 1625
Yosemite National Park, **19th:** 1624, 1707
Yosemite Valley, **19th:** 1625
Yoshida Mitsuyoshi, **17th:** 831
Yoshida, Shigeru, **20th:** 1702, 1965, 3646
Yoshida Tōgo, **MA:** 1154
Yoshihito. *See* Taishō
Yoshikazu, Ashikaga. *See* Ashikaga Yoshikazu
Yoshimitsu, Ashikaga. *See* Ashikaga Yoshimitsu
Yoshimochi, Ashikaga. *See* Ashikaga Yoshimochi
Yoshinaka, Minamoto. *See* Minamoto Yoshinaka
Yoshinori, Ashikaga. *See* Ashikaga Yoshinori
Yoshitomo, Minamoto. *See* Minamoto Yoshitomo
Yoshitsune, Minamoto. *See* Minamoto Yoshitsune
Yotsugi Soga (Chikamatsu), **18th:** 243
You, Dominique, **Notor:** 1117-1118
You Can't Go Home Again (Wolfe), **20th:** 4385
You Can't Keep a Good Woman Down (Walker), **20th:** 4197
You Can't Take It with You (film), **20th:** 3861
You Have Seen Their Faces (Caldwell and Bourke-White), **20th:** 462
You Must Set Forth at Dawn (Soyinka), **20th:** 3806
Youk, Thomas, **Notor:** 569
You'll Never Get Rich (film), **20th:** 1731
Young, Andrew, **Notor:** 890
Young, Brigham, **19th:** 832, 2474-2477; **Notor:** 664
Young, Charles, **19th:** 1257
Young, J. W. *See* Carto, Willis A.
Young, Lester, **20th:** 1853
Young, Loretta, **20th:** 1369
Young Duke, The (Disraeli), **19th:** 666
Young England movement, **19th:** 667
Young Europe, **19th:** 1531
Young Hegelians, **19th:** 119
Young Irelanders, **19th:** 1697
Young Italy, **19th:** 871, 922, 1531
Young King, The (Behn), **17th:** 42
Young Ladies of the Village (Courbet), **19th:** 560
Young Man in Chains (Mauriac), **20th:** 2657
Young Men's Christian Association, **19th:** 699, 1596, 1600; **20th:** 549
Young People's Concerts, **20th:** 339
Young Turk Movement, **19th:** 8
Young Turks Revolution (1908-1909), **20th:** 30, 162, 1157-1158
Young Woman Playing the Virginal (van Hemessen), **Ren:** 422
Younger, Cole, **19th:** 1211; **Notor:** 257-258, 524, 871, 994, 1118-1120
Younger, James, **19th:** 1211; **Notor:** 524, 871, 994, 1119
Younger, John, **Notor:** 524, 1119
Younger, Robert, **Notor:** 524, 1119
You're a Good Man, Charlie Brown (Gesner), **20th:** 3673
You're Only Old Once (Seuss), **20th:** 3712
Yousef, Ramzi, **Notor:** 744, 1121-1122
Youth (Gesell, Ilg, and Ames), **20th:** 1466
Youth League, **20th:** 2479
You've Got Mail (film), **20th:** 1163
Youx, Frederick. *See* You, Dominique

Ypsilantis, Alexander, **19th:** 2478-2480
Ypsilantis, Demetrios, **19th:** 2478-2480
Yuan Chung Huan, **17th:** 2
Yuan Dynasty, **MA:** 404, 626, 1147; emperors, 627
Yüan Shih-le'ai. *See* Yuan Shikai
Yuan Shikai, **20th:** 741, 3914, 4466; **Notor:** 1122-1124
Yuanzhang. *See* Mi Fei
Yudina, Maria Veniaminova, **20th:** 191
Yue di yanliu tu (Liu), **17th:** 541
Yüeh Fei. *See* Yo Fei
Yuezhi, **Anc:** 499, 959
Yūgen, **MA:** 1154
Yugoslavia. *See* Geographical Index
Yui Shōsetsu, **17th:** 998-1000
Yukawa, Hideki, **20th:** 4436-4438
Yukiguni. See *Snow Country*
Yukiie, Minamoto. *See* Minamoto Yukiie
Yume. See *Dreams*
Yunfa, **19th:** 2342
Yung-cheng. *See* Yongzheng
Yung-lo. *See* Yonglo
Yupanqui, Pachacutec Inca. *See* Pachacuti
Yuri (prince of Novgorod), **MA:** 998
Yurovsky, Yakov Mikhailovich, **Notor:** 1124-1125
Yūsuf ibn Tāshufīn, **MA:** 280
Yusuf Pasha Hasan al-Shallali, **19th:** 1474
Yusupov, Felix, **19th:** 1864; **Notor:** 887, 1126-1127
Yusupov, Irina, **Notor:** 1126
Yvain (Chrétien), **MA:** 268
Yverdon, **19th:** 1784

Z

Zabdas, **Anc:** 988
Zachariadis, Nikolaos, **Notor:** 493
Zadar, Siege of (1202), **MA:** 299, 1060
Zaddik, **18th:** 69
Zaghlūl, Saʿd, **20th:** 4439-4441
Zagwe Dynasty, **MA:** 632, 633
Zaharias, Babe Didrikson, **20th:** 4442-4445
Zahedi, Fazlollah, **20th:** 2846
Ẓ̄Êąččŭṟīr-ud-Dīn Muḥammad. *See* Bābur
Zaïde, une histoire espagnole. See *Zayde, a Spanish History*
Zakar-baal, **Anc:** 271
Zakharina, Anastasia Romanova, **Notor:** 517
Zakrzewska, Marie Elizabeth, **19th:** 249, 2481-2483
Zalinski, Edmund L., **19th:** 1114
Zama, Battle of (202 B.C.E.), **Anc:** 344, 384, 543, 759
Zambia. *See* Geographical Index
Zamora, Siege of (1072), **MA:** 279
Zamoyski, Jan, **Ren:** 911; **17th:** 854
Zampieri, Domenico. *See* Domenichino, Il
Zand Dynasty, **18th:** 552-553
Zangara, Giuseppe, **Notor:** 1128-1129
Zanuck, Darryl F., **20th:** 1760, 4230, 4445-4448
Zanzibar, **20th:** 3006
Zapata, Emiliano, **20th:** 3014, 4448-4451; **Notor:** 280, 1129-1131
Zapiski iz podpolya. See *Notes from the Underground*
Zapiski odnogo molodogo cheloveka (Herzen), **19th:** 1085
Zapiski okhotnika. See *Sportsman's Sketches, A*
Zápolya, János. *See* John I (1487-1540; king of Hungary)
Zar lässt sich photographieren, Der (Weill), **20th:** 4274
Zara Yaqob, **Ren:** 1006-1008
Zaria, Amina of. *See* Amina Sarauniya Zazzua
Zarqawi, Abu Musab al-, **Notor:** 1132-1134
Zarrin Taj. *See* Táhirih
Zashchita Luzhina. See *Defense, The*
Zastrozzi (Shelley), **19th:** 2092
Zauberberg, Der. See *Magic Mountain, The*
Zauberflöte, Die. See *Magic Flute, The*
Zawahiri, Ayman al-, **Notor:** 102, 1135-1136
Zayde, a Spanish History (La Fayette), **17th:** 478
Zayn al-ʿĀbidīn, **MA:** 452
Zaynab bint Jaḥsh, **MA:** 735
Zayyanid Dynasty, **Ren:** 80, 595
Zazzua, Hausaland, **Ren:** 37
Zboriv, Treaty of (1649), **17th:** 462
Ze Lan, **Anc:** 732
Ze Šumavy. See *From the Bohemian Forest*
Zealots, **Anc:** 459, 469
Zeami Motokiyo, **MA:** 1152-1155
"Zeami's Sixteen Treatises" (Yoshida), **MA:** 1154
Zedekiah, **Anc:** 336, 453, 582
Zeeman, Pieter, **20th:** 2432
Zeeman effect, **20th:** 3152
Zeit Konstantins des Grossen, Die. See *Age of Constantine the Great, The*
Zeitmasse (Stockhausen), **20th:** 3874
Zeitschrift für geschichtliche Rechtswissenschaft (journal), **19th:** 2004
Zelle, Margaretha Geertruida. *See* Mata Hari
Zemlya v snegu (Blok), **20th:** 394
Zen Buddhism, **MA:** 117, 758, 1087, 1155; **18th:** 450
Zend-Avesta (Fechner), **19th:** 771
Zeng Guofan, **19th:** 1363, 2483-2485
Zenger, Anna Catherine, **18th:** 1117
Zenger, John Peter, **18th:** 1116-1119
Zennichi-maru. *See* Nichiren

Zeno (Eastern Roman emperor), **MA:** 75, 782, 1012
Zeno of Citium, **Anc:** 70, 314, 690, 981-984
Zeno of Elea, **Anc:** 610, 984-986
Zeno the Stoic. *See* Zeno of Citium
Zenobia, **Anc:** 986-989
Zenshōbō Renchō. *See* Nichiren
Zephyrinus, **Anc:** 424
Zepp-LaRouche, Helga, **Notor:** 608
Zeppelin, Ferdinand von, **20th:** 1093, 4452-4455
Zeppelins, **20th:** 1093, 4453
Zerbrochene Krug, Der. See *Broken Jug, The*
Zerby, Karen "Maria," **Notor:** 87
Zero, concept of, **MA:** 314, 648
Zerubbabel, **Anc:** 339
Zetkin, Clara, **20th:** 4455-4458
Zeus, **Anc:** 635
Zewditu, **20th:** 1639
Zhang Chunqiao, **Notor:** 529
Zhang Geng, **17th:** 157
Zhang Jiuling, **MA:** 1085
Zhang Qian, **Anc:** 959
Zhang Xianzhong, **17th:** 849
Zhang Zhidong, **19th:** 2486-2488
Zhangsun Wuji, **MA:** 995
Zhao Gao, **Anc:** 781
Zhao Xiuye. *See* Zhao Ziyang
Zhao Ziyang, **20th:** 970, 1908, 2000, 2368, 4459-4461
Zhdanov, Andrei, **20th:** 2574, 3729; **Notor:** 1052, 1137-1138
Zheng. *See* Shi Huangdi
Zheng Chenggong, **17th:** 449, 1001-1003
Zheng He, **MA:** 1150, 1156-1158
Zheng Jing, **17th:** 449
Zheng Zhilong, **17th:** 161, 1001
Zhengde, **Ren:** 792, 1005, 1008-1010
Zhengwu (Wang Chong), **Anc:** 953
Zheyan, **Anc:** 345
Zhi Di. *See* Yonglo
Zhinga, N'. *See* Njinga
Zhirovich. *See* Kaganovich, Lazar
Zhitiye protopopa Avvakuma. See *Life of the Archpriest Avvakum, by Himself, The*
Zhong yong. See *Doctrine of the Mean, The*
Zhongzong, **MA:** 1128
Zhou Dynasty, **Anc:** 236, 379, 502
Zhou Enlai, **20th:** 969, 2367, 4459, 4461-4466
Zhou Shuren. *See* Lu Xun
Zhu De, **20th:** 1907, 2381, 3191, 4463, 4465-4469
Zhu Di. *See* Yonglo
Zhu Houzhao. *See* Zhengde
Zhu Xi, **MA:** 1159-1161; **Ren:** 986
Zhu Youjian. *See* Chongzhen
Zhu Youjiao. *See* Tianqi
Zhu Youlang, **17th:** 849
Zhu Youtang. *See* Xiaozong
Zhu Yuanzhang. *See* Hongwu
Zhuang Liedi. *See* Chongzhen
Zhuangzi, **Anc:** 989-992
Zhuangzi (Zhuangzi), **Anc:** 503, 950, 989
Zhukov, Georgy, **20th:** 4469-4473
Zhukovsky, Vasily, **19th:** 48, 937
Zhukovsky, Yegorovich, **20th:** 4108
Zhuo Wangsun, **Anc:** 786
Zhuo Wenjun, **Anc:** 786
Zia-ul-Haq, Mohammad, **20th:** 365, 369, 4473-4475
Zibhebhu, **19th:** 451
Zichu, **Anc:** 779
Ziegfeld Follies, **20th:** 3492
Ziegler, Karl, **20th:** 2920
Zigeunerbaron, Die (Strauss), **19th:** 2189
Zij. See *De scientia stellarum*
Zimbabwe. *See* Geographical Index
Zimbabwe African National Union, **20th:** 2858
Zimbabwe African People's Union, **20th:** 2858
Zimmerman, Robert Allen. *See* Dylan, Bob
Zimmermann Telegram, The (Tuchman), **20th:** 4106
Zimri-Lim, **Anc:** 376
Zingara, La (Donizetti), **19th:** 675
Zinjanthropus boisei. See *Australopithecus boisei*
Zinovyev, Grigory Yevseyevich, **Notor:** 990, 1080, 1138-1140
Zinzendorf, Count von, **18th:** 1119-1122
Zion College, **19th:** 2454
Zionism, **19th:** 1089; **20th:** 484, 555, 1120, 2993, 4280, 4377; criticism of, 1199
Zipporah, **Anc:** 573
Ziqqurats, **Anc:** 122, 914
Ziska, John. *See* Žižka, Jan
Života hmyzu, Ze. See *Insect Play, The*
Zixu fu (Sima Xiangru), **Anc:** 785
Zizhi tongjian (Sima Guang), **MA:** 945
Žižka, Jan, **MA:** 1162-1164
Zoë (Byzantine empress), **MA:** 863
Zohar (Moses de León), **MA:** 731
Zola, Émile, **19th:** 453, 2489-2492; **20th:** 780
Zolkiewski, Stanislaw, **17th:** 461, 855
Zolotoy petushok. See *Golden Cockerel, The*
Zonda, El, **19th:** 2000
Zong tragedy (1781), **18th:** 325
Zons, Michael, **19th:** 1715
Zoology, **MA:** Muslim, 570; **Ren:** 101, 375; **17th:** England, 783; Italy, 581; **19th:** 33, 1003, 1315; **20th:** 1335
Żórawno, Treaty of (1676), **17th:** 429, 452
Zorba the Greek (Kazantzakis), **20th:** 2087
Zoroaster, **Anc:** 992-995
Zoroastrianism, **Anc:** 252, 774, 992
Zoser, **Anc:** 439, 996-998
Zoshchenko, Mikhail, **Notor:** 1137
Zouche, William, **MA:** 308

Zrínyi, Peter, **17th:** 528
Zsitvatorok, Peace of (1606), **Ren:** 842
Zuccone (Donatello), **MA:** 321
Zug war pünktlich, Der. See *Train Was on Time, The*
Zuihitsu, **MA:** 932
Zukor, Adolph, **20th:** 1524, 3244; **Notor:** 32
Zulu War (1879), **19th:** 451
Zululand, **19th:** 450
Zum ewigen Frieden. See *Perpetual Peace*
Zunge zeigen. See *Show Your Tongue*
Zúñiga, Baltazar de, **17th:** 698
Zunis, **Ren:** 246
Zuo Zongfang, **19th:** 2484
Zuqāq al-Midaqq. See *Midaq Alley*
Zur Farbenlehre. See *Theory of Colors*
Zur Genealogie der Moral. See *On the Genealogy of Morals*
Zur Grundlegung der Ontologie (Hartmann), **20th:** 1697
Zur Kritik der politischen Ökonomie. See *Contribution to a Critique of Political Economy, A*
Zurbarán, Francisco de, **17th:** 671, 1003-1006
Zurich, Council of (1523), **Ren:** 1012
Zvonimir, **MA:** 639
Związek Walki Czynnej, **20th:** 3251
Zwicky, Fritz, **20th:** 184
Zwide, **19th:** 2081
Zwilich, Ellen Taaffe, **20th:** 4475-4479
Zwillingsbrüder, Die (Schubert), **19th:** 2026
Zwingli, Huldrych, **Ren:** 142, 375, 472, 584, 776, 1010-1014
Zworykin, Vladimir, **20th:** 4479-4481
Zygmunt II August. *See* Sigismund II Augustus
Zygmunt III Waza. *See* Sigismund III Vasa